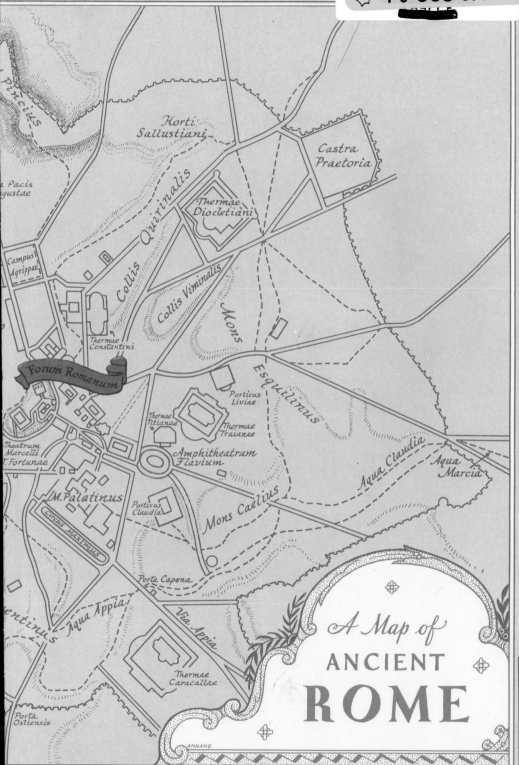

A Map of
ANCIENT
ROME

BY WILL DURANT

The Story of Philosophy
Transition
The Pleasures of Philosophy
Adventures in Genius

BY WILL AND ARIEL DURANT
THE STORY OF CIVILIZATION:

I. *Our Oriental Heritage*
II. *The Life of Greece*
III. *Caesar and Christ*
IV. *The Age of Faith*
V. *The Renaissance*
VI. *The Reformation*
VII. *The Age of Reason Begins*
VIII. *The Age of Louis XIV*
IX. *The Age of Voltaire*
X. *Rousseau and Revolution*
XI. *The Age of Napoleon*

The Lessons of History
Interpretations of Life

THE STORY OF CIVILIZATION: PART III

CAESAR AND CHRIST

*A History of Roman Civilization and of
Christianity from their beginnings to A.D. 325*

By Will Durant

SIMON AND SCHUSTER

NEW YORK

TO ARIEL

Preface

THIS volume, while an independent unit by itself, is Part III in a history of civilization, of which Part I was *Our Oriental Heritage*, and Part II was *The Life of Greece*. War and health permitting, Part IV, *The Age of Faith*, should be ready in 1950.

The method of these volumes is synthetic history, which studies all the major phases of a people's life, work, and culture in their simultaneous operation. Analytic history, which is equally necessary and a scholarly prerequisite, studies some separate phase of man's activity—politics, economics, morals, religion, science, philosophy, literature, art—in one civilization or in all. The defect of the analytic method is the distorting isolation of a part from the whole; the weakness of the synthetic method lies in the impossibility of one mind speaking with firsthand knowledge on every aspect of a complex civilization spanning a thousand years. Errors of detail are inevitable; but only in this way can a mind enchanted by philosophy—the quest for understanding through perspective—content itself with delving into the past. We may seek perspective through science by studying the relations of things in space, or through history by studying the relations of events in time. We shall learn more of the nature of man by watching his behavior through sixty centuries than by reading Plato and Aristotle, Spinoza and Kant. "All philosophy," said Nietzsche, "has now fallen forfeit to history." *

The study of antiquity is properly accounted worthless except as it may be made living drama, or illuminate our contemporary life. The rise of Rome from a crossroads town to world mastery, its achievement of two centuries of security and peace from the Crimea to Gibraltar and from the Euphrates to Hadrian's Wall, its spread of classic civilization over the Mediterranean and western European world, its struggle to preserve its ordered realm from a surrounding sea of barbarism, its long, slow crumbling and final catastrophic collapse into darkness and chaos—this is surely the greatest drama ever played by man; unless it be that other drama which began when Caesar and Christ stood face to face in Pilate's court, and continued until a handful of hunted Christians had grown by time and patience, and through persecution and terror, to be first the allies, then the masters, and at last the heirs, of the greatest empire in history.

---

* *Human, All Too Human*, Eng. tr., New York, 1911, vol. II, p. 17.

But that multiple panorama has greater meaning for us than through its scope and majesty: it resembles significantly, and sometimes with menacing illumination, the civilization and problems of our day. This is the advantage of studying a civilization in its total scope and life—that one may compare each stage or aspect of its career with a corresponding moment or element of our own cultural trajectory, and be warned or encouraged by the ancient aftermath of a modern phase. There, in the struggle of Roman civilization against barbarism within and without, is our own struggle; through Rome's problems of biological and moral decadence signposts rise on our road today; the class war of the Gracchi against the Senate, of Marius against Sulla, of Caesar against Pompey, of Antony against Octavian, is the war that consumes our interludes of peace; and the desperate effort of the Mediterranean soul to maintain some freedom against a despotic state is an augury of our coming task. *De nobis fabula narratur:* of ourselves this Roman story is told.

I wish to acknowledge the invaluable and self-sacrificing aid of Wallace Brockway at every step in the preparation of this book; the patience of my daughter, Mrs. David Easton, and of Miss Regina Sands, in typing 1200 pages from my minuscule script; and above all to the affectionate toleration and protective guidance accorded me by my wife through many years of dull and plodding and happy scholarship.

Table of Contents

INTRODUCTION: ORIGINS

Chapter I. ETRUSCAN PRELUDE: 800-508 B.C. 3

i. Italy 3
ii. Etruscan Life 5
iii. Etruscan Art 8
iv. Rome Under the Kings 11
v. The Etruscan Domination 14
vi. The Birth of the Republic 15

BOOK I: THE REPUBLIC: 508-30 B.C.

Chronological Table 20

Chapter II. THE STRUGGLE FOR DEMOCRACY: 508-264 B.C. 21

i. Patricians and Plebs 21
ii. The Constitution of the
    Republic 25
    1. The Lawmakers 25
    2. The Magistrates 28
3. The Beginnings of Roman
    Law 31
4. The Army of the
    Republic 33
iii. The Conquest of Italy 35

Chapter III. HANNIBAL AGAINST ROME: 264-202 B.C. 39

i. Carthage 39
ii. Regulus 43
iii. Hamilcar 45
iv. Hannibal 47
v. Scipio 51

Chapter IV. STOIC ROME: 508-202 B.C. 56

i. The Family 56
ii. The Religion of Rome 58
    1. The Gods 58
    2. The Priests 63
    3. Festivals 65
    4. Religion and Character.... 67
iii. Morals 67
iv. Letters 72
v. The Growth of the Soil 76
vi. Industry 77
vii. The City 81
viii. Post Mortem 83

Chapter V. THE GREEK CONQUEST: 201-146 B.C. 85

i. The Conquest of Greece 85
ii. The Transformation of
    Rome 87
iii. The New Gods 93
iv. The Coming of Philosophy.. 95
v. The Awakening of
    Literature 97
vi. Cato and the Conservative
    Opposition 102
vii. Carthago Deleta 105

ix

BOOK II: THE REVOLUTION: 145-30 B.C.

Chronological Table 110

Chapter VI. The Agrarian Revolt: 145-78 B.C. 111
  I. The Background of
     Revolution 111   IV. Marius 117
  II. Tiberius Gracchus 113   V. The Revolt of Italy 120
  III. Caius Gracchus 115   VI. Sulla the Happy 122

Chapter VII. The Oligarchic Reaction: 77-60 B.C. 128
  I. The Government 128
  II. The Millionaires 130   V. Spartacus 136
  III. The New Woman 134   VI. Pompey 138
  IV. Another Cato 135   VII. Cicero and Catiline 140

Chapter VIII. Literature under the Revolution: 145-30 B.C...146
  I. Lucretius 146
  II. *De Rerum Natura* 149   IV. The Scholars 158
  III. Lesbia's Lover 155   V. Cicero's Pen 161

Chapter IX. Caesar: 100-44 B.C. 167
  I. The Rake 167   Democracy 178
  II. The Consul 169   VI. Civil War 180
  III. Morals and Politics 172   VII. Caesar and Cleopatra 186
  IV. The Conquest of Gaul 174   VIII. The Statesman 190
  V. The Degradation of   IX. Brutus 194

Chapter X. Antony: 44-30 B.C. 198
  I. Antony and Brutus 198
  II. Antony and Cleopatra 203   III. Antony and Octavian 206

BOOK III: THE PRINCIPATE: 30 B.C.-A.D. 192

Chronological Table 210

Chapter XI. Augustan Statesmanship: 30 B.C.-A.D. 14...............211
  I. The Road to Monarchy 211   IV. The Augustan Reformation....221
  II. The New Order 215   V. Augustus Himself 227
  III. *Saturnia Regna* 218   VI. The Last Days of a God 229

Chapter XII. THE GOLDEN AGE: 30 B.C.-A.D. 18 233

I. The Augustan Stimulus 233
II. Virgil 235
III. The *Aeneid* 239
IV. Horace 244
V. Livy 250
VI. The Amorous Revolt 252

Chapter XIII. THE OTHER SIDE OF MONARCHY: A.D. 14-96............259

I. Tiberius 259
II. Gaius 265
III. Claudius 268
IV. Nero 274
V. The Three Emperors 284
VI. Vespasian 285
VII. Titus 288
VIII. Domitian 289

Chapter XIV. THE SILVER AGE: A.D. 14-96 295

I. The Dilettantes 295
II. Petronius 296
III. The Philosophers 299
IV. Seneca 301
V. Roman Science 307
VI. Roman Medicine 311
VII. Quintilian 313
VIII. Statius and Martial 315

Chapter XV. ROME AT WORK: A.D. 14-96 319

I. The Sowers 319
II. The Artisans 321
III. The Carriers 323
IV. The Engineers 326
V. The Traders 328
VI. The Bankers 330
VII. The Classes 332
VIII. The Economy and the State..336

Chapter XVI. ROME AND ITS ART: 30 B.C.-A.D. 96 338

I. The Debt to Greece 338
II. The Toilers' Rome 339
III. The Homes of the Great 343
IV. The Arts of Decoration 345
V. Sculpture 347
VI. Painting 351
VII. Architecture 355
  1. Principles, Materials, and Forms 355
  2. The Temples of Rome 357
  3. The Arcuate Revolution 359

Chapter XVII. EPICUREAN ROME: 30 B.C.-A.D. 96 363

I. The People 363
II. Education 367
III. The Sexes 369
IV. Dress 372
V. A Roman Day 374
VI. A Roman Holiday 377
  1. The Stage 377
  2. Roman Music 379
  3. The Games 381
VII. The New Faiths 388

Chapter XVIII. ROMAN LAW: 146 B.C.-A.D. 192 391

I. The Great Jurists 391
II. The Sources of the Law 393
III. The Law of Persons 394
IV. The Law of Property 399
V. The Law of Procedure 401
VI. The Law of the Nations 404

Chapter XIX. THE PHILOSOPHER KINGS: A.D. 96-180 407

I. Nerva 407
II. Trajan 408
III. Hadrian 413
  1. The Ruler 413

2. The Wanderer 417
3. The Builder 420
IV. Antoninus Pius 422
V. The Philosopher as Emperor..425

Chapter XX. LIFE AND THOUGHT IN THE SECOND CENTURY:
  A.D. 96-192 433

I. Tacitus 433
II. Juvenal 437
III. A Roman Gentleman 439

IV. The Cultural Decline 441
V. The Emperor as Philosopher..443
VI. Commodus 446

BOOK IV: THE EMPIRE: 146 B.C.-A.D. 192

Chronological Table 452

Chapter XXI. ITALY 453

I. A Roster of Cities 453
II. Pompeii 457

III. Municipal Life 460

Chapter XXII. CIVILIZING THE WEST 462

I. Rome and the Provinces 462
II. Africa 463
III. Spain 468

IV. Gaul 470
V. Britain 475
VI. The Barbarians 478

Chapter XXIII. ROMAN GREECE 482

I. Plutarch 482
II. Indian Summer 486

III. Epictetus 490
IV. Lucian and the Skeptics 494

Chapter XXIV. THE HELLENISTIC REVIVAL 498

I. Roman Egypt 498
II. Philo 501
III. The Progress of Science 502
IV. Poets in the Desert 507
V. The Syrians 510

VI. Asia Minor 513
VII. The Great Mithridates 516
VIII. Prose 520
IX. The Oriental Tide 522

Chapter XXV. ROME AND JUDEA: 132 B.C.-A.D. 135 528

I. Parthia 528
II. The Hasmoneans 530
III. Herod the Great 531
IV. The Law and Its Prophets 535

V. The Great Expectation 539
VI. The Rebellion 542
VII. The Dispersion 545

BOOK V

THE YOUTH OF CHRISTIANITY

4 B.C.-A.D. 325

Chronological Table 552

Chapter XXVI. JESUS: 4 B.C.-A.D. 30 553
    I. The Sources 553
    II. The Growth of Jesus 557   IV. The Gospel 564
    III. The Mission 560   V. Death and Transfiguration....570

Chapter XXVII. THE APOSTLES: A.D. 30-95 575
    I. Peter 575
    II. Paul 579   3. The Theologian 586
    1. The Persecutor 579   4. The Martyr 590
    2. The Missionary 581   III. John 592

Chapter XXVIII. THE GROWTH OF THE CHURCH: A.D. 96-305......596
    I. The Christians 596   IV. The Defenders of the Faith....611
    II. The Conflict of Creeds 603   V. The Organization of
    III. Plotinus 607   Authority 616

Chapter XXIX. THE COLLAPSE OF THE EMPIRE: A.D. 193-305 620
    I. A Semitic Dynasty 620   IV. The Twilight of Paganism 633
    II. Anarchy 627   V. The Oriental Monarchy 638
    III. The Economic Decline 631   VI. The Socialism of Diocletian..641

Chapter XXX. THE TRIUMPH OF CHRISTIANITY: A.D. 306-325 646
    I. The War of Church
        and State 646   III. Constantine and Christianity..655
    II. The Rise of Constantine 653   IV. Constantine and Civilization..661

EPILOGUE: 665
    I. Why Rome Fell 665   II. The Roman Achievement 670

Bibliography 673

Notes 681

Index 703

List of Illustrations

Following page 224

FIG. 1. Caesar (black basalt)

FIG. 2. An Etruscan Tomb at Cervetri

FIG. 3. Head of a Woman from an Etruscan Tomb at Corneto

FIG. 4. Apollo of Veii

FIG. 5. The Orator

FIG. 6. Pompey

FIG. 7. Caesar

FIG. 8. The Young Augustus

FIG. 9. Augustus Imperator

FIG. 10. Vespasian

FIG. 11. Relief from the Arch of Titus

FIG. 12. The Roman Forum

FIG. 13. Temple of Castor and Pollux

FIG. 14. Two Roman Mosaics

FIG. 15. The Gemma Augusta

FIG. 16. An Arretine Vase

Following page 416

FIG. 17. The Portland Vase

FIG. 18. Frieze from the Altar of Peace

FIG. 19. Frieze of Tellus from the Altar of Peace

FIG. 20. Portrait of a Young Girl

FIG. 21. "Clytie"

FIG. 22. "Spring," a Mural from Stabiae

FIG. 23. Details of Mural from the House of the Vettii

FIG. 24. Mural from the Villa Farnesina

FIG. 25. "Sappho"

FIG. 26. The Colosseum

FIG. 27. Interior of the Colosseum

FIG. 28. Roman Soldier and Dacian, from the Column of Trajan

FIG. 29. Antinoüs

FIG. 30. Altar Found at Ostia

FIG. 31. Arch of Trajan at Benevento
FIG. 32. Ruins of Timgad

Following page 544

FIG. 33. Pont du Gard at Nîmes
FIG. 34. Temple of Iuppiter Heliopolitanus at Baalbek
FIG. 35. Temple of Venus or Bacchus at Baalbek
FIG. 36. Arch of Septimius Severus, Rome
FIG. 37. Reconstruction of Interior of Baths of Caracalla
FIG. 38. Mithras and the Bull
FIG. 39. Sarcophagus of the Empress Helena

Maps of Ancient Rome and Ancient Italy and Sicily will be found on the inside covers. A map of the Roman Empire faces page 464.

INTRODUCTION

ORIGINS

CHAPTER I

Etruscan Prelude

800–508 B.C.

I. ITALY

QUIET hamlets in the mountain valleys, spacious pastures on the slopes, lakes upheld in the chalice of the hills, fields green or yellow verging toward blue seas, villages and towns drowsy under the noon sun and then alive with passion, cities in which, amid dust and dirt, everything from cottage to cathedral seems beautiful—this for two thousand years has been Italy. "Throughout the whole earth, and wherever the vault of heaven spreads, there is no country so fair": thus even the prosaic elder Pliny spoke of his fatherland.[1] "Here is eternal spring," sang Virgil, "and summer even in months not her own. Twice in the year the cattle breed, twice the trees serve us with fruit."[2] Twice a year the roses bloomed at Paestum, and in the north lay many a fertile plain like Mantua's, "feeding the white swans with grassy stream."[3] Like a spine along the great peninsula ran the Apennines, shielding the west coast from the northeast winds, and blessing the soil with rivers that hurried to lose themselves in captivating bays. On the north the Alps stood guard; on every other side protecting waters lapped difficult and often precipitous shores. It was a land well suited to reward an industrious population, and strategically placed athwart the Mediterranean to rule the classic world.

The mountains brought death as well as splendor, for earthquakes and eruptions now and then embalmed the labor of centuries in ashes. But here, as usually, death was a gift to life; the lava mingled with organic matter to enrich the earth for a hundred generations.[4] Part of the terrain was too steep for cultivation, and part of it was malarial marsh; the rest was so fertile that Polybius marveled at the abundance and cheapness of food in ancient Italy,[5] and suggested that the quantity and quality of its crops might be judged from the vigor and courage of its men. Alfieri thought that the "man-plant" had flourished better in Italy than anywhere else.[6] Even today the timid student is a bit frightened by the intense feelings of these fascinating folk—their taut muscles, swift love and anger, smoldering or blazing eyes; the pride and fury that made Italy great, and tore her to pieces, in the days of Marius and Caesar and the Renaissance, still run in Italian blood, only awaiting a good cause or argument. Nearly all the men are virile and handsome, nearly all the women beautiful, strong, and brave; what land can match the dynasty of genius that the mothers of Italy have poured forth through thirty centuries? No other country has been so long the hub of history—at first in government, then in religion, then in art. For seventeen hundred years, from Cato Censor to Michelangelo, Rome was the center of the Western world.

"Those who are the best judges in that country," says Aristotle, "report that when Italus became king of Oenotria, the people changed their name, and called themselves no longer Oenotrians but Italians." [7] Oenotria was the toe of the Italian boot, so teeming with grapes that the word meant "land of wine." Italus, says Thucydides, was a king of the Sicels, who had occupied Oenotria on the way to conquer and name Sicily.[8] Just as the Romans called all Hellenes *Graeci*, Greeks, from a few Graii who had emigrated from north Attica to Naples, so the Greeks gradually extended the name *Italia* to all the peninsula south of the Po.

Doubtless many chapters of Italy's story lie silent under her crowded soil. Remains of an Old Stone Age culture indicate that for at least 30,000 years before Christ the plains were inhabited by man. Between 10,000 and 6000 B.C. a neolithic culture appeared: a longheaded race called by ancient tradition Liguri and Siceli fashioned rude pottery with linear ornament, made tools and weapons of polished stone, domesticated animals, hunted and fished, and buried their dead. Some lived in caves, others in round huts of wattle and daub; from these cylindrical cottages architecture pursued a continuous development to the round "House of Romulus" on the Palatine, the Temple of Vesta in the Forum, and the Mausoleum of Hadrian—the Castel Sant' Angelo of today.

About 2000 B.C. northern Italy was invaded—presumably not for the first time—by tribes from central Europe. They brought with them the custom of building their villages upon piles sunk in water, for safety from animal or human attack. They settled on Garda, Como, Maggiore, and the other enchanted lakes that still lure aliens to Italy. Later they moved south and, finding fewer lakes, built their homes upon land, but still upon a foundation of piles. Their habit of surrounding these settlements with rampart and moat passed down to form features of Roman camps and medieval châteaux. They pastured flocks and herds, tilled the soil, wove clothing, fired pottery; and out of bronze, which had appeared in Italy toward the end of the Neolithic Age (about 2500 B.C.), they forged a hundred varieties of tools and weapons, including combs, hairpins, razors, tweezers, and other timeless implements.[9] They allowed their rubbish to accumulate so lavishly around the

villages that their culture has received the name of *terramare*—earth marl—
from the fertilizing potency of these remains. So far as we know, they were
the direct ancestors of the basic population of Italy in historical times.

In the valley of the Po the descendants of these *terramaricoli*, about 1000
B.C., learned from Germany the use of iron, made from it improved implements, and, so armed, spread their "Villanovan" culture from its center at
Villanova, near Bologna, far down into Italy. From them, we may believe,
came the blood, languages, and essential arts of the Umbrians, Sabines, and
Latins. Then, about 800 B.C., a new flood of immigrants arrived, subjugated
the Villanovan population, and established between the Tiber and the Alps
one of the strangest civilizations in the records of mankind.

II. ETRUSCAN LIFE

The Etruscans are among the irritating obscurities of history. They ruled
Rome for a hundred years or more, and left upon Roman ways so varied an
influence that Rome can hardly be understood without them; yet Roman
literature is as mute concerning them as a matron anxious to forget, publicly, the surrenders of her youth. Italian civilization, as literate provision,
begins with them: 8000 inscriptions, as well as many works of art, mingle
with their remains; and there are indications of a lost literature in poetry,
drama, and history.[10] But only a few unrevealing words of the language have
been deciphered, and scholarship stands in deeper darkness today before
the Etruscan mystery than that which shrouded the Egypt of the Pharaohs
before Champollion.

Consequently men still debate who the Etruscans were, and when and whence
they came. Perhaps the old tradition has been too readily set aside; pedants love
to disprove the accepted, which mischievously survives. Most Greek and Roman
historians took it for granted that the Etruscans had come from Asia Minor.[11]
Many elements in their religion, dress, and art suggest an Asiatic origin; many,
again, seem natively Italian. Most likely the civilization of Etruria was an out-
growth of the Villanovan culture, commercially influenced by Greece and the
Near East, while the Etruscans themselves, as they believed, were invaders from
Asia Minor, probably Lydia. In any case, their superior killing power made
them the ruling caste in Tuscany.

We do not know where they landed; but we know that they founded, conquered, or developed many cities—not mere villages of mud and straw as before
them, but walled towns with geometrically laid-out streets, and houses not only
of beaten earth, but often of baked brick or stone. Twelve of these communities
joined in a loose Etruscan Federation, dominated by Tarquinii (now Corneto),

Arretium (Arezzo), Perusia (Perugia), and Veii (Isola Farnese).* Hardships of transportation through mountains and forests collaborated with the jealous pugnacity of men, here as in Greece, to form independent city-states, seldom united against external foes; each cherished its separate security, often stood aside while others were attacked, and, one after another, succumbed to Rome. But through most of the sixth century B.C. these allied municipalities constituted the strongest political force in Italy, with a well-organized army, a famous cavalry, and a powerful navy that for a time ruled what is still called the Tyrrhene (i.e., Etruscan) Sea.†

As in the case of Rome, the government of the Etruscan cities began as a monarchy, became an oligarchy of "first families," and gradually gave over to an assembly of propertied citizens the right of choosing the annual magistrates. So far as we can make out from the tomb paintings and reliefs, it was a thoroughly feudal society, with an aristocracy owning the soil and enjoying in luxury the surplus product of Villanovan serfs and war-won slaves. Under this discipline Tuscany was reclaimed from forest and swamp, and a system of rural irrigation and urban sewage was developed beyond anything discoverable in contemporary Greece. Etruscan engineers built drainage tunnels to take the overflow of lakes, and cut drained roadways through rock and hill.[12] As early as 700 B.C. Etruscan industry mined the copper of the western coast and the iron of Elba, smelted the iron ore at Populonia, and sold pig iron throughout Italy.[13] Etruscan merchants traded up and down the Tyrrhene Sea, brought amber, tin, lead, and iron from northern Europe down the Rhine and the Rhone and over the Alps, and sold Etruscan products in every major port of the Mediterranean. About 500 B.C. Etruscan towns issued their own coins.

The people themselves are pictured on their tombs as short and stocky, with large heads, features almost Anatolian, complexion ruddy, especially in women; but rouge is as old as civilization.[14] The ladies were famous for their beauty,[15] and the men sometimes had faces of refinement and nobility. Civilization had already advanced to a precarious height, for specimens of dental bridgework have been found in the graves;[16] dentistry, like medicine and surgery, had been imported from Egypt and Greece.[17] Both sexes wore the hair long, and the men fondled beards. Garments followed the Ionian style: an inner shirt like the chiton, and an outer robe that became the Roman toga. Men as well as women loved ornament, and their tombs abounded in jewelry.

If we may judge from the gay pictures of the sepulchers, the life of the Etruscans, like that of the Cretans, was hardened with combat, softened with luxury, and brightened with feasts and games. The men waged war lustily, and practiced a variety of virile sports. They hunted, fought bulls in the arena, and

---

* The names given are Roman; the Etruscan names are unknown.

† The Greeks called the Etruscans *Tyrrheni* or *Tyrseni;* the Romans called them *Etrusci* or *Tusci.* Possibly, like *tyrant,* the Greek name came from Tyrrha, a fortress in Lydia. *Tower* is probably a kindred word.

drove their chariots, sometimes four horses abreast, around a dangerous course. They threw the discus and the javelin, pole-vaulted, raced, wrestled, boxed, and fought in gladiatorial bouts. Cruelty marked these games, for the Etruscans, like the Romans, thought it dangerous to let civilization get too far from the brute. Less heroic persons brandished dumbbells, threw dice, played the flute, or danced. Scenes of bibulous merriment relieve the paintings in the tombs. Sometimes they are symposia for men only, with vinous conversation; now and then they show both sexes, richly dressed, reclining in pairs on elegant couches, eating and drinking, waited on by slaves, and entertained by dancers and musicians.[18] Occasionally the meal is adorned with an amorous embrace.

Probably the lady in this case was a courtesan, corresponding to the Greek hetaira. If we may believe the Romans, the young women of Etruria, like those of Greek Asia and Samurai Japan, were allowed to obtain dowries by prostitution;[19] a character in Plautus accuses a girl of "seeking in the Tuscan way to earn her marriage by the shame of her body."[20] Nevertheless, women enjoyed a high status in Etruria, and the paintings represent them as prominent in every aspect of life. Relationship was traced through the mother in a manner suggesting again an Asiatic origin.[21] Education was not confined to the male, for Tanaquil, wife of the first Tarquin, was versed in mathematics and medicine as well as political intrigue.[22] Theopompus ascribed a communism of women to the Etruscan,[23] but no confirming evidence has come down to us of this Platonic utopia. Many of the pictures are scenes of marital concord and family life, with children romping about in happy ignorance.

Religion provided every incentive to a negative morality. The Etruscan pantheon was fully equipped to terrify the growing ego and ease the tasks of parentage. The greatest of the gods was Tinia, who wielded the thunder and the lightning. About him, as a committee pitilessly carrying out his commands, were the Twelve Great Gods, so great that it was sacrilege (and we may therefore neglect) to pronounce their names. Especially fearsome were Mantus and Mania, master and mistress of the Underworld, each with an executive horde of winged demons. Least appeasable of all was Lasa or Mean, goddess of fate, brandishing snakes or a sword, and armed with stylus and ink to write, and hammer and nails to affix, her unalterable decrees. Pleasanter were the Lares and Penates—little statuettes kept on the hearth, and symbolizing the spirits of field and home.

The sacred science of ascertaining the future by studying the livers of sheep or the flight of birds had probably come down to the Etruscans from Babylonia; but according to their own traditions it had been revealed to them by a divine boy, grandson of Tinia, who sprang to life from a furrow freshly turned, and at once spoke with the wisdom of a sage. Etruscan ritual culminated in the sacrifice of a sheep, a bull, or a man. Human victims were slaughtered or buried alive at the funerals of the great. In some cases prisoners of war were massacred as a propitiation of the gods; so the Phoceans taken at Alalia in 535 B.C. were stoned to death in the forum of Caere, and some 300 Romans captured in 358 B.C.

were sacrificed at Tarquinii. The Etruscan appears to have believed that for every enemy slain he could secure the release of a soul from hell.[24]

The belief in hell was the favorite feature of Etruscan theology. The dead spirit, as seen in the sepulchral representations, was conducted by genii to the tribunal of the Underworld, where in a Last Judgment it was given an opportunity to defend its conduct in life. If it failed, it was condemned to a variety of torments that left their mark on Virgil (reared on Mantua's Etruscan lore), on the early Christian conception of hell, and, through these and twenty centuries, on Tuscan Dante's *Inferno*. From such damnation the good were spared, and the sufferings of the damned might be shortened by the prayers or sacrifices of their living friends. The saved soul passed from the Underworld to the society of the gods above, there to enjoy feasts, luxuries, and powers depicted hopefully on the tombs.

Normally the Etruscans buried their dead. Those who could afford it were laid to rest in sarcophagi of terra cotta or stone, and the lid was topped with reclining figures carved partly in their likeness, partly in the smiling style of the archaic Greek *Apollos;* here, again, Etruscan traditions contributed to medieval art. Occasionally the dead were cremated and placed in cinerary urns, which also might be adorned with the figure of the deceased. In many cases the urn or tomb simulated a house; sometimes the tomb, cut into the rock, was divided into rooms, and was equipped for post-mortem living with furniture, utensils, vases, clothing, weapons, mirrors, cosmetics, and gems. In a tomb at Caere the skeleton of a warrior lay on a perfectly preserved bed of bronze, with weapons and chariots beside it; and in a chamber behind his were the ornaments and jewelry of a woman presumably his wife. The dust that had been her beloved body was clothed in her bridal robes.[25]

III. ETRUSCAN ART

Etruscan art is nearly all that we know of Etruscan history. We can trace in it the manners and morals of the people, the power of religion and caste, and the changing tides of economic and cultural contact with Asia Minor, Egypt, Greece, and Rome. It was an art fettered by ecclesiastical conventions and liberated by technical skill; it reflected a brutal and obscurantist civilization, but expressed it with character and force. Oriental influences—Ionic, Cypriot, Egyptian—dictated its earlier forms and styles, and Greek models dominated its later sculpture and pottery. In architecture and painting, however, in bronze statuary and the working of metals, Etruscan art spoke with its own voice and was unique.

The architectural remains are never more than fragments or tombs. Parts of Etruria's city walls still stand—heavy structures of uncemented masonry firmly and accurately joined. The homes of rich Etruscans defined the classic design of the Italian house: a deliberately forbidding external wall, a central atrium or reception room, an opening in the roof of the atrium to let rain fall into a cistern below, and a circuit of small chambers surrounding the atrium and often faced by a colonnaded porch. Vitruvius has described Etruscan temples, and the tombs sometimes take their form. Essentially they followed Greek models; but the "Tuscan style" modified the Doric by leaving the column unfluted, giving it a base, and planning the cella on a six-to-five proportion of length to breadth, instead of the more graceful Attic relation of six-to-three. A cella of brick, a peristyle of stone, architraves and pediments of wood, reliefs and ornaments in terra cotta, the whole resting on a podium or elevation, and brightly painted outside and within: this was the Etruscan temple. For secular mass architecture —for city gates and walls, aqueducts and drains—the Etruscans (so far as we know) introduced the arch and vault to Italy. Apparently they had brought these majestic forms from Lydia, which had taken them from Babylonia.* But they did not follow up this brilliant method of covering great spaces without a confusion of columns and an oppressive weight of architraves. For the most part they walked in the grooves worn by the Greeks, and left Rome to consummate the arcuate revolution.

The most renowned of Etruria's products is its pottery. Every museum abounds in it, setting the weary navigator of ceramic halls to wonder what unseen perfection exonerates these stores. Etruscan vases, when they are not clearly copies of Greek forms, are mediocre in design, crude in execution, barbarous in ornament. No other art has produced so many distortions of the human frame, so many hideous masks, uncouth animals, monstrous demons, and terrifying gods. But the black wares (*bucchero nero*) of the sixth century B.C. have an Italian vigor, and perhaps represent an indigenous development of Villanovan styles. Fine vases were found at Vulci and Tarquinii—imported from Athens or imitated from black-figured Attic shapes. The François Vase, a huge amphora discovered at Chiusi by a Frenchman of that name, was apparently the work of the Greek masters Clitias and Ergotimus. The later urns, red-figured on a black ground, are elegant, but again evidently of Greek manufacture; their abundance suggests that the Attic potters had captured the Etruscan market and driven the native workers into merely industrial production. All in all, the robbers were justified who, when they rifled Etruscan tombs, left so much of the pottery.

We cannot speak of Etruscan bronzes with such reckless irreverence. The bronze casters of Etruria were at the top of their craft. They almost rivaled the potters in productivity; one city alone is reported to have had two thousand statues in bronze. What remains to us from their hands belongs mostly to the period of Roman domination. Among these reliefs two masterpieces stand out: the *Orator* who now holds forth, with Roman dignity and bronze restraint, in the Archeological Museum at Florence; and—also at Florence—the *Chimera* found at Arezzo in 1553, and partly restored by Cellini. It is a disagreeable

---

* They were used in Egyptian tombs and temples, and in the palaces of Nineveh. Some Roman arches are as old as any that remain in Etruria.[26]

figure, presumably the monster slain by Bellerophon—head and body of a lion, a serpent for a tail, a goat's head growing anomalously out of the back; but its power and finish reconcile us to its biological extravagance. Etruscan bronze-workers produced, often for distant export, millions of statuettes, swords, helmets, cuirasses, spears, shields, utensils, urns, coins, locks, chains, fans, mirrors, beds, lamps, candelabra, even chariots. Greeting the visitor to the Metropolitan Museum of Art in New York is an Etruscan chariot: body and wheels of wood, sheathing and tires of bronze, the high front embossed with figures of considerable grace. Many bronze objects were delicately engraved. The surface was coated with wax, the design was etched in with a stylus, the piece was dipped into acid, the wax-freed lines were burned into the metal, and then the wax was melted away. In the working of silver and gold, bone and ivory, the Etruscan artist was the heir and peer of the Egyptian and the Greek.

Sculpture in stone was never popular in Etruria. Marble was scarce, and the quarries of Carrara were apparently unknown. Fine clays were at hand, however, and soon took shape in a profusion of terra-cotta reliefs, statuettes, and sepulchral or architectural ornaments. About the end of the sixth century an unknown Etruscan artist established a school of sculpture at Veii, and molded the chef-d'oeuvre of Etruscan art—that *Apollo of Veii* which was found on the site in 1916, and until lately stood in the Villa Giulia at Rome. Modeled on the Ionian and Attic *Apollos* of the time, this engaging statue shows an almost feminine Mona Lisa face, with delicate smile, archly slanting eyes, and a body of health, beauty, and life; the Italians call it *il Apollo che cammina*—"the Apollo that walks." In this, and in many excellent figures on sarcophagi, Etruscan sculptors carried to perfection the Asiatic stylization of hair and drapery, while in the *Orator* they or their Roman heirs established a tradition of realistic portraiture.

Etruscan painting collaborated with that of Greek Italy in transmitting another art to Rome. The elder Pliny described frescoes at Ardea "of older age than Rome itself"; and at Caere others of "still greater antiquity" and "supreme beauty." [27] The art used pottery, and the interiors of homes and tombs, for its surfaces; only tomb frescoes and vase pictures remain, but in such quantity that every stage of Etruscan painting can be traced in them, from Oriental and Egyptian, through Greek and Alexandrian, to Roman and Pompeian styles. In some tombs we find the first Italian examples of windows, portals, columns, porticoes, and other architectural forms mimicked by painting on inner walls, in the very manner of Pompeii. Often the colors of these frescoes are faded; a few are astonishingly fresh and brilliant after more than a score of centuries. The technique is mediocre. In the earlier pictures there is no perspective, no foreshortening, no use of light and shade to give fullness and depth; the figures are Egyptianly slender, as if seen in a horizontally convex mirror; the faces are regularly in profile, wherever the feet may point. In the later examples perspective and foreshortening appear, and the proportions of the body are represented with greater fidelity and skill. But in either case there is in these paintings a frolicsome and impish vivacity that makes one wonder how pleasant the life of the Etruscans must have been, if their tombs were so gay.

Here are men in battle, and enjoying it; or they play at war in the jousts of the arena. They hunt the boar or lion with all the bravery of men who have or expect an audience; they box or wrestle in the palaestra, while the spectators dispute more violently than the combatants; they ride their horses, or drive their chariots, around the amphitheater; sometimes, resigned to peace, they fish. One pleasant scene shows a couple idly boating on a quiet stream: so old is wisdom. In a grave at Caere the pictured man and his lady recline on a couch; garlanded with laurel, he pledges her his eternal fidelity with a goblet of wine; she smiles and believes him, though she knows he lies. In other burial chambers the Etruscan painter sketches his idea of paradise: endless revelry, with careless lasses dancing wildly to double-pipes and the lyre. Pipes and lyres, trumpets and syrinxes, were apparently essential to every banquet, wedding, and funeral; love of music and the dance is one of the gracious aspects of Etruscan civilization. In the Tomb of the Lioness at Corneto the figures whirl about in nude and Bacchic frenzy.[28]

It was the natural destiny of the Etruscans to expand north and south, to extend their sway to the foothills of the Alps and the Greek cities of Campania, and then to find themselves face to face, across the Tiber, with growing Rome. They established colonies at Verona, Padua, Mantua, Parma, Modena, Bologna, and beyond the Apennines at Rimini, Ravenna, and Adria; from this modest Etruscan outpost the Adriatic took its name. They hemmed in Rome with Etruscan settlements at Fidenae, Praeneste (Palestrina), and Capua, perhaps also at Cicero's Tusculum ("little Tuscany"). Finally—in 618 B.C., according to a precise and precarious tradition—an Etruscan adventurer captured the throne of Rome; and for a century the Roman nation was ruled and formed by Etruscan civilization and power.

IV. ROME UNDER THE KINGS

About 1000 B.C. Villanovan migrants crossed the Tiber and settled in Latium. No one knows whether they conquered, or exterminated, or merely married the neolithic population they found there. Slowly the agricultural villages of this historic region between the Tiber and the Bay of Naples coalesced into a few jealously sovereign city-states, loath to unite except in annual religious festivals or occasional wars. The strongest was Alba Longa, lying at the foot of Mt. Alban, probably where Castel Gandolfo now shelters the Pope on summer days. It was from Alba Longa, perhaps in the eighth century before Christ, that a colony of Latins—greedy for conquest, or driven by the pressure of the birth rate upon the land—moved some twenty miles to the northwest and founded the most famous of man's habitations.

This hazardously hypothetical paragraph contains all that history dares say about the origin of Rome. But Roman tradition was not so parsimonious. When the Gauls burned the city in 390 B.C. most historical records were presumably destroyed, and thereafter patriotic fancy could paint a free picture of Rome's birth. What we should call April 22, 753 B.C., was given as the date, and events were reckoned *A.U.C.—anno urbis conditae—*"in the year from the city's foundation." A hundred tales and a thousand poems told how Aeneas, offspring of Aphrodite-Venus, had fled from burning Troy, and how, after suffering many lands and men, he had brought to Italy the gods or sacred effigies of Priam's city. Aeneas had married Lavinia, daughter of the king of Latium; and eight generations later their descendant Numitor, said the story, held the throne of Alba Longa, Latium's capital. A usurper, Amulius, expelled Numitor and, to end the line of Aeneas, killed Numitor's sons and forced his only daughter, Rhea Silvia, to become a priestess of Vesta, vowed to virginity. But Rhea lay down by the banks of a stream and "opened her bosom to catch the breeze." [29] Too trustful of gods and men, she fell asleep; Mars, overcome with her beauty, left her rich with twins. Amulius ordered these to be drowned. They were placed on a raft, which kind waves carried to the land; they were suckled by a she-wolf (*lupa*) or—said a skeptical variant—by a shepherd's wife, Acca Larentia, nicknamed Lupa because, like a wolf's, her love-making knew no law. When Romulus and Remus grew up they killed Amulius, restored Numitor, and went resolutely forth to build a kingdom for themselves on the hills of Rome.

Archeology offers no confirmation to these stories of our youth; probably they contain a core of truth. Perhaps the Latins sent a colony to develop Rome as a strategic moat against the expanding Etruscans. The site was twenty miles from the sea, and not well adapted to maritime commerce; but in those days of marauding pirates it was an advantage to be a bit inland. For internal trade Rome was well placed at the crossroads of traffic on the river and the land route between north and south. It was not a healthy location; rains, floods, and springs fed malarial marshes in the surrounding plain and even in the lower levels of the city; hence the popularity of the seven hills. The first of these to be settled, tradition said, was the Palatine, possibly because an island near its foot made easier there the fording and bridging of the Tiber. One by one the neighboring slopes were peopled, until the human overflow crossed the river and built upon the Vatican and Janiculum.* The three tribes—Latins, Sabines, and Etruscans—that dwelt on the hills joined in

---

* There were more than seven of these modest elevations in Rome, and the "seven" varied from time to time. In Cicero's day they were the Palatine, Capitoline, Caelian, Esquiline, Aventine, Viminal, and Quirinal.

a federation, the Septimontium, and slowly merged into the city of Rome.

The ancient story goes on to tell how Romulus, to secure wives for his settlers, arranged some public games and invited the Sabines and other tribes to attend. During the races the Romans seized the Sabine women and drove off the Sabine men. Titus Tatius, King of the Sabine Curites tribe, declared war and advanced upon Rome. Tarpeia, daughter of the Roman who had charge of a fortress on the Capitoline, opened a gate to the invaders. They crushed her with their shields in fair recompense; and later generations gave her name to that "Tarpeian Rock" from which condemned men were hurled to death. As the troops of Tatius neared the Palatine, the Sabine women, not insensitive to the compliment of capture, secured an armistice on the plea that they would lose their husbands if the Curites won, and their brothers or fathers if the Curites lost. Romulus persuaded Tatius to share the kingdom with him and join his tribe with the Latins in a common citizenship; thereafter the freemen of Rome were called Curites or Quirites.[30] There may again be some elements of truth in this wholesale romance—or perhaps it patriotically concealed a Sabine conquest of Rome.

After a long reign Romulus was lifted up to heaven in a whirlwind, thereafter to be worshiped as Quirinus, one of Rome's favorite gods. Tatius too having died, the heads of the more important families chose a Sabine, Numa Pompilius, as king. Probably the real power of government, between the foundation of the city and the Etruscan domination, was in the hands of these elders, or *senatores,* while the functions of the king, like those of the *archon basileus* in coeval Athens, were chiefly those of the highest priest.[31] Tradition pictured Numa as a Sabine Marcus Aurelius, at once philosopher and saint. "He strove," says Livy,

> to inculcate fear of the gods as the most powerful influence that could act upon . . . a barbarous people. But as this effort would fail to impress them without some claim to supernatural wisdom, he pretended that he had nocturnal interviews with the divine nymph Egeria; and that it was on her advice that he was instituting the religious ritual most acceptable to Heaven, and was appointing special priests for each major deity.[32]

By establishing a uniform worship for the diverse tribes of Rome, Numa strengthened the unity and stability of the state;[33] by interesting the bellicose Romans in religion, Cicero thought, Numa gave his people forty years of peace.[34]

His successor, Tullus Hostilius, restored to the Romans their normal life. "Convinced that the vigor of the state was becoming enfeebled through inaction, he looked around for a pretext for war." [35] He chose Rome's mother city, Alba Longa, as an enemy, attacked it, and completely destroyed it. When the Alban king broke a promise of alliance, Tullus had him tied to two chariots and torn to pieces by driving the chariots in opposite directions.[36] His successor, Ancus Martius, agreed with his martial philosophy; Ancus understood, according to Dio Cassius,

> that it is not sufficient for men who wish to remain at peace to refrain from wrongdoing . . . but the more one longs for peace the more vulnerable one becomes. He saw that a desire for quiet was not a power for protection unless accompanied by equipment for war; he perceived also that delight in freedom from foreign broils very quickly ruined men who were unduly enthusiastic over it.[37]

V. THE ETRUSCAN DOMINATION

About 655 B.C., proceeds the tradition, Demaratus, a rich merchant banished from Corinth, came to live in Tarquinii, and married an Etruscan woman.[38] His son Lucius Tarquinius migrated to Rome, rose to high position there, and, on the death of Ancus, either seized the throne or, more probably, was chosen to it by a coalition of Etruscan families in the city. "He was the first," says Livy, "who canvassed for the crown, and delivered a set speech to secure the support of the plebs" [39]—i.e., those citizens who could not trace their ancestry to the founding fathers. Under this Tarquinius Priscus the monarchy increased its power over the aristocracy, and Etruscan influence grew in Roman politics, engineering, religion, and art. Tarquin fought successfully against the Sabines, and subjugated all Latium. He used the resources of Rome, we are told, to adorn Tarquinii and other Etruscan cities, but also he brought Etruscan and Greek artists to his capital and beautified it with majestic temples.* Apparently he represented the growing power of business and finance against the landed aristocracy.

After a reign of thirty-eight years the first Tarquin was assassinated by the patricians, who aimed to limit the kingship again to a religious role. But Tarquin's widow, Tanaquil, took charge of the situation and was able to transmit the throne to her son Servius Tullius. Servius, says Cicero, was the first "to hold the royal power without being chosen by the people" [41]—i.e., by the leading families. He governed well, and built a protective moat and wall around Rome; but the great landowners resented his rule and plotted to unseat him. Consequently he allied himself with the richer members of the plebs, and reorganized the army and the voters to strengthen his position.

---

* Perhaps also he cleansed it with sewers. Roman historians ascribed to him the Cloaca Maxima, or Supreme Sewer; but some scholars reserve this honor for the second century B.C.[40]

Taking a census of persons and property, he classified the citizens according to wealth rather than birth, so that while leaving the old aristocracy intact, he raised up as a balance to it a class of *equites*, literally, horsemen—men who could *equip* themselves with horse (*equus*) and armor to serve in the cavalry.* The census reported some 80,000 persons capable of bearing arms; reckoning one woman and one child for each soldier, and a slave for every fourth family, we may estimate at 260,000 the population of Rome and its subject environs about 560 B.C. Servius divided the people into thirty-five new tribes, arranging them according to place of residence rather than kinship or rank; thereby, like Cleisthenes a generation later in Attica, he weakened the political cohesion and voting power of the aristocracy—the class that rated itself supreme by birth. When another Tarquin, grandson of Tarquinius Priscus, charged Servius with ruling illegally, he submitted himself to a plebiscite and received, says Livy, "a unanimous vote." [42] Unconvinced, Tarquin had Servius assassinated, and announced himself king.†

Under Tarquinius Superbus ("the Proud") the monarchy became absolute, and Etruscan influence supreme. The patricians had thought of the *rex* as the executive of the Senate and chief priest of the national religion; they could not long consent to unlimited royal power. Therefore they had killed Tarquinius Priscus and had raised no hand to protect Servius. But this new Tarquin was worse than the first. He surrounded himself with a bodyguard, degraded freemen with months of forced labor, had citizens crucified in the Forum, put to death many leaders of the upper classes, and ruled with an insolent brutality that won him the hatred of all influential men.[44] ‡ Thinking to gain popularity by successful wars, he attacked the Rutuli and the Volscians. While he was with the army the Senate assembled and deposed him (508 B.C.), in one of the great turning points of Roman history.

VI. THE BIRTH OF THE REPUBLIC

Here the tradition becomes literature, and the prose of politics is fused into the poetry of love. One evening (says Livy), in the King's camp at

---

* As originally applied to cavalrymen, the term could bear the traditional English mistranslation into *knights;* but *equites* soon lost this early sense, and came to mean the upper middle, or business, class.

† Few students are inclined to follow the extreme skepticism of Ettore Pais, who rejects as legendary all Roman history before 443 B.C., and believes that the two Tarquins were one person, who never existed.[43] A tentative and modified acceptance of the traditional story after Romulus appears to "account for the phenomena" better than any other hypothesis.

‡ The traditional account of the Tarquins is probably darkened by aristocratic and anti-Etruscan propaganda. The history of early Rome was written chiefly by representatives or admirers of the patrician class, just as the history of the emperors was later written by senatorial partisans like Tacitus.

Ardea, his son, Sextus Tarquin, was debating with a relative, Lucius Tarquinius Collatinus, the comparative virtue of their wives. Collatinus proposed that they should take horse to Rome and surprise their ladies in the late hours of the night. They found the wife of Sextus feasting with intimates, but Lucretia, wife of Collatinus, was spinning wool for her husband's clothing. Sextus was inflamed with desire to try Lucretia's fidelity and enjoy her love. A few days later he returned secretly to the home of Lucretia and overcame her by wile and force. Lucretia sent for her father and her husband, told them what had happened, and then stabbed herself to death. Thereupon Lucius Junius Brutus, a friend of Collatinus, called upon all good men to drive the Tarquins from Rome. He himself was a nephew of the King; but his father and his brother had been put to death by Tarquin, and he had gained his cognomen Brutus—i.e., idiot—by pretending lunacy so that he might be spared for his revenge. Now he rode with Collatinus to the capital, told Lucretia's story to the Senate, and persuaded it to banish all the royal family. The King had meanwhile left the army and hurried to Rome; Brutus, apprised of this, rode out to the army, told Lucretia's story again, and won the soldiers' support. Tarquin fled north, and appealed to Etruria to restore him to his throne.[45] *

An assembly of the citizen-soldiers was now convened; and instead of a king chosen for life it elected two consuls,† with equal and rival powers, to rule for a year. These first consuls, says the tradition, were Brutus and Collatinus; but Collatinus resigned, and was replaced by Publius Valerius, who won the name Publicola—"friend of the people"—by putting through the Assembly several laws that remained basic in Rome: that any man who should try to make himself king might be killed without trial; that any attempt to take a public office without the people's consent should be punishable with death; and that any citizen condemned by a magistrate to death or flogging should have the right of appeal to the Assembly. It was Valerius who inaugurated the custom whereby a consul, upon entering the Assembly, must part the axes from the rods and lower them as a sign of the people's sovereignty and sole right, in peace, to impose a sentence of death.

The revolution had two main results: it freed Rome from Etruscan ascendancy and replaced the monarchy with an aristocracy that ruled Rome until Caesar. The political position of the poorer citizens was not improved; on the contrary, they were required to surrender the lands that Servius had given them, and they lost the modest measure of protection with which the

---

* Most students since Niebuhr consign Lucretia to legend and Shakespeare. We do not know where history retires and poetry enters. Some have thought even Brutus to be legend;[46] but here, again, skepticism has probably gone too far.

† Or, says another tradition, two praetors or generals.

monarchy had shielded them from aristocratic domination.[47] The victors called the revolution a triumph of liberty; but now and then liberty, in the slogans of the strong, means freedom from restraint in the exploitation of the weak.

The expulsion of the Tarquins from Rome, added to the defeat of the Etruscans by Greek colonists at Cumae in 524, threatened to end Etruscan leadership in central Italy. Responding for these reasons to Tarquin's appeal, Lars Porsena, chief magistrate of Clusium, collected an army from the federated cities of Etruria and advanced upon Rome. At the same time an attempt was made in Rome itself to restore Tarquin. The two sons of Brutus were among the arrested conspirators, and the fiery first consul provided an exemplar—perhaps a myth—for all later Romans when he witnessed in stoic silence the flogging and beheading of his children. The Romans destroyed the Tiber bridges before Porsena could reach them; it was in this defense of the bridgeheads that Horatius Cocles immortalized himself in Latin and English lays. Despite this and other legends with which defeat tried to cover itself with glory, Rome surrendered to Porsena,[48] and yielded portions of her territory to Veii and to the Latin towns that had been despoiled by Rome's kings.[49] Porsena showed his good taste by not demanding the restoration of Tarquin; in Etruria, too, by this time, aristocracy had driven out monarchy. Rome was weakened for a generation, but her revolution remained.

The Etruscan power had been expelled, but the marks and relics of Etruscan influence were to survive in Roman civilization to its end. That influence was apparently least on the Latin language; nevertheless, the Roman numerals are probably Etruscan,[50] and the name *Roma* may have come from the Etruscan *rumon*, river.[51] The Romans believed that they had taken from Etruria the ceremonies of a returning conqueror's triumph, the purple-hemmed robes and ivory curule (chariotlike) seat of the magistrates, and the rods and axes carried before each consul by twelve lictors in token of his authority to strike and kill.[52] * The coins of Rome, centuries before she had a fleet, were adorned with the prow of a ship—long used in the coinage of Etruria to symbolize her commercial activity and naval power. From the seventh to the fourth centuries B.C. it was a custom among Roman aristocrats to send their sons to Etruscan cities for higher education; there, among other

---

* In an Etruscan tomb at Vetulonia, dated back to the eighth century B.C., a double-headed iron ax was found, with its shaft enclosed by eight iron rods.[53] The double ax as a symbol of government is at least as old as Minoan Crete. The Romans gave to the bound rods and axes the name of *fasces*, bundles. The twelve lictors (*ligare*, to bind) owed their number to the twelve cities of the Etruscan Federation, each of which provided a lictor for the chief officer of the Federation.[54]

things, they learned geometry, surveying, and architecture.[55] Roman dress derived from the Etruscan, or both from a common source.

The first actors, and their name *histriones*, came to Rome from Etruria. It was Tarquinius Priscus, if we may believe Livy, who built the first Circus Maximus, and imported race horses and pugilists from Etruria for Roman games. The Etruscans gave Rome brutal gladiatorial contests, but they also transmitted to Rome a higher status of woman than could be found in Greece. Etruscan engineers built the walls and sewers of Rome, and turned it from a swamp into a protected and civilized capital. From Etruria Rome took most of her religious ritual, her augurs, haruspices, and soothsayers; as late as Julian (A.D. 363), Etruscan soothsayers were an official part of every Roman army. With Etruscan rites Romulus was believed to have laid out the limits of Rome. From the same source came the Roman wedding ceremony, with its symbolism of capture, and the Roman ceremonial funeral. Rome took her musical modes and instruments from Etruria.[56] Most of her artists were Etruscans, and the Roman street where the artists worked was called Vicus Tuscus; the arts themselves, however, may have filtered in through Latium from the Campanian Greeks. Sculptural portraiture in Rome was deeply influenced by the death masks made for the family gallery—a custom taken from Etruria. Etruscan sculptors adorned the temples and palaces of Rome with bronze statuary and terra-cotta figures and reliefs; Etruscan architects bequeathed to Rome a "Tuscan style" that still survives in the colonnade of St. Peter's Church; Etruscan kings at Rome seem to have built her first large edifices, and to have transformed Rome from an assemblage of earthen or wooden huts into a city of wood, brick, and stone. Not till Caesar would Rome see again so much building as under Etruscan rule.

We must not exaggerate. However much Rome learned from her neighbors, she remained, in all the basic features of life, distinctively herself. Nothing in Etruscan history quite suggests the Roman character, the grave self-discipline, the cruelty and courage, the patriotism and stoic devotion that patiently conquered, and then patiently ruled, the Mediterranean states. Now Rome was free, and the stage was cleared for the incomparable drama of the grandeur and decline of paganism in the ancient world.

BOOK I

THE REPUBLIC

508-30 B.C.

CHRONOLOGICAL TABLE

B.C.

813(?): Foundation of Carthage

558f: Carthage conquers western Sicily, Sardinia, Corsica, etc.

509: Establishment of Roman Republic

508: War with Etruscans; Horatius Cocles

500: Hanno explores west coast of Africa

494: First secession of the plebs; institution of the tribunate

492: Coriolanus (?)

485: Condemnation of Spurius Cassius

458,439: Cincinnatus, dictator

451: First Decemvirate

450: The Twelve Tables

449: Second secession of the plebs

445: *Lex Canuleia* on marriage

443: Institution of the censorship

432: First law to check electoral corruption

396: Romans capture Veii

390: Sack of Rome by the Gauls

367: *Lex Licinia* alleviates law of debt

343-341: First Samnite War

340-338: War with the Latins; dissolution of the Latin League

339: *Leges Publiliae* end veto power of Senate

327-304: Second Samnite War

326: *Lex Poetelia* alleviates law of debt

321: Romans defeated at Caudine Forks

312: Censorship of Appius Claudius; beginning of Appian Way

300: *Lex Valeria* on right of appeal; *lex Ogulnia* on eligibility to priesthood

298-290: Third Samnite War

287: Final secession of the plebs; *leges Hortensiae* on powers of the Assembly

283: Rome occupies most of Greek Italy

280-275: Pyrrhus in Italy and Sicily

280-279: "Pyrrhic victories" at Heraclea and Asculum

272: Rome takes Tarentum

264-241: First Punic War

248: Hamilcar Barca invades Sicily

241: Carthaginian fleet defeated off Aegadian Isles; Sicily a Roman province

B.C.

241-236: War of Mercenaries vs. Carthage

240: First play of Livius Andronicus

239: Carthage yields Sardinia and Corsica to Rome

237: Hamilcar in Spain

235: Naevius' first play

230: War on the Illyrian pirates

222: Rome takes Cisalpine Gaul

221: Hannibal commander in Spain

219-201: Second Punic War

218: Hannibal crosses the Alps and defeats Romans at the Ticinus and the Trebia

217: Hannibal defeats Romans at Lake Trasimene; Fabius Maximus dictator

216: Hannibal victorious at Cannae

215: Treaty between Hannibal and Philip V

214: *Fl.* Plautus

214-205: First Macedonian War

212: Romans capture Syracuse

210-209: Scipio Africanus Major in Spain

207: Hasdrubal defeated at the Metaurus

203: Hannibal recalled to Africa

202: Scipio defeats Hannibal at Zama; Quintus Fabius Pictor publishes first history of Rome

201: Spain a Roman province

200-197: Second Macedonian War

199: *Fl.* Ennius

189: Battle of Magnesia

186: Suppression of the worship of Bacchus

184: Censorship of Cato the Elder

171-168: Third Macedonian War

168: Battle of Pydna

167: Polybius in Rome

160: The *Adelphi* of Terence

155: Carneades lectures in Rome

155-138: War with the Lusitanians

150-146: Third Punic War

147-140: Successes of Viriathus against Rome in Spain

146: Scipio Africanus Minor destroys Carthage; Mummius sacks Corinth; extension of Roman rule over north Africa and Greece

CHAPTER II

The Struggle for Democracy

508-264 B.C.

I. PATRICIANS AND PLEBS

WHO were the patricians? Livy [1] thought that Romulus had chosen a hundred clan heads of his tribe to help him establish Rome and be his council or senate. These men were later called *patres*—"fathers"—and their descendants *patricii*—"derived from the fathers." Modern theory, which lives by nibbling at tradition, likes to explain the patricians as alien conquerors, perhaps Sabines, who invaded Latium and thereafter ruled the Latin plebs, or populace, as a lower caste. We may believe that they were composed of clans that through economic or military superiority had acquired the best lands, and had transformed their agricultural leadership into political mastery. These victorious clans—the Manlii, Valerii, Aemilii, Cornelii, Fabii, Horatii, Claudii, Julii, etc.—continued for five centuries to give Rome generals, consuls, and laws. When the three original tribes united, their clan heads made a senate of some three hundred members. They were not such lords of comfort and luxury as their descendants; often they put their own hands to the ax or the plow, lived vigorously on simple fare, and wore clothing spun in their homes. The plebs admired them even when it fought them, and applied to almost anything appertaining to them the term *classicus*, "classical"—i.e., of the highest rank or class.[2]

Close to them in wealth, but far below them in political power, were the *equites*, or businessmen. Some were rich enough to win their way into the Senate, and formed there the second part of its constituent *patres (et) conscripti*—i.e., "patricians and coinscribed men." These two classes were called the "orders," and were termed *boni*, "the good"; for early civilizations thought of virtue in terms of rank, ability, and power; *virtus* to the Roman meant manliness, the qualities that make a man (*vir*). *Populus*, "people," took in only these upper classes; and originally it was in this sense that those famous initials were used—S P Q R (*Senatus Populusque Romanus*)—which were to mark so proudly a hundred thousand monuments.[3] Gradually, as democracy fought its way, the word *populus* came to include the plebs.

This was the main body of Roman citizens. Some were artisans or tradesmen, some were freedmen, many were peasants; perhaps, in the beginning, they were the conquered natives of the city's hills. Some were attached as *clientes*, or dependents, to an upper-class *patronus;* in return for land and protection they helped him in peace, served under him in war, and voted in the assemblies as he told them.

Lowest of all were the slaves. Under the kings they had been costly and few, and therefore had been treated with consideration as valuable members of the family. In the sixth century B.C., when Rome began her career of conquest, war captives were sold in rising number to the aristocracy, the business classes, and even to plebeians; and the status of the slave sank. Legally he could be dealt with as any other piece of property; in theory, and according to the custom of the ancients, his life had been forfeited by defeat, and his enslavement was a merciful commutation of his death. Sometimes he managed his master's property, business, or funds; sometimes he became a teacher, writer, actor, craftsman, laborer, tradesman, or artist, and paid his master part of his earnings. In this or other ways he might earn enough to buy his freedom and become a member of the plebs.

Contentment is as rare among men as it is natural among animals, and no form of government has ever satisfied its subjects. In this system the businessmen were piqued by their exclusion from the Senate, the richer plebeians by their exclusion from the *equites;* and the poorer plebeians resented their poverty, their political disabilities, and their liability to enslavement for debt. The law of the early Republic allowed a creditor to imprison a persistently defaulting debtor in a private dungeon, to sell him into slavery, even to kill him. Joint creditors might, said the law, cut up the corpse of the defaulting debtor and divide it among them—a provision apparently never enforced.[4] The plebs demanded that these laws should be repealed and the burden of accrued debt reduced; that the lands won in war and owned by the state should be distributed among the poor instead of being given, or sold at nominal prices, to the rich; that plebeians should be eligible to the magistracies and the priesthoods, be permitted to intermarry with the "orders," and have a representative of their class among the highest officials of the government. The Senate sought to frustrate the agitation by fomenting wars, but it was shocked to find its calls to the colors ignored. In 494 B.C. large masses of the plebs "seceded" to the Sacred Mount on the river Anio, three miles from the city, and declared that they would neither fight nor work for Rome until their demands had been met. The Senate used every diplomatic or religious device to lure the rebels back; then, fearing that invasion from without might soon be added to revolt within, it agreed to a cancellation or reduction of debts, and the establishment of two tribunes and three aediles as the elected defenders of the plebs. The plebs returned, but only after taking a solemn oath to kill any man who should ever lay violent hands upon their representatives in the government.[5]

This was the opening battle in a class war that ended only with the Republic that it destroyed. In 486 the consul Spurius Cassius proposed an allotment of captured lands among the poor; the patricians accused him of currying popular favor with a view to making himself king, and had him killed; this was probably not the first in a long line of agrarian proposals and Senatorial assassinations, culminating in the Gracchi and Caesar. In 439 Spurius Maelius, who during a famine had distributed wheat to the poor at a low price or free, was slain in his home by an emissary of the Senate, again on the charge of plotting to be king.[6] In 384 Marcus Manlius, who had heroically defended Rome against the Gauls, was put to death on the same charge after he had spent his fortune relieving insolvent debtors.

The next step in the climb of the plebs was a demand for definite, written, and secular laws. Heretofore the patrician priests had been the recorders and interpreters of the statutes, had kept their records secret, and had used their monopoly, and the ritual requirements of the law, as weapons against social change. After a long resistance to the new demands, the Senate (454) sent a commission of three patricians to Greece to study and report on the legislation of Solon and other lawmakers. When they returned, the Assembly (451) chose ten men—*decemviri*—to formulate a new code, and gave them supreme governmental power in Rome for two years. This commission, under the presidency of a resolute reactionary, Appius Claudius, transformed the old customary law of Rome into the famous Twelve Tables, submitted them to the Assembly (which passed them with some changes), and displayed them in the Forum for all who would—and could—to read. This seemingly trivial event was epochal in Roman history and in the history of mankind; it was the first written form of that legal structure which was to be Rome's most signal achievement and her greatest contribution to civilization.

When the second year of the commission's tenure ended, it refused to restore the government to the consuls and tribunes, and continued to exercise supreme —and ever more irresponsible—authority. Appius Claudius, says a story suspiciously like Lucretia's, was stirred with a passion for the beautiful plebeian Virginia, and, to secure her for his pleasure, had her declared a slave. Her father, Lucius Virginius, protested; and when Claudius refused to hear him he slew his daughter, rushed out to his legion, and asked its aid in overthrowing the new despot. The enraged plebs once more "seceded" to the Sacred Mount, "imitating," says Livy, "the moderation of their fathers by abstaining from all injury." [7] Learning that the army was supporting the plebs, the patricians gathered in the senate house, deposed the Decemvirs, banished Claudius, restored the consulate, enlarged the tribunate, recognized the inviolability of the people's tribunes, and confirmed to the plebs the right of appealing to the Assembly of the Centuries from the decision of any magistrate.[8] Four years later (445) the tribune Caius Canuleius moved that the plebs should have the right of inter-marriage with patricians, and that plebeians should be eligible to the consulate. The Senate, again faced by threats of war from vengeful neighbors, yielded the first point, and averted the second by agreeing that thereafter six of the tribunes chosen by the Centurial Assembly should have the authority of consuls. The plebs responded handsomely by choosing all these *tribuni militum consulari potestate* from the patrician class.

The long war with Veii (405-396), and the assault of the Gauls upon Rome, unified the nation for a time, and stilled internal strife. But victory and disaster alike left the plebeians destitute. While they fought for their country their lands were neglected or ravaged, and the interest on their debts mounted beyond possible repayment. The lenders took no excuse, but demanded principal and interest, or the imprisonment and enslavement of the borrowers. In 376 the tribunes Licinius and Sextius proposed that interest already paid should be deducted from the principal, the balance to be met in three years; that no man should be allowed to own more than five hundred *iugera* (about three hundred acres) of land, or to use on them more than a certain proportion of slaves to free laborers; and that one of the two consuls should regularly be chosen from the plebs. For a decade the patricians resisted these proposals; meanwhile, says Dio Cassius, "they stirred up war after war, that the people might be too occupied to agitate about the land."[9] At last, threatened with a third secession, the Senate accepted the "Licinian laws," and Camillus, leader of the conservatives, celebrated the reconciliation of the classes by building a stately Temple of Concord in the Forum.

It was a major step in the growth of Rome's limited democracy. From that moment the plebs progressed rapidly towards a formal equality with the "orders" in politics and law. In 356 a plebeian was made dictator for a year; in 351 the censorship, in 337 the praetorship, and in 300 the priesthoods were opened to the plebs. Finally (287) the Senate agreed that the decisions of the Tribal Assembly should also have the force of law, even when contrary to the resolutions of the Senate. Since in this Assembly the patricians could easily be out-voted by the plebs, this *lex Hortensia* was the capstone and triumph of Roman democracy.

Nevertheless, the power of the Senate soon recovered after these defeats. The demand for land was quieted by sending Romans as colonists to conquered soil. The cost of winning and holding office—which was unpaid—automatically dis-qualified the poor. The richer plebeians, having secured political equality and opportunity, now co-operated with the patricians in checking radical legisla-tion; the poorer plebeians, shorn of financial means, ceased for two centuries to play a significant role in the affairs of Rome. Businessmen fell in with patrician policy because it gave them contracts for public works, openings for colonial and provincial exploitation, and commissions to collect taxes for the state. The Assembly of the Centuries, whose method of voting gave the aristocracy full control, continued to choose the magistrates, and therefore the Senate. The tribunes, dependent upon the support of rich plebeians, used their office as a conservative force. Every consul, even if chosen by the plebs, became by contagion a zealous conservative when, at the close of his year of office, he was received into the Senate for life. The Senate took the initiative in legislation, and custom sanctioned its authority far beyond the letter of the law. As foreign affairs became more important, the Senate's firm administration of them raised its prestige and power. When, in 264, Rome entered upon a century of war with Carthage for the mastery of the Mediterranean, it was the Senate that led the nation through every trial to victory; and an imperiled and desperate people yielded without protest to its leadership and domination.

II. THE CONSTITUTION OF THE REPUBLIC

1. The Lawmakers

Let us try to picture to ourselves this complex state, so formed after five centuries of development. By common consent it was one of the ablest and most successful governments that the world has yet seen; Polybius, indeed, considered it an almost literal realization of Aristotle's ideal constitution. It provided the framework, sometimes the battleground, of Roman history.

Who, among this people, were the citizens? Technically, those who had been born or adopted into one of the three original tribes of Rome. In practice this meant all males above fifteen years of age who were neither slaves nor aliens, and all aliens who had received a grant of Roman citizenship. Never before or since has citizenship been so jealously guarded or so highly prized. It meant membership in the relatively small group that was soon to rule the whole Mediterranean area; it brought immunity from legal torture or duress, and the right of appeal from any official in the Empire to the Assembly—or, later, the emperor—at Rome.

Obligations went with these privileges. The citizen, unless quite poor, was liable to military service at call from his sixteenth to his sixtieth year; and he could not hold political office until he had served ten years in the army. His political rights were so bound up with his military duties that his most important voting was done as a member of his regiment, or "century." In the days of the kings he had voted also in the *comitia curiata*; i.e., he and other heads of families had come together (*cum-ire*) in a gathering of the thirty *curiae*, or wards, into which the three tribes had been divided; and to the end of the Republic it was this Curial Assembly that conferred upon the elected magistrates the *imperium*, or authority to govern. After the fall of the monarchy the Curial Assembly rapidly lost its other powers to the *comitia centuriata*—the soldiers assembled in "centuries" originally of one hundred men. It was this Centurial Assembly that chose the magistrates, passed or rejected the measures proposed to it by officials or the Senate, heard appeals from the judgments of magistrates, tried all cases of capital crime charged to Roman citizens, and decided upon war or peace. It was the broad base of both the Roman army and the Roman government. Nevertheless, its powers were narrowly constrained. It could convene only at the call of a consul or a tribune. It could vote only upon such measures as were presented to it by the magistrates or the Senate. It could not discuss or amend these proposals; it could only vote Yes or No.

The conservative character of its decisions was guaranteed by the class arrangement of its members. At the top were eighteen centuries of patricians and businessmen (*equites*). Then came the "first class"—men owning 100,000 asses' worth of property;* these had eighty centuries, or 8000 men, in the Assembly. The second class embraced citizens owning between 75,000 and 100,000 asses; the third, between 50,000 and 75,000 asses; the fourth, between 25,000 and 50,000 asses; and each of these classes had twenty centuries. The fifth class included citizens owning between 11,000 and 25,000 asses, and had thirty centuries. All citizens possessing under 11,000 asses were formed into one century.[10] Each century cast one vote, determined by a majority of its members; a small majority in one century could cancel a large majority in another, and give the victory to a numerical minority. Since each century voted in the order of its financial rank, and its vote was announced as soon as taken, the agreement of the first two groups gave at once ninety-eight votes, a majority of the whole, so that the lower classes seldom voted at all. Voting was direct: citizens who could not come to Rome for the meeting had no representation in the Assembly. All this was no mere device to disfranchise the peasants and the plebs. The classification of centuries had been made by the census to distinguish men for taxation as well as for war; the Romans thought it just that the right to vote should be proportioned to taxes paid and military duties required. Citizens with less than 11,000 asses of property had altogether only one centurial vote; but correspondingly they paid a negligible tax and were in normal times exempt from military service.[11] Of the proletariat, till Marius' day, nothing was asked except prolific parentage. Despite some later changes, the Centurial Assembly remained a frankly conservative and aristocratic institution.

Doubtless as an offset to this, the plebs had from the beginning of the Republic held its own assemblies, the *concilia plebis*. Out of these councils, probably, came the *comitia populi tributa* which we find exercising legislative power

---

* An *as* would now be equivalent in purchasing power to approximately six cents of United States currency in 1942. Cf. p. 78.

as early as 357 B.C. In this Tribal Assembly of the People the voters were arranged according to tribe and residence, on the basis of the Servian census; each tribe had one vote, and the rich counted for no more than the poor. After the recognition of its legislative authority by the Senate in 287, the power of the Tribal Assembly grew until by 200 it had become the chief source of private law in Rome. It chose the tribunes (i.e., tribal representatives) of the people (*tribuni plebis*) as distinct from the *tribuni militares* elected by the centuries. Here, too, however, there was no discussion by the people; a magistrate proposed a law and defended it, another magistrate might speak against it; the Assembly listened, and voted Yes or No. Though by its constitution it was more progressive than the Centurial Assembly, it was far from radical. Thirty-one of its thirty-five tribes were rural, and their members, mostly owners of land, were cautious men. The urban proletariat, confined to four tribes, was politically powerless before Marius, and after Caesar.

The Senate remained supreme. Its original membership of clan heads was recruited by the regular admission of ex-consuls and ex-censors, and the censors were authorized to keep its numbers up to 300 by nominating to it men of patrician or equestrian rank. Membership was for life, but the Senate or a censor could dismiss any member detected in crime or serious moral offense. The august body convened at the call of any major magistrate in the *curia*, or senate house, facing the Forum. By a pleasant custom the members brought their sons with them to attend in silence, and to learn statesmanship and chicanery at first hand. Theoretically the Senate might discuss and decide only such issues as were presented to it by a magistrate, and its decisions were merely advice (*senatus consulta*), without the force of law. Actually its prestige was so great that the magistrates nearly always accepted its recommendations, and seldom submitted to the assemblies any measure not already sanctioned by the Senate. Its decisions were subject to veto by any tribune, and a defeated minority of the Senate might appeal to the assemblies; [12] but these procedures were rare except in revolution. The magistrates held power for a year only, while the senators were chosen for life; inevitably this deathless monarch dominated the bearers of a brief authority. The conduct of foreign relations, the making of alliances and treaties, the waging of war, the government of the colonies and provinces, the management and distribution of the public lands, the control of the treasury and its disbursements—all these were exclusive functions of the Senate, and gave it immense power. It was legislature, executive, and judiciary in one. It acted as judge in crimes like treason, conspiracy, or assassination, and appointed from its membership the judges in most major civil trials. When a crisis came it could issue its most formidable decree, the *senatus-consultum ultimum*, "that the consuls should see to it that no harm should come to the state"—a decree that established martial law and gave the consuls absolute command of all persons and property.

The Senate of the Republic * often abused its authority, defended corrupt officials, waged war ruthlessly, exploited conquered provinces greedily, and suppressed the aspirations of the people for a larger share in the prosperity of Rome. But never elsewhere, except from Trajan to Aurelius, have so much energy, wisdom, and skill been applied to statesmanship; and never elsewhere has the idea of service to the state so dominated a government or a people. These senators were not supermen; they made serious mistakes, sometimes vacillated in their policies, often lost the vision of empire in the lust for personal gain. But most of them had been magistrates, administrators, and commanders; some of them, as proconsuls, had ruled provinces as large as kingdoms; many of them came of families that had given statesmen or generals to Rome for hundreds of years; it was impossible that a body made up of such men should escape some measure of excellence. The Senate was at its worst in victory, at its best in defeat. It could carry forward policies that spanned generations and centuries; it could begin a war in 264 and end it in 146 B.C. When Cineas, the philosopher who had come to Rome as envoy of Pyrrhus (280), had heard the Senate's deliberations and observed its men, he reported to the new Alexander that here was no mere gathering of venal politicians, no haphazard council of mediocre minds, but in dignity and statesmanship veritably "an assemblage of kings." [13]

2. The Magistrates

The major officials were elected by the Centurial, the minor by the Tribal, Assembly. Each office was held by a *collegium* of two or more colleagues, equal in power. All offices except the censorship ran for only a year. The same office could be held by the same person only once in ten years; a year had to elapse between leaving one office and taking another; and in the interval the ex-official could be prosecuted for malfeasance. The aspirant to a political career, if he survived a decade in the army, might seek election as one of the quaestors who, under the Senate and the consuls, managed the expenditure of state funds, and assisted the praetors in preventing and investigating crime. If he pleased his electors or his influential supporters, he might later be chosen one of the four aediles charged with the care of buildings, aqueducts, streets, markets, theaters, brothels, saloons, police courts,

---

* The term *respublica* (the public property, or commonwealth) was applied by the Romans to all three forms of their state—monarchy, "democracy," and principate; historians now agree in limiting it to the period between 508 and 49 B.C.

and public games. If again successful, he might be made one of the four praetors who in war led armies, and in peace acted as judges and interpreters of the law.*

At about this point in the *cursus honorum*, or sequence of offices, the citizen who had made a name for integrity and judgment might become one of the two censors ("valuators") chosen every fifth year by the Centurial Assembly. One of them would take the quinquennial census of the citizens, and assess their property for political and military status and for taxation. The censors were required to examine the character and record of every candidate for office; they watched over the honor of women, the education of children, the treatment of slaves, the collection or farming of taxes, the construction of public buildings, the letting of governmental property or contracts, and the proper cultivation of the land. They could lower the rank of any citizen, or remove any member of the Senate, whom they found guilty of immorality or crime; and in this function the power of either censor was immune to the veto of the other. They could try to check extravagance by raising taxes on luxuries. They prepared and published a budget of state expenditures on a five-year plan. At the close of their eighteen-month term they would gather the citizens together in a solemn ceremony of national purification (*lustrum*), as a means of maintaining cordial relations with the gods. Appius Claudius Caecus (the Blind), great-grandson of the Decemvir, was the first to make the censorship rival the consulate in dignity. During his term (312) he built the Appian Aqueduct and the Appian Way, promoted rich plebeians to the Senate, reformed land laws and state finances, helped to break down the priestly and patrician monopoly and manipulation of the law, left his mark on Roman grammar, rhetoric, and poetry, and, by his deathbed speech against Pyrrhus, decided the Roman conquest of Italy.

Theoretically one of the two consuls ("consultants") had to be a plebeian; actually very few plebeians were chosen, for even the plebs preferred men of education and training for an office that would have to deal with every executive phase of peace and war throughout the Mediterranean. On the eve of the election the magistrate in charge of it observed the stars to see if they favored the presentation of the several candidates' names; presiding over the Centurial Assembly on the morrow, he might offer to its choice only those names that the auspices had approved; [14] in this way the aristocracy discouraged "upstarts" and demagogues, and in most cases the Assembly, awed or intimidated, submitted to the pious fraud. The candidate appeared in person, dressed in a plain white (*candidus*) toga to emphasize

---

* Quaestor from *quaerere*, to inquire—hence a trial was a *quaestio;* aedile from *aedes*, building; praetor from *prae-ire*, to go in advance, to lead—hence the cohort that watched over him was called the Praetorian Guard.

the simplicity of his life and morals, and perhaps the more easily to show the scars he had won in the field. If elected, he entered office on the ensuing March 15. The consul took on sanctity by leading the state in the most solemn religious rites. In peace he summoned and presided over the Senate and the Assembly, initiated legislation, administered justice, and in general executed the laws. In war he levied armies, raised funds, and shared with his fellow consul command of the legions. If both of them died or were captured during their year of office, the Senate declared an *interregnum*, and appointed an *interrex* (or interval-king) for five days, while a new election was being prepared. The word suggests that the consuls had inherited, for their brief term, the powers of the kings.

The consul was limited by the equal authority of his colleague, by the pressure of the Senate, and by the veto power of the tribune. After 367 B.C. fourteen military tribunes were chosen to lead the tribes in war, and ten "tribunes of the plebs" to represent them in peace. These ten were *sacrosancti*: it was a sacrilege, as well as a capital crime, to lay violent hands upon them except under a legitimate dictatorship. Their function was to protect the people against the government, and to stop by one word—*veto*, "I forbid" —the whole machinery of the state, whenever to any one of them this seemed desirable. As a silent observer the tribune could attend the meetings of the Senate, report its deliberations to the people, and, by his veto, deprive the Senate's decisions of all legal force. The door of his inviolable home remained open day and night to any citizen who sought his protection or his aid, and this right of sanctuary or asylum provided the equivalent of *habeas corpus*. Seated on his *tribunal* he could act as judge, and from his decision there was no appeal except to the Assembly of the Tribes. It was his duty to secure the accused a fair trial, and, when possible, to win some pardon for the condemned.

How did the aristocracy retain its ascendancy despite these obstructive powers? First, by limiting them to the city of Rome and to times of peace; in war the tribunes obeyed the consuls. Secondly, by persuading the Tribal Assembly to elect wealthy plebeians as tribunes; the prestige of wealth and the diffidence of poverty moved the people to choose the rich to defend the poor. Thirdly, by allowing the number of tribunes to be raised from four to ten; if only one of these ten would listen to reason or money, his veto could frustrate the rest.[15] In the course of time the tribunes became so dependable that they could be trusted to convene the Senate, take part in its deliberations, and become life members of it after their terms.

If all these maneuvers failed, a last bulwark of social order remained— dictatorship. The Romans recognized that in times of national chaos or peril their liberties and privileges, and all the checks and balances that they

had created for their own protection, might impede the rapid and united action needed to save the state. In such cases the Senate could declare an emergency, and then either consul could name a dictator. In every instance but one the dictators came from the upper classes; but it must be said that the aristocracy rarely abused the possibilities of this office. The dictator received almost complete authority over all persons and property, but he could not use public funds without the Senate's consent, and his term was limited to six months or a year. All dictators but two obeyed these restrictions, honoring the story of how Cincinnatus, called from the plow to save the state (456 B.C.), returned to his farm as soon as the task was done. When this precedent was violated by Sulla and Caesar, the Republic passed back into the monarchy out of which it had come.

3. The Beginnings of Roman Law

Within this unique constitution the magistrates administered a system of law based upon the Twelve Tables of the Decemvirs. Before that epochal enactment Roman law had been a mixture of tribal customs, royal edicts, and priestly commands. *Mos maiorum*—the way of the ancients—remained to the end of pagan Rome the exemplar of morals and a source of law; and though imagination and edification idealized the ruthless burghers of the early Republic, the tales told of them helped educators to form a stoic character in Roman youth. For the rest, early Roman law was a priestly rule, a branch of religion, surrounded with sacred sanctions and solemn rites. Law was both *lex* and *ius*—command and justice; it was a relation not only between man and man but between man and the gods. Crime was a disturbance of that relation, of the *pax deorum* or peace of the gods; law and punishment were in theory designed to maintain or restore that relation and peace. The priests declared what was right and wrong (*fas et nefas*), on what days the courts might open and the assemblies meet. All questions regarding marriage or divorce, celibacy or incest, wills or transfers, or the rights of children, required the priest as now so many of them require the lawyer. Only the priests knew the formulas without which hardly anything could be legally done. They were in Rome the first *iurisconsulti*, consultants in the law, counselors; they were the first to give *responsa*, or legal opinions. The laws were recorded in their books, and these volumes were so securely guarded from the plebs that suspicion charged the priests with altering the texts, on occasion, to suit ecclesiastical or aristocratic ends.

The Twelve Tables effected a double juristic revolution: the publication and secularization of Roman law. Like other codes of the sixth and fifth centuries—those of Charondas, Zaleucus, Lycurgus, Solon—they represented a change from uncertain unwritten custom to definite written law; they were a result of increasing literacy and democracy. The *ius civile*, or law of citizens, freed itself in these Tables from the *ius divinum*, or divine law; Rome decided not to be a theocracy. The priestly monopoly was further deflated when the secretary of Appius Claudius the Blind published (304) a calendar of court days (*dies fasti*—"days of utterance"), and a "formulary" of proper legal procedures, which had till then been known to few but the priests. Secularization took another step when Coruncanius (280) began the first known public instruction in Roman law; from that time onward the lawyer replaced the priest and dominated the mind and life of Rome. Soon the Tables were made the basis of education; till Cicero's day all schoolboys had to learn them by heart; and doubtless they had a share in forming the stern and orderly, litigious and legalistic, Roman soul. Amended and supplemented again and again—by legislation, praetorial edicts, *senatusconsulta*, and imperial decrees—the Twelve Tables remained for nine hundred years the basic law of Rome.

The law of procedure was already complex in this code. Almost any magistrate might act as a judge; but the praetors were the usual court, and their revisions and interpretations of the statutes kept Roman law a living growth instead of a corpse of precedents. Every year the *praetor urbanus*, or chief city magistrate, drew up a list or "white tablet" (*album*) of senators and *equites* eligible for jury service; the presiding judge in an action chose jurors from this list, subject to a limited number of rejections by plaintiff and defendant. Lawyers were permitted to advise clients and plead in court; and some senators gave legal advice in public sittings or at home. The law of Cincius (204 B.C.) forbade taking pay for legal services, but legal skill found ways of circumventing this counsel of perfection. Slaves were often tortured to elicit evidence.

The Twelve Tables constituted one of the severest codes in history. They retained the old paternal omnipotence of a military-agricultural society; allowed the father to scourge, chain, imprison, sell, or kill any of his children—merely adding that a son thrice sold was thereafter free from his father's rule.[16] Class division was preserved by forbidding the marriage of a patrician with a plebeian. Creditors received every right against debtors.[17] Owners could dispose freely of their property by will; property rights were held so sacred that a thief caught in the act was given as a slave to the man whom he had robbed. Penalties ranged from simple fines to exile, enslavement, or death. Several took the form of equivalent retaliation (*lex talionis*); many were fines delicately adjusted to the rank of the victim. "For breaking the bones of a freeman, 300 asses; of a slave, 150 asses."[18] Death was decreed for libel, bribery, perjury, harvest thiev-ing, nocturnal damage to a neighbor's crops, the defrauding of a "client" by a patron, "practicing enchantments," arson, murder, and "seditious gatherings in the city by night." [19] The parricide was tied in a sack, sometimes with a cock, a dog, a monkey, or a viper, and cast into the river.[20] Within the capital, however, appeal from any but a dictator's sentence of death could be taken by a citizen to the Assembly of the Centuries; and if the accused perceived that the vote there was going against him he was free to commute his sentence into exile by leaving Rome.[21] Consequently, despite the severity of the Twelve Tables, capital punishment of freemen was rare in republican Rome.

4. The Army of the Republic

The Roman constitution rested finally on the most successful military organization in history. The citizens and the army were one; the army assembled in its centuries was the chief lawmaking body in the state. The first eighteen centuries supplied the cavalry; the "first class" formed the heavy infantry, armed with two spears, a dagger, and a sword, and protected by bronze helmet, cuirass, greaves, and shield; the second class had all of these except the cuirass; the third and fourth had no armor; the fifth had only slings and stones.

A legion was a mixed brigade of some 4200 infantry, 300 cavalry, and various auxiliary groups; [22] two legions made a consul's army. Each legion was subdivided into centuries—originally of one hundred, later of two hundred, men—commanded by centurions. Every legion had its *vexillum*—its banner or colors; honor forbade that this should ever fall into hostile hands, and clever officers sometimes threw it into the enemy's ranks to stir their men to a desperate recovery. In battle the front ranks of the infantry hurled at the foe, ten to twenty paces away, a volley of javelins—short wooden lances with an iron point—while on the wings archers and slingers attacked with arrows and stones, and the cavalry charged with pikes and swords; hand-to-hand combats with short swords were the final and decisive action. In a siege massive wooden catapults, worked by tension or torsion, hurled ten-pound rocks over 300 yards; immense battering rams, suspended on ropes, were drawn back like a swing and then released against the enemy's walls; an inclined ramp of earth and timber was built, wheeled towers were pushed and hauled up this ramp, and from these towers missiles were discharged upon the foe.[23] Instead of the solid and unwieldy phalanx—six lines of 500 men each—which the early Republic seems to have taken over from Etruria, the legion was rearranged, about 366 B.C., into maniples * of two centuries each; free room was left between each maniple and its neighbors, and the maniples of each succeeding line stood behind these open spaces. This formation made possible a rapid reinforcement of one line by the next, and a quick veering of one or more maniples to face a flank attack; and it gave free

---

* *Manipulus* meant a handful of hay, ferns, etc.; attached to a pole this seems to have formed a primitive military standard; hence the word came to mean a body of soldiers serving under the same ensign.

play to that individual combat for which the Roman soldier was especially trained.

The major element in the success of this army was discipline. The young Roman was educated for war from his childhood; he studied the military art above all others, and spent ten formative years of his life in field or camp. Cowardice was in that army the unforgivable sin, punished by flogging the offender to death.[24] The general was empowered to behead any soldier or officer, not merely for flight from battle, but for any deviation from orders, however favorable the result. Deserters or thieves had their right hands cut off.[25] Food in camp was simple: bread or porridge, some vegetables, sour wine, rarely flesh; the Roman army conquered the world on a vegetarian diet; Caesar's troops complained when corn ran out and they had to eat meat.[26] Labor was so arduous and long that the soldiers begged for battle instead; valor became the better part of discretion. The soldier received no pay till 405 B.C., and little thereafter; but he was allowed to share, according to his rank, in the booty of the defeated—bullion and currency, lands and men and movable goods. Such training made not only brave and eager warriors but able and intrepid generals; the discipline of obedience developed the capacity to command. The army of the Republic lost battles, but it never lost a war. Men molded by stoic education and brutal spectacles to a contemptuous familiarity with death carved out the victories that conquered Italy, then Carthage and Greece, and then the Mediterranean world.

Such in outline was the "mixed constitution" that Polybius admired as "the best of all existing governments": a limited democracy in the legislative sovereignty of the assemblies, an aristocracy in the leadership of the patrician Senate, a Spartan "dyarchy" in the brief royalty of the consuls, a monarchy in occasional dictatorships. Essentially it was an aristocracy, in which old and rich families, through ability and privilege, held office for hundreds of years, and gave to Roman policy a tenacious continuity that was the secret of its accomplishments.

But it had its faults. It was a clumsy confusion of checks and balances in which nearly every command could in time of peace be nullified by an equal and opposite command. The division of power was an aid to liberty and—for a while—a restraint on malfeasance; on the other hand, it led to great military disasters like Cannae, it dissolved democracy into mob rule, and at last brought on the permanent dictatorship of the Principate. What astonishes us is that such a government could last so long (508 to 49 B.C.) and achieve so much. Perhaps it endured because of its muddling adaptability to change, and the proud patriotism formed in the home, the school, the temple, the army, the Assembly, and the Senate. Devotion to the state marked the zenith of the Republic, as unparalleled political corruption marked its fall. Rome remained great as long as she had enemies who forced her to unity, vision, and heroism. When she had overcome them all she flourished for a moment and then began to die.

III. THE CONQUEST OF ITALY

Never had Rome been so encompassed by enemies as when she emerged from the monarchy as a weak city-state ruling only 350 square miles —equivalent to a space nineteen by nineteen miles. While Lars Porsena advanced upon her, many of the neighboring communities that had been subjected by her kings resumed their liberty and formed a Latin League to withstand Rome. Italy was a medley of independent tribes or cities, each with its own government and dialect: in the north the Ligures, Gauls, Umbrians, Etruscans, and Sabines; to the south the Latins, Volscians, Samnites, Lucanians, Bruttians; along the western and southern coasts Greek colonists in Cumae, Naples, Pompeii, Paestum, Locri, Rhegium, Crotona, Metapontum, Tarentum. Rome was at the center of them all, strategically placed for expansion, but perilously open to attack from all sides at once. It was her salvation that her enemies seldom united against her. In 505, while she was at war with the Sabines, a powerful Sabine clan—the Claudian *gens* —came over to Rome and was granted citizenship on favorable terms. In 449 the Sabines were defeated; by 290 all their territory was annexed to Rome, and by 250 they had received the full Roman franchise.

In 496 the Tarquins persuaded some of the towns of Latium—Tusculum, Ardea, Lanuvium, Aricia, Tibur, and others—to join in a war against Rome. Faced with this apparently overwhelming combination, the Romans appointed their first dictator, Aulus Postumius; at Lake Regillus they won a saving victory, helped, they assure us, by the gods Castor and Pollux, who left Olympus to fight in their ranks. Three years later Rome signed a treaty with the Latin League in which all parties pledged that "between the Romans and the cities of the Latins there shall be peace as long as heaven and earth shall last. . . . Both shall share equally in all booty taken in a common war." [27] Rome became a member of the League, then its leader, then its master. In 493 she fought the Volscians; it was in this conflict that Caius Marcius won the name of Coriolanus by capturing Corioli, the Volscian capital. The historians add, probably with a touch of romance, that Coriolanus became a hard reactionary, was banished on the insistence of the plebs (491), fled to the Volscians, reorganized them, and led them in a siege of Rome. The starving Romans, we are told, sent embassy after embassy to dissuade him, to no avail, until his mother and wife went out to him and, failing in their pleas, threatened to block his advance with their bodies. Thereupon he withdrew his army, and was killed by the Volscians; or, says another story, he lived among them to a bitter ripe old age.[28] In 405 Veii and Rome entered upon a duel to the death for control of the Tiber. Rome besieged the city for nine years without success, and the emboldened towns of Etruria joined in the war. Attacked on every side, and their very existence challenged, the Romans appointed a dictator, Camillus, who raised a new army, captured Veii, and divided its lands among the citizens of Rome. In 351, after sundry further wars, southern Etruria was annexed to Rome under the almost modern name of Tuscia.

Meanwhile, in 390, a new and greater peril appeared, and that long duel had begun, between Rome and Gaul, which ended only with Caesar. While Etruria and Rome were fighting fourteen wars, Celtic tribes from Gaul and Germany had filtered down through the Alps and settled in Italy as far south as the Po. Ancient historians called the invaders Keltai or Celtae, Galatae or Galli, indifferently. Nothing is known of their origin; we may only describe them as that branch of the Indo-European stock which peopled western Germany, Gaul, central Spain, Belgium, Wales, Scotland, and Ireland, and formed the pre-Roman languages there. Polybius pictures them as "tall and handsome," relishing war, and fighting naked except for golden amulets and chains.[29] When the Celts of southern Gaul tasted Italian wine, they were so pleased with it that they decided to visit the land that produced such transporting fruit; probably they were moved more by the quest for fresh acres and new pasturage. Entering, they lived for a time in abnormal peace, tilling and herding, and taking over the Etruscan culture which they found in the towns. About 400 B.C. they invaded and plundered Etruria; the Etruscans resisted weakly, having sent most of their forces to defend Veii against Rome. In 391, 30,000 Gauls reached Clusium; a year later they met the Romans at the river Allia, routed them, and entered Rome unhindered. They sacked and burned large sections of the city, and for seven months besieged the remnants of the Roman army on the Capitol—the crest of the Capitoline hill. Finally the Romans yielded, and paid the Gauls a thousand pounds of gold to depart.* They left, but returned in 367, 358, and 350; repeatedly repulsed, they at last contented themselves with northern Italy, which now became Cisalpine Gaul.

The surviving Romans found their city so devastated that many of them wished to abandon the site and make Veii their capital. Camillus dissuaded them, and the government provided financial aid for rebuilding homes. This rapid reconstruction in the face of many enemies was a part cause of Rome's designlessness and the venturesome crookedness of her narrow streets. The subject peoples, seeing her so near destruction, revolted again and again, and half a century of intermittent war was required to cure their lust for freedom. The Latins, Aequi, Hernici, and Volscians attacked in turn or together; if the Volscians had succeeded they would have shut off Rome from southern Italy and

---

* Livy's story [30] that at the last moment Camillus refused to hand over the gold, and drove the Gauls out by force, is now by common consent rejected as an invention of Roman pride. No nation is ever defeated in its textbooks.

the sea, and perhaps have put an end to her history. In 340 the cities of the Latin League were defeated; two years later Rome dissolved the League and annexed nearly all Latium.*

Meanwhile the victories of Rome over the Volscians had brought her face to face with the powerful Samnite tribes. These held a large cross section of Italy from Naples to the Adriatic, with such rich cities as Nola, Beneventum, Cumae, and Capua. They had absorbed most of the Etruscan and Greek settlements of the west coast, and enough of Hellenism to produce a distinctive Campanian art; probably they were more civilized than the Romans. With them Rome fought three long and bloody wars for the control of Italy. At the Caudine Forks (321) the Romans suffered one of their greatest defeats, and their beaten army passed "under the yoke"—an arch of hostile spears—in token of submission. The consuls at the front signed an abject peace, which the Senate refused to ratify. The Samnites won the Etruscans and Gauls as allies, and for a time Rome faced nearly all Italy in arms. But the legions gained a decisive victory at Sentinum (295), and Rome added Campania and Umbria to her domain. Twelve years later she drove the Gauls back beyond the Po, and again reduced Etruria to a subject state.

Between the Gallic north and the Greek south, Rome was now master of Italy. Insatiate and insecure, she offered the cities of Magna Graecia a choice between alliance under Roman hegemony and war. Preferring Rome to further absorption by the "barbarian" (i.e., Italian) tribes who were multiplying around and within them, Thurii, Locri, and Crotona consented; probably they, too, like the towns of Latium, were troubled by class war, and received Roman garrisons as a protection of property owners against a rising plebs.[32] Tarentum was obstinate, and called over to her aid Pyrrhus, King of Epirus. This gallant warrior, fevered with memories of Achilles and Alexander, crossed the Adriatic with an Epirote force, defeated the Romans at Heraclea (280), and gave an adjective to European languages by mourning the costliness of his victory.[33] All the Greek cities of Italy now joined him, and the Lucanians, Bruttians, and Samnites declared themselves his allies. He dispatched Cineas to Rome with offers of peace, and freed his 2000 Roman prisoners on their word to return if Rome preferred war. The Senate was about to make terms when old blind Appius Claudius, who had long since retired from public life, had himself carried to the senate house and demanded that Rome should never make peace with a foreign army on Italian soil. The Senate sent back to Pyrrhus the prisoners whom he had released, and resumed the war. The young king won another victory; then, disgusted with the sloth and cowardice of his allies, he sailed with his

---

* This war was marked by two probably legendary deeds. One consul, Publius Decius, rode to his death amid the enemy as a sacrifice to win the aid of the gods for Rome; the other consul, Titus Manlius Torquatus, beheaded his son for winning an engagement by disobeying orders.[31]

depleted army to Sicily. He relieved the Carthaginian siege of Syracuse and drove the Carthaginians from nearly all their possessions on the island; but his imperious rule offended the Sicilian Greeks, who thought they could have freedom without order and courage; they withdrew their support, and Pyrrhus returned to Italy, saying of Sicily, "What a prize I leave to be fought for by Carthage and Rome!" His army met the Romans at Beneventum, where for the first time he suffered defeat (275); the light-armed and mobile maniples proved superior to the unwieldy phalanxes, and began a new chapter in military history. Pyrrhus appealed to his Italian allies for new troops; they refused, doubting his fidelity and persistence. He returned to Epirus, and died an adventurer's death in Greece. In that same year (272) Milo betrayed Tarentum to Rome. Soon all the Greek cities yielded, the Samnites sullenly surrendered, and Rome was at last, after two centuries of war, the ruler of Italy.

The conquest was quickly consolidated with colonies, some sent out by the Latin League, some by Rome. These colonies served many purposes: they relieved unemployment, the pressure of population upon the means of subsistence, and consequent class strife in Rome; they acted as garrisons or loyal nuclei amid disaffected subjects, provided outposts and outlets for Roman trade, and raised additional food for hungry mouths in the capital; conquests in Italy were completed with the plow soon after they had been begun by the sword. In these ways hundreds of Italian towns that still live today received their foundation or their Romanization. The Latin language and culture were spread throughout a peninsula still largely polyglot and barbarous, and Italy was slowly forged into a united state. The first step had been taken in a political synthesis brutal in execution, majestic in result.

But in Corsica, Sardinia, Sicily, and Africa, closing the western Mediterranean to Roman trade, and imprisoning Italy in her own seas, stood a power older and richer than Rome.

CHAPTER III

Hannibal Against Rome

264-202 B.C.

I. CARTHAGE

SOME eleven hundred years before our era the inquisitive traders of Phoenicia discovered the mineral wealth of Spain. Soon a fleet of merchant vessels plied between Sidon, Tyre, and Byblus, at one end of the Mediterranean, and Tartessus, at the mouth of the Guadalquivir, on the other. Since such voyages could not then be made without many stops, and the southern shores of the Mediterranean provided the shortest and safest route, the Phoenicians established intermediate posts and trading stations on the African coast at Leptis Magna (now Lebda), Hadrumetum (Sousse), Utica (Utique), Hippo Diarrhytus (Bizerte), Hippo Regius (Bone), and even beyond Gibraltar at Lixus (south of Tangier). The Semitic settlers at these posts married some of the natives and bribed the rest to peace. About 813 B.C. a new group of colonists, perhaps from Phoenicia, perhaps from expanding Utica, built their homes upon a promontory ten miles northwest of the modern Tunis. The narrow peninsula could be easily defended, and the land, watered by the Bagradas (Medjerda) River, was so fertile that it quickly recovered from repeated devastation. Classic tradition ascribed the founding of the city to Elissa, or Dido, daughter of the king of Tyre: her husband having been slain by her brother, she had sailed with other adventurous souls to Africa. Her settlement was called *Kart-hadasht*—Newtown—to distinguish it from Utica; the Greeks transformed the name into *Karchedon*, the Romans into *Carthago*. The Latins gave the name Africa to the region around Carthage and Utica, and followed the Greeks in calling its Semitic population *Poeni*—i.e., Phoenicians. The sieges of Tyre by Shalmaneser, Nebuchadrezzar, and Alexander drove many wealthy Tyrians to Africa. Most of them went to Carthage, and made it a new center of Phoenician trade. Carthage grew in power and splendor as Tyre and Sidon declined.

The strengthened city drove the African natives farther and farther inland, ceased to pay tribute to them, exacted tribute from them, and used them as slaves and serfs in its homes and fields. Large estates took form, some

with 20,000 men;[1] in the hands of the practical Phoenicians agriculture became a science and an industry, which the Carthaginian Mago summarized
in a famous manual. Irrigated with canals, the soil flowered into gardens,
cornfields, vineyards, and orchards of olives, pomegranates, pears, cherries,
and figs.[2] Horses and cattle, sheep and goats, were bred; asses and mules were
the beasts of burden, and the elephant was one of many domesticated animals. Urban industry was relatively immature, except for metalwork; the
Carthaginians, like their Asiatic forebears, preferred to trade what others
made. They led their pack mules east and west and across the Sahara to
find elephants, ivory, gold, or slaves. Their immense galleys carried goods
to and from a hundred ports between Asia and Britain, for they refused to
turn back, like most other mariners, at the Pillars of Hercules. It was presumably they who, about 490 B.C., financed Hanno's voyage of exploration
2600 miles down the Atlantic coast of Africa, and the voyage of Himilco
along the northern shores of Europe. Though their coinage was undistinguished, they were apparently the first to issue the equivalent of a paper
currency—leather strips stamped with signs of value, and accepted throughout the Carthaginian realm.

Probably it was the rich merchants, rather than the aristocratic landowners, who provided the funds for those armies and navies which transformed Carthage from a trading post into an empire. The African coast—
except Utica—was conquered from Cyrenaica to Gibraltar and beyond.
Tartessus, Gades (Cádiz), and other Spanish towns were captured, and
Carthage grew wealthy from the gold, silver, iron, and copper of Spain. It
took the Balearic Islands, and reached out even to Madeira; it conquered
Malta, Sardinia, Corsica, and the western half of Sicily. It treated these
subject lands with varying degrees of severity, charging them annual tribute,
conscripting their population for its army, and strictly controlling their
foreign relations and their trade. In return it gave them military protection,
local self-government, and economic stability. We may judge the wealth
of these dependencies from the fact that the town of Leptis Minor paid 365
talents ($1,314,000) a year into the Carthaginian treasury.

The exploitation of this empire and trade made Carthage, in the third
century B.C., the richest of Mediterranean cities. Tariffs and tribute brought
her annually 12,000 talents—twenty times the revenue of Athens at her
zenith. The upper classes lived in palaces, wore costly robes, and ate exotic
delicacies. The city, crowded with a quarter of a million inhabitants, became
famous for its gleaming temples, its public baths, above all for its secure
harbors and spacious docks. Each of the 220 docks was faced with two
Ionic pillars, so that the inner harbor ("cothon") presented a majestic circle
of 440 marble columns. Thence a broad avenue led to the Forum, a colon-

naded square adorned with Greek sculpture and containing administrative buildings, commercial offices, law courts, and temples; while the adjoining streets, Orientally narrow, teemed with a thousand shops plying a hundred crafts and resounded with bargaining. Houses rose to six stories, and often crowded a family into a single room. In the center of the city, providing one of many hints to the later builders of Rome, stood a hill or citadel— the Byrsa; here were the Treasury and the Mint, more shrines and colonnades, and the most brilliant of Carthaginian temples—to the great god Eshmun. Around the landward side of the city ran a threefold protective wall forty-five feet high, with still higher towers and battlements; within the wall were accommodations for 4000 horses, 300 elephants, and 20,000 men.[3] Outside the walls were the estates of the rich, and beyond these, the fields of the poor.

The Carthaginians were Semites, akin in blood and features to the ancient Jews. Their language now and then struck a Hebraic note, as when it called the chief magistrates *shofetes*—the Hebrew *shophetim*, or judges. The men grew beards, but usually shaved the upper lip with bronze razors. Most of them wore a fez or a turban, shoes or sandals, and a long loose gown; but the upper classes adopted the Greek style of dress, dyed their robes with purple, and fringed them with glass beads. The women led for the most part a veiled and secluded life; they could rise to high place in the priesthoods but otherwise had to be contented with the sovereignty of their charms. Both sexes used jewelry and perfume, and occasionally displayed a ring in the nose. We know little of their morals except from their enemies. Greek and Roman writers describe them as heavy eaters and drinkers, loving to gather in dinner clubs, and as loose in their sex relations as they were corrupt in their politics. The treacherous Romans employed *fides Punica*—Carthaginian faith—as a synonym for treachery. Polybius reported that "at Carthage nothing that results in profit is regarded as disgraceful."[4] Plutarch denounced the Carthaginians as "harsh and gloomy, docile to their rulers, hard to their subjects, running to extremes of cowardice in fear and of savagery in anger, stubborn in decisions, austere, and unresponsive to amusement or the graces of life."[5] But Plutarch, though usually fair, was always a Greek; and Polybius was bosom friend of the Scipio who burned Carthage to the ground.

The Carthaginians appear at their worst in their religion, which again we know only from their enemies. Their ancestors in Phoenicia had worshiped Baal-Moloch and Astarte as personifying the male and female principles in nature, and the sun and moon in the sky; the Carthaginians addressed similar devotions to corresponding deities—Baal-Haman and Tanith. Tanith above all aroused their loving piety; they filled her temples with gifts, and took her name in their oaths. Third in honor was the god Melkart, "Key of the City"; then Eshmun, god of wealth and health; then a host of minor gods—"baals" or lords; even Dido was worshiped.[6] To Baal-Haman, in great crises, living children were sacrificed, as many as three hundred in a day. They were placed upon the inclined and outstretched arms of the idol and rolled off into the fire beneath; their cries were drowned in the noise of trumpets and cymbals; their mothers were required to look upon the scene without moan or tear, lest they be accused of impiety and lose the credit due them from the god. In time the rich refused to sacrifice their own children and bought substitutes among the poor; but when Agathocles of Syracuse besieged Carthage, the upper classes, fearing that their subterfuge had offended the god, cast two hundred aristocratic infants into the fire.[7] It should be added that these stories are told us by Diodorus, a Sicilian Greek, who looked with equanimity upon the Greek custom of infanticide. It may be that the Carthaginian sacrifice solaced with piety an effort to control the excesses of human fertility.

When the Romans destroyed Carthage they presented the libraries they found there to their African allies. Of these collections nothing survives except Hanno's record of his voyage, and fragments of Mago on husbandry. Saint Augustine vaguely assures us that "in Carthage there were many things wisely handed down to memory,"[8] and Sallust and Juba made use of Carthaginian historians; but we have no native account of Carthage's history. Of its architecture the Romans left not a stone upon a stone. We are told that its style was a mixture of Phoenician and Greek, that its temples were massive and ornate; that the temple and statue of Baal-Haman were plated with gold valued at a thousand talents;[9] and that even the proud Greeks considered Carthage one of the world's most beautiful capitals. The museums of Tunis contain some pieces of sculpture from sarcophagi found in tombs near the site of Carthage; the finest is a strong and graceful figure, perhaps of Tanith, in a manner essentially Greek. Smaller statues, unearthed from Carthaginian graves in the Baleares, are crude and often repulsively grotesque, as if designed to impress children or frighten devils away. The surviving pottery is purely utilitarian; but we know that Carthaginian craftsmen did good work in textiles, jewelry, ivory, ebony, amber, and glass.

Any clear picture of Carthaginian government is now beyond our pens. Aristotle praised the constitution of Carthage as "in many respects superior to all others," for "a state is proved to be well ordered when the commons are steadily loyal to the constitution, when no civil conflict worth speaking of has arisen, and when no one has succeeded in making himself dictator."[10] The citizens met occasionally in an Assembly empowered to accept or reject, but not to discuss or amend, proposals referred to it by a Senate of three hundred elders; the Senate, however, was not obliged to submit to the Assembly any measures upon which it could itself agree.[11] The people elected the Senate, but open bribery reduced the virtue or danger of this democratic procedure, and replaced an aristocracy of birth with an oligarchy of wealth. From nominations presented by the Senate, the Assembly annually chose two *shofetes* to head the judicial and administrative branches of the state. Above all these bodies was a court of 104 judges, who, in contravention of the law, held office for life. As it was empowered to supervise all administration, and to require an accounting from every official at the end of his term, this court acquired, by the time of the Punic Wars, supreme control over every governmental agency and every citizen.

The commander of the armies was nominated by the Senate and chosen by the Assembly. He was in a better position than the Roman consul, for his command could be continued as long as the Senate desired. The Roman, however, led against Carthage legions of landowning patriots, whereas the Carthaginian army was a mercenary force of foreign—chiefly Libyan—origin, feeling no affection for Carthage, but loyal only to its paymaster and, occasionally, to its general. The Carthaginian navy was without question the most powerful of its time; 500 quinqueremes, gaily painted, slim and swift, ably protected Carthaginian colonies, markets, and trade routes. It was the conquest of Sicily by this army, and the closing of the western Mediterranean to Roman commerce by this navy, that brought on the century-long duel to the death known to us as the three Punic Wars.

II. REGULUS

The two nations had once been friends when one of them was strong enough to dominate the other. In 508 they had made a treaty that recognized the hegemony of Rome over the coast of Latium, but pledged the Romans not to sail the Mediterranean west of Carthage, nor to land in Sardinia or Libya except for the brief repair or provisioning of ships.[12] It became a common practice among the Carthaginians, says a Greek geographer, to drown any foreign sailor found between Sardinia and Gibraltar.[13] The Greeks of Massalia (Marseilles) had developed a peaceful coastal commerce between southern Gaul and northeastern Spain; Carthage, we are told, warred on this trade piratically, and Massalia was a faithful ally of Rome. (We do not know how much of this is war propaganda dignified as history.) Now that Rome controlled Italy she could not feel secure so long as two hostile powers—Greeks and Carthaginians—held Sicily, hardly a mile from the Italian coast. Besides, Sicily was fertile; it might supply half of Italy with grain. Sicily taken, Sardinia and Corsica would of themselves fall into Roman hands. Here was manifest destiny, the natural next step in the expansion of Rome.

How to find a *casus belli*? About 264 B.C. a band of Samnite mercenaries who called themselves Mamertines—i.e., "Men of Mars"—seized the town of

Messana, on the Sicilian coast nearest to Italy. They slew or expelled the Greek citizens, divided among themselves the women, children, and goods of the victims, and made a living by raiding the Greek cities near by. Hiero II, Dictator of Syracuse, besieged them; a Carthaginian force landed at Messana, drove Hiero back, and took possession of the city. The Mamertines appealed to Rome for help in expelling their saviors. The Senate hesitated, knowing the power and wealth of Carthage; but the rich plebeians who dominated the Centurial Assembly clamored for war and Sicily. Rome decided that at whatever cost she must keep the Carthaginians from so near and strategic a port. A fleet was fitted out and dispatched under Caius Claudius to rescue the Mamertines. But these had meanwhile been persuaded by the Carthaginians to withdraw their request for Roman aid, and a message from them to this effect reached Claudius at Rhegium. Ignoring it, he crossed the strait, invited the Carthaginian commander to a conference, imprisoned him, and sent word to the Carthaginian army that he would be killed if they resisted. The mercenaries welcomed so gallant an excuse for avoiding the legions, and Messana fell to Rome.

Two heroes were thrown up by this First Punic War: on the Roman side, Regulus; on the Carthaginian, Hamilcar. Perhaps we should add a third and fourth—the Senate and the Roman people. The Senate won Hiero of Syracuse to Rome's side, and thereby assured supplies for Roman troops in Sicily; it organized the nation with wisdom and resolution, and led it to victory through almost overwhelming disasters. The citizens provided money, materials, labor, and men to build Rome's first fleet—330 vessels, nearly all quinqueremes 150 feet long, each manned by 300 rowers and 120 soldiers, and most of them equipped with novel grappling irons and movable gangways for seizing and boarding enemy ships; by these means naval warfare, unfamiliar to the Romans, could be turned into hand-to-hand combat, in which the legionaries could use all their disciplined skill. "This fact," says Polybius, "shows us better than anything else how spirited and daring the Romans are when they are determined to do a thing. . . . They had never given a thought to a navy; yet when they had once conceived the project they took it in hand so boldly that before gaining any experience in such matters they at once engaged the Carthaginians, who for generations had held undisputed command of the sea."[14] Off Ecnomus, on the southern coast of Sicily, the hostile fleets, carrying 300,000 men, fought the greatest sea battle of antiquity (256). The Romans under Regulus won decisively and sailed on unhindered to Africa. Landing there without careful reconnaissance, they soon met a superior Carthaginian force, which almost annihilated them, and took their reckless consul prisoner. Shortly afterward the Roman fleet was dashed by a storm against a rocky coast, 284 vessels were wrecked,

and some 80,000 men were drowned; it was the worst naval calamity in the memory of men. The Romans showed their quality by building 200 new quinqueremes in three months, and training 80,000 men to man them.

After keeping Regulus a prisoner for five years, his captors allowed him to accompany a Carthaginian embassy sent to Rome to seek peace, but on his promise to return to captivity if the Senate refused the proffered terms. When Regulus heard these he advised the Senate to reject them and, despite the entreaties of his family and his friends, went back with the embassy to Carthage. There he was tortured to death by being prevented from sleeping.[15] His sons at Rome took two Carthaginian captives of high rank, bound them in a chest studded with spikes, and kept them awake till they died.[16] Neither tale seems credible, until we recall the barbarities of our time.

III. HAMILCAR

Of Hamilcars, Hasdrubals, and Hannibals Carthage had an abundance, for these names were given in almost every generation in their oldest families. They were pious names, formed from those of the gods: *Hamilcar* was "He whom Melkart protects"; *Hasdrubal* was "He whose help is Baal"; *Hannibal* was the very "Grace of Baal." Our present Hamilcar was surnamed Barca —"lightning"; it was his nature to strike swiftly, suddenly, anywhere. He was still a youth when (247) Carthage gave him supreme command of its forces. Taking a small fleet, he harassed the coast of Italy with surprise landings, destroying Roman outposts and taking many prisoners. Then, in the face of a Roman army holding Panormus (Palermo), he disembarked his troops and captured a height overlooking the town. His contingent was too small to risk a major engagement; but every time he led it forth it returned with spoils. He begged the Carthaginian Senate for reinforcements and supplies; it refused, hugged its hoards, and bade him feed and clothe his soldiers on the country that surrounded him.

Meanwhile the Roman fleet had won another victory, but had suffered a serious defeat at Drepana (249). Worn out almost equally, the two nations rested for nine years. But while in those years Carthage did nothing, relying upon the genius of Hamilcar, a number of Roman citizens voluntarily presented to the state a fleet of 200 men-of-war, carrying 60,000 troops. This new armada, sailing secretly, caught the Carthaginian fleet unprepared at the Aegadian Isles off the west coast of Sicily, and so overwhelmed it that Carthage sued for peace (241). Carthaginian Sicily was surrendered to Rome, an annual indemnity of 440 talents was pledged to Rome for ten years, and all Carthaginian restrictions on Roman trade were withdrawn.

The war had lasted nearly twenty-four years and had brought Rome so near to bankruptcy that its currency was debased eighty-three per cent. But it had proved the irresistible tenacity of the Roman character and the superiority of an army composed of free men over mercenaries seeking the greatest booty for the least blood.

Carthage was now to be all but destroyed by its own greed. It had withheld for some time the pay of its mercenaries, even of those who had served Hamilcar well. They poured into the city and demanded their money; and when the government temporized and tried to disperse them, they broke into mad revolt. Carthage's subject peoples, taxed beyond endurance during the war, joined the uprising, and the women of Libya sold their jewels to finance revolution. Twenty thousand mercenaries and rebels, led by Matho, a Libyan freeman, and Spendius, a Campanian slave, laid siege to Carthage at a time when hardly a soldier was there to defend it. The rich merchants trembled for their lives and appealed to Hamilcar to save them. Torn between affection for his mercenaries and his city, Hamilcar organized an army of 10,000 Carthaginians, trained them, led them forth, and raised the siege. The defeated mercenaries, retreating into the mountains, cut off the hands and feet of Gesco, a Carthaginian general, and 700 other prisoners, broke their legs, and then threw the still living victims into an indiscriminate grave.[17] Hamilcar maneuvered 40,000 of the rebels into a defile and blocked all exits so well that they began to starve. They ate their remaining captives, then their slaves; at last they sent Spendius to beg for peace. Hamilcar crucified Spendius and had hundreds of prisoners trampled to death under elephants' feet. The mercenaries tried to fight their way out, but were cut to pieces. Matho was captured and was made to run through the streets of Carthage while the citizens beat him with thongs and tortured him till he died.[18] This "War of the Mercenaries" lasted forty months (241-237), and "was by far," said Polybius, "the most bloody and impious war in history." [19] When the conflict was over, Carthage found that Rome had occupied Sardinia. Carthage protested, and Rome declared war. The desperate Carthaginians bought peace only by paying Rome an additional 1200 talents, and surrendering Sardinia and Corsica.

We may judge the fury of Hamilcar at this treatment of his country. He proposed to his government that it should provide him with troops and funds to re-establish the power of Carthage in Spain, as a steppingstone to an attack upon Italy. The landowning aristocracy opposed the plan, fearing further war; the mercantile middle class, resenting the loss of their foreign markets and ports, supported it. As a compromise Hamilcar was given a modest contingent, with which he crossed to Spain (238). He recaptured the cities whose allegiance to Carthage had lapsed during the war, built up his army with native recruits, financed and equipped it with the products of Spain's mines, and died while leading a charge against a Spanish tribe (229).

He left behind him in the camp his son-in-law Hasdrubal, and his sons Hannibal, Hasdrubal, and Mago—his "lion's-brood." The son-in-law was chosen commander, and for eight years governed wisely, winning the co-operation of the Spaniards and building near the silver mines a great city, known to Rome as Nova Carthago, or New Carthage—the Cartagena of today. When he was assassinated (221), the army elected as its leader Hamilcar's eldest son, Hannibal, then twenty-six years of age. Before leaving Carthage, his father had brought him, a boy of nine, to the altar of Baal-Haman and had bidden him swear that someday he would revenge his country against Rome. Hannibal swore, and did not forget.

IV. HANNIBAL

Why had Rome permitted the reconquest of Spain? Because she was harassed with class strife, was expanding in the Adriatic, and was at war with the Gauls. In 232 a tribune, Caius Flaminius, foreshadowed the Gracchi by carrying through the Assembly, against the violent opposition of the Senate, a measure distributing among the poorer citizens some lands recently won from the Gauls. In 230 Rome took her first step toward the conquest of Greece by clearing the Adriatic of pirates and seizing a part of the Illyrian coast as a further protection for Italian trade. Safe now on south and east, she resolved to drive the Gauls over the Alps and make Italy a completely united state. To secure herself on the west she signed a treaty with Hasdrubal by which the Carthaginians in Spain agreed to stay south of the Ebro River; and at the same time she made an alliance with the semi-Greek towns of Saguntum and Ampurias in Spain. In the following year (225) a Gallic army of 50,000 foot and 20,000 horse swept down the peninsula. The inhabitants of the capital were so frightened that the Senate returned to the primitive custom of human sacrifice and buried two Gauls alive in the Forum as an appeasement of the gods.[20] The legions met the invaders near Telamon, killed 40,000, took 10,000 prisoners, and marched on to subjugate all Cisalpine Gaul. In three years the task was completed; protective colonies were established at Placentia and Cremona, and from the Alps to Sicily Italy was one.

It was an untimely victory. Had the Gauls been left unmolested for a few years more they might have stopped Hannibal; but now all Gaul was aflame against Rome. Hannibal saw the opportunity he had longed for—

to cross Gaul with little opposition and to invade Italy with Gallic tribes as his allies.

The Punic leader was now twenty-eight years old, at his prime in body and mind. In addition to a Carthaginian gentleman's schooling in the languages, literatures, and history of Phoenicia and Greece,[21] he had received a soldier's training through nineteen years in camp. He had disciplined his body to hardship, his appetite to moderation, his tongue to silence, his thought to objectivity. He could run or ride with the swiftest, hunt or fight with the bravest; he was "the first to enter the battle," says the hostile Livy, "and the last to abandon the field."[22] The veterans loved him because in his commanding presence and piercing eyes they saw their old leader Hamilcar return to them in fresh youth; the recruits liked him because he wore no distinctive dress, never rested till he had provided for his army's needs, and shared with them all sufferings and gains. The Romans accused him of avarice, cruelty, and treachery, for he honored no scruples in seizing supplies for his troops, punished disloyalty severely, and laid many snares for his foes. Yet we find him often merciful, always chivalrous. "Nothing occurs in the accounts of him," says the judicious Mommsen, "which may not be justified under the circumstances, and according to the international law of the times."[23] The Romans could not readily forgive him for winning battles with his brains rather than with the lives of his men. The tricks he played upon them, the skill of his espionage, the subtlety of his strategy, the surprises of his tactics were beyond their appreciation until Carthage was destroyed.

In 219 B.C. Roman agents organized in Saguntum a *coup d'état* that set up a government patriotically hostile to Carthage. When the Saguntines molested tribes friendly to him, Hannibal ordered them to desist; when they refused he besieged the city. Rome protested to Carthage and threatened war; Carthage replied that since Saguntum was a hundred miles south of the Ebro, Rome had no right to interfere, and had, by signing an alliance with it, violated her treaty with Hasdrubal. Hannibal persisted in the siege, and Rome took up arms again, never dreaming that this Second Punic War was to be the most terrible in her history.

Hannibal spent eight months in subduing the Saguntines; he did not dare advance toward Italy while leaving to the Romans so excellent a port for landing in his rear. In 218 he crossed the Ebro, challenging fate as Caesar would at the Rubicon. He had an army of 50,000 infantry and 9000 cavalry, none of them mercenaries, most of them Spaniards and Libyans. Three thousand Spaniards deserted when they learned that he planned to cross the Alps, and Hannibal released 7000 others who protested against his enterprise as impossible.[24] It was hard enough to force a passage through the

Pyrenees; more unexpected was the fierce resistance of some Gallic tribes allied with Marseilles; a summer of fighting was required to reach the Rhone, and a major battle to cross it. He had hardly left its banks when a Roman army arrived at the mouth of the river.

Hannibal led his troops north toward Vienne and then struck eastward into the Alps. Celtic hordes had crossed those ranges before him, and he too might have done it without extraordinary hardship had it not been for the hostility of the Alpine tribes, and the difficulty of getting his elephants through narrow or precipitous passages. Early in September, after a climb of nine days, he reached the summit and found it covered with snow; there he let his men and animals rest for two days and then began the downward march through passes steeper than the ascent, over roads sometimes buried by landslides and often paved with ice. Many soldiers and beasts lost their footing and tumbled to their deaths. Hannibal spurred on his despairing forces by pointing out to them, in the distant south, the green fields and sparkling streams of Italy; that paradise, he promised them, would soon be theirs. After seventeen days in the Alps they reached the plain and rested. So many men and horses had been lost in the crossing that the army was now reduced to 26,000—less than half the force that had left New Carthage four months before. Had the Cisalpine Gauls resisted him as the Transalpine Gauls had done, Hannibal's progress might have ended there. But the Boii and other tribes welcomed him as a savior and joined him as allies, while the recently established Roman settlers fled southward across the Po.

Faced with this second threat in seven years to the very life of Rome, the Senate mobilized all its resources and called upon the states of Italy to unite in the defense of their land. With their help Rome raised armies totaling 300,000 foot, 14,000 horse, and 456,000 reserves. One army, under the first of many famous Scipios, met Hannibal along the Ticino—a small river flowing into the Po at Pavia. Hannibal's Numidian cavalry put the Romans to flight, and Scipio, dangerously wounded, was saved by the brave interposition of the son who was destined to meet Hannibal again at Zama sixteen years later. At Lake Trasimene Hannibal encountered another Roman army, 30,000 strong, led by the tribune Caius Flaminius, and accompanied by slave dealers bringing fetters and chains for the prospective prisoners whom they hoped to sell. With part of his forces Hannibal decoyed this army into a plain surrounded by hills and woods that concealed most of his troops; at his signal the hidden columns debouched upon the Romans from every side and killed nearly all of them, including Flaminius himself (217).

Hannibal now controlled all northern Italy, but he knew that he was still outnumbered ten to one by a resolute foe. His only hope lay in persuading at least some of the Italian states to revolt against Rome. He released all prisoners whom he had taken from Rome's allies, saying that he had come not to fight Italy but to set it free. He marched through flooded Etruria, where for four days no dry land could be found on which to pitch a camp; crossed the Apennines to the Adriatic, and there allowed his soldiers a long interval to refresh their energies and heal their wounds. He himself suffered from severe ophthalmia, took no time to treat it, and lost the use of one eye. Then he marched down the eastern coast, inviting the Italian tribes to join him. None did; on the contrary, every city closed its gates against him and prepared to fight. As he moved south, his Gallic allies, interested only in their northern homes, began to desert him. Plots against his life were so numerous that he had to assume ever new disguises. He begged his government to send him supplies and men by some Adriatic port; it refused. He asked his younger brother Hasdrubal, whom he had left in Spain, to organize an army and cross Gaul and the Alps to join him; but the Romans had invaded Spain, and Hasdrubal did not dare to leave it. Ten years were to pass before his coming.

Rome now adopted against her greatest adversary his own baffling policy of caution and attrition. Quintus Fabius Maximus, made dictator in 217, created an adjective by delaying as long as he could a direct engagement with Hannibal; in time, he believed, the invaders would be reduced by hunger, discord, and disease. After a year this "masterly inaction" irritated the Roman populace; the Assembly overruled the Senate, as well as all precedents and logic, by electing Minucius Rufus codictator with Fabius. Against Fabius' advice Minucius advanced against the enemy, fell into a trap, was severely beaten, and thereafter understood why Hannibal said that he feared Fabius, who would not fight, more than Marcellus, who would.[25] A year later Fabius was deposed, and the Roman armies were entrusted to Lucius Aemilius Paulus and Caius Terentius Varro. Paulus the aristocrat counseled caution; Varro of the plebs was all for action; and as usual, caution lost the argument. Varro sought and found the Carthaginians at Cannae, in Apulia, some ten miles from the Adriatic coast. The Romans had 80,000 infantry, 6000 cavalry; Hannibal had 19,000 veterans, 16,000 unreliable Gauls, 10,000 horse; and he had lured Varro to fight in a broad plain ideal for cavalry. He had placed the Gauls at his center, expecting that they would give way. They did; and when the Romans followed them into the pocket, the subtle Carthaginian, himself in the thick of the fray, ordered his veterans to close in upon the Roman flanks and bade his cavalry smash through the opposed horsemen to attack the legions from behind. The Roman army was surrounded, lost all chance of maneuvering, and was almost annihilated; 44,000 of them fell, including Paulus and eighty senators who had enlisted as soldiers; 10,000 escaped to Canusium, among them Varro and the Scipio who was to win the surname of Africanus Maior (216). Hannibal lost 6000 men, two thirds of them Gauls. It was a supreme example of generalship, never bettered in history. It ended the days of Roman reliance upon infantry, and set the lines of military tactics for two thousand years.

V. SCIPIO

The disaster shattered Rome's hegemony in southern Italy. Samnites, Bruttians, Lucanians, Metapontum, Thurii, Crotona, Locri, and Capua joined Cisalpine Gaul in attaching themselves to Hannibal; only Umbria, Latium, and Etruria remained firm. Hiero of Syracuse was loyal to the death, but his successors declared for Carthage. Philip V of Macedon, fearful of Roman expansion through Illyria into the east, allied himself with Hannibal and declared war upon Rome. Carthage herself became interested and sent Hannibal meager reinforcements and supplies. Some of the young Roman nobles among the survivors at Canusium thought the situation hopeless and meditated flight to Greece, but Scipio shamed them into courage. Rome was for a month hysterical with terror; only a small garrison remained to protect it against Hannibal. Matrons of high family ran weeping to the temples and cleansed with their hair the statues of the gods; some whose husbands and sons had fallen in battle cohabited with foreigners and slaves lest their strain should die. To regain the favor of obviously offended deities the Senate again sanctioned human sacrifice and buried alive two Gauls and two Greeks.[26]

But the Romans, says Polybius, "were most to be feared when they stood in real danger. . . . Though they were now so overwhelmingly defeated, and their military reputation had been destroyed, yet, by the peculiar virtues of their constitution, and by wise counsel, they not only recovered their supremacy in Italy . . . but in a few years made themselves masters of the world."[27] The class war ceased, and all groups rushed to the rescue of the state. Taxes had already risen apparently beyond tolerance; but now the citizens, even widows and children, voluntarily brought their secret savings to the Treasury. Every male who could bear arms was called to the colors; slaves were accepted in the levies and were promised freedom in the event of victory. Not a single soldier would consent to receive pay. Rome prepared to contest every inch of ground against the new lion of Carthage.

But Hannibal did not come. His 40,000 men were too small a force, he thought, to besiege a city to whose defense many armies would converge from still loyal states; and if he took it, how could he hold it? His Italian allies, instead of strengthening, weakened him; Rome and her friends were raising forces to attack them, and without his help they would succumb. His aides reproached his caution, and one of them remarked, sadly, "The gods have not given all their gifts to one man. You know how to win victory, Hannibal, but you do not know how to use it."[28] Hannibal decided to wait till Carthage, Macedon, and Syracuse could unite with him in a multiple offensive that would retake Sicily, Sardinia, Corsica, and Illyria, and compel Rome to confine her power to Italy. He released all captives except Romans, and offered these to Rome for a small ransom. When the Senate refused this he sent most of them to Carthage as slaves, and forced the rest, in Roman style, to amuse his men by gladiatorial combats, even to the death. He besieged and took several towns and then led his army to winter in Capua.

It was the most pleasant and dangerous place that he could have chosen. For this second city of Italy—some twelve miles north of Naples—had learned from the Etruscans and the Greeks the vices as well as the graces of civilization; and Hannibal's troops felt entitled to indulge for a season the flesh that had borne so many hardships and wounds. They were never again the invincible soldiers who had through many campaigns been formed in their master's Spartan image. In the next five years Hannibal led them to some minor successes; but while they were so engaged the Romans laid siege to Capua. Hannibal sought to relieve it by marching to within a few miles of Rome; the Romans raised twenty-five new legions—200,000 men— and Hannibal, still limited to 40,000, retired to the south. In 211 Capua fell; its leaders, who had let loose a massacre of Romans in the city, were beheaded or committed suicide; and the population, which had strongly supported Hannibal, was dispersed throughout Italy. A year before, Marcellus had taken Syracuse; and a year later Agrigentum yielded to Rome.

Meanwhile a Roman army under the two older Scipios had been sent to Spain to keep Hasdrubal occupied. They defeated him at the Ebro (215); but both of them were soon afterward killed in battle, and their gains were being lost when their son and nephew, Scipio Africanus, was dispatched to the Spanish command. He was but twenty-four, far below the legal age for so responsible a position; but the Senate was willing to stretch the constitution to save the state, and the Assembly was by this time voluntarily subordinating itself to the Senate. The people admired him not only because he was handsome and eloquent, intelligent and brave, but pious, courteous, and just. It was his custom, before undertaking an enterprise, to commune with the gods in the temples on the Capitol, and, after his victories, to reward them with hecatombs. He believed—or represented—himself to be a favorite of Heaven; his successes spread the belief and filled his followers with confidence. He soon restored discipline among the troops, captured Nova Carthago after a long siege, and scrupulously turned over to the Treasury the precious metal and stones that there fell into his hands. Most of the Spanish cities surrendered to him, and by 205 Spain had become a Roman province.

Nevertheless, Hasdrubal's main force had escaped and now crossed Gaul and the Alps into Italy. The young leader's message to Hannibal was intercepted, and his plan of campaign was revealed to Rome. A Roman army met his modest force at the Metaurus River (207) and defeated him despite his excellent generalship. Seeing the battle lost and all hope of reaching his brother gone, Hasdrubal leaped into the midst of the legions and took death in his stride. The Roman historians, perhaps romancing, tell us that the victor cut off the youth's head and sent it through Apulia to be cast over the ramparts into Hannibal's camp. Broken in spirit by the fate of a brother whom he had dearly loved, Hannibal withdrew his thinned-out forces to Bruttium. "No action was fought with him this year," says Livy, "nor did the Romans care to disturb him, so great was the reputation of his powers even while his cause was everywhere round him crumbling into ruin." [29] Carthage sent him a hundred ships laden with men and food, but a gale drove the vessels to Sardinia, where a Roman fleet sank or captured eighty of them; the rest fled home.

In 205 young Scipio, fresh from his victories in Spain, was chosen consul, raised a new army, and sailed for Africa. The Carthaginian government appealed to Hannibal to come to the help of the city that had so long refused to support him. How shall we imagine the feelings of the half-blind warrior, driven into a corner of Italy by an endless stream of enemies, seeing all his toil and hardships of fifteen years brought to nothing, and all his triumphs summing up to futility and flight? Half of his troops refused to embark with him for Carthage; according to hostile historians he had 20,000 of them killed for disobedience and for fear that Rome might add them to her legions.[30] Touching his native soil after an absence of thirty-six years, he hastily formed a new army and went out to face Scipio at Zama, fifty miles south of Carthage (202). The two generals met in a courteous interview, found agreement impossible, and joined battle. For the first time in his life Hannibal was defeated; the Carthaginians, mostly mercenaries, gave ground before the Roman infantry and the reckless cavalry of Masinissa, the Numidian king; 20,000 Carthaginians were left dead on the field. Hannibal, now forty-five, fought with the energy of youth, attacked Scipio in personal combat and wounded him, attacked Masinissa, re-formed his disordered forces again and again, and led them in desperate countercharges. When all hope fled he eluded capture, rode to Carthage, announced that he had lost not only a battle but the war, and advised the Senate to sue for peace. Scipio was generous. He allowed Carthage to retain her African empire but demanded the surrender of all her war vessels except ten triremes; she was not to make war outside of Africa or within it without Rome's consent; and she was to pay Rome 200 talents ($720,000) every year for fifty years. Hannibal pronounced the terms just and persuaded his government to accept them.

The Second Punic War changed the face of the western Mediterranean. It gave Spain and all its wealth to Rome, providing the funds for the Roman conquest of Greece. It reunited Italy under Rome's unquestioned mastery and threw open all routes and markets to Roman ships and goods. But it was the most costly of all ancient wars. It ravaged or injured half the farms of Italy, destroyed 400 towns, killed 300,000 men;[31] southern Italy has never quite recovered from it to this day. It weakened democracy by showing that a popular assembly cannot wisely choose generals or direct a war. It began the transformation of Roman life and morals by hurting agriculture and helping trade; by taking men from the countryside and teaching them the violence of battle and the promiscuity of the camp; by bringing the precious metals of Spain to finance new luxuries and imperialistic expansion; and by enabling Italy to live on the extorted wheat of Spain, Sicily, and Africa. It was a pivotal event for almost every phase of Roman history.

To Carthage it was the beginning of the end. With much of its commerce and empire left to it, it might have solved the problems of regeneration. But the oligarchical government was so corrupt that it threw upon the lower classes the burden of raising the annual indemnity for Rome and embezzled part of it to boot. The popular party called upon Hannibal to come out of his retirement and save the nation. In 196 he was elected suffete. He shocked the oligarchs by proposing that the judges of the Court of 104 should be elected for one year and should be ineligible for a second term until after a year's interval. When the Senate rejected the measure he brought it before the Assembly, and carried it; by this law and this procedure he established at one stroke a degree of democracy equal to Rome's. He punished and checked venality and pursued it to its source. He relieved the citizens of the extra taxes that had been laid upon them, and yet so managed the finances that by 188 Carthage was able to pay off the Roman indemnity in full.

To get rid of him the oligarchy secretly sent word to Rome that Hannibal was plotting to renew the war. Scipio used all his influence to protect his rival, but was overruled; the Senate accommodated the rich Carthaginians by demanding the surrender of Hannibal. The old warrior fled by night, rode 150 miles to Thapsus, and there took ship to Antioch (195).

He found Antiochus III hesitating between war and peace with Rome; he advised war and became one of the King's staff. When the Romans defeated Antiochus at Magnesia (189) they made it a condition of peace that Hannibal should be turned over to them. He escaped first to Crete, then to Bithynia. The Romans hunted him out and surrounded his hiding place with soldiers. Hannibal preferred death to capture. "Let us," he said, "relieve the Romans from the anxiety they have so long experienced, since they think it tries their patience too much to wait for an old man's death." [32] He drank the poison that he carried with him, and died, aged sixty-seven, in the year 184 B.C. A few months later his conqueror and admirer, Scipio, followed him to peace.

CHAPTER IV

Stoic Rome

508-202 B.C.

WHAT kind of human beings were these irresistible Romans? What institutions had formed them to such ruthless strength in character and policy?—what homes and schools, what religion and moral code? How did they take from the soil, and by what economic organization and skill did they mold to their uses, the wealth required to equip their growing cities and those ever new armies that never knew rest? What were they like in their streets and shops, their temples and theaters, their science and philosophy, their old age and death? Unless we visualize, scene by scene, this Rome of the early Republic, we shall never understand that vast evolution of customs, morals, and ideas which produced in one age the stoic Cato, in a later age the epicurean Nero, and at last transformed the Roman Empire into the Roman Church.

I. THE FAMILY

Birth itself was an adventure in Rome. If the child was deformed or female, the father was permitted by custom to expose it to death.[1] Otherwise it was welcomed; for though the Romans even of this period practiced some measure of family limitation, they were eager to have sons. Rural life made children assets, public opinion condemned childlessness, and religion promoted fertility by persuading the Roman that if he left no son to tend his grave his spirit would suffer endless misery. After eight days the child was formally accepted into the family and the clan by a solemn ceremony at the domestic hearth. A clan (*gens*) was a group of freeborn families tracing themselves to a common ancestor, bearing his name, united in a common worship, and bound to mutual aid in peace and war. The male child was designated by an individual first name (*praenomen*), such as Publius, Marcus, Caius; by his clan name (*nomen*), such as Cornelius, Tullius, Julius; and by his family name (*cognomen*), such as Scipio, Cicero, Caesar. Women were most often designated simply by the clan name— Cornelia, Tullia, Claudia, Julia. Since in classical days there were only

some fifteen first names for males, and these tended to be repeated confusingly in many generations of the same family, they were usually reduced
to an initial, and a fourth—or even a fifth—name was added for distinctiveness. So P. Cornelius Scipio Africanus Maior, the conqueror of Hannibal,
was differentiated from P. Cornelius Scipio Aemilianus Africanus Minor,
the destroyer of Carthage.

The child found itself absorbed into the most basic and characteristic
of Roman institutions—the patriarchal family. The power of the father
was nearly absolute, as if the family had been organized as a unit of an
army always at war. He alone of the family had any rights before the law
in the early Republic; he alone could buy, hold, or sell property, or make
contracts; even his wife's dowry, in this period, belonged to him. If his
wife was accused of a crime she was committed to him for judgment and
punishment; he could condemn her to death for infidelity or for stealing
the keys to his wine. Over his children he had the power of life, death, and
sale into slavery. All that the son acquired became legally his father's property; nor could he marry without his father's consent. A married daughter
remained under her father's power, unless he allowed her to marry *cum
manu*—gave her into the hand or power of her husband. Over his slaves
he had unlimited authority. These, and his wife and children, were *mancipia*
to him—literally, "taken in hand"; and no matter what their age or status,
they remained in his power until he chose to emancipate them—to let them
"out of hand." These rights of the *paterfamilias* were checked to some degree by custom, public opinion, the clan council, and praetorian law; otherwise they lasted to his death, and could not be ended by his insanity or
even by his own choice. Their effect was to cement the unity of the family
as the basis of Roman morals and government and to establish a discipline
that hardened the Roman character into stoic strength. They were harsher
in the letter than in practice; the most extreme of them were seldom used,
the rest seldom abused. They did not bar a deep and natural *pietas*, or reverential affection, between parents and children. The tomb stelae of Rome
are as tender as those of Greece or our own.

Since the greater urgency of the male supplies woman with charms more
potent than any law, her status in Rome must not be judged from her legal
disabilities. She was not allowed to appear in court, even as a witness. Widowed, she could not claim any dower right in her husband's estate; he
might, if he wished, leave her nothing. At every age of her life she was
under the tutelage of a man—her father, her brother, her husband, her son,
or a guardian—without whose consent she could not marry or dispose of
property. On the other hand, she could inherit, though not beyond 100,000
sesterces ($15,000), and she could own without limit. In many instances,

as the earlier passed into the later Republic, she became wealthy because her husband put his property in her name to escape bankruptcy obligations, damage suits, inheritance taxes, and other everlasting jeopardies. She played a role in religion as priestess; nearly every priest had to have a wife and lost his office when she died. Within the home (*domus*) she was honored mistress, *mea domina*, madame. She was not, like the Greek wife, confined to a gynaeceum, or woman's quarters; she took her meals with her mate, though she sat while he reclined. She did a minimum of servile work, for nearly every citizen had a slave. She might spin, as a sign of gentility, but her chief economic function was to superintend the servants; she made it a point, however, to nurse her children herself. They rewarded her patient motherhood with profound love and respect; and her husband seldom allowed his legal mastery to cloud his devotion.

The father and the mother, their house and land and property, their children, their married sons, their grandchildren by these sons, their daughters-in-law, their slaves and clients—all these constituted the Roman *familia*: not so much a family as a household; not a kinship group but an assembly of owned persons and things subject to the oldest male ascendant. It was within this miniature society, containing in itself the functions of family, church, school, industry, and government, that the Roman child grew up, in piety and obedience, to form the sturdy citizen of an invincible state.

II. THE RELIGION OF ROME

1. The Gods

The Roman family was both an association of persons with things and an association of persons and things with gods. It was the center and source of religion, as well as of morals, economy, and the state; every part of its property and every aspect of its existence were bound up in a solemn intimacy with the spiritual world. The child was taught, by the eloquent silence of example, that the undying fire in the hearth was the sign and substance of the goddess Vesta, the sacred flame that symbolized the life and continuity of the family; which therefore must never be extinguished, but must be tended with "religious" care, and fed with a portion of each meal. Over the hearth he saw the little icons, crowned with flowers, that represented the gods or spirits of the family: the Lar that guarded its fields and buildings, its fortune and destiny, and the Penates, or gods of the interior, who protected the accumulations of the family in its storerooms, cupboards, and barns. Hovering invisible but potent over the threshold was the god Janus, two-faced not as deceitful but as watching all entry and exit at every door. The child's father, he learned, was the ward and embodiment of an inner *genius*, or *gen*erative power, which would not die with the body, but must be nourished forever at the paternal grave. His mother was also the carrier of a deity and had likewise to be treated as divine; she had a *Juno* in her as the spirit of her capacity to bear, as the father enclosed a *genius* as the spirit of his power to beget. The child too had his *genius* or *Juno*, as both his guardian angel and his soul—a godly kernel in the mortal husk. Everywhere about him, he heard with awe, were the watchful *Di Manes*, or Kindly Shades, of those male forebears whose grim death masks hung on the household walls, warning him not to stray from the ways of his ancestors, and reminding him that the family was composed not merely of those few individuals that lived in his moment but also of those that had once been, or would someday be, members of it in the flesh, and therefore formed part of it in its spiritual multitude and timeless unity.

Other spirits came to his aid as he grew up: Cuba watched over his sleep, Abeona guided his first steps, Fabulina taught him to speak. When he left the house he found himself again and everywhere in the presence of gods. The earth itself was a deity: sometimes Tellus, or Terra Mater—Mother Earth; sometimes Mars as the very soil he trod, and its divine fertility; sometimes Bona Dea, the Good Goddess who gave rich wombs to women and fields. On the farm there was a helping god for every task or spot: Pomona for orchards, Faunus for cattle, Pales for pasturage, Sterculus for manure heaps, Saturn for sowing, Ceres for crops, Fornax for baking corn in the oven, Vulcan for making the fire. Over the boundaries presided the great god Terminus, imaged and worshiped in the stones or trees that marked the limits of the farm. Other religions may have looked to the sky, and the Roman admitted that there too were gods; but his deepest piety and sincerest propitiations turned to the earth as the source and mother of his life, the home of his dead and the magic nurse of the sprouting seed. Every December the Lares of the soil were worshiped in the joyful Feast of the Crossroads, or *Compitalia;* every January rich gifts sought the favor of Tellus for all planted things; every May the priests of the Arval (or Plowing) Brotherhood led a chanting procession along the boundaries of adjoining farms, garlanded the stones with flowers, sprinkled them with the blood of sacrificial victims, and prayed to Mars (the earth) to bear generous fruit. So religion sanctified property, quieted disputes, ennobled the labor of the fields with poetry and drama, and strengthened body and soul with faith and hope.

The Roman did not, like the Greek, think of his gods as having human form; he called them simply *numina*, or spirits; sometimes they were abstractions like Health, Youth, Memory, Fortune, Honor, Hope, Fear, Virtue, Chastity, Concord, Victory, or Rome. Some of them, like the Lemures or Ghosts, were spirits of disease, hard to propitiate. Some were spirits of the season, like Maia, the soul of May; others were water gods like Neptune, or woodland sprites like Silvanus, or the gods that dwelt in trees. Some lived in sacred animals, like the sacrificed horse or bull, or in the sacred geese that a playful piety preserved unharmed on the Capitol. Some were spirits of procreation; Tutumus supervised conception, Lucina protected menstruation and delivery. Priapus was a Greek god of fertility soon domiciled in Rome: maidens and matrons (if we may believe the indignant Saint Augustine) sat on the male member of his statue as a means of ensuring pregnancy; [2] scandalous figures of him adorned many a garden; little phallic images of him were worn by simple persons to bring fertility or good luck or to avert the "evil eye." [3] Never had a religion so many divinities. Varro reckoned them at 30,000, and Petronius complained that in some towns of Italy there were more gods than men. But *deus,* to the Roman, meant saint as well as god.

Under these basic concepts lurked a polymorphous mass of popular beliefs in animism, fetishism, totemism, magic, miracles, spells, superstitions, and taboos, most of them going back to the prehistoric inhabitants of Italy, and perhaps to Indo-European ancestors in their ancient Asiatic home. Many objects, places, or persons were sacred (*sacer*) and therefore taboo —not to be touched or profaned: e.g., newborn children, menstruating women, condemned criminals. Hundreds of verbal formulas or mechanical contraptions were used to achieve natural ends by supernatural means. Amulets were well-nigh universal; nearly every child wore a *bulla,* or golden talisman, suspended from his neck. Small images were hung upon doors or trees to ward off evil spirits. Charms or incantations were used to avert accidents, cure disease, bring rain, destroy a hostile army, wither an enemy's crops or himself. "We are all afraid," said Pliny, "of being transfixed by curses and spells." [4] Witches appear in Horace, Virgil, Tibullus, Lucian. They were believed to eat snakes, fly through the air at night, brew poisons from esoteric herbs, kill children, and raise the dead. All but a few skeptics seem to have believed in miracles and portents, in speaking or sweating statues,[5] in gods descending from Olympus to fight for Rome, in lucky odd and unlucky even days, and in the presaging of the future by strange events. Livy's history must contain several hundred such portents, reported with philosophic gravity; and the elder Pliny's volumes so abound in portents and magic cures that they might well have been called *Supernatural History.* The most serious business of commerce, government, or war could be deferred or ended by the priestly announcement of an unfavorable omen like abnormal entrails in a sacrificial victim or a roll of thunder in the sky.

The state did what it could to check these excesses—called them, indeed, precisely that, *superstitio*. But it sedulously exploited the piety of the people to promote the stability of society and government. It adapted the rural divinities to urban life, built a national hearth for the goddess Vesta, and appointed a college of Vestal Virgins to serve the city's sacred fire. Out of the gods of the family, the farm, and the village it developed the *di indigetes*—or native gods—of the state, and arranged for these a solemn and picturesque worship in the name of all the citizens.

Among these original national gods Jupiter or Jove was the favorite, though not yet, like Zeus, their king. In the early centuries of Rome he was still a half-impersonal force—the bright expanse of the sky, the light of the sun and the moon, a bolt of thunder, or (as Jupiter Pluvius) a shower of fertilizing rain; even Virgil and Horace occasionally use "Jove" as a synonym for rain or sky.[6] In time of drought the richest ladies of Rome walked in barefoot procession up the Capitoline hill to the Temple of Jupiter Tonans—Jove the Thunderer—to pray for rain. Probably his name was a corruption of Diuspater, or Diespiter, Father of the Sky. Perhaps primitively one with him was Janus, originally Dianus: first the two-faced spirit of the cottage door, then of the city gate, then of any opening or beginning, as of the day or year. The portals of his temple were open only in time of war, so that he might go forth with Rome's armies to overcome the gods of the foe. As old as Jupiter in the respect of the people was Mars, at first a god of tillage, then of war, then almost a symbol of Rome; every tribe in Italy named a month after him. Of like hoary antiquity was Saturn, the national god of the new-sown seed (*sata*). Legend pictured him as a prehistoric king who had brought the tribes under one law, taught them agriculture, and established peace and communism in the *Saturnia regna*— the Golden Age of Saturn's reign.

Less powerful but more deeply loved than these were the goddesses of Rome. Juno Regina was the queen of heaven, the protective genius of womanhood, marriage, and maternity; her month of June [7] was recommended as the luckiest for weddings. Minerva was the goddess of wisdom (*mens*) or memory, of handicrafts and guilds, of actors, musicians, and scribes; the *Palladium* on which the safety of Rome was believed to depend was an image of Pallas Minerva, fully armed, which Aeneas was said to have brought from Troy through love and war to Rome. Venus was the spirit of desire, mating, fertility; sacred to her was April, the month of opening buds (*aperire*); poets like Lucretius and Ovid saw in her the amorous origin of all living things. Diana was the goddess of the moon, of women and childbirth, of the hunt, of the woods and their wild denizens, a tree spirit brought from Aricia when that region of Latium came under Roman power. Near Aricia were the lake and grove of Nemi, and in that grove was a rich shrine of Diana, the resort of pilgrims who believed that the goddess had once mated there with Virbius, the first "King of the Woods." To ensure the fertility of Diana and the soil, the successors of Virbius—all priests and husbands of the huntress—were replaced, each in turn, by any vigorous slave who, having taken as a talisman a sprig of mistletoe (the Golden Bough) from the sacred oak tree of the grove, attacked and slew the king —a custom that endured till the second century of our era.[8]

These, then, were the major gods of the official Roman worship. There were lesser, but not less popular, national deities: Hercules, god of joy and wine, who was not above gambling gaily for a courtesan with the sacristan of his temple; [9] Mercury, the patron deity of merchants, orators, and thieves; Ops, goddess of wealth; Bellona, goddess of war; and countless more. As the city spread its rule it brought in new divinities—di novensiles. Sometimes it imported the god of a beaten city into the Roman pantheon as a sign and surety of conquest, as when the Juno of Veii was led captive to Rome. Conversely, when the citizens of a community were moved to the capital their gods were brought with them, lest the spiritual and moral roots of the new inhabitants should be too suddenly snapped short; so immigrants bring their gods to America today. The Romans did not question the existence of these foreign deities; most of them believed that when they led the statue away the god had to come with it; many believed that the statue was the god.[10]

But some of the di novensiles were not conquered but conquering; they seeped into Roman worship through commercial, military, and cultural contacts with Greek civilization—first in Campania, then in south Italy, then in Sicily, finally in Greece itself. There was something cold and impersonal in the gods of the state religion; they could be bribed by offerings or sacrifice, but they could seldom provide comfort or individual inspiration; by contrast the gods of Greece seemed intimately human, full of adventure, humor, and poetry. The Roman populace welcomed them, built temples for them, and willingly learned their ritual. The official priesthood, glad to enlist these new policemen in the service of order and content, adopted the Greek gods into the divine family of Rome, and merged them, when possible, with their nearest analogues in the indigenous deities. As far back as 496 B.C. came Demeter and Dionysus, who were attached to Ceres and Liber (god of the grape); twelve years later Castor and Pollux were received, to become the protectors of Rome; in 431 a temple was raised to Apollo the Healer in the hope that he might allay a plague; in 294 Aesculapius, the Greek god of medicine, was brought from Epidaurus to Rome in the form of a huge snake,[11] and a temple-hospital was built in his honor on an island in the Tiber. Cronus was accepted as substantially one with Saturn, Poseidon was identified with Neptune, Artemis with Diana, Hephaestus with Vulcan, Heracles with Hercules, Hades with Pluto, Hermes with Mercury. With the help of the poets Jupiter was elevated into another Zeus, a stern witness and guardian of oaths, a bearded judge of morals, a custodian of laws, a god of gods; and slowly the educated Roman was prepared for the monotheistic creeds of Stoicism, Judaism, and Christianity.

2. The Priests

To appease or enlist the aid of these gods Italy employed an elaborate clergy. In his home the father was priest; but public worship was conducted by several *collegia*—associations—of priests, each filling its own vacancies, but all under the lead of a *pontifex maximus* elected by the centuries. No special training was necessary for membership in these sacred colleges; any citizen might be enrolled in them or leave them; they formed no separate order or caste and were politically powerless except as tools of the state. They received the income of certain state lands for their support, with slaves to serve them; and grew rich through generations of pious legacies.

In the third century before Christ the main pontifical college had nine members. They kept historical annals, recorded laws, took auspices, offered sacrifices, and purified Rome with quinquennial lustrations. In performing the official ritual the pontiffs were aided by fifteen *flamines*—kindlers of the sacrificial flames. Minor pontifical colleges had special functions: the Salii, or Leapers, ushered in each New Year with a ritual dance to Mars; the *fetiales* sanctified the ratification of treaties and declarations of war; and the *Luperci*, or Brotherhood of the Wolf, carried on the strange rites of the *Lupercalia*. The college of the Vestal Virgins tended the state hearth, and sprinkled it daily with holy water from the fountain of the sacred nymph Egeria. These white-clad, white-veiled nuns were chosen from among girls six to ten years of age; they took a vow of virginity and service for thirty years, but in return they received many public honors and privileges. If any of them was found guilty of sexual relations she was beaten with rods and buried alive; Roman historians record twelve cases of such punishment. After thirty years they were free to leave and marry, but few took or found the opportunity.[12]

The most influential of the priestly colleges was that of the nine *augures* who studied the intent or will of the gods, in earlier times by watching the flight of birds,* later by examining the entrails of sacrificed animals. Before every im-

---

* Hence the words *augurs*—bird carriers (*aves-gero*)—and *auspices*—bird inspection (*aves-spicio*). Primitive man may actually have learned to forecast weather through the movements of birds.

portant act of policy, government, or war, the "auspices were taken" by the magistrates and interpreted by the augurs, or by special *haruspices*—liver inspectors—whose art went back through Etruria to Chaldea and beyond. As the priests were occasionally open to financial persuasion, their pronouncements were sometimes adjusted to the needs of the purchaser; for example, inconvenient legislation could be stopped by announcing that the auspices were unfavorable for further business on that day; or the Assembly might be induced by "favorable" auspices to vote a war.[13] In major crises the government professed to learn the pleasure of Heaven by consulting the Sibylline Books—the recorded oracles of the Sibyl, or priestess of Apollo, at Cumae. Through such means, and occasional deputations to the oracle at Delphi, the aristocracy could influence the people in any direction to almost any end.[14]

The ritual of worship aimed merely to offer the gods a gift or sacrifice to win their aid or avert their wrath. To be effective, said the priests, the ceremony had to be performed with such precision of words and movements as only the clergy could manage. If any mistake was made, the rite had to be repeated, even to thirty times. *Religio* meant the performance of ritual with religious care.[15] The essence of the ceremony was a sacrifice—literally making a thing *sacer*—i.e., belonging to a god. In the home the offering would normally be a bit of cake or wine placed on the hearth or dropped into the domestic fire; in the village it would be the first fruits of the crops, or a ram, a dog, or a pig; on great occasions, a horse, a hog, a sheep, or an ox; on supreme occasions the last three were slaughtered together in the *su-ove-taur-ilia*. Holy formulas pronounced over the victim turned it into the god who was to receive it; in this sense the god himself was sacrificed;[16] and since only the viscera were burned on the altar, while priests and people ate the rest, the strength and glory of the god (men hoped) passed into his feasting worshipers. Sometimes human beings were offered in sacrifice; it is significant that a law had to be passed as late as 97 B.C. forbidding this. By a variant of these ideas of vicarious atonement a man might offer his life for the state as the Decii had done, or Marcus Curtius, who, to propitiate angry subterranean powers, leaped into a chasm that an earthquake had opened in the Forum—whereupon, we are told, the chasm closed and all was well.[17]

Pleasanter was the ceremony of purification. This might be of crops or flocks, of an army or a city. A procession made the circuit of the objects to be purified, prayer and sacrifice were offered, evil influences were thereby dispelled, and misfortune was turned away. Prayer was still imperfectly evolved from magic incantations; the words for it—*carmen*—meant not only a chant but a *charm*; and Pliny frankly reckoned prayer as a form of magical utterance.[18] If the formula was properly recited, and was addressed to the correct deity according to the *indigitamenta*, or classified directory of the gods compiled and kept by the priests, the request was certain to be granted; if not granted there must have been an error in the ritual. Akin to magic were also the *vota*, or vowed offerings, with which the people sought to gain the help of the gods; sometimes great temples rose in fulfillment of such vows. The multitude of votive offerings found in Roman remains suggests that the religion of the people was warm and tender with piety and gratitude, a feeling of kinship with the hidden forces in nature, and an anxious desire to be in harmony with them all. By contrast the state religion was uncomfortably formal, a kind of legal and contractual relation between the government and the gods. When new cults flowed in from the conquered East it was this official worship that declined first, while the picturesque and intimate faith and ritual of the countryside patiently and obstinately survived. Victorious Christianity, half surrendering, wisely took over much of the faith and ritual; and, under new forms and phrases, they continue in the Latin world to this day.

3. Festivals

If the official worship was gloomy and severe, its festivals redeemed it, and showed men and gods in a lighter mood. The year was adorned with over a hundred holy days (*feriae*), including the first of every month and sometimes the ninth and fifteenth. Some of the *feriae* were sacred to the dead or to the spirits of the lower world; these were "apotropaic" in their ceremonies, aiming to appease the departed and turn away wrath. On May 11-13 Roman families commemorated with awe the feast of the *Lemures*, or dead souls; the father spat black beans from his mouth, and cried: "With these beans I redeem myself and mine. . . . Shades of my ancestors, depart!" [19] The *Parentalia* and the *Feralia*, in February, were similar attempts to propitiate the fearsome dead. But for the most part the festivals were occasions of feasting and jollity, often, among the plebs, of sexual freedom; on such days, says a character in Plautus, "you may eat what you like, go where you like . . . and love whom you like, provided you abstain from wives, widows, virgins, and free boys";[20] apparently he felt that a wide choice would still remain.

On February 15 came the strange Lupercalia, sacred to the God Faunus as averter of wolves (*lupercus*): goats and sheep were sacrificed; and the *luperci* —priests clad only in goatskin girdles—ran around the Palatine praying to Faunus to drive away evil spirits, and striking the women whom they encountered with thongs of hide from the sacrificed animals, to purify them and make them fertile; then puppets of straw were cast into the Tiber to appease or deceive the river god, who had perhaps, in wilder days, demanded living men. On March 15 the poor emerged from their hovels and, like the Jews on the Feast of Tabernacles, built themselves tents in the Field of Mars, celebrated the coming of the New Year, and prayed to the goddess Anna Perenna (Ring of the Years) for as many years as they quaffed cups of wine.[21] April alone had six festivals, culminating in the *Floralia*; this Feast of Flora, goddess of flowers and springs, continued for six days of bibulous and promiscuous revelry. The first of May was the Feast of the Good Goddess, Bona Dea. On May 9, 11, and 13 Liber and Libera, god and goddess of the grape, were celebrated in the *Liberalia;* the phallus, symbol of fertility, was frankly honored by gay crowds of men and women.[23] At the end of May the Arval Brethren led the people in the solemn and yet joyful *Ambarvalia.* The gods were neglected in the autumn months, after the crops were safely in, but December was again rich in feasts. The *Saturnalia* ran from the 17th to the 23rd; they celebrated the sowing of the seed for the next year and commemorated the happy classless reign of Saturn; gifts were exchanged, and many liberties were allowed; the distinction between slave and free was for a while abolished or even inverted; slaves might sit down with their owners, give orders to them, rail at them; the masters waited upon their slaves, and did not eat till all the slaves were filled.[24]

These festivals, though agricultural in origin, remained popular in the cities and survived through all vicissitudes of belief into the fourth and fifth centuries of our era. Their number was so confusing that one of the prime purposes of the Roman calendar was to list them for the guidance of the people. In early Italian custom the chief priest had convened the citizens at the beginning of every month and named the festivals to be observed in the next thirty days; this calling (*calatio*) gave a name (*calendae*) to the first day of each month. To the Romans, as in some measure to modern Catholics or orthodox Jews, a calendar meant a priestly list of holidays and business days, interspersed with scraps of sacred, legal, historical, and astronomical information. Tradition ascribed to Numa the calendar that governed Roman chronology and life till Caesar. It divided the year into twelve lunar months, with complex intercalations that summed up to an average of 366 days per year. To remedy the mounting excess the pontiffs were empowered (191 B.C.) to revise the intercalations; but they used their authority to lengthen or shorten magistracies pleasing or displeasing to them, so that by the end of the Republic the calendar, then three months amiss, was a monster of chaos and chicanery.

In the early days time had been measured simply by the height of the sun in the sky. In 263 B.C. a sundial was brought from Catana, in Sicily, and placed in the Forum; but as Catana was four degrees south of Rome, the dial was deceptive, and the priests were for a century unable to make the needed adjustments. In 158 B.C. Scipio Nasica set up a public clepsydra, or water clock. The month was divided into three periods by the kalends (first), the nones (fifth or seventh), and the ides (thirteenth or fifteenth); and the days were clumsily named by their distance before these dividing lines; so March 12 was "the fourth day before the ides of March." A loose economic week was marked out by the *nundinae*, or every ninth day, when the villagers came to market in the towns. The year began with the coming of spring, and the first month, Martius, bore the name of the god of sowing; next came Aprilis, sprouting; Maius, month of Maia, or perhaps of increase; Iunius, month of Juno, or possibly of thriving; then Quinctilis, Sextilis, September, October, November, and December, named from their numerical order in the year; then January for Janus, and February for the *februa*, or magic objects by which persons might be purified. The year itself was called *annus*, ring; as if to say that in reality there is no beginning and no end.

4. Religion and Character

Did this religion help Roman morals? In some ways it was immoral: its stress on ritual suggested that the gods rewarded not goodness but gifts and formulas; and its prayers were nearly always for material goods or martial victory. Ceremonies gave drama to the life of man and the soil, but they multiplied as if they, and not the devotion of the part to the whole, were the proper essence of religion. The gods were, with some exceptions, awesome spirits without moral aspect or nobility.

Nevertheless, the old religion made for morality, for order and strength in the individual, the family, and the state. Before the child could learn to doubt, faith molded its character into discipline, duty, and decency. Religion gave divine sanctions and support to the family: it instilled in parents and children a mutual respect and piety never surpassed, it gave sacramental significance and dignity to birth and death, encouraged fidelity to the marriage vow, and promoted fertility by making parentage indispensable to the peace of the dead soul. By ceremonies sedulously performed before each campaign and battle it raised the soldier's morale, and led him to believe that supernatural powers were fighting on his side. It strengthened law by giving it celestial origins and religious form, by making crime a disturbance of the order and peace of Heaven, and by placing the authority of Jove behind every oath. It invested every phase of public life with religious solemnity, prefaced every act of government with ritual and prayer, and fused the state into such intimate union with the gods that piety and patriotism became one, and love of country rose to a passion stronger than in any other society known to history. Religion shared with the family the honor and responsibility of forming that iron character which was the secret of Rome's mastery of the world.

III. MORALS

What kind of morality emerged from this life in the family and among the gods? Roman literature, from Ennius to Juvenal, idealized these earlier generations and mourned the passing of ancient simplicity and virtue. These pages too will suggest a contrast between the stoic Rome of Fabius and the epicurean Rome of Nero. But the contrast must not be exaggerated by a biased selection of the evidence. There were epicureans in Fabius' days and stoics in Nero's.

From beginning to end of Roman history the sexual morality of the common man remained essentially the same: coarse and free, but not incompatible with a successful family life. In all free classes virginity was demanded of young women, and powerful tales were told to exalt it; for the Roman had a strong sense of property and wanted a wife of such steady habits as would reasonably ensure him against leaving his goods to his rival's breed. But in Rome, as in Greece, premarital unchastity in men was not censured if it preserved a decent respect for the hypocrisies of mankind. From the elder Cato to Cicero [25] we find express justifications of it. What increases with civilization is not so much immorality of intent as opportunity of expression. In early Rome prostitutes were not numerous. They were forbidden to wear the matron's robe that marked the reputable wife, and were confined to the dark corners of Rome and Roman society. There were as yet no educated courtesans like the hetairai of Athens, nor such delicate drabs as posed for Ovid's verse.

Men married early—usually by twenty; not through romantic love but for the sound purposes of having a helpmate, useful children, and a healthy sexual life. In the words of the Roman wedding ceremony, marriage was *liberum quaerendorum causa*—for the sake of getting children; on the farm, children, like wives, were economic assets, not biological toys. Marriages were often arranged by the parents and engagements were sometimes made for couples in their infancy. In every case the consent of both fathers was required. Betrothal was formal and constituted a legal bond. The relatives gathered in a feast to witness the contract; a *stipula*, or straw, was broken between the parties as a sign of their agreement; the stipulations—especially those concerning the dowry—were put in writing; and the man placed an iron ring upon the fourth finger of the girl's left hand, because it was believed that a nerve ran thence to the heart.[26] The minimum age for legal marriage was twelve for the girl, fourteen for the man. Early Roman law made marriage compulsory;[27] but this law must have become a dead letter by 413 B.C., when Camillus as censor imposed a tax on bachelors.

Marriage was either *cum manu* or *sine manu*—with or without the handing over of the bride and her possessions to the authority of the husband or the father-in-law. Marriage *sine manu* dispensed with religious ceremony and required only the consent of the bride and groom. Marriage *cum manu* was by *usus*—a year's cohabitation; or by *coemptio*—purchase;

or by *confarreatio* (literally, eating a cake together), which required religious ceremony and was confined to patricians. Marriage by actual purchase disappeared at an early date, or was reversed; the bride's dowry often in effect bought the man. This dowry was usually at the husband's disposal, but its equivalent had to be returned to the wife in divorce or on the death of the male. Weddings were rich in folk ceremony and song. The two families feasted in the home of the bride; then they marched in colorful and frolicsome procession to the home of the groom's father, to an accompaniment of flutes, hymeneal chants, and Rabelaisian raillery. At the garlanded door the bridegroom asked the girl, "Who art thou?" and she answered with a simple formula of devotion, equality, and unity: "Where thou art Caius, there am I Caia." He lifted her over the threshold, presented her with the keys of the house, and put his neck with hers under a yoke to signify their common bond; hence marriage was called *coniugium* —a yoking together. In token of her joining the new family the bride then took part with the others in worshiping the household gods.

Divorce was difficult and rare in marriages by *confarreatio*; marriages *cum manu* could be dissolved only by the husband; in marriage *sine manu* divorce was open to either party at will, without asking consent of the state. The first recorded divorce in Roman history is dated 268 B.C.; a suspicious tradition claimed that no divorce had previously occurred since the foundation of the city.[28] Clan custom required a husband to divorce an unfaithful or childless wife. "If you find your wife in the act of adultery," said old Cato, "the law permits you to kill her without trial. If by chance she surprises you in the same condition she must not touch you even with the tips of her fingers; the law forbïds her." [29] Despite these distinctions there were apparently many happy marriages. The tombstones abound in post-mortem affection. One honored touchingly a lady who had served two husbands well:

> Thou wert beautiful beyond measure, Statilia, and true to thy husbands! . . . He who came first, had he been able to withstand the fates, would have set up this stone to thee; while I, alas, who have been blessed by thy pure heart these sixteen years, now have lost thee.[30]

The young women of early Rome were probably not quite so pretty as the later ladies whom the experienced Catullus would credit with *laneum latusculum manusque mollicellas* [31]—"little sides as smooth as wool, and soft little hands." Presumably in those rural days toil and care soon overlaid this adolescent loveliness. Feminine features were classically regular, nose small and thin, hair and eyes usually dark. Blondes were at a premium, as were the German dyes that made them. As for the Roman male, he was impressive rather than handsome. A stern education and years of military life, hardened his face, as later indulgence would soften it into flabbiness. Cleopatra must have loved Antony for something else than his wine-puffed cheeks, and Caesar for some other charm than his eagle's head and nose. The Roman nose was like the Roman character—sharp and devious. Beards and long hair were customary till about 300 B.C., when barbers began to ply their trade in Rome. Dress was essentially like the Greek. Boys, girls, magistrates, and the higher priests wore the *toga praetexta*, or purple-fringed robe; on attaining his sixteenth birthday the youth changed to the *toga virilis*—the white robe of manhood—as a symbol of his right to vote in the assemblies and his duty to serve in the army. Women wore, indoors, a dress (*stola*) bound with a girdle under the breasts, and reaching to the feet; outdoors they covered this with a *palla*, or cloak. Indoors, men wore a simple *tunica*, or shirt; outdoors they added a toga, and sometimes a cloak. The toga (*tegere*, to cover) was a woolen garment in one piece, twice the width and thrice in length the height of the wearer. It was wrapped around the body, and the surplus was thrown back over the left shoulder, brought forward under the right arm, and again thrown over the left shoulder. The folds at the breast served as pockets; the right arm remained free.

The Roman male cultivated a severe dignity (*gravitas*) as an uncomfortable necessity in an aristocracy that ruled a people, then a peninsula, then an empire. Sentiment and tenderness belonged to private life; in public a man of the upper classes had to be as stern as his statue, and hide behind a mask of austere calm the excitability and humor that cry out not only in the comedies of Plautus but in the speeches of Cicero. Even in private life the Roman of this age was expected to live Spartanly. Luxury of dress or table was reproved by the censor; even negligent tillage could bring some Cato down upon the farmer's head. In the First Punic War the Carthaginian ambassadors, returning from Rome, amused the rich merchants by telling how the identical set of silver plate had appeared in every house to which they had been invited; one set, secretly passed about, had sufficed the whole patriciate. In that age the Senate sat on hard wooden benches in a *curia*, or hall, never heated even in winter.

Nevertheless, between the First and Second Punic Wars, wealth and luxury made a good beginning. Hannibal gathered a peck of gold rings from the fingers of Romans slain at Cannae;[32] and sumptuary laws repeatedly—therefore vainly—forbade ornate jewelry, fancy dress, and costly meals. In the third century B.C. the menu of the average Roman was still simple: breakfast (*ientaculum*) of bread with honey or olives or cheese; luncheon (*prandium*) and dinner (*cena*) of grains, vegetables, and fruit;

only the rich ate fish or meat.[33] Wine, usually diluted, graced nearly every table; to drink undiluted wine was considered intemperance. Festivals and banquets were a necessary relaxation in this stoic age; those who could not unbend to them became too tense, and showed their nervous fatigue in the portrait statues they left to posterity.

Charity found little scope in this frugal life. Hospitality survived as a mutual convenience at a time when inns were poor and far between; but the sympathetic Polybius reports that "in Rome no one ever gives away anything to anyone if he can help it" [34]—doubtless an exaggeration. The young were kind to the old, but in general the graces and courtesies of life came to Rome only with the dying Republic. War and conquest molded morals and manners and left men often coarse and usually hard, prepared to kill without compunction and be killed without complaint. War captives were sold into slavery by the thousands, unless they were kings or generals; these were usually slaughtered at the victor's triumph or allowed to starve leisurely to death. In the business world these qualities took on a fairer aspect. The Romans loved money, but Polybius (about 160 B.C.) describes them as industrious and honorable men; a Greek, said the Greek, could not be prevented from embezzling, no matter how many clerks were set to watch him, while the Romans spent great sums of public money with only rare cases of ascertained dishonesty.[35] We note, however, that a law to check malpractice at elections was passed in 432 B.C. Roman historians report that political integrity was at its height in the first three centuries of the Republic; but they arouse suspicion by their high praise of Valerius Corvus, who, after occupying twenty-one magistracies, returned to his fields as poor as he had come; of Curius Dentatus, who kept no part of the spoils he had taken from the enemy; and of Fabius Pictor and his associates, who handed over to the state the rich presents they had received on an embassy to Egypt. Friends lent one another substantial amounts without interest. The Roman government was guilty of frequent treachery in dealing with other states, and perhaps in foreign relations the Empire was more honorable than the Republic. But the Senate refused to connive at the poisoning of Pyrrhus, and warned him of the plot. When, after Cannae, Hannibal sent ten prisoners to Rome to negotiate for the ransom of 8000 others, and drew from them a promise to return, all but one kept their word; the Senate apprehended the tenth, put him in irons, and turned him over to Hannibal, whose joy at his victory, says Polybius, "was not so great as his dejection when he saw how steadfast and high-spirited the Romans were." [27]

In summary, the typical educated Roman of this age was orderly, conservative, loyal, sober, reverent, tenacious, severe, practical. He enjoyed discipline, and would have no nonsense about liberty. He obeyed as a training for command. He took it for granted that the government had a right to inquire into his morals as well as his income, and to value him purely according to his services to the state. He distrusted individuality and genius. He had none of the charm, vivacity, and unstable fluency of the Attic Greek. He admired character and will as the Greek admired freedom and intellect; and organization was his forte. He lacked imagination, even to make a mythology of his own. He could with some effort love beauty, but he could seldom create it. He had no use for pure science, and was suspicious of philosophy as a devilish dissolvent of ancient beliefs and ways. He could not, for the life of him, understand Plato, or Archimedes, or Christ. He could only rule the world.

IV. LETTERS

The Roman was formed not only by the family, the religion, and the moral code, but, in less degree, by the school, the language, and the literature. Plutarch dates the first Roman school about 250 B.C.;[38] but Livy, perhaps romancing, describes Virginia, the desired of the Decemvir, as "going to a grammar school in the Forum" as early as 450.[39] The demand for written laws, and the publication of the Twelve Tables, suggest that by that date a majority of the citizens could read.

The teacher was usually a slave or freedman, employed by several families to instruct their children, or setting up his own private school and taking any pupil that came. He taught reading, writing, grammar, arithmetic, history, and obedience; moral education was fundamental and unceasing; disciple and discipline were almost the same word. Memory and character alike were trained by memorizing the Twelve Tables of the law. Heine remarked that "the Romans would not have had much time left for conquering the world if they had first had to learn Latin";[40] but they too had to conjugate irregular Latin verbs, and soon would be put to Greek. The boy familiarized himself, through poetry and prose, with the exploits of his country and its heroes, and received many a patriotic lesson conveyed through edifying episodes that had never occurred. No attention was given to athletics; the Romans thought it better to train and harden the body by useful work in the field or the camp rather than through contests in the palaestra or gymnasium.

The languagĕ, like the people, was practical and economical, martially sharp and brief; its sentences and clauses marched in disciplined subordination to a determined goal. A thousand similarities allied it, within the Indo-European family, with Sanskrit and Greek and the Celtic tongues of ancient Gaul, Wales, and Ireland. Latin was poorer than Greek in imagery, flexibility, and ready formation of compounds; Lucretius and Cicero complained of its limited vocabulary, its lack of subtle shadings. Nevertheless, it had a sonorous splendor and masculine strength that made it ideal for oratory, and a compactness and logical sentence form that made it an apt vehicle for Roman law. The Latin alphabet came from Euboean Chalcis via Cumae and Etruria.[41] In the oldest Latin inscription known to us, ascribed to the sixth century B.C., all the letters are Greek in form. *C* was sounded like our *K, J* like *Y, V* like *U* or *W*, the vowels as in Italian. Caesar's contemporaries knew him as *Yooleoos Keyssar*, and Cicero was *Keekero*.

The Romans wrote in ink with a slit metal reed (*calamus, stilus*), at first upon leaves (*folia*), whence our words *folio* and *leaf* (two pages); then upon strips of inner bark (*liber*); often upon white (*album*) tablets of waxed wood; later upon leather, linen paper, and parchment. As the written forms of Latin resisted change more than the spoken words, the language of literature diverged more and more from the speech of the people, as in modern America or France. The melodious Romance languages—Italian, Spanish, Portuguese, French, and Rumanian—evolved from the crude popular Latin brought to the provinces, not by poets and grammarians, but by soldiers, merchants, and adventurers. So the words for *horse* in the Romance languages—*caballo, cavallo, cheval, cal*—were taken from the spoken Latin *caballus*, not from the written *equus*. In popular Latin *ille* (he) was one syllable, like French and Italian *il*; and final *-s* and *-m* were, as in those languages, dropped or not pronounced. The best came from a corruption of the worst: *corruptio pessimi optima*.

What literature did the young Roman read in those first three centuries of the Republic? There were religious hymns and chants, such as the song of the Arval Brethren, and there were popular lays of Rome's historic or legendary past. There were official—usually priestly—records of elections, magistracies, events, portents, and holidays.* On the basis of these archives Q. Fabius Pictor compiled (202 B.C.) a respectable *History of Rome*—but in Greek; Latin was not yet thought fit for literary prose and was not used by historians until Cato. There were farragoes of prose called *saturae*—medleys of merry nonsense and erotic banter—out of which Lucilius would forge a new form for Horace and Juvenal. There were boisterously obscene burlesques or mimes, usually acted by players from Etruria; some of these performers, coming from the town of Istria, were named *istriones*, and gave the word *histrio* (actor) to Latin, and its

---

* *Fasti consulares, libri magistratuum, annales maximi, fasti calendares.*

derivatives to modern tongues. There were also, on holidays or market days, crude, half-impromptu farces that gave their stock characters to thousands of Italian comedies, ancient and modern: the rich and stupid father, the extravagant love-entangled youth, the maligned virgin, the clever intriguing servant, the glutton always maneuvering for a meal, the rollicking, tumbling clown. Already the last flaunted the gaily colored patches, the long expansive trousers, the large-sleeved doublet, and the shorn head, still familiar to our youth. An exact likeness of Punchinello, or Punch, has been found on the frescoes of Pompeii.[42]

Literature came formally to Rome about 272 B.C. in the person of a Greek slave. In that year Tarentum fell; many of its Greek citizens were slaughtered, but Livius Andronicus had the luck to be merely enslaved. Brought to Rome, he taught Latin and Greek to his master's children and some others, and translated the *Odyssey* for them into Latin "Saturnian" verse—lines of loose and irregular rhythm, scanned by accent rather than quantity. Freed for his services, he was commissioned by the aediles to produce a tragedy and a comedy for the *ludi*, or games, of 240 B.C. He composed them on Greek models, directed them, acted the main parts, and sang them to the accompaniment of a flute till his voice gave out; then he had another sing the lines while he acted them—a method followed in many later plays at Rome, and influential in generating the pantomime. The government was so well pleased by this introduction of the literary drama that in honor of Andronicus it gave poets the right to incorporate, and allowed them to hold their meetings in the Temple of Minerva on the Aventine. Henceforth it became the fashion to present such *ludi scenici*, or scenic plays, at the public festivals.[43]

Five years after this historic *première* a plebeian ex-soldier from Campania, Cnaeus Naevius, shocked the conservatives by producing a comedy in which he satirized with Aristophanic freedom the political abuses that were flourishing in the capital. The old families complained, and Naevius was jailed. He apologized and was freed, wrote another satire as sharp a the first, and was banished from Rome. In exile and old age he composed, with undiscourageable patriotism, an epic poem on the First Punic War, in which he had fought; it began with the founding of Rome by Trojan refugees, and provided Virgil with a theme and several scenes. His condemnation was a double misfortune: the vitality and originality of Roman comedy suffered from a censorship that made libel a capital crime, and Roman politics lost the purge of a public critique. Naevius wrote also a poetic drama based on Roman history; this experiment too ended with him, and thereafter Roman tragedy circled vainly in the cropped pastures

of Greek myth. Only a few fragments survive to reveal Naevius' quality.
One describes a coquettish girl:

> As if playing ball in a ring she skips from one to another, and is
> all things to all men with her words and winks, her caresses and em-
> braces; now a squeeze of the hand or a pressure of the foot; her ring
> to look at, her lips to blow an inviting kiss; here a song, there the lan-
> guage of signs.[44]

It is pleasant to see that women were then as charming as now, that not
all Romans were Catos, and that under the shadow of the Porch even virtue
might take a holiday.

Beyond the essentials of arithmetic, and enough geometry to plot a
farm or plan a temple, science played as yet no part in the education or
culture of the Roman citizen. The boy counted on his fingers (*digita*),
and the figures he used were imitations of an extended digit (I), a hand
(V), or two hands joined at their apexes (X); and he was content to form
the other numerals by repeating these symbols (II, III), and prefixing (IV,
IX) or suffixing (VI, XII) digits to V or X to lessen or increase them.
Out of this manual arithmetic came the decimal system, constructed on
parts and multiples of ten—i.e., the ten fingers. The Romans used geometry
well in building and engineering, but added not one theorem to that rounded
achievement of the Greek mind. We hear nothing of Roman astronomy
in this period except in its blundering calendar and its prosperous sister
or mother—astrology.

Medicine, till the third century, was largely a matter of family herbs,
magic, and prayer; the gods alone could heal; and to make cure certain
a special god was invoked for each disease [45]—as one now invokes a spe-
cialist. Against the mosquitoes of the Roman campagna appeal was made
to the goddesses Febris and Mephitis, as, until our century, the Romans
petitioned *La Madonna della Febbre*, Our Lady of the Fever.[46] Healing
shrines and sacred waters were as common as today. The temple of Aesculapius was a busy center of religious healing, where diet and hydrotherapy,
peaceful surroundings and a quiet routine, prayer and the soothing ritual
of worship, the aid of practical physicians and the cheerfulness of skilled
attendants, conspired to restore confidence and to effect apparently miraculous cures.[47] Nevertheless, there were slave doctors and quacks in Rome
five centuries before Christ; and some of these practiced dentistry, for the
Twelve Tables forbade the burial of gold with the dead except where
gold had been used to wire teeth.[48] In 219 we hear of the first freeman
physician in Rome—Archagathus the Peloponnesian. His surgical opera-

tions so delighted the patricians that the Senate voted him an official residence and the freedom of the city; later his "mania for cutting and burning" won him the name of Carnifex, butcher.[49] From that time onward Greek physicians flocked to Rome, and made the practice of medicine there a Greek monopoly.

V. THE GROWTH OF THE SOIL

The Roman of those centuries had little need of medicine, for his active life in farming or soldiering kept him healthy and strong. He took to the land as the Greek to the sea; he based his life on the soil, built his towns as meeting places for farmers and their products, organized his armies and his state on his readiness to defend and extend his holdings, and conceived his gods as spirits of the living earth and the nourishing sky.

As far back as we can reach into Rome's past we find private property.[50] Part of the land, however, was *ager publicus*—public acreage usually acquired by conquest and owned by the state. The peasant family of the early Republic owned two or three acres, tilled them with all hands and occasionally a slave, and lived abstemiously on the product. They slept on straw,[51] rose early, stripped to the waist,[52] and plowed and harrowed behind leisurely oxen whose droppings served as fertilizer, and their flesh as a religious offering and a festival food. Human offal was also used to enrich the soil, but chemical fertilizers were rare in Italy before the Empire. Manuals of scientific agriculture were imported from Carthage and Greece. Crops were rotated between grains and legumes, and lands were turned periodically to pasturage to prevent their exhaustion. Vegetables and fruits were grown in abundance, and formed, next to grains, the chief articles of food. Garlic was already a favorite seasoning. Some aristocratic families derived their names in part from the vegetables traditionally favored in their plantings: Lentuli, Caepiones, Fabii, from lentils, onions, beans. Culture of the fig, olive, and grape gradually encroached upon cereal and vegetable crops. Olive oil took the place of butter in the diet and of soap in the bath; it served as fuel in torches and lamps and was the chief ingredient in the unguents made necessary for hair and skin by the dry winds and fiery sun of the Mediterranean summer. Sheep were the favorite herd, for the Italians preferred clothing of wool. Swine and poultry were raised in the farmyard, and almost every family nursed a garden of flowers.[54]

War transformed this picture of rural toil. Many of the farmers who changed plowshares for swords were overcome by the enemy or the town and never returned to their fields; many others found their holdings so damaged by armies or neglect that they had not the courage to begin anew; others were broken by accumulated debt. Such men sold their lands at depression prices to aristocrats or agricultural capitalists who merged the little homesteads into *latifundia* (literally, broad farms), turned these vast areas from cereals to flocks and herds, orchards and vines, and manned them with war-captured slaves under an overseer who was often himself a slave. The owners rode in now and then to look at their property; they no longer put their hands to the work, but lived as absentee landlords in their suburban villas or in Rome. This process, already under way in the fourth century B.C., had by the end of the third produced a debt-ridden tenant class in the countryside, and in the capital a propertyless, rootless proletariat whose sullen discontent would destroy the Republic that peasant toil had made.

VI. INDUSTRY

The soil was poor in minerals—a fact that would write much economic and political history in Italy. There was no gold and little silver; there was a fair supply of iron, some copper, lead, tin, and zinc, but too scarce to support an industrial development. The state owned all mines in the empire, but leased them to private operators, who worked them profitably by using up the lives of thousands of slaves. Metallurgy and technology made few advances. Bronze was still employed more frequently than iron, and only the best and latest mines were equipped with the winches, windlasses, and chain buckets that Archimedes and others had set up in Sicily and Egypt. The chief fuel was wood; trees were cut also for houses and ships and furniture; mile by mile, decade by decade, the forest retreated up the mountainside to meet the timber line. The most prosperous industry was the manufacture of weapons and tools in Campania. There was no factory system, except for armament and pottery. Potters made not only dishes but bricks and tiles, conduits and pipes; at Arretium and elsewhere the potters were copying Greek models and learning to make artistic wares. As early as the sixth century the textile industry, in the design, preparation, and dyeing of linen and wool, had grown beyond the domestic stage despite the busy spinning of daughters, wives, and slaves; free and unfree weavers were brought together in small factories, which produced not only for the local market but also for export trade.

Industrial production for nonlocal consumption was arrested by difficulties of transport. Roads were poor, bridges unsafe, oxcarts slow, inns rare, robbers plentiful. Hence traffic moved by choice along canals and rivers, while coastal towns imported by sea rather than from their hinterland. By 202, however, the Romans had built three of their great "consular roads"—so called because usually named after the consuls or censors who began them. Soon these highways would far surpass in durability and extent the Persian and Carthaginian roads that had served them as models. The oldest of them was the *via Latina* which, about 370 B.C., brought Romans out to the Alban hills. In 312 Appius

Claudius the Blind, with the labor of thousands of criminals,[55] started the *via Appia*, or Appian Way, between Rome and Capua; later it reached out to Beneventum, Venusia, Brundisium, and Tarentum; its 333 English miles bound the two coasts, eased trade with Greece and the East, and collaborated with the other roads to make Italy one nation. In 241 the censor Aurelius Cotta began the Aurelian Way from Rome through Pisa and Genoa to Antibes. Caius Flaminius in 220 opened the Flaminian Way to Ariminum; and about the same time the Valerian Way connected Tibur with Corfinium. Slowly the majestic network grew: the Aemilian Way climbed north from Ariminum through Bononia and Mutina to Placentia (187); the Postumian Way linked Genoa with Verona (148); and the *via Popilia* led from Ariminum through Ravenna to Padua (132). In the following century roads would dart out from Italy to York, Vienna, Thessalonica, and Damascus, and would line the north African coast. They defended, unified, and vitalized the Empire by quickening the movement of troops, intelligence, customs, and ideas; they became great channels of commerce, and played no minor role in the peopling and enrichment of Italy and Europe.

Despite these highways, trade never flourished in Italy as in the eastern Mediterranean. The upper classes looked with contempt upon buying cheap and selling dear, and left trade to Greek and Oriental freedmen; while the country-side contented itself with occasional fairs, and "ninth-day" markets in the towns. Foreign commerce was similarly moderate. Sea transport was risky; ships were small, made only six miles an hour sailing or rowing, hugged the coast, and for the most part kept timidly in port from November to March. Carthage controlled the western Mediterranean, the Hellenistic monarchies controlled the east, and pirates periodically swept out of their lairs upon merchants relatively more honest than themselves. The Tiber was perpetually silting its mouth and blocking Rome's port at Ostia; two hundred vessels foundered there in one gale; besides, the current was so strong that the voyage upstream to Rome hardly repaid the labor and the cost. About 200 B.C. vessels began to put in at Puteoli, 150 miles south of Rome, and ship their goods overland to the capital.

To facilitate this external and internal trade it became necessary to establish a state-guaranteed system of coinage, measures, and weights.* Till the fourth century B.C. cattle were still accepted as a medium of exchange, since they were universally valuable and easily moved. As trade grew, rude chunks of copper (*aes*) were used as money (*ca.* 330 B.C.); *estimate* was originally *aes tumare*, to value copper. The unit of value was the *as* (one)—i.e., one pound of copper by weight; *ex-pend* meant weighed out. When, about 338 B.C., a copper coinage was issued by the state, it often bore the image of an ox, a sheep, or a hog, and was accordingly called *pecunia* (*pecus*, cattle). In the First Punic War, says Pliny, "the Republic, not having means to meet its needs, reduced the as to

---

* Some Roman measures: a *modius* was approximately a peck; a foot was 11 5/8 English inches; 5 Roman feet made a pace (*passus*); 1000 paces made a mile (*milia passuum*) of 1619 English yards; a *iugerum* was about 2/3 of an acre. Twelve ounces (*unciae*) made a pound.

two ounces of copper; by this contrivance a saving of five sixths was effected, and the public debt was liquidated." [56] By 202 the as had fallen to an ounce; and in 87 B.C. it was reduced to half an ounce to help finance the Social War. In 269 two silver coins were minted: the denarius, equal to ten asses, and corresponding to the Athenian drachma in the latter's depreciated Hellenistic'form; and the sestertius, representing two and a half asses, or a quarter of a denarius. In 217 appeared the first Roman gold coins—the aurei—with values of twenty, forty, and sixty sesterces. In metallic equivalence the as would equal two, the sesterce five, the denarius twenty, cents in the currency of the United States; but as precious metals were much less plentiful than now, and therefore had a purchasing power several times greater than today,[57] we shall, ignoring price fluctuations before Nero, roughly equate the as, sesterce, denarius, and talent (6000 denarii) of the Roman Republic with six, fifteen, and sixty' cents, and $3600 respectively, in terms of United States currency in 1942.*

The issuance of this guaranteed currency promoted the profession and operations of finance. The older Romans used temples as their banks, as we use banks as our temples; and the state continued to the end to use its strongly built shrines as repositories for public funds, perhaps on the theory that religious scruples would help discourage robbery. Moneylending was an old business, for the Twelve Tables had forbidden interest above eight and one third per cent per annum.[60] The legal rate was lowered to five per cent in 347, and to zero in 342, but this Aristotelian prohibition was so easily evaded that the actual minimum rate averaged twelve per cent. Usury (above twelve per cent) was widespread, and debtors had periodically to be rescued from their accumulating obligations by bankruptcy or legislation. In 352 B.C. the government used a very modern method of relief: it took over such mortgages as offered a fair chance of repayment, and persuaded mortgagees to accept a lower interest rate on the others.[61] One of the streets adjoining the Forum became a banker's row, crowded with the shops of the moneylenders (*argentarii*) and money-changers (*trapezitae*). Money could be borrowed on land, crops, securities, or government contracts, and for financing commercial enterprises or voyages. Co-operative lending took the place of industrial insurance; instead of one banker completely underwriting a venture, several joined in providing the funds. Joint-stock companies existed chiefly for the performance of government contracts let out on bids by the censor; they raised their capital by selling their stocks or bonds to the public in the form of *partes* or *particulae*

---

* In northern Italy, about 250 B.C., a bushel of wheat cost half a denarius (thirty cents); bed and board at an inn cost half an as (three cents) a day; [58] in Delos, in the second century B.C., a house of medium type rented for four denarii ($2.40) a month; in Rome, A.D. 50, a cup and saucer cost half an as (three cents).[59]

—"little parts," shares. These companies of "publicans"—i.e., men engaged on public or state undertakings—played an active role in supplying and transporting materials for the army and navy in the Second Punic War—not without the usual attempts to cheat the government.[62] Businessmen (*equites*) directed the larger of these enterprises, freedmen the smaller. Nongovernmental business was carried on by *negotiatores*, who usually provided their own funds.

Industry was in the hands of independent craftsmen, working in their separate shops. Most such men were freemen, but an increasing proportion were freedmen or slaves. Labor was highly differentiated, and produced for the market rather than for the individual customer. Competition by slaves depressed the wages of free workers, and reduced the proletariat to a bitter life in slums. Strikes among these men were impracticable and rare,[63] but slave uprisings were frequent; the "First Servile War" (139 B.C.) was not the first. When public discontent became acute, some cause could be found for a war that would provide universal employment, spread depreciated money, and turn the wrath of the people against a foreign foe whose lands would feed the Roman people victorious, or receive them defeated and dead.[64] The free workers had unions or guilds (*collegia*), but these seldom concerned themselves with wages, hours, or conditions of labor. Tradition credited Numa with having established or legalized them; in any case, the seventh century B.C. had organizations of flute players, goldsmiths, coppersmiths, fullers, shoemakers, potters, dyers, and carpenters.[65] The "Dionysian Artists"—actors and musicians—were among the most widespread associations in the ancient world. By the second century B.C. we find guilds of cooks, tanners, builders, bronzeworkers, ironworkers, ropemakers, weavers; but these were probably as old as the others. The chief aim of such unions was the simple pleasure of social intercourse; many of them were also mutual-benefit societies to defray the cost of funerals.

The state regulated not only the guilds, but many aspects of Rome's economic life. It supervised the operation of mines and other governmental concessions or contracts. It quieted agitation among the plebs by importing food and distributing it at nominal prices to the poor or to all applicants. It levied fines upon monopolists, and it nationalized the salt industry to end a monopoly that had raised the price of salt beyond the reach of the working class. Its commercial policy was liberal: after overcoming Carthage it opened the western Mediterranean to all trade; and it protected Utica and, later, Delos on condition that they remain free ports, permitting the entry and exit of goods without fee. At various times, however, it forbade the export of arms, iron, wine, oil, or cereals; it laid a customs duty, usually of two and a half per cent, upon the entry of most products into Rome, and afterward extended this modest tariff to other cities. Until 147 B.C. it required a *tributum*, or property tax, throughout Italy. All in all, its revenues were modest; and like other civilized states it used them chiefly for war.[66]

VII. THE CITY

Through taxes, spoils, indemnities, and inflowing population Rome was now (202 B.C.) one of the major cities of the Mediterranean ensemble. The census of 234 listed 270,713 citizens—i.e., free adult males; the figure fell sharply during the great war, but rose to 258,318 in 189, and 322,000 in 147. We may calculate a population of approximately 1,100,000 souls in the city-state in 189 B.C., of whom perhaps 275,000 lived within the walls of Rome. Italy south of the Rubicon had some 5,000,000 inhabitants.[67] Immigration, the absorption of conquered peoples, the influx, emancipation, and enfranchisement of slaves, were already beginning the ethnic changes that by Nero's time would make Rome the New York of antiquity, half native and half everything.

Two main cross streets divided the city into quarters, each with its administrative officials and tutelary deities. Chapels were raised at important intersections, and statues at lesser ones, to the *lares compitales*, or gods of the crossings —a pretty custom still found in Italy. Most streets were plain earth; some were paved with small smooth stones from river beds, as in many Mediterranean cities today; about 174 the censor began to surface the major thoroughfares with lava blocks. In 312 Appius Claudius the Blind built the first aqueduct, bringing fresh water to a city that had till then depended upon springs and wells and the muddy Tiber. Piping water from aqueduct-fed reservoirs, the aristocracy began to bathe more than once a week; and soon after Hannibal's defeat Rome opened its first municipal baths. At an unknown date Roman or Etruscan engineers built the *Cloaca Maxima*, whose massive stone arches were so wide that a wagon loaded with hay could pass under them.[68] Smaller sewers were added to drain the marshes that surrounded and invaded Rome. The city's refuse and rain water passed through openings in the streets into these drains and thence into the Tiber, whose pollution was a lasting problem of Roman life.

The embellishment of the city was almost confined to its temples. Houses adhered to the plain Etruscan style already described, except that the exterior was more often of brick or stucco, and (as a sign of growing literacy) was often defaced with *graffiti*—"scratchings" of strictly fugitive verse or prose. Temples were mostly of wood, with terra-cotta revetments and decorations, and followed Etruscan plans. A temple to Jupiter, Juno, and Minerva stood on the Capitoline hill; another to Diana on the Aventine; and others rose (before 201 B.C.) to Juno, Mars, Janus, Venus, Victory, Fortune, Hope, etc. In 303 Caius Fabius added to his leguminous clan name the cognomen of Pictor, painter, by executing frescoes in the Temple of Health on the Capitoline. Greek sculptors in Rome made statues of Roman gods and heroes in terra cotta, marble, or bronze. In 293 they erected on the Capitol a bronze Jupiter of such Olympian proportions that it could be seen from the Alban hills twenty miles away. About 296 the aediles set up a bronze she-wolf, to which later artists added the figures of Romulus and Remus. We do not know if this is the group described by Cicero, or if either of these is identical with the existing *Wolf of the Capital;* in any case, we have in this a masterpiece of the highest order, dead metal alive in every muscle and nerve.

While through painting and statuary the aristocracy commemorated its victories and recommended its lineage, the people consoled themselves with music and the dance, comedies and games. The roads and homes of Italy resounded with individual or choral song; men sang at banquets, boys and girls chorused hymns in religious processions, bride and groom were escorted with hymeneal chants, and every corpse was buried with song. The flute was the most popular instrument, but the lyre too had its devotees, and became the favorite accompaniment of lyric verse. When great holidays came, the Romans crowded to amphitheater or stadium, and pullulated under the sun while hirelings, captives, criminals, or slaves ran and jumped, or, better, fought and died. Two great amphitheaters—the Circus Maximus (attributed to the first Tarquin) and the Circus Flaminius (221 B.C.)— admitted without charge all free men and women who came in time to find seats. The expense was met at first by the state, then by the aediles out of their own purse, often, in the later Republic, by candidates for the consulate; the cost increased generation by generation, until in effect it barred the poor from seeking office.

Perhaps we should class with these spectacles the official "triumph" of a returning general. Only those were eligible for it who had won a campaign in which 5000 of the enemy had been slain; the unfortunate commander who had won with less slaughter received merely an *ovation*—for him no ox was sacrificed, but only a sheep (*ovis*). The procession formed outside the city, at whose borders the general and his troops were required to lay down their arms; thence it entered through a triumphal arch that set a fashion for a thousand monuments. Trumpeters led the march; after them came towers or floats representing the captured cities, and pictures showing the exploits of the victors; then wagons rumbled by, heavy with gold, silver, works of art, and other spoils. Marcellus' triumph was memorable for the stolen statuary of Syracuse (212); Scipio Africanus in 207 displayed 14,000 and, in 202, 123,000 pounds of silver taken from Spain and Carthage. Seventy white oxen followed, walking philosophically to their death; then the captured chiefs of the enemy; then lictors, harpers, pipers, and incense-bearers; then, in a flamboyant chariot, the general himself, wearing a purple toga and a crown of gold, and bearing an ivory scepter and a laurel branch as emblems of victory and the insignia of Jove. In the chariot with him might be his children; beside it rode his relatives; behind them his secretaries and aides. Last came the soldiers, some carrying the prizes awarded them, everyone wearing a crown; some praising their leaders, others deriding them; for it was an inviolable tradition that on these brief occasions the speech of the army should be free and unpunished, to remind the proud victors of their fallible mortality. The general mounted the Capitol to the Temple of Jupiter, Juno, and Minerva, laid his loot at the feet of the gods, presented an animal in sacrifice, and usually ordered the captive chieftains to be slain as an additional thank-offering. It was a ceremony well designed to stir military ambition and reward military effort; for man's vanity yields only to hunger and love.

VIII. POST MORTEM

War was the most dramatic feature of a Roman's life, but it did not play so absorbing a role as in the pages of Rome's historians. Perhaps even more than with us his existence centered about his family and his home. News reached him when it was old, so that his passions could not be stirred every day by the gathered turmoil of the world. The great events of his career were not politics and war, but anxious births, festal marriages, and somber deaths.

Old age was not then the abandoned desolation that so often darkens it in an individualistic age. The young never questioned their duty to care for the old; the old remained to the end the first consideration and the last authority; and after their death their graves were honored as long as a male descendant survived. Funerals were as elaborate as weddings. The procession was led by a hired band of wailing women, whose organized hysteria was cramped by a law of the Twelve Tables[71] forbidding them to tear out their hair. Then came the flute players, limited by a like Solonic law to ten; then some dancers, one of whom impersonated the dead. Then followed in strange parade actors wearing the death masks, or waxen images, of those ancestors of the corpse who had held some magistracy. The deceased came next, in splendor rivaling a triumph, clothed in the full regalia of the highest office he had held, comfortable in a bier overspread with purple and gold-embroidered coverlets, and surrounded by the weapons and armor of the enemies he had slain. Behind him came the dead man's sons, dressed and veiled in black, his daughters unveiled, his relatives, clansmen, friends, clients, and freedmen. In the Forum the procession stopped, and a son or kinsman pronounced a eulogy. Life was worth living, if only for such a funeral.

In the early centuries Rome's dead had been cremated; now, usually, they were buried, though some obstinate conservatives preferred combustion. In either case, the remains were placed in a tomb that became an altar of worship upon which pious descendants periodically placed some flowers and a little food. Here, as in Greece and the Far East, the stability of morals and society was secured by the worship of ancestors and by the belief that somewhere their spirits survived and watched. If they were very great and good, the dead, in Hellenized Roman mythology, passed to the Elysian Fields, or the Islands of the Blessed; nearly all, however, descended into the earth, to the shadowy realm of Orcus and Pluto. Pluto, the Roman form of the Greek god Hades, was armed with a mallet to stun the dead; Orcus (our *ogre*) was the monster who then devoured the corpse. Because Pluto was the most exalted of the underground deities, and because the earth was the ultimate source of wealth and often the repository of accumulated food and goods, he was worshiped also as the god of riches and plutocrats; and his wife Proserpina—the strayed daughter of Ceres—became the goddess of the germinating corn. Sometimes the Roman Hell was conceived as a place of punishment;[72] in most cases it was pictured as the abode of half-formless shades that had been men, not distinguished from one another by reward or punishment, but all equally suffering eternal darkness and final anonymity. There at last, said Lucian, one would find democracy.[73]

CHAPTER V

The Greek Conquest

201-146 B.C.

I. THE CONQUEST OF GREECE

WHEN Philip V of Macedon made an alliance with Hannibal against Rome (214) he hoped that all Greece would unite behind him to slay the growing young giant of the west. But rumors were about that he was planning, if Carthage won, to conquer all Greece with Carthage's aid. As a result, the Aetolian League signed a pact to help Rome against Philip, and the clever Senate, before dispatching Scipio to Africa, used Philip's discouragement by persuading him to a separate peace (205). The victory of Zama had hardly been won when the Senate, which never forgave an injury, began to plot revenge upon Macedon. Rome, the Senate felt, could never be secure with so strong a power at her back across a narrow sea. When the Senate moved for war, the Assembly demurred, and a tribune accused the patricians of seeking to divert attention from domestic ills.[1] The opponents of war were easily silenced by charges of cowardice and lack of patriotism; and in 200 B.C. T. Quinctius Flamininus sailed against Macedon.

He was a youth of thirty, one of that liberal Hellenizing circle which was gathering about the Scipios in Rome. After some careful maneuvering he met Philip at Cynoscephalae and overwhelmed him (197). Then he surprised all the Mediterranean nations, and perhaps Rome, by restoring the chastened Philip to a bankrupt and weakened throne, and offering freedom to all Greece. The imperialists in the Senate protested; but for a moment the liberals predominated, and in 196 the herald of Flamininus announced to a vast assemblage at the Isthmian games that Greece was to be free from Rome, from Macedon, from tribute, even from garrisons. So great a cheer rose from the multitude, says Plutarch, that crows flying over the stadium fell dead.[2] When a cynical world questioned the sincerity of the Roman general he answered by withdrawing his army to Italy. It was a bright page in the history of war.

But one war always invites another. The Aetolian League resented Rome's emancipation of Greek cities formerly subject to the League, and appealed to Antiochus III, the Seleucid king, to reliberate liberated Greece. Inflated with some easy victories in the East, Antiochus thought of extending his power over all western Asia. Pergamum, fearing him, called to Rome for help. The Senate sent Scipio Africanus and his brother Lucius with the first Roman army to touch Asiatic soil; the hostile forces met at Magnesia (189), and Rome's victory inaugurated her conquest of the Hellenistic East. The Romans marched north, drove back into Galatia (Anatolia) the Gauls who had threatened Pergamum, and earned the gratitude of all Ionian Greeks.

The Greeks of Europe were not so pleased. Roman armies had spared Greek soil, but they now encompassed Greece on east and west. Rome had freed the Greeks, but on condition that both war and class war should end. Freedom without war was a novel and irksome life for the city-states that made up Hellas; the upper classes yearned to play power politics against neighboring cities, and the poor complained that Rome everywhere buttressed the rich against the poor. In 171 Perseus, son and successor of Philip V as King of Macedon, having arranged an alliance with Seleucus IV and Rhodes, called upon Greece to rise with him against Rome. Three years later Lucius Aemilius Paulus, son of the consul who had fallen at Cannae, defeated Perseus at Pydna, razed seventy Macedonian towns, and led Perseus captive to grace a magnificent triumph at Rome.* Rhodes was punished by the emancipation of her tributary cities in Asia, and by the establishment of a competitive port at Delos. A thousand Greek leaders, including the historian Polybius, were taken as hostages to Italy, where, in sixteen years of exile, 700 of them died.

During the next decade the relations between Greece and Rome moved even nearer to open enmity. The rival cities, factions, and classes of Hellas appealed to the Senate for support, and gave cause for interferences that made Greece actually subject though nominally free. The partisans of the Scipios in the Senate were overruled by realists who felt that there would be no lasting peace or order in Greece until it was completely under Roman rule. In 146 the cities of the Achaean League, while Rome was in conflict with Carthage and Spain, announced a war of liberation. Leaders of the poor seized control of the movement, freed and armed the slaves, declared a moratorium on debts, promised a redistribution of land, and added revolu-

---

* It was on leaving for this campaign that Paulus paid his classic compliments to amateur strategists: "In all public places, and in private parties, there are men who know where the armies should be put in Macedonia, what strategical positions ought to be occupied. . . . They not only lay down what should be done, but when anything is decided contrary to their judgment they arraign the consul as though he were being impeached. . . . This seriously interferes with the successful prosecution of a war. . . . [If anyone] feels confident that he can give me good advice, let him go with me to Macedonia. . . . If he thinks this is too much trouble, let him not try to act as a pilot while he is on land." 3

tion to war. When the Romans under Mummius entered Greece they found a divided people and easily overcame the undisciplined Greek troops. Mummius burned Corinth, slew its males, sold its women and children into bondage, and carried nearly all its movable wealth and art to Rome. Greece and Macedon were made into a Roman province under a Roman governor; only Athens and Sparta were allowed to remain under their own laws. Greece disappeared from political history for two thousand years.

II. THE TRANSFORMATION OF ROME

Step by step the Roman Empire grew, not so much through conscious design as through the compulsions of circumstance and the ever receding frontiers of security. In bloody battles at Cremona (200) and Mutina (193) the legions again subdued Cisalpine Gaul and pushed the boundaries of Italy to the Alps. Spain, rewon from Carthage, had to be kept under control lest Carthage should win it again; besides, it was rich in iron, silver, and gold. The Senate exacted from it a heavy annual tribute in the form of bullion and coin, and the Roman governors reimbursed themselves liberally for spending a year away from home; so Quintus Minucius, after a brief pro-consulate in Spain, brought to Rome 34,800 pounds of silver and 35,000 silver denarii. Spaniards were conscripted into the Roman army; Scipio Aemilianus had 40,000 of them in the force with which he took Spanish Numantia. In 195 B.C. the tribes broke out in wild revolt, which Marcus Cato put down with a hard integrity that recalled the proud virtues of a vanishing Roman breed. Tiberius Sempronius Gracchus (179) adjusted his rule sympathetically to the character and civilization of the native population, made friends of the tribal chieftains, and distributed land among the poor. But one of his successors, Lucius Lucullus (151), violated the treaties made by Gracchus, attacked without cause any tribe that could yield plunder, and slaughtered or enslaved thousands of Spaniards without bothering to invent a pretext. Sulpicius Galba (150) lured 7000 natives to his camp by a treaty promising them land; when they arrived he had them surrounded and enslaved or massacred. In 154 the tribes of Lusitania (Portugal) began a sixteen-year war against Rome. An able leader, Viriathus, appeared among them, heroic in stature, endurance, courage, and nobility; for eight years he defeated every army sent against him, until at last the Romans purchased his assassination. The rebellious Celtiberians of central Spain bore a siege of fifteen months in Numantia, living on their dead; at last (133) Scipio Aemilianus starved them into surrender. In general the policy of the

Roman Republic in Spain was so brutal and dishonest that it cost more than it paid. "Never," said Mommsen, "had war been waged with so much perfidy, cruelty, and avarice."[4]

The plunder from the provinces provided the funds for that orgy of corrupt and selfish wealth which was to consume the Republic in revolution. The indemnities paid by Carthage, Macedon, and Syria, the slaves that poured into Rome from every field of glory, the precious metals captured in the conquest of Cisalpine Gaul and Spain, the 400,000,000 sesterces ($60,000,000) taken from Antiochus and Perseus, the 4503 pounds of gold and 220,000 pounds of silver seized by Manlius Vulso in his Asiatic campaigns[5]—these and other windfalls turned the propertied classes in Rome in half a century (202-146 B.C.) from men of means into persons of such opulence as hitherto only monarchs had known. Soldiers returned from these gigantic raids with their pouches full of coins and spoils. As currency multiplied in Italy faster than building, the owners of realty in the capital tripled their fortunes without stirring a muscle or a nerve. Industry lagged while commerce flourished; Rome did not have to produce goods; it took the world's money and paid with that for the world's goods. Public works were expanded beyond precedent and enriched the "publicans" who lived on state contracts; any Roman who had a little money bought shares in their corporations.[6] Bankers proliferated and prospered; they paid interest on deposits, cashed checks (*praescriptiones*), met bills for their clients, lent and borrowed money, made or managed investments, and fattened on such relentless usury that cutthroat (*sector*) and moneylender became one word.[7] Rome was becoming not the industrial or commercial, but the financial and political, center of the white man's world.

Equipped with such means, the Roman patriciate and upper middle class passed with impressive speed from stoic simplicity to reckless luxury; the lifetime of Cato (234-149) saw the transformation almost completed. Houses became larger as families became smaller; furniture grew lavish in a race for conspicuous expense; great sums were paid for Babylonian rugs, for couches inlaid with ivory, silver, or gold; precious stones and metals shone on tables and chairs, on the bodies of women, on the harness of horses. As physical exertion diminished and wealth expanded, the old simple diet gave way to long and heavy meals of meat, game, delicacies, and condiments. Exotic foods were indispensable to social position or pretense; one magnate paid a thousand sesterces for the oysters served at a meal; another imported anchovies at 1600 sesterces a cask; another paid 1200 for a jar of caviar.[8] Good chefs fetched enormous prices on the slave auction block. Drinking increased; goblets had to be large and preferably of gold; wine was less diluted, sometimes not at all. Sumptuary laws were passed by the Senate limiting expenditure on banquets and clothing, but as the senators ignored these regulations, no one bothered to observe them. "The citizens," Cato mourned, "no longer listen to good advice, for the belly has no ears."[9] The individual became rebelliously conscious of himself as against the state, the son as against the father, the woman as against the man.

Usually the power of woman rises with the wealth of a society, for when the stomach is satisfied hunger leaves the field to love. Prostitution flourished. Homosexualism was stimulated by contact with Greece and Asia; many rich men paid a talent ($3600) for a male favorite; Cato complained that a pretty boy cost more than a farm.[10] But women did not yield the field to these Greek and Syrian invaders. They took eagerly to all those supports of beauty that wealth now put within their reach. Cosmetics became a necessity, and caustic soap imported from Gaul tinged graying hair into auburn locks.[11] The rich bourgeois took pride in adorning his wife and daughter with costly clothing or jewelry and made them the town criers of his prosperity. Even in government the role of women grew. Cato cried out that "all other men rule over women; but we Romans, who rule all men, are ruled by our women."[12] In 195 B.C. the free women of Rome swept into the Forum and demanded the repeal of the Oppian Law of 215, which had forbidden women to use gold ornaments, varicolored dresses, or chariots. Cato predicted the ruin of Rome if the law should be repealed. Livy puts into his mouth a speech that every generation has heard:

> If we had, each of us, upheld the rights and authority of the husband in our own households, we should not today have this trouble with our women. As things are now, our liberty of action, which has been annulled by female despotism at home, is crushed and trampled on here in the Forum. . . . Call to mind all the regulations respecting women by which our ancestors curbed their license and made them obedient to their husbands; and yet with all those restrictions you can scarcely hold them in. If now you permit them to remove these restraints . . . and to put themselves on an equality with their husbands, do you imagine that you will be able to bear them? From the moment that they become your equals they will be your masters.[13]

The women laughed him down, and stood their ground until the law was repealed. Cato revenged himself as censor by multiplying by ten the taxes on the articles that Oppius had forbidden. But the tide was in flow, and could not be turned. Other laws disadvantageous to women were repealed or modified or ignored. Women won the free administration of their dowries, divorced their husbands or occasionally poisoned them, and doubted the wisdom of bearing children in an age of urban congestion and imperialistic wars.

Already by 160 Cato and Polybius had noted a decline of population and the inability of the state to raise such armies as had risen to meet Hannibal. The new generation, having inherited world mastery, had no time or inclination to defend it; that readiness for war which had characterized the Roman landowner disappeared now that ownership was being concentrated in a few families and a proletariat without stake in the country filled the slums of Rome. Men became brave by proxy; they crowded the amphitheater to see bloody games, and hired gladiators to fight before them at their banquets. Finishing schools were opened for both sexes, where young men and women learned to sing, play the lyre, and move gracefully.[14] In the upper classes manners became more refined as morals were relaxed. In the lower classes manners continued to be coarse and vigorous, amusements often violent, language freely obscene; we get the odor of this lusty *profanum vulgus* in Plautus, and understand why it wearied of Terence. When a band of flute players attempted a musical concert at a triumph in 167, the audience forced the musicians to change their performance into a boxing match.[15]

In the widening middle classes commercialism ruled unhindered. Their wealth was based no longer on realty but on mercantile investment or management. The old morality and a few Catos could not keep this new regime of mobile capital from setting the tone of Roman life. Everyone longed for money, everyone judged or was judged in terms of money. Contractors cheated on such a scale that many government properties—e.g., the Macedonian mines—had to be abandoned because the lessees exploited the workers and mulcted the state to a point where the enterprise brought in more tribulation than profit.[16] That aristocracy which (if we may believe the historians—and we must not) had once esteemed honor above life adopted the new morality and shared in the new wealth; it thought no longer of the nation, but of class and individual privileges and perquisites; it accepted presents and liberal bribes for bestowing its favor upon men or states, and found ready reasons for war with countries that had more wealth than power. Patricians stopped plebeians in the street and asked or paid for their votes. It became a common thing for magistrates to embezzle public funds and an uncommon thing to see them prosecuted; for who could punish robbery among his fellows when half the members of the Senate had joined in violating treaties, robbing allies, and despoiling provinces? "He who steals from a citizen," said Cato, "ends his days in fetters and chains; but he who steals from the community ends them in purple and gold."[17]

Nevertheless, the prestige of the Senate was higher than ever before. It had brought Rome successfully through two Punic Wars and three Macedonian Wars; it had challenged and overcome all of Rome's rivals, had won the subservient friendship of Egypt, and had captured so much of the world's wealth that in 146 Italy was freed from direct taxation. In the crises of war and policy it had usurped many powers of the assemblies and the magistrates, but victory sanctified its usurpations. The machinery of the *comitia* had been made ridiculous by empire; the turbulent peoples who now submitted to rule by a Senate largely composed of seasoned statesmen and triumphant generals would have protested passionately against having their affairs determined by the few thousand Italians who could attend the assemblies in Rome. The principle of democracy is freedom, the principle of war is discipline; each requires the absence of the other. War demands superior intelligence and courage, quick decisions, united action, immediate obedience; the frequency of war doomed democracy. By law the Centurial Assembly alone had the right to declare war or make peace; but by its power to conduct foreign relations the Senate could usually bring matters to a point where the Assembly had no longer any practical choice.[18] The Senate controlled the Treasury and all outlays of public funds; and it controlled the judiciary by the rule that all important juries had to be taken from the Senatorial list. The formulation and interpretation of the laws were in the hands of the patrician class.

Within this aristocracy there was an oligarchy of dominant families. Till Sulla, Roman history is a record of families rather than of individuals; no great statesman stands out, but generation after generation the same names occur in the higher offices of the state. Out of 200 consuls between 233 and 133 B.C., 159 belonged to twenty-six families, one hundred to ten. The most powerful family in this period was the Cornelii. From the Publius Cornelius Scipio who lost the battle of the Trebia (218), through his son Scipio Africanus who defeated Hannibal, to the latter's adoptive grandson, Scipio Aemilianus, who destroyed Carthage in 146, the history of Roman politics and war is largely the story of this family; and the revolution that destroyed the aristocracy was begun by the Gracchi, grandsons of Africanus. The saving victory at Zama made Africanus so popular with all classes that for a time Rome was ready to give him any office he desired. But when he and his brother Lucius returned from the war in Asia (187), the party of Cato demanded that Lucius should give an account of the money paid him by Antiochus as an indemnity to be transmitted to Rome. Africanus refused to let his brother answer; instead he tore the records to shreds before the Senate. Lucius was brought to trial before the Assembly and was convicted of embezzlement; he was saved from punishment by the tribunician veto of Africanus' son-in-law, Tiberius Sempronius Gracchus. Summoned to trial in his turn, Africanus disrupted the proceedings by inviting and leading the Assembly to the Temple of Jupiter to celebrate the anniversary of Zama. Summoned again, he refused to obey the call, retired to his estate at Liternum, and remained there unmolested till his death. The emergence of such individualism in politics corresponded with the growth of individualism in commerce and morals. The Roman Republic would soon be destroyed by the unfettered energy of its great men.

The redeeming feature of this aristocracy and this age was their awakened appreciation of the beautiful. Contact with Greek culture in Italy, Sicily, and Asia had acquainted the Romans not merely with the appurtenances of luxury but with the highest products of classic art. The conquerors brought back with them world-famous paintings and statues, cups and mirrors of chased metal, costly textiles and furniture. The older generation was shocked by Marcellus' adornment of Roman squares with the stolen sculptures of Syracuse; they complained not of the robbery, but of the "idleness and vain talk" among once industrious citizens who now stopped to "examine and criticize trifles." [19] Fulvius carried off 1015 statues from Pyrrhus' collection in Ambracia; Aemilius Paulus filled fifty chariots in his triumph with the art treasures he had taken from Greece as partial payment for liberating her; Sulla, Verres, Nero, and a thousand other Romans were to do likewise through two hundred years. Greece was denuded to clothe the Roman mind.

Overwhelmed with this invasion, Italian art abandoned its native quality and styles and, with one exception, surrendered to Greek artists, themes, and forms. Greek sculptors, painters, and architects, following the line of greatest gold, migrated to Rome and slowly Hellenized the capital of their conquerors. Rich Romans began to build their mansions in the Greek manner around an open court, and to adorn them with Greek columns, statuary, paintings, and furniture. Temples changed more slowly, lest the gods take offense; for them the short cella and high podium of the Tuscan style remained the rule; but as more Olympians were domiciled in Rome it seemed appropriate to design their homes on the slenderer Hellenic scale. In one vital respect, however, Roman art, while still taking hints from Greece, expressed with unique means and power the sturdy Italic soul. For triumphal and decorative monuments, basilicas and aqueducts, the Roman architect replaced the architrave with the arch. In 184 Cato built in stone the Basilica Porcia; five years later Aemilius Paulus gave its first form to that Basilica Aemilia which his descendants would repair and beautify through many generations.* The typical Roman basilica, designed for the transaction of business or law, was a long rectangle divided into nave and aisles

---

* The basilica (sc. *stoa*—i.e., royal portico) was a Hellenistic application of the arch to the Persian palace and the Egyptian hypostyle hall; Delos and Syracuse had raised such structures in the third century B.C.

by two internal rows of columns, and usually roofed with a coffered barrel vault—a development taken from Alexandria.[20] Since the nave was higher than the aisles, a clerestory of pierced stone trellises could be carved above each aisle for the admission of light and air. Here, of course, was the essential interior form of the medieval cathedral. With these vast edifices Rome began to take on that aspect of magnificence and strength which was to distinguish the city even after it ceased to be the capital of the world.

III. THE NEW GODS

How were the old gods faring in this age of reckless change? Apparently a rivulet of unbelief had trickled down from the aristocracy to the crowd; it is hard to understand how a people still faithful to the ancient pantheon could have accepted with such boisterous approval those comedies in which Plautus—with whatever excuse of following Greek models—made fun of Jupiter's labors with Alcmena, and turned Mercury into a buffoon. Even Cato, so anxious to preserve old forms, marveled at the ability of two augurs to keep from laughing when they met face to face.[21] Too long these takers of auspices had been suborned to political trickery; prodigies and portents had been concocted to mold public opinion, the vote of the people had been annulled by pious humbuggery, and religion had consented to turn exploitation into a sacrament. It was a bad omen that Polybius, after living seventeen years among the highest circles in Rome, could write, about 150 B.C., as if the Roman religion were merely a tool of government:

> The quality in which the Roman commonwealth is most distinctly superior is, in my judgment, the nature of its religion. The very thing that among other nations is an object of reproach—i.e., superstition— is that which maintains the cohesion of the Roman state. These matters are clothed in such pomp, and introduced to such an extent into public and private life, as no other religion can parallel. . . . I believe that the government has adopted this course for the sake of the common people. This might not have been necessary had it been possible to form a state composed of wise men; but as every multitude is fickle, full of lawless desires, unreasoned passion, and violent anger, it must be held in by invisible terrors and religious pageantry.[22]

Polybius could have justified himself, perhaps, by recent incidents tending to show that, despite Plautus and philosophy, superstition still was king. When the disaster of Cannae seemed to leave Rome defenseless against Hannibal, the excitable populace fell into a panic, and cried, "To what god must we pray to save Rome?" The Senate sought to still the commotion by human sacrifice; then·by prayers to Greek gods; then by applying the Greek ritual to all the gods, Roman and Greek alike. Finally the Senate decided that if it could not prevent superstition it would organize and control it. In 205 it announced that the Sibylline Books foretold that Hannibal would leave Italy if the Magna Mater—a form of the goddess Cybele—should be brought from Phrygian Pessinus to Rome. Attalus, King of Pergamum, consented; the black stone which was believed to be the incarnation of the Great Mother was shipped to Ostia, where it was received with impressive ceremony by Scipio Africanus and a band of virtuous matrons. When the vessel that bore it was grounded in the Tiber's mud, the Vestal Virgin Claudia freed it, and drew it upstream to Rome, by the magic power of her chastity. Then the matrons, each holding the stone tenderly in her turn, carried it in solemn procession to the Temple of Victory, and the pious people burned incense at their doors as the Great Mother passed. The Senate was shocked to find that the new divinity had to be served by self-emasculated priests; such men were found, but no Roman was allowed to be among them. From that time onward Rome celebrated, every April, the *Megalesia*, or Feast of the Great Goddess, first with wild sorrow and then with wild rejoicing. For Cybele was a vegetation deity, and legend told how her son Attis, symbol of autumn and spring, had died and gone to Hades, and then had risen from the dead.

In that same year (205) Hannibal left Italy, and the Senate complimented itself on its handling of the religious crisis. But the wars with Macedon opened the gates to Greece and the East; in the wake of soldiers returning with Eastern spoils, ideas, and myths came a flood of Greek and Asiatic captives, slaves, refugees, traders, travelers, athletes, artists, actors, musicians, teachers, and lecturers; and men in their migrations carry along their gods. The lower classes of Rome were pleased to learn of Dionysus-Bacchus, of Orpheus and Eurydice, of mystic rites that gave a divine inspiration and intoxication, of initiations that revealed the resurrected deity and promised the worshiper eternal life. In 186 the Senate was disturbed to learn that a considerable minority of the people had adopted the Dionysian cult, and that the new god was being celebrated by nocturnal bacchanalia whose secrecy lent color to rumors of unrestrained drinking and sexual revelry. "More uncleanliness was wrought with men than with women," says Livy; and he adds, probably turning gossip into history, that "whoever would not submit to defilement . . . was sacrificed as a victim."[23] The Senate suppressed the cult, arrested 7000 of the devotees, and sentenced hundreds to death. It was a temporary victory in the long war that Rome was to wage against Oriental faiths.

IV. THE COMING OF PHILOSOPHY

The Greek conquest of Rome took the form of sending Greek religion and comedy to the Roman plebs; Greek morals, philosophy, and art to the upper classes. These Greek gifts conspired with wealth and empire in that sapping of Roman faith and character which was one part of Hellas' long revenge upon her conquerors. The conquest reached its climax in Roman philosophy, from the stoic Epicureanism of Lucretius to the epicurean Stoicism of Seneca. In Christian theology Greek metaphysics overcame the gods of Italy. Greek culture triumphed in the rise of Constantinople as first the rival and then the successor of Rome; and when Constantinople fell, Greek literature, philosophy, and art reconquered Italy and Europe in the Renaissance. This is the central stream in the history of European civilization; all other currents are tributaries. "It was no little brook that flowed from Greece into our city," said Cicero, "but a mighty river of culture and learning."[24] Henceforth the mental, artistic, and religious life of Rome was a part of the Hellenistic world.*

The invading Greeks found a strategic opening in the schools and lecture halls of Rome. A swelling stream of *Graeculi—*"Greeklings," as the scornful Romans called them—followed the armies returning from the East. Many of them, as slaves, became tutors in Roman families; some, the *grammatici,* inaugurated secondary education in Rome by opening schools for instruction in the language and literature of Greece; some, the *rhetores,* gave private instruction and public lectures on oratory, literary composition, and philosophy. Roman orators—even the mishellenist Cato—began to model their addresses on the speeches of Lysias, Aeschines, and Demosthenes.

Few of these Greek teachers had any religious belief; fewer transmitted any; a small minority of them followed Epicurus and preceded Lucretius in describing religion as the chief evil in human life. The patricians saw where the wind was blowing, and tried to stop it; in 173 the Senate banished two Epicureans, and in 161 it decreed that "no philosophers or rhetors shall be permitted in Rome." The wind would not stop. In 159 Crates of Mallus, Stoic head of the royal library at Pergamum, came to Rome on an official embassy, broke a leg, stayed on, and, while convalescing, gave lectures on literature and philosophy. In 155 Athens sent as ambassadors to Rome the leaders of its three great philosophical schools: Carneades the Academic or Platonist, Critolaus the Peripatetic or Aristotelian, and Diog-

---

* Said Horace, in a now-trite line: *Graecia capta ferum victorem cepit:* "Conquered Greece took captive her barbarous conqueror." [24a]

enes the Stoic of Seleucia. Their coming was almost as strong a stimulus as Chrysoloras would bring to Italy in 1453. Carneades spoke on eloquence so eloquently that the younger set came daily to hear him.[25] He was a complete skeptic, doubted the existence of the gods, and argued that as good reasons could be given for doing injustice as for being just—a belated surrender of Plato to Thrasymachus.[26] When old Cato heard of this he moved in the Senate that the ambassadors be sent home. They were. But the new generation had tasted the wine of philosophy; and from this time onward the rich youth of Rome went eagerly to Athens and Rhodes to exchange their oldest faith for the newest doubts.

The very conquerors of Greece were in person the sponsors of Hellenistic culture and philosophy in Rome. Flamininus, who had loved Greek literature before invading Macedon and freeing Greece, was deeply moved by the art and drama he saw in Hellas. We must lay it to the credit side of Rome that some of its generals could understand Polycleitus and Pheidias, Scopas and Praxiteles, even if they carried their appreciation to the point of robbery. Of all the spoils that Aemilius Paulus brought back from his victories over Perseus, he kept for himself only the library of the King, as a heritage for his children. He had his sons instructed in Greek literature and philosophy as well as in the Roman arts of the chase and war; and so far as his public duties permitted he shared in these studies with his children.

Before Paulus died, his youngest son was adopted by his friend, P. Cornelius Scipio, son of Africanus. Following Roman custom, the lad took the name of his adoptive father and added the name of his father's clan; in this way he became the P. Cornelius Scipio Aemilianus whom we shall hereafter mean by Scipio. He was a handsome and healthy youth, simple in habits and moderate in speech, affectionate and generous, so honest that at his death, after having all the plunder of Carthage pass through his hands, he left only thirty-three pounds of silver and two of gold—though he had lived like a scholar rather than as a man of means. In his youth he met the Greek exile Polybius, who earned his gratitude and lifelong friendship by giving him good advice and good books. The boy won his spurs by fighting under his father at Pydna; in Spain he accepted the challenge of the enemy to single combat, and won.[27]

In private life he gathered about him a group of distinguished Romans interested in Greek thought. Chief among them was Gaius Laelius, a man of kindly wisdom and steadfast friendship, just in judgment and blameless in life, and second only to Aemilianus in eloquence of speech and purity of style. Cicero, across a century, fell in love with Laelius, named after him his essay on friendship, and wished he might have lived not in his own turbulent epoch but in that exalted circle of Rome's intellectual youth. Its influence on literature was considerable; through participation in it Terence developed the elegant precision of his language; and Gaius Lucilius (180-103) perhaps learned here to give a social purpose to the satires with which he lashed the vices and luxury of the age.

The Greek mentors of this group were Polybius and Panaetius. Polybius lived for years in Scipio's home. He was a realist and a rationalist, and had few illusions about men and states. Panaetius came from Rhodes and, like Polybius, belonged to the Greek aristocracy. For many years he lived with Scipio in affectionate intimacy and reciprocal influence: he stirred Scipio to all the nobility of Stoicism, and probably it was Scipio who persuaded him to modify the extreme ethical demands of that philosophy into a more practicable creed. In a book *On Duties* Panaetius laid down the central ideas of Stoicism: that man is part of a whole and must co-operate with it—with his family, his country, and the divine Soul of the World; that he is here not to enjoy the pleasures of the senses, but to do his duty without complaint or stint. Panaetius did not, like the earlier Stoics, require a perfect virtue, or complete indifference to the goods and fortunes of life. Educated Romans grasped at this philosophy as a dignified and presentable substitute for a faith in which they had ceased to believe, and found in its ethic a moral code completely congenial to their traditions and ideals. Stoicism became the inspiration of Scipio, the ambition of Cicero, the better self of Seneca, the guide of Trajan, the consolation of Aurelius, and the conscience of Rome.

V. THE AWAKENING OF LITERATURE

It was a basic purpose of the Scipionic circle to encourage literature as well as philosophy, to mold the Latin tongue into a refined and fluent literary medium, to lure the Roman muses to the nourishing springs of Greek poetry, and to provide an audience for promising writers of verse or prose. In 204 Scipio Africanus proved his character by welcoming to Rome a poet brought there by Cato, the strongest opponent of everything represented by the Scipios and their friends. Quintus Ennius had been born of Greek and Italian parentage near Brundisium (239). He had received his education in Tarentum, and his enthusiastic spirit had been deeply impressed by the Greek dramas presented on the Tarentine stage. His courage as a soldier in Sardinia attracted Cato, who was quaestor there. Arrived in Rome, he lived by teaching Latin and Greek, recited his verses to his friends, and found admittance to the circle of the Scipios.

There was hardly a poetic form that he did not try. He wrote a few comedies and at least twenty tragedies. He was in love with Euripides, flirted like him with radical ideas, and plagued the pious with such Epicurean quips as, "I grant you there are gods, but they don't care what men do; else it would go well with the good and ill with the bad—which rarely happens";[28] according to Cicero the audience applauded the lines.[29] He translated or paraphrased Euhemerus' *Sacred History*, which argued that the gods were merely dead heroes deified by popular sentiment. He was not immune to theology of a kind, for he announced that the soul of Homer, having passed through many bodies, including Pythagoras and a peacock, now resided in Ennius. He wrote with verve an epic history of Rome from Aeneas to Pyrrhus, and these *Annales* became, till Virgil, the national poem of Italy. A few fragments survive, of which the most famous is a line that Roman conservatives never tired of quoting:

Moribus antiquis stat res Romana virisque—

"the Roman state stands through its ancient morals and its great men." Metrically the poem was a revolution; it replaced the loose "Saturnian" verse of Naevius with the flowing and flexible hexameters of Greek epic poetry. Ennius molded Latin to new forms and powers, filled his lines with the meat of thought, and prepared for Lucretius, Horace, and Virgil in method, vocabulary, theme, and ideas. To crown his career he wrote a treatise on the pleasures of the palate, and died of gout at seventy, after composing a proud epitaph:

> Pay me no tears, nor for my passing grieve;
> I linger on the lips of men, and live.[30]

Ennius succeeded in everything but comedy; perhaps he took philosophy too seriously, forgetting his counsel that "one must philosophize, but not too much."[31] The people rightly preferred laughter to philosophy, and made Plautus rich and Ennius poor. For like reasons they gave little encouragement to the tragic drama in Rome. The tragedies of Pacuvius and Accius were acclaimed by the aristocracy, ignored by the people, and forgotten by time.

In Rome, as in Athens, plays were presented to the public by state officials as partial celebration of a religious festival or as the obsequies of some distinguished citizen. The theater of Plautus and Terence consisted of a wooden scaffolding supporting a decorated background (the *scaena*), and, in front of this, a circular *orchestra*, or platform for dancing; the rear half of this circle formed the *proscaenium*, or stage. These flimsy structures were torn down after each festival, like our reviewing stands today. The spectators stood, or sat on stools they had brought, or squatted on the ground under the sky. Not till 145 was a complete theater built in Rome, still of wood and roofless, but fitted with seats in the Greek semicircular style. No admission was charged; slaves might attend, but not sit; women were admitted only in the rear. The audience in this period was probably the roughest and dullest in dramatic history—a jostling, boisterous crowd of "groundlings"; it is sad to note how often the prologues beg for quiet and better manners, and how the crude jokes and stereotyped ideas must be repeated to be understood. Some prologues ask mothers to leave their babies at home, or threaten noisy children, or admonish women not to chatter so much; such petitions occur even in the midst of the published plays.[32] If an exhibition of prize fighting or rope walking happened to compete, the play, as like as not, would be interrupted until the more exciting performance was over. At the end of a Roman comedy the words, *Nunc plaudite omnes*, or some variant, made plain that the play was finished and that applause was in order.

The best feature of the Roman stage was the acting. The leading part was usually played by the manager, a freeman; the other performers were mostly Greek slaves. Any citizen who became an actor forfeited his civic rights—a custom that lasted till Voltaire. Female parts were taken by men. As audiences were small, actors in this age did not wear masks, but contented themselves with paint and wigs. About 100 B.C., as audiences grew larger, the mask became necessary to distinguish the characters; it was called *persona*, apparently from the Etruscan word for mask, *phersu;* and the parts were called *dramatis personae*—masks of the play. Tragedians wore a high shoe, or "buskin" (*cothurnus*), comedians a low shoe, or "sock" (*soccus*). Parts of the play were sung to the *obbligato* of a flute; sometimes singers sang the parts while actors performed them in pantomime.

The Plautine comedies were written in rough and ready iambic verse, imitating the meter as well as the matter of their Greek models. Most of the Latin comedies that have come down to us were taken directly, or by combination, from one or more Greek dramas; usually from Philemon, Menander, or other practitioners of the New Comedy in Athens. The author and title of the Greek original were usually named on the title page. Adaptations of Aristophanes and the Old Comedy were ruled out by a law of the Twelve Tables punishing political satire with death.[33] It was probably fear of this lethal legislation that led the Latin playwrights to keep the Greek scenes, characters, customs, names, even coins, of their originals; but for Plautus Roman law would have banished Roman life almost completely from the Roman stage. This police supervision did not exclude coarseness and obscenity; the aedile wished to amuse the crowd, not to elevate it; and the Roman government was never displeased by the ignorance of the multitude. The audience preferred broad humor to wit, buffoonery to subtlety, vulgarity to poetry, Plautus to Terence.

T. Maccius Plautus—literally, Titus the flat-footed clown—had made his first entrance in Umbria in 254. Coming to Rome, he worked as a stage hand, saved his money, invested it eagerly, and lost it. To eat he wrote plays; his adaptations from the Greek pleased by the Roman allusions scattered through them; he made money again and was given the citizenship of Rome. He was a man of the people and the earth, exuberantly jolly, Rabelaisianly robust; he laughed with everyone at everyone, but felt a hearty good will toward all. He wrote or refurbished 130 plays, of which twenty survive. The *Miles Gloriosus* is a jolly picture of a braggart soldier, whose servant feeds him hopefully with lies:

> *Servant:* You saw those girls who stopped me yesterday?
> *Captain:* What did they say?
> *Servant:* Why, when you passed, they asked me,
>   "What! is the great Achilles here?" I answered,
>   "No, it's his brother." Then says the other one,
>   "Troth, he *is* handsome! What a noble man!
>   What splendid hair!" . . . and begged me, both of them,
>   . . . To make you take a walk again today,
>   That they might get a better sight of you.
> *Captain:* 'Tis a great nuisance being so very handsome! [34]

The *Amphitryon* turns the laugh upon Jove, who, disguised as Alcmena's husband, calls upon himself to witness his own oath and offers pious sacrifice to Jupiter.[35] The day after he seduces the lady she bears twins. At the end Plautus asks the god to forgive him and to take the lion's share of the applause. The story proved as popular in the Rome of Plautus as in the Athens of Menander, the Paris of Molière, or the New York of our own time. The *Aulularia* is the tale of a miser's hoard, told with more sympathy than in Molière's *Avare;* the miser collects the parings of his nails, and laments the wasted water in the tears he has shed. The *Menaechmi* is the old story of twins and their climactic recognition—a source for Shakespeare's *Comedy of Errors.* Lessing thought the *Captivi* the best play ever staged;[36] Plautus, too, liked it, and made its prologue say:

> It is not hackneyed or just like the rest;
> It has no filthy lines one must not quote,
> No perjured pander, and no wicked wench.

It is true; but the plot is so intricate, so dependent upon improbable coincidences and revelations, that a mind allergic to dead history may be forgiven for passing it by. What made these comedies succeed was not their ancient plots but their wealth of humorous incident, their rollicking puns as bad as Shakespeare's, their boisterous indecency, their gallery of precipitate women, and their occasional sentiment; in every play the audience could rely upon finding a love affair, a seduction, a handsome and virtuous hero, and a slave with more brains than all the rest of the characters put together. Here, almost at its outset, Roman literature touches the common man, and reaches, through

Greek disguises, to the realities of daily life as Latin poetry would never do again.

Probably in the year of Plautus' death (184), Publius Terentius Afer was born at Carthage of Phoenician, perhaps also of African, blood. We know nothing more of him until he appears as the slave of Terentius Lucanus in Rome. This senator recognized the shy lad's talent, gave him an education, and freed him; the youth in gratitude took his master's name. We get a pleasant note of Roman manners when we hear how Terence, "poor and meanly clad," came to the house of Caecilius Statius—whose comedies, now lost, were then dominating the Roman stage—and read him the first scene of the *Andria*. Caecilius was so charmed that he invited the poet to dinner and listened admiringly to the rest.[37] Terence soon won a hearing from Aemilianus and Laelius, who sought to form his style in the polished Latin so dear to their hearts. Hence gossip said that Laelius was writing Terence's plays—a report which the author, with tact and prudence, neither confirmed nor denied.[38] Moved perhaps by the respectful Hellenism of the Scipionic circle, Terence adhered faithfully to his Greek originals, gave his plays Greek titles, avoided allusions to Roman life, and called himself merely a translator[39]—a modest understatement of his work.

We do not know the fate of the play that Caecilius liked so well. The *Hecyra*, which Terence wrote next, failed because its audience slipped away to watch a bear fight. Fortune smiled in 162 when he produced his most famous play—the *Heauton Timoroumenos*, or "Self-Tormentor." It told the story of a father who had forbidden his son to marry the girl of his choice; the son married her nevertheless; the father disowned and banished him, and then, in self-punishing remorse, refused to touch his wealth, but lived in hard labor and poverty. A neighbor proposes to mediate; the father asks why he takes so kindly an interest in the troubles of others; and the neighbor replies in a world-renowned line which all the audience applauded:

Homo sum; humani nihil a me alienum puto—

"I am a man; I consider nothing human alien to me." In the following year *The Eunuch* was so well received that it was performed twice in the same day (then a rare event), and earned Terence 8000 sesterces ($1200) between morning and night.[40] A few months later appeared the *Phormio*, named from the witty servant who saved his master from paternal ire, and became the model for Beaumarchais' lusty Figaro. In 160 Terence's last play, the *Adelphi*, or "Brothers," was performed at the funeral games of Aemilius Paulus. Soon afterward the playwright sailed for Greece. On the way back he died of illness in Arcadia, in his twenty-fifth year.

His later plays had suffered in popularity because Hellenism had won in him too full a victory. He lacked the vivacity and abounding humor of Plautus; he never thought to deal with Roman life. There were no lusty villains in his comedies, no reckless strumpets; all his feminine characters were handled with tenderness, and even his prostitutes hovered on the brink of virtue. There were fine pithy lines and memorable phrases: *hinc illae lacrimae* ("hence those tears"), *fortes fortuna adiuvat* ("fortune favors the brave"), *quot homines tot sententiae* ("as many opinions as men"), and a hundred more; but they required for their appreciation a philosophical intelligence or literary sensitivity which the African slave found wanting in the Roman plebs. It did not care for his comedies that were half tragedies, his well-built but slowly moving plots, his subtle studies of strange characters, his quiet dialogue and too even style, and the almost insulting purity of his language; it was as if the audience felt that a breach, never to be healed, had been opened between the people and the literature of Rome. Cicero, too near to Catullus to see him, and too prudent to relish Lucretius, thought Terence the finest poet of the Republic. Caesar estimated him more justly when he praised the "lover of pure speech," but deplored the lack of *vis comica*—the power of laughter—in Terence, and called him *dimidiatus Menander*—"half a Menander." One thing, nevertheless, Terence had achieved: this Semitic alien, inspired by Laelius and Greece, had molded the Latin language at last into a literary instrument that would in the next century make possible the prose of Cicero, and Virgil's poetry.

VI. CATO AND THE CONSERVATIVE OPPOSITION

This Greek invasion, in literature, philosophy, religion, science, and art, this revolution in manners, morals, and blood, filled old-fashioned Romans with disgust and dread. Out on a Sabine farm a retired senator, Valerius Flaccus, fretted over the decay of the Roman character, the corruption of politics, the replacement of the *mos maiorum* with Greek ideas and ways. He was too old to fight the tide himself. But on a near-by homestead, just outside Reate, was a young plebeian peasant who showed all the old Roman qualities, loved the soil, worked hard, saved carefully, lived with conservative simplicity, and yet talked as brilliantly as a radical. He bore the names Marcus Porcius Cato: *Porcius* because his family had for generations raised pigs; *Cato* because they had been shrewd. Flaccus encouraged him to study law; Cato did, and won his neighbors' cases in the local courts. Flaccus advised him to go to Rome; Cato went, and by the age of thirty obtained the quaestorship (204). By 199 he was aedile, by 198 praetor, by 195 consul; in 191 tribune, in 184 censor. Meanwhile he served twenty-six years in the army as a fearless soldier and an able and ruthless general. He considered discipline the mother of character and freedom; he despised a soldier "who plied his hands in marching and his feet in fighting, and whose snore was louder than his battle cry"; but he won the respect of his troops by marching beside them on foot, giving each of them a pound of silver from the spoils, and keeping nothing for himself.[41]

In the intervals of peace he denounced rhetors and rhetoric, and became the most powerful orator of his time. The Romans listened in reluctant fascination, for no one had ever spoken to them with such obvious honesty and stinging wit; the lash of his tongue might fall upon any man present, but it was pleasant to see it descend upon one's neighbor. Cato fought corruption recklessly, and seldom let the sun set without having made new enemies. Few loved him, for his scar-covered face and wild red hair disconcerted them, his big teeth threatened them, his asceticism shamed them, his industry left them lagging, his green eyes looked through their words into their selfishness. Forty-four times his patrician enemies tried to destroy him by public indictments; forty-four times he was saved by the votes of farmers who, like him, resented venality and luxury.[42] When their votes made him censor, all Rome shuddered. He carried out the threats with which he had won the campaign; laid heavy taxes upon luxuries, fined a senator for extravagance, and excluded from the Senate six members in whose record he found malfeasance. He expelled Manilius for kissing his wife in public; as for himself, he said, he never embraced his wife except when it thundered—though he was glad when it thundered. He completed the drainage system of the city, cut the pipes that had clandestinely tapped water from the public aqueducts or conduits, compelled owners to demolish the illegal projections of their buildings upon or over the public right of way, forced down the price paid by the state for public works, and frightened the tax collectors into remitting a larger share of their receipts to the Treasury.[43] After five years of heroic opposition to the nature of man, he retired from office, made successful investments, manned his now vast farm with slaves, lent money at usurious rates, bought slaves cheap and—after training them in some skill—sold them dear, and became so rich that he could afford to write books—an occupation he despised.

Cato was the first great writer of Latin prose. He began by publishing his own speeches. Then he issued a manual of oratory, demanded a rugged Roman style instead of the Isocratean smoothness of the rhetors, and set a theme for Quintilian by defining the orator as *vir bonus dicendi peritus*[44]—"a good man skilled in speaking" (but was there ever union so rare?). He put his farming experiences to use by composing a treatise *De agri cultura*—the only work of Cato, and the oldest literary Latin, that time has saved. It is written in a simple and vigorous style, pithily compact; Cato wastes no words, and seldom condescends to a conjunction. He gives detailed advice on buying and selling slaves (old ones should be sold before they become a loss), on renting land to share-croppers, on viticulture and aboriculture, on domestic management and industries, on making cement and cooking dainties, on curing constipation and diarrhea, on healing snakebite with the dung of swine, and offering sacrifice to the gods. Asking himself what is the wisest use of agricultural land, he answers, "Profitable cattle raising." The next best? "Moderately profitable cattle raising." The third best? "Very unprofitable cattle raising." The fourth? "To plow the land." This was the argument that gave the *latifundia* to Italy.

The most important of his books was probably the lost *Origines*, a brave attempt to deal with the antiquities, ethnology, institutions, and history of Italy from the beginnings to the very year of Cato's death. Nearly all that we know of it is that, to spite the aristocracy through its touted ancestors, the author named no generals in it, but lauded by name an elephant that had fought well against Pyrrhus.[45] Cato designed this work, and his essays on oratory, agriculture, sanitation, military science, and law, to form an encyclopedia for the education of his son. By writing in Latin he hoped to displace the Greek textbooks that were in his judgment warping the minds of Roman youth. Though he himself studied Greek, he seems to have been sincere in his conviction that an education in Greek literature and philosophy would so rapidly dissolve the religious beliefs of young Romans that their moral life would be left defenseless against the instincts of acquisition, pugnacity, and sex. His condemnation, like Nietzsche's, took in Socrates; that prattling old midwife, Cato thought, had been rightly poisoned for undermining the morals and laws of Athens.[46] Even Greek physicians irked him; he preferred the old household remedies, and distrusted the ever-ready surgeons.

> The Greeks [he wrote to his son] are an intractable and iniquitous race. You may take my word for it that when this people bestows its literature upon Rome it will ruin everything. . . . And all the sooner if it sends us its physicians. They have conspired among themselves to murder all "barbarians." . . . I forbid you to have anything to do with physicians.[47]

Having these ideas, he was a natural antagonist of the Scipionic circle, which thought the spread of Greek literature in Rome a necessary ferment in lifting Latin letters and the Roman mind to a fuller growth. Cato lent his aid to the prosecution of Africanus and his brother; the laws against embezzlement should be no respecters of persons. Toward foreign states, with one exception, he advocated a policy of justice and nonintervention. Despising Greeks, he respected Greece; and when the imperialistic plunderers in the Senate were for waging war upon rich Rhodes, he made a decisive speech in favor of conciliation. The exception, as all the world knows, was Carthage. Sent there on an official mission in 175, he had been shocked by the rapid recovery of the city from the effects of the Hannibalic war, the fruitful orchards and vineyards, the wealth that poured in from revived commerce, the arms that mounted in the arsenals. On his return he held up before the Senate a bundle of fresh figs that he had plucked in Carthage three days before, as an ominous symbol of her prosperity and her nearness to Rome; and he predicted that if Carthage were left unchecked, she would soon be rich and strong enough to renew the struggle for the mastery of the Mediterranean. From that day, with characteristic pertinacity, he ended all his speeches in the Senate, on whatever subject, with his dour conviction: *Ceterum censeo delendam esse Carthaginem*—"Besides, I think that Carthage must be destroyed." The imperialists in the Senate agreed with him, not so much because they coveted Carthage's trade, as because they saw in the well-irrigated fields of north Africa a new investment for their money, new *latifundia* to be tilled by new slaves. They awaited eagerly a pretext for the Third Punic War.

VII. *CARTHAGO DELETA*

Their cue came from the most extraordinary ruler of his time. Masinissa, King of Numidia, lived ninety years (238-148), begot a son at eighty-six,[48] and by a vigorous regimen kept his health and strength almost to the end. He organized his nomad people into a settled agricultural society and a disciplined state, ruled them ably for sixty years, adorned Cirta, his capital, with lordly architecture, and left as his tomb the great pyramid that still stands near the town of Constantine, in Tunisia. Having won the friendship of Rome, and knowing the political weakness of Carthage, he repeatedly raided and appropriated Carthaginian terrain, took Great Leptis and other cities, and finally controlled all land approaches to the harassed metropolis. Bound by treaty to make no war without Rome's consent, Carthage sent ambassadors to the Senate to protest against Masinissa's encroachments. The Senate reminded them that all Phoenicians were interlopers in Africa and had no rights there which any well-armed nation was obliged to respect. When Carthage paid the last of her fifty annual indemnities of 200 talents to Rome, she felt herself released from the treaty signed after Zama. In 151 she declared war against Numidia, and a year later Rome declared war against her.

The latter declaration, and the news that the Roman fleet had already sailed for Africa, reached Carthage at the same time. The ancient city, however rich in population and trade, was quite unprepared for a major war. She had a small army, a smaller navy, no mercenaries, no allies. Rome controlled the sea. Utica therefore declared for Rome, and Masinissa blocked all egress from Carthage to the hinterland. An embassy hastened to Rome with authority to meet all demands. The Senate promised that if Carthage would turn over to the Roman consuls in Sicily 300 children of the noblest families as hostages, and would obey whatever orders the consuls would give, the freedom and territorial integrity of Carthage would be preserved. Secretly the Senate bade the consuls carry out the instructions that they had already received. The Carthaginians gave up their children with forebodings and laments; the relatives crowded the shores in a despondent farewell; at the last moment the mothers tried by force to prevent the ships from sailing; and some swam out to sea to catch a last glimpse of their children. The consuls sent the hostages to Rome, crossed to Utica with army and fleet, summoned the Carthaginian ambassadors, and required of Carthage the surrender of her remaining ships, a great quantity of grain, and all her engines and weapons of war. When these conditions had been fulfilled, the consuls further demanded that the population of Carthage should retire to ten miles from the city, which was then to be burned to the ground. The ambassadors argued in vain that the destruction of a city which had surrendered hostages and its arms without striking a blow was a treacherous atrocity unknown to history. They offered their own lives as a vicarious atonement; they flung themselves upon the ground and beat the earth with their heads. The consuls replied that the terms were those of the Senate and could not be changed.

When the people of Carthage heard what was demanded of them they lost their sanity. Parents mad with grief tore limb from limb the leaders who had advised surrendering the child hostages; others killed those who had counseled the surrender of arms; some dragged the returning ambassadors through the streets and stoned them; some killed whatever Italians could be found in the city; some stood in the empty arsenals and wept. The Carthaginian Senate declared war against Rome and called all adults—men and women, slave or free—to form a new army, and to forge anew the weapons of defense. Fury gave them resolution. Public buildings were demolished to provide metal and timber; the statues of cherished gods were melted down to make swords, and the hair of the women was shorn to make ropes. In two months the beleaguered city produced 8000 shields,

18,000 swords, 30,000 spears, 60,000 catapult missiles, and built in its inner harbor a fleet of 120 ships.[49]

Three years the city stood siege by land and sea. Again and again the consuls led their armies against the walls, but always they were repulsed; only Scipio Aemilianus, one of the military tribunes, proved resourceful and brave. Late in 147 the Roman Senate and Assembly made him consul and commander, and all men approved. Soon afterward Laelius succeeded in scaling the walls. The Carthaginians, though weakened and decimated by starvation, fought for their city street by street, through six days of slaughter without quarter. Harassed by snipers, Scipio ordered all captured streets to be fired and leveled to the ground. Hundreds of concealed Carthaginians perished in the conflagration. At last the population, reduced from 500,000 to 55,000, surrendered. Hasdrubal, their general, pleaded for his life, which Scipio granted, but his wife, denouncing his cowardice, plunged with her sons into the flames. The survivors were sold as slaves, and the city was turned over to the legions for pillage. Reluctant to raze it, Scipio sent to Rome for final instructions; the Senate replied that not only Carthage, but all such of her dependencies as had stood by her were to be completely destroyed, that the soil should be plowed and sown with salt, and a formal curse laid upon any man who should attempt to build upon the site. For seventeen days the city burned.

There was no treaty of peace, for the Carthaginian state no longer existed. Utica and other African cities that had helped Rome were left free under a protectorate; the remainder of Carthage's territory became the province of "Africa." Roman capitalists came in to divide the land into *latifundia*, and Roman merchants fell heir to Carthaginian trade. Imperialism became now the frank and conscious motive of Roman politics. Syracuse was absorbed into the province of Sicily, southern Gaul was subdued as a necessary land route to completely subjected Spain, and the Hellenistic monarchies of Egypt and Syria were quietly induced—like Antiochus IV by Popilius—to submit to the wishes of Rome. From the moral standpoint, which is always a window dressing in international politics, the destruction of Carthage and Corinth in 146 must rank among the most brutal conquests in history; from the standpoint of empire—of security and wealth—it laid simultaneously the two cornerstones of Rome's commercial and naval supremacy. From that moment the political history of the Mediterranean flowed through Rome.

In the midst of the war its chief instigators had died in the fullness of victory—Cato in 149, Masinissa in 148. The old censor had left a deep mark upon Roman history. Men would look back to him for many centuries as the typical Roman of the Republic: Cicero would idealize him in *De Senectute;* his great-great-grandson would reincarnate his philosophy without his humor; Marcus Aurelius would mold himself upon his example; Fronto would call upon Latin literature to return to the simplicity and directness of his style. Nevertheless, the destruction of Carthage was his only success. His war against Hellenism completely failed; every department of Roman letters, philosophy, oratory, science, art, religion, morals, manners, and dress surrendered to Greek influence. He hated Greek philosophers; his famous descendant would surround himself with them. The religious faith that he had lost continued to decline despite his efforts to reanimate it. Above all, the political corruption that he had fought in his youth grew wider and deeper as the stakes of office rose with the Empire's spread; every new conquest made Rome richer, more rotten, more merciless. She had won every war but the class war; and the destruction of Carthage removed the last check to civil division and strife. Now through a hundred bitter years of revolution Rome would pay the penalty of gaining the world.

BOOK II

THE REVOLUTION

145-30 B.C.

CHRONOLOGICAL TABLE

B.C.

139: First Servile War in Sicily
133: Tribunate and assassination of Tiberius Gracchus
132: *Fl.* Lucilius; Panaetius in Rome
124-123: Caius Gracchus tribune
122: C. Gracchus introduces state distribution of corn
121: Suicide of C. Gracchus
119: Marius tribune; 116: praetor
113-101: Wars against Cimbri and Teutones
112-105: The Jugurthine War
107, 104-100, 87: Marius consul
106: Birth of Cicero and Pompey
105: Cimbri defeat Romans near Arausio
103-99: Second Servile War in Sicily
103-100: Saturninus tribune
102: Marius defeats Cimbri at Aquae Sextiae
100: Marius suppresses Saturninus; birth of Julius Caesar
91: Reforms and assassination of M. Livius Drusus
91-89: The Social War in Italy
88: Sulla consul; flight of Marius
88-84: First Mithridatic War
87: Rebellion of Cinna and Marius; radical reign of terror
86: Sulla takes Athens and defeats Archelaus at Chaeronea
86: Marius and Cinna depose Sulla; death of Marius
85-84: Third and fourth consulates, and death of Cinna
83-81: Second Mithridatic War
83: Sulla lands at Brundisium
82: Sulla takes Rome; reactionary reign of terror
81: *Leges Corneliae* of Sulla
80-72: Revolt of Sertorius in Spain
79: Resignation and, 78: death, of Sulla
76: *Fl.* Varro
75-63: Third Mithridatic War; victories of Lucullus and Pompey
75: Cicero quaestor in Sicily
73-71: Third Servile War; Spartacus
70: First consulate of Crassus and Pompey; trial of Verres; Virgil b.
69: Titus Pomponius Atticus
68: Caesar quaestor in Spain
67: Pompey subdues the pirates
66: Cicero *Pro lege Manilia*
63: Cicero exposes Catiline; Octavius b.
63-12: M. V. Agrippa, engineer
62: Caesar praetor; misconduct of Clodius

B.C.

61: Caesar gov. of Further Spain; return and triumph of Pompey
60: First Triumvirate: Caesar, Crassus, Pompey
60-54: Poems of Catullus; Cornelius Nepos
59: Caesar consul; Lucretius' *De rerum natura*
58: Clodius, tribune, exiles Cicero; Caesar defeats Helvetii and Ariovistus in Gaul
57: Return of Cicero; Caesar defeats Belgae
56: Meeting of triumvirs at Luca
55: Pompey and Crassus consuls; theater of Pompey; Caesar in Germany and Britain
54: Caesar's second invasion of Britain
53: Violence of Clodius and Milo in Rome; defeat of Crassus at Carrhae
52: Murder of Clodius; trial of Milo; Pompey sole consul; revolt of Vercingetorix
51: Cicero governor of Cilicia; Cicero's *De re publica;* Caesar's *De bello Gallico*
49: Caesar crosses Rubicon and takes Rome
48: Battles of Dyrrachium and Pharsalus
48-47: Caesar in Egypt and Syria; Vitruvius, architect; Columella, botanist
47: Caesar's victories at Zela and Thapsus; suicide of Cato the Younger
46: Caesar appointed dictator for ten years; revision of calendar; Sallust, historian; Cicero *Pro Marcello*
45: Caesar defeats the Pompeians in Spain; Cicero's *Academica* and *De finibus*
44: Assassination of Caesar; Cicero's *Disputationes Tusculanae, De natura deorum, De officiis*
43: Second Triumvirate: Antony, Octavian, Lepidus; murder of Cicero
42: Brutus and Cassius die at Philippi
41: Antony and Cleopatra at Tarsus
40: Reconciliation of Antony and Octavian at Brundisium; Virgil's Fourth Eclogue
36: Antony invades Parthia
32: Antony marries Cleopatra
31: Octavian defeats Antony at Actium
30: Suicide of Antony and Cleopatra; Egypt annexed to the Empire; Octavian sole ruler of Rome

CHAPTER VI

The Agrarian Revolt

145-78 B.C.

I. THE BACKGROUND OF REVOLUTION

THE causes of revolution were many, the results were endless, the personalities thrown up by the crisis, from the Gracchi to Augustus, were among the most powerful in history. Never before, and never again till our own time, were such stakes fought for, never was the world drama more intense. The first cause was the influx of slave-grown corn from Sicily, Sardinia, Spain, and Africa, which ruined many Italian farmers by reducing the price of domestic grains below the cost of production and marketing. Second, was the influx of slaves, displacing peasants in the countryside and free workers in the towns. Third, was the growth of large farms. A law of 220 forbade senators to take contracts or invest in commerce; flush with the spoils of war, they bought up extensive tracts of agricultural land. Conquered soil was sometimes sold in small plots to colonists, and eased urban strife; more of it was given to capitalists in part payment of their war loans to the state; most of it was bought or leased by senators or businessmen on terms fixed by the Senate. To compete with these *latifundia* the little man had to borrow money at rates that insured his inability to pay; slowly he sank into poverty or bankruptcy, tenancy or the slums. Finally, the peasant himself, after he had seen and looted the world as a soldier, had no taste or patience for the lonely labor and unadventurous chores of the farm; he preferred to join the turbulent proletariat of the city, watch without cost the exciting games of the amphitheater, receive cheap corn from the government, sell his vote to the highest bidder or promiser, and lose himself in the impoverished and indiscriminate mass.

Roman society, once a community of free farmers, now rested more and more upon external plunder and internal slavery. In the city all domestic service, many handicrafts, most trade, much banking, nearly all factory labor, and labor on public works, were performed by slaves, reducing the wages of free workers to a point where it was almost as profitable to be idle as to toil. On the *latifundia* slaves were preferred because they were not subject to military service, and their number could be maintained, generation after generation, as a by-product of their only pleasure or their master's vice. All the Mediterranean region was raided to produce living machines for these industrialized farms; to the war prisoners led in after every victorious campaign were added the victims of pirates who captured slaves or freemen on or near the coasts of Asia, or of Roman officials whose organized man hunts impressed into bondage any provincial whom the local authorities did not dare protect.[1] Every week slave dealers brought their human prey from Africa, Spain, Gaul, Germany, the Danube, Russia, Asia, and Greece to the ports of the Mediterranean and the Black Sea. It was not unusual for 10,000 slaves to be auctioned off at Delos in a single day. In 177, 40,000 Sardinians, in 167, 150,000 Epirotes, were captured by Roman armies and sold as slaves, in the latter case at approximately a dollar a head.[2] In the city the lot of the slave was mitigated by humanizing contacts with his master and by hope of emancipation; but on the large farms no human relation interfered with exploitation. There the slave was no longer a member of the household, as in Greece or early Rome; he seldom saw his owner; and the rewards of the overseer depended upon squeezing every possible profit from the chattels entrusted to his lash. The wages of the slave on the great estates were as much food and clothing as would enable him to toil from sunrise to sunset every day—barring occasional holidays—until senility. If he complained or disobeyed, he worked with chains about his ankles and spent the night in an *ergastulum*—a subterranean dungeon that formed a part of nearly every *latifundium*. It was a wasteful as well as a brutal system, for it supported hardly a twentieth of the families that once had lived on the same acreage as freemen.

If we remember that at least half these slaves had once been free (for slaves seldom fought in the wars), we can surmise the bitterness of these broken lives, and must marvel at the rarity of their revolts. In 196 the rural slaves and free workers of Etruria rebelled; they were beaten down by Roman legions and, Livy tells us, "many were killed or taken prisoners; others were scourged and crucified." [3] In 185 a like uprising occurred in Apulia; 7000 slaves were captured and condemned to mines.[4] In the mines of New Carthage alone 4000 Spaniards worked as slaves. In 139 the "First Servile War" broke out in Sicily. Four hundred slaves accepted the call of Eunus and massacred the free population in the town of Enna; slaves poured from the farms and private dungeons of Sicily and swelled the number of the rebels to 70,000. They occupied Agrigentum, defeated the forces of the Roman praetor, and held nearly all the island till 131, when a consular army penned them into Enna and starved them into surrender. Eunus was taken to Rome, dropped into an underground cell, and allowed to die of hunger and lice.[5] In 133 lesser uprisings resulted in the execution of 150 slaves in

Rome, 450 in Minturnae, 4000 in Sinuessa. In that year Tiberius Gracchus passed the agrarian law that opened the Roman Revolution.

II. TIBERIUS GRACCHUS

He was the son of the Tiberius Sempronius Gracchus who had earned the gratitude of Spain by his generous administration, had served twice as consul and once as censor, and had saved the brother and married the daughter of Scipio Africanus. Cornelia gave him twelve children, all but three of whom died in adolescence; and his own death left upon her the burden of rearing Tiberius and Caius and a daughter—also named Cornelia—who became the wife of Scipio Aemilianus. Both parents shared in the Hellenistic culture and sympathies of the Scipionic circle. Cornelia gathered about her a literary *salon*, and wrote letters of so pure and elegant a style that they were reckoned as a distinguished contribution to Latin literature. An Egyptian king, says Plutarch, offered her his hand and throne in her widowhood, but she refused; she preferred to remain the daughter of one Scipio, the mother-in-law of another, and the mother of the Gracchi.

Brought up in the atmosphere of statesmanship and philosophy, Tiberius and Caius Gracchus knew both the problems of Roman government and the speculations of Greek thought. They were particularly influenced by Blossius, a Greek philosopher from Cumae, who helped to inspire in them a passionate liberalism that underestimated the power of the conservatives in Rome. The brothers were almost equally ambitious, proud, sincere, eloquent beyond reason, and brave without stint. Caius tells how Tiberius had the agrarian tragedy borne in upon him when, passing through Etruria, he "noted the dearth of inhabitants, and observed that those who tilled the soil and tended the flocks were foreign slaves." [6] Knowing that at that time only property holders could serve in the army, Tiberius asked himself how Rome could preserve its leadership or independence if the sturdy peasants that had once filled its legions were displaced by desolate and alien bondsmen. How could Roman life and democracy ever be healthy with a city proletariat festering in poverty, instead of a proud yeomanry owning and tilling the land? A distribution of land among the poorer citizens seemed the obvious and necessary solution of three problems: rural slavery, urban congestion and corruption, and military decay.

Early in 133 Tiberius Gracchus, elected a tribune of the people, announced his intention to submit to the Tribal Assembly three proposals: (1) that no citizen should be permitted to hold more than 333—or, if he had two sons, 667—acres of land bought or rented from the state; (2) that all other public lands that had been sold or leased to private individuals should be returned to the state for the purchase or rental price plus an allowance for improvements made; and (3) that the returned lands should be divided into twenty-acre lots among poor citizens, on condition that they agree never to sell their allotment, and to pay an annual tax on it to the Treasury. It was not a utopian scheme; it was merely an attempt to implement the Licinian laws passed in 367 B.C., which had never been repealed and never enforced. "The beasts of the field and the birds of the air," said Tiberius to the poorer plebeians in one of the epochal orations in Roman history,

> have their holes and their hiding places; but the men who fight and die for Italy enjoy only the light and the air. Our generals urge their soldiers to fight for the graves and shrines of their ancestors. The appeal is idle and false. You cannot point to a paternal altar. You have no ancestral tomb. You fight and die to give wealth and luxury to others. You are called the masters of the world, but there is not a foot of ground that you can call your own.[7]

The Senate denounced the proposals as confiscatory, charged Tiberius with seeking a dictatorship, and persuaded Octavius, another tribune, to prevent by his veto the submission of the bills to the Assembly. Gracchus thereupon moved that any tribune who acted contrary to the wishes of his constituents should be immediately deposed. The Assembly passed the measure, and Octavius was forcibly removed from the tribune's bench by the lictors of Tiberius. The original proposals were then voted into law; and the Assembly, fearing for Gracchus' safety, escorted him home.[8]

His illegal overruling of the tribunician veto, which the Assembly itself had long ago made absolute, gave his opponents a handle with which to frustrate him. They declared their purpose to impeach him at the end of his one-year term, as having violated the constitution and used force against a tribune. To protect himself he flouted the constitution further by seeking re-election to the tribunate for 132. As Aemilianus and Laelius and other senators who had defended his proposals now withdrew their support, he turned more completely to the plebs. He promised, if re-elected, to shorten the term of military service, to abolish the exclusive right of senators to act as jurors, and to admit the Italian allies to Roman citizenship. Meanwhile the Senate refused funds to the agrarian commission that had been appointed to execute Tiberius' laws. When Attalus III of Pergamum bequeathed his kingdom to Rome (133), Gracchus proposed to the Assembly that the personal and movable property of Attalus should be sold and the proceeds distributed to the recipients of state lands to finance the equipment of their farms. The proposal infuriated the Senate, which saw its authority over the provinces and the public purse being transferred to an unmanageable and unrepresentative Assembly largely of servile origin and alien stock. When election day came, Gracchus appeared in the Forum with armed guards and in mourning costume, implying that his defeat would mean his impeachment and death. As the voting proceeded, violence broke out on both sides. Scipio Nasica, crying that Tiberius wished to make himself king, led the senators, armed with clubs, into the Forum. The supporters of Gracchus, awed by patrician robes, gave way; Tiberius was killed by a blow on the head, and several hundred of his followers perished with him. When his younger brother Caius asked permission to bury him he was refused, and the bodies of the dead rebels were thrown into the Tiber, while Cornelia mourned.

The Senate sought to mollify the bitter plebs by consenting to the enforcement of the Gracchan laws. An increase of 76,000 in the register of citizens from 131 to 125 suggests that a large number of land allotments was actually made. But the agrarian commission found itself faced by many difficulties. Much of the land in question had been obtained from the state years or generations back and its present possessors claimed rights established and sanctified by time. Many parcels had been bought by new owners, for a substantial price, from those who had bought them cheaply from the government. The landowners in Italian allied states, whose squatter rights were imperiled by the laws, appealed to Scipio Aemilianus to defend them against the land board; and through his influence its operations were suspended. Public opinion flamed out against him; he was denounced as a traitor to the already sacred memory of Gracchus; and one morning in 129 he was discovered dead in his bed, apparently the victim of an assassin, who was never found.

III. CAIUS GRACCHUS

Ruthless gossip accused Cornelia of conspiring with her daughter, Scipio's deformed and unloved wife, to murder him. In the face of these calamities she sought consolation by devoting herself to her surviving son, the last of her "jewels." The murder of Tiberius aroused in Caius no mere spirit of vengeance, but a resolve to complete his brother's work. He had served with intelligence and courage under Aemilianus at Numantia, and he had won the admiration of all groups by the integrity of his conduct and the simplicity of his life. His passionate temperament, all the more vehement on occasion because so long controlled, made him the greatest of Roman orators before Cicero, and opened almost any office to him in a society where eloquence served only next to bravery in the advancement of men. In the fall of 124 he was elected tribune.

More realistic than Tiberius, Caius understood that no reform can endure which is opposed by the balance of economical or political power in the state. He aimed to bring four classes to his support: the peasantry, the army, the proletariat, and the businessmen. He won the first by renewing the agrarian legislation of his brother, extending its application to state-owned land in the provinces, restoring the land board, and personally attending to its operations. He fed the ambitions of the middle classes by establishing new colonies in Capua, Tarentum, Narbo, and Carthage, and by developing these as thriving centers of trade. He pleased the soldiers by passing a bill that they should be clothed at the public expense. He gained the gratitude of the urban masses by his *lex frumentaria*, or corn law, which committed the government to distribute wheat at six and one third asses per modius (thirty-nine cents a peck—half the market price) to all who asked for it. It was a measure shocking to old Roman ideas of self-reliance, and destined to play a vital role in Roman history. Caius believed that the grain dealers were charging the public twice the cost of production, and that his measure, through the economy of unified operation, would involve no loss to the state. In any case, the law turned the poor freemen of Rome from client supporters of the aristocracy into defenders of the Gracchi, as later of Marius and Caesar; it was the foundation stone of that democratic movement which would reach its peak in Clodius, and die at Actium.

Caius' fifth measure sought to assure the power of his party by ending the tradition whereby the richer classes in the Centurial Assembly voted first; hereafter the centuries were on each occasion to vote in an order determined by lot. He appeased the business class by giving them the exclusive right to serve as jurors in trials for provincial malfeasance; i.e., they were hereafter to be in large measure their own judges. He whetted their appetites by proposing a tax of one tenth, to be collected by them, on all the produce of Asia Minor. He enriched contractors, and reduced unemployment, by a program of road building in every part of Italy. Altogether these laws, despite the political trickery that colored some of them, formed the most constructive body of legislation offered to Rome before Caesar.

Armed with such varied support, Caius was able to override custom and win election to a second and successive tribunate. Probably it was now that he sought to "pack" the Senate by adding to its 300 members 300 more to be chosen from the business class by the Assembly. He proposed also to extend the full franchise to all the freemen of Latium, and a partial franchise to the remaining freemen of Italy. This, his boldest move toward a broader democracy, was his first strategic error. The voters showed no enthusiasm for sharing their privileges, even with men of whom only a small minority could have attended their assemblies in Rome. The Senate acted on its opportunity. Almost ignored by Caius, and reduced to apparent impotence, it saw in the brilliant tribune only a demagogic tyrant extending his personal power through the reckless distribution of state property and funds. Suddenly finding an ally in the jealous proletariat of Rome, and taking advantage of Caius' absence in establishing his colony at Carthage, the Senatorial party suggested to another tribune, Marcus Livius Drusus, that he should win over the new peasantry by a bill canceling the tax laid upon their lands in the Gracchan laws; and that he should at once please and weaken the proletariat by proposing the formation of twelve new colonies in Italy, each to take 3000 men from Rome. The Assembly readily passed the bills; and when Caius returned he found his leadership challenged at every step by the popular Drusus. He sought a third term as tribune but was defeated; his friends charged that he had been elected but that the ballots had been falsified. He counseled his followers against violence and retired to private life.

In the following year the Senate proposed the abandonment of the colony at Carthage; all sides interpreted the measure, openly or privately, as the first move in a campaign to repeal the Gracchan laws. Some of Caius' adherents attended the Assembly armed, and one of them cut down a conservative who threatened to lay hands upon Caius. On the morrow the senators appeared in full battle array, each with two armed slaves, and attacked the popular party entrenched on the Aventine. Caius did his best to quiet the tumult and avert further violence. Failing, he fled across the Tiber; overtaken, he ordered his servant to kill him; the slave obeyed and then killed himself. A friend cut off Caius' head, filled it with molten lead, and brought it to the Senate, which had offered a reward of its weight in gold.[9] Of Caius' supporters 250 fell in the fight, 3000 more were put to death by Senatorial decree. The city mob that he had befriended made no protest when his corpse, and those of his followers, were flung into the river; it was busy plundering his house.[10] The Senate forbade Cornelia to wear mourning for her son.

IV. MARIUS

The triumphant aristocracy devoted its subtlest intelligence to undoing the constructive, rather than the demagogic, elements in Caius' legislation. It did not dare eject the business class from the juries, or the contractors and publicans from their happy hunting ground in Asia; and it allowed the corn dole to stand as insurance against revolution. Into an otherwise attractive measure it inserted a clause permitting the recipients of the new lands to sell them; soon thousands of holders sold to the great slaveowners, and the *latifundia* resumed their growth. In 118 the land board was abolished. The masses in the capital raised no objection; they had decided that to eat state corn in the city was better than to sweat on the land or toil in pioneer colonies. Sloth combined with superstition (for the soil of Carthage had been cursed) to frustrate till Caesar the attempt to mitigate urban poverty by emigration. Wealth mounted, but it did not spread; in 104 B.C. a moderate democrat reckoned that only 2000 Roman citizens owned property.[11] "The condition of the poor," says Appian, "became even worse than before. . . . The plebeians lost everything. . . . The number of citizens and soldiers continued to decline." [12] More and more the legions had to be filled out with conscripts from the Italian states; but these men had no stomach for fighting or no love for Rome. Desertions multiplied, discipline deteriorated, and the defense of the Republic sank to its lowest ebb.

Consequently it was soon attacked, almost at the same time, on north and south. In 113 two Germanic tribes, the Cimbri and the Teutones, as if to give Rome a foretaste of its final fate, rolled down through Germany in a frightening avalanche of covered wagons—300,000 fighting men, with their wives, children, and animals. Perhaps the word had gone up over the Alps that Rome was in love with wealth and weary of war. The newcomers were tall and strong and fearless, so blond that the Italians described the children as having the white hair of old men. They met a Roman army at Noreia (now Neumarkt, in Carinthia) and destroyed it. They crossed the Rhine and defeated another Roman army; they poured west into southern Gaul and overcame a third, fourth, and fifth Roman army; at Arausio (Orange) 80,000 legionnaires and 40,000 camp followers were left dead on the field.[13] All Italy lay open to the invaders; and a terror rose in Rome such as it had not known since Hannibal.

Almost at the same time war broke out in Numidia. When Jugurtha, grandson of Masinissa, tortured his brother to death, and tried to deprive his cousins of their share in the kingdom, the Senate declared war upon him (111), with a view to making Numidia a province and opening it to Roman commerce and capital. Jugurtha bought patricians to defend his cause and crimes before the Senate, and bribed the generals sent against him into harmless activities or a favorable peace. Summoned to Rome, he opened his royal purse more lavishly, and was able to return unhindered to his capital.[14]

Only one officer emerged from these campaigns with credit. Gaius Marius, born like Cicero at Arpinum, son of a day laborer, had enlisted in the army at an early age, had won his scars at Numantia, had married an aunt of Caesar, and despite, or because of, his lack of education or manners, had been chosen a tribune of the plebs. In the fall of 108 he returned from his services as lieutenant to the incompetent Quintus Metellus in Africa, and ran for the consulate on a platform proposing that he should replace Metellus and bring the Jugurthine War to a successful end. He was elected, took command, and forced Jugurtha's surrender (106). The people did not learn at this time that the chief agent of this victory was a reckless young aristocrat, Lucius Sulla; they would hear from him later. Marius enjoyed a splendid triumph, and was so loved that the Assembly, ignoring a dying constitution, elected him consul year after year (104-100). The business classes supported him partly because his victories opened new fields for their enterprises, partly because he was clearly the only man who could repel the Celtic hordes. Rome already recognized in Caesar's uncle the uses of Caesarism; the dictatorship of a popular leader backed by a devoted army seemed to many weary Romans the only alternative to the oligarchic abuses of liberty.

After their victory at Arausio, the Cimbri had reprieved Rome by crossing the Pyrenees and ravaging Spain. But in 102 they returned to Gaul, greater in number than before, and entered into an agreement with the Teutones for a simultaneous assault by separate routes upon the rich plains of northern Italy. To meet the peril Marius resorted to a new form of military enrollment, which revolutionized first the army and then the state. He invited the enlistment of any citizen, property owner or not; offered attractive pay, and promised to release volunteers, and give them lands, after a completed campaign. The army now formed was composed chiefly of the city proletariat; its sentiments were hostile to the patrician Republic; it fought not for its country, but for its general and for booty; in this way, probably without knowing it, Marius laid the military basis of the Caesarian revolution. He was a soldier, not a statesman; he had no time to weigh distant political consequences. He led his recruits over the Alps, hardened their bodies with marches and drills, and developed their courage with attacks upon objectives that could be easily won; until they were trained he could not risk an engagement. The Teutones marched unhindered by his camp, asking the Romans derisively if they had messages for their wives in Rome, with whom the invaders proposed soon to refresh themselves; the number of the Teutones could be judged from the six days they took to pass the Roman camp. When they had all filed by, Marius ordered his army to fall upon their rear. In the great battle that ensued at Aquae Sextiae (Aix in Provence), the new legions slew or captured 100,000 men (102). "They say," Plutarch reports, "that the inhabitants of Marseilles made fences round their vineyards with the bones, and that the soil, after the bodies had rotted and the winter rains had fallen, was so fertilized with the putrefied matter which sank into it, that in the following season it yielded an unprecedented crop." [15] After resting his army for several months, Marius led it back into Italy, and met the Cimbri at Vercellae, near the Po (101), on the very field where Hannibal had won his first battle against Rome. The barbarians, to show their strength and courage, went naked in the snow, climbed over ice and through deep drifts to summits from which they tobogganed gaily along steep descents, using their shields as sleds.[16] In the battle that followed they were nearly all slain.

Marius was received in the rejoicing capital as a "second Camillus" who had turned back a Celtic invasion, and another Romulus who had refounded Rome. Part of the spoils he brought was bestowed upon him as a personal reward; thereby he became a rich man, with estates big "enough for a kingdom." In 100 he was elected consul for the sixth time. The tribune was Lucius Saturninus, a fiery radical who was resolved to achieve the goals of the Gracchi by law if possible, otherwise by force. He pleased Marius with a bill that bestowed colonial lands upon the veterans of the recent campaign, and Marius raised no objection when he lowered the price of state-doled corn from six and one third asses (thirty-nine cents) to five sixths of an as (five cents) per modius, or peck. The Senate sought to protect the Treasury and itself by having a tribune forbid the submission of these measures to a vote, but Saturninus proceeded with the voting nevertheless. Violence flared up on both sides. When Saturninus' bands killed Caius Memmius, one of the most respected of the aristocracy, the Senate took its final resort and, by a *senatusconsultum de re publica defendenda*, ordered Marius, as consul, to suppress the revolt.

Marius faced the bitterest choice of his life. It seemed a miserable end to his long career of service to the common people of Rome that he should now attack their leaders and his former friends. And yet he too distrusted the appeal to violence, and saw in revolution more ills than it could cure. He led a force against the rebels, let Saturninus be stoned to death, and then fled to a gloomy retirement, despised alike by the people he had championed and the aristocracy he had saved.

V. THE REVOLT OF ITALY

The revolution was now passing into civil war. When the Senate asked for help against the Cimbri from the eastern kings allied with Rome, Nicomedes of Bithynia replied that all men of military value in his kingdom had been sold into slavery to satisfy the extortions of the Roman tax collectors. Preferring an army for the moment, the Senate decreed that all males enslaved for unpaid taxes should be freed. Hearing of this order, hundreds of slaves in Sicily, many of them Greeks from the Hellenistic East, left their masters and, gathering before the palace of the Roman praetor, demanded their freedom. Their owners protested, and the praetor suspended the operation of the decree. The slaves organized themselves under a religious impostor, Salvius, and attacked the town of Morgantia. The citizens there secured the loyalty of most of their slaves by promising to liberate them if they repelled the attack; they repelled it, but were not freed; and many of them joined the revolt. About the same time (103), some 6000 slaves in the western end of the island rose under Athenion, a man of education and resolution. This force defeated army after army sent against it by the praetor, and moving eastward, merged with the rebels under Salvius. Together they mastered an army dispatched from Italy, but Salvius died in the moment of victory. Still other legions crossed the straits, under the consul Manius Aquilius (101); Athenion engaged him in single combat and was killed; the leaderless slaves were overwhelmed; thousands of them died in the field, thousands were returned to their masters, hundreds were shipped to Rome to fight wild beasts in the games that celebrated Aquilius' triumph. Instead of fighting, the slaves plunged their knives into one another's hearts until all lay dead.

A few years after this Second Servile war all Italy was in arms. For almost two centuries now Rome—a tiny nation between Cumae and Caere, between the Apennines and the sea—had ruled the rest of Italy as subject states. Even some cities close to Rome, like Tibur and Praeneste, had no representation in the government that ruled them. The Senate, the assemblies, and the consuls meted out decrees and laws to the Italian communities with the same high hand as to alien and conquered provinces. The resources and man power of the "allies" were drained by wars whose chief effect was to enrich a few families in Rome. Those states that had remained loyal to Rome in the ordeal with Hannibal had received scant reward; those that had helped him in any way had been punished with so servile a subjection that many of their freemen joined the slave revolts. A few rich men in the cities had been granted Roman citizenship; and the power of Rome had everywhere been used to support the rich against the poor. In 126 the Assembly forbade the inhabitants of the Italian towns to migrate to Rome; and in 95 a decree of the jealous capital expelled all residents whose citizenship was not Roman but merely Italian.

A member of the aristocracy paid with his life for trying to improve this situation. M. Livius Drusus was the son of the tribune who had rivaled Tiberius Gracchus; since his adopted son became the father-in-law of Augustus, the family bound the beginnings of the revolution with its end. Elected tribune in 91, he proposed three measures: (1) to divide more state lands among the poor; (2) to restore to the Senate its exclusive jury rights, but at the same time add 300 *equites*, or businessmen, to the Senate; and (3) to confer Roman citizenship upon all the freemen of Italy. The Assembly passed the first bill with pleasure, the second with indifference; the Senate rejected both and declared them void. The third never reached a vote, for an unknown assassin stabbed Drusus to death in his home.

Aroused to hope by Drusus' bill, and convinced by his fate that neither the Senate nor the Assembly would ever peaceably consent to share its privileges, the Italian states prepared for revolt. A federal republic was formed, Corfinium was named the capital, and the government was vested in a senate of 500 men chosen from all the Italian tribes except the Etruscans and Umbrians, who refused to join. Rome at once declared war upon the secessionists. All parties in the capital co-operated in what seemed to them a defense of the union; and every Roman dreaded the revenge the rebel states would take if they won this fratricidal "Social War." * Marius emerged from his solitude, took command, and won victory after victory while all other Roman generals but Sulla met defeat. In three years of war 300,000 men fell, and central Italy was devastated. When Etruria and Umbria were on the verge of going over to the rebels, Rome pacified them by a grant of full Roman citizenship; and in 90 the Roman franchise was offered to all Italian freemen or freedmen who would swear fealty to Rome. These belated concessions weakened the allies; one town after another laid down its arms; and in 89 this ferocious and costly war ended in a sullen peace. The Romans nullified the franchise they had granted by enrolling the new citizens in ten new tribes, which voted only after the existing thirty-five, and therefore usually to no use; besides, only a few of the new citizens could attend the assemblies in Rome. The deceived and desolate communities bided their time. Forty years later they would open their gates in welcome to a Caesar who offered them citizenship in a democracy that was dead.

VI. SULLA THE HAPPY

After a few years of peace the strife of Italians against Italians was resumed, merely changing its name from "Social" to "Civil," and its scene from the towns to Rome. Lucius Cornelius Sulla was chosen one of the consuls for 88, and took command of the army that was being prepared to march against Mithridates of Pontus. Sulpicius Rufus, a tribune, unwilling to put a conservative like Sulla in charge of so powerful a force, persuaded the Assembly to transfer the command to Marius, who, though fat and sixty-nine, was still rumbling with military ambition. Sulla refused to let his long-awaited chance for leadership slip by through what seemed to him the whim of an assembly spellbound by a demagogue and bribed, he was sure, by the merchants who liked Marius. He fled to Nola, won the army to his support, and marched at its head against Rome.

Sulla was unique in his origins, character, and fate. Born poor, he became the defender of the aristocracy, as the aristocratic Gracchi, Drusi, and

---

* This is the time-honored mistranslation of *Bellum Sociale*—the War of the Allies (*socii*) against Rome.

Caesar became leaders of the poor. He took his revenge upon life for having made him at once patrician and penniless; when he conquered money he made it serve his appetites without qualm or restraint. He was unprepossessing—glaring blue eyes in a white face mixed with rough blotches of fiery red, "like a mulberry sprinkled over with flour." [17] His education belied his looks. He was well versed in Greek as well as Roman literature, was a discriminate collector of art (usually by military means), had the works of Aristotle brought from Athens to Rome as part of his richest spoils, and found time, between war and revolution, to write his *Memoirs* for the misguidance of posterity. He was a jolly companion and a generous friend, devoted to wine, women, battle, and song. "He lived extravagantly," says Sallust, "yet pleasure never interfered with his duties, except that his conduct as a husband might have been more honorable." [18] He made his way rapidly, above all in the army, his happiest medium; he treated his soldiers as comrades, shared their work, their marches, and their dangers; "his only effort was not to allow anyone to surpass him in wisdom or bravery." [19] He believed in no gods, but many superstitions. Otherwise he was the most realistic as well as the most ruthless of the Romans; his imagination and his feelings were always under the control of his intellect. It was said of him that he was half lion and half fox, and that the fox in him was more dangerous than the lion.[20] Living half the time on battlefields, spending the last decade of his life in civil war, he nevertheless preserved his good humor to the end, graced his brutalities with epigrams, filled Rome with his laughter, made a hundred thousand enemies, achieved all his purposes, and died in bed.

Such a man seemed chemically compounded of the virtues and vices needed to subdue revolution at home and Mithridates abroad. His 35,000 trained men easily overcame the haphazard cohorts that Marius had improvised in Rome. Seeing his situation helpless, Marius escaped to Africa. Sulpicius was killed, betrayed by his servant; Sulla had the head of the tribune affixed to the rostrum that had lately rung with its eloquence; he rewarded the slave with freedom for his services, and death for his treachery. While his soldiers dominated the Forum he decreed that henceforth no measure should be offered to the Assembly except by permission of the Senate, and that the order of voting should be as in the "Servian constitution," which gave priority and advantage to the upper classes. He had himself chosen proconsul, allowed Cnaeus Octavius and Cornelius Cinna to be elected consuls (87), and then marched off to encounter Mithridates the Great.

He had hardly left Italy when the struggle of the plebeian *populares* and the patrician and equestrian *optimates* was resumed. The conservative supporters of Octavius fought in the Forum with the radical followers of Cinna, and in one day 10,000 men were killed. Octavius won, and Cinna fled to organize revolt in the neighboring towns. Marius, after a winter in hiding, sailed back to Italy, proclaimed freedom to slaves, and led a force of 6000 men against Octavius in Rome. The rebels won, slaughtered thousands, adorned the rostra with the heads of slain senators, and paraded the streets with noble heads on their pikes as a model for later revolutions. Octavius accepted death calmly as he sat in his robes of office on his tribune's chair. The carnage continued for five days and nights, the rebel terror for a year. A revolutionary tribunal subpoenaed patricians, condemned them if they had opposed Marius, and seized their property. A nod from Marius sufficed to send any man to death, usually by execution there and then. All of Sulla's friends were slain; his property was confiscated; he was deposed from his command and was declared a public enemy. The dead were refused burial and were left in the streets to be devoured by birds and dogs. The freed slaves plundered, raped, and killed indiscriminately, until Cinna gathered 4000 of them together, surrounded them with Gallic soldiery, and had them butchered to death.[21]

Cinna was now (86) chosen consul for the second time, Marius for the seventh. In the first month of his new term Marius died, aged seventy-one, worn out with hardships and violence. Valerius Flaccus, elected in his stead, passed a bill canceling seventy-five per cent of all debts, and then left for the East with an army of 12,000 men to depose Sulla from command. Enjoying undivided power at Rome, Cinna changed the Republic into a dictatorship, nominated all successful candidates for major offices, and had himself elected consul for four successive years.

When Flaccus left Italy, Sulla was besieging Athens, which had joined Mithridates in revolt. Receiving nothing from the Senate for the pay of his troops, he had financed his campaign by pillaging the temples and treasuries of Olympia, Epidaurus, and Delphi. In March, 86, his soldiers broke through a gate in Athens' walls, poured in, and revenged themselves for the city's long-delayed welcome by a riot of slaughter and robbery. Plutarch tells us that "there was no numbering the slain; . . . blood flowed through the streets and far out into the suburbs." [22] At last Sulla called a halt to the massacre, remarking generously that he would "forgive the living for the dead." He led his refreshed troops northward, defeated a great force at Chaeronea and Orchomenus, pursued its remnants across the Hellespont into Asia, and prepared to meet the main army of the Pontic king. But meanwhile Flaccus and his legions had also reached Asia, and Sulla was again informed that he must give up his command. He persuaded Flaccus to let him complete the campaign; thereupon Flaccus was killed by his lieutenant, Fimbria, who now declared himself commander of all Roman armies and advanced north against Sulla. Faced with this folly, Sulla made a peace with Mithridates (85), by which the King was to restore all the conquests that he had made in the war, surrender eighty galleys to Rome, and pay an indemnity of 2000 talents. Then Sulla turned south and met Fimbria in Lydia. Fimbria's soldiers went over to Sulla, and Fimbria committed suicide. Master now of the Greek East, Sulla exacted 20,000 talents as indemnities and accrued taxes from the revolted cities of Ionia. He sailed with his army to Greece, marched to Patrae, and arrived at Brundisium in 83. Cinna tried to stop him but was killed by his troops.

Sulla was bringing to the Treasury 15,000 pounds of gold and 115,000 pounds of silver, in addition to money and works of art which he credited to his personal account. But the democratic leaders, still in power in Rome, continued to brand him as a public enemy, and denounced his treaty with Mithridates as a national humiliation. Reluctantly Sulla led his 40,000 troops to the gates of Rome. Many of the aristocracy went out to join him; one of them, Cnaeus Pompey, brought a legion recruited entirely from his father's clients and friends. The son of Marius led an army out to encounter Sulla, was defeated, and fled to Praeneste, after sending instructions to the *populares* praetor to put to death all leading patricians still left in the capital. The praetor convoked the Senate, and the marked men were killed in their seats or their flight. The democratic forces then evacuated Rome, and Sulla entered it unhindered; but meanwhile a Samnite army of 100,000 men intent on avenging the Social War, marched up from the south and joined the democratic remnants. Sulla went out to meet them, and at the Colline Gate his 50,000 men won one of the bloodiest victories of ancient times. Sulla ordered 8000 prisoners shot down with arrows, on the ground that they could make more trouble alive than dead. The severed heads of the captured generals were displayed on pikes before the walls of Praeneste, where the last democratic army was standing siege. Praeneste fell, the young Marius killed himself, and his head was nailed up in the Forum—a procedure which frequent precedents had now made constitutional.

Sulla had no trouble in persuading the Senate to make him dictator. At once he issued a proscription list condemning to death forty senators and 2600 businessmen; these last had supported Marius against him, and had bought in at bargains the property of senators slain during the radical regime. He offered rewards to informers, and prizes up to 12,000 denarii ($7200) to those who should bring him the proscribed men, alive or dead. The Forum was adorned festively with the heads of the slain and with periodically renewed proscription lists which the citizens had to read at frequent intervals to know if they might still live. Massacre, banishment, and confiscation spread their horrors from Rome to the provinces and fell upon

Italian rebels and the followers of Marius everywhere. Some 4700 persons died in this aristocratic terror. "Men were butchered in the embraces of their wives," says Plutarch, "sons in the arms of their mothers." Many persons who had been neutral, or even conservative, were proscribed, exiled, or slain; Sulla, it was said, needed their money for his troops, his pleasures, or his friends. Confiscated property was sold to the highest bidder or to Sulla's favorites, and became the foundation of many fortunes, like those of Crassus and Catiline.

Using his powers as dictator, Sulla issued a series of edicts—known from his clan name as the Cornelian Laws—by which he hoped to establish a permanently aristocratic constitution. To replace dead citizens he enfranchised many Spaniards and Celts and some former slaves. He weakened the assemblies by adding these new members indebted to him and by again ruling that no measure should be put before the Assembly except by consent of the Senate. To stop the flocking of poor Italians to Rome he suspended the state distribution of corn; at the same time he eased the pressure of population in the city by distributing land to 120,000 veterans. To prevent the use of successive consulships as in effect a dictatorship, he re-emphasized the old requirement of a ten-year interval before the same office could be held a second time by the same man. He lowered the prestige of the tribunate by limiting its right of veto and making ex-tribunes ineligible for any higher office. He took from the business class, and restored to the Senate, the exclusive right to serve as jurors in the higher courts; and he replaced the farming of taxes to publicans with direct payments from the provinces to the Treasury. He reorganized the courts, increased their number for quicker trials, and carefully specified their functions and fields. All the legislative, judicial, executive, social, and sartorial privileges enjoyed by the Senate before the Gracchan revolt were returned to it, for Sulla was certain that only a monarchy or an aristocracy could wisely administer an empire. To renew the full membership of the Senate he allowed the Tribal Assembly to promote to it 300 members of the "equestrian" class. To show his confidence in this thoroughgoing restoration, he disbanded his legions and decreed that no army should be permitted in Italy. After two years of dictatorship, he resigned all his powers, re-established consular government, and retired to private life (80).

He was safe, for he had killed nearly all who could plan his assassination. He dismissed his lictors and guards, walked unharmed in the Forum, and offered to give an account of his official actions to any citizen who should ask for it. Then he went to spend his last years in his villa at Cumae. Tired of war, of power and glory, perhaps of men, he surrounded himself with singers, dancers, actors, and actresses; wrote his *Commentarii*, hunted and fished, ate and drank. Men had long since called him Sulla Felix, Sulla the Happy, because he had won every battle, known every pleasure, reached every power, and lived without fear or regret. He married five wives, divorced four, and eked out their inadequacy with mistresses. At 58 he developed an ulcer of the colon so severe that "the corrupted flesh," says Plutarch, "broke out into lice. Many men were employed day and night in destroying them, but they so multiplied that not only his clothes, baths, and basins, but his very food was polluted with them." [23] He died of intestinal hemorrhage, after hardly a year of retirement (78). He had not neglected to dictate his epitaph: "No friend ever served me, and no enemy ever wronged me, whom I have not repaid in full." [24]

CHAPTER VII

The Oligarchic Reaction

77-60 B.C.

I. THE GOVERNMENT

NEVERTHELESS, Sulla had erred twice on the side of generosity. He had spared the son and nephew of his enemies, the gay and brilliant Caius Julius Caesar, who was entering his twenties in the proscription years; Sulla had nominated him for death, but let him go on the importuning of their common friends; his judgment, however, was not mistaken when he remarked, "In that young man go many Mariuses." [1] And perhaps he erred in resigning too soon and enjoying himself to an early end. Had his patience and insight equaled his ruthlessness and courage, he might have saved Rome a half century of chaos and given her in 80 B.C. the peace and security, order and prosperity, that Augustus would bring back from Actium. He restored the old when he should have created the new.

Within a decade after his death his work was in ruins. Relaxed in the arms of victory, the patricians neglected the tasks of government to seek wealth in business and spend it in luxury. The struggle between the *optimates* and the *populares* continued with a bitterness that passionately awaited another opportunity for violence. The *optimates*, or "best people," made *nobilitas* their creed; not in the sense of *noblesse oblige*, but on the theory that good government required the restriction of major magistracies to men whose ancestors had held high office. Anyone who ran for office without such forebears was scorned as *novus homo*—a "new man," or upstart; such were Marius and Cicero. The *populares* demanded "career open to talent," all power to the assemblies, and free land for veterans and the poor. Neither party believed in democracy; both aspired to dictatorship, and both practiced intimidation and corruption without conscience or concealment. The *collegia* that had once been mutual-benefit societies became agencies for the sale of great blocks of plebeian votes. The business of vote buying reached a scale where it required a high specialization of labor: there were *divisores*, who bought votes, *interpretes*, or go-betweens, and *sequestres*, who held the money until the votes had been delivered.[2] Cicero describes candidates as going about purse in hand among the electors in the Field of Mars.[3] Pompey had his mediocre friend Afranius made consul by inviting the leaders of the tribes to his gardens and there paying them for the ballots of their groups.[4] So much money was borrowed to finance candidacies that the campaigns raised the interest rate to eight per cent per month.[5]

The courts, now pre-empted by senators, rivaled the polls in corruption. Oaths had lost all value as testimony; perjury was as common as bribery. Marcus Messala, being indicted for buying his election to the consulate (53), was unanimously acquitted, though even his friends acknowledged his guilt.[6] "Trials are now managed so venally," wrote Cicero to his son, "that no man will ever be condemned hereafter except for murder." [7] He should have said "no man of means"; for "without money and a good lawyer," said another advocate at this period, "a plain, simple defendant may be accused of any crime which he has not committed, and will certainly be convicted." [8] Lentulus Sura, having been acquitted by two votes, mourned the extra expense he had gone to in bribing one more judge than he had needed.[9] When Quintus Calidus, praetor, was convicted by a jury of senators, he calculated that "they could not honestly require less than 300,000 sesterces to condemn a praetor." [10]

Protected by such courts, the Senatorial proconsuls, the tax gatherers, the moneylenders, and the business agents milked the provinces at a rate that would have angered their predecessors with envy. There were several honorable and competent provincial governors, but what could be expected of the majority? They served without pay, usually for a year's term; in that brief time they had to accumulate enough to pay their debts, buy another office, and set themselves up for life in the style befitting a great Roman. The sole check upon their venality was the Senate; and the senators could be trusted as gentlemen not to raise a fuss, since nearly all of them had done, or hoped soon to do, the same. When Caesar went to Farther Spain as proconsul in 61 he owed $7,500,000; when he returned in 60 he cleared off these debts at one stroke. Cicero thought himself a painfully honest man; he made only $110,000 in his year as governor of Cilicia and filled his letters with wonder at his own moderation.

The generals who conquered the provinces were the first to profit from them. Lucullus, after his campaigns in the East, became a synonym for luxury. Pompey brought in from the same region $11,200,000 for the Treasury and $21,000,000 for himself and his friends; Caesar took literally untold millions from Gaul. After the generals came the publicans, who collected from the people twice the amount which they remitted to Rome. When a province or city could not raise enough from its subjects to pay the demanded tribute or tax, Roman financiers or statesmen would lend them the necesssary funds at from twelve to forty-eight per cent interest, to be collected, if need be, by the Roman army through siege, conquest, and pillage. The Senate had forbidden its members to take part in such loans, but pompous aristocrats like Pompey, and saints like Brutus, skirted the law by lending through intermediaries. In some years the province of Asia paid Romans twice as much in interest on loans as it paid to the publicans and the Treasury.[11] The paid and unpaid interest on money borrowed by the cities of Asia Minor to meet Sulla's exactions in 84 had swelled by 70 to six times the principal. To meet the charges on this debt communities sold their public buildings and statuary, and parents sold their children into slavery, for defaulting debtors could be stretched on the rack.[12] If any wealth still remained, a flock of entrepreneurs came in from Italy, Syria, and Greece, with Senatorial contracts for "developing" the mineral, timber, or other resources of the province; trade followed the flag. Some bought slaves, some sold or bought goods, others purchased land and set up provincial *latifundia* larger than those of Italy. "No Gaul," said Cicero in 69, with his customary exaggeration, "carries through any business without the intervention of a Roman citizen; not a penny changes hands there without passing through the ledgers of a Roman."

Antiquity had never known so rich, so powerful, and so corrupt a government.

II. THE MILLIONAIRES

The business classes reconciled themselves to the rule of the Senate because they were better prepared than the aristocracy to exploit the provinces. That "concord of the orders," or co-operation of the two upper classes, which Cicero was to preach as an ideal, was already a reality in his youth; they had agreed to unite and conquer. Businessmen and their aggressive agents crowded the basilicas and streets of Rome and swarmed into provincial markets and capitals. Bankers issued letters of exchange on their provincial affiliates,[13] and lent money for everything, even political careers. Merchants and financiers swung their influence to the *populares* when the Senate proved selfish, and back to the *optimates* when democratic leaders tried to keep their pre-election promises to the proletariat.

Crassus, Atticus, and Lucullus typify the three phases of Roman wealth: acquisition, speculation, luxury. Marcus Licinius Crassus was of aristocratic lineage. His father, a famous orator, consul, and censor, had fought for Sulla and had killed himself rather than yield to Marius. Sulla rewarded the son by letting him buy at bargain prices the confiscated properties of proscribed men. As a youth Marcus had studied literature and philosophy and had assiduously practiced law; but now the smell of money intoxicated him. He organized a fire brigade—something new to Rome; it ran to fires, sold its services on the spot, or bought endangered buildings at nominal sums and then put out the fire; in this way Crassus acquired hundreds of houses and tenements, which he let at high rentals. He bought state mines when Sulla denationalized them. Soon he had inflated his fortune from 7,000,000 to 170,000,000 sesterces ($25,500,000)—a sum nearly equal to the total yearly revenue of the Treasury. No man should consider himself rich, said Crassus, unless he could raise, equip, and maintain his own army; [14] it was his destiny to perish by his definition. Having become the wealthiest man in Rome, he was still unhappy; he itched for public office, for a province, for the leadership of an Asiatic campaign. He solicited votes humbly in the streets, memorized the first names of countless citizens, lived in conspicuous simplicity, and, to tether influential politicians to his star, lent them money without interest but payable on demand. With all his eager ambitions he was a kindly man, accessible to everyone, generous without limit to his friends, and contributing to both political parties with that bilateral wisdom which has always distinguished his kind. He fulfilled all his dreams: he became consul in 70 and again in 55, governed Syria, and helped to raise the great army that he led against Parthia. He was defeated at Carrhae, treacherously captured, and barbarously slain (53); his head was cut off, and into the mouth his conqueror poured molten gold.

Titus Pomponius Atticus, though of equestrian birth, was a truer aristocrat than Crassus and a higher type of millionaire: as honest as Meyer Anschel of the *rot Schild*, as learned as Lorenzo de' Medici, as financially astute as Voltaire. We hear of him first as a student in Athens, when his conversation, and his reading of Greek and Latin poetry, so charmed Sulla that the bloodstained commander wished, in vain, to take him back to Rome as a personal companion. He was a scholar and a historian, wrote an outline of universal history,[15] lived most of his life in the philosophical circles of Athens, and earned his cognomen from his Attic erudition and philanthropies. His father and his uncle left him some $960,000; he invested it in a great cattle ranch in Epirus, in buying and letting houses in Rome, in training gladiators and secretaries and hiring them out, and in publishing books. When good openings came he lent money at profitable rates; but to Athens and his friends he lent without interest.[16] Men like Cicero, Hortensius, and the younger Cato entrusted him with their savings and the management of their affairs, and honored him for his caution, his integrity, and his dividends. Cicero was glad to have his advice not only in purchasing houses, but in choosing statuary to adorn them and books to fill his library. Atticus entertained frugally and lived with the modesty of a true Epicurean; but his genial friendship and his cultivated conversation made his house in Rome the *salon* of all political celebrities. He contributed to all parties and was spared in all proscriptions. At the age of seventy-seven, finding himself afflicted with a painful and incurable disease, he starved himself to death.

Lucius Licinius Lucullus, of high patrician family, sallied forth in 74 to complete Sulla's war against Mithridates. For eight years he led his inadequate forces with courage and skill; then, as his campaign was nearing full success, his tired troops mutinied, and he guided their retreat from Armenia to Ionia through perils as great as those that had immortalized Xenophon. Relieved of his command by political intrigue, he returned to Rome and, with his patrimony and his spoils, spent the rest of his life in quiet but ornate luxury. He built on the Pincian hill a palace with spacious halls, loggias, libraries, and gardens; at Tusculum his estate extended for many miles; he bought a villa at Misenum for 10,000,000 sesterces ($1,500,000); and he turned the entire island of Nisida into his summer resort. His various gardens were famous for their horticultural innovations; it was he, for example, who introduced the cherry tree from Pontus to Italy, whence it was carried to north Europe and America. His dinners were the culinary events of the Roman year. Cicero tried once to find out how Lucullus ate when alone; he asked Lucullus to invite him and some friends to dinner that evening, but pledged Lucullus to send no word of warning to his servants. Lucullus agreed, merely stipulating that he be allowed to notify his staff that he would eat in the "Apollo Room" that evening. When Cicero and the rest came they found a lavish repast. Lucullus had several dining rooms in his city palace, each selected according to the splendor of the feast; the Apollo Room was reserved for meals costing 200,000 sesterces or more.[17] But Lucullus was no gourmand. His houses were galleries of well-chosen art; his libraries were the resort of scholars and his friends; he himself was learned in both the classical literatures and in all the philosophies—naturally favoring that of Epicurus. He smiled at Pompey's strenuous life; one campaign seemed to him enough for one life; anything more was mere vanity.

His example spread without his taste among the rich of Rome; soon patricians and magnates were competing in luxurious display, while revolt brewed in bankrupt provinces and men starved in the slums. Senators lounged in bed till noon and seldom attended sessions. Some of their sons dressed and walked like courtesans, wore frilled robes and women's sandals, decked themselves with jewelry, sprinkled themselves with perfume, deferred marriage or avoided parentage, and emulated the bisexual impartiality of the Greeks. Senatorial houses cost up to 10,000,000 sesterces; Clodius, leader of the plebs, built a mansion costing 14,800,000. Lawyers like Cicero and Hortensius, despite the Cincian law against legal fees, competed in palaces as well as in oratory; the gardens of Hortensius contained the largest zoological collection in Italy. All men of any pretension had villas at or near Baiae, where the aristocracy took the baths, enjoyed the Bay of Naples, and declared a moratorium on monogamy. Other villas rose on the hills outside of Rome; rich men had several, moving from one to another as the season changed. Fortunes were spent on interior decoration, furniture, or silver plate. Cicero paid 500,000 sesterces for a table of citrus wood; a million sesterces might be paid for one of cypress wood; even the younger Cato, pillar of all Stoic virtues, was alleged to have paid 800,000 sesterces for some table spreads from Babylon.[18]

A horde of specialized slaves formed the staff of these palaces—valets, letter carriers, lamplighters, musicians, secretaries, doctors, philosophers, cooks. Eating was now the chief occupation of upper-class Rome; there, as in the ethics of Metrodorus, "everything good had reference to the belly." At a repast given in 63 by a high priest, and attended incongruously by Vestal Virgins and Caesar, the hors d'oeuvres consisted of mussels, spondyles, fieldfares with asparagus, fattened fowls, oyster pastries, sea nettles, ribs of roe, purple shellfish, and songbirds. Then came the dinner—sows' udders, boar's head, fish, duck, teals, hares, fowl, pastries, and sweets.[19] Delicacies were imported from every part of the Empire and beyond: peacocks from Samos, grouse from Phrygia, cranes from Ionia, tunnyfish from Chalcedon, muraenas from Gades, oysters from Tarentum, sturgeons from Rhodes. Foods produced in Italy were considered a bit vulgar, fit only for plebeians. The actor Aesopus gave a dinner at which songbirds were eaten to the cost of $5000.[20] Sumptuary laws continued to denounce expensive meals, and to be ignored. Cicero tried to obey, ate the legally permitted vegetables, and suffered ten days of diarrhea.[22]

Some of the new wealth disported itself in enlarged theaters and extended games. In 58 Aemilius Scaurus built a theater with 8000 seats, 360 pillars, 3000 statues, a three-storied stage, and three colonnades—one of wood, one of marble, and one of glass; his slaves, rebelling against the hard labor he had exacted of them, burned down the theater soon afterward, netting him a loss of 100,000,000 sesterces.[23] In 55 Pompey provided funds for the first permanent stone theater in Rome—with 17,500 seats, and a spacious porticoed park for entr'acte promenades. In 53 Scribonius Curio, one of Caesar's generals, erected two wooden theaters, each a semicircle, back to back; in the morning the two stages presented plays; then, while the spectators were still in their seats, the two structures were turned on pivots and wheels, the semicircles formed an amphitheater and the united stages became an arena for gladiatorial games.[24] Never had such games been so frequent, costly, or prolonged. In a single day of the games given by Caesar 10,000 gladiators took part, many of whom were killed. Sulla exhibited a fight involving a hundred lions, Caesar four hundred, Pompey six hundred. Beasts fought men, men fought men; and the vast audience waited hopefully for the sight of death.

III. THE NEW WOMAN

The increase of wealth conspired with the corruption of politics to loosen morals and the marriage bond. Despite increasing competition from women and men, prostitution continued to flourish; brothels and the taverns that usually housed them were so popular that some politicians organized votes through the *collegium lupanariorum,* or guild of brothelkeepers.[25] Adultery was so common as to attract little attention unless played up for political purposes, and practically every well-to-do woman had at least one divorce. This was not the fault of women; it resulted largely from the subordination of marriage, in the upper classes, to money and politics. Men chose wives, or youths had wives chosen for them, to get a rich dowry or make advantageous connections. Sulla and Pompey married five times. Seeking to attach Pompey to him, Sulla persuaded him to put away his first wife and marry Aemilia, Sulla's stepdaughter, who was already married and with child; Aemilia reluctantly agreed, but died in childbirth shortly after entering Pompey's house. Caesar gave his daughter Julia to Pompey in marriage as an item in their triumviral alliance. The Empire, growled Cato, had become a matrimonial agency.[25a] Such unions were *mariages de politique;* as soon as their utility ended, the husband looked for another wife as a steppingstone to higher place or greater wealth. He did not need to give a reason; he merely sent his wife a letter announcing her freedom and his. Some men did not marry at all, alleging distaste for the forwardness and extravagance of the new woman; many lived in free unions with concubines or slaves. The censor Metellus Macedonicus (131) had begged men to marry and beget children as a duty to the state, however much of a nuisance (*molestia*) a wife might be; [26] but the number of celibates and childless couples increased more rapidly after he spoke. Children were now luxuries which only the poor could afford.

Under these circumstances women could hardly be blamed for looking lightly upon their marriage vows and seeking in liaisons the romance or affection that political matrimony had failed to bring. There was, of course, a majority of good women, even among the rich; but a new freedom was breaking down the old *patria potestas* and the ancient family discipline. Roman women now moved about almost as freely as men. They dressed in diaphanous silks from India and China, and ransacked Asia for perfumes and jewelry. Marriage *cum manu* disappeared, and women divorced their husbands as readily as men their wives. A growing proportion of women sought expression in cultural pursuits: they learned Greek, studied philosophy, wrote poetry, gave public lectures, played, sang, and danced, and opened literary *salons;* some engaged in business; a few practiced medicine or law.

Clodia, the wife of Quintus Caecilius Metellus, was the most prominent of those ladies who in this period supplemented their husbands with a succession of *cavalieri serventi.* She had a gay passion for the rights of women; shocked the older generation by going about unchaperoned with her male friends after her marriage; accosted people whom she met and knew, and sometimes publicly kissed them, instead of lowering her eyes and crouching in her carriage as proper women were supposed to do. She invited her male friends to dine with her while her husband absented himself with the chivalry of the Marquis du Châtelet. Cicero, who cannot be trusted, describes "her loves, adulteries, and lecheries, her songs and symphonies, her suppers and carousing, at Baiae on land and sea." [27] She was a clever woman, who could sin with irresistible grace, but she underestimated the selfishness of men. Each lover demanded her entirely until his appetite waned, and each became her shocked enemy when she found a new friend. So Catullus (if she was his Lesbia) besmeared her with ribald epigrams; and Caelius, alluding to the price paid for the poorest prostitutes, called her in open court the *quadrantaria*—the quarter-of-an-as (one-and-a-half-cent) woman. She had accused him of trying to poison her; he hired Cicero to defend him; and the great orator did not hesitate to charge her with incest and murder, protesting, however, that he was "not the enemy of women, still less of one who was the friend of all men." Caelius was acquitted, and Clodia paid some penalty for being the sister of that Publius Clodius who was the most radical leader in Rome and Cicero's implacable enemy.

IV. ANOTHER CATO

Amid all this corruption and laxity one man stood out as an exemplar and professor of the ancient ways. Marcus Porcius Cato the Younger had violated a precept of his great-great-grandfather by studying Greek; from it he derived that Stoic philosophy which shared with his republican convictions the inflexible devotion of his life. He inherited 120 talents ($432,000), but lived in sedulous simplicity. He lent money, but took no interest. He lacked his ancestor's rough humor, and frightened people by what seemed to them his obstinate incorruptibility and his untimely addiction to principles. His life was an unforgivable indictment of theirs; they wished he would sin a little, if only out of a decent respect for the habits of mankind. They must have rejoiced when, with an almost Cynical conception of woman as a biological instrument, he "lent" his wife Marcia to his friend Hortensius— i.e., divorced her and assisted at her marriage to the orator—and later, when Hortensius died, took her again to wife.[28] He could not be popular, for he was the relentless enemy of all dishonesty, the stern defender of the *patria potestas*, a more merciless *censor moralium* than Cato Censor himself. He seldom laughed or smiled, made no effort to be affable, and sharply reprimanded any who dared to flatter him. He was defeated for the consulship, said Cicero, because he acted like a citizen in Plato's republic instead of a Roman living among "the dregs of Romulus' posterity." [29]

As quaestor Cato made himself a terror to all incompetence and malfeasance, and guarded the Treasury ferociously from all political raids; nor did his watchfulness abate when his term expired. His indictments fell upon all parties and left him with a thousand admirers but hardly a friend. As praetor he persuaded the Senate to issue an order that all candidates, soon after election, must come into court and give under oath a detailed account of their expenses and proceedings in the campaign. The measure disturbed so many politicians, most of whom depended upon bribery, that they and their clients, when Cato next appeared in the Forum, reviled and stoned him; whereupon he climbed to the rostrum, faced the crowd resolutely, and talked them into submission. As tribune he led a legion into Macedonia; his attendants rode on horseback, he went on foot. He scorned the business classes and defended aristocracy, or rule by birth, as the only alternative to plutocracy, or rule by wealth. He warred without truce upon the men who were corrupting Roman politics with money, and Roman character with luxury; and he stood out to the last against every move, by either Pompey or Caesar, toward dictatorship. When Caesar had overthrown the Republic Cato died by his own hand, with a volume of philosophy by his side.

V. SPARTACUS

Misgovernment now reached a height, and democracy a depth, rare in the history of states. In 98 B.C. the Roman general Didius repeated the exploit of Sulpicius Galba: he lured a whole tribe of troublesome natives into a Roman camp in Spain by pretending to register them for a distribution of land; when they had entered, with their wives and children, he had them all slaughtered. On his return to Rome he was awarded a public triumph.[30] Shocked by the brutalities of empire, a Sabine officer in the Roman army, Quintus Sertorius, went over to the Spaniards, organized and drilled them, and led them to victory after victory over the legions sent to subdue him. For eight years (80-72) he ruled a rebel kingdom, winning the affection of the people by his just administration and by his establishment of schools for the education of native youth. Metellus, the Roman general, offered a hundred talents ($360,000) and 20,000 acres of land to any Roman who should kill him. Perpenna, a Roman refugee in Sertorius' camp, invited him to dinner, assassinated him, and made himself master of the army that Sertorius had trained. Pompey was sent against Perpenna and easily defeated him; Perpenna was executed, and the exploitation of Spain was resumed.

The next act of the revolution came not from the free but from the slave. Lentulus Batiates kept at Capua a school of gladiators—slaves or condemned criminals trained to fight animals, or one another, to the death in public arenas or private homes. Two hundred of them tried to escape; seventy-eight succeeded, armed themselves, occupied a slope of Vesuvius, and raided the adjoining towns for food (73). As their leader they chose a Thracian, Spartacus, "a man not only of high spirit and bravery," says Plutarch, "but also in understanding and gentleness superior to his condition." [31] He issued a call to the slaves of Italy to rise in revolt; soon he had 70,000 men, hungering for liberty and revenge. He taught them to manufacture their own weapons, and to fight with such order and discipline that for years they outmatched every force sent to subdue them. His victories filled the rich men of Italy with fear, and its slaves with hope; so many of these tried to join him that after raising his army to 120,000 he refused further recruits, finding it difficult to care for them. He marched his horde toward the Alps, "intending, when he had passed them, that every man should go to his own home." [32] But his followers did not share these refined and pacific sentiments; revolting against his leadership, they began to loot the towns of northern Italy. The Senate now sent both consuls, with heavy forces, against the rebels. One army met a detachment that had seceded from Spartacus, and slaughtered it; the other attacked the main rebel body, and was defeated. Moving again toward the Alps, Spartacus encountered a third army, led by Cassius, and decimated it; but finding his way blocked by still other legions, he turned south and marched toward Rome.

Half the slaves of Italy were on the verge of insurrection, and in the capital no man could tell when the revolution would break out in his very home. All that opulent society, which had enjoyed every luxury slavery could produce, trembled at the thought of losing everything—mastery, property, life. Senators and millionaires cried out for a better general; few offered themselves, for all feared this strange new foe. At last Crassus came forward and was given the command, with 40,000 men; and many of the nobility, not all forgetting the traditions of their class, joined him as volunteers. Knowing that he had an empire against him, and that his men could never administer either the Empire or the capital, Spartacus passed Rome by and continued south to Thurii, marching the length of Italy in the hope of transporting his men to Sicily or Africa. For a third year he fought off all attacks. But again his impatient soldiers rejected his authority and began to ravage the neighboring towns. Crassus came upon a horde of these marauders and slew them, 12,300 in number, every man fighting to the last. Meanwhile Pompey's legions, returning from Spain, were sent to swell the forces of Crassus. Despairing of victory over such a multitude, Spartacus flung himself upon the army of Crassus and welcomed death by plunging into the midst of the foe. Two centurions fell by his hand; struck down and unable to rise, he continued the fight on his knees; at last he was so cut to pieces that his body could not later be identified. The great majority of his followers perished with him; some fled, and became hunted men in the woods of Italy; 6000 captives were crucified along the Appian Way from Capua to Rome (71). There their rotting bodies were left to hang for months, so that all masters might take comfort, and all slaves take heed.

VI. POMPEY

When Crassus and Pompey returned from this campaign they did not, as the Senate wished and law required, disband or disarm their troops at the gates. Camping outside the walls, they asked permission to stand for the consulate without entering the city—again a violation of precedent; in addition Pompey demanded land for his soldiers and a triumph for himself. The Senate refused, hoping to play one general against the other. But Crassus and Pompey joined hands, made a sudden alliance with the *populares* and the business class, and by generous bribery won election as consuls for 70 B.C. The magnates entered the partnership for two immediate ends: to recapture power in the juries that tried them, and to replace Lucullus—who had ruled the Roman East with unprofitable integrity—by a man of their own class and views. In Pompey they recognized their man.

Pompey was now thirty-five, and already the veteran of many campaigns. Born of a rich equestrian family, he had won universal admiration by his courage and temperance, and his skill in every branch of sport and war. He had cleared Sicily and Africa of Sulla's enemies, and by his victories and his pride had earned from the humorous dictator the cognomen Magnus, the Great. He had achieved a triumph almost before a beard.[33] He was so handsome that the courtesan Flora declared she could never part from him without a bite.[34] He was sensitive and shy, and blushed when he had to address a public gathering, but in battle he was in these days impetuously brave; in later life timidity and corpulence burdened his generalship, and he hesitated till lost. His mind had neither brilliance nor depth; his policies were made for him, not by him—first by the politicians of the *populares*, then by the Senatorial oligarchy. His great wealth lifted him above the coarser temptations of politics; amid the selfishness and corruption of his time he shone by his patriotism and his integrity; he seems to have sincerely sought the public good as well as his own. His outstanding fault was vanity. His early successes led him to overrate his abilities, and he wondered why Rome waited so long to make him in everything but name a king.

The two favorites of Sulla, now consuls together, devoted themselves to overthrowing the Sullan constitution. Pompey and Crassus paid their debt to the *populares* by passing a bill that restored all the power of the tribunes. They consolidated their alliance with business by directing Lucullus to give the publicans full charge of tax collections in the East; and they supported legislation that required juries to be drawn equally from the Senate, the equestrian class, and the tribunes of the Treasury. Crassus had to wait fifteen years for his reward—the privilege of drinking gold in Asia; Pompey received his in 67, when the Assembly voted him almost limitless authority to proceed against the pirates of Cilicia. Once Rhodes had kept the Aegean free of such marauders; but Rhodes, humiliated and impoverished by Rome and Delos, could no longer maintain the fleet required for such a service; and the landed aristocracy that controlled the Senate had no keen interest in making the channels of maritime commerce secure. Merchants and plebs felt the results more sharply: trade became almost impossible in the Aegean, even in the central Mediterranean; and imports of grain fell so rapidly that the price of wheat at Rome rose to twenty sesterces per modius, or three dollars a peck. The pirates flaunted their success with gilded masts, purple sails, and silver-plated oars on their thousand ships; they took and held 400 coastal towns, plundered temples in Samothrace, Samos, Epidaurus, Argos, Leucas, and Actium, kidnaped Roman officials, and assailed even the shores of Apulia and Etruria.

To meet this situation Pompey's friend Gabinius proposed a bill giving him for three years absolute control of all Roman fleets, and all persons within fifty miles of any Mediterranean shore. Every senator but Caesar opposed this extraordinary measure, but the Assembly passed it with enthusiasm, voted Pompey an army of 125,000 men and a navy of 500 vessels, and ordered the Treasury to place 144,000,000 sesterces at his disposal. In effect the bill deposed the Senate, ended the Sullan restoration, and established a provisional monarchy as a prelude and lesson to Caesar. The outcome strengthened the precedent. The very day after Pompey's appointment the price of wheat began to fall. Within three months he accomplished his task—captured the pirate ships, took their strongholds, executed their leaders—and yet without abusing his unusual authority. Commerce took heart and sailed again, and a river of cereals flowed into Rome.

While Pompey was still in Cilicia, his friend Manilius offered the Assembly a bill transferring to him full command of the armies and provinces then (66) under Lucullus, and prolonging the powers conferred upon him by the Gabinian Law. The Senate resisted, but the merchants and moneylenders gave strong support to the proposal. Pompey, they hoped, would be less lenient than Lucullus to their Asiatic debtors; he would restore the tax collections to the publicans; he would conquer not only Bithynia and Pontus, but Cappadocia, Syria, and Judea; and these rich fields would be thrown open to Roman trade and finance under the protection of Roman arms. A "new man," Marcus Tullius Cicero, who had been elected praetor for that year with the aid of the business class, spoke "For the Manilian Law," and attacked the Senatorial oligarchy with a rash eloquence unheard in Rome since the Gracchi, and with a candor shocking in a politician:

> The whole system of credit and finance which is carried on here at Rome is inextricably bound up with the revenues of the Asiatic provinces. If these revenues are destroyed, our system of credit will crash. . . . If some lose their entire fortunes they will drag many more down with them. Save the state from such a calamity. . . . Prosecute with all your energies the war against Mithridates, by which the glory of the Roman name, the safety of our allies, our most valuable revenues, and the fortunes of innumerable citizens will be effectively preserved.[35]

The measure was readily passed by the Assembly. The plebs cared little for the fortunes of the financiers; but it rejoiced in having found, through the issuance of extraordinary powers to a general, a means of annulling the Sullan legislation and deposing its ancient enemy, the Senate. From that moment the days of the Republic were numbered. The Roman revolution, helped by the oratory of its greatest foe, had taken another step toward Caesar.

VII. CICERO AND CATILINE

Plutarch thought that Marcus Tullius was called Cicero because of a wart, shaped like a vetch (*cicer*), on an ancestor's nose; more probably his forebears had earned the cognomen by raising renowned crops of chick-peas.

In his *Laws* Cicero describes with engaging tenderness the modest villa that had seen his birth near Arpinum, halfway between Rome and Naples, in the foothills of the Apennines. His father was just rich enough to give his son the best education that the age could provide. He engaged the Greek poet Archias to tutor Marcus in literature and Greek and then sent the youth to study law with Q. Mucius Scaevola, the greatest jurist of his time. Cicero listened eagerly to the trials and debates in the Forum, and rapidly learned the arts and tricks of forensic speech. "To succeed in the law," he said, "a man must renounce all pleasures, avoid all amusements, say farewell to recreation, games, entertainment, almost to intercourse with his friends." [36]

Soon he was practicing law himself and making speeches whose brilliance and courage won him the gratitude of the middle classes and the plebs. He prosecuted a favorite of Sulla and denounced the proscriptions in the midst of the Sullan terror (80 B.C.).[37] Shortly afterward, perhaps to avoid the dictator's revenge, he went to Greece, and continued there his studies of oratory and philosophy. After three happy years in Athens he passed over to Rhodes, where he heard the lectures of Apollonius, son of Molon, on rhetoric, and those of Poseidonius on philosophy. From the first he learned the periodic sentence structure and purity of speech that were to distinguish his style; and from the other that mild Stoicism which he would later expound in his essays on religion, government, friendship, and old age.

Returning to Rome at the age of thirty, he married Terentia, whose ample dowry now enabled him to go into politics. In 75 he distinguished himself by his just administration of a quaestorship in Sicily. In 70, having resumed the practice of law, he raised a furor among the aristocracy by accepting a retainer from the cities of Sicily and bringing suit against the senator Caius Verres, on the charge that as propraetor there (73-71) Verres had sold his appointments and decisions, had lowered individual tax assessments in inverse proportion to bribes received, had despoiled Syracuse of nearly all its statuary, had assigned the revenues of a whole city to his mistress, and all in all had carried injustice, extortion, and robbery to such a pitch as to leave the island more desolate than after two Servile Wars. Worse yet, Verres had kept for himself some of the spoils that usually went to the publicans. The business class supported Cicero in the indictment, while Hortensius, aristocratic leader of the Roman bar, led the defense for Verres. Cicero was allowed some hundred days to gather evidence in Sicily; he took only fifty, but he presented so much damaging testimony in his opening address that Hortensius—who had decorated his gardens with part of Verres' sculptural loot—abandoned his client. Condemned to pay a fine of 40,000,000 sesterces, Verres fled into exile. Cicero published the five additional speeches that he had prepared; they constituted an unsparing attack upon Roman malfeasance in the provinces. His energy and courage won him such support that when he ran for the consulate for 63 B.C. he was elected by acclamation.

Born of modest equestrian rank, Cicero had naturally sided with the middle class and had resented the pride, privileges, and misrule of the aristocracy. But far more deeply he feared those radical leaders whose program, he thought, threatened all property with mob rule. He therefore made it his policy, now that he was in office, to promote a "concord of the orders"— i.e., a co-operation of the aristocracy and the business class—against the returning tide of revolt.

The causes and forces of discontent, however, were too deep and varied to be easily dissolved. Many of the poor were listening to preachers of utopia, and some who listened were ripe for violence. A little above them were plebeians who had forfeited their property through defaulted mortgages. Some of Sulla's veterans had failed to make their land allotments pay and were ready for any disturbance that might give them loot without toil. Among the upper classes were insolvent debtors and ruined speculators who had lost all hope or wish to meet their obligations. Others had political ambitions and saw their road to advancement cluttered with conservatives who took too long to die. A few revolutionists were sincere idealists, convinced that only a complete overturn could mitigate the corruption and inequity of the Roman state.

One man sought to unite these scattered groups into a coherent political force. We know Lucius Sergius Catiline only through his enemies—through the history of his movement by the millionaire Sallust, and through the violent vituperation of Cicero's orations *Against Catiline*. Sallust describes him as a "guilt-stained soul at odds with gods and men, who found no rest either waking or sleeping, so cruelly did conscience ravage his overwrought mind. Hence his pallid complexion, his bloodshot eyes, his gait now fast now slow; in short, his face and every glance showed the madman." [38] Such a description suggests the pictures that a people struggling for life or power paints of its enemies in war; when the battle is over the pictures are gradually revised, but in the case of Catiline we have no revision. In youth he had been charged with deflowering a Vestal Virgin, a half sister of Cicero's first wife; the court had acquitted the Virgin, but gossip had not acquitted Catiline; on the contrary, it added that he had killed his son to please his jealous mistress. [39] In the scale against these stories we can only say that for four years after Catiline's death the common people of Rome—"the miserable, starveling rabble," Cicero called them—strewed flowers upon his tomb. [40] Sallust quotes what purports to be one of his speeches:

> Ever since the state fell under the sway of a few powerful men . . .
> all influence, rank, and wealth have been in their hands. To us they
> have left danger, defeat, prosecutions, poverty. . . . What have we
> left save only the breath of life? . . . Is it not better to die valiantly
> than to lose our wretched and dishonored lives after being the sport
> of other men's insolence? [41]

The program on which he proposed to unite the heterogeneous elements
of revolution was simple: *novae tabulae*—"new records"—i.e., a clean sweep
and abolition of all debts. He labored for this purpose with all the energy of
a Caesar; indeed, for a time he had the sympathy, if not the secret support,
of Caesar. "There was nothing," said Cicero, "that he could not undergo, no
pains that he would spare of co-operation, vigilance, and toil. He could bear
cold, hunger, and thirst." [42] We are assured by his enemies that he organized
a band of 400 men who planned to kill the consuls and seize the government
on the first day of 65. The day came, and nothing unusual transpired. At the
end of 64 Catiline stood against Cicero for the consulate and waged a vigorous campaign.* Capital took fright and began to leave Italy. The upper classes
united in support of Cicero; for a year the *concordia ordinum* that he had
asked for was a reality, and he was its perfect voice.

Blocked politically, Catiline turned to war. Secretly his followers organized an army of 20,000 men in Etruria, and gathered together in Rome a
group of conspirators that included representatives of every class from
senators to slaves, and two urban praetors—Cethegus and Lentulus. In the
following October Catiline again ran for the consulate. To make sure of
his election, conservative historians tell us, he planned to have his rival murdered during the campaign, and to have Cicero assassinated at the same time.
Claiming that he had been apprised of these plans, Cicero filled the Field of
Mars with armed guards and superintended the voting. Despite the enthusiastic support of the proletariat, Catiline was again defeated. On November 7,
says Cicero, several conspirators knocked at his door, but were driven away
by his guards. On the morrow, seeing Catiline in the Senate, Cicero flung at
him that superb excoriation which once every schoolboy mouthed. As the
oration proceeded, the seats around Catiline were emptied one by one, until
he sat alone. Silently he bore the torrent of accusations, the sharp, relentless
phrases falling like whips upon his head. Cicero played upon every emotion;
he spoke of the nation as the common father, and of Catiline as in intent a
parricide; he charged him—not with evidence given, but by innuendo and

---

* It was in this campaign that Cicero's brother Quintus drew up for him a manual of
electioneering technique. "Be lavish in your promises," Quintus advised; "men prefer a false
promise to a flat refusal. . . . Contrive to get some new scandal aired against your rivals for
crime, corruption, or immorality." [43]

implication—with conspiracy against the state, with theft, adultery, and sexual abnormality; finally he petitioned Jove to protect Rome, and to devote Catiline to eternal punishment. When Cicero had finished, Catiline walked out unhindered, and joined his forces in Etruria. His general, L. Manlius, sent a last appeal to the Senate:

> We call gods and men to witness that it is not against our country that we have taken up arms, nor against the safety of our fellow citizens. We, wretched paupers, who through the violence and cruelty of usurers are without a country, condemned to scorn and indigence, are actuated by only one wish: to guarantee our personal security against wrong. We demand neither power nor wealth, those great and external causes of strife among mankind. We only ask for freedom, a treasure that no man will surrender except with life itself. We implore you, senators, have pity on your miserable fellow citizens! [44]

The next day, in a second oration, Cicero described the rebel's following as centering around a coterie of perfumed perverts, and indulged without stint his genius for sarcasm and invective, ending again on a religious note. In the following weeks he presented evidence to the Senate purporting to show that Catiline had tried to stir up revolution in Gaul. On December 3 he had Lentulus, Cethegus, and five other adherents of Catiline arrested. In a third oration he declared their guilt, announced their imprisonment, and told the Senate and the people that the conspiracy was broken and that they might retire to their homes in security and peace. On December 5 he convoked the Senate and asked what should be done with the prisoners. Silanus voted that they should be executed. Caesar advised mere imprisonment, recalling that the execution of a Roman citizen was forbidden by the Sempronian Law. In a fourth oration Cicero gently advised death. Cato gave the opinion the sanction of his philosophy, and death won the day. Some young aristocrats tried to kill Caesar as he left the senate chamber, but he escaped. Cicero, with armed men, went to the jail and had the sentence carried out with a minimum of delay. Marcus Antonius, co-consul with Cicero, and father of a famous son, was sent north with an army to destroy Catiline's force. The Senate promised pardon and 200,000 sesterces to every man who would leave the rebel ranks; but, says Sallust, "not one deserted from Catiline's camp." On the plains of Pistoia battle was joined (61). The 3000 insurgents, far outnumbered, fought to the end around their treasured standards, the eagles of Marius. None surrendered or took flight; every one of them died on the field, among them Catiline.

Being essentially a man of thought rather than of action, Cicero was surprised and impressed by the skill and courage he had shown in suppressing a dangerous revolt. "The direction of so great an enterprise," he told the Senate, "seems scarcely possible to merely human wisdom." [45] He compared himself with Romulus, but considered it a greater deed to have preserved Rome than to have founded it.[46] Senators and magnates smiled at his language, but they knew that he had saved them. Cato and Catulus hailed him as *pater patriae*, father of his country. When, at the end of 63, he laid down his office, all the propertied classes in the community, he tells us, gave him thanks, named him immortal, and escorted him in honor to his home.[47] The proletariat did not join in these demonstrations. It could not forgive him for violating the laws of Rome by putting citizens to death without appeal; it felt that he had made no effort to remove the causes of Catiline's revolt, or to mitigate the poverty of the masses. It refused to let him address the Assembly on that last day, and listened in anger when he swore that he had preserved the city. The revolution was not over. With Caesar's consulate it would begin again.

CHAPTER VIII

Literature Under the Revolution

145-30 B.C.

I. LUCRETIUS

AMID this turbulent transformation of economy, government, and morals, literature was not forgotten, and did not quite escape the fever and stimulus of the age. Varro and Nepos found safety in antiquarian scholarship or historical research; Sallust retired from his campaigns to defend his party and disguise his morals with brilliant monographs; Caesar stooped from empire to grammar and continued his wars in his *Commentaries;* Catullus and Calvus sought refuge from politics in the pursuit and poetry of love; timid and sensitive spirits like Lucretius hid themselves in the gardens of philosophy; and Cicero retreated now and then from the heat of the Forum to cool his blood with books. But not one of them found peace. War and revolution touched them with pervasive infection; and even Lucretius must have known the restlessness which he describes:

> There is a weight on their minds, and a mountain of misery lies on their hearts. . . . For each, not knowing what he wants, seeks always to change his place, as if he could drop his burden. Here is one who, bored to death at home, goes forth every now and then from his palace; but feeling no better abroad, suddenly returns. Off he courses, driving his nags to his country house in headlong haste. . . . He has hardly crossed the threshold when he yawns, or seeks oblivion in a heavy sleep, or even hurries back to the city. So each man flees from himself; but, as one might expect, the self which he cannot escape cleaves to him all the more against his will. He hates himself because, a sick man, he does not know the cause of his complaint. Any man who could see that clearly would cast aside his business, and before all else would seek to understand the nature of things.[1]

His poem is our only biography of Titus Lucretius Carus; it is proudly reticent about its author; and outside of it, barring a few allusions, Roman literature is strangely silent about one of its greatest men. Tradition placed his birth at 99 or 95, his death at 55 or 51, B.C. He lived through half a century of the Roman revolution: through the Social War, Marian massacres, and Sullan proscriptions; through Catiline's conspiracy and Caesar's consulate. The aristocracy to which he probably belonged was in obvious decay; the world in which he lived was falling apart into a chaos that left no life or fortune secure. His poem is a longing for physical and mental peace.

Lucretius sought refuge in nature, philosophy, and poetry. Perhaps also he had a round of love; he must have fared badly, for he writes ungallantly of women, denounces the lure of beauty, and advises itching youth to appease the flesh with calm promiscuity.[2] In woods and fields, in plants and animals, in mountain, river, and sea, he found a delight only rivaled by his passion for philosophy. He was as impressionable as Wordsworth, as keen of sense as Keats, as prone as Shelley to find metaphysics in a pebble or a leaf. Nothing of nature's loveliness or terror was lost upon him; he was stirred by the forms and sounds, odors and savors, of things; felt the silences of secret haunts, the quiet falling of the night, the lazy waking of the day. Everything natural was a marvel to him—the patient flow of water, the sprouting of seeds, the endless changes of the sky, the imperturbable persistence of the stars. He observed animals with curiosity and sympathy, loved their forms of strength or grace, felt their sufferings, and wondered at their wordless philosophy. No poet before him had so expressed the grandeur of the world in its detailed variety and its congregated power. Here at last nature won the citadels of literature, and rewarded her poet with a force of descriptive speech that only Homer and Shakespeare have surpassed.

So responsive a spirit must have been deeply moved in youth by the mystery and pageantry of religion. But the ancient faith, which had once served family discipline and social order, had lost its hold on the educated classes of Rome. Caesar smiled indulgently as he played *pontifex maximus*, and the banquets of the priests were the holydays of Roman epicures. A small minority of the people were open atheists; now and then some Roman Alcibiades nocturnally mutilated the statues of the gods.[3] No longer inspired or consoled by the official ritual, many among the lower classes were flocking to the bloodstained shrines of the Phrygian Great Mother, or the Cappadocian goddess Ma, or some of the Oriental deities that had entered Italy with soldiers or captives from the East. Under the influence of Greek or Asiatic cults the old Roman idea of "Orcus" as a colorless subterranean abode of all the indiscriminate dead had developed into belief in a literal Hell—a "Tartarus" or "Acheron" of endless suffering for all but a "reborn" initiated few.[4] The sun and the moon were conceived as gods, and every eclipse sent terror into lonely villages and teeming tenements. Chaldean fortunetellers and astrologers were overrunning Italy, casting horoscopes for paupers and millionaires, revealing hidden treasures and future events, interpreting omens and dreams with cautious ambiguity and profitable flattery. Every unusual occurrence in nature was examined as the warning of a god. It was this mass of superstition, ritualism, and hypocrisy that Lucretius knew as religion.

No wonder that he rebelled against it, and attacked it with all the ardor of a religious reformer. We may judge from the bitterness of his resentment the depth of his youthful piety and the distress of his disillusionment. Seeking for some alternative faith, he passed through the skepticism of Ennius to the great poem in which Empedocles had expounded evolution and the conflict of opposites. When he discovered the writings of Epicurus it seemed to him that he had found the answers to his questions; that strange mixture of materialism and free will, of joyful gods and a godless world, appealed to him as a free man's answer to doubt and fear. A breath of liberation from supernatural terrors seemed to come out of Epicurus' garden, revealing the omnipresence of law, the self-ruled independence of nature, the forgivable naturalness of death. Lucretius resolved to take this philosophy out of the ungainly prose in which Epicurus had expressed it, fuse it into poetic form, and offer it to his generation as the way, the truth, and the life. He felt in himself a rare and double power—the objective perception of the scientist and the subjective emotion of the poet; and he saw in the total order of nature a sublimity, and in nature's parts a beauty, that encouraged and justified this marriage of philosophy and poetry. His great purpose aroused all his powers, lifted him to a unique intellectual exuberance, and left him, before its completion, exhausted and perhaps insane. But his "long and delightful toil" gave him a consuming happiness, and he poured into it all the devotion of a profoundly religious soul.

He chose for his work a philosophical rather than a poetic title—*De Rerum Natura*, "On the Nature of Things"—a simple translation of the *Peri Physeos* ("About Nature") which the pre-Socratics had used as a common name for their treatises. He offered it to the sons of Caius Memmius, praetor in 58, as a road from fear to understanding. He took as his model the Empedoclean epic of exposition, as his speech the quaint bluntness of Ennius, as his medium the mobile and versatile hexameter. And then, forgetting for a moment the distant carelessness of the gods, he began with a fervent apostrophe to Venus conceived, like Empedocles' Love, as a symbol of creative desire and the ways of peace:

> Mother of Aeneas' race, delight of men and gods, O nurturing Venus! . . . Through thee every kind of life is conceived and born, and looks upon the sun; before thee and thy coming the winds flee, and the clouds of the sky depart; to thee the miraculous earth lifts up sweet flowers; for thee the waves of the sea laugh, and the peaceful heavens shine with overspreading light. For as soon as the springtime face of day appears, and the fertilizing south wind makes all things

fresh and green, then first the birds of the air proclaim thee and thy advent, O divine one, pierced to the heart by thy power; then the wild herds leap over the glad pastures, and cross the swift streams; so, held captive by thy charm, each one follows thee wherever thou goest to lead. Then through seas and mountains and rushing rivers, and the leafy dwellings of the birds, and the verdant fields, thou strikest soft love into the breasts of all creatures, and makest them to propagate their generations after their kinds. Since, therefore, thou alone rulest the nature of things; since without thee nothing rises to the shining shores of light, nothing joyful or lovely is born; I long for thee as partner in the writing of these verses. . . . Grant to my words, O goddess, an undying beauty. Cause, meanwhile, the savage works of war to sleep and be still. . . . As Mars reclines upon thy sacred form, bend thou around him from above, pour sweet coaxings from thy mouth, and beg for thy Romans the gift of peace.[5]

II. *DE RERUM NATURA*

If we try to reduce to some logical form the passionate disorder of Lucretius' argument, his initial thesis lies in a famous line:

Tantum religio potuit suadere malorum—

"to so many evils religion has persuaded men." [6] He tells the story of Iphigenia in Aulis, of countless human sacrifices, of hecatombs offered to gods conceived in the image of man's greed; he recalls the terror of simplicity and youth lost in a jungle of vengeful deities, the fear of lightning and thunder, of death and Hell, and the subterranean horrors pictured in Etruscan art and Oriental mysteries. He reproaches mankind for preferring sacrificial ritual to philosophical understanding:

> O miserable race of men, to impute to the gods such acts as these, and such bitter wrath! What sorrow did men [through such creeds] prepare for themselves, what wounds for us, what tears for our children! For piety lies not in being often seen turning a veiled head to stones, nor in approaching every altar, nor in lying prostrate . . . before the temples of the gods, nor in sprinkling altars with the blood of beasts . . . but rather in being able *to look upon all things with a mind at peace.*[7]

There are gods, says Lucretius, but they dwell far off in happy isolation from the thought or cares of men. There, "beyond the flaming ramparts of the world" (*extra flammantia moenia mundi*),[8] beyond the reach of our sacrifices and prayers, they live like followers of Epicurus, shunning worldly affairs, content with the contemplation of beauty and the practices of friend-ship and peace.[9] They are not the authors of creation, nor the causes of events; who would be so unfair as to charge them with the wastefulness, the disorder, the sufferings, and the injustices of earthly life? No, this infinite universe of many worlds is self-contained; it has no law outside itself; nature does everything of her own accord. "For who is strong enough to rule the sum of things, to hold in hand the mighty bridle of the unfathomable deep? —who to turn all the heavens around at once . . . to shake the serene sky with thunder, to launch the lightning that often shatters temples, and cast the bolt that slays the innocent and passes the guilty by?" [10] The only god is Law; and the truest worship, as well as the only peace, lies in learning that Law and loving it. "This terror and gloom of the mind must be dispelled not by the sun's rays . . . but by the aspect and law of nature." [11]

And so, "touching with the honey of the Muses" the rough materialism of Democritus, Lucretius proclaims as his basic theorem that "nothing exists but atoms and the void" [12]—i.e., matter and space. He proceeds at once to a cardinal principle (and assumption) of modern science—that the quantity of matter and motion in the world never varies; no thing arises out of nothing, and destruction is only a change of form. The atoms are indestructible, unchangeable, solid, resilient, soundless, odorless, tasteless, colorless, infinite. They interpenetrate one another to produce endless com-binations and qualities; and they move without cease in the seeming stillness of motionless things.

> For often on a hill . . . woolly sheep go creeping wherever the dew-sparkling grass tempts them, and the well-fed lambs play and butt their heads in sport; yet in the distance all these are blurred to-gether and seem but a whiteness resting on a green hill. Sometimes great armies cover wide fields in maneuvers mimicking war; the bril-liant bronze of their shields illumines the countryside and is mirrored in the sky; the ground trembles and thunders under their marching feet and their galloping steeds; and the mountains, buffeted by the sound, hurl it back to the very stars: and yet there is a place on the peaks from which these armies appear to be motionless, a little bright-ness resting on the plain.[13]

The atoms * have parts—*minima*, or "least things"—each *minimum* being solid, indivisible, ultimate. Perhaps because of the different arrangement of these parts, the atoms vary in size and shape, and so make possible the re-freshing diversity of nature. The atoms do not move in straight or uniform

---

* Lucretius never uses this word, but calls his primordial particles *primordia, elementa,* or *semina* (seeds).

lines; there is in their motion an incalculable "declination" or deviation, an elemental spontaneity that runs through all things and culminates in man's free will.*

All was once formless; but the gradual assortment of the moving atoms by their size and shape produced—without design—air, fire, water, and earth, and out of these the sun and moon, the planets and stars. In the infinity of space new worlds are ever being born, and old worlds are wasting away. The stars are fires set in the ring of ether (a mist of thinnest atoms) that surrounds each planetary system; this cosmic wall of fire constitutes the "flaming ramparts of the world." A portion of the primeval mist broke off from the mass, revolved separately, and cooled to form the earth. Earthquakes are not the growling of deities, but the expansion of subterranean gases and streams. Thunder and lightning are not the voice and breath of a god, but natural results of condensed and clashing clouds. Rain is not the mercy of Jove, but the return to earth of moisture evaporated from it by the sun.

Life does not differ essentially from other matter; it is a product of moving atoms which are individually dead. As the universe took form by the inherent laws of matter, so the earth produced by a purely natural selection all the species and organs of life.

> Nothing arises in the body in order that we may use it, but what arises brings forth its own use.[14] . . . It was no design of the atoms that led them to arrange themselves in order with keen intelligence . . . but because many atoms in infinite time have moved and met in all manner of ways, trying all combinations. . . . Hence arose the beginnings of great things . . . and the generations of living creatures.[15] . . . Many were the monsters that the earth tried to make: . . . some without feet, and others without hands or mouth or face, or with limbs bound to their frames. . . . It was in vain; nature denied them growth, nor could they find food or join in the way of love. . . . Many kinds of animals must have perished then, unable to forge the chain of procreation . . . for those to which nature gave no [protective] qualities lay at the mercy of others, and were soon destroyed.[16]

Mind (*animus*) is an organ precisely like feet or eyes; it is, like them, a tool or function of that soul (*anima*) or vital breath which is spread as a very fine matter throughout the body, and animates every part. Upon the highly sensitive atoms that form the mind fall the images or films that perpetually emanate from the surfaces of things; this is the source of sensation. Taste, smell, hearing, sight, and touch are caused by particles coming from

---

* Cf. the "indeterminacy" ascribed to the electrons by some physicists of our time.

objects and striking tongue or palate, nostrils, ears, eyes, or skin; all senses are forms of touch. The senses are the final test of truth; if they seem to err, it is only through misinterpretation, and only another sense can correct them. Reason cannot be the test of truth, for reason depends upon experience—i.e., sensation.

The soul is neither spiritual nor immortal. It could not move the body unless it too were corporeal; it grows and ages with the body; it is affected like the body by disease, medicine, or wine; its atoms are apparently dispersed when the body dies. Soul without body would be senseless, meaningless; of what use would soul be without organs of touch, taste, smell, hearing, and sight? Life is given us not in freehold but on loan, and for so long as we can make use of it. When we have exhausted our powers we should leave the table of life as graciously as a grateful guest rising from a feast. Death itself is not terrible; only our fears of the hereafter make it so. But there is no hereafter. Hell is here in the suffering that comes from ignorance, passion, pugnacity, and greed; heaven is here in the *sapientum templa serena*—"the serene temples of the wise." [17]

Virtue lies not in the fear of the gods, nor in the timid shunning of pleasure; it lies in the harmonious operation of senses and faculties guided by reason. "Some men wear out their lives for the sake of a statue and fame"; but "the real wealth of man is to live simply with a mind at peace" (*vivere parce aequo animo*).[18] Better than living stiffly in gilded halls is "to lie in groups upon the soft grass beside a rivulet and under tall trees," [19] or to hear gentle music, or lose one's ego in the love and care of our children. Marriage is good, but passionate love is a madness that strips the mind of clarity and reason. "If one is wounded by the shafts of Venus—whether it be a boy with girlish limbs who launches the shaft, or a woman radiating love from her whole body—he is drawn toward the source of the blow, and longs to unite." [20] No marriage and no society can find a sound basis in such erotic befuddlement.

As Lucretius, exhausting his passions on philosophy, finds no room for romantic love, so he rejects the romantic anthropology of Greek Rousseauians who had glorified primitive life. Men were hardier then, to be sure; but they dwelt in caves without fire, they mated without marriage, killed without law, and died of starvation as frequently as people in civilization die of overeating.[21] How civilization developed, Lucretius tells in a pretty summary of ancient anthropology. Social organization gave man the power to survive animals far stronger than himself. He discovered fire from the friction of leaves and boughs, developed language from gestures, and learned song from the birds; he tamed animals for his use, and himself with marriage and law; he tilled the soil, wove clothing, molded metals into tools; he observed the heavens, measured time, and learned navigation; he improved the art of killing, conquered the weak, and built cities and states. History is a procession of states and civilizations rising, prospering, decaying, dying; but each in turn transmits the civilizing heritage of customs, morals, and arts; "like runners in a race they hand on the lamps of life" (*et quasi cursores vitai lampada tradunt*).[22]

All things that grow decay: organs, organisms, families, states, races, planets, stars; only the atoms never die. The forces of creation and development are balanced by the forces of destruction in a vast diastole and systole of life and death. In nature there is evil as well as good; suffering, even unmerited, comes to every life, and dissolution dogs the steps of every evolution. Our earth itself is dying: earthquakes are breaking it up. The land is becoming exhausted, rains and rivers erode it, and carry even the mountains at last into the sea. Someday our whole stellar system will suffer a like mortality; "the walls of the sky will be stormed on every side, and will collapse into a crumbling ruin."[23] But the very moment of mortality betrays the invincible vitality of the world. "The wailing of the newborn infant is mingled with the dirge sung for the dead."[24] New systems form, new stars and planets, another earth, and fresher life. Evolution begins again.

Looking back over this "most marvelous performance in all antique literature,"[25] we may first recognize its shortcomings: the chaos of its contents, left unrevised by the poet's early death; the repetition of phrases, lines, whole passages; the conception of sun, moon, and stars as no larger than we see them;[26] the inability of the system to explain how dead atoms became life and consciousness; the insensitiveness to the insights, consolations, inspirations, and moving poetry of faith, and the moral and social functions of religion. But how light these faults are in the scale against the brave attempt at a rational interpretation of the universe, of history, of religion, of disease; * the picture of nature as a world of law, in which matter and motion are never diminished or increased; the grandeur of the theme and the nobility of its treatment; the sustained power of imagination that feels everywhere "the majesty of things," and lifts the visions of Empedocles, the science of Democritus, and the ethics of Epicurus into some of the loftiest poetry that any age has known. Here was a language still rough and immature, almost devoid as yet of philosophical or scientific terms; Lucretius does not merely create a new vocabulary, he forces the old speech into new channels of

---

* "There are many seeds of things that support our life; and on the other hand there must be many flying about that make for disease and death."[27]

rhythm and grace; and, while molding the hexameter into an unequaled masculinity of power, reaches now and then the mellow tenderness and fluency of Virgil. The sustained vitality of his poem shows Lucretius as one who amid all sufferings and disappointments enjoyed and exhausted life almost from birth to death.

How did he die? Saint Jerome reports that "Lucretius was driven mad by a love philter, after he had written several books. . . . He died by his own hand in his forty-fourth year." [28] The story is uncorroborated, and has been much doubted; no saint could be trusted to give an objective account of Lucretius. Some critics have found support for the story in the unnatural tension of the poem, its poorly organized contents, and its sudden end; [29] but one need not be a Lucretius to be excitable, disorderly, or dead.

Like Euripides, Lucretius is a modern; his thought and feeling are more congenial to our time than to the century before Christ. Horace and Virgil were deeply influenced by him in their youth, and recall him without name in many a lordly phrase; but the attempt of Augustus to restore the old faith made it unwise for these imperial protégés to express too openly their admiration and their debt. The Epicurean philosophy was as unsuited to the Roman mind as epicurean practices suited Roman taste in the age of Lucretius.* Rome wanted a metaphysic that would exalt mystic powers rather than natural law; an ethic that would make a virile and martial people rather than humanitarian lovers of quiet and peace; and a political philosophy that, like those of Virgil and Horace, would justify Rome's imperial mastery. In the resurrection of faith after Seneca, Lucretius was almost forgotten. Not till Poggio rediscovered him in 1418 did he begin to influence European thought. A physician of Verona, Girolamo Fracastoro (1483-1553) took from the poet the theory of disease as due to noxious "seeds" (*semina*) floating in the air; and in 1647 Gassendi revived the atomic philosophy. Voltaire read the *De Rerum Natura* devotedly, and agreed with Ovid that its rebel verses would last as long as the earth.[30]

In the endless struggle of East and West, of "tender-minded" and consoling faiths vs. a "tough-minded" and materialistic science, Lucretius waged alone the most vigorous battle of his time. He is, of course, the greatest of philosophical poets. In him, as in Catullus and Cicero, Latin literature came of age, and leadership in letters passed at last from Greece to Rome.

---

* The words *Epicurean* and *Stoic* will be used in these volumes as meaning a believer in the metaphysics and ethics of Epicurus, or of Zeno; *epicurean* and *stoic* as meaning one who practices, or avoids, soft living and sensual indulgence.

III. LESBIA'S LOVER

In 57 B.C. the Caius Memmius to whom Lucretius dedicated his poem left Rome to serve as propraetor in Bithynia. After the growing custom of Roman governors he took with him an author—not Lucretius, but a poet different from the other in everything but the strength of his passion. Quintus (or Caius) Valerius Catullus had come to Rome some five years before from his native Verona, where his father was of sufficient standing to be frequent host to Caesar. Quintus himself must have had a substantial competence, for he owned villas near Tibur and on Lake Garda and had an elegant house in Rome. He speaks of these properties as choked with mortgages, and repeatedly proclaims his poverty; but the picture we form of him from his poems is that of a polished man of the world who did not bother to earn a living, but enjoyed himself unstintingly among the wilder set in the capital. The keenest wits, the cleverest young orators and politicians belonged to this circle: Marcus Caelius, the impecunious aristocrat who was to become a communist; Licinius Calvus, brilliant in poetry and in law; and Helvius Cinna, a poet whom Antony's mob would mistake for one of Caesar's assassins and beat to death. These men opposed Caesar with every epigram at their disposal, unaware that their literary revolt reflected the revolution in which they lived. They were tired of old forms in literature, of the crudity and bombast of Naevius and Ennius; they wished to sing the sentiments of youth in new and lyric meters, and with a refinement and delicacy of execution known once in the Alexandria of Callimachus, but never yet seen in Rome. And they were resentful of old morals, of the *mos maiorum* perpetually preached upon them by their exhausted elders; they announced the sanctity of instinct, the innocence of desire, and the grandeur of dissipation. They and Catullus were no worse than other young literary blades of their generation and the next; Horace, Ovid, Tibullus, Propertius, even the shy Virgil in his youth, made life and verse revolve around any woman, married or not, who fed their muses with facile casual love.

The liveliest lady in this group was Clodia, of the proud old Claudian gens that even now had emperors in its loins.* Apuleius [31] assures us that it was she whom Catullus named Lesbia in memory of the Sappho whose poems he occasionally translated, often imitated, and always loved. Arriving in Rome at the age of twenty-two, he cultivated her friendship while her husband governed Cisalpine Gaul. He was fascinated the moment she "set her shining foot on the well-worn threshold"; he called her his "lustrous goddess of the

---

* Cf. p. 135.

delicate step"; and indeed a woman's walk, like her voice, may be in itself a sufficient seduction. She accepted him graciously as one of her worshipers; and the enraptured poet, unable to match otherwise the gifts of his rivals, laid at her feet the most beautiful lyrics in the Latin tongue. For her he translated perfectly Sappho's description of the lover's frenzy that now raged in him;[32] and to the sparrow that she pressed to her bosom he indited a jewel of jealousy:

> Sparrow, delight of my beloved,
> Who plays with you, and holds you to her breast;
> Who offers her forefinger to your seeking,
> And tempts your sharp bite;
> I know not what dear jest it pleases my shining one
> To make of my desire! . . .*

For a while he was consumed with happiness, played attendance upon her daily, read his poems to her, forgot everything but his infatuation.

> Let us live, Lesbia mine, and love,
> And all the mumbling of harsh old men
> We shall reckon as a pennyworth.
> Suns may sink and return;
> For us, when once our brief sun has set,
> There comes the long sleep of everlasting night.
> Give me a thousand kisses, then a hundred,
> Then another thousand, then a second hundred,
> Then still another thousand, then a hundred.
> And when we shall have reached many thousands
> We shall confuse the count, lest we should ever know,
> Or some mean soul should envy us,
> Learning the great sum of our kisses.†

---

* No one has yet transformed Catullus' poems into equivalent English verse. The foregoing is an almost literal translation of

> Passer, deliciae meae puellae,
> quicum ludere, quem in sinu tenere,
> cui primum digitum dare adpetenti
> et acris solet incitari morsus,
> cum desiderio meo nitenti
> carum nescio quid libet iocari. . . .[33]

† Vivamus, mea Lesbia, atque amemus,
> rumoresque senum severiorum
> omnes unius aestimemus assis.
> Soles occidere et redire possunt;
> nobis cum semel occidit brevis lux,
> nox est perpetua una dormienda.
> Da mi basia mille, deinde centum
> dein mille altera, dein secunda centum. . . .[34]

We do not know how long this ecstasy lasted; probably his thousands wearied her, and she who had betrayed her husband for him found it a relief to betray him for another. Her benefactions now ranged so widely that Catullus madly fancied her "embracing at once three hundred adulterers." [35] In the very heat of his love he came to hate her (*odi et amo* [36]) and rejected with a Keatsian image her protestations of fidelity:

> A woman's words to hungry lover said
> Should be upon the flowing winds inscribed,
> Upon swift streams engraved.[37]

When sharp doubt became dull certainty his passion turned to bitterness and coarse revenge; he accused her of yielding to tavern habitués, denounced her new lovers with obscene abandon, and meditated suicide, poetically. At the same time he was capable of nobler feelings: he addressed to his friend Manlius a touching epithalamium or wedding song, envying him the wholesome comradeship of marriage, the security and stability of a home, and the happy tribulations of parentage. He snatched himself from the scene by accompanying Memmius to Bithynia, but he was disappointed in his hopes of restoring there his spirits or his purse. He went out of his way to find the grave of a brother who had died in the Troad; over it he performed reverently the ancestral burial rites; and soon afterward he composed tender lines that gave the world a famous phrase:

> Dear brother, through many states and seas
> Have I come to this sorrowful sacrifice,
> Bringing you the last gift for the dead. . . .
> Accept these offerings wet with fraternal tears;
> And forever, brother, hail and farewell.*

His sojourn in Asia changed and softened him. The skeptic who had written of death as "the sleep of an eternal night" was moved by the old religions and ceremonies of the East. In the rich and flowing verse of his greatest poem, "Atys," he described with vivid intensity the worship of Cybele, and caught an exotic fervor in the lament of the self-emasculated devotee over the joys and friends of his youth. In "Peleus and Thetis" he retold the tale of Peleus and Ariadne in hexameters of such melodious delicacy as even Virgil would hardly equal. In a small yacht bought at Amastris he sailed through the Black Sea, the Aegean, and the Adriatic, and

---

* Multas per gentes et multa per aequora vectus
advenio has miseras, frater, ad inferias,
ut te postremo donarem munere mortis. . . .
Accipe fraterno multum manantia fletu,
atque in perpetuum, frater, ave atque vale.[38]

up the Po to Lake Garda and his villa at Sirmio. "Oh, what happier way is there to escape the cares of the world," he asked, "than to return to our own homes and altars, and rest on our own beloved bed?" [39] Men begin by seeking happiness and are content at last with peace.

We know Catullus more intimately than most Roman poets, because his subject is nearly always himself. These lyric cries of love and hate reveal a sensitive and kindly spirit, capable of generous feeling even for relatives, but unpleasantly self-centered, deliberately obscene, and merciless to his enemies. He published their most private peculiarities, their pederastic propensities, their bodily odor. One of them washes his teeth with urine, after an old Spanish custom; [40] another is so foul of breath that if he should open his mouth all persons near him would fall dead. [41] Catullus oscillates easily between love and offal, kisses and fundaments; he rivals Martial as a guide to the street-corner urology of Rome, and suggests in his contemporaries and his class a mixture of primitive coarseness with civilized refinement, as if educated Romans, however versed in the literature of Greece, could never quite forget the stable and the camp. Catullus pleads, like Martial, that he must salt his lines with dirt to hold his audience.

He atoned for these faults by the conscientious perfection of his verse. His hendecasyllabics leap with a naturalness and spontaneity that escape the artifices of Horace and occasionally rise above all the graces of Virgil. It took much art to conceal his art, and Catullus more than once refers to the painful toil and care that produced his quick intelligibility and apparent ease. His vocabulary helped him to this end; he molded the words of popular speech into poetry, and enriched the Latin of literature with affectionate diminutives as well as tavern slang. He avoided inversions and obscurities, and gave to his lines a limpid fluidity grateful to the ear. He pored over the poets of Hellenistic Alexandria and ancient Ionia: mastered the smooth technique and varied meters of Callimachus, the lusty directness of Archilochus, the vinous exuberance of Anacreon, the amorous ecstasy of Sappho; indeed, it is largely through him that we must guess how these poets wrote. He learned their lessons so thoroughly that he became, from their pupil, their equal. He did for Latin poetry what Cicero did for Latin prose: he took it as crude potency and lifted it to an art that only Virgil would surpass.

IV. THE SCHOLARS

How were Latin books written, illustrated, bound, published, sold? For school exercises, short letters, transient commercial records, the Romans through antiquity wrote with a stylus upon waxed tablets and erased with the thumb.

The oldest literary Latin known to us was written with quill and ink upon paper manufactured in Egypt from the pressed and glued leaves of the papyrus tree. In the first centuries of our era parchment made from the dried skins of animals began to rival papyrus as a receptacle of literature and important documents. A folded sheet of membrane, or *vellum*, constituted a *diploma*, or twofold. Usually a literary work was issued as a roll (*volumen*, "wound up"), and was read by unrolling as the reading progressed. The text was customarily written two or three narrow *columnae* to a page, often without punctuation of clauses or even separation of words. Some manuscripts were illustrated by ink drawings; Varro's *Imagines*, e.g., consisted of 700 portraits of famous men, each picture accompanied by a biographical note. Anyone could publish a manuscript by hiring slaves to make copies, and selling the copies. Rich men had clerks who copied for them any book they wished to own. Since copyists were fed rather than paid, books were cheap. First "printings" were usually of a thousand copies. Booksellers bought wholesale from publishers like Atticus, and sold at retail in arcade bookstalls. Neither publisher nor bookseller gave the author anything except courtesy and occasional gifts; royalties were unknown. Private libraries were now numerous; and about 40 B.C. Asinius Pollio made his great collection the first public library in Rome. Caesar planned a still larger one, and made Varro its director; but this, like so many of his ideas, waited upon Augustus for its fulfillment.

Stimulated by these facilities, Roman literature and scholarship began to equal the industry of the Alexandrians. Poems, pamphlets, histories, textbooks rivaled the Tiber's floods; every aristocrat adorned his escapades with verse, every lady composed words and music, every general wrote memoirs. It was an age of "outlines"; summaries on every subject struggled to meet the needs of a hurried commercial age. Marcus Terentius Varro, despite many military campaigns, found time during his eighty-nine years (116-26 B.C.) to synopsize nearly every branch of knowledge; his 620 "volumes" (some seventy-four books) constituted a one-man encyclopedia for his time. Fascinated by the pedigrees of words, he wrote an essay *On the Latin Language*, now our chief guide to early Roman speech. Perhaps in co-operation with the aims of Augustus, he tried in his treatise *On Country Life* (*De Re Rustica*, 36 B.C.) to encourage a return to the land as the best refuge from the disorder of civil strife. "My eightieth year," said his introduction, "warns me that I must pack up and prepare to leave this life"; [42] he would make his last testament a guide to rural happiness and peace. He admired the sturdy women who were delivered of children in the fields and soon resumed work.[43] He mourned the low native birth rate that was transforming the population of Rome; "formerly the blessing of children was woman's pride; now she boasts with Ennius that she 'would rather face battle three times than bear one child.'" In his *Divine Antiquities* he concluded that the fertility, order, and courage of a nation require moral commandments supported by religious belief. Adopting the distinction of the great jurist Q. Mucius Scaevola between two kinds of religion—one for philosophers and one for the people [44]—he argued that the second must be upheld regardless of its intellectual defects; and though he himself accepted only a vague pantheism,* he proposed a vigorous attempt to restore the worship of Rome's ancient deities. Influenced by Cato and Polybius, he in his turn decisively affected the religious policy of Augustus and the pious ruralism of Virgil.

As if to complete the work of the elder Cato in every field, Varro continued the censor's *Origines* in his *Life of the Roman People*—a history of Roman civilization. It is a pity that time has scuttled this and nearly all of Varro's work, while preserving the schoolboy biographies of Cornelius Nepos. In Rome history was an art, never also a science; not even in Tacitus did it rise to a critical scrutiny and summary of sources. History as rhetoric, however, found in this age a brilliant practitioner—Caius Sallustius Crispus (86-35 B.C.). He played a vigorous role as politician and warrior on Caesar's side, governed Numidia, stole with skill, and spent a fortune on women; then he retired to a life of luxury and letters in a Roman villa that became famous for its gardens and was to be the home of emperors. His books, like politics, were a continuation of war by other means; his *Histories, Jugurthine War*, and *Catiline* were able defenses of the *populares*, powerful attacks upon the "old guard." He exposed the moral decay of Rome,† charged the Senate and the courts with placing property rights above human rights, and put into the mouth of Marius a speech asserting the natural equality of all classes and demanding a career open to talent wherever born.[46] He deepened his narratives with philosophical commentary and psychological analysis of character, and carved out a style of epigrammatic compactness and vivid rapidity which became a model for Tacitus.

That style, like almost all Roman prose of Sallust's century and the next, took its color and tone from the oratory of the Forum and the courts. The development of the legal profession, and the growth of a talkative democracy, had widened the demand for public speaking. Schools of rhetoric were multiplying despite governmental hostility; "rhetoricians," said Cicero, "are everywhere." Great masters of the art appeared in the first half of the first century before Christ: Marcus Antonius (father of Mark), Lucius Crassus, Sulpicius Rufus, Quintus Hortensius. We may imagine the strength of their lungs when we hear of audiences that overflowed from the Forum into neighboring temples and balconies. The flamboyant eloquence and purchasable conscience of Hortensius made him the darling of the aristocracy and one of Rome's richest men; he left his heirs 10,000 casks of wine.[46b] His delivery was so animated that famous actors like Roscius and Aesopus attended the trials at which he pleaded, to perfect their acting by studying his gestures and his delivery. Following the example of old Cato, he revised and published his speeches—an art which his rival Cicero perfected, and which furthered the influence of rhetoric upon all Roman prose. It

---

* "The soul of the world is God, and its parts are the true divinities." [45]

† Varro claims that Sallust "was taken in adultery by Annius Milo, soundly beaten with thongs, and permitted to escape only after paying a sum of money"; [46a] but this, too, may be politics.

was through oratory that the Latin language reached its full height of colorful eloquence, masculine power, and almost Oriental grace. Indeed, the younger orators who came after Hortensius and Cicero condemned the luxurious adornment and passionate turbulence of what they called the "Asianic" style; and Caesar, Calvus, Brutus, and Pollio pledged themselves to a calmer, chaster, sparer "Attic" speech. Here, so long ago, the battle lines formed between "romanticism" and "classicism"—between the emotional and the intellectual view of life and domination of style. Even in oratory, the young classicists complained, the East was conquering Rome.

V. CICERO'S PEN

Proud of his speeches, and aware that they were making literature, Cicero felt keenly the criticism of the "Attic" school, and defended himself in a long series of treatises on oratorical art. In lively dialogues he sketched the history of Roman eloquence and laid down the rules for composition, prose rhythm, and delivery. He did not admit that his own style was "Asian"; he had modeled it, he claimed, upon that of Demosthenes; and he reminded the Atticists that their cold and passionless speech drove audiences to sleep or flight.

The fifty-seven orations that have come down to us from Cicero illustrate all the tricks of successful eloquence. They excel in the passionate presentation of one side of a question or a character, the entertainment of the auditors with humor and anecdote, the appeal to vanity, prejudice, sentiment, patriotism, and piety, the ruthless exposure of the real or reported, public or private, faults of the opponent or his client, the skillful turning of attention from unfavorable points, the barrage of rhetorical questions framed to make answer difficult or damaging, the heaping up of charges, in periodic sentences whose clauses are lashes, and whose torrent overwhelms. These speeches do not pretend to be fair; they are defamations rather than declamations, briefs that take every advantage of that freedom of abuse which, though forbidden to the stage, was allowed in the Forum and the courts. Cicero does not hesitate to apply to his victims terms like "swine," "pest," "butcher," "filth"; he tells Piso that virgins kill themselves to escape his lechery, and excoriates Antony for being publicly affectionate to his wife. Audiences and juries enjoyed such vituperation, and no one took it too seriously. Cicero corresponded amiably with Piso a few years after the brutal attack of the *In Pisonem*. It is to be admitted, further, that Cicero's orations abound rather in egotism and rhetoric than in moral sincerity, philosophical wisdom, or even legal acumen or depth. But what eloquence! Even Demosthenes was not so vivid, vital, exuberantly witty, so full of the salt and tang of the human fray. Certainly no man before or after Cicero spoke a Latin so seductively charming and fluent, so elegantly passionate; this was the zenith of Latin prose. "You have discovered all the treasures of oratory," said the generous Caesar in dedicating his book *On Analogy* to Cicero; "and you have been the first to employ them. Thereby you have laid the Roman people under a mighty obligation, and you honor your fatherland. You have gained a triumph to be preferred to that of the greatest generals. For it is a nobler thing to enlarge the boundaries of human intelligence than those of the Roman Empire." [47]

The speeches betray the politician; the letters of Cicero bare the man, and make even the politician forgivable. Nearly all of them were dictated to a secretary and never revised by Cicero; most of them were written with no thought of publication; seldom, therefore, has a man's secret soul been so completely exposed. "He who reads these letters," said Nepos, "will not much need a history of those times"; [48] in them the most vital part of the revolutionary drama is seen from within, all blinds removed. Usually their style is artless and direct and dances with humor and wit; [49] their language is an attractive mixture of literary grace and colloquial ease. They are the most interesting of Cicero's remains; indeed, of all extant Latin prose. It is natural that we should find in so large a correspondence (864 letters, ninety of them to Cicero) occasional contradictions and insincerities. There is no sign here of the religious piety and belief that appear so frequently in Cicero's essays or in those speeches in which he plays up the gods as his last trump. His private opinion of various men, especially of Caesar, does not always conform with his public protestation. [50] His incredible vanity appears more amiably here than in his orations, where he seems to be carrying his own statue with him wherever he goes; he smilingly confesses that "my own applause has the greatest weight with me." [51] He assures us, with charming innocence, that "if ever any man was a stranger to vainglory it is myself." [52] We are amused to find so many letters about money and so much ado about so many homes. Besides modest villas at Arpinum, Asturae, Puteoli, and Pompeii, Cicero had an estate at Formiae valued at 250,000, another at Tusculum worth 500,000, and a palace on the Palatine that cost him 3,500,000 sesterces.* Such comfort seems outrageous in a philosopher.

But which of us is so virtuous that his reputation could survive the publication of his intimate correspondence? Indeed, as we continue to read these letters, we almost come to like the man. He had no more faults, perhaps no

---

* This last sum had been raised by a loan from a client; we do not know if it was repaid. Forbidden by law to receive fees, lawyers received loans instead. Another way of being paid was to be remembered in a client's will. Through bequests of this sort or another Cicero inherited 20,000,000 sesterces in thirty years.[53] The constitution of man always rewrites the constitutions of states.

greater vanity, than we; he made the mistake of immortalizing them with
perfect prose. At his best he was a hard worker, a tender father, a good
friend. We see him in his home, loving his books and his children, and trying
to love his wife, the rheumatic and irritable Terentia, whose wealth and
eloquence equaled his own. They were too rich to be happy; their worries
and quarrels were always in large figures; at last, in their old age, he divorced
her over some financial dispute. Soon afterward he married Publilia, who
attracted him by having more money than years; but when she showed dis-
like for his daughter Tullia he sent Publilia away, too. Tullia he loved hu-
manly beyond reason; he grieved almost to madness at her death and wished
to build a temple to her as a deity. Pleasanter are the letters to and about
Tiro, his chief secretary, who took his dictation in shorthand and managed his
finances so ably and honestly that Cicero rewarded him with freedom. Most
numerous are the letters to Atticus, who invested Cicero's savings, extricated
him from financial difficulties, published his writings, and gave him excellent
unheeded advice. To Atticus, wisely absent in Greece at the height of the
revolution, Cicero writes a letter of typical cordiality and charm:

> There is nothing of which I so much feel the want as of him with
> whom I can communicate everything that concerns me; who loves me,
> who is prudent; to whom I can speak without flattery, dissimulation,
> or reserve. My brother, who is all candor and kindness, is away. . . .
> And you, who have so often relieved my cares and anxieties by your
> counsel, who used to be my companion in public matters, my confi-
> dant in all private ones, the partaker of all my words and thoughts—
> where are you?[54]

In those turbulent days when Caesar crossed the Rubicon, conquered
Pompey, and made himself dictator, Cicero retired for a moment from political life and sought solace in reading and writing philosophy. "Remember,"
he begged Atticus, "not to give up your books to anybody, but to keep
them, as you promised, for me. I entertain the strongest affection for them,
as I now feel disgust for everything else."[55] In his youth, defending the poet
Archias in the most modest and amiable of his speeches, he had praised the
study of literature as "nourishing our adolescence, adorning our prosperity,
and delighting our old age."[56] Now he took his own counsel, and in little
more than two years wrote almost a library of philosophy.* The dissolution
of religious belief in the higher classes had left a moral vacuum, by which
Rome seemed to be drawn into a disintegration of character and society.

---

* *De Republica*, 54 B.C.; *De Legibus*, 52; *Academica*, *De Consolatione*, and *De Finibus*, 45;
De Natura Deorum, *De Divinatione*, *De Fato*, *De Virtutibus*, *De Officiis*, *De Amicitia*, *De
Senectute*, *De Gloria*, *Disputationes Tusculanae*, all 44 B.C. In these same two years, 45-44,
Cicero wrote five books on oratory.

Cicero dreamed that philosophy might serve as a substitute for theology in providing for these classes a guide and stimulus to right living. He resolved not to construct one more system, but to summarize the teachings of the Greek sages and offer them as his last gift to his people.[57] He was honest enough to confess that he was for the most part adapting, sometimes translating, the treatises of Panaetius, Poseidonius, and other recent Greeks.[58] But he transformed the dull prose of his models into limpid and graceful Latin, enlivened his discourse with dialogue, and passed quickly over the deserts of logic and metaphysics to the living problems of conduct and statesmanship. Like Lucretius he had to invent a philosophical terminology; he succeeded, and put both language and philosophy heavily in his debt. Not since Plato had wisdom worn such prose.

It was from Plato above all that his ideas stemmed. He did not relish the dogmatism of the Epicureans, who "talk of divine things with such assurance that you would imagine they had come directly from an assemblage of the gods"; nor yet that of the Stoics, who so labor the argument from design that "you would suppose even the gods had been made for human use" [59]—a theory that Cicero himself, in other moods, would not find incredible. His starting point is that of the New Academy—a lenient skepticism which denied all certainties and found probability sufficient for human life. "In most things," he writes, "my philosophy is that of doubt.[60] . . . May I have your leave not to know what I do not know?" [61] "Those who seek to learn my personal opinion," he says, "show an unreasonable degree of curiosity"; [62] but his coyness soon yields to his talent for expression. He scorns sacrifices, oracles, and auguries, and devotes an entire treatise to disproving divination. Against the widespread cult of astrology he asks if all the men slain at Cannae had been born under the same star.[63] He even doubts that a knowledge of the future would be a boon; the future may be as unpleasant as much else of the truth that we so recklessly chase. He vainly thinks to make short work of old beliefs by laughing them out of court: "When we call corn Ceres and wine Bacchus we use a common figure of speech; but do you imagine that anybody is so insane as to believe that the thing he feeds upon is a god?" [63a] Nevertheless, he is as skeptical of atheism as of any other dogma. He rejects the atomism of Democritus and Lucretius; it is as unlikely that unguided atoms—even in infinite time—could fall into the order of the existing world as that the letters of the alphabet should spontaneously form the *Annales* of Ennius.[64] Our ignorance of the gods is no guarantee of their nonexistence; and indeed, Cicero argues, the general agreement of mankind establishes a balance of probability in favor of Providence. He concludes that religion is indispensable to private morals and public order and that no man of sense will attack it.[65] Hence, while writing against divination, he continued to fulfill the functions of official augur. It was not quite hypocrisy; he would have called it statesmanship. Roman morals, society, and government were bound up with the old religion and could not safely let it die. (The emperors would reason so in persecuting Christianity.) When his beloved Tullia died, Cicero inclined more strongly than ever to the hope of personal immortality. Many years before, in the "Dream of Scipio" with which he ended his *Republic,* he had borrowed from Pythagoras, Plato, and Eudoxus a complex and eloquent myth of a life beyond the grave, in which the good great dead enjoyed eternal bliss. But in his private correspondence—even in the letters that condoled with bereaved friends—there is no mention of an afterlife.

Knowing the skepticism of his age, he based his moral and political treatises on purely secular grounds, independent of supernatural sanctions. He begins (in *De Finibus*) by inquiring for the road to happiness, and hesitantly agrees with the Stoics that virtue alone suffices. Therefore (in *De Officiis*) he examines the way of virtue, and by the charm of his style succeeds for a time in making duty interesting. "All men are brothers," he writes, and "the whole world is to be considered as the common city of gods and men." [66] The most perfect morality would be a conscientious loyalty to this whole. More immediately a man owes it to himself and society, first of all, to establish a sound economic basis to his life, and then to fulfill his duties as a citizen. Wise statesmanship is nobler than the subtlest philosophy.[67]

Monarchy is the best form of government when the monarch is good, the worst when he is bad—a truism soon to be illustrated in Rome. Aristocracy is good when the really best rule; but Cicero, as a member of the middle class, could not quite admit that the old entrenched families were the best. Democracy is good when the people are virtuous, which, Cicero thought, is never; besides, it is vitiated by the false assumption of equality. The best form of government is a mixed constitution, like that of pre-Gracchan Rome: the democratic power of the assemblies, the aristocratic power of the Senate, the almost royal power of the consuls for a year. Without checks and balances monarchy becomes despotism, aristocracy becomes oligarchy, democracy becomes mob rule, chaos, and dictatorship. Writing five years after Caesar's consulate, Cicero cast a dart in his direction:

> Plato says that from the exaggerated license which people call liberty, tyrants spring up as from a root . . . and that at last such liberty reduces a nation to slavery. Everything in excess is changed into its opposite. . . . For out of such an ungoverned populace one is usually chosen as leader . . . someone bold and unscrupulous . . . who curries favor with the people by giving them other men's property. To such a man, because he has much reason for fear if he remains a private citizen, the protection of public office is given, and continually renewed. He surrounds himself with an armed guard, and emerges as a tyrant over the very people who raised him to power.[68]

Nevertheless, Caesar won; and Cicero thought it best to bury his discontent in melodious platitudes on law, friendship, glory, and old age. *Silent leges inter arma*, he said—"laws are silent in time of war"; but at least he could muse on the philosophy of law. Following the Stoics, he defined law as "right reason in agreement with nature"; [69] i.e., law seeks to make orderly and stable the relations that rise out of the social impulses of men. "Nature has inclined us to love men" (society), "and this is the foundation of law." [70] Friendship should be based not upon mutual advantage but upon common interests cemented and limited by virtue and justice; the law of friendship should be "neither to ask dishonorable things, nor to do them if asked." [71] An honorable life is the best guarantee of a pleasant old age. An indulgent and intemperate youth delivers to age a body prematurely worn out; but a life well spent can leave both body and mind sound to a hundred years; witness Masinissa. Devotion to study may make one "unaware of the stealthy approach of old age." [72] Age as well as youth has its glories—a tolerant wisdom, the respectful affection of children, desire and ambition's fever cooled. Age may fear death, but not if the mind has been formed by philosophy. Beyond the grave there will be, at the best, a new and happier life; and at the worst there will be peace.[73]

All in all, Cicero's essays in philosophy are meager in result. Like his statesmanship they clung too anxiously to orthodoxy and tradition. He had all the curiosity of a scientist and all the timidity of a bourgeois; even in his philosophy he remained a politician, reluctant to offend any vote. He collected the ideas of others, and balanced pros and cons so well that we come out from his sessions by the same door wherein we went. Only one thing redeems these little books—the simple beauty of their style. How pleasant Cicero's Latin is, how easy to read, how smoothly and clearly the stream of language flows! When he narrates events he catches some of the vivacity that made his speeches chain attention; when he describes a character it is with such skill that he mourns that he has no time to be Rome's greatest historian; [74] when he lets himself go he flowers into the balanced clauses and crashing periods which he had learned from Isocrates, and with which he had made the Forum resound. His ideas are those of the upper classes, but his style aims to reach the people; for them he labors to be clear, toils to make his truisms thrilling, and salts abstractions with anecdote and wit.

He re-created the Latin language. He extended its vocabulary, forged from it a flexible instrument for philosophy, fitted it to be the vehicle of learning and literature in western Europe for seventeen hundred years. Posterity remembered him more as an author than as a statesman. When, despite all his reminders, men had almost forgotten the glory of his consulate, they cherished his conquests in letters and eloquence. And since the world honors form as well as substance, art as well as knowledge and power, he achieved, of all Romans, a fame second only to Caesar's. It was an exception that he could never forgive.

CHAPTER IX

Caesar

100-44 B.C.

I. THE RAKE

CAIUS JULIUS CAESAR traced his pedigree to Iulus Ascanius, son of Aeneas, son of Venus, daughter of Jupiter: he began and ended as a god. The Julian gens, though impoverished, was one of the oldest and noblest in Italy. A Caius Julius had been consul in 489, another in 482, a Vopiscus Julius in 473, a Sextus Julius in 157, another in 91.[1] From his uncle-in-law Marius he derived by a kind of avuncular heredity an inclination toward radical politics. His mother Aurelia was a matron of dignity and wisdom, frugally managing her small home in the unfashionable Subura—a district of shops, taverns, and brothels. There Caesar was born 100 B.C., allegedly by the operation that bears his name.*

"Now was this Caesar," says Holland's Suetonius, "wondrous docible and apt to learn." His tutor in Latin, Greek, and rhetoric was a Gaul; with him Caesar unconsciously began to prepare himself for his greatest conquest. The youth took readily to oratory and almost lost himself in juvenile authorship. He was saved by being made military aide to Marcus Thermus in Asia. Nicomedes, ruler of Bithynia, took such a fancy to him that Cicero and other gossips later taunted him with having "lost his virginity to a king."[2] Returning to Rome in 84, he married Cossutia to please his father; when, soon afterward, his father died, he divorced her and married Cornelia, daughter of that Cinna who had taken over the revolution from Marius. When Sulla came to power he ordered Caesar to divorce Cornelia; when Caesar refused, Sulla confiscated his patrimony and Cornelia's dowry, and listed him for death.

Caesar fled from Italy and joined the army in Cilicia. On Sulla's death he returned to Rome (78), but finding his enemies in power he left again for Asia. Pirates captured him on the way, took him to one of their Cilician lairs, and offered to free him for twenty talents ($72,000); he reproached

---

* It was already an ancient mode of birth, being mentioned in the laws ascribed to Numa. Caesar's cognomen was not derived from the operation (*caesus ab utero matris*); long before him there had been Caesars among the Julii.

them for underestimating his value, and volunteered to give them fifty. Having sent his servants to raise the money, he amused himself by writing poems and reading them to his captors. They did not like them. He called them dull barbarians and promised to hang them at the earliest opportunity. When the ransom came he hurried to Miletus, engaged vessels and crews, chased and caught the pirates, recovered the ransom, and crucified them; but being a man of great clemency, he had their throats cut first.[3] Then he went to Rhodes to study rhetoric and philosophy.

Back again in Rome, he divided his energies between politics and love. He was handsome, though already worried about his thinning hair. When Cornelia died (68) he married Pompeia, granddaughter of Sulla. As this was a purely political marriage, he did not scruple to carry on liaisons in the fashion of his time; but in such number and with such ambigendered diversity that Curio (father of his later general) called him *omnium mulierum vir et omnium virorum mulier*—"the husband of every woman and the wife of every man."[4] He would continue these habits in his campaigns, dallying with Cleopatra in Egypt, with Queen Eunoe in Numidia, and with so many ladies in Gaul that his soldiers in fond jest called him *moechus calvus*, the "bald adulterer"; in his triumph after conquering Gaul they sang a couplet warning all husbands to keep their wives under lock and key as long as Caesar was in town. The aristocracy hated him doubly—for undermining their privileges and seducing their wives. Pompey divorced his wife for her intimacy with Caesar. Cato's passionate hostility was not all philosophical: his half sister Servilia was the most devoted of Caesar's mistresses. When Cato, suspecting Caesar's complicity with Catiline, challenged him in the Senate to read aloud a note just brought to him, Caesar passed it to Cato without comment; it was a love letter from Servilia.[5] Her passion for him continued throughout his life, and merciless gossip, in her later years, charged her with surrendering her daughter Tertia to Caesar's lust. During the Civil War, at a public auction, Caesar "knocked down" some confiscated estates of irreconcilable aristocrats to Servilia at a nominal price; when some expressed surprise at the low figure, Cicero remarked, in a pithy pun that might have cost him his life, *Tertia deducta*, which could either mean "a third off," or refer to the rumor that Servilia had brought her daughter to Caesar. Tertia became the wife of Caesar's prime assassin, Cassius. So the amours of men mingle with the commotions of states.

Probably these diversified investments helped Caesar's rise as well as his fall. Every woman he won was an influential friend, usually in the enemy's camp; and most of them remained his devotees even when his passion had cooled to courtesy. Crassus, though his wife Tertulla was reported to be Caesar's mistress, lent him vast sums to finance his candidacies with bribes and games; at one time Caesar owed him 800 talents ($2,880,000). Such loans were not acts of generosity or friendship; they were campaign contributions, to be repaid with political favors or military spoils. Crassus, like Atticus, needed protection and opportunities for his millions. Most Roman politicians of the time incurred similar "debts": Mark Antony owed 40,000,-000 sesterces, Cicero 60,000,000, Milo 70,000,000—though these figures may be conservative slanders. We must think of Caesar as at first an unscrupulous politician and a reckless rake, slowly transformed by growth and responsibility into one of history's most profound and conscientious statesmen. We must not forget, as we rejoice at his faults, that he was a great man notwithstanding. We cannot equate ourselves with Caesar by proving that he seduced women, bribed ward leaders, and wrote books.

II. THE CONSUL

Caesar began as the secret ally of Catiline and ended as the remaker of Rome. Hardly a year after Sulla's death he prosecuted Gnaeus Dolabella, a tool of the Sullan reaction; the jury voted against Caesar, but the people applauded his democratic offensive and his brilliant speech. He could not rival Cicero's verve and wit, passionate periods, and rhetorical flagellations; indeed, Caesar disliked this "Asianic" style and disciplined himself to the masculine brevity and stern simplicity that were to distinguish his *Commentaries* on the Gallic and Civil Wars. Nevertheless, he was soon ranked as second only to Cicero in eloquence.[6]

In 68 he was chosen quaestor and was assigned to serve in Spain. He led military expeditions against the native tribes, sacked towns, and collected enough plunder to pay off some of his debts. At the same time he won the gratitude of Spanish cities by lowering the interest charges on the sums that had been lent them by the Roman bankers. Coming at Gades upon a statue of Alexander, he reproached himself for having accomplished so little at an age when the Macedonian had conquered half the Mediterranean world. He returned to Rome and plunged again into the race for office and power. In 65 he was elected aedile, or commissioner of public works. He spent his money—i.e., the money of Crassus—in adorning the Forum with new buildings and colonnades, and courted the populace with unstinted games. Sulla had removed from the Capitol the trophies of Marius—banners, pictures, and spoils representing the features and victories of the old radical; Caesar had these restored, to the joy of Marius' veterans; and by that act alone he announced his rebel policy. The conservatives protested and marked him out as a man to be broken.

In 64, as president of a commission appointed to try cases of murder, he summoned to his tribunal the surviving agents of Sulla's proscriptions and sentenced several of them to exile or death. In 63 he voted in the Senate against the execution of Catiline's accomplices and remarked casually, in his speech, that human personality does not outlive death;[7] it was apparently the only part of his speech that offended no one. In that same year he was elected *pontifex maximus*, head of the Roman religion. In 62 he was chosen praetor, and prosecuted a leading conservative for embezzling public funds. In 61 he was appointed propraetor for Spain, but his creditors prevented his departure. He admitted that he needed 25,000,000 sesterces in order to have nothing.[8] Crassus came to his rescue by underwriting all his obligations. Caesar proceeded to Spain, led militarily brilliant campaigns against tribes with a passion for independence, and came back to Rome with spoils enough to pay off his debts and yet so enrich the Treasury that the Senate voted him a triumph. Perhaps the *optimates* were subtle; they knew that Caesar wished to stand for the consulate, that the law forbade candidacy in absence, and that the *triumphator* was required by law to remain outside the city until the day of his triumph—which the Senate had set for after the election. But Caesar forewent his triumph, entered the city, and campaigned with irresistible energy and skill.

His victory was obtained by his clever attachment of Pompey to the liberal cause. Pompey had just returned from the East after a succession of military and diplomatic achievements. By clearing the sea of pirates he had restored security to Mediterranean trade, and prosperity to the cities it served. He had pleased the capitalists of Rome by conquering Bithynia, Pontus, and Syria; he had deposed and set up kings and had lent them money from his spoils at lush rates of interest; he had accepted a huge bribe from the king of Egypt to come and quell a revolt there, and then had refrained from carrying out the compact on the ground that it was illegal;[9] he had pacified Palestine and made it a client state of Rome; he had founded thirty-nine cities and had established law, order, and peace; all in all he had behaved with judgment, statesmanship, and profit. Now he had brought back to Rome such wealth in taxes and tribute, goods captured and slaves ransomed or sold, that he was able to contribute 200,000,000 sesterces to the Treasury, add 350,000,000 to its annual revenues, distribute 384,000,000 among his soldiers, and yet keep enough for himself to rival Crassus as one of the two richest men in Rome.

The Senate was more frightened than pleased at these accomplishments. It trembled when it heard that Pompey had landed at Brundisium (62) with an army personally devoted to him and capable at his word of making him dictator. He magnanimously relieved its fears by disbanding his troops and entering Rome with no other retinue than his personal staff. His triumph lasted two days, but even that time proved insufficient for all the floats that pictured his victories and displayed his garnerings. The ungrateful Senate rejected his request that state lands be given his soldiers, refused to ratify his agreements with conquered kings, and restored those arrangements that Lucullus had made in the East and which Pompey had ignored. The effect of these actions was to break down Cicero's *concordia ordinum*, or alliance of the higher classes, and throw Pompey and the capitalists into a flirtation with the *populares*. Taking full advantage of the situation, Caesar formed with Pompey and Crassus the First Triumvirate (60), by which each pledged himself to oppose legislation unsatisfactory to any one of them. Pompey agreed to support Caesar for the consulate, and Caesar promised, if elected, to carry through the measures in which Pompey had been rebuffed by the Senate.

The campaign was bitter, and bribery flourished on both sides. When Cato, leader of the conservatives, heard that his party was buying votes, he unbent and approved the procedure as in a noble cause. The *populares* elected Caesar, the *optimates* Bibulus. Caesar had hardly entered upon his consulate (59) when he proposed to the Senate the measures asked for by Pompey: a distribution of land to 20,000 of the poorer citizens, including Pompey's soldiers; the ratification of Pompey's arrangements in the East; and a one-third reduction of the sum which the publicans had pledged themselves to raise from the Asiatic provinces. As the Senate opposed each of these measures by every means, Caesar, like the Gracchi, offered them directly to the Assembly. The conservatives induced Bibulus to use his veto power to forbid a vote, and had omens declared unfavorable. Caesar ignored the omens and persuaded the Assembly to impeach Bibulus; and an enthusiastic *popularis* emptied a pot of ordure upon Bibulus' head. Caesar's bills were carried. As in the case of the Gracchi, they combined an agrarian policy with a financial program pleasing to the business class. Pompey was impressed by Caesar's performance of his pledges. He took Caesar's daughter Julia as his fourth wife, and the entente between plebs and *bourgeoisie* became a feast of love. The Triumvirs promised the radical wing of their following that they would support Publius Clodius for the tribunate in the fall of 59. Meanwhile they kept the voters in good humor with profuse amusements and games.

In April Caesar submitted his second land bill, by which the areas owned by the state in Campania were to be distributed among poor citizens who had three children. The Senate was again ignored, the Assembly passed the bill, and, after a century of effort, the Gracchan policy triumphed. Bibulus kept to his house and contented himself with periodical announcements that the omens were unpropitious to legislation. Caesar administered public affairs without consulting him, so that the town wits referred to the year as "the consulate of Julius and Caesar." To bring the Senate under public scrutiny, he established the first newspaper by having clerks make a record of Senatorial and other public proceedings and news, and post these *Acta Diurna*, or "Daily Doings," on the walls of the forums. From these walls the reports were copied and sent by private messengers to all parts of the Empire.[10]

Toward the end of this historic consulate Caesar had himself appointed governor of Cisalpine and Narbonese Gaul for the ensuing five years. As no troops could lawfully be stationed in Italy, the command over the legions stationed in north Italy gave its possessor military power over the whole peninsula. To guarantee the maintenance of his legislation, Caesar secured the election of his friends Gabinius and Piso as consuls for 58 and married Piso's daughter Calpurnia. To ensure continued support from the plebs he lent his decisive aid to the election of Clodius as tribune for 58. He did not let his plans be influenced by the fact that he had recently divorced his third wife, Pompeia, on suspicion of adultery with Clodius.

III. MORALS AND POLITICS

Publius Clodius Pulcher (the Handsome) was a scion of the Claudian gens, a young aristocrat whose courage knew no fear and his morals no restraint. Like Catiline and Caesar he descended from his rank to lead the poor against the rich. To be eligible as a tribune of the people he had himself adopted into a plebeian family. To redistribute the concentrated wealth of Rome and to destroy Cicero—who had abused his sister Clodia and stood for the sanctity of property—he served as a subaltern to Caesar until he could take power into his own hands. He admired Caesar's policies and loved Caesar's wife. To gain access to her he disguised himself as a woman, entered the house of Caesar, then (62) high priest, took part in the ceremonies offered by women alone to the Bona Dea, was detected, accused, and publicly tried (61) for having violated the mysteries of the Good Goddess. Caesar, called as a witness, said that he had no charge to make against Clodius. Why, then, asked the prosecutor, had he divorced Pompeia? "Because," said Caesar, "my wife must be above suspicion." It was a clever answer, which neither exonerated nor condemned a valuable political aide. Various witnesses—perhaps bribed—told the court that Clodius had had relations with Clodia and had seduced his sister Tertia after her marriage to Lucullus. Clodius protested that he had been away from Rome on the day of the alleged sacrilege; Cicero, however, testified that Clodius had on that day been with him in Rome. The populace thought the whole affair a Senatorial plot to destroy a *populares* leader and cried out for acquittal. Crassus—some say at Caesar's behest—bribed a number of judges for Clodius. The radicals for once had the more money, and Clodius was freed. Caesar took advantage of the situation to exchange an inconveniently conservative wife for the daughter of a senator allied to the popular cause.

He had hardly retired from office when some conservatives proposed the complete annulment of his legislation. Cato did not conceal his opinion that these "Julian laws" should be wiped off the statute books. The Senate hesitated to fling so open a challenge to Caesar armed with legions and to Clodius wielding the tribunate. In 63 Cato had wooed the populace for the conservatives by renewing the state distribution of cheap corn; now (58) Clodius countered by making the dole completely free to all who came for it. He passed bills through the Assembly forbidding the use of religious vetoes against legislative procedures and restoring the legality of the *collegia*, which the Senate had tried to disband. He reorganized these guilds into voting blocs and won such fealty from them that they provided him with an armed guard. Fearing that after his year as tribune had expired Cato or Cicero might attempt to undo Caesar's work, Clodius persuaded the Assembly to send Cato as commissioner to Cyprus, and to pass a decree banishing any man who had put Roman citizens to death without securing, as law required, the Assembly's consent. Cicero saw that the measure was aimed at him and fled to Greece, where cities and dignitaries rivaled one another in offering him hospitality and honors. The Assembly decreed that Cicero's property should be confiscated, and his house on the Palatine was razed to the ground.

It was Cicero's good fortune that Clodius, overcome with success, now attacked both Pompey and Caesar, and planned to make himself sole leader of the plebs. Pompey retaliated by supporting the petition of Cicero's brother Quintus for the orator's recall. The Senate appealed to all Roman citizens in Italy to come to the capital and vote on the proposal. Clodius brought an armed gang into the Field of Mars to supervise the balloting, and Pompey engaged a needy aristocrat, Annius Milo, to organize a rival band. Riot and bloodshed ensued, many men were killed, and Quintus barely escaped with his life. But his measure carried, and after months of exile Cicero returned in triumph to Italy (57). Multitudes greeted him as he passed from Brundisium to Rome; there the welcoming crowd was so great that Cicero feigned fear that he would be accused of having contrived his banishment for the sake of this glorious restoration.[11]

Apparently he had pledged himself to Pompey, and perhaps to Caesar, as the price of his recall. Caesar lent him large sums to recoup his finances and refused to take interest.[12] For several years now Cicero became the advocate of the Triumvirs in the Senate. When a dearth of grain threatened Rome (57), he secured for Pompey an extraordinary commission with full power for six years over all the food supply of Rome and over all ports and trade. Pompey again acquitted himself well, but the constitution of the Republic suffered another blow, and government by men continued to replace government by laws. In 56 Cicero persuaded the Senate to vote a substantial amount for the payment of Caesar's troops in Gaul. In 54 he unsuccessfully defended the extortionate provincial administration of Aulus Gabinius, a friend of the Triumvirs. In 55 he canceled all the favor he had gained with Caesar by an abusive attack upon another provincial governor, Calpurnius Piso. He remembered too vividly that Piso had voted for his banishment; he forgot that Piso's daughter was Caesar's wife.

Upon Cato's return (57) from his brilliant reorganization of Cyprian affairs, the conservatives re-formed their lines. Clodius, now the enemy of Pompey, accepted the invitation of the aristocracy to lend it the assistance of his popularity and his thugs. Literature took on an anti-Caesarian tint; the epigrams of Calvus and Catullus flew like poisoned darts into the camp of the Triumvirs. As Caesar moved farther and farther into Gaul, and news came of the many dangers that he faced, hope sprung anew in noble breasts; after all, said Cicero, there are many ways in which a man may die. If we may believe Caesar, several conservatives opened negotiations with Ariovistus, the German leader, for the assassination of Caesar.[13] Domitius, running for the consulate, announced that if elected he would at once move for Caesar's recall—which meant Caesar's indictment and trial. Veering with the wind, Cicero proposed that on May 25, 56, the Senate should consider the abrogation of Caesar's land laws.

IV. THE CONQUEST OF GAUL

In the spring of 58 Caesar took up his duties as governor of Cisalpine and Narbonese Gaul—i.e., northern Italy and southern France. In 71 Ariovistus had led 15,000 Germans into Gaul at the request of one Gallic tribe seeking assistance against another. He had provided the desired aid and then had remained to establish his rule over all the tribes of northeastern Gaul. One of these, the Aedui, appealed to Rome for help against the Germans (61); the Senate authorized the Roman governor of Narbonese Gaul to comply, but almost at the same time it listed Ariovistus among rulers friendly to Rome. Meanwhile 120,000 Germans crossed the Rhine, settled in Flanders, and so strengthened Ariovistus that he treated the native population as subject peoples and dreamed of conquering all Gaul.[14] At the same time the Helvetii, centering about Geneva, began migrating westward, 368,000 strong, and Caesar was warned that they planned to cross his province of Narbonese Gaul on their way to southwestern France. "From the sources of the Rhine to the Atlantic Ocean," says Mommsen, "the German tribes were in motion; the whole line of the Rhine was threatened by them; it was a movement like that when the Alemanni and the Franks threw themselves upon the falling empire of the Caesars . . . five hundred years afterward."[15] While Rome plotted against him, Caesar plotted to save Rome.

At his own expense, and without the authority he should have sought from the Senate, he raised and equipped four extra legions besides the four already provided him. He sent a peremptory invitation to Ariovistus to come and discuss the situation; as he had expected, Ariovistus refused. Deputations came now to Caesar from many Gallic tribes, asking for his protection. Caesar declared war against both Ariovistus and the Helvetii, marched northward, and met the Helvetian avalanche in a bloody battle at Bibracte, capital of the Aedui, near the modern Autun. Caesar's legions won, but by a narrow margin; in these matters we must for the most part follow his own account. The Helvetii offered to return to their Swiss homeland; Caesar agreed to give them safe passage, but on condition that their territory should accept the rule of Rome. All Gaul now sent him thanks for its deliverance, and begged his aid in expelling Ariovistus. He met the Germans near Ostheim,* and slew or captured (he tells us) nearly all of them (58). Ariovistus escaped, but died soon afterward.

Caesar took it for granted that his liberation of Gaul was also a conquest of it: he began at once to reorganize it under Roman authority, with the excuse that in no other way could it be protected against Germany. Some Gauls, unconvinced, rebelled, and invoked the aid of the Belgae, a powerful tribe of Germans and Celts inhabiting north Gaul between the Seine and the Rhine. Caesar defeated their army on the banks of the Aisne; then, with a celerity of movement that never allowed his foes to unite, he moved in succession against the Suessiones, Ambiani, Nervii, and Aduatici, conquered them, despoiled them, and sold the captives to the slave merchants of Italy. Somewhat prematurely he announced the conquest of Gaul; the Senate proclaimed it a Roman province (56), and the common people of Rome, as imperialistic as any general, shouted the praises of their distant champion. Caesar recrossed the Alps into Cisalpine Gaul, busied himself with its internal administration, replenished his legions, and invited Pompey and Crassus to meet him at Luca to plan a united defense against the conservative reaction.

---

* Ten miles west of the Rhine, 160 miles south of Cologne.

To forestall Domitius they agreed that Pompey and Crassus should run against him for the consulate for 55 B.C.; that Pompey should be made governor of Spain, and Crassus of Syria, for five years (54-50); that Caesar should be continued for another five years (53-49) as governor of Gaul; and that at the end of this term he should be allowed to seek a second consulate. He furnished his colleagues and friends, from the booty of Gaul, with funds to finance their campaigns; he sent great sums to Rome to provide work for the unemployed, commissions for his supporters, and prestige for himself, by an extensive program of public buildings; and he so oiled the palms of the senators who came to sample his loot that the movement to repeal his laws collapsed. Pompey and Crassus were elected consuls after the usual bribery, and Caesar returned to the task of persuading the Gauls that peace is sweeter than freedom.

Trouble was brewing on the Rhine below Cologne. Two German tribes had crossed into Belgic Gaul as far as Liége, and the nationalist party in Gaul was seeking their help against the Romans. Caesar met the invaders near Xanten (55), drove them back to the Rhine, and slew such of them—women and children as well as men—as were not drowned in the river. His engineers then built in ten days a bridge over the great stream, there 1400 feet wide; Caesar's legions crossed, and fought long enough on German soil to establish the Rhine as a secure frontier. After two weeks he retraced his steps into Gaul.

We do not know why he now invaded Britain. Possibly he was lured by rumors that gold or pearls abounded there; or he wished to capture the tin and iron deposits of Britain for Roman exportation; or he resented the aid that Britons had sent to the Gauls, and thought that Roman power in Gaul must be made secure in every direction. He led a small force across the Channel at its narrowest point, defeated the unprepared Britons, took a few notes, and returned (55). A year later he crossed again, overcame the British under Cassivelaunus, reached the Thames, exacted promise of tribute, and sailed back to Gaul.

Perhaps he had heard that revolt was once more agitating the Gallic tribes. He suppressed the Eburones and marched again into Germany (53). Returning, he left his main army in northern Gaul, while with his remaining troops he went to winter in north Italy, hoping to devote a few months to mending his fences in Rome. But early in 52 word came to him that Vercingetorix, the ablest of the Gallic chieftains, had united nearly all the tribes in a war for independence. Caesar's situation was precarious in the extreme. Most of his legions were in the north, and the country between them and himself was in rebel hands. He led a small detachment over the snow-covered Cevennes against Auvergne; when Vercingetorix brought up his forces to defend it, Caesar left Decimus Brutus in command and, with a few horse-men, rode in disguise across all Gaul from south-to north, rejoined his main army, and at once led them to the attack. He besieged, captured, and sacked Avaricum (Bourges) and Cenabum (Orléans), massacred their populations, and replenished his depleted supplies with their treasuries. He moved on to assail Gergovia; there, however, the Gauls resisted so resolutely that he was compelled to withdraw. The Aedui, whom he had rescued from the Germans, and who heretofore had remained his allies, now deserted him, captured his base and stores at Soissons, and prepared to drive him back into Narbonese Gaul.

It was the lowest ebb of Caesar's fortunes, and for a time he considered himself lost. He staked everything upon a siege of Alesia (Alise Ste.-Reine), where Vercingetorix had gathered 30,000 troops. Caesar had hardly dis-tributed a like number of soldiers around the city when word came that 250,000 Gauls were marching down upon him from the north. He ordered his men to raise two concentric walls of earth around the city, one before them, the other behind them. Against these walls and the desperate Romans the armies of Vercingetorix and his allies threw themselves in repeated vain attacks. After a week the army of relief broke up in disorder for lack of discipline and supplies, and melted into ineffectual bands at the very moment when the Romans had reached the end of their stores. Soon thereafter the starving city sent Vercingetorix at his own suggestion as a prisoner to Caesar, and then surrendered to the Roman's mercy (52). The town was spared, but all its soldiers were given to the legionaries as slaves. Vercinge-torix was led in chains to Rome; there he later graced Caesar's triumph and paid with his life for his devotion to liberty.

The siege of Alesia decided the fate of Gaul and the character of French civilization. It added to the Roman Empire a country twice the size of Italy and opened the purses and markets of 5,000,000 people to Roman trade. It saved Italy and the Mediterranean world for four centuries from barbarian invasion; and it lifted Caesar from the verge of ruin to a new height of repu-tation, wealth, and power. After another year of sporadic revolts, which the angry general put down with uncharacteristic severity, all Gaul accepted subjection to Rome. Once his victory was certain Caesar became again the generous conqueror; he treated the tribes with such lenience that in all the ensuing Civil War, when he and Rome would have been helpless to retaliate, they made no move to throw off the yoke. For three hundred years Gaul remained a Roman province, prospered under the Roman peace, learned and transformed the Latin language, and became the channel through which the culture of classic antiquity passed into northern Europe. Doubtless neither Caesar nor his contemporaries foresaw the immense consequences of his bloody triumph. He thought he had saved Italy, won a province, and forged an army; he did not suspect that he was the creator of French civilization.

Rome, which had known Caesar only as a spendthrift, rake, politician, and reformer, was amazed to find him also a tireless administrator and a resourceful general. At the same time it discovered in him a major historian. In the midst of his campaigns, disturbed by the attacks upon him in Rome, he had recorded and defended his conquest of Gaul in *Commentaries* whose military conciseness and artful simplicity raised them, despite a thousand *milia passuum*, from a partisan pamphlet to a high place in Latin literature. Even Cicero, shifting again, sang a paean in his praise, and anticipated the verdict of history:

> It is not the ramparts of the Alps, nor the foaming and flooding Rhine, but the arms and generalship of Caesar which I account our true shield and barrier against the invasion of the Gauls and the barbarous tribes of Germany. It is to him we owe it that, should the mountains be leveled with the plain and the rivers be dried up, we should still hold our Italy fortified not by nature's bulwarks but by the exploits and victories of Caesar.[16]

To which should be added the tribute of a great German:

> That there is a bridge connecting the past glory of Hellas and Rome with the prouder fabric of modern history, that western Europe is Romanic, and Germanic Europe classic . . . all this is the work of Caesar; and while the creation of his great predecessor in the East has been almost wholly reduced to ruin by the tempests of the Middle Ages, the structure of Caesar has outlasted those thousands of years which have changed religions and states.[17]

V. THE DEGRADATION OF DEMOCRACY

During the second quinquennium of Caesar in Gaul, Roman politics had become an unparalleled chaos of corruption and violence. Pompey and Crassus, as consuls, pursued their policies by the bribery of votes, the intimidation of juries, and occasional murder.[18] When their year of office ended, Crassus recruited and conscripted a large army and sailed for Syria. He crossed the Euphrates and met the Parthians at Carrhae. Their superior cavalry defeated him, and his son fell in the battle. Crassus was withdrawing his forces in good order when the Parthian general invited him to a conference. He went and was treacherously slain. His head was sent to play the part of Pentheus in a performance of Euripides' *Bacchae* at the Parthian court; and his leaderless army, long wearied of the campaign, disappeared in a disorderly rout (53).

Meanwhile Pompey too had levied an army, presumably to complete the conquest of Spain. Had Caesar's plans matured, Pompey would have brought Farther Spain, and Crassus Armenia and Parthia, within the orbit of Roman power at the same time that Caesar was extending the frontier to the Thames and the Rhine. Instead of leading his legions to Spain, Pompey kept them in Italy, except for one which he lent to Caesar in the crisis of the Gallic revolt. In 54 the strongest tie that held him to Caesar was cut by the death of his wife Julia in childbirth. Caesar offered him his grandniece Octavia, now Caesar's nearest female relative, and asked for the hand of Pompey's daughter; but Pompey refused both proposals. The debacle of Crassus and his army in the following year removed another balancing force, for a vic-torious Crassus would have opposed the dictatorship of either Caesar or Pompey. Henceforth Pompey openly allied himself with the conservatives. His plan to secure supreme power through legal forms had now only one obstacle—the ambition and army of Caesar. Knowing that Caesar's command would expire in 49, Pompey secured decrees continuing his own command to the end of 46, and requiring all Italians capable of bearing arms to take an oath of military fealty to him personally; in this way, he trusted, time itself would make him master of Rome.[19]

While the potential dictators maneuvered for position, the capital filled with the odor of a dying democracy. Verdicts, offices, provinces, and client kings were sold to the highest bidders. In the year 53 the first voting division in the Assembly was paid 10,000,000 sesterces for its vote.[20] When money failed, murder was available;[21] or a man's past was raked over, and black-mail brought him to terms. Crime flourished in the city, brigandage in the country; no police force existed to control it. Rich men hired bands of gladiators to protect them, or to support them in the *comitia*. The lowest elements in Italy were attracted to Rome by the smell of money or the gift of corn, and made the meetings of the Assembly a desecration. Any man who would vote as paid was admitted to the rolls, whether citizen or not; sometimes only a minority of those who cast ballots were entitled to vote. The privilege of addressing the Assembly had on several occasions to be won by storming the rostrum and holding it by main force. Legislation came to be determined by the fluctuating superiority of rival gangs; those who voted the wrong way were, now and then, beaten to within an inch of their lives, after which their houses were set afire. Following one such meeting Cicero wrote: "The Tiber was full of the corpses of citizens, the public sewers were stuffed with them, and slaves had to mop up with sponges the blood that streamed from the Forum."[22]

Clodius and Milo were Rome's most distinguished experts in this brand of parliament. They organized rival bands of ruffians for political purposes, and hardly a day passed without some test of their strength. One day Clodius assaulted Cicero in the street; another day his warriors burned down Milo's house; at last Clodius himself was caught by Milo's gang and killed (52). The proletariat, not privy to all his plots, honored Clodius as a martyr, gave him a mighty funeral, carried the body to the senate house, and burned the building over him as his funeral pyre. Pompey brought in his soldiers and dispersed the mob. As reward he asked from the Senate, and received, appointment as "consul without colleague," a phrase that Cato recommended as more pleasant than "dictator." Pompey then put through the Assembly—cowed by his troops—several measures aimed at political corruption, and another repealing the right (which his bill of 55 had granted to Caesar) to stand for the consulate while absent from Rome. He impartially supervised, with military force, the operation of the courts; Milo was tried for the murder of Clodius, was condemned despite Cicero's defense,* and fled to Marseilles. Cicero went off to govern Cilicia (51), and acquitted himself there with a degree of competence and integrity which surprised and offended his friends. All the elements of wealth and order in the capital resigned themselves to the dictatorship of Pompey, while the poorer classes hopefully awaited the coming of Caesar.

VI. CIVIL WAR

A century of revolution had broken down a selfish and narrow aristocracy, but had put no other government in its place. Unemployment, bribery, bread and circuses had corrupted the Assembly into an ill-informed and passion-ridden mob obviously incapable of ruling itself, much less an empire. Democracy had fallen by Plato's formula: liberty had become license, and chaos begged an end to liberty.[24] Caesar agreed with Pompey that the Republic was dead; it was now, he said, "a mere name, without body or form";[25] dictatorship was unavoidable. But he had hoped to establish a leadership that would be progressive, that would not freeze the *status quo*, but would lessen the abuses, inequities, and destitution which had degraded democracy. He was now fifty-four, and surely weakened by his long campaigns in Gaul; he did not relish a war against his fellow citizens and

---

* The speech as it has come down to us was much revised. It differed so much from the actual address—which had been confused by hostile disturbances—that when Milo read it he exclaimed: "O Cicero! If you had only spoken as you have written I should not now be eating the very excellent fish of Marseilles." [23]

his former friends. But he saw the snares that had been prepared for him, and resented them as an ill-reward for one who had saved Italy. His term as governor of Gaul would end on March 1, 49; he could not run for the consulship until the fall of that year; in the interval he would lose the immunity of an officeholder, and could not enter Rome without subjecting himself to those proscriptions which were among the favorite weapons of party warfare in Rome. Already Marcus Marcellus had proposed to the Senate that Caesar should be deposed from his governorship before its expiration—which meant self-exile or trial. The tribunes of the plebs had saved him by their veto, but the Senate clearly favored the motion. Cato frankly expressed the hope that Caesar would be accused, tried, and banished from Italy.

Caesar made every effort at conciliation. When, at Pompey's suggestion, the Senate asked both generals to release to it a legion for use against Parthia, Caesar at once complied, though his force was small; and when Pompey asked Caesar for the return of the legion sent him a year before, Caesar dispatched it to him without delay. His friends informed him, however, that instead of being sent to Parthia these legions were being kept at Capua. Through his supporters in the Senate Caesar requested a renewal of the Assembly's earlier decree permitting him to stand for the consulship in absence. The Senate refused to submit the motion and demanded that Caesar dismiss his troops. Caesar felt that his legions were his only protection; perhaps he had nourished their personal loyalty with a view to just such a crisis as this. Nevertheless, he proposed to the Senate that both he and Pompey should lay down their commissions—an offer which seemed to the people of Rome so reasonable that they garlanded his messenger with flowers. The Senate favored the plan, 370 to 22, but Pompey balked at it. In the last days of the year 50 the Senate declared Caesar a public enemy unless he should abandon his command by July 1. On the first day of 49 Curio read to the Senate a letter in which Caesar agreed to disband all but two of his ten legions if he might retain the governorship till 48; but he spoiled the offer by adding that he would look upon its rejection as a declaration of war. Cicero spoke for the proposal, and Pompey agreed to it; but the consul Lentulus intervened and drove Caesar's lieutenants, Curio and Antony, from the senate house.[26] After a long debate the reluctant Senate, persuaded by Lentulus, Cato, and Marcellus, gave Pompey orders and powers to "see that no harm should come to the state"—the Roman phrase for dictatorship and martial law.

Caesar hesitated more than was his wont. Legally the Senate was right, he had no authority to name the conditions under which he would resign his command. He knew that civil war might bring Gaul to revolt and Italy to ruin. But to yield was to surrender the Empire to incompetence and reaction. Amid his deliberations he learned that one of his nearest friends and ablest lieutenants, Titus Labienus, had gone over to Pompey. He summoned the soldiers of his favorite Thirteenth Legion and laid the situation before them. His first word won them: *Commilitones!*—"fellow soldiers." They who had seen him share their hardships and perils, who had had to complain that he risked himself too readily, recognized his right to use this word; he had always addressed them so rather than with the curt *Milites!* of less gracious commanders. Most of his men came from Cisalpine Gaul, to which he had extended Roman citizenship; they knew that the Senate had refused to recognize this grant and that one senator had flogged a Cisalpine Gaul just to show his contempt for Caesar's enfranchisement; it was illegal to flog a Roman citizen. They had learned to respect Caesar—even, in their rough mute way, to love him—during their many campaigns. He had been severe with cowardice and indiscipline, but he had been lenient with their human faults, had winked at their sexual escapades, had spared them unnecessary dangers, had saved them by skillful generalship, had doubled their pay, and had spread his spoils among them handsomely. He told them of his proposals to the Senate and how these had been received; he reminded them that an idle and corrupt aristocracy was unfit to give Rome order, justice, and prosperity. Would they follow him? Not one refused. When he told them that he had no money with which to pay them they emptied their savings into his treasury.

On January 10, 49, he led one legion across the Rubicon, a small stream, near Ariminum, that marked the southern boundary of Cisalpine Gaul. *Iacta est alea*, he is reported to have said—"the die is cast." [27] It seemed an act of folly, for the remaining nine legions of his army were still distant in Gaul and could not reach him for weeks to come; while Pompey had ten legions, or 60,000 troops, authority to levy as many more as he pleased, and funds to arm and feed them. Caesar's Twelfth Legion joined him at Picenum, the Eighth at Corfinium; he formed three legions more from prisoners, volunteers, and levies upon the population. He had little difficulty in getting recruits; Italy had not forgotten the Social War (88), and saw in Caesar a champion of Italian rights; one by one its cities opened their gates to him, some turned out en masse to welcome him; [28] "the towns," wrote Cicero, "salute him as a god." [29] Corfinium resisted briefly, then surrendered; Caesar protected it from sack by his soldiers, freed all captured officers, and sent to Pompey's camp the money and baggage that Labienus had left behind. Though almost penniless, he refrained from confiscating those estates of his opponents that fell into his hands—a characteristically wise measure, which won to neutrality most of the middle class. It would be his policy, he announced, to consider all neutrals his friends. At every new advance he tried again for reconciliation. He sent a message to Lentulus begging him to use his consular influence for peace. In a letter to Cicero he offered to retire to private life and leave the field to Pompey, provided he should be allowed to live in security.[30] Cicero labored to effect a compromise, but found his logic helpless before the rival dogmatisms of revolution.[31]

Though his forces still far outnumbered Caesar's, Pompey withdrew with them from the capital, and a disorderly stream of aristocrats followed him, leaving their wives and children to Caesar's mercy. Rejecting every overture of peace, Pompey declared that he would consider as an enemy any senator who did not abandon Rome and join his camp. The majority of the Senate remained in Rome, and vacillating Cicero, despising Pompey's vacillations, divided himself among his rural estates. Pompey marched to Brundisium and ferried his troops across the Adriatic. He knew that his undisciplined army needed further training before it could stand up to Caesar's legions; meanwhile, he hoped, the Roman fleet under his control would starve Italy into destroying his rival.

Caesar entered Rome (March 16) unresisted and unarmed, having left his troops in near-by towns. He proclaimed a general amnesty and restored municipal administration and social order. The tribunes convoked the Senate; Caesar asked it to name him dictator, but it refused; he asked it to send envoys to Pompey to negotiate peace, but it refused. He sought funds from the national Treasury; the tribune Lucius Metellus barred his way, but yielded when Caesar remarked that it was harder for him to utter threats than to execute them. Henceforth he made free use of the state's money; but with unscrupulous impartiality he deposited in the Treasury the booty from his later campaigns. Then he returned to his soldiers, and prepared to meet the three armies that the Pompeians were organizing in Greece, Africa, and Spain.

To secure the grain supply upon which Italy's life depended, he sent the impetuous Curio with two legions to take Sicily. Cato surrendered the island and withdrew to Africa; Curio pursued him with the recklessness of Regulus, gave battle prematurely, was defeated, and died in action, mourning not his own death, but the injury he had done to Caesar. Meanwhile Caesar had led an army to Spain, partly to ensure the renewal of its grain exports to Italy, partly to forestall a rear attack when he marched to meet Pompey. In Spain, as in Gaul, he made serious blunders in strategy.[32] For a time his outnumbered army faced starvation and defeat; but, as usual, he redeemed himself by brilliant improvisation and personal bravery.[33] By altering the course of a river he turned blockade into counterblockade; he waited patiently for the entrapped army to surrender, though his troops fretted for action; at last the Pompeians gave in, and all Spain came over to Caesar (August, 49). Returning toward Italy by land, he found his way blocked at Marseilles by an army under Lucius Domitius, whom he had captured and released at Corfinium. Caesar took the town after a hard siege, reorganized the administration of Gaul, and by December was back in Rome.

His political position had been strengthened by this campaign, which had reassured the worried bellies of the capital. The Senate now named him dictator, but he surrendered that title after being elected one of the two consuls for 48. Finding Italy in a credit crisis due to the fact that the hoarding of currency had depressed prices, and debtors were refusing to pay in dear money what they had borrowed in cheap money, he decreed that debts might be paid in goods valued by state arbitrators at prewar prices; this, he thought, was "the most suitable way both of maintaining the honor of the debtors and of removing or diminishing the fear of that general repudiation of debts which is apt to follow war." [34] It is a revelation of how slowly reform had moved in Rome that he was compelled again to forbid enslavement for debt. He permitted the interest already paid on debts to be deducted from the principal, and limited interest to one per cent per month. These measures satisfied most creditors, who had feared confiscation; correspondingly they disappointed the radicals, who had hoped that Caesar would continue Catiline by abolishing all debts and redividing the land. He distributed corn to the needy, canceled all sentences of banishment except Milo's, and pardoned all returning aristocrats. No one thanked him for his moderation. The forgiven conservatives resumed their plotting against his life; and while he was facing Pompey in Thessaly the radicals abandoned him for Caelius, who promised them a complete abolition of debts, the confiscation of large properties, and the reallotment of all land.

Near the end of 49 Caesar joined the troops and fleet that his aides had collected at Brundisium. A winter crossing of the Adriatic by an army was in those days unheard of; the twelve vessels at his disposal could carry over only a third of his 60,000 men at one time; and Pompey's superior squadrons patrolled all islands and harbors along the opposite coast. Nevertheless, Caesar set sail and crossed to Epirus with 20,000 men. On their way back to Italy his ships were wrecked. Wondering what delayed the remainder of his army, Caesar tried to recross in a small skiff. The sailors rowed out against the surf and were nearly drowned. Caesar, dauntless amid their terror, encouraged them with the possibly legendary exhortation: "Fear not; you carry Caesar and his fortune." [35] But wind and wave tossed the boat back upon the shore, and Caesar had to abandon the attempt. Meanwhile Pompey, with 40,000 men, seized Dyrrhachium and its rich stores; then, with the indecision that marked his obese years, he failed to attack

Caesar's depleted and starving force. During this delay Mark Antony gathered another fleet and brought over the rest of Caesar's army.

Ready now to join battle, but still loath to turn Roman against Roman, Caesar sent an envoy to Pompey proposing that both leaders should lay down their commands. Pompey gave no reply.* Caesar attacked and was repulsed; but Pompey failed to follow his victory with pursuit. Against Pompey's advice his officers put all captives to death, while Caesar spared his [37]—a contrast that raised the morale of Caesar's troops and lowered that of Pompey's. Caesar's men begged him to punish them for the cowardice they had shown in this their first fight against Roman legions. When he refused, they besought him to lead them back to battle; but he thought it wiser to retreat into Thessaly and let them rest.

Pompey now made the decision that cost him his life. Afranius advised him to return and recapture undefended Italy; but the majority of his counselors urged him to pursue and destroy Caesar. The aristocrats in Pompey's camp exaggerated the victory at Dyrrhachium and supposed that the great issue had there been decided. Cicero, who had finally joined them, was shocked to hear them dispute as to their respective shares in the coming restoration, and to see with what luxury they lived in the midst of war—their meals served on silver plate, their tents comfortable with carpets, brilliant with hangings, garlanded with flowers.

> Excepting Pompey himself [Cicero wrote], the Pompeians carried on the war with such rapacity, and breathed such principles of cruelty in their conversation, that I could not contemplate even their success without horror. . . . There was nothing good among them but their cause. . . . A proscription was proposed not only individually but collectively. . . . Lentulus had promised himself Hortensius' house, Caesar's gardens, and Baiae.[38]

Pompey would have preferred a more Fabian strategy, but taunts of cowardice prevailed upon him, and he gave orders to march.

At Pharsalus, August 9, 48, the decisive battle was fought to the bitter end. Pompey had 48,000 infantry, 7000 horse; Caesar had 22,000 and 1000.[39] "Some few of the noblest Romans," says Plutarch, "standing as spectators outside the battle . . . could not but reflect to what a pass private ambition had brought the Empire. . . . The whole flower and strength of the same city, meeting here in collision with itself, offered plain proof how blind and mad a thing human nature is when passion is aroused." [40] Near relatives, even brothers, fought in the opposed armies. Caesar bade his men spare all Romans who should surrender; as to the young aristocrat Marcus Brutus,

---

* Our only authority for this embassy is Caesar.[36]

he said, they were to capture him without injuring him, or, if this proved impossible, they were to let him escape.[41] The Pompeians were overwhelmed by superior leadership, training, and morale; 15,000 of them were killed or wounded, 20,000 surrendered, the remainder fled. Pompey tore the insignia of command from his clothing and took flight like the rest. Caesar tells us that he lost but 200 men [42]—which casts doubt upon all his books. His army was amused to see the tents of the defeated so elegantly adorned, and their tables laden with the feast that was to celebrate their victory. Caesar ate Pompey's supper in Pompey's tent.

Pompey rode all night to Larissa, thence to the sea, and took ship to Alexandria. At Mytilene, where his wife joined him, the citizens wished him to stay; he refused courteously, and advised them to submit to the conqueror without fear, for, he said, "Caesar was a man of great goodness and clemency." [43] Brutus also escaped to Larissa, but there he dallied and wrote to Caesar. The victor expressed great joy on hearing that he was safe, readily forgave him, and at his request forgave Cassius. To the nations of the East, which—controlled by the upper classes—had supported Pompey, he was likewise lenient. He distributed Pompey's hoards of grain among the starving population of Greece, and to the Athenians asking pardon he replied with a smile of reproof: "How often will the glory of your ancestors save you from self-destruction?" [44]

Probably he had been warned that Pompey hoped to resume the contest with the army and resources of Egypt, and the forces that Cato, Labienus, and Metellus Scipio were organizing at Utica. But when Pompey reached Alexandria, Pothinus, eunuch vizier of young Ptolemy XII, ordered his servants to kill Pompey, presumably in expectation of reward from Caesar. The general was stabbed to death as he stepped upon the shore, while his wife looked on in helpless terror from the ship in which they had come. When Caesar arrived, Pothinus' men presented him with the severed head. Caesar turned away in horror and wept at this new proof that by diverse means men come to the same end. He established his quarters in the royal palace of the Ptolemies and set himself to regulate the affairs of the ancient kingdom.

VII. CAESAR AND CLEOPATRA

Since the death of Ptolemy VI (145) Egypt had rapidly decayed. Her kings were no longer able to maintain social order or national freedom; the Roman Senate increasingly dictated their policy, and garrisoned Alexandria with Roman troops. By the will of Ptolemy XI, whom Pompey and Gabinius had established on the throne, the government had descended to his son

Ptolemy XII and his daughter Cleopatra, who were to marry each other and reign together.

Cleopatra was a Macedonian Greek by origin, and more probably blonde than brunette.[45] She was not particularly beautiful; but the grace of her carriage, the vivacity of her body and her mind, the variety of her accomplishments, the suavity of her manners, the very melody of her voice, combined with her royal position to make her a heady wine even for a Roman general. She was acquainted with Greek history, literature, and philosophy; she spoke Greek, Egyptian, Syrian, and allegedly other languages, well; she added the intellectual fascination of an Aspasia to the seductive abandon of a completely uninhibited woman. Tradition credits her with a treatise on cosmetics and another on the alluring subject of Egyptian measures, weights, and coins.[46] She was an able ruler and administrator, effectively promoted Egyptian commerce and industry, and was a competent financier even when making love. With these qualities went an Oriental sensuality, an impetuous brutality that dealt out suffering and death, and a political ambition that dreamed of empire and honored no code but success. If she had not borne the intemperate blood of the later Ptolemies in her veins she might have achieved her purpose of being the queen of a unified Mediterranean realm. She saw that Egypt could no longer be independent of Rome and knew no reason why she should not dominate their union.

Caesar was not pleased to learn that Pothinus had banished Cleopatra and now ruled as regent for young Ptolemy. Secretly he sent for her, and secretly she came. To reach him she had herself concealed in some bedding which her attendant Apollodorus carried into Caesar's apartment. The amazed Roman, who never let his victories in the field outnumber his conquests in love, was captivated by her courage and wit. He reconciled her with Ptolemy, and re-established her with her brother on the throne of Egypt. Learning from his barber that Pothinus and the Egyptian general Achillas were plotting to kill him and slaughter the small force that he had brought with him, he delicately arranged the assassination of Pothinus. Achillas escaped to the Egyptian army and roused it to insurrection; soon all Alexandria was alive with soldiers vowing death to Caesar. The Roman garrison which had been stationed in the city by the Senate was inspired by its officers to join in rising against this treasonable interloper who presumed to settle the succession to the throne of the Ptolemies, and even to beget an heir for its future.

In this emergency Caesar acted with his customary resourcefulness. He turned the royal palace and the near-by theater into fortresses for himself and his men, and sent for reinforcements from Asia Minor, Syria, and Rhodes. When he saw that his defenseless fleet would soon fall into the hands of his enemies, he ordered it burned; in the fire an uncertain portion of the Alexandrian library was consumed. By desperate sallies he captured, lost, and recaptured the island of Pharos, as being essential to the entry of the relief he awaited; in one of these engagements he swam for his life, amid a storm of arrows, when the Egyptians drove him and 400 of his men off the connecting mole into the sea. Thinking the rebels victorious, Ptolemy XII left the royal palace, joined them, and disappeared from history. When reinforcements arrived, Caesar routed the Egyptians and the Senatorial garrison in the Battle of the Nile. He rewarded Cleopatra for her fidelity to him in this crisis by making her younger brother Ptolemy XIII coregent with her, which left her in effect the supreme ruler of Egypt.

It is hard to understand why Caesar remained nine months in Alexandria while hostile armies were being organized against him near Utica, and while Rome, stirred to radical revolt by Caelius and Milo, longed for his fine administrative hand. Perhaps he felt that he deserved a little rest and play after ten years of war. He "often feasted with Cleopatra till daybreak," says Suetonius, "and would have gone through Egypt with her in her royal barge almost to Ethiopia, had not his soldiers threatened mutiny"; [47] they had not all found queans. Perhaps he gallantly waited to share the pains of her confinement. A child was born to her in 47 and was named Caesarion; according to Mark Antony, Caesar acknowledged the boy as his son.[48] It is not impossible that she whispered to him the pleasant thought of making himself king, marrying her, and uniting the Mediterranean world under one bed.

This, however, is conjectural as well as scandalous; nothing but circumstantial evidence supports it. Certainly Caesar flew to action when he learned that Pharnaces, son of Mithridates, had recaptured Pontus, Lesser Armenia, and Cappadocia, and was inviting the East to rise once more against divided Rome. His wisdom in "pacifying" Spain and Gaul before meeting Pompey was now apparent; had the West revolted at one time with the East the Empire would probably have broken up, the "barbarians" would have moved southward, and Rome might never have known an Augustan age. Re-forming his three legions, Caesar set out in June of 47, marched with characteristic speed along the coast of Egypt through Syria and Asia Minor into Pontus, defeated Pharnaces at Zela (August 2), and sent to a friend at Rome the laconic report, *Veni, vidi, vici*—"I came, I saw, I conquered." [49]

At Tarentum (September 26) he was met by Cicero, who asked forgiveness for himself and other conservatives. Caesar consented amiably. He was shocked to find that during his twenty months' absence from Rome the Civil War had become a social revolution: that Cicero's son-in-law Dolabella had joined forces with Caelius, and had proposed to the Assembly a bill canceling all debts; that Antony had let loose his soldiers upon Dolabella's armed prolétaires, and 800 Romans had been killed in the Forum. Caelius, as praetor, had recalled Milo; together they had organized an army in southern Italy and had invited the slaves to unite with them in a thorough-going revolution. They had met with small success, but their spirit was in the air. At Rome the radicals were celebrating the memory of Catiline and again garlanding his tomb. Meanwhile the Pompeian army in Africa had grown as large as the one that had been beaten at Pharsalus. Pompey's son Sextus had organized a new army in Spain, and the grain supply of Italy was once more hanging in the balance. Such was the situation in October, 47, when Caesar reached Rome and Calpurnia, bringing with him Cleopatra, her boy husband-brother, and Caesarion.

In the few months permitted him between campaigns he set about restoring order. Having been reappointed dictator, he appeased the radicals for a moment by repealing the last of Sulla's laws and canceling for a year all rents below 2000 sesterces in Rome; at the same time he tried to comfort the conservatives by making Marcus Brutus governor of Cisalpine Gaul, assuring Cicero and Atticus that he would abet no war against property, and ordering the re-erection of the statues of Sulla, which the prolétaires had knocked down. When he turned his thoughts to the Pompeians he was discouraged to hear that his most trusted legions were in revolt because of long-overdue pay and were refusing to embark for Africa. As the Treasury was nearly empty, he raised funds by confiscating and selling the property of rebel aristocrats; he had learned, he said, that soldiers depend upon money, money upon power, and power upon soldiers.[50] He suddenly appeared among the rebellious legions, called them together, and quietly told them that they were released from service and might go to their homes; he added that he would make up all arrears to them when he had triumphed in Africa "with other soldiers." "At this expression," says Appian, "shame seized upon them all, that they were abandoning their commander in this moment when enemies surrounded him on every side. . . . They cried out that they repented of their revolt, and besought him to keep them in his service." [51] He yielded with charming reluctance, and sailed with them for Africa.

At Thapsus, on April 6, 46, he met the combined forces of Metellus Scipio, Cato, Labienus, and Juba I, the Numidian king. Again he lost the first encounter; again he re-formed his lines, attacked, and won. His blood-crazed soldiers, blaming his clemency at Pharsalus for having to fight this second battle, slaughtered 10,000 of the 80,000 Pompeians, giving no quarter; they did not propose to meet these men again. Juba committed suicide; Scipio fled and died in an engagement at sea; Cato with a small division escaped to Utica. When the officers wished to defend the city against

Caesar, Cato persuaded them that it was impossible. He provided funds for those who planned flight, but advised his son to submit to Caesar. He himself rejected both courses. He spent the evening in philosophical discussion; then he retired to his room and read Plato's *Phaedo*. Suspecting that he would kill himself, his friends took his sword from his bedside. When they had relaxed their vigil he compelled his servant to bring back the weapon. For a while he feigned sleep; then suddenly he took the sword and plunged it into his abdomen. His friends rushed in; a physician put back the extruding intestines and sewed and bandaged the wound. As soon as they had left the room Cato removed the bandage, tore open the wound, pulled out his entrails, and died.

When Caesar came he mourned that he had no chance to pardon Cato; he could only pardon the son. The Uticans gave the dead Stoic a magnificent funeral, as if knowing that they were burying a republic almost five centuries old.

VIII. THE STATESMAN

After appointing Sallust governor of Numidia, and reorganizing the provinces of Africa, Caesar in the fall of 46 returned to Rome. The frightened Senate, recognizing the advent of monarchy, voted him the dictatorship for ten years, and such a triumph as Rome had never seen before. He paid each of his soldiers 5000 Attic drachmas ($3000), much more than he had promised them. He feasted the citizens at 22,000 tables, and for their amusement provided a sham sea battle involving 10,000 men. Early in 45 he left for Spain, and at Munda defeated the last Pompeian army. When, in October, he reached Rome, he found all Italy in chaos. Oligarchic misrule and a century of revolution had disordered agriculture, industry, finance, and trade. The exhaustion of the provinces, the hoarding of capital, and the precariousness of investment had disturbed the flow of money. Thousands of estates had fallen into ruin; 100,000 men had been drawn from production into war; peasants beyond number had been driven by the competition of foreign grain or *latifundia* slaves to join the proletariat in the towns and listen hungrily to promising demagogues. The surviving aristocracy, unmelted by Caesar's clemency, plotted against him in their clubs and palaces. He appealed to them in the Senate to recognize the necessity of dictatorship, and to co-operate with him in a healing reconstruction. They scorned the advances of the usurper, denounced the presence of Cleopatra as his guest in Rome, and whispered that he was planning to make himself king and move the seat of the Empire to Alexandria or Ilium.

Caesar alone, therefore, though prematurely old at fifty-five, set himself with Roman energy to remake the Roman state. He knew that his victories would be meaningless if he could not build something better than the wreckage that he had cleared away. When, in 44, his dictatorship for ten years was extended for life, he did not much exaggerate the difference, though he could hardly foresee that in five months he would be dead. The Senate heaped adulation and titles upon him, perhaps to make him odious to a people that hated the very name of king. It let him wear the laurel wreath, with which he hid his baldness, and carry even in peace the *imperator*'s powers. Through these he controlled the Treasury, and as *pontifex maximus*, the priesthoods; as consul he could propose and execute laws; as tribune his person was inviolable; as censor he could make or unmake senators. The assemblies kept the right to vote on proposed measures, but Caesar's lieutenants, Dolabella and Antony, managed the assemblies, which in general favored his policies. Like other dictators he sought to base his power upon popularity with the people.

He subordinated the Senate almost to the role of an advisory council. He enlarged it from 600 to 900 members and permanently transformed it with 400 new appointees. Many of these were Roman businessmen; many were leading citizens of Italian or provincial cities; some had been centurions, soldiers, or sons of slaves. The patricians were alarmed to see the chieftains of conquered Gaul enter the Senate and join the rulers of the Empire; even the wags of the capital resented this and circulated a satiric couplet:

Gallos Caesar in triumphum ducit, idem in curiam;
Galli braccas deposuerunt, latum clavum sumpserunt—

"Caesar leads Gauls in his triumph, then into the Senate; the Gauls have removed their breeches, and put on the broad-rimmed toga" of the senators.[52]

Perhaps Caesar purposely made the new Senate too cumbersome a body for effective deliberation or unified opposition. He chose a group of friends—Balbus, Oppius, Matius, and others—as an informal executive cabinet, and inaugurated the bureaucracy of the Empire by delegating the clerical details of his government, and the minutiae of administration, to his household of freedmen and slaves. He allowed the Assembly to elect half the city magistrates; he chose the rest by "recommendations" which the Assembly regularly approved. As tribune he could veto the decisions of other tribunes or consuls. He increased the praetors to sixteen, and the quaestors to forty, to expedite municipal and judicial business. He kept a personal eye on every aspect of the city's affairs, and tolerated no incompetence or waste. In the city charters that he granted he placed severe injunctions and penalties against electoral corruption and official malfeasance. To end the domination of politics by organized vote buying, and perhaps to secure his power against proletarian revolt, he abolished the *collegia*, except some of ancient origin and the essentially religious associations of the Jews. He restricted jury service to the two upper classes and reserved for himself the right to try the most vital cases; frequently he sat as judge, and none could deny the wisdom and impartiality of his decisions. He proposed to the jurists of his time an orderly codification of existing Roman law, but his early death frustrated the plan.

Resuming the work of the Gracchi, he distributed lands to his veterans and the poor; this policy, continued by Augustus, for many years pacified the agrarian agitation. To forestall the rapid reconcentration of landowner-ship he ruled that the new lands could not be sold within twenty years; and to check rural slavery he passed a measure requiring that a third of the laborers on ranches should be freemen. Having turned many idle prolétaires into soldiers and then into peasant proprietors, he further diminished their ranks by sending 80,000 citizens as colonists to Carthage, Corinth, Seville, Arles, and other centers. To provide work for the remaining unemployed in Rome he spent 160,000,000 sesterces in a great building program. He had a new and more spacious meeting place for the assemblies set up in the Field of Mars, and relieved the congestion of business in the Forum by adding, near it, a Forum Iulium. He embellished likewise many cities in Italy, Spain, Gaul, and Greece. Having so eased the pressure of poverty, he required a means test for eligibility to the state dole of grain. At once the number of applicants fell from 320,000 to 150,000.

So far he had remained true to his role as a champion of the *populares*. But since the Roman revolution was more agrarian than industrial, and was aimed chiefly at the landed slave-driving aristocracy, then at the money-lenders, and only mildly at the business classes, Caesar continued the Gracchan policy of inviting businessmen to support the agrarian and fiscal revolution. Cicero sought to unite the middle classes with the aristocracy; Caesar sought to unite them with the plebs. Many of the great capitalists, from Crassus to Balbus, helped to finance him, as similar men helped the American and French Revolutions. Nevertheless, Caesar ended one of the richest sources of financial profiteering—the collection of provincial taxes through corporations of publicans. He scaled down debts, enacted severe laws against excessive interest rates, and relieved extreme cases of insolvency by establishing the law of bankruptcy essentially as it stands today. He restored the stability of the currency by basing it upon gold and issuing a golden *aureus*, equivalent in purchasing power to the British pound sterling in the nineteenth century. The coins of his government were stamped with his own features and were designed with an artistry new to Rome. A novel order and competence entered the administration of the Empire's finances, with the result that when Caesar died the Treasury contained 700,000,000 sesterces, and his private treasury 100,000,000.

As a scientific basis for taxation and administration, he had a census taken of Italy, and planned a like census of the Empire. To replenish a citizenry decimated by war, he granted the Roman franchise widely—among others, to physicians and teachers in Rome. Long disturbed by the fall in the birth rate, he had in 59 given precedence in land allotments to fathers of three children; now he promulgated rewards for large families and forbade childless women under forty-five to ride in litters or wear jewelry—the weakest and most futile part of his varied legislation.

Still an agnostic, though not quite free from superstitions,[53] Caesar remained high priest of the state religion and provided it with the usual funds. He restored old temples and built new ones, honoring above all his *alma mater* Venus. But he allowed full liberty of conscience and worship, withdrew old prohibitions against the Isis cult, and protected the Jews in the exercise of their faith. Noting that the calendar of the priests had lost all concord with the seasons, he commissioned the Alexandrian Greek Sosigenes to devise, on Egyptian models, the "Julian calendar": henceforth the year was to consist of 365 days, with an added day in every fourth February. Cicero complained that Caesar, not content with ruling the earth, was now regulating the stars; but the Senate accepted the reform graciously, and gave the dictator's family name, Julius, to the month Quinctilis—which had been fifth when March opened the year.

As impressive as these things done are the works begun or planned by Caesar but postponed by his assassination. He laid the foundations of a great theater, and of a temple to Mars proportioned to that god's voracity. He appointed Varro to head an organization for the establishment of public libraries. He designed to free Rome from malaria by draining Lake Fucinus and the Pontine marshes, and reclaiming these acres for tillage. He proposed to raise dykes to control the Tiber's floods; by diverting the course of that stream he hoped to improve the harbor at Ostia, periodically ruined by the river's silt. He instructed his engineers to prepare plans for building a road across central Italy and for cutting a canal at Corinth.

The most resented of his undertakings was to make the freemen of Italy equal citizens with those of Rome, and the provinces ultimately equal with Italy. In 49 he had enfranchised Cisalpine Gaul; now (44) he drew up a municipal charter, apparently for all the cities of Italy, equalizing their rights with Rome's; probably he was planning some representative government by which they would have had a democratic share in his constitutional monarchy.[55] He took the appointment of provincial governors out of the hands of the corrupt Senate and himself named to these posts men of proved ability, who remained at every moment subject to recall at his will. He reduced provincial taxes by a third, and entrusted their collection to special officials responsible to himself. He overrode ancient curses to restore Capua, Carthage, and Corinth—completing again the work of the Gracchi. To the colonists whom he sent to found or people a score of cities from Gibraltar to the Black Sea, he gave Roman or Latin rights, and evidently hoped to extend Roman citizenship to all free adult males in the Empire; the Senate was then to represent not a class in Rome, but the mind and will of every province. This conception of government, and Caesar's reorganization of Rome and Italy, completed the miracle whereby the youthful spendthrift and roisterer had become one of the ablest, bravest, fairest, and most enlightened men in all the sorry annals of politics.

Like Alexander he did not know where to stop. Contemplating his reordered realm, he resented its exposure to attack at the Euphrates, the Danube, and the Rhine. He dreamed of a great expedition to capture Parthia and avenge his old pocketbook Crassus; of a march around the Black Sea and the pacification of Scythia; of the exploration of the Danube and the conquest of Germany.[56] Then, having made the Empire secure, he would return to Rome laden with honor and spoils, rich enough to end economic depression, powerful enough to ignore all opposition, free at last to name his successor, and to die with the *pax Romana* as his supreme legacy to the world.

IX. BRUTUS

When news of this plan trickled through Rome the common people, who love glory, applauded; the business classes, smelling war orders and provincial loot, licked their chops; the aristocracy, foreseeing its extinction on Caesar's return, resolved to kill him before he could go.

He had treated these bluebloods with such generosity as to stir Cicero's eloquence in his praise. He had forgiven all surrendering foes and had condemned to death only a few officers who, defeated and pardoned, had fought against him again. He had burned unread the correspondence he had found in the tents of Pompey and Scipio. He had sent the captured daughter and grandchildren of Pompey to Pompey's son Sextus, who was still in arms against him; and he had restored the statues of Pompey which his followers had thrown down. He had given provincial governorships to Brutus and Cassius, and high office to many others of their class. He bore silently a thousand slanders, and instituted no proceedings against those whom he suspected of plotting against his life. To Cicero, who had trimmed his wind to every sale, he offered not only pardon but honor, and refused nothing that the orator asked for himself or his Pompeian friends; he even forgave, at Cicero's urging, the unrepentant Marcus Marcellus. In a pretty speech *For Marcellus* (46) Cicero acclaimed Caesar's "unbelievable liberality," and admitted that Pompey, victorious, would have been more vengeful. "I have heard with regret," he said, "your celebrated and highly philosophical remark, *Iam satis vixi*, 'I have lived enough, whether for nature or for fame.' . . . Put aside, I beg you, that wisdom of the sage; do not be wise at the cost of our peril. . . . You are still far from the completion of your greatest labors; you have not yet laid their foundations." And he solemnly promised Caesar, in the name of all the Senate, that they would watch over his safety and oppose with their own bodies any attack upon him.[57] Cicero now prospered so well that he planned to buy still another palace—no less than that of Sulla himself. He enjoyed the dinners to which he was invited by Antony, Balbus, and others of Caesar's aides; never before had his letters been so gay.[58] Caesar was not deceived; he wrote to Matius: "If anyone is gracious, it is Cicero; but I doubt not that he hates me bitterly." [59] When reassured Pompeians resumed their opposition, this unctuous Talleyrand of the pen fell in with their hopes and wrote a eulogy of the younger Cato that should have put Caesar on his guard. Caesar contented himself with writing a reply, the *Anti-Cato*, which did not show the dictator at his best; in this duel he had given Cicero the choice of weapons, and the orator had won. Public opinion praised Cicero's style, and the mildness of a ruler who composed a pamphlet when he might have signed a death warrant.

Men who have been deprived of wonted power cannot be mollified by pardoning their resistance; it is as difficult to forgive forgiveness as it is to forgive those whom we have injured. The aristocrats fretted in a Senate that dared not reject the proposals that Caesar so constitutionally submitted to them. They patriotically denounced the destruction of a liberty that had fattened their purses, and would not admit that the restoration of order required the limitation of their freedom. They looked with horror upon the presence of Cleopatra and Caesarion in Rome; it was true that Caesar was living with his wife Calpurnia apparently in mutual affection; but who could say—who would not say—what happened on his frequent visits to the gorgeous queen? Rumors persisted that he would make himself king, marry her, and place the capital of their united empires in the East. Had he not ordered his statue to be erected on the Capitol next to those of Rome's ancient kings? Had he not stamped his own image upon Roman coins—an unprecedented insolence? Did he not wear robes of purple, usually reserved for kings? At the Lupercalia, on February 15, 44, the consul Antony, sacerdotally naked * and impiously drunk, tried thrice to place a royal crown upon Caesar's head. Thrice Caesar refused; but was it not because the crowd murmured disapproval? Did he not dismiss from office the tribunes who removed from his statue the royal diadem placed upon it by his friends? When the Senate approached him as he sat in the Temple of Venus, he did not rise to receive them. Some explained that he had been overcome by an epileptic stroke; others, that he was suffering from diarrhea and had remained seated to avoid a movement of his bowels at so unpropitious a moment.[60] But many patricians feared that any day might see him proclaimed a king.

Shortly after the Lupercalia, Gaius Cassius, a sickly man—"pale and lean," as Plutarch describes him [61]—approached Marcus Brutus and suggested the assassination of Caesar. He had already won to his plan several senators, some capitalists whose provincial pillage had fallen with Caesar's restriction of the publicans, even some of Caesar's generals, who felt that the spoils and offices awarded them had not quite equaled their deserts. Brutus was needed as the front of the conspiracy, for he had won a wide reputation as the most virtuous of men. He was supposedly descended from the Brutus who had expelled the kings 464 years before. His mother Servilia was Cato's half sister; his wife Portia was Cato's daughter and the widow of Caesar's enemy Bibulus. "It was thought," says Appian, "that Brutus was Caesar's son, as Caesar was the lover of Servilia about the time of Brutus' birth"; [62] Plutarch adds that Caesar believed Brutus to be his son.[63] Possibly Brutus himself shared this opinion, and hated the dictator for having seduced his mother and made him, in the gossip of Rome, a bastard instead of a Brutus. He had always been moody and taciturn, as if brooding over a secret wrong; at the same time he carried himself proudly, as one who in any case bore noble blood in his veins. He was a master of Greek and a devotee of philosophy; in metaphysics a follower of Plato, in ethics, of Zeno. It was not lost upon him that Stoicism, like Greek and Roman opinion, approved tyrannicide. "Our ancestors," he wrote to a friend, "thought that we ought not to endure a tyrant even if he were our own father." [64] He composed a treatise on Virtue and was later confused with that abstraction. Through intermediaries he lent money at forty-eight per cent to the citizens of Cyprian Salamis; when they balked at paying the accumulated interest he urged Cicero, then proconsul in Cilicia, to enforce the collection with Roman arms.[65] He governed Cisalpine Gaul with integrity and competence and, returning to Rome, was made urban praetor by Caesar (45).

Every generous element in his nature rebelled against Cassius' proposal.

* Cf. p. 65.

Cassius reminded him of his rebel ancestry, and perhaps Brutus felt challenged to prove it by imitation. The sensitive youth blushed when he saw, affixed to statues of the older Brutus, such inscriptions as "Brutus, are you dead?"—or, "Your posterity is unworthy of you." [66] Cicero dedicated to him several treatises written in these years. Meanwhile it was whispered among the patricians that at the next meeting of the Senate, on March 15, Lucius Cotta would move that Caesar be made king, on the ground that according to the Sibylline oracle the Parthians would be conquered only by a king. [67] A Senate half filled with Caesar's appointees, said Cassius, would pass the measure, and all hope of restoring the Republic would be lost. Brutus yielded, and the conspirators then made definite plans. Portia drew the secret from her husband by stabbing her thigh to show that no physical injury could make her speak against her will. In a moment of unprophetic sentiment Brutus insisted that Antony should be spared.

On the evening of March 14, to a gathering at his home, Caesar proposed as topic of conversation, "What is the best death?" His own answer was, "A sudden one." The next morning his wife begged him not to go to the Senate, saying that she had dreamed of seeing him covered with blood. A like-minded servant sought to provide a deterrent omen by causing an ancestral picture to fall from the wall. But Decimus Brutus, who was one of his closest friends and was also one of the conspirators—urged him to attend the Senate if only to adjourn it courteously in person. A friend who had learned of the plot came to warn him, but Caesar had already left. On his way to the Senate he met a soothsayer who had once whispered to him, "Beware the ides of March"; Caesar remarked, smiling, that the ides had come and all was well. "But they have not passed," answered Spurinna. While Caesar was offering the usual presession sacrifice before Pompey's theater, where the Senate was to meet, a tablet informing him of the conspiracy was put into his hands. He ignored it, and tradition says that it was found in his hand after his death.*

Trebonius, a conspirator who had been a favored general of Caesar, detained Antony from the meeting by conversation. When Caesar entered the theater and took his seat, the "Liberators" flung themselves upon him without delay. "Some have written," reports Suetonius, "that when Marcus Brutus rushed at him he said, in Greek, *kai su teknon*—'You, too, my child?'" [69] When Brutus struck him, says Appian, Caesar ended all resistance; drawing his robe over his face and head, he submitted to the blows and fell at the foot of Pompey's statue. [70] One wish had been granted to the most complete man that antiquity produced.

---

* These stories of the ides of March appear in Suetonius, Plutarch, and Appian; [68] but they may be legend nevertheless.

CHAPTER X

Antony

44-30 B.C.

I. ANTONY AND BRUTUS

THE assassination of Caesar was one of the major tragedies of history. Not merely in the sense that it interrupted a great labor of statesmanship and led to fifteen years more of chaos and war; civilization survived, and Augustus completed what Caesar had begun. It was a tragedy also in the sense that probably both parties were right: the conspirators in thinking that Caesar meditated monarchy, Caesar in thinking that disorder and empire had made monarchy inevitable. Men have divided on the issue ever since the Senate sat for a moment in consternation at the deed and then fled in tumult and terror from the hall. Antony, arriving after the event, saw valor in discretion and fortified himself in his house. Cicero's eloquence lost its tongue, even when Brutus, dagger in hand, hailed him as "Father of His Country." Emerging, the conspirators found an excited populace in the square; they tried to win it with catchwords of Liberty and the Republic, but the dazed crowd had no homage for phrases so long used to cover greed. Fearing for their lives, the assassins took refuge in the buildings on the Capitol and surrounded themselves there with their personal gladiatorial guards. Toward evening Cicero joined them. Antony, approached by their emissaries, sent a friendly reply.

The next day a larger crowd gathered in the Forum. The conspirators sent agents to buy its support and organize it into a legal assembly; then they ventured down from the Capitol, and Brutus delivered an oration which he had prepared for the Senate. The speech failed to move its hearers. Cassius tried and was met with cold silence. The Liberators returned to the Capitol, and as the crowd thinned out they stealthily departed to their homes. Antony, thinking himself Caesar's heir, obtained from the stunned Calpurnia all the papers and funds that the dictator had left in his palace; at the same time he secretly summoned Caesar's veterans to Rome. On the 17th, by his authority as tribune, he convened the Senate and astonished all parties by his amiability and calm. He accepted Cicero's proposal for a general amnesty, and agreed that Brutus and Cassius should receive provincial governorships (i.e., flight with safety and power), on condition that the Senate should ratify all the decrees, legislation, and appointments of Caesar. Since a majority of the Senate owed office or emoluments to these acts, it consented; and when it adjourned Antony was acclaimed as a statesman who had snatched peace out of the jaws of war. That evening he entertained Cassius for dinner. On the 18th the Senate met again, recognized Caesar's will, voted him a public funeral, and appointed Antony to deliver the customary eulogy.

On the 19th Antony secured the will from the Vestal Virgins, with whom it had been deposited, and read it, first to a small, then to a larger gathering. It bequeathed Caesar's private fortune to three grandnephews and (to the astonishment and anger of Antony) named one of them, Caius Octavius, as adoptive son and heir. The dictator had devised his gardens to the people as a public park and had left 300 sesterces to every citizen of Rome. The news of these benefactions sped through the city; and when, on the 20th, Caesar's body, which had been embalmed in his home, was brought into the Forum for the last rites, a great concourse of people, including Caesar's veterans, gathered to do him reverence. Antony seems to have spoken at first with cautious restraint; but as he went on, his pent-up feelings flared into eloquence. When he raised from the ivory bier the torn and bloody robe through which Caesar had been stabbed, the emotions of the crowd were stirred beyond control. Amid weird wailing and frenzied cries men gathered wood anywhere and built a fire beneath the corpse. Veterans threw their weapons upon the pyre as an offering, actors threw their costumes, musicians their instruments, women their most precious ornaments. Taking brands from the fire, some enthusiasts sought to burn down the houses of the conspirators; but these buildings were well guarded, and their masters had fled from Rome. A large part of the crowd stayed all night long by the smoldering pyre; many Jews, grateful for Caesar's sympathetic legislation, remained there three days, intoning their ancient funeral chants. During those days riot surged through the capital; at last Antony directed his soldiers to restore order and to fling persistent marauders from the Tarpeian rock.

Antony was one half of what Caesar had been, as Augustus would be the other half; Antony was a good general, Augustus a superlative statesman; neither would be both. Born in 82 B.C., Antony had spent a large part of his life in camps and more in the quest of wine, women, good food, and fun. Though of high lineage and handsome features, he had the characteristic virtues of the common man: strength of body, animal spirits, good nature, generosity, courage, and loyalty. He had scandalized even Caesar by keeping a harem of both sexes in Rome, and traveling with a Greek courtesan in his litter.[1] He had bought in Pompey's house at auction, occupied it, and then refused payment.[2] Now he found in Caesar's papers, or (some said) placed there, whatever it suited him to find—appointments for his friends, decrees for his purposes, perquisites for himself; in two weeks' time he had paid off $1,500,000 in debts and had become a rich man. He seized the $25,000,000 that Caesar had deposited in the Temple of Ops and took another $5,000,000 from Caesar's private treasury. Noting that Decimus Brutus, whom Caesar had appointed governor of Cisalpine Gaul, had assumed that lucrative office despite sharing in the assassination of Caesar, Antony passed through the Assembly a bill giving himself that strategic province and consoling Decimus with Macedonia. Likewise Marcus Brutus and Cassius were to surrender Macedonia to Decimus and Syria to Dolabella, and were to content themselves with sharing Cyrene and Crete.

Alarmed by Antony's spreading power, the Senate invited to Rome, as a foil to him, Caesar's adopted son. Caius Octavius, who was to make himself the greatest statesman in Roman history, was eighteen years old in 44. By natural custom he took his adoptive father's name; adding his own as a modifier, he became Caius Julius Caesar Octavianus, until, seventeen years later, he received that lofty name of Augustus by which the centuries have known him. His grandmother was Caesar's sister Julia; his grandfather had been a banker of plebeian stock at Velitrae, in Latium; his father had served as plebeian aedile, then praetor, then governor of Macedonia. The boy was trained to Spartan simplicity, and educated in the literature and philosophy of Greece and Rome. In the last three years he had lived a good part of the time in Caesar's palace. It was one of the sorrows of Caesar's life that he had no legitimate son and one of his profoundest insights that he adopted Octavius. He took the boy with him to Spain in 45 and was pleased to see the courage with which the frail and nervous invalid endured the perils and hardships of the campaign. He had him carefully instructed in the arts of war and government.[3] Many statues have made his features familiar: refined, delicate, serious, at once diffident and resolute, yielding and tenacious; an idealist forced to be a realist, a man of thought painfully learning to be a man of action. He was thin and pale and suffered from a poor digestion. He ate little, drank less, and outlived the strong men around him by abstinence and the regularity of his life.

Late in March of 44 a freedman arrived at Apollonia, in Illyria, where Octavian was stationed with the army, and brought the news of Caesar's death and will. The sensitive youth was horrified at men's ingratitude; all his love for the great-uncle who had so cherished him, and had worked so feverishly to rebuild a shattered state, welled up in him and filled him with a silent resolve to complete the labors of Caesar and avenge his death. He rode down to the sea, crossed to Brundisium, and hastened to Rome. His relatives there advised him to stay in hiding lest Antony destroy him; his mother likewise recommended inaction; but when he scorned such a course she rejoiced, merely suggesting that whenever possible he should use patience and subtlety rather than open war. He followed this wise counsel to the end.

He visited Antony and inquired what was being done against Caesar's enemies. He was shocked to find Antony busy planning to lead an army against Decimus Brutus, who had refused to surrender Cisalpine Gaul. He asked Antony to disburse Caesar's legacies according to will, especially the forty-five dollars bequeathed to every citizen. Antony saw many reasons for delay. Octavian thereupon distributed the money to Caesar's veterans out of funds borrowed by him from Caesar's friends, and with this approach, organized his own army.

Infuriated by the insolence of this "boy," as he called him, Antony announced that an attempt had been made upon his life and that the would-be assassin had named Octavian as the instigator of his plan. Octavian protested his innocence. Cicero took advantage of the quarrel to persuade him that Antony was a ruffian, who must be defeated. Octavian agreed, joined his two legions with those of the consuls Hirtius and Pansa, and marched with them northward to battle Antony. Cicero lent this new civil war the aid of his invective in fourteen powerful "Philippics" against the public policy and private life of Antony, some delivered to the Senate or the Assembly, the rest published as propaganda broadcasts in the best tradition of martial blackening. In the ensuing engagement at Mutina (Modena), Antony lost and fled (44); but Hirtius and Pansa fell, and Octavian returned to Rome sole commander of the Senate's legions as well as his own. With this force behind him he compelled the Senate to name him consul, to repeal its amnesty to the conspirators, and to sentence them all to death. Discovering that Cicero and the Senate were now his enemies, and were merely using him as a temporary tool against Antony, he composed his differences with Antony and formed with him and Lepidus the Second Triumvirate (43-33). Their combined armies marched into Rome and took it without resistance. Many of the senators and conservatives fled to south Italy and the provinces. The Assembly ratified the Triumvirate and gave it full power for five years.

To pay their troops, replenish their coffers, and revenge Caesar, the three men now let loose the bloodiest reign of terror in Roman history. They listed 300 senators and 2000 businessmen for execution, and offered 25,000 drachmas ($15,000) to any freeman, and 10,000 to any slave, who would bring in the head of a person proscribed.[4] To have money became a capital crime; children to whom fortunes had been left were condemned and killed;

widows were shorn of their legacies; 1400 rich women were required to turn over a large share of their property to the Triumvirs; at last even the savings deposited with the Vestal Virgins were seized. Atticus was spared because he had helped Antony's wife Fulvia; while acknowledging the courtesy, he sent great sums to Brutus and Cassius. The Triumvirs set their soldiers to guard all exits from the city. The proscribed hid in wells, sewers, attics, chimneys. Some died resisting, some submitted quietly to their slayers; some starved, hanged, or drowned themselves; some leaped from a roof or into a fire; some were killed by mistake; some, not proscribed, committed suicide on the bodies of slain relatives. Salvius the tribune, knowing himself doomed, gave a last feast to his friends; the emissaries of the Triumvirs entered, cut off his head, left his body at the table, and bade the feast go on. Slaves took the opportunity to get rid of hard masters, but many fought to the death to protect their owners; one disguised himself as his master and suffered decapitation in his stead. Sons died to protect their fathers, others betrayed their fathers to inherit a part of their fortunes. Adulterers or deceived wives surrendered their husbands. The wife of Coponius secured his safety by sleeping with Antony. Antony's wife Fulvia had tried to buy the mansion of her neighbor Rufus; he had refused to sell; now, though he offered it to her as a gift, she had him proscribed and nailed his severed head to his front door.[5]

Antony placed Cicero high on the list of those who should be killed. Antony was the husband of Clodius' widow and the stepson of the Catalinarian Lentulus whom Cicero had slain in jail; and he resented with some reason the unstinted vituperation of the "Philippics." Octavian protested, but not too long; he could not forget Cicero's glorification of Caesar's assassins and the pun by which that reckless wit had excused to the conservatives his dalliance with Caesar's heir.* Cicero tried to escape; but being buffeted and sickened by the sea, he disembarked and spent the night in his villa at Formiae. The next day he wished to stay there and await his executioners, preferring them to a choppy sea; but his slaves forced him into a litter and were carrying him toward the ship when Antony's soldiers came upon them. The servants wished to resist, but Cicero bade them set the litter down and yield. Then, "his person covered with dust, his beard and hair untrimmed, and his face worn with his troubles,"[7] he stretched his head out so that the soldiers might more conveniently decapitate him (43). By Antony's command Cicero's right hand was also cut off and brought with the head to the Triumvir. Antony laughed in triumph, gave the assassins 250,000 drachmas, and had head and hand hung up in the Forum.[8]

---

* Cicero had said of Octavian: *laudandum adolescentem, ornandum, tollendum*—"the boy is to be praised, decorated, and exalted"; but *tollendum* also meant "to be killed." [6]

Early in 42 the Triumvirs led their forces across the Adriatic and marched through Macedonia into Thrace. There Brutus and Cassius had massed the last republican army, financed by exactions beyond even Roman precedent. From the Eastern cities of the Empire they demanded, and received, ten years' taxes in advance. When the Rhodians proved reluctant, Cassius stormed the great port, ordered all citizens to surrender their wealth, killed those who hesitated, and carried away $10,000,000. In Cilicia he quartered his soldiers in the homes of Tarsus till it paid him $9,000,000 to leave; to raise this sum the citizens auctioned off all municipal lands, melted down all temple vessels and ornaments, and sold free persons into slavery—first boys and girls, then women and old men, finally youths; many, on learning that they had been sold, killed themselves. In Judea Cassius levied $4,200,000 and sold the inhabitants of four towns into slavery. Brutus, too, could raise money by force. When the citizens of Lycian Xanthus refused his demands, he besieged them until, starving but obdurate, they committed suicide en masse.[9] For the most part Brutus, loving philosophy, tarried in Athens; but the city was filling with young Roman nobles clamoring for a war of restoration. When sufficient funds had been raised Brutus closed his books, joined his troops with those of Cassius, and took the field.

The rival armies met at Philippi in September of 42. Brutus' wing forced back Octavian's and captured his camp; but Antony's routed the legions of Cassius. Cassius ordered his shield-bearer to kill him and was obeyed. Antony could not follow up his success at once; Octavian was confined to his tent with illness, and his troops were in disorder. Antony reorganized the whole army and after a few days' rest led them against Brutus and put the last remnants of the republican forces to flight. Seeing his men yield, Brutus realized, perhaps with relief, that all was lost; he threw himself upon the sword of a friend and died. Antony, coming upon the body, covered it with his own purple robe. They had once been friends.

II. ANTONY AND CLEOPATRA

The old aristocracy fought its last land battle at Philippi. Many of them —Cato's son, Hortensius' son, Quintilius Varus, and Quintus Labeo—joined Brutus and Cassius in suicide. The victors divided the Empire between them: Lepidus was given Africa, Octavian took the West, Antony, having his choice, took Egypt, Greece, and the East. Always needing money, Antony forgave the Eastern cities their contributions to his enemies on condition that they give him a like sum—ten years' taxes within a year. His old geniality returned as victory made him seemingly secure. He reduced his demands upon the Ephesians when their women, dressed as Bacchantes, greeted him as the god Dionysus; but he gave his cook the house of a Magnesian magnate as reward for a distinguished supper. He called an assembly of the Ionian cities at Ephesus and settled the boundaries and affairs of these states with such good judgment that Augustus a decade later found little to change. He pardoned all who had fought against him except those who had shared in killing Caesar. He gave relief to the cities that had suffered most severely from Cassius and Brutus, released several of them from every Roman tax, freed many who had been sold into slavery by the conspirators, and liberated the cities of Syria from the despots who had overthrown their democracies.[10]

While displaying these graces of his simple character, Antony surrendered to such exuberant sensuality that his subjects lost respect for his authority. He surrounded himself with dancers, musicians, courtesans, and roisterers, and took wives and concubines whenever a fair woman struck his Olympian fancy. He had sent messengers to bid Cleopatra present herself before him at Tarsus and answer charges that she had aided Cassius to raise money and troops. She came, but in her own time and way. While Antony sat on a throne in the forum, waiting for her to plead and be judged, she sailed up the river Cydnus in a barge with purple sails, gilded stern, and silver oars that beat time to the music of flutes and fifes and harps. Her maids, dressed as sea nymphs and graces, were the crew, while she herself, dressed as Venus, lay under a canopy of cloth of gold. When the news of this seductive apparition spread among the people of Tarsus they flocked to the shore, leaving Antony solitary on his throne. Cleopatra invited him to dine with her on her ship. He came with an overawing retinue; she feted them with every luxury, and corrupted his generals with gifts and smiles. Antony had almost fallen in love with her as a girl in Alexandria; now he found her, at twenty-nine, in the full maturity of her charms. He began by reproving her, and ended by presenting her with Phoenicia, Coele-Syria, Cyprus, and parts of Arabia, Cilicia, and Judea.[11] She rewarded him according to his desire and invited him to Alexandria. There he spent a carefree winter (41-40), drinking the Queen's love, listening to lectures at the Museum, and forgetting that he had an empire to rule. She herself was not in love. She knew that Egypt, rich but weak, would soon attract the cupidity of omnipotent Rome; the only salvation for her country and her throne lay in marriage with Rome's lord. She had sought this with Caesar; she sought it now with Antony. And he, who had no policy but Caesar's, was tempted to realize the dream of uniting Rome and Egypt and making his capital in the fascinating East.

While Antony frolicked in Alexandria, his wife Fulvia and his brother

Lucius were plotting to overthrow Octavian's power in Rome. Octavian had found no happiness there: the Senate was a rump of adventurers and generals, labor was restless with unemployment, the *populares* were disorganized, Sextus Pompey was blocking the import of food, business was petrified with fear, taxation and spoliation had ruined nearly every fortune, and many men were living in a reckless and sensual riot on the ground that the morrow might in any case bring repudiation of the currency, or further spoliation, or death. Octavian himself was anything but an exemplar of chastity at this time. To perfect the confusion, Fulvia and Lucius raised an army and called upon Italy to oust him. Marcus Agrippa, Octavian's general, besieged Lucius in Perusia and starved him out (March, 40). Fulvia died of illness, frustrated ambition, and grief over Antony's neglect of her. Octavian pardoned Lucius in the hope of maintaining peace with Antony, but Antony crossed the sea and besieged Octavian's troops in Brundisium. The armies, showing more sense than their leaders, refused to fight each other, and compelled them to a peaceable agreement (40). As a pledge of good behavior Antony married Octavian's sister, the gentle and virtuous Octavia. Everybody was briefly happy; and Virgil, writing now his Fourth Eclogue, predicted the return of Saturn's utopian reign.

In 38 Octavian fell in love with Livia, the pregnant wife of Tiberius Claudius Nero. He divorced his first wife Scribonia, persuaded Nero to release Livia, married her, and found, in her persuasive counsel and her aristocratic connections as a member of the Claudian gens, a passage to reconciliation with the propertied classes. He reduced taxes, returned 30,000 runaway slaves to their masters, and set himself patiently to restoring order in Italy. With the help of Agrippa, and of 120 ships contributed by Antony, he destroyed the fleet of Sextus Pompey, secured Rome's food supply, and ended the resistance of the Pompeians (36). The Senate by acclamation named him tribune for life.

After marrying Octavia in a state ceremony at Rome, Antony went with her to Athens. There for a time he enjoyed the novel experience of living with a good woman. He put aside politics and war and, with Octavia at his side, attended the lectures of philosophers. Meanwhile, however, he studied the plans that Caesar had left for conquering Parthia. Labienus, son of Caesar's general, had entered the services of the Parthian king and had led Parthian armies victoriously into Cilicia and Syria—lucrative provinces of Rome (40). To meet this threat Antony needed soldiers; to pay soldiers he needed money; and of this Cleopatra had plenty. Suddenly tiring of virtue and peace, he sent Octavia back to Rome and asked Cleopatra to meet him at Antioch. She brought him a few troops, but she disapproved of his grandiose plans and apparently gave him little of her fabulous treasury. He invaded Parthia with 100,000 men (36), tried in vain to capture its citadels, and lost almost half his forces in a heroic retreat through 300 miles of hostile country. On the way he annexed Armenia to the Empire. He awarded himself a triumph and shocked Italy by celebrating it at Alexandria. He sent a letter of divorce to Octavia (32), married Cleopatra, confirmed her and Caesarion as joint rulers of Egypt and Cyprus, and bequeathed the Eastern provinces of the Empire to the son and daughter that Cleopatra had borne him. Knowing that he would soon have to square accounts with Octavian, he abandoned himself to a year of frolic and luxury. Cleopatra encouraged him to dare the last gamble for omnipotence, helped him to raise an army and a fleet, and chose as her favorite oath, "As surely as I shall one day give judgment in the Capitol."[13]

III. ANTONY AND OCTAVIAN

Octavia bore her rejection silently, lived quietly in Antony's house at Rome, and brought up faithfully his children by Fulvia and the two daughters that she herself had given him. The daily sight of her mute desolation inflamed Octavian's conviction that both Italy and he were doomed if Antony's plans succeeded. He saw to it that Italy should realize the situation: Antony had married the Queen of Egypt, had assigned to her and her illegitimate offspring the most tribute-yielding of Rome's provinces, was seeking to make Alexandria the capital of the Empire, and would reduce Rome and Italy to subordinate roles. When Antony sent a message to the Senate (which he had for years ignored) proposing that he and Octavian should retire to private life, and that the institutions of the Republic should be restored, Octavian escaped a difficult situation by reading to the Senate what he claimed was Antony's will, which he had taken by force from the Vestal Virgins. It named Antony's children by Cleopatra his sole heirs, and directed that he should be buried beside the Queen in Alexandria.[14] The last clause was as decisive for the Senate as it should have proved suspicious; instead of raising doubts that a will filed in Rome should have made such provisions, it convinced the Senate and Italy that Cleopatra was scheming to absorb the Empire through Antony. With characteristic subtlety Octavian declared war (32) against her rather than Antony, and made the conflict a holy war for the independence of Italy.

In September, 32, the fleet of Antony and Cleopatra sailed into the Ionian Sea, 500 warships strong; no such armada had been seen before. Supporting it was an army of 100,000 infantry and 12,000 cavalry, mostly supplied by Eastern princes and kings in the hope of making this a war of liberation from

Rome. Octavian crossed the Adriatic with 400 vessels, 80,000 foot, 12,000 horse. For almost a year the rival forces prepared and maneuvered; then, on September 2, 31, they fought at Actium, in the Ambracian Gulf, one of the decisive battles of history. Agrippa proved the better tactician, and his light ships more manageable than Antony's heavy-towered leviathans. Many of these were consumed by fires set by burning brands cast upon them by Octavian's crews. "Some sailors," says Dio Cassius,

> perished by the smoke before the flames could reach them; others were cooked in their armor, which became red hot; others were roasted in their vessels as though in ovens. Many leaped into the sea; of these some were mangled by sea monsters, some were shot by arrows, some were drowned. The only ones to obtain an endurable death were those who killed one another.[15]

Antony saw that he was losing, and signaled to Cleopatra to carry out their prearranged plan for retreat. She headed her squadron southward and waited for Antony; unable to extricate his flagship, he abandoned it and rowed out to hers. As they sailed for Alexandria he sat alone on the prow, his head between his hands, conscious that everything was lost, even honor.

From Actium Octavian went to Athens; thence to Italy to quell a mutiny among his troops, who clamored for the plunder of Egypt; then to Asia to depose and punish Antony's adherents and raise new funds from long-suffering cities; then to Alexandria (30). Antony had left Cleopatra and was staying on an island near Pharos; thence he sent offers of peace, which Octavian ignored. Unknown to Antony, Cleopatra sent Octavian a golden scepter, crown, and throne as tokens of her submission; according to Dio he replied that he would leave her and Egypt untouched if she would kill Antony.[16] The beaten Triumvir wrote to Octavian again, reminding him of their former friendship and of "all the wanton pranks in which they had shared as youths"; and agreed to kill himself if the victor would spare Cleopatra. Again Octavian made no reply. Cleopatra gathered all that she could of the Egyptian treasury into a palace tower and informed Octavian that she would destroy it all, and herself, unless he granted an honorable peace. Antony led what small forces remained to him in a last fight; his desperate courage won a temporary victory; but on the next day, seeing Cleopatra's mercenaries surrender, and receiving a report that Cleopatra was dead, he stabbed himself. When he learned that the report was false he begged to be brought to the tower in whose upper chambers the Queen and her attendants had locked themselves; they drew him up through the window, and he died in her arms. Octavian allowed her to come forth and bury her lover; then he granted her an audience and, immune to what lure survived in a broken woman of thirty-nine, he gave her terms that made life seem worth-less to one who had been a queen. Convinced that he intended to take her as captive to adorn a Roman triumph, she arrayed herself in her royal robes, put an asp to her breast, and died. Her handmaidens Charmion and Iris followed her in suicide.[18]

Octavian permitted her to be buried beside Antony. Caesarion, and Antony's eldest son by Fulvia, he slew; the children of Antony and the Queen he spared and sent to Italy, where Octavia reared them as if they were her own. The victor found the Egyptian treasury intact and as abundant as he had dreamed. Egypt escaped the indignity of being named a Roman province; Octavian merely mounted the throne of the Ptolemies, succeeded to their possessions, and left a *praefectus* to administer the country in his name. Caesar's heir had conquered those of Alexander, and absorbed Alexander's realm; the West again, as at Marathon and Magnesia, had triumphed over the East. The battle of the giants was over, and an invalid had won.

The Republic died at Pharsalus; the revolution ended at Actium. Rome had completed the fatal cycle known to Plato and to us: monarchy, aristocracy, oligarchic exploitation, democracy, revolutionary chaos, dictatorship. Once more, in the great systole and diastole of history, an age of freedom ended and an age of discipline began.

BOOK III

THE PRINCIPATE

30 B.C.-A.D. 192

CHRONOLOGICAL TABLE

B.C.

30: Octavian receives tribunician power for life; Horace's 2nd book of *Satires*
29: Virgil's *Georgics;* Horace's *Epodes*
27: Octavian becomes Augustus
27-A.D. 68: JULIO-CLAUDIAN DYNASTY
27-A.D. 14: *Principate of Augustus*
25: Agrippa's Pantheon; *fl.* Tibullus
23: First 3 books of Horace's *Odes*
20: First book of Horace's *Epistles*
19: Death of Virgil; *fl.* Propertius
18: *Lex Iulia de adulteriis*
13: Theater of Marcellus; fourth book of Horace's *Odes*
12-9: Campaigns of Drusus in Germany; Tiberius subjugates Pannonia
9: *Fl.* Livy; *Ara Pacis* of Augustus
8: Death of Maecenas and Horace
6: Tiberius in Rhodes
2: Banishment of Julia

A.D. 4: Augustus adopts Tiberius
8: Ovid banished to Tomi
9: Defeat of Varus in Germany; *lex Papia Poppaea* and *lex Iulia de maritandis ordinibus*
14: Death of Augustus
14-37: *Principate of Tiberius*
14-16: Germanicus and Drusus in Germany
17-18: Germanicus in the Near East
18: Death of Ovid
19: Death of Germanicus; trial of Piso
20: *Lex maiestatis;* rise of informers
23-31: Rule of Sejanus
27: Tiberius settles at Capraea
29: Death of Livia; banishment of Agrippina
30: *Fl.* Celsus, encyclopedist
31: Death of Sejanus
37-41: *Principate of Gaius (Caligula)*
41-54: *Principate of Claudius*
41-49: Exile of Seneca
43: Conquest of Britain
48: Death of Messalina; Claudius marries Agrippina the Younger
49: Seneca praetor, and tutor to Nero
54-68: *Principate of Nero*
55: Seneca dedicates *De Clementia* to Nero; Nero poisons Britannicus
59: Nero orders death of his mother Agrippina
62: Fall of Seneca; death of Persius; Nero kills Octavia and marries Poppaea
64: Burning of Rome; first persecution of Christians in Rome

A.D.

65: Execution of Seneca and Lucan
66: Death of Petronius and Thrasea Paetus
68-69: *Principate of Galba*
69 (Jan.-Apr.): *Principate of Otho*
69 (July-Dec.): *Principate of Vitellius*
69-96: FLAVIAN DYNASTY
69-79: *Principate of Vespasian*
70: The Colosseum; Quintilian fills first state professorship
71: Vespasian banishes philosophers
72: Suicide of Helvidius Priscus
79-81: *Principate of Titus*
79: Eruption of Vesuvius; death of the elder Pliny
81: Arch of Titus
81-96: *Principate of Domitian; fl.* Martial and Statius
81-84: Campaigns of Agricola in Britain
93: Persecution of Jews, Christians, and philosophers
96-98: *Principate of Nerva*
98: Tacitus consul
98-117: *Principate of Trajan*
101-2: Trajan's first war against the Dacians
105: Tacitus' *Histories*
105-7: Trajan's second war against the Dacians
111: Pliny the Younger *curator* of Bithynia
113: Forum and column of Trajan
114-6: Trajan's campaigns against Parthia
116: Tacitus' *Annals;* Juvenal's *Satires*
117-38: *Principate of Hadrian*
119: Suetonius' *Lives of the Caesars*
121-34: Hadrian's tour of the Empire
134: *Fl.* Salvius Julianus, jurist
138-61: *Principate of Antoninus Pius*
139: Mausoleum of Hadrian
161-80: *Principate of Marcus Aurelius Antoninus*
161-9: Co-reign of Lucius Verus
161: *Institutiones* of Gaius
162-5: War against Parthia
166-7: Plague spreads through the Empire
166-80: War with the Marcomanni
174 (?): Marcus writes the *Meditations*
175: Rebellion of Avidius Cassius
180: Death of Marcus Aurelius
180-92: *Principate of Commodus*
183: Conspiracy of Lucilla
185: Execution of Perennis
189: Famine; execution of Cleander
190: Pertinax, prefect
193 (Jan. 1): Murder of Commodus

CHAPTER XI

Augustan Statesmanship

30 B.C.–A.D. 14

I. THE ROAD TO MONARCHY

FROM Alexandria Octavian passed to Asia and continued the reallotment of kingdoms and provinces. Not till the summer of 29 did he reach Italy. There almost all classes welcomed and feted him as a savior and joined in a triumph that lasted three days. The Temple of Janus was closed as a sign that for a moment Mars had had his fill. The lusty peninsula was worn out with twenty years of civil war. Its farms had been neglected, its towns had been sacked or besieged, much of its wealth had been stolen or destroyed. Administration and protection had broken down; robbers made every street unsafe at night; highwaymen roamed the roads, kidnaped travelers, and sold them into slavery. Trade diminished, investment stood still, interest rates soared, property values fell. Morals, which had been loosened by riches and luxury, had not been improved by destitution and chaos, for few conditions are more demoralizing than poverty that comes after wealth. Rome was full of men who had lost their economic footing and then their moral stability: soldiers who had tasted adventure and had learned to kill; citizens who had seen their savings consumed in the taxes and inflation of war and waited vacuously for some returning tide to lift them back to affluence; women dizzy with freedom, multiplying divorces, abortions, and adulteries. Childlessness was spreading as the ideal of a declining vitality; and a shallow sophistication prided itself upon its pessimism and cynicism. This was not a full picture of Rome, but a dangerous disease burning in its blood. On the sea piracy had returned, rejoicing in the suicide of states. Cities and provinces licked their wounds after the successive exactions of Sulla, Lucullus, Pompey, Gabinius, Caesar, Brutus, Cassius, Antony, and Octavian. Greece, which had been the battlefield, was ruined; Egypt was despoiled; the Near East had fed a hundred armies and bribed a thousand generals; their peoples hated Rome as a master who had destroyed their freedom without giving them security or peace. What if some leader should arise among them, discover the exhaustion of Italy, and unite them in another war of liberation against Rome?

Once a virile Senate would have faced these dangers, raised sturdy legions, found for them able captains, and guided them with far-seeing statesmanship. But the Senate was now only a name. The great families that had been its strength had died out in conflict or sterility, and the traditions of statecraft had not been transmitted to the businessmen, soldiers, and provincials who had succeeded them. The new Senate gratefully yielded its major powers to one who would plan, take responsibility, and lead.

Octavian hesitated before abolishing the old constitution, and Dio Cassius represents him as discussing the matter at great length with Maecenas and Agrippa. Since in their judgment all governments were oligarchies, the problem could not present itself to them as a choice among monarchy, aristocracy, and democracy; they had to decide whether, under the given conditions of space and time, oligarchy was to be preferred in a monarchical form based upon an army, or an aristocratic form rooted in heredity, or a democratic form resting on the wealth of the business class. Octavian combined them all in a "principate" that mingled the theories of Cicero, the precedents of Pompey, and the policies of Caesar.

The people accepted his solution philosophically. They were no longer enamored of freedom, but wearily wished for security and order; any man might rule them who guaranteed them games and bread. Vaguely they understood that their clumsy *comitia*, clogged with corruption and racked with violence, could not govern the Empire, could not restore health to Italy, could not even administer Rome. The difficulties of freedom multiply with the area it embraces. When Rome ceased to be a city-state, empire drove it inexorably toward the imitation of Egypt, Persia, and Macedon. Out of the collapse of freedom into individualism and chaos a new government had to be created to forge a new order for a widened realm. All the Mediterranean world lay in disorder at Octavian's feet, waiting for statesmanship.

He succeeded where Caesar had failed, because he was more patient and devious, because he understood the strategy of words and forms, because he was willing to move cautiously and slowly where his great-uncle had been forced by the brevity of time to wound living traditions and crowd a generation of changes into half a year of life. Moreover, Octavian had money. When he brought the treasury of Egypt to Rome, says Suetonius, "money became so abundant that the interest rate fell" from twelve to four per cent, and "the value of real estate rose enormously." As soon as Octavian made it clear that property rights were again sacred, that he was through with proscriptions and confiscations, money came out of hiding, investment took courage, trade expanded, wealth resumed its accumulation, and some of it trickled down to the workers and the slaves. All ranks in Italy were pleased to learn that Italy was to remain the beneficiary, and Rome the capital, of the Empire; that the threat of a resurrected East had for a time been laid; and that Caesar's dream of a commonwealth with equal rights had been replaced by a quiet return to the privileges of the master race.

From this bountiful rapine Octavian first paid his debts to his soldiers. He kept 200,000 men in service, each bound to him by an oath of personal loyalty; the remaining 300,000 he discharged with an allotment of agricultural land; and to each soldier he gave a substantial gift of money. He lavished presents upon his generals, his supporters, and his friends. On several occasions he made up deficits in the public treasury from his private funds. To provinces suffering from political depredations or acts of God he remitted a year's tribute and sent large sums for relief. He forgave property owners all tax arrears and publicly burned the records of their debts to the state. He paid for the corn dole, provided prodigal spectacles and games, and presented cash to every citizen. He undertook great public works to end unemployment and beautify Rome, and paid for them out of his purse. Was it any wonder that the nations looked upon him as a god?

While all this money slipped through his hands this *bourgeois empereur* lived simply, shunning the luxuries of the nobles and the emoluments of office, wearing the garments woven by the women in his home, and sleeping always in one small room of what had been the palace of Hortensius. When this burned down after he had occupied it for twenty-eight years, he built his new palace on the plan of the old, and slept in the same narrow *cubiculum* as before. Even when away from the eyes of the city he lived like a philosopher rather than a prince. His sole indulgence was to escape from public affairs by sailing leisurely along the Campanian coast.

Step by step he persuaded, or graciously permitted, the Senate and the assemblies to grant him powers that in their total made him in all but name a king. He kept always the title of *imperator*, as commander in chief of all the armed forces of the state. As the army remained for the most part outside the capital and usually outside Italy, the citizens could forget, while they went through all the forms of the dead Republic, that they were living under a military monarchy in which force was hidden so long as phrases could rule. Octavian was chosen consul in 43 and 33, and in every year from 31 to 23. By the tribunician authority conferred upon him in 36, 30, and 23, he had for life the inviolability of a tribune, the right to initiate legislation in the Senate or the Assembly, and the power to veto the actions of any official in the government. No one protested against this amiable dictatorship. The businessmen who were making hay under the sun of peace, the senators who sniffed Octavian's Egyptian spoils, the soldiers who held their lands or status by his bounty, the beneficiaries of Caesar's laws, appointments, and will— all were now agreed with Homer that the rule of one man is best, at least if he should be so free with his funds as Octavian, so industrious and competent, and so visibly devoted to the good of the state.

In 28, as co-censor with Agrippa, he took a census of the people, revised the membership of the Senate, reduced it to 600, and was himself named permanently *princeps senatus*. The title had meant "first on the roll call of the Senate"; soon it would mean "prince" in the sense of ruler, just as *imperator*, through Octavian's life tenure of the name, would come to mean "emperor." History rightly calls his government, and that of his successors for two centuries, a "principate" rather than strictly a monarchy; for until the death of Commodus all the "emperors" recognized, at least in theory, that they were only the leaders (*principes*) of the Senate. To make the constitutional façade of his authority more imposing, Octavian in 27 surrendered all his offices, proclaimed the restoration of the Republic, and expressed his desire (at thirty-five) to retire to private life. Perhaps the drama had been arranged; Octavian was one of those cautious men who believe that honesty is the best policy, but that it must be practiced with discrimination. The Senate countered his abdication with its own, returned to him nearly all his powers, implored him to continue his guidance of the state, and conferred upon him the title of *Augustus* which history has mistaken as his name. Hitherto the word had been applied only to holy objects and places, and to certain creative or augmenting divinities (*augere*, to increase); applied to Octavian it clothed him with a halo of sanctity, and the protection of religion and the gods.

The people of Rome seem to have thought for a while that the "restoration" was real, and that they were receiving back the Republic in return for an adjective. Did not the Senate and the assemblies still make the laws, still elect the magistrates? It was so; Augustus or his agents merely "proposed" the laws and "nominated" the more important candidates. As *imperator* and consul he ruled the army and the Treasury and administered the laws; and by his tribunician privileges he controlled all other activities of the government. His powers were not much greater than those of Pericles or Pompey, or any energetic American president; the difference lay in their permanence. In 23 he resigned the consulate, but received from the Senate a "proconsular authority" that gave him control of all officials in all provinces. Again no one objected; on the contrary, when a scarcity of grain threatened, the people besieged the Senate with demands that Augustus be made dictator. They had fared so ill under the Senatorial oligarchy that they were inclined toward a dictatorship, which would presumably cultivate their favor as a foil to the power of wealth. Augustus refused; but he took charge of the *annona*, or food supply, quickly ended the shortage, and earned such gratitude that Rome looked on with complacency as he remolded its institutions in his image.

II. THE NEW ORDER

Let us study this principate government in some detail, for in many ways it was one of the subtlest political achievements in history.

The powers of the prince were at once legislative, executive, and judicial: he could propose laws or decrees to assemblies or Senate, he could administer and enforce them, he could interpret them, he could penalize their violation. Augustus, says Suetonius, regularly sat as a judge, sometimes till nightfall, "having a litter placed upon the tribunal if he was indisposed. . . . He was highly conscientious and very lenient." [1] Bearing the duties of so many offices, Augustus organized an informal cabinet of counselors like Maecenas, executives like Agrippa, generals like Tiberius, and an incipient clerical and administrative bureaucracy chiefly composed of his freedmen and slaves.

Caius Maecenas was a wealthy businessman who devoted half his life to helping Augustus in war and peace, in politics and diplomacy, at last, unwillingly, in love. His palace on the Esquiline was famous for its gardens and its swimming pool of heated water. His enemies described him as an effeminate epicurean, for he flaunted silks and gems and knew all the lore of a Roman gourmet. He enjoyed and generously patronized literature and art, restored Virgil's farm to him and gave another to Horace, inspired the *Georgics* and the *Odes*. He refused public office, though he might have had almost any; he labored for years over principles and details of administration and foreign policy; he had the courage to reprove Augustus when he thought him seriously wrong; and when he died (8 B.C.) the Prince mourned his loss as beyond repair.

Perhaps it was on his advice that Augustus—himself of middle-class origin, and free from the aristocrat's contempt of trade—named so many businessmen to high administrative posts, even to provincial governorships. To a Senate offended by this innovation he made amends by many obeisances, by giving exceptional powers to Senatorial commissions, and by gathering about him a *concilium principis* of some twenty men, nearly all senators. In the course of time the decisions of this council acquired the force of *senatusconsulta*, or decrees of the Senate; its powers and functions grew as those of the Senate waned. However he might lavish courtesies upon it, the Senate was merely his highest instrument. As censor he four times revised its membership; he could, and did, eject individuals from it for official incompetence or private immorality; most of its new members were nominated by him; and the quaestors, praetors, and consuls who entered it after their term of office had been chosen by him or with his consent. The richest businessmen of Italy were enrolled in the Senate, and the two orders were in some measure brought together in that *concordia* of united domination which

Cicero had proposed. The power of wealth checked the pride and privilege of birth, and an hereditary aristocracy checked the abuses and irresponsibility of wealth.

At the suggestion of Augustus the meetings of the Senate were confined to the first and fifteenth of each month and usually lasted but a day. As the *princeps senatus* presided, no measure could be submitted without his consent; and in fact all measures presented had been prepared by himself or his aides. The judicial and executive functions of the Senate now outweighed its lawmaking. It served as a supreme court, governed Italy through commissions, and directed the performance of various public works. It ruled those provinces which required no extensive military control, but foreign relations were now controlled by the Prince. Shorn in this way of its ancient authority, the Senate grew negligent in even its limited functions, and yielded ever more responsibility to the Emperor and his staff.

The assemblies still met, though with decreasing frequency; they still voted, but only on measures or nominations approved by the Prince. The right of the plebs to hold office was practically ended in 18 B.C. by a law restricting office to men having a fortune of 400,000 sesterces ($60,000) or more.[2] Augustus ran for the consulate thirteen times and canvassed for votes like the rest; it was a gracious concession to dramatic technique. Corruption was hindered by requiring every candidate to deposit, before election, a financial guarantee that he would abstain from bribery.[3] Augustus himself, however, once distributed a thousand sesterces to each voting member of his tribe to make sure that its vote would be correct.[4] Tribunes and consuls continued to be elected till the fifth century A.D.;[5] but as their major powers had fallen to the Prince, these offices were administrative rather than executive and finally became mere dignities. The actual government of Rome was placed by Augustus in the hands of salaried regional officials, equipped with a force of 3000 police under a *praefectus urbi*, or municipal police commissioner. Further to assure order of the desired kind, and support his own power, Augustus, seriously violating precedent, kept six cohorts of a thousand soldiers each near Rome and three cohorts within it. These nine cohorts became the Praetorian Guard—i.e., guard of the *praetorium*, or headquarters of the commander in chief. It was this body that in A.D. 41 made Claudius emperor and began the subjection of the government to the army.

From Rome the administrative care of Augustus passed to Italy and the provinces. He conferred Roman citizenship, or the limited franchise of "Latin rights," upon all Italian communities that had borne their share in the war against Egypt. He helped the Italian cities with gifts, embellished them with new buildings, and devised a plan whereby their local councilors might vote by mail in the assembly elections at Rome. He divided the provinces into two classes: those that required active defense, and those that did not. The latter (Sicily, Baetica, Narbonese Gaul, Macedonia, Achaea, Asia Minor, Bithynia, Pontus, Cyprus, Crete and Cyrene, and north Africa) he allowed the Senate to rule; the others —"imperial provinces"—were governed by his own legates, procurators, or prefects. This pleasant arrangement allowed him to keep control of the army, which was mostly quartered in the "endangered" provinces; it gave him the lush revenue of Egypt; and it enabled him to keep an eye on the Senatorial governors through the procurators whom he appointed to collect the tribute in all the provinces. Each governor now received a fixed salary, so that his temptation to mulct his subjects was moderately reduced; furthermore, a body of civil servants provided a continuing administration and a check upon the malfeasance of their temporary superiors. The kinglets of client states were treated with wise courtesy and gave Augustus full allegiance. He persuaded most of them to send their sons to live in his palace and receive a Roman education; by this generous arrangement the youths served as hostages until their accession, and then as unwitting vehicles of Romanization.

In the flush aftermath of Actium, and possessed of an enormous army and navy, Augustus apparently planned to extend the Empire to the Atlantic, the Sahara, the Euphrates, the Black Sea, the Danube, and the Elbe; the *pax Romana* was to be maintained not by passive defense but by an aggressive policy on every frontier. The Emperor in person completed the conquest of Spain and so ably reorganized the administration of Gaul that it remained at peace for nearly a century. In the case of Parthia he contented himself with the return of the standards and surviving captives taken from Crassus in 53; but he restored to the throne of Armenia a Tigranes favorable to Rome. He sent abortive expeditions to conquer Ethiopia and Arabia. In the decade from 19 to 9 B.C. his stepsons Tiberius and Drusus subjugated Illyria, Pannonia, and Raetia. Agreeably provoked by German invasions of Gaul, Augustus ordered Drusus to cross the Rhine, and rejoiced to learn that the brilliant youth had fought his way to the Elbe. But Drusus suffered internal injuries from a fall, lingered in pain for thirty days, and died. Tiberius, who loved Drusus with all the intensity of a restrained but passionate nature, rode 400 miles on horseback from Gaul into Germany to hold his brother in his arms in the final hours; then he conveyed the body to Rome, walking before the cortege all the way (9 B.C.). Returning to Germany, Tiberius in two campaigns (8-7 B.C., A.D. 4-5) forced the submission of the tribes between the Elbe and the Rhine.

Two disasters, coming almost together, changed this fever of expansion into a policy of peace. In A.D. 6 the lately won provinces of Pannonia and Dalmatia revolted, massacred all the Romans in their territory, organized an army of 200,000 men, and threatened to invade Italy. Tiberius quickly made peace with the German tribes and led his depleted forces into Pannonia. With patient and ruthless strategy he captured or destroyed the crops that could supply the enemy, and by guerrilla warfare prevented new plantings, while he saw to it that his own troops were well fed. For three years he persisted in this policy despite universal criticism at home; at last he had the satisfaction of seeing the starving rebels disband, and of re-establishing the Roman power. But in that same year (A.D. 9) Arminius organized a revolt in Germany, lured the three legions of Varus, the Roman governor, into a trap, and killed every man of them except those who, like Varus, fell upon their own swords. When Augustus heard of this he was "so deeply affected," says Suetonius, "that for several months he cut neither his beard nor his hair; and sometimes he would dash his head against a door, and cry out, 'Quintilius Varus, give me back my legions!' " [6] Tiberius hastened to Germany, reorganized the army there, stood off the Germans, and, by Augustus' orders, withdrew the Roman boundary to the Rhine.

It was a decision costly to the Emperor's pride but creditable to his judgment. Germany was surrendered to "barbarism"—i.e., to a nonclassic culture—and was left free to arm its growing population against Rome. However, the same reasons that had argued for the conquest of Germany would have demanded the subjection of Scythia—southern Russia. Somewhere the Empire had to stop; and the Rhine was a better frontier than any other west of the Urals. Having annexed northern and western Spain, Raetia, Noricum, Pannonia, Moesia, Galatia, Lycia, and Pamphylia, Augustus felt that he had sufficiently earned his title of "the increasing god." At his death the Empire covered 3,340,000 square miles, more than the mainland of the United States, and over a hundred times the area of Rome before the Punic Wars. Augustus advised his successor to be content with this, the greatest empire yet seen; to seek rather to unite and strengthen it within than to extend it without. He expressed his surprise "that Alexander did not regard it as a greater task to set in order the empire that he had won than to win it." [7] The *Pax Romana* had begun.

III. *SATURNIA REGNA*

It could not be said that Augustus had made a desert and called it peace. Within a decade after Actium the Mediterranean knew such economic quickening as no tradition could parallel. The restoration of order was in itself a stimulus to recovery. The renewed safety of the seas, the stability of government, the conservatism of Augustus, the consumption of Egypt's hoarded treasure, the opening of new mines and mints, the reliability and accelerated circulation of the currency, the easing of congested population into agricultural allotments and colonial settlements—how could prosperity resist so unanimous an invitation? A group of Alexandrian sailors, landing at Puteoli when Augustus was near by, approached him in festal dress and offered him incense as to a deity. It was because of him, they said, that they could voyage in safety, trade in confidence, and live in peace.[8]

Augustus was convinced, as became the grandson of a banker, that the best economy was one that united freedom with security. He protected all classes with well-administered laws, guarded the highways of trade, lent money without interest to responsible land-owners,[9] and mollified the poor with state grain, lotteries, and occasional gifts; for the rest he left enterprise, production, and exchange freer than before. Even so, the works directed by the state were now of unprecedented magnitude, and played some part in restoring economic life. Eighty-two temples were built; a new forum and basilica were added to facilitate the operations of finance and the courts; a new senate house replaced the one that had incinerated Clodius; colonnades were erected to temper the sun; the theater that Caesar had begun was completed and named after Marcellus, son-in-law of Augustus; and rich men were prodded by the Emperor into spending part of their fortunes in adorning Italy with basilicas, temples, libraries, theaters, and roads. "Those that celebrated triumphs," says Dio Cassius, "he commanded to erect out of their spoils some public work to commemorate their deeds." [9a] Augustus hoped to make the majesty of Rome enhance and symbolize her power and his own. Toward the close of his life he remarked that he had found Rome a city of brick and had left it a city of marble.[9b] It was a forgivable exaggeration: there had been much marble there before, and much brick remained. But seldom had any man done so much for a city.

His indispensable aide in the reconstruction of Rome was Marcus Vipsanius Agrippa. This perfect friend had shared with Maecenas the guidance of Augustus' policy. In his year as aedile (33 B.C.) Agrippa had won the public to Octavian by opening 170 public baths, distributing free oil and salt, presenting games for fifty-five successive days, and providing free barbers for all citizens for a year—apparently all at his own expense. His ability might have made him another Caesar; he preferred to serve Augustus for a generation. So far as we know, his life was unstained by public or private scandal; Roman gossip, which sooner or later besmirched everyone else, left him untouched. He was the first Roman to realize the importance of sea power. He planned, built, and commanded the fleet, defeated Sextus Pompey, suppressed piracy, and won a world for Augustus at Actium. After these victories and his pacification of Spain, Gaul, and the Bosporan kingdom, he was thrice offered a triumph and always refused. Enriched by a grateful prince, he continued to live without luxury, and devoted himself as ardently to public works as he had done to the preservation of the state. Out of his own purse he hired hundreds of laborers to repair roads, buildings, and sewers, and reopen the Marcian aqueduct. He constructed a new aqueduct, the Julian, and further improved the water supply of Rome with 700 wells, 500 fountains, and 130 reservoirs. When the people complained of the high price of wine Augustus slyly remarked, "My son-in-law Agrippa has seen to it that Rome shall not go thirsty." [10] This greatest of Roman engineers created a spacious harbor and shipbuilding center by connecting the Lucrine and Avernian lakes with the sea. He built the first of the imposing public baths that were to distinguish Rome among the cities. He constructed, again out of his own funds, a temple to Venus and Mars, which was rebuilt by Hadrian, is known to us as the Pantheon, and still bears on its portico the words, M. AGRIPPA . . . FECIT. He organized a thirty-year survey of the Empire, wrote a treatise on geography, and made in painted marble a map of the world. Like Leonardo he was a scientist, an engineer, an inventor of military projectiles, and an artist. His early death at the age of fifty (12 B.C.) was among the many sorrows that darkened the later years of Augustus, who had given him his daughter Julia in marriage, and had hoped to bequeath the Empire to him as the man best fitted to govern it honestly and well.

Costly public works combined with extended governmental services to raise state expenditures beyond precedent. Salaries were now paid to provincial and municipal officials, bureaucrats and police; a large army and navy were maintained; buildings were put up or restored without number; corn and games bribed the populace to peace. Since expenses were met out of current revenue, and no national debt was laid upon the future, taxation under Augustus became a science and an unremitting industry. Augustus was not relentless; often he forgave taxes to harassed individuals and cities or paid them out of his personal funds. He returned to the municipalities 35,000 pounds of gold offered him as a "coronation gift" on the occasion of his fifth consulate; and he refused many other donations.[12] He abolished the land tax laid upon Italy in the Civil War; in its stead he levied upon all citizens in the Empire a five per cent tax on bequests to any persons except near relatives and the poor.[13] A tax of one per cent was placed upon auction sales, four per cent upon the sale of slaves, five per cent upon their manumission; and custom dues from two and a half to five per cent were collected on nearly all ports of entry. All citizens were subject also to municipal taxes, and Roman realty did not share in Italy's exemption from the tax on land. Taxes were paid for water supplied from the public mains. Considerable revenue came from the leasing of public lands, mines, and fisheries, from the state monopoly of salt, and the fines imposed by the courts. The provinces paid a *tributum soli*, or land tax, and a *tributum capitis*—literally a head or poll tax, actually a tax on personal property. Taxes flowed into two coffers at Rome, both stored in temples: the national Treasury (*aerarium*) controlled by the Senate, and the imperial Treasury (*fiscus*) owned and managed by the

Emperor.* To the latter came the income not only from his vast personal properties, but bequests from well-wishers and friends. Such legacies, in the lifetime of Augustus, amounted to 1,400,000,000 sesterces.

All in all, taxation under the Principate was not oppressive, and until Commodus the results were worth the cost. The provinces prospered and raised altars of gratitude or expectation to Augustus the god; even in sophisticated Rome he had to censure the people for the extravagance of their eulogies. One enthusiast ran through the streets calling upon men and women to "devote" themselves to Augustus—i.e., promise to kill themselves when he died. In 2 B.C. Messala Corvinus, who had captured Octavian's camp at Philippi, proposed that the title of *pater patriae* should be conferred upon Augustus. The Senate, pleased to have so little responsibility while retaining honors and wealth, gladly heaped upon the Emperor this and other titles of praise. The business classes, now richer than ever, celebrated his birthday with a two-day festival year after year. "All sorts and conditions of men," says Suetonius,[14] "brought him gifts on the kalends of January"— New Year's Day. When fire destroyed his old palace every city, apparently every tribe and guild, in the Empire sent him a contribution to rebuild it; he refused to take more than a denarius from any individual, but nevertheless he had more than enough. All the Mediterranean world, after its long ordeal, seemed happy; and Augustus might believe that his patience and labor had accomplished his great task.

IV. THE AUGUSTAN REFORMATION

He destroyed his own happiness by trying to make people good as well as happy; it was an imposition that Rome never forgave him. Moral reform is the most difficult and delicate branch of statesmanship; few rulers have dared to attempt it; most rulers have left it to hypocrites and saints.

Augustus began modestly enough by seeking to check the racial transformation of Rome. Population there was not declining; on the contrary, it was growing by mass and dole attraction and the import of wealth and slaves. Since freedmen were included in the dole, many citizens freed old or sickly slaves to have them fed by the state; kinder motives freed more, and many slaves saved enough to buy their liberty. As the sons of freedmen automatically became citizens, the emancipation of slaves and the fertility of aliens combined with the low birth rate of the native stocks to

---

* The *fisci* were, in the Republic, the sealed baskets in which the provincial money tribute was brought to Rome.

change the ethnic character of Rome. Augustus wondered what stability there could be in so heterogeneous a population, and what loyalty to the Empire might be expected of men in whose veins ran the blood of subject peoples. By his urging, the *lex Fufia Caninia* (2 B.C.) and later measures enacted that an owner of not more than two slaves might free them all, the owner of from three to ten slaves might free half of them, the owner of from eleven to thirty one-third, the owner of from thirty-one to one hundred one-fourth, the owner of from 101 to 300 one-fifth; and no master might free more than a hundred.

One might wish that Augustus had limited slavery instead of freedom. But antiquity took slavery for granted, and would have contemplated with horror the economic and social effects of a wholesale emancipation, just as the employers of our time fear the sloth that might come from security. Augustus was thinking in terms of race and class; he could not conceive a strong Rome without the character, courage, and political ability that had marked the old Roman; above all, the old aristocracy. The decay of the ancient faith among the upper classes had washed away the supernatural supports of marriage, fidelity, and parentage; the passage from farm to city had made children less of an asset, more of a liability and a toy; women wished to be sexually rather than maternally beautiful; in general the desire for individual freedom seemed to be running counter to the needs of the race. To accentuate the evil, legacy hunting had become the most profitable occupation in Italy.[16] Men without children were sure to be courted in their declining years by expectant ghouls; and so large a number of Romans relished this esurient courtesy that it became an added cause of childlessness. Protracted military service drew a considerable proportion of young men from marriage in their most nubile years. A large number of native-stock Romans avoided wedlock altogether, preferring prostitutes or concubines even to a varied succession of wives. Of those who married, a majority appear to have limited their families by abortion, infanticide, *coitus inter-ruptus*, and contraception.[18]

Augustus was disturbed by these insignia of civilization. He began to feel that a movement backward to the old faith and morals was necessary. Respect for the *mos maiorum* revived in him as the years cleared his vision and tired his frame. It was not good, he felt, for the present to break too sharply with the past; a nation must have a continuity of traditions to be sane, as a man must have memory. He read with aging seriousness the historians of Rome, and envied the virtues they ascribed to the ancients. He relished the speech of Quintus Metellus on marriage, read it to the Senate, and recommended it to the people by imperial proclamation. A large part of the older generation agreed with him; it formed a kind of puritan party eager to reform morals by law; and probably Livia lent them her influence. By his powers as censor and tribune Augustus promulgated—or passed through the Assembly—a series of laws of now uncertain date and sequence, aimed at restoring morals, marriage, fidelity, parentage, and a simpler life. They forbade adolescents to attend public entertainments except in the company of an adult relative; excluded women from athletic exhibitions, and restricted them to the upper seats at gladiatorial games; limited expenditure on homes, servants, banquets, weddings, jewels, and dress. The most important of these "Julian laws" * was the *lex Iulia de pudicitia et de coercendis adulteriis* (18 B.C.)—"The Julian law of chastity and repressing adultery." Here for the first time in Roman history marriage was brought under the protection of the state, instead of being left to the *patria potestas*. The father retained the right to kill an adulterous daughter and her accomplice as soon as he discovered them; the husband was allowed to kill his wife's paramour if caught in the husband's house, but he might kill his wife only if he found her sinning in his own home. Within sixty days of detecting a wife's adultery, the husband was required to bring her before the court; if he failed to do this, the woman's father was required to indict her; if he too failed, any citizen might accuse her. The adulterous woman was to be banished for life, was to lose a third of her fortune and half her dowry, and must not marry again. Like penalties were decreed for a husband conniving at his wife's adultery. A wife, however, could not accuse her husband of adultery, and he might with legal impunity have relations with registered prostitutes. The law applied only to Roman citizens.

Probably at the same time Augustus passed another law, usually named *lex Iulia de maritandis ordinibus*, from its chapter on marriage in the "orders" —i.e., the two upper classes. Its purpose was threefold: to encourage and yet restrict marriage, to retard the dilution of Roman with alien blood, and to restore the old conception of marriage as a union for parentage. Marriage was to be obligatory upon all marriageable males under sixty and women under fifty. Bequests conditional on the legatee remaining unmarried were made void. Penalties were imposed upon celibates: they could not inherit, except from relatives, unless they were married within a hundred days after the testator's death; and they could not attend public festivals or games. Widows and divorcees might inherit only if remarried within six months after the death or divorce of the husband. Spinsters and childless wives could not inherit after fifty, nor before if they possessed 50,000 sesterces ($7500). Men of the Senatorial class could not marry a freedwoman, an actress, or a prostitute; and no actor or freedman could marry a senator's daughter.

---

* So named from the clan to which Augustus belonged by adoption.

Women owning above 20,000 sesterces were to pay a one per cent annual tax till married; after marriage this tax decreased with each child until the third, with whose coming it ceased. Of the two consuls the one with more children was to have precedence over the other. In appointments to office the father of the largest family was as far as feasible to be preferred to his rivals. The mother of three children acquired the *ius trium liberorum*—the right to wear a special garment, and freedom from the power of her husband.

These laws offended every class, even the puritans—who complained that the "right of three children" dangerously emancipated the mother from male authority. Others excused their celibacy on the score that the "modern woman" was too independent, imperious, capricious, and extravagant. The exclusion of bachelors from public shows was considered too severe and impossible to enforce; Augustus had the clause rescinded in 12 B.C. In A.D. 9 the *lex Papia Poppaea* further softened the Julian laws by easing the conditions under which celibates might inherit, doubling the period in which widows and divorcees must remarry to inherit, and increasing the amount that childless heirs could receive. Mothers of three children were freed from those limits which the *lex Voconia* (169 B.C.) had placed upon bequests to women. The age at which a citizen might stand for the various offices was lowered in proportion to the size of his family. After the law was passed men noted that the consuls who had framed it and given it their names were childless celibates. Gossip added that the reform laws had been suggested to Augustus, who had only one child, by Maecenas, who had none; and that while the laws were being enacted Maecenas was living in sybaritic luxury, and Augustus was seducing Maecenas' wife.[19]

It is difficult to estimate the effectiveness of this, the most important social legislation in antiquity. The laws were loosely drawn, and recalcitrants found many loopholes. Some men married to obey the law and divorced their wives soon afterwards; others adopted children to secure offices or legacies and then "emancipated"—i.e., dismissed—them.[20] Tacitus, a century later, pronounced the laws a failure; "marriages and the rearing of children did not become frequent, so powerful are the attractions of a childless state." [21] Immorality continued, but was more polite than before; in Ovid we see it becoming a fine art, the subject of careful instructions from experts to apprentices. Augustus himself doubted the efficacy of his laws, and agreed with Horace that laws are vain when hearts are unchanged.[22] He struggled heroically to reach people's hearts: in his box at the games he displayed the numerous children of the exemplary Germanicus; gave a thousand sesterces to parents of large families; [23] raised a monument to a slave girl who (doubtless without patriotic premeditation) had borne quintuplets; [24] and rejoiced when a peasant marched into Rome with eight children, thirty-six grand-

FIG. 1—*Caesar* (*black basalt*)
Altes Museum, Berlin

Fig. 2.—*An Etruscan Tomb at Cervetri*

FIG. 3—*Head of a Woman*
From an Etruscan tomb at Corneto

FIG. 4—*Apollo of Veii*
Villa di Papa Giulio, Rome

FIG. 5—*The Orator*
Museo Archeologico, Florence

FIG. 6—*Pompey*
Ny Carlsberg Glyptotek, Copenhagen

FIG. 7—*Caesar*
Museo Nazionale, Naples

FIG. 8—*The Young Augustus*
Vatican, Rome

Fig. 9—*Augustus Imperator, from the Villa of Livia at Prima Porta*
Vatican, Rome

FIG. 10—*Vespasian*
Museo Nazionale, Naples

Fig. 11—*Relief from the Arch of Titus*

Fig. 12—*The Roman Forum*

FIG. 13—*Temple of Castor and Pollux*
Roman Forum

FIG. 14—*Two Roman Mosaics*
Top, Museo Nazionale, Naples. Bottom, Capitoline Museum, Rome

FIG. 15—*The Gemma Augusta*
Vienna Museum

FIG. 16—*An Arretine Vase*
From the Loeb Collection, Harvard University

children, and nineteen great-grandchildren in his train.[25] Dio Cassius pictures him making public addresses denouncing "race suicide." [26] He enjoyed, perhaps inspired, the moral preface of Livy's history. Under his influence the literature of the age became didactic and practical. Through Maecenas or in person he persuaded Virgil and Horace to lend their muses to the propaganda of moral and religious reform; Virgil tried to sing the Romans back to the farm in the *Georgics,* and to the old gods in the *Aeneid;* and Horace, after a large sampling of the world's pleasures, tuned his lyre to stoic themes. In 17 B.C. Augustus presented the *ludi saeculares* *– three days of ceremonies, contests, and spectacles, celebrating the return of Saturn's Golden Age; and Horace was commissioned to write the *carmen saeculare* to be chanted in procession by twenty-seven boys and as many girls. Even art was used to point a moral: the lovely *Ara Pacis* showed in relief the life and government of Rome; magnificent public buildings rose to represent the strength and glory of the Empire; scores of temples were erected to stir again a faith that had almost died.

In the end Augustus, skeptic and realist, became convinced that moral reform awaited a religious renaissance. The agnostic generation of Lucretius, Catullus, and Caesar had run its course, and its children had discovered that the fear of the gods is the youth of wisdom. Even the cynical Ovid would soon write, Voltaireanly: *expedit esse deos, et ut expedit esse putemus:* "it is convenient that there should be gods, and that we should think they exist." [27] Conservative minds traced the Civil War, and the sufferings it had brought, to neglect of religion and the consequent anger of Heaven. Everywhere in Italy a chastened people was ready to turn back to its ancient altars and thank the deities who, it felt, had spared it for this happy restoration. When, in 12 B.C., Augustus, having waited patiently for the tepid Lepidus to die, succeeded him as *pontifex maximus,* "such a multitude from all Italy assembled for my election," the Emperor tells us, "as is never recorded to have been in Rome before." [28] He both led and followed the revival of religion, hoping that his political and moral reconstruction would win readier acceptance if he could entwine it with the gods. He raised the four priestly colleges to unprecedented dignity and wealth, chose himself to each of them, took upon himself the appointment of new members, attended their meetings faithfully, and took part in their solemn pageantry. He banned Egyptian and Asiatic cults from Rome, but he made an exception in favor of the Jews, and permitted religious freedom in the provinces. He lavished gifts upon the temples and renewed old religious ceremonies, processions, and festivals. The *ludi saeculares* were not secular; every day of

---

* Literally, century games, because given only at long intervals.

them was marked with religious ritual and song; their chief significance was the return of a happy friendship with the gods. Nourished with such sovereign aid, the ancient cult took on fresh life, and touched again the dramatic impulses and supernatural hopes of the people. Amid the chaos of competing faiths that flowed in upon Rome after Augustus, it held its own for three centuries more; and when it died it was at once reborn, under new symbols and new names.

Augustus himself became one of the chief competitors of his gods. His great-uncle had set the example: two years after being murdered, Caesar had been recognized by the Senate as a deity, and his worship spread throughout the Empire. As early as 36 B.C. some Italian cities had given Octavian a place in their pantheon; by 27 B.C. his name was added to those of the gods in official hymns at Rome; his birthday became a holy day as well as a holiday; and after his death the Senate decreed that his *genius,* or soul, was thereafter to be worshiped as one of the official divinities. All this seemed quite natural to antiquity; it had never recognized an impassable difference between gods and men; the gods had often taken human form, and the creative *genius* of a Heracles, a Lycurgus, an Alexander, a Caesar, or an Augustus seemed, especially to the religious East, miraculous and divine. The Egyptians had thought of the Pharaohs, of the Ptolemies, even of Antony, as deities; they could hardly think less of Augustus. The ancients were not in these cases such simpletons as their modern counterparts would like to believe. They knew well enough that Augustus was human; in deifying his *genius,* or that of others, they used *deus* or *theos* as equivalent to our "canonized saint"; indeed, canonization is a descendant of Roman deification; and to pray to such a deified human being seemed no more absurd then than prayer to a saint seems now.

In Italian homes the worship of the Emperor's *genius* became associated with the adoration given to the Lares of the household and the *genius* of the paterfamilias; there was nothing difficult in this for a people which through centuries had deified their dead parents, built altars to them, and given the name of temples to the ancestral tombs. When Augustus visited Greek Asia in 21 B.C. he found that his cult had made rapid headway there. Dedications and orations hailed him as "Savior," "Bringer of Glad Tidings," "God the Son of God"; some men argued that in him the long-awaited Messiah had come, bringing peace and happiness to mankind.[29] The great provincial councils made his worship the center of their ceremonies; a new priesthood, the *Augustales,* was appointed by provinces and municipalities for the service of the new divinity. Augustus frowned upon all this, but finally accepted it as a spiritual enhancement of the Principate, a valuable cementing of church and state, a uniting common worship amid diverse and dividing creeds. The moneylender's grandson consented to become a god.

V. AUGUSTUS HIMSELF

What sort of man was this who was heir to Caesar at eighteen, master of the world at thirty-one, ruler of Rome for half a century, and architect of the greatest empire in ancient history? He was at once dull and fascinating; no one more prosaic, yet half the world adored him; a physical weakling not particularly brave, but able to overcome all enemies, regulate kingdoms, and fashion a government that would give the vast realm an unexampled prosperity for two hundred years.

Sculptors spent much marble and bronze in making images of him: some showing him in the timid pride of a refined and serious youth, some in the somber pose of a priest, some half covered with the insignia of power, some in military garb—the philosopher unwillingly and uneasily playing the general. These effigies do not reveal, though sometimes they suggest, the ailments that made his war against chaos depend precariously at every step upon his fight for health. He was unprepossessing. He had sandy hair, a strangely triangular head, merging eyebrows, clear and penetrating eyes; yet his expression was so calm and mild, says Suetonius, that a Gaul who came to kill him changed his mind. His skin was sensitive and intermittently itched with a kind of ringworm; rheumatism weakened his left leg and made him limp a bit; a stiffness akin to arthritis occasionally incapacitated his right hand. He was one of many Romans attacked in 23 B.C. by a plague resembling typhus; he suffered from stones in the bladder, and found it hard to sleep; he was troubled each spring by "an enlargement of the diaphragm; and when the wind was in the south he had catarrh." He bore cold so poorly that in winter he wore "a woolen chest protector, wraps for his thighs and shins, an undershirt, four tunics (blouses), and a heavy toga." He dared not expose his head to the sun. Horseback riding tired him, and he was sometimes carried in a litter to the battlefield.[30] At thirty-five, having lived through one of the most intense dramas in history, he was already old— nervous, sickly, easily tired; no one dreamed that he would live another forty years. He tried a variety of doctors, and richly rewarded one, Antonius Musa, for curing an uncertain illness (abscess of the liver?) with cold fomentations and baths; in Musa's honor he exempted all Roman physicians from taxation.[31] But for the most part he doctored himself. He used hot salt water and sulphur baths for his rheumatism; he ate lightly and only the plainest food—coarse bread, cheese, fish, and fruit; he was so careful of his diet that "sometimes he ate alone either before a dinner party or after it, taking nothing during its course." [32] In him, as in some medieval saints, the soul bore its body like a cross.

His essence was nervous vitality, inflexible resolution, a penetrating, calculating, resourceful mind. He accepted an unheard-of number of offices, and took upon himself responsibility only less than Caesar's. He fulfilled the duties of these positions conscientiously, presided regularly over the Senate, attended innumerable conferences, judged hundreds of trials, suffered ceremonies and banquets, planned distant campaigns, governed legions and provinces, visited nearly every one of them, and attended to infinite administrative detail. He made hundreds of speeches, and prepared them with proud attention to clarity, simplicity, and style; he read them instead of speaking extemporaneously, lest he should utter regrettable words. Suetonius would have us believe that for the same reason he wrote out in advance, and read, important conversations with individuals, even with his wife.[33]

Like most skeptics of his time, he retained superstitions long after losing his faith. He carried a sealskin about him to protect against lightning; he respected omens and auspices and sometimes obeyed warnings derived from dreams; he refused to begin a journey on what he reckoned to be unlucky days.[34] At the same time he was remarkable for the objectivity of his judgment and the practicality of his thought. He advised young men to enter soon upon an active career, so that the ideas they had learned from books might be tempered by the experience and necessities of life.[35] He kept to the end his bourgeois good sense, conservatism, parsimony, and caution. *Festina lente*—"make haste slowly"—was his favorite saw. Far more than most men of such power, he could take advice and bear reproof humbly. Athenodorus, a philosopher who was returning to Athens after living with him for years, gave him some parting counsel: "Whenever you get angry do not say or do anything before repeating to yourself the twenty-four letters of the alphabet." Augustus was so grateful for the caution that he begged Athenodorus to stay another year, saying, "No risk attends the reward that silence brings." [36]

Even more surprising than Caesar's development from a roistering politician into a great general and statesman was the transformation of the merciless and self-centered Octavian into the modest and magnanimous Augustus. He grew. The man who had allowed Antony to hang Cicero's head in the Forum, who had moved without scruple from one faction to another, who had run the gamut of sexual indulgence, who had pursued Antony and Cleopatra to the death unmoved by friendship or chivalry—this tenacious and unlovable youth, instead of being poisoned by power, became in his last forty years a model of justice, moderation, fidelity, magnanimity, and toleration. He laughed at the lampoons that wits and poets wrote about him. He advised Tiberius to be content with preventing or prosecuting hostile actions and not seek to suppress hostile words. He did not insist upon others living as simply as himself; when he invited guests to dinner he would retire early to leave their appetite and merriment unrestrained. He had no pretentiousness; he buttonholed voters to ask their suffrages; he substituted for his lawyer friends in court; he left or entered Rome secretly, abhorring pomp; in the reliefs of the *Ara Pacis* he is not set apart from the other citizens by any mark of distinction. His morning receptions were open to all citizens, and all were affably received. When one man hesitated to present a petition he jokingly chided him for offering the document "as if he were giving a penny to an elephant." [37]

In his senile years, when disappointments had embittered him, and he had grown accustomed to omnipotence, even to being a god, he lapsed into intolerance, prosecuted hostile writers, suppressed histories of too critical a stamp, and gave no ear to Ovid's penitent verse. Once, it is said, he had the legs of his secretary Thallus broken for taking 500 denarii to reveal the contents of an official letter; and he forced one of his freedmen to kill himself when found guilty of adultery with a Roman matron. All in all, it is hard to love him. We must picture the frailty of his body and the sorrows of his old age before our hearts can go out to him as to the murdered Caesar or the beaten Antony.

VI. THE LAST DAYS OF A GOD

His failures and his tragedies were almost all within his home. By his three wives—Claudia, Scribonia, Livia—he had but one child: Scribonia unwittingly avenged her divorce by giving him Julia. He had hoped that Livia would bear him a son whom he might train and educate for government; but though she had rewarded her first husband with two splendid children —Tiberius and Drusus—her marriage with Augustus proved disappointingly sterile. Otherwise their union was a happy one. She was a woman of stately beauty, firm character, and fine understanding; Augustus rehearsed his most vital measures with her and valued her advice as highly as that of his maturest friends. Asked how she had acquired such influence over him, she replied, "by being scrupulously chaste . . . never meddling with his affairs, and pretending neither to hear of nor to notice the favorites with whom he had amours." [38] She was a model of the old virtues, and perhaps expounded them too persistently. In her leisure she devoted herself to charity, helping parents of large families, providing dowries for poor brides, and maintaining many orphans at her own expense. Her palace itself was almost an orphanage; for there, and in the home of his sister Octavia, Augustus supervised the education of his grandsons, nephews, nieces, and even the six surviving children of Antony. He sent the boys off early to war, saw to it that the girls should learn to spin and weave, and "forbade them to do or say anything except without concealment, and such as might be recorded in the household diary." [39]

Augustus learned to love Livia's son Drusus, adopted and reared him, and would gladly have left him his wealth and power; the youth's early death was one of the Emperor's first bereavements. Tiberius he respected but could not love, for his future successor was a positive and imperious character, inclined to sullenness and secrecy. But the comeliness and vivacity of his daughter Julia must have given Augustus many happy moments in her childhood. When she had reached the age of fourteen he persuaded Octavia to allow the divorce of her son Marcellus, and induced the youth to marry Julia. Two years later Marcellus died; and Julia, after brief mourning, set out to enjoy a freedom she had long coveted. But soon the matchmaking Emperor, craving a grandson as heir, coaxed the reluctant Agrippa to divorce his wife and marry the merry widow (21 B.C.). Julia was eighteen, Agrippa forty-two; but he was a good and great man and agreeably rich. She made his town house a *salon* of pleasure and wit, and became the soul of the younger and gayer set in the capital as against the puritans who took their lead from Livia. Rumor accused Julia of deceiving her new husband, and ascribed to her an incredible reply to the incredible question why, despite her adulteries, all the five children she gave Agrippa resembled him: *Numquam nisi nave plena tollo vectorem.*[40] When Agrippa died (12 B.C.) Augustus turned his hopes to Julia's oldest sons, Gaius and Lucius, overwhelmed them with affection and education, and had them promoted to office far sooner than was legally warranted by their years.

Again a widow, Julia, richer and lovelier than ever, entered with saucy abandon upon a succession of amours which became at once the scandal and the joy of a Rome that fretted under the "Julian laws." To quiet this gossip, and perhaps to reconcile his daughter with his wife, Augustus made a third match for Julia. Livia's son Tiberius was compelled to divorce his pregnant wife, Vipsania Agrippina, daughter of Agrippa, and to marry the equally reluctant Julia (9 B.C.). The young old Roman did his best to be a good husband; but Julia soon gave up the effort to adjust her epicurean to his stoic ways, and resumed her illicit loves. Tiberius bore the infamy for a time in furious silence. The *lex Iulia de adulteriis* required the husband of an adulteress to denounce her to the courts; Tiberius disobeyed the law to protect its author, and perhaps himself, for he and Livia had hoped that Augustus would adopt him as his son and transmit to him the leadership of the Empire. When it became clear that the Emperor favored, instead, Julia's children by Agrippa, Tiberius resigned his official posts and retired to Rhodes. There for seven years he lived as a simple private citizen, devoting himself to solitude, philosophy, and astrology. Freer than ever, Julia passed from one lover to another, and the revels of her set filled the Forum with turmoil at night.[41]

Augustus, now (2 B.C.) an invalid of sixty, suffered all that a father and ruler could bear from the simultaneous collapse of his family, his honor, and his laws. By these laws the father of an adulteress was bound to indict her publicly if her husband had failed to do so. Proofs of her misconduct were laid before him, and the friends of Tiberius let it be known that unless Augustus acted they would accuse Julia before the court. Augustus decided to anticipate them. While the merrymaking was at its height, he issued a decree banishing his daughter to the island of Pandateria, a barren rock off the Campanian coast. One of her lovers, a son of Antony, was forced to kill himself, and several others were exiled. Julia's freedwoman Phoebe hanged herself rather than testify against her; the distraught Emperor, hearing of the act, said, "I would rather have been Phoebe's father than Julia's." The people of Rome begged him to forgive his daughter, Tiberius added his request to theirs, but pardon never came. Tiberius, enthroned, merely changed her place of residence to a less narrow confinement at Rhegium. There, broken and forgotten after sixteen years of imprisonment, Julia died.

Her sons Gaius and Lucius had long preceded her in death: Lucius of an illness in Marseilles (A.D. 2), Gaius of a wound received in Armenia (A.D. 4). Left without aide or successor at a time when Germany, Pannonia, and Gaul were threatening revolt, Augustus reluctantly recalled Tiberius (A.D. 2), adopted him as son and coregent, and sent him off to put down the rebellions. When he returned (A.D. 9), after five years of arduous and successful campaigning, all Rome, which hated him for his stern puritanism, resigned itself to the fact that though Augustus was still prince, Tiberius had begun to rule.

Life's final tragedy is unwilling continuance—to outlive one's self and be forbidden to die. When Julia went into exile Augustus was not in years an old man; others were still vigorous at sixty. But he had lived too many lives, and died too many deaths, since he had come to Rome, a boy of eighteen, to avenge Caesar's murder and execute his will. How many wars and battles and near-defeats, how many pains and illnesses, how many conspiracies and perils, and bitter miscarriages of noble aims, had befallen him in those crowded forty-two years—and the snatching away of one hope and helper after another, until at last only this dour Tiberius remained! Perhaps it had been wiser to die like Antony, at the peak of life and in the arms of love. How sadly pleasant must have seemed, in retrospect, the days when Julia and Agrippa were happy, and grandchildren frolicked on the palace floor. Now another Julia, daughter of his daughter, had grown up and was following her mother's morals as if resolved to illustrate all the amatory arts of her friend Ovid's verse. In A.D. 8, having received proofs of her adultery, Augustus exiled her to an isle in the Adriatic, and at the same time banished Ovid to Tomi on the Black Sea. "Would that I had never married," mourned the feeble and shrunken Emperor, "or that I had died without offspring!" Sometimes he thought of starving himself to death.

All the great structure that he had built seemed to be in ruins. The powers that he had assumed for order's sake had weakened into degeneration the Senate and the assemblies from which he had taken them. Tired of ratifications and adulations, the senators no longer came to their sessions, and a mere handful of citizens gathered in the *comitia*. Offices that had once stirred creative ambition by the power they brought were now shunned by the able as empty and expensive vanities. The very peace that Augustus had organized, and the security that he had won for Rome, had loosened the fibre of the people. No one wanted to enlist in the army, or recognize the inexorable periodicity of war. Luxury had taken the place of simplicity, sexual license was replacing parentage; by its own exhausted will the great race was beginning to die.

All these things the old Emperor keenly saw and sadly felt. No one then could tell him that despite a hundred defects and half a dozen idiots on the throne, the strange and subtle principate that he had established would give the Empire the longest period of prosperity ever known to mankind; and that the *Pax Romana*, which had begun as the *Pax Augusta*, would in the perspective of time be accounted the supreme achievement in the history of statesmanship. Like Leonardo, he thought that he had failed.

Death came to him quietly at Nola in the seventy-sixth year of his age (A.D. 14). To the friends at his bedside he uttered the words often used to conclude a Roman comedy: "Since well I've played my part, clap now your hands, and with applause dismiss me from the stage." He embraced his wife, saying, "Remember our long union, Livia; farewell"; and with this simple parting he passed away.[42] Some days later his corpse was borne through Rome on the shoulders of senators to the Field of Mars, and there cremated while children of high degree chanted the lament for the dead.

CHAPTER XII

The Golden Age

30 B.C.–A.D. 18

I. THE AUGUSTAN STIMULUS

IF peace and security are more favorable than war to the production of literature and art, yet war and profound social disturbances turn up the earth about the plants of thought and nourish the seeds that mature in peace. A quiet life does not make great ideas or great men; but the compulsions of crisis, the imperatives of survival, weed out dead things by the roots and quicken the growth of new ideas and ways. Peace after successful war has all the stimulus of a rapid convalescence; men then rejoice at mere being, and sometimes break into song.

The Romans were grateful to Augustus because he had cured, even if by a major operation, the cancer of chaos that had been consuming their civic life. They were astonished to find themselves rich so soon after devastation; and they were elated to note that despite their recent defenseless disorder they were still masters of what seemed to them the world. They looked back upon their history, from the first to this second Romulus, from creator to restorer, and judged it epically wonderful; they were hardly surprised when Virgil and Horace put their gratitude, their glory, and their pride into verse, and Livy into prose. Better still, the region they had conquered was only partly barbarous; a large area of it was the realm of Hellenistic culture—of refined speech, subtle literature, enlightening science, mature philosophy, and noble art. This spiritual wealth was now pouring into Rome, stirring imitation and rivalry, compelling language and letters to spruce up and grow. Ten thousand Greek words slipped into the Latin vocabulary, ten thousand Greek statues or paintings entered Roman forums, temples, streets, and homes.

Money was passing down, even to poets and artists, from the captors of Egypt's treasure, the absentee owners of Italy's soil, and the exploiters of the Empire's resources and trade. Writers dedicated their works to rich men in the hope of receiving gifts that would finance their further toil; so Horace addressed his odes to Sallust, Aelius Lamia, Manlius Torquatus, and Munatius, Plancus. Messala Corvinus gathered about him a coterie of authors whose star was Tibullus, and Maecenas redeemed his wealth and poetry by presents to Virgil, Horace, and Propertius. Until his final irascible years, Augustus followed a liberal policy toward literature; he was glad to have letters and art take up the energies that had disturbed politics; he would pay men to write books if they would let him govern the state. His generosity to poets became so renowned that a swarm of them buzzed around him wherever he went. When a Greek persisted, day after day, in pressing verses into his hand as he left his palace, Augustus retaliated by stopping, composing some lines of his own, and having an attendant give them to the Greek. The latter offered the Emperor a few denarii and expressed his regret that he could not give more. Augustus rewarded his wit, not his poetry, with 100,000 sesterces.[1]

The stream of books swelled now to proportions unknown before. Everyone from fool to philosopher wrote poetry.[2] Since all poetry, and most literary prose, were designed to be read aloud, gatherings were formed at which authors read their productions to invited or general audiences or, in rare moments of tolerance, to one another. Juvenal thought that a compelling reason for living in the country was to escape the poets who infested Rome.[3] In the bookshops that crowded a district called the Argiletum, writers assembled to compute literary genius, while impecunious bibliophiles furtively read snatches of the books they could not buy. Placards on the walls announced new titles and their cost. Small volumes sold for four or five sesterces, average volumes for ten ($1.50); elegant editions like Martial's epigrams, usually illustrated with a portrait of the author, brought some five denarii ($3).[4] Books were exported to all parts of the Empire, or were published simultaneously in Rome, Lyons, Athens, and Alexandria;[4a] Martial was pleased to learn that he was bought and sold in Britain. Even poets now had private libraries; Ovid affectionately describes his.[5] We gather from Martial that there were already book fanciers who collected de luxe editions, or rare manuscripts. Augustus established two public libraries; Tiberius, Vespasian, Domitian, Trajan, and Hadrian built others; by the fourth century there were twenty-eight in Rome. Foreign students and writers came to study in these libraries and in public archives; so Dionysius came from Halicarnassus, and Diodorus from Sicily. Rome was now the rival of Alexandria as the literary center of the Western world.

This efflorescence transformed both literature and society. Letters and the arts took on new dignity. Grammarians lectured on living authors; people sang snatches from them in the streets. Writers mingled with statesmen and highborn ladies in luxurious *salons* such as history would never know again until the flowering of France. The aristocracy became literary, literature became aristocratic. The lusty vigor of Ennius and Plautus, Lucretius and Catullus, was exchanged for a delicate beauty, or a teasing complexity, in expression and thought. Writers ceased to mingle with the people, ceased therefore to describe their ways or speak their language; a divorce set in between literature and life that finally sucked the sap and spirit out of Latin letters. Forms were set by Greek models, themes by Greek tradition or Augustus' court. Poetry, when it could spare time from Theocritean shepherds or Anacreontic love, was to sing didactically the joys of agriculture, the morality of ancestors, the glory of Rome, and the splendor of its gods. Literature became a handmaiden of statesmanship, a polyphonic sermon calling the nation to Augustan ideas.

Two forces opposed this conscription of letters by the state. One was Horace's hated and "profane crowd," which liked the salty tang and independence of the old satires and plays rather than the curled and perfumed beauty of the new. The other was that demimonde of jollity and sin to which Clodia and Julia belonged. This younger set was in full rebellion against the Julian laws, wanted no moral reform, had its own poets, circles, and norms. In letters as in life the two forces fought each other, crossing in Tibullus and Propertius, matching the chaste piety of Virgil with the obscene audacities of Ovid, crushing two Julias and one poet with exile, and at last exhausting each other in the Silver Age. But the ferment of great events, the releasing leisure of wealth and peace, the majesty of a world acknowledging Rome's sway, overcame the corrosion of state subsidies and produced a Golden Age whose literature was the most perfect, in form and utterance, in all the memory of men.

II. VIRGIL

The most lovable of Romans was born in 70 B.C. on a farm near Mantua, where the river Mincio wanders slowly toward the Po. The capital would henceforth give birth to very few great Romans; they would come from Italy in the century that was divided by the birth of Christ, and thereafter from the provinces. Perhaps Virgil's veins contained some Celtic blood, for Mantua had long been peopled by Gauls; technically he was a Gaul by birth, for it was only twenty-one years later that Cisalpine Gaul received the Roman franchise from Caesar. The man who most eloquently sang the majesty and destiny of Rome would never show the hard masculinity of the Roman stock, but would touch Celtic strings of mysticism, tenderness, and grace rare in the Roman breed.

His father saved enough as a court clerk to buy a farm and raise bees.

In that murmurous quietude the poet spent his boyhood; the full foliage of the well-watered north lingered in his later memory, and he was never really happy away from those fields and streams. At twelve he was sent to school at Cremona, at fourteen to Milan, at sixteen to Rome. There he studied rhetoric and allied subjects under the same man who was to teach Octavian. Probably after this he attended the lectures of Siro the Epicurean at Naples. Virgil tried hard to accept the philosophy of pleasure, but his rural background had ill-equipped him. He seems to have returned north after his education, for in 41 B.C. we find him swimming for life to escape a soldier who seized by force his father's farm; Octavian and Antony had confiscated it because the region had favored their enemies. Asinius Pollio, the learned governor of Cisalpine Gaul, tried to have the farm returned, but failed. He atoned by giving his patronage to the young man, and encouraging him to continue the *Eclogues* he was composing.

By the year 37 Virgil was drinking in the wine of fame in Rome. The *Eclogues* ("Selections") had just been published and had been well received; some verses had been recited on the stage by an actress and had been enthusiastically applauded.[6] The poems were pastoral sketches in the manner, sometimes the phrases, of Theocritus, beautiful in style and rhythm, the most melodious hexameters that Rome had yet heard, full of pensive tenderness and romantic love. The youth of the capital had been long enough detached from the soil to idealize country life; everyone was pleased to imagine himself a shepherd moving with his flocks up and down the Apennine slopes, and breaking his heart with love unreturned.

Realer than these Theocritan ghosts were the rural scenes. Here, too, Virgil idealized, but he did not have to imitate. He had heard the woodman's lusty song and the hovering restlessness of bees;[8] and he had known the emptyhearted despair of the farmer who, like thousands then, had lost his land.[9] Above all, he felt intensely the hopes of the age for an end to faction and war. The Sibylline Books had predicted that after the Age of Iron the Golden Age of Saturn would return. When, in 40 B.C., a son was born to Virgil's patron, Asinius Pollio, the poet announced in his *Fourth Eclogue* that this birth would usher in utopia:

> Ultima Cumaei venit iam carminis aetas;
> magnus ab integro saeclorum nascitur ordo.
> Iam redit et Virgo, redeunt Saturnia regna;
> iam nova progenies, caelo demittitur alto.
> Tu modo nascenti puero, quo ferrea primum
> desinet, ac toto surget gens aurea mundo,
> casta fave Lucina; tuus iam regnat Apollo—

"Now comes the final age [announced] in the Cumean [Sibyl's] chant; the great succession of epochs is born anew. Now the Virgin * returns, the reign of Saturn returns; now a new race descends from heaven on high. O chaste Lucina [goddess of births]! smile upon the boy just born, in whose time the race of iron shall first cease, and a race of gold shall arise throughout the world. Thine own Apollo is now king."

Ten years later these prophecies were fulfilled. The iron tools of war were laid aside; a new generation took charge, armed and infatuated with gold. Through the brief remainder of Virgil's life Rome would know no further turmoil; prosperity and happiness increased, and Augustus was hailed as a savior, though not an Apollo. The quasi-royal court welcomed the optimism of the poet's verse; Maecenas invited him, liked him, and saw in him a popular instrument of Octavian's reforms. This judgment showed insight; for to all appearances Virgil, now thirty-three, was an awkward rustic, shy to the point of stammering, shunning any public place where he might be recognized and pointed out, ill at ease in the voluble and aggressive fashionable society of Rome. Besides, even more than Octavian, he was an invalid, suffering from headaches, throat ailments, stomach disorders, and frequent spitting of blood. Virgil never married, and seems to have felt no more than his Aeneas the full abandon of love. Apparently he consoled himself for a time with the affection of a boy slave; for the rest he was known, at Naples, as "the virgin." [10]

Maecenas treated the youth generously, had Octavian restore his farm, and suggested to him some poems glorifying agricultural life. At that moment (37 B.C.) Italy was paying a penalty for letting so much of her soil go to pasturage, orchards, and vines; Sextus Pompey was blocking the import of food from Sicily and Africa, and a shortage of grain threatened another revolution. City life was enervating the young manhood of Italy; from every standpoint the health of the nation seemed to require the restoration of farming. Virgil readily agreed; he knew rural life; and though too frail now to bear its hardships, he was just the man to paint its attractive features with affectionate memory. He hid himself in Naples, and after seven years of file work emerged with his most perfect poems, the *Georgics* —literally "the labor of the land." Maecenas was delighted, and brought Virgil south with him to meet Octavian, then (29 B.C.) returning from his victory over Cleopatra. At the little town of Atella the weary general rested and listened for four enchanted days to the 2000 lines. They fell in with his policies more completely than even Maecenas had foreseen. For he proposed now to disband the larger part of the immense armies that had

---

* Astraea, or Justice, the last immortal to leave the earth in the legend of the Saturnian age.

won the world for him, to settle his veterans on the land, and at once to quiet them, feed the cities, and preserve the state, through rural toil. From that moment Virgil was free to think only of poetry.

In the *Georgics* a great artist deals with the noblest of the arts—the cultivation of the earth. Virgil borrows from Hesiod, Aratus. Cato Varro; but he transforms their rough prose or limping lines into finely chiseled verse. He covers dutifully the diverse branches of husbandry—the variety and treatment of soils, the seasons for sowing and reaping, the culture of the olive and the vine, the raising of cattle, horses, and sheep, and the care of bees. Every aspect of farming interests and beguiles him; he has to caution himself to get on;

> Sed fugit interea, fugit irreparabile tempus,
> Singula dum capti circum vectamur amore—[11]

"But meanwhile time flies, flies irreparably, while we, charmed with love [of our theme], linger around each single detail." He has a word about the diseases of animals and how to treat them. He describes the common farm animals with understanding and sympathy; he is never through admiring the simplicity of their instincts, the power of their passions, the perfection of their forms. He idealizes rural life, but he does not ignore the hardships and vicissitudes, the crippling toil, the endless struggle against insects, the torturing pendulum of drought and storm. Nevertheless, *labor omnia vincit;* [12] there is in such toil a purpose and result that give it dignity; no Roman need feel ashamed to guide a plow. Moral character, says Virgil, grows on the farm; all the old virtues that made Rome great were planted and nourished there; and hardly any process of seed sowing, protection, cultivation, weeding, and harvesting but has its counterpart in the development of the soul. And out of the fields, where the miracle of growth and the whims of the sky bespeak a thousand mystic forces, the soul, more readily than in the city, perceives the presence of creative life, and is deepened with religious intuition, humility, and reverence. Here Virgil breaks into his most famous lines, beginning with a noble echo of Lucretius, but passing into a pure Virgilian strain:

> Felix qui potuit rerum cognoscere causas,
> atque metus omnis et inexorabile fatum
> subiecit pedibus strepitumque Acherontis avari;
> fortunatus et ille deos qui novit agrestis,
> Panaque Silvanumque senem Nymphasque sorores—[13]

"Happy the man who has been able to learn the causes of things, and has put under foot all fear and inexorable fate, and the noise of a greedy Hell.

But happy too he who knows the rural deities, Pan and old Silvanus and the sister Nymphs." The peasant is right in seeking to propitiate the gods with sacrifice and enlist their good will; these exercises of piety brighten the round of toil with festivals and clothe earth and life with meaning, drama, and poetry.

Dryden considered the *Georgics* "the best poem of the best poet." [14] It shares with the *De Rerum Natura* the rare distinction of being at once didactic and beautiful. Rome did not take it seriously as a handbook of agriculture; we do not hear that anyone, having read it, exchanged the Forum for a farm; indeed, as Seneca thought, Virgil may have written these rural ecstasies precisely to please an urban taste. In any case, Augustus felt that Virgil had performed Maecenas' assignment marvelously well. He called the poet to his palace and suggested a harder task, a vastly larger theme.

III. THE *AENEID*

At first the plan was to sing the battles of Octavian.[15] But the supposed descent of his adoptive father from Venus and Aeneas led the poet—perhaps the Emperor—to conceive an epic on the founding of Rome. As the theme developed it came to include, by preview through prophecy, the expansion of Rome into the Augustan empire and peace. It would also show the role of Roman character in these achievements and seek to make the ancient virtues popular; it would picture its hero as reverent of the gods and guided by them, and would fall in with the Augustan reformation of morals and faith. Virgil retired to various lairs in Italy and spent the next ten years (29-19) on the *Aeneid*. He wrote slowly, with the devotion of a Flaubert, dictating a few lines in the fresh morning and rewriting them in the afternoon. Augustus waited impatiently for the poem's completion, repeatedly inquired about its progress, and importuned Virgil to bring him any finished fragment. Virgil put him off as long as he could, but finally read to him the second, fourth, and sixth books. Octavia, Antony's widow, fainted at the passage describing her son Marcellus, but lately dead.[16] The epic was never completed, never finally revised. In 19 B.C. Virgil visited Greece, met Augustus in Athens, was sunstruck in Megara, started home, and died soon after reaching Brundisium. On his deathbed he begged his friends to destroy the manuscript of his poem, saying that at least three years more would have been necessary to give it finished form. Augustus forbade them to carry out the request.

Every schoolboy knows the story of the *Aeneid*. As Troy burns, the ghost of the slain Hector appears to the leader of his Dardanian allies, the "pious Aeneas," and bids him resume from the Greeks the "holy things and household gods" of Troy—above all, the *Palladium*, or image of Pallas Athene, on the retention of which the preservation of the Trojans was believed to depend. "Seek for these" sacred symbols, says Hector, "the city which, when you have wandered over the sea, you shall at last establish." [17] Aeneas escapes with his old father Anchises and his son Ascanius. They set sail and stop at divers places; but always the voices of the gods command them to go on. Winds drive them ashore near Carthage, where a Phoenician princess, Dido, is founding a city. (When Virgil wrote this, Augustus was carrying out Caesar's plan for rebuilding Carthage.) Aeneas falls in love with her. A convenient storm enables them to take refuge in the same cave and to consummate what Dido considers their marriage. For a time Aeneas accepts her interpretation, and shares with her and his willing men the tasks of construction. But the relentless gods—who, in classic myth, never cared much for marriage—warn him to depart; this is not the capital that he must make. Aeneas obeys, and leaves the mourning queen with a theme song in his words:

> I will never deny, O Queen, that thou hast deserved of me the utmost thou canst set forth in speech. . . . I never held out the bridegroom's torch, nor took the marriage vow. . . . But now Apollo has bidden me sail. . . . Cease then to consume thyself and me with these complaints. Not of my own will do I seek Italy.[18]

Italiam non sponte sequor: this is the secret of the tale. We who, after eight centuries of sentimental literature, judge Virgil and his hero in its terms, attach far more significance to romantic love, and to extramarital relations, than did either Greece or Rome. Marriage was to the ancients a union of families rather than of bodies or souls; and the demands of religion or fatherland were placed above the rights or whim of the individual. Virgil treats Dido sympathetically, and rises to one of his finest passages in telling how she flings herself upon a funeral pyre and is burned alive; then he follows Aeneas to Italy.

Landing at Cumae, the Trojans march into Latium and are welcomed by its king, Latinus. His daughter Lavinia is betrothed to Turnus, the handsome chief of the neighboring Rutuli. Aeneas alienates her affection and her father; Turnus declares war upon him and Latium, and mighty battles ensue. To refresh and encourage Aeneas the Cumaean Sibyl takes him through the grotto of Lake Avernus into Tartarus. As Virgil writes an *Odyssey* of Aeneas' wanderings and a short *Iliad* of his wars, so now he takes a lead from Odysseus' tour of Hades, and becomes in turn an exemplar and guide for Dante. *Facilis descensus Averni*—"easy is the descent to Hell"—says Virgil; [19]

but his hero finds the way tortuous, and the lower world confusingly complex. There he meets Dido, who scorns his protestations of love; there he sees the varied torments with which earthly sin is punished and the prison house where suffer, Lucifer-like, rebellious demigods. Then the Sibyl takes him through mystic passages to the Blissful Groves where those who led good lives bask in green valleys and endless joys. His father Anchises, who has died en route, expounds to him here the Orphic doctrine of heaven, purgatory, and hell, and reveals to him in panoramic vision the future glory and heroes of Rome. In a later vision Venus shows him the battle of Actium and the triumphs of Augustus. His spirits revived, Aeneas returns to the living world, kills Turnus, and scatters death about him with epic hand. He marries the shadowy Lavinia, and when her father dies he inherits the throne of Latium. Soon afterward he falls in battle and is transported to the Elysian Fields. His son Ascanius or Iulus builds Alba Longa as the new capital of the Latin tribes, and thence his descendants Romulus and Remus go forth to establish Rome.

It seems unmannerly to criticize so gentle a soul as Virgil for all these grateful flatteries to his country and his Emperor, or to find flaws in a work that perhaps he had never wished to write and never lived to complete. Of course it imitates Greek models; so does practically all Roman literature except the satire and the essay. The battle scenes are weak echoes of the *Iliad*'s clanging frays, and Aurora rises as often as Homer's rosy-fingered Dawn. Naevius, Ennius, and Lucretius lend the poet episodes and phrases, sometimes whole lines; and Apollonius of Rhodes, through his *Argonautica*, provides a model for Dido's tragic love. Such borrowings were judged legitimate in Virgil's as in Shakespeare's days; all Mediterranean literature was viewed as the heritage and storehouse of every Mediterranean mind. The mythological background tires us, now that we are making our own; but these divine allusions and interpositions were familiar and pleasant even to skeptical readers of Roman poetry. We miss in the smooth epic of the ailing Virgil the torrential narrative of Homer, the life-and-blood reality that moves the giants of the *Iliad* or the homely folk of Ithaca. Virgil's story often lags, and his characters are almost all anemic except those whom Aeneas abandons or destroys. Dido is a living woman, gracious, subtle, passionate; Turnus is a simple and honest warrior, betrayed by Latinus, and doomed to an unmerited death by ridiculous gods. After ten cantos of cant we resent the "piety" of Aeneas, which leaves him no will of his own, excuses his treachery, and brings him success only by supernatural intervention. We do not enjoy the windy speeches with which he kills good men, adding a rhetorical boredom to that competitive perforation which is humanity's final test of truth.

To understand and appreciate the *Aeneid* we must at every turn remind ourselves that Virgil was writing not a romance, but a sacred scripture for Rome. Not that he offers any clear theology. The gods who pull the strings of his drama are as vicious as Homer's and not as humorously human; indeed, all the mischief and suffering in the story are caused not by men and women but by deities. Probably Virgil conceived these divinities as poetical machinery, symbols of tyrannous circumstance and disruptive chance; in general he oscillates between Jove and an impersonal Fate as the ruler of all things. He likes the gods of the village and the field better than those of Olympus; he loses no opportunity to commemorate them and describe their rites; and he wishes that his fellow men could recapture the *pietas*—the reverence toward parents, fatherland, and gods—which was nourished by that primeval rural creed. *Heu pietas! heu prisca fides!* he mourns—"alas for the old piety and faith!" But he rejects the traditional conception of a Hades in which all the dead bear alike a gloomy fate; he plays with Orphic and Pythagorean ideas of reincarnation and a future life, and makes as vivid as he can the notion of a rewarding heaven, a cleansing purgatory, and a punishing hell.

The real religion of the *Aeneid* is patriotism, and its greatest god is Rome. The destiny of Rome moves the plot, and all the tribulations of the tale find meaning in "the heavy task of establishing the Roman race"—*tantae molis erat Romanam condere gentem.* The poet is so proud of the Empire that he looks with no envy upon the superior culture of the Greeks. Let other peoples transform into living figures marble and bronze, and chart the courses of the stars:

> But thou, O Roman, must the peoples rule.
> Thine arts shall be to teach the ways of peace,
> To spare the humbled, and throw down the proud.[20]

Nor does Virgil resent the death of the Republic; he knows that class war, not Caesar, killed it; at every stage of his poem he foreshadows the restorative rule of Augustus, hails it as Saturn's reign returned, and promises him, as reward, admission to the company of the gods. No man ever fulfilled a literary commission more perfectly.

Why do we retain a warm affection for this pietistic, moralistic, chauvinistic, imperialistic propagandist? Partly because the gentleness of his spirit is on every page; because we feel that his sympathies have spread from his own fair Italy to all men, even to all life. He knows the sufferings of the lowly and the great, the obscene ghastliness of war, the brief mortality that stalks the noblest men, the griefs and pains, the *lacrimae rerum,* or "tears in things," that mar and accentuate the sunshine of our days. He is not merely imitating

Lucretius when he writes of "the nightingale mourning beneath the poplar's shade the loss of her young ones, whom some hard plowman has seen and torn unfledged from their nest; all night long she cries, and perched on a spray, renews her pitiful song, filling the woods with her sad lament." [21] But what draws us back to Virgil again and again is the persistent loveliness of his speech. It is not in vain that he pored over every line, "licking it into shape as the she-bear does her cubs"; [22] and only the reader who has tried to write can guess the toil that made this narrative so smooth and adorned it with so many passages of sonorous melody that every second page cries out for quotation, and tempts the tongue. Perhaps the poem is too uniformly beautiful; even beauty palls upon us if its eloquence is prolonged. There is a delicate feminine charm in Virgil, but seldom the masculine power and thought of Lucretius or the surging tide of that "many-billowed sea" called Homer. We begin to understand the melancholy ascribed to Virgil when we picture him preaching beliefs that he could never recapture, writing for ten years an epic whose every episode and line required the effort of artificial art, then dying with the haunting thought that he had failed, that no spark of spontaneity had set his imagination on fire or spurred his figures into life. But over his medium, if not over his subject, the poet won a complete victory. Artifice has seldom achieved a brighter miracle.

Two years after his death his executors gave the poem to the world. There were some detractors: one critic published an anthology of his defects, another listed his pilferings, another printed eight volumes of *Resemblances* between lines in Virgil and in earlier poetry.[23] But Rome soon forgave this literary communism. Horace ranked Virgil fondly with Homer, and schools inaugurated nineteen hundred years of memorizing the *Aeneid*. Plebeian and aristocrat mouthed him; artisans and shopkeepers, tombstones and scribbled walls, quoted him; temple oracles gave responses through ambiguous verses of his epic; the custom began—and lasted till the Renaissance— of opening Virgil at random and finding some counsel or prophecy in the first passage that struck the eye. His fame grew until in the Middle Ages he was considered a magician and a saint. Had he not, in the *Fourth Eclogue*, predicted the coming of the Saviour and, in the *Aeneid*, described Rome as the Holy City, from which the power of religion would uplift the world? Had he not in that terrible Book VI pictured the Last Judgment, the sufferings of the wicked, the cleansing fire of purgatory, the happiness of the blessed in paradise? Virgil too, like Plato, was *anima naturaliter Christiana*, despite his pagan gods. Dante loved the elegance of his verse, and took him as guide not only through hell and purgatory, but also in the art of flowing narrative and beautiful speech. Milton thought of him when writing *Paradise Lost* and the pompous orations of devils and men. And Voltaire, of whom we should have expected a harsher judgment, ranked the *Aeneid* as the finest literary monument left us by antiquity.[24]

IV. HORACE

One of the pleasantest pictures in the world of letters—where jealousy is only less rife than in love—is Virgil introducing Horace to Maecenas. The two poets had met in 40 B.C., when Virgil was thirty and Horace twenty-five. Virgil opened the doors of Maecenas to him a year later, and all three remained fast friends till death.

In 1935 Italy celebrated the two thousandth birthday of Quintus Horatius Flaccus. He was born in the little town of Venusia, in Apulia. His father was an ex-slave who had risen to the dignity of a tax collector—or, some said, a fishmonger.[25] Flaccus meant flap-eared; Horatius was probably the name of the master whom the father had served. Somehow the freedman prospered, sent Quintus to Rome for rhetoric, and to Athens for philosophy. There the youth joined the army of Brutus, and received command of a legion. It was *dulce et decorum pro patria mori*—"sweet and honorable to die for one's country"; [26] but Horace, who often imitated Archilochus, dropped his shield in the midst of battle and took to his heels. After the war was over he found himself shorn of all property and patrimony, and "bare-faced poverty drove me to writing verses." [27] Actually, however, he buttered his bread by being a quaestor's clerk.

He was short and stout, proud and shy, disliking the common crowd and yet not having the garb or means to move in circles whose education might equal his own. Too cautious to marry, he contented himself with courtesans who may have been real or may have been forms of poetic license invented to demonstrate maturity. He wrote of prostitutes with scholarly restraint and intricate prosody, and thought he deserved much for not seducing married women.[28] Too poor to ruin himself sexually, he took to books and composed Greek and Latin lyrics in the most recondite of Greek meters. Virgil saw one of these poems and praised it to Maecenas. The kindly epicure was complimented by Horace's stammering timidity and found a sly relish in his sophisticated thought. In 37 Maecenas took Virgil, Horace, and some others on a jaunt by canal boat, stagecoach, litter, and foot across Italy to Brundisium. Shortly afterward he introduced Horace to Octavian, who proposed that Horace should become his secretary. The poet excused himself, having no passion for work. In 34 Maecenas gave him a house and income-producing farm in the Sabine valley of Ustica, some forty-five miles from Rome. Horace was now free to live in the city or the country, and to write as authors dream of writing—with lazy leisure and laborious care.*

For a while he stayed in Rome, enjoying the life of an amused spectator of the hurrying world. He mingled with all ranks, studying the types that made up Rome, contemplating with clinical pleasure the follies and vices of the capital. He pictured some of these types in two books of *Satires* (34 and 30 B.C.) modeled at first on Lucilius and later in a milder and more tolerant strain. He called these poems *sermones*—not by any means sermons, but informal conversations, sometimes intimate dialogues, in almost colloquial hexameters; he confessed that they were prose in everything but meter, "for you would not call one a poet who writes, as I do, lines more akin to prose." In these racy verses we meet the living men and women of Rome and hear them talking as Romans talked: not the shepherds, peasants, and heroes of Virgil, nor the legendary lechers and heroines of Ovid, but the saucy slave, the vain poet, the pompous lecturer, the greedy philosopher, the gabbing bore, the eager Semite, the businessman, the statesman, the streetwalker: this at last, we feel, is Rome. With homicidal playfulness Horace lays down for the hunter of legacies the rules for success in that ghoulish game.[29] He laughs at the gourmets who feast on delicacies and limp with gout.[30] He reminds the *laudator temporis acti*—the "praiser of times past"—that "if some god were for taking you back to those days you would refuse every time"; [31] the chief charm of the past is that we know we need not live it again. He wonders, like Lucretius, at the restless souls who in the city long for the country, and there long for the city; who can never enjoy what they have because there is someone who has more; who, not content with their wives, hanker with too great and yet too little imagination for the charms of other women who have in turn become prose to other men. Money-madness, he concludes, is the basic disease of Rome. He asks the itching gold-seeker, "Why do you laugh at Tantalus, from whose thirsty lips the water always moves away? Change the name, and the story is about you": *mutato nomine, de te fabula narratur.*[32] He satirizes himself, too: he represents his slave telling him to his face that he, the moralist, is hot-tempered, never knows his own mind or purpose, and is the menial of his passions like anybody else. It is doubtless to himself, as well as to others, that he recommends the golden mean, *aurea mediocritas;* [33] *est modus in rebus,* he says—"there's a limit, a measure in things," [34] which the intelligent man will neither fall short of

---

* Horace's estate, unearthed in 1932, turned out to be a spacious mansion, 363 by 142 feet, with twenty-four rooms, three bathing pools, several mosaic floors, and a large formal garden surrounded by a covered and enclosed portico. Beyond this was an extensive farm, worked by eight slaves and five families of leasehold *coloni.*[28a]

nor exceed. In opening his second series of *Satires* he complains to a friend that the first group were criticized as too savage and too weak. He asks advice and is told, "Take a rest." "What?" the poet objects, "not write verses at all?" "Yes." "But I can't sleep." [35]

He would have done well to take the advice for a time. His next publication, the *Epodes*, or "Refrains" (29 B.C.), is the least worthy of his works: harsh and coarse, ungenerous, tastelessly and bisexually obscene, forgivable only as an experiment in the iambic meters of Archilochus. Perhaps his disgust with the "smoke and wealth and noise of Rome" [36] had mounted to bitterness; he could not bear the pressure of the "ignorant and evil-thinking crowd." He pictures himself jostled and jostling in the human flotsam of the capital, and cries out: "O rural home! when shall I behold you? When shall I be able, now with the books of the ancients, now with sleep and idle hours, to quaff sweet forgetfulness of life's cares? When will beans, the very brethren of Pythagoras, be served to me, and greens well larded with fat bacon? O nights and feasts divine!" [37] His stays in Rome became shorter; he spent so much time in his Sabine villa that his friends, even Maecenas, complained that he had cut them out of his life. After the heat and dust of the city he found the pure air, the peaceful routine, and the simple workmen on his farm a cleansing delight. His health was poor, and like Augustus he lived for the most part on a vegetarian diet. "My stream of pure water, my few acres of woodland, my sure trust in a crop of corn, bring me more blessing than the lot of the dazzling lord of fertile Africa." [39] In him, as in the other Augustan poets, the love of country life finds a warm expression rare in the literature of Greece. *Beatus ille qui procul negotiis*—

> Happy is he who far from business cares,
>   Even as the oldest race of men,
> Tills with his own oxen his patrimonial fields,
>   Freed from every debt. . . .
> How sweet it is to lie under the ancient ilex tree,
>   Or on the matted grass,
> While the stream flows on between high banks,
>   And the woodland birds sing,
> And springs with leaping waters plash,
>   Inviting to soft sleep! [40]

It should be added, however, that these lines are put with Horatian irony into the mouth of a city moneylender, who, having uttered them, at once forgets them and loses himself in his coins.

Probably it was in those quiet haunts that he labored with "painstaking happiness"—*curiosa felicitas* *—over those odes by which he knew that his name would live or die. He was tired of hexameters, the endless march of their measured feet, the sharp caesura cleaving the line like some inexorable guillotine. He had enjoyed in his youth the subtle and vivacious meters of Sappho, Alcaeus, Archilochus, and Anacreon; he proposed now to transplant these "sapphics" and "alcaics," these iambics and hendecasyllabics, into Roman lyric form, to express his thoughts on love and wine, religion and the state, life and death, in stanzas refreshingly new, epigrammatically compact, modeled for music, and teasing the mind with the complex skein of their weaving. He did not intend them for simple or hurried souls; indeed, he warned such away by the bluenosed opening of the third group:

> Odi profanum vulgus et arceo.
> Favete linguis. Carmina non prius
>   audita Musarum sacerdos
>   virginibus puerisque canto:—

"I hate and shun the profane crowd. Be silent! I, priest of the Muses, sing for maidens and youths songs never heard before."

The maidens, if they had cared to tread and skip their way through Horace's playful inversions of speech and desire, might have been pleasantly shocked by the chiseled epicureanism of these odes. The poet pictures the pleasures of friendship, eating and drinking, and making love; one would hardly surmise from such lauds that their author was a recluse who ate little and drank less. Why disturb ourselves with Roman politics and distant wars? he asks (anticipating the reader of these pages). Why plan so carefully a future whose shape will laugh at our plans? Youth and beauty touch us and flit away; let us enjoy them now, "reclining under the pine trees, our gray locks garlanded with roses and perfumed with Syrian nard." [42] Even as we speak, envious time runs out; seize the occasion, *carpe diem*, "snatch the day." [43] He intones a litany of loose ladies whom he claims to have loved: Lalage, Glycera, Neaera, Inacha, Cinara, Candia, Lyce, Pyrrha, Lydia, Tyndaris, Chloe, Phyllis, Myrtale. We need not believe all his protestations of guilt; these were literary exercises almost compulsory among the poets of the day; the same ladies or names had served other pens. The now virtuous Augustus was not deceived by these iambic fornications; he was pleased to find, among them, stately praises of his reign, his victories, his aides, his moral reforms, and the Augustan peace. Horace's famous drinking song—*Nunc est bibendum* [44]—was composed on receipt of the news that Cleopatra was dead and Egypt taken; even his sophisticated soul thrilled at the thought of

---

* This is the curious and happy phrase applied to Horace by Petronius.[41]

the Empire victorious and expanding as never before. He warned his readers
that new laws could not take the place of old morals; mourned the spread
of luxury and adultery, of frivolity and cynical unbelief. "Alas!" he says,
referring to the latest war, "the shame of our scars and crimes, and of
brothers slain! What have we of this hard generatioɩ shrunk from? What
iniquity have we left untouched?" [45] Nothing could save Rome but a
return to the simplicity and steadfastness of ancient ways. The skeptic who
found it difficult to believe anything bent his hoary head before the ancient
altars, acknowledged that without a myth the people perish, and lent his
pen graciously to the ailing gods.

There is nothing in the world's literature quite like these poems—delicate
and yet powerful, exquisite and masculine, subtle and intricate, hiding their
art with perfect art, and their toil with seeming ease. This is music in another
scale than Virgil's, less melodious and more intellectual, meant not for youths
and maidens but for artists and philosophers. There is rarely any passion
here, or enthusiasm, or "fine writing"; the diction is simple even where the
sentence stands on its head. But in the greater odes there is a pride and
majesty of thought, as if an emperor were speaking and not in letters but
in bronze:

> Exegi monumentum aere perennius
> regalique situ pyramidum altius,
> quod non imber edax, non Aquilo impotens
> possit diruere, aut innumerabilis
> annorum series et fuga temporum.
> Non omnis moriar.[46]

> I have raised a monument more lasting than bronze,
> Loftier than the royal peak of pyramids;
> No biting storm can bring it down,
> No impotent north wind, nor the unnumbered series
> Of the years, nor the swift course of time.
> I shall not wholly die.

The slandered crowd ignored the *Odes*, the critics denounced them as
tiresome artifice, the puritans declaimed against the songs of love. Augustus
pronounced the poems immortal, asked for a fourth group that would celebrate the exploits of Drusus and Tiberius in Germany, and chose Horace
to write the *carmen saeculare* for the Secular Games. Horace complied, but
without inspiration. The effort of the *Odes* had exhausted him. In his final
work he relaxed into the conversational hexameters of the *Satires*, and wrote
his *Epistles* as from an easy chair. He had always wanted to be a philosopher;
now he abandoned himself to wisdom, even while remaining a *causeur*. Since

a philosopher is a dead poet and a dying theologian, Horace, old at forty-five, was ripe to discuss God and man, morals and literature and art.

The most famous of these letters, named by later critics "The Art of Poetry," was addressed *Ad Pisones*—to some uncertain members of the Piso clan; it was no formal treatise, but a bit of friendly advice on how to write. Choose a subject suited to your powers, Horace says; beware of laboring like a mountain and producing a mouse.[47] The ideal book is that which at the same time instructs and entertains; "he who has mingled the useful with the pleasant wins every vote"—*omne tulit punctum qui miscuit utile dulci.*[48] Avoid words that are new, obsolete, or "sesquipedalian"—foot-and-a-half words. Be as brief as clarity allows. Go straight to the heart of the matter—in *medias res*. In writing poetry do not imagine that emotion is everything. It is true that you must feel an emotion yourself if you wish the reader to feel it (*si vis me flere, dolendum est primum ipsi tibi*).[49] But art is not feeling; it is form (here again is the challenge of the classic to the romantic style).* To achieve form, study the Greeks day and night; erase almost as much as you write; delete every "purple patch" (*purpureus pannus*); submit your work to a competent critic, and beware of your friends. If it survives all this, put it away for eight years; if then you do not perceive the uses of oblivion, publish it, but remember that it can never be recalled except by time: *verba volant, scripta manent*. If you write drama let the action, not your words, tell the story and delineate the characters. Do not represent horror on the stage. Obey the unities of action, time, and place: let the story be one and occur within a brief time in one place. Study life and philosophy, for without observation and understanding even a perfect style is an empty thing. *Sapere aude:* dare to know.

Horace himself had obeyed all these precepts but one—he had not learned to weep. Because his feelings were too thin, or had been stifled into silence, he seldom rose to the high art that gives form to sincere sympathy, or to "emotion remembered in tranquillity." He was too urbane. *Nil admirari*, "to marvel at nothing," [50] was poor advice; to the poet everything should be a miracle, even when, like the sunrise or a tree, it greets him every day. Horace observed life, but not too deeply; he studied philosophy, but kept so persistently an "even mind" [51] that only his *Odes* rise above a "golden mediocrity." [52] He honored virtue like a Stoic, and respected pleasure like an Epicurean. "Who, then, is free?" he asks, and answers, like Zeno, "The wise man, he who is lord over himself, whom neither poverty nor death

---

* Almost neglected in the Middle Ages, Horace came into his own in the seventeenth and eighteenth centuries, the age of modern classicism, when every statesman and pamphleteer, above all in England, turned the poet's phrases into prose clichés. Boileau's *L'Art poétique* revived Horace's *Ad Pisones* and formed and chilled the French drama till Hugo; Pope's *Essay on Criticism* attempted a similar refrigeration in England, but was thawed by Byron's fire.

nor bonds affright, who defies his passions, scorns ambition, and is in himself a whole." [53] One of his noblest poems sings a Stoic strain:

Iustum et tenacem propositi virum
si fractus inlabatur orbis
impavidum ferient ruinae—

"If a man is just and resolute, the whole world may break and fall upon him and find him, in the ruins, undismayed." [54] But despite all this he calls himself, with engaging honesty, "a pig from Epicurus' sty." [55] Like Epicurus he placed more store on friendship than on love; like Virgil he lauded the reforms of Augustus, and remained a bachelor. He did his best to preach religion, but he had none. Death, he felt, ends all. [56]

His last days were clouded with this thought. He had his share of pains— stomach trouble, rheumatism, and much else. "The years as they pass," he mourned, "rob us of all joys, one by one." [57] And to another friend: "Alas, O Postumus, the fleeting years slip by; nor shall piety hold back our wrinkles, or pressing age, or indomitable death." [58] He recalled how, in his first satire, he had hoped, when his time came, to quit life contentedly, "like a guest who has had his fill." [59] Now he told himself: "You have played enough, eaten enough, drunk enough; it is time for you to go." [60] Fifteen years have passed since he had told Maecenas that he would not long survive the financier. [61] In 8 B.C. Maecenas died, and a few months later Horace followed him. He left his property to the Emperor, and was laid to rest near Maecenas' tomb.

V. LIVY

Augustan prose achieved no triumphs equal to those of Augustan verse. Oratory subsided as the making of laws and decisions passed in reality if not in form from Senate and assemblies to the secret chambers of the prince. Scholarship continued its quiet course, sheltered from present storms by its ghostly interests. It was only in the writing of history that the age achieved a masterpiece in prose.

Born in Patavium (Padua) in 59, Titus Livius came to the capital, devoted himself to rhetoric and philosophy, and gave the last forty years of his life (23 B.C.–A.D. 17) to writing a history of Rome. That is all we know of him; "Rome's historian has no history." [63] Like Virgil he came from the region of the Po, retained the old virtues of simplicity and piety, and— perhaps through the pathos of distance—developed a passionate reverence for the Eternal City. His work was planned on a majestic scale and was completed; of its 142 "books" only thirty-five have come down to us; as these fill six volumes we may judge the magnitude of the whole. Apparently it was published in parts, each with a separate title, and all under the general heading, *Ab urbe condita*—"From the city's foundation." Augustus could forgive its republican sentiments and heroes, since its religious, moral, and patriotic tone accorded well with the Emperor's policies. He took Livy into his friendship and encouraged him as a prose Virgil who was beginning where the poet had left off. Halfway on his long journey from 753 to 9 B.C., Livy thought of stopping, on the ground that he had already won lasting fame; he went on, he says, because he found himself restless when he ceased to write.[64]

Roman historians looked upon history as a hybrid child of rhetoric and philosophy: if we may believe them, they wrote to illustrate ethical precepts with eloquent narrative—to adorn a moral with a tale. Livy was trained as an orator; finding oratory censured and dangerous, "he took to history," says Taine, "so that he could still be an orator." [65] He began with a stern preface, denouncing the immorality, luxury, and effeminacy of the age; he buried himself in the past, he tells us, to forget the evils of his time, "when we can bear neither our diseases nor their remedies." He would set forth, through history, the virtues that had made Rome great—the unity and holiness of family life, the *pietas* of children, the sacred relation of men with the gods at every step, the sanctity of the solemnly pledged word, the stoic self-control and *gravitas*. He would make that stoic Rome so noble that its conquest of the Mediterranean would appear as a moral imperative, a divine order and law cast over the chaos of the East and the barbarism of the West. Polybius had ascribed Rome's triumph to its form of government; Livy would make it a corollary of the Roman character.

The chief faults of his work derive from this moral intent. He gives many signs of being privately a rationalist; but his respect for religion is so great that he accepts almost any superstition, and litters his pages with omens, portents, and oracles, until we feel that here too, as in Virgil, the real actors are the gods. He expresses his doubts concerning the myths of early Rome; he gives the less credible ones with a smile; but as he goes on he ceases to distinguish legend from history, follows his predecessors with scant discrimination, and accepts at their face value the laudatory romances that earlier historians had composed to ennoble their ancestry.[66] He rarely consults original sources or monuments, and never bothers to visit the scene of an action. Sometimes he paraphrases Polybius for pages.[67] He adopts the old priestly method of annals, narrating events by consulates; consequently there is in him, aside from his moral theme, no tracing of causes, but only a succession of brilliant episodes. He makes no distinction between the rude *patres* of the early Republic and the aristocracy of his day, nor between the virile plebs that had created Roman democracy and the venal mob that had destroyed it. His prejudices are always patrician.

The patriotic pride that makes Rome forever right in Livy was the secret of his greatness. It gave him an enduring happiness in his long toil; seldom has any writer executed so vast a plan so faithfully. It gave his readers, and still gives us, a sense of Rome's grandeur and destiny. This imperial consciousness contributed to the energy of Livy's style, the vigor of his characterizations, the brilliance and power of his descriptions, the majestic march of his prose. The invented speeches in which his history abounds are masterpieces of oratory, and became models for the schools. The charm of good manners pervades the work: Livy never shouts, never severely condemns; his sympathy is broader than his scholarship and deeper than his thought. It fails him forgivably when he comes to Hannibal; but he atones with a sweep and splendor of narrative that reaches its zenith in describing the Second Punic War.

His readers did not mind his inaccuracies or his bias. They liked his style and story, and gloried in the vivid picture that he had drawn of their past. They took the *Ab urbe condita* as a prose epic, one of the noblest monuments of the Augustan age and mood. From that time onward it was Livy's book that would color for eighteen centuries men's conception of Rome's history and character. Even readers in subject lands were impressed by this massive record of unprecedented conquests and titanic deeds. The younger Pliny tells of a Spaniard who was so moved by Livy's work that he traveled from far Cádiz to Rome in the hope of seeing him. Having accomplished his purpose and tendered his worship, he neglected other sights and returned content to his Atlantic home.[68]

VI. THE AMOROUS REVOLT

Meanwhile poetry continued to flourish, but not quite on the lines of Augustus' desire. Only supreme artists like Virgil or Horace can produce good verse to governmental specifications; greater men would refuse, lesser men are unable to comply. Of the three major sources of poetry—religion, nature, love—two had been brought under imperial sway; the third remained lawless, even in Horace's *Odes*. Now, mildly in Tibullus and Propertius, recklessly in Ovid, poetry escaped from the bureau of propaganda and staged a rebellion that proceeded with mounting gaiety to a tragic end.

Albius Tibullus (54-19), like Virgil, lost his ancestral lands when the Civil War reached the little town of Pedum—near Tibur—that had seen his birth. Messala rescued him from poverty and took him in his train to the East, but Tibullus fell ill on the way and returned to Rome. He was happy to be free from war and politics; now he could give himself to genderless love and the polishing of elegiac verse in the manner of the Alexandrian Greeks. To Delia (otherwise unknown, and perhaps one name for many) he addressed the usual supplications, "sitting like a gatekeeper [*ianitor*] before her stubborn doors" [69] and reminding her, as so many maids have been reminded, that youth comes but once and soon steals away. It did not disturb him that Delia was married; he put the husband to sleep with undiluted wine—but fumed when her new lover played the same trick upon him.[70] These ancient themes might not have harassed Augustus; what made Tibullus, Propertius, and Ovid really disagreeable to a government that was finding it hard to enlist recruits for the army was the persuasive anti-militarism of this love-loose set. Tibullus laughs at warriors who forage for death when they might have been seducing women. He mourns for the age of Saturn, when, he imagines,

> there were no armies, no hatred, and no war. . . . There was no war when men drank from wooden cups. . . . Give me but love, and let others go to war. . . . The hero is he whom, when his children have been begotten, old age overtakes in his humble cottage. He follows his sheep, his son follows the lambs, while the good wife heats the water for his weary limbs. So let me live till the white hairs glisten on my head, and I tell in my old man's fashion of the days gone by.[71]

Sextus Propertius (49-15) sang less simply and tenderly, and with more learned ornaments, the same idyl of peaceful lechery. Born in Umbria, educated in Rome, he soon lapsed into verse; and though few readers could fetch his thought from the wells of his pedantry, Maecenas took him into his circle on the Esquiline. He describes with pride and pleasure the dinners there on the banks of the Tiber, when he would drink the wine of Lesbos in cups chiseled by great artists, and, "seated as on a throne amid merry women," would watch the vessels gliding by on the river below.[72] To please his patron and his prince Propertius now and then plucked his lyre in praise of war; but to his mistress Cynthia he sang another tune: "Why should I raise sons for Parthian triumphs? No child of ours shall be a soldier." [73] Not all the martial glory in the world, he assured her, could equal one night with Cynthia.[74]

Of all these epicureans, light of heart and head, who spent their lives climbing and descending the mount of Venus, Publius Ovidius Naso was the happy model and poet laureate. Sulmo (Soloma) saw his birth (43 B.C.) in a pleasant valley of the Apennines some ninety miles east of Rome; how beautiful, from the cold exile of his later years, would seem Sulmo's vineyards, olive groves, cornfields, and streams! His rich middle-class father sent him to Rome to study law, and was shocked to hear that the boy wished to be a poet; he held up to the lad the awful fate of Homer, who, according to the best authorities, had died blind and poor. So warned, Ovid managed to rise to the post of a judge in the praetorial courts. Then, to his father's dismay, he refused to run for the quaestorship (from which he would have emerged a senator), and retired to the cultivation of literature and love. He pleaded that he could not help being a poet; "I lisped in numbers and the numbers came." [75]

Ovid traveled leisurely to Athens, the Near East, and Sicily, and, returning, joined the loosest circles in the capital. Possessed of charm, wit, education, and money, he was able to open all doors. He married twice in early manhood, was twice divorced, and then grazed for a time in public pastures. "Let the past please others," he sang; "I congratulate myself on being born into this age, whose morals are so congenial to my own." [76] He laughed at the *Aeneid*, and merely concluded from it that since the son of Venus had founded Rome, it should, if only out of piety, become the city of love. [77] He lost his head to a pretty courtesan, whose anonymity or multiplicity he hides under the name of Corinna. His racy couplets about her had no trouble in finding a publisher; under the title of *Amores* they were soon (14 B.C.) on the lips and lyres of youthful Rome. "On every hand people want to know who is this Corinna that I sing about." [78] He mystified them, in a second series of *Amores*, by writing a pronunciamento of promiscuity:

> It is no fixed beauty that calls my passion forth; there are a hundred
> causes to keep me always in love. If it is some fair one with modest
> eyes downcast upon her lap, I am aflame, and her innocence is my en-
> snaring; if it is some saucy jade, I am smitten because she is not rustic
> simple, and gives me hope of enjoying her supple embrace on the
> soft couch. If she seems austere, and affects the rigid Sabine dame, I
> judge she would yield, but is deep in her conceit. If you are versed in
> books you win me by your rare accomplishments. . . . One treads
> softly, and I fall in love with her step; another is hard, but can be
> softened by the touch of love. Because this one sings sweetly . . . I
> would snatch kisses as she sings; this other runs with nimble fingers
> over the complaining strings—who could but fall in love with such
> cunning hands? Another takes me by her movement, swaying her
> arms in rhythm and curving her tender side with supple art—to say
> naught of myself, who take fire from every cause; put Hippolytus in
> my place, and he will be Priapus! . . . Tall and short are after the
> wish of my heart; I am undone by both. . . . My love is candidate
> for the favors of them all. [79]

Ovid apologizes for not chanting the glory of war; Cupid came and stole a foot from his verse and left it lame.[80] He wrote a lost play, *Medea*, which was well received, but for the most part he preferred "the slothful shade of Venus," and was content to be called "the well-known singer of his worthless ways." [81] Here are the lays of the troubadours a thousand years beforetime, addressed like them to married ladies, and making flirtation the main business of life. Ovid instructs Corinna how to communicate with him by signs as she lies on her husband's couch.[82] He assures her of his eternal fidelity, his strictly monogamous adultery: "I am no fickle philanderer, not one of those who love a hundred women at a time." At last he wins her and intones a paean of victory. He commends her for having denied him so long, and advises her to deny him again, now and then, so that he may love her forever. He quarrels with her, strikes her, repents, laments, and loves her more madly than before. Romeo-like he begs the dawn to delay, and hopes some blessed wind will break the axle of Aurora's car. Corinna deceives him in his turn, and he is furious on finding that she holds her favors insufficiently rewarded by the homage of his verse. She kisses him into forgiveness, but he cannot pardon the new skill of her loving; some other master has been teaching her.[83] A few pages later he is "in love with two maids at once, each beautiful, each tasteful in dress and accomplishment." [84] Soon, he fears, his simultaneous duties will undo him; but he will be happy to die on the field of love.[85]

These poems were tolerantly received by Roman society four years after the passing of the Julian reform laws. Great Senatorial families like the Fabii, the Corvini, the Pomponii continued to entertain Ovid in their homes. Buoyant with success, the poet issued a manual of seduction called *Ars amatoria* (2 B.C.). "I have been appointed by Venus," he says, "as tutor to tender love." [86] He chastely warns readers that his precepts must be applied only to courtesans and slaves; but his pictures of whispered confidences, secret assignations, billets-doux, raillery and wit, deceived husbands, and resourceful handmaids suggest the middle and upper classes of Rome. Lest his lessons should prove too apt, he added another treatise, *Remedia amoris*, on curing love. The best remedy is hard work; next, hunting; third, absence; "it is also useful to surprise your lady in the morning, before she has completed her toilette." [90] Finally, to make the balance even, he wrote *De medicamina faciei feminineae*, a metrical manual of cosmetics, pilfered from the Greeks. These little volumes sold so well that Ovid soared to heights of insolent fame. "So long as I am celebrated all the world over, it matters not to me what one or two pettifoggers say about me." [91] He did not know that one of these pettifoggers was Augustus, that the Prince resented his poems as an insult to the Julian laws, and would not forget the insult when imperial scandal should touch the poet's careless head.

About the third year of our era Ovid married a third time. His new wife belonged to one of the most distinguished families in Rome. Now forty-six, the poet settled down to domestic life and seems to have lived in mutual faith and happiness with Fabia. Age did to him what law could not; it cooled his fires and made his poetry respectable. In the *Heroides* he told again the love stories of famous women—Penelope, Phaedra, Dido, Ariadne, Sappho, Helen, Hero; told them, perhaps, at too great length, for repetition can make even love a bore. Startling, however, is a sentence in which Phaedra expresses Ovid's philosophy: "Jove decreed that virtue is whatever brings us pleasure." [92] About A.D. 7 the poet published his greatest work, the *Metamorphoses*. These fifteen "books" recounted in engaging hexameters the renowned transformations of inanimate objects, animals, mortals, and gods. Since almost everything in Greek and Roman legend changed its form, the scheme permitted Ovid to range through the whole realm of classical mythology from the creation of the world to the deification of Caesar. These are the old tales that until a generation ago were *de rigueur* in every college, and whose memory has not yet been erased by the revolution of our time: Phaëthon's chariot, Pyramus and Thisbe, Perseus and Andromeda, the Rape of Proserpine, Arethusa, Medea, Daedalus and Icarus, Baucis and Philemon, Orpheus and Eurydice, Atalanta, Venus and Adonis, and many more; here is the treasury from which a hundred thousand poems, paintings, and statues have taken their themes. If one must still learn the old myths there is no more painless way than by reading this kaleidoscope of men and gods— stories told with skeptical humor and amorous bent, and worked up with such patient art as no mere trifler could ever have achieved. Little wonder that at the end the confident poet announced his own immortality: *per saecula omnia vivam*—"I shall live forever."

He had hardly written the words when news came that Augustus had banished him to cold and barbarous Tomi on the Black Sea—even today unalluring as Constanta. It was a blow for which the poet, rounding fifty-one, was wholly unprepared. He had just composed, toward the close of the *Metamorphoses*, an elegant tribute to the Emperor, whose statesmanship he now recognized as the source of that peace, security, and luxury which Ovid's generation had enjoyed. He had half completed, under the title of *Fasti*, an almost pious poem celebrating the religious feasts of the Roman year. In these verses he was on the way to making an epic out of a calendar, for he applied to the tales of the old religion, and to the honoring of its shrines and gods, the same lucid facility, delicacy of word and phrase, and even flow of racy narrative that he had devoted to Greek mythology and

Roman love. He had hoped to dedicate the work to Augustus as a contribution to the religious restoration and as an apologetic palinode to the faith he once had scorned.

The Emperor gave no reason for his edict, and no one today can fathom its causes confidently. He offered some hint, however, by at the same time banishing his granddaughter Julia, and ordering that Ovid's works should be removed from the public libraries. The poet had apparently played some role in Julia's misconduct—whether as witness, accomplice, or principal. He himself declared that he was punished for "an error" and his poems, and implied that he had been the unwilling observer of some indecent scene.[93] He was given the remaining months of the year (A.D. 8) to arrange his affairs. The decree was *relegatio*, softer than exile in allowing him to retain his property, harsher in commanding him to stay in one city. He burned his manuscripts of the *Metamorphoses*, but some readers had made copies, and preserved them. Most of his friends avoided him;[94] a few dared the lightning by staying with him till his departure; and his wife, who remained behind at his bidding, supported him with affection and loyalty. Otherwise Rome took no notice as the bard of its joys sailed out of Ostia on the long voyage from everything that he had loved. The sea was rough nearly all the days of that trip, and the poet thought once that the waves would engulf the vessel. When he saw Tomi he regretted that he had survived, and gave himself over to grief.

On the voyage he had begun those verses which we know as *Tristia*, "Sorrows." Now he continued them, and sent them to his wife, his daughter, his stepdaughter, and his friends. Probably the sensitive Roman exaggerated the horrors of his new home: a treeless rock where nothing would grow, and yet shut out from the sun by the Euxine mists; the cold so bitter that in some years the snow remained all summer long; the Black Sea stiff with ice through gloomy winters, and the Danube so frozen that it offered no bar to the raids of hinterland barbarians upon the city's mixture of knife-wearing Getae and half-breed Greeks. When he thought of Roman skies and Sulmo's fields his heart broke, and his poetry, still beautiful in form and phrase, took on a depth of feeling that it had never fathomed before.

These *Tristia*, and the poetic letters to his friends *Ex Ponto*—"From the Pontus" or Black Sea—have nearly all the charms of his greater works. A simple vocabulary that made him a pleasure even in school, scenes vividly realized by insight and imagery, characters brought to life by touches of psychological subtlety, phrases compact with experience or thought,* an

---

* E.g., *video meliora proboque, deteriora sequor*—"I see and approve the better, I follow the worse"; *est deus in nobis agitante calescimus illo*—"there is a god in us, and by his action we have the warmth of life."

unfailing grace of speech and flowing ease of line: all these stayed with him in his exile, attended by a seriousness and tenderness whose absence makes the earlier poems unworthy of a man. Strength of character never came to him; as once he had spoiled his verse with superficial sensuality, so now he flooded his lines with tears and suppliant adulation of the Prince.

He envied these poems which could go to Rome. "Go, my book, and in my name greet the places I love" and "the dear soil of my native land";[95] perhaps, he tells it, some brave friend will hand it to a relenting emperor. In every letter he still hopes for pardon, or pleads for at least some milder home. He thinks each day of his wife and calls her name in the night; he prays that he may kiss her whitened hairs before he dies.[96] But no pardon came. After nine years of exile the broken man of sixty welcomed death. His bones, as he had begged, were brought to Italy and buried near the capital.

His prediction of lasting fame was justified by time. His hold on the Middle Ages rivaled Virgil's; his *Metamorphoses* and *Heroides* became rich sources of medieval romance; Boccaccio and Tasso, Chaucer and Spenser, drew upon him without stint; and the painters of the Renaissance had a treasure trove of subjects in his sensuous verse. He was the great romanticist of a classic age.

With his passing ended one of the great flowering epochs in the history of letters. The Augustan was not a supreme literary age, like the Periclean or Elizabethan; even at its best there is in its prose a pompous rhetoric, and in its verse a formal perfection, that seldom come from soul to soul. We find no Aeschylus here, no Euripides, no Socrates, not even a Lucretius or a Cicero. Imperial patronage inspired and nourished, repressed and narrowed, the literature of Rome. An aristocratic age—like that of Augustus, or Louis XIV, or eighteenth-century England—exalts moderation and good taste and tends in letters to a "classic" style in which reason and form dominate feeling and life. Such literature is more finished and less powerful, more mature and less influential, than the literature of passionately creative periods or minds. But within the classic range this age deserved the compliment of its name. Never had sober judgment found expression in such perfect art; even the madcap revelry of Ovid was cooled into a classic mold. In him and Virgil and Horace the Latin language as a poetic medium reached its zenith. It would never be so rich and resonant, so subtle and compact, so pliant and melodious again.

CHAPTER XIII

The Other Side of Monarchy

A.D. 14-96*

I. TIBERIUS

WHEN great men stoop to sentiment the world grows fonder of them; but when sentiment governs policy empires totter. Augustus had chosen Tiberius wisely, but too late. When Tiberius was saving the state with patient generalship the Emperor had almost loved him. "Farewell," one of his letters ended, "most agreeable of men . . . most valiant of men, most conscientious of commanders." [1] Then the pathos of propinquity blinded Augustus, as later Aurelius; he set Tiberius aside for his pretty grandsons; compelled him to renounce a fortunate marriage to become the cuckold of Julia; resented his resentment, and let him grow old with philosophy in Rhodes. When at last Tiberius reached the principate he was already fifty-five, a disillusioned misanthrope who found no happiness in power.

To understand him we must remember that he was a Claudian; with him began the Claudian branch of that Julio-Claudian dynasty which ended with Nero. Through both parents he inherited the proudest blood in Italy, the narrowest prejudices, the strongest will. He was tall, powerful, and well featured; but acne accentuated his shyness, his awkward manners, his moody diffidence, and his love of seclusion.[2] The fine head of Tiberius in the Boston Museum shows him as a young priest, with broad forehead, large deep eyes, and pensive countenance; he was so serious in youth that wags called him "the old man." He received all the education that Rome, Greece, environment, and responsibility could afford; he learned the two classic languages and literatures well, wrote lyrics, dabbled in astrology, and "neglected the gods." [3] He loved his brother Drusus despite the young man's superior popularity; he was a devoted husband to Vipsania, and so generous to his friends that they could safely give him presents in the expectation of a fourfold return. The severest as well as the ablest general of his time, he gained the admiration and affection of his soldiers because he watched over

---

* All further dates will be A.D. unless otherwise noted.

every detail of their welfare, and won his battles by strategy rather than by blood.

His virtues ruined him. He believed the stories told about the *mos maiorum*, and wished to see the stern qualities of old Rome reborn in the new Babylon; he approved the moral reforms of Augustus and made clear his intention to enforce them. He had no liking for the ethnic farrago that steamed in the caldron of Rome; he gave it bread but no circuses, and offended it by not attending the games presented by rich men. He was convinced that Rome could be saved from a vulgar degeneration only by an aristocracy stoic in conduct and refined in taste. But the aristocracy could no more than the people bear his "stiff neck" and sober countenance, his long silences and slow speech, his visible awareness of his own excellence, and, worst of all, his grim husbanding of the public funds. He had been misborn a stoic in an epicurean age, and he was too coldly honest to learn Seneca's art of preaching the one doctrine in beautiful language and practicing the other with graceful constancy.

Four weeks after the death of Augustus, Tiberius appeared before the Senate and asked it to restore the Republic. He was unfit, he told them, to rule so vast a state; "in a city so well provided with men of illustrious character . . . the several departments of public business could be better filled by a coalition of the best and ablest citizens." [4] Not daring to take him at his word, the Senate exchanged bows with him until at last he accepted power "as a wretched and burdensome slavery," and in the hope that someday the Senate would permit him to retire to privacy and freedom.[5] The play was well acted on both sides. Tiberius wanted the principate, or he would have found some way to evade it; the Senate feared and hated him, but shrank from re-establishing a republic based, like the old, upon theoretically sovereign assemblies. It wanted less democracy, not more; and it was pleased when Tiberius (A.D. 14) persuaded it to take over from the *comitia centuriata* the power of choosing the public officials. The citizens complained for a time, mourning the loss of the sums they had received for their votes. The only political power now left to the common man was the right of electing the emperor by assassination. After Tiberius democracy passed from the assemblies to the army, and voted with the sword.

He seems to have sincerely disliked monarchy and to have considered himself the administrative head and arm of the Senate. He refused all titles that savored of royalty, contented himself with that of *princeps senatus*, stopped all efforts to deify him or offer worship to his *genius*, and made evident his distaste for flattery. When the Senate wished to name a month after him, as it had done for Caesar and Augustus, he turned the compliment aside with dry humor: "What will you do if there should be thirteen

Caesars?" [6] * He rejected a proposal that he should revise the Senatorial list. Nothing could surpass his courtesy to this ancient "assembly of kings"; he attended its meetings, referred "even the smallest matters" to its judgment, sat and spoke as merely a member, was often in the minority, and made no protest when decrees were passed contrary to his expressed opinion.[7] "He was self-contained and patient," according to Suetonius, "in the face of abuse, slander, and lampoons against himself and his family; in a free country, he said, there should be freedom of speech and thought." [8] His nominations, the hostile Tacitus admits,

> were made with judgment. The consuls and the praetors enjoyed the ancient honors of their rank. The subordinate officials exercised their functions free from imperial control. The laws, if we except those of violated majesty, flowed in their regular channel. . . . The revenues were administered by men of distinguished probity. . . . In the provinces no new burdens were imposed, and the old duties were collected without cruelty or extortion. . . . Good order prevailed among his slaves. . . . In all questions of right between the emperor and individuals the courts of justice were open, and the law decided.[9]

This Tiberian honeymoon lasted nine years, during which Rome, Italy, and the provinces enjoyed government as good as any in their history. Without additional taxes, despite many benefactions to stricken families and cities, the careful repair of all public property, the absence of booty-yielding wars, and the rejection of bequests made to the Prince by persons with children or near relatives, Tiberius, who had found 100,000,000 sesterces in the Treasury on his accession, left 2,700,000,000 there at his death. He tried to check extravagance by example rather than by law. He labored carefully on every aspect of domestic and foreign affairs. To provincial governors anxious to collect more revenues he wrote that "it was the part of a good shepherd to shear his flock, not fleece it." [10] Though skilled in the art of war, he denied himself, as Prince, the glories of the battlefield; and after the third year of his long reign he kept the Empire at peace.

It was this pacific policy that marred the progress of his rule. His handsome and popular nephew, Germanicus, whom he had adopted as his son at Drusus' death, had won some victories in Germany and wished to go on to its conquest. Tiberius advised against it, to the disgust of the imperialistic populace. Because Germanicus was a grandson of Mark Antony, those who still dreamed of restoring the Republic used him as a symbol for their cause.

---

* The Senate should have taken him at his word and divided the year into thirteen months of twenty-eight days each, with an intercalary holiday (in leap years two) at the end.

When Tiberius transferred him to the East, half of Rome called the young commander a martyr to the Prince's jealousy; and when Germanicus suddenly took sick and died (19), nearly all Rome suspected that Tiberius had had him poisoned. Cnaeus Piso, an appointee of Tiberius in Asia Minor, was accused of the crime and was tried by the Senate; foreseeing condemnation, he killed himself to save his property for his family. No facts appeared to indicate Tiberius' innocence or guilt; we know only that he asked the Senate to give Piso a fair trial, and that Germanicus' mother, Antonia, remained to the end of her life the most faithful friend of Tiberius.[11]

The excited participation of the public in the celebrated case, the scurrilous tales circulated about the Emperor, and the agitation now aroused against him by Germanicus' widow, Agrippina, induced Tiberius to avail himself of that *lex Iulia de maiestate*, or law of treason, which Caesar had passed to define crimes against the state. Since Rome had no public prosecutor or attorney general, and (before Augustus) no police, every citizen was empowered and requested to accuse before the courts any person whom he knew to have violated a law. If the accused was condemned, the *delator* or informer was awarded a fourth of the convicted man's goods, while the state confiscated the rest. Augustus had used this dangerous procedure to enforce his marriage laws. Now, as plots multiplied against Tiberius, *delatores* sprang up to profit from denouncing them; and the supporters of the Prince in the Senate were ready to prosecute such accusations vigorously. The Emperor sought to restrain them. He interpreted the law strictly in the case of persons charged with defaming the memory or statues of Augustus; but "personalities leveled against himself," says Tacitus, "were to be let pass unpunished." He assured the Senate that his mother Livia wished a similar leniency shown to assailants of her good name.[12]

Livia herself was now a major problem of state. Tiberius' failure to remarry left him with no protection against a strong-minded woman accustomed to exercise authority over him. She felt that her maneuvers had cleared his way to the throne, and she gave him to understand that he held it only as her representative.[13] During the earlier years of Tiberius' reign, though he was approaching sixty, his official letters were signed by her as well as by himself. "But not satisfied to rule on equal terms with him," says Dio, "she wished to assert a superiority over him . . . and undertook to manage everything like a sole ruler." [14] Tiberius long bore this situation patiently; but as Livia survived Augustus fifteen years, he at last built himself a separate palace and left his mother in undisputed possession of that which Augustus had raised. Gossip accused him of cruelty to her, and of having starved his exiled wife. Meanwhile Agrippina was pushing her son Nero to succeed—if possible, to replace—Tiberius.[15] This, too, he bore with hot patience, merely chiding her with a Greek quotation: "Do you think a wrong is done you, dear daughter, if you are not empress?" * Hardest of all for him to bear was the realization that his only son, Drusus, borne to him by his first wife, was a worthless rake, cruel, ill-mannered, and lecherous.

The self-control with which Tiberius supported these tribulations left his nerves on edge. He retired more and more into himself, and developed a gloom of countenance and severity of speech that scattered all but his most hopeful friends. One man seemed unfailingly loyal to him—Lucius Aelius Sejanus. As prefect of the Praetorian Guard, Sejanus professed it his duty to protect the Prince; soon no one was admitted to the Emperor's presence except through the hands and under the watch of the crafty vizier. Gradually Tiberius entrusted to him more and more of the government. Sejanus persuaded him that the imperial safety required the closer presence of the Praetorian Guard. Augustus had stationed six of its nine cohorts outside the city limits; Tiberius now allowed all nine to pitch their camp at the Viminal Gate, only a few miles from the Palatine and the Capitol; there they became first the protectors, then the masters, of the emperors. So supported, Sejanus exercised his powers with increasing boldness and venality. He began by recommending men for office, he advanced his fortune by selling offices to the highest bidders, he ended by aspiring to the principate. A senate of real Romans would soon have overthrown him; but the Senate had, with many exceptions, become an epicure's club too listless to wield competently even the authority that Tiberius had urged it to retain. Instead of unseating Sejanus, it crowded Rome with statues voted by it in his image and honor, and at his suggestion it banished one after another of Agrippina's followers. When Tiberius' son Drusus died, Rome whispered that Sejanus had poisoned him.

Overcome with disappointment and bitterness, Tiberius, now a lonely and melancholy man of sixty-seven, left the hectic capital and removed to the inaccessible privacy of Capri. But gossip followed him without impediment. People said that he wished to conceal his emaciated figure and scrofulous face, and to indulge himself in drink and unnatural vice.[16] Tiberius drank considerably, but was no drunkard; the story of his vices was probably calumny;[17] most of his companions on Capri, says Tacitus, "were Greeks distinguished in nothing but literature." [18] He continued to administer carefully the affairs of the Empire, except that he communicated his views and desires to officials and the Senate through Sejanus. Since the Senate increasingly feared him, or Sejanus, or the hovering Guard, it accepted the wishes

---

* Agrippina, daughter of Julia by Agrippa, was Tiberius' stepdaughter through his marriage with Julia, and his daughter-in-law through his adoption of Germanicus. Her son Nero was the uncle, her daughter Agrippina the Younger the mother, of the Emperor Nero.

of the Emperor as commands; and without any change in the constitution, and with no clear insincerity on Tiberius' part, the principate became a monarchy under the man who had proposed to restore the Republic.

Sejanus took advantage of his position to exile more of his enemies by having them accused under the "law of majesty," and the weary Emperor no longer interfered. If we may believe Suetonius, Tiberius was now often guilty of cruelty;[19] and we have the word of the unreliable Tacitus that he asked and obtained the death penalty for Poppaeus Sabinus on the ground that spies had overheard him plot against the government.[20] A year later (27) Livia died, sad and lonely in the home of her former husband; Tiberius, who had seen her but once since leaving Rome, did not attend her funeral. Freed from the restraint that the "Mother of her Country" might have exercised, Sejanus now persuaded Tiberius that Agrippina and her son Nero had been involved in the conspiracy of Sabinus. The mother was banished to Pandateria, and the son to the island of Pontia, where shortly afterward he killed himself.

Having won everything else, Sejanus now reached for the throne. Irked by a letter which Tiberius had written to the Senate recommending Gaius, son of Agrippina, as successor to the principate, Sejanus formed a plot to kill the Emperor (31). Tiberius was saved by Germanicus' mother, Antonia, who risked her life to send him a warning. The old Prince, not yet destitute of resolution, secretly placed a new prefect over the Praetorians, had Sejanus arrested, and accused him to the Senate. Never had that body so gladly complied with the imperial wishes. It condemned Sejanus with expedition and had him strangled that very night. A reign of terror followed, led partly by senators whose interests, relatives, or friends had been injured by Sejanus, and partly by Tiberius, whom fear and anger, topping an accumulation of disillusionments, had plunged into a fury of revenge. Every important agent or supporter of Sejanus was put to death; even his young daughter was condemned; and since the law forbade the execution of a virgin, she was first deflowered and then strangled. Apicata, his divorced wife, committed suicide, but only after she had sent Tiberius a letter assuring him that Antonia's daughter Livilla had joined with Sejanus in poisoning her husband Drusus, the Emperor's son. Tiberius ordered Livilla tried, but she refused food until she died. Two years later (33) Agrippina killed herself in exile; and another of her sons, having been imprisoned, starved himself to death.

Tiberius lingered for six years after the fall of Sejanus. Probably his mind was now disordered; only on this supposition can we explain the incredible cruelties attributed to him. We are told that he now supported, instead of checked, accusations for *maiestas;* all in all sixty-three persons were indicted on this charge during his reign. He begged the Senate to provide protection for "an old and lonely man." In 37 he left Capri after nine years of self-imprisonment, and visited some cities in Campania. While stopping at Lucullus' villa in Misenum he fell in a fainting fit, and seemed dead. The courtiers at once flocked about Gaius, soon to be Emperor, and then were shocked to learn that Tiberius was recovering. A friend of all concerned ended the embarrassment by smothering Tiberius with a pillow (37).[21]

He was, said Mommsen, "the ablest ruler the Empire ever had." [22] Almost every misfortune had come to him during his life; and after his death he fell upon the pen of Tacitus.

II. GAIUS

The populace celebrated the old Emperor's passing with cries of "Tiberius to the Tiber!" and hailed the Senate's ratification of Gaius Caesar Germanicus as his successor. Born to Agrippina as she was accompanying Germanicus on his northern campaigns, Gaius had been brought up among soldiers, had imitated their dress, and had been affectionately named Caligula, or Little Boot, from the half boot (*caliga*) worn in the army. He now announced that he would follow the principles of Augustus in his policy and would co-operate respectfully with the Senate in everything. He distributed among the citizens the 90,000,000 sesterces that Livia and Tiberius had bequeathed them, and added a gift of 300 sesterces to each of the 200,000 recipients of state corn. He restored to the *comitia* the power to choose the magistrates, promised low taxes and rich games, recalled the banished victims of Tiberius, and brought his mother's ashes piously to Rome. He seemed to be in all ways the opposite of his predecessor—prodigal, cheerful, humane. Within three months of his accession the people had sacrificed 160,000 victims to the gods in gratitude for so charming and beneficent a prince.[23]

They had forgotten his lineage. His father's mother was the daughter of Antony, his mother's mother was the daughter of Augustus; in his blood the war between Antony and Octavian was renewed, and Antony won. Caligula was proud of his skill as a dueler, a gladiator, and a charioteer; but he was "troubled with the falling sickness," and at times was "hardly able to walk or collect his thoughts." [24] He hid under the bed when it thundered, and fled in terror from the sight of Aetna's flames. He found it hard to sleep and would wander through his enormous palace at night crying for the dawn. He was tall, huge, hairy, except for a bald crown; his hollow eyes and temples made him look forbidding, to his delight; he "practiced all kinds of fearsome expressions before a mirror." [25] He had received a good schooling, was an eloquent orator, had a keen wit, and a sense of humor that knew no scruple and no law. Infatuated with the theater, he subsidized many performers and himself privately acted and danced; desiring an audience, he summoned the leaders of the Senate as if to some vital conference, and then displayed his steps before them.[26] A quiet life of responsible labor might have steadied him, but the poison of power made him mad. Sanity, like government, needs checks and balances; no mortal can be omnipotent and sane. When Caligula's grandmother Antonia gave him some advice he rebuked her with the remark, "Remember that I have the right to do anything to anybody." In the midst of a banquet he reminded his guests that he could have them all killed where they reclined; and while embracing his wife or mistress he would say pleasantly, "Off comes this beautiful head whenever I give the word." [27]

Soon therefore the young Prince who had been so respectful of the Senate began to give it orders and exact an Oriental subservience. He let senators kiss his feet in homage, and senators thanked him for the honor.[28] He admired Egypt and its ways, introduced many of these to Rome, and longed to be worshiped, Pharaoh-like, as a god. He made the religion of Isis one of the official cults of the Roman state. He did not forget that his great-grandfather had planned to unite the Mediterranean region under an Oriental monarchy; he too thought of making his capital at Alexandria, but distrusted the wit of its people. Suetonius describes him as living in "habitual incest with all his sisters";[29] it seemed to him an excellent Egyptian custom. Ill, he made his sister Drusilla heir to his throne; when she married he made her divorce her husband, and "treated her as his lawful wife." [30] To other desired women he sent letters of divorce in their husbands' names, and invited them to his embraces; there was scarcely one woman of rank whom he did not approach. Amid these and some homosexual amours he found time for four marriages. Attending the wedding of Livia Orestilla and Gaius Piso, he took the bride to his own house, married her, and in a few days divorced her. Hearing that Lollia Paulina was very beautiful, he sent for her, divorced her from her husband, married her, divorced her, and forbade her to have relations with any man thereafter. His fourth wife, Caesonia, was pregnant by her husband when he married her. She was neither young nor fair, but he loved her faithfully.

In this imperial frolic government was an aside, and could usually be left to inferior minds. Caligula ably revised the roster of the business class and promoted its best members to the Senate. But his extravagance soon exhausted the full treasuries left him by Tiberius. He took his baths not in water but in perfumes; on one banquet he spent 10,000,000 sesterces.[31] He built great pleasure barges with colonnades, banquet halls, baths, gardens, fruit trees, and gem-set sterns. He had his engineers span Baiae's bay with a bridge resting on so many boats that Rome suffered famine for lack of ships to import corn. When the bridge was completed a great celebration took place, illuminated by flood lights in the modern manner; the people drank merrily, boats overturned, and many were drowned. From the roof of the Basilica Julia he would scatter gold and silver coins among the people below and watch with glee their fatal scrambling. He was so devoted to the green faction at the races that he gave a charioteer 2,000,000 sesterces. He built a marble stall and an ivory manger for the race horse Incitatus, invited it to dinner, and proposed to make it consul.

To raise funds for his lifelong Saturnalia, Caligula restored the custom of presenting gifts to the emperor; he accepted these in person, on his palace terrace, from all who came to give. He encouraged citizens to name him heir in their wills. He levied taxes upon everything: a sales tax on all food, a tax on all legal processes, a twelve and a half per cent tax on the wages of porters. "On the earnings of prostitutes," Suetonius avers, he laid a tax of "as much as each received for one embrace; and the law provided that those who had ever been prostitutes should remain subject to this tax even after they married." [32] He had rich men accused of treason and condemned to death as an aid to the Treasury. He personally auctioned off gladiators and slaves, and forced aristocrats to attend and bid; when one of these slept, Caligula interpreted his nods as bids, so that the sleeper, waking, found himself richer by thirteen gladiators and poorer by 9,000,000 sesterces. [33] He compelled senators and knights to fight as gladiators in the arena.

After three years a conspiracy was formed to end this humiliating buffoonery. Caligula detected it and revenged himself by a reign of terror enhanced by his maniac joy in inflicting pain. The executioners were instructed to kill his victims "by numerous slight wounds, so that they may feel that they are dying." [34] If we may believe Dio Cassius, he forced his saintly grandmother Antonia to kill herself. [35] Suetonius recounts that when meat ran short for feeding the beasts kept for gladiatorial games, Caligula ordered "all bald-headed" prisoners to be fed to the animals for the public good; that he had men of high rank branded with irons, condemned to mines, thrown to beasts, or shut up in cages and then sawn in two. [36] These are stories that we have no means of disproving and must record as the tradition; but Suetonius loved gossip, the senator Tacitus hated the emperors, and Dio Cassius wrote two centuries after the event. [37] More credible is the report that Caligula began the war between the principate and philosophy by exiling Carrinas Secundus and sentencing two other teachers to death. The young Seneca was marked for execution, but was spared because he was sickly and might be relied upon to die without prodding. Claudius, uncle of Caligula, escaped because he was, or pretended to be, an insignificant book-ridden dolt.

Caligula's final pleasantry was to announce himself as a god, equal to Jupiter himself. Famous statues of Jove and other deities were decapitated and crowned with heads of the Emperor. He enjoyed sitting on a throne in the Temple of Castor and Pollux and receiving divine worship. At times he would converse with an image of Jupiter, often in terms of reproof; and he had a contrivance made by which he could reply to Jove's thunder and lightning peal for peal and stroke for stroke.[39] He set up a temple to his godhead, with a corps of priests and a supply of select victims, and he appointed his favorite horse as one of the priests. He pretended that the moon-goddess had come down to embrace him, and asked Vitellius could he not see her. "No," answered that wise courtier, "only you gods can see one another." [40] The people were not deceived. When a Gallic cobbler saw Caligula masquerading as Jupiter, and was asked what he thought of the Emperor, he said, simply, "A big humbug." Caligula heard, but did not punish such refreshing courage.[41]

At twenty-nine this god was an old man, worn out by excesses, probably venereally diseased, with a small and half-bald head upon a fat body, with a livid complexion, hollow eyes, and a sinister glance. His fate came suddenly, and from that Praetorian Guard whose support he had long purchased with gifts. A tribune of the Guard, Cassius Chaerea, insulted by the obscenities that Caligula gave him as passwords day after day, killed him in a secret passage of the palace (41). When the news went out, the city hesitated to believe it; men feared that this was a trick of the imperial prankster to find out who would rejoice at his death. To clarify the issue the assassins killed Caligula's final wife and dashed out his daughter's brains against a wall. On that day, says Dio, Caligula learned that he was not a god.[42]

III. CLAUDIUS

Caligula had left the Empire in a dangerous condition: the Treasury empty, the Senate decimated, the people alienated, Mauretania in rebellion, Judea in arms at his insistence on placing his cult statue in the Temple of Jerusalem. No one knew where to find a ruler fit to face these problems. The Praetorians, coming upon the apparently imbecile Claudius hiding in a corner, proclaimed him *imperator*. The Senate, in terror of the army, and perhaps relieved by the prospect of dealing with a harmless pedant instead of a reckless lunatic, confirmed the choice of the Guard; and Tiberius Claudius Caesar Augustus Germanicus hesitantly mounted the throne.

He was the son of Antonia and Drusus, the brother of Germanicus and Livilla, the grandson of Octavia and Antony, of Livia and Tiberius Claudius

Nero. He had been born at Lugdunum (Lyons) in the year 10 B.C. and was now fifty years old. He was tall and stout, with white hair and an amiable face; but infantile paralysis and other diseases had weakened his frame. His legs were precariously thin and gave him a shambling gait; his head wobbled as he walked. He loved good wines and rich food and suffered from gout. He stuttered a bit, and his laughter seemed too boisterous for an emperor. In anger, says the merciless gossiper, "he would foam at the mouth and trickle at the nose." [43] He had been brought up by women and freedmen, had developed a timidity and sensitivity hardly advantageous to a ruler, and had had few opportunities to practice government. His relatives had looked upon him as a feeble-minded invalid; his mother, who had inherited Octavia's gentleness, called him "an unfinished monster," and when she wished to stress a man's dullness she would term him "a bigger fool than my Claudius." Scorned by all, he lived in safe obscurity, absorbed in gambling, books, and drink. He became a philologist and antiquarian, learned in "ancient" art, religion, science, philosophy, and law. He wrote histories of Etruria, Carthage, and Rome, treatises on dice and the alphabet, a Greek comedy, and an autobiography. Scientists and savants corresponded with him and dedicated their tomes to him; Pliny the Elder cites him four times as an authority. As Emperor he told his people how to cure snakebite, and forestalled superstitious fears by predicting a solar eclipse on his birthday and explaining its cause. He spoke Greek well, and wrote several of his works in that language. He had a good mind; perhaps he was sincere when he told the Senate that he had pretended stupidity in order to save his head.

His first act as Emperor was to reward with a donative of 15,000 sesterces every soldier of that Guard which had raised him to the throne. Caligula had given such gifts, but not so clearly in payment for the Empire; now Claudius acknowledged the sovereignty of the army, while canceling again the power of the Assembly to choose the magistrates. With wiser generosity he ended accusations *de maiestate*, released persons imprisoned on such charges, recalled all exiles, restored confiscated property, returned to Greece the statues that Gaius had stolen, and abolished the taxes that Gaius had introduced. But he put to death Caligula's assassins, on the theory that it was unsafe to condone the murder of an emperor. He ended the practice of prostration, and announced simply that he was not to be worshiped as a god. Like Augustus he repaired the temples and with antiquarian fervor sought to reanimate the old religion. He applied himself personally and conscientiously to public affairs; he even "made the rounds of those who sold goods and let buildings, and corrected whatever he deemed to be abuses." [44] But in truth, though he emulated the moderation of Augustus, his actual policies went beyond that cautious conservatism to the bold and varied plans of Caesar: the reform of government and law, the construction of public works and services, the elevation of the provinces, the enfranchisement of Gaul, and the conquest and Romanization of Britain.

He surprised everyone by showing will and character as well as learning and intellect. Like Caesar and Augustus, he was convinced that the local magistrates were too few and untrained, the Senate too proud and impatient to do the complex work of municipal and imperial administration. He bowed to the Senate, and left it many powers and more dignities; but the real labor of government was performed by himself, a cabinet of his appointees, and a civil service gradually organized, as under Caesar, Augustus, and Tiberius, out of the freedmen of the Emperor's household, and using "public" slaves for clerical and minor tasks. Four cabinet members headed this bureaucracy: a secretary of state (*ab epistulis*—"for communications"), a treasurer (*a rationibus*—"for accounts"), another secretary (*a libellis*—for petitions), and an attorney general (*a cognitionibus*—"for actions at law"). Able freedmen—Narcissus, Pallas, and Callistus—held the first three posts. Their rise to power and wealth was the symbol of a wide elevation of the freedman class, which had been going on for centuries and reached a new height in Claudius' reign. When the aristocracy protested against the empowerment of these parvenus, Claudius revived the office of censor, had himself chosen to it, revised the list of persons eligible to the Senate, eliminated the chief opponents of his policies, and added new members from the knights and the provinces.

Equipped with these administrative organs, he set himself an ambitious program of construction and reform. He improved the procedure of the courts, decreed penalties for the law's delays, sat patiently as judge many hours every week, and forbade the application of torture to any citizen. To prevent the floods that endangered Rome all the more frequently as the Apennines were being denuded of timber, he had an additional channel dug for the lower course of the Tiber. To expedite the import of grain he had a new harbor (Portus) built near Ostia, with commodious warehouses and docks, two great moles to break the fury of the sea, and a channel connecting the harbor with the Tiber above the river's silted mouth. He finished the "Claudian" aqueduct begun by Caligula, and constructed another, the Anio Novus, both immense works and notable for the beauty of their lofty arches. Observing that the lands of the Marsians were periodically swamped by the overflow of Lake Fucinus, he provided state funds for the labor of 30,000 men during eleven years, digging a three-mile tunnel from the lake through a mountain to the river Ciris. Before releasing the waters of the lake he staged on it a sham naval battle between two fleets manned by 19,000 condemned criminals, before spectators gathered from all Italy upon the slopes of the surrounding hills. The combatants saluted the Emperor with a historic phrase: *Ave Caesar! morituri salutamus te*—"Hail Caesar! we who are about to die salute you." [45]

The provinces prospered under him as in Augustan days. He punished decisively the malfeasance of officials, except in the case of Felix, procurator of Judea, whose misrule was concealed from him by Pallas, brother of Saint Paul's inquisitor. He busied himself with every phase of provincial affairs; his edicts and inscriptions, found throughout the Empire, are marked by his characteristic fussiness and prolixity, but they show a mind and will intelligently devoted to the public good. He labored to improve communication and transport, to protect travelers from brigandage, and to reduce the cost of the official post to the communities it served. Like Caesar he wished to raise the provinces to the level of Italy in a Roman commonwealth. He carried out Caesar's design in granting full citizenship to Transalpine Gaul; if he had had his way he would have enfranchised all freemen in the Empire.[46] A bronze tablet unearthed at Lyons in 1524 has preserved for us part of the rambling speech in which he persuaded the Senate to admit to its membership and to imperial office those Gauls who held the Roman franchise. Meanwhile he did not allow the army to deteriorate or the frontiers to be infringed; his legions were kept busy and fit, and great generals like Corbulo, Vespasian, and Paulinus developed under his choice and encouragement. Again deciding to complete Caesar's plans, he invaded Britain in 43, conquered it, and was back in Rome within six months of setting out. In the triumph accorded him he violated precedent by pardoning the captured British king, Caractacus. The people of Rome laughed at their strange Emperor, but loved him; and when, on one of his absences from the capital, a false rumor spread that he had been killed, so great a turmoil of sorrow swept the city that the Senate had to issue official assurances that Claudius was safe and would soon be in Rome.

From that great height he fell because he had built a government too complex for his personal supervision, and because his amiable spirit was too easily deceived by his freedmen and his family. The bureaucracy had improved administration and had made a thousand new openings for corruption. Narcissus and Pallas were excellent executives, who considered their salaries unequal to their merits. To make up the difference they sold offices, extorted bribes by threats, and brought charges against men whose estates they wished to confiscate. They ended by being the richest individuals in all antiquity. Narcissus had 400,000,000 sesterces ($60,000,000); Pallas was miserable because he had only 300,000,000.[47] When Claudius complained of a deficit in the imperial Treasury, Roman wags remarked that he would have enough and to spare if he would take his two freedmen into partnership.[48] The old aristocratic families, now comparatively poor, looked with horror upon these accumulations and powers, and burned with anger when they had to court ex-slaves to obtain a word with the Emperor,

Claudius was busy writing to appointees and scholars, preparing edicts and speeches, and attending to the needs of his wife. Such a man should have lived like a monk and barricaded himself against love; his wives proved a ruinous distraction, and his domestic policy was not as successful as his foreign. Like Caligula he married four times. His first wife died on her wedding day, the next two he divorced; then, aged forty-eight, he married Valeria Messalina, sixteen. She was not unusually pretty: her head was flat, her face florid, her chest malformed;[49] but a woman need not be beautiful to commit adultery. When Claudius became Emperor she assumed the rights and manners of a queen, rode in his triumph, and had her birthday celebrated throughout the Empire. She fell in love with the dancer Mnester; when he rejected her advances she begged her husband to bid him to be more obedient to her requests; Claudius complied, whereupon the dancer yielded to her patriotically. Messalina rejoiced at the simplicity of her formula, and adopted it with other men; those who still refused her were accused of invented crimes by officials pliant to her influence, and found themselves deprived of their property and their liberty, sometimes of their lives.[50]

Perhaps the Emperor tolerated these irregularities to secure indulgence for his own. "He was immoderate in his passion for women," says Suetonius, who adds, as a startling distinction, that Claudius "was wholly free from unnatural vice." [51] Messalina, says Dio, "gave him some attractive housemaids for bedfellows." [52] Needing funds for her escapades, the Empress sold offices, recommendations, and contracts. Juvenal has handed down the story that she would disguise herself, enter a brothel, receive all comers, and gladly pocket their fees; the tale was probably taken from the lost memoirs of Messalina's successor and foe, the younger Agrippina. While Claudius, says Tacitus, "devoted all his time to the duties of his censorial office" [53]— including the supervision and improvement of Roman morals—Messalina "gave a loose to love," and at last, while her husband was in Ostia, formally married a handsome youth, Caius Silius, "with pomp and all accustomed rites." [54] Narcissus informed the Emperor through the latter's concubines [55] and told him that an uprising was being planned to kill him and put Silius on the throne. Claudius rushed back to Rome, summoned the Praetorian Guard, had Silius and other lovers of Messalina slain, and then retired in nervous exhaustion to his rooms. The Empress hid herself in those gardens of Lucullus which she had confiscated for her pleasure. Claudius sent her a message inviting her to come and plead her cause. Fearing that the Emperor would forgive her and turn against him, Narcissus dispatched some soldiers with instructions to kill her. They found her alone with her mother, slew her with one blow, and left her corpse in her mother's arms (48). Claudius told the Praetorian Guard that if he should every marry again they would be justified in killing him. He never mentioned Messalina again.*

Within a year he was hesitating whether to marry Lollia Paulina or the younger Agrippina. Lollia, ex-wife of Caligula, was rich; sometimes, we are told, she wore jewelry worth 40,000,000 sesterces;[59] perhaps Claudius admired her money more than her taste. Agrippina was the daughter of the elder Agrippina and Germanicus; she too, had in her the unreconciled blood of Octavian and Antony, and had succeeded to the beauty, ability, resolution, and unscrupulous vindictiveness of her mother. She was already twice a widow. By her first husband, Cnaeus Domitius Ahenobarbus, she had a son Nero, whose enthronement became the ruling passion of her life; and from her second husband Caius Crispus, whom rumor accused her of poisoning, she inherited the wealth that sinewed her aims. Her problem was to become the wife of Claudius, to get rid of his son Britannicus, and make Nero, by adoption, heir to the Empire. The fact that she was Claudius' niece did not deter her, but gave her opportunities for fond intimacies that stirred the aging ruler in no avuncular way. Suddenly he appeared before the Senate and asked it to bid him marry again for the good of the state. The Senate complied, the Praetorians laughed, and Agrippina reached the throne (48).

She was thirty-two, Claudius fifty-seven. His energies were failing; hers were at their height. Playing upon him with all her charms, she persuaded him to adopt Nero as his son, and to give his thirteen-year-old daughter Octavia to the sixteen-year-old youth in marriage (53). She assumed more and more political power with each year, and finally sat beside him on the imperial dais. She recalled the philosopher Seneca from the exile to which Claudius had condemned him, and made him the tutor of her son (49); and she had her friend Burrus appointed prefect of the Praetorian Guard. So poised, she ruled with a virile hand and established order and economy in the imperial household. Her ascendancy might have been a boon to Rome had she not indulged her avarice and her revenge. She had Lollia Paulina put to death because Claudius, in a careless moment which no wife forgives, remarked on the elegance of Lollia's figure. She had Marcus Silanus poisoned because she feared that Claudius might name him his heir. She conspired with Pallas to overthrow Narcissus, and this moneyed potentate, as faithful as he was corrupt, ended his career in a dungeon. The Emperor, weakened by ill-health, many labors, and sexual enterprise, allowed Pallas and Agrippina to establish another reign of terror. Men were accused, exiled, or killed because

---

* Ferrero [56] and Bury [57] have tried to explain away Messalina's bigamy, but Tacitus vouches for the story as "well attested by writers of the period, and by grave and elderly men who lived at the time, and were informed of every circumstance." [58]

the Treasury was exhausted by public works and games and needed replenishment by confiscated wealth. Thirty-five senators and 300 knights were condemned to death in the thirteen years of Claudius' reign. Some of these executions may have been justified by actual conspiracy or crime; we do not know. Nero later claimed that he had examined all the papers of Claudius, and that from these it appeared that not one prosecution had been set on foot by the Emperor's order.[60]

After five years of his fifth marriage Claudius awakened to what Agrippina was doing. He resolved to put an end to her power, and circumvent her plans for Nero, by naming Britannicus his heir. But Agrippina had more determination and less scruple. Perceiving the Emperor's intentions she risked everything: she fed Claudius poisonous mushrooms, and he died after twelve hours of agony, without being able to utter a word (54). When the Senate deified him, Nero, already enthroned, remarked that mushrooms must be the food of the gods, since by eating them Claudius had become divine.[61]

IV. NERO

On his father's side Nero belonged to the Domitii Ahenobarbi—so named from the bronzelike beards that ran in the family. For five hundred years they had been famous in Rome for ability, recklessness, haughtiness, courage, and cruelty. Nero's paternal grandfather had a passion for games and the stage; drove a chariot in the races, spent money with open hand on wild beasts and gladiatorial shows, and had to be reproved by Augustus for barbarous treatment of his employees and slaves. He married Antonia, daughter of Antony and Octavia. Their son Cnaeus Domitius enhanced the reputation of the family by adultery, incest, brutality, and treason. In A.D. 28 he married the second Agrippina, then thirteen years old. Knowing his wife's ancestry and his own, he concluded that "no good man can possibly be born from us." [62] They named their only child Lucius, and added the cognomen Nero, meaning, in the Sabine tongue, valiant and strong.

The chief authors of his education were Chaeremon the Stoic, who taught him Greek, and Seneca, who taught him literature and morals but not philosophy. Agrippina forbade the last on the ground that it would unfit Nero for government;[63] the result was creditable to philosophy. Like many a teacher, Seneca complained that his labors were thwarted by the mother: the boy would run to her when reproved, and was sure to be comforted. Seneca sought to train him in modesty and courtesy, simplicity and stoicism. If he could not retail to him the doctrines and disputes of the philosophers, he could at least dedicate to him the eloquent philosophical treatises that he was composing, and hope that someday his pupil might read them. The young prince was a good student, wrote forgivable poetry, and addressed the Senate in the graceful manner of his master. When Claudius died, Agrippina had no great difficulty in securing the confirmation of her son on the throne, especially since her friend Burrus brought to him the full support of the Guard.

Nero rewarded the soldiers with a donative, and gave 400 sesterces to every citizen. He pronounced over his predecessor a eulogy composed by the same Seneca [64] who would soon publish, anonymously, a pitiless satire (*Apocolocyntosis* or *Pumpkinification*) on the late Emperor's ejection from Olympus. Nero made the usual obeisance to the Senate, modestly excused his youth, and announced that of the powers heretofore taken by the prince he would keep only the command of the armies—a highly practical choice for the pupil of a philosopher. The promise was probably sincere, since Nero kept it faithfully for five years [65]—that *quinquennium Neronis* which Trajan later accounted the best period in the history of the imperial government.[66] When the Senate proposed that statues of gold and silver should be raised in his honor, the seventeen-year-old Emperor rejected the offer; when two men were indicted for favoring Britannicus, he had the accusations withdrawn; and in a speech to the Senate he pledged himself to observe throughout his reign that virtue of mercy which Seneca was then extolling in an essay *De clementia*. Asked to sign a death warrant for a condemned criminal, he sighed, "Would that I had never learned to write!" He abolished or reduced oppressive taxes, and gave annuities to distinguished but impoverished senators. Recognizing his immaturity, he allowed Agrippina to administer his affairs; she received embassies, and had her image engraved beside his own on the imperial coins. Alarmed by this matriarchate, Seneca and Burrus conspired, by playing upon Nero's pride, to win from her the administration of his powers. The infuriated mother announced that Britannicus was the true heir to the throne, and threatened to unmake her son as decisively as she had made him. Nero countered by having Britannicus poisoned. Agrippina retired to her villas and wrote her *Memoirs* as a last vindictive stroke—blackening all the enemies of herself and her mother, and providing Tacitus and Suetonius with that museum of horrors from which they drew the darker colors for their portraits of Tiberius, Claudius, and Nero.

Under the guidance of the philosopher-premier, and on the impetus of the administrative organization already devised, the Empire prospered within and without. The frontiers were well guarded, the Black Sea was cleared of pirates, Corbulo brought Armenia back under Rome's protectorate, and Parthia signed a peace that endured for fifty years. Corruption was reduced in the courts and the provinces, bureaucratic personnel was improved, the

Treasury was managed with economy and wisdom. Probably at Seneca's suggestion Nero made the far-reaching proposal to abolish all indirect taxes, especially the customs duties collected at frontiers and ports, and so establish free trade throughout the Empire. The measure was defeated in the Senate through the influence of the tax-gathering corporations—a defeat which indicates that the Principate was still recognizing its constitutional limits.

To divert Nero from interference with state affairs, Seneca and Burrus allowed him to indulge his sensuality unrestrained. "At a time when vice had charms for all orders of men," says Tacitus,[67] "it was not expected that the sovereign should lead a life of austerity and self-denial." Nor could religious belief encourage Nero to morality; a smattering of philosophy had liberated his intellect without maturing his judgment. "He despised all cults," says Suetonius, "and voided his bladder upon an image of the goddess whom he most respected, Cybele." [68] His instincts inclined him to excessive eating, exotic desires, extravagant banquets where the flowers alone cost 4,000,000 sesterces;[69] only misers, he said, counted what they spent. He admired and envied Caius Petronius, for that rich aristocrat taught him new ways of combining vice with taste. Petronius, says Tacitus in a classic description of the epicurean's ideal,

> passed his days in sleep, and his nights in business, joy, and revelry. Indolence was at once his passion and his road to fame. What others did by vigor and industry, he accomplished by his love of pleasure and luxurious ease. Unlike the men who profess to understand social enjoyment, and ruin their fortunes, he led a life of expense without profusion; an epicure, yet not a prodigal; addicted to his appetites, but with refinement and judgment; an educated and elegant voluptuary. Gay and airy in his conversation, he charmed by a certain graceful negligence, the more engaging as it flowed from the natural frankness of his disposition. With all his delicacy and careless ease, he showed, when he was governor of Bithynia, and again when consul, that vigor of mind and softness of manners may unite in the same person. . . . From his public offices he returned to his usual gratifications, fond of vice, or of pleasures that bordered on it. . . . Cherished by Nero and his companions . . . he was allowed to be the arbiter of taste and elegance. Without his sanction nothing was exquisite, nothing delightful or rare.[70]

Nero was not subtle enough to achieve this artistic epicureanism. He disguised himself and visited brothels; he roamed the streets and frequented taverns at night with the comrades of his mood, robbing shops, insulting women, "practicing lewdness on boys, stripping those whom they encountered, striking, wounding, murdering." [71] A senator who defended himself vigorously against the disguised Emperor was soon afterward forced to kill himself. Seneca sought to divert the royal lust by condoning Nero's relations with an ex-slave, Claudia Acte. But Acte was too faithful to him to keep his affections; he soon exchanged her for a woman of superlative refinement in all the ways of love. Poppaea Sabina was of high family and great wealth; "she had everything," says Tacitus, "except an honest mind"; she was one of those women who spend all the day in adorning their persons, and exist only when they are desired. Her husband, Salvius Otho, boasted of her beauty to Nero; the Emperor at once commissioned him to govern Lusitania (Portugal), and laid siege to Poppaea. She refused to be his mistress, but agreed to be his wife if he would divorce Octavia.

Octavia had borne the transgressions of Nero silently, and had preserved her own modesty and chastity amid the stream of sexual license in which she had been forced to live from her birth. It is to the honor of Agrippina that she lost her life in defending Octavia against Poppaea. She used every plea against the proposed divorce, even, says Tacitus, to offering her own charms to her son. Poppaea fought back with hers and won; youth was served. She taunted Nero with being afraid of his mother, and led him to believe that Agrippina was plotting his fall. Finally, in the madness of his infatuation, he consented to kill the woman who had borne him and given him half the world. He thought of poisoning her, but she had guarded against this by the habitual use of antidotes. He tried to have her drowned, but she swam to safety from the shipwreck he had arranged. His men pursued her to her villa; when they seized her she bared her body and said, "Plunge your sword into my womb." It took many blows to kill her. The Emperor, viewing the uncovered corpse, remarked, "I did not know I had so beautiful a mother." [72] Seneca, it is said, had no share in the plot; but the saddest lines in the history of philosophy tell how he penned the letter in which Nero explained to the Senate how Agrippina had plotted against the Prince and, being detected, had killed herself.[73] The Senate gracefully accepted the explanation, came in a body to greet Nero returning to Rome, and offered thanks to the gods for having kept him safe.

It is hard to believe that this matricide was a youth of twenty-two with a passion for poetry, music, art, drama, and athletic games. He admired the Greeks for their varied contests of physical and artistic ability, and sought to introduce like competitions to Rome. In 59 he instituted the *ludi iuvenales*, or Youth Games; and a year later he inaugurated the *Neronia* on the model of the quadrennial festival at Olympia, with contests in horse racing, athletics, and "music"—which included oratory and poetry. He built an amphitheater, a gymnasium, and a magnificent public bath. He practiced gymnastics with skill, became an enthusiastic charioteer, and finally decided to compete in the games. To his philhellenic mind this seemed not only proper, but in the best tradition of Greek antiquity. Seneca thought it ridiculous, and tried to confine the imperial exhibitions to a private stadium. Nero overruled him and invited the public to witness his performance. It came, and applauded lustily.

But what this uninhibited satyr really wanted was to be a great artist. Having every power, he longed also for every accomplishment. It is to his credit that he applied himself with painstaking seriousness to engraving, painting, sculpture, music, and poetry.[74] To improve his singing "he used to lie upon his back with a leaden plate upon his chest, purge himself by a syringe or by vomiting, and deny himself fruits and all foods injurious to the voice";[75] on certain days, for the same purpose, he ate nothing but garlic and olive oil. One evening he summoned the foremost senators to his palace, showed them a new water organ, and lectured to them on its theory and construction.[76] He was so fascinated by the music which Terpnos drew from the harp that he spent entire nights with him in practicing on that instrument. He gathered artists and poets about him, competed with them in his palace, compared his paintings with theirs, listened to their poetry, and read his own. He was deceived by their praise, and when an astrologer predicted that he would lose his throne he replied cheerfully that he would then make a living by his art. He dreamed of performing publicly in one day on the water organ, the flute, and the pipes, and then appearing as actor and dancer in the part of Virgil's Turnus. In 59 he gave a semipublic concert as a harpist (*citharoedus*) in his gardens on the Tiber. For five years more he controlled his longing for a larger audience; at last he dared it in Naples; there the Greek spirit ruled, and the people would forgive and understand him. The auditorium was so overcrowded for his exhibition that it crumbled to pieces shortly after the audience had left. Encouraged, the young Emperor appeared as singer and harpist in the great theater of Pompey at Rome (65). In these recitals he sang poems apparently composed by himself;* some fragments have survived and show a moderate talent. Besides many lyrics, he wrote a long epic on Troy (with Paris as hero), and began a still longer one on Rome. To complete his versatility, he came upon the boards as an actor, playing the roles of Oedipus, Heracles, Alcmaeon, even the matricide Orestes. The populace was delighted to have an emperor entertain it and kneel on the stage, as custom required, to ask for its applause. It took up the songs that Nero sang and repeated them in the taverns and the streets. His

---

* Suetonius claims to have seen the royal manuscripts, with text and corrections in Nero's hand.[77]

enthusiasm for music spread through all ranks. His popularity, instead of waning, grew.

The Senate was more horrified by these displays than by all the gossip of sexual license and perversion that ran about the palace. Nero replied that the Greek custom of confining athletic and artistic competitions to the citizen class was better than the Roman custom of leaving these to the slaves; certainly the contests should not take the form of slowly executing criminals. The young murderer decreed that so long as he ruled, no combat in the arenas should be carried to the death.[78] To restore the Greek tradition and dignify his own performances, he persuaded or compelled certain senators to compete in public as actors, musicians, athletes, gladiators, and charioteers. Some patricians, like Thrasea Paetus, showed their disapproval of his ways by absenting themselves from the Senate when Nero came to address it; some others, like Helvidius Priscus, denounced him violently in those aristocratic salons that had become the last refuge of free speech; and the Stoic philosophers in Rome spoke ever more openly against this impish epicurean on the throne. Plots were laid to depose him. His spies discovered them, and like his predecessors he countered with a reign of terror. The law of *maiestas* was revived (62), and accusations were brought against men whose opposition or wealth made their deaths culturally or financially desirable. For Nero, like Caligula, had now exhausted the Treasury with his extravagance, his gifts, and his games. He announced his intention to confiscate completely the estates of citizens whose wills left insufficient sums to the Emperor. He stripped many temples of their votive offerings, and melted down their images of silver or gold. When Seneca protested and privately criticized his conduct—worse, his poetry—Nero dismissed him from the court (62), and the old philosopher spent the remaining three years of his life in the seclusion of his villas. Burrus had died some months before.

Nero now surrounded himself with new aides, mostly of coarser strain. Tigellinus, urban prefect, became his chief adviser, and smoothed the Prince's path to every indulgence. In 62 Nero divorced and dismissed Octavia on the ground of barrenness, and twelve days later married Poppaea. The people protested mutely by throwing down the statues that Nero had raised to Poppaea and crowning those of Octavia with flowers. The angry Poppaea convinced her lover that Octavia was planning to remarry, and that a revolution was being organized to replace him in power with Octavia's new mate. If we may follow Tacitus, Nero invited Anicetus, who had killed Agrippina, to confess adultery with Octavia and implicate her in a plot to overthrow the Prince. Anicetus played his part as commanded, was banished to Sardinia, and lived out his life in ease and wealth. Octavia was exiled to Pandateria. There, a few days after her arrival, imperial agents came to murder her. She was still but twenty-two, and could not believe that life must end so soon for one so guiltless. She pleaded with her slayers, saying that she was now only Nero's sister and could do him no harm. They cut off her head and brought it to Poppaea for their reward. The Senate, informed that Octavia was dead, thanked the gods for having again preserved the Emperor.[79]

Nero himself was now a god. After the death of Agrippina a consul-elect had proposed a temple "to the deified Nero." When, in 63, Poppaea bore him a daughter who died soon afterward, the child was voted a divinity. When Tiridates came to receive the crown of Armenia he knelt and worshipped the Emperor as Mithras. When Nero built his Golden House he prefaced it with a colossus 120 feet high, bearing the likeness of his head haloed with solar rays that identified him as Phoebus Apollo. Actually he was now, at twenty-five, a degenerate with swollen paunch, weak and slender limbs, fat face, blotched skin, curly yellow hair, and dull gray eyes.

As a god and an artist he fretted over the flaws of the palaces he had inherited, and planned to build his own. But the Palatine was crowded, and at its base were on one side the Circus Maximus, on another the Forum, and on the others slums. He mourned that Rome had grown so haphazardly, instead of being scientifically designed like Alexandria or Antioch. He dreamed of rebuilding Rome, of being its second founder, and renaming it Neropolis.

On July 18, 64, a fire broke out in the Circus Maximus, spread rapidly, burned for nine days, and razed two thirds of the city. Nero was at Antium when the conflagration started; he hurried to Rome and arrived in time to see the Palatine palaces consumed. The Domus Transitoria, which he had just built to connect his palace with the gardens of Maecenas, was one of the first structures to fall. The Forum and the Capitol escaped, and the region west of the Tiber; throughout the remainder of the city countless homes, temples, precious manuscripts, and works of art were destroyed. Thousands of people lost their lives amid falling tenements in the crowded streets; hundreds of thousands wandered shelterless through the nights, crazed with horror, and listening to rumors that Nero had ordered the fire, was scattering incendiaries to renew it, and was watching it from the tower of Maecenas while singing his lines on the sack of Troy and accompanying himself on the lyre.* He energetically guided attempts to control or localize the flames and to provide relief; he ordered all public buildings and the imperial gardens to be thrown open to the destitute; he raised a city of tents on the

---

* Tacitus (xv, 38), Suetonius ("Nero," 38), and Dio Cassius (LXII, 16) all agree in accusing Nero of starting and renewing the fire in order to rebuild Rome. There is no proof of his guilt or innocence.

Field of Mars, requisitioned food from the surrounding country, and arranged for the feeding of the people.[80] He bore without remonstrance the accusatory lampoons and inscriptions of the infuriated populace. According to Tacitus (whose Senatorial prejudice must always be remembered), he cast about for some scapegoat, and found one in

> a race of men detested for their evil practices, and commonly called *Chrestiani*. The name was derived from Chrestus, who, in the reign of Tiberius, suffered under Pontius Pilate, Procurator of Judea. By that event the sect of which he was the founder received a blow which for a time checked the growth of a dangerous superstition; but it revived soon after, and spread with recruited vigor not only in Judea . . . but even in the city of Rome, the common sink into which everything infamous and abominable flows like a torrent from all quarters of the world. Nero proceeded with his usual artifice. He found a set of profligate and abandoned wretches who were induced to confess themselves guilty; and on the evidence of such men a number of Christians were convicted, not indeed on clear evidence of having set the city on fire, but rather on account of their sullen hatred of the whole human race. They were put to death with exquisite cruelty, and to their sufferings Nero added mockery and derision. Some were covered with skins of wild beasts, and left to be devoured by dogs; others were nailed to crosses; numbers of them were burned alive; many, covered with inflammable matter, were set on fire to serve as torches during the night. . . . At length the brutality of these measures filled every breast with pity. Humanity relented in favor of the Christians.[81]

When the debris had been cleared away Nero undertook with visible pleasure the restoration of the city along the lines of his dream. Contributions for this purpose were solicited or elicited from every city in the Empire, and those whose homes had been destroyed were enabled to rebuild out of these funds. The new streets were made wide and straight, the new houses were required to have their façades and first stories of stone, and had to be sufficiently separated from other buildings to oppose a protective gap to the spread of fire. The springs that flowed beneath the city were channeled into a reserve water supply in case of future conflagrations. Out of the imperial Treasury Nero built porticoes along the main thoroughfares, providing a shaded porch for thousands of homes. Antiquarians and old men missed the picturesque, time-hallowed sights of the old city; but soon all agreed that a healthier, safer, and fairer Rome had risen from the fire.

Nero might have earned forgiveness for his crimes had he now molded his life as he had remade his capital. But Poppaea died in 65, in advanced pregnancy, allegedly from a kick in the stomach; rumor said this had been

Nero's answer to her reproaches for having come home late from the races.[82] He grieved bitterly over her passing, for he had eagerly awaited an heir. He had her body embalmed with rare spices, gave her a pompous funeral, and delivered a eulogy over the corpse. Having found a youth, Sporus, who closely resembled Poppaea, he had him castrated, married him by a formal ceremony, and "used him in every way like a woman"; whereupon a wit expressed the wish that Nero's father had had such a wife.[83] In the same year he began the building of his Golden House; and its extravagant decoration, cost, and extent—covering an area that once had sheltered many thousands of the poor—renewed the resentment of the aristocracy and the suspicions of the plebs.

Suddenly Nero's spies brought him word of a widespread conspiracy to put Calpurnius Piso on the throne (65). His agents seized some minor personages in the plot, and by torture or threat drew from them confessions implicating, among others, Lucan the poet and Seneca. Bit by bit the whole plan was laid bare. Nero's revenge was so savage that Rome credited the rumor that he had vowed to wipe out the whole Senatorial class. When Seneca received the command to kill himself he argued for a while and then complied; Lucan likewise opened his veins and died reciting his poetry. Tigellinus, jealous of Petronius' popularity with Nero, bribed one of the epicure's slaves to testify against his master, and induced Nero to order Petronius' death. Petronius died leisurely, opening his veins and then closing them, conversing in his usual light manner with his friends and reading poetry to them; after a walk and a nap he opened his veins again and passed away quietly.[84] Thrasea Paetus, the leading exponent of the Stoic philosophy in the Senate, was condemned not for taking part in the plot, but on the general ground of deficient enthusiasm for the Emperor, for not enjoying Nero's singing, and for composing a laudatory life of Cato. His son-in-law Helvidius Priscus was merely banished, but two others were put to death for writing in their praise. Musonius Rufus, Stoic philosopher, and Cassius Longinus, a great jurist, were exiled; two brothers of Seneca—Annaeus Mela, father of Lucan, and Annaeus Novatus, the Gallio who in Corinth had freed Saint Paul—were ordered to commit suicide.

Having cleared the lines in his rear, Nero left in 66 to compete in the Olympic games and make a concert tour of Greece. "The Greeks," he remarked, "are the only ones who have an ear for music." [85] At Olympia he drove a *quadriga* in the races; he was thrown from the car and was nearly crushed to death; restored to his chariot he continued the contest for a while, but gave up before the end of the course. The judges, however, knew an emperor from an athlete and awarded him the crown of victory. Overcome with happiness when the crowd applauded him, he announced

that thereafter not only Athens and Sparta but all Greece should be free—
i.e., exempt from any tribute to Rome. The Greek cities accommodated
him by running the Olympian, Pythian, Nemean, and Isthmian games in one
year; he responded by taking part in all of them as singer, harpist, actor,
or athlete. He obeyed the rules of the various competitions carefully, was
all courtesy to his opponents, and gave them Roman citizenship as consolation for his invariable victories. Amid his tour he received news that Judea
was in revolt and that all the West was hot with rebellion. He sighed and
continued his itinerary. When he sang in a theater, says Suetonius, "no one
was allowed to leave, even for the most urgent reasons. And so it was that
some women gave birth there, while some feigned death to be carried out." [86]
At Corinth he ordered work started on a canal to cut the Isthmus as Caesar
had planned; the task was begun, but was laid aside during the turmoil of
the following year. Alarmed by further reports of uprisings and plots, Nero
returned to Italy (67), entered Rome in a formal triumph, and showed, as
trophies, the 1808 prizes he had won in Greece.

Tragedy was rapidly catching up with his comedy. In March, 68, the
Gallic governor of Lyons, Julius Vindex, announced the independence of
Gaul; and when Nero offered 2,500,000 sesterces for his head, Vindex
retorted, "He who brings me Nero's head may have mine in return." [87] Preparing to take the field against this virile antagonist, Nero's first care was
to choose wagons to carry along with him his musical instruments and
theatrical effects.[88] But in April word came that Galba, commander of the
Roman army in Spain, had joined fortunes with Vindex and was marching
toward Rome. Hearing that the Praetorian Guard was ready to abandon
Nero for proper remuneration, the Senate proclaimed Galba emperor. Nero
put some poison into a small box and, so armed, fled from his Golden House
to the Servilian Gardens on the road to Ostia. He asked such officers of the
Guard as were in the palace to accompany him; all refused, and one quoted
to him a line of Virgil: "Is it, then, so hard to die?" He could not believe
that the omnipotence which had ruined him had suddenly ceased. He sent
appeals for help to various friends, but none replied. He went down to the
Tiber to drown himself, but his courage failed him. Phaon, one of his
freedmen, offered to conceal him in his villa on the Via Salaria; Nero grasped
at the proposal, and rode through the dark four miles out from the center
of Rome. He spent that night in Phaon's cellar, clad in a soiled tunic, sleep-
less and hungry, and trembling at every sound. Phaon's courier brought
word that the Senate had declared Nero a public enemy, had ordered his
arrest, and had decreed that he should be punished "after the ancient
manner." Nero asked what this was. "The condemned man," he was told,
"is stripped, is fastened to a post by a fork passing through his neck, and is

then beaten to death." Terrified, he tried to stab himself; but he made the mistake of testing the poniard's point first and found it disconcertingly sharp. *Qualis artifex pereo!* he mourned—"What an artist dies in me!"

As a new day dawned he heard the clatter of horses: the Senate's soldiers had tracked him down. Quoting a verse of poetry—"Hark! now strikes upon my ear the trampling of swift couriers"—he drove a dagger into his throat; his hand faltered, and his freedman Epaphroditus helped him to press the blade home. He had begged his companions to keep his corpse from being mutilated, and Galba's agents granted the wish. His old nurses, and Acte his former mistress, buried him in the vaults of the Domitii (68). Many of the populace rejoiced at his death and ran about Rome with liberty caps on their heads. But many more mourned him, for he had been as generous to the poor as he had been recklessly cruel to the great. They lent eager hearing to the rumor that he was not really dead but was fighting his way back to Rome; and when they had reconciled themselves to his passing they came for many months to strew flowers before his tomb.[89]

V. THE THREE EMPERORS

Servius Sulpicius Galba reached Rome in June of 68. He was of noble birth, for he traced his lineage on his father's side to Jupiter, and on his mother's to Pasiphaë, wife of Minos and the bull. In this year of his exaltation he was already bald, and his hands and feet were so crooked with gout that he could not wear a shoe or hold a book.[90] He had the usual vices, normal and abnormal, but it was not these that made his reign so brief. What shocked army and populace were his economy of the public funds and his strict administration of justice.[91] When he ruled that those who had received gifts or pensions from Nero must return nine tenths to the Treasury, a thousand new enemies arose, and Galba's days ran out.

A bankrupt senator, Marcus Otho, announced that he could pay his debts only by becoming emperor.[92] The Guards declared for him, marched into the Forum, and met Galba riding in a litter. Galba offered his neck unresisting to their swords; they cut off his head, his arms, his lips; one of them carried the head to Otho, but as he could not hold it well by the sparse and blood-wet hair, he thrust his thumb into the mouth. The Senate hastened to accept Otho, just as Roman armies in Germany and Egypt were hailing as emperors their respective generals—Aulus Vitellius and Titus Flavius Vespasianus. Vitellius invaded Italy with his hardy legions, and swept away the weak resistance of the northern garrisons and the Praetorian Guard.

Otho killed himself after a reign of ninety-five days, and Vitellius mounted the throne.

It does not speak well for the Roman military system that so senile a man as Galba should have commanded in Spain, or so slothful an epicurean as Vitellius in Germany. He was a gourmand who thought of the Principate chiefly as a feast, and made a banquet of every meal. He governed in the intervals; and as these grew shorter he left state affairs to his freedman Asiaticus, who in four months became one of the richest men in Rome. When Vitellius learned that Vespasian's general Antonius was leading an army into Italy to dethrone him, he delegated his defense to subordinates and continued to feast. In October of 69 the troops of Antonius defeated the defenders of Vitellius at Cremona in one of the bloodiest battles of ancient times. They marched into Rome, where the remnants of Vitellius' legions fought bravely for him while he took refuge in his palace. The populace, says Tacitus, "flocked in crowds to behold the conflict, as if a scene of carnage were no more than a public spectacle exhibited for their amusement"; while the battle raged some of them plundered shops and homes, and prostitutes plied their trade.[93] The soldiers of Antonius triumphed, killed without quarter, and pillaged without stint; and the mob, as ready as history to applaud the victors, helped them to ferret out their enemies. Vitellius, dragged from his concealment, was led half naked through the city with a noose around his neck, was pelted with dung, was tortured without haste, and at last, in a moment of mercy, was slain (December, 69). The corpse was drawn through the streets with a hook and flung into the Tiber.[94]

VI. VESPASIAN

What a relief to meet a man of sense, ability, and honor! Vespasian, busy directing the war against Judea, took his time in coming to occupy the dangerous eminence that his soldiers had won for him, and which the Senate hurriedly confirmed. When he arrived (October, 70), he set himself with inspiring energy to restore order to a society disturbed in every aspect of its life. Perceiving that he would have to repeat the labors of Augustus, he modeled his behavior and policy upon those of that prince. He made his peace with the Senate and re-established constitutional government; he freed or recalled those who had been convicted of lèse-majesté under Nero, Galba, Otho, and Vitellius; he reorganized the army, limited the number and power of the Praetorian Guard, appointed competent generals to suppress revolts in the provinces, and was soon able to close the Temple of Janus as a sign and pledge of peace.

He was sixty, but in the unimpaired vigor of his powerful frame. He was built foursquare in body and character, with a broad, bald, and massive head, coarse but commanding features, and small sharp eyes that pierced every sham. He had none of the stigmata of genius; he was merely a man of firm will and practical intelligence. He had been born in a Sabine village near Reate, of purely plebeian stock. His accession was a fourfold revolution: a commoner had reached the throne, a provincial army had overcome the Praetorians and crowned its candidate, the Flavians had succeeded the Julio-Claudians, and the simple habits and virtues of the Italian bourgeois replaced, at the court of the emperor, the epicurean wastefulness of the city-bred descendants of Augustus and Livia. Vespasian never forgot, or sought to conceal, his modest ancestry. When expectant genealogists traced his family back to a companion of Hercules he laughed them into silence. Periodically he returned to the home of his birth to enjoy its rustic ways and fare, and he would not allow anything there to be changed. He scorned luxury and laziness, ate the food of peasants, fasted one day in each month, and declared war upon extravagance. When a Roman whom he had nominated for office came to him smelling of perfume, he said, "I would rather you smelled of garlic," and withdrew the nomination. He made himself easily accessible, talked and lived on a footing of equality with the people, enjoyed jokes at his own expense, and allowed everyone great freedom in criticizing his conduct and his character. Having discovered a conspiracy against him he forgave the plotters, saying that they were fools not to realize what a burden of cares a ruler wore. He lost his good temper in one case only. Helvidius Priscus, restored to the Senate from the exile into which Nero had sent him, demanded the restoration of the Republic, and reviled Vespasian without concealment or restraint. Vespasian asked him not to attend the Senate if he proposed to continue such abuse; Helvidius refused. Vespasian banished him and tarnished an excellent reign by ordering him put to death. He regretted the action later, and for the rest, says Suetonius, showed "the greatest patience under the frank language of his friends . . . and the impudence of philosophers." [95] These latter were not so much Stoics as Cynics, philosophical anarchists who felt that all government was an imposition and attacked every emperor.

To get fresh blood into a Senate depleted by family limitation and civil war, Vespasian secured appointment as censor, brought to Rome a thousand distinguished families from Italy and the western provinces, enrolled them in the patrician or equestrian orders, and over many bitter protests filled out the Senate from their ranks. The new aristocracy, under the stimulus of his example, improved Roman morals and society. It was not spoiled yet by idle wealth, nor yet so removed from labor and the soil as to disdain the routine tasks of life and administration; and it had something of the Emperor's order and decency of life. Out of it came those rulers who, after Domitian, gave Rome good government for a century. Conscious of the evils that had flowed from the use of freedmen as imperial executives, Vespasian replaced most of them with men from this provincial infiltration and from Rome's expanding business class. With their help he accomplished in nine years a miracle of rehabilitation.

He calculated that 40,000,000,000 sesterces were needed to transform bankruptcy into solvency.[96] * To raise this sum he taxed almost everything, raised the provincial tribute, reimposed it upon Greece, recaptured and let public lands, sold royal palaces and estates, and insisted upon such economy that the citizens denounced him as a miserly peasant. A tax was placed even upon the use of the public urinals that adorned ancient like modern Rome; his son Titus protested against such undignified revenue, but the old Emperor held some coins of it to the youth's nose and said, "See, my child, if they smell." [97] Suetonious accuses him of adding to the imperial income by selling offices, and by promoting the most rapacious of his provincial appointees so that they might be swollen with spoils when he suddenly summoned them, examined their transactions, and confiscated their gains. The crafty financier, however, used none of the proceeds for himself, but poured them all into the economic recovery, architectural adornment, and cultural advancement of Rome.

It remained for this blunt soldier to establish the first system of state education in classical antiquity. He ordered that certain qualified teachers of Latin and Greek literature and rhetoric should thereafter be paid out of public funds and should receive a pension after twenty years of service. Perhaps the old skeptic felt that teachers had some share in forming public opinion and would speak better of a government that paid their way. Probably for like reasons he restored many of the ancient temples, even in rural districts. He rebuilt the Temple of Jupiter, Juno, and Minerva, which had been burned down by the Vitellians over his soldiers' heads; raised a majestic shrine to Pax, the goddess of peace; and began the most renowned of Roman buildings, the Colosseum. The upper classes mourned as they saw their fortunes taxed to provide public works for the state and wages for prolétaires; and the workers were not particularly grateful. He roused the people to an energetic campaign for clearing away the debris left by the recent war, and he himself carried the first load. When an inventor showed him plans for a hoisting machine that would greatly reduce the need for human labor in these enterprises of removal and construction, he refused to use it, saying,

---

* The figure given by Suetonius is often rejected as incredible; but probably it was reckoned in a depreciated currency.

"I must feed my poor." [98] In this moratorium on invention Vespasian recognized the problem of technological unemployment, and decided against an industrial revolution.

The provinces prospered as never before. Their wealth was now twice as great—at least in monetary terms—as under Augustus, and they bore the increased tribute without injury. Vespasian sent the able Agricola to govern Britain, and delegated to Titus the task of ending the revolt of the Jews. Titus captured Jerusalem and returned to Rome with all the honors that usually crown superior killing. A spectacular triumph led a long procession of captives and spoils through the streets, and a famous arch was raised to commemorate the victory. Vespasian was proud of his son's success but disturbed by the fact that Titus had brought home a pretty Jewish princess, Berenice, as his mistress, and wished to marry her; again *capta ferum victorem cepit*. The Emperor could not see why one should marry a mistress; he himself, after the death of his wife, lived with a freedwoman without troubling to wed her; and when this Caenis died he distributed his love among several concubines.[99] He was convinced that the succession to his power must be settled before his death, as the alternative to anarchy. The Senate agreed, but demanded that he should name and adopt "the best of the best"—presumably a senator; Vespasian answered that he reckoned that Titus was the best. To ease the situation the young conqueror dismissed Berenice, and sought consolation in promiscuity.[100] The Emperor thereupon associated Titus with himself on the throne and delegated to him an increasing share in the government.

In 79 Vespasian again visited Reate. While in the Sabine country he drank copiously the purgative waters of Lake Cutilia and was seized with severe diarrhea. Though confined to his bed he continued to receive embassies and perform the other duties of his office. Feeling the hand of death upon him he nevertheless kept his bluff humor. *Vae! puto deus fio*, he remarked—"Alas, I think I am becoming a god." [101] Almost fainting, he struggled to his feet with the help of attendants, saying, "An emperor should die standing." With these words he concluded a full life of sixty-nine years and a beneficent reign of ten.

VII. TITUS

His older son, named like himself Titus Flavius Vespasianus, was the most fortunate of emperors. Titus died in the second year of his rule and the forty-second of his age, while still "the darling of mankind"; time did not suffice him for the corruptions of power or the disillusionment of desire.

As a youth he had distinguished himself in ruthless war and tarnished his name with loose living; now, instead of letting omnipotence intoxicate him, he reformed his morals and made his government a model of wisdom and honor. His greatest fault was uncontrollable generosity. He counted that day lost on which he had not made someone happy with a gift; he spent too much on shows and games; and he left the replenished Treasury almost as low as his father had found it. He completed the Colosseum and built another municipal bath. No one suffered capital punishment during his brief reign; on the contrary, he had informers flogged and banished. He swore that he would rather be killed than kill. When two patricians were detected in a conspiracy to depose him he contented himself with sending them a warning; then he dispatched a courier to relieve the anxiety of a conspirator's mother by telling her that her son was safe.

His misfortunes were disasters over which he could have little control. A three-day fire in the year 79 destroyed many important buildings, including again the Temple of Jupiter, Juno, and Minerva; in the same year Vesuvius buried Pompeii and thousands of Italians; and a year later Rome was stricken with a plague more deadly than any her history had yet recorded. Titus did all he could to lessen the sufferings caused by these calamities; "he showed not merely the concern of an emperor, but a father's surpassing love." [102] He died of a fever in 81, in the same farmhouse in which his father had recently passed away. All Rome mourned him except the brother who succeeded to his throne.

VIII. DOMITIAN

Of Domitian it is harder to paint an objective portrait than even of Nero. Our chief sources for his reign are Tacitus and the younger Pliny; they prospered under him, but belonged to the senatorial party that engaged with him in a war almost of mutual extermination. To set against these hostile witnesses we have the poets Statius and Martial, who ate or sought Domitian's bread and literally praised him to the skies. Perhaps all four were right, for the last of the Flavians, like many of the Julio-Claudians, began like Gabriel and ended like Lucifer. In this respect Domitian's soul walked with his body: in youth he was modest, graceful, handsome, tall; in later years he had "a protruding belly, spindle legs, and a bald head"— though he had written a book *On the Care of the Hair*.[103] In adolescence he composed poetry; in obsolescence he distrusted his own prose and let others write his speeches and proclamations. He might have been happier had not Titus been his brother; but only the noblest spirits can bear with equanimity the success of their friends. Domitian's jealousy soured into a taciturn gloom, then into secret machinations against his brother; Titus had to beg his father to forgive the younger son. When Vespasian died, Domitian claimed that he had been left partner in the imperial power but that the Emperor's will had been tampered with. Titus replied by asking him to be his partner and successor; Domitian refused, and continued to plot. When Titus fell ill, says Dio Cassius, Domitian hastened his death by packing him about with snow.[104] We cannot assess the truth of these stories, nor of those tales of sexual license that have come down to us—that Domitian swam with prostitutes, made the daughter of Titus one of his concubines, and "was most profligate and lewd toward women and boys alike." [105] All Latin historiography is present politics, a partisan blow struck for contemporary ends.

When we come to the actual policies of Domitian we find him, in his first decade, surprisingly puritan and competent. As Vespasian had modeled himself on Augustus, so Domitian seemed to take over the policies and manners of Tiberius. Having made himself censor for life, he stopped the publication of scurrilous lampoons (though he winked at the epigrams of Martial), enforced the Julian laws against adultery, tried to end child prostitution and reduce unnatural vice, forbade the performance of pantomimes because of their indecency, ordered the execution of a Vestal Virgin convicted of incest or adultery, and put an end to the practice of castration, which had spread with the rising price of eunuch slaves. He shrank from any form of bloodshed, even the ritual sacrifice of oxen. He was honorable, liberal, and free from avarice. He refused legacies from those who had children, canceled all tax arrears more than five years old, and discountenanced delation. He was a strict but impartial judge. He had freedmen secretaries, but kept them on their good behavior.

His reign was one of the great ages of Roman building. The fires of 79 and 82 having caused much destruction and destitution, Domitian organized a program of public works to provide employment and distribute wealth.[106] He, too, hoped to reanimate the old faith by beautifying or multiplying its shrines. He raised the Temple of Jupiter, Juno, and Minerva once more, and spent $22,000,000 on its gold-plated doors and gilded roof; Rome admired the result and mourned the extravagance. When Domitian built for himself and his administrative staff an enormous palace, the Domus Flavia, the citizens reasonably complained of the cost; but they raised no voice against the expensive games with which he sought to moderate his Tiberian unpopularity. He dedicated a temple to his father and his brother; he restored the Baths and Pantheon of Agrippa, the Portico of Octavia, the temples of Isis and Serapis; he added to the Colosseum, finished the Baths of Titus, and began those that were completed by Trajan.

At the same time he did his dour best to encourage arts and letters. Flavian portrait sculpture reached its zenith in his principate; his coins are of outstanding excellence. To stimulate poetry he established in 86 the Capitoline games, which included contests in literature and music; and for these he built a stadium and a music hall in the Field of Mars. He gave modest help to the modest talent of Statius and the immodest talent of Martial. He rebuilt the public libraries, which had been destroyed by fire, and had their contents renewed by sending scribes to copy the manuscripts in Alexandria —another proof that the great library there had lost only a small part of its treasures in the fire started by Caesar.

He managed the Empire well. He had Tiberius' grim resolution as an administrator, pounced upon peculation, and kept strict watch on all appointees and developments. As Tiberius had restrained Germanicus, so Domitian withdrew Agricola from Britain after that enterprising general had led his armies, and pushed the frontier, to Scotland; apparently Agricola wished to go farther, and Domitian demurred. The recall was attributed to jealousy, and the Emperor paid a heavy price for it when the history of his reign was written by Agricola's son-in-law. He was equally unfortunate in war. In 86 the Dacians crossed the Danube, invaded the Roman province of Moesia, and defeated Domitian's generals. The Prince took command, planned his campaign well, and was about to enter Dacia when Antoninus Saturninus, Roman governor of Upper Germany, persuaded two legions at Mainz to proclaim him emperor. The revolt was suppressed by Domitian's aides, but it disconcerted his strategy by allowing the enemy time to prepare. He crossed the Danube, met the Dacians, and apparently suffered a reverse. He made peace with Decebalus, the Dacian king, sent him an annual *douceur*, and returned to Rome to celebrate a double triumph over the Chatti and the Dacians. He contented himself thereafter with the building of a *limes*, or fortified road, between the Rhine and the Danube, and another between the northward turn of the Danube and the Black Sea.

The revolt of Saturninus was the turning point in Domitian's reign, the dividing line between his better and worse selves. He had always been coldly severe; now he slipped into cruelty. He was capable of good government, but only as an autocrat; the Senate rapidly lost power under him; and his tenacious authority as censor made that body at once subservient and vengeful. Vanity, which flourishes even in the humble, had no check in Domitian's status: he filled the Capitol with statues of himself, announced the divinity of his father, brother, wife, and sisters as well as his own, organized a new order of priests, the *Flaviales*, to tend the worship of these new deities, and required officials to speak of him, in their documents, as *Dominus et Deus Noster*—"Our Lord and God." He sat on a throne, encouraged visitors to embrace his knees, and established in his ornate palace the etiquette of an Oriental court. The Principate had become, through the power of the army and the decay of the Senate, an unconstitutional monarchy.

Against this new development rebellion rose not only in the aristocracy but among the philosophers and in the religions that were flowing into Rome from the East. The Jews and the Christians refused to adore the godhead of Domitian, the Cynics decried all government, and the Stoics, though they accepted kings, were pledged to oppose despots and honor tyrannicides. In 89 Domitian expelled the philosophers from Rome, in 95 he banished them from Italy. The earlier edict applied also to the astrologers, whose predictions of the Emperor's death had brought new terrors to a mind empty of faith and open to superstition. In 93 Domitian executed some Christians for refusing to offer sacrifice before his image; according to tradition these included his nephew Flavius Clemens.[107]

In the last years of his reign the Emperor's fear of conspiracy became almost a madness. He lined with shining stone the walls of the porticoes under which he walked, so that he might see mirrored in them whatever went on behind him. He complained that the lot of rulers was miserable since no man believed them when they alleged conspiracy, unless the conspiracy succeeded. Like Tiberius he listened more readily to informers as he grew older; and as the *delatores* multiplied, no citizen of any prominence could feel safe from spies, even in his home. After Saturninus' revolt indictments and convictions rapidly increased; aristocrats were exiled or killed, suspected men were tortured, even by having "fire inserted into their private parts." [108] The terrified Senate, including the Tacitus who recounts these events most bitterly, was the agent of trial and condemnation; and at each execution it thanked the gods for the salvation of the Prince.

Domitian made the mistake of frightening his own household. In 96 he ordered the death of his secretary Epaphroditus because, twenty-seven years before, he had helped Nero to commit suicide. The other freedmen of the imperial household felt themselves threatened. To protect themselves they resolved to kill Domitian, and the Emperor's wife Domitia joined in the plot. On the night before his last he leaped from his bed in fright. When the appointed moment came, Domitia's servant struck the first blow; four others took part in the assault; and Domitian, struggling madly, met death in the forty-fifth year of his age and the fifteenth of his reign (96). When the news reached the senators they tore down and shattered all images of him in their chamber, and ordered that all statues of him, and all inscriptions mentioning his name, should be destroyed throughout the realm.

History has been unfair to this "age of despots" because it has spoken here chiefly through the most brilliant and most prejudiced of historians. It is true that the gossip of Suetonius often confirms—or follows—the invective of Tacitus; but the study of literature and inscriptions has condemned them both as mistaking the vices of ten emperors for the record of an empire and a century. There was something good in the worst of these rulers—devoted statesmanship in Tiberius, a charming gaiety in Caligula, a plodding wisdom in Claudius, an exuberant aestheticism in Nero, a stern competence in Domitian. Behind the adulteries and the murders an administrative organization had formed which provided, through all this period, a high order of provincial government. The emperors themselves were the chief victims of their power. Some disease in the blood, fired by the heat of loosed desire, had pursued the Julio-Claudians as fatally as the children of Atreus; and some flaw in the system had debased the Flavians in one generation from patient statesmanship to terrified cruelty. Seven of these ten men met a violent end; nearly all of them were unhappy, surrounded by conspiracy, dishonesty, and intrigue, trying to govern a world from the anarchy of a home. They indulged their appetites because they knew how brief was their omnipotence; they lived in the daily horror of men condemned to an early and sudden death. They went under because they were above the law; they became less than men because power had made them gods.

But we must not absolve the age or the principate of its ignominy and its crimes. It had given peace to the Empire, but terror to Rome; it had injured morals by the high example of cruelty and lust; it had torn Italy with a civil war more ferocious than that of Caesar and Pompey; it had filled the islands with exiles and had killed off the best and bravest men. It had suborned the treachery of relatives and friends by rewarding avaricious spies. It had, in Rome, replaced a government of laws with a tyranny of men. It had raised gigantic edifices by accumulating tribute, but it had dwarfed the soul by frightening talented or creative minds into servility or silence. Above all, it had made the army supreme. The power of the prince over the Senate lay not in his superior genius, nor in custom, nor in prestige; it rested upon the pikes of the Guard. When provincial armies saw how emperors were made, how rich were the donatives and spoils of the capital, they deposed the Praetorians and themselves entered upon the business of making kings. For a century yet the wisdom of great rulers chosen by adoption rather than by heredity, violence, or wealth would hold the legions in check and keep the frontiers safe. But when, through a philosopher's love, idiocy would again reach the throne, the armies would run riot, chaos would break through the fragile film of order, and civil war would join hands with the waiting barbarians to topple down the noble and precarious structure of government that the genius of Augustus had built.

CHAPTER XIV

The Silver Age

A.D. 14-96

I. THE DILETTANTES

TRADITION has given to Latin letters from A.D. 14 to 117 the name of Silver Age, implying a fall from the cultural excellence of the Augustan Age. Tradition is the voice of time, and time is the medium of selection; a cautious mind will respect their verdict, for only youth knows better than twenty centuries. We may be permitted, however, to suspend judgment, to give Lucan, Petronius, Seneca, the elder Pliny, Celsus, Statius, Martial, Quintilian—and, in later chapters, Tacitus, Juvenal, Pliny the Younger, and Epictetus—an unbiased hearing, and enjoy them as if we had never heard that they belonged to a decadent period. In every epoch something is decaying and something is growing. In epigram, satire, the novel, history, and philosophy the Silver Age marks the zenith of Roman literature, as it represents in realistic sculpture and mass architecture the climax of Roman art.

The speech of the common man re-entered literature, diminishing inflections, relaxing syntax, and dropping final consonants with Gallic impertinence. About the middle of the first century the Latin *V* (which had been pronounced like our *W*) and *B* (between vowels) were both softened into a sound like the English *V*; so *habere*, to have, became in sound *havere*, and prepared for Italian *avere* and French *avoir;* while *vinum*, wine, began to approximate, by lazy slurring of the changing final consonant, the Italian *vino* and the French *vin*. The Latin language was preparing to mother Italian, Spanish, and French.

It must be admitted that rhetoric had now grown at the expense of eloquence, grammar at the expense of poetry. Able men devoted themselves beyond precedent to studying the form, evolution, and niceties of the language, editing already "classical" texts, formulating the august rules of literary composition, forensic oratory, poetic meter, and prose rhythm. Claudius tried to reform the alphabet; Nero made poetry fashionable by his almost Japanese example; and the elder Seneca wrote manuals of rhetoric on the ground that eloquence gives to every power a double power. Without eloquence only generals could rise in Rome; and even generals had to be orators. The mania for rhetoric seized all forms of literature: poetry became rhetorical, prose became poetical, and Pliny himself wrote an eloquent page in the six volumes of his *Natural History*. Men began to worry about the balance of their phrases and the melody of their clauses; historians wrote declamations, philosophers itched for epigrams, and every one wrote *sententiae*—concentrated pills of wisdom. All the polite world was writing poetry, and reading it to friends in hired halls or theaters, at table, even (Martial complained) in the bath. Poets engaged in public competitions, won prizes, were feted by municipalities and crowned by emperors; aristocrats and princes welcomed dedications or tributes and paid for them with dinners or denarii. The passion for poetry gave a pleasant aspect of amateur authorship to an age and city darkened with sexual license and periodic terror.

Terror and poetry met in the life of Lucan. The older Seneca was his grandfather, the philosopher Seneca his uncle. Born in Corduba in 39, and named Marcus Annaeus Lucanus, he was brought in infancy to Rome and grew up in aristocratic circles where poetry and philosophy rivaled amorous and political intrigues as the foci of life. At twenty-one he competed in the Neronian Games with a poem "In Praise of Nero," and won a prize. Seneca introduced him at court, and soon the poet and the Emperor were bandying epics. Lucan made the mistake of winning first prize in a poetic contest with the Prince; Nero ordered him to publish no more, and Lucan withdrew to avenge himself in private with a vigorous but rhetorical epic, *Pharsalia*, which viewed the Civil War from the standpoint of the Pompeian aristocracy. Lucan is fair to Caesar, and writes of him an illuminating phrase: *nil actum credens cum quid superesset agendum*—"thinking nothing done while anything remained to do." [1] But the real hero of the book is the younger Cato, whom Lucan equals with the gods in a famous line: *victrix causa deis placuit, sed victa Catoni*—"the winning cause pleased the gods, but the lost one pleased Cato." [2] Lucan too loved a lost cause and died for it. He joined in the conspiracy to replace Nero with Piso, was arrested, broke down (he was only twenty-six), and revealed the names of other conspirators, even, we are told, of his mother. When Nero confirmed his death sentence he recovered his courage, summoned his friends to a feast, ate with them heartily, opened his veins, and recited his lines against despotism as he bled to death (65).

II. PETRONIUS

We are not certain—it is only the general opinion—that the Petronius whose *Satyricon* still finds many readers was the Caius Petronius who died by Nero's orders a year after Lucan. The book itself contains not a word to serve as a clue; and Tacitus, who describes the *arbiter elegantiarum* with pithy eloquence, makes no mention of the disreputable masterpiece. Some forty epigrams are ascribed to a Petronius, including a line that almost sums up Lucretius: *primus in orbe deos fecit timor*—"it was fear that first in the world made gods"; [3] but these fragments too are silent about the author's identity.

The *Satyricon* was a collection of satires, probably in sixteen books, of which only the last two remain, themselves incomplete. They are *saturae* in the Latin sense of medleys—here of prose and verse, adventure and philosophy, gastronomy and venery. The form owes something to the satires of Menippus, a Syrian Cynic who wrote in Gadara about 60 B.C., and to the "Milesian Tales," or love romances, that had become popular in the Hellenistic world. As all extant examples of these are later than Petronius, the *Satyricon* has the distinction of being the oldest known novel.

It is hardly credible that an aristocratic lord of luxury, and master of fine taste, should have fathered a book so profusely vulgar as the *Satyricon*. All its active characters are plebeians, ex-slaves, or slaves, and all the scenes are of low life; here the Augustan preoccupation of literature with the upper classes is violently ended. Encolpius, who tells the tale, is an adulterer, a homosexual, a liar, and a thief, and takes it for granted that all sensible men are the same. "We had it understood between ourselves," he says of himself and his friend, "that whenever opportunity came we would pilfer whatever we could lay our hands upon, for the improvement of our common treasury." [4] The story begins in a brothel, where Encolpius meets Ascyltos, who has taken refuge there from a lecture on philosophy. Their escapades among the towns and trolls of southern Italy form the thread of the wandering narrative; their rivalry for the handsome slave boy Giton unites and divides them in picaresque romance. At last they come to the house of the merchant Trimalchio; and the rest of the extant work is given over to describing the *Cena Trimalchionis*, the most astounding dinner in literature.

Trimalchio is an ex-slave who has made a fortune, has bought enormous *latifundia*, and lives in parvenu luxury with the appointments of a palace and the atmosphere of a stew. His estates are so vast that a daily gazette must be written to keep him abreast of his earnings. He begs his guests to drink:

> If the wine don't please you I'll change it. I don't have to buy it, thank the gods. Everything here that makes your mouth water was produced on one of my country places, which I've never yet seen; but they tell me it's down Terracina and Tarentum way. I've got a notion to add Sicily to my other little holdings, so in case I want to go to Africa I'll be able to sail along my own coasts. . . . When it comes to silver I'm a connoisseur; I have goblets as big as wine jars. . . . I own a thousand bowls that Mummius left to my patron. . . . I buy cheap and sell dear; others may have different ideas.[5]

He is a kindly fellow withal; he shouts at his slaves, but he pardons them readily. He has so many that only a tenth of them know him by sight. "Slaves are men," he says, generously remembering his origin; "they sucked the same milk that we did . . . and mine will drink the water of freedom if they live." To prove his intentions he has his will brought in and reads it to his guests. It includes specifications for his epitaph, which is to end with the proud claim that he "grew rich from little, left 30,000,000 sesterces, and never heard a philosopher." [6]

Forty pages describe the dinner; a few sentences will convey its aroma:

> There was a circular tray around which were displayed the signs of the zodiac, and upon each sign the caterer had placed the food best in keeping with it. Ram's vetches on Aries, beef on Taurus . . . the womb of an unfarrowed sow on Virgo . . . on Libra a balance holding a tart in one pan and a cake in the other. . . . Four dancers ran in to music, and removed the upper part of the tray. Beneath it . . . stuffed capons and sows' bellies, and in the middle a hare. At the corners four figures of Marsyas spouted from their bladders a highly spiced sauce upon fish which were swimming about. . . . A tray followed on which was served a wild boar; from its tusks hung baskets loaded with dates; around it were little suckling pigs made of pastry. . . . When the carver plunged his knife into the boar's side, thrushes flew out, one for each guest. [7]

Three white hogs walk into the room, and the guests choose which one they will have cooked for them; while they eat, the winning hog is roasted; soon it re-enters; when it is carved, sausages and meat puddings emerge from its belly. When the dessert arrives Encolpius has no stomach for it; but Trimalchio urges his guests onward by assuring them that the dessert has been made entirely out of a hog. A hoop is lowered from the ceiling, bringing to each diner an alabaster jar filled with perfume, while slaves replenish empty glasses with ancient wines. Trimalchio gets drunk and makes love to a boy; his fat wife protests, and he throws a cup at her head. "This Syrian dancing whore," he says of her, "has a poor memory. I took her off the auction block and made her a woman, and now she puffs herself up like a frog. . . . But that's the way it is: if you're born in an attic you can't sleep in a palace." [8] And he bids his major-domo keep her statue off his tomb, "else I'll be nagged even after I'm dead."

It is a powerful and savage satire; realistic only in its details, and probably true of only a small segment of Roman life. If Nero's Petronius wrote it we must count it the merciless caricature of the *nouveau riche* freedman by a patrician who had never earned his keep. There is no mercy in the book, no tenderness, no ideal; immorality and corruption are taken for granted, and the life of the underworld is presented with gusto, without indignation, and without comment. Here the gutter flows directly into classic literature, bringing its own judgments and taste, its own lusty vocabulary and hilarious vitality. Sometimes the story rises to those sublime heights of nonsense, obscenity, and vituperation which crown the epic of Gargantua and Pantagruel. Apuleius' *Golden Ass* would follow in its steps; *Gil Blas*, seventeen centuries later, would rival it; *Tristram Shandy* and *Tom Jones* would continue its meandering tradition. It is the strangest book in the literature of Rome.

III. THE PHILOSOPHERS

In this loose and complex age, when freedom was so limited and life was so free, philosophy flourished alongside of sensuality, and the two were not above joining hands. The decay of the native religion had left a moral vacuum which philosophy sought to fill. Parents sent their sons, and themselves often went, to hear the lectures of men who offered to provide a rational code of civilized conduct, or a formal dress for naked desire. Those who could afford it paid philosophers to live with them, partly as educators, partly as spiritual counselors, partly as learned company; so Augustus had Areus, consulted him on almost everything, and for his sake (if we may believe a ruler) was lenient to Alexandria. When Drusus died Livia called in "her husband's philosopher"—so Seneca phrases it—"to help her bear her grief." [9] Nero, Trajan, and of course Aurelius had philosophers residing with them at court, as kings have chaplains now. In their last moments men would summon philosophers to chart their passing, as centuries later they would ask for a priest. [10]

The public never forgave these teachers of wisdom for taking salaries or fees. Philosophy was esteemed a sufficient substitute for food and drink, and philosophers who had a less exalted opinion of their profession were the butt of popular jokes, of Quintilian's criticism, of Lucian's satire, and of imperial hostility. Many of them deserved it, for they put on the philosopher's coarse cloak, and grew a profound beard, to give a learned front to gluttony, avarice, and vanity. "A short survey of life," says a character in Lucian,

> had convinced me of the absurdity and meanness . . . that pervade all worldly purposes. . . . In this state of mind the best I could think of was to get at the truth of it all from the . . . philosophers. So I selected the best of them—if solemnity of visage, pallor of complexion, and length of beard are a criterion . . . I placed myself in their hands. For a considerable sum down, and more to be paid when they had perfected me in wisdom, I was to be . . . instructed in the order of the

universe. Unfortunately, so far from dispelling my previous ignorance, they perplexed me more and more with their daily drenches of
beginnings and ends, atoms and voids, matters and forms. My greatest
difficulty was that, though they differed among themselves, and all
they said was full of contradictions, they expected me to believe
them, each pulling me in his own direction. . . . Often one of them
could not tell you correctly the number of miles from Megara to
Athens, but had no hesitation about the distance in feet from the sun
to the moon.[11]

Most of the Roman philosophers followed the Stoic creed. The epicureans
were too busy pursuing wine, woman, and food to have much time for theory.
Here and there in Rome were mendicant preachers of the Cynic philosophy,
ignoring speculation, and calling men to a simple and soapless life; they acceded
to the popular demand that philosophers should be poor, and were in consequence the least respected of the schools. Seneca, however, made one of them
his intimate friend. "Why should I not hold Demetrius in high esteem?" he
asked. "I have found that he lacks nothing;" and the millionaire sage marveled
when the nearly naked Cynic refused a gift of 200,000 sesterces from Caligula.[12]

Since the Roman Stoic was a man of action rather than of contemplation, he
eschewed metaphysics as a hopeless quest, and sought in Stoicism a philosophy of
conduct that would support human decency, family unity, and social order
independently of supernatural surveillance and command. The essence of his
code was self-control: he would subordinate passion to reason, and train his will
to desire nothing that would make his peace of soul contingent upon external
goods. In politics he would recognize the universal brotherhood of man under
the fatherhood of God; at the same time he would love his country and hold
himself ready to die at any time to avert its disgrace or his own. Life itself was
always to remain within his choice; he was free to leave it whenever it should
become an evil rather than a boon. A man's conscience was to be higher than
any law. Monarchy was a sad necessity for the rule of wide and diverse realms;
but to kill a despot was an excellent thing.

Roman Stoicism had at first profited from the Principate; the limitations on
political freedom had driven men from the forum to the study, and had inclined
the finest of them to a philosophy that made the self-controlled subject more
sovereign than the impassioned king. The government did not check freedom
of thought or speech so long as these made no public attack upon the emperor,
his family, or the official gods. But when the professors and their Senatorial
patrons began to denounce tyranny, there arose between philosophy and autocracy a war that lasted till the adoptive emperors united them on the throne.
When Nero ordered Thrasea to die (65), he at the same time exiled Thrasea's
friend Musonius Rufus, the most sincere and consistent of the Stoic philosophers
in first-century Rome. Rufus had defined philosophy as inquiry into right
conduct, and had taken his quest seriously. He denounced concubinage despite
its legality, and demanded of men the same standard of sexual morality that they

required of women. Sexual relations, said this ancient Tolstoian, were permissible only in marriage and for procreation. He believed in equal educational opportunities for both sexes and welcomed women to his lectures; but he bade them seek from education and philosophy the means of perfecting themselves as women.[13] Slaves, too, attended his classes; one of them—Epictetus—honored his teacher by surpassing him. When civil war flared in Rome after Nero's death, Musonius went out to the attacking army and lectured it on the blessings of peace and the horrors of war. Antonius' troops laughed at him and resumed the ultimate arbitrament. Vespasian, in expelling the philosophers from Rome, excepted Rufus; but he kept his concubines.

IV. SENECA

The Stoic philosophy found its most doubtful expression in the life, its most perfect expression in the writings, of Lucius Annaeus Seneca. Born at Corduba about 4 B.C., he was soon taken to Rome, and received all the education available there. He imbibed rhetoric from his father, Stoicism from Attalus, Pythagoreanism from Sotion, and practical politics from his aunt's husband, the Roman governor of Egypt. He tried vegetarianism for a year, then gave it up, but remained always abstemious in food and drink; he was a millionaire in his surroundings rather than in his habits. He suffered so much from asthma and weak lungs that he often contemplated suicide. He practiced law, and was chosen quaestor about A.D. 33. Two years later he married Pompeia Paulina, with whom he lived in remarkable continuity until his death.

On inheriting his father's fortune he abandoned the law and indulged himself in writing. When Cremutius Cordus was forced by Caligula to kill himself (40), Seneca addressed to Cordus' daughter Marcia a *consolatio* —an essay of condolence which was a regularly practiced form in the schools of rhetoric and philosophy. Caligula wished to have him executed for his impertinence, but Seneca's friends saved his life by arguing that he would presently die of consumption in any case. Soon afterward Claudius accused him of improper relations with Julia, daughter of Germanicus; the Senate condemned him to death, but Claudius commuted this to exile in Corsica. On that rugged isle, amid a population as primitive as in Ovid's Tomi, the philosopher spent eight lonely years (41-49). At first he took his misfortune with true stoic calm, and comforted his mother with a touching *Consolatio ad Helviam;* but as the bitter years crawled on, his spirit broke, and he addressed to Claudius' secretary a *Consolatio ad Polybium* in a humble appeal for pardon. When this failed he tried to dull his sufferings by composing tragedies.

These strange productions, in which almost every character is an orator, were probably intended for the study rather than the stage; we do not hear of any of them being played; at most some brilliant episodes or resounding speeches were put to music and acted by a mime. The gentle philosopher incarnadines the stage with violence, as if he would rival in the theater the blood feasts of the games. Despite these heroic efforts he is too much of a thinker to be a good dramatist: he prefers ideas to men, and loses no chance for reflection, sentiment, or epigram. His plays contain some fine lines, but for the rest they may be forgotten with impunity. It should be added, however, that many good judges have not agreed with this verdict. Scaliger, lord of Renaissance critics, preferred Seneca to Euripides. When ancient literature came back to life it was Seneca who served as model for the first dramas in modern speech; from him came the classic form and unities that marked the plays of Corneille and Racine and dominated the French stage till the nineteenth century. In England, which felt his influence less, the translation of Seneca's dramas by Heywood (1559) gave an exemplar to the first English tragedy, *Gorboduc,* and left its mark on Shakespeare.

In 48 the younger Agrippina replaced Messalina in power over Claudius and Rome. Anxious to turn her eleven-year-old son Nero into an Alexander, she looked about for an Aristotle and found him in Corsica. She had Seneca recalled and restored to his seat in the Senate. For five years he tutored the youth and for five more he guided the Emperor and the state. During this decade he wrote for the edification of Nero and sundry some genial expositions of the Stoic philosophy—*On Anger, On the Brevity of Life, On the Tranquillity of the Soul, On Clemency, On the Happy Life, On the Constancy of the Sage, On Benefits, On Providence.* These formal treatises do not show him at his best. Like his plays they gleam with epigrams; but these, sent forth page after page in a staccato jet, at last weary the mind and lose their charm. Seneca's public, however, read these essays at intervals, and did not resent the gay wit that displeased the austere Quintilian,[14] or the "sugar plums" and "glaring patches" that would offend Fronto's archaic taste; it was pleased that their rich premier spoke so amiably, and, like his pupil, tried so hard to win its applause. For many years Seneca was the leading author, statesman, and vinegrower of Italy.

He multiplied his patrimony by investments that apparently took full advantage of his official position and knowledge. If we may believe Dio, he lent money to provincials at such high interest that panic and insurrection broke out in Britain when he suddenly called in his loans there in the sum of 40,000,000 sesterces.[15] His fortune, we are told, rose to 300,000,000 ($30,000,000).[16] In 58 an old delator friend of Messalina, Publius Suilius, publicly attacked the premier as a "hypocrite, an adulterer, and a wanton; a man who denounces courtiers and never leaves the palace; who denounces luxury, and displays 500 dining tables of cedar and ivory; who denounces wealth, and sucks the provinces dry by usury." [17] Like Caesar, Seneca contented himself with a rebuttal when he might have arranged an execution. In his essay *On the Happy Life* he repeated the charges, and replied that the sage is not bound to poverty; if wealth comes to him honestly he may take it; but he must be capable of abandoning it at any time without serious regret.[18] Meanwhile he lived ascetically amid his fine furniture, slept on a hard mattress, drank only water, and ate so sparingly that when he died his body was emaciated through undernourishment.[19] "Abundance of food," he wrote, "dulls the wits; excess of food strangles the soul." [20] The charges of sexual irregularity were probably true of his youth, but he was noted for his unfailing tenderness to his wife. In truth he never made up his mind which he loved better—philosophy or power, wisdom or pleasure; and he was never convinced of their incompatibility. He admitted that he was a very imperfect sage. "I persist in praising not the life that I lead, but that which I ought to lead. I follow it at a mighty distance, crawling" [21]—of which of us is this not true? If he is not sincere in saying that "mercy becomes no man so well as the king or the prince," [22] he at least phrases the sentiment almost as well as Portia. He condemned gladiatorial combats to the death,[24] and Nero forbade them. He disarmed much criticism by what Tacitus calls "the grace with which he imparted wisdom." [25] He did not demand, any more than he practiced, perfection.

We have seen that he ruled the Empire well, and that he tarnished his record by condoning the worst of Nero's crimes, "letting much evil pass in order to have the power of doing a little good." [27] He felt disgraced, and longed to free himself from his imperial servitude; he described the Emperor's palace as *triste ergastulum*—"an unhappy prison for slaves." He began to wish that he had devoted all his life to the study of wisdom and had shunned the dark labyrinths of power. With pleasure he would put aside, now and then, the cares of politics, and at sixty attend like an eager youth the lectures of Metronax on philosophy.[28] In the year 62, aged sixty-six, he begged leave to resign his reduced place in the government, but Nero would not let him go. After the great fire of 64, when Nero asked all the Empire to send contributions for the rebuilding of Rome, Seneca donated the greater part of his fortune. Gradually he succeeded in withdrawing from the court; more and more he lived in his Campanian villas, hoping by an almost monastic seclusion to escape the attentions and spies of the Emperor. For a time he lived on wild apples and running water for fear of poison in his food.

It was in this atmosphere of leisurely terror that he wrote (63-65) his studies in natural science (*Quaestiones Naturales*), and the most lovable of his works, the *Epistulae Morales*. They were casual, intimate causeries addressed to his friend Lucilius—rich governor of Sicily, poet, philosopher, and frank Epicurean. There are few books in Roman literature more pleasant than these urbane attempts to adapt Stoicism to the needs of a millionaire. Here begins the informal essay, which would be the favorite medium of Plutarch and Lucian, Montaigne and Voltaire, Bacon and Addison and Steele. To read these letters is to be in correspondence with an enlightened, humane, and tolerant Roman who has reached the heights and known the depths of literature, statesmanship, and philosophy. They are Zeno speaking with Epicurus' lenience and Plato's charm. Seneca apologizes to Lucilius for the carelessness of his style (it is nevertheless delectable Latin): "I want my letters to you to be just what my conversation would be if you and I were sitting or walking together." [30] "I write this," he adds, "not for the many but for you; each of us is sufficient audience to the other" (*satis magnum alter alteri theatrum sumus*) [31]—though the old diplomat doubtless hoped that posterity would eavesdrop on his talk. He describes his asthma vividly but without self-pity; he cheerfully calls it "practicing how to die" by taking "last gasps" for an hour. He is sixty-seven now, but only in body: "my mind is strong and alert; it takes issue with me on the subject of old age; it declares that old age is its period of bloom." [32] He rejoices that he has time at last to read the good books he has had so long to put aside. Apparently he now reread Epicurus, for he quotes him with a frequency and an enthusiasm scandalous in a Stoic. He is frightened by the excesses of individualism and self-indulgence in Caligula, Nero, and thousands more; he wishes to offer some counterweight to the temptations that beset minds liberated before moral maturity; and he seems resolved to confute the epicureans out of the mouth of the master whose name they abused and whose doctrine they dared not understand.

The first lesson of philosophy is that we cannot be wise about everything. We are fragments in infinity and moments in eternity; for such forked atoms to describe the universe, or the Supreme Being, must make the planets tremble with mirth. Therefore Seneca has little use for metaphysics or theology. One may prove out of his writings that he was a monotheist, a polytheist, a pantheist, a materialist, a Platonist, a monist, a dualist. Sometimes God is to him a personal Providence who watches over all, "loves good men," [33] answers their prayers, and helps them by divine grace; [34] in other passages God is the First Cause in an unbroken chain of causes and effects, and the ultimate force is Fate, "an irrevocable cause which carries along human and divine affairs equally . . . leading the willing and dragging the unwilling along." [36] A like indecision obscures his conception of the soul: it is a finely material breath animating the body; but it is also "a god dwelling as a guest" in the human frame.[37] He speaks hopefully of a life beyond death, where knowledge and virtue will be perfected; [38] and again he calls immortality "a beautiful dream." [39] In truth Seneca has never thought these matters out to a consistent (or public) conclusion; he talks of them with the cautious inconsistency of a politician who agrees with everybody. He has followed too successfully his father's oratorical lessons, and expresses every point of view with irresistible eloquence.

The same hesitations mar and grace his moral philosophy. He is too Stoic to be practical, and too lenient to be Stoic. He sees about him an immorality that exhausts the body and debases the soul, never satisfying either; avarice and luxury have destroyed peace and health, and power has made man only an abler brute. How shall one free himself from this ignominious agitation?

> I read in Epicurus today: "If you would enjoy real freedom you must be the slave of philosophy." The man who submits to her is emancipated there and then. . . . The body, once cured, often ails again . . . but the mind, once healed, is healed for good and all. I shall tell you what I mean by health: if the mind is content and confident; if it understands that those things for which all men pray, all the benefits that are sought or bestowed, are of no importance in relation to a life of happiness. . . . I shall give you a rule by which to measure yourself and your development: in that day you will come into your own when you realize that the successful are of all men most miserable.[40]

Philosophy is the science of wisdom, and wisdom is the art of living. Happiness is the goal, but virtue, not pleasure, is the road. The old ridiculed maxims are correct and are perpetually verified by experience; in the long run honesty, justice, forbearance, kindliness, bring us more happiness than ever comes from the pursuit of pleasure. Pleasure is good, but only when consistent with virtue; it cannot be a wise man's goal; those who make it their end in life are like the dog that snaps at every piece of meat thrown to it, swallows it whole, and then, instead of enjoying it, stands with jaws agape anxiously awaiting more.[41]

But how does one acquire wisdom? By practicing it daily, in however modest a degree; by examining your conduct of each day at its close; by being harsh to your own faults and lenient to those of others; by associating with those who excel you in wisdom and virtue; by taking some acknowledged sage as your invisible counselor and judge. You will be helped by reading the philosophers; not outline stories of philosophy, but the original works; "give over hoping that you can skim, by means of epitomes, the wisdom of distinguished men." [44] "Every one of these men will send you away happier and more devoted, no one of them will allow you to depart empty-handed. . . . What happiness, and what a noble old age, await him who has given himself into their patronage!" [45] Read good books many times, rather than many books; travel slowly, and not too much; "the spirit cannot mature into unity unless it has checked its curiosity and its wanderings." [46] "The primary sign of a well-ordered mind is a man's ability to remain in one place and linger in his own company." [47] Avoid crowds. "Men are more wicked together than separately. If you are forced to be in a crowd, then most of all you should withdraw into yourself." [48]

The final lesson of the Stoic is contempt and choice of death. Life is not always so joyful as to merit continuance; after life's fitful fever it is well to sleep. "What is baser than to fret at the threshold of peace?" [49] If a man finds life grievous, and can leave it without serious injury to others, he should feel free to choose his own time and way. Seneca preaches suicide to Lucilius as if he were Lucilius' heir:

> This is one reason why we cannot complain of life, it keeps no one against his will. . . . You have had veins cut for the purpose of reducing your weight. If you would pierce your heart, a gaping wound is not necessary; a lancet will open the way to freedom, and tranquillity can be purchased at the cost of a pinprick.[50] . . . Wherever you look, there is an end to troubles. Do you see that precipice?—it is a descent to liberty. Do you see that river, that cistern, that sea?— freedom is in their depths.[51] . . . But I am running on too long. How can a man end his life if he cannot end a letter? [52] . . . As for me, my dear Lucilius, I have lived long enough. I have had my fill. I await death. Farewell.[53]

Life took him at his word. Nero sent a tribune to seek his answer to the charge that he had plotted to make Piso emperor; Seneca replied that he was no longer interested in politics, and sought nothing but peace and the opportunity to attend to "a weak and crazy constitution." "He showed no symptom of fear," reported the tribune, "no sign of sorrow . . . his words and looks bespoke a mind serene, erect, and firm." "Return," said Nero, "and tell him to die." "Seneca heard the message," says Tacitus, "with calm composure." He embraced his wife, and bade her be comforted by the honorableness of his life and the lessons of philosophy. But Paulina refused to outlive him; when his veins were opened she had hers opened too. He called for a secretary and dictated a letter of farewell to the Roman people. He asked and received a drink of hemlock, as if resolved to die like Socrates. As the physician placed him in a warm bath to ease his pain he sprinkled the nearest servants with the water, saying "a libation to Jove the Deliverer", and after much suffering he passed away (65). At Nero's command the physician forcibly bound Paulina's wrists and stopped the flow of her blood; she survived her husband a few years, but her perpetual pallor recalled her stoic resolution.

Death glorified Seneca and made one generation forget his poses and his inconsistencies. Like all Stoics he underestimated the power and value of feeling and passion, exaggerated the worth and reliability of reason, and trusted too much to a nature in whose soil grow all the flowers of evil as well as of good. But he made Stoicism human, brought it down livably within the scope of men, and formed it into a spacious vestibule to Christianity. His pessimism, his condemnation of the immorality of his time, his counsel to return anger with kindness,[54] and his preoccupation with death [55] made Tertullian call him "ours," [56] and led Augustine to exclaim, "What more could a Christian say than this pagan has said?" [57] He was not a Christian; but at least he asked for an end to slaughter and lechery, called men to a simple and decent life, and reduced the distinctions between freeman, freedman, and slave to "mere titles born of ambition or of wrong." [58] It was a slave in Nero's court, Epictetus, who profited most from his teaching. Nerva and Trajan were in some measure molded by his writings and inspired by his example to conscientious and humanitarian statesmanship. To the end of antiquity and through the Middle Ages he remained popular; and when the rebirth came Petrarch placed him next to Virgil and upon Seneca's prose devotedly modeled his own. Montaigne's brother-in-law translated him into French, and Montaigne quoted him as fondly as Seneca quoted Epicurus. Emerson read him again and again [59] and became an American Seneca. There are few original ideas in him; but that may be forgiven, for in philosophy all truth is old, and only error is original. With all his faults he was the greatest of Rome's philosophers and, at least in his books, one of the wisest and kindliest of men. Next to Cicero he was the most lovable hypocrite in history.

V. ROMAN SCIENCE

Therefore we have given him too much space; nevertheless, we have not finished with him yet, for he was also a scientist. In those fertile years between his retirement and his death he amused himself with *Quaestiones Naturales*, and sought natural explanations of rain, hail, snow, wind, comets, rainbows, earthquakes, rivers, springs. In his drama *Medea* he had suggested the existence of another continent beyond the Atlantic.[60] With similar intuition, contemplating the overwhelming multitude of stars, he wrote, "How many an orb, moving in the depths of space, has never yet reached the eyes of men!" [61] And he adds, clairvoyantly, "How many things our sons will learn that we cannot now suspect!—what others await centuries when our names will be forgotten! . . . Our descendants will marvel at our ignorance." [62] We do. Seneca, though always eloquent, adds little to Aristotle and Aratus, and borrows abundantly from Poseidonius. He believes in divination despite Cicero, lapses into ludicrous teleology despite Lucretius, and interrupts his science at every turn to inculcate morality; he passes skillfully from mussels to luxury, and from comets to degeneration. The Fathers of the Church liked this mixture of meteorology and morals, and made the *Quaestiones Naturales* the most popular textbook of science in the Middle Ages.

There were a few men of scientific mind and interest in Rome, like Varro, Agrippa, Pomponius Mela, and Celsus; but they were scarce outside of geography, horticulture, and medicine. For the rest, science had not yet detached itself from magic, superstition, theology, and philosophy; it consisted of collected observations and traditions, seldom of fresh inquiry into facts, and rarely of experiment. Astronomy remained as Babylonia and Greece had left it. Time was still told by water clocks and sundials, and by the great obelisk that Augustus had stolen from Egypt and set up in the Field of Mars; its shadow, falling upon a pavement marked off in brass, indicated both the hour and the season.[63] Day and night were variably defined by the rising and setting of the sun; each had twelve hours, so that an hour of the day was longer, and an hour of the night shorter, in summer than in winter. Astrology was almost universally accepted. Pliny noted that in his time (A.D. 70) both learned and simple believed that a man's destiny was determined by the star under which he was born.[64] They argued plausibly that vegetation, and perhaps the mating season in animals, depend upon the sun;* that the physical and moral qualities of people are affected by climatic factors themselves determined by the sun; and that individual character and fate, like these general phenomena, are the result of celestial conditions inadequately known. Astrology was rejected only by the skeptics of the later Academy, who denied its pretended knowledge, and by the Christians, who scorned it as idolatry. Geography was studied more realistically, for navigation's sake. Pomponius Mela (A.D. 43) published maps on which the surface of the globe was divided into a central torrid zone and north and south temperate zones. Roman geographers knew Europe, southwestern and southern Asia, and northern Africa; of the remainder they had vague ideas and fantastic legends. Spanish and African skippers reached Madeira and the Canary Islands,[65] but no Columbus rose to test Seneca's dream.

The most extensive, industrious, and unscientific product of Italian science was the *Historia Naturalis* (77) of Caius Plinius Secundus. Though busy nearly all his life as soldier, lawyer, traveler, administrator, and head of the western Roman fleet, he wrote treatises on oratory, grammar, and the javelin, a history of Rome, another of Rome's wars in Germany, and—

---

* Many farmers today plant according to the phases of the moon.

sole survivor of this flood—thirty-seven "books" of natural history. How he managed all this in fifty-five years is explained in a letter of his nephew's:

> He had a quick apprehension, incredible zeal, and an unequaled capacity to go without sleep. He would rise at midnight or at one, and never later than two in the morning, and begin his literary work. . . . Before daybreak he used to wait upon Vespasian, who likewise chose that season to transact business. When he had finished the affairs which the Emperor committed to his charge, he returned home to his studies. After a short light repast at noon . . . he would frequently, in the summer, repose in the sun; but during that time some author was read to him, from whom he made extracts and notes . . . as was his method with whatever he read. . . . Thereafter he generally went into a cold bath, took a light refreshment, and rested for a while. Then, as if it were a new day, he resumed his studies till dinner, when again a book was read to him, and he made notes. . . . Such was his manner of life amid the noise and hurry of the town. But in the country his whole time was devoted to study, except when he was actually bathing; all the while he was being rubbed and wiped he was employed in hearing some book read to him, or in dictating. In his journeys a stenographer constantly attended him in his chariot or sedan chair. . . . He once reproved me for walking; "you need not have lost those hours," he said, for he counted all time lost that was not given to study.[66]

His book, so sheared and sewn, was a one-man encyclopedia summarizing the science and errors of his age. "My purpose," he says, "is to give a general description of everything that is known to exist throughout the earth." [67] He deals with 20,000 topics and apologizes for omitting others; he refers to 2000 volumes by 473 authors, and admits his indebtedness by name with a candor exceptional in ancient literature; he notes, in passing, that he found many authors transcribing their predecessors word for word without acknowledgment. His style is dull, though sometimes purple, but we must not expect encyclopedias to be fascinating.

Pliny begins by rejecting the gods; they are, he thinks, merely natural phenomena, or planets, or services, personified and deified. The sole god is Nature, i.e., the sum of natural forces; and this god apparently pays no special attention to mundane affairs.[68] Pliny modestly refuses to measure the universe. His astronomy is a galaxy of absurdities (e.g., "In the war of Octavian against Antony the sun remained dim for almost a year" [69]); but he notes the aurora borealis,[70] states with approximate modernity the orbital period of Mars, Jupiter, and Saturn as respectively two, twelve, and thirty years, and argues for the spherical form of the earth.[71] He tells of islands rising from the Mediterranean in his time, and surmises that Sicily and Italy, Boeotia and Euboea, Cyprus and Syria, were gradually sundered by the patience of the sea.[72] He treats of the laborious and servile mining of precious metals and regrets that "many hands are worn down that one little joint may be adorned." [73] He wishes that iron had never been found, since it has made war more terrible; "as if to bring death upon man more swiftly, we have given wings to iron and taught it to fly" [74]—referring to iron missiles equipped with leather feathers to help them keep their course. Following Theophrastus, he mentions under the name of *anthracitis* a "stone that burns," [75] but says no more about coal. He speaks of "an incombustible linen," called by the Greeks *asbestinon*, "which is used to embalm the cadavers of kings." [76] He describes or lists many animals, lauds their sagacity, and tells how to predetermine their sex: "If you wish to have females, let the dams face north while being covered." [77] He has twelve wondrous books on medicine—i.e., on the curative value of various minerals and plants. Books xx-xxv are a Roman herbal, which the Middle Ages passed down to form the initial plant lore of modern medicine. He offers cures for everything from intoxication and halitosis [78] to "a pain in the neck";[79] he provides "stimulants for the sexual passion," [80] and warns women against sneezing after coitus, lest they abort there and then.[81] He recommends coitus for physical weariness, hoarseness, pains in the loins, dim eyesight, melancholy, and "alienation of the mental faculties";[82] here is a panacea rivaling Bishop Berkeley's tar water. Amid such nonsense occurs much useful information, especially about ancient industry, manners, or drugs; with interesting references to atavism, petroleum, and change of sex after birth. "Mucianus informs us that he once saw at Argos a person whose name was then Arescon, but had formerly been Arescusa; that this person had been married to a man, but that shortly afterward he developed a beard and other male characteristics, upon which he took a wife." [83] Here and there valuable hints occur; e.g., Himly (1800) was led to investigate the action of jusquiamus and belladonna on the pupil by reading in Pliny a passage [84] about the use of anagallis juice before operations for cataract.[85] There are precious chapters on painting and sculpture, which constitute our oldest and principal account of ancient art.

Pliny was not content with natural history; he wished also to be a philosopher; and throughout his pages he scatters comments on mankind. The life of animals, he thinks, is preferable to man's, for "they never think about glory, money, ambition, or death"; [86] they can learn without being taught and never have to dress; and they do not make war upon their own species. The invention of money was fatal to human happiness; it made interest possible, by which some could live in idleness while others worked";[87] hence the rise of great estates owned by absentee landlords, and the ruinous re-placement of tillage with pasturage. Life, in Pliny's estimate, gives us much more grief and pain than happiness, and death is our supreme boon.[88] After death there is nothing.[89]

The *Natural History* is a lasting monument to Roman ignorance. Pliny gathers superstitions, portents, love charms, and magic cures as assiduously as anything else, and apparently believes in most of them. He thinks that a man, especially if fasting, can kill a snake by spitting into its mouth.[90] "It is well known that in Lusitania the mares become impregnated by the west wind" [91]—a point missed in Shelley's ode. Pliny condemns magic; but "on the approach of a menstruating woman," he informs us, "must will sour and seeds touched by her will become sterile; and fruit will fall from the tree under which she sits. Her look will blunt the edge of steel and take the polish from ivory; if it falls upon a swarm of bees they will die at once." [92] Pliny rejects astrology and then fills pages with "prognostics" derived from the behavior of the sun and the moon.[93] "In the consulship of M. Acilius, and frequently at other times, it rained milk and blood." [94] When we reflect that this book, and Seneca's *Quaestiones*, were the chief legacy of Roman natural science to the Middle Ages, and compare them with the corresponding works and temper of Aristotle and Theophrastus four hundred years earlier, we begin to feel the slow tragedy of a dying culture. The Romans had con-quered the Greek world, but they had already lost the most precious part of its heritage.

VI. ROMAN MEDICINE

They did better in medicine. Medical science too they borrowed from the Greeks, but they formulated it well, and applied it ably to personal and public hygiene. Rome, almost surrounded by marshes, and subject to mephitic floods, had particular need of public sanitation. About the second century B.C. we hear of malaria in Rome; the anopheles mosquito had settled down in the Pontine swamps.[95] Gout spread as luxury increased; the younger Pliny tells how his friend Corellius Rufus suffered its pains from his thirty-third to his sixty-seventh year before committing suicide, just to have the pleasure of outliving by one day "that brigand Domitian." [96] Some passages in the Roman satirists suggest the appearance of syphilis in the first century A.D.[97] Great epidemics swept central Italy in 23 B.C., A.D. 65, 79, and 166.

The people had of old tried to meet disease and plague with magic and prayer; even now they begged the skeptical but complaisant Vespasian to heal their blindness with his spittle and their lameness with the touch of his foot.[98] They brought their illnesses and votive offerings to the temples of Aesculapius and Minerva and many left gifts in gratitude for cures. But in the first century B.C. they turned more and more to secular medicine. There was as yet no state regulation of medical practice; shoemakers, barbers, carpenters, added it to their operations as they pleased, called in magic to their aid, and compounded, touted, and sold their own drugs.[99] There were the usual satires and complaints. Pliny repeated old Cato's imprecations upon Greek physicians who "seduce our wives, grow rich by feeding us poisons, learn by our suffering, and experiment by putting us to death." [100] Petronius, Martial, and Juvenal joined in the assault; and a century later Lucian would score incompetent practitioners who hide their incapacity under the elegance of their apparatus.[101]

Nevertheless, medicine, as we shall see, had made great progress in Alexandria, Cos, Tralles, Miletus, Ephesus, and Pergamum; and from these centers came Greek physicians who so raised the level of Roman practice that Caesar enfranchised the profession in Rome, and Augustus exempted it from taxation. Asclepiades of Prusa won the friendship of Caesar, Crassus, and Antony. He declared that the heart pumps blood and air through the body; rarely prescribed drugs or drastic purges; and accomplished impressive cures by hydrotherapy (baths, fomentations, enemas), massage, sunshine, exercise (walking, horseback riding), diet, fasting, and abstinence from meat. He was distinguished for his treatment of malaria, his operations on the throat, and his humane handling of the insane.[102] He gathered pupils about him and took some of them with him on his rounds. After his death they and similar students formed themselves into *collegia* and built for themselves a meeting place, on the Esquiline, called *Schola Medicorum*.

Under Vespasian *auditoria* were opened for the teaching of medicine, and recognized professors were paid by the state. Greek was the language of instruction, as Latin is now the language of prescription, and for a like reason— its intelligibility to persons of diverse tongues. Graduates of these state schools received the title of *medicus a republica*, and after Vespasian they alone could legally practice medicine in Rome.[103] The *lex Aquilia* provided for state supervision of physicians, and held them responsible for negligence; and the *lex Cornelia* severely punished practitioners whose carelessness or culpable ignorance caused the death of a patient.[104] Quacks continued, but sound practice increased. Midwives saw most Romans into the world, but many of these women were well trained.[105] About A.D. 100 military medicine reached its ancient zenith: every legion had twenty-four surgeons, first-aid and field-ambulance service were well organized, and hospitals were maintained near every important encampment.[106] Private hospitals (*valetudinaria*) were opened by physicians; from these evolved the public hospitals of the Middle Ages. Doctors were appointed and paid by the state to give free treatment to the poor.[107] Rich men kept their own physicians, and well-paid *archiatri* ("chief healers") took care of the emperor, his family, his servants, and his aides. Sometimes families would contract with a doctor to attend to their health and illnesses for a period of time; in this way Quintus Stertinius made 600,000 sesterces a year.[108] The surgeon Alcon, fined 10,000,000 sesterces by Claudius, paid it with a few years' fees.[109]

The profession now reached a high degree of specialization. There were urologists, gynecologists, obstetricians, ophthalmologists, eye and ear specialists, veterinarians, dentists. Romans could have gold teeth, wired teeth, false teeth, bridgework, and plates.[110] There were many women physicians; some of them wrote manuals of abortion, which were popular among great ladies and prostitutes. Surgeons were divided into further specialities and seldom engaged in general practice. Mandragora juice or atropin was used as an anesthetic.[111] Over 200 different surgical instruments have been found in the ruins of Pompeii. Dissection was illegal, but the examination of wounded or dying gladiators offered a frequent substitute. Hydrotherapy was popular; in a measure the great *thermae* were hydrotherapeutic institutes. Charmis of Marseilles made a fortune by administering cold baths. Consumptives were sent to Egypt or north Africa. Sulphur was used as a skin specific and to fumigate rooms after an infectious disease.[112] Drugs were a final but frequent resort. Physicians made them by processes kept secret from the public and charged for them all that patients could be persuaded to pay.[113] Repulsive drugs were held in high honor: the offal of lizards was used as a purgative, human entrails were sometimes prescribed, Antonius Musa recommended the excreta of dogs for angina, Galen applied a boy's dung to swellings of the throat.[114] In compensation for all this a cheerful quack offered to cure almost any ailment with wine.[115]

Of the known medical writers in this age only one was a Roman, and he was not a physician. Aurelius Cornelius Celsus was an aristocrat who about A.D. 30 gathered into an encyclopedia *De Artibus* his studies in agriculture, war, oratory, law, philosophy, and medicine; only the section *De Medicina* survives. It is the greatest work on medicine that has come down to us from the six centuries between Hippocrates and Galen; it has also the distinction of being written in such pure and classical Latin that Celsus was dubbed *Cicero medicorum*. The Latin terms into which he translated the nomenclature of Greek medicine have ruled the science ever since. The sixth book shows considerable knowledge, in antiquity, of venereal disease. The seventh is an illuminating description of surgical methods; it contains the earliest known account of ligature, and describes tonsillectomy, lateral lithotomy, plastic surgery, and operations for cataract. Altogether this is the soundest achievement in Roman scientific literature, and suggests that we might have a better opinion of Roman science if Pliny had not been preserved. It is a pity that scholarship has concluded that Celsus' treatise is largely a compilation or paraphrase of Greek texts.[116] Lost in the Middle Ages, it was rediscovered in the fifteenth century, was printed before Hippocrates or Galen, and took a leading part in stimulating the reconstruction of medicine in modern times.

VII. QUINTILIAN

When Vespasian established a state professorship of rhetoric in Rome he appointed to it a man who, like so many authors of this Silver Age, was of Spanish birth. Marcus Fabius Quintilianus was born at Calagurris (A.D. 35?), went to Rome to study oratory, and opened a school of rhetoric there which numbered Tacitus and the younger Pliny among its pupils. Juvenal describes him in his prime as handsome, noble, wise, well bred, with a fine voice and delivery, and a senatorial dignity. In old age he retired to write for the guidance of his son the classic treatment of his subject, the *Institutio Oratoria* (96).

> I thought that this work would be the most precious part of the inheritance of my son, whose ability was so remarkable that it called for the most anxious cultivation on the part of his father. . . . Night and day I pursued this design, and hastened its completion in the fear that death might cut me off with my task unfinished. Then misfortune overwhelmed me with such suddenness that the success of my labors now interests no one less than myself. . . . I have lost him of whom I had formed the highest expectations, and in whom I reposed all the hopes that should solace my old age.[117]

His wife had died at nineteen, leaving him two sons; one of these had died at the age of five, "robbing me, as it were, of one of my two eyes"; now the other went, leaving the old teacher "to outlive all my nearest and dearest."

He defines rhetoric as the science of speaking well. The training of the orator should begin before birth: it is desirable that he should come of educated parents, so that he may receive correct speech and good manners from the very air he breathes; it is impossible to become both educated and a gentleman in one generation. The future orator should study music, to give him an ear for harmony; the dance, to give him grace and rhythm; drama, to animate his eloquence with gesture and action; gymnastics, to keep him in health and strength; literature, to form his style, train his memory, and arm him with a treasury of great thoughts; science, to acquaint him with some understanding of nature; and philosophy, to mold his character on the dictates of reason and the precepts of wise men. For all preparations will be of no avail unless integrity of conduct and nobility of spirit are present to generate an irresistible sincerity of speech. Then the student must write as much as possible and with the utmost care. It is a hard training, and "I trust," says Quintilian, "that no one among my readers would think of calculating its monetary value." [118]

The oration itself has five phases: conception, arrangement, style, memory, and delivery. Having chosen his subject and clearly conceived his purpose, let the orator gather his material, from observation, inquiry, and books, and arrange it both logically and psychologically—so that each part will be in its proper place and lead as naturally to the next as in geometry.[119] A well-organized address will consist of introduction (*exordium*), proposition, proof, refutation, and peroration. The speech should be written out only if it is to be fully memorized; otherwise fragmentary memories of the written form will obstruct and confuse an extempore style. If it is written it must be with care. "Write quickly and you will never write well; write well, and you will soon write quickly"; shun the lazy "luxury of dictation now so fashionable among writers." [120] "Clearness is the first essential," then brevity, beauty, and vigor. Correct repeatedly and stoically:

> Erasure is as important as writing. Prune what is turgid, elevate what is commonplace, arrange what is disorderly, introduce rhythm where the language is harsh, modify where it is too absolute. . . . The best method of correction is to put aside for a time what we have written, so that when we come to it again it may have an aspect of novelty, as of being another man's work; in this way we may preserve ourselves from regarding our writings with the affection that we lavish upon a newborn child.[121]

Delivery, like composition, should touch the emotions, but avoid exuberant gesticulation. "It is feeling and force of imagination that makes us eloquent," but "shout and bellow with uplifted hand, pant, wag your head, smite your hands together, slap your thigh, your breast, your forehead, and you will go straight to the heart of the dingier members of your audience." [122]

To all this excellent counsel Quintilian adds, in his twelfth book, the best literary criticism that has survived from antiquity. He enters with zest into the ancient and modern war between the ancients and the moderns, and finds truth precariously in the middle. He does not, like Fronto, wish to return to the rude simplicity of Cato and Ennius, but still more he would shun the "voluptuous and affected" fluency of Seneca; he prefers, as a model for students, the virile yet polished speech of Cicero, the one Roman writer who had in his line surpassed the Greeks.[123] Quintilian's own style is often that of a schoolmaster, moribund with definitions, classification, and distinctions, and rising to eloquence only in denouncing Seneca; but it is a vigorous style, whose dignity is lightened now and then with touches of humanity and wit. Behind the good sense of the words we feel always the quiet goodness of the man; it is a moral stimulus to read him. Perhaps the Romans who had the privilege of his instruction took from it some part of the moral renovation that, more than any brilliance of letters, ennobled the age of the younger Pliny and Tacitus.

VIII. STATIUS AND MARTIAL

We have left to the last two poets who belonged to the same epoch, sought the favor of the same emperor and the same patrons, and yet never mention each other: one the purest, the other the coarsest, poet in the history of imperial Rome. Publius Papinius Statius was the son of a Neapolitan poet and grammarian; his environment and his education gave him everything but money and genius. He lisped in numbers, startled *salons* with poetical improvisations, and wrote an epic, the *Thebaid*, on the war of the Seven against Thebes. We cannot read it today, for its movement is obstructed with dead gods, and its smooth verses have an overpowering *virtus dormitiva*. But his contemporaries liked it; crowds gathered to hear him recite it in a Naples theater; they understood his mythological machinery, welcomed the delicacy of his sentiment, and found that his lines ran trippingly on the tongue. The judges in the Alban poetry contest gave him the first prize; rich men became his friends and helped him stave off penury;[124] Domitian himself invited him to dinner in the *domus Flavia*, and Statius repaid him by describing the palace as heaven and the Emperor as god.

To Domitian and other patrons, to his father and his friends, he addressed the most pleasing of his poems, the *Silvae*, modest idyls and eulogies in light and happy verse. In the Capitoline games, however, another poet won the crown, Statius' star waned in fickle Rome, and he persuaded his reluctant wife to return with him to his boyhood home. In Naples he began another epic, the *Achilleid;* then suddenly, in 96, he died, a youth of thirty-five. He was not a great poet; but he struck a welcome note of kindliness and tenderness amid a literature too often sarcastic and bitter, and a society corrupt and coarse beyond any precedent. He would have been as famous as Martial if he had been as obscene.

Marcus Valerius Martialis was born at Bilbilis in Spain in the fortieth year of our era. At twenty-four he came to Rome and won the friendship of Lucan and Seneca. Quintilian advised him to butter his bread by practicing law, but Martial preferred to starve on poetry. His friends were suddenly swept away in the conspiracy of Piso, and he was reduced to addressing his poems to rich men who might give him a dinner for an epigram. He lived in a third-floor garret, probably alone; for though he indites two poems to a woman whom he calls his wife, they are so foul that she must have been an invention or a bawd.[126]

His poems, he lets us know, were read throughout the Empire, even among the Goths; he rejoices to learn that he was almost as famous as a racehorse, but he fretted to see his publisher enriched while he himself received nothing from the sale of his books. He descended to suggesting, in an epigram, that he badly needed a toga; the Emperor's rich freedman Parthenius sent him one; he replied in two stanzas, one of which celebrated the newness of the garment, the other its cheap worthlessness. In time he found some more generous patrons; one gave him a little farm at Nomentum, and somehow he raised funds to buy a simple home on the Quirinal hill. He became a "client" or retainer to one rich man after another, waited upon them in the morning, and received an occasional gift; but he felt the shame of his situation and mourned that he did not have the courage to be contentedly poor and therefore free.[127] He could not afford to be poor, for he had to mingle in the society of men who could reward his verse. He showered Domitian with lauds and announced that if Jupiter and Domitian were to invite him to dinner on the same day he would turn down the god; but the Emperor preferred Statius. Martial became jealous of the younger poet and suggested that a live epigram was worth more than a dead epic.[128]

The epigram had till now been a pretty conceit on any passing subject, sometimes a dedication, a compliment, an epitaph; Martial molded it into a briefer, sharper form, barbed with satiric sting. We do him injustice when we read these 1561 epigrams in a few sittings; they were issued in twelve books at divers times, and the reader was expected to use them in small portions as *hors d'oeuvres*, not as a prolonged feast. Most of them seem trivial today; their allusion was local and temporary, too well timed to endure. Martial does not take them very seriously; the bad ones, he agrees, outnumber the good, but he had to fill a volume.[129] He is a master of versification, knows all the meters and all the tricks of the poetic trade; but he avoids rhetoric as proudly as his prose patrician analogue, Petronius. He cares nothing for the mythological furniture that littered the literature of his age; he is interested in real men and women and their intimate life and describes them with relish and spite; "my pages," he says, "taste of men."[130] He can "take down" some stiff aristocrat or stingy millionaire, some pompous lawyer or famous orator; but he likes better to tell of barbers, cobblers, hawkers, jockeys, acrobats, auctioneers, poisoners, perverts, and prostitutes. His scenes are laid not in ancient Greece but in the baths, the theaters, the streets, the circus, the homes, and tenements of Rome. He is the poet laureate of worthless men.

He is more interested in money than in love, and most often thinks of the latter in one gender. There is some sentiment in him, and he speaks very tenderly of a friend's child just dead; but there is no gallant line in his books, not even a noble wrath. He chants a litany of evil smells, and adds, "All these stenches I prefer to yours, Bassa."[131] He describes one of his mistresses:

> Your tresses, Galla, are manufactured far away; you lay aside your teeth at night as you do your silk dresses; you lie stored away in a hundred caskets, and your face does not sleep with you; you wink with an eyebrow brought to you in the morning. No respect moves you for your outworn carcass, which you may now count as one of your ancestors.[132]

He writes with unmanly vengefulness of the women who have refused him, and flings his epigrammatic mud at them with the delicacy of a scavenger. His love lyrics are addressed to boys; he climbs to ecstasy over the fragrance of "thy kisses, cruel lad." [133] One of his love poems begot a famous English counterpart:

> I do not love you, Sabidius, the reason I cannot tell;
> This only I can say—I dislike you very well.*

Indeed there are many whom Martial does not like. He describes them under transparent pseudonyms and in language that can be found today only on the most private public walls.[135] He is always libeling his enemies, as Statius is always celebrating his friends. Some of his victims retaliated by publishing under his name poems filthier than his own, or attacking the men whom Martial was anxious to please. From these technically perfect epigrams one could construct a full vocabulary of barroom urology.

But Martial's obscenity sits on him lightly. He shares it with his time, and never doubts that even highborn maidens in palace bowers will like it. "Lucretia blushed and laid down my volume, but Brutus was present. Brutus, go away; she will read it." [136] The poetic license of the age allowed indecencies, provided the meter and diction were correct. Sometimes Martial boasts of his lubricity; "no page of mine is without wantonness." [137] More often he is a bit ashamed of it, and begs us to believe that his life is cleaner than his verse.

At last he tired of purveying compliments and insults as a source of food; he began to long for a quieter, wholesomer life, and the haunts of his native Spain. He was now fifty-seven, with gray head and bushy beard, so swarthy that anyone, he tells us, could see at a glance that he had been born near the Tagus. He addressed a poetical bouquet to the younger Pliny and received in return a sum that paid his fare to Bilbilis. The little town welcomed him, forgiving his morals for his fame; he found simpler patrons there, but more open-handed than those at Rome. A kindly lady presented him with a modest villa, and there he spent his few remaining years. In 101 Pliny wrote: "I have just heard of Martial's death. The news has deeply grieved me. He was a man of wit, piquant and mordant, who mixed in his verse salt and honey, and not least of all, candor." [138] There must have been some secret virtue in the man if Pliny loved him.

---

* Non amo te, Sabidi, nec possum dicere quare;
Hoc tantum possum dicere, non amo te.[134]

CHAPTER XV

Rome at Work

A.D. 14-96

I. THE SOWERS

TO the Silver Age belongs the classic Roman work on agriculture—the *De Re Rustica* (65) of Junius Columella. Like Quintilian, Martial, and the Senecas, he came from Spain; he farmed several estates in Italy and retired to a residence in Rome. The best lands, he found, were taken up by the villas and grounds of the rich; the next best by olive orchards and vineyards; only inferior soils were left for tillage. "We have abandoned the husbanding of our soil to our lowest slaves, and they treat it like barbarians." The freemen of Italy, he thought, were degenerating in cities when they should have been hardening themselves by working the earth; "we ply our hands in circuses and theaters rather than among crops and vines." Columella loved the soil, and felt that the physical culture of the earth is saner than the literary culture of the town; farming "is a blood relative of wisdom" (*consanguinea sapientiae*). To lure men back to the fields he adorned his subject with polished Latin, and when he came to speak of gardens and flowers he fell into enthusiastic verse.

It was in this period that Pliny the naturalist pronounced a premature epitaph: *latifundia perdidere Italiam*—"the large farms have ruined Italy." Similar judgments occur in Seneca, Lucan, Petronius, Martial, and Juvenal. Seneca described cattle ranches wider than kingdoms, cultivated by fettered slaves; some estates were so large, said Columella, that their masters could never ride around them.[1] Pliny mentions an estate with 4117 slaves, 7200 oxen, and 257,000 other animals.[2] Land distributions by the Gracchi, Caesar, and Augustus had raised the number of small holdings, but many of these had been abandoned during the wars and bought in by the rich. When imperial administration reduced plunder in the provinces, much patrician wealth went into large farms. The latifundia spread because greater profits flowed from producing cattle, oil, and wine than from growing cereals and vegetables, and the discovery that ranching, to be most profitable, required the operation of large areas under one management. By the close of the first Christian century these advantages were being offset by the rising cost of slaves and their slow and uninventive work.[3] The long transition now began from slavery to serfdom. As peace diminished the flow of war captives into bondage, some owners of large estates, instead of operating them with slaves, divided them into small holdings and leased these to free tenants (*coloni*, cultivators) who paid in rent and labor. Most of the *ager publicus* belonging to the government was now worked in this way. So were the extensive properties of the younger Pliny, who describes his tenants as healthy, sturdy, good-natured, talkative peasants—precisely such as one finds throughout Italy today, unchanged after all changes.

The modes and tools of tillage were essentially as they had been for centuries. Plow, spade, hoe, pick, pitchfork, scythe, rake, have preserved their forms almost unaltered for 3000 years. Corn was ground in mills turned by water or by beasts. Screw pumps and water wheels raised water out of mines or into irrigation canals. Soils were protected by crop rotation, and fertilized by manure, alfalfa, clover, rye, or beans.[4] Seed selection was highly developed. Skillful care drew three, sometimes four, harvests per year from the rich fields of the Campagna and the valley of the Po;[5] from one planting of alfalfa four to six crops could be cut yearly for ten years.[6] All but the rarest European vegetables were grown, some of them in greenhouses for the winter trade. Fruit and nut trees of every sort abounded, for Roman generals and merchants, and alien merchants and slaves, had brought in many new species: the peach from Persia, the apricot from Armenia, the cherry from Pontic Cerasus (whence its name), the grape from Syria, the damson (*pruna damascena*) from Damascus, the plum and filbert from Asia Minor, the walnut from Greece, the olive and fig from Africa. . . . Clever arboriculturists had grafted the walnut upon the arbutus, the plum upon the plane tree, the cherry upon the elm. Pliny enumerates twenty-nine varieties of figs grown in Italy.[7] "Through the zeal of our farmers," said Columella, "Italy has learned to produce the fruits of almost the whole world." [8] In turn it transmitted these arts to western and northern Europe. Our rich dietary has a wide geography and a long history behind it, and the very food that we eat may be part of our Oriental and classical heritage.

Olive orchards were numerous, but vineyards were everywhere, beautifully terraced on the slopes. Italy produced fifty famous kinds of wine, and Rome alone drank 25,000,000 gallons per year—two quarts per week for each man, woman, and child, slave or free. Most wines were produced by capitalistic organization—by large-scale operations financed from Rome.[9] Much of the product was exported and taught the graces of wine to beer-drinking countries like Germany and Gaul. During this first century Spain, Africa, and Gaul began to grow their own grapes; Italian vintners lost one provincial outlet after another, and glutted their domestic market in one of the few "overproduction" crises of Roman economy. Domitian tried to ease the situation, and restore cereal culture, by prohibiting the further plantings of vines in Italy and ordering half of all vineyards in the provinces destroyed.[10] These edicts aroused a fury of protest and could not be enforced. In the second century the wines of Gaul and the oil of Spain, Africa, and the East began to crowd Italian products out of Mediterranean markets, and the economic decline of Italy began.

A large part of the peninsula was given over to grazing. The cheapest soils and slaves could be used for the raising of cattle, sheep, and swine. Careful attention was paid to scientific breeding. Horses were bred chiefly for war, hunting, and sport, seldom as draft animals; oxen drew the plow and the cart, mules bore burdens on their backs. Cows, sheep, and goats gave three kinds of milk, from which the Italian made delectable cheeses then as now. Swine were herded in woods rich with acorns and nuts; Rome, said Strabo, lived chiefly on pork fattened in the oak forests of northern Italy. Poultry fertilized the farmyard and helped feed the family, while bees provided the ancient and honorable substitute for sugar. If we add some acres of flax and hemp, a little hunting and much fishing, we get a picture of the Italian countryside as it was nineteen hundred years ago, and is today.

II. THE ARTISANS

There was not in Roman life—and perhaps there would not be in a healthy economy—so geographical a division between agriculture and industry as in our modern states. The ancient rural home—cottage, villa, or estate—was literally a manufactory, where the hands of men carried on a dozen vital industries, and the skill of women filled the house and its environs with a score of wholesome arts. There the woods were turned into shelter, fuel, and furniture, cattle were slain and dressed, grain was milled and baked, oil and wine were pressed, food was prepared and preserved, wool and flax were cleaned and woven; sometimes clay was fired into vessels, bricks, and tiles, and metal was beaten into tools; life there had an educative fullness and variety that come to few of us in our time of wider movement and narrowing specialties. Nor was this diversity of occupation the sign of a poor and primitive economy; the wealthiest households were the most self-sufficient, and prided themselves on making the largest part of what they needed. A family was an organization of economic helpmates engaged in the united agriculture and industry of a home.

When an artisan undertook to do a certain task for several families, and set up his shop at some center within reach of them all, village economy supplemented, but did not supersede, domestic industry. So the miller took and ground the grain of many fields; later he baked the bread, and finally he delivered it. Forty bakeries were unearthed at Pompeii, and at Rome the pastrymakers were a separate guild. There were likewise contractors who bought an olive crop on the trees and gathered the fruit;[11] most estates, however, continued to process their own oil and bake their own bread. The clothing of peasants and philosophers was homespun, but the well-to-do wore garments that, though woven at home, were carded, cleaned, bleached, and cut in a fullery. Some delicate woolen fabrics were woven in factories; and such flax as was not made into sails or nets was turned by factories into linen garments for women and handkerchiefs for men.[12] In its next stage the cloth might be sent to a dyer, who not only colored it but impressed upon it such delicate designs as we find on the costumes in Pompeian murals. Tanning of leather had also reached the factory stage, but shoemakers were usually individual craftsmen, making shoes to order; some were specialists who made only fancy slippers for feminine feet.

The extractive industries were manned almost wholly by slaves or criminals. The gold and silver mines of Dacia, Gaul, and Spain, the lead and tin of Spain and Britain, the copper of Cyprus and Portugal, the sulphur of Sicily, the salt beds of Italy, the iron of Elba, the marble of Luna, Hymettus, and Paros, the porphyry of Egypt, and in general all subsoil natural resources, were owned by the state, were operated by it or on lease from it, and provided a main source of the national revenue; the gold of Spain alone yielded Vespasian $44,000,000 a year.[13] The quest for minerals was a chief source of imperialist conquest; the mineral wealth of Britain, says Tacitus, was "the prize of victory" in Claudius' campaign.[14] Wood and charcoal were the chief fuels. Petroleum was known in Commagene, Babylonia, and Parthia,[15] and the defenders of Samosata threw it in flaming torches upon Lucullus' troops; but there is no sign of its commercial use as a fuel.* Coal was found in the Peloponnesus and northern Italy, but was used chiefly by smiths.[16] The art of carburizing iron into steel had now spread from Egypt throughout the Empire. Most ironworkers, coppersmiths, goldsmiths, and silversmiths had a single forge and worked with one or two apprentices. At Capua, Minturnae, Puteoli, Aquileia, Como, and elsewhere several forges and smelters were united in factories; those at Capua were apparently large-scale capitalist enterprises externally financed.

The building trades were well organized and specialized. *Dendrophoroi* ("tree-bearers") cut and delivered the wood, *fabri lignarii* ("woodworkers") made houses and furniture, *caementarii* mixed the cement, *structores* laid the foundations, *arcuarii* built the arches, *parietarii* raised the walls, *tectores* applied plaster, *albarii* whitewashed it, *artifices plumbarii* inserted the plumbing—usually with pipes of lead (*plumbum*), and *marmorii* paved marble floors; we may imagine the jurisdictional disputes. Bricks and tiles were provided by potteries, many of which had reached the factory stage. Trajan, Hadrian, and Marcus Aurelius owned such factories and made fortunes from them.[17] The kilns of Arretium, Mutina, Puteoli, Surrentum, and Pollentia supplied the ordinary tableware of all the European and African provinces as well as Italy. This wholesale production laid no claim to artistic excellence; the emphasis was now frankly on quantity; and the *terra sigillata* ("signed earthenware") that now crowded the Italian market was distinctly inferior to the earlier product of Arretium. Outstanding work, as we shall see, was done in glass.

---

* In the fourth century a fire dart filled with flaming naphtha, and shot from a bow or a catapult, was among the weapons of war. "It burns persistently wherever it falls," says Ammianus Marcellinus; "and water poured upon it rouses the fire to greater heat; and there is no way of extinguishing it except by sprinkling it with dust." [15a]

The factory production of glass, brick, tiles, pottery, and metalware does not warrant us in ascribing an industrial capitalism to ancient Italy. Rome itself had only two large factories—a paper mill and a dyeing establishment;[18] probably neither metals nor fuels were at hand in quantity, and the profits of politics seemed more honorable than the proceeds of industry. In the factories of central Italy almost all the workers, and some of the managers, were slaves; in those of north Italy there was a greater proportion of freemen. Slaves were still sufficiently available to discourage the development of machinery; listless slave labor, with small stake in the product, was not likely to make inventions; some labor-saving devices were rejected because they might have caused technological unemployment; and the purchasing power of the people was too low to stimulate or support mechanized production.[19] There were of course many simple machines, common to Italy, Egypt, and the Greek world: screw presses, screw pumps, water wheels, animal-driven grain mills, spinning wheels, looms, the crane and pulley, the revolving mold for pottery. . . . But Italian life was now (A.D. 96) as highly industrialized as life was ever to be until the nineteenth century. It would hardly go further on the basis of slavery and a high concentration of wealth. Roman law contracepted large organizations by requiring every sharer in an industrial undertaking to be a legally responsible partner; it forbade "limited liability" companies and allowed joint-stock corporations only for the performance of governmental contracts. Since similar restrictions affected banks, these could seldom provide capital for large-scale enterprise. At no time would the industrial development of Rome or Italy equal that of Alexandria or the Hellenistic East.

III. THE CARRIERS

From Caesar to Commodus wheeled vehicles were forbidden in Rome by day; people then walked, or were carried in slave-borne chairs or litters. For longer distances they traveled on horseback or in horse-drawn carriages or chariots. Travel by public stagecoach averaged some sixty miles a day. Caesar once rode by carriage 800 miles in eight days; messengers bearing the news of Nero's death to Galba in Spain covered 332 miles in thirty-six hours; Tiberius, hurrying day and night, rode in three days 600 miles to stand beside his dying brother. The public post, by carriage or horse at all hours, averaged one hundred miles a day. Augustus had modeled it on the Persian system, as indispensable to imperial administration. It was called *cursus publicus* as serving the *res publica*, or commonwealth, by carrying official correspondence. Private individuals could use it only by rare and special permission through a government *diploma* ("*double-folded*") or passport entitling the bearer to certain privileges and introducing him en route to persons of diplomatic importance. A more rapid means of communication was sometimes arranged by semaphores flashing signals from point to point; by this primitive telegraph the arrival of the grain ships at Puteoli was quickly made known to worried Rome. Nonofficial correspondence went by special courier or merchants or traveling friends; some traces suggest the existence, under the Empire, of private companies arranging to transmit private mail. Fewer letters were written than now, and better. Nevertheless, the movement of intelligence over western and southern Europe was as rapid in Caesar's day as at any time before the railway. In 54 B.C. Caesar's letter from Britain reached Cicero at Rome in twenty-nine days; in 1834 Sir Robert Peel, hurrying from Rome to London, required thirty days.[20]

Communication and transport were immensely aided by the consular roads. These were the tentacles of Roman law, the members by which the mind of Rome became the will of the realm. They achieved in the ancient world a commercial revolution comparable in kind with that which the railroads effected in the nineteenth century. Until steam transportation came, the roads of medieval and modern Europe were inferior to those of the Empire under the Antonines. Italy alone had then 372 main routes, and 12,000 miles of paved thoroughfares; the Empire had 51,000 miles of paved highways and a pervasive network of secondary roads. Highways ran over the Alps to Lyons, Bordeaux, Paris, Rheims, Rouen, and Boulogne; others to Vienna, Mainz, Augsburg, Cologne, Utrecht, and Leiden; and from Aquileia a road skirted the Adriatic to connect with the Via Egnatia to Thessalonica. Magnificent bridges replaced the ferries that had crept across a thousand impeding streams. At every mile on the consular roads stone markers gave the distance to the next town; 4000 of these survive. At intervals seats were placed for tired travelers. At every tenth mile a *statio* offered a stopping place, where fresh horses could be hired; at every thirty miles was a *mansio*—an inn that was also a store, a saloon, and a brothel.[21] The main halting points were the *civitates*, cities, usually equipped with fair hotels, which were in some cases owned and managed by the municipal government.[22] Most innkeepers robbed their guests whenever convenient, and other thieves made the highways unsafe at night despite a garrison of soldiers at each *statio*. "Itineraries" could be bought, showing routes, stations, and intermediate distances.[23] Rich men, disdaining the inns, brought their equipage and slaves with them, and slept in their guarded carriages or in the homes of friends or officials on the way.

Despite all difficulties, there was probably more traveling in Nero's day than at any time before our birth. "Many people," says Seneca, "make long voyages to see some remote sight";[24] and Plutarch speaks of "globe-trotters who spend the best part of their lives in inns and on boats." [25] Educated Romans flocked to Greece and Egypt and Greek Asia, scratched their names on historic monuments, sought healing waters or climates, ambled by art collections in the temples, studied under famous philosophers, rhetors, or physicians, and doubtless used Pausanias as their Baedeker.[26]

These "grand tours" usually involved a voyage on one or more of the merchant vessels that cut the Mediterranean with a hundred routes of trade. "Look at the harbors and seas," exclaimed Juvenal, "filled with great keels, more peopled than the land." [27] Rome's rival ports, Puteoli, Portus, and Ostia, were alive with *fabri navales* building ships, *stuppatores* calking them, *saburarii* loading sand into them as ballast, *sacrarii* unloading grain in sacks, *mensores* weighing it, *lenuncularii* operating tenders between large ships and the shore, and *urinatores* diving for goods fallen into the sea. Of corn barges alone twenty-five were drawn up the Tiber every working day; if we add the transport of building stone, metals, oil, wine, and a thousand other articles, we picture a river teeming with commerce and noisy with loading and carrying machines, with dockmen, porters, stevedores, traders, brokers, and clerks.

Ships were driven with sails, aided by one or more banks of oars. They were larger, on the average, than before; Athenaeus describes a grain cargo vessel as 420 feet long with a fifty-seven-foot beam;[29] but this was highly exceptional. Some vessels had three decks; many took 250, several took a thousand, tons of freight. Josephus tells of one that carried 600 persons—passengers and crew;[30] another carried an Egyptian obelisk as large as that in Central Park, New York, together with 200 sailors, 1300 passengers, 93,000 bushels of wheat, and a load of linen, pepper, paper, and glass.[31] Nevertheless, voyages except along the coasts were still dangerous, as Saint Paul found; between November and March only a few vessels ventured across the open Mediterranean, and in midsummer eastward voyages were made almost impossible by the etesian winds. Night sailing was now frequent, and every harbor of any pretense had a good lighthouse. Danger of piracy had almost disappeared from the Mediterranean. To discourage it, and starve rebellion, Augustus had stationed two main war fleets at Ravenna on the Adriatic and at Misenum on the Bay of Naples, besides minor squadrons at ten other points in the Empire. We may judge what Pliny called "the immense majesty of the Roman peace" by the fact that for two centuries we hardly hear of these fleets.

Passenger schedules were largely indefinite, as sailings were determined by weather and commercial convenience. Rates were low—e.g., two drachmas ($1.20) from Athens to Alexandria; but passengers brought their own food, and probably most of them slept on deck. Speed was as moderate as the fares, and varied with the winds, averaging six knots per hour; one might cross the Adriatic in a day, or, like Cicero, take three weeks from Patrae to Brundisium. A swift cruiser might make 230 knots in twenty-four hours.[32] With favorable winds, six days carried one from Sicily to Alexandria or from Gades to Ostia, and four from Utica to Rome.[33] The longest and most dangerous voyage was the six-month sail from Aden, in Arabia, to India, for monsoons forced vessels to hug the pirate-breeding coast all the way. At some time before A.D. 50 an Alexandrian Greek skipper, Hippalus, charted the periodicity of the monsoon winds and found that in certain seasons he could sail directly and safely across the Indian Ocean. The discovery was almost as important for that sea as the voyage of Columbus was for the Atlantic. From Egyptian ports on the Red Sea ships thereafter sailed to India in forty days. About A.D. 80 another Alexandrian captain, of unknown

name, wrote a *Periplus of the Erythrean Sea* as a handbook for merchants trading
along the east African coast and with India. Meanwhile other mariners had
developed routes through the Atlantic to Gaul, Britain, Germany, even to
Scandinavia and Russia.[34] Never before in human memory had the seas borne
so many vessels, products, and men.

IV. THE ENGINEERS

The ships and roads that carried goods, the bridges that bound the roads, the
harbors and docks that received the ships, the aqueducts that brought clean water
to Rome, the sewers that drained the rural marshes and the city's waste, were the
work of Roman, Greek, and Syrian engineers operating with armies of free
labor, legionaries, and slaves. They raised or drew heavy loads or stones by
pulleys on cranes or vertical beams, worked by windlasses on treadmills turned
by animals or men.[35] They banked the treacherous Tiber with walls set back in
three stages, so that low water would not expose the muddy bed.* They dredged
a multiple harbor at Ostia for Claudius, Nero, and Trajan, opened lesser havens
at Marseilles, Puteoli, Misenum, Carthage, Brundisium, and Ravenna, and renewed the greatest of all at Alexandria. They emptied the Fucine Lake and
reclaimed its bed for cultivation by boring a tunnel through a mountain of rock.
They lined the subsoil of Rome with sewers of concrete, brick, and tile which
lasted for hundreds of years. They drained the swamps of Campania sufficiently
to make it habitable, for many sumptuous palaces are indicated by the ruins
there.[36]† They executed the astonishing public works by which Caesar and the
emperors mitigated unemployment and beautified Rome.

The consular roads were among their simpler achievements. How did these
highways compare with those of today? They were from sixteen to twenty-four
feet wide, but near Rome part of this width was taken up with sidewalks (*mar-
gines*) paved with rectangular stone slabs. They went straight to their goal in
brave sacrifice of initial economy to permanent saving: they overleaped countless
streams with costly bridges, crossed marshes with long, arched viaducts of brick
and stone, climbed up and down steep hills with no use of cut and fill, and crept
along mountainsides or high embankments secured by powerful retaining walls.
Their pavement varied with locally available material. Usually the bottom layer
(*pavimentum*) was a four- to six-inch bed of sand, or one inch of mortar. Upon
this were imposed four strata of masonry: the *statumen*, a foot deep, consisting
of stones bound with cement or clay; the *rudens*, ten inches of rammed concrete;
the *nucleus*, twelve to eighteen inches of successively laid and rolled layers of

---

* In 1870 the Italian government built embankments at a uniform width, with unpleasant
results in the dry season.

† Apparently the Volsci had drained the Pontine marshes before 600 B.C. Their Roman conquerors neglected the drainage canals, and the region again became swampy and malarial.
Caesar planned its reclamation, and Augustus and Nero made some progress on the work; but
the task was not accomplished till 1931.

concrete; and the *summa crusta* of silex or lava polygonal slabs, one to three feet in diameter, and eight to twelve inches thick. The upper surface of the slabs was smoothed, and the joints were so well fitted as to be hardly discernible. Occasionally the surface was of concrete; on less important roads it might be of gravel; in Britain it was composed of flint stones laid in cement upon a gravel bed. The substructure was so deep that little attention was given to drainage. All in all, these were the most durable roads in history. Many of them are still in use; but their steep gradients, designed for pack mules and small vehicles, have compelled their abandonment by modern traffic.[37]

The bridges that carried these roads were themselves high exemplars of wedded science and art. The Romans inherited from Ptolemaic Egypt the principles of hydraulic engineering; they employed them on an unprecedented scale, and the methods they transmitted remained unchanged till our time. They carried to its ancient limit the building of foundations and piers under water. They drove into the bed a double cylinder of piles, boarded each cylinder tightly, drained the water from between them, covered the exposed bottom with rock or lime, and on this basis raised the pier. Eight bridges crossed the Tiber at Rome: some sacredly ancient like the Pons Sublicius, on which no metal might be used; some so well built that like the Pons Fabricius they are functioning to this day. From these spans the Roman arch would go forth to bridge a hundred thousand streams in the white man's world.

Pliny thought that the aqueducts were Rome's greatest achievement. "If one will note the abundance of water skillfully brought into the city for many public and private uses; if he will observe the lofty aqueducts required to maintain a proper elevation and grade, the mountains that had to be pierced, the depressions that had to be filled—he will conclude that the whole globe offers nothing more marvelous." [38] From distant springs fourteen aqueducts, totaling 1300 miles, brought through tunnels and over majestic arches into Rome some 300,000,000 gallons of water daily—as large a quantity per capita as in any modern city.[39] These structures had their faults; leaks developed in the lead pipes and required frequent repair; by the end of the Western Empire all the aqueducts had gone out of use.* But when we consider that they fed ample water to homes, tenements, palaces, fountains, gardens, parks, and public baths where thousands bathed at once, and that enough remained to create artificial lakes for naval battles, we begin to see that despite terror and corruption Rome was the best managed capital of antiquity and one of the best equipped cities of all time.

At the head of the water department at the close of the first century was Sextus Julius Frontinus, whose books have made him the most famous of Roman engineers. He had already served as praetor, as governor of Britain, and several terms as consul. Like modern British statesmen he found time to write books as well as to govern states; he published a work on military science, of which the

---

* One of them, the Aqua Virgo, now feeds the Fontana di Trevi; three others have been restored, and supply Rome with water today.

concluding portion, *Stratagemata*, remains,* and left us his personal account of the water system of Rome (*De aquis urbis Romae*). He describes the corruption and malfeasance that he found in his department on taking office, and how palaces and brothels secretly tapped the water mains, and so greedily that once Rome ran out of water.[41] He describes his resolute reforms; tells in proud detail the sources, length, and function of each aqueduct; and concludes like Pliny: "Who will venture to compare with these mighty conduits the idle Pyramids, or the famous but useless works of the Greeks?"[42] We sense here the frankly utilitarian Roman with little taste for beauty apart from use; we can understand him and admit that a city should have clean water before it has Parthenons. Through these artless books we perceive that even in the age of the despots there were Romans of the old type, men of ability and integrity, conscientious administrators who made the Empire prosper under the lords of misrule and opened a way for monarchy's golden age.

V. THE TRADERS

The improvement of government and transport expanded Mediterranean trade to an unprecedented amplitude. At one end of the busy process of exchange were peddlers hawking through the countryside everything from sulphur matches to costly imported silks; wandering auctioneers who served also as town criers and advertised lost goods and runaway slaves; daily markets and periodical fairs; shopkeepers haggling with customers, cheating with false or tipped scales, and keeping a tangential eye for the aedile's inspectors of weights and measures. A little higher in the commercial hierarchy were shops that manufactured their own merchandise; these were the backbone of both industry and trade. At or near the ports were wholesalers (*magnarii*) who sold, to retailers or consumers, goods recently brought in from abroad; sometimes the owner or captain of a vessel would sell his cargo directly from the deck.

For two centuries Italy enjoyed an "unfavorable" balance of trade—cheerfully bought more than she sold. She exported some Arretine pottery, some wine and oil, some metalware, glass, and perfumes from Campania; for the rest her products were kept at home. Meanwhile the wholesalers had agents buying goods for Italy in all parts of the Empire, and foreign merchants had Greek or Syrian drummers touting and placing their goods in Italy. By this double process the delicacies of half the planet came to please the palate, clothe the flesh, and adorn the home of the Roman optimate. "Whoever wishes to see all the goods of the world," said Aelius Aristides, "must either journey throughout the world or stay in Rome."[43] From Sicily came corn, cattle, hides, wine, wool, fine woodwork, statuary, jewelry; from north Africa corn and oil; from Cyrenaica silphium; from central Africa wild beasts for the arena; from Ethiopia and east Africa ivory, apes, tortoise shell, rare marbles, obsidian, spices, and Negro slaves; from

---

* Book III opens with an instructive remark: "The invention of engines of war has long since reached its limit, and I see no further hope for any improvement in the art." [40]

west Africa oil, beasts, citron, wood, pearls, dyes, copper; from Spain fish, cattle. wool, gold, silver, lead, tin, copper, iron, cinnabar, wheat, linen, cork, horses, ham, bacon, and the finest olives and olive oil; from Gaul clothing, wine, wheat, timber, vegetables, cattle, poultry, pottery, cheese; from Britain tin, lead, silver, hides, wheat, cattle, slaves, oysters, dogs, pearls, and wooden goods. From Belgium flocks of geese were driven all the way to Italy to supply goose livers for aristocratic bellies. From Germany came amber, slaves, and furs; from the Danube wheat, cattle, iron, silver, and gold; from Greece and the Greek isles cheap silk, linen, wine, oil, honey, timber, marble, emeralds, drugs, artworks, perfumes, diamonds, and gold. From the Black Sea came corn, fish, furs, hides, slaves; from Asia Minor fine linen and woolen fabrics, parchment, wine, Smyrna and other figs, honey, cheese, oysters, carpets, oil, wood; from Syria wine, silk, linen, glass, oil, apples, pears, plums, figs, dates, pomegranates, nuts, nard, balsam, Tyrian purple, and the cedar of Lebanon; from Palmyra textiles, perfumes, drugs; from Arabia incense, gums, aloes, myrrh, laudanum, ginger, cinnamon, and precious stones; from Egypt corn, paper, linen, glass, jewelry, granite, basalt, alabaster, and porphyry. Finished products of a thousand kinds came to Rome and the West from Alexandria, Sidon, Tyre, Antioch, Tarsus, Rhodes, Miletus, Ephesus, and the other great cities of the East, while the East received raw materials and money from the West.

In addition to all this there was a substantial import trade from outside the Empire. From Parthia and Persia came gems, rare essences, morocco leather, rugs, wild beasts, and eunuchs. From China—through Parthia, or India, or the Caucasus—came silk, raw or manufactured; the Romans thought it a vegetable product combed from trees and valued it at its weight in gold.[44] Much of this silk came to the island of Cos, where it was woven into dresses for the ladies of Rome and other cities; in A.D. 91 the relatively poor state of Messenia had to forbid its women to wear transparent silk dresses at religious initiations; it was with such garments that Cleopatra touched the hearts of Caesar and Antony.[45] In return the Chinese imported from the Empire carpets, jewels, amber, metals, dyes, drugs, and glass. Chinese historians speak of an embassy coming by sea to the Emperor Huan-ti in 166 from the Emperor "An-Tun"—Marcus Aurelius Antoninus; more probably it was a band of merchants posing as ambassadors. Sixteen Roman coins, dating from Tiberius to Aurelius, have been found in Shansi. From India came pepper, spikenard, and other spices (the same that Columbus would seek), herbs, ivory, ebony, sandalwood, indigo, pearls, sardonyx, onyx, amethyst, carbuncle, diamonds, iron products, cosmetics, textiles, tigers, and elephants. We may judge the extent of this trade, and the Roman hunger for luxuries, by noting that Italy imported more from India than from any other country except Spain.[46] From one Egyptian port alone, Strabo avers, 120 ships sailed every year for India and Ceylon.[47] In exchange India took a modest quantity of wine, metals, and purple, and the rest—over 100,000,000 sesterces per year —in bullion or coin. A like amount went to Arabia and China, and probably to Spain.[48]

This immense trade produced prosperity for two centuries, but its unsound basis ruined Roman economy in the end. Italy made no attempt at equaling imports with exports; she appropriated the mines, and taxed the people, of half a hundred states to provide her with the money to meet her international balances. As the richer veins of the mines gave out, and the zest for exotic luxuries continued, Rome tried to stave off the breakdown of her import system by conquering new mineral regions like Dacia, and by debasing her once incorruptible currency—turning ever less bullion into ever more coin. When the costs of administration and war mounted nearer to the profits of empire, Rome had to pay for goods with goods, and could not. Italy's dependence upon imported food was her vital weakness; the moment she could not force other countries to send her food and soldiers she was doomed. Meanwhile the provinces recovered not only prosperity but economic initiative: Italian merchants, in this first century A.D., almost disappeared from Eastern ports, while Syrian and Greek traders established themselves at Delos and Puteoli and multiplied in Spain and Gaul. In the leisurely oscillation of history the East was preparing once more to dominate the West.

VI. THE BANKERS

How were production and commerce financed? First by the maintenance of a comparatively reliable currency internationally honored. All Roman coins had suffered gradual depreciation since the First Punic War, for the Treasury had found it convenient to pay off governmental war debts by permitting the inflation that naturally comes from the multiplication of money and the diminution of goods. The as, originally a pound of copper, had been reduced to two ounces in 241, one ounce in 202, half an ounce in 87 B.C., and a quarter ounce in A.D. 60. During the final century of the Republic the generals had issued their own coinage, usually in *aurei*, gold coins, normally worth one hundred sesterces. From this military coinage that of the emperors was descended, and the emperors followed Caesar's custom of stamping their effigies on their issues as symbols of the state's guarantee. The sesterce was now made from copper instead of silver and was revalued at four asses.* Nero lowered the silver content of the denarius to ninety per cent of its former quantity, Trajan to eighty-five per cent, Aurelius to seventy-five, Commodus to seventy, Septimius Severus to fifty. Nero re-

---

* In referring to the period after Nero, Roman currency will be equated at two thirds its general value under the Republic: the as at two and a half, the sesterce at ten, the denarius at forty, cents, and the talent at $2400, in terms of United States currency of 1942. Since lesser variations will again be ignored, the reader will remember that all equivalents are very loosely approximate.

duced the aureus from one fortieth of a pound of gold to one forty-fifth, Caracalla to one fiftieth. A general rise of prices accompanied these deprecia- tions, but income seems to have risen commensurately until Aurelius; per- haps this controlled inflation was a simple way of relieving debtors at the expense of creditors whose superior ability and opportunity, unchecked, would have concentrated wealth to the point of economic coagulation and political revolution. Despite these changes we must consider the Roman fiscal system one of the most successful and stable in history. For two cen- turies a single monetary standard was honored throughout the Empire; and with this stable medium investment and trade flourished as never before in the memory of men.

Consequently bankers were everywhere. They served as money-changers, accepted checking accounts and interest-bearing deposits, issued travelers' checks and bills of exchange, managed, bought, and sold realty, placed in- vestments and collected debts, and lent money to individuals and partner- ships. This banking system had come from Greece and the Greek East, and was mostly in the hands of Greeks and Syrians even in Italy and the West; in Gaul the words for Syrian and banker were synonyms.[49] Interest rates, which had sunk to four per cent under the weight of Augustus' Egyptian spoils, rose to six per cent after his death, and reached their legal maximum of twelve per cent by the age of Constantine.

The famous "panic" of A.D. 33 illustrates the development and complex interdependence of banks and commerce in the Empire. Augustus had coined and spent money lavishly, on the theory that its increased circulation, low interest rates, and rising prices would stimulate business. They did; but as the process could not go on forever, a reaction set in as early as 10 B.C., when this flush minting ceased. Tiberius rebounded to the opposite theory— that the most economical economy is the best. He severely limited the governmental expenditures, sharply restricted new issues of currency, and hoarded 2,700,000,000 sesterces in the Treasury. The resulting dearth of circulating medium was made worse by the drain of money eastward in exchange for luxuries. Prices fell, interest rates rose, creditors foreclosed on debtors, debtors sued usurers, and moneylending almost ceased. The Senate tried to check the export of capital by requiring a high percentage of every senator's fortune to be invested in Italian land; senators thereupon called in loans and foreclosed mortgages to raise cash, and the crisis rose. When the senator Publius Spinther notified the bank of Balbus and Ollius that he must withdraw 30,000,000 sesterces to comply with the new law, the firm an- nounced its bankruptcy. At the same time the failure of an Alexandrian firm, Seuthes and Son—due to their loss of three ships laden with costly spices— and the collapse of the great dyeing concern of Malchus at Tyre, led to rumors that the Roman banking house of Maximus and Vibo would be broken by their extensive loans to these firms. When its depositors began a "run" on this bank it shut its doors, and later on that day a larger bank, of the Brothers Pettius, also suspended payment. Almost simultaneously came news that great banking establishments had failed in Lyons, Carthage, Corinth, and Byzantium. One after another the banks of Rome closed. Money could be borrowed only at rates far above the legal limit. Tiberius finally met the crisis by suspending the land-investment act and distributing 100,-000,000 sesterces to the banks, to be lent without interest for three years on the security of realty. Private lenders were thereby constrained to lower their interest rates, money came out of hiding, and confidence slowly returned.[50]

VII. THE CLASSES

Nearly everybody in Rome worshiped money with mad pursuit, and all but the bankers denounced it. "How little you know the age you live in," says a god in Ovid, "if you fancy that honey is sweeter than cash in hand!" [51] —and a century later Juvenal sarcastically hails the *sanctissima divitiarum maiestas*, "the most holy majesty of wealth." To the end of the Empire Roman law forbade the Senatorial class to invest in commerce or industry; and though they evaded the prohibition by letting their freedmen invest for them, they despised their proxies and upheld rule by birth as the sole alternative to rule by money, or myths, or the sword. After all the revolutions and the decimations the old class divisions remained, with brand-new titles: members of the Senatorial and equestrian orders, magistrates and officials, were called *honestiores*, i.e., "men of honors" or offices; all the rest were *humiliores*, "lowly," or *tenuiores*, "weak." A sense of honor often mingled with the proud gravity of the senator: he served in a succession of public posts without pay and at much personal expense; he administered important functions with a fair degree of competence and integrity; he provided for public games, helped his clients, freed some of his slaves, and shared a part of his fortune with the people through benefactions before or after his death. Because of the obligations his position entailed, he was required to have a million sesterces to enter or remain in the Senatorial class.

One senator, Gnaeus Lentulus, had 400,000,000 sesterces; but with this exception the greatest fortunes in Rome were those of businessmen who did not disdain to handle money or trade. While reducing the powers of the Senate, the emperors had favored the business class with high office, had protected industry, commerce, and finance, and had based upon equestrian support the security of the Principate against patrician intrigue. Membership in this second order required 400,000 sesterces and specific nomination by the prince. Consequently many men of means belonged to the plebs.

The plebs was now a motley receptacle of such innominate businessmen, freeborn workers, peasant proprietors, teachers, doctors, artists, and freedmen. The census defined the *proletarii* not by their occupation but by their offspring (*proles*); an old Latin treatise called them "plebeians who offer nothing to the state but children." [52] Most of them found employment in the shops, factories, and commerce of the city at an average wage of a denarius (forty cents) a day; this rose in later centuries, but not faster than prices. [53] Exploitation of the weak by the strong is as natural as eating and differs from it only in rapidity; we must expect to find it in every age and under every form of society and government; but rarely has it been so thorough and unsentimental as in ancient Rome. Once all men had been poor, and had not known their poverty; now penury rubbed elbows with wealth, and suffered from consciousness. Absolute destitution, however, was prevented by the dole, the occasional gifts of patrons to clients, and the lordly legacies of rich men like Balbus, who left twenty-five denarii to every citizen of Rome. Class divisions verged upon caste; yet an able man might free himself from slavery, make a fortune, and rise to high office in the service of the prince. The freedman's son became a fully enfranchised freeman, and his grandson could become a senator; soon a freedman's grandson, Pertinax, would be emperor.

During the first century many high offices were filled by freedmen. They often had charge of the imperial finances in the provinces, the waterways of Rome, the mines and quarries and estates of the emperor, and the provisioning of the army camps. Freedmen and slaves, nearly all of Greek or Syrian origin, managed the imperial palaces and held vital positions in the imperial cabinet. Petty industry and trade fell increasingly into the control of freedmen. Some of them became great capitalists or landowners; some accumulated the largest fortunes of their time. Their past had seldom given them moral standards or elevated interests; after their liberation money became the absorbing interest of their lives; they made it without scruple and spent it without taste. Petronius savagely excoriated them in Trimalchio, and Seneca, less bitter, smiled at the new rich who bought books in ornamental sets but never read them. [54] Probably these satires were in part the jealous reactions of a caste that saw its ancient prerogatives of exploitation and luxury encroached upon, and could not forgive the men who were rising to share its perquisites and power.

The success of the freedmen must have given some consoling hope to the class that did most of the manual work in Italy. Beloch estimated the slaves in Rome about 30 B.C. at some 400,000, or nearly half the population; in

Italy at 1,500,000. If we may believe the table gossipers of Athenaeus, some Romans had 20,000 slaves.[55] A proposal that slaves be required to wear a distinctive dress was voted down in the Senate lest they should realize their numerical strength.[56] Galen reckoned the proportion of slaves to freemen at Pergamum about A.D. 170 as one to three—i.e., twenty-five per cent; probably this proportion was not much different in other cities.[56a] Human prices varied from 330 sesterces for a farm slave to the 700,000 ($105,000) paid by Marcus Scaurus for Daphnis the grammarian;[57] the average price was now 4000 sesterces ($400). Eighty per cent of the employees in industry and retail trade were slaves, and most of the manual or clerical work in government was performed by *servi publici*—"public slaves." Domestic slaves were of every variety and condition: personal servants, handicraftsmen, tutors, cooks, hairdressers, musicians, copyists, librarians, artists, physicians, philosophers, eunuchs, pretty boys to serve at least as cupbearers, and cripples to provide amusement by their deformities; there was a special market at Rome where one might buy legless, armless, or three-eyed men, giants, dwarfs, or hermaphrodites.[58] Household slaves were sometimes beaten, occasionally killed. Nero's father killed his freedmen because they refused to drink as much as he wished.[59] In an angry passage of his essay on anger Seneca describes the "wooden racks and other instruments of torture, the dungeons and other jails, the fires built around imprisoned bodies in a pit, the hook dragging up the corpses, the many kinds of chains, the varied punishments, the tearing of limbs, the branding of foreheads";[59a] all these, apparently, entered into the life of the agricultural slave. Juvenal describes a lady as having slave after slave thrashed while her hair was being curled,[60] and Ovid pictures another mistress jabbing hairpins into her maidservant's arms;[61] but these tales have the earmarks of literary concoctions and must not be taken for history.

We are in danger of exaggerating the cruelty of the past for the same reason that we magnify the crime and immorality of the present—because cruelty is interesting by its very rarity. By and large the lot of a domestic slave under the Empire was lightened by a growing acceptance into the family, by mutual loyalty, by the pretty custom of owners waiting on the slaves at certain feasts, and by a security and permanence of employment exceptional in modern times. The joys of family life were not denied them, and their tombstones reveal as much tenderness as those of the free. One reads: "His parents have raised this monument to Eucopion, who lived six months and three days; the sweetest and most delightful babe, who, though he could not yet speak, was our greatest happiness." [62] Other epitaphs show the most affectionate relations between masters and slaves: one owner declares that a dead servant was as dear to him as his son; a young noble mourns the death of his nurse; a nurse expresses her grief over a dead charge; a

learned lady raises an elegant memorial to her librarian.[63] Statius writes a
"Poem of Consolation to Flavius Ursus on the Death of a Favorite Slave." [64]
It was not unusual for slaves to risk their lives to protect their masters; many
voluntarily accompanied them into exile; several gave their lives for them.
Some owners freed their slaves and married them; some treated them as
friends; Seneca ate with his.[65] The refinement of manners and sensitivity,
the absence of a color line between master and slave, the tenets of the Stoic
philosophy, and the classless faiths coming in from the East had a share in the
mitigation of slavery; but the basic factors were the economic advantage of
the owner, and the rising cost of slaves. Many slaves were respected as having
high cultural abilities—stenographers, research aides, financial secretaries and
managers, artists, physicians, grammarians, and philosophers. A slave could
in many cases go into business for himself, giving a share of his earnings to
his owner and keeping the rest as his *peculium*, a "little money" peculiarly
his own. With such earnings, or by faithful or exceptional service, or by
personal attractiveness, a slave could usually achieve freedom in six years.[66]

The condition of the workers, and even of the slaves, was in some measure
relieved by the *collegia*, or workers' organizations. By this period we hear of
these in great number and in proud specialization; there were separate guilds of
trumpeters, horn players, clarion blowers, tuba players, flutists, bagpipers, etc.
Usually the *collegia* were modeled on the Italian municipality: they had a
hierarchy of magistrates and one or more favorite deities whom they honored
with a temple and an annual feast. Like the cities, they asked and found rich men
and women to be their patrons, and to repay compliments by helping to finance
their outings, their assembly halls, and their shrines. It would be an error to think
of these associations as corresponding to the labor unions of our time; we can
picture them better in terms of our fraternal orders, with their endless offices
and titles of honor, their brotherly hilarity and jaunts, and their simple mutual
aid. Rich men often encouraged the formation of these guilds and remembered
them in their wills. In the *collegium* all the men were "brothers" and all the
women "sisters," and in some of them the slave could sit at table or in council
with freeborn men. Every "member in good standing" was guaranteed a fancy
funeral.

In the last century of the Republic demagogues of all orders discovered that
many *collegia* could be persuaded to vote almost to a man for any giving candidate. In this way the associations became political instruments of patricians,
plutocrats, and radicals; and their competitive corruption helped to destroy
Roman democracy. Caesar outlawed them, but they revived; Augustus dissolved
all but a few useful ones; Trajan again forbade them; Aurelius tolerated them;
obviously they persisted throughout, within or beyond the law. In the end they
became vehicles through which Christianity entered and pervaded the life of
Rome.

VIII. THE ECONOMY AND THE STATE

How far did the government, under the Empire, attempt to control the economic life? It tried, and largely failed, to restore peasant proprietorship; here the emperors were more enlightened than the Senate, which was dominated by the owners of the latifundia. Domitian sought to encourage the planting of cereals in Italy, but without success; in consequence Italy was always in fear of starvation. Vespasian forced the Senate to accept him as emperor by holding Egypt, then the chief source of Italy's wheat; Septimius Severus would do the same by seizing north Africa. The state had to assure, and therefore supervise, the importation and distribution of grain; it offered privileges to merchants bringing grain to Italy; Claudius guaranteed them against loss, and Nero freed their ships from the property tax. The delay or wrecking of the grain fleet was now the only cause that could stir the Roman populace to revolt.

The Roman economy was a system of *laissez faire* tempered with state ownership of natural resources—mines, quarries, fisheries, salt deposits, and considerable tracts of cultivated land.[68] The legions made the bricks and tiles needed for their buildings, and were often used on public construction, especially in the colonies. The manufacture of arms and machines of war was probably reserved for state arsenals; and there may have been, in the first century, such governmentally owned factories as we hear of in the third.[69] Public works were normally let out to private contractors under such strict state supervision that they were usually well done, and with a minimum of corruption.[70] About A.D. 80 such enterprises were increasingly carried out by the emperor's freedmen with the labor of governmental slaves. At all times, apparently, the mitigation of unemployment was one purpose of these state undertakings.[71]

Trade was moderately burdened with a one per cent sales tax, light custom dues, and occasional tolls for the passage of goods over bridges and through towns. The aediles supervised retail trade under an excellent system of regulations, but, if we may believe an irate character in Petronius, they were no better than similar officials in other times; "they graft with the bakers and other such scoundrels . . . and the jaws of the capitalists are always open."[72] Finance was subject to governmental manipulation of the currency, and to the competition of the Treasury, which appears to have been the largest banker in the Empire; it lent money at interest to farmers on the pledge of their crops, and to city dwellers on the security of their furniture.[73] Commerce was aided by wars, which opened new resources and markets and won control of trade routes; so the expedition of Gallus into

Arabia secured the passage to India against the competition of Arabs and Parthians. Pliny complained that campaigns had been undertaken that Roman ladies and dandies might have a wider choice of perfumes.[74]

We must not exaggerate the wealth of ancient Rome. The total annual revenue of the state under Vespasian was at most 1,500,000,000 sesterces ($150,000,000)—less than a fifth of the budget of New York City today. The means of amassing great fortunes by large-scale production were unknown or ignored, and had not developed the immense and taxable industry and commerce of the modern world. The Roman government spent little on the navy, and nothing on servicing a national debt; it lived on its income, not on its debts. Industry being largely domestic, its products passed to the consumer with less intervening trade and taxation than today. Men produced for their own localities rather than for the general market. They did more for themselves, less for unseen others, than we do. They used their bodies more, worked longer hours less intensely, and did not miss a thousand luxuries that lay outside their dreams. They could not begin to rival the wealth of even our less affluent years; but they enjoyed a degree of prosperity such as the Mediterranean nations had not known before and, as a whole, have never known again. It was the material zenith of the ancient world.

CHAPTER XVI

Rome and Its Art

30 B.C.–A.D. 96

I. THE DEBT TO GREECE

THE Romans were not of themselves an artistic people. Before Augustus they were warriors, after him they were rulers; they counted the establishment of order and security through government a greater good and nobler task than the creation or enjoyment of beauty. They paid great sums for the works of dead masters, but looked down upon living artists as menials. "While we adore images," said the kindly Seneca, "we despise those who fashion them." [1] Only law and politics, and, of manual arts, only agriculture (by proxy), seemed honorable ways of life. Barring the architects, most artists in Rome were Greek slaves or freedmen or hirelings; nearly all worked with their hands and were classed as artisans; Latin authors seldom thought of recording their lives or their names. Hence Roman art is almost wholly anonymous; no vivid personalities humanize its history as Myron, Pheidias, Praxiteles, and Protogenes light up the aesthetic story of Greece. Here the historian is constrained to speak of things, not men, to catalogue coins, vases, statues, reliefs, pictures, and buildings in the desperate hope that their accumulation may laboriously convey the crowded majesty of Rome. The products of art appeal to the soul through eye or ear or hand rather than through the intellect; their beauty fades when it is diluted into ideas and words. The universe of thought is only one of many worlds; each sense has its own; each art has therefore its characteristic medium, which cannot be translated into speech. Even an artist writes about art in vain.

A special misfortune clouds Roman art: we come to it from Greek art, which seems at first its model and master. As the art of India disturbs us by strange shapes, so that of Rome chills us by the monotonous repetition of familiar forms. We have seen long since these Doric, Ionic, Corinthian columns and capitals, these smooth idealized reliefs, these busts of poets, rulers, and gods; even the astonishing frescoes of Pompeii, we are told, were copies of Greek originals; only the "Composite" order is indigenously Roman, and it offends our notions of classic unity, simplicity, and restraint. Certainly the art of the Augustan Age in Rome was overwhelmingly Greek. Through

Sicily and Greek Italy, through Campania and Etruria, finally through Greece, Alexandria, and the Hellenic East, the aesthetic forms, methods, and ideals of Hellas passed into Roman art. When Rome became mistress of the Mediterranean, Greek artists poured into the new center of wealth and patronage and made countless copies of Greek masterpieces for Roman temples, palaces, and squares. Every conqueror brought home examples, every magnate scoured the cities for the surviving treasures, of Greek workmanship. Gradually Italy became a museum of bought or stolen paintings and statuary that set the tone of Roman art for a century. Artistically Rome was swallowed up in the Hellenistic world.

All this is half the truth. In one aspect, as we shall see, the history of Roman art is a conflict between the architrave and the arch; in another it is the struggle of native Italian realism to recover from the invasion of the peninsula by a Greek art that had pictured gods rather than men, the type or Platonic idea rather than the earthly individual, and had sought a noble perfection of form rather than truth of perception and utterance. That virile indigenous art which had helped to carve the figures on Etruscan tombs hibernated between the Greek conquest and Nero's philhellenic ecstasy; but at last it broke the Hellenistic mold, and revolutionized classic art with realistic sculpture, impressionistic painting, and an architecture of arch and vault. Through these, as well as by her borrowed beauty, Rome became for eighteen centuries the art capital of the Western world.

II. THE TOILERS' ROME

The ancient traveler bent on making a tour of Flavian Rome, and coming northward up the Tiber from Ostia, would first of all have noted the swiftness of the muddy current, carrying along the soil of hills and valleys to the sea. In this simple fact lay the leisurely tragedy of erosion, the difficulty of two-way commerce on the river, the periodical silting of the Tiber's mouth, and the floods that almost every spring inundated the lower levels of Rome, confined the residents to upper stories reached by boats, and often destroyed the corn stored in granaries on the wharves. When the waters fell they carried houses to ruin, and men and animals to death.[2]

As he neared the city * the visitor's eye would be caught by the Emporium, which ran for a thousand feet along the river's eastern edge, and was noisy with workers, warehouses, markets, and moving goods. Beyond it rose that Aventine hill on which the angry plebs had staged its "sit-down strikes" of

---

* Cf. the map of Rome on the flyleaf of this volume.

494 and 449 B.C. On the left bank at this point were the gardens that Caesar had bequeathed to the people, and behind them the Janiculum. Near the eastern shore at the beautiful Pons Aemilius lay the Forum Boarium or Cattle Market, with its (still standing) temples to Fortune and Mater Matuta, the Goddess of the Dawn. Farther north on the right loomed the Palatine and Capitoline hills, thick with palaces and temples. On the left bank were Agrippa's gardens, and beyond them the Vatican hill. North of the city's center, off the eastern shore, stretched the spacious lawns and decorative buildings of the Campus Martius, or Field of Mars; here were the theaters of Balbus and Pompey, the Circus of Flaminius, the Baths of Agrippa, and Domitian's stadium; here the legions practiced, athletes competed, chariots raced, the people played ball,[3] and the Assembly gathered, under the emperors, to go through the motions of democracy's ghost.

Disembarking at the city's northern limits, the visitor saw some remains of the wall ascribed to Servius Tullius. Rome had probably rebuilt it after the Gallic raid of 390 B.C., but the power of Roman arms, and the apparent security of the capital, allowed the rampart to lapse into ruins; not till Aurelian (A.D. 270) would another wall rise, a symbol of security gone. Gates had been cut in the wall, usually as single or triple archways, to permit the passage of the great roads from which they took their names. Touring the boundary of the city east and then south, the visitor would see the luxuriant gardens of Sallust, the dusty camp of the Praetorians, the arches of the Marcian, Appian, and Claudian aqueducts, and on his right, in turn, the Pincian, Quirinal, Viminal, Esquiline, and Caelian hills. Leaving the walls and walking northwest on the Appian Way, he would pass through the Porta Capena along the southern slope of the Palatine to the Nova Via ("New Street"), and then northward through a maze of arches and buildings to stand in the ancient Forum, the head and heart of Rome.

Originally it had been a market place, some 600 by 200 feet; now (A.D. 96) the sellers had retired into the near-by streets or into other forums, but in the adjoining basilicas men sold shares in the publicans' corporations, made contracts with the government, defended themselves in the courts, or consulted lawyers on how to escape the law. Around the Forum had been built, as around New York's Wall Street, some modest temples to the gods, and some larger ones to Mammon. A population of statues adorned it, and the colonnades of great edifices provided the shade that could hardly come from a few ancient trees. From 145 B.C. till Caesar it had been the meeting place of the assemblies. At either end stood a speaker's platform, named *rostrum* because an earlier stand had been decorated with the *rostra* or prows of ships captured from Antium in 338 B.C. At the western end was the Millenarium Aureum, or Golden Milestone, a column of gilded bronze set up by Augustus to mark the junction and origin of several consular roads; on it were inscribed the major towns reached and their distances from Rome. Along the south-west side ran the Sacra Via, or Sacred Way, which led up to the temples of Jupiter and Saturn on the Capitoline hill. North of this Forum the visitor would find a larger one, the Forum Iulium, built by Caesar to relieve the older area; near by were additional forums laid out for Augustus and Vespasian; and soon Trajan would clear and adorn the greatest of them all.

Even in so hasty a circuit the ancient tourist would have felt the crowded diversity of the city's population and the tortuous inadequacy of its hap-hazard streets. A few of these were from sixteen to nineteen feet wide; most of them were meandering alleys in the Oriental style. Juvenal complained that carts rumbling over the uneven pavements at night made sleep im-possible, while the jostling crowds made daytime walking a form of war. "Hurry as we may, we are blocked by a surging host in front, and by a dense mass of people pressing upon us from behind. One digs an elbow into me, another a sedan pole; one bangs a beam, another a wine cask, against my head. My legs are beplastered with mud; huge feet trample upon me from every side; a soldier plants his hobnail boot squarely upon my toes." [4] The main thoroughfares were paved with large pentagonal blocks of lava stone, sometimes so firmly set in concrete that a few have remained in place till our time. There was no street lighting; whoever ventured out after dark carried a lantern, or followed a torchbearing slave; in either case he ran the gauntlet of many thieves. Doors were fastened with locks and keys; windows were bolted at night, and those on the ground floor were guarded—as now—by iron bars. To these perils Juvenal adds the objects, solid or liquid, thrown from upper-floor windows. All in all, he thought, only a fool would go out to dinner without making his will.[5]

Since there were no public vehicles to transport workers from their homes to their toil, most of the plebs lived in brick tenements near the heart of the town, or in rooms behind or above their shops. A tenement usually covered an entire square, and was therefore called an *insula*, or island. Many of these buildings were six or seven stories high, and so flimsily built that several collapsed, killing hundreds of occupants. Augustus limited the frontal height of buildings to seventy Roman feet, but apparently the law permitted greater elevations in the rear, for Martial tells of "a poor devil whose attic is 200 steps up." [6] Many tenements had shops on the ground floor; some had balconies on the second; a few were connected at the top with tenements across the street by arched passages containing additional rooms—precarious penthouses for particular plebeians. Such *insulae* almost filled the Nova Via, the Clivus Victoriae (Victory Hill) on the Palatine, and the Subura—a noisy brothel-ridden district between the Viminal and the Esquiline. In them dwelt the longshoremen of the Emporium, the butchers of the Macellum, the fishmongers of the Forum Piscatorium, the cattlemen of the Forum Boarium, the vegetable vendors of the Forum Holitorium, and the workers in Rome's factories, clerkships, and trades. The slums of Rome lapped the edges of the Forum.

The streets off the Forum were lined with shops and resounded with labor and bargaining. Fruit sellers, booksellers, perfumers, milliners, dyers, florists, cutlers, locksmiths, apothecaries, and other caterers to the needs, foibles, and vanities of mankind blocked the thoroughfares with their projecting booths. Barbers plied their trade in the open air, where all could hear; wine taverns were so numerous that Rome seemed to Martial one vast saloon.[7] Each trade tended to center in some quarter or street and often gave the locality a name; so the sandalmakers were gathered in the Vicus Sandalarius, the harnessmakers in the Vicus Lorarius, the glassblowers in the Vicus Vitrarius, the jewelers in the Vicus Margaritarius.

In such shops the artists of Italy did their work—all but the greatest of them, who drew high fees and lived in peripatetic luxury. Lucullus gave Arcesilaus a million sesterces to make a statue of the goddess Felicitas, and Zenodorus received 400,000 for a colossus of Mercury.[8] Architects and sculptors were ranked with physicians, teachers, and chemists as pursuing *artes liberales*, arts of freemen; but the men who did most of the artwork of Rome were or had been slaves. Some owners had their bondsmen trained in carving, painting, and like skills, and sold their products in Italy and abroad. In such shops labor was sharply divided: some specialized in votive figures, others in decorative cornices; some cut glass eyes for statues; different painters made arabesques or flowers or landscapes or animals or men, and worked in turn on the same picture. Several artists were expert forgers, producing antiques of any marketable age.[9] The Romans of the last century B.C. were easily deceived in these matters, for, like most *nouveaux riches*, they tended to value objects according to cost and rarity rather than by beauty and use. During the Empire, when it was no longer a distinction to be wealthy, taste improved, and a sincere love of excellence brought to many thousands of families a refinement of utensils and ornaments such as only a very few had known in Egypt, Mesopotamia, and Greece. Art was to antiquity what industry is to modernity. Men could not then enjoy the lavish abundance of useful products now poured forth by our machines; but they could, if they cared enough, gradually surround themselves with objects whose zealously finished form gave to all who lived with them the subtle and quiet happiness of beautiful things.

III. THE HOMES OF THE GREAT

The visitor seeking to study the dwellings of the middle class would have found them away from the city's center on the main diverging roads. Their brick-and-stucco exteriors were still built, as before, in the plain and solid style dictated by insecurity and heat; the Roman bourgeois wasted no art on passers-by. Few houses rose to more than two stories. Cellars were rare; roofs sparkled with red tiles; windows were fitted with shutters or, occasionally, panes of glass. The entrance was usually a double door, each half turning on metal pivots. Floors were of concrete or tile, often of mosaic squares; there were no carpets. Around the central atrium were grouped the main rooms of the house: this is the architectural origin of the cloister and the college quadrangle. In the richer houses one or more rooms would be used for bathing, usually in tubs much like our own. Plumbing was carried by the Romans to an excellence unmatched before the twentieth century. Lead pipes brought water from the aqueducts and mains into most tenements and homes; fittings and stopcocks were of bronze, and some were molded into highly ornamental designs.[10] Leaders and gutters of lead carried rain from the roof. Most rooms were heated, if at all, by portable charcoal braziers; a few homes, many villas and palaces, and the public baths enjoyed central heating from wood- or charcoal-burning furnaces supplying hot air to various rooms through tile pipes or passages in floors and walls.*

In the early Empire a Hellenistic addition was made to the rich Roman's house. To provide a privacy not always possible in the atrium, he built behind it a *peristylium,* a court open to the sky, planted with flowers and shrubs, adorned by statues, surrounded by a portico, and centering about a fountain or a bathing pool. Around this court he raised a new set of rooms: a *triclinium* or dining room, an *oecus* ("house") for the women, a *pinacotheca* for his art collection, a *bibliotheca* for his books, and a *lararium* for his household gods; there might also be extra bedrooms, and little alcoves called *exedrae*—"sitting-out" nooks. Less expensive homes substituted a garden for the *peristylium;* and if even that could find no ground, the Romans placed flower boxes in the windows or grew flowers and shrubs on the roof. Some large roofs, says Seneca, had grape arbors, fruit trees, and shade trees planted in boxes of soil;[12] not a few had *solaria* for baking bellies in the sun.

Many Romans wearied of the roar and rush of Rome and fled to the peace and boredom of the countryside. Rich and poor alike developed a feeling for nature beyond anything discernible in ancient Greece. Juvenal thought a man foolish to live in the capital when, for the annual rental of a dark garret in Rome, he might buy a pretty house in some quiet Italian town and surround it with "a trim garden fit to feast a hundred Pythagoreans." [13] The well to do moved out of

---

* Vitruvius describes these *hypocausta* as introduced about 100 B.C.[11] By A.D. 10 they were fairly common, particularly in the north, and even in Britain, which is slowly recapturing the idea.

Rome in early spring to villas in the foothills of the Apennines or on the shores of lakes or the sea. The younger Pliny has left us a pleasant description of his country house at Laurentum on the coast of Latium. He calls it "large enough for my convenience, without being expensive to maintain"; but as he goes on we suspect a pose in his modesty. He describes "a small porch sheltered by glazed windows and overhanging eaves . . . a handsome dining room gently washed by the edge of the last breakers," and so bright with spacious windows as to give "a view in three directions, as if of three different seas"; an atrium "whence the prospect ends in woods and mountains"; two drawing rooms; a "semicircular library whose windows receive the sun all day long"; a bedchamber, and several rooms for servants. In an opposite wing were "an elegant parlor," a second dining room, and four small rooms; a bathroom suite consisting of "a pleasant undressing room," a frigidarium or cold bath, a tepidarium with three pools heated to different degrees, and a calidarium or hot bath; all centrally heated by hot-air pipes. Outside were a swimming pool, a ball court, a storehouse, a variegated garden, a private study and banquet hall, and an observation tower with two apartments and a dining room. "Tell me now," Pliny concludes, "have I not just cause to bestow my time and affection upon this agreeable retreat?" [14]

If a senator could have such a villa on the sea, and another on Como, we may begin to imagine the sprawling luxury of Tiberius' estate at Capri, or Domitian's at Alba Longa—not to speak of the one that Hadrian would soon build at Tibur. To match this cubicular extravagance the visitor would have to find entry to the palaces of millionaires and emperors on the Palatine. In domestic architecture the Romans did not care to imitate classic Greece, where homes were modest and only temples were great; they modeled their palaces upon the residences of the half-Orientalized Hellenistic kings; Ptolemaic styles came to Rome with Cleopatra's gold, and royal architecture accompanied monarchical politics. The *palace* of Augustus, receiving the name from the hill it stood on, spread with extensions as the administrative functions of the imperial household increased. Most of his successors built additional palaces for themselves and their staffs: Tiberius his *domus Tiberiana*, Caligula his *domus Gaiana*, Nero his *domus aurea*.

This Golden House became the passing wonder of Rome. Its buildings alone covered 900,000 square feet, and yet were but a small part of a mile-square villa that overflowed from the Palatine upon the neighboring hills. A great park surrounded the palace, with gardens, meadows, fish ponds, game preserves, aviaries, vineyards, streams, fountains, waterfalls, lakes, imperial galleys, pleasure houses, summerhouses, flower houses, and porticoes 3000 feet long. An angry wit scratched a representative comment on a wall: "Rome has become the habitation of one man. It is time, citizens, to emigrate to Veii—unless, indeed, Veii itself is to be comprised in Nero's home." [15]

The interior of the palace gleamed with marble, bronze, and gold, with the gilded metal of countless Corinthian capitals, and with thousands of statues, reliefs, paintings, and objects of art bought or looted from the classic world; among them was the *Laocoön*. Some of the walls were inlaid with mother-of-pearl and various costly gems. The ceiling of the banquet hall was covered with ivory flowers from which, at a nod of the emperor, a perfumed spray would fall upon his guests. The dining room had a spherical ceiling of ivory painted to represent the sky and the stars, which was kept in constant slow rotation by hidden machines. A suite of rooms provided hot baths, cold baths, tepid baths, salt-water baths, and sulphur baths. When the Roman architects Celer and Severus had nearly finished the immense structure and Nero moved in, he remarked, "At last I am lodged." A generation later this Roman Versailles, too costly and dangerous to maintain amid surrounding poverty, had fallen into neglect. Over its ruins Vespasian built the Colosseum, Titus and Trajan their enormous public baths.

Domitian shared Nero's architectural madness. For him Rabirius raised the *domus Flavia*, not quite as elephantine as Nero's museum, but yielding little to it in gaudy splendor and decoration. One wing alone contained a vast basilica, probably the court where the Emperor tried cases of final appeal; the same wing enclosed a *peristylium* covering 30,000 square feet. Adjoining this was a banquet hall, whose pavement of red porphyry and green serpentine survives; gone are the delicate marble screens and beautifully columned windows through which the diners might watch the waters splashing over the marble basins of the *nymphaea* or fountains outside. It should be added that Domitian used this building only for receptions and administration; usually he lived in the more modest quarters of Augustus' palace. Doubtless these royal edifices were part of the façade of empire, designed to impress natives, visitors, and embassies, while the emperors themselves, perhaps excepting Caligula and Nero, fled from the constraining formality of these ceremonial rooms to the ease and intimacy of their family quarters, and enjoyed, as Antoninus Pius would put it, "the pleasure of being men." [16]

IV. THE ARTS OF DECORATION

In these palaces, and in the homes of the rich, a hundred arts were employed to make everything if not beautiful, at least expensive. The floors were often of polychrome marble, or mosaics whose patient combination of tiny varicolored cubes (*tesserae*) resulted in paintings of remarkable realism and permanence. Furniture was less abundant and comfortable than among ourselves, but of generally superior design and workmanship. Tables, chairs, benches, couches, beds, lamps, and utensils were made of lasting materials, and lavishly adorned; the best wood, ivory, marble, bronze, silver, and gold were carefully turned and finished, decorated with plant or animal forms, or inlaid with ivory, tortoise shell, chased bronze, or precious stones. Tables were sometimes cut from costly cypress or citrus woods; some were of gold or silver; many were of marble or bronze. Chairs were of every sort from folding stool to throne, but less calculated than ours to deform the spine. Beds were of wood or metal, with slim but sturdy legs often ending in an animal's head or foot; a bronze web, instead of a spring, supported a mattress filled with straw or wool. Bronze tripods of elegant form took the place of our end tables; and here and there were cabinets with pigeon-holes for rolled books. Bronze braziers warmed the rooms, and bronze lamps lighted them. Mirrors too were of bronze, highly polished, embossed or engraved with floral or mythical designs; some were made horizontally or vertically convex or concave to distort reflections into a humorous slenderness or rotundity.[17]

The factories of Campania, working with the rich output of Spanish mines, produced silverware on a large scale for a wide market; silver services were now common in the middle and upper classes. In 1895 an excavator found in the cistern of a villa at Boscoreale a remarkable collection of silver, apparently deposited there by its owner before his unsuccessful flight from the embers of Vesuvius in A.D. 79. One of the sixteen cups bears an almost perfect representation of simple foliage; two depict skeletons in high relief; another pictures Augustus enthroned between Venus and Mars, the rival deities of mankind; the sliest shows Zeno the Stoic pointing with scorn at Epicurus, who is helping himself to a huge piece of cake, while a pig, with uplifted foreleg, politely asks for a share.

The coins and gems of the early Empire prove the progress of the engraver's art. Those of Augustus show the same good taste, sometimes the same designs, as the Altar of Peace. Precious stones imported from Africa, Arabia, and India were cut and set into rings, brooches, necklaces, bracelets, cups, even into walls. A ring on at least one finger was a social necessity; a few fops wore rings on all fingers but one. The Roman sealed his signature with his ring and therefore liked to have the seal individually designed. Some of the best-paid artists in Rome were gem cutters, like the Dioscurides who made Augustus' seal. In cutting cameos the Golden Age reached a level never surpassed; the *gemma Augusta* in Vienna is among the finest in existence. To collect gems and cameos became a hobby of rich Romans—Pompey, Caesar, Augustus; by inheritance the imperial gem cabinet grew till Marcus Aurelius sold it to help pay for his war against the Marcomanni. From the official guardian of the imperial seals and gems England derived her Keeper of the Great, or Privy, Seal.

Meanwhile the potters of Capua, Puteoli, Cumae, and Arretium were filling Italian homes with every variety of ceramic art. Arretium had mixing vats with a capacity of 10,000 gallons. Its red-glazed tableware was for a century the most widely spread product of Italy; specimens of it have been found almost everywhere. Iron stamps, hollowed out in relief, were used to impress upon each vase, lamp, or tile the name of the maker, sometimes also the names of the year's consuls, as a date. To this degree the ancients knew the art of printing; they left it undeveloped because slave copyists were cheap.[18]

From pottery the workers of Cumae, Liternum, and Aquileia turned to the production of artistic glass.* The Portland Vase is a famous example of its kind;† finer still is the "Blue Glass Vase" found at Pompeii, depicting in lively and graceful action a vintage feast of Bacchus.[19] In the reign of Tiberius, say Pliny and Strabo,[20] the art of glass blowing was brought from Sidon or Alexandria to Rome, and soon produced polychrome phials, cups, bowls, and other forms of such delicate beauty that they became for a time the favorite prey of art collectors and millionaires. In Nero's reign 6000 sesterces were paid for two small cups of blown glass now known as *millefiori*, or "thousand flowers," produced by fusing together differently colored glass rods. Even more prized were the "Murrhine" vases imported from Asia and Africa. They were made by placing white and purple glass filaments side by side to form a desired pattern, and then firing them; or pieces of colored glass were embedded in a transparent white body. Pompey brought some to Rome after his victory over Mithridates; Augustus, though he melted down Cleopatra's gold plate, kept for himself her goblet of Murrhine glass. Nero paid a million sesterces for one such cup; Petronius, dying, broke another lest it should fall into Nero's hands. All in all, the Romans have had no superior in making glass; and there are few art collections in the world more precious than those of Roman glass in the British Museum and the Metropolitan Museum of Art.

V. SCULPTURE

Pottery passed into sculpture through baked clay—terra-cotta reliefs and statuettes, toys, imitations of fruit, grapes, fish—at last full-sized statues. Glazed terra cotta—majolica—abounded in the ruins of Pompeii. Temple pediments and eaves were adorned with terra-cotta palmettes, acroteria,

---

* The Syrians and Egyptians, some 200 years before Christ, had discovered that the fusion of sand with an alkaline substance at a high temperature produced a semitransparent liquid of greenish color (due to the iron oxide in the sand); that the addition of manganese and lead oxide rendered the product colorless and fully transparent; and that different shades could be induced by different chemicals—blue, for example, by cobalt. The fluid paste was shaped by hand or blown into molds; or the paste was allowed to harden, and then cut on a wheel.

† This vase of superimposed layers of glass was probably of Greek origin. It was found near Rome in 1770, was bought by the Duke of Portland, and was lent to the British Museum in 1810. In 1845 a maniac smashed it into 250 pieces, but it was so successfully restored that when the then Duke offered it for sale in 1929 he received a bid of $152,000. The bid was rejected as too low.[18a]

gargoyles, and reliefs. The Greeks laughed at these ornaments, and under the Empire they went out of fashion; Augustus was no friend of clay.

It was probably through his Attic taste that relief and sculpture attained in Rome an excellence comparable with the best Hellenistic work. For a generation the artists of Rome carved fountains, tombstones, arches, and altars with a refinement of feeling, a precision of execution, a quiet dignity of form, a measure of modeling and perspective, that rank Roman reliefs among the masterpieces of the world's art. In 13 B.C. the Senate celebrated the return of Augustus from the pacification of Spain and Gaul by decreeing that an *Ara Pacis Augustae*, or "Altar of the Augustan Peace," should be erected in the Field of Mars. This is the noblest of all the sculptural remains of Rome. Perhaps the monument owed its form to the altar at Pergamum, and its processional motif to the Parthenon frieze; the altar was raised on a platform in an enclosure whose surrounding walls were partly carved in marble relief; the extant pieces are slabs from these walls.* One slab represents Tellus—Mother Earth—with two children in her arms, corn and flowers growing beside her, and animals lying contentedly at her feet. These were the leading ideas of the Augustan reformation: the family restored to parentage, the nation to agriculture, the Empire to peace. The central figure is unsurpassed; indeed, in its union of mature motherhood and womanly beauty, tenderness, and grace, there is a soft perfection unmatched by the stately goddesses of the Parthenon. The frieze of the outer wall had a lower panel of acanthus scrolls, broad-petaled peonies and poppies, and rich clusters of ivy berries; this too is unequaled in its class. Another panel showed two processions moving in opposite directions to meet before the altar of the Goddess of Peace. In these groups are grave and quiet figures, probably of Augustus, Livia, and the imperial family, with nobles, priests, Vestal Virgins, and children. These last are engagingly real in their shy innocence. One is a baby toddling along with no taste for ceremony; another is a boy already proud of his years; another a little girl with a nosegay; another, after some mischief, is being gently admonished by his mother. Henceforth children would play a rising role in Italian art. But never again would Roman sculpture show such mastery of drapery, such natural and effective grouping, such modulations of light and shade. Here, as in Virgil, propaganda had found a perfect medium.

The only Roman rivals of these reliefs are the carvings on the arches raised for the entry of triumphing generals. The finest survivor is the Arch of Titus, begun by Vespasian and completed by Domitian to commemorate

---

* The largest fragments were till recently in the Museo delle Terme at Rome; others were in the Vatican, the Uffizi Gallery at Florence, and in the Louvre.

the capture of Jerusalem. One relief shows the burning city, its walls in ruins, its people wild with fear, its wealth looted by legionaries; another pictures Titus riding into Rome in his chariot amid soldiers, animals, magistrates, priests, and prisoners, followed by the holy candelabra of the Temple, and varied spoils of war. The artists here experimented bravely: they cut different figures to different levels, and distributed them on diverse planes; they chiseled the background to give an illusion of depth; and they painted the whole to convey additional shades of fullness and distance. The action was shown not in separate episodes but in continuity, as on the friezes of Mesopotamia and Egypt, and later on the columns of Trajan and Aurelius; so the sense of motion and life was better conveyed. The figures were not idealized and softened into a mood of Attic repose as in the Hellenistic *Ara Pacis;* they were taken from the flesh and the dirt, and carved in the earthy tradition of Italian realism and vitality. The subject was not perfect gods but living men.

It is this vigorous realism that distinguishes Roman sculpture from the Greek; but for this recurrent fidelity to their own bent the Romans would have added little to art. About 90 B.C. a Greek from south Italy, Pasiteles, went to Rome, lived there for sixty years, did excellent work in silver, ivory, and gold, introduced silver mirrors, made skillful copies of Greek masterpieces, and wrote five volumes on the history of art; he was both the Vasari and the Cellini of his time. Another Greek, Arcesilaus, made for Caesar a famous statue of his distant relative, Venus Genetrix. Apollonius of Athens, probably in Rome, carved the powerful *Torso Belvedere* of the Vatican: a work conceived with moderation, proclaiming no bulging muscles, but showing a man in the fullness of healthy strength; we can only say of it that it is perfect so far as it goes. For a time the studios busied themselves giving Greek form to Italian gods, even to divine abstractions like Chance and Chastity. Presumably in this period and in Rome Glycon of Athens carved the *Farnese Hercules.* We cannot tell to what age or country the *Apollo Belvedere* belongs; perhaps it was a Roman copy of an original by Leochares of Athens. Every student knows how its calm beauty stirred Winckelmann to Uranian ecstasy.[21] Juno received now two renowned embodiments: the porphyry *Farnese Juno* of the Naples Museum and the *Ludovisi Juno* of the Terme—cold and stern, righteous and just; one begins to understand Jove's wanderings.

All these, and the graceful *Perseus and Andromeda* of the Capitoline Museum, were in the Greek style, idealized and generalized, and tiresomely divine. More arresting are the portrait busts that constitute a bronze-and-marble dictionary of Roman physiognomy from Pompey to Constantine. Some of these too are idealized, particularly the Julio-Claudian heads; but the old Etruscan realism, and the ever-present example of unflattering death masks, reconciled the Romans to being represented as ugly, provided they were shown as strong. So many of them bequeathed their effigies to public places that at times Rome seemed to belong less to the quick than to the dead. Some worthies could not bide their end, but erected themselves as statues before their death, until the jealous emperors, to make room for the living, forbade such premature immortality.

The greatest of the portrait busts is the so-named *Head of Caesar*, of black basalt, in Berlin. We do not know whom it represents; but the sparse hair and sharp chin, the thin and bony face, the heavy lines of weary thought, the resolution yielding to disillusionment, accord well with the traditional attribution. Only second to it is the colossal head of Caesar in Naples: here the wrinkles have set almost into bitterness, as if the giant had at last discovered that no mind is broad enough to understand, much less to rule, the world. Realistic to repulsiveness is the Pompey of the Ny Carlsberg Glyptotek in Copenhagen: all the brave triumphs of his youth forgotten in the dull obesity of a beaten man. Of Augustus we have half a hundred statues, many of them masterly: Augustus the boy (in the Vatican), serious, keen, noble—the finest portrait of an actual youth in any age; Augustus at thirty (in the British Museum)—a bronze figure of burning determination, reminding us of Suetonius' statement that the Emperor could quell a mutiny with a glance; Augustus the priest (in the Terme), a profound and pensive face emerging from a prison of drapery; and Augustus *imperator*, found in the ruins of Livia's villa at Prima Porta, and now in the Vatican. The breastplate of this famous figure is covered with esoteric and distracting reliefs,* the pose is stiff, the legs are too mighty for such an invalid; but the head has a quiet and self-confident power that reveals the hand and soul of a great artist—who could not quite forget the *Doryphoros* of Polycleitus.

Livia herself was fortunate in the artist who made the head now in Copenhagen. The hair is stately, the bent Roman nose smacks of character, the eyes are thoughtful and tender, the lips pretty but firm; this is the woman who stood quietly behind Augustus' throne, overthrew all her rivals and enemies, and mastered everybody but her son. Tiberius too fared well; idealized though it is, the seated figure in the Lateran Museum is a chef-d'oeuvre worthy of the hand that carved the diorite *Chephren* in Cairo. Claudius was not so lucky; surely the sculptor was making fun of him, or illustrating Seneca's *Pumpkinification*, when he carved him up as a worried Jupiter, fat and amiable and dumb. Nero tried hard to develop a sense of

---

* They portray the return of the Parthian standards, the submission of the conquered provinces, the fertility of the earth (Terra Mater) at peace, and the mantle of protection spread over all by Jove.

beauty, but his real passion was for fame and size; he saw no better function for Zenodotus, the Scopas of this age, than to consume his time in making a colossus of Nero as Apollo, 117 feet high.* Hadrian had it removed to the foreground of the Flavian Amphitheater, which thence derived its name of Colosseum.[22]

With the honest Vespasian sculpture returned to reality. He let himself be represented frankly as a veritable plebeian, with coarse features, wrinkled brow, bald head, and enormous ears. Kinder is the bust in the Terme, showing a spirit harassed with affairs of state, or the businesslike face of the massive head in Naples. Titus comes down to us with a like cubical cranium and homely countenance; it is hard to think of this stout street vendor as the darling of mankind. Domitian had the good sense, in the realistic Flavian age, to have himself so hated in life that all his images were ordered destroyed after his death.

When the artist left the palace and roamed the streets he could give free play to the Italic imp of humorous truth. Some old man, surely less equipped with wisdom and denarii than the philosopher-premier, posed for the disheveled scarecrow once labeled *Seneca*. Athletes had their muscles immortalized for a moment by famous artists; and gladiators, as statues, found entry into the best homes, from patrician villas to Farnese palaces. The Roman sculptors relented when they handled the figures of women; now and then they carved an irascible shrew, but also they molded some Vestal Virgins of a graceful gravity, occasional incarnations of tenderness like the *Clytie* of the British Museum, and aristocratic ladies as fragilely charming as the dolls of Watteau or Fragonard.[23] They were adept in the portrayal of children, as in the bronze *Boy* of the Metropolitan Museum, or the *Innocenza* of the Capitoline. They could chisel or cast the forms of animals with startling vividness, as in the wolves' heads found at Nemi in 1929, or the prancing horses of St. Mark's. They seldom achieved the smooth perfection of the Periclean schools; but that was because they loved the individual more than the type, and relished the life-giving imperfections of the real. With all their limitations they stand supreme in the history of portrait art.

VI. PAINTING

The ancient visitor would have found painting even more popular than sculpture in Rome's temples and dwellings, porticoes and squares. He would have come upon many works of old masters there—Polygnotus, Zeuxis,

---

* With its pedestal, 153. The Statue of Liberty, without its base, is 104 feet in height.

Apelles, Protogenes, and others—as dear to the opulent Empire as the paintings of the Renaissance are to rich America; and he would have seen in greater abundance, through their better preservation, the products of Alexandrian and Roman schools. The art was old in Italy, where every wall craved ornament. Once even Roman nobles had practiced it; but the Hellenistic invasion had made painting Greek and servile, and at last Valerius Maximus marveled that Fabius Pictor should have stooped to paint murals in the Temple of Health.[24] There were exceptions: toward the end of the Republic Arellius made a name for himself by hiring prostitutes to pose for his goddesses; in the time of Augustus a dumb aristocrat, Quintus Pedius, took up painting because his defect closed most professions to him; and Nero employed for the interior of his Golden House one Amulius, who "painted with the greatest gravity, always in his toga." [25] But such men were *rari nantes* in the crowd of Greeks who, at Rome and Pompeii and throughout the peninsula, made copies or variations of Greek paintings on Greek or Egyptian themes.

The art was practically limited to fresco and tempera. In fresco a freshly plastered wall was painted with water-moistened colors; in tempera the pigments were mixed with an adhesive sizing and laid upon a dry surface. Portrait painters sometimes employed an encaustic process in which the tints were fused in hot wax. Nero had his picture painted on a canvas 120 feet high—the first known use of this material. Painting, as we have seen, was applied to statues, temples, stage scenery, and great linen pictures intended for exhibition in triumphs or in the Forum; but its favored receptacle was the external or internal wall. The Romans seldom placed furniture against a wall or hung pictures there; they preferred to use the entire space for one painting, or for a group of related designs. In this way the mural became a part of the house, an integral item in the architectural design.

The caustic humor of Vesuvius has preserved for us some 3500 frescoes— more paintings at Pompeii than can be found in all the rest of the classic world. Since Pompeii was a minor town we may imagine how many such murals brightened the homes and shrines of classic Italy. The best survivors have been removed to the Naples Museum; even there their lithe grace impresses us; but only the ancients knew them in the full depth of their color and in the architectural framework that gave each picture a function and a place. In the House of Vettii the murals have been left *in situ:* in a dining room Dionysus surprises the sleeping Ariadne; on the opposite wall Daedalus displays his wooden cow to Pasiphaë; at the farther end Hermes looks on calmly as Hephaestus fastens Ixion to the torturing wheel; and in another room a succession of humorous frescoes shows carefree

Cupids parodying the industries of Pompeii, including the wine business of the Vettii. The bite of time has gnawed into these once brilliant surfaces, but enough remains to shock the visitor into modesty; the figures are almost perfectly drawn, and so colorful with the flesh of life that they can still make the blood stir lustily in living veins.

It is by reference to these Pompeian paintings that connoisseurs have tried to understand the nature, and classify the periods and styles, of pictorial art in ancient Italy. The method is precarious, for Pompeii was more Greek than Latin; but what remains of classic painting in Rome and its suburbs falls in tolerably well with the Pompeian development. In the First or In-crustation Style (second century B.C.) walls were often colored to resemble inlaid marble slabs (*crustae*), as in the "House of Sallust" at Pompeii. In the Second or Architectural Style (first century B.C.) the wall was painted to simulate a building or façade or colonnade. Often the columns were repre-sented as seen from within, and open country was pictured between them; in this way the artist gave to a probably windowless room cool vistas of trees and flowers, fields and streams, peaceful or playful animals; the im-prisoned dweller could fancy himself in Lucullus' gardens by merely look-ing at the wall; he might fish or row or hunt, or indulge a fondness for birds without suffering their untimeliness; nature was taken into the house. The Third or Ornate Style (A.D. 1-50) employed architectural forms purely for ornament, and subordinated landscape to figures. In the Fourth or Intri-cate Style (A.D. 50-79) the artist let his fancy riot, invented fantastic struc-tures and shapes, placed them in positions gaily scornful of gravity, piled gardens and columns, villas and pavilions, upon one another in modernistic disarray,[26] and occasionally achieved the impressionistic effect of a picture supplemented by unconscious memory and suffused with light. In all these kindred styles architecture was handmaid and mistress to painting, served it and used it, and gave body to a tradition that reawoke, after sixteen cen-turies, in Nicolas Poussin.

It is a pity that the subjects of the major extant paintings so seldom venture beyond Greek myth. We tire of these same gods and satyrs, heroes and sinners—Zeus and Mars, Dionysus and Pan, Achilles and Odysseus, Iphigenia and Medea; though a like charge could be brought against the Renaissance. There are a few pictures of still life, and here and there a fuller, an innkeeper, or a butcher shines on Pompeian walls. Love often dominates the scene: a girl sits brooding over some secret longing not unrelated to the Eros who stands beside her; young men and women gambol amorously on the grass; Psyches and Cupids frolic as if the town had never known any-thing but love and wine. If we may judge from their representation in these murals, the women of Pompeii deserved to have life center about their

comeliness. We see them engrossed in the game of "knucklebones," or lean-
ing gracefully over a lyre, or composing poetry with a meditative stylus at
the lips; their faces are quiet with maturity, their forms are healthily full,
their robes fall about them with Pheidian amplitude and rhythm, they walk
like Helens conscious of their divinity. One of them performs a Bacchic
dance, apparently in thin air; her right arm, hand, and foot are as lovely
as anything in the history of painting. Some male characters must be included with these masterpieces: Theseus victor over the Minotaur, Hercules
rescuing Deianira or adopting Telephus, Achilles angrily surrendering the
reluctant Briseis; in this last picture every figure nears perfection and
Pompeian painting is at its best. Humor is represented, too: a disheveled
pedagogue stumbles forward on his staff; a jolly satyr shakes his shanks
in sardonic revelry, a bald ribald Silenus is caught in a mood of musical
ecstasy. Taverns and brothels came in for appropriate decoration, and no
eager tourist need be told that Priapus still flaunts his precious powers on
Pompeian walls. At the other end of the gamut, in the Villa Item, is a series
of religious pictures, suggesting the use of the place for celebrating the
Dionysian mysteries: in one fresco a little girl, palsied with piety, reads
from an apparently sacred book; in another a procession of damsels advances,
blowing pipes and bringing sacrifice; in a third a nude lady dances on tip-
toe while a neophyte kneels exhausted by some ritualistic whipping.[27] Finer
than any of these is a mural found in the ruins of Stabiae, presaging Botticelli and called *Spring:* a woman walks slowly through a garden, gathering
flowers; only her back is seen, and the graceful turning of her head; but
seldom has any art conveyed so movingly the poetry of this simple theme.

The most powerful of all the pictures recovered from these ruins is the
Medea found at Herculaneum, and preserved in the Naples Museum—a
brooding woman, magnificently draped, meditating the murder of her children; apparently this is a copy of the painting for which Caesar paid the
artist, Timomachus of Byzantium, forty talents ($144,000).[27a]

Few pictures of such quality have been found in Rome. But in the
suburban villa of Livia at Prima Porta a supreme example was discovered of
that landscape painting in which Italy so far excels Greece. The eye is lured
as if across a court to a marble trellis, beyond which is a jungle of plants
and flowers so accurately reproduced that botanists can now identify and
catalogue them; every leaf is carefully drawn and colored; birds perch here
and there as if for a moment, and insects creep amid the foliage. Only less
masterly is the *"Aldobrandini" Wedding* found on the Esquiline in 1606,
and enthusiastically studied by Rubens, Vandyke, and Goethe. Perhaps
it is a copy of a Greek work; perhaps it is an original by a Roman Greek,
or by a Roman; we can only say that these figures—the quiet and timid bride,

the goddess who counsels her, the mother absorbed in preparations, the maidens waiting to play the lyre and sing—are all done with a delicacy and sensitivity that make this mural a distinguished relic of classic art.

Roman painting laid no claim to originality; Greek artists carried with them everywhere the same traditions and methods; and even the vague impressionism of these pictures may be offshoots of Alexandrian skills. But there is in them a fineness of line, and a richness of color, that explain why painters like Apelles and Protogenes were held in as high repute as sculptors like Polycleitus and Praxiteles. Sometimes the color is as full as if Giorgione had laid it on; sometimes the subtle gradations of light and shade suggest Rembrandt; sometimes a crude figure catches the ungainly realism of Van Gogh. Perspective here is often faulty, and hasty workmanship limps behind mature conception. But a fresh vitality redeems these faults, the rhythm of the drapery lures the eye, and the woodland scenes must have been a delight to dwellers in a crowded town. Our taste today is more restrained; we like to leave a wall its own significance, and have hesitated, till yesterday, to cover it with paint. But to the Italian a wall was a prison, seldom opening through a window upon the world; he wished to forget the barrier, and be deluded by art into some verdant peace. Perhaps he was right: better a pictured tree on a wall than a magic casement's prospect of a thousand unkempt rooftops blaspheming the sky and festering in the sun.

VII. ARCHITECTURE

1. Principles, Materials, and Forms

We have reserved for the climactic edification of our forgotten visitor the greatest of Rome's arts, that in which she most ably defended herself against the Greek invasion, and displayed all her originality, courage, and power. Originality, however, is not parthenogenesis; it is, like parentage, a novel combination of pre-existing elements. All cultures are eclectic in their youth, as education begins with imitation; but when the soul or nation comes of age it stamps its character, if it has any, upon all its works and words. Rome, like other Mediterranean cities, took the Doric, Ionic, and Corinthian orders from Egypt and Greece; but also she took the arch, the vault, and the dome from Asia, and with them made such a city of palaces, basilicas, amphitheaters, and baths as the earth had not yet beheld. Roman architecture became the art expression of the Roman spirit and state: boldness, organization, grandeur, and brutal strength raised these unparalleled structures upon the hills. They were the Roman soul in stone.

Most of the leading architects in Rome were Romans, not Greeks. One of them, Marcus Vitruvius Pollio, wrote a world classic *On Architecture* (*ca.* 27 B.C.).* Having served as military engineer under Caesar in Africa, and as an architect under Octavian, Vitruvius retired in old age to formulate the principles of Rome's most honored art. "Nature has not given me stature," he confessed, "my face is homely with years, and illness has stolen my strength; therefore I hope to win favor by my knowledge and my book." [29] As Cicero and Quintilian made philosophy a prerequisite for the orator, so Vitruvius required it of the architect; it would improve his purposes while science improved his means; it would make him "high-minded, urbane, just, loyal, and without greed; for no true work can be done without good faith and clean hands." [30] He described the materials of architecture, the orders and their elements, and the diverse types of building in Rome; and added discourses on machinery, water clocks, speedometers,† aqueducts, town planning, and public sanitation. As against the rectangular design established by Hippodamus in many Greek cities, Vitruvius recommended the radial arrangement used in Alexandria (and modern Washington); the Romans, however, continued to lay out their towns on the rectangular plan of their camps. He warned Italy that in several localities its drinking water led to goiter, and declared that poisoning could come from working with lead. He explained sound as a vibratory motion of the air, and wrote our oldest extant discussion of architectural acoustics. His book, rediscovered in the Renaissance, deeply influenced Leonardo, Palladio, and Michelangelo.

The Romans, says Vitruvius, built with wood, brick, stucco, concrete, stone, and marble. Bricks were the usual substance of walls, arches, and vaults, and served as a frequent facing for concrete. Stucco too was often used as a facing. It was made of sand, lime, marble dust, and water, took a high polish, and was laid on in several coats, often to a thickness of three inches; hence it could keep its form for nineteen centuries, as in some parts of the Colosseum. In making and using concrete the Romans were unrivaled until our time. They took the volcanic ash abounding near Naples, mixed it with lime and water, threw in fragments of brick, pottery, marble, and stone, and produced, from the second century B.C. onward, an *opus caementicum* as hard as rock, and capable of being poured into almost any shape. They cast it as we do, in troughs formed of boards. By its means they could cover large unsupported spaces with rigid domes free from the lateral thrust of an arched roof; in this way they topped the Pantheon and the

---

* Some students suspect the work of being a third-century forgery, but the evidence inclines toward authenticity.[28]

† More accurately, odometers. A peg attached to the axle of the wheel advanced by a cog a smaller wheel, whose much slower revolution caused a pebble to fall into a box.[31]

great baths. Stone was employed for most temples and the more pretentious homes. One variety from Cappadocia was so translucent that a temple built with it was adequately lighted with all its openings closed.[32] The conquest of Greece brought a taste for marble, which was satisfied first by importing columns, then marble, and finally by working the Carrara quarries near Luna. Before Augustus marble was largely confined to columns and slabs; in his time it was used as a facing for brick and concrete; only in this superficial sense did he leave Rome, here and there, a city of marble; walls of solid marble were rare. The Romans liked to mingle in the same building the red and gray granite of Egypt, the green *cipollino* of Euboea, the black and yellow marbles of Numidia, with their own white Carrara, and with basalt, alabaster, and porphyry. Never had architectural material been so complex or so colorful.

To the Doric, Ionic, and Corinthian orders Rome added the Tuscan and Composite styles, and certain modifications. Columns were often monoliths instead of superimposed drums. The Doric column received an Ionic base and took on a new, unfluted slenderness; the Ionic capital was sometimes given four volutes to offer the same appearance from every side; the Corinthian column and capital were developed to a delicate beauty beyond any Greek example, but in later decades this style was spoiled by undue elaborations. A like excess poured flowers over the Ionic volutes to make the Composite capital, as in the Arch of Titus; sometimes the volutes ended in animal or human forms suggestive of gargoyles and presaging medieval forms. The lavish Romans often mixed several orders in the same building, as in the theater of Marcellus; and then again, with perverse economy, they left the side columns attached to the cella, as in the Maison Carrée at Nîmes. Even when the development of the arch had taken from columns their old supporting role the Romans added them as functionless ornaments—a custom that has survived into our own uncertain age.

2. The Temples of Rome

For nearly all her temples Rome kept the Greek trabeate principle—architraves (i.e., master beams) upheld by columns and carrying the roof. Augustus was conservative in art as in everything else, and most of the shrines built by his order clung to the orthodox tradition. From his time onward the emperors multiplied homes for their Olympic rivals and clothed their lechery with an architectural piety that crowded the hills and blocked the streets with tiled and gilded fanes. Jupiter, of course, was their favorite recipient. Among many he had one as Jupiter Tonans, the Thunderer; another as Jupiter Stator, who had stayed the flight of the Romans in battle; and he shared with Juno and Minerva the holiest of Rome's sanctuaries, atop the Capitoline hill. There in the central cell, flanked by a three-storied Corinthian colonnade, was the gold-and-ivory colossus of Jupiter Optimus Maximus—Jove the Best and Greatest. Tradition ascribed the first form of this supreme house of Roman worship to Tarquinius Priscus; it was several times burned down and rebuilt; Stilicho (A.D. 404) stole its gold-plated bronze doors to pay his soldiers, and the Vandals carried off the gold-plated tiles of the roof. Some fragments of the pavement remain.

On the northern summit of the same hill rose the Temple of Juno Moneta, Juno the Monitor or Guardian; here was the Roman mint, and from its name, of course, comes our word for the root of much ambition. On the south side of the hill was the shrine of Saturn, the oldest god of the Capitol; the Romans dated its first dedication at 497 B.C.; eight Ionic columns and an architrave survive. In the Forum, at the foot of the hill, was the little Temple of Janus, god of all beginnings; its doors were opened only in time of war, and were closed but three times in Rome's ancient history. At the southeast corner of the Forum stood the Temple of Castor and Pollux, erected in 495 B.C.; three slender Corinthian columns have come down to us from the reconstruction by Tiberius; they are by common consent the finest columns in Rome.

In his own forum Augustus added a Temple of Mars Ultor—the Avenger—vowed before Philippi; three of its majestic columns stand. One end of its cella was a semicircular apse, an architectural form destined to become the chancel of early Christian churches. On the Palatine Augustus built entirely of marble a sumptuous temple to Apollo for the god's help at Actium; he adorned it with sculptures by Myron and Scopas, added a splendid library and an art gallery to its enclosure, and did all he could to make men feel that the god had left Greece for Rome and had brought with him the spiritual and cultural leadership of the world. It was even whispered by Augustus' friends, now that his mother was safely dead, that Apollo, disguised as an agile snake, had begotten the subtle prince.

In the northwest part of the city was a great shrine to Isis, and on the Palatine a spacious sanctuary for Cybele. Handsome shelters were provided for personified abstractions—Health, Honor, Virtue, Concord, Faith, Fortune, and many more. Nearly all of these contained galleries of statuary and painting. In his great Temple of Peace Vespasian gathered for the general eye many of the art treasures of Nero's Golden House, and some of the relics of Jerusalem. The Temple of Fortuna Virilis, in the Forum Boarium, has the distinction of being the most completely preserved of the pre-Augustan buildings in Rome. The ladies of the capital frequently worshipped there, for the goddess, they believed, would teach them how to conceal their defects from men.

To these and a hundred other temples in the classic rectangular style the architects of Rome added several circular temples, which revealed a new mastery of the problems presented by a dome. Tradition derived this type from the round hut of Romulus, religiously preserved on the Palatine for many centuries. Almost as old was the pretty *Aedes Vestae,* or House of Vesta, near the Temple of Castor and Pollux; its circular cella, faced with white marble, was enclosed by handsome Corinthian columns, and its roof was a dome of gilded brass. Adjoining it was the Palace of the Vestals—eighty-four rooms built cloisterwise around a peristyled court, the *Atrium Vestae.* The Pantheon was not yet a circular temple; as built by Agrippa it was rectangular, but had a circular plaza before it; Hadrian's architects raised over this space the round temple and mighty dome which are still among the bravest works of man.

3. The Arcuate Revolution

Rome was greater in her secular than in her sacred architecture. For here she could escape the bondage of tradition and unite engineering with art—utility and power with beauty and form—in a manner all her own. The principle of Greek architecture had been the straight line (however delicately modulated as in the Parthenon): the vertical column, the horizontal architrave, the triangular pediment. The principle of specifically Roman architecture was to be the curve. The Romans wanted grandeur, audacity, size; but they could not roof their vast buildings on rectilinear and trabeate principles except by a maze of impeding columns. They solved the problem with the arch, usually in its rounded form; with the vault, which is a prolonged arch; and with the dome, which is a rotated arch. Perhaps Roman generals and their aides had brought from Egypt and Asia a growing familiarity with arcuate shapes, and had reawakened early Roman and Etruscan traditions long overwhelmed by orthodox Greek styles. Now Rome employed the arch on so great a scale that the whole art of building took from this form a new and lasting name. By laying a web of brick ribs along the lines of strain before pouring concrete into the wooden frame of the roof, the Romans developed the articulated vault; by crossing two cylindrical or barrel vaults at right angles they produced a network of ribs and groins that could sustain a heavier superstructure and bear more lateral thrust. These were the principles of Rome's arcuate revolution.

It was in the great baths and amphitheaters that the new style reached its completion. The baths of Agrippa, Nero, and Titus were the first of a long series that culminated in the Baths of Diocletian. They were monumental buildings of concrete faced with stucco or brick, and rising to majestic heights. The interiors were richly decorated with marble and mosaic pavements, varicolored columns, coffered ceilings, paintings, and statuary. They were equipped with dressing rooms, hot and cold baths, an intermediate room of warm air, swimming pools, palaestras, libraries, reading rooms, research rooms, lounges, and probably art galleries. Most of the chambers were centrally heated by large clay pipes running under floors and within the walls. These *thermae* were the most spacious and sumptuous public buildings ever erected, and they have never been equaled in their class. They were part of that socialism of recreation with which the principate excused its growing monarchy.*

This same paternalism built the greatest theaters in history. Those of Rome were much fewer but larger than those of modern capitals. The smallest was that which Cornelius Balbus built in the Field of Mars (13 B.C.), seating 7700; Augustus rebuilt Pompey's theater, seating 17,500; he completed another, named for Marcellus, seating 20,500. Unlike Greek theaters, these were walled, and the stands were supported by arched and vaulted masonry instead of resting on the slope of a hill. Only the stage was roofed; but often the audience was sheltered from the sun by a linen awning (*velarium*), which in Pompey's theater covered a space 550 feet wide. Over the entrances were boxes for dignitaries and magnates. Some stages had curtains which, when the play began, were not raised aloft, but lowered into a groove. The stage was elevated some five feet. Its background usually took the form of an elaborate building which, extending from wing to wing, helped the actors to throw their voices out over the immense audiences. Seneca speaks of "stage mechanics who invent scaffolding that goes aloft of its own accord, or floors that rise silently into the air." [32a] A change of scene was effected by revolving prisms, or by moving a set into the wings or into the loft, thereby exposing the next. Acoustics were aided by sinking hollow jars into the floor and walls of the stage.[32b] The auditorium was cooled by rivulets of water running along the passages; sometimes a mixture of water, wine, and crocus juice was conducted by pipes to the highest tiers and thence scattered over the audience as a perfumed spray.[32c] Statues adorned the interior, and large pictures were painted as scenery. Probably no theater or opera house in the world today could equal the size and splendor of Pompey's.

More popular still were the circus, the stadium, and the amphitheater. Rome had several stadiums, used chiefly for athletic contests. Horse or chariot races, and some spectacles, were presented at the Circus Flaminius in the Field of Mars, or, more usually, at the Circus Maximus as rebuilt by Caesar between the Palatine and Aventine hills. This was an immense ellipse

---

* The Roman baths provided models for many modern structures faced with like problems of covering great spaces with a minimum of obstruction. The Pennsylvania Station and Grand Central Terminal in New York are outstanding examples.

2200 feet long and 705 feet wide, with wooden seats on three sides for 180,000 spectators.[33] We may judge the wealth of Rome by noting that Trajan rebuilt these seats in marble.

By comparison the Colosseum was a modest structure, seating only 50,000. Its plan was not new; the cities of Greek Italy had long since had amphitheaters; Curio, as we have seen, *composed* one in 53 B.C.; Caesar built another in '46, Statilius Taurus another in 29 B.C. The Flavian Amphitheater, as Rome called the Colosseum, was begun by Vespasian and finished by Titus (A.D. 80); the architect's name is unknown. Vespasian chose as its site the lake in the gardens of Nero's Golden House, between the Caelian and Palatine hills. It was constructed of travertine stone in an ellipse 1790 feet around. Its external wall rose 157 feet and was divided into three stories, the first partly supported by Tuscan-Doric, the second by Ionic, the third by Corinthian, columns, with an arch in each intercolumnar space. The main corridors were roofed with barrel vaults, sometimes crossed in the style of medieval cloisters. The interior was also divided into three tiers, each upheld by arches, divided into concentric rings of boxes or seats, and cut by stairways into *cunei*, "wedges." The aspect of the interior today is that of a mass of masonry into which some giant artisan has cut the arches, passages, and seats. Statues and other decorations adorned the whole, and many rows of seats were in marble. There were eighty entrances, two of them reserved for the emperor and his suite; these entrances and the exits (*vomitoria*) could empty the gigantic bowl in a few minutes. The arena, 287 by 180 feet, was surrounded by a fifteen-foot wall topped with an iron grating to protect brutes from beasts. The Colosseum is not a beautiful building, and its very immensity reveals a certain coarseness, as well as grandeur, in the Roman character. It is only the most imposing of all the ruins left by the classic world. The Romans built like giants; it would have been too much to ask that they should finish like jewelers.

Roman art had taken over in eclectic confusion the Attic, Asiatic, and Alexandrian styles—restraint, immensity, and elegance; it never quite combined them into that organic unity which is one requisite of beauty. There is something Oriental in the crude strength of the typically Roman buildings; they are awe-inspiring rather than beautiful; even Hadrian's Pantheon is a structural marvel rather than an artistic whole. Except in certain moments, as in the Augustan reliefs and the glass, we must not look here for delicacy of feeling or refinement of execution; we must expect an engineer's art that seeks the perfection of stability, economy, and use, a parvenu's infatuation with immensity and ornament, a soldier's insistence on realism, a warrior's art of overwhelming force. The Romans did not finish like jewelers because conquerors do not become jewelers. They finished like conquerors.

Without doubt they created the most influential and fascinating city in history. They made a plastic, pictorial, and structural art that every man could understand, and a city that every citizen could use. The free masses were poor, but in some measure they owned much of the wealth of Rome: they ate the corn of the state, they sat at almost no cost in the theaters, the circuses, the amphitheaters, and the stadiums; they exercised, refreshed, amused, and educated themselves in the baths, they enjoyed the shade of a hundred colonnades, and walked under decorated porticoes that covered many miles of street and three miles in the Field of Mars alone. Never had the world seen such a metropolis. At its center a tumultuous Forum busy with business, resounding with oratory, alive with empire-shaking debates; then a ring of majestic temples, basilicas, palaces, theaters, and baths, in a profusion without parallel; then a ring of humming shops and teeming tenements; still another ring of homes and gardens, again with temples and public baths; and last of all, a circle of villas and estates pushing the city into the countryside and binding the mountains with the sea: this was the Rome of the Caesars—proud, powerful, brilliant, materialistic, cruel, iniquitous, chaotic, and sublime.

CHAPTER XVII

Epicurean Rome

30 B.C.–A.D. 96

I. THE PEOPLE

LET us enter these dwellings, temples, theaters, and baths, and see how these Romans lived; we shall find them more interesting than their art. We must at the outset recall that by Nero's time they were only geographically Roman. The conditions that Augustus had failed to check—celibacy, childlessness, abortion, and infanticide among the older stocks, manumission and comparative fertility among the new—had transformed the racial character, the moral temper, even the physiognomy, of the Roman people.

Once the Romans had been precipitated into parentage by the impetus of sex, and lured to it by anxiety for the post-mortem care of their graves; now the upper and middle classes had learned to separate sex from parentage, and were skeptical about the afterworld. Once the rearing of children had been an obligation of honor to the state, enforced by public opinion; now it seemed absurd to demand more births in a city crowded to the point of redolence. On the contrary, wealthy bachelors and childless husbands continued to be courted by sycophants longing for legacies. "Nothing," said Juvenal, "will so endear you to your friends as a barren wife." [1] "Crotona," says a character in Petronius, "has only two classes of inhabitants—flatterers and flattered; and the sole crime there is to bring up children to inherit your money. It is like a battlefield at rest: nothing but corpses and the crows that pick them." [2] Seneca consoled a mother who had lost her only child by reminding her how popular she would now be; for "with us childlessness gives more power than it takes away." [3] The Gracchi had been a family of twelve children; probably not five families of such abundance could be found in Nero's age in patrician or equestrian Rome. Marriage, which had once been a lifelong economic union, was now among a hundred thousand Romans a passing adventure of no great spiritual significance, a loose contract for the mutual provision of physiological conveniences or political aid. To escape the testatory disabilities of the unmarried some women took eunuchs as contraceptive husbands; [4] some entered into sham wedlock with poor men on the understanding that the wife need bear no children and might have as many lovers as she pleased.[5] Contraception was practiced in both its mechanical and chemical forms.[6] If these methods failed there were many ways of procuring abortion. Philosophers and the law condemned it, but the finest families practiced it. "Poor women," says Juvenal, "endure the perils of childbirth, and all the troubles of nursing . . . but how often does a gilded bed harbor a pregnant woman? So great is the skill, so powerful the drugs, of the abortionist!" Nevertheless, he tells the husband, "rejoice; give her the potion . . . for were she to bear the child you might find yourself the father of an Ethiopian." [7] In so enlightened a society infanticide was rare.*

The infertility of the moneyed classes was so offset by immigration and the fecundity of the poor that the population of Rome and the Empire continued to grow. Beloch estimated it at 800,000 for the Rome of the early Empire, Gibbon at 1,200,000, Marquardt at 1,600,000.† Beloch computed the population of the Empire at 54,000,000, Gibbon at 120,000,000.[11] The aristocracy was as numerous as before, but it was almost wholly altered in origin. We hear no more of the Aemilii, Claudii, Fabii, Valerii; only the Cornelii remained of the proud clans that, as late as Caesar, had strutted their Rome. Some had vanished through war or political execution; others had faded out through family limitation, physiological degeneration, or an impoverishment that had lowered them into the plebeian mass. Their places had been taken by Roman businessmen, Italian municipal dignitaries, and provincial nobles. In A.D. 56 a senator declared that "most of the knights, and many of the senators, were descendants of slaves." [12] After a generation or two the new optimates adopted the ways of their predecessors, had fewer children and more luxuries, and surrendered to inundation from the East.

First had come the Greeks—not so much from the mainland as from Cyrenaica, Egypt, Syria, and Asia Minor. They were eager, clever, facile semi-Orientals; many of them small traders or import merchants; some of them scientists, writers, teachers, artists, physicians, musicians, actors; some sincerely, some venally, devoted to philosophy; some of them able administrators and financiers, many of them without moral scruple, nearly all without religious belief. The majority had come as slaves and were not an ideal selection; freed, they kept their external servility, their internal hatred and scorn of the rich Roman who lived intellectually on the cultural leavings of ancient Hellas. The streets of the capital were now noisy with restless

---

* Sometimes, in the first century, girls or illegitimate children were exposed, usually at the base of the Columna Lactaria—so named because the state provided wet nurses to feed and save the infants found there.[10] The abandonment of unwanted babies, however, is a custom to be found in all but the most uncivilized societies.

† In 1937 the population of Rome was 1,178,000.

and voluble Greeks; the Greek language was more often heard there than the Latin; if one wished to be read by all classes he had to write in Greek. Nearly all the early Christians in Rome spoke Greek; so did the Syrians, the Egyptians, and the Jews. A large colony of Egyptians—traders, artisans, artists—lived in the Field of Mars. Syrians, thin, affable, shrewd, were everywhere in the capital, busy with trade, handicrafts, secretarial work, finance, and chicanery.

The Jews were already in Caesar's time a substantial element in the population of the capital. A few had come as early as 140 B.C.;[13] many had been brought to Rome as war captives after Pompey's campaign of 63 B.C. They were rapidly emancipated, partly by their industry and thrift, partly because their strict adherence to their religious customs was inconvenient for their masters. By 59 B.C. there were so many Jewish citizens in the assemblies that Cicero represented opposition to them as political temerity.[14] In general the republican party was hostile to the Jews, the *populares* and the emperors were friendly.[15] * By the end of the first century they numbered some 20,000 in the capital.[18] They lived mostly on the west side of the Tiber, where they suffered periodically from the floods. They worked on the near-by docks, engaged in handicrafts and retail business, and peddled goods through the city. There were some rich men among them, but only a few great merchants; Syrians and Greeks dominated international commerce. Synagogues were numerous in Rome, and each had its school, its scribes, and its *gerousia*, or senate of elders.[19] The separatism of the Jews, their scorn of polytheism and image worship, the severity of their morals, their refusal to attend the theaters or the games, their strange customs and ceremonies, their poverty and resultant uncleanliness, led to the usual racial antagonisms. Juvenal denounced their fertility, Tacitus their monotheism, Ammianus Marcellinus their fondness for garlic.[20] Bad feeling was heightened by the bloody capture of Jerusalem, and the procession of Jewish captives and sacred spoils featured in the triumph of Titus and in the reliefs on his arch. Vespasian heaped insult upon injury by ordering that the half shekel paid annually by the Jews of the Dispersion for the upkeep of the Temple at Jerusalem should henceforth be contributed yearly to the rebuilding of

---

* They supported Caesar consistently and were in turn protected by him. Augustus followed suit; but Tiberius, hostile to all foreign faiths, conscripted 4000 of them for almost suicidal soldiering in Sardinia, and expelled the rest from Rome (A.D. 19).[16] Twelve years later, convinced that he had been misled in this matter by Sejanus, he withdrew his edict and ordered that the Jews should be unmolested in the practice of their religion and the pursuit of their customs.[17] Caligula protected them in Rome and oppressed them abroad. Claudius exiled some because of riots, but by a general edict (42) confirmed the right of the Jews throughout the Empire to live by their own laws. In 94 Domitian banished the Jews of Rome to the valley of Egeria; in 96 Nerva brought them back, restored their civic rights, and allowed them a generation of peace.

Rome. Nevertheless, many educated Romans admired Jewish monotheism; some were converted to Judaism, and several, even of high family, observed the Jewish Sabbath as a day of worship and rest.[21]

If we add to the Greeks, the Syrians, the Egyptians, and the Jews some Numidians, Nubians, and Ethiopians from Africa; a few Arabs, Parthians, Cappadocians, Armenians, Phrygians, and Bithynians from Asia; powerful "barbarians" from Dalmatia, Thrace, Dacia, and Germany; mustachioed nobles from Gaul, poets and peasants from Spain, and "tattooed savages from Britain" [22]—we get an ethnic picture of a very heterogeneous and cosmopolitan Rome. Martial marveled at the pliable facility with which the courtesans of Rome readjusted their language and their charms to so varied and polyglot a clientele.[23] Juvenal complained that the Orontes, Syria's great river, was flowing into the Tiber,[24] and Tacitus described the capital as "the cesspool of the world." [25] Oriental faces, ways, dress, words, gestures, quarrels, ideas, and faiths made up a great part of the city's seething life. By the third century the government would be an Oriental monarchy; by the fourth the religion of Rome would be an Oriental creed, and the masters of the world would kneel to the god of the slaves.

There were elements of nobility in this motley crowd. It showed its contempt of Nero's mistress Poppaea when angry senators dared not speak, and it stormed the senate house to protest the wholesale slaughter of Pedanius Secundus' slaves.[26] The simple virtues of the common man were not wanting in it; the family life of the Jews was exemplary, and the little Christian communities were troubling the pleasure-mad pagan world with their piety and their decency. But most of the inflowing peoples had literally been demoralized by uprootage from their native surroundings, cultures, and moral codes; years of slavery had destroyed in them that self-respect which is the backbone of upright conduct; and daily friction with groups of different customs had worn away still more of their custom-made morality. If Rome had not engulfed so many men of alien blood in so brief a time, if she had passed all these newcomers through her schools instead of her slums, if she had treated them as men with a hundred potential excellences, if she had occasionally closed her gates to let assimiliation catch up with infiltration, she might have gained new racial and literary vitality from the infusion, and might have remained a Roman Rome, the voice and citadel of the West. The task was too great. The victorious city was doomed by the vastness and diversity of her conquests, her native blood was diluted in the ocean of her subjects, her educated classes were drawn down by the power of numbers to the culture of those who had been her slaves. Much breeding overcame good breeding; the fertile conquered became masters in the sterile master's house.

II. EDUCATION

We do not know much of Roman childhood, but we can judge from Roman art and epitaphs that when children came they were loved not wisely but too well. Juvenal interrupts his wrath to write a tender passage on the good examples we must place before our children's eyes, the evil sights and sounds we must keep from them, the respect that we should show them even in the excesses of our love.[27] Favorinus, in a discourse premimicking Rousseau, begged mothers to nurse their babes.[28] Seneca and Plutarch spoke to the same effect, which was slight indeed; wet-nursing was the rule in all families that could afford it, with no evident tragedies ensuing.*

Early education came from the nurse, who was usually Greek. There were fairy tales beginning, "Once upon a time a king and a queen . . ." Primary schooling was still entrusted to private enterprise. Rich men often hired tutors for their children, but Quintilian, like Emerson, warned against this as depriving the child of formative friendships and stimulating rivalries. Ordinarily the boy and girl of the free classes entered at the age of seven an elementary school, accompanied each way by a *paedagogus* ("child-leader") to guard his safety and his morals. Such schools existed everywhere in the Empire, even in small country towns; the wall scribblings at Pompeii suggest a general literacy, and probably education was then as widespread in the Mediterranean world as at any time before or since. Both the *paedagogus* and the teacher (*ludi magister*, "schoolmaster") were usually Greek freedmen or slaves. In Horace's youth and native town each pupil paid the teacher eight asses (forty-eight cents) monthly; [30] 350 years later Diocletian fixed the maximum fee for the elementary teacher at fifty denarii ($20) per month per pupil; we may judge from this the rise of the teacher and the fall of the as.

About the age of thirteen the successful student, of either sex, was graduated into a secondary or high school; Rome had twenty of these in A.D. 130. Here the scholars studied more grammar, the Greek language, Latin and Greek literature, music, astronomy, history, mythology, and philosophy, generally through lecture-commentaries on the classic poets. Up to this point the girls seem to have taken the same courses as the boys, but they often sought additional instruction in music and dancing. Since the secondary teachers (*grammatici*) were nearly always Greek freedmen, they naturally emphasized Greek literature and history; Roman culture took on a Greek tint, until by the end of the second century almost all higher education was given in Greek, and Latin literature was swallowed up in the general Hellenic *koiné* and culture of the age.

The Roman equivalent of our college and university education was provided in the schools of the rhetors. The Empire bristled with rhetoricians who spoke

---

* Toys and games were much as today. Roman children played hopscotch, tug-of-war, pitch and toss, blindman's buff, hide-and-seek; and with dolls, hoops, skipping ropes, hobbyhorses, and kites. Roman youth played five distinguishable games of ball. One resembled our football, except that (or in that) it was played rather with arms and hands than with legs and feet.[29]

for their clients in court, or wrote speeches for them, or gave public lectures, or taught their art to pupils, or did all four. Many of them traveled from city to city, speaking on literature, philosophy, or politics, and giving exhibitions of how to handle any subject with oratorical skill. The younger Pliny tells of the Greek Isaeus, then sixty-three years old:

> He proposes several questions for discussion, gives his audience liberty to call for any they please, and sometimes even to say what side of it he should defend; whereupon he rises, dons his gown, and begins. . . . He introduces his theme with great propriety, his narrative is clear, his controversy ingenious, his logic forcible, and his rhetoric sublime.[31]

Such men might open a school, employ assistants, and gather a large student body. Pupils entered about their sixteenth year, and paid fees as high as 2000 sesterces per course. The chief subjects were oratory, geometry, astronomy, and philosophy—which included much that is now termed science. These constituted a "liberal education"—i.e., one designed for a well-to-do freeman (*homo liber*), who would presumably have no physical work to perform. Petronius complained, as every generation does, that education unfitted youth for the problems of maturity: "The schools are to blame for the gross foolishness of our young men, since in them they see or hear nothing at all of the affairs of everyday life." [32] We can only say that they gave the assiduous student that clarity and quickness of thought which have distinguished the legal profession in all ages, and that capacity for unscrupulous eloquence which marked the orators of Rome. Apparently no degrees were granted in these schools. The student might stay as long, and take as many courses, as he liked; Aulus Gellius remained till he was twenty-five. Women also attended, some after marriage. Those who wished further instruction went to Athens for philosophy at its bubbling source, to Alexandria for medicine, or to Rhodes for the last subtleties of rhetoric. Cicero spent $4000 a year maintaining his son in the university of Athens.

By Vespasian's time the schools of rhetoric had so grown in number and influence that the wily Emperor thought it advisable to bring the more important ones in the capital under governmental control by paying their head professors a state salary—the highest being 100,000 sesterces ($10,000) a year. We do not know to how many teachers or cities Vespasian extended this subsidy. We hear of private endowments for higher education, such as the younger Pliny established at Comum.[33] Trajan provided scholarships for 5000 boys who had less money than brains. By the reign of Hadrian governmental financing of secondary schools had been adopted in many municipalities throughout the Empire, and a pension fund had been set aside for retired teachers. Hadrian and Antoninus exempted the leading professors of each city from taxation and other civic burdens. Education reached its height while superstition grew, morals declined, and literature decayed.

III. THE SEXES

The moral life of youth was carefully guarded in the girl, leniently supervised in the young man. The Roman, like the Greek, readily condoned the resort of men to prostitutes. The profession was legalized and restricted; brothels (*lupanaria*) were by law kept outside the city walls and could open only at night; prostitutes (*meretrices*) were registered by the aediles and were required to wear the toga instead of the stola. Some women enrolled as prostitutes to avoid the legal penalties of detected adultery. Fees were adjusted to bring promiscuity within the reach of every pocketbook; we have heard of the "quarter-of-an-as woman." But there was now a rising number of educated courtesans who sought to win patrons by poetry, singing, music, dancing, and cultured conversation. One did not have to go outside the walls to find these or other ladies of easy persuasion; Ovid assures us that they could be met under the porticoes, at the circus, in the theater, "as numerous as stars in the sky";[34] and Juvenal found them in the precincts of temples, particularly that of Isis, a goddess lenient to love.[35] Christian authors charged that prostitution was practiced within the cellas and between the altars of Roman temples.[36]

Male prostitutes were also available. Condemned by law, tolerated by custom, homosexualism flourished with Oriental abandon. "I am stricken with the heavy dart of love," sings Horace—and for whom?—"for Lyciscus, who claims in tenderness to outdo any woman"; from this passion he can be freed "only by another flame for some fair maid or slender youth."[37] Martial's choicest epigrams turn upon pederasty; and one of Juvenal's least publishable satires represents the complaint of a woman against this outrageous competition.[38] Erotic poetry of indifferent worth and gender, the *Priapeia*, circulated freely among sophisticated youths and immature adults.

Marriage contended bravely with these rival outlets and, helped by anxious parents and matrimonial brokers, managed to find at least temporary husbands for nearly every girl. Unmarried women above nineteen were considered "old maids," but they were rare. The betrothed couple seldom saw each other; there was no courtship, not even a word for it; Seneca complained that everything else was tested before purchase, but not the bride by the groom.[39] Sentimental attachment before marriage was uncommon; love poetry was addressed to married women or to women whom the poet never thought of marrying; and women's escapades came after marriage, as under similar conditions in medieval and modern France. The elder Seneca assumed widespread adultery among Roman women,[40] and his philosopher son thought that a married woman content with two lovers was a paragon of fidelity.[41] "Pure women," sang the cynical Ovid, "are only those who have not been asked; and a man who is angry at his wife's amours is a mere rustic." [42] These may be literary conceits; more reliable is the simple epitaph of Quintus Vespillo to his wife: "Seldom do marriages last without divorce until death; but ours continued happily for forty-one years." [43] Juvenal tells of a woman who married eight times in five years.[44] Having been wed for property or politics rather than for love, some women considered their duty fulfilled if they surrendered their dowries to their husbands and their persons to their lovers. "Did we not agree," an adulteress in Juvenal explained to her unexpected husband, "that we should both do as we liked?" [45] The "emancipation" of women was as complete then as now, barring the formalities of the franchise and the letter of dead laws. Legislation kept women subject, custom made them free.

In a number of cases emancipation, as in our time, meant industrialization. Some women worked in shops or factories, especially in the textile trades; some became lawyers and doctors;[46] some became politically powerful; the wives of provincial governors reviewed and addressed troops.[47] The Vestal Virgins secured political appointments for their friends, and the women of Pompeii announced their political preferences on the walls. Conservatives moaned and gloated over the apparent fulfillment of Cato's warning that if women achieved equality they would turn it into mastery. Juvenal was horrified to find women actresses, athletes, gladiators, poets;[48] Martial describes them as fighting wild beasts, even lions, in the arena;[49] Statius tells of women dying in such jousts.[50] Ladies rode through the streets in sedan chairs, "exposing themselves on every side to the view";[51] they conversed with men in porticoes, parks, gardens, and temple courts; they accompanied them to private or public banquets, to the amphitheater and the theater, where "their bare shoulders," said Ovid, "give you something charming to contemplate." [52] It was a gay, colorful, multisexual society that would have astonished the Periclean Greeks. In the spring fashionable women filled the boats, shores, and villas of Baiae and other resorts with their laughter, their proud beauty, their amorous audacities, and political intrigue. Old men denounced them longingly.

Frivolous or immoral women were then, as now, a conspicuous minority. Quite as numerous—though not always distinct—were the ladies who fell in love with art, religion, or literature. Sulpicia's verses were thought worthy of being handed down with those of Tibullus; they were highly erotic, but as they were addressed to her husband they were almost virtuous.[53] Martial's friend Theophila was a philosopher, a real expert on the Stoic and Epicurean systems. Some women busied themselves in philanthropy and social service, gave temples, theaters, and porticoes to their towns, and contributed as patronesses to *collegia*. An inscription at Lanuvium speaks of a *curia mulierum*, "an assembly of women"; Rome had a *conventus matronarum;* perhaps Italy had a national federation of women's clubs. In any case, after reading Martial and Juvenal, we are disconcerted to find so many good women in Rome. Octavia faithful to Antony through every betrayal, and rearing devotedly his exotic children; Antonia her loving daughter, the chaste widow of Drusus, and the perfect mother of Germanicus; Mallonia, who publicly reproved Tiberius for his wickedness and then killed herself; Arria Paeta, who, when Caecina Paetus was ordered by Claudius to die, plunged a dagger into her breast and, dying, handed the weapon to her husband with the assuring words, "It does not hurt";[54] Paulina, who tried to die with Seneca; Politta, who, when Nero had her husband executed, began to starve herself, and, when the same sentence came to her father, joined him in suicide;[55] Epicharis, the freedwoman who suffered every torture rather than betray the conspiracy of Piso; the unnumbered women who concealed and protected their husbands in the proscriptions, went with them into exile, or like Fannia, wife of Helvidius, defended them at great risk and cost: these alone would tip the scale against all the trollops of Martial's epigrams and Juvenal's stings.

Behind such heroines were the nameless wives whose marital fidelity and maternal sacrifices sustained the whole structure of Roman life. The old Roman virtues—*pietas, gravitas, simplicitas*—the mutual devotion of parents and children, a sober sense of responsibility, an avoidance of extravagance or display—still survived in Roman homes. The refined and wholesome families described in Pliny's letters did not suddenly begin with Nerva and Trajan; they had existed quietly through the age of the despots; they had survived the espionage of emperors, the debasement of a helpless populace, the vulgarity of the demimonde. We catch glimpses of such homes in the epitaphs of mate to mate and of parents to children. "Here," reads one, "lie the bones of Urbilia, wife of Primus. She was dearer to me than life. She died at twenty-three, beloved of all. Farewell, my consolation!" And another: "To my dear wife, with whom I passed eighteen happy years. For love of her I have sworn never to remarry." [56] We can picture these women in their homes—spinning wool, scolding and educating their children, directing servants, carefully administering their modest funds, and sharing with their husbands in the immemorial worship of the household gods. Despite her immorality it was Rome, not Greece, that raised the family to new heights in the ancient world.

IV. DRESS

If we may judge from a few hundred statues, the Roman males of Nero's day were stouter and softer in figure and features than the men of the young Republic. World rule kept many of them characteristically hard and stern, fearful rather than lovable; but food and wine and sloth had rounded many others into shapes that would have scandalized the Scipios. They still shaved, or, more usually, were shaved by barbers (*tonsores*). A youth's first shave was a holyday in his life; often he piously dedicated his original whiskers to a god.[57] Common Romans continued the republican tradition and had their hair cut close, or even cropped, but an increasing number of dandies had theirs curled; Mark Antony and Domitian are so represented. Many men wore wigs, some had the semblance of hair painted on their pates.[58] All classes, indoors and out, now dressed in a simple tunic or blouse; the toga was donned only for formal occasions, by clients at receptions and by patricians in the Senate or at the games. Caesar wore a purple toga as a sign of office; many dignitaries imitated him; but soon the purple robe became a prerogative of the emperors. There were no irksome trousers, no elusive buttons, no drooping hose; but in the second century men began to wrap their legs with *fasciae*, or bands. Footwear ranged from the sandal—a leather or cork sole attached Nipponwise by a thong between the big and second toes—to the high shoe of full leather, or of leather and cloth, usually worn with the toga in *synthesis* or full dress.

Roman women of the early Empire, as seen in frescoes and statuary and on coins, were much like the women of the United States at the beginning of the twentieth century, except that they were nearly all brunette. Their figures were moderately slender, and their robes gave their carriage a hypnotic grace. They knew the value of sunshine, exercise, and fresh air; some brandished dumbbells, some swam assiduously, some dieted; others reined in their bosoms with stays.[59] Feminine hair was usually combed back and bound in a knot behind the neck, often enclosed in a net, and tied with a band or ribbon over the head. Later fashions demanded a loftier coiffure, supported by wire and elaborated with a wig of blonde hair imported from German maids.[60] A woman of fashion might occupy several slaves for hours in manicuring her nails and dressing her hair.[61]

Cosmetics were as varied as today. Juvenal describes "beautification" as one of the most important technologies of the age; physicians, queens, and poets wrote volumes on the subject.[62] A Roman lady's boudoir was an arsenal of cosmetic instruments—tweezers, scissors, razors, files, brushes, combs, strigils, hair nets, wigs—and jars or phials of perfumes, creams, oils, pastes, pumice stone, soaps. Depilatories were used to remove hair, scented ointments to wave it or fix it. Many women applied to their faces a nocturnal mask of dough and asses' milk in a mixture concocted by Poppaea, who found it helpful in repairing a bad complexion; therefore asses followed her in all her travels; sometimes she took a

whole herd with her and bathed in asses' milk.[63] Faces were whitened or rouged
with paint, brows and eyelashes were dyed black or painted over, sometimes the
veins of the temple were traced with delicate lines of blue.[64] Juvenal complained
that a rich woman "reeks of Poppaean ointments that stick to the lips of her
unfortunate husband," who never sees her face. Ovid found these arts disillusion-
ing and advised the ladies to conceal them from their lovers—all but the combing
of their hair, which entranced him.[66]

Delicate lingerie was now added to the simple feminine garments of pre-
Hannibalic Rome. Scarfs fell over the shoulders, and veils made an alluring
mystery of the face. In winter soft furs caressed affluent forms. Silk was so common that men as well as women wore it. Silk and linen were colored with costly
dyes; Romans often paid a thousand denarii for a pound of double-dyed Tyrian
wool.[67] Embroideries of gold and silver thread decorated dresses, curtains,
carpets, and coverlets. Women's shoes were made of soft leather or cloth,
sometimes elaborately cut into an openwork pattern; they might be trimmed
with gold and beset with jewelry; [68] and high heels were often added to remedy
the shortcomings of nature.

Jewelry was an important part of a woman's equipment. Rings, earrings, necklaces, amulets, bracelets, breast chains, brooches, were necessities of life. Lollia
Paulina once wore a dress covered from head to foot with emeralds and pearls,
and carried with her the receipts showing that they cost 40,000,000 sesterces.[69]
Pliny describes over a hundred varieties of precious stones used in Rome. Expert
imitations of these provided a busy industry; Roman "emeralds" of glass were
superior to modern forgeries and were sold as genuine by jewelers as late as
the nineteenth century.[70] Men as well as women were fond of large and conspicuous stones. One senator had in his ring an opal as big as a filbert. Hearing
of it, Antony had him proscribed; he escaped, carrying 2,000,000 sesterces on
his finger; doubtless jewelry was then, as often, a hedge against inflation or
revolution. Silver plate was now common in all but the lower classes. Tiberius
and later emperors issued edicts against luxury, but these could not be enforced
and were soon ignored. Tiberius yielded, and confessed that the extravagance of
patricians and parvenus gave employment to the artisans of Rome and the East,
and allowed provincial tribute to flow back from the capital. "Without luxury,"
he said, "how could Rome, how could the provinces, live?"

Roman dress was not more luxurious than that of modern women, and far less
gorgeous and costly than the garb of medieval lords. Fashion did not change in
Rome as rapidly as in modern cities; a good garment might be worn a lifetime
and remain in style. But compared with the standards of the Republic before
Lucullus and Pompey had brought in the loot and hedonism of the East, upper-
class Rome was now an epicurean paradise of fine clothing, varied food, elegant
furniture, and stately homes. Shorn of political leadership, almost of political
power, the aristocracy retired from the *curia* to its palaces, and abandoned itself,
with no morals but philosophy, to the pursuit of pleasure and the art of life.

V. A ROMAN DAY

The luxuries of the home far outran the luxuries of dress. Floors of marble and mosaic; columns of polychrome marble, alabaster, onyx; walls painted with brilliant murals or encrusted with costly stones; ceilings sometimes coffered in gold [71] or plate glass; [72] tables with citrus wood standing on ivory legs; divans decorated with tortoise shell, ivory, silver, or gold; Alexandrian brocades or Babylonian coverings for which common millionaires paid 800,000, Nero 4,000,000, sesterces;[73] beds of bronze fitted with mosquito netting; candelabra of bronze, marble, or glass; statues and paintings and objects of art; vases of Corinthian bronze or Murrhine glass—these were some of the ornaments that crowded the mansions of Nero's age.

In such a home the master lived as in a museum. Slaves had to be bought to guard this wealth, and others to guard these. Some houses had 400 of them, engaged in attendance, supervision, or industry; the life of the great man, even in the privacy of his rooms, was spent in the publicity of his slaves. To eat with a servant at each elbow, to undress with a slave at each boot, to relax with a menial at every door—this is not paradise. To assure the misery of wealth the great man began his day, about seven, by receiving his "clients" and parasites and offering his cheeks to their kisses. After two hours of this he might breakfast. Then he received and returned formal visits of his friends. Etiquette required that one must repay the calls of every friend, help him in his lawsuits and candidacies, attend the betrothal of his daughter, the coming of age of his son, the reading of his poems, the signing of his will. These and other social obligations were performed with a grace and courtesy not exceeded in any civilization. Then the great man went to the Senate, or labored on some governmental commission, or attended to his personal affairs.

For the man of modest means life was simpler, but not less arduous. After the social calls of the early morning he gave himself to his business till noon. Humble folk were at their work by sunrise; as there was little night life, the Roman took full advantage of the day. A light luncheon came at noon, dinner at three or four—the higher the class, the later the hour. After luncheon and a siesta, the peasant and the employed prolétaire returned to work till nearly sunset; others sought recreation outdoors or in the public baths. The Romans of the Empire took their bathing more religiously than their gods. Like the Japanese, they could bear public better than private smells, and no ancient people but the Egyptians rivaled them in cleanliness. They carried handkerchiefs (*sudaria*) to wipe away their sweat,[74] and brushed their teeth with powders and paste. In the early Republic a bath every eighth day had sufficed; now one had to bathe daily or risk a Martial's epigram; even the rustic, says Galen, bathed every day.[75] Most homes had bathtubs, rich houses had bathroom suites sparkling with marble, glass, or silver fixtures and taps.[76] But the majority of free Romans relied on the public baths.

Ordinarily these were privately owned. In 33 B.C. there were 170 in Rome; in the fourth century A.D. there were 856, besides 1352 public swimming pools.[77] More popular than such establishments were the great baths built by the state, managed by concessionaires and staffed by hundreds of slaves. These *thermae*—"hot [waters]"—erected by Agrippa, Nero, Titus, Trajan, Caracalla, Alexander Severus, Diocletian, and Constantine, were monuments of state-socialistic splendor. The Baths of Nero had 1600 marble seats and accommodated 1600 bathers at one time; the Baths of Caracalla and those of Diocletian accommodated 3000 each. Admission was open to any citizen for a quadrans (1½ cents);[78] the government met the balance of the cost, and apparently oil and service were included in the fee. The baths were open from daybreak to one P.M. for women, from two to eight P.M. for men; but mixed bathing was allowed by most of the emperors. Normally the visitor went first to a dressing room to change his clothes; then to the palaestra to box, wrestle, run, jump, hurl the disk or the spear, or play ball. One ball game was like our "medicine ball"; in another two opposed groups scrambled for a ball, and carried it forward against each other with all the enterprise of a modern university.[79] Sometimes professional ballplayers would come to the baths and give exhibitions.[80] Oldsters who preferred to take their exercise by proxy went to massage rooms and had a slave rub away their fat.

Passing to the baths proper, the citizen entered the tepidarium—in this case a warm-air room; thence he went on to the calidarium, or hot-air room; if he wished to perspire still more freely, he moved into the laconicum, and gasped in superheated steam. Then he took a warm bath and washed himself with a novelty learned from the Gauls—soap, made from tallow and the ashes of the beech or the elm.[81] These warm rooms were the most popular and gave the baths their Greek name; probably they were Rome's attempt to forestall or mitigate rheumatism and arthritis.[82] The bather progressed to the frigidarium and took a cold bath; he might also dip into the *piscina*, or swimming pool. Then he had himself rubbed with some oil or ointment, usually made from the olive; this was not washed off, but merely scraped off with a strigil and dried with a towel, so that some oil might be returned to the skin in place of that which the warm baths had removed.

The bather seldom left the *thermae* at this point. For these were clubhouses as well as baths; they provided rooms for games like dice and chess,[83] galleries of painting and statuary, *exedrae* where friends might sit and converse, libraries and reading rooms, and halls where a musician or a poet might give a recital or a philosopher might explain the world. In these afternoon hours after the bath Roman society found its chief meeting point; both sexes mingled freely in gay but polite association, flirtation, or discussion; there, and at the games and in the parks, the Romans could indulge their passion for talk, their fondness for gossip, and learn all the news and scandal of the day.

If they wished they could have dinner in the restaurant at the baths, but most of them dined at home. Perhaps because of the lassitude caused by exercise and warm bathing, the custom was to recline at meals. Once the women had sat apart while the men reclined; now the women reclined beside the men. The triclinium, or dining room, was so named because it usually contained three couches, arranged in square-magnet form around a serving table. Each couch normally accommodated three persons. The diner rested his head on his left arm, and his arm on a cushion, while the body extended diagonally away from the serving table.

The poorer classes continued to live chiefly on grains, dairy products, vegetables, fruits, and nuts. Pliny lists a wide assortment of vegetables in the Roman dietary, from garlic to rape. The well to do ate meat, with the usual superabundance of reckless carnivores. Pork was the favorite flesh food; Pliny praises the pig for furnishing fifty different dainties.[84] Pork sausages (*botuli*) were hawked through the streets in portable ovens, as on our highways today.

When one dined at a banquet he expected rarer foods. The banquet began at four and lasted till late in the night or till the next day. The tables were strewn with flowers and parsley, the air was scented with exotic perfumes, the couches were soft with cushions, the servants were stiff with livery. Between the appetizer (*gustatio*) and the dessert (*secunda mensa*, "second table") came the luxury dishes on which the host and his chef prided themselves. Rare fish, rare birds, rare fruit, appealed to the curiosity as well as the palate. Mullets were bought at a thousand sesterces a pound; Asinius Celer paid 8000 for one; Juvenal growled that a fisherman cost less than a fish. As an added delight for the guests, the mullet might be brought in alive and boiled before their eyes, that they might enjoy the varied colors it took in the agony of death.[85] Vedius Pollio raised these sesquipedalian fish in a large tank and fed them with unsatisfactory slaves.[86] Eels and snails were considered dainties, but the law forbade the eating of dormice.[87] The wings of ostriches, the tongues of flamingoes, the flesh of songbirds, the livers of geese, were favorite dishes. Apicius, a famous epicure under Tiberius, invented the *pâté de fois gras* by fattening the livers of sows with a diet of figs.[88*] Custom allowed the diner to empty his stomach with an emetic after a heavy banquet. Some gluttons performed this operation during the meal and then returned to appease their hunger; *vomunt ut edant, edunt ut vomant,* said Seneca—"they vomit to eat, and eat to vomit." [90] Such behavior was exceptional, and no worse than the braggart drunkenness of American conventioneers. Pleasanter was the custom of presenting gifts to the guests, or letting flowers or perfumes fall upon them from the ceiling, or entertaining them with music, dancing, poetry, or drama. Conversation, loosened with wine and stimulated by the presence of the other sex, would conclude the evening.

We must not think of such banquets as the customary end of a Roman day, or as more frequent in a Roman's life than the dinners-*cum*-oratory so popular today. History, like the press, misrepresents life because it loves the exceptional and shuns the newsless career of an honest man or the quiet routine of a normal day. Most Romans were like our neighbors and ourselves: they rose reluctantly, ate too much, worked too much, played too little, loved much, seldom hated, quarreled a bit, talked a great deal, dreamed waking dreams, and slept.

VI. A ROMAN HOLIDAY

1. The Stage

Having many gods to worship, and many provinces to milk, Rome had many holidays, once solemn with religious pageantry, now gay with secular delight. In summer many of the poor fled from the humid heat to suburban or riverside taverns or groves, drinking, dining, dancing, and loving in the open air. Those who could afford it might go to the bathing resorts that lined the western coast, or sport with the rich on Baiae's bay. In winter it was the ambition of every caste-conscious Roman to go south, if possible to Rhegium or Tarentum, and return with a coat of tan as a certificate of class. But those who stayed in Rome found entertainment plentiful and cheap. Recitations, lectures, concerts, mimes, plays, athletic contests, prize fights, horse races, chariot races, mortal combats of men with men or beasts, not-quite-sham naval battles on artificial lakes—never was a city more bountifully amused.

In the early Empire there were in the Roman year seventy-six festival days on which *ludi* were performed. Of these, fifty-five were *ludi scenici,*

---

* Apicius squandered a huge fortune in extravagant living; then, being reduced to 10,000,000 sesterces ($1,500,000), he committed suicide.[89] Two hundred years later a classic of gastronomy—*De re coquinaria*—was attributed to him by a device permitted in antiquity.

devoted to plays or mimes; twenty-two were games in the circus, the stadium, or the amphitheater. The number of *ludi* increased until by A.D. 354 they were presented on 175 days in the year.[91] This meant no growth in the Roman drama; on the contrary, the drama decayed while the stage prospered. Original dramas were now written to be read rather than played; the theater contented itself with old Roman and Greek tragedies, old Roman comedies, and mimes. Stars dominated the stage and made huge fortunes. Aesopus the tragedian, after a life of assiduous extravagance, left 20,000,-000 sesterces. Roscius the comic actor made 500,000 sesterces a year and became so rich that for several seasons he acted without pay—a scorn of money that made this ex-slave the lion of aristocratic gatherings. The games of the circus and the amphitheater absorbed the interest and coarsened the taste of the public, and the Roman drama died in the arena, another martyr to Roman holidays.

Through emphasis on acting and scenery rather than plot or thought, the drama gradually yielded the stage to mimes and pantomimes. The mime contained little dialogue, chose its themes from lowly life, and relied on character sketches presented with skillful mimicry. Freedom of speech, having disappeared from the assemblies and the Forum, survived for a moment in these brief farces, when a mime would risk his head to earn applause by a *double-entendre* aimed at an emperor or his favorites. Caligula had an actor burned alive in the amphitheater for such an allusion.[92] On the day when the parsimonious Vespasian was buried a mime imitated the obsequies. During the procession the corpse sat up and asked how much this funeral was costing the state. "Ten million sesterces," was the answer. "Give me 100,000," said the imperial cadaver, "and throw me into the Tiber." [93] The mime alone admitted women as actors; and as these were thereby automatically classed as prostitutes, they had nothing to lose by obscenity. On special occasions like the *Floralia* the audience called upon these performers to remove every garment.[94] Both sexes attended these performances, as in our time. Cicero found brides there, and they found him.

By suppressing speech altogether, and raising the theme to subjects from classic literature, the pantomime ("all mimicry") was evolved out of the mime. There was a profit in foregoing language; the polyglot population of Rome, of which a considerable part could understand only the simplest Latin, followed the action better when unburdened with words. In 21 B.C. two actors, Pylades of Cilicia and Bathyllus of Alexandria, came to Rome and introduced the pantomime—already popular in the Hellenistic East—by performing one-act plays composed only of music, action, gesture, and dance. Tired of dramas in ancient and pompous verse, Rome welcomed the new art, thrilled to the grace and skill of the actors, enjoyed the gorgeousness of their costumes, the splendor or humor of their masks, the trained and dieted perfection of their figures, the Oriental expressiveness of their hands, their quick and versatile impersonation of diverse characters, their sensuous enactment of erotic scenes. Audiences divided into frantic cliques and claques in support of rival favorites; women of high station fell in love with the actors, and pursued them with gifts and embraces, until one literally lost his head over Domitian's wife. The pantomime gradually drove all rivals but the mime from the Roman stage. The drama succumbed to the ballet.

2. Roman Music

Such a triumph was made possible by the high development of music and the dance. Under the Republic dancing had been looked upon as disgraceful; the younger Scipio had compelled the closing of schools that taught music and dancing,[95] and Cicero had remarked that "only a lunatic would dance when sober." [96] But the pantomimes made dancing a fashion, then a passion; nearly every private home, says Seneca, had a dancing platform, echoing to the feet of men and women; rich households now had a dancing master, as well as a chef and a philosopher, as part of their equipment. As practiced in Rome the dance involved the rhythmical movement of the hands and the upper body even more than of legs and feet. Women cultivated the art not only for its own attractiveness, but because it gave them flexibility and grace.

The Romans loved music only less than power, money, women, and blood. Like nearly everything else in Rome's cultural life, her music came from Greece and had to fight its way against a conservatism that identified art with degeneration. In 115 B.C. the censors had forbidden the playing of any instrument except the short Italian flute. A century later the elder Seneca still considered music unmanly; but meanwhile Varro had devoted a book to De Musica, and this treatise, together with its Greek sources, became the support of many Roman works on musical theory.[97] Finally the rich and sensuous Greek modes and instruments won the day over Roman awkwardness and simplicity, and music became a regular element in the education of women, and frequently of men. By A.D. 50 it had captured all classes and sexes; men as well as women spent whole days in hearing, composing, or singing airs; at last even emperors climbed and descended scales, and the philosophic Hadrian, as well as the effeminate Nero, was proud of his skill on the lyre. Lyric poetry was intended to be sung with music, and music was seldom composed except for poetry; ancient music was subordinated to the verse, whereas with us the music tends to overwhelm the words. Choral music was popular and was frequently heard at weddings, games, religious ceremonies, and funerals. Horace was deeply moved by the sight and sound of youths and maidens singing his *carmen saeculare*. In such choruses all the voices sang the same note, though in different octaves; part singing was apparently unknown.

The basic instruments were the flute and the lyre. Our wind and string orchestras are still variations of these forms: the most heroic symphony is a judicious combination of puffing, plucking, scraping, and beating. The flute accompanied drama and was supposed to arouse emotion; the lyre attended song and was expected to elevate the soul. The flute was long, had many openings, and a greater range of expression than the modern instrument. The lyre and the cithara were like our harp, but took a greater variety of shapes. Among the Greeks they had been of modest size, but the Romans magnified them until Ammianus described citharas "as large as carriages"; [98] in general the Roman instruments, like ours, improved upon earlier ones chiefly in sonorousness and size. The strings of the lyre were made of gut or sinew and numbered up to eighteen; they were plucked with a plectrum or with the fingers—which alone could execute the quicker runs. From Alexandria, early in the first century, came the hydraulic organ, with several registers, stops, and orders of pipes. Nero fell in love with it, and the calm Quintilian was impressed by its versatility and power.

Formal concerts were given, and musical contests played a part in some public games. Even modest dinners required a bit of music; Martial promises his guest at least a flute player;[99] as for Trimalchio's feast, the tables are wiped in rhythm with song. Caligula had an orchestra and a chorus on his pleasure boat. At the pantomimes *symphoniae* were performed—i.e., a chorus sang and danced to the accompaniment of an orchestra. Sometimes the actor would sing the solo parts, sometimes a professional singer (*cantor*) sang the words while the actor gestured or danced. It was not unheard of for a pantomime to be accompanied by 3000 singers and 3000 dancers.[100] The orchestra was led by flutes, aided by lyres, cymbals, pipes, trumpets, "syringes," and scabella—boards fastened to the players' feet and capable of producing a pandemonium even more frightful than that of a modern orchestra at the height of its powers. Seneca mentions harmony in the playing of individuals,[101] but there is no sign that ancient orchestras used harmony contrapuntally. The accompaniment was usually on a higher note than the song, but it did not, so far as we know, pursue a distinct sequence.

Virtuosi were plentiful and minor performers abounded. Talent converged from all provinces upon the center of the world's gold, while the institution of slavery permitted the training of choruses and orchestras on a large but inexpensive scale. Many rich establishments had their own musicians, and sent the most promising to famous teachers for advanced instruction. Some became *citharoedi* and gave concerts in which they sang and played the lyre; some specialized in singing, usually composing their own songs; some gave concerts on the organ or the flute like Cannus, who boasted, in the style of Beethoven, that his music could alleviate sorrow, increase joy, elevate piety, and fan the flame of love.[102] These professionals went on extended concert tours throughout the Empire, earning plaudits, fees, public monuments, and infatuations; some, says Juvenal, sold their love for an added honorarium.[103] Women fought for the plectra with which famous players had touched the strings, and offered sacrifice at the altars for the victory of their musical favorites in the Neronian and Capitoline games. We can faintly picture the imposing scene when musicians and poets from all the realm competed before great throngs, and the breathless winners received the crown of oak leaves from the emperor's hands.

We do not know enough of Roman music to describe its quality. Apparently it was louder, fuller, wilder than the Greek; a weird Oriental quality had entered it from Egypt, Asia Minor, and Syria. Old men mourned that recent composers were abandoning the restraint and dignity of the classic style, and were disordering the soul and nerves of youth with extravagant airs and noisy instruments. Certainly no people ever loved music more. The songs of the stage were caught up by a lively and volatile populace and rang through the streets and windows of Rome; the complex airs of the pantomimes were so fondly remembered that devotees could tell from the first notes of a strain to what play and scene it belonged. Rome made no real contribution to music, except perhaps through the better organization of performers into larger groups. But it honored music with exuberant usage and resilient response; it gathered the musical heritage of the ancient world into its temples, theaters, and homes; and when it passed it left to the Church the instruments and elements of the music that moves and deepens us today.

3. The Games

Now that war seemed banished, the great games were the most exciting event of the Roman year. They took place chiefly in celebration of religious festivals—of the Great Mother, of Ceres, of Flora, of Apollo, of Augustus; they might be the "Plebeian Games" to appease the plebs, or "Roman Games" in honor of the city and its goddess Roma; they might be offered in connection with triumphs, candidacies, elections, or imperial birthdays; they might, like the *ludi saeculares*, commemorate some cycle in Roman history. Like the games of Achilles in honor of Patroclus, those of Italy had originally been offered as a sacrifice to dead men. At the funeral of

Brutus Pera in 264 B.C. his sons gave a "spectacle" of three duels; at the funeral of Marcus Lepidus in 216 B.C. twenty-two combats were fought; and in 174 B.C. Titus Flaminius celebrated his father's death with gladiatorial games in which seventy-four men fought.

The simplest public games were athletic contests, usually held in a stadium. The performers, mostly professionals and aliens, ran foot races, threw the discus, wrestled, and boxed. The Roman public, accustomed to sanguinary gladiatorial exhibitions, only mildly favored athletics, but relished the prize fights in which massive Greeks fought almost to the death with gloves reinforced at the knuckles with an iron band three quarters of an inch thick. The gentle Virgil describes a milder pugilistic feast in almost modern terms:

> Then the son of Anchises brought out hide gloves of equal weight, and bound the hands of the antagonists. . . . Each took his stand, poised on tiptoe and raising one arm. . . . Drawing their heads back from the blows they spar, hand against hand. They aim many hard blows, wildly pummeling each other's sides and chests, ears and brows and cheeks, making the air resound with their strokes. . . . Entellus puts forth his right; Dares slips aside in a nimble dodge. . . . Entellus furiously drives Dares headlong over the arena, redoubling his blows, now with the right hand, now with the left. . . . Then Aeneas put an end to the fray, Dares' mates led him to the ships with his knees shaking, his head swaying from side to side, his mouth spitting teeth and blood.[104]

Still more exciting were the races at the Circus Maximus. On two successive days forty-four races were run, some of horses and jockeys, some of light two-wheeled chariots drawn by two, three, or four horses abreast. The cost was met by rival stables owned by rich men; the jockeys, drivers, and chariots of each stable were costumed or painted in distinctive colors— white, green, red, or blue; and all Rome, as the time for these contests approached, divided into factions named from these colors, and particularly the red and the green. At home, in school, at lectures, in the forums, half the talk was about favorite jockeys and charioteers; their pictures were everywhere, their victories were announced in the *Acta Diurna*; some of them made great fortunes, some had statues raised to them in public squares. On the appointed day 180,000 men and women moved in festive colors to the enormous hippodrome. Enthusiasm rose to a mania. Excited partisans smelled the dung of the animals to assure themselves that the horses of their favorite drivers had been properly fed.[105] The spectators passed by the shops and brothels that lined the outer walls; they filed through hundreds of entrances and sorted themselves with the sweat of anxiety into the great horseshoe of seats. Vendors sold them cushions, for the seats were mostly of hard wood, and the program would last all day. Senators and other dignitaries had special seats of marble, ornamented with bronze. Behind the imperial box was a suite of luxurious rooms, where the emperor and his family might eat, drink, rest, bathe, and sleep. Gambling was feverish, and fortunes passed from hand to hand as the day advanced. From openings under the stands emerged the horses, the jockeys and drivers, and the chariots; and each faction shook the stands with applause as its favorite color appeared. The charioteers, mostly slaves, wore bright tunics and shining helmets; in one hand was a whip, and in their belts a knife to cut, in accident, the traces tied to their waists. Along the middle of the elliptical arena ran the *spina* ("thorn," "spine"), an island a thousand feet long, adorned with statues and obelisks; at one end were the *metae* ("measures"), circular pillars that served as goals. The usual length of a chariot race was seven circuits, about five miles. The test of skill lay in making the turns at the goals as swiftly and sharply as safety would allow; collisions were frequent there, and men, chariots, and animals mingled in fascinating tragedy. As the horses or chariots clattered to the final post the hypnotized audience rose like a swelling sea, gesticulated, waved handkerchiefs, shouted and prayed, groaned and cursed, or exulted in almost supernatural ecstasy. The applause that greeted the winner could be heard far beyond the limits of the city.

The most stupendous of all the spectacles offered at Roman celebrations was the sham naval battle. The first large *naumachia* was given by Caesar in a basin excavated for the purpose on the outskirts of the city. Augustus marked the dedication of his temple to Mars the Avenger by presenting 3000 fighters in a replica of the battle of Salamis on an artificial lake 1800 by 1200 feet. Claudius, as already noted, celebrated the completion of the Fucine tunnel with a conflict of triremes and quadriremes involving 19,000 men. They fought with a disappointing courtesy, and soldiers had to be sent among them to ensure a proper shedding of blood.[106] At the dedication of the Colosseum Titus had its arena flooded, and reproduced that battle of the Corinthians and Corcyreans which had brought on the Peloponnesian War. The combatants in these engagements were war captives or condemned criminals. They butchered one another until one side or the other was killed off; the victors, if they had cut bravely, might be granted freedom.

The games reached their climax in the contests of animals and gladiators in the amphitheater—after Vespasian, in the Colosseum. The arena was an immense wooden floor strewn with sand; parts of this floor could be lowered and then quickly raised with a change of scene; and at brief notice the whole floor could be covered with water. Large chambers beneath it held the animals, machines, and men scheduled for the program of the day. Just above the arena's guard wall was a podium or marble terrace on whose ornate seats sat senators, priests, and high officials; above this was the *suggestum*, a high loge where the emperor and empress sat on thrones of ivory and gold, surrounded by their family and retinue. Behind this aristocratic circle sat the equestrian order, in twenty tiers of seats. A lofty intervening wall, decorated with statuary, separated the upper orders from the lower classes in the stands above. Any free person, male or female, could come, and apparently no admission was charged. The crowd took advantage of the emperor's presence, here and at the circus, to shout its wishes to him—for the pardon of a prisoner or a fallen fighter, the emancipation of a courageous slave, the appearance of favorite gladiators, or some minor reform. From the topmost wall awnings could be unrolled to the arena railing to shade such parts of the assemblage as might suffer from the sun. Here and there fountains threw up jets of scented water to cool the air. When noon came most of the spectators hurried below to eat lunch; concessionaires were on hand to sell them food and sweets and drinks. On occasion the entire multitude might be fed by the order and bounty of the emperor, or dainties and presents might be scattered among the scrambling crowd. If, as sometimes occurred, contests were presented at night, a circle of lights could be lowered over the arena and the spectators. Bands of musicians performed in the interludes and accompanied the crises of the combats with exciting crescendo strains.

The simplest event in the amphitheater was an exhibition of exotic animals. Gathered from all the known world, elephants, lions, tigers, crocodiles, hippopotami, lynxes, apes, panthers, bears, boars, wolves, giraffes, ostriches, stags, leopards, antelopes, and rare birds were kept in the zoological gardens of emperors and rich men, and were trained to skillful exploits or merry pranks; apes were taught to ride dogs, drive chariots, or act in plays; bulls let boys dance on their backs; sea lions were conditioned to bark in answer to their individual names; elephants danced to cymbals struck by other elephants, or they walked a rope, or sat down to table, or wrote Greek or Latin letters. Animals might be merely paraded in bright or humorous costumes; usually, however, they were made to fight one another, or with men, or they were hunted to death with arrows and javelins. In one day, under Nero, 400 tigers fought with bulls and elephants; on another day, under Caligula, 400 bears were slain; at the dedication of the Colosseum 5000 animals died.[107] If the animals wished to compromise they were stung to combat by lashes, darts, and hot irons. Claudius made a division of the Praetorian Guard fight panthers; Nero made them fight 400 bears and 300 lions.[108]

Combats of a bull with a man, long popular in Crete and Thessaly, were introduced into Rome by Caesar and were a frequent spectacle in the amphitheater.[109] Condemned criminals, sometimes dressed in skins to resemble animals, were thrown to beasts made ravenous for the occasion; death in such cases came with all possible agony, and wounds were so deep that physicians used such men to study internal anatomy. All the world knows the story of Androcles, the runaway slave; captured, he was flung into the arena with a lion; but this lion, we are told, remembered that Androcles had once drawn a thorn from its paw, and refused to injure him. Androcles was pardoned, and made a living by exhibiting his civilized lion in taverns.[110] The condemned man was sometimes required to play in no make-believe way some famous tragic role: he might represent Medea's rival, and be garbed in a handsome robe that would suddenly burst into flame and consume him; he might be burned to death on a pyre as Heracles; he might (if we may believe Tertullian) be publicly castrated as Atys; he might play Mucius Scaevola and hold his hand over burning coals until it was shriveled up; he might be Icarus and fall from the sky into no merciful ocean but a crowd of wild beasts; he might be Pasiphaë, and bear the embraces of a bull. One victim was dressed as Orpheus; he was sent with his lyre into an arena set as a pleasant grove of trees and brooks; suddenly hungry animals emerged from recesses and tore him to pieces.[111] Laureolus, a robber, was crucified in the arena for the amusement of the populace; but as he took too long in dying, a bear was brought in and was persuaded to eat him, piece by piece, as he hung upon the cross. Martial describes the spectacle with fascination and approval.[112]

The supreme events were the combats of armed men, in duels or en masse. The contestants were war captives, condemned criminals, or disobedient slaves. The right of victors to slaughter their prisoners was generally accepted throughout antiquity, and the Romans thought themselves generous in giving captives a chance for their lives in the arena. Men convicted of capital crimes were brought to Rome from all parts of the Empire, were sent to gladiatorial schools, and soon appeared in the games. If they fought with exceptional bravery they might win immediate freedom; if they merely survived they had to fight again and again as holidays recurred; if they lasted three years they were released into slavery; if then they satisfied their masters for two years they were freed. Crimes entailing condemnation to a gladiatorial career were limited to murder, robbery, arson, sacrilege, and mutiny, but sedulous governors responsive to imperial needs might override these restrictions if the arena ran short of men.[113] Even knights and senators might be sentenced to fight as gladiators, and sometimes a passion for applause led members of the equestrian order to offer themselves as volunteers.

Not a few men, under the lure of adventure and danger, enlisted in the gladiatorial schools.

Such schools had existed in Rome as early as 105 B.C. Under the Empire there were four of them there, several more in Italy, and one in Alexandria. Rich men, in Caesar's day, had their own schools for preparing slaves to be gladiators. They used the graduates as bodyguards in peace and as aides in war, hired them out to fight at private banquets, and lent them to the games. On entering a professional gladiatorial school many a novice took an oath "to suffer himself to be whipped with rods, burned with fire, and killed with steel." [114] Training and discipline were rigorous; diet was supervised by physicians, who prescribed barley to develop muscle; violation of rules was punished by scourging, branding, and confinement in chains. Not all of these candidates for death were discontented with their lot. Some were elated with victories and thought of their prowess rather than their peril; some complained that they were not allowed to fight often enough; [115] such men hated Tiberius for giving so few games. They had the stimulus and consolation of fame; their names were daubed by admirers upon public walls; women fell in love with them, poets sang of them, painters portrayed them, sculptors carved for posterity their iron biceps and terrifying frowns. Many, however, were despondent at their imprisonment, their brutalizing routine, and their brief expectation of life. Several committed suicide; one by stuffing his throat with a sponge used to clean privies, another by inserting his head between the spokes of a moving wheel, several by hara-kiri in the arena.[116]

On the eve of their combat they were given a rich banquet. The rougher ones ate and drank heartily; others took sad leave of their wives and children; those who were Christians joined in a last *agapé*, or "supper of love." The next morning they entered the arena in festal dress and paraded from one end of it to the other. They were usually armed with swords, or spears, or knives, and armored with bronze helmets, shields, shoulderplates, breastplates, and greaves. They were classified according to their weapons: *retiarii*, who entangled their opponents with nets and dispatched them with daggers; *secutores*, skilled in pursuit with shield and sword; *laqueatores*, slingshooters; *dimachae*, with a short sword in each hand; *essedarii*, who fought in chariots; *bestiarii*, who contended with beasts. Besides these enterprises the gladiators engaged in duels, in pairs or in groups. If a dueler in a single combat was seriously wounded, the provider of the games asked the spectators for their will; they held thumbs up—or waved handkerchiefs—as signs of mercy, or turned thumbs down (*pollice verso*) to signify that the victor was to kill the defeated forthwith.[117] Any combatant who betrayed a reluctance to die aroused the resentment of the people and was prodded to bravery by hot irons.[118] Richer slaughter was furnished by mass battles in which thousands of men fought with desperate ferocity. In the eight spectacles given by Augustus 10,000 men took part in such wholesale conflicts. Attendants in the garb of Charon probed the fallen with sharp rods to see if they were feigning death, and killed such actors with mallet blows on the head. Other attendants, dressed like Mercury, dragged the bodies away with hooks, while Moorish slaves gathered up the bloodied ground in shovels and spread fresh sand for the next death.

Most Romans defended the gladiatorial games on the ground that the victims had been condemned to death for serious crimes, that the sufferings they endured acted as a deterrent to others, that the courage with which the doomed men were trained to face wounds and death inspired the people to Spartan virtues, and that the frequent sight of blood and battle accustomed Romans to the demands and sacrifices of war. Juvenal, who denounced everything else, left the games unscathed; the younger Pliny, a highly civilized man, praised Trajan for providing spectacles that impel men "to noble wounds and the scorn of death"; [119] and Tacitus reflected that the blood spilled in the arena was in any case *vilis sanguis*—the "cheap gore" of common men.[120] Cicero was revolted by the slaughter; "what entertainment," he asks, "can possibly arise, to a refined and humanized spirit, from seeing a noble beast struck to the heart by its merciless hunter, or one of our own weak species cruelly mangled by an animal of far greater strength?" But, he added, "when guilty men are compelled to fight, no better discipline against suffering and death can be presented to the eye." [121] Seneca, dropping in at the games during the noon recess, when most of the assemblage had left for luncheon, was shocked to see hundreds of criminals driven into the arena to amuse the remaining audience with their blood.

> I come home more greedy, more cruel and inhuman, because I have been among human beings. By chance I attended a midday exhibition, expecting some fun, wit, and relaxation . . . whereby men's eyes may have respite from the slaughter of their fellow men. But it was quite the contrary. . . . These noon fighters are sent out with no armor of any kind; they are exposed to blows at all points, and no one ever strikes in vain. . . . In the morning they throw men to the lions; at noon they throw them to the spectators. The crowd demands that the victor who has slain his opponent shall face the man who will slay him in turn; and the last conqueror is reserved for another butchering. . . . This sort of thing goes on while the stands are nearly empty. . . . Man, a sacred thing to man, is killed for sport and merriment.[122]

VII. THE NEW FAITHS

Religion accepted the games as proper forms of religious celebration and inaugurated them with solemn processions. The Vestal Virgins and the priests occupied seats of honor in the theaters, at the circus, and before the arena. The emperor who presided was the high priest of the state religion.

Augustus and his successors had done everything they could to revitalize the old faith, except to live moral lives; even the declared atheists among them, like Caligula and Nero, had carried out all the ritual traditionally due the official gods. The Luperci priests still danced through the streets on their festival day; the Arval Brethren still mumbled prayers to Mars in old Latin that no one could understand. Divination and augury were assiduously practiced and widely trusted; all but a few philosophers believed in astrology, and the emperors who banished astrologers consulted them. Magic and sorcery, witchcraft and superstition, charms and incantations, "portents" and the interpretation of dreams were deeply woven into the tissue of Roman life. Augustus studied his dreams with the diligence of a modern psychologist; Seneca saw women sitting on the steps of the Capitol waiting the pleasure of Jupiter because their dreams had told them they were desired of the god.[123] Every consul celebrated his inauguration by sacrificing steers; Juvenal, who could laugh at everything else, piously slit the throats of two lambs and a young ox in gratitude for the safe voyage of a friend. Temples were rich with gold and silver offerings; candles burned before the altars; the lips, hands, and feet of divine images were worn by the kisses of the devout. The old religion seemed still vigorous; it created new gods like Annona (gatherer of the world's corn for Rome), put new life into the worship of Fortuna and Roma, and gave powerful support to law, order, and tyranny. If Augustus had returned a year after his death he might well have claimed that his religious revival had proved a happy success.

Despite these appearances the ancient faith was diseased at the bottom and at the top. The deification of the emperors revealed not how much the upper classes thought of their rulers, but how little they thought of their gods. Among educated men philosophy was whittling away belief even while patronizing it. Lucretius had not been without effect; men did not mention him, but merely because it was easier to practice epicureanism than to study Epicurus or his passionate expositor. The rich youths who went to Athens, Alexandria, and Rhodes for higher education found no sustenance there for the Roman creed. Greek poets made fun of the Roman pantheon, and Roman poets leaped to imitate them. The poems of Ovid assumed that the gods were fables; the epigrams of Martial assumed that they were jokes; and no one seems to have complained. Many of the mimes ridiculed the gods; one whipped Diana off the stage, another showed Jove making his will in expectation of death.[124] Juvenal, like Plato five centuries before him and ourselves eighteen centuries after him, noted that the fear of a watchful deity had lost its power to discourage perjury.[125] Even on the tombstones of the poor we note increasing skepticism, and some candid sensuality. *Non fui, fui, non sum, non curo*, reads one—"I was not, I was, I am not, I care not"; and another, *Non fueram, non sum, nescio*—"I had not been, I am not, I know not"; and another, "What I have eaten and drunk is my own; I have had my life." [126] "I believe in nothing beyond the grave," says one tombstone; "There is no Hades, no Charon, no Cerberus," asserts another. "Now," a harassed soul wrote, "I need never fear hunger, need never pay rent, and am at least free from gout"; and a somber Lucretian writes of the buried flesh: "The elements out of which he was formed take possession of their own again. Life is only lent to man; he cannot keep it forever. By his death he pays his debt to Nature." [127]

But doubt, however honest, cannot long take the place of belief. Amid all its pleasures this society had not found happiness. Its refinements wearied it, its debaucheries exhausted it; rich and poor were still subject to pain and grief and death. Philosophy—least of all so coldly superior a doctrine as Stoicism—could never give the common man a faith to grace his poverty, encourage his decency, solace his sorrows, and inspire his hopes. The old religion had fulfilled the first of these functions; it had failed in the rest. Men wanted revelation, and it gave them ritual; they wanted immortality, and it gave them games. Men who had come, enslaved or free, from other states felt excluded from this nationalistic worship; therefore they brought their own gods with them, built their own temples, practiced their own rites; in the very heart of the West they planted the religions of the East. Between the creeds of the conquerors and the faith of the defeated a war took form in which the weapons of the legions were useless; the needs of the heart would determine the victory.

The new deities came with war captives, returning soldiers, and merchants. Traders from Asia and Egypt set up temples in Puteoli, Ostia, and Rome for the cult of their traditional gods. The Roman government treated these alien faiths for the most part with toleration; since it would not admit foreigners to its own worship it preferred that they should practice their imported rites rather than have no religion at all. In return it required that each new faith should exercise a similar tolerance towards other creeds, and should include in its ritual some obeisance to the emperor's "genius" and the goddess Roma, as an expression of loyalty to the state. Encouraged by this lenience, the Oriental faiths already domiciled in Rome became major religions of the populace. Hoping to civilize the cult, Claudius removed the restrictions that had harassed the worship of the Great Mother; he allowed Romans to become her ministrants, and established her feast around the vernal equinox, from March 15 to 27. Her chief rival in this first Christian century was Isis, the Egyptian goddess of motherhood, fertility, and trade. Again and again the government had forbidden the cult in Rome, but it always returned; the piety of the devotees overcame the power of the state, and Caligula marked the surrender by building with public funds an immense shrine to her in the Field of Mars. Otho and Domitian took part in the Isiac festivals; Commodus, with shaven head, walked humbly behind the priests, holding reverently in his arms a statue of Anubis, the Egyptian monkey god.

The divine invasion swelled from year to year. From southern Italy came the worship of Pythagoras—vegetarianism and reincarnation. From Hierapolis came Atargatis, known to the Romans as *dea Syria*, "the Syrian goddess," Aziz the "Zeus of Doliche," and other strange gods; their worship was spread by Syrian merchants and slaves; and at last a young priest of a Syrian Baal ascended the throne as Elagabalus—worshiper of the god of the sun. From hostile Parthia came the cult of another sun-god, Mithras; its devotees were enlisted as soldiers in the great cosmic war of Light against Darkness, of Good against Evil; it was a virile faith that won men rather than women, and pleased the Roman legions stationed on distant frontiers where they could hardly hear the voices of their native gods. From Judea came Yahweh, an uncompromising monotheist who commanded the most difficult life of piety and regulation, but gave his followers a moral code and courage that supported them well in tribulation, and clothed with a certain nobility the life of the humblest poor. Among the Roman Jews who prayed to him were some, as yet obscurely distinguished from the rest, who worshiped his incarnate and resurrected son.

CHAPTER XVIII

Roman Law*

146 B.C.–A.D. 192

I. THE GREAT JURISTS

LAW was the most characteristic and lasting expression of the Roman spirit. As Greece stands in history for freedom, so Rome stands for order; and as Greece bequeathed democracy and philosophy as the foundations of individual liberty, so Rome has left us its laws, and its traditions of administration, as the bases of social order. To unite these diverse legacies, to attune their stimulating opposition into harmony, is the elemental task of statesmanship.

Since law is the essence of Roman history it has been impossible to keep them separate, and this chapter can only be a structural and synoptic supplement to preceding and subsequent details. The Roman constitution was like the British—no set of permanently binding rules, but a stream of precedent giving direction without preventing change. As wealth increased, and life became more complex, new legislation issued from assemblies, Senate, magistrates, and princes; the body of the law grew as rapidly as the Empire and reached out to ever new frontiers. The education of lawyers, the guidance of judges, and the protection of the citizen from illegal judgments demanded the organization and formulation of the law into some orderly and accessible form. Amid the turmoil of the Gracchan and Marian revolution Publius Mucius Scaevola (consul, 133 B.C.) and his son Quintus (consul, 95 B.C.) labored to reduce the laws of Rome to an intelligible system. Cicero, pupil of another Quintus Mucius Scaevola (consul, 117 B.C.), wrote eloquently on the philosophy of law, and constructed an ideal code designed to preserve the fortune that he had gained and the faith that he had lost. The contradictory enactments of Marius and Sulla, the unprecedented powers of Pompey, the revolutionary legislation of Caesar, and the new constitution of Augustus created fresh problems for minds that struggled to make a logic of the law; and the brilliant jurist Antistius Labeo confounded confusion by declaring the decrees of Caesar and Augustus

---

* This chapter will be of no use to lawyers, and of no interest to others.

void, as the expression of usurped and illegal authority. Not till the Principate had established itself, first by the use of force and then by the force of use, could the new legislation win acceptance in the minds of men as well as in the courts of power. To the second and third centuries of our era belongs the honor of giving Roman law its final formulation in the West—an achievement comparable to the formulation of science and philosophy in Greece.

Here, too, Caesar had set the goal; but the actual work did not begin till Hadrian (A.D. 117). This best educated of the emperors gathered about him a corps of jurists as his Privy Council, and commissioned them to replace the variable annual edicts of the praetors with a Perpetual Edict to be observed by all future judges in Italy. The Greeks had produced since Solon no masterpiece of jurisprudence, and never a codified system of law; but the Greek cities of Asia and Italy had developed excellent municipal codes. The much-traveled Hadrian knew these cities well and was perhaps inspired by their constitutions to improve and co-ordinate the laws of Rome. Under his successors, the Antonines, the work of codification continued, and the half-official repute enjoyed by the Stoic philosophy permitted a profound Greek influence upon Roman law. The Stoics declared that law should accord with morality, and that guilt lay in the intention of the deed, not in the results. Antoninus, a product of the Stoic school, decreed that cases of doubt should be resolved in favor of the accused, and that a man should be held innocent until proved guilty [1]—two supreme principles of civilized law.

Favored by imperial patronage, the science of jurisprudence nurtured a succession of geniuses. Salvius Julianus, a Roman of African birth, showed so much learning and industry as *quaestor Augusti*, or legal adviser to the emperor, that the Senate voted him double the usual salary of that office. His *responsa* were acclaimed for their logic and clarity; his *Digesta* presented a systematic arrangement of civil and praetorian law; it was he who, as the leading member of Hadrian's Council, formulated the Praetorian Perpetual Edict. Another jurist is known to us only by his first name, Gaius; his famous *Institutiones* was discovered by Niebuhr in 1816 on a faded palimpsest overwritten with some essays by Saint Jerome; it is now our fullest authority for pre-Justinian Roman law. It was issued (*ca.* A.D. 161) not as a creative work but as an elementary manual for students; if we find it a masterpiece of orderly exposition, we may imagine the intellectual stature of the men whose lost treatises it summarized. Sixty years later Papinian, Paulus, and Ulpian brought Roman jurisprudence to its height; while the administration of the law fell a victim to violence and chaos, they gave it a rational formulation and consistency. After them the great science sank in the general ruin.

II. THE SOURCES OF THE LAW

As the terminology of science and philosophy comes mostly from the Greek, betraying their source, so the language of the law comes mostly from the Latin. Law in general was *ius*, justice or right; *lex* meant a specific law.* Jurisprudence— wisdom in the law—was defined in the *Digest* of Justinian (A.D. 533) as both a science and an art: the "science of the just and the unjust," and the "art [i.e., administration] of the good and the equitable." [2] *Ius* included unwritten law, or custom, as well as written law. The latter was composed of *ius civile*—the "law of [Roman] citizens"—and *ius gentium*—"the law of the nations." Civil law was "public law" when it related to the state or the official worship, and "private law" when it dealt with the legal interrelations of the citizens.

Roman law as a whole flowed from five sources. 1. Under the Republic the ultimate source of law was the will of the citizens, expressed as *leges* in the Curial and Centurial Assemblies, and as *plebiscita* ("decided by the plebs") in the Tribal Assembly. The Senate acknowledged *leges* only when they had been proposed to the assemblies with the proper formalities and by a magistrate of Senatorial rank. When Senate and assembly agreed in passing a measure, it was proclaimed in the name of *Senatus Populusque Romanus*.

2. The Senate itself, in theory, had no lawmaking power under the Republic; its *senatusconsulta* were, formally, recommendations to the magistrates; gradually they became directives, then imperatives, until in the later Republic and under the Empire they took on the force of laws. Altogether the laws passed by the assemblies or the Senate were so few in the course of six centuries as to astonish one accustomed to the legislative flux of modern states.

3. The need for minor or more specific laws was met by the *edicta* of the municipal officials. Each new urban praetor (our "chief city magistrate") issued an *edictum praetorium*, announced by a herald in the Forum and inscribed upon a wall, and stating the legal principles on which the praetor proposed to act and judge during his year's term. Similar edicts could be put forth by circuit judges (*praetores peregrini*) and provincial praetors. Through their power of *imperium*, or rule, the praetors were allowed not only to interpret existing laws, but to make new ones. In this way Roman law combined the stability of its basic legislation with the flexibility of praetorian judgments. When a law or clause was carried down from one praetorian edict to the next for many years, it became a definite part of the *ius honorarium;* by the time of Cicero this "law of the offices" had displaced the Twelve Tables as the main text of legal instruction in Rome. Nevertheless, a praetor often reversed the decisions, and sometimes contradicted the principles, of a predecessor, so that uncertainties of law and arbitrariness of judgment were added to the abuses natural in every judicial system operated by men. It was to end this uncertainty that Hadrian instructed Julianus

---

* Cf. French *droit* and *loi*, German *Recht* and *Gesetz*.

to unify all preceding *ius honorarium* in a Perpetual Edict alterable only by the emperor.

4. The *constitutiones principum*, or statutes of the princes, became themselves in the second century a varied source of law. They took four forms. (*a*) The prince issued *edicta* by virtue of his *imperium* as an official of the city; these were valid for the whole Empire, but apparently lapsed after his death. (*b*) His *decreta* as a judge, like those of other magistrates, had the force of law. (*c*) Imperial *rescripta* were his answers to inquiries. Usually they were *epistulae*—letters —or *subscriptiones*, brief replies "written under" a question or petition. The wise and pithy letters in which Trajan answered the requests of governmental appointees for instruction were incorporated into the laws of the Empire and kept their validity long after his death. (*d*) The *mandata* of the emperors were their directives to officials; in the course of time these came to constitute a detailed code of administrative law.

5. Under certain circumstances law could be created by the *responsa prudentium*. It must have been a pleasant sight when learned jurists sat in chairs in the open Forum (or, in later decades, in their homes), and gave legal opinions to all who asked, taking their chances on some indirect remuneration. Often their advice was solicited by lawyers or municipal judges. Like the great rabbis of the Jews they reconciled contradictions, drew subtle distinctions, interpreted and adjusted the ancient law to the needs of life or the exigencies of politics. Their written replies, by unwritten custom, had an authority only less than the law's. Augustus gave such opinions full legal force on two conditions; that the jurist should have received from the Emperor the *ius respondendi*, or right of giving legal opinions; and that the reply should be sent under seal to the judge trying the case in point. By the time of Justinian these *responsa* had become a vast school and literature of law, the fountain and foundation of his culminating *Digest* and *Code*.

III. THE LAW OF PERSONS

"All law," says the precise Gaius, "pertains to persons, to property, or to procedure." [3] The word *persona* had signified an actor's mask; later it was applied to the part played by a man in life; finally it came to mean the man himself—as if to say that we can never know a man, but only the parts he plays, the mask or masks that he wears.

The first person in Roman law was the citizen. He was defined as anyone who had been accepted into a Roman tribe by birth, adoption, emancipation, or governmental grant. Within this franchise were three grades: (1) full citizens, who enjoyed the fourfold right of voting (*ius suffragii*), of holding office (*ius honorum*), of marriage with a freeborn person (*ius connubii*), and of engaging in commercial contracts protected by Roman law (*ius commercii*); (2) "citizens without suffrage," who had the rights of marriage and contract, but not of voting or office; and (3) freedmen, who had the rights of voting and contract, but not of marriage or office. The full citizen had, furthermore, certain exclusive rights in private law: the power of the father over his children (*patria potestas*), of the husband over his wife (*manus*), of an owner over his property, including his slaves (*dominium*), and of a freeman over another by contract (*mancipium*). A kind of potential citizenship, called *Latinitas* or *ius Latii*, was conferred by Rome upon the free inhabitants of favored towns and colonies, whereby they acquired the right of contract, but not of intermarriage, with Romans, and their magistrates received full Roman citizenship upon completing their terms of office. Each city of the Empire had its own citizens and conditions of citizenship; and by a unique tolerance a man might be a citizen—and enjoy the civic rights—of several cities at once. The most precious privilege of a Roman citizen was the safeguarding of his person, property, and rights by the law, and his immunity from torture or violence in the trying of his case. It was the glory of Roman law that it protected the individual against the state.

The second person in Roman law was the father. The *patria potestas* had been weakened by the spread of law into areas formerly governed by custom; but we may judge its surviving force from the fact that when Aulus Fulvius set out to join Catiline's army, his father called him back and put him to death. In general, however, the power of the father declined as that of the government rose; democracy entered the family when it left the state. In the early Republic the fathers had been the state; the family heads formed the Curial Assembly, and the clan heads probably constituted the Senate. Rule through family and clan diminished as population became more abundant and diverse, and life more mobile, commercial, and complex; kinship, status, and custom were replaced by contract and law.[4] Children won greater freedom from their parents, wives from their husbands, individuals from their groups. Trajan compelled a father to emancipate a son whom he had maltreated; Hadrian took from the father the right of life and death over his household and transferred it to the courts; Antoninus forbade a father to sell his children into slavery.[5] Custom had long since reduced the use of these old powers to rare occurrences. Law tends to lag behind moral development, not because law cannot learn, but because experience has shown the wisdom of testing new ways in practice before congealing them into law.

The Roman woman gained new rights as the man lost old ones; but she was clever enough to disguise her freedom under continuing legal disabilities. The law of the Republic assumed that she was never *sui iuris*, "of her own right," but always dependent upon some male guardian; "according to our ancestors," said Gaius, "even women of mature age must be kept in tutelage because of the lightness of their minds." [6] In the later Republic and under the Empire this legal dependence was largely annulled by feminine charms and willfulness, abetted by male susceptibility and affection. From Cato the Elder to Commodus Roman society, legally patriarchal, was ruled by women, with all the graceful mastery of Renaissance Italian or Bourbon French *salons*. The laws of Augustus made some obeisance to the facts by releasing from *tutela* any woman who had borne three legitimate children.[7] Hadrian decreed that women might dispose of their property as they liked, provided they obtained the consent of their guardians; but actual procedure soon dispensed with this consent. By the end of the second century all compulsory tutelage was ended in law for free women over twenty-five.

The consent of both fathers was still required for legal marriage.[8] Marriage by *confarreatio* was now (A.D. 160) confined to a few Senatorial families. Marriage by purchase (*coemptio*) lingered as a form; the bridegroom paid for the bride by weighing an as or an ingot of bronze in a scale before five witnesses, her father or her guardian having consented.[9] Most marriages were now by *usus*, i.e., cohabitation. To avoid falling under the *manus* or proprietory power of her husband, the wife absented herself three nights in each year; thereby she retained control of her property, excepting her dowry. Indeed, the husband often put his property in his wife's name to avoid suits for damages or the penalties of bankruptcy.[10] Such marriage *sine manu* could be ended by either party at will; marriage by other forms could be ended only by the husband. Adultery was still a minor offense in the man; in the woman it was a major offense against the institutions of property and inheritance. But the husband no longer had the right to kill his wife taken in adultery; this right was now vested technically in her father, actually in the courts; and the penalty was banishment. Concubinage was recognized by the law as a substitute for marriage, but not as an accompaniment to it; and a man could not legally have two concubines at once. Children by a concubine were classed as illegitimate and could not inherit—which made concubinage all the more attractive to men who liked to be courted by hunters of legacies. Vespasian, Antoninus Pius, and Marcus Aurelius lived in concubinage after the death of their wives.[11]

The law struggled to encourage parentage among the freeborn, but with negligible results. Infanticide was forbidden except in the case of infants deformed or incurably diseased. The detected procurer of abortion was banished and lost part of his property; if the woman died he was to be put to death; [12] these laws, of course, were largely evaded then as now. Children of any age remained under the authority of the father except when thrice sold by him into bondage, or when formally emancipated, or when the son held a public office or became a *flamen dialis,* or when a daughter married *cum manu* or became a Vestal Virgin. If a son married in the lifetime of his father, the *patria potestas* over the grandchildren resided in the grandfather.[13] By the legislation of Augustus the earnings of a son in the army, in public office, in priestly orders, or in the liberal professions were freed from the old rule that such gains belonged to the father. A son might still be sold into bondage (*mancipium*); but this differed from slavery (*servitus*) in leaving the bondsman with his former civic rights.

The slave had no legal rights whatever; indeed, Roman law hesitated to apply the term *persona* to him and compromised by calling him an "impersonal man." [14] It is only by a considerate error that Gaius discusses him under the law of persons; logically the slave came under the rubric of property (*res*). He could not own, inherit, or bequeath; he could not make a legal marriage; his children were all classed as illegitimate, and the children of a slave woman were classed as slaves even if the father was free.[15] Slaves male or female might be seduced by their master without legal redress. The slave could not bring action in the courts against those who injured him; he could proceed in such a case only through his owner. The latter, under the law of the Republic, could beat him, imprison him, condemn him to fight beasts in the arena, expose him to die of starvation, or kill him, with cause or without, and with no other control than a public opinion formed by slaveowners. If a slave ran away and was caught he could be branded or crucified; Augustus boasted that he had recaptured 30,000 runaway slaves and had crucified all who had not been claimed.[16] If, under these or other provocations, a slave killed his master, law required that all the slaves of the murdered man should be put to death. When Pedanius Secundus, urban prefect, was so slain (A.D. 61), and his 400 slaves were condemned to die, a minority in the Senate protested, and an angry crowd in the streets demanded mercy; but the Senate ordered the law to be carried out, in the belief that only by such measures could a master be secure.[17]

It is to the credit of the Empire—or perhaps of the diminishing supply of slaves—that their condition was progressively improved under the emperors. Claudius prohibited the killing of a useless slave and ruled that an abandoned sick slave who recovered should become automatically free. The *lex Petronia,* probably under Nero, forbade owners, without a magistrate's approval, to condemn slaves to fight in the arena. Nero allowed maltreated slaves to use his statue as an asylum and appointed a judge to hear their complaints— a modest advance that seemed revolutionary to Rome, since it opened the courts to slaves. Domitian made it a criminal offense to mutilate slaves for sensual purposes. Hadrian ended the right of the owner to kill a slave without magisterial sanction. Antoninus Pius permitted an abused slave to take sanctuary in any temple and had him sold to another master if he could prove injury. Marcus Aurelius encouraged owners to bring before the courts, rather than themselves punish, damages sustained by them from their slaves; in this way, he hoped, law and judgment would gradually replace brutality and private revenge.[18] Finally a great jurist of the third century, Ulpian, proclaimed what only a few philosophers had dared suggest— that "by the law of Nature all men are equal." [19] Other jurists laid it down as a maxim that where the freedom or slavery of a man was in question, all doubts should favor liberty.[20]

Despite these mitigations, the legal subjection of slaves is the worst blot on Roman law. The last indignity was the tax and restrictions upon emancipation. Many owners evaded the *lex Fufia Canina* by informally freeing a slave without official witness or legal ceremony; such liberation, however, conferred not citizenship but only *Latinitas*. The slave freed by process of law became a citizen with limited civic rights; but custom required him to pay his respects to his former owner every morning, attend him when needed, vote for him at every opportunity, and, in some cases, pay him a portion of all money earned. If the freedman died intestate, his property went automatically to his living patron; if he made a will he was expected to leave him a part of his estate.[21] Only when the master was dead, dutifully mourned, and safely buried could the freedman really breathe the air of freedom.

To these general divisions of the law of persons must be added the legislation which in modern codes is separately known as criminal law. Roman jurisprudence recognized crimes against the individual, the state, and social or business groups considered as juridical persons. Against the state one might be guilty of *maiestas*, treason by act or word; *vis publica*, sedition; *sacrilegium*, offenses against the state religion; *ambitus*, bribery; *crimen repetundarum*, extortion or corruption in public administration; *peculatus*, embezzlement of state funds; and *corruptio judicis*, bribery of a judge or juryman; from this partial list we may see that corruption has an ancient pedigree and a probable future. Against the individual one could commit *iniuria*, physical injury; *falsum*, deception; *stuprum*, indecency; and *caedes*, murder. Cicero mentions a *lex Scantinia* against pederasty; [22] Augustus corrected the error with a fine, Martial with epigrams, Domitian with death. Personal injury was no longer punished with equivalent retaliation, as in the Twelve Tables, but by a fine. Suicide was no crime; on the contrary, before

Domitian, it was in some sense rewarded; a man condemned to death could usually, by suicide, ensure the validation of his will and the unimpeded trans- mission of his property to his heirs. The law left the last choice free.

IV. THE LAW OF PROPERTY

Problems of ownership, obligation, exchange, contract, and debt took up by far the largest part of Roman law. Material possession was the very life of Rome, and the increase of wealth and the expansion of trade demanded a body of law immeasurably more complex than the simple code of the Decemvirs.

Ownership (*dominium*) came by inheritance or acquisition. Since the father owned as agent and trustee of the family, the children and grandchildren were potential owners—*sui heredes* in the law's queer phrase—"their own heirs." [23] If the father died intestate they succeeded automatically to the family property, and the oldest father among the sons inherited the *dominium*. The making of valid wills was hedged about with hundreds of legal restrictions, and their com- position required, as now, a gorgeous and sonorous tautology. Every testator was compelled to leave a specified portion of his estate to his children, another part to a wife who had borne him three children, and (in some cases) parts to his brothers, sisters, and ascendants. No heir might take any part of an estate with- out assuming all the debts and other legal obligations of the deceased; not infre- quently a Roman found himself saddled with a *damnosa hereditas*—a legacy, so to speak, in the red. Where an owner died without children and without a will, his property and his debts passed automatically to the nearest "agnate," or relative descended from a common ancestor exclusively through males. In the later Em- pire this male conceit abated, and by the time of Justinian agnates and cognates (relatives through male or female lines of ascent) inherited with equal right. An old law passed on the urging of Cato (169 B.C.) had forbidden any Roman who owned 100,000 sesterces ($15,000) or more to bequeath any part of his estate to a woman. This *lex Voconia* was still on the statute books in Gaius' time, but love had found a way. The testator left property on trust (*fideicommissum*) to a qualified heir, and bound him by a solemn request to transfer the property before a stated date to the woman named. By this and other channels much of the wealth of Rome passed into the hands of women. Gifts offered another escape from testamentary law; but gifts made in prospect of death were subject to legal scrutiny, and under Justinian they were liable to the same laws as those that harassed legacies.

Acquisition came by transfer, or by legal conveyance resulting from a suit at law. Transfer (*mancipatio*, "taking in hand") was a formal gift or sale before witnesses and with scales struck by a copper ingot as token of a sale; without this ancient ritual no exchange had the sanction or protection of the law. An intermediate or potential ownership was recognized under the name of *possessio—*

the right to hold or use property; e.g., tenants on state lands were *possessores* ("sitters," squatters), not *domini;* but their prescriptive right (*usucapio,* "taking by use") became *dominium,* and could no longer be questioned after two years of unchallenged occupancy. Probably this lenient conception of occupation as so soon generating ownership came from patricians who were in this manner acquiring public lands.[24] By the same right of *usucapio* a woman who lived with a man through a year without three nights' absence became the property (*in manu*) of the man.

Obligation was any compulsion by law to the performance of an act. It could arise by delict or by contract. Delicts or torts—noncontractual wrongs committed against a person or his property—were in many cases punished by an obligation to pay the injured person a sum of money in compensation. A contract was an agreement enforceable at law. It did not have to be written; indeed, until the second century A.D. the verbal agreement made by uttering the word *spondeo*— "I promise"—before a witness was considered more sacred than any written compact. The many witnesses and solemn ceremony once required for legal contract were no longer necessary; business was quickened by the legal recognition of any clear agreement—usually entries made by the parties in their account books (*tabulae*). But the law guarded transactions carefully: it warned the seller with a *caveat venditor,* as well as the buyer with a *caveat emptor,* against the myriad forms of cheating natural to civilized life. Any seller of slaves or cattle, for example, was required by law to disclose their physical defects to the purchaser and was held accountable despite a plea of ignorance.[25]

Debt was contracted by loan, mortgage, deposit, or trust. Loans for consumption were usually secured by a mortgage on realty or movable goods. A default in principal entitled the mortgagee to take over the property. In early republican law, as we have seen, such default permitted the lender to attach the person of the borrower as a bondsman.* The *lex Poetelia* (326 B.C.) modified this rule by allowing the debtor to work off his obligation while retaining his freedom. After Caesar, defaulted mortgages were usually satisfied by the sale of the debtor's property without jeopardy to his person; but cases of enslavement to a creditor occur as late as Justinian. Commercial defaults were mitigated by a law of bankruptcy which sold the bankrupt's property to pay his debts, but permitted him to keep as much of his later acquisitions as his subsistence required.

The chief crimes against property were damage, theft, and rapine—theft with violence. The Twelve Tables had condemned a detected thief to be flogged and then delivered as a bondsman to his victim; if the thief was a slave he was to be scourged and flung from the Tarpeian rock. Increased social security permitted praetorian law to soften these severities to a twofold, threefold, or fourfold restitution.[26] In its final form the law of property was the most perfect part of the Roman code.

---

* The mortgagor was in law bound (*nexus*) to the mortgagee; but the obscure term *nexum* was apparently applied to any solemnly sworn obligation.

V. THE LAW OF PROCEDURE

Of all ancient peoples the Romans were the most prone to litigation, despite the discouraging complexity, technicality, and confusing fictions of their procedural law. Doubtless our own legal actions would have seemed to them equally devious and prolonged. The older the civilization, the longer the lawsuits. Any man, as noted above, could make himself a prosecutor in a Roman court. In the patrician Republic the accuser, the defendant, and the magistrate were required to follow a form called *legis actio*, or process of law, and the slightest deviation invalidated the action. "Thus," says Gaius, "a man who sued another for cutting his vines, and in his action called them 'vines,' lost his case because he should have called them 'trees,' since the Twelve Tables speak generally of trees, and not particularly of vines." [27] Each party deposited with the magistrate a sum of money (*sacramentum*), which was forfeited by the losing party to the state religion. The defendant also had to give bail (*vadimonium*) as security for his subsequent appearances. The magistrate then turned over the dispute to a person on the list of those qualified to act as judges. In some cases the judge issued an interim *interdictum*, requiring one or more of the parties in the case to perform or refrain from certain actions. If the defendant lost, his property—sometimes his person—could be seized by the plaintiff until the judgment was satisfied.

About 150 B.C. the *lex Aebutia* abolished the necessity of using this ritual *legis actio*, and accepted in its place a procedure *per formulam*. Specific acts and words were no longer required; the parties shared with the magistrate in determining the form under which the matter was to be submitted to the judge; and the magistrate then wrote to the judge an instruction (*formula*) on the factual and legal questions involved; it was partly in this way that the praetor, as magistrate, made "praetorian law." In the second century A.D. a third mode of action—*cognitio extraordinaria*—came into use: the magistrate decided the case himself. By the end of the third century the formulary procedure had disappeared, and the summary judgment of a magistrate responsible only to the emperor, and usually owing his office to him, reflected the coming of absolute monarchy.

The litigants could conduct their case, and the praetor or judge decide it, without the help of lawyers if they wished; but as the *iudex* was not often a professional trained in the law, and the litigants might at every step stumble over a technicality, all parties to a dispute usually sought the aid of trial lawyers (*advocati*), legal technicians (*pragmatici*), consultants (*iurisconsulti*), or jurists (*iurisprudentes*). There was no lack of legal talent, for every fond parent yearned to see his son an advocate, and the law, then as now, was the vestibule to public office. A character in Petronius gives his son a collection of red-backed books (*codices*) "to learn a little law," as "it spells money." [28] A law student began by learning the elements from some private instructor; in his second stage he attended the consultations of eminent jurists; thereafter he apprenticed himself to a practicing lawyer. Early in the second century A.D. certain *iurisconsulti* set up in various parts of Rome schools (*stationes*) at which they gave instruction or advice in the law; Ammianus complains of their high fees, saying that they charged even for their yawns and made matricide venial if the client paid enough.[29] These teachers were called *iuris civilis professores;* apparently the title of *professor* came from the fact that they were required by law to declare (*profiteri*) their intention of teaching, and to secure a license therefor from the public authority.[30]

Out of the many lawyers so trained there were inevitably some who sold their learning to sordid causes,[31] accepted bribes to present their client's case weakly,[32] found loopholes in the law for any crime, fomented disputes among rich men, dragged on suits to any lucrative length,[33] and shook the courts or the Forum with their intimidating questioning and their vituperative summations. Forced to compete for cases, some lawyers sought to build a reputation by walking hurriedly through the streets with bundles of documents in their hands, borrowed rings on their fingers, dependents attending them, and hired *claqueurs* to applaud their speech.[34] So many ways had been found of circumventing the old Cincian law against fees that Claudius legalized them up to 10,000 sesterces per case; any fee above this figure was to be recoverable by law.[35] This restriction was easily evaded, for we hear of a lawyer in Vespasian's reign amassing a fortune of 300,000,-000 sesterces ($30,000,000).[36] As in every generation, there were attorneys and judges whose clear and disciplined minds were at the service of truth and justice regardless of fee; and the lowest practitioners were redeemed by the great jurists whose names are the highest in the history of the law.

Courts for the trial of offenders varied from the hearings held by individual judges or magistrates to the assemblies, the Senate, and the emperor. Instead of a single judge the praetor might choose by lot (subject to a number of challenges by accuser and defendant) a jury of almost any size, usually fifty-one or seventy-five, from the 850 Senatorial or equestrian names on the jury list. Two special courts were permanently maintained: the *decemviri*, or Ten Men, to try cases of civil status; and the *centumviri*, or Hundred Men, to hear suits in property and bequest. The proceedings of these bodies were open to the public, for the younger Pliny describes the great crowd that came to hear him address the larger court.[37] Juvenal [38] and Apuleius [39] complain of judicial procrastination and venality, but their very indignation suggests exceptional cases.

Trials were marked by a freedom of speech and action seldom known in modern courts. Several lawyers might appear on each side; some specialized in preparing the evidence, some in presenting it. The proceedings were recorded by various clerks (*notarii, actuarii, scribae*), and were sometimes taken down in shorthand; Martial says of certain scribes, "However fast the words may run, their hands are quicker still." [41] Plutarch tells how stenographers took down the speeches of Cicero, often to his discomfort. Witnesses were dealt with according to time-honored precedents. Says the exemplary Quintilian:

> In the examination of a witness the first essential is to know his type. For a timid witness may be terrorized, a fool outwitted, an irascible man provoked, and vanity flattered. The shrewd and self-possessed witness must be dismissed at once as malicious and obstinate; or . . . if his past life admits of criticism, his credit may be overthrown by the scandalous charges that can be brought against him.[42]

Almost any kind of argument might be made by the advocate. He could show the court pictures of the alleged crime, painted on canvas or wood; he could hold a child in his arms while arguing a point; he could bare the scars of an accused soldier or the wounds of a client. Defenses were contrived against these weapons. Quintilian tells how one attorney, when his opponent illustrated a summation by bringing his client's children into court, threw dice among them; the children scrambled for the *tesserae* and ruined a peroration.[43] The slaves of either party to a suit might be tortured to elicit evidence, but such evidence was not admissible against their owners. Hadrian decreed that slaves should be tortured for evidence only as a last resort and under the strictest regulations, and he warned the courts that evidence secured by torture could never be trusted. Legal torture nevertheless persisted, and was extended in the third century to freemen.[44] The jury voted by depositing marked tablets in an urn; a majority sufficed for a decision. In most cases the loser might appeal to a higher court, and finally, if he could afford it, to the emperor.

Penalties were fixed by law rather than left to the discretion of the judge. They varied with the rank of the offender, being severest for the slave; he might be crucified, the citizen might not; and no Roman citizen, as every reader of the Acts of the Apostles knows, could be scourged, tortured, or put to death over his appeal to the emperor. Different penalties were laid upon *honestiores* and *humiliores* for the same crime; they varied also according as the offender was freeborn or freeman, solvent or bankrupt, soldier or civilian. The simplest punishment was a fine. Since the value of currency changed more rapidly than the penalties named in the law, certain anomalies ensued. The Twelve Tables exacted a fine of twenty-five asses (originally twenty-five pounds of copper) for striking a freeman; when rising prices had lowered the as to six cents Lucius Veratius went about striking freemen in the face, followed by a slave who counted out twenty-five asses to each victim.[45] Some offenses resulted in *infamia* ("speechlessness"), chiefly the inability to appear, or be represented by another, in an action at law. A more stringent punishment was loss of civic rights (*capitis deminutio*), which took the progressive forms of incapacity to inherit, deportation, and enslavement. Deportation was the harshest form of exile: the condemned man was put in chains, confined in some inhospitable place, and deprived of all his property. *Exilium* was milder in allowing the victim to live in freedom wherever he pleased outside of Italy; *relegatio*, as in the case of Ovid, involved no confiscation, but compelled the outcast to stay in a specified town, usually far from Rome. Imprisonment was seldom used as a permanent punishment, but men might be condemned to menial labor on public works, or in the mines, or in the quarries of the state. Under the Republic a freeman sentenced to death could escape the penalty by leaving Rome or Italy; under the Empire the death penalty was imposed with increasing frequency and ruthlessness. Prisoners of war, and in some cases other condemned men, might be thrown into the *Carcer Tullianum*, to die of starvation, rodents, and lice in underground darkness and irremovable filth.[46] There Jugurtha died, and Simon Ben-Giora, heroic defender of Jerusalem against Titus. There, said tradition, Peter and Paul had languished before their martyrdom, and had written their last addresses to the young Christian world.

VI. THE LAW OF THE NATIONS

The most difficult problem of Roman law was to adjust itself as an intelligent master to the varied codes and customs of the lands that Roman arms or diplomacy had won. Many of these states were older than Rome; what they had lost in military courage they made up in proud traditions and a jealous fondness for their peculiar ways. Rome met the situation ably. A *praetor peregrinus* was appointed at first for the foreigners in Rome, then for Italy, then for the provinces; and power was given him to make some viable union between Roman and local law. The annual edicts of this praetor and the provincial governors and aediles gradually created the *ius gentium* by which the Empire was ruled.

This "Law of the Nations" was not an international law—not a body of commitments accepted by the generality of states as governing their interrelations. In a sense not much more tenuous than today there was in antiquity an international law, insofar as certain common customs were honored in peace and war—the mutual safeguarding of international merchants and diplomats, the granting of truce for the burial of the dead, abstention from the use of poisoned arrows, etc. The jurists of Rome, by a patriotic fiction, described the *ius gentium* as law common to all nations. But they were too modest about Rome's part in it. Actually it was local law adapted to Roman sovereignty, and designed to govern the peoples of Italy and the provinces without giving them Roman citizenship and the other rights of the *ius civile*.

By a corresponding fiction the philosophers attempted to identify the Law of the Nations with the "Law of Nature." The Stoics defined the latter as a moral code implanted in man by "natural reason." Nature, they held, was a system of reason, a logic and order in all things; this order, spontaneously developing in society, and coming to consciousness in man, was natural law. Cicero phrased the fancy in a famous passage:

> True law is right reason in agreement with nature, world-wide in scope, unchanging, everlasting. . . . We may not oppose or alter that law, we cannot abolish it, we cannot be freed from its obligations by any legislature, and we need not look outside ourselves for an expounder of it. This law does not differ for Rome and for Athens, for the present and for the future; . . . it is and will be valid for all nations and all times. . . . He who disobeys it denies himself and his own nature.[47]

It was a perfect statement of an ideal that grew in force as Stoicism reached the throne in the Antonines. Ulpian developed it into the far-reaching principle that class distinctions and privileges are accidental and artificial; and from this it was but a step to the Christian conception of all men as fundamentally equal. But when Gaius defined the *ius gentium* as simply "the law which natural reason has established among all mankind," [48] he was mistaking Roman arms for Divine Providence. Roman law was the logic and economy of force; the great codes of *ius civile* and *ius gentium* were the rules by which a wise conqueror gave order, regularity, and time's sanctity to a sovereignty based upon the legions' strength. They were natural, but only in the sense that it is natural for the strong to use and abuse the weak.

Nevertheless, there is something noble in this imposing architecture of government called Roman law. Since the victor must rule, it is a boon that the rules of his mastery should be clearly expressed; in this sense law is the consistency of power. It was natural that the Romans should create the greatest system of law in history: they loved order and had the means to enforce it; upon the chaos of a hundred diverse nations they laid an imperfect but sublime authority and peace. Other states had had laws, and legislators like Hammurabi and Solon had issued small bodies of humane legislation; but no people had yet achieved that immense co-ordination, unification, and codification which occupied the highest legal minds of Rome from the Scaevolas to Justinian.

The flexibility of the *ius gentium* facilitated the transmission of Roman law to medieval and modern states. It was a happy accident that while the chaos of barbarian invasion was mutilating the legal heritage in the West, the *Code, Digest*, and *Institutes* of Justinian were collected and formulated in Constantinople, in the comparative security and continuity of the Empire in the East. Through those labors, and a hundred lesser channels, and the silent tenacity of useful ways, Roman law entered into the canon law of the medieval Church, inspired the thinkers of the Renaissance, and became the basic law of Italy, Spain, France, Germany, Hungary, Bohemia, Poland, even—within the British Empire—of Scotland, Quebec, Ceylon, and South Africa. English law itself, the only legal edifice of comparable scope, took its rules of equity, admiralty, guardianship, and bequests from Roman canon law. Greek science and philosophy, Judeo-Greek Christianity, Greco-Roman democracy, Roman law—these are our supreme inheritance from the ancient world.

CHAPTER XIX

The Philosopher Kings

A.D. 96-180

I. NERVA

WITH the assassination of Domitian the principle of heredity disappeared for a century from Roman monarchy. The Senate had never recognized inheritance as a source of sovereignty; now, after 123 years of submission, it reasserted its authority; and as in Rome's beginnings it had chosen the king, now it named one of its own members princeps and imperator. It was an act of courage intelligible only when we remember that the vigor of the Flavian family was exhausted in that same generation which had seen the vitality of the Senate renewed by Italian and provincial blood.

Marcus Cocceius Nerva was sixty-six when supremacy surprised him. The colossal *Nerva* of the Vatican shows a handsome and virile face; no one would suppose that this was a respectable jurist with a bad stomach, a mild and amiable poet who had once been hailed as "the Tibullus of our time." [1] Perhaps the Senate had chosen him for his gray harmlessness. He consulted it on all policies, and kept his pledge never to be the cause of death to any of its members. He recalled Domitian's exiles, restored their property, and moderated their revenge. He distributed 60,000,000 sesterces' worth of lands among the poor, and established the *alimenta*—a state fund to encourage and finance parentage among the peasantry. He annulled many taxes, lowered the inheritance dues, and freed the Jews from the tribute that Vespasian had laid upon them. At the same time he repaired the finances of the state by economy in his household and his government. With reason he thought that he had been just to all classes, and remarked that "I have done nothing that could prevent me from laying down the imperial office and returning to private life in safety." [2] But a year after his accession the Praetorian Guard, which had been forestalled in his nomination and resented his economy, besieged his palace, demanded the surrender of Domitian's assassins, and killed several of Nerva's councilors. He offered his throat to the swords of the soldiers, but they spared him. Humiliated, he wished to abdicate, but his friends persuaded him, instead, to return to Augustus' example and adopt as his son and successor a man acceptable to the Senate and capable of ruling not only the Empire, but the Guard as well. The greatest debt that Rome owed Nerva was that he chose Marcus Ulpius Traianus to succeed him. Three months later, after a reign of sixteen months, he passed away (98).

The principle of adoption thus accidentally restored meant that each emperor, as he felt his powers decline, would associate with himself in rule the ablest and fittest man he could find, so that when death came there would be neither the absurdity of a Praetorian elevation, nor the risk of a natural but worthless heir, nor a civil war among competitors for the throne. It was a lucky chance that no son was born to Trajan, Hadrian, or Antoninus Pius, and that each could apply the adoptive plan without slighting his offspring or his own parental love. While the principle was maintained it gave Rome "the finest succession of good and great sovereigns the world has ever had." [3]

II. TRAJAN

Trajan received word of his accession while he was in charge of a Roman army in Cologne. It was characteristic of him that he went on with his work at the frontier and postponed his coming to Rome for nearly two years. He had been born in Spain of an Italian family long settled there; in him and in Hadrian Roman Spain arrived at political hegemony, as it had reached literary leadership in Seneca, Lucan, and Martial. He was the first in a long line of generals whose provincial birth and training seemed to give them the will-to-life that had gone from the native Roman stock. That Rome made no protest against this enthronement of a provincial was in itself an event and omen in Roman history.

Trajan never ceased to be a general. His carriage was military, his presence commanding; his features were undistinguished but strong. Tall and robust, he was wont to march on foot with his troops and ford with full armament the hundred rivers they had to cross. His courage showed a stoic impartiality between life and death. Told that Licinius Sura was plotting against him, he went to Sura's house for dinner, ate without scrutiny whatever food was offered him, and had himself shaved by Sura's barber.[4] He was not in any technical sense a philosopher. He used to take Dio Chrysostom, the "golden-mouthed" rhetor, with him in his chariot to discourse to him on philosophy, but he confessed that he could not understand a word of Dio's talk [5]—the worse for philosophy. His mind was clear and direct; he uttered an amazing minimum of nonsense for a man. He was vain, like all human beings, but completely unassuming; he took no advantage of his office, joined his friends at table and the hunt, drank with them copiously, and indulged in occasional pederasty as if out of deference to the customs of his time. Rome thought it worthy of praise that he never disturbed his wife Plotina by making love to another woman.

When, in the forty-second year of his age, Trajan reached Rome, he was at the height of his faculties. His simplicity, geniality, and moderation readily won a people so lately acquainted with tyranny. The younger Pliny was chosen by the Senate to pronounce the "panegyric" of greeting. About the same time Dio Chrysostom delivered before the Emperor a discourse on the duties of a monarch as viewed by the Stoic philosophy. Both Pliny and Dio distinguished between *dominatio* and *principatus*: the prince was to be not lord of the state but its first servant, the executive delegate of the people, chosen through their representatives, the senators. *Imperaturus omnibus elegi debet ex omnibus*, said Pliny: "He who is to command all should be elected by all." [6] The general listened courteously.

Such fair beginnings were not new in history; what astonished Rome was that Trajan fulfilled their promise abundantly. He gave to his aides or associates the villas in which his predecessors had stayed for a few weeks in the year; "he regarded nothing as his own," said Pliny, "unless his friends possessed it"; [7] as for himself he lived as simply as Vespasian. He asked the Senate's opinion on all matters of moment, and discovered that he might wield nearly absolute power if he never used absolute speech. The Senate was willing to let him rule if he would observe the forms that maintained its dignity and prestige; like the rest of Rome, it now loved security too much to be capable of freedom. Perhaps also it was pleased to find Trajan a conservative, who had no intention of mulcting the rich to appease the poor.

Trajan was an able and tireless administrator, a sound financier, a just judge. To him the *Digest* of Justinian ascribes the principle, "It is better that the guilty should remain unpunished than that the innocent should be condemned." [8] By careful supervision of expenditures (and some lucrative conquests) he was able to complete extensive public works without increasing taxation; on the contrary, he lowered taxes and published a budget to expose the revenues and outlays of the government to examination and criticism. He required from the senators who enjoyed his comradeship an administrative devotion almost as meticulous as his own. The patricians entered the bureaucracy and worked as well as played; Trajan's extant correspondence with them suggests how carefully they labored under his watchful and inspiring leadership. Many of the Eastern cities had mismanaged their finances to the point of bankruptcy, and Trajan sent *curatores* like the younger Pliny to help and check them. The procedure weakened municipal independence and institutions, but it was unavoidable; self-government, by extravagance and incompetence, had brought its own end.

Nurtured on war, the Emperor was a frank imperialist who preferred order to liberty and power to peace. Hardly a year after his arrival in Rome he set out for the conquest of Dacia. Roughly corresponding to the Rumania of 1940, Dacia plunged like a fist into the heart of Germany, and would therefore be of great military value in the struggle that Trajan foresaw between the Germans and Italy. Its annexation would give Rome control of the road that ran down the Save to the Danube and thence to Byzantium—an invaluable land route to the East. Besides, Dacia had gold mines. In a campaign brilliantly planned and swiftly executed, Trajan led his legions through all obstacles and resistance to the Dacian capital, Sarmizegetusa, and forced its surrender. A Roman sculptor has left us an impressive portrait of the Dacian king Decebalus—a face noble with strength and character. Trajan reinstated him as a client king and returned to Rome (102); but Decebalus soon broke his agreements and resumed his independent sway. Trajan marched his army back into Dacia (105), bridged the Danube with a structure that was one of the engineering marvels of the century, and again stormed the Dacian capital. Decebalus was killed, a strong garrison was left to hold Sarmizegetusa, and Trajan went back to Rome to celebrate his victory with 10,000 gladiators (probably war captives) in 123 days of public games. Dacia became a Roman province, received Roman colonists, married them, and corrupted the Latin language in its own Rumanian way. The gold mines of Transylvania were put under the direction of an imperial procurator and soon paid for the material cost of the war. To reimburse himself for his labors Trajan took out of Dacia a million pounds of silver and half a million pounds of gold—the last substantial booty that the legions would win for Roman sloth.

With these spoils the Emperor distributed 650 denarii ($260) to all such citizens as applied for the gift—probably some 300,000; and enough remained to remedy the unemployment of demobilization with the greatest program of public works, governmental aid, and architectural adornment that Italy had seen since Augustus. Trajan improved the older aqueducts and built a new one which is still in operation. At Ostia he constructed a spacious harbor connected by canals with the Tiber and the harbor of Claudius, and decorated it with warehouses that were models of beauty as well as of use. His engineers repaired old roads, carried a new one across the Pontine marshes, and laid the Via Traiana from Beneventum to Brundisium. They reopened the Claudian tunnel that had drained the Fucine Lake, dredged harbors at Centumcellae and Ancona, gave Ravenna an aqueduct, and Verona an amphitheater. Trajan supplied the funds for new roads, bridges, and buildings throughout the Empire. But he discouraged the architectural rivalry of the cities and urged them to spend their surplus on improving the condition and environment of the poor. He was always ready to help any city that had suffered from earthquake, fire, or storm. He tried to promote agriculture in Italy by requiring senators to invest a third of their capital in Italian land; and when he saw that this was extending the latifundia, he encouraged small proprietors by advancing them state funds at low interest for the purchase and improvement of their lands and homes.[9] To raise the birth rate he enlarged the *alimenta*, or feeding fund: the state made mortgage loans at five per cent (half the usual rate) to Italian peasants, and allowed local charity boards to distribute the interest to poor parents at sixteen sesterces ($1.60) monthly for each boy raised by them, and twelve for each girl. The sums seem small, but contemporary testimony indicates that from sixteen to twenty sesterces sufficed for a month's care of a child on a first-century Italian farm.[10] With a similar hope Trajan allowed the children of Rome to receive the corn dole in addition to that given to their parents. The system of *alimenta* was enlarged by Hadrian and the Antonines, was extended to several parts of the Empire, and was supplemented by private philanthropy; so the younger Pliny gave 30,000 sesterces a year as *alimenta* to the children of Comum, and Caelia Macrina left a million to like purpose for the children of Tarracina in Spain.

Trajan, like Augustus, favored Italy over the provinces, and Rome over Italy. He used to the full the architectural genius of Apollodorus, a Damascene Greek who had designed the new roads and aqueduct, and the Danube bridge. The Emperor now commissioned him to clear away large blocks of houses, cut 130 feet from the base of the Quirinal hill, lay out in this and the adjoining space a new forum equal in area to all preceding forums combined, and surround it with buildings of a majesty fit for a world capital that had reached the height of its power and opulence. The *Forum Traianum* was entered through the Triumphal Arch of Trajan. The interior, 370 by 354 feet, was paved with smooth stone and surrounded by a high wall and portico; east and west walls were indented with hemicycle *exedrae* formed of Doric columns. In the center rose the Basilica Ulpia, named after Trajan's clan and intended as an office building for commerce and finance; its exterior was adorned with fifty monolithic columns, its floor was of marble, its immense nave was enclosed by granite colonnades, its roof of massive beams was covered with bronze. Near the northern end of the new forum two libraries were built, one for Latin works, the other for Greek. Between them rose the column, behind them the temple, of Trajan. When the forum was complete it was accounted one of the architectural wonders of the world.

The column, still standing, was first of all an achievement in transportation. It was cut from eighteen cubes of marble, each weighing some fifty tons; the blocks were brought by ship from the island of Paros, were transferred to barges at Ostia, were drawn against the current up the river, and were moved on rollers up the bank and through the streets to their site. The cubes were recut into thirty-two blocks. Eight formed the pedestal; three sides of this were decorated with sculptures; the fourth opened into a spiral stairway of 185 marble steps. The shaft, twelve feet in diameter at the bottom, and ninety-seven feet high, was composed of twenty-one blocks and was topped by a statue of Trajan holding a globe of the world. Before being raised into position the blocks were carved with reliefs picturing the campaigns in Dacia. These reliefs are the culmination of Flavian realism and of ancient historical sculpture. They do not aim at the calm beauty or idealized types of Greek sculpture; they seek rather to convey a vivid impression of living individuals in the actual scenes and turmoil of war; they are Balzac and Zola after Corneille and Racine. In the 2000 figures of these 124 spiral panels we follow the conquest of Dacia step by step: the Roman cohorts issuing from their stations in full armor; the crossing of the Danube on a pontoon bridge; the pitching of a Roman camp in the enemy's land; the confused conflict of spears, arrows, sickles, and stones; a Dacian village set to the torch, with women and children begging Trajan for mercy; Dacian women torturing Roman prisoners; soldiers displaying before the Emperor the heads of slain enemies; surgeons treating the wounded; the Dacian princes drinking one after another the cup of poison; the head of Decebalus brought as a trophy to Trajan; the long file of captive men, women, and children snatched from their homes into foreign settlement or Roman slavery—this and more the dark column tells in the most masterly narrative relief in sculptural history. These artists and their employers were not chauvinists; they showed Trajan's acts of clemency, but also they revealed the heroic aspects of a nation's struggle for freedom; and the finest figure in the scroll is the Dacian king. It is a strange document, too crowded for full effectiveness; some figures so crude that one wonders if a Dacian warrior carved them; superposition primitively substituted for perspective; and the whole observable, like Pheidias' frieze, only by some skylark scorner of the ground. But it was an interesting deviation from a classic style whose placidity had never expressed the overwhelming energy of the Roman character. Its "method of continuity" [11]—making each scene melt into the next—carried on the suggestions of Titus' arch and prepared for medieval reliefs. Despite its defects the spiral story was imitated again and again, from the column of Aurelius in Rome, and that of Arcadius in Constantinople, to the Napoleonic shaft in the Place Vendôme in Paris.

Trajan completed his building program by finishing in the grand manner the baths begun by Domitian. Meanwhile six years of peace had wearied him; administration was a task that did not awaken his reserve energies as war did; he did not feel alive in a palace. Why not take up Caesar's plans where Antony had failed, settle the Parthian question once and for all, establish a more strategic frontier in the East, and capture control of the trade routes across Armenia and Parthia to Central Asia, the Persian Gulf, and India?

After careful preparation he set out again with his legions (113). A year later he had taken Armenia; yet another year and he had marched down through Mesopotamia, captured Ctesiphon, and reached the Indian Ocean— the first and last Roman general to stand before that sea. The population at home learned geography by following his victories; the Senate was amused to be informed, almost weekly, of another nation conquered or hastily submitting: the Bosporus, Colchis, Asiatic Iberia, Asiatic Albania, Osrhoene, Messenia, Media, Assyria, Arabia Petrea, at last even Parthia. Parthia, Armenia, Assyria, and Mesopotamia were constituted provinces, and the new Alexander had the glory of naming and crowning a client king over the ancient enemies of Rome. Standing on the shores of the Red Sea, Trajan mourned that he was too old to repeat the Macedonian's advance to the Indus. He contented himself with building a Red Sea fleet to control the passage and commerce to India; left garrisons at all strategic points, and turned back reluctantly toward Rome.

Like Antony he had gone too fast and too far and had neglected to consolidate his victories and his lines. On reaching Antioch he was informed that the Parthian king Osroes, whom he had deposed, had gathered another army and had reconquered central Mesopotamia; that rebellion had broken out in all the new provinces; that the Jews of Mesopotamia, Egypt, and Cyrene were in revolt; and that disaffection was flaring up in Libya, Mauretania, and Britain. The old warrior wished to take the field again, but his flesh refused. He had worn himself out by living as actively in the hot East as in the West; dropsy set in, and a paralytic stroke left the great will helpless in a broken frame. Sadly he commissioned Lucius Quietus to put down the uprisings in Mesopotamia, sent Marcius Turba to suppress the Jews in Africa, and left his nephew Hadrian in command of the main Roman army in Syria. He had himself carried down to the Cilician coast, hoping to sail thence to Rome, where the Senate was preparing for him the greatest triumph since Augustus. He died at Selinus on the way (117), aged sixty-four, after a reign of nineteen years. His ashes were taken to the capital, and were buried under the great column that he had chosen as his tomb.

III. HADRIAN

1. The Ruler

Probably we shall never know whether the most brilliant of the Roman emperors won his throne by amorous connivance or by Trajan's conviction of his worth. "His appointment," says Dio Cassius, "was due to the fact that when Trajan died without an heir, his widow Plotina, who was in love with Hadrian, conspired to secure him the succession." [12] Spartianus repeats the story.[13] Plotina and Hadrian denied the rumor, which nevertheless persisted to the end of his reign. He settled the matter by distributing a generous donative among the troops.

Publius Aelius Hadrianus traced his cognomen and family to the town of Adria, on the Adriatic coast; thence, said his autobiography, his ancestors had migrated to Spain. The same Spanish town, Italica, that had seen the birth of Trajan in 52 saw that of his nephew Hadrian in 76. When the boy's father died (86) he was placed under the guardianship of Trajan and Caelius Attianus. The latter tutored him and instilled in him so warm a fondness for Greek literature that the youth was nicknamed Graeculus. He studied also singing, music, medicine, mathematics, painting, and sculpture, and later dabbled in half a dozen arts. Trajan called him to Rome (91) and gave him his niece in marriage (100). Vivia Sabina, as preserved in portrait busts that may have idealized her, was a woman of distinguished and conscious beauty, in whom Hadrian found no lasting happiness. Possibly he loved dogs and horses too keenly, and spent too much time hunting with them, and building tombs for them when they died. Perhaps he was unfaithful, or seemed so. In any case, she bore him no children, and though she accompanied him on many of his travels, they lived in lifelong estrangement. He showed her every favor and courtesy, and gave her every kindness but affection. When Suetonius, one of his secretaries, spoke disrespectfully of her he dismissed him.

Hadrian's first decision as emperor was to revise the imperialistic policy of his uncle. He had counseled Trajan against the Parthian expedition as too great an expenditure of men and means so soon after the Dacian Wars, and as promising, at best, gains difficult to hold; and Trajan's generals, eager for glory, had never pardoned his opposition. Now he withdrew the legions from Armenia, Assyria, Mesopotamia, and Parthia, made Armenia a client kingdom instead of a province, and accepted the Euphrates as the eastern boundary of the Empire; he played Augustus to Trajan's Caesar, and consolidated with peaceful administration as much as he could of the unprecedented realm that reckless arms had won. The generals who had led Trajan's forces—Palma, Celsus, Quietus, Nigrinus—thought this policy cowardly and unwise; to cease to attack, they felt, was merely to defend, and merely to defend was to begin to die. While Hadrian was with his legions on the Danube the Senate announced that the four generals had been detected in a conspiracy to overthrow the government and had been executed by the Senate's orders. Rome was shocked to find that the men had received no trial; and though Hadrian, returning hurriedly to Rome, protested that he had had nothing to do with the matter, no one believed him. He vowed to put no senator to death except at the Senate's bidding, distributed a gift of money among the people, amused them with abundant games, canceled tax arrears to the amount of 900,000,000 sesterces, publicly burned the tax records in a fiscal auto-da-fé, and for twenty years governed with wisdom, justice, and peace. But his unpopularity remained complete.

His ancient biographer describes him as tall and elegant, with hair curled, and "a full beard to hide the natural blemishes of his face";[14] thenceforth all Rome wore beards. He was strongly built and kept himself in vigor by frequent exercise, above all by hunting; on several occasions he killed a lion with his own hands.[15] So many elements were mingled in him that description is baffled. We are told that he was "stern and cheerful, humorous and grave, sensual and cautious, hard and liberal, severe and merciful, deceptively simple, and always in all things various." [16] He had a quick, impartial, skeptical and penetrating mind, but he respected tradition as the connective tissue of generations. He read and admired the Stoic Epictetus, but he sought pleasure with shamelessness and taste. He was irreligious and superstitious, laughed at oracles, played with magic and astrology, encouraged the national faith, and sedulously performed the duties of *pontifex maximus*. He was courteous and obstinate, sometimes cruel, usually kind; perhaps his contradictions were merely adaptations to circumstance. He visited the sick, helped the unfortunate, extended existing charities to orphans and widows, and was a generous patron to artists, writers, and philosophers. He was a good singer, dancer, and harpist, a competent painter, a middling sculptor. He wrote several volumes—a grammar, an autobiography, poems decent and indecent,[17] in Latin and Greek. He preferred Greek to Latin literature, and old Cato's simple Latin to Cicero's smooth eloquence; under his example many authors now affected an archaic style. He organized the state-paid professors into a university, paid them well, and built for them a magnificent Athenaeum to rival the Museum of Alexandria. It delighted him to gather scholars and thinkers about him, to puzzle them with questions, and laugh at their contradictions and disputes. Favorinus of Gaul was the wisest of this philosophic court; when his friends rallied him for yielding to Hadrian in argument, he answered that any man with thirty legions behind him must be right.[18]

Along with these multiple intellectual interests went an unerring sense for the practical. Following Domitian's lead, Hadrian reduced his freedmen to subordinate functions, chose businessmen of tried ability to administer the government, and formed from them and senators and jurists a *concilium* to meet in regular sessions for the consideration of policies. He appointed an *advocatus fisci,* or Attorney for the Treasury, to detect corruption or deceit in the payment of taxes, with the illuminating result that while taxes remained as before, revenues were decidedly increased. He himself kept watch on each department and, like Napoleon, astonished its heads by detailed knowledge of their field. "His memory was vast," says Spartianus; "he wrote, dictated, listened, and conversed with his friends, all at the same time" [19]—though the frequency of this tale invites suspicion. Under his care, and with the help of an extended civil service, the Empire was probably better governed than ever before or afterward. The price of this zealous order was a swelling bureaucracy, and a "mania of regulation" that moved the principate still closer to absolute monarchy. Hadrian observed all the forms of co-operation with the Senate; nevertheless, his appointees and their executive orders encroached more and more upon the functions of what had once seemed "an assembly of kings." He was too close to his problems to foresee that his efficient but proliferating bureaucracy might become in time an unbearable burden upon the taxpayers. On the contrary, he believed that within the framework of law and ordinance which his government had established every person in the Empire would find career open to talent and any man could rise rapidly from class to class.

His clear and logical mind resented the chaos of accumulated, obscure, and contradictory laws. He commissioned Julianus to co-ordinate the enactments of past praetors into a Perpetual Edict, and encouraged further codifications that paved the way for Justinian. He acted as a supreme court both in Rome and on his journeys, and earned the reputation of a fair and learned judge, always as lenient as the reign of law would permit. He issued innumerable decrees, usually in favor of the weak against the strong, the slave against the master, the small farmer against the large estate, the tenant against the landlord, the consumer against the deceptions of retailers and the multiplication of middlemen.[20] He rejected accusations for *maiestas,* refused bequests from parents, or persons unknown to him, and ordered a tolerant application of the laws against Christians.[21] By his own example on state lands he encouraged the practice of emphyteusis ("implanting"), by which owners rented rough acres to tenants to be planted with orchards and remain rent-free till fruit grew. He was not a radical reformer; he was only a superlative administrator seeking, within the limits and inequalities of human nature, the greatest good of the whole. He preserved old forms, but he quietly poured new content into them according to the needs of the time. Once, when his passion for administration flagged, he refused audience to a petitioning woman with the plea, "I haven't time." "Don't be emperor, then," she cried. He granted her a hearing.[22]

FIG. 17—*The Portland Vase*
British Museum

FIG. 18—*Frieze from the Altar of Peace*
Uffizi Gallery, Florence

FIG. 19—*Frieze of Tellus from the Altar of Peace*
Uffizi Gallery, Florence

FIG. 20—*Portrait of a Young Girl*
Museo delle Terme, Rome

FIG. 21—"*Clytie*"
British Museum

FIG. 22—"*Spring*"
A Mural from Stabiae

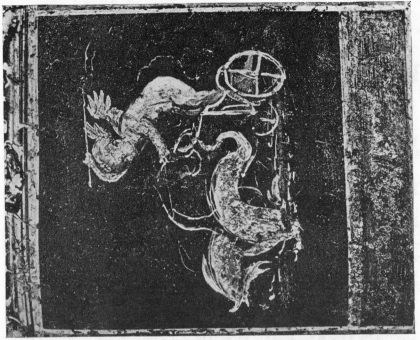

Fig. 23—*Details of Mural*
From the House of the Vettii, Pompeii

FIG. 24—*Mural from the Villa Farnesina*
Museo delle Terme, Rome

FIG. 25—*"Sappho"*
Museo Nazionale, Naples

FIG. 26—*The Colosseum*

FIG. 27—*Interior of the Colosseum*

FIG. 28—*Roman Soldier and Dacian*
Relief from the Column of Trajan

FIG. 29—*Antinoüs*
Museo Nazionale, Naples

FIG. 30—*Altar Found at Ostia*
Museo delle Terme, Rome

FIG. 31—*Arch of Trajan at Benevento*

FIG. 32—*Ruins of Timgad*

2. The Wanderer

Unlike his predecessors Hadrian was as interested in the Empire as in the capital. Following the wholesome precedent of Augustus, he decided to visit every province, examining its conditions and needs and alleviating them with the expedition and resources available to an emperor. He was curious, too, about the ways and arts, dress and beliefs, of the diverse peoples in his realm; he wished to see the famous places of Greek history, to steep himself in that Hellenic culture which was the background and adornment of his mind. "He loved," says Fronto, "not only to govern, but to perambulate, the world." [23] In 121 he set out from Rome, accompanied not by the pomp and trappings of royalty, but by experts, architects, builders, engineers, and artists. He went first to Gaul and "came to the relief of all the communities with various acts of generosity." [24] He passed into Germany and astonished everyone by the thoroughness with which he inspected the defenses of the Empire against its future destroyers. He reorganized, extended and improved the *limes* between the Rhine and the Danube. A man of peace, he knew the arts of war and was resolved that his pacific temper should neither weaken his armies nor misguide his enemies. He issued severe regulations to maintain military discipline and obeyed these rules while visiting the camps; there he lived the life of the soldiers, eating their fare, never using a vehicle, walking with full equipment twenty miles on a march, and showing such endurance that no one could have guessed that he was at heart a scholar and a philosopher. At the same time he rewarded excellence, raised the legal and economic status of the legionaries, gave them better weapons and ample supplies, and relaxed the discipline of their free hours, merely insisting that their amusements should not unfit them for their tasks. The Roman army was never in better condition than in his reign.

He now traveled down the Rhine to its mouth and sailed across to Britain (122). We are not informed of his activities there, except that he ordered a wall built from the Solway Firth to the mouth of the Tyne "to divide the barbarians from the Romans." Returning to Gaul he passed leisurely through Avignon, Nîmes, and other towns of the *provincia*, and settled down for the winter at Tarragona in northern Spain. While he was strolling alone in the gardens of his host a slave rushed upon him with drawn sword and tried to kill him. Hadrian overpowered him and quietly handed him over to the servants, who found that he was insane.

In the spring of 123 he led some legions against the Moors of northwest Africa, who had been raiding the Roman towns of Mauretania. Having defeated them and driven them back into their hills, he took ship for Ephesus.

After wintering there he visited the cities of Asia Minor, listening to petitions and complaints, punishing malfeasance, rewarding competence, and providing money, designs, and workmen for municipal temples, baths, and theaters. Cyzicus, Nicaea, and Nicomedia had suffered a severe earthquake; Hadrian had the damage made good by imperial funds, and built at Cyzicus a temple that was at once ranked among the seven wonders of the world.[25] He pushed eastward along the Euxine to Trapezus, ordered the governor of Cappadocia—the historian Arrian—to examine and report to him the condition of all the ports on the Black Sea, moved southwest through Paphlagonia, and spent a winter at Pergamum. In the fall of 125 he sailed to Rhodes and thence to Athens. He passed a happy winter there and then turned homeward. Still curious at fifty, he stopped in Sicily, and climbed Mt. Etna to see the sunrise from a perch 11,000 feet above the sea.

It is worthy of note that he could leave his capital for five years and trust to his subordinates to carry on; like a good manager, he had organized and trained an almost automatic government. He stayed in Rome something more than a year. But the lust for travel was in his blood, and so much of the world remained to rebuild! In 128 he set out again, this time to Utica, Carthage, and the flourishing new cities of northern Africa. Returning to Rome in the fall, he left soon afterward and spent another winter in Athens (128-29). He was made archon, presided happily at games and festivals, and enjoyed being called Liberator, Helios, Zeus, and Savior of the World. He mingled with philosophers and artists, imitating the graces, without the follies, of Nero and Antony. Distressed by the free chaos of Athens' laws, he commissioned a corps of jurists to codify them. Always skeptically interested in religion, he had himself initiated into the Eleusinian mysteries. Finding Athens beset with unemployment, and resolved to restore the city to the splendor of Periclean days, he summoned architects, engineers, and skilled artisans, and began a building program more extensive than his public works in Rome. In a square enclosed by an extensive colonnade his workmen raised a library with marble walls, 120 columns, a gilded roof, and spacious rooms sparkling with alabaster, paintings, and statuary. They built a gymnasium, an aqueduct, a temple to Hera, and another to Zeus Panhellenicos—god "of all the Greeks." The most ambitious of these architectural undertakings was the completion (131) of the Olympieum—that lordly temple to Zeus the Olympian which Peisistratus had begun six centuries before and Antiochus Epiphanes had failed to finish. When Hadrian left Athens it was a cleaner, more prosperous, and more beautiful city than ever before in its history.[26]

In the spring of 129 he sailed to Ephesus and traveled again in Asia Minor, spawning buildings and cities as he went. He sallied into Cappadocia and reviewed the garrisons there. At Antioch he provided funds for an aqueduct, a temple, a theater, and public baths. In the fall he visited Palmyra and Arabia, and in 130 he journeyed to Jerusalem. The Holy City was still in ruins, almost as Titus had left it sixty years before; a handful of destitute Jews lived in lairs and hovels amid the rocks. Hadrian's heart was touched by the desolation; and his imagination was moved by the empty site. He had hoped, by his restoration of Greece and the Hellenistic East, to raise higher than before the barriers between Greco-Roman civilization and the Oriental world; now he dreamed of transforming Zion itself into a pagan citadel. He ordered that Jerusalem should be rebuilt as a Roman colony and renamed Aelia Capitolina in memory of Hadrian's gens and Jupiter's Capitol in Rome. It was an astonishing error of psychology and statesmanship in one of the wisest statesmen in history.

He passed on to Alexandria (130), smiled tolerantly at its disputatious populace, enriched the Museum, rebuilt Pompey's tomb, and then, surpassing Caesar, abandoned himself to a leisurely sail up the Nile with his wife Sabina and his beloved Antinoüs. He had come upon the young Greek some years before in Bithynia; he had been stirred by the youth's rounded beauty, soft eyes, and curly head; he had made him his favored page and had formed for him a tender and passionate attachment. Sabina made no protest that has come down to us, but the gossip of the cities assumed that the boy played Ganymede to the new Zeus; possibly, however, the childless Emperor loved him as a heaven-sent son. Now, at the height of Hadrian's happiness, Antinoüs, still but eighteen, died—apparently by drowning in the Nile. The monarch of the world "wept like a woman," says Spartianus; he ordered a temple to be raised on the shore, buried the lad there, and offered him to the world as a god. Around the shrine he built a city, Antinoöpolis, destined to be a Byzantine capital. While Hadrian returned sadly to Rome, legend began to remold the story: the Emperor, it said, had learned by magic divination that his greatest plans would succeed only if that which he loved most should die; Antinoüs had heard of the prophecy and had gone voluntarily to his death. Perhaps the legend formed soon enough to embitter Hadrian's declining years.

Back in Rome (131), he could feel that he had made the Empire better than he had found it. Never before, not even under Augustus, had it been so prosperous, and never has the Mediterranean world reached that fullness of life again; never has it again been the home of so advanced a civilization so widely spread and so deeply shared. And no man had so beneficently ruled it as Hadrian. Augustus had thought of the provinces as a lucrative appendage to Italy, to be husbanded for Italy's sake; now for the first time the ideas of Caesar and Claudius reached fulfillment, and Rome became not a tax collector for Italy, but the responsible administrator of a realm in which all parts alike received the care of the government, and in which the Greek spirit ruled the East and the mind as openly as the Roman spirit ruled the state and the West. Hadrian had seen it all and had made it one. He had promised that he "would manage the commonwealth as conscious that it was the people's property, not his own";[27] and he had kept his promise.

3. The Builder

Only one thing remained—to make Rome, too, more beautiful than before. The artist in Hadrian was ever competing with the governor; he rebuilt the Pantheon while reorganizing Roman law. No other man ever built so plentifully, no other ruler so directly. The structures erected for him were sometimes designed by him, and were always subject to his expert inspection as they progressed. He had a hundred edifices repaired or restored and inscribed his name on none of them. Rome in all quarters benefited from his rare union of wisdom with power. *Si jeunesse savait et vieillesse pouvait* was in him a riddle solved.

His most famous reconstruction was the Pantheon—the best-preserved building of the ancient world. The rectangular temple reared by Agrippa had been destroyed by fire; apparently only the frontal Corinthian portico remained. North of this remnant Hadrian had his architects and engineers raise a circular temple, in the most indigenous of Roman styles. His Hellenic tastes inclined him to prefer Greek to Roman forms in the architecture of his capital. The new temple did not form with the portico a harmonious whole; but the interior—a circle 132 feet in diameter, with no impeding supports—gave a sense of space and freedom equaled only by the Gothic cathedrals. The walls were twenty feet thick, of brick externally faced in the lower section with marble, in the rest with stucco relieved by pilasters. The ceiling of the portico was of bronze plates so thick that when they were removed by Pope Urban VIII they sufficed to cast 110 cannon and to form the baldachin over the high altar in St. Peter's.[29] The massive bronze doors were originally covered with gold. Seven niches were cut into the lower section of the windowless interior wall and were adorned with lofty marble columns and entablatures; once these niches served as alcoves for statuary, now they are modest chapels in a magnificent church. A higher section of the wall was plated with panels of costly stone, separated by pillars of porphyry. The coffered dome, rising inward from the top of the walls, was the supreme triumph of Roman engineering. It was erected by pouring concrete into ribbed sections and letting the whole congeal into one solid mass. Its monolithic character did away with lateral thrust, but to make security doubly sure the architect built buttresses into the walls. At the top of the dome an opening (the *oculus*, or "eye"), twenty-six feet in diameter, gave the interior its sole and sufficient illumination. From this majestic dome, the largest in history, an architectural lineage descends through Byzantine and Roman-esque variations to the dome of St. Peter's, and to that of the Capitol in Washington.

Probably Hadrian himself designed the double-apsed temple to Venus and Roma which rose opposite the Colosseum, for legend tells how he sent his plans for it to Apollodorus and had the old architect put to death for returning a scornful comment.[30] The temple was notable in several particu-lars: it was the largest in Rome; it had two cellas, one for each of its gods, who sat back to back on incommunicative thrones; and its vaulted roof of gold-plated bronze tiles was among the most brilliant sights of the city. For himself the Emperor built a yet ampler home—the villa whose remains still draw visitors to the pleasant suburb known to him as Tibur, to us as Tivoli. There, in an estate seven miles in circumference, rose a palace with every variety of room, and gardens so crowded with famous works of art that every major museum in Europe has enriched itself from the ruins. The designer showed here the usual Roman indifference to symmetry; he added building to building as need or fancy prompted, and made no greater at-tempt at harmony than we find in the architectural chaos of the Forum; perhaps the Romans, like the Japanese, were tired of symmetry and pleased with the surprises of irregularity. Besides porticoes, libraries, temples, a theater, a music hall, and a hippodrome, the profuse architect added small replicas of Plato's Academy, Aristotle's Lyceum, and Zeno's Stoa—as if the Emperor, amid all this vain wealth, would make some amends to philosophy.

The villa was finished in the last years of Hadrian's life. We do not know that he found happiness there. The revolt of the Jews in 135 embittered him; he put it down without mercy and fretted that he could not end his reign without war. In that same year, still only fifty-nine, he was stricken with a painful and wasting illness—akin to tuberculosis and dropsy—which slowly crushed his body, his spirit, and his mind. His temper became sharper, his manner querulous; he suspected his oldest friends of conspiring to kill and replace him; at last—perhaps in an illucid interval, and how justly we cannot say—he ordered that several of them should be put to death.

To end the war of succession that was forming in his court, he adopted as heir his friend Lucius Verus. When, soon after, Lucius died, Hadrian called to his bedside at Tibur a man with an unblemished reputation for integrity and wisdom, Titus Aurelius Antoninus, and adopted him as his son and suc-cessor. Looking far ahead, he advised Antoninus to adopt in turn, and educate for government, two youths then growing up at the court: Marcus Annius Verus, then seventeen, and Lucius Aelius Verus, then eleven, respectively the nephew of Antoninus and the son of Lucius Verus. The title of *Caesar*, heretofore borne by the emperors and their agnatic descendants, was conferred by Hadrian upon Antoninus; and thereafter, while the emperors kept for themselves the title of *Augustus*, they granted the name *Caesar* to each heir presumptive to the throne.

Hadrian's sickness and sufferings had now increased; blood often gushed from his nostrils; and in his distress he began to long for death. He had already prepared his own tomb beyond the Tiber—that huge mausoleum whose gloomy remains are today the Castel Sant' Angelo, still reached by the Pons Aelius that Hadrian built. He was impressed by the example of the Stoic philosopher Euphrates, then in Rome, who, weary with illness and old age, asked Hadrian's permission to kill himself and, receiving it, drank hemlock.[31] The Emperor begged for poison or a sword, but no attendant would accommodate him. He bade a Danubian slave stab him, but the slave fled; he commanded his physician to poison him, but the physician committed suicide.[32] He found a dagger and was about to kill himself when it was taken from him. He mourned that he, who had the power to put anyone to death, was not himself permitted to die. Dismissing his doctors, he withdrew to Baiae and deliberately fed on foods and drinks that would hasten his end. At last, exhausted and maddened with pain, he died (138), after sixty-two years of life and twenty-one of rule. He left behind him a little poem that expressed like Dante the sadness of recalling in grief the days of our happiness:

> Animula vagula, blandula,   Soul of mine, pretty one, flitting one,
> Hospes comesque corporis,   Guest and partner of my clay,
> Quae nunc abibis in loca,   Whither wilt thou hie away—
> Pallidula, rigida, nudula,   Pallid one, rigid one, naked one,
> Nec ut soles dabis iocos?   Never to play again, never to play?[33]

IV. ANTONINUS PIUS

Of Antoninus there is no history, for he had almost no faults and committed no crimes. His ancestors had come from Nîmes two generations before, and his family was one of the wealthiest in Rome. Reaching the throne at fifty-one, he gave the Empire the most equitable, and not the least efficient, government it would ever have.

He was the most fortunate man that ever wore a crown. We are told that he was tall and handsome, healthy and serene, gentle and resolute, modest and omnipotent, eloquent and a despiser of rhetoric, popular and immune to flattery. If we are.to believe his adopted son Marcus we should have to reject him as "that faultless monster whom the world ne'er knew." The Senate called him *Pius* as a model of the milder Roman virtues, and *Optimus Princeps* as the best of princes. He had no enemies and hundreds of friends. But he was not unacquainted with grief. His elder daughter died as he was setting out as proconsul to Asia; his younger daughter proved a dubious wife to Aurelius; and scandal accused his own wife of being as faithless as she was beautiful. Antoninus bore these rumors silently; and after Faustina's death he established in her name and honor a fund for the support and education of girls and raised to her memory one of the loveliest temples in the Forum. He did not marry again, lest he mar the happiness and inheritance of his children, but contented himself with a concubine.

He was not a man of intellect in the narrower sense of that term. He had no learning and looked with an aristocrat's indulgence upon men of letters, philosophy, or art; nevertheless, he helped such men richly and invited them often to his home. He preferred religion to philosophy, worshiped the old gods with apparent sincerity, and gave his adopted sons an example of piety that Marcus never forgot. "Do everything as a disciple of Antoninus," Marcus bade himself; "remember his constancy in every reasonable act, his evenness in all things, his piety, and the serenity of his countenance, and his disregard of empty fame . . . with how little he was satisfied; how laborious and patient, how religious without superstition." [34] Yet he was tolerant of non-Roman creeds, moderated Hadrian's measures against the Jews, and continued his predecessor's lenience toward the Christians. He was no killjoy; he loved a jest and made many a good one; he played, fished, and hunted with his friends, and from his behavior none could have guessed that he was emperor. He preferred the quiet of his villa at Lanuvium to the luxury of his official palace and nearly always spent the evenings in the intimacy of his family. When he inherited the throne he put aside all thought of that careless ease to which he had looked forward as the consolation of old age. Perceiving that his wife anticipated increased splendor he reproved her: "Do you not understand that we have now lost what we had before?" [35] He knew that he had succeeded to the cares of the world.

He began his reign by pouring his immense personal fortune into the imperial treasury. He canceled arrears of taxes, made gifts of money to the citizens, paid for many festival games, and relieved scarcities of wine, oil, and wheat by buying these and distributing them free. He carried on, but with moderation, the building program of Hadrian in Italy and the provinces. Yet he managed the national finances so ably that at his death the combined treasuries of the state had 2,700,000,000 sesterces. He gave a public accounting of all his receipts and expenditures. He behaved toward the Senate as merely one of it and never took important measures without consulting its leaders. He devoted himself to the chores of administration as well as to problems of policy; "he cared for all men and all things as his own." [36] He continued Hadrian's liberalization of the law, equalized the penalties of adultery for men and women, deprived ruthless masters of their slaves, restricted the torture of slaves in trials, and decreed severe punishment for any owner who killed a slave. He encouraged education with state funds, provided for the education of poor children, and extended to recognized teachers and philosophers many privileges of the Senatorial class.

He ruled the provinces as well as he could without traveling. In all his long reign he was never absent for a day from Rome or its environs. He was content to appoint to provincial governorships men of tried competence and honor. He was anxious to keep the Empire safe without war; "he was continually quoting the saying of Scipio, that he would rather save a single citizen than slay a thousand foes." [37] He had to wage some minor wars in order to suppress revolts in Dacia, Achaea, and Egypt, but he left these tasks to subordinates and was satisfied with Hadrian's cautious frontiers. Some tribes in Germany interpreted his mildness as weakness and perhaps were encouraged by it to prepare those invasions which rocked the Empire after his death; this is the one flaw in his statesmanship. For the rest the provinces were happy under him and accepted the Empire as the only alternative to chaos and strife. They showered him with petitions, which he almost always granted; and they could rely upon him to repair the ravages of any public calamity. Provincial authors—Strabo, Philo, Plutarch, Appian, Epictetus, Aelius Aristides—sang the praises of the *pax Romana;* and Appian assures us that he had seen at Rome the envoys of foreign states vainly asking admission for their countries to the boons of the Roman yoke.[38] Never had monarchy left men so free, or so respected the rights of its subjects.[39] "The world's ideal seemed to have been attained. Wisdom reigned, and for twenty-three years the world was governed by a father." [40]

It only remained for Antoninus to crown a good life with a peaceful death. In his seventy-fourth year he fell sick of a stomach disturbance and was seized with a high fever. He called Marcus Aurelius to his bedside and committed to him the care of the state. He instructed his servants to transfer to Marcus' room the golden statue of Fortuna that had for many years stood in the bedchamber of the Prince. To the officer of the day he gave as watchword *aequanimitas;* soon afterward he turned as if to sleep, and died (161). All classes and cities vied with one another in honoring his memory.

V. THE PHILOSOPHER AS EMPEROR

Antoninus, said Renan, "would have been without competition for the reputation of being the best of sovereigns, had he not designated Marcus Aurelius as his heir." [41] "If," said Gibbon, "a man were called upon to fix the period in the history of the world during which the condition of the human race was most happy and prosperous, he would without hesitation name that which elapsed from the accession of Nerva to the death of Aurelius. Their united reigns are possibly the only period of history in which the happiness of a great people was the sole object of government." [42]

Marcus Annius Verus was born in Rome in 121. The Annii had come a century before from Succubo, near Cordova; there, it seems, their honesty had won them the cognomen *Verus*, "true." Three months after the boy's birth his father died, and he was taken into the home of his rich grandfather, then consul. Hadrian was a frequent visitor there; he took a fancy to the boy and saw in him the stuff of kings. Seldom has any lad had so propitious a youth, or so keenly appreciated his good fortune. "To the gods," he wrote fifty years later, "I am indebted for having good grandparents, good parents, a good sister, good teachers, good kinsmen and friends, nearly everything good";[43] time struck a balance by giving him a questionable wife and a worthless son. His *Meditations* lists the virtues these people had, and the lessons he received from them in modesty, patience, manliness, abstemiousness, piety, benevolence, and "a simplicity of life far removed from the habits of the rich"[44]—though wealth surrounded him on every side.

Never was a boy so persistently educated. He was attached in boyhood to the service of temples and priests; he committed to memory every word of the ancient and unintelligible liturgy; and though philosophy later shook his faith, it never diminished his sedulous performance of the old exacting ritual. Marcus liked games and sports, even bird snaring and hunting, and some efforts were made to train his body as well as his mind and character. But seventeen tutors in childhood are a heavy handicap. Four grammarians, four rhetors, one jurist, and eight philosophers divided his soul among them. The most famous of these teachers was M. Cornelius Fronto, who taught him rhetoric. Though Marcus loved him, lavished upon him all the kindnesses of an affectionate and royal pupil, and exchanged with him letters of intimate charm, the youth turned his back upon oratory as a vain and dishonest art, and abandoned himself to philosophy.

He thanks his instructors for sparing him logic and astrology, thanks Diognetus the Stoic for freeing him from superstition, Junius Rusticus for acquainting him with Epictetus, and Sextus of Chaeronea for teaching him to live in conformity with nature. He is grateful to his brother Severus for telling him about Brutus, Cato of Utica, Thrasea, and Helvidius; "from him I received the idea of a state in which there is the same law for all, a polity of equal rights and freedom of speech, and the idea of a kingly government that most of all respects the freedom of the governed";[45] here the Stoic ideal of monarchy takes possession of the throne. He thanks Maximus for teaching him "self-government, and not to be led aside by anything; cheerfulness in all circumstances, and a just admixture of gentleness and dignity, and to do appointed tasks without complaining." [46] It is clear that the leading philosophers of the time were priests without religion rather than metaphysicians without life. Marcus took them so seriously that for a time he almost ruined a naturally weak constitution with ascetic devotions. At the age of twelve he took on the rude cloak of a philosopher, slept on a little straw strewn over the floor, and long resisted the entreaties of his mother to use a couch. He was a Stoic before he became a man. He offers thanks "that I preserved the flower of my youth; that I took not upon me to be a man before my time, but rather put it off longer than I needed . . . that I never had to do with Benedicta . . . and afterwards, when I fell into some fits of love, I was soon cured." [47]

Two influences diverted him from professional philosophy and sanctity. One was the succession of minor political offices to which he was appointed; the realism of an administrator was crossed with the idealism of a meditative youth. The other was his close association with Antoninus Pius. He did not fret at Antoninus' longevity, but continued his life of stoic simplicity, philosophical study, and official duties, while living in the palace and serving his protracted apprenticeship; and the example of his adoptive father's devotion and honesty in government became a powerful influence in his development. The name by which we know him, Aurelius, was the clan name of Antoninus, which both Marcus and Lucius, on their adoption, had taken as their own. Lucius became a gay man of the world, a graceful adept in the pleasures of life. When, in 146, Pius desired a colleague to share the government with him, he named Marcus only and left to Lucius the empire of love. On the death of Antoninus, Marcus became sole emperor; but remembering Hadrian's wish, he at once made Lucius Verus his full colleague and gave him his daughter Lucilla in marriage. At the outset of his reign, as at the end, the philosopher erred through kindness. The division of rule was a bad precedent, which, in the heirs of Diocletian and Constantine, would divide and weaken the realm.

Marcus asked the Senate to vote Pius divine honors, completed with perfect taste the temple that Pius had raised to his wife, and rededicated it to Antoninus and Faustina both.* He paid the Senate every courtesy and rejoiced to see that many of his philosopher friends had found their way into its membership. All Italy and all the provinces acclaimed him as Plato's dream come true: the philosopher was king. But he had no thought of attempting a Utopia. Like Antoninus he was a conservative; radicals do not grow up in palaces. He was a philosopher-king in the Stoic rather than the Platonic sense. "Never hope," he admonished himself, "to realize Plato's Republic. Let it be sufficient that you have in some degree ameliorated mankind, and do not think such improvement a matter of small importance. Who can change the opinions of men? And without a change of sentiments what can you make but reluctant slaves and hypocrites?" He had discovered that not all men wished to be saints; and he sadly reconciled himself to a world of corruption and wickedness. "The immortal gods consent for countless ages to endure without anger, and even to surround with blessings, so many and such evil men; but thou, who hast so short a time to live, art thou already weary?" [48] He decided to rely on example rather than law. He made himself in fact a public servant; he carried all the burdens of administration and judgment, even that part which Lucius had agreed to take but was neglecting; he allowed himself no luxury, treated all men with simple fellowship, and wore himself out by being easy of access. He was not a great statesman: he spent too much of the public funds in cash gifts to the people and the army, gave each member of the Praetorian Guard 20,000 sesterces, increased the number of those who could apply for free corn, provided frequent and costly games, and remitted large sums in unpaid taxes and tribute; it was generosity with many precedents, but unwise at a time when rebellion or war visibly threatened, or was breaking out, in several provinces and on far-spread frontiers.

Marcus continued sedulously that reform of law which Hadrian had begun. He increased the number of court days and reduced the length of trials. He himself often sat as judge, inflexible against grave offenses, but usually merciful. He devised legal protection for wards against dishonest guardians, for debtors against creditors, for provinces against governors. He connived at the rejuvenation of the forbidden *collegia*, legalized those associations which were chiefly burial societies, made them legal persons eligible for bequests, and established a fund for the interment of poor citizens. He gave the *alimenta* the widest extension in their history. After the death of his wife he created an endowment for the aid of young women; a pretty bas-relief shows us such girls crowding around the younger Faustina,

---

* Its ten Corinthian monolithic columns are among the finest remains in the Forum. The portico is intact, and the cella, though shorn of its marble facing, has survived as the Church of San Lorenzo in Miranda.

who pours wheat into their laps. He abolished mixed bathing, forbade extravagant remuneration to actors and gladiators, restricted according to their wealth the expenditures of the cities on games, required the use of foiled weapons in gladiatorial contests, and did all that sanguinary custom would allow to banish death from the arena. The people loved him but not his laws. When he enlisted gladiators in his army for the Marcomannic Wars the populace cried out in good-humored anger: "He is taking our amusement from us; he wants to force us to be philosophers." [49] Rome was preparing, but not quite ready, to be puritan.

It was his misfortune that his fame as a philosopher, and the long peace under Hadrian and Antoninus, encouraged rebels within and barbarians without. In 162 revolt broke out in Britain, the Chatti invaded Roman Germany, and the Parthian king Vologases III declared war upon Rome. Marcus chose able generals to put down the revolt in the north, but he delegated to Lucius Verus the major task of fighting Parthia. Lucius got no farther than Antioch. For there lived Panthea, so beautiful and accomplished that Lucian thought all the perfections of all sculptural masterpieces had come together in her; to which were added a voice of intoxicating melody, fingers skilled on the lyre, and a mind enriched with literature and philosophy. Lucius saw her, and, like Gilgamesh, forgot when he was born. He abandoned himself to pleasure, to hunting, at last to debauchery, while the Parthians rode into terror-stricken Syria. Marcus made no comment on Lucius but sent to Avidius Cassius, second in charge in Lucius' army, a plan of campaign whose military excellence helped the general's own ability not only to drive the Parthians back across Mesopotamia, but to plant the Roman standards once more in Seleucia and Ctesiphon. This time the two cities were burned to the ground lest they serve again as bases for Parthian campaigns. Lucius returned from Antioch to Rome and was awarded a triumph, which he magnanimously insisted that Marcus should share.

Lucius brought with him the invisible victor of the war—pestilence. It had appeared first among the troops of Avidius in captured Seleucia; it spread so rapidly that he withdrew his army into Mesopotamia, while the Parthians rejoiced at the vengeance of their gods. The retreating legions carried the plague with them to Syria; Lucius took some of these soldiers to Rome to march in his triumph; they infected every city through which they passed and every region of the Empire to which they were later assigned. The ancient historians tell us more of its ravages than of its nature; their descriptions suggest exanthematous typhus or possibly bubonic plague.[52] Galen thought it similar to the disease that had wasted the Athenians under Pericles: in both cases black pustules almost covered the body, the victim was racked with a hoarse cough, and his "breath stank." [53] Rapidly it swept through

Asia Minor, Egypt, Greece, Italy, and Gaul; within a year (166-67) it had killed more men than had been lost in the war. In Rome 2000 died of it in one day, including many of the aristocracy;[54] corpses were carried out of the city in heaps. Marcus, helpless before this intangible enemy, did all he could to mitigate the evil; but the medical science of his day could offer him no guidance, and the epidemic ran its course until it had established an immunity or had killed all its carriers. The effects were endless. Many localities were so despoiled of population that they reverted to jungle or desert; food production fell, transport was disorganized, floods destroyed great quantities of grain, and famine succeeded plague. The happy *hilaritas* that had marked the beginning of Marcus' reign vanished; men yielded to a bewildered pessimism, flocked to soothsayers and oracles, clouded the altars with incense and sacrifice, and sought consolation where alone it was offered them—in the new religions of personal immortality and heavenly peace.

Amid these domestic difficulties news came (167) that the tribes along the Danube—Chatti, Quadi, Marcomanni, Iazyges—had crossed the river, overwhelmed a Roman garrison of 20,000 men, and were pouring unhindered into Dacia, Raetia, Pannonia, Noricum; that some had made their way over the Alps, had defeated every army sent against them, were besieging Aquileia (near Venice), were threatening Verona, and were laying waste the rich fields of northern Italy. Never before had the German tribes moved with such unity or so closely threatened Rome. Marcus acted with surprising decisiveness. He put away the pleasures of philosophy and determined to take the field in what he foresaw would be the most momentous of Roman wars since Hannibal. He shocked Italy by enrolling policemen, gladiators, slaves, brigands, and barbarous mercenaries into legions depleted by war and pestilence. Even the gods were conscripted to his purpose: he bade the priests of alien faiths to offer sacrifice for Rome according to their various rites; and he himself burned such hecatombs at the altars that a wit circulated a message sent him by white oxen, begging him not to be too victorious; "if thou shouldst conquer, we are lost." [55] To raise war funds without levying special taxes he auctioned off in the Forum the wardrobes, art objects, and jewels of the imperial palaces. He took careful measures of defense—fortified the border towns from Gaul to the Aegean, blocked the passes into Italy, and bribed German and Scythian tribes to attack the invaders in the rear. With energy and courage all the more admirable in a man who hated war, he trained his army into disciplined strength, led them through a hard campaign mapped out with strategic skill, drove the besiegers from Aquileia, and routed them even to the Danube, until nearly all were captured or dead.

He understood that this action had not ended the German danger; but thinking the situation safe for a time, he returned with his colleague to Rome. On the way Lucius died of an apoplectic stroke, and gossip, which, like politics, has no bowels of mercy, whispered that Marcus had poisoned him. From January to September, 169, the Emperor rested at home from efforts that had strained his frail body close to the breaking point. He suffered from a stomach ailment that often left him too weak to talk; he controlled it by eating sparingly, one light meal a day. Those who knew his condition and his diet marveled at his labors in the palace and the field and could only say that he made up in resolution what he lacked in strength. On several occasions he called in the most famous physician of the age, Galen of Pergamum, and praised him for the unpretentious remedies he prescribed.[56]

Perhaps a succession of domestic disappointments co-operated with political and military crises to aggravate his illness and make him old at forty-eight. His wife Faustina, whose pretty face has come down to us in many a sculptured portrait, may not have relished sharing bed and board with incarnate philosophy; she was a lively creature, who longed for a gayer life than his sober nature could give her. The talk of the town assumed her infidelity; the mimes satirized him as a cuckold and even named his rivals.[57] Like Antoninus with Faustina the mother, Marcus said nothing; instead, he promoted the supposed paramours to high office, gave Faustina every sign of tenderness and respect, had her deified when she died (175), and thanked the gods, in his *Meditations*, for "so obedient and affectionate a wife." [58] No evidence exists upon which to condemn her.[59] Of the four children that she gave him—and whom he loved with a passion still warm in his letters to Fronto—one girl died in childhood; the surviving daughter was saddened by Lucius' life, and widowed by his death. Twin sons came in 161; one died at birth, the other was Commodus. Scandalmongers called him a gladiator's gift to Faustina,[60] and he strove all his life long to confirm the tale. But he was a handsome and vigorous lad; Marcus forgivably doted on him, presented him to the legions in a manner symbolic of naming a successor, and engaged the best teachers in Rome to fit him for rule. The youth preferred to model cups, dance, sing, hunt, and fence; he developed an understandable aversion to books, scholars, and philosophers, but enjoyed the company of gladiators and athletes. Soon he surpassed all comrades in lying, cruelty, and coarse speech. Marcus was too good to be great enough to discipline him or renounce him; he kept on hoping that education and responsibility would sober him and make him grow into a king. The lonely Emperor, emaciated, beard untended, eyes weary with anxiety and sleeplessness, turned back from his wife and son to the tasks of government and war.

The assaults of the central European tribes against the frontier had stopped only for a breathing spell; in this struggle to destroy an Empire and make barbarism free, peace was but an armistice. In 169 the Chatti invaded the Roman regions of the upper Rhine. In 170 the Chauci attacked Belgica, and another force besieged Sarmizegetusa; the Costoboii crossed the Balkans into Greece and plundered the Temple of the Mysteries at Eleusis, fourteen miles from Athens; the Mauri or Moors invaded Spain from Africa, and a new tribe, the Longobardi or Lombards, made its first appearance on the Rhine. Despite a hundred defeats, the fertile barbarians were growing stronger, the barren Romans weaker. Marcus saw that it was now a war to the death, that one side must destroy the other or go under. Only a man schooled in the Roman and Stoic sense of duty could have transformed himself so completely from a mystic philosopher into a competent and successful general. The philosopher remained, hidden under the imperator's armor; in the very tumult of this Second Marcomannic War (169-75), in his camp facing the Quadi on the river Granna,* Marcus wrote that little book of *Meditations* by which the world chiefly remembers him. This glimpse of a frail and fallible saint, pondering the problems of morality and destiny while leading a great army in a conflict on which the fate of the Empire turned, is one of the most intimate pictures that time has preserved of its great men. Pursuing the Sarmatians by day he could write with sympathy of them at night: "A spider, when it has caught a fly, thinks it has done a great deed. So does one who has run down a hare . . . or who has captured Sarmatians. . . . Are they not all alike robbers?" [61]

Nevertheless, he fought the Sarmatians, the Marcomanni, the Quadi, the Iazyges, through six hard years, defeated them, and marched his legions as far north as Bohemia. It was apparently his plan to use the Hercynian and Carpathian ranges as a new frontier; if he had succeeded, Roman civilization might have made Germany, like Gaul, Latin in speech and classical in heritage. But at the height of his successes he was shocked to learn that Avidius Cassius, after putting down a revolt in Egypt, had declared himself emperor. Marcus surprised the barbarians with a hasty peace, merely annexing a ten-mile strip on the north bank of the Danube and leaving strong garrisons on the southern side. He summoned his soldiers, told them that he would gladly yield his place to Avidius if Rome wished it, promised to pardon the rebel, and marched into Asia to encounter him. Meanwhile a centurion killed Cassius, and the rebellion collapsed. Marcus passed through Asia Minor and Syria to Alexandria, mourning like Caesar that he had been cheated of a chance for clemency. At Smyrna, Alexandria, and Athens he

---

* Probably the Gran, a tributary of the Danube.

walked the streets without a guard, wore the mantle of a philosopher, attended the lectures of the leading teachers, and joined with them in discussion, speaking Greek. During his stay at Athens he endowed professorships in each of the great schools of doctrine—Platonic, Aristotelian, Stoic, and Epicurean.

In the fall of 176, after almost seven years of war, Aurelius reached Rome and was accorded a triumph as the savior of the Empire. The Emperor associated Commodus with himself in the victory and now made him, a lad of fifteen, his colleague on the throne. For the first time in nearly a century the principle of adoption was put aside and the hereditary principate was resumed. Marcus knew what perils he was inviting for the Empire; he chose them as a lesser evil than the civil war that Commodus and his friends would wage if he were denied the throne. We must not judge him with hindsight; neither did Rome anticipate the consequences of this love. There the plague had burned itself out, and men were beginning to be happy again. The capital had suffered little from the wars, which had been financed with remarkable economy and little extra taxation; while battle raged on the frontiers trade flourished within, and money jingled everywhere. It was the height of Rome's tide and of its Emperor's popularity; all the world acclaimed him as at once a soldier, a sage, and a saint.

But his triumph did not deceive him; he knew that the problem of Germany had not been solved. Convinced that further invasions could be prevented only by an active policy of extending the frontier to the mountains of Bohemia, he set forth with Commodus, in 178, on the Third Marcomannic War. Crossing the Danube, he again defeated the Quadi after a long and arduous campaign. No resistance remained, and he was about to annex the lands of the Quadi, the Marcomanni, and the Sarmatians (roughly Bohemia and Danubian Galicia) as new provinces, when sickness struck him down in his camp at Vindobona (Vienna). Feeling death's hand, he called Commodus to his side and warned him to carry through the policy which was now so near fulfillment, and realize the dream of Augustus by pushing the boundary of the Empire to the Elbe.* Then he refused all further food or drink. On the sixth day he rose with his last strength and presented Commodus to the army as the new emperor. Returning to his couch he covered his head with the sheet and soon afterward died. When his body reached Rome the people had already begun to worship him as a god who for a while had consented to live on the earth.

---

* "We must not merely acknowledge the resolution and tenacity of the ruler," says the impartial Mommsen, "but must also admit that he did what right policy enjoined." 62

CHAPTER XX

Life and Thought in the Second Century

A.D. 96-192

I. TACITUS

THE policies of Nerva and Trajan liberated the suppressed mind of Rome, and gave to the literature of their reigns a note of fierce resentment against a despotism that had gone but might come again. Pliny's *Panegyric* voiced it in welcoming the first of three great Spaniards to the throne; Juvenal seldom sang any other note; and Tacitus, the most brilliant of historians, became a *delator temporis acti*, an accuser of times past, and excoriated a century with his pen.

We do not know the date or place of Tacitus' birth, nor even his given name. Probably he was the son of Cornelius Tacitus, procurator of imperial revenue in Belgic Gaul; through this man's advancement the family was raised from the equestrian class into the new aristocracy.[1] Our first definite fact about the historian is his own statement: "Agricola, during his consulship (78) . . . agreed to a marriage between myself and his daughter, who might certainly have looked for a prouder connection."[2] He had received the usual education, and had learned to the full those oratorical arts which enliven his style, that skill in pros and cons which marks the speeches in his histories. The younger Pliny often heard him in the courts, admired his "stately eloquence," and acclaimed him as the greatest orator in Rome.[3] In 88 Tacitus was praetor; thereafter he sat in the Senate and confesses with shame[4] that he failed to speak out against tyranny, and joined in the Senatorial condemnation of Domitian's Senatorial victims. Nerva made him consul (97), and Trajan appointed him proconsul of Asia. He was evidently a man of affairs and practical experience; his books were the afterthought of a full life, the product of a leisurely old age, and of a mature and profound mind.

One theme unites them—hatred of autocracy. His *Dialogue on Orators* (if it is his) attributes the decline of eloquence to the suppression of liberty. His *Agricola*—the most perfect of those brief monographs to which the ancients confined biography—proudly recounts the achievements of his father-in-law as general and governor, and then bitterly records Domitian's dismissal and neglect of him. The little essay *On the Situation and Origin of the Germans* contrasts the virile virtues of a free people with the degeneration and cowardice of Romans under the despots. When Tacitus praises the Germans for considering infanticide an infamy, and giving no advantage to childlessness, he is not describing Germans but denouncing Romans. The philosophical purpose destroys the objectivity of the study, but allows a remarkable breadth of view in a Roman official praising the German power of resisting Rome.[5] *

The success of these essays induced Tacitus to illustrate the evils of tyranny by indicting the record of the despots in ruthless detail. He began with what was freshest in his memory and in the testimony of his older friends—the period from Galba to the death of Domitian; and when these *Historiae* were acclaimed by a grateful aristocracy as the best historical writing since Livy, he continued his story *a fronte* by describing, in the *Annales*, the reigns of Tiberius, Caligula, Claudius, and Nero. Of the fourteen (some say thirty) "books" of the *Histories* four and a half remain, all devoted to the years 69 and 70; of the *Annals* twelve books survive from an original sixteen or eighteen. Even in this mutilated form they are the most powerful works in extant Roman prose; we may vaguely imagine the grandeur and impress of the whole. Tacitus had hoped to chronicle also the reigns of Augustus, Nerva, and Trajan, mitigating the gloom of his published works with some commemoration of constructive statesmanship. But the years were not given him; and posterity has judged him, as he judged the past, from a somber aspect alone.

"The chief duty of the historian," he thought, "is to judge the actions of men, so that the good may meet with the reward due to virtue, and pernicious citizens may be deterred by the condemnation that awaits evil deeds at the tribunal of posterity." [6] It is a strange conception, which turns history into a Last Judgment and the historian into God. So conceived, history is a sermon—ethics teaching by horrible examples—and falls, as Tacitus assumed, under the rubric of rhetoric. It is easy for indignation to be eloquent but hard for it to be fair; no moralist should write history. Tacitus remembered tyranny too intimately to view tyrants calmly; he saw nothing in Augustus but the destruction of freedom and supposed that all Roman genius had ended with Actium.[7] He seems never to have thought of tempering his indictments by recording the excellent administration and growing prosperity of the provinces under the imperial monsters; no one would

---

* It was probably written in 98, before Trajan's campaign against the Dacians.

suspect, from reading him, that Rome was an empire as well as a city. Perhaps the lost "books" viewed the provincial world; those that remain make Tacitus a deceptive guide, who never lies but never reveals the truth. He often cites, and sometimes critically examines, his sources—histories, speeches, letters, *Acta Diurna, Acta Senatus*, and the traditions of old families; but for the most part he has heard only the stories of the persecuted nobility, and never imagines that the executions of senators and the assassinations of emperors were incidents in a long contest between vicious, cruel, and competent monarchs and a decadent, cruel, and incompetent aristocracy. He is fascinated by striking personalities and events rather than by forces, causes, ideas, and processes; he draws the most brilliant and unjust character portraits in history, but he has no conception of economic influences upon political events, no interest in the life and industry of the people, the stream of trade, the conditions of science, the status of woman, the vicissitudes of belief, the achievements of poetry, philosophy, or art. In Tacitus Seneca, Lucan, and Petronius die, but they do not write; the emperors kill, but they do not build. Perhaps the great historian was limited by his audience; probably he read parts of his work—following the custom of the time—to the aristocratic friends whom Pliny describes as crowding to his receptions; he would have told us that these men and women knew Roman life, industry, literature, and art, and did not have to be reminded of them; what they wanted to hear, again and again, was the exciting story of the evil emperors, the heroic deeds of stoic senators, the long war of their noble class against tyrannical power. We cannot condemn Tacitus for not succeeding in what he did not attempt; we can only regret the narrowness of his great purpose and the limitations of his powerful mind.

He does not pretend to be a philosopher. He praises Agricola's mother for dissuading her son, who "had acquired a keener zest for philosophy than became a Roman and a senator." [8] His imagination and art, like Shakespeare's, were too creatively active to let him ponder quietly the meaning and possibilities of life. He is as rich in illuminating comment as in unverified scandal; but it is difficult to find in him any consistent view of God, or man, or the state. He is cautiously ambiguous on matters of faith, and suggests [9] that it is wiser to accept one's native religion than to try to replace it with knowledge. He rejects most astrologers, auguries, portents, and miracles, but accepts some; he is too much of a gentleman to deny the possibility of what so many have affirmed. In general, events seem to prove "the indifference of the gods to good and bad alike," [10] and the existence of some unknown, perhaps capricious, force that drives men and states fatally onward to their destiny [11]—*urgentibus imperii fatis*.[12] He hopes that Agricola has departed to a happy life, but he obviously doubts it, and contents himself with the last delusion of great minds—an immortality of fame.[13]

Nor does any utopian aspiration console him. "Most plans of reformation are at first embraced with ardor; but soon the novelty ceases, and the scheme ends in nothing." [14] Matters are temporarily better in his time, he reluctantly admits; but not even the genius of Trajan will prevent renewed deterioration.[15] Rome is rotten literally to the core, in the hearts of men, of a populace whose disorder of soul has made an anarchy of freedom,[16] a rabble "fond of innovation and change, and ever ready to shift to the side of the strongest." [17] He mourns the "malignity of the human mind," [18] and scorns like Juvenal the alien stocks in Rome. After blackening the Empire he does not dream of returning to the Republic, but hopes that the adoptive emperors will reconcile the Principate with liberty.[19] In the end, he thinks, character is more important than government; what makes a people great is not its laws but its men.

If, despite our surprise in finding a sermon and a drama where we had looked for history, we must nevertheless rank Tacitus among the greatest of historians, it is because the power of his art redeems the limitations of his view. Above all he sees intensely, sometimes deeply, always vividly. The portraits he draws stand out more clearly, stride the stage more livingly, than any others in historical literature. Here, too, however, there are blemishes. Tacitus composes speeches for his varied personages, all in his own fashion and majestic prose; he describes Galba as a simpleton and makes him talk like a sage.[20] And he does not rise to the difficult art of making his characters develop in time. Tiberius is the same at the beginning of his reign as at the end; and if he appeared to be human at the outset it was, Tacitus thinks, pure dissimulation.

First and last in Tacitus is the splendor of his style. No other author has ever said so much so compactly. This does not mean that he is brief; on the contrary, he is desultory and diffuse and takes 400 pages of the *Histories* to chronicle two years of time. Sometimes the condensation is extreme to the point of affectation or obscurity; every second word then requires a sentence to translate it; verbs and conjunctions are disdained as crutches for crippled minds. This is the culmination of Sallust's concise rapidity, of Seneca's pithy epigrams, of the balanced clauses taught in the schools of rhetoric. In a long work such a style, unrelieved with passages of a more even tenor, becomes an exhausting excitement to the reader, who nevertheless returns to it with mounting fascination. This martial brusqueness, more economical of words than of men, this scorn of the props of syntax, this passion of feeling and clearness of visualization, this tang of a novel vocabulary and murderous pungency of unhackneyed phrase, give to the writing of Tacitus a swiftness, color, and force which no ancient author has equaled. The color is dark, the mood is gloomy, the sarcasm stings, and the tone of the whole is that of a Dante without tenderness; but the cumulative effect is overwhelming. Along this black river of relentless exposure we are carried, despite our reservations and objections, by a narrative at once dignified and turbulent, stately and impetuous. Character after character rises upon the stage and is struck down; scene after scene rushes on until all Rome seems ruined and all the participants are dead. We can hardly believe, when we emerge from this chamber of horrors, that this period of despotism, cowardice, and immorality flowed into the zenith of monarchy under Hadrian and the Antonines, and the quiet decency of Pliny's friends.

Tacitus was wrong in scorning philosophy—that is, perspective; all his faults were due to lack of it. If he could have disciplined his pen to the service of an open mind, he would have placed his name first on the list of those who have labored to give form and permanence to the memory and heritage of mankind.

II. JUVENAL

Unfortunately, Juvenal corroborates Tacitus. What the one writes in mordant prose about princes and senators, the other chants in bitter verse about women and men.

Decimus Iunius Iuvenalis, son of a rich freedman, was born at Aquinum in Latium (59). He came to Rome for his education and practiced law there "for his own amusement." His satires betray the shock of rural tastes struck by the loose turmoil of city life; yet he appears to have been friends with Martial, whose epigrams show no prejudice in favor of morality. Shortly before Domitian's death, says an uncertain tradition, Juvenal composed, and circulated among his friends, a satire on the influence of dancers at court; the pantomime actor Paris, we are told, took offense and had him exiled to Egypt. We cannot say if the story is true, nor when Juvenal returned; in any case he published nothing till after Domitian's death. The first volume of his sixteen satires appeared in 101, the remainder in four volumes at intervals in a long life. Probably they were unforgiving memories of Domitian's time; but the indignation that makes them so vivid and unreliable suggests that a few years of "the good emperors" had not cured the evils he denounced. Perhaps, again, he chose the satire as a characteristic Roman form, found models and some material in Lucilius, Horace, and Persius, and molded his fulminations and his wrath on the rhetorical principles that he had learned in the schools. We shall never know how darkly

our picture of imperial Rome has been colored by the pleasures of denunciation.

Juvenal takes everything for his subject, and has no trouble in finding
in everything some aspect that can bear condemning. "We are arrived at
the zenith of vice," he thinks, "and posterity will never be able to surpass
us"; [21] so far, so true. The root of the evil is the unscrupulous pursuit of
wealth. He scorns the plebs that once ruled armies and unmade kings but
can now be bought with *panem et circenses,* bread and circuses; [23] this is
one of a hundred phrases to which Juvenal's vitality gave lasting life. He
resents the influx of Oriental faces, dress, ways, smells, and gods; protests
against the clannishness of the Jew, and likes least of all the "greedy little
Greek" (*Graeculus esuriens*)—the degenerate descendant of a people once
great but never honest. He loathes the informers who, like Pliny's Regulus,
get rich by reporting "unpatriotic" remarks; the legacy hunters who flutter
around childless old men; the proconsul living in lifelong luxury on the
profits of a term in the provinces; the clever lawyers who spin out lawsuits like an excreted web. He is disgusted above all by sexual excesses and
perversions: by the roué who on marrying finds that his lechery has left him
impotent; by the dandies whose manners, perfumes, and desires make them
indistinguishable from women; and by the women who think that emancipation means that they should be indistinguishable from men.

His sixth and bitterest satire is devoted to the gentler sex. Postumus is
thinking of marriage; don't do it, Juvenal warns him; and then the poet por-
trays the women of Rome as selfish, shrewish, superstitious, extravagant,
quarrelsome, haughty, vain, litigious, adulterous, equaling every marriage
with a divorce, substituting lapdogs for children,[24] going in for athletics,
worse yet for literature, quoting Virgil at you, spouting rhetoric and philosophy [25]—"oh, may the gods save us from a learned wife!" [26] He concludes
that there is hardly a woman in the city worth marrying. A good wife is a
rare bird (*rara avis*), stranger than a white crow. He marvels that Postumus
should think of marriage when "there are so many halters to be had, so many
high and dizzy windows are accessible, and the Aemilian Bridge is close at
hand." No; stay single. And get out of this nerve-wearying bedlam called
Rome and live in some quiet Italian town where you will meet honest men
and be safe from criminals, poets, collapsing tenements, and Greeks.[27] Put
ambition behind you; the goal is not worth the striving, so long is labor and so
brief is fame. Live simply, cultivate your garden, desire only so much as
hunger and thirst, cold and heat demand;[28] learn pity, be kind to children,
keep a sane mind in a healthy body (*mens sana in corpore sano* [29]). But only
a fool will pray for a long life.

We can understand such a mood; it is pleasant to contemplate the imperfections of our neighbors and the despicable inferiority of the world as compared with our dreams. Our enjoyment in this case is sharpened by Juvenal's street-corner vocabulary, his easy-moving colloquial hexameters, his grim humor, and his lusty style. But we must not take him literally. He was angry; he had not made his way in Rome as rapidly as he had hoped; it was sweet revenge to lay about him with the bludgeon of a hatred that never feigned to be fair. His moral standard was high and sound, though tinged with conservative prejudices and delusions about the virtuous past; by those standards, used without mercy or modesty, we could indict any generation anywhere. Seneca knew how old a pastime this is. "Our forefathers," he wrote, "complained, we complain, and our descendants will complain, that morals are corrupt, that wickedness holds sway, that men are sinking deeper and deeper into sinfulness, that the condition of mankind is going from bad to worse." [30] Around the immoral hub of any society is a spreading wheel of wholesome life, in which the threads of tradition, the moral imperatives of religion, the economic compulsions of the family, the instinctive love and care of children, the watchfulness of women and policemen, suffice to keep us publicly decent and moderately sane. Juvenal is the greatest of Roman satirists, as Tacitus is the greatest of Roman historians; but we should err as much in taking their picture as accurate as we should were we to accept without scrutiny the pleasant and civilized scene that rises before us as we read the letters of Pliny.

III. A ROMAN GENTLEMAN

When he was born at Como in 61 he was named Publius Caecilius Secundus. His father owned a farm and villa near the lake and held high office in the town. Orphaned early, Publius was adopted and educated first by Virginius Rufus, governor of Upper Germany, and then by his uncle Caius Plinius Secundus, author of the *Natural History*. This busy scholar made the boy his son and heir and died soon afterward. According to custom, the youth took his adoptive father's name, causing confusion for 2000 years. At Rome he studied under Quintilian, who formed his taste on Cicero and must receive some of the credit for the Ciceronian fluency of Pliny's style. At 18 he was admitted to the bar; at 39 he was chosen to deliver an address of welcome to Trajan. In the same year he was made consul; in 103, augur; in 105, "Curator of the Bed and Banks of the Tiber and the City Sewers." He took no fees or gifts for his legal services, but he was a rich man and could afford to be magnanimous. He had properties in

Etruria, at Beneventum, Como, and Laurentum, and offered 3,000,000 sesterces for another.[31]

Like many aristocrats of his time, he amused himself by writing: at first a Greek tragedy, then some poems, lighthearted and occasionally obscene. Reproved by some, he confessed his fault impenitently, and proposed again "to indulge in mirth, wit, and gaiety, and enter into the spirit of the most wanton muse." [32] Hearing his letters praised, he composed some for publication and issued them at intervals from 97 to 109. Intended not only for the public but for the pleasure of the circles he described, they avoided the darker aspects of Roman life and passed by as too serious for his purpose the larger problems of philosophy and statesmanship. Their worth is in their graceful intimacy, and in the rosy light they shed upon Roman character and patrician ways.

Pliny reveals himself with half the candor and all the felicity of Montaigne. He has an author's inevitable vanity, but so openly that it hardly offends. "Nothing, I confess, so strongly affects me as the desire of a lasting name." [33] He speaks appreciatively of others as well as of himself, adding that "one may be sure a man has many virtues if he admires those of others"; [34] in any case it is a relief, coming from Juvenal and Tacitus, to hear an author speak well of his fellow men. He was as generous in act as in words, ever ready with favors, loans, or gifts, from finding a husband for a friend's niece to enriching his native town. Finding that Quintilian could not give his daughter a dowry befitting the high station of the man she was marrying, he sent her 50,000 sesterces, excusing the smallness of the gift.[35] He gave an old schoolmate 300,000 to make him eligible for the equestrian class; when the daughter of a friend inherited a legacy of debts he paid them off; and at some risk he lent a considerable sum to a philosopher banished by Domitian. To Como he gave a temple, a secondary school, an institute for poor children, a municipal bath, and 11,000,000 sesterces for a public library.

What is especially pleasing in him is his love for his home, or his homes. He does not denounce Rome, but he is happier in Como or Laurentum, near the lake or the sea. There his chief enterprises are reading and doing nothing. He loves his gardens, and the mountain scenery behind them; he did not have to wait for Rousseau to make him enjoy nature. He speaks with the greatest tenderness of his third wife, Calpurnia, her sweet temper and pure mind, her fond delight in his success and his books. She read them all (he believed) and learned many of his pages by heart; she set his poems to music and sang them, and had a private corps of couriers to keep her informed of every development when he was trying an important case. She was but one of many good women in his circle. He tells of the modesty, patience, and courage of a fourteen-year-old girl who, just betrothed, learned that she had an incurable illness, and cheerfully awaited death;[36] of Pompeius Saturninus' wife, whose letters to her husband were lyrics of affection and fine Latin;[37] of Thrasea's daughter Fannia, who uncomplainingly bore exile for defending her husband Helvidius, nursed a relative through a dangerous illness, caught it, and died of it; "How complete," he exclaims, "is her virtue, her sanctity, her sobriety, her courage!" [38]

He had a hundred friends, some great, many good. He joined with Tacitus in prosecuting Marius Priscus for dishonesty and cruelty as proconsul in Africa; the two orators corrected each other's speeches and invested in mutual compliments; Tacitus lifted Pliny to heaven by reporting that the literary world was pairing them as the leading writers of the age.[39] He knew Martial, but from an aristocratic distance. He took Suetonius with him to Bithynia and helped him to get the "right of three children" without having any. His circle buzzed with literary and musical amateurs, with public recitals of poetry and speeches. "I do not believe," says the learned Boissier, "that in any other period has literature been so greatly loved." [40] Homer and Virgil were being studied on the banks of the Danube and the Rhine, and the Thames was trembling with rhetoric.[41] It was, in its upper half, an elegant and amiable society, rich in loving marriages, parental affection, humane masters, sincere friendships, and fine courtesies. "I accept your invitation to supper," reads one letter, "but I must make this agreement beforehand, that you dismiss me soon, and treat me frugally. Let our table abound only in philosophical conversation, and let us enjoy even that within limits." [42]

Most of the men whom Pliny describes were members of the new aristocracy stemming from the provinces; they were not idlers, for nearly every one of them held public office and shared in the admirable administration of the Empire under Trajan. Pliny himself was sent as propraetor to Bithynia to restore the solvency of some cities there. His letters include some inquiries addressed to the Prince, and Trajan's pithy replies; they show Pliny accomplishing his mission with ability and honor, though with a strangely detailed dependence upon the Emperor's advice. His final letter begs forgiveness for sending his sick wife home by the coaches of the imperial post. Thereafter Pliny disappears from literature and history, leaving behind him a redeeming picture of a Roman gentleman, and of Italy in her happiest age.

IV. THE CULTURAL DECLINE

We should obscure these outstanding figures if we were to surround them with lesser lights. After them there were no giants in pagan Latin letters. Reason had made its great effort from Ennius to Tacitus and had spent itself. It is a shock to pass from the grandeur of the *Histories* and the *Annals* to the scandalous chronicle of Suetonius' *Lives of Illustrious Men* (110); history is here degenerating into biography, and biography into anecdote; portents and miracles and superstitions crowd the pages, and only the Elizabethan English of Philemon Holland's translation (1606) has raised the book to the level of literature. Less disturbing is the descent from Pliny to the letters of Fronto. Perhaps these were not meant for publication, and cannot be fairly compared with Pliny's; some were spoiled by a search for archaic phraseology, but many are touched by real affection of the teacher for his pupil. Aulus Gellius supported the archaizing movement in his *Attic Nights* (169)—the largest collection of worthless trifles in ancient literature; and Apuleius brought it to a climax in *The Golden Ass*. Apuleius and Fronto came from Africa, and the fad may have had partial source in the fact that written Latin there had departed less than in Rome from the language of the people and the Republic. Fronto rightly believed in strengthening literature with popular speech, as one freshens a plant by turning over the earth at its roots. But youth does not come twice to a man, a nation, a literature, or a language. Orientalization had set in and could not be stopped. The common Greek tongue of the Hellenistic East and Oriental Rome was becoming the language of literature as well as of life; Fronto's pupil chose it for his *Meditations*. Appian, an Alexandrian Greek living at Rome, chose Greek for his vivid *Histories* of Rome's wars (*ca.* 160); so did Claudius Aelian, a Roman by birth and blood; a half century later Dio Cassius, a Roman senator, would write his history of Rome in Greek. Leadership in literature was passing back from Rome to the Greek East; not to the Greek spirit, but to the Oriental soul using Hellenic speech. There would be giants again in Latin; but they would be Christian saints.

Roman art declined more slowly than Roman letters. Technical ability lingered on and produced good architecture, sculpture, painting, and mosaic. The head of Nerva, in the Vatican, carries on the vivid realism of Flavian portraits, and the Column of Trajan is an impressive relief despite much crudity. Hadrian labored to revive Hellenic classicism, but found no one to play Pheidias to his Pericles; the inspiration that had stirred Greece after Marathon, and Rome after Actium, was missing in an age of self-limitation, contentment, and peace. The busts of Hadrian lose character by their smooth Hellenistic lines; the heads of Plotina and Sabina are pretty; but the portraits of Antinoüs repel us by their sleek effeminate insipidity. Probably Hadrian's classical reaction was a mistake: it ended the forceful naturalism and individuation of Flavian and Trajanic sculpture, which had had indigenous roots in Italian tradition and character. Nothing reaches maturity except through the fulfillment of its own nature.

Under the Antonines Roman sculpture had its penultimate fling. Once at least it achieved perfection, in the figure of a young woman whose veiled head and modest robes are molded with a bewitching delicacy and firmness of line.[43] Almost as good is the portrait of Marcus' Faustina, aristocratically refined, and sensuous enough to accord with the innuendoes of history. Aurelius himself was carved or cast in a thousand forms, from the meditative and guileless yet eagerly sensitive youth of the Capitoline bust to the curly-headed professor in armor of that same collection. Every tourist knows the stately bronze of *Aurelius Imperator* on horseback, which, since Michelangelo restored it, has dominated the piazza of Rome's Capitol.

Relief remained to the end a favorite Roman art. The Etruscan and Hellenistic custom of carving mythological or historical scenes upon sarcophagi returned in Hadrian's time as the hope of immortality took more personal and even physical form, and burial replaced cremation. Eleven panels surviving from triumphal arches erected to commemorate the campaigns of Aurelius * show the naturalistic style in perfection: no one is idealized, every participant is individualized; Marcus, receiving without pride the submission of a fallen enemy, is an appealingly human figure; and the defeated are shown not as barbarians but as men worthy of their long struggle for freedom. In 174 the Senate and people of Rome raised that Column of Aurelius which still adorns the Piazza Colonna; inspired by Trajan's Column, it pictured the Marcomannic Wars with a sympathetic art that honored conquerors and conquered alike.

The spirit of the Emperor had helped to form the art and morals of his time. The games were less cruel, the laws more considerate of the weak; marriage was apparently more lasting and content. Immorality continued, openly in a minority, clandestinely in the majority, as at all times; but it had passed its peak with Nero and had ceased to be fashionable. Men as well as women were returning to the old religion or devoting themselves to new ones; and the philosophers approved. Rome was now teeming with them, invited, welcomed, or tolerated by Aurelius; they took full advantage of his generosity and his power, crowded his court, received appointments and emoluments, delivered countless lectures, and opened many schools. In their imperial pupil they gave the world the culmination and disintegration of ancient philosophy.

V. THE EMPEROR AS PHILOSOPHER

Six years before his death Marcus Aurelius sat down in his tent to formulate his thoughts on human life and destiny. We cannot be sure that the *Ta eis heauton*—"to himself"—was intended for the public eye; probably so, for even saints are vain, and the greatest man of action has moments of weakness in which he aspires to write a book. Marcus was not an expert author; most of the training that Fronto had given him in Latin was wasted now, since he wrote in Greek; besides, these "Golden Thoughts" were penned in the intervals of travel, battles, revolts, and many tribulations; we must forgive them for being disconnected and formless, often repetitious,

---

* Eight adorn the Arch of Constantine; three are in the Museo de' Conservatori.

sometimes dull. The book is precious only for its contents—its tenderness and candor, its half-conscious revelations of a pagan-Christian, ancient-medieval soul.

Like most thinkers of his time, Aurelius conceived philosophy not as a speculative description of infinity, but as a school of virtue and a way of life. He hardly bothers to make up his mind about God; sometimes he talks like an agnostic, acknowledging that he does not know; but having made that admission, he accepts the traditional faith with a simple piety. "Of what worth is it to me," he asks, "to live in a universe without gods or Providence?" [44] He speaks of deity now in the singular, now in the plural, with all the indifference of Genesis. He offers public prayer and sacrifice to the old divinities, but in his private thought he is a pantheist, deeply impressed with the order of the cosmos and the wisdom of God. He has a Hindu's sense of the interdependence of the world and man. He marvels at the growth of the child out of a little seed, the miraculous formation of organs, strength, mind, and aspiration out of a little food.[45] He believes that if we could understand we should find in the universe the same order and creative power as in man. "All things are implicated with one another, and the bond is holy. . . . There is a common reason in all intelligent beings; one god pervades all things, one substance, one law, one truth. . . . Can a clear order subsist in thee, and disorder in the All?" [46]

He admits the difficulty of reconciling evil, suffering, apparently unmerited misfortune, with a good Providence; but we cannot judge the place of any element or event in the scheme of things unless we see the whole; and who shall pretend to such total perspective? It is therefore insolent and ridiculous for us to judge the world; wisdom lies in recognizing our limitations, in seeking to be harmonious parts of the universal order, in trying to sense the Mind behind the body of the world, and co-operating with it willingly. To one who has reached this view "everything that happens happens justly"—i.e., as in the course of nature; [47] nothing that is according to nature can be evil; [48] everything natural is beautiful to him who understands.[49] All things are determined by the universal reason, the inherent logic of the whole; and every part must welcome cheerfully its modest role and fate. "Equanimity" (the watchword of the dying Antoninus) "is the voluntary acceptance of the things that are assigned to thee by the nature of the whole." [50]

> Everything harmonizes with me that harmonizes with thee, O universe. Nothing for me is too early or too late which is in due time for thee. Everything is fruit to me that thy seasons bring, O Nature. From thee are all things, in thee are all things, to thee all things return.[51]

Knowledge is of value only as a tool of the good life. "What, then, can direct a man? One thing only—philosophy" [52]—not as logic or learning, but as a persistent training in moral excellence. "Be thou erect, or be made erect." [53] God has given every man a guiding *daimon*, or inner spirit—his reason. Virtue is the life of reason.

> These are the principles of the rational soul. It traverses the whole universe, and surveys its form, and extends itself into the infinity of time, and embraces the cyclical renewal of all things, and comprehends that those who come after us will see nothing new, nor have those before us seen anything more; but in a manner he who is forty years old, if he has any understanding at all, has seen, by virtue of this uniformity, all things that have been or will be.[54]

Marcus thinks his premises compel him to puritanism. "Pleasure is neither good nor useful." [55] He renounces the flesh and all its works, and talks at times like some Anthony in the Thebaid:

> Observe how ephemeral and worthless human things are, and what was yesterday a little mucus, tomorrow will be a mummy or ashes. . . . The whole space of man's life is but little, and yet with what troubles it is filled . . . and with what a wretched body it must be passed! . . . Turn it inside out, and see what kind of thing it is.[56]

The mind must be a citadel free from bodily desires, passions, anger, or hate. It must be so absorbed in its work as hardly to notice the adversities of fortune or the barbs of enmity. "Every man is worth just so much as the things about which he busies himself." [57] He reluctantly concedes that there are bad men in this world. The way to deal with them is to remember that they, too, are men, the helpless victims of their own faults by the determinism of circumstance.[58] "If any man has done thee wrong, the harm is his own; it is thy duty to forgive him." [59] If the existence of evil men saddens you, think of the many fine persons you have met, and the many virtues that are mingled in imperfect characters.[60] Good or bad, all men are brothers, kinsmen in one God; even the ugliest barbarian is a citizen of the fatherland to which we all belong. "As Aurelius I have Rome for my country; as a man, the world." [61] Does this seem an impracticable philosophy? On the contrary, nothing is so invincible as a good disposition, if it be sincere.[62] A really good man is immune to misfortune, for whatever evil befalls him leaves him still his own soul.

> Will this [evil] that has happened prevent thee from being just, magnanimous, temperate, prudent . . . modest, free? . . . Suppose that men curse thee, kill thee, cut thee in pieces: what can these things do to prevent thy mind from remaining pure, wise, sober, and just?

If a man stand by a limpid, pure spring and curse it, the spring never ceases to send up clean water; if he cast dirt into it, or filth, it will speedily wash them out and be unpolluted again. . . . On every occasion that brings thee trouble, remember to apply this principle: that this is not a misfortune, but that to bear it nobly is good fortune. . . . Thou seest how few the things are to which if a man lays hold of, he is able to live a life that flows on quietly and is like the existence of the gods.[63]

Marcus' life, however, did not flow on quietly; he had to kill Germans while writing this Fifth Gospel, and in the end he faced death with no consolation in the son who would succeed him, and no hope of happiness beyond the grave. Soul and body alike return to their original elements.

For as the mutation and dissolution of bodies make room for other bodies doomed to die, so the souls that are removed into the air, after life's existence, are transmuted and diffused . . . into the seminal intelligence of the universe, and make room for new souls.[64] . . . Thou hast existed as a part; thou shalt disappear in that which produced thee. . . . This, too, nature wills. . . . Pass, then, through this little space of time conformably to nature, and end thy journeys in content, just as an olive falls when it is ripe, blessing the nature that produced it, and thanking the tree on which it grew.[65]

VI. COMMODUS

When the officer of the guard asked the dying Marcus for the watchword of the day he answered: "Go to the rising sun; my sun is setting." The rising sun was then nineteen, a robust and dashing youth without inhibitions, morals, or fear. One would have expected of him, rather than of Marcus the ailing saint, a policy of war to victory or death; instead, he offered the enemy immediate peace. They were to withdraw from the vicinity of the Danube, to surrender most of their arms, return all Roman prisoners and deserters, pay Rome an annual tribute of corn, and persuade 13,000 of their soldiers to enlist in the Roman legions.[66] All Rome condemned him except the people; his generals fumed at allowing the trapped prey to escape and fight again another day. During the reign of Commodus, however, no trouble came from the Danubian tribes.

The young prince, though no coward, had seen enough of war; he needed peace to enjoy Rome. Back in the capital, he snubbed the Senate and loaded the plebs with unprecedented gifts—725 denarii to each citizen. Finding no field in politics for his exuberant strength, he hunted beasts on the imperial estates and developed such skill with sword and bow that he decided to perform publicly. For a time he left the palace and lived in the gladiators' school; he drove chariots in the races, and fought in the arena against animals and men.[67] Presumably the men who opposed him took care to let him win; but he thought nothing of fighting, unaided and before breakfast, a hippopotamus, an elephant, and a tiger, which made no distinctions for royalty.[68] He was so perfect a bowman that with a hundred arrows he killed a hundred tigers in one exhibition. He would let a panther leap upon some condemned criminal and then slay the animal with one arrow, leaving the man unhurt to die again.[69] He had his exploits recorded in the *Acta Diurna* and insisted on being paid, out of the Treasury, for each of his thousand combats as a gladiator.

The historians upon whom we must here depend wrote, like Tacitus, from the viewpoint and traditions of the offended aristocracy; we cannot tell how much of the marvels they relate are history, how much are revenge. We are assured that Commodus drank and gambled, wasted the public funds, kept a harem of 300 women and 300 boys, and liked to vary his sex occasionally, at least by using a woman's garb, even at the public games. Tales of unbelievable cruelty are transmitted to us: Commodus ordered a votary of Bellona to amputate an arm in proof of piety; forced some women devotees of Isis to beat their breasts with pine cones till they died; killed men indiscriminately with his club of Hercules; gathered cripples together and slew them one by one with arrows. . . .[70] One of his mistresses, Marcia, was apparently a Christian; for her sake, we are told, he pardoned some Christians who had been condemned to the Sardinian mines. Her devotion to him suggests that in this man, described as more bestial than any beast, there was some lovable element unrecorded by history.

Like his predecessors, he was aroused to the wildest ferocity by fear of assassination. His aunt Lucilla formed a conspiracy to kill him; he discovered it, had her executed, and on proof or suspicion of participation put so many men of rank to death that soon hardly any survived who had been prominent in Marcus' reign. Delators, who had almost disappeared for a century, returned to activity and favor, and a new terror raged in Rome. Appointing Perennis as praetorian prefect, Commodus yielded the reins of government to him, and (the tradition says) abandoned himself to sexual dissipation. Perennis ruled efficiently but mercilessly; he organized his own terror and had all his opponents slain. The Emperor, suspecting that Perennis planned to replace him, surrendered this second Sejanus to the Senate, which reenacted its role of glowing revenge. Cleander, a former slave, succeeded Perennis (185) and surpassed him in corruption and cruelty; any office might be had for a proper bribe, any decision of any court could be reversed. Under his orders senators and knights were put to death for treason or criticism. In 190 a mob besieged the villa where Commodus was staying and demanded Cleander's death. The Emperor accommodated them. Cleander's successor, Laetus, after holding power for three years, judged that his time had come. One day he chanced upon a proscription list that contained the names of his supporters and friends, and of Marcia. On the last day of 192 Marcia gave Commodus a cup of poison; and when it worked too slowly the athlete whom he had kept to wrestle with strangled him in his bath. He was a youth of thirty-one.

When Marcus died Rome had reached the apex of her curve and was already touched with decay. Her boundaries had been extended beyond the Danube, into Scotland and the Sahara, into the Caucasus and Russia, and to the gates of Parthia. She had accomplished for that confusion of peoples and faiths a unity not of language and culture, but at least of economy and law. She had woven it into a majestic commonwealth, within which the exchange of goods moved in unprecedented plenty and freedom; and for two centuries she had guarded the great realm from barbarian inroads and had given it security and peace. All the white man's world looked to her as the center of the universe, the omnipotent and eternal city. Never had there been such wealth, such splendor, or such power.

Nevertheless, amid the prosperity that made Rome brilliant in this second century, all the seeds were germinating of the crisis that would ruin Italy in the third. Marcus had contributed heavily to the debacle by naming Commodus his heir and by wars that centralized ever more authority in the hands of the Emperor. Commodus kept in peace the prerogatives assumed by Aurelius in war. Private and local independence, initiative, and pride withered as the power and functions of the state increased; and the wealth of nations was drained away by ever-rising taxation to support a self-multiplying bureaucracy and the endless offensives of defense. The mineral wealth of Italy was diminishing,[71] pestilence and famine had taken bitter toll, the system of tillage by slaves was failing, governmental expenditures and doles had exhausted the Treasury and debased the currency. Italian industry was losing its markets in the provinces through provincial competition, and no economic statesmanship appeared to make up for a languishing foreign trade by a wider distribution of buying power at home. Meanwhile the provinces had recovered from the exactions of Sulla, Pompey, Caesar, Cassius, Brutus, and Antony; their ancient skills had revived, their industries were flourishing, their new wealth was financing science, philosophy, and art. Their sons replenished the legions, their generals led them; soon their armies would hold Italy at their mercy and make their generals emperors. The process of conquest was finished and was to be reversed; henceforth the conquered would absorb the conquerors.

As if conscious of these omens and problems, the mind of Rome, at the close of the Antonine age, sank into a cultural and spiritual fatigue. The practical disfranchisement of first the assemblies and then the Senate had removed the mental stimulus that comes from free political activity and a widespread sense of liberty and power. Since the prince had almost all authority, the citizens left him almost all responsibility. More and more of them, even in the aristocracy, retired into their families and their private affairs; citizens became atoms, and society began to fall to pieces internally precisely when unity seemed most complete. Disillusionment with democracy was followed by disillusionment with monarchy. The "Golden Thoughts" of Aurelius were often leaden thoughts, weighted down with the suspicion that Rome's problems could not be solved, that the multiplying barbarians could not long be held back by a sterile and pacific breed. Stoicism, which had begun by preaching strength, was ending by preaching resignation. Almost all the philosophers had made their peace with religion. For 400 years Stoicism had been to the upper classes a substitute for religion; now the substitute was put aside, and the ruling orders turned back from the books of the philosophers to the altars of the gods. And yet paganism, too, was dying. Like Italy, it was flushed only with governmental aid and was nearing exhaustion. It had conquered philosophy; but already its temple precincts heard reverently the names of invading deities. The age was heavy with the resurrection of the provinces and the incredible victory of Christ.

BOOK IV

THE EMPIRE
146 B.C.–A.D. 192

CHRONOLOGICAL TABLE

B.C.

1200: Goidelic Celts invade England
900: Brythonic and Belgic Celts invade England
350: Pytheas of Marseilles explores the North Sea
248: Arsacid Dynasty begins in Parthia
241-10: Sicily becomes a province
238: Sardinia and Corsica acquired
211-190: Arsaces II of Parthia
197: Spain acquired
170-38: Mithridates I of Parthia
168: Macedonia acquired
167: Illyricum
146: Achaea, "Africa," Epirus
145-130: Ptolemy VII
135-105: John Hyrcanus, King of Judea
135-51: Poseidonius
133: Attalus III bequeaths Pergamum
124-88: Mithridates II of Parthia
121: Gallia Narbonensis
112-05: The Jugurthine War
110: Philo of Byzantium, physicist
104-78: Alexander Jannaeus, King of Judea
102: Cilicia; Pamphylia
88-4: First Mithridatic War
88: Massacre of Romans in Near East
83-1: Second Mithridatic War
78-69: Alexandra, Queen of Judea
76: Timomachus of Byzantium, painter
75-63: Third Mithridatic War
74: Bithynia
74-67: Cyrene and Crete
69-63: Aristobulus II, King of Judea
64: Syria
63: Pontus and Judea become Roman provinces
63-40: Hyrcanus II, King of Judea
58: Cyprus
58-50: Caesar conquers Gaul
55,54: Caesar in Britain
50: Hero of Alexandria; Meleager of Gadara
46: Numidia
40: Parthians invade Syria
37-4: Herod the Great
30: Egypt
25: Galatia

B.C.

25-4: Aelius Gallus' expedition into Arabia Felix
17: Upper and Lower Germany acquired
15: Noricum; Raetia
14: Maritime Alps
11: Moesia
7: *Fl.* Strabo, geographer
4(?): Birth of Christ

B.C. 4-6 A.D.: Archelaus, King of Judea; Herod Antipas, Tetrarch of Galilee

A.D. 17: Cappadocia
40: Mauretania
43: Britain
47: Revolt of Caractacus
50: Dioscorides, pharmacologist
51-63: War between Parthia and Rome
55-60: Corbulo subjugates Armenia
61. Revolt of Boudicca
64: Cottian Alps
70-80: Roman conquest of Wales
77-84: Agricola, governor of Britain
72: Extinction of Seleucid Dynasty
89: Plutarch in Rome
90: Epictetus
95: Dio Chrysostom
100: Apollodorus of Damascus, architect
105: Arabia Petrea
107: Dacia
114: Armenia, Assyria, Mesopotamia
115: Soranus of Ephesus, physician
117: Hadrian relinquishes Armenia and Assyria
120: Marinus of Tyre, geographer
122: Hadrian's Wall in England
130: Aelia Capitolina founded on site of Jerusalem; Theon of Smyrna, mathematician; Arrian of Nicomedia, historian; Claudius Ptolemy, astronomer
142: Wall of Antoninus Pius in England
147-91: Vologeses III of Parthia
150: Lucian; Aelius Aristides
160: Galen, physician; Pausanias, geographer
190: Sextus Empiricus, philosopher
227: End of the Arsacid Dynasty

CHAPTER XXI

Italy

I. A ROSTER OF CITIES

LET us stop at this precarious zenith and try to realize that the Empire was greater than Rome. We have lingered unduly at this brilliant center, which hypnotizes historians as it fascinated provincials. In truth the vitality of the great realm no longer dwelt in the corrupt and dying capital; its surviving health and strength, much of its beauty, most of its mental life lay in the provinces and in Italy. We can have no just idea of what Rome meant, nor of its astonishing achievement in organization and pacification, until we leave it and surrender ourselves to a tour of the thousand cities that made up the Roman world.*

"How shall I commence this undertaking?" the elder Pliny asked as he began his description of Italy, "so vast is the number of places—what man could enumerate them all?—and so great is their individual renown!" [1] Around and south of Rome lay Latium, once her mother, then her enemy, then her granary, then a paradise of suburbs and villas for Romans who had both money and taste. South and west from the capital fine roads and the Tiber led to the rival harbors of Portus and Ostia on the Tyrrhenian Sea. Ostia had its great age in the second and third centuries of our era. Merchants and longshoremen crowded its streets and filled its theaters; its homes and apartment houses were remarkably like those of Rome today; as late as the fifteenth century a Florentine traveler marveled at the wealth of the town and its sumptuous adornment. Some surviving columns, and an altar elegantly designed and carved with delicate floral reliefs, show that even this commercial population had absorbed the classic conception of the beautiful.

Southward on the coast rose Antium (Anzio), where the richest Romans, many emperors, and favored gods had palaces or temples reaching out into the Mediterranean to catch any passing breeze; in its three miles of ruins were found such master sculptures as the *Borghese Gladiator* and the *Apollo Belvedere*. Near by an extant monument reminds "excellent citizens," now nineteen centuries dead, that they have recently had the pleasure of seeing eleven gladiators die in combat with ten ferocious bears.[2] To the north, beyond the coastal hills, Aquinum gave birth to Juvenal, and Arpinum plumed itself on Marius and Cicero. Twenty

---

* The reader may follow this pilgrimage on the end maps of this book.

miles from Rome was the old town of Praeneste (Palestrina), its pretty homes built upon terraces in the mountain slopes, its gardens famous for their roses, its peak crowned with a celebrated temple to the goddess Fortuna Primigenia, who gave good luck to women in childbirth, and exchanged oracles for cash. Tusculum, ten miles from Rome, was similarly rich in gardens and villas; here old Cato was born, and Cicero placed his *Tusculan Disputations*.* Most renowned of Rome's suburbs was Tibur (Tivoli), where Hadrian spread his country house and Zenobia, Queen of Palmyra, spent her captive years.

North of Rome, Etruria experienced under the Principate a modest resurrection. Perusia was largely destroyed and partly restored by Augustus, whose artists beautified there an old Etruscan arch. Arretium gave Maecenas to Rome and pottery to the world. Pisae was already hoar with age: it traced its name and origin to a colony of Greeks from Pisa in the Peloponnesus, and made a living by organizing the lumber business along the Arnus River. Farther up the same stream was a young Roman colony, Florentia, rare among cities because it probably underestimated its future. At the northwestern extremity of Etruria were the quarries of Carrara; Rome's finest marble was conveyed thence to the port of Luna, and went by ship to the capital. Genua had long served as an outlet for the goods of northwestern Italy; as far back as 209 B.C. we hear of the Carthaginians destroying it in a ruthless commercial war; it has been destroyed many times since, and has always achieved a fairer reincarnation.

Under the Alps lay Augusta Taurinorum, founded by the Taurini Gauls and made a Roman colony by Augustus; its ancient pavements and drains can still be seen under the streets of Turin; and a massive gate survives from Augustan days to remind us that the city was once a fortress against invaders from the north. Here the lazy Padus (Po), rising in the Cottian Alps, turns eastward 250 miles to divide north Italy into what the early Republic knew as Transpadane and Cispadane Gaul. In all the peninsula the valley of the Po was the region most fertile, populous, and prosperous. At the foot of the Alps were those lakes—Verbanus (Maggiore), Larius (Como), and Benacus (Garda)—whose splendor feasted the eye and soul of those generations as well as ours. From the younger Pliny's Comum a main trade route led south to Mediolanum (Milan). Settled by the Gauls in the fifth century B.C., it was already a metropolis and educational center in the days of Virgil; by A.D. 286 it would replace Rome as the capital of the Western Empire. Verona controlled the trade over the Brenner Pass and was rich enough to have an amphitheater (recently restored) seating 25,000 spectators. Along the winding Po rose Placentia (Piacenza), Cremona, Mantua, and Ferrara—originally frontier towns designed to hold the Gauls at bay.

North of the Po and east of the Adige lay Venetia. The district took its name from the Veneti, early immigrants from Illyria. Herodotus tells how the leaders of these tribes annually brought together the marriageable lasses in their villages, put a price upon each according to her beauty, wed her to the man who paid

---

* Tusculum's heir, Frascati, is still the resort of the Italian rich; there are the villas Aldobrandini, Torlonia, Mondragone, etc.[3]

the price, and used the money to provide alluring dowries for the less alluring girls.[4] Venice itself was not yet born, but at Pola on the Istrian peninsula, at Tergeste (Trieste), Aquileia, and Patavium (Padua), substantial cities crowned the head of the Adriatic. Pola still has from Roman days a stately arch, a pretty temple, and an amphitheater only less impressive than its model, the Colosseum. South of the Po a line of important cities ran from Placentia through Parma, Mutina (Modena), Bononia (Bologna), and Faventia (Faenze) to Ariminum. Here, at Rimini, is one of the most perfectly preserved of the countless bridges built by Roman engineers; it carried the Flaminian Way into the city through an arch as strong and dominating as the Roman character. A branch road led from Bononia to Ravenna, the Venice of Roman days, built upon piles in marshes made by several rivers emptying into the Adriatic; Strabo describes it as "provided with thoroughfares by means of bridges and ferries." [5] Augustus stationed there his Adriatic fleet, and several emperors in the fifth century made the city their official residence. The superior fertility of northern Italy, its healthier and more stimulating climate, its mineral resources, varied industries, and cheaply-borne river trade, raised the region to economic supremacy over central Italy in the first century of our era and to political leadership in the third.

South of Ariminum the eastern coast, rocky, stormy, and harborless, developed few cities of moment north of Brundisium. And yet there were in Umbria, Picenum, Samnium, and Apulia many small towns whose wealth and art can be judged only by studying Pompeii. Asisium gave birth to Propertius as well as Saint Francis; Sarsina to Plautus, Amiternum to Sallust, Sulmo to Ovid, Venusia to Horace. Beneventum was famous not only for a Pyrrhic defeat but for the great arch erected there by Trajan and Hadrian; on its virile reliefs Trajan told the story of his achievements in war and peace. On the southeastern coast Brundisium commanded traffic with Dalmatia, Greece, and the East. Within the "heel" Tarentum, once a proud city-state, was now a declining winter resort for Roman magnates and aristocrats. In southern Italy large estates had absorbed most of the land and turned it to pasture; the cities lost their peasant patronage, and their business classes waned. The Greek communities that had sported their sybaritic wealth in earlier times had been ruined by barbarian infiltration and the Second Punic War, and were now reduced to small towns in which Latin was slowly replacing Greek. On the "toe" Rhegium (Reggio) had a good harbor and flourished on the trade with Sicily and Africa. Up the west coast Velia could hardly remember the days when Parmenides and Zeno had made it, as Elea, ring with metaphysical poetry and impish paradox. Poseidonia, which still amazes visitors with its majestic temples, had been renamed Paestum by its Roman colony, and its Greek stock was melting in a flux of "barbarian"—here Italian—blood from the countryside. Only in Campania was Greek civilization alive in Italy.

Geographically Campania—the mountains and coast around Naples—was part of Samnium; economically and culturally it was a world by itself, industrially more advanced than Rome, financially powerful, and crowding into a little space an intense life of political turmoil, literary competition, artistic exuberance, epicurean luxury, and exciting public games. The land was fertile and produced the finest olives and grapes in Italy; hence came the famous Surrentine and Falernian wines. Probably Varro was thinking of Campania when he challenged the world: "You who have wandered over many lands, have you ever seen any better cultivated than Italy? . . . Is not Italy so stocked with fruit trees as to seem one great orchard?" [6] At the southern end of Campania a precipitous peninsula ran out from Salernum to Surrentum. Villas nestled among the vines and orchards on the hills and garlanded the shore. Surrentum was as beautiful as Sorrento is now; the elder Pliny called it "Nature's own delight," upon which she had poured out all her gifts.[7] Hardly anything seems to have changed there in two thousand years; the people and their customs are probably the same, almost the same their gods; and the cliffs still stand the sea's unending siege.

Facing this promontory lay the buffeted isle of Capreae (Capri). On the southern side of the gulf Vesuvius smoked, while Pompeii and Herculaneum slept under their lava coat. Then came Neapolis, "Newtown," the most Greek of Italian cities in Trajan's day; in Naples' laziness we watch an echo of its ancient addiction to love and sport and art. The people were Italian; the culture, customs, games, were Greek. Here were fine temples, palaces, and theaters; here, every fifth year, were held those contests in music and poetry at which Statius had won a prize. In the western corner of the gulf was the port of Puteoli (Pozzuoli), named from the stench of its sulphur pools; [8] it throve on Rome's trade and on manufactures of iron, pottery, and glass; an amphitheater here shows us, by its well-preserved underground passages, how gladiators and beasts were introduced into the arena. Across the harbor of Puteoli sparkled the villas of Baiae, doubly attractive in their setting between mountains and sea; here Caesar, Caligula, and Nero played and rheumatic Romans came to bathe in mineral springs. The place profited from its reputation for gambling and immorality; Varro reports that maidens there were common property, and many boys were girls; [9] Claudius thought Cicero irremediably disgraced for having gone there once.[10] "Do you suppose," asks Seneca, "that Cato would ever have dwelt in a pleasure palace, so that he might count the lewd women as they sailed past, the many kinds of barges painted in all sorts of colors, the roses wafted about the lake?" [11]

A few miles north of Baiae, in the crater of a dead volcano, Lake Avernus emitted sulphurous fumes of such potency that legend said no bird could fly above it and live. Near it was the cave through which Aeneas, in Virgil's epic, had made his *facilis descensus Averni* into Tartarus. North of the lake was the old city of Cumae, now slowly dying through the superior attractions of her daughter-city Neapolis, the better harbors of Puteoli and Ostia, and the industries of Capua. Capua lay thirty miles inland, in a fertile region that sometimes harvested four crops in a year; [12] and its bronze and iron works were unrivaled in Italy. Rome had so severely punished it for helping Hannibal that for two centuries it failed to recover, and Cicero spoke of it as the "abode of the politically dead." [13] Caesar restored it with thousands of new colonists, and in Trajan's time it was prospering again.

Listed so rapidly, these major cities of classic Italy are merely names; we mistake them for words on a map and hardly feel that they were the noisy abodes of sensitive men eagerly pursuing food and drink, women and gold. Let us turn over the ashes of one Roman habitation, and from its strangely preserved vestiges try to recapture some movement of the life that ran in those ancient streets.

II. POMPEII

Pompeii was one of the minor towns of Italy, hardly noticed in Latin literature except for its fish sauces, its cabbage, and its burial. Founded by Oscans perhaps as early as Rome, peopled by Greek immigrants, captured by Sulla and turned into a Roman colony, it was partly destroyed by an earthquake in A.D. 63 and was being rebuilt when Vesuvius destroyed it again. On August 24, A.D. 79, the volcano exploded and hurled dust and rock high into the air amid clouds of smoke and flashes of flame. A heavy rainfall turned the erupted matter into a torrent of mud and stone, which in six hours covered Pompeii and Herculaneum to a depth of eight or ten feet. All that day and the next the earth shook and buildings fell. Audiences were buried in the ruins of theaters,[14] hundreds were choked by dust or fumes, and tidal waves shut off escape by sea. The elder Pliny was at that time commanding the western fleet at Misenum, near Puteoli. Moved by appeals for help and by curiosity to observe the phenomenon at closer range, he boarded a small vessel, landed on the southern shore of the gulf, and rescued several persons; but as the party ran from the advancing hail and smoke, the old scientist was overcome, fell in his tracks, and died.[15] The next morning his wife and his nephew joined the desperate crowd that fled down the coast, while from Naples to Sorrento the continuing eruption blackened the day into night. Many refugees, separated in the darkness from their husbands, wives, or children, made the terror worse with their laments and shrieks. Some prayed to divers gods for help; some cried out that all gods were dead and that the long-predicted end of the world had come.[16] When, on the third day, the sky cleared at last, lava and mud had covered everything of Pompeii but the rooftops, and Herculaneum had completely disappeared.

Of approximately 20,000 population in Pompeii, probably some 2000 lost their lives. Several of the dead were preserved by a volcanic embalmment: the rain and pumice stone that fell upon them made a cement that hardened as it dried; and the filling of these impromptu molds has made some gruesome plaster casts. A few of the survivors dug into the ruins to recover valuables; thereafter the site was abandoned and was slowly covered by the detritus of time. In 1709 an Austrian general sank a shaft at Herculaneum, but the tufa layer was so thick (in some places sixty-five feet) that excavations had to proceed by slow and costly tunneling. The exhuming of Pompeii began in 1749 and has gone on at intervals since. Today most of the ancient town has been uncovered and has revealed so many houses, objects, and inscriptions that in some ways we know ancient Pompeii better than ancient Rome.

The center of its life, as in every Italian city, was the forum. Once, doubtless, it had been the gathering point for farmers and their produce on market days; games were held there, and dramas were performed. There the citizens had raised shrines to their gods; at one end to Jupiter, at the other to Apollo, and near by to Venus Pompeiana, the patron goddess of the town. But they were not a religious people; they were too busy with industry and politics, games and venery, to have much time for worship; and even in worship they honored the phallus as the crown of their Dionysian ritual.[17] When economic and state affairs swelled in volume and dignity, great buildings rose around the forum for administration, negotiation, and exchange.

We may judge from modern Italian towns how the adjoining streets throbbed with the hawking of peddlers, the disputes of buyers and sellers, the noise of crafts by day and revelry by night. In the ruins of the shops excavators found some of the charred and petrified nuts, loaves, and fruits that so narrowly escaped a purchaser. Farther down the streets were the taverns, gambling houses, and brothels, each zealous to be all in one.

We might not have guessed the keenness of Pompeii's life had not its people scratched their sentiments upon public walls. Three thousand such *graffiti* have been copied there, and presumably there were thousands more. Sometimes the authors merely inscribed their names or obscene audacities, as men still love to do; sometimes they gave hopeful instructions to enemies, as *Samius Cornelio, suspendere*—"Samius to Cornelius: go hang yourself." Many of the inscriptions are love messages, often in verse: Romula notes that she "tarried here with Stephylus"; and a devoted youth writes, *Victoria vale, et ubique es, suaviter sternutas*—"Good-by, Victoria, and wherever you are may you sneeze pleasantly." [18]

Quite as numerous as these messages are the carved or painted announcements of public events or private offerings. Landlords advertised vacancies, losers described missing articles; guilds and other groups declared themselves for promising candidates in the municipal campaigns. So "the fishermen have named Popidius Rufus for aedile"; "the lumbermen and the charcoal sellers ask you to elect Marcellinus." [19] Some *graffiti* announced gladiatorial games, others proclaimed the valor of famous gladiators like Celadus, *suspirium puellarum*, "the maidens' sigh," or breathed devotion to a favorite actor—"Actius, darling of the people, come back soon!" [20] Pompeii lived to be amused. It had three public baths, a palaestra, a small theater seating 2500, a larger one accommodating 5000, and an amphitheater where 20,000 persons could enjoy by proxy the agony of death. One inscription reads: "Thirty pairs of gladiators furnished by the duumvir . . . will fight at Pompeii on November 24, 25, and 26. There will be a hunt [*venatio*]. Hurrah for Maius! Bravo, Paris!" Maius was duumvir or city magistrate; Paris was the leading gladiator.

The remains of the domestic interiors suggest a life of solid comfort and varied art. Windows were exceptional, central heating was rare; bathrooms appear in the richer homes, and a few houses had an outdoor pool in a peristyled garden. Floors were of cement or stone, sometimes of mosaic. One frank moneymaker had the words *Salve lucrum*—"Hail, gain!" lettered in his floor; another inscribed his with *Lucrum gandium*—"Gain is joy." [21] Little has been found of the ancient furniture; nearly all was of wood, and perished; but a few tables, couches, chairs, and lamps of marble or bronze have survived. In the museums at Pompeii and Naples may be seen the miscellanea of domestic life: pens, inkstands, scales, kitchen utensils, toilet articles, and musical instruments.

The art recovered from Pompeii or near it suggests that not only the aristocrats of the villas, but the merchants of the city enjoyed the cultural accessories of life. A private library unearthed at Herculaneum had 1756 volumes or rolls. We must not repeat what we have said of the Boscoreale cups, or the rich vistas and graceful women painted upon the walls of Pompeian homes. Many dwellings had excellent sculptures, and the forum contained 150 statues. In the Temple of Jupiter a head of the god was found which Pheidias himself might have carved—strength and justice framed in the curls of abounding hair and beard. In the Temple of Apollo was a statue of Diana, equipped with a hole in the back of the head through which a hidden ministrant might utter oracles. In one Herculanean villa enough first-class bronzes were found to fill a famous room at the Naples Museum. Presumably the masterpieces in this collection—the *Resting Mercury*, the *Narcissus* or *Dionysus*, the *Drunken Satyr*, and the *Dancing Faun*—were of Greek origin or workmanship; they reveal the skillful technique, and the shameless joy in the healthy body, characteristic of Praxitelean art. One of them, however, a bravely realistic bust in bronze, shows the bald head and sharp but not unkindly face of L. Caecilius Iucundus, a Pompeian auctioneer whose accounts, inscribed upon 154 wax tablets, were found in his house at Pompeii. Supremely human in its mixture of coarseness and intelligence, wisdom and warts, this work of a contemporary—perhaps Italian—sculptor is a welcome foil to the unwrinkled gods and goddesses who surround it in the Naples Museum, and who confess by their smooth and placid features that they never lived.

III. MUNICIPAL LIFE

Life, private and public, individual and corporate, has never been lived more intensely than in ancient Italy. But the events of our own time are too vital and absorbing to let us spare interest for the details of municipal organization under the Caesars; the confusing diversities of constitution and the jealous gradations of franchise are no longer a part of that living past which is our matrix and our theme.

It was a basic feature of the Roman Empire that though divided into provinces it was organized into an assemblage of relatively self-governed city-states each owning an extensive hinterland. Patriotism meant love of one's city rather than of the Empire. Normally the freemen of each community were content to exercise a purely local franchise; and those non-Romans who had won Roman citizenship rarely went to Rome to vote. As the example of Pompeii shows, the decay of the assemblies in the capital was not accompanied by a similar debasement in the cities of the Empire. Most Italian municipalities had a senate (*curia*)—and most Eastern cities had a council (*boulé*)—that formulated ordinances, and an assembly (*comitia, ekklesia*) that chose the magistrates. Each magistrate was expected to give his city a substantial sum (*summa honoraria*, from *honos*, office) for the privilege of serving it, and custom required him also to make incidental donations for public benefits or games. As no pay attached to office, the democracy— or aristocracy—of freemen issued almost everywhere in an oligarchy of wealth and power.

For two hundred years, from Augustus to Aurelius, the municipalities of Italy prospered. There was a majority of poor in them, of course; nature and privilege had seen to this; but never before or since, so far as history tells, have the rich done so much for the poor. Practically all the expenses of operating the city, of financing dramas, spectacles, and games, of building temples, theaters, stadiums, palaestras, libraries, basilicas, aqueducts, bridges, and baths, and adorning these with arches, porticoes, painting, and statuary, fell upon men of means; and in the first two centuries of the Empire these philanthropies were carried out with a competitive patriotism that in some cases bankrupted the families that contributed, or the cities that maintained, the benefactions. In time of famine it was usual for the wealthy to buy food and distribute it gratis among the poor; on occasion they furnished free oil or wine, or a public banquet, or a gift of money, to all citizens, sometimes to all inhabitants. Extant inscriptions abound in commemorations of such generosity. A millionaire gave Altinum, in Venetia, 1,600,-000 sesterces for public baths; a rich lady built a temple and an amphitheater for Casinum; Desumius Tullus gave Tarquinii baths costing 5,000,000 sesterces; Cremona, destroyed by Vespasian's troops, was rapidly rebuilt by the contributions of private citizens; and two physicians exhausted their fortunes in gifts to Naples. At populous Ostia, Lucilius Gemala invited all the inhabitants to dinner, paved a long and spacious avenue, repaired or restored seven temples, rebuilt the municipal baths, and donated 3,000,000 sesterces to the city treasury.[22] It was the custom of many rich men to invite a considerable portion of the citizenry to a feast on the occasion of their birthday, their election to office, their daughter's marriage, their son's assumption of the *toga virilis* of manhood, or the dedication of a building which they had presented to the community. In return for such favors the city voted the giver an office, a statue, a panegyric, or an inscription. The poor were not overwhelmed with all these gifts; they accused the rich of deriving the means of philanthropy from exploitation, and they demanded less ornate buildings and cheaper corn, less statuary and more games.[23]

When we add to private munificence the donations of the emperors to the towns, the buildings erected, and the catastrophes mitigated, in them by imperial funds, and the public works and functions financed by the municipal treasury, we begin to feel the splendor and pride of the Italian cities under the Principate. Streets were paved, drained, policed, and adorned, free medical service was maintained for the poor, clean water was piped into private homes for a small fee, food was offered to the poor at a low price, public baths were often free through private subsidies, *alimenta* were paid to straitened families to help them rear their children, schools and libraries were built, plays were presented, concerts were given, games were arranged in reckless emulation of Rome. Civilization in the Italian towns was not so materialistic as in the capital. They rivaled one another in erecting amphitheaters, but also they raised noble temples, sometimes equaling Rome's best,[24] and made the months gay with picturesque religious festivals. They spent freely on works of art and provided halls for lecturers, poets, sophists, rhetors, philosophers, and musicians. They supplied their citizens with facilities for health, cleanliness, recreation, and a vigorous cultural life. From them, not from Rome, came most of the great Latin authors, and some of the finest sculptural masterpieces in our museums, like the *Nike* of Naples, the *Eros* of Centumcellae, the *Zeus* of Otricoli. They supported as large a population as their modern successors before our century, and gave it an unparalleled security from war. The first two hundred years of our era saw the zenith of the great peninsula.

CHAPTER XXII

Civilizing the West

I. ROME AND THE PROVINCES

THE blot on Italian prosperity—aside from a system of slavery common to ancient states—was its partial dependence upon provincial exploitation. Italy was free of taxation because the provinces had yielded so much in plunder and tribute; and to them could be traced some of the wealth that came to flower in the Italian towns. Rome, before Caesar, frankly classed the provinces as conquered territory; all their inhabitants were Roman subjects, only a few were Roman citizens; all their land was the property of the Roman state and was held by the possessors on revocable grants from the imperial government. To lessen the likelihood of revolt Rome cut conquered regions into smaller states, forbade any province to have direct political dealings with another, and favored the business classes against the lower classes everywhere. *Divide et impera* was the secret of Roman rule.

Cicero perhaps exaggerated when, in excoriating Verres, he pictured the Mediterranean nations as desolate under the Republic: "All the provinces mourn, all free peoples cry out, all kingdoms protest against our cruelty and greed; from one ocean to another there is no place, however hidden or remote, that has not felt our lust and our iniquity." [1] The Principate dealt more liberally with the provinces, not from generosity so much as from husbandry. Taxation was made bearable, local religions, languages, and customs were respected, freedom of speech was allowed except for attacks against the sovereign power, and local laws were retained so far as they did not conflict with Roman profit and mastery. A wise flexibility created a useful diversity of rank and privilege among and within the subject states. Certain municipalities, like Athens and Rhodes, were "free cities"; they paid no tribute, were not subject to the provincial governor, and managed their domestic affairs without Roman interference so long as they maintained social order and peace. Some old kingdoms, like Numidia and Cappadocia, were allowed to keep their kings, but these were "clients" of Rome—dependent upon her protection and her policy and required to aid her with men and materials at her call. In the provinces the governor (proconsul or propraetor) combined in himself the power to legislate, to administer, and to judge; his power was limited only by the free cities, by a Roman citizen's right of appeal to the emperor, and by the financial supervision exercised by the provincial quaestor or procurator. Such near-omnipotence invited abuse; and though the lengthening of the governor's term under the Principate, his ample salary and allowance, and his financial responsibility to the emperor considerably lessened malfeasance, we may see from the letters of Pliny and some passages in Tacitus [2] that extortion and corruption were still no rarities at the end of the first century.

Taxation was a primary industry of the governor and his aides. Under the Empire a census was taken of every province for the purpose of assessing the tax on land and the tax on property—which included animals and slaves. To stimulate production a fixed tribute was substituted for the tithe. "Publicans" no longer gathered these taxes, but they collected port duties and managed some state forests, mines, and public works. The provinces were expected to contribute towards a golden crown for each new emperor, pay the cost of provincial administration, and in some cases send heavy shipments of grain to Rome. The old custom of liturgies was maintained in the East, and spread through the West, by which the local or the Roman government might "ask" rich men to provide loans for war, ships for the navy, buildings for public purposes, food for famine victims, or choruses for festivals and plays.

Cicero, having joined the Ins, contended that the taxes paid by the provinces barely covered the cost of administration and defense; [3] "defense" included the suppression of revolts, and "administration" presumably embraced the perquisites that made so many Roman millionaires. We must reconcile ourselves to the probability that whatever power establishes security and order will send taxgatherers to collect something more than the cost. Despite all levies the provinces prospered under the Principate. The emperor and the Senate exercised a more careful supervision over provincial staffs and severely punished those who stole beyond their station. Ultimately the excess taken from the provinces flowed back to them in payment for their goods; and in the end the industries so supported made the provinces stronger than a precariously parasitic Italy. A government, said Plutarch, ought to give a people two boons above all: liberty and peace. "As to peace," he wrote, "there is no need to occupy ourselves, for all war has ceased. As to liberty, we have that which the government [Rome] leaves us; and perhaps it would not be good if we had any more." [4]

II. AFRICA

Corsica and Sardinia were classed together as a province, not as parts of Italy. Corsica was for the most part a mountainous wilderness, in which Romans hunted the natives with dogs to sell them as slaves.[5] Sardinia provided slaves, silver, copper, iron, and grain; it had a thousand miles of road and one excellent harbor, Carales (Cagliari). Sicily had been reduced to an almost purely agricultural province as one of the "frumentary supports" of Rome; its arable soil was largely taken up with latifundia devoted to cattle raising, and manned by slaves so poorly clothed and fed that they periodically revolted and escaped to form robber bands. The island had in Augustus' days some 750,000 souls. (In 1930 it had 3,972,000.) Of its sixty-five cities the most flourishing were Catania, Syracuse, Tauromenium (Taormina), Messana, Agrigentum, and Panormus (Palermo). Syracuse and Tauromenium had magnificent Greek theaters, still in use today. Despite Verres' depredations Syracuse was so full of impressive architecture, famous sculptures, and historic sites that professional guides prospered on the tourist trade,[6] and Cicero considered it the finest city in the world. Most well-to-do urban families had farms or orchards in the suburbs, and the whole Sicilian countryside was fragrant with fruit trees and vineyards, as it is today.

All that Sicily lost through Roman domination Africa gained. It gradually replaced Sicily as an unwilling granary for Rome; but in return Roman soldiers, colonists, businessmen, and engineers made it blossom into a hardly credible affluence. Doubtless the new conquerors had found certain regions thriving when they came; between the mountains that frowned upon the Mediterranean, and the Atlas range that kept out the Sahara, ran a semitropical valley sufficiently watered by the Bagradas (Medjerda) River, and two months of rain, to repay the patient husbandry that Mago had taught and Masinissa had enforced. But Rome improved and expanded what she found. Her engineers built dams across the rivers that flowed down from the southern hills; they gathered the surplus water in reservoirs in the rainy season, and poured it into irrigation canals in the hot months when the streams ran dry.[7] Rome asked no heavier taxes than native chiefs had levied, but her legion and fortifications gave better protection against nomad raiders from the mountains; mile by mile new soil was won from desert or savagery for cultivation and settlement. The valley produced so much olive oil that when in our seventh century the Arabs came, they were amazed to find that they could ride from Tripoli to Tangier without ever moving from the shade of olive trees.[8] Towns and cities multiplied, architecture exalted them, and literature found new voice. The ruins of Roman forums, temples, aqueducts, and theaters on now arid wastes reveal the reach and wealth of Roman Africa. Those fields decayed and became dead sand not through a change in climate but through a change in government—from a state that gave economic security, order, and discipline to one that allowed chaos and negligence to ruin the roads, reservoirs, and canals.

At the head of this restored prosperity was the resurrected city of

Carthage. After the battle of Actium Augustus took up the frustrated project of Caius Gracchus and Caesar and sent to Carthage as colonists some of the soldiers whose fidelity and victories he wished to reward with land. The geographical advantages of the site, the perfect harbor, the fertile Bagradas delta, the excellent roads opened or reopened by Roman engineers, soon enabled Carthage to recapture from Utica the export and import trade of the region; within a century of its refounding it had become the largest city in the western provinces. Rich merchants and landowners built mansions on the historic Byrsa, or villas in the flowering suburbs, while peasants driven from the soil by the competition of latifundia joined prolétaires and slaves in slums whose fetid poverty would welcome the egalitarian gospel of Christianity. Houses rose to six or seven stories, public buildings gleamed with marble, and statuary of good Greek style abounded in the streets and squares. Temples were built again to the old Carthaginian gods, and Melkart enjoyed till our second century the sacrifice of living children.[9] The people rivaled the Romans in their passion for luxuries, cosmetics, jewelry, dyed hair, chariot races, and gladiatorial games. Among the sights of the city were the great public baths presented by Marcus Aurelius. There were lecture halls, schools of rhetoric, philosophy, medicine, and law; Carthage ranked only after Athens and Alexandria as a university town. Here Apuleius and Tertullian came to study everything, and Saint Augustine marveled at the pranks and immorality of the students, whose favorite philanthropy was to break into a lecture room and dismiss both the professor and his class.[10]

Carthage was the capital of the province called "Africa," now eastern Tunisia. South of it commerce bedecked the eastern coast with cities whose ancient wealth was reviving after twelve centuries when war struck them in our time: Hadrumetum (Sousse), Leptis Minor, Thapsus, and Tacapae (Gabes). Farther east on the Mediterranean lay a district named Tripolis from its federation of three cities: Oea (Tripoli), founded by the Phoenicians in 900 B.C., Sabrata, and Leptis Magna (Lebda). In this last city the Emperor Septimius Severus was born (A.D. 146); he rewarded it with a basilica and municipal bath whose ruins astonish the traveler or warrior today. Paved roads busy with camel caravans connected these ports with the towns of the interior: Sufetula, now a tiny village with the remains of a great Roman temple; Thysdrus (El Djem), which had an amphitheater seating 60,000; and Thugga (Dougga), whose ruined theater attests, by its graceful Corinthian columns, the wealth and taste of its citizens.

North of Carthage was her ancient mother and implacable rival, Utica (Utique). We catch a hint of its Roman opulence when we learn that in 46 B.C. 300 Roman bankers and wholesalers had branch offices there.[11] Its territory reached northward to Hippo Diarrhytus, now Bizerte; thence a road led along the coast westward to Hippo Regius (Bone), soon to be Augustine's episcopal

see. South and inland lay Cirta (Constantine), capital of the province of Numidia. Westward lay Thamugadi (Timgad), almost as well preserved as Pompeii,
with paved and colonnaded streets, covered drains, an elegant arch, a forum,
senate house, basilica, temples, baths, theater, library, and many private homes.
On the pavement of the forum is a checkerboard engraved with the words,
Venari, lavari, ludere, ridere, hoc est vivere—"to hunt, bathe, play, and laugh,
this is to live." [12] Thamugadi was founded about A.D. 117 by the Third Legion,
sole guard of the African provinces. About 123 the legion took up more permanent headquarters a few miles to the west, and raised the city of Lambaesis (Lambèse). The soldiers married and settled there, and lived in their homes more than
in the camp; but even their *praetorium* was a stately and ornate edifice, whose
baths were as fine as any in Africa. Outside the camp they helped to build a
capitol, temples, triumphal arches, and an amphitheater where struggle and
death might mitigate the monotony of their peaceful lives.

That a single legion could protect all north Africa from the marauding tribes
of the interior was made possible by a network of roads, military in purpose but
commercial in result, binding Carthage with the Atlantic, and the Sahara with
the Mediterranean. The main road went westward through Cirta to Caesarea,
capital of Mauretania (Morocco). Here King Juba II taught civilization to the
Mauri or Moors from whom the province took its ancient and modern names.
Son of the Juba who had died at Thapsus, he had been taken as a child to grace
Caesar's triumph in Rome; he was spared, remained as a student, and became one
of the most learned scholars of his time. Augustus made him client king of Mauretania and bade him spread among his people the classic culture he had so zealously
acquired. He succeeded, being favored with a long reign of forty-eight years;
his subjects marveled that a man could write books and yet rule so well. His son
and heir was brought to Rome and starved to death by Caligula. Claudius annexed the kingdom and divided it into two provinces: Mauretania Caesariensis
and Mauretania Tingitana, named from its capital Tingis—our Tangier.

In these African cities there were many schools, open to the poor as well
as to the rich. We hear of courses in stenography, [13] and Juvenal calls Africa
nutricula causidicorum—the nurse of barristers. [14] It produced in this period
one minor and one major author—Fronto and Apuleius; only in its Christian
heyday would African literature lead the world. Lucius Apuleius was a
strange and picturesque character, far more than Montaigne "undulant and
diverse." Born at Madaura of high family (A.D. 124), he studied there, at
Carthage, and in Athens, spent a large inheritance recklessly, wandered from
city to city and from faith to faith, had himself initiated into various religious
mysteries, played with magic, wrote many works on subjects ranging from
theology to tooth powder, lectured at Rome and elsewhere on philosophy
and religion, returned to Africa, and married at Tripoli a lady considerably
richer than himself in both purse and years. Her friends and heirs-apparent

sued to annul the marriage, charging that he had persuaded the widow by magic arts; he defended himself before the court in an *Apologia* that has come down to us in refurbished form. He won his case and bride, but the people persisted in believing him a magician, and their pagan posterity sought to belittle Christ by recounting the miracles of Apuleius. He spent the remainder of his days at Madaura and Carthage, practicing law and medicine, letters and rhetoric. Most of his writings were on scientific and philosophical subjects; his native city raised a monument to him labeled *Philosophus Platonicus;* and he would be chagrined, if he could return, to find himself remembered only for his *Golden Ass.*

It is a work akin to the *Satyricon* of Petronius and even more bizarre. Originally entitled *Metamorphoseon Libri XI—Eleven Books of Transformations*—it expanded fantastically a story that Lucius of Patras had told of a man changed into an ass. It is a loose concatenation of adventures, descriptions, and extraneous episodes, seasoned with magic, horror, ribaldry, and deferred piety. The Lucius of the tale tells how he wandered into Thessaly, amused himself with various maidens, and sensed everywhere around him an atmosphere of sorcery.

> As soon as night was past and a new day began to spring, I fortuned to awake, and rose out of my bed as half amazed, and indeed desirous to know and see some strange and marvelous things. . . . Neither was there anything which I saw that I did believe to be the same which it was indeed, but everything seemed to me transformed into other shapes by the wicked power of enchantment, in so much that I thought the stones against which I might stumble were indurate and turned from men into that figure, and that the birds which I heard chirping, and the trees and the running waters were changed into such feathers and leaves and fountains. And further I thought that the statues and images would by and by move, and that the walls would talk, and the kine and other brute beasts would speak and tell strange news, and that immediately I should hear some oracle from heaven and from the ray of the sun.[15]

Ready now for any adventure, Lucius rubs himself with a magic ointment, meanwhile mightily wishing to be changed into a bird; but as he rubs he becomes a perfect ass. Thenceforth the story records the tribulations of an ass with "the sense and understanding of a man." His single consolation lies in his "long ears, whereby I might hear all things that were even afar off." He will be restored to human shape, he is told, if he can find and eat a rose. He achieves this consummation after a long *Asineid* of vicissitudes. Disenamored of life, he turns first to philosophy, then to religion, and composes a prayer of thanksgiving to Isis astonishingly like a Christian apostrophe to the Mother of God.[16] He shaves his head, is received into the third order of Isiac initiates, and paves a road back to earth by revealing a dream in which Osiris, "greatest of the gods," bids him go home and practice law.

Few books embrace so much nonsense, but fewer still have phrased it so pleasantly. Apuleius tries every manner of style and manages each successfully; he loves most a rich and fanciful verbiage ornate with alliteration and assonance, picturesque slang and archaic speech, sentimental diminutives, rhythmic and sometimes poetic prose. An Oriental warmth of coloring accompanies here an Oriental mysticism and sensuality. Perhaps Apuleius wished to suggest, from the background of his experience, that sensual indulgence is an intoxicating ferment which changes us into beasts, and that we can become human again only through the rose of wisdom and piety. He is at his best in the incidental stories caught by his powerful and perambulating ears; so an old woman comforts a kidnaped maiden by recounting the romance of Cupid and Psyche—[17] how the son of Venus fell in love with a pretty maid, gave her every joy but that of seeing him, aroused his mother to cruel jealousy, and came to a happy ending in the skies. No artist's brush, in many an effort, has bettered the hoar shrew's tongue in telling the ancient tale.

III. SPAIN

Crossing the straits from Tangier, we pass from one of the newest to one of the oldest provinces of Rome. Standing strategically at the door of the Mediterranean, blessed and cursed with precious minerals that soaked her soil with the blood of greed, crossed with mountain ranges that hindered communications, assimilation, and unity, Spain has felt the full fever of life from the days when Old Stone Age artists painted bisons on the cave walls of Altamira down to our own disordered time. For thirty centuries the Spaniards have been a proud and warlike people, lean and tough, stoically brave, passionate and obstinate, sober and melancholy, frugal and hospitable, courteous and chivalrous, easily provoked to hatred, more easily to love. When the Romans came they found a population even then inextricably diverse: Iberians from Africa (?), Ligurians from Italy, Celts from Gaul, and a layer of Carthaginians at the top. If we may believe their conquerors, the pre-Roman Spaniards were close to barbarism, some living in towns and houses, some in hamlets and huts and caves, sleeping on the floor or the earth, and washing their teeth with urine carefully aged.[18] The men wore black cloaks, the women "long mantles and gay-colored gowns." In some parts, Strabo reprovingly adds, "the women dance promiscuously with men, taking hold of their hands." [19]

As early as 2000 B.C. the inhabitants of southeastern Spain—Tartessus, the Phoenician "Tarshish"—had developed a bronze industry whose products were sold throughout the Mediterranean. On this basis Tartessus evolved in the sixth century B.C. a literature and art that claimed an antiquity of 6000 years. Little remains of it except a few crude statues and a strange polychrome bust in sandstone, *The Lady of Elche*, carved on Greek models in a strong and flowing Celtic style. About 1000 B.C. the Phoenicians began to tap the mineral wealth of Spain, and by 800 they had taken Cádiz and Malaga, and built great temples there. Towards 500 B.C. Greek colonists settled along the northeastern coast. About the same time the Carthaginians, summoned by their Phoenician kin to help suppress a revolt, conquered Tartessus and all south and eastern Spain. The rapid exploitation of the peninsula by Carthage between the First and Second Punic Wars opened the eyes of the Romans to the resources of what they then called "Iberia," and the passage of Hannibal into Italy was finally outweighed by the movement of the Scipios into Spain. The disunited tribes fought fiercely for their independence; women killed their children rather than let them fall into Roman hands, and captive natives sang their war songs while dying on the cross.[20] The conquest took two centuries, but once completed it proved more fundamental than in most other provinces. The Gracchi, Caesar, and Augustus changed the Republic's policy of ruthlessness to one of courtesy and consideration, with good and lasting results. Romanization proceeded rapidly; Latin was adopted and adapted, the economy expanded and prospered, and soon Spain was contributing poets, philosophers, senators, and emperors to Rome.

From Seneca to Aurelius Spain was the economic mainstay of the Empire. Having enriched Tyre and then Carthage, Spanish minerals now enriched Rome; Spain became to Italy what Mexico and Peru would be to Spain. Gold, silver, copper, tin, iron, lead were mined with modern thoroughness; at Rio Tinto one may still see Roman shafts sunk to great depths through solid quartz, and Roman slag with an astonishingly low percentage of copper left in it.[21] In these mines slaves and prisoners worked day after day, in many cases never seeing the light of the sun for months.[22] Great metallurgical industries rose near the mines. Meanwhile the soil of Spain, despite mountains and arid wastes, produced esparto grass for cord, rope, baskets, bedding, and sandals, nourished prize sheep and a renowned woolen industry, and gave to the Empire the best olives, oil, and wine that antiquity knew. The Guadalquivir, the Tagus, the Ebro, and lesser streams helped a web of Roman roads to carry the products of Spain to her ports and innumerable towns.

Indeed, the most remarkable and characteristic result of Roman rule, here as elsewhere, was the multiplication or expansion of cities. In the province of Baetica (Andalusia) were Carteia (Algeciras), Munda, Malaca, Italica (birthplace of Trajan and Hadrian), Corduba, Hispalis (Seville), and Gades (Cádiz). Corduba, founded 152 b.c. was a literary center famous for its schools of rhetoric; here were born Lucan, the Senecas, and Saint Paul's Gallio; this tradition of scholarship would last through the Dark Ages and make Cordova the most learned city in Europe. Gades was the most populous of Spanish towns, and notoriously rich; situated at the mouth of the Guadalquivir, it commanded the Atlantic trade with western Africa, Spain, Gaul, and Britain. Its sensuous dancing girls (*puellae Gaditanae*) contributed modestly to its fame.

Rome knew Portugal as the province of Lusitania, and Lisbon as Olisipo. At Norba Caesarina, to which the Arabs gave its present name of Alcantara (The Bridge), Trajan's engineers threw across the Tagus the most perfect of existing Roman bridges; its majestic arches, 100 feet wide and 180 above the stream, still carry a busy four-lane road. The capital of Lusitania was Emerita (Mérida), which boasted many temples, three aqueducts, a circus, a theater, a naumachia, and a bridge 2500 feet long. Farther east, in the province of Tarraconensis, Segovia still enjoys the pure water brought in by an aqueduct built in Trajan's reign. South of it was Toletum (Toledo), known in Roman times for its ironworks. On the eastern coast rose the great city of Nova Carthago (Cartagena), rich with mining, fisheries, and trade. Out in the Mediterranean lay the Baleares, where Palma and Pollentia were already old and flourishing cities. Northward on the coast were Valentia, Tarraco (Tarragona), Barcino (Barcelona), and, just below the Pyrenees, the old Greek town of Emporiae. A short sail around the eastern end of the mountains, and the traveler found himself in Gaul.

IV. GAUL

In those days, when all ships were of moderate draught, even ocean-going vessels could navigate the Rhone from Marseilles to Lyons; smaller boats could continue to within thirty miles of the upper Rhine; after a short haul over level land goods could sail by a hundred cities and a thousand villas into the North Sea. Similar overland leaps led from the Rhone and the Saône to the Loire and the Atlantic, from the Aude to the Garonne and Bordeaux, from the Saone to the Seine and the English Channel. Trade followed these waterways and created cities at their meeting points. France, like Egypt, was the gift of her streams.

In a sense French civilization began with "Aurignacian man" 30,000 years before Christ; for even then, as the caves of Montignac attest, there were artists capable of rich color and vivid line. From that Old Stone Age of hunting and herding, France passed, about 12,000 B.C., to the settled life and tillage of the Neolithic Age, and, after ten long millenniums, to the Age of Bronze. About 900 B.C. a new race, "Alpine" and roundheaded, began to filter in from Germany and spread across France to Britain and Ireland and down into Spain. These "Celts" brought with them the Halstatt iron culture of Austria, and about 550 B.C. they imported from Switzerland the more developed iron technology of La Tène. When Rome became conscious of France she named it *Celtica;* only in Caesar's time was this changed to *Gallia,* Gaul.

The immigrants displaced some native groups and settled down in in-dependent tribes whose names still lurk in the cities they built.* The Gauls, said Caesar, were tall, muscular, and strong;[23] they combed their rich blond hair back over their heads and down the nape of their necks; some had beards, many had powerful mustaches curling around their mouths. They had brought from the East, perhaps from the ancient Iranians, the custom of wearing breeches; to these they added tunics dyed in many colors and embroidered with flowers, and striped cloaks fastened at the shoulders. They loved jewelry and wore gold ornaments—even if nothing else—in war.[24] They liked abundant meat, beer, and undiluted wine, being "intemperate by nature" if we may believe Appian.[25] Strabo calls them "simple and high-spirited, boastful . . . insufferable when victorious, scared out of their wits when defeated";[26] but it is not always a boon that our enemies should write a book. Poseidonius was shocked to find that they hung the severed heads of their foes from the necks of their horses.[27] They were easily aroused to argument and combat, and sometimes, to amuse themselves at banquets, they fought duels to the death. "They were," says Caesar, "our equals in valor and warlike zeal."[28] Ammianus Marcellinus describes them as

> at all ages fit for military service. The old man marches out on a campaign with courage equal to that of the man in the prime of life.
> . . . In fact a whole band of foreigners will be unable to cope with one Gaul if he call in his wife, who is usually far stronger and fiercer than he, above all when she swells her neck, gnashes her teeth, and poising her huge arms, begins to rain down blows and kicks like shots from a catapult.[29]

The Gauls believed in a variety of gods, now too dead to mind anonymity. Belief in a pleasant life after death was so keen as to be in Caesar's judgment an important source of Gallic bravery. On the strength of it, says Valerius

---

* The Ambiani in Amiens, Bellovaci in Beauvais, Bituriges in Bourges, Carnutes in Chartres, Parisii in Paris, Pictones in Poitiers, Remi in Rheims, Senones in Sens, Suessiones in Soissons, etc.

Maximus, men lent money to be repaid in heaven; and Poseidonius claimed to have seen Gauls at a funeral write letters to their friends in the other world and throw them upon the pyre so that the dead man might deliver them;[30] we should enjoy a Gaul's opinion of these Roman tales. A priestly class, the Druids, controlled all education and vigorously inculcated religious belief. They conducted a colorful ritual, in sacred groves more often than in temples; and to appease the gods they offered human sacrifice of men condemned to death for crime; the custom will appear barbarous to those who have not seen an electrocution. The Druids were the only learned, perhaps the only literate, part of the community. They composed hymns, poems, and historical records; they studied "the stars and their movements, the size of the universe and the earth, and the order of nature," [31] and formulated a practicable calendar. They served as judges and had great influence at the courts of the tribal kings. Pre-Roman, like medieval, Gaul was a political feudalism clothed in theocracy.

Under these kings and priests Celtic Gaul reached its zenith in the fourth century B.C. Population expanded with the productivity of the La Tène techniques, and the result was a series of wars for land. About 400 B.C. the Celts, who already held most of central Europe as well as Gaul, conquered Britain, Spain, and north Italy. In 390 they pushed south to Rome; in 278 they pillaged Delphi and conquered Phrygia. A century later their vigor began to wane, partly through the softening influence of wealth and Greek ways, partly through the political atomism of feudal barons. Just as in medieval France the kings broke the power of the barons and established a unified state, conversely, in the century before Caesar, the lords of the manors broke the power of the kings and left Gaul more fragmentary than before. The Celtic front was pushed back everywhere except in Ireland; the Carthaginians subdued the Celts in Spain, the Romans drove them out of Italy, the Cimbri and Teutones overran them in Germany and southern Gaul. In 125 B.C. the Romans, eager to control the road to Spain, conquered southern Gaul and made it a Roman province. In 58 B.C. the Gallic leaders begged Caesar to help them repel a German invasion. Caesar complied and named his own reward.

Caesar and Augustus reorganized Gaul into four provinces: Gallia Narbonensis in the south, known to the Romans as *provincia*, and to us as Provence, then largely Hellenized through the Greek settlements on the Mediterranean coast; Aquitania in the southwest, chiefly Iberian in population; in the center Gallia Lugdunensis, overwhelmingly Celtic; and in the northeast Belgica, predominantly German. Rome recognized and abetted these ethnic divisions to forestall united revolt. The tribal cantons were retained as administrative areas; the magistrates were chosen by owners of property, whose allegiance was secured by Rome's support of them against the lower classes; and Roman citizenship was granted as a prize to loyal and useful Gauls. A provincial assembly of representatives chosen from every canton met each year in Lyons; at first it limited itself cautiously to the ritual of Augustan worship, but soon it passed on to sending requests to the Roman governors, then recommendations,.then demands. The administration of justice was taken out of the hands of the Druids, who were suppressed, and France received Roman law. For almost a century Gaul submitted peacefully to the new yoke; for a moment in A.D. 68, and again in 71, revolt flared under Vindex and Civilis; but the people gave scant support to these movements, and the love of liberty yielded to the enjoyment of prosperity, security, and peace.

Under the *Pax Romana* Gaul became one of the richest parts of the Empire. Rome marveled at the wealth of the Gallic nobles who entered the Senate under Claudius, and a century later Florus contrasted the flourishing economy of Gaul with the decline of Italy.[33] Forests were cleared, swamps were drained, agriculture was improved even to the introduction of a mechanical reaper,[34] and the grape and the olive spread into every canton of Gaul. Already in the first century Pliny and Columella praised the wines of Burgundy and Bordeaux. There were large estates tilled by serfs and slaves and owned by the forerunners of medieval feudal lords; but there were also many small proprietors, and wealth was more evenly distributed in ancient Gaul, as in modern France, than in almost any other civilized state. Progress was especially rapid in industry. By A.D. 200 Gallic potters and ironworkers were stealing the markets of Germany and the West from Italy, Gallic weavers were doing the largest textile business in the Empire, and the factories of Lyons were turning out not only commercial glass, but wares of artistic excellence.[35] Industrial techniques were handed down from father to son and formed a precious part of the classical heritage. Over 13,000 miles of road, built or improved by Roman engineers, teemed with transport and trade.

Enriched with this expanded economic life, the towns of ancient Celtica became the cities of Roman Gaul. In Aquitania the capital, Burdigala (Bordeaux), was one of the busiest of Atlantic ports; Limonum (Limoges), Avaricum (Bourges), and Augustonemetum (Clermont-Ferrand) were already rich; the last paid Zenodotus 400,000 sesterces for a colossus of Mercury.[36] In Gallia Narbonensis there were so many cities that Pliny described it as "more like Italy than a province." [37] Farthest west was Tolosa (Toulouse), famous for its schools. Narbo (Narbonne), capital of the province, was in our first century the greatest city of Gaul, the chief port of exit for Gallic goods to Italy and Spain; "here," Sidonius Apollinaris would say, "are walls, promenades, taverns, arches, porticoes, a forum, a theater, temples, baths, markets, meadows, lakes, a bridge, and the sea." [38] Farther east, on the great Via Domitia from Spain to Italy, lay Nemausus (Nîmes). Its pretty Maison Carrée was raised by Augustus and the town to commemorate his grandsons Lucius and Caius Caesar; its inner colonnade is lamentably sunk into the cella wall, but its free Corinthian columns are as lovely as any in Rome. The amphitheater, which seated 20,000, is still the scene of periodical pageantry. The Roman aqueduct that brought Nîmes fresh water became in time the Pont du Gard, or Bridge of the Gard River; standing today as a gigantic ruin in the rugged countryside beyond the city, its massive lower arches contrast to fine effect with the smaller arches above them to make the structure a revealing witness of Rome's engineering art.

Eastward on the Mediterranean, at the mouth of the Rhone, Caesar founded Arelate (Arles), in the hope that it would replace rebellious Massalia as a ship-building center and port. Massalia (Marseilles), already old when Caesar was born, remained Greek in language and culture until his death. Through its harbor Hellenic agriculture, arboriculture, viticulture, and culture had entered Gaul; here, above all, western Europe exchanged its goods for those of the classic world. It was one of the great university centers of the Empire, especially re-nowned for its school of law. It declined after Caesar, but maintained its ancient status as a free city, independent of the provincial governor. Farther east were Forum Iulii (Fréjus), Antipolis (Antibes), and Nicaea (Nice)—this in the little province of the Maritime Alps. Sailing up the Rhone from Arelate the traveler came to Avenio (Avignon) and Arausio (Orange); here a powerful arch sur-vives from Augustus' days, and an immense Roman theater still hears ancient plays.

The largest of the Gallic provinces was Gallia Lugdunensis, named from Lug-dunum (Lyons), its capital. Situated at the confluence of the Rhone and the Saône, and at the crossing of great highways built by Agrippa, the city became the trading center of a rich region and the capital of all Gaul. Iron, glass, and ceramic industries helped to sustain a population of 200,000 in our first century.[40] Northward lay Cabillonum (Chalon-sur-Saône), Caesarodunum (Tours), Au-gustodunum (Autun), Cenabum (Orléans), and Lutetia (Paris). "I have spent the winter" (357-58), writes the Emperor Julian, "in our beloved Lutetia, for so the Gauls term the little town of the Parisii, a small island in the river. . . . Good wine is grown here."[41]

Belgica, which included parts of France and Switzerland, was almost entirely agricultural; its industry was for the most part attached to the villas whose numerous remains suggest a baronial life of comfort and luxury. Here Augustus founded the cities now known as Soissons, St. Quentin, Senlis, Beauvais, and Trèves. The last, Augusta Trevirorum, rose to prominence as the headquarters of the army defending the Rhine; under Diocletian it replaced Lyons as the capital of Gaul, and in the fifth century it was the greatest city north of the Alps. It is still rich in classic remains—the Porta Nigra in its Roman wall, the Baths of St. Barbara, the Tomb of the Secundini family at nearby Igel, and the crude reliefs on the fortress blocks of neighboring Neumagen.

In and around these towns life slowly changed its surface and obstinately renewed its elements. The Gauls kept their character, their breeches, and for three centuries their language. Latin triumphed in the sixth century, chiefly through its use by the Roman Church, but it was already being clipped and nosed into French. In Gaul Rome achieved her greatest triumph in the transmission of civilization. Great French historians like Jullian and Funck-Brentano [43] have thought that France would have fared better without the Roman conquest, but a still greater historian believed that the Roman conquest was the sole alternative to a German conquest of Gaul. If Caesar had not won there, says Mommsen,

> the migration of peoples would have occurred 400 years sooner than it did, and would have come at a time when Italian civilization had not become naturalized either in Gaul, or on the Danube, or in Africa and Spain. Inasmuch as the great Roman general and statesman with sure glance perceived in the German tribes the rival antagonists of the Romano-Greek world; inasmuch as with firm hand he established the new system of aggressive defense, down even to its details, and taught men to protect the frontiers of the Empire by rivers and artificial ramparts . . . he gained for the Greco-Roman culture the interval necessary to civilize the West.[44]

The Rhine was the frontier between classic and primitive civilization. Gaul could not defend that frontier; Rome did; and that fact determined the history of Europe to this day.

V. BRITAIN

About 1200 B.C. a branch of the Celts crossed over from Gaul and settled in England. They found there a mingled population of dark-haired people, possibly Iberian, and light-haired Scandinavians. They conquered these natives, married them, and spread through England and Wales. About 100 B.C. (for so the egocentric foreshortening of history telescopes eventful centuries, and erases vital generations from a crowded memory) another branch of Celts came from the Continent and dispossessed their kinsmen of southern and eastern Britain. When Caesar came he found the island peopled by several independent tribes, each with its expansive king. He gave to all the population the name *Britanni*, from a Gallic tribe, so called, just south of the Channel, in the belief that the same tribe inhabited both shores.

Celtic Britain was in customs, language, and religion essentially like Celtic Gaul, but its civilization was less advanced. It passed from bronze to iron some six centuries before Christ, three centuries after Gaul. Pytheas, the Massiliot explorer, sailing the Atlantic to England about 350 B.C., found the

Cantii of Kent already prosperous with agriculture and trade. The soil was fertile from abundant rain and contained rich ores of copper, iron, tin, and lead. By Caesar's time domestic industry was able to supply an active commerce among the tribes and with the Continent, and coins were minted in bronze and gold.[45] His invasions were reconnaissance raids; he brought back the double assurance that the tribes were incapable of united resistance and that the crops were adequate to feed an invading army coming at the proper time. A century later (A.D. 43) Claudius crossed the Channel with 40,000 men whose discipline, armament, and skill proved too much for the natives; Britain in her turn became a Roman province. In 61 a British tribal queen, Boudicca or Boadicea, led a furious revolt, alleging that Roman officers had ravished both her daughters, plundered her realm, and sold many of its freemen into slavery. While the Roman governor Paulinus was busy conquering the Isle of Man, Boudicca's army overcame the single legion that opposed it and marched upon Londinium—already, says Tacitus, "the chief residence of merchants, and a great mart of trade." [46] Every Roman found there or in Verulamium (St. Albans) was killed; 70,000 Romans and their allies were slain before Paulinus and his legions caught up with the rebel force. Boudicca, standing with her daughters in a chariot, fought heroically in defeat. She drank poison, and 80,000 Britons were put to the sword.

Tacitus tells how his father-in-law Agricola, as governor of Britain (A.D. 78-84), brought civilization to a "rude, scattered, and warlike people" by establishing schools, spreading the use of Latin, and encouraging cities and rich men to build temples, basilicas, and public baths. "By degrees," says the caustic historian, "the charms of vice gained admission to British hearts; baths, porticoes, and elegant banquets grew into vogue; and the new manners, which in reality only served to sweeten slavery, were by the unsuspecting Britons called the arts of polished humanity." [47] In swift campaigns Agricola carried these arts, and Roman rule, to the Clyde and the Forth, defeated an army of 30,000 Scots, and wished to go farther when Domitian recalled him. Hadrian built a wall (122-27) seventy miles across the island from Solway Firth to the mouth of the Tyne as a defense against not-unsuspecting Scots; and twenty years later Lollius raised farther north the thirty-three-mile Wall of Antoninus between the firths of Clyde and Forth. For over two centuries these fortifications kept Britain safe for Rome.

As Rome's rule achieved stability it became more lenient. The cities were managed by native senates, assemblies, and magistrates, and the countryside was left, as in Gaul, to tribal chieftains amenable to Roman surveillance. It was not so urban a civilization as Italy's, nor so rich as Gaul's; but it was under Roman stimulus and protection that most British cities now took form. Four of them were Roman "colonies," whose freemen enjoyed Roman citizenship: Camulodunum (Colchester), the first Roman capital of Britain, and the seat of the provincial council; Lindum, whose modern name Lin*coln* declares its ancient privilege; Eboracum (York), an important military post; and Glevum, whose name Gloucester merges Glevum with *chester*, the Anglo-Saxon word for town.* Chester, Winchester, Dorchester, Chichester, Leicester, Silchester, and Manchester appear to have had their beginnings in the first two centuries of Roman rule. These were small towns, each with some 6000 souls; but they had paved and drained streets, forums, basilicas, temples, and houses with stone foundations and tiled roofs. Viroconium (Wroxeter) had a basilica accommodating 6000 persons, and public baths where hundreds could bathe at once. The hot springs of Aquae Salis ("Salt Waters"), now Bath, made it a fashionable resort in ancient days, as its surviving *thermae* show. Londinium rose to economic and military importance because of its position on the Thames and its radiating roads. It grew to a population of 60,000 and soon replaced Camulodunum as Britain's capital.[49]

Most of the homes in Roman London were of brick and stucco, in smaller towns, of wood. Climate determined their architecture: a gable roof to shed rain and snow, and many windows to let in whatever sun might shine; for even "on clear days," said Strabo, "the sun is to be seen only for three or four hours." [50] But interiors followed the Roman style—mosaic floors, large bathrooms, muraled walls, and (far more than in Italian homes) central heating by hot-air conduits in walls and floors. Coal—mined from surface veins—was used not only for warming houses but for industrial processes like smelting lead. Apparently the mines of ancient Britain were owned by the state, but were leased to private entrepreneurs.[51] There was a factory (*fabrica*) at Bath for the manufacture of iron weapons,[52] and probably the making of pottery, bricks, and tiles had reached the factory stage; but most industries were carried on in homes, small shops, and villas. Five thousand miles of Roman roads, and innumerable waterways, were the arteries of a brisk internal trade. A modest foreign commerce, inverting the custom of Britain today, exported raw materials for manufactured goods.

How deeply did Roman civilization, in its four centuries of domination, penetrate the life and soul of Britain? Latin became the language of politics, law, literature, and the educated minority, but in the countryside and among many workers in the towns the Celtic tongue survived; even now, in Wales and the Isle of Man, it holds its own. Roman schools in Britain spread literacy and determined the Roman form of the English alphabet; and a stream of Latin words poured into English speech. Temples were built to Roman gods, but the common man cherished his Celtic deities and feasts. Even in the cities Rome sank no lasting roots. The people submitted apathetically to a rule that brought them a fructifying peace and such prosperity as the island would not experience again until the Industrial Revolution.

---

* So Haverfield;[48] the more widely accepted derivation is from the Latin *castrum*, fortress, or *castra*, camp. Most Roman-British towns were designed on the chessboard plan of a Roman camp.

VI. THE BARBARIANS

The decisions of Augustus and Tiberius not to attempt the conquest of Germany were among the pivotal events of European history. Had Germany been conquered and Romanized like Gaul, nearly all Europe west of Russia would have had one organization, one government, one classic culture, perhaps one tongue; and central Europe might have served as a buffer against those eastern hordes whose pressure upon the Germans caused the Germanic invasions of Italy.

We call them Germans, but they themselves have never used this name, and no one knows when it came.* They were in classic days a medley of independent tribes occupying Europe between the Rhine and the Vistula, between the Danube and the North and Baltic Seas. Gradually, in the two centuries from Augustus to Aurelius, they passed from migratory hunting and herding to agriculture and village life; but they were still so far nomadic that they rapidly exhausted the land they tilled and then moved on to conquer new acres by the sword. If we may believe Tacitus, war was the German's meat and drink:

> To cultivate the earth, and wait the regular produce of the seasons, is not the maxim of a German; you will more readily persuade him to attack the enemy and provoke honorable wounds on the field of battle. To earn by the sweat of your brow what you might gain at the price of your blood is in the opinion of a German a sluggish principle, unworthy of a soldier.[53]

The Roman historian, lamenting the deterioration of his own people under luxury and peace, described with the exaggeration of a moralist the martial qualities of the Germans, and the ardor with which the women spurred them into battle, often fighting by their side. Flight from the enemy meant lifelong disgrace, in many cases suicide. Strabo described the Germans as "wilder and taller than the Gauls," [54] and Seneca, as if he had read Tacitus, drew ominous conclusions: "To those vigorous bodies, to those souls unwitting of pleasures, luxury, and wealth, add but a little more tactical skill and discipline—I say no more; you [Romans] will only be able to hold your own against them by returning to the virtues of your sires." [55]

In peace, Tacitus reports, these warriors were correspondingly indolent. The men spent their time (presumably after hunting or harvesting) in eating heavy meals of meat and drinking rivers of beer, while the women and children did the work of the home.[56] The German bought his wife from her father by a gift of cattle or weapons; he had the power of life and death over her and their children, subject to the approval of the tribal assembly; nevertheless, women were held in

---

* Rome used the adjective *germanus* (from *germen*, offspring) to mean born of the same parents; and in applying it to the Germans they may have had in mind the kinship organization of the Teutonic tribes.

high honor, were often asked to decide tribal disputes, and were as free to divorce their husbands as these were to divorce them.[57] Some chieftains had several wives, but the usual German family was monogamous and maintained (we are assured) a lofty level of marital morality. Adultery was "seldom heard of" and was punished in the woman by cutting off her hair and driving her naked through the streets to be flogged as she fled. The wife was allowed to practice abortion if she wished,[58] but normally she bore many children. A man without children was so rare that wills were not made; it was assumed that the property of the family would go down from father to son, generation after generation.[59]

Four classes composed the population: (1) bondsmen, some of them slaves, most of them serfs bound to the soil and obliged to pay the landowner in produce; (2) freedmen—unfranchised renters; (3) freemen—landowners and warriors; and (4) nobles—landowners who traced their pedigrees to the gods, but based their power upon substantial patrimonies and armed bodyguards (comites, companions, "counts"). The tribal assembly was composed of nobles, guards, and freemen; they came in arms, chose the chief or king, approved the proposals submitted to them by clashing their spears, or rejected them by a majority of grunts. The second and third classes were partly engaged in handicrafts and the metallurgical industries, in which the Germans excelled; the fourth provided the lords and knights and chivalry of feudal Germany.

Very little cultural superstructure was added to this simple social organization. Religion had at this time barely emerged from nature worship into the cult of anthropomorphic deities. Tacitus calls them Mars, Mercury, and Hercules—probably Tiu (Tyr), Wodin (Odin), and Donar (Tor); we still unwittingly commemorate them, and Freya, the goddess of love, on four days of every week. There was a virgin goddess Hertha (Mother Earth), impregnated by a sky-god; and every imagination and need was supplied by a varied population of fairies, elves, cobolds, nixes, giants, and dwarfs. Human sacrifice was offered to Wodin, perhaps tastier animals to other gods. Worship was conducted in the open air in forests and groves, for the Germans thought it absurd to confine a nature spirit in an abode built by human hands. There was no powerful sacerdotal class like the Druids of Gaul or Britain, but there were priests and priestesses who presided over religious ceremonies, sat as judges in criminal cases, and divined the future by studying the motions and neighings of white horses. As in Gaul, there were bards who sang in rude verse the legends and history of their tribes. A small minority could read and write, and adapted the Latin characters to form the "runes" that serve for their alphabet. Art was primitive, but skillful work was done in gold.

When Rome withdrew her legions from Germany she retained control of the Rhine from source to mouths and divided the majestic valley into two provinces—Upper and Lower Germany. The latter included Holland and the Rhineland south to Cologne. This once lovely city, known to the Romans as Colonia Agrippinensis, had been made a colony (A.D. 50) in honor of Nero's mother, who had been born there; half a century later it was the most opulent settlement on the

Rhine. The province of Upper Germany followed the Rhine southward through Moguntiacum (Mayence), Aquae Aureliae (Baden-Baden), Argentoratum (Strasbourg), and Augusta Rauricorum (Augst) to Vindonissa (Windisch). Nearly all these towns had the usual array of temples, basilicas, theaters, baths, and public statuary. Many of the legionaries sent by Rome to guard the Rhine lived outside their camps, married German girls, and remained as citizens when their term of service was complete. The Rhineland was probably as thickly settled and affluent in Roman days as at any time before the nineteenth century.

Between the Rhine and the Danube, as we have seen, Rome's military engineers built a fortified road (*limes*), with a fortress every nine miles, and 300 miles of wall. It served Rome for a century, but availed little when the Roman birth rate fell too far below the German. Still weaker as a frontier was the Danube, which the ancients considered the longest river in the world. South of it lay the half-barbarous provinces of Raetia, Noricum, and Pannonia, approximately composing what our youth knew as Austria-Hungary and Serbia. On the site of modern Augsburg (i.e., Augustus' town) the Romans established a colony, Augusta Vindelicorum, as a main station on the road from Italy over the Brenner Pass to the Danube. On the river they built two fortress cities—at Vindobona, now Vienna, and at Aquincum on the heights from which Buda looks down upon Pesth. In southeastern Pannonia, on the Save River west of the modern Belgrade, the city of Sirmium (Mitrovica) rose to be in Diocletian's time one of the four imperial capitals. South of Pannonia, in the province of Dalmatia, the commercial energy of Greeks, Romans, and natives had developed the Adriatic ports of Salona (Spalato), Apollonia (near Valona), and Dyrrhachium (Durazzo). From these provinces below the Danube came imperial Rome's sturdiest soldiers and, in the third century, the martial emperors who would for 200 years hold back the barbarian avalanche. East of Pannonia lay Dacia (Rumania), with its now vanished capital of Sarmizegetusa. South and east of this Moesia (parts of Yugoslavia, Rumania, and Bulgaria) boasted two cities on the Danube—Singidunum (Belgrade) and Troesmis (Iglitza); one near the Isker—Sardica (Sofia); and three major towns on the Black Sea—Istrus, Tomi (Constanta), and Odessus (Varna). In these harassed settlements Greek civilization and Roman arms struggled in vain to maintain themselves against the Goths, Sarmatians, Huns, and other barbarian tribes breeding and wandering north of the great stream.

It was Rome's inability to civilize these provinces south of the Danube that led to her fall. The task was too great for a people suffering from old age; the vitality of the master race was ebbing in sterile comfort while the tribes of the north were advancing in reckless health. When Trajan subsidized the Sarmatians to keep the peace it was the beginning of the end; when Marcus Aurelius brought thousands of Germans into the Empire as settlers, the dikes were down. German soldiers were welcomed into the Roman army and rose to positions of command; German families multiplied in Italy while Italian families died. In this process the movement of Romanization was reversed: the barbarians were barbarizing Rome.

Nevertheless, it was a magnificent and precious achievement that the West, if not the North, had been won for the classical heritage. There, at least, the arts of peace had emerged from the travail of war, and men could turn their swords into plowshares without decaying in urban ease and slums. Out of the earthy vigor of Spain and Gaul a new civilization would rise when the barbarian flood would fall; and the seed of despot centuries would come to fruit and pardon in the lands where the merciless legions had brought the law of Rome and the enkindling light of Greece.

CHAPTER XXIII

Roman Greece

I. PLUTARCH

ROME tried hard to be generous to Greece and did not quite fail. No garrisons were placed in the new province of Achaea; less was exacted from it than its own taxgatherers had claimed before; the city-states were allowed to govern themselves by their old constitutions and laws; and many of them—Athens, Sparta, Plataea, Delphi, and others—were "free cities" exempt from all restrictions except the right to wage foreign or class war.

Nevertheless, hungry for its ancient liberties, and bled by Roman generals, moneylenders, and businessmen skilled in buying cheap and selling dear, Greece joined in Mithridates' revolt and paid the heaviest penalty. Athens suffered a devastating siege, and Delphi, Elis, and Epidaurus were pillaged of their sanctuary hoards. A generation later Caesar and Pompey, then Antony and Brutus, fought their duels on Greek territory, conscripted Greek men, requisitioned Greek crops and gold, levied twenty years' taxes in two, and left the cities destitute. Under Augustus Greek Asia recovered, but Greece herself remained poor, ruined not so much by the Roman conquest as by a stifling despotism in Sparta, a chaotic freedom in Athens, a blighting sterility in soil and men. Her most enterprising sons deserted her for younger and richer lands. The rise of new powers in Egypt, Carthage, and Rome, and the development of industry in the Hellenistic East, left the homeland of the classic spirit outmoded and forlorn. Rome loaded Greece with compliments and ravaged her art: Scaurus took 3000 statues for his theater, Caligula ordered the husband of his mistress to comb Greece for statuary, and Nero alone took half the sculptures of Delphi. Not till Hadrian would Athens smile again.

Epirus bore the brunt of Rome's anger in the Macedonian Wars; the Senate delivered it to the rapine of the soldiers, and 150,000 Epirots were sold as slaves. Augustus built a new capital for Epirus at Nicopolis to celebrate his triumph at near-by Actium; civilization must have had some homage there, since the City of Victory gave Epictetus an audience and a home. Macedonia fared better than its loyal neighbor; it was rich in minerals and timber, and its commercial life was quickened by the Via Egnatia that spanned it and Thrace from Apollonia and Dyrrhachium to Byzantium. On this great highway, still in part preserved, lay the chief cities of the province—Edessa, Pella, and Thessalonica. This last—known to us as Salonika, but to modern Greeks by its ancient name (Victory of Thessaly)—was the capital of the province, seat of the provincial council, and one of the great ports of trade between the Balkans and Asia. Thrace, farther east, devoted itself to agriculture, herding, and mining; but it had considerable cities at Serdica (Sofia), Philippopolis its capital, Adrianople, Perinthus, and Byzantium (Istanbul). Here at the Golden Horn the merchants and fishmongers grew rich while the Greek settlers of the hinterland gave way to the encroaching barbarians; all the grain of the interior came down to its docks, all the commerce of Scythia and the Black Sea paid toll as it passed by, and the fish almost leaped into the net as they poured through the narrow Bosporus. Soon Constantine would recognize this site as the key city of the classic world.

Thessaly, south of Macedonia, specialized in wheat and fine horses. Euboea, the great island named of old (like Boeotia) for its fine cattle, was described by Dio Chrysostom [1] as reverting to barbarism in our second century; here, above all, the discouragement of the poor by the concentration of land and wealth in the hands of a few families, the discouragement of the rich by ever-rising taxes and liturgies, and the discouragement of parentage by selfish wealth and desperate poverty had almost wiped out a once thriving agricultural population, and cattle grazed within the walls of Chalcis and Eretria. Boeotia had not recovered from the death and taxes laid upon it by Sulla's campaigns; "Thebes," said Strabo, "is only a village," huddled into what had once been merely its Cadmea or citadel. A century of peace, however, brought some prosperity to Plataea; and Chaeronea, on whose plains Philip and Sulla had won empires, retained enough charm to keep its most famous citizen; it had become so small, said Plutarch, that he would not make it smaller by leaving it.[2] In his calm career and genial thought we find a fairer side of a somber scene, a decent middle class clinging to ancient virtues, capable of civic devotion, warm friendship, and parental love. There is no more pleasant character in our tale than Plutarch of Chaeronea.

He was born there about A.D. 46, and died there about 126. He was a student at Athens when Nero collected triumphs in Greece. He must have had a fair income, for he traveled in Egypt and Asia Minor and twice in Italy; he lectured in Greek at Rome and seems to have served his country in some diplomatic role. He liked the great capital and the good manners and honorable life of its new aristocracy; he admired their stoic code, and agreed with Ennius that Rome had been made by morality and character. As he contemplated these living nobles and the noble dead, the thought came to him of comparing the heroes of Rome with those of Greece. He proposed not merely to write history or even biography, but to teach virtue and heroism by historic exemplars; even his *Parallel Lives* were in his mind *Moralia*. He was always a teacher and never lost a chance to tie a moral to a tale; but who has ever done it more gracefully? He warns us, in his "Alexander," that he is more interested in character than in history; he hopes that by pairing and comparing great Romans with great Greeks he will pass on some moral stimulus, some heroic impulse, to his readers. With disarming candor he confesses that he himself has become a better man through keeping company so long with distinguished men.[3]

We must not expect to find in him the conscience and accuracy of a proper historian; he is rich in errors of name and place and date and occasionally (if we may judge) misunderstands events; he even fails in two major tasks of the biographer—to show the derivation of his subject's character and work from heredity, environment, and circumstance, and the development of character through growth, responsibility, and crisis; in Plutarch, as in Heracleitus, a man's character is his fate. But no one who has read the *Lives* can feel their shortcomings; these are lost in the vivid narrative, the exciting episodes, the fascinating anecdotes, the wise comments, the noble style. In all these 1500 pages there is not a line of padding; every sentence counts. A hundred eminent men—generals, poets, and philosophers—have borne witness to the book; "it is," said Mme Roland, "the pasture of great souls." [4] "I can hardly do without Plutarch," wrote Montaigne; "it is my breviary." [5] Shakespeare takes many stories here, and his view of Brutus goes back through Plutarch to Roman aristocrats. Napoleon carried the *Lives* with him almost everywhere; and Heine, reading them, could hardly restrain himself from leaping upon a horse and riding forth to conquer France. Greece has not left us a more precious book.

Having seen the Mediterranean world Plutarch returned to Chaeronea, raised four sons and a daughter, lectured and wrote, journeyed now and then to Athens, but for the most part shared to the end of his days the simple life of his native town. He thought it an obligation to combine public office with his scholarly pursuits. His fellow citizens elected him building inspector, then chief magistrate, then Boeotarch—member of the national council. He presided over municipal ceremonies and festivals, and became in his spare moments a priest of the revived oracle at Delphi. He thought it unwise to reject the old faith because of its intellectual incredibility; the vital thing was not the creed but the support it gave to man's weak morality, the reinforcing bond it wove among the members and generations of a family and a state. The thrill of religious emotion was in his judgment the most deepening experience of life. Tolerant as well as pious, he almost founded the study of comparative religion by his treatises on Roman and Egyptian cults.[6] All deities, he argued, are aspects of one supreme being, timeless, indescribable, so far removed from earthly and temporal affairs that intermediary spirits (*daimones*) must create and regulate the world. There are also evil spirits, marshaled by some master demon who is the source and soul of all the chaos, irrationality, and viciousness in nature and man. It is good, Plutarch thought, to believe in personal immortality—a rewarding Heaven, a cleansing Purgatory, a punishing Hell; he was comforted by the possibility that a stay in Purgatory might purify even Nero, and that only a few would suffer eternal damnation.[7] He denounced the terrors of superstition as worse than atheism, but he accepted divination, oracles, necromancy, and the prophetic power of dreams. He did not pretend to be an original philosopher; like Apuleius and so many others of that age, he described himself as an adapter of Plato. He condemned the Epicureans for replacing the fear of Hell with the gloom of annihilation, and criticized the "repugnances" of Stoicism; but he held, like a Stoic, that "to follow God and to obey reason are the same thing." [8]

His lectures and essays have properly been collected under the title *Moralia*, for most of them are simple and genial preachments on the wisdom of life. They discuss everything, from the advisability of keeping old men in public office to the priority of the chicken or the egg. Plutarch is fond of his library, but confesses that good health is more precious than good books:

> Some men, led by gluttony, rush off to join in drinking bouts, as if they were laying in provisions for a siege. . . . The less expensive foods are always more helpful. . . . When, in a precipitate retreat, Artaxerxes Memnon had nothing to eat but barley-bread and figs, he exclaimed, "What a pleasure is this, which has never been mine before!" . . . Wine is the most beneficial of beverages, provided there is a happy combination of it with the occasion as well as with water. . . . Especially to be feared are indigestions arising from meats, for they are depressing at the outset, and a pernicious residue from them remains behind. It is best to accustom the body not to require meat in addition to other food. For the earth yields in abundance many things not only for nourishment but for comfort and enjoyment. But since custom has become a sort of unnatural second nature, our use of meat should be . . . as a prop and support of our diet; we should use other foods . . . more in accord with nature, and less dulling to the reasoning faculty, which, as it were, is kindled from plain and light substances.[9]

He follows Plato in advocating equal opportunity for women, and gives many examples of cultured ladies in antiquity (there were some in his own circle); but he views adultery by the man with all the lenience of a pagan male:

> If a man in private life, who is incontinent and dissolute in regard to his pleasures, commit some peccadillo with a paramour or maidservant, his wedded wife ought not to be indignant or angry, but she should reason that it is respect for her that leads him to share his licentiousness with another woman.[10]

Nevertheless, we rise from these charming essays warmed by the fellowship of a man humane, essentially wholesome, and complete. We are not offended by the commonness of his ideas; his moderation is a welcome antidote to the ideological hysteria of our time; his good sense, his kindly humor, and his engaging illustrations carry us on unresisting, even over the shoals of his platitudes. It is refreshing to find a philosopher who is wise enough to be happy. Let us be thankful, he counsels us, for the common boons and graces of life, and feel them none the less gladly for their permanence:

> We must not forget those blessings and comforts which we share with many more, but must . . . joy in this, that we live, that we have our health, that we behold the light of the sun. . . . Will not the good man consider every day a festival? . . . For the world is the most august of temples, and most worthy of its Lord. Into this temple man is introduced at his birth, into the presence not of statues made with hands and motionless, but such as the Divine Mind has manifested to our senses . . . even the sun, moon, and stars, and the rivers ever pouring forth fresh water, and the earth producing food. . . . As this life is the most perfect of initiations into the most exalted of mysteries, we should ever be filled with good cheer and rejoicing.[11]

II. INDIAN SUMMER

Plutarch exemplifies two movements of his time: the return to religion and the passing renaissance of Greek literature and philosophy. The former was universal, the latter was confined to Athens and the Greek East. Six cities of the Peloponnesus prospered, but contributed little to Greek thought. Western commerce and a busy textile industry kept Patrae alive through Roman and medieval history even to our day. Olympia throve on the leavings of tourists coming to see Pheidias' *Zeus* or the Olympic games. It is one of the pleasantest aspects of Greek history that these quadrennial contests continued from 776 B.C. to A.D. 394, when Theodosius ended them. As in the days of Prodicus and Herodotus, philosophers and historians came to harangue the crowd assembling for the festival. Dio Chrysostom describes authors reading "their stupid compositions" to transient listeners, poets reciting their verses, rhetoricians thumping the air, and "sophists in great number, like gorgeous peacocks," coming to blow their wind over the multitude;[12] he proved no more silent than the rest. Epictetus pictures the spectators cramped and sweltering in the unshaded stands, burned by the sun or drenched by the rain, but forgetting everything in the tumult and the shouting that marked the final moments of each bout or race.[13] The old Nemean, Isthmian, Pythian, and Panathenaic games continued; new ones were added like the Pan-hellenia of Hadrian; and many of them included competitions in poetry, oratory, or music. "Can you not hear classical music at the great festivals?" asks a character in Lucian.[14] Gladiatorial combats were introduced to Greece by the Roman colony at Corinth; thence they spread to other cities until even the Theater of Dionysus was befouled with butchery. Many Greeks—Dio Chrysostom, Lucian, Plutarch—protested against the desecration; Demonax, the Cynic philosopher, begged the Athenians not to allow the innovation until they had thrown down the altar of Pity at Athens;[15] but the Roman games continued in Greece till predominantly Christian times.

Sparta and Argos were still moderately alive, and Epidaurus grew rich on the visits of sick bodies and souls to the shrine of Asclepius. Corinth, controlling the trade across the isthmus, became, within half a century of its re-establishment by Caesar, the wealthiest city in Greece. Its heterogeneous population of Romans, Greeks, Syrians, Jews, and Egyptians, most of them uprooted from their native lands and morals, was notorious for commercialism, epicureanism, and immorality. The old Temple of Aphrodite Pandemos carried on an undiminished trade as the shrine and center of Corinthian prostitutes. Apuleius describes a gorgeous ballet that he saw in Corinth, representing the judgment of Paris. "Venus appeared all naked, save that her fine and comely middle was lightly covered with a thin silken smock; and this the wanton wind blew hither and thither." [16] Corinth had not mended her ways since Aspasia.

Passing through Megara into Attica, the rural scene was one of great poverty. Deforestation, erosion, and mineral depletion had been added to war, emigration, taxation, and race suicide to make a desert of the Roman peace. Two cities alone in Attica were prosperous: Eleusis, whose sacramental Mysteries drew lucrative crowds to her every year; and Athens, the educational and intellectual center of the classic world. Its ancient institutions—council, assembly, and archons—still functioned, and Rome had restored the Areopagus to its primeval authority as the seat of judgment and the citadel of property rights. Rulers like Antiochus IV, Herod the Great, Augustus, and Hadrian rivaled millionaires like Herodes Atticus in benefactions to the city. Herodes rebuilt the stadium in marble, almost exhausting Pentelicus, and raised an odeon, or music hall, at the foot of the Acropolis. Hadrian provided funds to complete the Olympieum, and Zeus, who now had one foot in the grave, received a home worthy of his Casanova prime.

Meanwhile the unrivaled fame of Athens in letters, philosophy, and education brought a stream of rich youths and needy scholars to her schools. The University of Athens consisted of ten professorships endowed by the city or the emperor, and a host of private lecturers and tutors. Instruction was given in literature, philology, rhetoric, philosophy, mathematics, astronomy, medicine, and law—usually in gymnasia or theaters, sometimes in temples or homes. Except in oratory or law the curriculum had no thought of equipping the student to earn a living; it sought rather to sharpen his mind, deepen his understanding, and provide him with a moral code. It produced many brilliant intellects, but also it generated thousands of cobweb-spinners who would turn both philosophy and religion into a maze of controversial theories.

As Athens depended for a considerable part of its income on the students, it put up patiently with their hilarious ways. "Freshmen" were hazed with practical jokes that sometimes injured citizens; the students of rival professors became ardent partisans and attacked one another in occasional riots like the "cane rushes" of our youth. Some students felt that they could learn more from the courtesans and gamblers of the town than from all teachers of philosophy; and we gather from Alciphron that the ladies in question looked upon the professors as dull and incompetent competitors.[17] But there was often a pleasant bond of friendship between learners and teachers; many of these invited students to dinner, guided their reading, visited them in illness, and kept their parents misinformed about their progress. Most of the lecturers lived on fees paid by each disciple; a small number of professors drew a salary from the state; and the heads of the four schools of philosophy received 10,000 drachmas ($6000) a year from the imperial Treasury.

Under these stimuli the period of the "Second Sophistic" developed—a revival of the orator-philosopher passing from city to city as honorariums might beckon, delivering addresses, teaching pupils, pleading cases in the courts, living in rich homes as spiritual counselors, and sometimes acting as honored emissaries of their city-states. The movement flourished throughout the Empire, but especially in the Greek world, in the first three centuries of our era; philosophers were then, says Dio, as numerous as cobblers.[18] The new sophists, like the old, had no common doctrine, phrased their teaching eloquently, drew large audiences, and attained in many cases high social status, imperial favor, or great wealth. They differed from the earlier Sophists in seldom questioning religion or morality; they were more interested in form and style, in oratorical technique and skill, than in the great questions that had shaken the beliefs and morals of the world; indeed, the new sophists were warm defenders of the ancient faith. Philostratus has preserved for us the lives of the leading sophists of this age; let one example suffice. Adrian of Tyre studied rhetoric at Athens and rose to the state chair of rhetoric there; he opened his inaugural address with the proud words, "Once again letters have come from Phoenicia." He rode to his lectures in a carriage with silver

harness, in rich attire, and gleaming with gems. When Marcus Aurelius visited Athens he tested Adrian by asking him to improvise an oration on a difficult theme; Adrian carried the matter off so well that Marcus loaded him with honors, silver and gold, houses and slaves. Promoted to the chair of rhetoric at Rome, Adrian's lectures, though in Greek, proved so alluring that senators adjourned their sessions, and the populace deserted the pantomimes, to go and hear him.[19] Such a career almost announces the death of philosophy; it had been swallowed up in an ocean of rhetoric, and had ceased to think when it learned to speak.

At the other extreme were the Cynics. We have described them else-where—their tattered cloak, their unkempt hair and beard, their wallet and staff, their reduction of life to simplicities, sometimes obscenities. They lived like mendicant friars, had a hierarchical organization with novices and su-periors,[20] avoided marriage and work, scorned the conventions and arti-ficialities of civilization, denounced all governments as thieves and super-fluities, laughed at all oracles, "mysteries," and gods. Everyone satirized them, Lucian most savagely; yet even Lucian admired Demonax, a cultured Cynic who had abandoned his wealth to live in philosophical poverty. He gave his century of life (A.D. 50-150) to helping others, reconciling hostile individuals and cities; and Athens, which ridiculed everything, respected him. Indicted before an Athenian court for refusing to offer sacrifice to the gods, he won acquittal by saying simply that the gods had no need of offer-ings, and that religion consisted in kindness to all. When the Athenian as-sembly was engaged in a quarrel of factions, his mere appearance sufficed to quiet the dispute; whereupon he left without having uttered a word. It was his custom, in old age, to enter any house uninvited and eat and sleep there; and every home in Athens sought the honor.[21] Lucian speaks with less sympathy of Peregrinus, who tried Christianity, abandoned it for the Cynic regimen, denounced Rome, called all Greece to revolt, and astonished an assemblage at Olympia by making and lighting his own funeral pyre, leap-ing into it, and allowing himself to be consumed in the flames (A.D. 165).[22] In such scorn of wealth and life the Cynics were paving a way for the monks of the Christian Church.

When Vespasian, Hadrian, and Marcus Aurelius established chairs of philosophy at Athens they ignored the Cynics and the Skeptics, and recog-nized only four schools of thought: the Platonic Academy, the Aristotelian Lyceum, the Stoics, and the Epicureans. The Academy had diluted Plato's proud faith in reason into the universal doubt of Carneades; but after the latter's death the school reacted toward orthodoxy, and Antiochus of As-calon, who taught Cicero at the Academy (79 B.C.), returned to Plato's con-ceptions of reason, immortality, and God. The Lyceum was now devoting

itself to natural science in the tradition of Theophrastus, or to pious commentaries on Aristotle's works. The school of Epicurus was declining in this
religious age; few men dared profess its doctrines without diplomatic reservations. In most of Greek Asia the words *Epicurean, atheist,* and *Christian* were
synonyms expressive of horror and desecration.[23]

The dominant philosophy had long since been Stoicism. The rigorous
perfectionism of its early forms had been softened by Panaetius and Poseidonius, both citizens of Rhodes. Returning to Athens after Scipio's death
(129 B.C.), Panaetius, now head of the Stoa, defined God as a material spirit
or breath (*pneuma*) permeating all things, appearing in plants as the power
of growth, in animals as soul (*psyche*), in man as reason (*logos*). His successors developed this vague pantheism into a more definitely religious philosophy. The Stoic theory of moral discipline moved closer to Cynic asceticism; and in the second century A.D. Cynicism, as one observer put it,
differed from Stoicism only by a torn cloak. In Epictetus, as in Marcus
Aurelius, we see both movements advancing toward Christianity.

III. EPICTETUS

Epictetus was born at Hierapolis in Phrygia about A.D. 50, a slave woman's
son, and therefore himself a slave. He had little chance of education, for he
was passed from one owner and city to another, until he found himself the
property of Epaphroditus, a powerful freedman in Nero's court. He was of
feeble health and lame, apparently through the brutality of one of his masters, but he lived the normal threescore years and ten. Epaphroditus allowed
him to attend the lectures of Musonius Rufus and later freed him. Epictetus
must himself have set up as a teacher in Rome, for when Domitian banished
the philosophers Epictetus was among those who fled. He settled in Nicopolis and drew to his lectures there students from many parts. One was Arrian
of Nicomedia, later governor of Cappadocia; Arrian took down the words of
Epictetus, probably in shorthand, and published them as *Diatribai*—"rub-
bings" or copies—now on all lists of the world's best books as the *Discourses.**
It is no dull formal treatise, but a classic of simple speech and bluff humor,
intimately expressing a modest and kindly, yet sharp and vigorous character.
Epictetus applied his lusty sarcasms to himself and others impartially, and
gaily mocked his rough-and-tumble style. He made no complaint when
Demonax, hearing that the old bachelor counseled marriage, sarcastically
petitioned for his daughter's hand; he excused himself on the ground that
teaching wisdom is as great a service as begetting "two or three pug-nosed

---

* Arrian later issued an *Encheiridion,* or synoptic "Handbook" of Epictetus.

children." [24] In later years he took a wife to help him care for an infant that he had rescued from exposure. In those years his fame compassed the Empire, and Hadrian counted him among his friends.

Epictetus, resembling Socrates in this as in so many other ways, cared too little about physics or metaphysics to construct a system of thought; his one subject and passion was the good life. "What do I care," he asks, "whether all existing things are composed of atoms . . . or of fire and earth? Is it not enough to learn the true nature of good and evil?" [25] Philosophy does not mean reading books about wisdom, it means training oneself in the practice of wisdom. The essence of the matter is that a man should so mold his life and conduct that his happiness shall depend as little as possible upon external things. This does not require a hermit's solitude; on the contrary, "Epicureans and blackguards" are to be condemned for detaching men from public service; the good man will take his part in civic affairs. But he will accept with equanimity all vicissitudes of fortune—poverty, bereavement, humiliation, pain, slavery, imprisonment, or death; he will know how to "endure and renounce."

> Never say about anything, "I have lost it," but only "I have given it back." Is your child dead? It has been given back. Is your wife dead? She has been returned. "I have had my farm taken away." Very well; this, too, has been given back. So long as God gives it to you take care of it as something not your own. . . . "Alas, that I should be lame in one leg!" Slave! do you then, because of one paltry leg, blame the universe? Will you not make a free gift of it to the whole? . . . I must go into exile: does anyone keep me from going with a smile, serene? . . . "I will throw you into prison." It is only my body you imprison. I must die; must I then die complaining? . . . These are the lessons that philosophy ought to rehearse, and write down daily, and practice. . . . A platform or a prison are places, one high, the other low; but your moral purpose can be kept the same in either place.[27]

The slave can be spiritually free, like Diogenes; the prisoner can be free, like Socrates; the emperor can be a slave, like Nero.[28] Even death is a minor incident in the good man's life; he may advance its coming if he finds that evil too heavily outweighs good;[29] in any case he will receive it calmly as part of the secret wisdom of Nature.

> If heads of grain had feeling, ought they to pray that they should never be harvested? . . . I would have you know that it is a curse never to die. . . . The ship goes down. What, then, am I to do? Whatever I can . . . I drown without fear, neither shrinking nor crying out against God, but recognizing that what is born must also

perish. For I am a part of the whole, as an hour is part of a day. I must come on as the hour, and like an hour pass away.[30] . . . Regard yourself as but a single thread of all that go to make up the garment.[31] . . . Seek not that the things which happen to you should happen as you wish, but wish the things that happen to be as they are, and you will find tranquillity.[32]

Though he often speaks of Nature as an impersonal force, Epictetus as frequently infuses his conception with personality, intelligence, and love. The atmosphere of religion pervading his age warms his philosophy to a self-surrendering piety akin to that of the Stoic emperor who would soon read him and echo his thought. He speaks with a fine eloquence of the majestic order prevailing in time and space, and the evidences of design in nature, but he proceeds to explain that "God has created some animals to be eaten, others to serve in farming, others to produce cheese." [33] The human mind itself, he thinks, is so marvelous an instrument that only a divine creator could have brought it into being; indeed, so far as we possess reason we are parts of the World Reason. If we could trace our ancestry back to the first man we should find him begotten by God; God is therefore literally the father of us all, and all men are brothers.[34]

> He who has once observed with understanding the administration of the world, and has learned that the greatest and most comprehensive community is the system [*systema*, standing together] of men and God, and that from God came the seeds whence all things, and especially rational beings, spring—why should not that man call himself a citizen of the world . . . nay, a son of God? . . . If a man could only subscribe heart and soul to this doctrine . . . I think he would entertain no mean or ignoble thought in himself. . . . Bear in mind, then, when you eat, who you are that eat, and whom you are nourishing; when you cohabit with women, who you are that do this. . . . You are bearing God about with you, you poor wretch, and know it not! [35]

In a passage that Saint Paul might have written, Epictetus exhorts his students not only to submit their wills trustingly to God's, but to be the apostles of God among mankind:

> God says, "Go and bear witness for me." [36] . . . Think what it is to be able to say, "God has sent me into the world to be his soldier and witness, to tell men that their sorrows and fears are vain, that to a good man no evil can befall, whether he live or die. God sends me at one time here, at another time there; he disciplines me by poverty and imprisonment, that I may be the better witness to him among men. With such a ministry committed to me, can I any longer

care in what place I am, or who my companions are, or what they say about me? Nay, rather, does not my whole nature strain after God, his laws and commandments?" [37]

As for himself, he is filled with awe and gratitude by the mystery and splendor of things, and he intones to the Creator a pagan *Magnificat* that is one of the supreme passages in the history of religion:

> What language is adequate to praise all the works of Providence? . . . If we had sense, ought we to be doing anything else, publicly or privately, than hymning and praising the Deity, and rehearsing his benefits? Ought we not, as we dig and plow and eat, to sing a hymn of praise to God? . . . What then?—since most of you have become blind, ought there not to be someone to fulfill this office for you, and in behalf of all sing hymns of praise to God? [38]

Though we have here no word for immortality, and can trace all these ideas back to the Stoics and the Cynics, we find in these pages remarkable parallels to many attitudes of early Christianity. Epictetus, indeed, sometimes advances beyond Christianity: he denounces slavery, condemns capital punishment, and wishes to have criminals treated as sick men. [39] He advocates a daily examination of conscience [40] and announces a kind of Golden Rule: "What you shun to suffer, do not make others suffer"; [41] and he adds: "If a man is reported to have spoken ill of you, make no defense, but say, "He did not know the rest of my faults, else he would not have mentioned only these." [42] He advises men to return good for evil, [43] and to "submit when reviled"; [44] to fast now and then and "abstain from the things you desire." [45] Sometimes he speaks of the body with the blasphemous contempt of an unscoured anchorite: "The body is of all things the most unpleasant and most foul. . . . It is astonishing that we should love a thing to which we perform such strange services every day. I fill this bag, and then I empty it; what is more troublesome?" [46] There are passages that breathe the piety of Augustine and the eloquence of Newman: "Use me henceforward, O God, as thou wilt; I am of one mind with thee. I am thine. I ask exemption from nothing that seems good in thy sight. Where thou wilt, lead me; in what raiment thou wilt, clothe me." [47] And like Jesus he bids his disciples take no care of the morrow:

> To have God as our maker, father, and guardian—shall not this suffice to keep us from grief and fear? And wherewithal shall I be fed, asks one, if I have nothing? But what shall we say of . . . the animals, every one of which is sufficient to itself, and lacks neither its own proper food nor that way of life which is appropriate to it, and in harmony with nature? [48]

Is it any wonder that Christians like Saint John Chrysostom and Augustine lauded him, and that his *Encheiridion* was adopted, with minor changes, as a rule and guide for the monastic life?[49] Who knows but that Epictetus had read in some form the sayings of Jesus and was, without knowing it, a convert to Christianity?

IV. LUCIAN AND THE SKEPTICS

Nevertheless, in this final stage of Hellenistic culture, there were skeptics who recalled all the doubts of Protagoras, and a Lucian who laughed at belief with the insolence of Aristippus and almost Plato's charm. The school of Pyrrho was not dead; Aenesidemus of Cnossus rephrased its denials in the Alexandria of our first century, by propounding the famous "Ten Modes" (*tropoi*), or contradictions, that made knowledge impossible.* Towards the end of the second century Sextus Empiricus, of unknown date or place, gave the skeptical philosophy its final formulation in several destructive volumes of which three survive. Sextus takes all the world for his enemy; he divides philosophers into diverse species and slays each breed in turn. He writes with the vigor necessary to an executioner, the good order and clarity characteristic of ancient philosophy, occasional sarcastic humor, and much dreary chopping of logic.

To every argument, says Sextus, an equal argument can be opposed, so that in the end there is nothing so superfluous as reasoning. Deduction is untrustworthy unless based upon complete induction; but complete induction is impossible, for we can never tell when a "negative instance" will turn up.[51] "Cause" is merely a regular antecedent (as Hume would repeat), and all knowledge is relative.[52] Similarly there is no objective good or evil; morality changes across every frontier,[53] and virtue has a different definition in every age. All the arguments of the nineteenth century against the possibility of knowing whether God exists or not are stated here, and all the contradictions between benevolent omnipotence and worldly suffering.[54] But Sextus is a

---

* Some of them: (1) The sense organs (e.g., eyes) of different animals, even of different men, vary in form and structure, and presumably give diverse pictures of the world; how do we know which picture is true? (2) The senses convey only a fraction of the object—e.g., a limited range of colors, sounds, and smells; clearly the conception that we form of the object is partial and unreliable. (3) One sense sometimes contradicts another. (4) Our physical and mental condition colors and perhaps discolors our perceptions—awake or sleeping, youth or age, motion or rest, hunger or satiety, hatred or love. (6) The appearance of an object varies according to the condition of the surrounding media—light, air, cold, heat, moisture, etc.; which appearance is "real"? (8) Nothing is known by itself or absolutely, but only in relation to something else, *ta pros ti*. (10) An individual's beliefs depend upon the customs, religion, institutions, and laws amid which he was reared; no individual can think objectively.[50]

more complete agnostic than the agnostics, for he affirms that we cannot know that we cannot know; agnosticism is a dogma.[55] But, he consoles us, we do not need certainty. Probability is enough for all practical purposes, and the suspension of judgment (*epoché*, holding back; *aphasia*, saying nothing) in philosophical questions, instead of disturbing the mind, brings it a careless peace (*ataraxia*).[56] Meanwhile, since nothing is certain, let us accept the conventions and beliefs of our time and place, and modestly worship our ancient gods.[57]

Lucian would have belonged to the Skeptic school if he had been so unwise as to fetter his judgment with a label. Like Voltaire, whom he resembled in all but pity, he wrote philosophy so brilliantly that no one supposed that he was writing philosophy. As if to show the spread of Hellenism, he was born at Samosata, in distant Commagene; "I am a Syrian from the Euphrates," he said; his native tongue was Syriac, his blood probably Semitic.[58] He was apprenticed to a sculptor, but deserted to a rhetor. After a stay in Antioch practicing law he took to the road as a "dependent scholar," living by lecturing, especially in Rome and Gaul; then (A.D. 165) he settled down in Athens. In his later years he was rescued from poverty by the pious but tolerant Marcus Aurelius, who appointed the irreverent skeptic to an official post in Egypt. There, at a date unknown, he died.

Time has preserved seventy-six of Lucian's little books, and many of them are as fresh and pertinent today as when he read them to friends and audiences eighteen centuries ago. He tried his hand at a variety of forms, until he found a congenial medium in the dialogue. His *Dialogues of the Hetairai* were free enough to win a large audience. But at least in his works he is more absorbed in the gods than in courtesans; he is never through mishandling them. "When I was a boy," says his Menippus, "and heard the tales of Homer and Hesiod about the gods—adulterous gods, rapacious gods, violent, litigious, incestuous gods—I found it all quite proper and, indeed, was intensely interested. When, however, I came to man's estate I observed that the laws flatly contradicted the poets, forbidding adultery and rapacity." Perplexed, Menippus went to the philosophers for an explanation; but they were so busy refuting one another that they only confounded his confusion. So he made himself wings, flew up to heaven, and examined matters for himself. Zeus received him magnanimously and allowed him to watch Olympus functioning. Zeus himself was listening to prayers as they came up to him through "a row of openings with lids like well covers. . . . Of those at sea one prayed for a north, another for a south, wind. The farmer asked for rain, the fuller for sun. . . . Zeus seemed puzzled; he did not know which prayer to grant, and experienced a truly Academic suspension of judgment, showing a reserve and equilibrium worthy of Pyrrho himself." [59] The great god rejects some petitions, grants others, and then arranges the day's weather: rain for Scythia, snow for Greece, a storm in the Adriatic, and "about a thousand bushels of hail for Cappadocia." Zeus is disturbed by the new and outlandish gods who have stolen into his pantheon; he issues a decree that, whereas Olympus is crowded with polyglot aliens, who have caused a great rise in the price of nectar, and the old and only true gods are being squeezed out, a committee of seven shall be appointed to sit on claims. In "Zeus Cross-Examined" an Epicurean philosopher asks Zeus are the gods also subject to Fate? Yes, answers the genial Jove. "Why, then, should men sacrifice to you?" asks the philosopher; and "if Fate rules men and gods, why should we be held responsible for our actions?" "I see," says Zeus, "that you have been with that accursed race, the sophists." [60] In "Zeus Tragoedus" the god is in a gloomy mood, for he observes a great crowd gathering in Athens to hear Damis the Epicurean deny, and Timocles the Stoic affirm, the existence and solicitude of the gods. Timocles breaks down and runs away, and Zeus despairs about his own future. Hermes comforts him: "There are plenty of believers left—a majority of Greeks, the body and dregs of the people, and the barbarians to a man." [61] That such a piece should have brought no indictment on Lucian's head proves either the tolerance of the times or the twilight of the Greek gods.

But Lucian was as skeptical of rhetoric and philosophy as of the old religion. In one of his *Dialogues of the Dead* Charon commands a rhetorician, whom he is ferrying to the other world, to "strip off that boundless length of sentences that is wrapped around you, and those antitheses, and balanced clauses"—otherwise the boat will surely sink.[62] In "Hermotimus" a student enters with enthusiasm upon the study of philosophy, hoping that it will give him some substitute for faith; but he is shocked by the vanity and greed of the rival teachers, and is left intellectually and morally naked by their mutual refutations; henceforth, he concludes, "I shall turn aside from a philosopher as from a mad dog." [63] Lucian himself defines philosophy as an attempt to "get an elevation from which you may see in every direction." [64] From such an elevation life seems to him a ridiculous confusion, a chaotic chorus in which all the dancers move and shout each at his own individual will, "until the impresario dismisses them one by one from the stage." [65] In "Charon" he paints a dark picture of the human scene as witnessed by superhuman eyes from some celestial peak: men plowing, toiling, disputing, suing in the courts, lending at usury, cheating and being cheated, running after gold or pleasure; over their heads a cloud of hopes, fears, follies, and hates; over these the Fates spinning the web of life for each human atom; one man is lifted high from the mass and then has a resounding fall; and each in turn is drawn away by some messenger of death. Charon observes two armies fighting in the Peloponnesus; "Fools!" he comments, "not to know that though each of them should win a whole Peloponnesus he will get but a bare foot of ground in the end." [66] Lucian is as impartial as nature; he satirizes the rich for their greed, the poor for their envy, the philosophers for their cobwebs, the gods for their nonexistence. In the end he concludes with Voltaire that one must cultivate his garden. Menippus, finding Teiresias in the lower world, asks him, What is the best life? The old prophet answers:

> The life of the ordinary man is the best and most prudent choice. Cease from the folly of metaphysical speculation and inquiry into origins and ends; count all this clever logic as idle talk, and pursue one end alone—how you may do what your hand finds to do, and go your way with never a passion and always a smile.[67]

If we sum up Greek thought in the first two centuries of our era, we find it, despite Lucian, overwhelmingly religious. Men had once lost faith in faith and taken to logic; now they were losing faith in logic and were flocking back to faith. Greek philosophy had completed the circuit from primitive theology through the skepticism of the early Sophists, the atheism of Democritus, the reconciliatory blandishments of Plato, the naturalism of Aristotle, and the pantheism of the Stoa back to a philosophy of mysticism, submission, and piety. The Academy had passed from the utilitarian myths of its founder through the skepticism of Carneades to the learned devotion of Plutarch; soon it would culminate in the heavenly visions of Plotinus. The scientific achievements of Pythagoras were forgotten, but his notion of reincarnation was having another life; Neo-Pythagoreans were exploring the mysticism of number, were practicing a daily examination of conscience, and were praying that after a minimum of avatars they might pass—if necessary through Purgatory—into a blessed union with God.[68] Stoicism was ceasing to be the proud and scornful philosophy of aristocrats, and had found its final and most eloquent voice in a slave; its doctrine of a final conflagration of the world, its rejection of all pleasures of the flesh, its humble surrender to the hidden will of God, were preparing for the theology and ethics of Christianity. The Oriental mood was capturing the European citadel.

CHAPTER XXIV

The Hellenistic Revival

I. ROMAN EGYPT

EGYPT should have been the happiest of lands, for not only was the earth freely nourished by the Nile, but the country was the most self-sufficient in the whole Mediterranean basin—rich in cereals and fruits, cutting three crops a year, unexcelled in its industries, exporting to a hundred nations, and seldom disturbed by foreign or civil war. And yet—perhaps for these reasons—"The Egyptians," Josephus notes, "appear never in all their history to have enjoyed one day of freedom." [1] Their wealth tempted, their semitropical lassitude suffered, one despot or conqueror after another through fifty centuries.

Rome classed Egypt not as a province but as the property of the emperor, and ruled it through a prefect responsible only to him. Native Greek officials administered the three divisions—Lower, Middle, and Upper Egypt, and the thirty-six "nomes" or counties; and the official language remained Greek. No attempt was made to urbanize the population, for Egypt's imperial function was to be the granary of Rome. Large tracts of land were taken from the priests and turned over to Roman or Alexandrian capitalists to be worked as latifundia by fellaheen accustomed to merciless exploitation. The state capitalism of the Ptolemies was continued in reduced form. Every step in the agricultural process was planned and controlled by the state: proliferating bureaucrats determined what crops should be sown and in what quantities, annually allotted the requisite seed, received the product into government warehouses (*thesauroi*, treasuries), exported Rome's quota, took out taxes in kind, and sold the rest to the market. Corn and flax were state monopolies from seed to sale; so, at least in the Fayum, was the production of bricks, perfumes, and sesame oil.[2] Private enterprise was permitted in other fields, but under ubiquitous regulation. All mineral resources were owned by the state, and the quarrying of marble and precious stones was a governmental privilege.

Domestic industry, already old in Egypt, now expanded in the towns—Ptolemaïs, Memphis, Thebes, Oxyrhynchus, Saïs, Bubastis, Naucratis, Heliopolis; in Alexandria it was half the life of the vibrant capital. Apparently the paper industry had reached the capitalist stage, for Strabo tells how the owners of the papyrus plantations limited production to lift the price.[3] Priests used the temple precincts as factories and turned out fine linens for their own use and for the market. Slaves outside of domestic service were few in Egypt, since "free" workers were paid only a notch above nudity and starvation. Sometimes the workers went on strike (*anachoresis*, secession)—they left their tasks and took sanctuary on temple grounds, whence they were coaxed by hunger or fair words. Occasionally wages were raised, prices went up, and all was as before. Guilds were permitted, but they were mostly of tradesmen and managers; the government used them as agents for the collection of taxes and for the organization of forced labor on dikes, canals, and other public works.

Internal trade was active but slow. Roads were poor, and land transport moved on men, donkeys, or camels—which now replaced horses as draft animals in Africa. Much traffic went by inland waterways. A great canal, 150 feet wide, completed in Trajan's reign, bound the Mediterranean and the Indian Ocean through the Nile and the Red Sea, from whose ports at Arsinoë, Myos Hormos, and Berenice ships left daily for Africa or India. The banking system that financed production and trade was under full governmental control. Each nome capital had a state bank, which acted as a receiver of taxes and repository of public funds. Loans were made to farmers, industry, and business by the government, by priests from temple treasuries, and by private lending associations.[4] Taxes were laid upon every product, process, sale, export, or import, even upon graves and burials; and additional assessments were levied from time to time, in kind from the poor, in liturgies from the rich. From Augustus to Trajan the country—or its masters—prospered; after that zenith it succumbed to the discouragement and exhaustion of endless tribute and taxation and the lethargy of a regimented economy.

Outside of Alexandria and Naucratis Egypt remained sullenly, silently Egyptian; Romanization hardly touched it beyond the mouths of the Nile; and even Alexandria, which had been the greatest of Greek cities, was assuming in our second century the character, languages, and odor of an Oriental metropolis. Of Egypt's 8,500,000 population its capital had now some 800,-000 [5] (in 1930, 573,000), second only to Rome; in industry and commerce it was first. Everyone in Alexandria is busy, says a letter questionably Hadrian's; everyone has a trade; even the lame and the blind find work to do.[6] Here, among a thousand other articles, glass, paper, and linen were produced on a large scale. Alexandria was the clothing and fashion center of the age, setting the styles and making the goods. Its great harbor had nine miles of wharves, from which its merchant fleet wove a web of commerce over many seas. It was also a tourist center, equipped with hotels, guides, and interpreters for visitors coming to see the Pyramids and the majestic temples of Thebes. The main avenue, sixty-seven feet wide, was lined for three miles with colonnades, arcades, and alluring shops displaying the fanciest products of ancient crafts. At many intersections there were spacious squares or circles named *plateai*, "broad" (ways)—whence the Italian *piazza* and our *plaza* and *place*. Imposing structures adorned the central thorough-fares—a large theater, an Emporium or exchange, temples to Poseidon, Caesar, and Saturn, a celebrated Serapeum or Temple of Serapis, and a group of university buildings known over the world as the Museum, or Home of the Muses. Of the five sections into which the city was divided, one was almost wholly given to the palaces, gardens, and administrative buildings of the Ptolemies, now used by the Roman prefect. Here, in a pretty mausoleum, lay the city's founder, Alexander the Great, preserved in honey and encased in glass.

Greeks, Egyptians, Jews, Italians, Arabs, Phoenicians, Persians, Ethiopi-ans, Syrians, Libyans, Cilicians, Scythians, Indians, Nubians—nearly every Mediterranean people had its quota in Alexandria. They made a volatile and inflammable mixture, quarrelsome and disorderly, intellectually clever and irreverently witty, shameless in speech, skeptical and superstitious, loose in morals and gay in mood, fanatically fond of the theater, music, and public games. Dio Chrysostom describes life there as "a continuous revel . . . of dancers, whistlers, and murderers." [8] The canals were alive with merry-makers in gondolas at night on their five-mile sail to the amusement suburb at Canopus. There were musical contests that rivaled the horse races in raising excitement and claques.

If we may believe Philo,[9] forty per cent of the city's population was Jewish. Most Alexandrian Jews were employed in industry and trade, and lived in great poverty;[10] many were merchants, a few were moneylenders, some were rich enough to win enviable places in the government. Originally confined to one fifth of the city, they had now overflowed to occupy two fifths. They were governed by their own laws and elders, and Rome con-firmed the privileges that the Ptolemies had given them to ignore any ordi-nance that conflicted with their religion. They gloried in their magnificent central synagogue, a colonnaded basilica so vast that a system of signals had to be used to secure proper response at proper times from worshipers too distant from the sanctuary to hear the words of the priest.[11] According to Josephus the moral life of the Alexandrian Jews was exemplary compared with the sexual looseness of the "pagan" population.[12] They had an active intellectual culture and contributed substantially to philosophy, historiog-raphy, and science. Racial hostility agitated the city at various times; we find in Josephus' tract *Against Apion* (an anti-Semitic leader) all the causes, arguments, and legends that disturb the relations of Jew and gentile today. In A.D. 38 a mob of Greeks invaded the synagogues and insisted on placing in each of them a statue of Caligula as a god. The Roman prefect, Avillius Flaccus, annulled the Alexandrian citizenship of the Jews and ordered those of them who lived outside the original Jewish section to return to it within a few days. When these had elapsed the Greek populace burned down 400 Jewish homes, and killed or clubbed Jews, outside the ghetto; and thirty-eight members of the Jewish *gerousia* or senate were arrested and publicly scourged in a theater. Thousands of Jews lost their homes, their businesses, or their savings. Flaccus' successor submitted the matter to the Emperor, and two separate delegations—five Greeks and five Jews—went to Rome (A.D. 40) to plead their causes before Caligula. He died before he could judge. Claudius restored the rights of the Jews in Alexandria, confirmed them in their municipal citizenship, and sternly bade both factions keep the peace.

II. PHILO

The leader of the Jewish delegation to Caligula was the philosopher Philo, brother of the arabarch, or manager of the Jewish export trade in Alexandria. Eusebius describes him as belonging to an ancient priestly family.[13] We know hardly anything else of his life; but his pious and generous character stands out in the many works that he wrote to expound Judaism to the Greek world. Brought up in a sacerdotal atmosphere, intensely loyal to his people, and yet fascinated by Greek philosophy, he made it the aim of his life to reconcile the Scriptures and customs of the Jews with Greek ideas and above all with the philosophy of "the most holy" Plato. He adopted for his purpose the principle that all events, characters, doctrines, and laws in the Old Testament have an allegorical as well as a literal meaning and symbolize certain moral or psychological truths; by this method he was able to prove anything. He wrote indifferently in Hebrew, but so well in Greek that his admirers said, "Plato writes like Philo." [14]

He was a theologian rather than a philosopher, a mystic whose intense piety presaged Plotinus and the medieval mind. God, in Philo, is the essential being of the world, incorporeal, eternal, indescribable; reason can know his existence, but can ascribe no quality to him, since every quality is a limitation. To conceive him as having human form is a concession to the sensuous imagination of men. God is everywhere; "what place can a man find where God is not?" [15] But he is not everything: matter is also eternal and increate; however, it has no life, motion, or form until infused with the divine force. To create the world by giving form to matter, and to establish relations with man, God used a host of intermediary beings, called angels by the Jews, *daimones* by the Greeks, and Ideas by Plato. These, says Philo, may popularly be conceived as persons, though really they exist only in the Divine Mind, as the thoughts and powers of God.[16] Together these powers constitute what the Stoics called the Logos, or Divine Reason creating and guiding the world. Fluctuating between philosophy and theology, between ideas and personifications, Philo sometimes thinks of the Logos as a person; in a poetic moment he calls the Logos "the first-begotten of God," [17] son of God by the virgin Wisdom,[18] and says that through the Logos God has revealed himself to man. Since the soul is part of God, it can through reason rise to a mystic vision not quite of God, but of the Logos. Perhaps, if we could free ourselves from the taint of matter and sense, and by ascetic exercises and long contemplation become for a moment pure spirit, we might for an ecstatic moment see God himself.[19]

Philo's Logos was one of the most influential ideas in the history of thought. Its antecedents in Heracleitus, Plato, and the Stoics are obvious; presumably he knew the recent Jewish literature that had made a distinct person of the Wisdom of God as creator of the world; and he must have been impressed by those lines in Proverbs (VIII, 22) where Wisdom says, "The Lord possessed me in the beginning of his way, before his works of old. I was set up from everlasting . . . or ever the earth was." Philo was a contemporary of Christ; he apparently never heard of him; but he shared unknowingly in forming Christian theology. The rabbis frowned upon his allegorical interpretations as likely to be used as an excuse for neglecting literal obedience to the Law; they suspected the Logos doctrine as a retreat from monotheism; and they saw in Philo's passion for Greek philosophy a threat of cultural assimilation, racial dilution, and consequent disappearance, of the dispersed Jews. But the Fathers of the Church admired the Jew's contemplative devotion, made abundant use of his allegorical principles to answer the critics of the Hebrew Scriptures, and joined with Gnostics and Neo-Platonists in accepting the mystical vision of God as the crown of human enterprise. Philo had tried to mediate between Hellenism and Judaism. From the Judaic point of view he had failed; from the historical point of view he had succeeded; and the result was the first chapter of the Gospel of John.

III. THE PROGRESS OF SCIENCE

In science Alexandria was the unchallenged head of the Hellenistic world. Claudius Ptolemy must be ranked among the most influential astronomers of antiquity, for despite Copernicus the world is still Ptolemaic in its speech. Born at Ptolemais on the Nile (whence his name), he lived most of his life at Alexandria, where he made observations from A.D. 127 to 151. The world remembers him chiefly for his rejection of Aristarchus' theory that the earth revolves around the sun. This immortal error was enshrined in Ptolemy's *Mathematiké Syntaxis*, or "Mathematical Arrangement" of the stars. The

Arabs referred to the work with a Greek superlative as *Al-megisté*, "The Greatest"; and the Middle Ages corrupted the phrase into *Almagest*, by which the book is known to history. It ruled the skies till Copernicus upset the world. And yet Ptolemy did not claim to do more than systematize the work and observation of previous astronomers, Hipparchus above all. He pictured the universe as spherical and as daily revolving around a spherical, motionless earth. Strange as this view seems to us (though there is no telling what some future Copernicus will do to our present Ptolemies), the geocentric hypothesis made it possible to compute the position of the stars and planets more accurately than the heliocentric conception could do in the state of astronomic knowledge at the time.[20] Ptolemy suggested further a theory of eccentrics to explain the orbits of the planets, and discovered the evection, or orbital aberration, of the moon. He measured the moon's distance from the earth by the parallax method still in use, and calculated it as fifty-nine times the earth's radius. This is approximately our current reckoning; but Ptolemy followed Poseidonius in underestimating the diameter of the earth.

Just as the *Syntaxis* gathered ancient astronomy into its final form, so Ptolemy's *Geographical Outline* summarized antiquity's knowledge of the earth's surface. Here, too, his industrious tables of latitude and longitude for the major cities of the globe were vitiated by accepting Poseidonius' modest estimate of the earth; but to this encouraging mistake, as transmitted by Ptolemy, Columbus owed his belief in the possibility of reaching the Indies in a practicable time by sailing west.[21] Ptolemy was the first to use the terms *parallels* and *meridians* in geography; and in his maps he successfully projected a spherical upon a flat surface. But he was a mathematician rather than an astronomer or a geographer; his work consisted chiefly in mathematical formulations. In the *Syntaxis* he drew up an excellent table of chords. He divided the radius of the earth into sixty *partes minutae primae* ("first small parts"), which became our "minutes," and subdivided each of these into sixty *partes minutae secundae* ("second small parts"), now our "seconds."

Though he made many mistakes, Ptolemy had the temper and patience of a true scientist. He tried to rest all conclusions upon observation—too seldom his own. In one field he carried out a long series of experiments: his *Optica*, a study of refraction, has been acclaimed as "the most remarkable experimental research of antiquity." [22] It is significant that this greatest astronomer, geographer, and mathematician of his age wrote also a *Tetrabiblios*, or "Four Books," on the control of human life by the stars.

Meanwhile a minor Archimedes was giving the classic world a second chance to stage an industrial revolution. A brilliant inventor or compiler, of whom we know only the one name, Hero, issued in this age* at Alexandria a long succession of treatises on mathematics and physics, of which several have been preserved through Arabic translations. He warned his readers frankly that the theorems and inventions which he presented were not necessarily his own, but were the accumulations of centuries. In the *Dioptra* he described an instrument like the theodolite, and formulated principles for measuring, by surveying, the distances to inaccessible points. In the *Mechanica* he considered the uses and combinations of simple devices like the wheel, axle, lever, pulley, wedge, and screw. In the *Pneumatica* he studied air pressure in seventy-eight experiments, most of them playful tricks; e.g., he showed how either wine or water could be made to flow from the same small orifice in the bottom of a jug by closing one or the other of the air holes at the top of the divided container.

From these amusements he was led on to make a force pump, a fire-engine pump with piston and valves, a hydraulic clock, a water organ, and a steam engine. In this contraption the steam from heated water was passed into a globe by a tube, and escaped through curved outlets at opposite sides, causing the globe to revolve in a direction contrary to that of the expelled steam. Hero's keen sense of humor kept him from developing this invention to industrial uses. He employed steam to support a ball in mid-air, to make a mechanical bird sing, to cause a statue to blow a horn. So in the *Catoptrica* he studied the reflection of light and showed how to construct mirrors that would enable a person to see his back, or appear with head downward, or with three eyes, two noses, etc. He told magicians how to perform tricks by concealed apparatus. He made water pour from a font when a coin was inserted in the slot. He constructed a hidden machine by which heated water overflowed into a bucket, whose increasing weight, by pulleys, opened temple doors. In these and a hundred other ways Hero succeeded in being a thaumaturgist, and failed to become a Watt.

Alexandria had long since been the chief center of medical education. There were famous schools of medicine at Marseilles, Lyons, Saragossa, Athens, Antioch, Cos, Ephesus, Smyrna, and Pergamum; but medical students came to the Egyptian capital from every province. Even as late as the fourth century, when Egypt was in decline, Ammianus Marcellinus wrote that "it is enough to commend a physician's skill if he can say that he was trained at Alexandria." [24] Specialization was progressing; "no one can be a universal physician," said Philostratus (*ca.* A.D. 225); "there must be specialists for wounds, fevers, eyes, consumption." [25] Dissection of cadavers was practiced at Alexandria, and there seem to have been cases of human vivi-

---

* His date is disputed. Pauly-Wissowa place him about 50 B.C.; Heiberg, Diels, and Heath about A.D. 225.[23]

section.[26] Surgery was probably as well developed there in the first century A.D. as anywhere in Europe before the nineteenth century. Women physicians were not rare; one of them, Metrodora, wrote an extant treatise on diseases of the womb.[27] Great names adorned the medical history of this age: Rufus of Ephesus, who described the anatomy of the eye, distinguished between motor and sensory nerves, and improved methods for stopping the flow of blood in surgery; Marinus of Alexandria, famous for his operations on the skull; and Antyllus, the greatest ophthalmologist of the time. Dioscorides of Cilicia (A.D. 40-90) wrote a *Materia Medica* which scientifically described 600 medical plants so well that his book remained the chief authority on its subject until the Renaissance. He recommended medicated pessaries for contraception;[28] and his recipe for wine of mandragora to produce surgical anesthesia was successfully applied in 1874.[29]

Soranus of Ephesus, about A.D. 116, published a treatise on the diseases of women and the birth and care of children; it ranks only below the Hippocratic collection and the works of Galen among the extant products of ancient medicine. He describes a vaginal speculum and an obstetric chair, gives an excellent anatomy of the uterus, offers almost modern dietetic and operative advice, such as bathing the eyes of the newborn child with oil,[30] suggests half a hundred contraceptive devices, mostly by vaginal medication,[31] and (unlike Hippocrates) allows abortion where delivery would endanger the mother's life.[32] Soranus was the greatest gynecologist of antiquity; no advance was made on his work till Paré, fifteen centuries after him. If all his forty treatises were extant we should probably rank him with Galen.

The most famous physician of the period was the son of a Pergamese architect, who named him Galenus, i.e., quiet and peaceable, in the hope that he would not take after his mother.[33] At fourteen the youth found his first love in philosophy, from whose dangerous lure he was never freed. At seventeen he turned to medicine, studied in Cilicia, Phoenicia, Palestine, Cyprus, Crete, Greece, and Alexandria (a mobility typical of ancient scholars), served as a surgeon in the gladiatorial school at Pergamum, and practiced for a time in Rome (A.D. 164-68). There his successful cures brought him many rich patients, and his lectures drew distinguished audiences. His repute rose to such a point that people wrote to him from every province for medical advice; and he confidently prescribed by mail. His good father, forgetting the purpose of his name, had counseled him to join no sect or party and always to tell the truth. Galen obeyed, exposed the ignorance and venality of many physicians in Rome, and in a few years had to flee from his enemies. Marcus Aurelius called him back to care for young Commodus (169) and tried to take him on a Marcomannic campaign; but Galen was clever enough to be soon back in Rome. Thereafter we know nothing of him except his works.

He was almost as voluminous as Aristotle. Of 500 volumes ascribed to him some 118 have survived, covering in 20,000 pages all branches of medicine and several fields of philosophy. They are of little medical value today, but they abound in incidental information and in the vitality of a vigorous and controversial spirit. His fondness for philosophy had given him a bad habit of drawing large deductions from small inductions; his faith in his own knowledge and powers often betrayed him into a dogmatism impossible to a scientific mind; and his great authority prolonged for centuries the life of serious errors. Nevertheless, he was an accurate observer and the most experimental of ancient physicians. "I confess the disease from which I have suffered all my life—to trust . . . no statements until, so far as possible, I have tested them for myself." [34] Forbidden by the Roman government to dissect the human body alive or dead, he dissected and vivisected animals, and sometimes too readily concluded to human anatomy from a study of apes, dogs, cows, and pigs.

Despite his limitations Galen made more contributions to anatomy than any other observer in antiquity. He described accurately the bones of the cranium and the spinal column, the muscular system, the lacteal vessels, the ducts of the lingual and submaxillary glands, and the valves of the heart. He showed that an excised heart can continue to beat outside the body; he proved that the arteries contain blood, not air (as the Alexandrian school had taught for 400 years). He missed anticipating Harvey; he thought that most of the blood traveled forth as well as back in the veins, while the remainder, mixed with air from the lungs, moved to and fro in the arteries. He was the first to explain the mechanism of respiration, and brilliantly conjectured that the principal element in the air we breathe is also that which is active in combustion.[35] He differentiated pleurisy and pneumonia, described aneurism, cancer, and tuberculosis, and recognized the infectious nature of the last. Above all, he founded experimental neurology. He made the first experimental sections of the spinal cord, determined the sensory and motor functions of each segment, understood the sympathetic system, recognized seven of the twelve pairs of cranial nerves, and caused aphasia at will by cutting the laryngeal nerve. He showed that injuries to one side of the brain produce derangements in the opposite side of the body. He cured the sophist Pausanias of numbness in the fourth and fifth fingers of the left hand by stimulating the brachial plexus in which the ulnar nerve arises that controls those fingers.[36] He was so skilled in symptomatology that he preferred to diagnose without questioning the patient.[37] He made much use of diet, exercise, and massage, but he was also an expert on drugs and traveled widely to secure rare medicines. He condemned the prescription of offal and urine, still popular with some of his contemporaries,[38] recommended dried cicadas for colic, applied goat dung to a tumor, and gave a long list of illnesses that could be cured by theriac—a famous drug made as an antidote for Mithridates the Great, daily imbibed by Marcus Aurelius, and containing the flesh of snakes.[39]

He tarnished his record as an experimentalist by a torrent of precipitate theory. He ridiculed magic and spells, accepted divination by dreams, and thought that the phases of the moon affected the condition of patients. He took up Hippocrates' notion of the four humors (blood and phlegm, black and yellow bile),* added a dash of Pythagoras' doctrine of four elements (earth, air, fire, and water), and tried to reduce all diseases to derangement of these humors or these elements. He was a firm vitalist, convinced that a *pneuma*, a vital breath or spirit, pervaded and activated every part of the body. Mechanistic interpretations of biology had been advanced by several physicians, as for example by Asclepiades, who held that physiology should be treated as a branch of physics; Galen objected that whereas a machine is merely the sum of its parts, an organism implies the purposive control of the parts by the whole. And just as purpose alone can explain the origin, structure, and function of organs, so the universe, Galen thought, can be understood only as the expression and instrument of some divine plan. God, however, operates solely through natural laws; there are no miracles, and the best revelation is Nature herself.

Galen's teleology and monotheism won him favor with Christians, as later with Moslems. Nearly all his writings were lost to Europe in the chaos of the barbarian invasions, but in the East they were preserved by Arab scholars, and were translated from Arabic into Latin from the eleventh century onward. Galen became then an uncriticized authority, an Aristotle for medieval medicine.

The last creative age of Greek science ended with Ptolemy and Galen. Experiment ceased, dogma ruled; mathematics relapsed into restatements of geometry, biology into Aristotle, natural science into Pliny; and medicine marked time until the Arab and Jewish physicians of the Middle Ages renewed the noblest of the sciences.

IV. POETS IN THE DESERT

Across the Red Sea from Egypt lay Arabia. Neither the Pharaohs nor the Achaemenids nor the Seleucids nor the Ptolemies nor the Romans had been able

---

* Cf. the emphasis of current medicine on glandular secretions.

to conquer the mysterious peninsula. Arabia Deserta knew only Arab nomads, but in the southwest a mountain range and its streams gave milder temperatures and fruitful vegetation to Arabia Felix, the Yemen of today. In those recesses the little kingdom of Saba hid, the Sheba of the Bible, so rich in frankincense and myrrh, cassia and cinnamon, aloes and nard, senna and gum and precious stones that the Sabateans could build at Mariaba and elsewhere cities proud with temples, palaces, and colonnades.[40] Arab merchants not only sold Arab products at high prices, but carried on a caravan trade with northwestern Asia and an active commerce by sea with Egypt, Parthia, and India. In 25 B.C. Augustus sent Aelius Gallus to absorb the kingdom into the Empire; the legions failed to take Mariaba and returned to Egypt decimated by disease and heat. Augustus contented himself with destroying the Arab port at Adana (Aden) and thereby secured control of the trade between Egypt and India.

The main commercial route running north from Mariaba went through the northwest corner of the peninsula, known to the ancients as Arabia Petraea from its capital at Petra, some forty miles south of Jerusalem. The city had been named from the circle of steep crags within which it was strategically placed. There, in the second century B.C., the Nabatean Arabs established a kingdom that slowly grew rich on passing caravans, until its rule extended from Leuce Come on the Red Sea along the eastern border of Palestine through Gerasa and Bostra to Damascus. Under King Aretas IV (9 B.C.–A.D. 40) the country reached its zenith; Petra became a Hellenistic city, Aramaic in speech, Greek in art, Alexandrian in the splendor of its streets. To this time belong the finest of the giant tombs that were carved into the rocks outside the city—crude but powerful façades of double-tiered Greek colonnades, sometimes a hundred feet in height. After Trajan annexed Arabia Petraea into the Empire (106), Bostra became the capital of the province of Arabia, and raised in its turn the architectural symbols of wealth and power. Petra decayed as Bostra and Palmyra became the crossroads of the desert caravans, and the great tombs lapsed into "the nightstalls of nomad flocks." [41]

The most striking feature of the great Empire was its numerous and populous cities. Never again till our own century has urbanization been so pronounced. Lucullus, Pompey, Caesar, Herod, Hellenistic kings and Roman emperors prided themselves on founding new cities and embellishing old ones. So, moving northward along the eastern Mediterranean coast, one could hardly go twenty miles without encountering a city—Raphia (Rafa), Gaza, Ascalon, Joppa (Jaffa) Apollonia, Samaria-Sebaste, and Caesarea (Kaisaria). These cities, though in Palestine, were half Greek in population and predominantly Greek in language, culture, and institutions; they were Hellenistic bridgeheads in the pagan invasion of Judea. Herod spent large sums making Caesarea worthy of Augustus, for whom it was named; he provided it with a fine harbor, a lofty temple, a theater, an amphitheater, "sumptuous palaces, and many edifices of white stone." [42] Farther inland were other Greek Palestinian cities—Livias, Philadelphia, Gerasa

(Djerasch), and Gadara (Katra). At Gerasa stand a hundred columns of the colonnade that lined the main street; and the ruins of temples, theater, baths, and aqueduct proclaim the affluence of the town in the second century A.D.

Gadara, where the remains of two theaters echo with memories of Greek plays, was famous for its schools, professors, and authors. Here, in the third century B.C., had lived Menippus, the Cynic philosopher and humorist whose satires taught that everything is vain except an upright life, and gave a model to Lucilius, Varro, and Horace. Here in his "Syrian Athens," some hundred years before Christ, Meleager, the Anacreon of the age, polished epigrams to fair ladies and handsome boys and wore out his pen with love.

> Brightly the goblet smiles since rested here
>   Zenophila's sweet mouth, to Love so dear.
> How blest would she to mine her rose-lips place,
> And drink my soul out in a long embrace.[43]

One of these flames, too soon snuffed out, burned with especial brightness in his memory—Heliodora, whom he loved in Tyre.

> I'll twine white violets, and the myrtle green;
> Narcissus will I twine, and lilies sheen;
> I'll twine sweet crocus, and the hyacinth blue;
> And last I'll twine the rose, love's token true:
> That all may form a wreath of beauty, meet
> To deck my Heliodora's tresses sweet.[44]

Now "Hades has snatched her, and the dust has tarnished her flower in bloom. O Mother Earth, I pray thee, clasp her gently to thy breast." [45]

Meleager immortalized himself by gathering into a "garland" (*stephanos*) the elegiac verse of Greece from Sappho to Meleager; out of this and like collections grew, by merger, the *Greek Anthology*.* Here is the Greek epigram at its best and worst, polished like a jewel or empty as a pose; it was unwise to pluck these 4000 "flowers" from their branches to make this fading wreath. Some of the verses commemorate forgotten great men, or famous statues, or dead relatives; some, so to speak, are autotaphs, as when a woman who died of triplets says pithily, "After this let women pray for children." [46] Some are barbs aimed at physicians, shrews, undertakers, pedagogues, cuckolds; or the miser who, fainting, is revived by the smell of a penny; or the grammarian whose grandchild displayed successively all three genders; [47] or the pugilist who retires, marries, and gets more blows than he ever

---

* Meleager's *Stephanos* was combined in our sixth century with the *Musa Paidiké*, a homosexual anthology compiled by Strabo of Sardis (50 B.C.). Subsequent additions were made, chiefly of Christian verse; and the *Anthology* was given its present form at Constantinople about A.D. 920.

received in the ring; or the dwarf who, carried off by a mosquito, thinks he is suffering the rape of Ganymede. A single epigram celebrates "that famous woman who slept with only one man." Others dedicate offerings to the gods: Lais hangs up her mirror as useless now that it does not show her as she was; Nicias, after fifty years of serving men, surrenders her complaisant girdle to Venus. Some stanzas glorify the arterial dilation of wine as wiser than wisdom. One honors the unceasing monogamy of the adulterer who was buried by a wreck in the arms of his mistress. Some are pagan dirges on the brevity of life; some are Christian assurances of a happy resurrection. Most of them, of course, toast the beauty of women and boys and sing the painful ecstasy of love: everything that later literature has said about amorous itching is here said in brief and in full, with more than Elizabethan conceits. Meleager makes a mosquito his pander by charging it with a message to his lady of the hour. And his townsman Philodemus, philosophic mentor of Cicero, tunes a melancholy note to his Xantho:

> White waxen cheeks, soft scented breast,
> Deep eyes wherein the Muses nest,
> Sweet lips that perfect pleasure bring—
> Sing me your song, pale Xantho, sing. . . .
> Too soon the music ends. Again,
> Again repeat the sad, sweet strain,
> With perfumed fingers touch the string;
> O Love's delight, pale Xantho, sing.[48]

V. THE SYRIANS

Northward along the coast lay the ancient cities of Phoenicia, part, with Palestine, of the province of Syria. Their industrious workers skilled in handicrafts, their favored position as traditional ports of trade, their rich and subtle merchants sending ships and agents everywhere, had kept them alive through all the vicissitudes of a thousand years. Tyre (Sur) had taller dwellings than Rome's [49] and worse slums; it stank with the smell of its dyeing establishments, but it consoled itself with the thought that the whole world bought its richly colored textiles, above all its purple silks. Sidon had probably discovered the art of blowing glass and now specialized in glass and bronze. Berytus (Beirut) was distinguished for its schools of medicine, rhetoric, and law; very likely from this university the great jurists Ulpian and Papinian went to Rome.

No province of the Empire surpassed Syria in industry and prosperity. Where now 3,000,000 inhabitants find a precarious existence, 10,000,000 lived in Trajan's time.[50] Half a hundred cities here enjoyed the pure water, the public baths, the underground drainage system, the clean markets, the gymnasia and palaestras, the lectures and music, the schools and temples and basilicas, the porticoes and arches, the public statuary and picture galleries, characteristic of the Hellenistic cities in the first century after Christ.[51] The oldest of them was Damascus, over the Lebanons from Sidon, fortified by the surrounding desert, and turned almost into a garden by the spreading arms and tributaries of a stream gratefully called "the river of gold." Many caravan routes converged here, and poured into the bazaars the products of three continents.

Returning over the Anti-Lebanon hills and moving north over dusty roads, the modern traveler is astonished to find, in the tiny village of Baalbek, the ruins of two majestic temples and a propylaeum, once the pride of Heliopolis, the Greco-Roman-Syrian City of the Sun. Augustus planted a small colony there, and the town grew as the sacred seat of Baal the Sun-God and as the meeting point of roads to Damascus, Sidon, and Beirut. Under Antoninus Pius and his successors Roman, Greek, and Syrian architects and engineers raised, on the site of an old Phoenician temple to Baal, an imposing shrine to Iuppiter Heliopolitanus. It was built of huge monoliths from a quarry a mile away; one block measures sixty-two by fourteen by eleven feet, and contains enough stone for a commodious house. Fifty-one marble steps 150 feet wide lead up to the propylaeum, a Corinthian portico. Beyond a colonnaded forecourt and court rose the main temple, of which fifty-eight columns still tower sixty-two feet into the air. Near it are the remains of a smaller temple, variously attributed to Venus, Bacchus, and Demeter; nineteen of its columns survive, and a handsome portal delicately carved. Resplendent in their solitary grandeur under the unclouded sun, the columns of these temples are among the fairest extant works of man. Seeing them we feel, better than in Italy, the grandeur that was Rome, the wealth and courage, skill and taste that could build, in so many scattered cities, temples greater and more majestic than the crowded capital ever knew.

A similar sight meets the traveler who strikes eastward across the desert from Homs, the ancient Emesa, to Tadmor, which the Greeks translated into Palmyra, City of a Myriad Palms. Its fortunate position and fertile soil around two gushing springs on the roads from Emesa and Damascus to the Euphrates made it grow in affluence until it was one of the major cities of the East; and its distance from other settlements enabled it to maintain practical independence despite nominal allegiance to Seleucid kings or Roman emperors. Its wide central thoroughfare was flanked by shady porticoes containing 454 columns; and at the four main crossings were stately arches, of which one remains to let us judge the rest. The glory of the city was the Temple of the Sun, dedicated (A.D. 30) to the supreme trinity of Bel (Baal), Yarhibol (the sun), and Aglibol (the moon). Its size continued Assyrian traditions of immensity. Its court, the largest in the Empire, had an unrivaled colonnade 4000 feet long, much of it composed of Corinthian columns running four abreast. Within the court and the temple were paintings and sculptures whose extant examples reveal the approach of Palmyra to Parthia in art as in geography.

A main route eastward from Palmyra reached the Euphrates at Dura-Europus. There (A.D. 100) the merchants shared their gains with the Palmyrene trinity by rearing a temple half Greek and half Indian; and an eastern painter adorned the walls with frescoes that vividly illustrate the Oriental origin of Byzantine and early Christian art.[52] Farther north on the great river were other important crossing towns at Thapsacus and Zeugma. Turning westward from Thapsacus the traveler passed through Beroea (Aleppo) and Apamea to the Mediterranean at Laodicea—still keeping its ancient name as Latakia, and still an active port. Between it and Apamea the river Orontes flowed north, between shores largely pre-empted by rich estates, to Antioch (Antakia), capital of Syria. The river, and a great network of roads, brought the goods of the East to Antioch, while its Mediterranean port, Seleucia Pieria, fourteen miles down the stream, brought in the products of the West. Most of the city rose on a mountain slope and had the Orontes at its feet; it was a picturesque location, that helped Antioch rival Rhodes as the most beautiful city of the Hellenic East. It had a system of street lighting that made it safe and brilliant at night. The main avenue, four and a half miles long, was paved with granite and had a covered colonnade on either side, so that people could walk from one end of the town to the other immune to rain and sun. Pure water was supplied in abundance to every home. The complex population of 600,000 Greeks, Syrians, and Jews was notoriously gay, pursuing pleasure relentlessly, laughing at the pompous Romans who came to govern them, oscillating between the circus and the amphitheater, the brothels and the baths, and taking full advantage of Daphne, their famous suburban park. Festivals were numerous, and Aphrodite had a share in all of them. During the feast of Brumalia, lasting through most of December, the whole city, says a contemporary, resembled a tavern, and the streets rang all night with song and revelry.[53] There were schools of rhetoric, philosophy, and medicine, but Antioch was not a center of learning. Its populace lived intensely for the day; and when it needed religion it flocked to astrologers, magicians, miracle-workers, and charlatans.

The general picture of Syria under Roman rule is one of prosperity more continuous than in any other province. Most of the workers were freemen, except in domestic service. The upper classes were Hellenized, the lower remained Oriental; in the same town Greek philosophers rubbed elbows with temple prostitutes and emasculated priests; and even till Hadrian children were now and then offered as sacrifices to the gods.[54] Sculpture and painting took on a semi-Oriental, half-medieval face and form. The Greek language prevailed in government and literature, but native tongues—chiefly Aramaic—remained the speech of the people. Scholars were plenty and made the world ring with their moment's fame. Nicolaus of Damascus, besides mentoring Antony, Cleopatra, and Herod, undertook the weary task of writing a universal history—a labor, he tells us, that Hercules himself would have shunned.[55] Time in its tenderness has buried all his works, as at its leisure it will cover ours.

VI. ASIA MINOR

North of Syria was the client kingdom—later the province—of Commagene, with a populous capital at Samosata, Lucian's childhood home. Across the Euphrates stood the little realm of Osrhoene; Rome fortified its capital, Edessa (Urfa), as a base against Parthia; we shall hear more of it in Christian days. Westward from Syria one passed into Cilicia (as now into Turkey) at Alexandria Issi (Alexandretta). This, Cicero's province, was highly civilized along the southern Asia Minor coast, but still barbarous in the Taurus hills. Tarsus (Tersous), the capital, was "no mean city," said its son Saint Paul, but was renowned for its schools and philosophers.

Over against Cilicia, in the Mediterranean, the island of Cyprus pursued its immemorial life of mining copper, cutting cypress, building ships, and bearing patiently a succession of conquerors. The lucrative mines were owned by Rome and worked by slaves. Galen describes how in his time a mine there collapsed and crushed hundreds of workers—a periodical incident in the geological basis of human comforts and powers.

North of Cilicia lay arid and mountainous Cappadocia, mining precious metals, and raising wheat, cattle, and slaves for export. West of it, Lycaonia would enter into history with the visits of Saint Paul to Derbe, Lystra, and Iconium. Again north was Galatia, settled and named by the Gauls in the third century, B.C.; its most famous product was the Black Stone of Pessinus, sent to Rome as a symbol of Cybele; its chief city was Ancyra, capital of the Hittites 3500 years ago, and of Turkey today. West of Cilicia, the province of Pisidia counted fine cities within its borders, like Xanthus, now recovering from its mass suicide before Brutus, and Aspendus, whose theater is so well preserved that one easily imagines it filling again to hear Menander or Euripides.

West and north of Pisidia was the province of "Asia," divided into Phrygia, Caria, Lydia, and Mysia. Here, where the civilization of Ionia still flourished after a thousand years, Philostratus counted 500 towns, with a total population far greater than the region supports today. The countryside was fertile, the crafts had grown in skill from age to age, and the ports profited from the development of rich markets in Italy, Africa, Spain, and Gaul. Phrygia was mountainous, but it boasted large cities like Apamea Celaenae—ranked by Strabo as second only to Ephesus in "Asia"—and Laodicea, fortunate in its philanthropic philosophers and millionaires. Cnidus was yet important enough to make an alliance with Rome; but Halicarnassus had declined from Herodotus to Dionysius —an excellent literary critic, an uncritical historian. Miletus was no longer in its prime, though still an active port; the oracle of Apollo in the temple at near-by

Didyma continued to answer questions with puzzles; and the storytellers of the region were weaving those amorous picaresque "Milesian tales" that would soon develop into the Greek novel. Priene was a minor town, but its citizens vied honorably in making it fair with fine buildings. Here, in the first century B.C., a woman, Phile, was elected to the highest municipal office; the influence of wealth and Rome was raising the status of woman in Hellenic lands. Magnesia on the Maeander had what many rated as the most nearly perfect temple in Asia—dedicated to Artemis (129 B.C.), and designed by Hermogenes, the supreme architect of the age. At Mycale the *koinon*, or Commons, still met annually as a general council and religious union for Ionia.

Of the islands lying off the Carian coast Cos prospered with its silk industry and its medical school, rich with traditions of Hippocrates, and Rhodes (i.e., the Rose) was even in her decline the most beautiful city of the Greek world. When, after the Civil War, Augustus sought to relieve the distress of the eastern cities by allowing the cancellation of all debts, Rhodes refused to avail herself of the expedient and met all her obligations faithfully. As a result she rapidly regained her place as banker to the Aegean trade and became again a halfway port for vessels plying between Asia and Egypt. The city was celebrated for its fallen Colossus, its handsome buildings, its famous statuary, its clean and orderly streets, its competent aristocratic government, its celebrated schools of rhetoric and philosophy. Here Apollonius Molo taught Caesar and Cicero those arts of style which through them influenced all later Latin prose.

The most famous Rhodian of this period was Poseidonius, the last great synthetic mind of antiquity. Born at Syrian Apamea (135 B.C.), he first earned fame as a long-distance runner. After studying under Panaetius in Athens he made Rhodes his home, served her as magistrate and ambassador, traveled into many provinces, returned to Rhodes, and drew such men as Pompey and Cicero to his lectures on the Stoic philosophy. At 83 he went to live in Rome and died there a year later. His lost *Universal History*—covering Rome and its possessions from 144 to 82 B.C.—was ranked by ancient scholars as equal to the work of Polybius. His report of his travels in Gaul and his treatise *On the Ocean* were basic sources for Strabo. His calculation of the sun's distance from the earth— 52,000,000 miles—was closer than that of any other ancient student to our modern reckoning. He went to Cádiz to study the tides, and explained them by the joint action of the sun and the moon. He underestimated the distance across the Atlantic and predicted that one sailing from Spain would come to India after 8000 miles. Despite his wide acquaintance with natural science, he accepted many of the spiritualistic ideas of his time—*daimones*, divination, astrology, telepathy, and the power of the soul to rise to a mystic union with God, whom he defined as the Life-Force of the world. Cicero too generously ranked him as the greatest of the Stoics; we might also consider him a forerunner of the Neo-Platonists, a bridge from Zeno to Plotinus.

Following the coast of Asia northward from Caria, the traveler entered Lydia and its greatest city, Ephesus. It flourished under the Romans as never before. Though Pergamum was the formal capital of "Asia," Ephesus became the seat of the Roman proconsul and his staff; it was also the main port of the province and the meeting place of the provincial assembly. Its polyglot population of 225,000 ranged from philanthropic sophists to a noisy and superstitious rabble. The streets were well paved and lighted and had miles of shady porticoes. There were the usual public buildings, some unearthed as late as 1894: a "museum" or scientific center, a medical school, a library with a strangely baroque façade, and a theater that seated 56,000 persons; here Demetrius the image-maker would arouse the populace against Saint Paul. The center (and chief bank) of the city was the Temple of Artemis, surrounded by 128 columns each the gift of a king. The eunuch priests were attended by virgin priestesses and a swarm of slaves; the rites were a mixture of Oriental and Greek; the barbarous statue that represented the goddess had two rows of supernumerary breasts, symbolizing fertility. The Festival of Artemis made all May a month of rejoicing, feasting, and games.

Smyrna, despite its fishermen, had a better atmosphere. Apollonius of Tyana, who traveled far and wide, called it "the most beautiful city under the sun." [59] It was proud of its long, straight streets, its double-tiered colonnades, its library, and its university. One of its most famous sons, Aelius Aristides (A.D. 117-187), described it in terms that reveal the splendor of these Roman-Hellenistic cities.

> Go from east to west, and you will pass from temple to temple and from hill to hill along a street fairer than its name (the Golden Way). Stand on the acropolis: the sea flows beneath you, the suburbs lie about you, the city through three lovely views fills the goblet of your soul. . . . Everything to the very shore is a shining mass of gymnasia, markets, theaters . . . baths—so many that you hardly know where to bathe . . . fountains and public walks, and running water in every home. The abundance of her spectacles, contests, and exhibitions is beyond telling, and the variety of her handicrafts. Of all cities this is best suited for those who like to live at ease and be philosophers without guile.[60]

Aelius was one of many rhetors and sophists whose fame drew students to Smyrna from all Hellas. His teacher Polemo was so great (says Philostratus) "that he talked with cities as his inferiors, with emperors as not his superiors, and with the gods as his equals." [61] When he lectured in Athens Herodes Atticus, his greatest rival in opulent eloquence, attended as an admiring pupil. In payment for the privilege Herodes sent him 150,000 drachmas ($90,000); when Polemo failed to thank him a friend suggested that he felt underpaid; Herodes sent 100,000 more, which Polemo quietly accepted as his due. Polemo used his fortune to embellish his adopted city; he took part in its government, harmonized its factions, and served it as ambassador. Tradition says that finding his arthritis unbearable he shut himself up in the tomb of his ancestors at Laodicea and died of voluntary starvation at the age of fifty-six.[62]

Sardis, Croesus' ancient capital, was still "a great city" in Strabo's time. Cicero was impressed by the splendor and refinement of Mytilene, and in the third century Longus described it in terms suggestive of Venice.[63] Pergamum shone with the great altar and costly buildings raised by the Attalid kings out of a treasury fattened by the labor of slaves in state forests, fields, mines, and factories. Attalus III anticipated Roman expansion and social revolution by bequeathing his realm to Rome in 133 B.C. Aristonicus, son of King Eumenes II by a concubine, denounced the bequest as forced, called the slaves and the free poor to revolt, defeated a Roman army (132), captured many cities, and planned a socialist state with the help of Blossius, teacher of the Gracchi. The neighboring kings of Bithynia and Pontus, and the business classes of the occupied cities, joined Rome in suppressing the rebellion, and Aristonicus died in a Roman dungeon. This uprising, and the Mithridatic Wars, interrupted the cultural life of Pergamum for half a century, and Antony despoiled its famous library to reimburse Alexandria for the volumes burned during Caesar's stay. Pergamum must have recovered by Vespasian's time, for the elder Pliny judged it the most brilliant city in Asia. It enjoyed a new flurry of building under the Antonines, and developed in its Asclepieum a medical school from which Galen went forth to cure the world.

Farther north Alexandria Troas was made a Roman colony by Augustus in memory of Rome's supposed Trojan origin—which gave Rome a convenient claim to all these parts. On a near-by hill (Hissarlik) old Troy was rebuilt as new Ilium, and became a goal for tourists to whom guides pointed out the exact spot of every exploit in the *Iliad*, and the cave where Paris had judged Hera, Aphrodite, and Athena. On the Propontis Cyzicus built ships and sent out a ubiquitous merchant fleet rivaled only by that of Rhodes. Here Hadrian built a Temple of Persephone which was one of the glories of Asia. Its columns, says Dio Cassius, were six feet in diameter and seventy-five feet high, yet each was a single block of stone.[64] Rising from a hill, it towered so high that Aelius counted the harbor's lighthouse superfluous.

From the Red to the Black Sea a hundred cities flourished under the Roman peace.

VII. THE GREAT MITHRIDATES

Along the northern shores of Asia Minor sprawled Bithynia and Pontus, mountainous in the interior, but rich in timber and minerals. Here a mixture of Thracians, Greeks, and Iranians overlay an antique Hittite stock. A line of Greco-Thracian kings ruled Bithynia, built a capital at Nicomedia (Is-nikmid), and major cities at Prusa and Nicaea (Is-nik). About 302 B.C.

a Persian noble, piously called Mithridates, carved a kingdom for himself out of Cappadocia and Pontus, and founded a dynasty of virile Hellenizing monarchs, with capitals at Comana Pontica and Sinope. Their rule spread until it impinged upon Roman economic and political interests. The resulting Mithridatic Wars are fitly named from the redoubtable king who united western Asia and European Greece in a revolt which, if it had succeeded, would have changed the face of history.

Mithridates VI had inherited the throne of Pontus as a boy of eleven. His mother and his guardians, seeking to supplant him, tried to kill him. He fled from the palace, disguised himself, and for seven years lived in the woods as a hunter, dressed in skins. About 115 B.C. a *coup d'état* deposed his mother and restored him to power. Surrounded by the conspiracies characteristic of Oriental courts, he took the precaution of drinking a little poison every day, until he had developed immunity to most of the varieties available to his intimates. In the course of his experiments he discovered many antidotes. From these his interest spread to medicine, on which he compiled data of such value that Pompey had them translated into Latin. His wild and exacting life had given him strength of body as well as of will; he grew to so large a frame that he sent his suit of armor to Delphi to amuse the worshipers. He was an expert horseman and warrior, could (we are assured) run fast enough to overtake a deer, drove a sixteen-horse chariot, and rode 120 miles in a day.[65] He prided himself on being able to outeat and outdrink any man, and he attended to a numerous harem. Roman historians tell us that he was cruel and treacherous and slew his mother, his brother, three sons, and three daughters;[66] but Rome has not transmitted his side of this tale. He was a man of some culture, could speak twenty-two languages, and never used an interpreter;[67] he studied Greek literature, was fond of Greek music, enriched Greek temples, and had Greek scholars, poets, and philosophers at his court; he collected works of art and issued coins of surpassing excellence. But he shared in the sensuality and coarseness of his half-barbarian environment and accepted the superstitions of his time. He defended himself against Rome not with the far-seeing maneuvers of a great general or statesman, but with the impromptu courage of an animal at bay.

Such a man could not be content with the reduced kingdom relinquished by his mother. With the help of Greek officers and mercenaries he conquered Armenia and the Caucasus, passed over the Kuban River and the Strait of Kerch into the Crimea, and brought under his sway all the Greek cities on the east, north, and west coast of the Black Sea. As the collapse of Greek military power had left these communities almost defenseless against the barbarians of their hinterland, they received the Greek phalanxes of

Mithridates as saviors. The subject cities included Sinope (Sinob), Trapezus (Trebizond), Panticapaeum (Kerch), and Byzantium; but Bithynian control of the Hellespont (Dardanelles) left the Mediterranean commerce of Pontus at the mercy of hostile kings. When Nicomedes II of Bithynia died (94 B.C.), his two sons contested the succession. One of them sought the aid of Rome, the other, Socrates, appealed to the Pontic king. Mithridates took advantage of the factional strife in Italy to invade Bithynia and enthrone Socrates. Rome, unwilling to see the Bosporus in hostile hands, ordered Mithridates and Socrates out of Bithynia. Mithridates complied, Socrates refused. The Roman governor of Asia deposed him and crowned Nicomedes III. The new ruler, encouraged by the Roman proconsul Manius Aquilius, invaded Pontus, and the First Mithridatic War began (88-84 B.C.).

Mithridates felt that his sole chance of survival lay in arousing the Hellenic East to revolt against its Italian overlords. He announced himself as the liberator of Hellas and sent troops to free the Greek cities of Asia, if necessary by force. Opposed by the business classes of the towns, he courted the democratic parties with promises of semisocialistic reforms. Meanwhile his navy of 400 ships destroyed the Roman Black Sea fleet, and his army of 290,000 men overwhelmed the forces of Nicomedes and Aquilius. To express his scorn of Roman avarice,[68] the victorious king poured molten gold down the throat of the captured Aquilius—fresh from his triumph over the revolted slaves of Sicily. The Greek cities of Asia Minor, shorn of Roman defense, opened their gates to the armies of Mithridates and declared their allegiance to his cause. At his suggestion, on an appointed day, they slew all Italians—80,000 men, women, and children—whom they found within their walls (88 B.C.). Says Appian:

> The Ephesians tore away the fugitives who had taken refuge in the Temple of Artemis and were clasping the images of the goddess, and slew them. The Pergamenes shot with arrows the Romans who had sought sanctuary in the Temple of Aesculapius. The people of Adramyttium followed into the sea those who sought to escape by swimming, and killed them and drowned their children. The inhabitants of Caunus (in Caria) pursued the Italians who had taken refuge about the statue of Vesta, killed the children before their mothers' eyes, then the mothers, then the men. . . . By which it was made plain that it was as much hatred of the Romans as fear of Mithridates that impelled these atrocities.[69]

Doubtless the poorer classes, who had borne the brunt of Roman domination, took the lead in this mad massacre; the propertied classes, long protected by Rome, must have trembled at so wild an uprising of revenge.

Mithridates sought to appease the well to do by exempting the Greek cities from taxes for five years and giving them complete home rule. At the same time, however, he "proclaimed the canceling of debts," says Appian,[70] "freed the slaves, confiscated many estates, and redistributed the land." Leading men in the communities formed a conspiracy against him; he discovered it and had 1600 of them killed. The lower classes, aided by philosophers and university professors,[71] seized power in many Greek cities, even in Athens and Sparta, and declared war against both Rome and wealth. The Greeks of Delos, in an ecstasy of freedom, slaughtered 20,000 Italians in one day. The fleet of Mithridates captured the Cyclades, and his armies took possession of Euboea, Thessaly, Macedonia, and Thrace. The defection of rich "Asia" stopped the flow of tribute to the Roman treasury and of interest to Roman investors, and plunged Italy into a financial crisis that had something to do with the revolutionary movement of Saturninus and Cinna. Italy itself was divided, for the Samnites and Lucanians sent offers of alliance to the Pontic king.

Faced with war and revolution everywhere, the Senate sold the accumulated gold and silver of Rome's temples to finance Sulla's troops. We must not tell again how Sulla captured Athens, defeated the rebel armies, saved the Empire for Rome, and gave Mithridates a lenient peace. The King withdrew to his Pontic capital and quietly organized another army and fleet. Murena, the Roman legate in Asia, decided to attack him before he grew stronger. When, in this Second Mithridatic War (83-81), Murena was defeated, Sulla reprimanded him for violating the treaty and ordered hostilities ended. Six years later Nicomedes III bequeathed Bithynia to Rome. Mithridates realized that his own kingdom would soon be swallowed up if the Roman power, already controlling the Bosporus, should reach the borders of Paphlagonia and Pontus. In the Third Mithridatic War (75-63) he made a last effort, fought for twelve years against Lucullus and Pompey, was betrayed by his allies and aides, and fled to the Crimea. There the old warrior, now in his sixty-ninth year, tried to organize an army to cross the Balkans and invade Italy from the north. His son Pharnaces revolted against his authority, his army refused the venture, and the deserted king tried to kill himself. The poison that he took failed to work because he had inured his system to it, and his hands were too weak to press home the blade from whose point he invited death. His friends and protégés, commissioned by his son to kill him, ended his life with their swords and spears.

VIII. PROSE

It speaks well for Roman rule that the cities of Asia Minor recovered so rapidly from the intermittent fever of these wars. Nicomedia became the capital of the province of Bithynia-Pontus and later the imperial seat of Diocletian; Nicaea would be immortalized by the most important council in the history of the Christian Church. The two cities so rivaled one another in building that Trajan had to send the younger Pliny to draw them back from bankruptcy. Nicomedia made her offering to literature in Flavius Arrianus, whom we have seen recording the discourses of Epictetus. Governor of Cappadocia for six years, archon of Athens for one, Arrian yet found time to write many histories, of which only the *Anabasis of Alexander* remains, with an appendix of *Indica*. It was written in clear and simple Greek, for Arrian took Xenophon as his exemplar in style as well as life. "This work," he says, with the bold vanity of the ancients, "is, and has been from my youth up, equivalent to native land, and family, and public office for me; and therefore I do not deem myself unworthy to rank among the greatest authors in the Greek language." [72]

Other cities along the Black Sea had goodly buildings and famous scholars. Myrlea had 320,000 inhabitants; [73] Amastris (Amasra) impressed Pliny as "a neat and lovely city," known for its fine box trees; Sinope flourished as a fishing center and an outlet for the timber and minerals of its countryside; Amisus (Samsun) and Trapezus made a living by trading across the waters with Scythia (southern Russia); and Amasea (Amasia) gave birth and a home to antiquity's most celebrated geographer.

Strabo came of a rich family, related, he assures us, to the Pontic kings. He suffered from a peculiar squint still known by his name.[74] He traveled extensively, apparently on diplomatic missions, and used every opportunity to gather geographical or historical information. He wrote a lost history continuing Polybius; and in 7 B.C. he issued his great *Geography*, of whose seventeen books time has preserved nearly all. Like Arrian he begins by proclaiming the virtues of his work:

> I ask pardon of my readers, and appeal to them not to fasten the blame for the length of my discussion upon me rather than upon those who earnestly desire knowledge of things famous and ancient. . . . In this work I must leave untouched what is small, and devote my attention to what is noble and great . . . useful or memorable or entertaining. And just as, in judging the merits of colossal statues, we do not examine each individual part with minute care, but rather

> consider the general effect . . . so should this my book be judged.
> For it, too, is a colossal work . . . worthy of a philosopher.[75]

He borrows frankly from Polybius and Poseidonius, less frankly from Eratosthenes, brings them all sharply to account for their errors, and suggests that his own should be blamed on his sources.[76] But he acknowledges his sources with rare candor and usually selects them with discrimination. He notes that the extension of the Roman Empire has widened geographical knowledge, but believes that there are whole continents still unknown—possibly in the Atlantic. He believes that the earth is spheroidal (but the word probably meant spherical), and that if one were to sail westward from Spain he would in time come to India. He describes coastlines as always changing through erosion or eruption and conjectures that subterranean disturbances may someday sever Suez and unite the seas. His work was a brave summary of the global knowledge of his age and must be ranked as one of the major achievements of ancient science.

Far more renowned than Strabo in his time was Dio Chrysostom—Dio of the Golden Mouth (A.D. 40-120). His family had long been distinguished in Prusa; his grandfather had exhausted a fortune in gifts to the Bithynian city and then had made another; his father had gone through the same experience; and Dio followed in their steps.[77] He became an orator and a sophist, went to Rome, was converted to Stoicism by Musonius Rufus, and was banished from Italy and Bithynia by Domitian (82). Forbidden the use of his property or income, he wandered for thirteen years from country to country as a penniless philosopher, refusing money for his discourses, and earning his bread for the most part by the work of his hands. When Domitian was succeeded by Nerva, Dio's exile was changed into honors; Nerva and Trajan befriended him and gave his city many favors at his request. He returned to Prusa and devoted most of his wealth to beautifying it. Another philosopher accused him of embezzling public funds; he was tried by Pliny and appears to have been exonerated.

Dio left behind him eighty orations. For us today they contain more wind than meat; they suffer from empty amplification, deceptive analogies, and rhetorical tricks; they stretch half an idea to half a hundred pages; no wonder a weary listener complained, "You are letting the sun go down with your interminable questions." [78] But the man had charm and eloquence, else he could hardly have become the most celebrated orator of the century, for whose speeches men would interrupt a war. "I don't know what you mean," said the honest Trajan, "but I love you as myself." [79] The barbarians on the Borysthenes (Dnieper) heard him as gladly as the Greeks gathered at Olympia, or the excitable Alexandrians; an army about to revolt against Nerva was mollified into acceptance by the impromptu address of the half-naked exile.

Probably what drew people to him was not his fine Attic Greek, but the courage of his denunciations. Almost alone in pagan antiquity he condemned prostitution; and few writers of his time so openly attacked the institution of slavery. (He was a bit vexed, however, when he found that his slaves had run away.)[80] His address to the Alexandrians was a castigation of their luxury, superstition, and vice. He chose Ilium as the scene of an oration in which he argued that Troy had never existed and that "Homer was the boldest liar in history." In the heart of Rome he expounded the case of the countryside against the city, painted in vivid narrative a touching picture of rural poverty, and warned his audience that the land was being neglected and the agricultural basis of civilization was in decay. At Olympia, amid a multitude of fanatical worldlings, he reproved the atheists and epicureans of the day. Though popular conceptions of deity may be absurd, said Dio, the wise man will understand that the simple mind needs simple ideas and pictorial symbols. In truth no man can conceive the form of the Supreme Being, and even Pheidias' noble statue was an anthropomorphic assumption as unwarrantable as the primitive identification of God with a star or a tree. We cannot know what God is, but we have an innate conviction that he exists, and we feel that philosophy without religion is a dark and hopeless thing. The only real freedom is wisdom—i.e., the knowledge of what is right and what is wrong; the road to freedom lies not through politics or revolution, but through philosophy; and true philosophy consists not in the speculations of books, but in the faithful practice of honor and virtue according to the dictates of that inmost voice which is, in some mystic sense, the word of God in the heart of man.[81]

IX. THE ORIENTAL TIDE

Religion, which had bided its time and nourished its roots through all the learned or ribald skepticism of the Periclean and Hellenistic periods, now in the second century resumed its immemorial sway as philosophy, baffled by infinity and human hope, confessed its limitations and abdicated its authority. The people themselves had never lost their faith; most of them accepted in outline the Homeric description of the afterlife,[82] sacrificed religiously before undertaking a voyage, and still placed an obol in the mouth of the dead to pay his passage across the Styx. Roman statecraft welcomed the aid of established priesthoods and sought popular support by building costly temples to local gods. Throughout Palestine, Syria, and Asia Minor, the wealth of the clergy continued to grow. Hadad and Atargatis were still worshiped by the Syrians and had an awesome shrine at Hierapolis; the resurrection of the god Tammuz was still hailed in the towns of Syria with the cry, "Adonis [i.e., the Lord] is risen," and his ascension into heaven was celebrated in the closing scenes of his festival.[83] Similar ceremonies commemorated in Greek ritual the agony, death, and resurrection of Dionysus. From Cappadocia the worship of the goddess Ma had spread into Ionia and Italy; her priests (called *fanatici* as belonging to the *fanum*, or temple) danced dizzily to the sound of trumpets and drums, slashed themselves with knives, and sprinkled the goddess and her devotees with their blood.[84] The making of new deities went on assiduously; Caesar and the emperors, Antinoüs and many local worthies, were deified (i.e., canonized) in life or death. Cross-fertilized by trade and war, pantheons were everywhere in flower, and prayers rose hopefully in a thousand tongues to a thousand gods. Paganism was not one religion; it was a jungle of rival creeds, often merging in eclectic confusion.

The worship of Cybele held its ground in Lydia and Phrygia, Italy and Africa and elsewhere, and its priests, as before, emasculated themselves in imitation of her beloved Attis. At her spring festival her worshipers fasted, prayed, and mourned the death of Attis; her priests cut their arms and drank their own blood; and a solemn procession bore the young god to his grave. But on the morrow the streets rang with exultant shouts as the people celebrated the resurrection of Attis and the renewal of the earth. "Take courage, O mystics," cried the priests, "the god is saved; and for you also will come salvation." [85] On the last day of the feast the image of the Great Mother was carried in triumph through crowds that hailed her, at Rome, as *Nostra Domina*, "Our Lady." [86]

Even more widely honored than Cybele was the Egyptian goddess Isis, the sorrowing mother, the loving comforter, the bearer of the gift of eternal life. All the Mediterranean peoples knew how her great spouse Osiris had died and had risen from the dead; in nearly every great city on that historic sea this happy resurrection was commemorated with gorgeous pageantry, and jubilant worshipers sang, "We have found Osiris again." [87] Isis was represented in pictures and statues as holding her divine child Horus in her arms, and devout litanies hailed her as "Queen of Heaven," "Star of the Sea," and "Mother of God." [88] Of all pagan cults this came nearest to Christianity in the tenderness of its story, the refinement of its ritual, the solemnity and yet joyful atmosphere of its chapels, the moving music of its vespers, the conscientious ministry of its white-robed and tonsured priests,[89] the honors and opportunities with which it charmed and comforted women, the universal welcome it gave to every nationality and every class. The religion of Isis spread from Egypt to Greece in the fourth century B.C., to Sicily in the third, to Italy in the second, and then to all parts of the Empire; her icons have been found on the Danube, the Rhine, and the Seine, and a temple to her has been unearthed in London.[90] The Mediterranean soul has never ceased to worship the divine creativeness and maternal solicitude of woman.

Meanwhile the masculine cult of Mithras was passing from Persia to the most distant Roman frontiers. In the later Zoroastrian theology Mithras was the son of Ahura-Mazda, the God of Light. He, too, was the god of light, of truth, purity, and honor; sometimes he was identified with the sun and led the cosmic war against the powers of darkness, always he mediated between his father and his followers, protecting and encouraging them in life's struggle with evil, lies, uncleanliness, and the other works of Ahriman, Prince of Darkness. When Pompey's soldiers brought this religion from Cappadocia to Europe a Greek artist pictured Mithras as kneeling on the back of a bull and plunging a poniard into its neck; this representation became the universal symbol of the faith. The seventh day of each week was held sacred to the sun-god; and towards the end of December his followers celebrated the birthday of Mithras "the Invincible Sun," who, at the winter solstice, had won his annual victory over the forces of darkness, and day by day would now give longer light.[91] Tertullian speaks of a Mithraic priesthood with a "high pontiff," and of celibates and virgins serving the god; daily sacrifice was offered at his altar, worshipers partook of consecrated bread and wine, and the climax of the ceremony was signaled by the sounding of a bell.[92] A flame was kept ever burning before the crypt in which the young god was represented felling the bull. Mithraism preached a high morality and pledged its "soldiers" to a lifelong war against evil in every form. After death, said its priests, all men must appear before the judgment seat of Mithras; then unclean souls would be handed over to Ahriman for eternal torment, while the pure would rise through seven spheres, shedding some mortal element at each stage, until they would be received into the full radiance of heaven by Ahura-Mazda himself.[93] This invigorating mythology spread in the second and third centuries of our era through western Asia and Europe (skipping Greece), and built its chapels as far north as Hadrian's Wall. Christian Fathers were shocked to find so many parallels between their own religion and Mithraism; they argued that these were thefts from Christianity, or confusing stratagems of Satan (a form of Ahriman). It is difficult to say which faith borrowed from the other; perhaps both absorbed ideas current in the religious air of the East.

Each of the great cults of the Mediterranean region had "mysteries," which were usually ceremonies of purification, sacrifice, initiation, revelation, and regeneration, centering about the death and resurrection of the god. New members were admitted into the worship of Cybele by being placed naked in a pit over which a bull was slain; the blood of the sacrificed animal, falling upon the candidate, purified him of sin and gave him a new spiritual and eternal life. The genitals of the bull, representing his sacred fertility, were placed in a consecrated vessel and were dedicated to the goddess.[94] Mithraism had a similar rite, known to the classic world as the *taurobolium*, or throwing of the bull. Apuleius described in ecstatic terms the degrees of initiation into the service of Isis—the long novitiate of fasting, continence, and prayer, the purifying submersion in holy water, and at last the mystic vision of the goddess offering everlasting bliss. At Eleusis the candidate was required to confess his sins (which discouraged Nero), abstain for a time from certain foods, bathe in the bay for spiritual as well as physical cleansing, and then offer sacrifice, usually of a pig. For three days, at the Feast of Demeter, the initiates mourned with her the snatching of her daughter into Hades, and meanwhile lived on consecrated cakes and a mystic mixture of flour, water, and mint. On the third night a religious drama represented the resurrection of Persephone, and the officiating priest promised a like rebirth to every purified soul.[95] Varying the theme under Hindu or Pythagorean influence, the Orphic sect throughout Greek lands taught that the soul is imprisoned in a succession of sinful bodies and can be released from this degrading reincarnation by rising to ecstatic union with Dionysus. At their gatherings the members of the Orphic brotherhood drank the blood of a bull sacrificed to—and identified with—the dying and atoning savior. Communal partaking of sacred food or drink was a frequent feature of these Mediterranean faiths. Often the food was thought to take on, by sanctification, the powers of the god, which were then magically conveyed to the communicant.[96]

All sects assumed the possibility of magic. The Magi had disseminated their art through the East and had given a new name to old jugglery. The Mediterranean world was rich in magicians, miracleworkers, oracles, astrologers, ascetic saints, and scientific interpreters of dreams. Every unusual occurrence was widely hailed as a divine portent of future events. *Askesis*, which the Greeks had used to denote the athletic training of the body, came now to mean the spiritual taming of the flesh; men scourged themselves, mutilated themselves, starved themselves, or bound themselves to one place with chains; some of them died through self-torture or self-denial.[97] In the Egyptian desert near Lake Mareotis a group of Jews and non-Jews, male and female, lived in solitary cells, avoided sexual relations, met on the Sabbath for common prayer, and called themselves *Therapeutae*, healers of the soul.[98] Millions believed that the writings ascribed to Orpheus, Hermes, Pythagoras, the sibyls, etc., had been dictated or inspired by a god. Preachers claiming divine inspiration traveled from city to city, performing apparently miraculous cures. Alexander of Abonoteichus trained a serpent to hide its head under his arm and allow a half-human mask to be affixed to its tail; he announced that the serpent was the god Asclepius come to earth to serve as an oracle; and he amassed a fortune by interpreting the sounds made by reeds inserted in the false head.[99]

Beside such charlatans there were probably thousands of sincere preachers of the pagan faiths. Early in the third century Philostratus painted an idealized picture of such a man in his *Life of Apollonius* of Tyana. At sixteen Apollonius adopted the strict rule of the Pythagorean brotherhood, renouncing marriage, meat, and wine, never shaving his beard, and keeping silence for five years.[100] He distributed his patrimony among his relatives and wandered as a penniless monk through Persia, India, Egypt, western Asia, Greece, and Italy. He imbibed the lore of the Magi, the Brahmans, and the Egyptian ascetics. He visited temples of any creed, implored the priests to abandon the sacrifice of animals, worshiped the sun, accepted the gods, and taught that behind them there was one supreme unknowable deity. His life of abnegation and piety led his followers to claim that he was the son of a god, but he described himself simply as the son of Apollonius. Tradition credited him with many miracles: he walked through closed doors, understood all languages, cast out demons, and raised a girl from the dead.[101] But he was a philosopher rather than a magician. He knew and loved Greek literature and expounded a simple but exacting morality. "Grant me," he prayed the gods, "to have little and to desire nothing." Asked by a king to choose a gift, he answered, "Dried fruit and bread." [102] Preaching reincarnation, he bade his followers injure no living creature and eat no flesh. He exhorted them to shun enmity, slander, jealousy, and hatred; "if we are philosophers," he told them, "we cannot hate our fellow men." [103] "Sometimes," says Philostratus, "he discussed communism and taught that men ought to support one another." [104] He was accused of sedition and witchcraft, came of his own accord to Rome to answer these charges before Domitian, was imprisoned, and escaped. He died about A.D. 98, at an advanced age. His followers claimed that he had appeared to them after his death and had then ascended bodily into heaven.[105]

What were the qualities that won half of Rome, half the Empire, to these new faiths? Partly their classless, raceless character; they accepted all nationalities, all freemen, and all slaves, and rode with consoling indifference over inequalities of pedigree and wealth. Their temples were made spacious to welcome the people as well as to enshrine the god. Cybele and Isis were mother-goddesses acquainted with grief, who mourned like millions of bereaved women; they could understand what the Roman deities seldom knew—the emptied hearts of the defeated. The desire to return to the mother is stronger than the impulse to depend upon the father; it is the mother name that comes spontaneously to the lips in great joy or distress; therefore men as well as women found comfort and refuge in Isis and Cybele. Even today the Mediterranean worshiper appeals more often to Mary than to the Father or the Son; and the lovely prayer that he most frequently repeats is addressed not to the Virgin but to the Mother, blessed in the fruit of her womb.

The new faiths not only entered more deeply into the heart; they appealed more colorfully to the imagination and the senses with processions and chants alternating between sorrow and rejoicing, and a ritual of impressive symbolism that brought fresh courage to spirits heavy with the prose of life. The new priesthoods were filled not by politicians occasionally donning sacerdotal garb, but by men and women of all ranks, graduating through an ascetic novitiate to continual ministration. By their help the soul conscious of wrongdoing could be purified; sometimes the body racked with illness could be healed by an inspiring word or ritual; and the mysteries at which they officiated symbolized the hope that even death might be overcome.

Once men had sublimated their longing for grandeur and continuance in the glory and survival of their family and their clan, and then of a state that was their creation and collective self. Now the old clan lines were melting away in the new mobility of peace; and the imperial state was the spiritual embodiment only of the master class, not of the powerless multitude of men. Monarchy at the top, frustrating the participation and merger of the citizen in the state, produced individualism at the bottom and through the mass. The promise of personal immortality, of an endless happiness after a life of subjection, poverty, tribulation, or toil, was the final and irresistible attraction of the Oriental faiths and of the Christianity that summarized, absorbed, and conquered them. All the world seemed conspiring to prepare the way for Christ.

CHAPTER XXV

Rome and Judea

132 B.C.-A.D.135

I. PARTHIA

BETWEEN Pontus and the Caucasus rose the troubled mountains of Armenia, on whose crest, story told, Noah's ark had found a mooring. Through the fertile valleys ran the roads that led from Parthia and Mesopotamia to the Black Sea; hence empires competed for Armenia. The people were Indo-European, akin to the Hittites and the Phrygians, but they had never surrendered their sweeping Anatolian nose. They were a vigorous race, patient in agriculture, skilled in handicraft, unequaled in commercial acumen; they made the best of a difficult terrain and raised enough wealth to keep their kings in luxury if not in power. Darius I, in the Behistun inscription (521 B.C.), named Armenia among the satrapies of Persia; later it gave a nominal allegiance to the Seleucids and then alternately to Parthia and Rome; but its remoteness allowed it a practical independence. Its most famous king, Tigranes the Great (94-56 B.C.), conquered Cappadocia, added a second capital, Tigranocerta, to Artaxata, and joined Mithridates' revolt against Rome. When Pompey accepted his apologies he gave the victorious general 6000 talents ($21,600,000), 10,000 drachmas ($6000) to each centurion, and fifty to each soldier, in the Roman army.[1] Under Caesar, Augustus, and Nero Armenia acknowledged the suzerainty of Rome, and under Trajan it was for a time a Roman province; nevertheless, its culture was Iranian, and its usual orientation was toward Parthia.

The Parthians had for centuries occupied the region south of the Caspian Sea as subjects of the Achaemenid, then of the Seleucid, kings. They were of Scythian-Turanian stock—i.e., they belonged racially with the peoples of southern Russia and Turkestan. About 248 B.C. a Scythian chief, Arsaces, revolted against the Seleucid authority, made Parthia a sovereign state, and established the Arsacid dynasty. The Seleucid kings, weakened by Rome's defeat of Antiochus III (189 B.C.), were unable to defend their territory against the reckless, half-barbarous Parthians, and by the end of the second century B.C. all Mesopotamia and Persia were absorbed into a new Parthian Empire. Three capitals, according to the season, entertained the new royalty: Hecatompylus in Parthia, Ecbatana in Media, and Ctesiphon on the lower Tigris. Across from Ctesiphon lay the former Seleucid capital Seleucia, which remained for centuries a Greek city in a Parthian realm. The Arsacid rulers kept the administrative structure built up by the Seleucids, but overlaid it with a feudalism derived from the Achaemenid kings. The mass of the population was composed of agricultural serfs and slaves; industry was backward, but the Parthian ironworkers made a fine steel, and "the brewing trade was highly profitable."[2] The wealth of the state came partly from the trade that passed along the great rivers, partly from the caravans that crossed Parthia on the way between farther Asia and the West. From 53 B.C., when the Parthians defeated Crassus at Carrhae, to A.D. 217, when Macrinus bought peace from Artabanus, Rome fought war after war for the control of these routes and the Red Sea.

The Parthians were too rich or too poor to indulge in literature. The aristocrats, as in all ages, preferred the art of life to the life of art, and the serfs were too illiterate, the artisans too busy, the merchants too commercial, to produce great art or great books. The people spoke Pahlavi and wrote in Aramaic on parchment, which now replaced cuneiform; but not a line of Parthian literature has been preserved. We know that Greek plays were enjoyed in Ctesiphon as well as in Seleucia, for the head of Crassus played a part there in the *Bacchae* of Euripides. The paintings and sculptures discovered at Palmyra, Dura-Europus, and Ashur were probably the work of Iranian artists; their crude amalgam of Greek and Oriental styles affected later art from China to Byzantium. A vivid relief of a mounted archer has come down to us to suggest that we might have a higher opinion of Parthian art if more of it remained.[2a] At Hatra, near Mosul, an Arabian feudatory of the Parthian king built (88 B.C.?) a limestone palace of seven arched and vaulted halls, in a powerful but barbarous style. Good Parthian work has survived in engraved silverware and jewelry.

The Parthians excelled in man's favorite art—personal adornment. Both sexes curled their hair; the men nursed frizzed beards and flowing mustaches, and clothed themselves in tunic and baggy trousers, usually covered with a many-colored robe; the women swathed themselves in delicate embroideries and decked their hair with flowers. Free Parthians amused themselves with hunting, ate and drank abundantly, and never went on foot when they could ride. They were brave warriors and honorable foes, treated prisoners decently, admitted foreigners to high office, and gave asylum to refugees; sometimes, however, they mutilated dead enemies, tortured witnesses, and corrected trifling offenses with the scourge. They practiced polygamy according to their means, veiled and secluded their women, severely punished the infidelity of their wives, but permitted divorce to either sex almost at will.[3] When the Parthian general Surena led an army against Crassus he took with him 200 concubines and a thousand camels for his baggage.[4] All in all the Parthians impress us as less civilized than the Achaemenid Persians and more honorable gentlemen than the Romans. They were tolerant of religious diversities, allowing the Greeks, Jews, and Christians among them to practice their rituals unhindered. They themselves, veering from Zoroastrian orthodoxy, worshiped the sun and the moon, and preferred Mithras to Ahura-Mazda, much as the Christians preferred Christ to Yahveh. The Magi, neglected by the later Arsacid kings, abetted the overthrow of the dynasty.

On the death of Vologases IV (A.D. 209) his sons Vologases V and Artabanus IV fought for the throne. Artabanus won, and then defeated the Romans at Nisibis. Three centuries of war between the empires ended in a modified victory for Parthia; on the Mesopotamian plains the Roman legions were at a disadvantage against the Parthian cavalry. Artabanus in turn fell in civil war. His conqueror, Ardashir or Artaxerxes, feudal lord of Persia, made himself King of Kings (A.D. 227) and established the Sassanid dynasty. The Zoroastrian religion was restored, and Persia entered upon a greater age.

II. THE HASMONEANS

In 143 B.C. Simon Maccabee, taking advantage of the struggles among the Parthians, Seleucids, Egyptians, and Romans, wrested the independence of Judea from the Seleucid king. A popular assembly named him general and high priest of the Second Jewish Commonwealth (142 B.C-A.D. 70), and made the latter office hereditary in his Hasmonean family. Judea became again a theocracy, under the Hasmonean dynasty of priest-kings. It has been a characteristic of Semitic societies that they closely associated the spiritual and temporal powers, in the family and in the state; they would have no sovereign but God.

Recognizing the weakness of the little kingdom, the Hasmoneans spent two generations widening its borders by diplomacy and force. By 78 B.C. they had conquered and absorbed Samaria, Edom, Moab, Galilee, Idumea, Transjordania, Gadara, Pella, Gerasa, Raphia, and Gaza, and had made Palestine as extensive as under Solomon. The descendants of those brave Maccabees who had fought for religious freedom enforced Judaism and circumcision upon their new subjects at the point of the sword.[5] At the same time the Hasmoneans lost their religious zeal and, over the bitter protests of the Pharisees, yielded more and more to the Hellenizing elements in the population. Queen Salome Alexandra (78-69 B.C.) reversed this trend and made peace with the Pharisees, but even before her death her sons Hyrcanus II and Aristobulus II began a war of succession. Both parties submitted their claims to Pompey, who now (63 B.C.) stood with his victorious legions at Damascus. When Pompey decided for Hyrcanus, Aristobulus fortified himself with his army in Jerusalem. Pompey laid siege to the capital and gained its lower sections; but the followers of Aristobulus took refuge in the walled precincts of the Temple and held out for three months. Their piety, we are told, helped Pompey to overcome them; for perceiving that they would not fight on the Sabbath, he had his men prepare unhindered on each Sabbath the mounds and battering rams for the next day's assault. Meanwhile the priests offered the usual prayers and sacrifices in the Temple. When the ramparts fell 12,000 Jews were slaughtered; few resisted, none surrendered, many leaped to death from the walls.[6] Pompey ordered his men to leave the treasures of the Temple untouched, but he exacted an indemnity of 10,000 talents ($3,600,000) from the nation. The cities that the Hasmoneans had conquered were transferred from the Judean to the Roman power; Hyrcanus II was made high priest and nominal ruler of Judea, but as the ward of Antipater the Idumean, who had helped Rome. The independent monarchy was ended, and Judea became part of the Roman province of Syria.

In 54 B.C. Crassus, on his way to play the part of Pentheus at Ctesiphon, robbed the Temple of the treasures that Pompey had spared, amounting to some 10,000 talents. When news came that Crassus had been defeated and killed, the Jews took the opportunity to reclaim their freedom. Longinus, successor of Crassus as governor of Syria, suppressed the revolt and sold 30,000 Jews into slavery (43 B.C.).[7] In that same year Antipater died; the Parthians swept across the desert into Judea and set up, as their puppet king, Antigonus, the last of the Hasmoneans. Antony and Octavian countered by naming Herod—son of Antipater—king of Judea and financing his Jewish army with Roman funds. Herod drove out the Parthians, protected Jerusalem from pillage, sent Antigonus to Antony for execution, slew all Jewish leaders who had supported the puppet, and so auspiciously entered upon one of the most colorful reigns in history (37-4 B.C.).

III. HEROD THE GREAT

His character was typical of an age that had produced so many men of intellect without morals, ability without scruple, and courage without honor. He was in his lesser way the Augustus of Judea: like Augustus he overlaid the chaos of freedom with dictatorial order, beautified his capital with Greek architecture and sculpture, enlarged his realm, made it prosper, achieved more by subtlety than by arms, married widely, was broken by the treachery of his offspring, and knew every good fortune but happiness. Josephus describes him as a man of great physical bravery and skill, a perfect marksman with arrow and javelin, a mighty hunter who in one day caught forty wild beasts, and "such a warrior as could not be withstood." [8] He must have added some charm of personality to these qualities, for he was always able to outtalk or outbribe the enemies who sought to discredit him with Antony, Cleopatra, or Octavian. From every crisis with the Triumvirs he emerged with larger powers and territory than before, until Augustus judged him "too great a soul for so small a dominion," restored the cities of Hasmonean Palestine to his kingdom, and wished Herod might rule Syria and Egypt too.[9] "The Idumean" was a generous as well as a ruthless man, and the benefits he conferred upon his subjects were equaled only by the injuries he did them.

He was molded in part by the hatred of those whom he had defeated or whose relatives he had slain, and by the scornful hostility of a people that resented his harsh autocracy and his alien descent. He had become king by the help and money of Rome, and remained to the end of his life a friend and vassal of the power from which the people night and day plotted to regain their liberty. The modest economy of the country bent and at last broke under the taxes imposed upon it by a luxurious court and a building program out of proportion to the national wealth. Herod sought in various ways to appease his subjects, but failed. He forgave taxes in poor years, persuaded Rome to reduce the tribute it exacted, secured privileges for Jews abroad, relieved famine and other calamities promptly, maintained internal order and external security, and developed the natural resources of the land. Brigandage was ended, trade was stimulated, the markets and ports were noisy with life. At the same time the King alienated public sentiment by the looseness of his morals, the cruelty of his punishments, and the "accidental" drowning, in the bath, of Aristobulus, grandson of Hyrcanus II and therefore the legitimate heir to the throne. The priests whose power he had ended, and whose leaders he appointed, conspired against him, and the Pharisees abominated his apparent resolution to make Judea a Hellenistic state.

Ruling many cities that were more Greek than Jewish in population and culture, and impressed with the refinement and variety of Hellenic civilization, Herod, himself not by origin or conviction a Jew, naturally sought a cultural unity for his realm, and an imposing façade for his rule, by encouraging Greek ways, dress, ideas, literature, and art. He surrounded himself with Greek scholars, entrusted to them high affairs of state, and made Nicolas of Damascus, a Greek, his official counselor and historian. He raised at great expense a theater and an amphitheater in Jerusalem, adorned them with monuments to Augustus and other pagans, and introduced Greek athletic and musical contests and Roman gladiatorial combats.[10] He beautified Jerusalem with other buildings in what seemed to the people a foreign architectural style, and set up in public places Greek statuary whose nudity startled the Jews as much as the nakedness of the wrestlers in the games. He built himself a palace, doubtless on Greek models, filled it with gold and marble and costly furniture, and surrounded it with extensive gardens after the manner of his Roman friends. He shocked the people by telling them that the Temple which Zerubbabel had set up five centuries before was too small, and proposing to tear it down and erect a larger one on its site. Despite their protests and their fears he realized his plan and reared the lordly Temple that Titus would destroy.

On Mt. Moriah an area was cleared 750 feet square. Along its boundaries cloisters were built roofed with cedar "curiously graven," and supported by multiple rows of Corinthian columns, each a marble monolith so large that three men could barely join hands around it. In this main court were the booths of the money-changers, who for the convenience of pilgrims changed foreign coins into those acceptable to the Sanctuary; here, too, were the stalls where one might buy animals to offer in sacrifice, and the rooms or porticoes where teachers and pupils met to study Hebrew and the Law, and the noisy beggars inevitable in Oriental scenes. From this "Outer Temple" a broad flight of steps led up to an inner walled space which non-Jews were forbidden to enter; here was the "Court of the Women," where "such men as were pure came in with their wives." [11] From this second enclosure the worshiper passed up another flight of steps, and through gates plated with silver and gold, into the "Court of the Priests," where stood, in the open air, the altar upon which burnt sacrifice was offered to Yahveh. Still other steps led through bronze doors seventy-five feet high and twenty-four wide, overhung with a famous golden vine, into the temple proper, open only to priests. It was built entirely of white marble, in set-back style, and its façade was plated with gold. The interior was divided crosswise by a great embroidered veil, blue and purple and scarlet. Before the veil were the golden seven-branched candlestick, the altar of incense, and the table bearing the unleavened "shewbread" that the priests laid before Yahveh. Behind the veil was the Holy of Holies, which in the earlier temple had contained a golden censer and the Ark of the Covenant, but in this temple, says Josephus, contained "nothing whatever." Here human foot trod only once a year, on the Day of Atonement, when the high priest entered alone. The main structures of this historic edifice were finished in eight years; the work of adornment, however, continued for eighty years, and was just completed when Titus' legions came.[12]

The people were proud of the great shrine, which was ranked among the marvels of the Augustan world; for its splendor they almost forgave the Corinthian columns of the porticoes and the golden eagle that—defying the Jewish prohibition of graven images—symbolized at the very entrance to the Temple the power of Judea's enemy and master, Rome. Meanwhile Jews who traveled brought back news of the completely Greek buildings with which Herod was remaking the other cities of Palestine, and told how he was spending national funds, and (rumor said) the gold that had been hidden in David's tomb,[13] in constructing a great harbor at Caesarea, and lavishing gifts upon such foreign cities as Damascus, Byblus, Berytus, Tyre, Sidon, Antioch, Rhodes, Pergamum, Sparta, and Athens. Herod, it became clear, wished to be the idol of the Hellenic world, not merely the King of the Jews. But the Jews lived by their religion, by their faith that Yahveh would someday rescue them from bondage and oppression; the triumph of the Hellenic over the Hebraic spirit in the person of their ruler foreboded to them a disaster as great as the persecutions of Antiochus. Plots were formed against Herod's life; he discovered them, arrested the conspirators, tortured and killed them, and in some cases put their entire families to death.[14] He set spies among the people, disguised himself to eavesdrop on his subjects, and punished every hostile word.[15]

He foiled all his enemies except his wives and his children. Of wives he had ten, once nine at a time; of children, fourteen. His second wife, Mariamne, was the grandaughter of Hyrcanus II and the sister of Aristobulus, both of whom Herod had slain. She was, says Josephus, "a chaste woman, but somewhat rough by nature, and treated her husband imperiously because she saw he was so fond of her as to be her slave. . . . She would also expose his mother and sister openly, on account of the meanness of their birth, and would speak unkindly of them, insomuch that there was an unpardoning hatred among the women" of the royal household. Herod's sister persuaded him that Mariamne was plotting to poison him. He accused his wife before the members of his court; they condemned her, and she was executed. Doubtful of her guilt, Herod was for a time mad with remorse; he called out her name repeatedly, sent his servants to summon her, gave up public affairs, went into the desert, "afflicted himself bitterly," and was brought to his palace in a state of fever and insanity. Mariamne's mother joined with others in an attempt to depose him; he suddenly recovered his powers of mind and throne, and put the plotters to death. Soon thereafter Antipater, his son by his first wife, laid proofs before him of an attempted conspiracy by Alexander and Aristobulus, his sons by Mariamne; he submitted the matter to a council of 150 men, who sentenced the youths to die (6 B.C.). Two years later Nicolas of Damascus convicted Antipater himself of scheming to replace his father. Herod had the youth brought before him and "began to weep, lamenting the misfortunes he had suffered from his children." [16] In a moment of mercy he ordered Antipater jailed.

Meanwhile the old king was breaking down with disease and grief. He suffered from dropsy, ulcer, fever, convulsions, and loathsome breath. After frustrating so many attempts against his life he tried to kill himself, but was prevented. Hearing that Antipater had sought to bribe the guard to free him, Herod had him slain. Five days afterward he too died (4 B.C.), in the sixty-ninth year of his age, hated by all his people. It was said of him by his enemies that "he stole to the throne like a fox, ruled like a tiger, and died like a dog." [17]

IV. THE LAW AND ITS PROPHETS

Herod's will divided his kingdom among three remaining sons. To Philip went the eastern region known as Batanea, containing the cities of Bethsaida, Capitolias, Gerasa, Philadelphia, and Bostra. To Herod Antipas went Peraea (the land beyond the Jordan) and, in the north, Galilee, where lay Esdraela, Tiberias, and Nazareth. To Archelaus fell Samaritis, Idumea, and Judea. In this last were many famous cities or towns: Bethlehem, Hebron, Beersheba, Gaza, Gadara, Emmaus, Jamnia, Joppa, Caesarea, Jericho, and Jerusalem. Some Palestinian cities were predominantly Greek, some Syrian; the Gadarene swine attest the non-Jews of Gadara. The gentiles were in the majority in all the coast towns except Joppa and Jamnia, and in the "Decapolis" or ten cities of the Jordan; in the interior the villages were almost entirely Jewish. In this racial division, not unpleasing to Rome, lay the tragedy of Palestine.

We must go back to the Puritans of England to understand the repulsion aroused in pious Jews by the polytheism and immorality of pagan society. Religion was to the Jews the source of their law, their state, and their hope: to let it melt away in the swelling river of Hellenism would, they thought, be national suicide. Hence that mutual hatred of Jew and gentile which kept the little nation in a kind of undulating fever of racial strife, political turbulence, and periodic war. Moreover, the Jews of Judea scorned the people of Galilee as ignorant backsliders, and the Galileans scorned the Judeans as slaves caught in the cobwebs of the Law. Again, a perpetual feud burned between Judeans and Samaritans; for the latter claimed that their hill of Gerizim, and not Zion, had been chosen by Yahveh as his home, and they rejected all the Scriptures except the Pentateuch.[18] All these factions agreed in hating the Roman power, which made them pay a heavy price for the unwelcome privilege of peace.

There were now in Palestine some 2,500,000 souls, of whom perhaps 100,000 lived in Jerusalem.[19] Most of them spoke Aramaic; priests and scholars understood Hebrew; officials and foreigners and most authors used Greek. The majority of the people were peasants, tilling and irrigating the soil, tending the orchard, the vine, and the flock. In the time of Christ Palestine grew enough wheat to export a modest surplus: [20] its dates, figs, grapes and olives, wine and oil were prized and bought throughout the Mediterranean. The old command was still obeyed to let the land lie fallow in each sabbatical year.[21] Handicrafts were largely hereditary and were usually organized in guilds. Jewish opinion honored the worker, and most scholars plied their hands as well as their tongues. Slaves were fewer than in any other Mediterranean country. Petty trade flourished, but there were as yet few Jewish merchants of large means and range. "We are not a commercial people," said Josephus; "we live in a country [eastern Judea] without a seaboard, and have no inclination to [foreign] trade." [22] Financial operations were of minor scope until Hillel, perhaps at Herod's suggestion, abrogated the law of Deuteronomy (xv, 1-11) requiring the cancellation of debts every seventh year. The Temple itself was the national bank.

Within the Temple was the hall Gazith, meeting place of the Sanhedrin or Great Council of the Elders of Israel. Probably the institution arose in the period of Seleucid rule (*ca.* 200 B.C.), to replace the earlier council mentioned in Numbers (xi, 16) as advising Moses. Originally selected by the high priest from the sacerdotal aristocracy, it had come in Roman times to co-opt into its membership a rising number of Pharisees and a few professional Scribes.[23] These seventy-one men, under the presidency of the high priest, claimed supreme power over all Jews everywhere, and orthodox Jews everywhere acknowledged it; but the Hasmoneans, Herod, and Rome recognized their authority only in violations of Jewish law by a Judean Jew. They could pass sentence of death upon Jews in Judea for religious offenses, but could not execute it without confirmation by the civil power.[24]

In this assembly, as in most, two factions fought for predominance—a conservative group led by the higher priests and the Sadducees, and a liberal group led by Pharisees and Scribes. Most of the upper clergy and upper classes belonged to the Sadducees (*Zadokim*), so named after their founder Zadok; they were nationalistic in politics and orthodox in religion; they stood for the enforcement of the Torah or written Law, but rejected the additional ordinances of the oral tradition and the liberalizing interpretations of the Pharisees. They doubted immortality and were content to possess the good things of the earth.

The Pharisees (*Perushim*, separatists) were so named by the Sadducees as meaning that they separated themselves (like good Brahmans) from those who contracted religious impurity by neglecting the requirements of ritual cleanliness.[25] They were a continuation of the Chasidim, or Devotees, of the Maccabean age, who had upheld the strictest application of the Law. Josephus, himself a Pharisee, defined them as "a body of Jews who profess to be more religious than the rest, and to explain the laws more precisely." [26] For this purpose they added to the written Law of the Pentateuch the oral tradition of interpretations and decisions made by recognized teachers of the

Law. These interpretations were necessary, in the judgment of the Pharisees, to clarify the obscurities of the Mosaic Code, to specify its application in particular cases, and to modify its letter, occasionally, in adaptation to the changed needs and conditions of life. They were at once rigorous and lenient, softening the Law here and there as in Hillel's decree on interest, but demanding the full observation of the oral tradition as well as of the Torah. Only through this full obedience, they felt, could the Jews escape assimilation and extinction. Reconciled to Roman domination, the Pharisees sought consolation in the hope of a physical and spiritual immortality. They lived simply, condemned luxury, fasted frequently, washed sedulously, and were now and then irritatingly conscious of their virtue; but they represented the moral strength of Judaism, won the middle classes to their support, and gave their followers a faith and rule that saved them from disintegration when catastrophe came. After the Temple was destroyed (A.D. 70), the priesthood lost influence, the Sadducees disappeared, the synagogue replaced the temple, and the Pharisees, through the rabbis, became the teachers and shepherds of a scattered but undefeated people.

The most extreme of the Jewish sects was that of the Essenes. They derived their piety from the Chasidim, their name probably from the Chaldaic *aschai* (bather), their doctrine and practice from the stream of ascetic theory and regimen circulating through the world of the last century before Christ; possibly they were influenced by Brahmanic, Buddhist, Parsee, Pythagorean, and Cynic ideas that came to the crossroads of trade at Jerusalem. Numbering some 4000 in Palestine, they organized themselves into a distinct order, observed both the written and the oral Law with passionate exactitude, and lived together as almost monastic celibates tilling the soil in the oasis of Engadi amid the desert west of the Dead Sea. They dwelt in homes owned by their community, had their meals in common and in silence, chose their leaders by a general vote, mingled their goods and earnings in a common treasury, and obeyed the Chasidic motto, "Mine and thine belong to thee." [27] Many of them, says Josephus, "lived more than a hundred years because of their simple diet and regular life." [28] Each clothed himself in white linen, carried a little hoe to cover his droppings, washed himself like a Brahmin afterward, and considered it a sacrilege to evacuate on the Sabbath.[29] A few of them married and lived in towns, but practiced the Tolstoian rule of cohabiting with their wives only to beget children. The members of the sect avoided all sensual pleasure and sought through meditation and prayer a mystic union with God. They hoped that by piety, abstinence, and contemplation they might acquire magic powers and foresee the future. Like most people of their time they believed in angels and demons, thought of diseases as possession by evil spirits, and tried to exorcise these by magical formulas; from their "secret doctrine" came some parts of the Cabala.[30] They looked for the coming of a Messiah who would establish a communistic egalitarian Kingdom of Heaven (*Malchuth Shamayim*) on earth; into that Kingdom only those would enter who had led a spotless life.[31] They were ardent pacifists and refused to make implements of war; but when the legions of Titus attacked Jerusalem and the Temple the Essenes joined other Jews in defending their city and its shrine and fought till nearly all of their order were dead. As Josephus describes their customs and their sufferings we enter into the atmosphere of Christianity:

> Although they were tortured and racked, burnt and torn to pieces, and went through every torment to force them either to blaspheme their legislator, or to eat what was forbidden them, yet could they not be made to do either of them; no, nor once to flatter their tormentors, or to shed a tear. But they smiled in their very pains, and laughed those to scorn who tortured them, and gave up their souls in great cheerfulness, as expecting to receive them again.[32]

These—Sadducees, Pharisees, Essenes—were the chief religious sects of Judea in the generation before Christ. The Scribes (*Hakamin*, learned) whom Jesus so often bracketed with the Pharisees were not a sect but a profession; they were scholars learned in the Law, who lectured on it in synagogues, taught it in schools, debated it in public and private, and applied it in judgment on specific cases. A few of them were priests, some were Sadducees, most were Pharisees; they were in the two centuries before Hillel what the rabbis were after him. They were the *iurisprudentes* of Judea, whose legal opinions, selected by time and transmitted by word of mouth from teacher to pupil, became part of that oral tradition which the Pharisees honored along with the written Law. Under their influence the Code of Moses proliferated into thousands of detailed precepts designed to meet every circumstance.

The earliest definite figure among these lay teachers of the Law is that of Hillel, and even he is nearly lost in the web of legend that a fond posterity wove about his name. We are told that he was born in Babylon (75 B.C.?) of a distinguished but impoverished family. He came as a grown man to Jerusalem, where he supported his wife and children by manual labor. Half his daily wage he paid for admission to the school where two famous masters, Shemaya and Abtolim, expounded the Law. Lacking the fee one day, and denied entry, he climbed upon a window sill "that he might hear the words of the living God." Frozen with the cold, story says, he fell into the snow and was found there half dead the next morning.[33] He became in his turn a revered *rabbi* or teacher, renowned for his modesty, patience, and gentleness.

One account tells how a man wagered he could anger Hillel, and lost.[34] He laid down three principles for the guidance of life: love of man, of peace, and of the Law and the knowledge of it. When a would-be proselyte asked him to explain the Law in as little time as a man could stand on one foot, Hillel answered: "What is hateful to thyself do not do to another";[35]* it was a cautiously negative form of that Golden Rule which had long before been phrased positively in Leviticus. Again Hillel taught: "Judge not thy neighbor until thou art in his place." [37] He sought to quiet the quarreling sects by laying down seven rules for interpreting the Law. His own interpretations were liberal; most notably, he facilitated the lending of money and the procurement of divorce. He was a pacifier, not a reformer; "separate not thyself from the congregation," he advised the young rebels of his day. He accepted Herod as an inescapable evil and was appointed by him president of the Sanhedrin (30 B.C.). Its Pharisean majority loved him so well that he remained head of the Great Council until his death (A.D. 10). Out of respect for his memory the office was made hereditary in his family for 400 years.

The Council gave its second place of honor to Hillel's rival, the conservative rabbi Shammai. He taught a much stricter interpretation of the Law, rejected divorce, and demanded the literal application of the Torah, regardless of new conditions. This division of Jewish teachers into conservative and liberal groups had existed for a century before Hillel, and continued until the destruction of the Temple.

V. THE GREAT EXPECTATION

The Jewish literature that has come down to us from this period is almost entirely religious. Just as it seemed to the orthodox Hebrew a profanation to make images of the deity, or to adorn his temples with plastic art, so it seemed to him an error to write philosophy or literature for any other ultimate purpose than to praise God and glorify the Law. There were of course many exceptions, of which the pretty story of Susannah may serve as an instance. It tells of a fair Jewess falsely accused of unchastity by two unsatisfied elders, and freed through the skillful cross-examination of witnesses by a youth named Daniel. Even this romance found its way into some editions of the Book of Daniel.

The book of Joshua son of Sirach, which we know as Ecclesiasticus, may be as late as this period; it is one of many Apocrypha—"hidden" or unau-

---

* The Talmud attributes to Hillel's reply the additional words, "This is all the Law, the rest is commentary." [36]

thentic compositions not accepted into the Jewish canon of the Old Testament; rich in beauty and wisdom, it did not deserve to be excluded from the company of Ecclesiastes and Job. In its twenty-fourth chapter we find again, as in the eighth chapter of Proverbs, the doctrine of the Logos or Incarnate Word: "Wisdom the first product of God, created from the beginning of the world." Between 130 B.C. and A.D. 40 an Alexandrian Jew—or a number of Hellenistic Jews—published a Book of the Wisdom of Solomon, which sought, like Philo, to harmonize Judaism and Platonism, and called Hellenizing Jews back to the Law in prose as noble as any since Isaiah. A lesser work, the Psalms of Solomon (*ca.* 50 B.C.), is rich in anticipation of a Redeemer for Israel.

This hope of salvation from Rome and earthly suffering through the coming of a divine Redeemer rings through nearly all the Jewish literature of this age. Many productions took the form of apocalypses or revelations, whose aim was to make the past intelligible and forgivable by presenting it as a prelude to a triumphant future revealed to some seer by God. The Book of Daniel, written about 165 B.C. to encourage Israel against Antiochus Epiphanes, was still circulating among Jews who could not believe that Yahveh would let them long remain under pagan domination. The Book of Enoch, probably the work of several authors between 170 and 66 B.C., took the form of visions vouchsafed to the patriarch who, in Genesis (v, 24), had "walked with God." It recounted the fall of Satan and his cohorts, the consequent intrusion of evil and suffering into human life, the redemption of mankind by a Messiah, and the coming of the Kingdom of Heaven. About 150 B.C. Jewish writers began to publish Sibylline Oracles, in which various sibyls or prophetesses were represented as defending Judaism against paganism and foretelling the final victory of the Jews over their enemies.

The idea of the saving god had probably come to western Asia from Persia and Babylonia.[38] In the Zoroastrian creed all history and life were represented as a war between the holy forces of light and the diabolical powers of darkness; in the end a savior would come—Shaosyant or Mithras—to judge all men and establish an everlasting reign of righteousness and peace. To many Jews the rule of Rome seemed part of the transient victory of evil. They denounced the greed, treachery, brutality, and idolatry of "gentile" civilization and the "atheistic" hedonism of an epicurean world. According to the Book of Wisdom

the ungodly said: Our life is short and tedious, and in the death of a man there is no remedy; neither was there any man known to return from the grave. . . . For the breath in our nostrils is as smoke, and a little spark in the moving of our heart; which being extinguished, our body shall be turned into ashes, and our spirit shall

> vanish as the soft air, and our name shall be forgotten, and our life
> shall pass away as the trace of a cloud, as a mist dispersed by the
> beams of the sun. . . . Come on, let us enjoy the good things that
> are present . . . let no flower of the spring pass us by; let us crown
> ourselves with rosebuds before they be withered; let us leave tokens
> of our joyfulness in every place.[39]

These epicureans reason falsely, says the author; they hitch their wagon to a
falling star, since pleasure is a vain and transitory thing.

> For the hope of the ungodly man is as chaff swept away by the wind,
> and as thin hoar-frost scattered by the tempest; it passeth as the
> remembrance of a guest who tarrieth but a day. But the righteous
> shall live forever, and the care of them is with the Most High. There-
> fore shall they receive a glorious kingdom, and a diadem of beauty
> from the hand of the Lord.[40]

The reign of evil will be brought to an end, according to the apocalyptic
books, either by the direct intervention of God himself or the earthly coming of his son or representative, the Messiah or Anointed One.* Had not
the prophet Isaiah, a century back foretold him?

> For unto us a child is born, a son is given; and the government shall
> be upon his shoulder, and his name shall be called . . . the mighty
> God, the Prince of Peace.[41]

Many Jews agreed with Isaiah (xi, 1) in describing the Messiah as an earthly
king who would be born of the royal house of David; others, like the authors
of Enoch and Daniel, called him the Son of Man, and pictured him as coming down from heaven. The philosopher of Proverbs and the poet of the
Wisdom of Solomon,[42] perhaps influenced by Plato's Ideas or the Stoic
anima mundi, saw him as incarnate Wisdom, the first-begotten of God, the
Word or Reason (*logos*) that would soon play so great a role in Philo's philosophy. Nearly all the apocalyptic authors thought that the Messiah would
triumph speedily; but Isaiah in a remarkable passage had conceived him as

> despised and rejected of men, a man of sorrows and acquainted with
> grief. . . . Surely he hath borne our griefs, and carried our sorrows
> . . . he was wounded for our transgressions, bruised for our iniqui-
> ties . . . and with his stripes we are healed. The Lord hath laid upon
> him the iniquity of us all. . . . He was taken from prison and from
> judgment, and was cut off out of the land of the living. . . . He
> bare the sin of many, and made intercession for the transgressors.[43]

---

* The word *Messiah* (Heb. *mahsiah*) occurs frequently in the Old Testament. The Jews
who made the Septuagint (*ca.* 280 B.C.) translated it into the Greek *Christos,* the Anointed, he
upon whom has been poured a chrism or holy oil.

All, however, agreed that in the end the Messiah would subdue the heathen, free Israel,[44] make Jerusalem his capital, and win all men to accept Yahveh and the Mosaic Law.[45] Thereafter a "Good Time" would come of happiness for the whole world: all the earth would be fertile, every seed would bear a thousandfold, wine would be plentiful, poverty would disappear, all men would be healthy and virtuous, and justice, good fellowship, and peace would reign over the earth.[46] Some seers thought that this joyful age would be interrupted, that the powers of darkness and evil would make a last assault upon the happy kingdom, and that the world would be consumed in chaos and conflagration. In the final "Day of God" the dead would rise and be judged by the "Ancient of Days" (Yahveh), or by the "Son of Man," to whom absolute and everlasting dominion would then be given over a reno-vated world, the Kingdom of God. The wicked would be cast down head-long and speechless "into Hell," [47] but the good would be received into unending blessedness.

Essentially the movement of thought in Judea was parallel with that in the pagan theology of the time: a people that had once thought of the future in terms of its national destiny lost its trust in the state and thought of salva-tion in spiritual and individual terms. The mystery religions had brought this hope to many millions in Greece, the Hellenic East, and Italy; but nowhere was the hope so earnest, or its need so great, as in Judea. The poor or be-reaved, the oppressed or scorned of the earth, looked for some divine re-deemer of their subjection and their suffering. Soon, said the apocalypses, a savior would come, and in his triumph all just men would be lifted up, even out of the grave, into a paradise of eternal bliss. Old saints like Simeon, mystic women like Anna daughter of Phanuel, passed their lives about the Temple, fasting, waiting, praying that they might look upon the Redeemer before they died. A great expectation filled the hearts of men.

VI. THE REBELLION

No people in history has fought so tenaciously for liberty as the Jews, nor any people against such odds. From Judas Maccabee to Simeon Bar Cocheba, and even into our own time, the struggle of the Jews to regain their freedom has often decimated them, but has never broken their spirit or their hope.

When Herod the Great died the nationalists, spurning the pacific counsels of Hillel, declared a revolt against Herod's successor Archelaus, and encamped in tents about the Temple. Archelaus' troops slew 3000 of them, many of whom had come to Jerusalem for the Passover festival (4 B.C.). At the following feast of

Pentecost the rebels gathered again, and once more suffered great slaughter; the Temple cloisters were burned to the ground, the treasures of the sanctuary were plundered by the legions, and many Jews killed themselves in despair. Patriot bands took form in the countryside, and made life precarious for any supporter of Rome; one such band, under Judas the Gaulonite, captured Sepphoris, the capital of Galilee. Varus, governor of Syria, entered Palestine with 20,000 men, razed hundreds of towns, crucified 2000 rebels, and sold 30,000 Jews into slavery. A delegation of leading Jews went to Rome and begged Augustus to abolish the kingship in Judea. Augustus removed Archelaus, and made Judea a Roman province of the second class, under a procurator responsible to the governor of Syria (A.D. 6).

Under Tiberius the troubled land knew a moment's peace. Caligula, wishing to make the worship of the emperor a unifying religion throughout the Empire, ordered all cults to include a sacrifice to his image, and bade the Jerusalem officials to install his statue in the Temple. The Jews had compromised, under Augustus and Tiberius, by sacrificing to Yahveh in the name of the emperor; but they were so averse to setting up the graven image of a pagan in their Temple that thousands of them, we are told, went to the governor of Syria and asked to be slain in cold blood before the edict should be carried out.[49] Caligula eased the situation by dying. Impressed by Herod's grandson Agrippa, Claudius made him king of nearly all Palestine (41); but Agrippa's sudden death released another outburst of disorder, and Claudius restored the procuratorial rule (44).

The men whom his mercenary freedmen chose for this office were mostly incompetents or scoundrels. Felix, made procurator by his brother Pallas, "governed Judea," says Tacitus, "with the powers of a king and the soul of a slave." [50] Festus ruled more justly, but died in the attempt. Albinus, if we may believe Josephus, plundered and taxed assiduously, and made a fortune by releasing criminals from jail for a consideration; "nobody remained in prison but those who gave him nothing." [51] Florus, says the same friend and admirer of the Romans, behaved "like an executioner rather than a governor," despoiled whole cities, and not only stole on his own account, but connived at other robberies if allowed to share the loot. These reports retain some odor of war propaganda; doubtless the procurators complained that the Jews were a very troublesome people to oppress.

Bands of "Zealots" and "Dagger-men" (*Sicarii*) were formed in protest against this misrule. Their members, pledged to kill any disloyal Jew, mingled in street gatherings, stabbed their appointed victims from behind, and disappeared in the chaos of the crowd.[52] When Florus took seventeen talents ($61,200) from the Temple treasury, an angry mob collected before the shrine and cried out for his dismissal; some youths went about with baskets begging alms for him as suffering from poverty. Florus' legions dispersed the assemblage, plundered hundreds of homes, and slew the occupants; the leading rebels were scourged and crucified; on that day, says Josephus, 3600 Jews were slain.[53] The old or well-to-do Hebrews counseled patience, arguing that revolt against so powerful an empire would be national suicide; the young or poor accused them of connivance and cowardice. The two factions divided the city and nearly every family; one seized the upper part of Jerusalem, the other the lower, and each attacked the other with every weapon at hand. In 68 a pitched battle was fought between the groups; the radicals won, and killed 12,000 Jews, including nearly all the rich;[54] the revolt had become a revolution. A rebel force surrounded the Roman garrison at Masada, persuaded it to disarm, and then slaughtered every man of it. On that day the gentiles of Caesarea, the Palestinian capital, rose in a pogrom that slew 20,000 Jews; other thousands were sold into slavery. In one day the gentiles of Damascus cut the throats of 10,000 Jews.[55] The enraged revolutionists laid waste many Greek cities in Palestine and Syria, burned some of them to the ground, and killed and were killed in great number. "It was then common," says Josephus, "to see cities filled with dead bodies . . . unburied, those of old men mixed with infants, and women lying among them without any cover." [56] By September of 66 the revolution had won Jerusalem and nearly all of Palestine. The peace party was discredited, and most of its members now joined in the revolt.

Among them was a priest named Josephus, then a young man of thirty, energetic, brilliant, and endowed with an intellect capable of transforming every desire into a virtue. Commissioned by the rebels to fortify Galilee, he defended its stronghold, Jotopata, against Vespasian's siege, until only forty Jewish soldiers remained alive, hiding with him in a cave. Josephus wished to surrender, but his men threatened to kill him if he tried it. Since they preferred death to capture, he persuaded them to draw lots to fix the order in which each should die by the hand of the next; when all were dead but himself and one other, he induced him to join him in surrender. They were about to be sent to Rome in chains when Josephus prophesied that Vespasian would be emperor. Vespasian released him, and gradually accepted him as a useful adviser in the war against the Jews. When Vespasian left for Alexandria, Josephus accompanied Titus to the siege of Jerusalem.

The approach of the legions brought the defenders to a belated and fanatical unity. Tacitus reckons that 600,000 rebels had gathered in the city. "All who were capable of serving appeared in arms," and the women were not less martial than the men.[57] Josephus, from the Roman lines, called upon the besieged to surrender; they branded him as a traitor, and

FIG. 33—*Pont du Gard at Nîmes*

FIG. 34—*Temple of Iuppiter Heliopolitanus at Baalbek*

FIG. 35—*Temple of Venus or Baachus at Baalbek*

Fig. 36—*Arch of Septimius Severus, Rome*

FIG. 37—Reconstruction of Interior of Baths of Caracalla

FIG. 38—*Mithras and the Bull*
British Museum

FIG. 39—*Sarcophagus of the Empress Helena*
Vatican, Rome

fought to the last. Starving Jews made desperate sorties to forage for food; thousands of them were captured by the Romans, and were crucified; "the multitude of these was so great," Josephus reports, "that room was wanting for the crosses, and crosses were wanting for the bodies." In the later stages of the five-month siege the streets of the city were clogged with corpses; ghouls wandered about despoiling and stabbing the dead; we are told that 116,000 bodies were thrown over the walls. Some Jews swallowed gold pieces and slipped out from Jerusalem; Romans or Syrians, capturing them, slit open their bellies, or searched their offal, to find the coins.[58] Having taken half the city, Titus offered what he thought were lenient terms to the rebels; they rejected them. The flaming brands of the Romans set fire to the Temple, and the great edifice, much of it of wood, was rapidly consumed. The surviving defenders fought bravely, proud, says Dio, to die on Temple grounds.[59] Some killed one another, some fell upon their own swords, some leaped into the flames. The victors gave no quarter, but slew all Jews upon whom they could lay their hands; 97,000 fugitives were caught and sold as slaves; many of them died as unwilling gladiators in the triumphal games that were celebrated at Berytus, Caesarea Philippi, and Rome. Josephus numbered at 1,197,000 the Jews killed in this siege and its aftermath; Tacitus calculated them at 600,000 (A.D. 70).[60]

Resistance continued here and there till 73, but essentially the destruction of the Temple marked the end of the rebellion and of the Jewish state. The property of those who had shared in the revolt was confiscated and sold. Judea was almost shorn of Jews, and those that remained lived on the edge of starvation. Even the poorest Jew had now to pay to a pagan temple at Rome the half shekel that pious Hebrews had formerly paid each year for the upkeep of the Temple at Jerusalem. The high-priesthood and the Sanhedrin were abolished. Judaism took the form that it has kept till our own time: a religion without a central shrine, without a dominant priesthood, without a sacrificial service. The Sadducees disappeared, while the Pharisees and the rabbis became the leaders of a homeless people that had nothing left but its synagogues and its hope.

VII. THE DISPERSION

The flight or enslavement of a million Jews so accelerated their spread through the Mediterranean that their scholars came to date the *Diaspora* from the destruction of Herod's Temple. We have seen that this Dispersion had begun six centuries before in the Babylonian Captivity, and had been renewed in the settling of Alexandria. Since fertility was commanded and infanticide sternly forbidden by Jewish piety and law, the expansion of the Jews was due to biological as well as economic causes; Hebrews still played a very minor role in the commerce of the world. Fifty years before the fall of Jerusalem, Strabo, with anti-Semitic exaggeration, reported that "it is hard to find a single place on the habitable earth that has not admitted this tribe of men, and is not possessed by it." [61] Philo, twenty years before the Dispersion, described "the continents . . . full of Jewish settlements, and likewise the . . . islands, and nearly all Babylonia." [62] By A.D. 70 there were thousands of Jews in Seleucia on the Tigris, and in other Parthian cities; they were numerous in Arabia, and crossed thence into Ethiopia; they abounded in Syria and Phoenicia; they had large colonies in Tarsus, Antioch, Miletus, Ephesus, Sardis, Smyrna; they were only less numerous in Delos, Corinth, Athens, Philippi, Patrae, Thessalonica. In the west there were Jewish communities in Carthage, Syracuse, Puteoli, Capua, Pompeii, Rome, even in Horace's native Venusia. All in all we may reckon 7,000,000 Jews in the Empire—some seven per cent of the population, twice their proportion in the United States of America today.[63]

Their number, dress, diet, circumcision, poverty, ambition, prosperity, exclusiveness, intelligence, aversion to images, and observation of an inconvenient Sabbath aroused an anti-Semitism that ranged from jokes in the theater and slurs in Juvenal and Tacitus to murders in the street and wholesale pogroms. Apion of Alexandria made himself the chief mouthpiece of these attacks, and Josephus answered him in an incisive pamphlet.*

After the fall of Jerusalem Josephus sailed to Rome with Titus, and accompanied the conqueror of his people in a triumphal procession that exhibited captive Jews and Jewish spoils. Vespasian gave him Roman citizenship, a pension, an apartment in his palace, and profitable lands in Judea.[65] In return Josephus took Vespasian's family name Flavius, and wrote The Wars of the Jews (ca. 75) to defend the actions of Titus in Palestine, to exonerate his own defection, and to discourage further revolt by showing forth the might of Rome. In his later years (ca. 93), feeling more keenly his isolation, he wrote The Antiquities of the Jews to regain the good will of his people by giving gentiles a more favorable view of Jewish achievements, customs, and character. His narratives are clear and forceful, and his account of Herod the Great is as engaging as Plutarch, but his bias and his aims impair his objectivity. The Antiquities required many years and exhausted the author's strength; the last four of the twenty books were written by his secretaries from his notes.[66] Josephus was still but fifty-six when the work appeared, but he was already worn out by a life of adventure, controversy, and moral solitude.

With their characteristic resilience the Jews gradually rebuilt their economic

---

* Josephus rejoiced to learn that an ulcer had compelled Apion to be circumcized.[64]

and cultural life in Palestine. Amid the siege of Jerusalem an aged pupil of Hillel, Johanan ben Zakkai, fearful lest the carnage should destroy all teachers and transmitters of the oral tradition, escaped from the city, and set up an academy in a vineyard at Yabne, or Jamnia, near the Mediterranean coast. When Jerusalem fell Johanan organized a new Sanhedrin at Jamnia, composed not of priests, politicians, and rich men, but of Pharisees and rabbis—i.e., teachers of the Law. This *Bet Din* or Council had no political power, but most Palestinian Jews recognized its authority in all matters of religion and morals. The patriarch whom the Council chose as its head appointed the administrative officers of the Jewish community, and had the power to excommunicate recalcitrant Jews. The stern discipline of the Patriarch Gamaliel II (*ca.* 100) welded into unity first the Council, then the Jews of Jamnia, then the Jews of Palestine. Under his leadership the contradictory interpretations of the Law transmitted by Hillel and Shammai were reviewed and voted on; those of Hillel were for the most part approved, and were made binding upon all Jews.

Since the Law was now the indispensable cement of scattered and stateless Jewry, the teaching of the Law became the chief occupation of the synagogue throughout the *Diaspora;* the synagogue replaced the temple, prayer replaced sacrifice, the rabbi replaced the priest. *Tannaim*—expositors —interpreted one or another of the orally transmitted laws (*Halacha*) of the Jews, usually supported it with scriptural quotation, sometimes added to it, and illustrated it with stories, homilies, or other material (*Haggada*). The most famous of the *Tannaim* was Rabbi Akiba ben Joseph. At the age of forty (*ca.* A.D. 80) he joined his five-year-old son at school, and learned to read. Soon he could recite the whole Pentateuch by heart. After thirteen years of study he opened his own school under a fig tree in a village near Jamnia. His enthusiasm and idealism, his courage and humor, even his lusty dogmatism, brought him many students. When, in 95, word came that Domitian was planning new measures against the Jews, Akiba was chosen with Gamaliel and two others to make a personal appeal to the Emperor. While they were in Rome Domitian died. Nerva heard their plea favorably, and ended the *fiscus Iudaicus*—the tax laid upon Jews for rebuilding Rome. On his return to Jamnia Akiba set himself the lifelong task of codifying the *Halacha;* his pupil Rabbi Meir and their successor Judah the Patriarch (*ca.* 200) completed the undertaking. Even in this classified form the *Halacha* remained part of the oral tradition, handed down from generation to generation by scholars and professional memorizers—living textbooks of the Law. Akiba's methods were as absurd as his conclusions were sound; he derived liberal principles from a weird exegesis in which every letter of the Torah, or written law, was held to have a mysterious meaning; perhaps he had observed that men will accept the rational only in the form of the mystical.

From Akiba came that painstaking organization and exposition of theology and ethics which passed down through the Talmud to Maimonides, and ultimately to the methods of the Scholastic philosophers.

In his ninetieth year, when he had grown weak and reactionary, Akiba found himself, as in his youth, surrounded by revolution. In 115-16 the Jews of Cyrene, Egypt, Cyprus, and Mesopotamia rose once more against Rome; the massacre of gentiles by Jews, and of Jews by Gentiles, became the order of the day; 220,000 men, says Dio, were killed in Cyrene, 240,000 in Cyprus; the figures are incredible, but we know that Cyrene never recovered from the devastation, and that for centuries thereafter no Hebrew was allowed in Cyprus. The uprisings were suppressed, but the surviving Jews kept fiercely alive their hope of a Messiah who would rebuild the Temple and restore them in triumph to Jerusalem. Roman stupidity reanimated the revolt. In 130 Hadrian declared his intention to raise a shrine to Jupiter on the site of the Temple; in 131 he issued a decree forbidding circumcision and public instruction in the Jewish Law.[67] Under the leadership of Simeon Bar Cocheba, who claimed to be the Messiah, the Jews made their last effort in antiquity to recover their homeland and their freedom (132). Akiba, who all his life had preached peace, gave his blessing to the revolution by accepting Bar Cocheba as the promised Redeemer. For three years the rebels fought valiantly against the legions; finally they were beaten by lack of food and supplies. The Romans destroyed 985 towns in Palestine, and slew 580,000 men; a still larger number, we are told, perished through starvation, disease, and fire; nearly all Judea was laid waste. Bar Cocheba himself fell in defending Bethar. So many Jews were sold as slaves that their price fell to that of a horse. Thousands hid in underground channels rather than be captured; surrounded by the Romans, they died one by one of hunger, while the living ate the bodies of the dead.[68]

Resolved to destroy the recuperative virility of Judaism, Hadrian forbade not merely circumcision, but the observance of the Sabbath or any Jewish holyday, and the public performance of any Hebrew ritual.[69] A new and heavier poll tax was placed upon all Jews. They were allowed in Jerusalem only on one fixed day each year, when they might come and weep before the ruins of their Temple. The pagan city of Aelia Capitolina rose on the site of Jerusalem, with shrines to Jupiter and Venus, and with palaestras, theaters, and baths. The Council at Jamnia was dissolved and outlawed; a minor and powerless Council was permitted at Lydda, but public instruction in the Law was prohibited on pain of death. Several rabbis were executed for disobeying this injunction. Akiba, now ninety-five, insisted on teaching his pupils; he was imprisoned for three years, but taught even in jail; he was tried and condemned, and died, we are told, with the basic tenet of Judaism on his lips: "Hear, O Israel! The Lord is our God, the Lord is one." [70]

Though Hadrian's decrees were softened by Antoninus Pius, the Jews did not for centuries recover from the disaster of Bar Cocheba's revolt. From this moment they entered their Middle Ages, abandoning all secular learning except medicine, renouncing every form of Hellenism, and taking comfort and unity only from their rabbis, their mystic poets, and their Law. No other people has ever known so long an exile, or so hard a fate. Shut out from their Holy City, the Jews were compelled to surrender it first to paganism, then to Christianity. Scattered into every province and beyond, condemned to poverty and humiliation, unbefriended even by philosophers and saints, they retired from public affairs into private study and worship, passionately preserving the words of their scholars, and preparing to write them down at last in the Talmuds of Babylonia and Palestine. Judaism hid in fear and obscurity while its offspring, Christianity, went out to conquer the world.

BOOK V

THE YOUTH OF CHRISTIANITY

4 B.C.–A.D. 325

CHRONOLOGICAL TABLE

All dates except the first are A.D.; and all dates before 150 are uncertain.

B.C. 4: Birth of Christ
A.D.30: Crucifixion; conversion of Paul
45-47: First mission of Paul
50-53: Second mission of Paul
51: Paul in Athens
53-57: Third mission of Paul
58-60: Paul imprisoned by Felix
61-64: Paul imprisoned in Rome
64: Neronic persecution; d. of Peter and Paul
65: Linus, Bishop of Rome
77: Cletus, Bishop of Rome
60-100: The Four Gospels
89: Clement I, Bishop of Rome
90: The Johannine epistles
98: Evaristus, Bishop of Rome
106: Alexander I, Bishop of Rome
116: Xystus I, Bishop of Rome
126: Telesphorus, Bishop of Rome
137: Hyginus, Bishop of Rome
141: Pius I, Bishop of Rome
150: Justin's First Apology
156: Anicetus, Bishop of Rome
166: Martyrdom of Polycarp
175: Eleutherius, Bishop of Rome
177: Martyrdoms at Lyons
178: Irenaeus, Bishop of Lyons
190: Victor I, Bishop of Rome
193: Pertinax and Didius Julianus, emperors
193-211: Septimius Severus, emperor
194: Montanus; Clement of Alexandria
200: Tertullian's *Liber Apologeticus*
202: Zephyrinus, Bishop of Rome
203: Arch of Sept. Severus; Origen
205-70: Plotinus
211-17: Caracalla
212: Caracalla extends citizenship
215: Baths of Caracalla; Mani
218: Callistus I, Bishop of Rome
218-22: Elagabalus, emperor
222: Urban I, Bishop of Rome
222-35: Alexander Severus, emperor
228: Murder of Ulpian
235-58: Maximinus, emperor
236: Fabian, Bishop of Rome
238-44: Gordianus I, II, III, emperors
241-72: Shapur I, King of Persia
244-49: Philip the Arab, emperor
248: Cyprian, Bishop of Carthage; Origen's *Contra Celsum*

249-51: Decius, emperor; Diophantus, mathematician
251: Cornelius, Bishop of Rome
251-53: Gallus, emperor
253-60: Valerianus, emperor
253-68: Gallienus, emperor
254: Marcomanni raid north Italy
255: Shapur invades Syria
257: Edict of Valerian against Christians
259: Goths overrun Asia Minor
260: First edict of toleration
260-66: Odenathus at Palmyra
266-73: Zenobia and Longinus at Palmyra
268-70: Claudius II, emperor
270-75: Aurelian, emperor
271: Barbarians invade Italy
275-76: Tacitus, emperor
276-82: Probus, emperor
282-83: Carus, Carinus, Numerianus, emperors
284-305: Diocletian, emperor
286-305: Maximianus co-*Augustus*
292: Galerius and Constantius, Caesars
295: Baths of Diocletian
296: Marcellinus, Bishop of Rome
301: Price Edict of Diocletian
303-11: Diocletian persecution
306: Constantine becomes a Caesar
307: Maxentius and Maximian, *Augusti*; basilica of Maxentius
307-09: Marcellus I, Bishop of Rome
307-10: Lactantius' *Divinae Institutiones*
307-13: Constantine and Licinius, *Augusti*
309-10: Eusebius, Bishop of Rome
312: Battle of the Mulvian Bridge; Edict of Milan (?)
313: Eusebius' *Church History*
313-23: Constantine and Licinius divide the Empire
314: Council of Arles
314-36: Sylvester I, Bishop of Rome
315: Arch of Constantine
323: Licinius defeated at Adrianople
324-37: Constantine sole emperor
325: Council of Nicaea
326: Constantine kills son, nephew, and wife
330: Constantinople made the capital
337: Death of Constantine

CHAPTER XXVI

Jesus

4 B.C.–A.D. 30

I. THE SOURCES

DID Christ exist? Is the life story of the founder of Christianity the product of human sorrow, imagination, and hope—a myth comparable to the legends of Krishna, Osiris, Attis, Adonis, Dionysus, and Mithras? Early in the eighteenth century the circle of Bolingbroke, shocking even Voltaire, privately discussed the possibility that Jesus had never lived. Volney propounded the same doubt in his *Ruins of Empire* in 1791. Napoleon, meeting the German scholar Wieland in 1808, asked him no petty question of politics or war, but did he believe in the historicity of Christ? [1]

One of the most far-reaching activities of the modern mind has been the "Higher Criticism" of the Bible—the mounting attack upon its authenticity and veracity, countered by the heroic attempt to save the historical foundations of Christian faith; the results may in time prove as revolutionary as Christianity itself. The first engagement in this two-hundred-year war was fought in silence by Hermann Reimarus, professor of Oriental languages at Hamburg; on his death in 1768 he left, cautiously unpublished, a 1400-page manuscript on the life of Christ. Six years later Gotthold Lessing, over the protests of his friends, published portions of it as the *Wolfenbüttel Fragments*. Reimarus argued that Jesus can only be regarded and understood not as the founder of Christianity, but as the final and dominant figure in the mystical eschatology of the Jews— i.e., Christ thought not of establishing a new religion, but of preparing men for the imminent destruction of the world, and God's Last Judgment of all souls. In 1796 Herder pointed out the apparently irreconcilable difference between the Christ of Matthew, Mark, and Luke, and the Christ of the Gospel of St. John. In 1828 Heinrich Paulus, summarizing the life of Christ in 1192 pages, proposed a rationalistic interpretation of the miracles—i.e., accepted their occurrence but ascribed them to natural causes and powers. In an epoch-marking *Life of Jesus* (1835-36) David Strauss rejected this compromise; the supernatural elements in the Gospels, he thought, should be classed as myths, and the actual career of Christ must be reconstructed without using these elements in any form. Strauss's massive volumes made Biblical criticism the storm center of German thought for a generation. In the same year Ferdinand Christian Baur attacked the Epistles of Paul, rejecting as unauthentic all but those to the Galatians, Corinthians, and Romans. In 1840 Bruno Bauer began a series of passionately controversial works aiming to show that Jesus was a myth, the personified form of a cult that evolved in the second century from a fusion of Jewish, Greek, and Roman theology. In 1863 Ernest Renan's *Life of Jesus*, alarming millions with its rationalism and charming millions with its prose, gathered together the results of German criticism, and brought the problem of the Gospels before the entire educated world. The French school reached its climax at the end of the century in the Abbé Loisy, who subjected the New Testament to such rigorous textual analysis that the Catholic Church felt compelled to excommunicate him and other "Modernists." Meanwhile the Dutch school of Pierson, Naber, and Matthas carried the movement to its farthest point by laboriously denying the historical reality of Jesus. In Germany Arthur Drews gave this negative conclusion its definitive exposition (1906); and in England W. B. Smith and J. M. Robertson argued to a like denial. The result of two centuries of discussion seemed to be the annihilation of Christ.

What evidence is there for Christ's existence? The earliest non-Christian reference occurs in Josephus' *Antiquities of the Jews* (A.D. 93?):

> At that time lived Jesus, a holy man, if man he may be called, for he performed wonderful works, and taught men, and joyfully received the truth. And he was followed by many Jews and many Greeks. He was the Messiah.[2]

There may be a genuine core in these strange lines; but the high praise given to Christ by a Jew uniformly anxious to please either the Romans or the Jews—both at that time in conflict with Christianity—renders the passage suspect, and Christian scholars reject it as almost certainly an interpolation.[3] There are references to "Yeshu'a of Nazareth" in the Talmud, but they are too late in date to be certainly more than counterechoes of Christian thought.[4] The oldest known mention of Christ in pagan literature is in a letter of the younger Pliny (*ca.* 110),[5] asking the advice of Trajan on the treatment of Christians. Five years later Tacitus [6]* described Nero's persecution of the *Chrestiani* in Rome, and pictured them as already (A.D. 64) numbering adherents throughout the Empire; the paragraph is so Tacitean in style, force, and prejudice that of all Biblical critics only Drews questions its authenticity.[7] Suetonius (*ca.* 125) mentions the same persecution,[8] and reports Claudius' banishment (*ca.* 52) of "Jews who, stirred up by Christ [*impulsore Chresto*], were causing public disturbances,"[9] the passage accords well with the Acts of the Apostles, which mentions a decree of Claudius that "the Jews should leave Rome." [10] These references prove the existence

---

* Quoted on p. 281.

of Christians rather than of Christ; but unless we assume the latter we are driven to the improbable hypothesis that Jesus was invented in one generation; moreover, we must suppose that the Christian community in Rome had been established some years before 52, to merit the attention of an imperial decree. About the middle of this first century a pagan named Thallus, in a fragment preserved by Julius Africanus,[11] argued that the abnormal darkness alleged to have accompanied the death of Christ was a purely natural phenomenon and coincidence; the argument took the existence of Christ for granted. The denial of that existence seems never to have occurred even to the bitterest gentile or Jewish opponents of nascent Christianity.

The Christian evidence for Christ begins with the letters ascribed to Saint Paul. Some of these are of uncertain authorship; several, antedating A.D. 64, are almost universally accounted as substantially genuine. No one has questioned the existence of Paul, or his repeated meetings with Peter, James, and John; and Paul enviously admits that these men had known Christ in the flesh.[12] The accepted epistles frequently refer to the Last Supper[13] and the crucifixion.[14]

Matters are not so simple as regards the Gospels. The four that have come down to us are survivors from a much larger number that once circulated among the Christians of the first two centuries. Our English term *gospel* (Old English *godspel*, good news) is a rendering of the Greek *euangelion*, which is the opening word of Mark, and means "glad tidings"—that the Messiah had come, and the Kingdom of God was at hand. The Gospels of Matthew, Mark, and Luke are "synoptic": their contents and episodes allow of being arranged in parallel columns and "viewed together." They were written in the Greek *koiné* of popular speech, and were no models of grammar or literary finish; nevertheless, the directness and force of their simple style, the vivid power of their analogies and scenes, the depth of their feeling, and the profound fascination of the story they tell give even the rude originals a unique charm, immensely enhanced for the English world by the highly inaccurate but lordly version made for King James.

The oldest extant copies of the Gospels go back only to the third century. The original compositions were apparently written between A.D. 60 and 120, and were therefore exposed to two centuries of errors in transcription, and to possible alterations to suit the theology or aims of the copyist's sect or time. Christian writers before 100 quote the Old, but never the New, Testament. The only reference to a Christian gospel before 150 is in Papias, who, about 135, reports an unidentified "John the Elder" as saying that Mark had composed his gospel from memories conveyed to him by Peter.[15] Papias adds: "Matthew transcribed in Hebrew the *Logia*"—apparently an early Aramaic collection of the sayings of Christ. Probably Paul had some such document, for though he mentions no gospels he occasionally quotes the direct words of Jesus.* Criticism generally agrees in giving the Gospel of Mark priority, and in dating it between 65 and 70. Since it sometimes repeats the same matter in different forms,[16] it is widely believed to have been based upon the *Logia*, and upon another early narrative which may have been the original composition of Mark himself. Our Gospel of Mark was apparently circulated while some of the apostles, or their immediate disciples, were still alive; it seems unlikely, therefore, that it differed substantially from their recollection and interpretation of Christ.[17] We may conclude, with the brilliant but judicious Schweitzer, that the Gospel of Mark is in essentials "genuine history." [18]

Orthodox tradition placed Matthew's Gospel first. Irenaeus [19] describes it as originally composed in "Hebrew"—i.e., Aramaic; but it has come down to us only in Greek. Since in this form it apparently copies Mark, and probably also the *Logia*, criticism inclines to ascribe it to a disciple of Matthew rather than to the "publican" himself; even the most skeptical students, however, concede to it as early a date as A.D. 85-90.[20] Aiming to convert Jews, Matthew relies more than the other evangelists on the miracles ascribed to Jesus, and is suspiciously eager to prove that many Old Testament prophecies were fulfilled in Christ. Nevertheless, it is the most moving of the four Gospels, and must be ranked among the unconscious masterpieces of the world's literature.

The Gospel according to St. Luke, generally assigned to the last decade of the first century, announces its desire to co-ordinate and reconcile earlier accounts of Jesus, and aims to convert not Jews but gentiles. Very probably Luke was himself a gentile, the friend of Paul, and the author of the Acts of the Apostles.[21] Like Matthew he borrows much from Mark.[22] Of the 661 verses in the received text of Mark over 600 are reproduced in Matthew, and 350 in Luke, mostly word for word.[23] Many passages in Luke that are not in Mark occur in Matthew, again nearly verbatim; apparently Luke borrowed these from Matthew, or Luke and Matthew took them from a common source, now lost. Luke works up these candid borrowings with some literary skill; Renan thought this Gospel the most beautiful book ever written.[24]

The Fourth Gospel does not pretend to be a biography of Jesus; it is a presentation of Christ from the theological point of view, as the divine Logos or Word, creator of the world and redeemer of mankind. It contradicts the synoptic gospels in a hundred details and in its general picture of Christ.[25] The half-Gnostic character of the work, and its emphasis on metaphysical ideas, have led many Christian scholars to doubt that its author was the apostle John.[26] Experience suggests, however, that an old tradition must not be too quickly rejected; our ancestors were not all fools. Recent studies tend to restore the Fourth Gospel

---

* In 1897 and 1903 Grenfell and Hunt discovered in the ruins of Oxyrhynchus, in Egypt, twelve fragments of *logia* loosely corresponding to passages in the Gospels. These papyri are not older than the third century, but they may be copies of older manuscripts.

to a date near the end of the first century. Probably tradition was correct in assigning to the same author the "Epistles of John"; they speak the same ideas in the same style.

In summary, it is clear that there are many contradictions between one gospel and another, many dubious statements of history, many suspicious resemblances to the legends told of pagan gods, many incidents apparently designed to prove the fulfillment of Old Testament prophecies, many passages possibly aiming to establish a historical basis for some later doctrine or ritual of the Church. The evangelists shared with Cicero, Sallust, and Tacitus the conception of history as a vehicle for moral ideas. And presumably the conversations and speeches reported in the Gospels were subject to the frailties of illiterate memories, and the errors or emendations of copyists.

All this granted, much remains. The contradictions are of minutiae, not substance; in essentials the synoptic gospels agree remarkably well, and form a consistent portrait of Christ. In the enthusiasm of its discoveries the Higher Criticism has applied to the New Testament tests of authenticity so severe that by them a hundred ancient worthies—e.g., Hammurabi, David, Socrates—would fade into legend.* Despite the prejudices and theological preconceptions of the evangelists, they record many incidents that mere inventors would have concealed—the competition of the apostles for high places in the Kingdom, their flight after Jesus' arrest, Peter's denial, the failure of Christ to work miracles in Galilee, the references of some auditors to his possible insanity, his early uncertainty as to his mission, his confessions of ignorance as to the future, his moments of bitterness, his despairing cry on the cross; no one reading these scenes can doubt the reality of the figure behind them. That a few simple men should in one generation have invented so powerful and appealing a personality, so lofty an ethic and so inspiring a vision of human brotherhood, would be a miracle far more incredible than any recorded in the Gospels. After two centuries of Higher Criticism the outlines of the life, character, and teaching of Christ, remain reasonably clear, and constitute the most fascinating feature in the history of Western man.

II. THE GROWTH OF JESUS

Both Matthew and Luke assign Jesus' birth to "the days when Herod was king of Judea" [27]—consequently before 3 B.C. Luke, however, describes

---

* Says a great Jewish scholar, perhaps too strongly: "If we had ancient sources like those in the Gospels for the history of Alexander or Caesar, we should not cast any doubt upon them whatsoever."—Klausner, J., *From Jesus to Paul*, 260.

Jesus as "about thirty years old" when John baptized him "in the fifteenth year of Tiberius" [27a]—i.e., A.D. 28-29; this would place Christ's birth in the year 2-1 B.C. Luke adds that "in those days there went out a decree of Caesar Augustus that all the world should be taxed . . . when Quirinius was governor of Syria." Quirinius is known to have been legate in Syria between A.D. 6 and 12; Josephus notes a census by him in Judea, but ascribes it to A.D. 6-7;[28] we have no further mention of this census. Tertullian[29] records a census of Judea by Saturninus, governor of Syria 8-7 B.C.; if this is the census that Luke had in mind, the birth of Christ would have to be placed before 6 B.C. We have no knowledge of the specific day of his birth. Clement of Alexandria (ca. 200) reports diverse opinions on the subject in his day, some chronologists dating the birth April 19, some May 20; he himself assigned it to November 17, 3 B.C. As far back as the second century the Eastern Christians celebrated the Nativity on January 6. In 354 some Western churches, including those of Rome, commemorated the birth of Christ on December 25; this was then erroneously calculated as the winter solstice, on which the days begin to lengthen; it was already the central festival of Mithraism, the *natalis invicti solis,* or birthday of the unconquered sun. The Eastern churches clung for a time to January 6, and charged their Western brethren with sun worship and idolatry, but by the end of the fourth century December 25 had been adopted also in the East.[30]

Matthew and Luke place the birth of Christ in Bethlehem, five miles south of Jerusalem; thence, they tell us, the family moved to Nazareth in Galilee. Mark makes no mention of Bethlehem, but merely names Christ "Jesus of Nazareth." * His parents gave him the quite common name Yeshu'a (our Joshua), meaning "the help of Yahveh"; the Greeks made this into *Iesous,* the Romans into *Iesus.*

He was apparently one of a large family, for his neighbors, marveling at his authoritative teaching, asked, "Where did he get this wisdom, and the power to do these wonders? Is he not the carpenter's son? Is not his mother named Mary, and are not his brothers named James, Joseph, Simon, and Judas? And do not his sisters live here among us?" [31] Luke tells the story of the Annunciation with some literary art, and puts into the mouth of Miriam—Mary—that *Magnificat* which is one of the great poems embedded in the New Testament.

Next to her son, Mary is the most touching figure in the narrative: rearing him through all the painful joys of motherhood, proud of his youthful learning, wondering later at his doctrine and his claims, wishing to withdraw him

---

* Critics suspect Matthew and Luke of choosing Bethlehem to strengthen the claim that Jesus was the Messiah, and descended, as Jewish prophecy required, from David—whose family had dwelt in Bethlehem; but the suspicion falls far short of proof.

from the exciting throng of his followers and bring him back to the healing quiet of his home ("thy father and I have sought thee sorrowing"), helplessly witnessing his crucifixion, and receiving his body into her arms; if this is not history it is supreme literature, for the relations of parents and children hold deeper dramas than those of sexual love. The tales later circulated, by Celsus and others, about Mary and a Roman soldier are by critical consent "clumsy fabrications." [32] Not so awkward are the stories, chiefly contained in the apocryphal or uncanonical gospels, about the birth of Christ in a cave or stable, the adoration of the shepherds and the Magi, the massacre of the innocents, and the flight into Egypt; the mature mind will not resent this popular poetry. The virgin birth is not mentioned by Paul or John; and Matthew and Luke, who tell of it, trace Jesus back to David through Joseph, by conflicting genealogies; apparently the belief in the virgin birth rose later than that in the Davidic descent.

The evangelists tell us little of Christ's youth. When he was eight days old he was circumcized. Joseph was a carpenter, and the occupational heredity usual in that age suggests that Jesus followed that pleasant trade for a time. He knew the craftsmen of his village, and the landlords, stewards, tenants, and slaves of his rural surroundings; his speech is studded with them. He was sensitive to the natural beauties of the countryside, to the grace and color of flowers, and the silent fruitfulness of trees. The story of his questioning the scholars in the temple is not incredible; he had an alert and curious mind, and in the Near East a boy of twelve already touches maturity. But he had no formal education. "How is it," his neighbors asked, "that this man can read when he has never gone to school?" [33] He attended the synagogue, and heard the Scriptures with evident delight; the Prophets and the Psalms above all sank deep into his memory, and helped to mold him. Perhaps he read also the books of Daniel and Enoch, for his later teaching was shot through with their visions of the Messiah, the Last Judgment, and the coming Kingdom of God.

The air he breathed was tense with religious excitement. Thousands of Jews awaited anxiously the Redeemer of Israel. Magic and witchcraft, demons and angels, "possession" and exorcism, miracles and prophecies, divination and astrology were taken for granted everywhere; probably the story of the Magi was a necessary concession to the astrological convictions of the age.[34] Thaumaturgists—wonder-workers—toured the towns. On the annual journeys that all good Palestinian Jews made to Jerusalem for the Passover festival, Jesus must have learned something of the Essenes, and their half-monastic, almost Buddhistic, life; * possibly he heard also of a sect

---

* Ashoka had sent his Buddhist missionaries as far west as Egypt and Cyrene; [35] very likely, therefore, to the Near East.

called "Nazarenes," who dwelt beyond the Jordan in Peraea, rejected Temple worship, and denied the binding character of the Law.[36] But the experience that aroused him to religious fervor was the preaching of John, the son of Mary's cousin Elizabeth.

Josephus tells John's story in some detail.[37] We tend to picture the Baptist as an old man; on the contrary, he was apparently of the same age as Jesus. Mark and Matthew describe him as garbed in haircloth, living on dried locusts and honey, standing beside the Jordan, and calling people to repentance. He shared the asceticism of the Essenes, but differed from them in holding one baptism to be enough; his name "the Baptist" may be a Greek equivalent of "Essene" (bather).[38] To his rite of symbolic purification John added a menacing condemnation of hypocrisy and loose living, warned sinners to prepare themselves for the Last Judgment, and proclaimed the early coming of the Kingdom of God.[39] If all Judea should repent and be cleansed of sin, said John, the Messiah and the Kingdom would come at once.

In or shortly after "the fifteenth year of Tiberius," says Luke, Jesus came down to the Jordan to be baptized by John. This decision, by a man now "about thirty years old," [40] attested Christ's acceptance of John's teaching; his own would be essentially the same. His methods and character, however, were different: he would himself never baptize anyone,[41] and he would live not in the wilderness but in the world. Soon after this meeting Herod Antipas, tetrarch ("ruler of four cities") of Galilee, ordered the imprisonment of John. The Gospels ascribe the arrest to John's criticism of Herod's acts in divorcing his wife and marrying Herodias while she was still the wife of his half brother Philip. Josephus attributes the arrest to Herod's fear that John was fomenting a political rebellion in the guise of a religious reformation.[42] Mark [43] and Matthew [44] tell here the story of Salome, Herodias' daughter, who danced so alluringly before Herod that he offered her any reward she might name. At her mother's urging, we are told, she asked for the head of John, and the tetrarch reluctantly accommodated her. There is nothing in the Gospels about Salome loving John, nor anything in Josephus about her share in John's death.

III. THE MISSION

When John was imprisoned Jesus took up the Baptist's work, and began to preach the coming of the Kingdom.[45] He "returned to Galilee," says Luke, "and taught in the synagogues." [46] We have an impressive picture of the young idealist taking his turn at reading the Scriptures to the congregation at Nazareth, and choosing a passage from Isaiah:

The spirit of the Lord is upon me, because he hath anointed me to preach glad tidings to the poor; he hath sent me to heal the broken-hearted, to preach deliverance to captives, and recovery of sight to the blind, to set the down-trodden free.[47]

"The eyes of everyone in the synagogue," Luke adds, "were fixed upon him. And he began by saying to them, 'This passage of Scripture has been fulfilled here in your hearing today.' And they all spoke well of him, and were astonished at the winning words that fell from his lips."[48] When the news came that John had been beheaded, and his followers sought a new leader, Jesus assumed the burden and the risk, at first retiring cautiously to quiet villages, always refraining from political controversy, then more and more boldly proclaiming the gospel of repentance, belief, and salvation. Some of his hearers thought he was John risen from the dead.[49]

It is difficult to see him objectively, not only because the evidence is derived from those who worshiped him, but even more because our own moral heritage and ideals are so closely bound up with him and formed on his example that we feel injured in finding any flaw in his character. His religious sensitivity was so keen that he condemned severely those who would not share his vision; he could forgive any fault but unbelief. There are in the Gospels some bitter passages quite out of key with what else we are told about Christ. He seems to have taken over without scrutiny the harshest contemporary notions of an everlasting hell where unbelievers and unrepentant sinners would suffer from inextinguishable fire and insatiable worms.[50] He tells without protest how the poor man in heaven was not permitted to let a single drop of water fall upon the tongue of the rich man in hell.[51] He counsels nobly, "Judge not, that ye be not judged," but he cursed the men and cities that would not receive his gospel, and the fig tree that bore no fruit.[52] He may have been a bit harsh to his mother.[53] He had the puritan zeal of the Hebrew prophet rather than the broad calm of the Greek sage. His convictions consumed him; righteous indignation now and then blurred his profound humanity; his faults were the price he paid for that passionate faith which enabled him to move the world.

For the rest he was the most lovable of men. We have no portrait of him, nor do the evangelists describe him; but he must have had some physical comeliness, as well as spiritual magnetism, to attract so many women as well as men. We gather from stray words [54] that, like other men of that age and land, he wore a tunic under a cloak, had sandals on his feet, and probably a cloth headdress falling over his shoulders to shield him from the sun.[55] Many women sensed in him a sympathetic tenderness that aroused in them an unstinted devotion. The fact that only John tells the story of the woman taken in adultery is no argument against its truth; it does not help John's theology, and is completely in character with Christ.* Of like beauty, and hardly within the inventive powers of the evangelists, is the account of the prostitute who, moved by his ready acceptance of repentant sinners, knelt before him, anointed his feet with precious myrrh, let her tears fall upon them, and dried them with her hair; of her Jesus said that her sins were forgiven "because she loved much." [57] We are told that mothers brought their children to be touched by him, and "he took the children in his arms, laid his hands upon them, and blessed them." [58]

Unlike the prophets, the Essenes, and the Baptist, he was no ascetic. He is represented as providing abundant wine for a marriage feast, as living with "publicans and sinners," and receiving a Magdalene into his company. He was not hostile to the simple joys of life, though he was unbiologically harsh on the desire of a man for a maid. Occasionally he partook of banquets in the homes of rich men. Generally, however, he moved among the poor, even among the almost untouchable *Amhaarez* so scorned and shunned by Sadducees and Pharisees alike. Realizing that the rich would never accept him, he built his hopes upon an overturn that would make the poor and humble supreme in the coming Kingdom. He resembled Caesar only in taking his stand with the lower classes, and in the quality of mercy; otherwise what a world of outlook, character, and interests separated them! Caesar hoped to reform men by changing institutions and laws; Christ wished to remake institutions, and lessen laws, by changing men. Caesar too was capable of anger, but his emotions were always under the control of his clear-eyed intellect. Jesus was not without intellect; he answered the tricky questions of the Pharisees with almost a lawyer's skill, and yet with wisdom; no one could confuse him, even in the face of death. But his powers of mind were not intellectual, did not depend upon knowledge; they were derived from keenness of perception, intensity of feeling, and singleness of purpose. He did not claim omniscience; he could be surprised by events; only his earnestness and enthusiasm led him to overestimate his capacities, as in Nazareth and Jerusalem. That his powers were nevertheless exceptional seems proved by his miracles.

Probably these were in most cases the result of suggestion—the influence of a strong and confident spirit upon impressionable souls. His presence was itself a tonic; at his optimistic touch the weak grew strong and the sick were made well. The fact that like stories have been told of other characters in legend and history [59] does not prove that the miracles of Christ were myths.

---

* John, VII, 52 f. The episode is found also in some old manuscripts of Mark and Luke; it was expunged from later texts, perhaps through fear of encouraging immorality.[56]

With a few exceptions they are not beyond belief; similar phenomena may be observed almost any day at Lourdes, and doubtless occurred in Jesus' time at Epidaurus and other centers of psychic healing in the ancient world; the apostles too would work such cures. The psychological nature of the miracles is indicated by two features: Christ himself attributed his cures to the "faith" of those whom he healed; and he could not perform miracles in Nazareth, apparently because the people there looked upon him as "the carpenter's son," and refused to believe in his unusual powers; hence his remark that "a prophet is not without honor, save in his own country, and in his own house." [60] We are told of Mary Magdalene that "seven demons had been driven out of her"; i.e., she suffered from nervous diseases and seizures (the word recalls the theory of "possession"); these seemed to abate in the presence of Jesus; therefore she loved him as one who had restored her to life, and whose nearness was indispensable to her sanity. In the case of Jairus' daughter Christ said frankly that the girl was not dead but asleep —perhaps in a cataleptic state; in calling upon her to awake he used not his wonted gentleness but the sharp command, "Little girl, get up!" [61] This is not to say that Jesus considered his miracles to be purely natural phenomena; he felt that he could work them only through the help of a divine spirit within him. We do not know that he was wrong, nor can we yet set limits to the powers that lie potential in the thought and will of man. Jesus himself seems to have experienced a psychical exhaustion after his miracles. He was reluctant to attempt them, forbade his followers to advertise them, reproved men for requiring a "sign," and regretted that even his apostles accepted him chiefly because of the "wonders" he performed.

These men were hardly of the type that one would have chosen to remold the world. The Gospels realistically differentiate their characters, and honestly expose their faults. They were frankly ambitious; to quiet them Jesus promised that at the Last Judgment they would sit upon twelve thrones and judge the twelve tribes of Israel.[62] When the Baptist was imprisoned one of his followers, Andrew, attached himself to Jesus, and brought with him his brother Simon, whom Christ called Cephas—"the rock"; the Greeks translated the name into *Petros*. Peter is a thoroughly human figure, impulsive, earnest, generous, jealous, at times timid to the point of a forgivable cowardice. He and Andrew were fishermen on the Lake of Galilee; so were the two sons of Zebedee—James and John; these four forsook their work and their families to become an inner circle about Christ. Matthew was the collector of customs at the frontier town of Capernaum; he was a "publican"—i.e., a man engaged in public or state business, therefore in this case serving Rome, and hated by every Jew who longed for freedom. Judas of Kerioth was the only one of the apostles who did not come from Galilee.

The Twelve pooled their material possessions, and entrusted Judas with their common funds. As they followed Christ in his missionary wandering they lived on the country, taking their food now and then from the fields they passed, and accepting the hospitality of converts and friends. In addition to the Twelve Jesus appointed seventy-two others as disciples, and sent two of them to each town that he intended to visit. He bade them "carry no purse, nor wallet, nor shoes." [63] Kindly and pious women joined the apostles and disciples, contributed to their support, and performed for them those solicitous domestic functions which are the supreme consolation of male life. Through that little band, lowly and letterless, Christ sent his gospel into the world.

IV. THE GOSPEL

He taught with the simplicity required by his audiences, with interesting stories that insinuated his lessons into the understanding, with pungent aphorisms rather than with reasoned argument, and with similes and metaphors as brilliant as any in literature. The parable form that he used was customary in the East, and some of his fetching analogies had come down to him, perhaps unconsciously, from the prophets, the psalmists, and the rabbis; [64] nevertheless, the directness of his speech, the vivid colors of his imagery, the warm sincerity of his nature lifted his utterances to the most inspired poetry. Some of his sayings are obscure, some seem at first sight unjust,[65] some are sharp with sarcasm and bitterness; nearly all of them are models of brevity, clarity, and force.

His starting point was the Gospel of John the Baptist, which itself went back to Daniel and Enoch; *historia non facit saltum*. The Kingdom of Heaven was at hand, he said; soon God would put an end to the reign of wickedness on earth; the Son of Man would come "on the clouds of the sky" to judge all humanity, living and dead.[66] The time for repentance was running out; those who repented, lived justly, loved God, and put their faith in his messenger would inherit the Kingdom, would be raised to power and glory in a world at last freed from all evil, suffering, and death.

As these ideas were familiar to his hearers, Christ did not define them clearly, and many difficulties obscure his conception now. What did he mean by the Kingdom? A supernatural heaven? Apparently not, for the apostles and the early Christians unanimously expected an earthly kingdom. This was the Jewish tradition that Christ inherited; and he taught his followers to pray to the Father, "Thy Kingdom come, thy will be done on earth as it is in heaven." Only after that hope had faded did the Gospel of John make Jesus say, "My kingdom is not of this world." [67] Did he mean a spiritual condition, or a material utopia? At times he spoke of the Kingdom as a state of soul reached by the pure and sinless [68]—"the Kingdom of God is within you"; [69] at other times he pictured it as a happy future society in which the apostles would be rulers, and those who had given or suffered for Christ's sake would receive a hundredfold reward. [70] He seems to have thought of moral perfection as only metaphorically the Kingdom, as the preparation and price for the Kingdom, and as the condition of all saved souls in the Kingdom when realized. [71]

When would the Kingdom come? Soon. "I will drink no more of the fruit of the vine until I drink it new in the Kingdom of God." [72] "Ye shall not have gone over the cities of Israel," he told his followers, "till the Son of Man is come." [73] Later he deferred it a bit: "There be some standing here that shall not taste of death till they see the Son of Man coming in the Kingdom"; [74] and "this generation shall not pass till all these things be done." [75] In more politic moments he warned his apostles: "Of that day and hour knoweth no man, no, not the angels in heaven, neither the Son, but the Father." [76] Certain signs would precede the coming: "wars and rumors of war . . . nation will rise against nation . . . there will be famines and earthquakes . . . many shall be offended, and . . . shall hate one another. Many false prophets will appear, many will be misled by them; and because of the increase of wickedness most men's love will grow cold." [77] Sometimes Jesus made the advent of the Kingdom depend and wait upon the conversion of man to God and justice; usually he made its coming an act of God, a sudden and miraculous gift of divine grace.

Many have interpreted the Kingdom as a communist utopia, and have seen in Christ a social revolutionist. [78] The Gospels provide some evidence for this view. Christ obviously scorned the man whose chief purpose in life is to amass money and luxuries. [79] He promised hunger and woe to the rich and filled, and comforted the poor with Beatitudes that pledged them the Kingdom. To the rich youth who asked what he should do besides keeping the commandments, Christ answered: "Sell your property, give your money to the poor, and . . . follow me." [80] Apparently the apostles interpreted the Kingdom as a revolutionary inversion of the existing relationships between the rich and the poor; we shall find them and the early Christians forming a communistic band which "had all things in common." [81] The charge on which Jesus was condemned was that he had plotted to make himself "King of the Jews."

But a conservative can also quote the New Testament to his purpose.

Christ made a friend of Matthew, who continued to be an agent of the Roman power; he uttered no criticism of the civil government, took no known part in the Jewish movement for national liberation, and counseled a submissive gentleness hardly smacking of political revolution. He advised the Pharisees to "render unto Caesar the things that are Caesar's, and unto God the things that are God's." [82] His story of the man who, before going on a journey, "called on his slaves, and put his property in their hands," [83] contains no complaint against interest or slavery, but takes these institutions for granted. Christ apparently approves of the slave who invested the ten minas ($600) that the master had entrusted to him, and made ten more; he disapproves of the slave who, left with one mina, held it in unproductive safekeeping against the master's return; and he puts into the master's mouth the hard saying that "to him who has, more will be given, and from him who has nothing, even that which he has will be taken away" [84]—an excellent summary of market operations, if not of world history. In another parable workers "grumbled at their employer," who paid as much to one who had labored an hour as to those who had toiled all day; Christ makes the employer answer: "Is it not lawful for me to do what I will with my own?" [85] Jesus does not seem to have thought of ending poverty; "the poor ye have always with you." He takes for granted, like all ancients, that a slave's duty is to serve his master well; "blessed is the slave whom his master, returning, finds performing his charge." [86] He is not concerned to attack existing economic or political institutions; on the contrary, he condemns those ardent souls who would "take the Kingdom of Heaven by storm." [87] The revolution he sought was a far deeper one, without which reforms could only be superficial and transitory. If he could cleanse the human heart of selfish desire, cruelty, and lust, utopia would come of itself, and all those institutions that rise out of human greed and violence, and the consequent need for law, would disappear. Since this would be the profoundest of all revolutions, beside which all others would be mere *coups d'état* of class ousting class and exploiting in its turn, Christ was in this spiritual sense the greatest revolutionist in history.

His achievement lay not in ushering in a new state, but in outlining an ideal morality. His ethical code was predicated on the early coming of the Kingdom,[88] and was designed to make men worthy of entering it. Hence the Beatitudes, with their unprecedented exaltation of humility, poverty, gentleness, and peace; the counsel to turn the other cheek, and be as little children (no paragons of virtue!); the indifference to economic provision, property, government; the preference of celibacy to marriage; the command to abandon all family ties: these were not rules for ordinary life, they were a semimonastic regimen fitting men and women for election by God into an imminent Kingdom in which there would be no law, no marriage, no sexual relations, no property, and no war. Jesus praised those who "leave house, or parents, or brethren, or wife, or children," even those "who make themselves eunuchs, for the Kingdom of Heaven's sake"; [89] obviously this was intended for a devoted religious minority, not for a continuing society. It was an ethic limited in purpose but universal in its scope, for it applied the conception of brotherhood and the Golden Rule to foreigners and enemies as well as to neighbors and friends. It visioned a time when men would worship God not in temples but "in spirit and truth," in every deed rather than in passing words.

Were these moral ideas new? Nothing is new except arrangement. The central theme of Christ's preaching—the coming Judgment and Kingdom —was already a century old among the Jews. The Law had long since inculcated brotherhood: "Thou shalt love thy neighbor as thyself," said Leviticus; even "the stranger that dwelleth with you shall be unto you as one born among you, and thou shalt love him as thyself." [90] Exodus had commanded the Jews to do good to their enemies: a good Jew will restore the straying ox or ass even of the "enemy that hateth thee." [91] The prophets, too, had ranked a good life above all ritual; and Isaiah [94] and Hosea [95] had begun to change Yahveh from a Lord of Hosts into a God of Love. Hillel, like Confucius, had phrased the Golden Rule. We must not hold it against Jesus that he inherited and used the rich moral lore of his people.

For a long time Christ thought of himself purely as a Jew, sharing the ideas of the prophets, continuing their work, and preaching like them only to Jews. In dispatching his disciples to spread his gospel he sent them only to Jewish cities; "go not into the way of the gentiles, nor into the city of the Samaritans"; [96] hence the apostles, after his death, hesitated to bring the Good News to the "heathen" world. [97] When he met the Samaritan woman at the well he told her, "Salvation is of the Jews" [98]—though we must not judge him from words perhaps put into his mouth by one who was not present, and who wrote sixty years after the event. When a Canaanite woman asked him to heal her daughter, he at first refused, saying "I was sent only to the lost sheep of Israel." [99] He told the leper whom he had cured to "go to the priest and . . . offer the gift that Moses prescribed." [100] "Do everything that the scribes and Pharisees tell you, and observe it all; but do not do as they do." [101] In suggesting modifications and mitigations of the Judaic Law Jesus, like Hillel, did not think that he was overthrowing it; "I came not to destroy the Law of Moses but to fulfill

it." [102] "It is easier for heaven and earth to pass away than for one tittle *
of the Law to fail." [103] †

Nevertheless, he transformed everything by the force of his character
and his feeling. He added to the Law the injunction to prepare for the
Kingdom by a life of justice, kindliness, and simplicity. He hardened the
Law in matters of sex and divorce,[105] but softened it toward a readier forgiveness,[106] and reminded the Pharisees that the Sabbath was made for man.[107]
He relaxed the code of diet and cleanliness, and omitted certain fasts. He
brought religion back from ritual to righteousness, and condemned conspicuous prayers, showy charities, and ornate funerals. He left the impression, at times, that the Judaic Law would be abrogated by the coming
of the Kingdom.[108]

Jews of all sects except the Essenes opposed his innovations, and especially
resented his assumption of authority to forgive sins and to speak in the name
of God. They were shocked to see him associate with the hated employees
of Rome, and with women of low repute. The priests of the Temple and
the members of the Sanhedrin watched his activity with suspicion; like
Herod with John, they saw in it the semblance or cover of a political revolution; they feared lest the Roman procurator should accuse them of neglecting their responsibility for maintaining social order. They were a bit
frightened by Christ's promise to destroy the Temple, and not quite sure
that it was only a metaphor. For his part Christ denounced them in sharp
and bitter terms:

> The scribes and Pharisees . . . put heavy loads of the Law upon
> men's shoulders, but they will not lift a finger to move them. They
> do everything they do to have men see it. They wear wide Scripture
> texts as charms, and large tassels, and they like the best places at din-
> ners and the front seats in the synagogues. . . . But alas for you
> hypocritical scribes and Pharisees . . . you blind guides . . . blind
> fools! . . . You let the weightier matters of the Law go—justice,
> mercy, and integrity. . . . You clean the outside of the cup and the
> dish, but inside they are full of greed and self-indulgence. . . . You
> hypocritical scribes and Pharisees are like whitewashed tombs! . . .
> Outwardly you appear to men to be upright, but within you are full
> of hypocrisy and wickedness. . . . You are descended from the mur-
> derers of the prophets. Go on and fill up the measure of your fore-
> fathers' guilt! You serpents! You brood of snakes! How can you

---

* A vowel point placed over a Hebrew consonant.
† These passages may have been interpolated by Judaic Christians anxious to discredit
Paul; [104] but we may not arbitrarily assume so.

escape being sentenced to the pit? . . . The publicans and the harlots go into the Kingdom of God before you.[109]

Was Jesus just to the Pharisees? Probably there were some among them who deserved this castigation, many who, like numberless Christians a few centuries later, substituted outward piety for inward grace. But there were also many Pharisees who agreed that the Law should be softened and humanized.[110] Very likely a large number of the sect were sincere men, reasonably decent and honorable, who felt that the ceremonial laws neglected by Jesus should be judged not in themselves but as part of a code that served to hold the Jews together, in pride and decency, amid a hostile world. Some of the Pharisees sympathized with Jesus, and came to warn him that plots were being made to kill him.[111] Nicodemus, one of the defenders of Jesus, was a rich Pharisee.

The final break came from Jesus' growing conviction and clear announcement that he was the Messiah. At first his followers had looked upon him as the successor to John the Baptist; gradually they came to believe that he was the long-awaited Redeemer who would raise Israel out of Roman bondage and establish the reign of God on earth. "Lord," they asked him, "will you at this time restore the kingdom to Israel?" [112] He put them off by saying, "It is not for you to know the times and seasons which the Father has set"; and he gave an equally vague answer to emissaries of the Baptist who asked him, "Art thou he that was to come?" To turn his followers from their conception of him as a political Messiah, he repudiated all claim to Davidic descent.[113] Gradually, however, the intense expectations of his followers, and his discovery of his unusual psychic powers, seem to have persuaded him that he had been sent by God, not to restore the sovereignty of Judea, but to prepare men for the reign of God on earth. He did not (in the synoptic Gospels) identify or equate himself with the Father. "Why do you call me good?" he asked; "there is none good but one, that is God." [114] "Not as I will," he prayed in Gethsemane, "but as thou wilt." [115] He took the phrase "Son of Man," which Daniel [116] had made a synonym for the Messiah, used it at first without clearly meaning himself, and ended by applying it to himself in such statements as "The Son of Man is master of the Sabbath" [117]—which seemed high blasphemy to the Pharisees. He called God "Father" at times in no exclusive sense; occasionally, however, he spoke of "my Father," apparently signifying that he was the son of God in an especial manner or degree.[118] For a long time he forbade the disciples to call him the Messiah; but at Caesarea Philippi he approved Peter's recognition of him as "the Christ, the Son of the living God." [119] When, on the last Monday before his death, he approached Jerusalem to make a final appeal to the people, "the whole throng of his disciples" greeted him with the words, "Blessed is the *king* who comes in the name of the Lord"; and when some Pharisees asked him to reprove this salutation, he answered, "I tell you, if they keep silence, the stones will cry out." [120] The Fourth Gospel reports that the crowd hailed him as "King of Israel." [121] Apparently his followers still thought of him as a political Messiah, who would overthrow the Roman power and make Judea supreme. It was these acclamations that doomed Christ to a revolutionist's death.

V. DEATH AND TRANSFIGURATION

The Feast of the Passover was at hand, and great numbers of Jews were gathering in Jerusalem to offer sacrifice in the Temple. The outer court of the shrine was noisy with vendors selling doves and other sacrificial animals, and with money-changers offering locally acceptable currency for the idolatrous coins of the Roman realm. Visiting the Temple on the day after his entry into the city, Jesus was shocked by the clamor and commercialism of the booths. In a burst of indignation he and his followers overthrew the tables of the money-changers and the dove merchants, scattered their coins on the ground, and with "a scourge of rods" drove the traders from the court. For several days thereafter he taught in the Temple, unhindered; [122] but at night he left Jerusalem and stayed on the Mount of Olives, fearing arrest or assassination.

The agents of the government—civil and ecclesiastical, Roman and Jewish—had kept watch on him probably from the time when he had taken up the mission of John the Baptist. His failure to secure a large following had inclined them to ignore him; but his enthusiastic reception in Jerusalem seems to have set the Jewish leaders wondering whether this excitement, working upon the emotional and patriotic Passover throngs, might flare up into an untimely and futile revolt against the Roman power, and issue in the suppression of all self-government and religious freedom in Judea. The high priest called a meeting of the Sanhedrin, and expressed the opinion "that one man should die for the people, instead of the whole nation being destroyed." [123] The majority agreed with him, and the Council ordered the arrest of Christ.

Some news of this decision seems to have reached Jesus, perhaps through members of the Sanhedrin minority. On the fourteenth day of the Jewish month of Nisan (our April third), probably in the year 30,* Jesus and his

---

* There is much dispute about the duration of Christ's mission, and the year of his death. We have seen Luke dating Christ's baptism in the year 28-29. The chronology of Paul, as based

apostles ate the Seder, or Passover supper, in the home of a friend in Jerusalem. They looked to the Master to free himself by his miraculous powers; he, on the contrary, accepted his fate, and perhaps hoped that his death would be received by God as a sacrificial atonement for the sins of his people.[124] He had been informed that one of the Twelve was conspiring to betray him; and at this last supper he openly accused Judas Iscariot.* In accord with Jewish ritual Jesus blessed (in Greek, *eucharistisae*) the wine that he gave the apostles to drink; and then they sang together the Jewish ritual song *Hallel*.[127] He told them, says John, that he would be with them "only a little longer. . . . I give you a new command: Love one another. . . . Let not your hearts be troubled. Believe in God and believe in me. In my Father's house are many mansions . . . I go to prepare a place for you." [128] It seems quite credible that in so solemn a moment he should ask them to repeat this supper periodically (as Jewish custom required), in commemoration of him; and not improbable that, with Oriental intensity of feeling and imagery, he asked them to think of the bread they ate as his body, and of the wine they drank as his blood.

That night, we are told, the little band hid in the Garden of Gethsemane, outside Jerusalem. There a detachment of Temple [129] police found them, and arrested Jesus. He was taken first to the house of Annas, a former high priest, then to that of Caiaphas; according to Mark the "Council"—probably a committee of the Sanhedrin—had already gathered there. Various witnesses testified against him, especially recalling his threat to destroy the Temple. When Caiaphas asked him whether he was "the Messiah, the Son of God," Jesus is reported to have answered "I am he." [130] In the morning the Sanhedrin met, found him guilty of blasphemy (then a capital crime), and decided to bring him before the Roman procurator, who had come to Jerusalem to keep an eye on the Passover crowds.

Pontius Pilate was a hard man, who would later be summoned to Rome, accused of extortion and cruelty,[131] and removed from office. Nevertheless, it did not seem to him that this mild-mannered preacher was a real danger to the state. "Are you the King of the Jews?" he asked. Jesus, says Matthew,[132] answered ambiguously, "You have said it (*sù eipas*)." Such details, reported presumably from hearsay and long after the event, must be held suspect; if we accept the text we must conclude that Jesus had resolved to die, and that Paul's theory of atonement had some support in Christ. John

---

upon his own statements in Galatians I-II, the chronology of the procurators who tried him, and the tradition of his death in 64, apparently require the dating of Paul's conversion in 31. Cf. Chapter XXVII.

* Many arguments have been raised against the story of Judas,[125] but they are unconvincing.[126]

quotes Jesus as adding: "For this I was born . . . to give testimony for the truth." "What is truth?" asked the procurator [133]—a question perhaps due to the metaphysical propensities of the Fourth Gospel, but well revealing the chasm between the sophisticated and cynical culture of the Roman and the warm and trustful idealism of the Jew. In any case, after Christ's confession, the law required conviction, and Pilate reluctantly issued the sentence of death.

Crucifixion was a Roman, not a Jewish, form of punishment. It was usually preceded by scourging, which, carried out thoroughly, left the body a mass of swollen and bloody flesh. The Roman soldiers crowned Christ with a wreath of thorns, mocking his royalty as "King of the Jews," and placed upon his cross an inscription in Aramaic, Greek, and Latin: *Iesus Nazarathaeus Rex Ioudaeorum*. Whether or not Christ was a revolutionist he was obviously condemned as one by Rome; Tacitus, too, understood the matter so.[134] A small crowd, such as could gather in Pilate's courtyard, had called for Christ's execution; now, however, as he climbed the hill of Golgotha, "he was followed by a great crowd of the people," says Luke,[135] and of women who beat their breasts and mourned for him. Quite clearly the condemnation did not have the approval of the Jewish people.

All who cared to witness the horrible spectacle were free to do so; the Romans, who thought it necessary to rule by terror, chose, for capital offenses by other than Roman citizens, what Cicero called "the most cruel and hideous of tortures." [136] The offender's hands and feet were bound (seldom nailed) to the wood; a projecting block supported the backbone or the feet; unless mercifully killed, the victim would linger there for two or three days, suffering the agony of immobility, unable to brush away the insects that fed upon his naked flesh, and slowly losing strength until the heart failed and brought an end. Even the Romans sometimes pitied the victim, and offered him a stupefying drink. The cross, we are told, was raised "at the third hour"—i.e., at nine in the morning. Mark reports that two robbers were crucified with Jesus, and "reviled him"; [137] Luke assures us that one of them prayed to him.[138] Of all the apostles only John was present; with him were three Marys—Christ's mother, her sister Mary, and Mary Magdalene; "there were also some women watching from a distance." [139] Following the Roman custom,[140] the soldiers divided the garments of the dying men; and as Christ had but one, they cast lots for it. Possibly we have here an interpolated remembrance of Psalm XXII, 18: "They part my garments among them, and cast lots upon my vesture." The same Psalm begins with the words: "My God, my God, why hast thou forsaken me?"—and this is the desperately human utterance that Mark and Matthew attribute to the dying Christ. Can it be that in those bitter moments the great faith that had sustained him before Pilate faded into black doubt? Luke, perhaps finding such words repugnant to the theology of Paul, substitutes for them: "Father, into thy hands I commend my spirit"—which in turn echoes Psalm XXXI, 5 with suspicious accuracy.

A soldier, pitying Christ's thirst, held up to his mouth a sponge soaked in sour wine. Jesus drank, and said, "It is consummated." At the ninth hour —at three in the afternoon—he "cried out with a loud voice, and gave up the ghost." Luke adds—again revealing the sympathy of the Jewish populace—that "all the people that came together to that sight . . . smote their breasts and returned" to the town.[141] Two kindly and influential Jews, having secured Pilate's permission, took the body down from the cross, embalmed it with aloes and myrrh, and placed it in a tomb.

Was he really dead? The two robbers beside him were still alive; their legs were broken by the soldiers so that the weight of the body would hang upon the hands, constricting the circulation and soon stopping the heart. This was not done in Jesus' case, though we are told that a soldier pierced his breast with a lance, drawing forth first blood and then lymph. Pilate expressed surprise that a man should die after six hours of crucifixion; he gave his consent to Christ's removal from the cross only when the centurion in charge assured him of Christ's death.

Two days later Mary Magdalene, whose love of Jesus partook of that nervous intensity which characterized all her feelings, visited the tomb with "Mary the mother of James, and Salome." They found it empty. "Frightened and yet overjoyed," they ran to tell the news to the disciples. On the way they met one whom they thought to be Jesus; they bowed down before him and clasped his feet. We can imagine the hopeful incredulity with which their report was greeted; the thought that Jesus had triumphed over death, and had thereby proved himself Messiah and Son of God, filled the "Galileans" with such excitement that they were ready for any miracle and any revelation. That same day, we are told, Christ appeared to two disciples on the road to Emmaus, talked with them, and ate with them; for a long time "they were prevented from recognizing him"; but when "he took the bread and blessed it . . . their eyes were opened, and they knew him, and he vanished from them." [142] The disciples went back to Galilee, and soon thereafter "saw him and bowed down before him, though some were in doubt." [143] While they were fishing they saw Christ join them; they cast their nets, and drew in a great haul.[144]

Forty days after his appearance to Mary Magdalene, says the beginning of the Book of Acts, Christ ascended physically into heaven. The idea of a saint being so "translated" into the sky in body and life was familiar to the

Jews; they told it of Moses, Enoch, Elijah, and Isaiah. The Master went as mystically as he had come; but most of the disciples seem to have been sincerely convinced that he had, after his crucifixion, been with them in the flesh. "They went back with great joy to Jerusalem," says Luke,[145] "and were constantly in the Temple, blessing God."

CHAPTER XXVII

The Apostles

A.D. 30-95

I. PETER

CHRISTIANITY arose out of Jewish apocalyptic—esoteric revelations of the coming Kingdom; it derived its impetus from the personality and vision of Christ; it gained strength from the belief in his resurrection, and the promise of eternal life; it received doctrinal form in the theology of Paul; it grew by the absorption of pagan faith and ritual; it became a triumphant Church by inheriting the organizing patterns and genius of Rome.

The apostles were apparently unanimous in believing that Christ would soon return to establish the Kingdom of Heaven on earth.* "The end of all things is near," says the first epistle of Peter; "be serious and collected, therefore, and pray." [3] "Children," says the first epistle of John, "it is the last hour. You have heard that Antichrist was coming, and many Antichrists" (Nero, Vespasian, Domitian?) "have indeed appeared. So we may be sure that it is the last hour." [4] The belief in the Messianic mission, bodily resurrection, and earthly return of Christ formed the basic faith of early Christianity. This creed did not prevent the apostles from continuing to accept Judaism. "Day after day," says Acts, "they all went regularly to the Temple"; [5] they obeyed the dietetic and ceremonial laws; [6] they proclaimed their faith at first only to Jews, and often preached it in the Temple courts. [7]

---

* Our chief guide for this period is the Acts of the Apostles. It is universally agreed that this book and the Third Gospel are by the same author; but there is far less general acceptance of the tradition that both were written by Luke, the gentile friend of Paul. As Acts makes no mention of Paul's death, the original work may have been composed about 63 as an effort to mollify Roman hostility to Christianity and Paul; but it was probably expanded by a later hand. It abounds in the supernatural, but its basic narrative may be accepted as history.[1] In the second century various apocryphal "Acts" and "Epistles" rounded out with legend the story of the Apostles after Christ. These "Acts" were the historical novels of the age, not necessarily attempts at deception; the Church rejected them, but the pious accepted them, and increasingly confused them with history.

Of the seven letters ascribed in the New Testament to the Twelve Apostles, criticism inclines to accept the first of Peter as substantially genuine,[2] to identify the author of the epistles of John with the disputed author of the Fourth Gospel; and to reject the rest as of doubtful authenticity.

They believed that they had received from Christ or the Holy Spirit miraculous powers of inspiration, healing, and speech. Many sick and infirm persons came to them; some were cured, says Mark,[8] by anointing with oil —always a popular treatment in the East. The author of Acts draws a touching picture of the trustful communism in which these early Christians lived:

> There was but one heart and soul in the multitude who had become believers, and not one of them claimed anything that belonged to him as his own, but they shared everything they had with one another. . . . No one among them was in any want, for any who owned lands or houses would sell them and bring the proceeds and put them at the disposal of the Apostles; then they were shared with everyone in proportion to his need.[9]

As the number of proselytes increased, the apostles, by a laying on of hands, ordained seven deacons to administer the affairs of the community. For some time the Jewish authorities tolerated the sect as small and harmless; but as the "Nazarenes" multiplied in a few years from 120 to 8000,[10] the priests became alarmed. Peter and others were arrested and questioned by the Sanhedrin; the Sadducees wished to condemn them to death, but a Pharisee named Gamaliel—probably the teacher of Paul—advised a suspended judgment; as a compromise the prisoners were flogged and released. A little later (A.D. 30?) Stephen, one of the ordained deacons, was summoned before the Sanhedrin on the charge that he had "used abusive language about Moses and about God." [11] He defended himself with reckless vehemence:

> You stubborn people, with heathen hearts and ears, you are always opposing the Holy Spirit, just as your forefathers did! Which of the prophets did not your forefathers persecute? They killed the men who foretold the coming of the righteous one, whom you have now betrayed and killed—you who had the Law given you by angels, and did not obey it! [12] *

The Sanhedrin, in a rage, had him dragged outside the city and stoned to death. A young Pharisee named Saul aided the attack; thereafter he went from house to house in Jerusalem, seized adherents of "the Way," and put them in jail.[13]

The Jewish converts of Greek name and culture, who had had Stephen as their leader, fled to Samaria and Antioch, where they established strong Christian communities. Most of the apostles, apparently spared in this persecution

---

* The speeches of Stephen, Peter, Paul, and others in Acts may have been invented by the author, after the general custom of ancient historians.

because they still observed the Law, remained in Jerusalem with the Judaic Christians. While Peter carried the Gospel to the towns of Judea, James "the Just," "the brother of the Lord," became the head of the now reduced and impoverished church in Jerusalem. James practiced the Law in all its severity, and rivaled the Essenes in asceticism; he ate no meat, drank no wine, had only one garment, and never cut his hair or beard. For eleven years, under his guidance, the Christians were left undisturbed. About 41 another James, the son of Zebedee, was beheaded; Peter was arrested, but escaped. In 62 James the Just was himself put to death. Four years later the Jews revolted against Rome. The Jerusalem Christians, too convinced of the coming "end of the world" to care about politics, left the city and established themselves in pagan and pro-Roman Pella, on the farther bank of the Jordan. From that hour Judaism and Christianity parted. The Jews accused the Christians of treason and cowardice, and the Christians hailed the destruction of the Temple by Titus as a fulfillment of Christ's prophecy. Mutual hatred enflamed the two faiths, and wrote some of their most pious literature.

Thereafter Judaic Christianity waned in number and power, and yielded the new religion to be transformed by the Greek mind. Galilee, where Christ had lived nearly all his life, and where the Magdalene and the other women who had been among the first to follow him were now lost in obscurity, turned a deaf ear to the preachers who proclaimed the Nazarene as the Son of God. The Jews, who thirsted for liberty, and reminded themselves daily that "the Lord is One," were repelled by a Messiah who ignored their struggle for independence, and were scandalized by the announcement that a god had been born in a cave or stable in one of their villages. Judaic Christianity survived for five centuries in a little group of Syriac Christians called *Ebionim* ("the poor"), who practiced Christian poverty and the full Jewish Law. At the end of the second century the Church condemned them as heretics.

Meanwhile the apostles and disciples had spread the Good News, chiefly among the Jews of the Dispersion,[14] from Damascus to Rome. Philip made converts in Samaria and Caesarea, John developed a strong church in Ephesus, and Peter preached in the cities of Syria. Like most of the apostles, Peter took a "sister" with him on his missions to serve as his wife and aide.[15] He healed the sick so successfully that at Samaria a magician, Simon Magus, offered him money for a share in his mysterious powers. At Joppa he raised Tabitha from apparent death; at Caesarea he won a Roman centurion to Christianity. A vision, says the Book of Acts, convinced him that he should accept pagan as well as Jewish converts; and from this time forward, with some amiable vacillations, he contented himself with baptizing, rather than also circumcizing, non-Jewish proselytes. We feel some of the ardor of these early missionaries in the first epistle of Peter:

Peter, an apostle of Jesus Christ, to those [Christian Jews] who are scattered as foreigners over Pontus, Galatia, Cappadocia, Asia, and Bithynia . . . God bless you and give you perfect peace. . . . My dearly beloved, I pray you as aliens and exiles, to live upright lives among the gentiles so that . . . they may, from observing the uprightness of your conduct, come to praise God. . . . Submit to all human authority for the Master's sake. . . . Live like free men, but do not make your freedom an excuse for wrong doing. . . . Servants, be submissive to your masters, and perfectly respectful to them; not only to those who are kind and considerate, but also to those who are unreasonable. You married women, likewise, must be submissive to your husbands, so that any who refuse to believe . . . may be won over when they see how chaste and submissive you are. You must not adopt the external attractions of arranging your hair or wearing jewelry; you must be a quiet and gentle spirit. You married men also must be considerate to your wives; show deference to women as the weaker sex, sharing the gift of life with you. . . . Return not evil for evil. . . . Above all keep your love for one another strong, for love covers a multitude of sins.[16]

We do not know when and by what stages Peter made his way to Rome. Jerome (*ca.* 390) dates his first arrival there as early as 42. The tradition that he played a leading role in establishing the Christian community in the capital has survived all criticism.[17] Lactantius speaks of Peter's coming to Rome in Nero's reign;[18] probably the apostle visited the city on divers occasions. He free and Paul in prison labored as rivals to win converts there, until both of them suffered martyrdom, perhaps in the same year 64.[19] Origen reports that Peter "was crucified head downward, for he had asked that he might suffer that way,"[20] perhaps hoping that in that position death would come sooner, or (said the opinion of the faithful) holding himself unworthy to die in the same manner as Christ. Ancient texts testify that his wife was killed with him and that he had to see her led to execution.[21] A later story named Nero's Circus, on the Vatican field, as the place of his death. Over the site the Cathedral of St. Peter rose, and claimed to enshrine his bones.

His missions in Asia Minor and Rome must have helped to preserve many Judaic elements in Christianity. Through him and the other apostles it inherited Jewish monotheism, puritanism, and eschatology. Through them and Paul the Old Testament became the only Bible that first-century Christianity knew. Till 70 Christianity was preached chiefly in synagogues or among Jews. The form, ceremony, and vestments of Hebrew worship passed down into Christian ritual. The Paschal lamb of sacrifice was sublimated in the *Agnus Dei*—the expiatory Lamb of God—of the Catholic Mass. The appointment of elders (*presbyteri*, priests) to govern the churches was adopted from Jewish methods of administering the synagogue. Many Judaic festivals—e.g., Passover and Pentecost—were accepted into the Christian calendar, however altered in content and date. The Jewish Dispersion aided the rapid dissemination of Christianity; the frequent movement of Jews from city to city, and their connections throughout the Empire, co-operated with commerce, Roman roads, and the Roman peace, to open a path for the Christian faith. In Christ and Peter Christianity was Jewish; in Paul it became half Greek; in Catholicism it became half Roman. In Protestantism the Judaic element and emphasis were restored.

II. PAUL

1. The Persecutor

The founder of Christian theology was born at Tarsus, in Cilicia, about the tenth year of our era. His father was a Pharisee, and brought up the youth in the fervent principles of that sect; the Apostle of the Gentiles never ceased to consider himself a Pharisee, even after he had rejected the Judaic Law. The father was also a Roman citizen, and transmitted the precious franchise to his son. Probably the name Paul was the Greek equivalent of the Hebrew Saul, so that both names belonged to the apostle from infancy.[22] He did not receive a classical education, for no Pharisee would have permitted such outright Hellenism in his son, and no man with Greek training would have written the bad Greek of the Epistles. Nevertheless, he learned to speak the language with sufficient fluency to address an Athenian audience, and he occasionally referred to famous passages in Greek literature. We may believe that some Stoic theology and ethics passed from the university environment of Tarsus into the Christianity of Paul. So he uses the Stoic term *pneuma* (breath) for what his English translators call spirit. Like most Greek cities, Tarsus had followers of the Orphic or other mystery religions, who believed that the god they worshiped had died for them, had risen from the grave, and would, if appealed to by lively faith and proper ritual, save them from Hades, and share with them his gift of eternal and blessed life.[23] The mystery religions prepared the Greeks for Paul, and Paul for the Greeks.

After the youth had learned the trade of tentmaking, and had received instruction in the local synagogue, his father sent him to Jerusalem, where, Paul tells us, he was "educated at the feet of Gamaliel according to the strict manner of the Law." [24] Gamaliel was reputedly the grandson of Hillel; he succeeded Hillel as president of the Sanhedrin, and carried on the tradition of interpreting the Law with a lenient regard for the frailty of mankind. Stricter Pharisees were shocked to find him gazing appreciatively even upon pagan women.[25] He was so learned that the Jews, who keenly honor scholarship, called him "the beauty of the Law," and gave to him first, as to only six men after him, the title of *rabban*, "our master." From him and others Paul learned that shrewd and subtle, sometimes casuistic and sophistical, manner of Biblical interpretation which was to disport itself in the Talmud. Despite Paul's initiation into Hellenism he remained to the end a Jew in mind and character, uttered no doubt of the Torah's inspiration, and proudly maintained the divine election of the Jews as the medium of man's salvation.

He describes himself as "insignificant in appearance," [26] and adds: "to keep me from being too much elated, a bitter physical affliction was sent me"; [27] he does not further specify. Tradition pictured him at fifty as a bent and bald and bearded ascetic, with vast forehead, pale face, stern countenance, and piercing eyes; Dürer imagined him so in one of the greatest drawings of all time; but in truth these representations are literature and art, not history.

His mind was of a type frequent among Jews: penetrating and passionate rather than genial and urbane; emotional and imaginative rather than objective and impartial; he was powerful in action because he was narrow in thought. Even more than Spinoza he was a "God-intoxicated man," consumed with religious enthusiasm in the literal sense of this word—holding "a god within." He believed himself divinely inspired, and endowed with the ability to work miracles. He was also a practical soul, capable of laborious organization, impatiently patient in founding and preserving Christian communities. As in so many men, his faults and virtues were near allied and mutually indispensable. He was impetuous and courageous, dogmatic and decisive, domineering and energetic, fanatical and creative, proud before man and humble before God, violently wrathful and capable of the tenderest love. He advised his followers to "bless them that persecute you," but he could hope that his enemies—"the party of circumcision"—"would get themselves emasculated." [28] He knew his failings, struggled against them, and begged his converts to "put up with a little folly from me." [29] The postscript to his first epistle to the Corinthians sums him up: "This farewell I, Paul, add in my own hand. A curse upon anyone who has no love for the Lord! Lord, come quickly! The blessing of the Lord Jesus be with you! My love be with you all." He was what he had to be to do what he did.

He began by attacking Christianity in the name of Judaism, and ended by rejecting Judaism in the name of Christ; at every moment he was an apostle. Shocked by Stephen's disrespect for the Law, he joined in killing him, and led the first persecution of Christians in Jerusalem. Hearing that the new faith had made converts in Damascus, he obtained authorization from the high priest to go there, arrest all "who belonged to the Way," and bring them in chains to Jerusalem (A.D. 31?).[30] It may be that the fervor of his persecution was due to secret doubts; he could be cruel, but not without remorse; possibly the vision of Stephen stoned to death, perhaps even some youthful glimpse of Golgotha, troubled his memory and his journey, and fevered his imagination. As his party neared Damascus, says the Acts,

> a sudden light flashed upon him from heaven, and he fell to the ground. Then he heard a voice saying to him, "Saul, Saul, why do you persecute me?" "Who are you, sir?" he asked. "I am Jesus,". . . said the voice. . . . Saul's fellow-travelers stood speechless, for they heard the voice but could not see anyone. When he got up from the ground and opened his eyes he could see nothing. They had to take him by the hand and lead him into Damascus. For three days he could not see.[31]

No one can say what natural processes underlay this pivotal experience The fatigue of a long journey, the strength of the desert sun, perhaps a stroke of heat lightning in the sky, acting by accumulation upon a frail and possibly epileptic body, and a mind tortured by doubt and guilt, may have brought to culmination the half-conscious process by which the passionate denier became the ablest preacher of Stephen's Christ. His Greek environment in Tarsus had spoken of a *Soter* or Saviour who redeemed mankind; his Jewish lore had told of a Messiah to come; how could he be sure that this mysterious and fascinating Jesus, for whom men were ready to die, was not the promised one? When, weak and still blind at the end of his journey, he felt upon his face the kindly, soothing hands of a converted Jew, "something like scales dropped from his eyes, and his sight was restored; he got up and was baptized, and after taking some food, regained his strength." [32] A few days later he entered the synagogues of Damascus, and told their congregations that Jesus was the Son of God.

2. *The Missionary*

The governor of Damascus, urged by the offended Jews, issued an order for Paul's arrest; Paul's new friends lowered him in a basket over the city walls. For three years, he tells us, he preached Christ in the hamlets of Arabia. Returning to Jerusalem, he won the forgiveness and friendship of Peter, and lived with him for a while. Most of the apostles distrusted him, but Barnabas, himself a recent convert, gave him a cordial hand, and persuaded the Jerusalem church to commission its persecutor as a bearer of the Good News that the Messiah had come and would soon establish the Kingdom. The Greek-speaking Jews to whom he brought the Gospel tried to kill him, and the apostles, perhaps fearing that his ardor would endanger them all, sent him to Tarsus.

For eight years he was lost to history in his native city; and perhaps again he felt the influence of the mystic salvation theology popular among the Greeks. Then Barnabas came and asked his aid in ministering to the church at Antioch. Working together (43-44?), they made so many converts that Antioch soon led all other cities in the number of its Christians. There for the first time the "Believers," "Disciples," "Brethren," or "Saints," as they had called themselves, received from the pagans, perhaps in scorn, the name *Christianoi*—followers of the Messiah or Anointed One. There too, for the first time, gentiles (i.e., people of the *gentes* or nations) were won to the new faith. Most of these were "God-fearers," predominantly women, who had already accepted the monotheism, and in some part the ritual, of the Jews.

The Antioch converts were not as poor as those in Jerusalem; a considerable minority belonged to the merchant class. With the enthusiasm of a youthful and growing movement, they raised a fund to spread the Gospel. The elders of the church "laid their hands upon" Barnabas and Paul, and sent them out on what history, unduly belittling Barnabas, calls the "first missionary journey of Saint Paul" (45-47?). They sailed to Cyprus, and met with encouraging success among the many Jews of that island. From Paphos they took ship to Perga in Pamphylia, and traveled over dangerous mountain roads to Antioch in Pisidia. The synagogue gave them a courteous hearing; but when they began to preach to gentiles as well, the orthodox Jews persuaded the municipal officers to banish the missionaries. Similar difficulties developed at Iconium; and at Lystra Paul was stoned, dragged out of the town, and left for dead. Still "full of the joy of the Holy Spirit," Paul and Barnabas carried the Gospel to Derbe. Then they returned by the same route to Perga, and sailed to Syrian Antioch. There they found themselves faced by the most crucial problem in the history of Christianity.

For some leading disciples of Jerusalem, hearing that the two preachers were accepting gentile converts without requiring circumcision, had come to Antioch "to teach the brethren that unless they were circumcized as Moses prescribed, they could not be saved." [33] To the Jew circumcision was not so much a ritual of health as a holy symbol of his people's ancient covenant with God; and the Christian Jew was appalled at the thought of breaking that covenant. For their part Paul and Barnabas realized that if these emissaries had their way, Christianity would never be accepted by any significant number of gentiles; it would remain "a Jewish heresy" (as Heine was to call it), and would fade out in a century. They went down to Jerusalem (50?) and fought the matter out with the apostles, nearly all of whom were still faithful worshipers in the Temple. James was reluctant to consent; Peter defended the two missionaries; finally it was agreed that pagan proselytes should be required only to abstain from immorality and from the eating of sacrificial or strangled animals.[34] Apparently Paul eased the way by promising financial support for the impoverished community at Jerusalem from the swelling funds of the Antioch church.[35]

The issue, however, was too vital to be so easily laid. A second group of orthodox Jewish Christians came from Jerusalem to Antioch, found Peter eating with gentiles, and persuaded him to separate himself, with the converted Jews, from the uncircumcized proselytes. We do not know Peter's side of this episode; Paul tells us that "he withstood Peter to his face" at Antioch,[36] and accused him of hypocrisy; perhaps Peter had merely wished, like Paul, to be "all things to all men."

Probably in the year 50 Paul left on his second missionary journey. He had quarreled with Barnabas, who now disappeared from history in his native Cyprus. Revisiting his churches in Asia Minor, Paul attached to himself at Lystra a young disciple named Timothy, whom he came to love with a profound affection that had long been starved for an object. Together they went through Phrygia and Galatia as far north as Alexandria Troas. Here Paul made the acquaintance of Luke, an uncircumcized proselyte to Judaism, a man of good mind and heart, probably the author of the Third Gospel and the Book of Acts—both designed to soften the conflicts that from the beginning marked the history of Christianity. From Troas Paul, Timothy, and another aide, Silas, sailed to Macedonia, for the first time touching European soil. At Philippi, where Antony had conquered Brutus, Paul and Silas were arrested as disturbers of the peace, were scourged and jailed, but were freed on the discovery that they were Roman citizens. Passing on to Thessalonica, Paul went to the synagogue, and for three Sabbaths preached to the Jews. A few were convinced, and organized a church; others roused the town against Paul on the ground that he was proclaiming a new king; and his friends had to spirit him away to Beraea during the night. There "the Jews received the message with great eagerness"; but the Thessalonians came to denounce Paul as an enemy of Judaism, and he took ship for Athens (51?), discouraged and alone.

Here, in the heart of pagan religion, science, and philosophy, he found himself quite friendless. There were few Jews to give him a hearing; he had to take his stand in the market place, like any modern haranguer of city crowds, and compete with a dozen rivals for passing ears. Some listeners argued with him; some laughed at him, and asked, "What is this ragpicker trying to make out?" [37] Several were interested, and led him up to the Areopagus, or Hill of Mars, for a quieter hearing. He told them how he had noted, in Athens, an altar inscribed "To an Unknown God"; this dedication, which probably expressed the desire of the donors to thank, appease, or enlist the aid of a god of whose name they were not certain, Paul interpreted as a confession of ignorance concerning the nature of God. He proceeded with high eloquence:

> Whom therefore ye worship though ye know him not, him I declare unto you. God, who made the world and all things therein . . . dwells not in temples made with hands. . . . It is he that giveth life and breath unto all. . . . And he made of one blood all the nations of mankind . . . that they should seek God, if haply they might feel after him, though he be not far from us; for in him we live and move and have our being, as certain also of your own poets have said.* . . . Forasmuch, then, as we are the offspring of God, we ought not to think that the Godhead is like unto gold, or silver, or stone, graven by the art and device of man. Howbeit, those past times of ignorance God hath overlooked; but now he commandeth all men everywhere to repent, because he hath appointed a day wherein he will judge the world . . . by that Man whom he hath ordained; whereof he hath given assurance unto all, in that he hath raised him from the dead.[38]

It was a brave effort to reconcile Christianity with Greek philosophy.† Nevertheless, it impressed only a few; the Athenians had heard too many ideas to have much enthusiasm for any. Paul left the city in disappointment and went to Corinth, where commerce had gathered a substantial community of Jews. He stayed there eighteen months (51-52?), earning his living as a tentmaker, and preaching every Sabbath in the synagogue. The leader of the synagogue was converted, and so many others that the alarmed Jews indicted Paul before the Roman governor, Gallio, on the charge of "trying to induce people to worship God in ways that are against the law." Gallio replied: "As it is only a question of words and titles and your own law, you must look after it yourselves; I will not decide such matters"; and he dismissed them from the court. The two parties fell to blows, "but Gallio paid no attention." [39] Paul offered his gospel to the gentiles of Corinth, and made many converts among them. Christianity may have seemed to

---

* Paul quotes the line from Cleanthes' *Hymn to Zeus*, or from Aratus' *Phainomena*.
† Perhaps we should credit the speech to the Hellenized author of the Acts.

them an acceptable variation of the mystery faiths that had so often told them of resurrected saviors; possibly in accepting it they assimilated it to these beliefs, and influenced Paul to interpret Christianity in terms familiar to the Hellenistic mind.

From Corinth Paul went to Jerusalem (53?) to "salute the church." Soon, however, he was off on his third missionary journey, visiting the Christian communities in Antioch and Asia Minor, and reinvigorating them with his fervor and confidence. At Ephesus he spent two years, and "did such extraordinary wonders" that many looked upon him as a miracle-worker, and sought to cure ailments by applying to the sick the linens Paul had used. The manufacturers of the images that pagan worshipers dedicated in the Temple of Artemis found their trade slackening; perhaps Paul had repeated here his Athenian indictment of image worship, or idolatry. One Demetrius, who made silver models of the great shrine for pious pilgrims, organized a protest against Paul and the new faith, and led to the city theater a crowd of Greeks whose catchword, repeated for two hours, was "Great is Artemis of the Ephesians!" A local official dissolved the gathering, but Paul thought it the better part of valor to leave for Macedonia.

He spent some happy months with the little congregations he had founded in Philippi, Thessalonica, and Beraea. Hearing that dissension and immorality were disordering the church at Corinth, he not only reprimanded it in several epistles, but went down to it in person (56?) to face his detractors. They had accused him of profiting materially from his preaching, laughed at his visions, and renewed the demand that all Christians should obey the Jewish Law. Paul reminded the turbulent community that he had everywhere earned his living with the work of his hands; and as to material profit, what had he not suffered from his missions?—eight floggings, one stoning, three shipwrecks, and a thousand dangers from robbers, patriots, and streams.[40] Amid this turmoil word was brought him that the "party of the circumcision," apparently violating the Jerusalem agreement, had gone into Galatia and demanded of all converts the full acceptance of the Jewish Law. He wrote to the Galatians a wrathful epistle in which he broke completely with the Judaizing Christians, and declared that men were to be saved not by adherence to the Mosaic Law, but by an active faith in Christ as the redeeming Son of God. Then, not knowing what sharper tribulations awaited him there, he left for Jerusalem, eager to defend himself before the Apostles, and wishing to celebrate in the Holy City the ancient feast of Pentecost. From Jerusalem, he hoped, he might go to Rome, even to Spain, and never rest till every province of the Empire had heard the news and promise of the risen Christ.

3. *The Theologian*

The leaders of the mother church gave him "a hearty welcome" (57?);
but privately they admonished him:

> You see, brother, how many thousand believers there are among
> the Jews, all of them zealous upholders of the Law. They have been
> told that you teach all Jews who live among the heathen to turn away
> from Moses, that you tell them not to circumcize their children, nor
> to observe the old customs. . . . They will be sure to hear that you
> have come. So do what we tell you. We have four men here who are
> under a vow. Join them, undergo the rites of purification with them,
> and pay their expenses. . . . Then everybody will understand that
> there is no truth in the stories told about you, but that you yourself
> observe the Law.[41]

Paul took the advice in good spirit, and went through the rites of purification. But when some Jews saw him in the Temple they raised an outcry
against him as "the man who teaches everybody everywhere against our
people and the Law." A mob seized him, dragged him from the Temple,
and "were trying to kill him" when a squad of Roman soldiers rescued him
by arrest. Paul turned to speak to the crowd, and affirmed both his Judaism
and his Christianity. They shouted for his death. The Roman officer ordered
him to be flogged, but desisted when he learned of Paul's Roman citizenship.
The next day he brought the prisoner before the Sanhedrin. Paul addressed
it, proclaimed himself a Pharisee, and won some support; but his excited
opponents again sought to do him violence, and the officer withdrew him
into the barracks. That night a nephew of Paul came to warn him that forty
Jews had vowed not to eat or drink until they had killed him. The officer,
fearing a disturbance that would compromise him, sent Paul in the night to
the procurator Felix at Caesarea.

Five days later the high priest and some elders came up from Jerusalem,
and accused Paul of being "a pest and a disturber of the peace among Jews
all over the world." Paul admitted that he was preaching a new religion,
but added: "I believe everything that is taught in the Law." Felix dismissed
the accusers; nevertheless, he kept Paul under house arrest—accessible to
friends—for two years (58-60?), hoping, perhaps, for a substantial bribe.

When Festus succeeded Felix he suggested that Paul should stand trial
before him at Jerusalem. Fearing that hostile environment, Paul exercised
his rights as a Roman citzen, and demanded trial before the emperor. King
Agrippa, passing through Caesarea, gave him another hearing, and judged

him "mad with great learning," but otherwise innocent; "he might be let go," said Agrippa, "if he had not appealed to the emperor." Paul was put on a trading vessel, which sailed so leisurely that it encountered a winter storm before it could reach Italy. Through fourteen days of tempest, we are told, he gave crew and passengers an encouraging example of a man superior to death and confident of rescue. The ship broke to pieces on Malta's rocks, but all on board swam safely to shore. Three months later Paul arrived in Rome (61?).

The Roman authorities treated him leniently, awaiting his accusers from Palestine, and Nero's leisure to hear the case. He was allowed to live in a house of his choosing, with a soldier to guard him; he could not move about freely, but he could receive whomever he wished. He invited the leading Jews of Rome to come to him; they heard him patiently, but when they perceived that in his judgment the observance of the Jewish Law was not necessary to salvation, they turned away; the Law seemed to them the indispensable prop and solace of Jewish life. "Understand, then," said Paul, "that this message of God's salvation has been sent to the heathen. They will listen to it!" [42] His attitude offended also the Christian community that he found in Rome. These converts, chiefly Jews, preferred the Christianity that had been brought to them from Jerusalem; they practiced circumcision, and were hardly distinguished by Rome from the orthodox Jews; they welcomed Peter, but were cold to Paul. He made some converts among the gentiles, even in high place; but a bitter sense of frustration darkened the loneliness of his imprisonment.

He found some solace in sending long and tender letters to his distant flocks. For ten years now he had written such epistles; there were doubtless many more than have come down to us under his name.* They did not come directly from his pen; he dictated them, often adding a postscript in his own rough hand; he left them apparently unrevised, with all their repetitions, obscurities, and bad grammar on their head. Nevertheless, the depth and sincerity of their feeling, their angry devotion to a great cause, their profusion of noble and memorable speech make them the most forceful and eloquent letters in all literature; even Cicero's charm seems slight beside this passionate faith. Here are strong words of love from one to whom his churches were his fiercely protected children; violent attacks upon his numberless enemies; reprimands to sinners, backsliders, and divisive disputants; and everywhere tender exhortations.

---

* Of these we may regard the letters to the Galatians, Corinthians, and Romans as authentic; probably also those to the Thessalonians, Philippians, Colossians, and Philemon; perhaps even the epistle to the Ephesians.[43]

Be filled with thanksgiving. Let the presence of Christ dwell in you,
a well-spring of abounding wisdom; teach and encourage one another
with hymns and songs of the spiritual life; make music in your hearts
in gratitude to God.[44]

Here are great phrases that all Christendom quotes and cherishes: "the letter
kills, the spirit gives life";[45] "evil communications corrupt good manners";[46]
"to the pure all things are pure";[47] "the love of money is the root of all evil."[48]
Here are frank confessions of his faults, even of his statesmanlike hypocrisies:

I have made myself everyone's slave, so as to win over all the more.
To the Jews I have become like a Jew to win Jews . . . to those
without the Law I have become like a man without any law . . . I
have become all things to all men, that I might save some of them.
I do it all for the sake of the Good News, that I may share its blessings
with the rest.[49]

These epistles were preserved, and often publicly read, by the congregations to which they were addressed. By the end of the first century many
of them were widely known; Clement of Rome refers to them in 97,
Ignatius and Polycarp soon afterwards; gradually they entered into the
subtlest theology of the Church. Moved by his own somber spirit and
remorse, and his transforming vision of Christ; influenced perhaps by
Platonist and Stoic denunciations of matter and the body as evil; recalling,
it may be, Jewish and pagan customs of sacrificing a "scapegoat" for the
sins of the people, Paul created a theology of which none but the vaguest
warrants can be found in the words of Christ: that every man born of woman
inherits the guilt of Adam, and can be saved from eternal damnation only
by the atoning death of the Son of God.* [50] Such a conception was more
agreeable to the pagans than to the Jews. Egypt, Asia Minor, and Hellas
had long since believed in gods—Osiris, Attis, Dionysus—who had died to
redeem mankind; such titles as *Soter* (Savior) and *Eleutherios* (Deliverer)
had been applied to these deities; and the word *Kyrios* (Lord), used by Paul
of Christ, was the term given in Syrian-Greek cults to the dying and redeeming Dionysus.[52] The gentiles of Antioch and other Greek cities, never having

---

* The ancient Jews shared with the Canaanites, Moabites, Phoenicians, Carthaginians, and
other peoples the custom of sacrificing a child, even a beloved son, to appease the wrath of
Heaven. In the course of time a condemned criminal might be substituted. In Babylonia he
was dressed in royal robes to represent the son of the king, and was then scourged and
hanged. A similar sacrifice took place in Rhodes at the feast of Cronus. The offering of a
lamb or kid at the Passover was probably a civilized mitigation of ancient human sacrifice.
"On the day of atonement," says Frazer, "the Jewish high priest laid both his hands on the head
of a live goat, confessed over it all the iniquities of the children of Israel, and having thereby
transferred the sins of the people to the beast, sent it away into the wilderness." [51]

known Jesus in the flesh, could only accept him after the manner of their
savior gods. "Behold," said Paul, "I show you a mystery." [53]

Paul added to this popular and consoling theology certain mystic con-
ceptions already made current by the Book of Wisdom and the philosophy
of Philo. Christ, said Paul, is "the wisdom of God," [54] the first-born Son
of God; "he is before all things, in him all things exist . . . through him
all things have been created." [55] He is not the Jewish Messiah who will deliver
Israel from bondage; he is the Logos whose death will deliver all men.
Through these interpretations Paul could neglect the actual life and sayings
of Jesus, which he had not directly known, and could stand on an equality
with the immediate apostles, who were no match for him in metaphysical
speculation; he could give to the life of Christ, and to the life of man, high
roles in a magnificent drama that embraced all souls and all eternity. Moreover, he could answer the troublesome questions of those who asked why
Christ, if very god, had allowed himself to be put to death: Christ had died
to redeem a world lost to Satan by Adam's sin; he had to die to break the
bonds of death and open the gates of heaven to all who should be touched
by the grace of God.

Two factors, said Paul, determine who shall be saved by Christ's death:
divine election and humble faith. God chooses from all eternity those whom
he will bless with his grace, and those whom he will damn.[56] Nevertheless,
Paul bestirred himself to awaken faith as a rod to catch God's grace; only
through such "assurance of things longed for," such "confidence in things
unseen," [57] can the soul experience that profound change which makes a
new man, unites the believer with Christ, and allows him to share in the
fruits of Christ's death. Good works and the performance of all the 613
precepts of the Jewish Law will not suffice, said Paul; they cannot remake
the inner man, or wash the soul of sin. The death of Christ had ended the
epoch of the Law; now there should no more be Jew and Greek, slave and
freeman, male and female, for "in union with Christ Jesus you are all one." [58]
As to good works combined with faith, Paul never tired of inculcating
them; and the most famous words ever spoken about love are his own:

> Though I speak with the tongues of men and angels, and have not
> love, I am become as sounding brass or tinkling cymbal. And though
> I have the gift of preaching, and understand all mysteries, and have
> all knowledge; and though I have all faith, so that I can move moun-
> tains; if I have not love I am nothing. And though I give away every-
> thing that I am, and give myself, but do it in pride, not love, it profits
> me nothing. Love is patient and kind. It is not envious or boastful.
> . . . It does not insist on its rights. . . . It never fails. So faith, hope
> and love endure, these three; and the greatest of these is love.[59]

To sexual love, and marriage, Paul gives the most discouraging toleration. One passage [60] suggests, but does not prove, that he was married: "Have we not" (he and Barnabas) "a right to take a Christian wife about with us, like the rest of the apostles, and the Lord's brothers, and Peter?"—but in another [61] he calls himself single. Like Jesus, he had no sympathy for physical desire.[62] He was horrified when he heard of promiscuity and perversions.[63] "Do you not know," he asked the Corinthians, "that your body is a temple of the Holy Spirit that is within you? . . . Honor God with your bodies." [64] Virginity is better than marriage, but marriage is better than concupiscence. The marriage of divorced persons is forbidden, except after mixed unions. Women are to be obedient to their husbands, slaves to their masters. "Everyone ought to remain in the station in which he was called" (i.e., converted to Christianity). "If you were a slave when you were called, never mind. Even if you can gain your freedom, make the most of your present condition instead. For a slave who has been called to union with the Lord is a freedman of the Lord, just as a freeman who had been called is a slave of Christ." [65] Freedom and slavery meant little if the world was soon coming to an end. By the same token national liberty was unimportant. Let "every soul be in subjection to the higher powers, for there is no power but God, and the powers that be are ordained by God." [66] It was ungracious of Rome to destroy so accommodating a philosopher.

4. The Martyr

"Do your best to come to me soon," runs the doubtful second letter to Timothy,

> for Demas has deserted me for love of the present world . . . Crescens has gone, and Titus; no one but Luke is with me. . . . At my first appearance in court no one came to help me; everybody deserted me. . . . But the Lord stood by me, and gave me strength, so that I might make a full presentation of the message and let all the heathen hear it. So I was saved from the jaws of the lion. . . . My life is already being poured out, and the time has come for my departure. I have had a part in the great contest. I have run my race, I have preserved the faith.[66a]

He spoke bravely, but he was desolate. One ancient tradition said that he was freed, went to Asia and Spain, preached again, and once more found himself a prisoner in Rome; probably he was never freed. Without wife or children to comfort him, with all friends gone but one, only his faith could support him; and perhaps that too was shaken. Like the other Christians of his age, he had lived on the hope of seeing Christ return. He had written to the Philippians: "We are eagerly awaiting the coming of a savior, the Lord Jesus Christ. . . . The Lord is coming soon." [67] And to the Corinthians: "The appointed time has grown very short. From now on, those who have wives should live as though they had none . . . and those who buy anything as if they did not own it. . . . For the present shape of the world is passing away . . . *Maranatha!* Lord, come quickly!" [68] But in his second epistle to the Thessalonians he reproved them for neglecting the affairs of this world in expectation of Christ's early advent; the coming will be delayed until the "Adversary"—Satan—"makes his appearance and proclaims himself to be God." [69] We surmise from his last letters that he had struggled, during his imprisonment, to reconcile his early faith with the long delay in the *Parousia* or Second Appearance. More and more he put his hope beyond the grave, and made for his own solace the great adjustment that saved Christianity—the transformation of the belief in Christ's earthly return into the hope of union with him in heaven after death. Apparently he was tried again, and convicted; Caesar and Christ came face to face, and Caesar won for a day. We do not know the precise charge; probably now, as at Thessalonica, Paul was accused of "disobeying the emperor's decrees, and claiming that someone else called Jesus is king." [70] This was a crime of *maiestas*, punishable with death. We have no ancient record of the trial; but Tertullian, writing about 200, reports that Paul was beheaded at Rome; and Origen, about 220, writes that "Paul suffered martyrdom in Rome under Nero." [71] Probably, as a Roman citizen, he had the honor of a distinct execution, and was not mingled with the Christians crucified after the fire of 64. Tradition united him with Peter in a simultaneous, though separate, martyrdom; and a touching legend pictured the great rivals meeting in friendship on the road to death. Over the place on the Via Ostia, where the Church believed that Paul had found peace, a shrine was raised in the third century. Remade in ever fairer form, it stands today as the basilica of San Paolo fuori le Mura—St. Paul beyond the Walls.

It is a fit symbol of his victory. The emperor who condemned him died a coward's death, and soon nothing survived of his inordinate works. But from the defeated Paul came the theological structure of Christianity, as from Paul and Peter the astonishing organization of the Church. Paul had found a dream of Jewish eschatology, confined in Judaic Law; he had freed and broadened it into a faith that could move the world. With the patience of a statesman he had interwoven the ethics of the Jews with the metaphysics of the Greeks, and had transformed the Jesus of the Gospels into the Christ of theology. He had created a new mystery, a new form of the resurrection drama, which would absorb and survive all the rest. He had replaced conduct with creed as the test of virtue, and in that sense had begun the Middle Ages. It was a tragic change, but perhaps humanity had willed it so; only a few saints could achieve the imitation of Christ, but many souls could rise to faith and courage in the hope of eternal life.

The influence of Paul was not immediately felt. The communities that he had established were tiny isles in a pagan sea. The church at Rome was Peter's, and remained faithful to his memory. For a century after Paul's death he was almost forgotten. But when the first generations of Christianity had passed away, and the oral tradition of the apostles began to fade, and a hundred heresies disordered the Christian mind, the epistles of Paul provided the framework for a stabilizing system of belief that united the scattered congregations into a powerful Church.

Even so, the man who had detached Christianity from Judaism was still so essentially Jewish in intensity of character and sternness of morality that the Middle Ages, adopting paganism into a colorful Catholicism, saw no kindred spirit in him, built few churches to him, seldom sculptured his figure or used his name. Fifteen centuries went by before Luther made Paul the Apostle of the Reformation, and Calvin found in him the somber texts of the predestinarian creed. Protestantism was the triumph of Paul over Peter; Fundamentalism is the triumph of Paul over Christ.

III. JOHN

The accidents of history have transmitted Paul to us in comparative clarity, and have left the apostle John in obscurity and mystery. Besides three epistles, two major works have come down to us under his name. Criticism tentatively assigns the Book of Revelation to the year 69-70,[72] and to another John, "the Presbyter" mentioned by Papias (135).[73] Justin Martyr (135) attributes this powerful Apocalypse to the "beloved" apostle;[74] but as early as the fourth century Eusebius [75] noted that some scholars doubted its authenticity. The author must have been a man of considerable prominence, for he addresses the churches of Asia in a tone of menacing authority. If the apostle wrote it (and we may provisionally continue to think so), we can understand why, like his brother James, he was called *Boanerges,* Son of Thunder. In Ephesus, Smyrna, Pergamum, Sardis, and other cities of Asia Minor, John, rather than Peter or Paul, was looked upon as the highest head of the Church. Tradition as reported by Eusebius [76] held that John had been banished to Patmos by Domitian, and had on that Aegean isle written both the Fourth Gospel and the Apocalypse. He lived to so great an age that people said he would never die.

In form Revelation resembles the books of Daniel and Enoch. Such prophetic-symbolic visions were a literary device frequently used by the Jews of the age; there were several other apocalypses ("hidden things revealed"), but this one surpassed all the rest in lurid eloquence. Starting from the common belief that the coming of the Kingdom of God would be preceded by the reign of Satan and the heyday of evil, the author describes the principate of Nero as precisely this Satanic age. Satan and his followers, having revolted against God, are defeated by Michael's angelic hosts, are cast down upon the earth, and there lead the pagan world in the attack upon Christianity. Nero is the Beast and Antichrist of the book, a Messiah from Satan as Jesus was from God. Rome is described as "the harlot who sits on the great waters, with whom the kings of the earth have committed fornication"; she is the "whore of Babylon," the source and center and summit of all iniquity, immorality, perversion, idolatry; there the blasphemous and bloodstained Caesars demand the worship that Christians must reserve for Christ.

In a succession of visions the author sees the punishments that will fall upon Rome and its empire. A plague of locusts will for five months torture all inhabitants except the 144,000 Jews who have on their foreheads the sign of Christianity.[77] Other angels will empty "the seven vials of God's wrath" upon the earth, afflicting men with terrible sores, and turning the sea "into blood like a dead man's," so that "every living thing in the sea" will die. Another angel will let loose the full heat of the sun upon all unrepentant men; another will cover the earth with darkness; four angels will lead "twice 10,000 times 10,000" knights to slaughter a third of mankind. Four horsemen will ride forth to "kill the people with sword, famine, death, and the wild animals of the earth." [78] A great earthquake will tumble the planet into ruins; huge hailstones will fall upon the surviving infidels, and Rome will be utterly destroyed. The kings of the earth will come together on the plains of Armageddon to make their last stand against God; but they will be overwhelmed in death. Satan and his cohorts, everywhere defeated, will be plunged into Hell. Only true Christians will be saved from these calamities; and those who have suffered for Christ's sake, who have been "washed in the blood of the Lamb," [79] will receive abounding reward.

After a thousand years Satan will be released to prey again upon mankind; sin will mount again in an unbelieving world; and the forces of evil will make a last effort to undo the work of God. But they will once more be overcome, and this time Satan and his followers will be cast into Hell forever. Then will come the Last Judgment, when all the dead will be raised from their graves, and the drowned will be drawn up out of the seas. On that dread day all "whose names are not found in the Book of Life" will be "flung into . . . a burning lake of fire and brimstone." [80] The faithful will "gather for God's great banquet, and will eat the bodies of kings, commanders, mighty men . . . the bodies of all men, slaves or freemen, high or low," [81] who have not heeded the call of Christ. A new heaven and earth will be formed, and a New Jerusalem will come down from the hand of God to be a paradise on earth. It will have a foundation of precious stones, buildings of translucent silver or gold, walls of jasper, and each gate a single pearl; through it will run a "river of living water," on whose bank will grow the "tree of life." The reign of evil will be ended for all time; the faithful of Christ will inherit the earth; "there will be no death any longer, nor night, nor any grief or pain." [82]

The influence of the Book of Revelation was immediate, enduring, and profound. Its prophecies of salvation for loyal believers, and of punishment for their enemies, became the sustenance of a persecuted Church. Its theory of the millennium solaced those who mourned the long delay in the second coming of Christ. Its vivid images and brilliant phrases entered into both the popular and the literary speech of Christendom. For nineteen centuries men have interpreted the events of history as fulfillments of its visions; and in some recesses of the white man's world it still gives its dark colors and bitter flavor to the creed of Christ.

It seems incredible that the Apocalypse and the Fourth Gospel should have come from the same hand. The Apocalypse is Jewish poetry, the Fourth Gospel is Greek philosophy. Perhaps the apostle wrote Revelation in justifiable wrath after Nero's persecution, and the Gospel in the mellow metaphysics of his old age (A.D. 90?). His memories of the Master may by this time have faded a bit, so far as one could ever forget Jesus; and doubtless in the isles and cities of Ionia he had heard many an echo of Greek mysticism and philosophy. Plato had set a theme by picturing the Ideas of God as the patterns on which all things were formed; the Stoics had combined these Ideas into the *Logos Spermatikos* or fertilizing wisdom of God; the Neo-Pythagoreans had made the Ideas a divine person; and Philo had turned them into the Logos or Reason of God, a second divine principle, through which God created, and communicated with, the world. If we reread the famous exordium of the Fourth Gospel with all this in mind, and retain the *Logos* of the Greek original in place of the translation *Word*, we perceive at once that John has joined the philosophers:

> In the beginning was the Logos; the Logos was with God, and the Logos was God. . . . All things were made by the Logos; without

him nothing was made that was made. It was by him that all things came into existence. . . . So the Logos became flesh and blood, and dwelt amongst us.

Just as Philo, learned in Greek speculation, had felt a need to rephrase Judaism in forms acceptable to the logic-loving Greeks, so John, having lived for two generations in a Hellenistic environment, sought to give a Greek philosophical tinge to the mystic Jewish doctrine that the Wisdom of God was a living being,[83] and to the Christian doctrine that Jesus was the Messiah. Consciously or not, he continued Paul's work of detaching Christianity from Judaism. Christ was no longer presented as a Jew, living more or less under the Jewish Law; he was made to address the Jews as "you," and to speak of their Law as "yours"; he was not a Messiah sent "to save the lost sheep of Israel," he was the coeternal Son of God; not merely the future judge of mankind, but the primeval creator of the universe. In this perspective the Jewish life of the man Jesus could be put into the background, faded almost as in Gnostic heresy; and the god Christ was assimilated to the religious and philosophical traditions of the Hellenistic mind. Now the pagan world—even the anti-Semitic world—could accept him as its own.

Christianity did not destroy paganism; it adopted it. The Greek mind, dying, came to a transmigrated life in the theology and liturgy of the Church; the Greek language, having reigned for centuries over philosophy, became the vehicle of Christian literature and ritual; the Greek mysteries passed down into the impressive mystery of the Mass. Other pagan cultures contributed to the syncretist result. From Egypt came the ideas of a divine trinity, the Last Judgment, and a personal immortality of reward and punishment; from Egypt the adoration of the Mother and Child, and the mystic theosophy that made Neoplatonism and Gnosticism, and obscured the Christian creed; there, too, Christian monasticism would find its exemplars and its source. From Phrygia came the worship of the Great Mother; from Syria the resurrection drama of Adonis; from Thrace, perhaps, the cult of Dionysus, the dying and saving god. From Persia came millennarianism, the "ages of the world," the "final conflagration," the dualism of Satan and God, of Darkness and Light; already in the Fourth Gospel Christ is the "Light shining in the darkness, and the darkness has never put it out." [84] The Mithraic ritual so closely resembled the eucharistic sacrifice of the Mass that Christian fathers charged the Devil with inventing these similarities to mislead frail minds.[85] Christianity was the last great creation of the ancient pagan world.

CHAPTER XXVIII

The Growth of the Church

A.D. 96-305

I. THE CHRISTIANS

THEY met in private rooms or small chapels, and organized themselves on the model of the synagogue.[1] Each congregation was called an *ekklesia*—the Greek term for the popular assembly in municipal governments. Slaves were welcomed, as in the Isiac and Mithraic cults; no attempt was made to liberate them, but they were comforted by the promise of a Kingdom in which all could be free. The early converts were predominantly proletarian, with a sprinkling of the lower middle classes and an occasional conquest among the rich. Nevertheless, they were far from being the "dregs of the people," as Celsus would claim; they lived for the most part orderly and industrious lives, financed missions, and raised funds for impoverished Christian communities. Little effort was made as yet to win over the rural population; these came in last, and it was in this strange way that their name *pagani* (villagers, peasants) came to be applied to the pre-Christian inhabitants of the Mediterranean states.

Women were admitted to the congregations, and rose to some prominence in minor roles; but the Church required them to shame the heathen by lives of modest submission and retirement. They were bidden to come to worship veiled, for their hair was considered especially seductive, and even angels might be distracted by it during the service;[2] Saint Jerome thought it should be entirely cut off.[3] Christian women were also to avoid cosmetics and jewelry, and particularly false hair; for the blessing of the priest, falling upon dead hair from another head, would hardly know which head to bless.[4] Paul had instructed his communities sternly:

> Women should keep quiet in church. They must take a subordinate place. If they want to find out anything they should ask their husbands at home, for it is disgraceful for a woman to speak in church. . . . A man ought not to wear anything on his head in church, for he is the image of God and reflects God's glory, while woman is a reflection of man's glory. For man was not made from

woman, but woman from man; and man was not created for woman, but woman for man. That is why she ought to wear upon her head something to symbolize her subjection.[5]

This was the Judaic and Greek view of woman, not the Roman; perhaps it represented a reaction against the license into which some women had debased their growing liberty. We may believe, from these very fulminations, that despite the lack of jewels and scents, and with the help of veils, Christian women succeeded in being attractive, and exercised their ancient powers in their subtle ways. For unmarried or widowed women the Church found many useful tasks. They were organized as "sisters," performed works of administration or charity, and created in time the divers orders of those nuns whose cheerful kindliness is the noblest embodiment of Christianity.

Lucian, about 160, described "those imbeciles," the Christians, as "disdaining things terrestrial, and holding these as belonging to all in common." [6] A generation later Tertullian declared that "we" (Christians) "have all things in common except our wives," and added, with his characteristic bite: "at that point we dissolve our partnership, precisely where the rest of men make it effective." [7] We should not take these statements literally; as another passage in Tertullian [8] suggests, this communism meant merely that each Christian would contribute according to his means to the congregation's common fund. The expectation of an early end to the existing order of things doubtless facilitated giving; the richer members may have been persuaded that they must not let the Last Judgment surprise them in the arms of Mammon. Some early Christians agreed with the Essenes that the prosperous man who does not share his surplus is a thief.[9] James, "brother of the Lord," attacked wealth with words of revolutionary bitterness:

> Come, now, you rich people, weep aloud and howl over the miseries that shall overtake you! Your wealth has rotted, your clothes are moth-eaten, your gold and silver are rusted . . . and their rust will eat into your very flesh, for you have stored up fire for the last days. The wages you have withheld from the laborers who have reaped your harvests cry aloud, and their cries have reached the ears of the Lord of Hosts. . . . Has not God chosen the world's poor to possess the Kingdom? [10]

In that Kingdom, he adds, the rich will wither like flowers under a scorching sun.[11]

An element of communism entered into the custom of the common meal. As the Greek and Roman associations had met on occasion to dine together, so the early Christians gathered frequently in the *agapé* or love feast, usually on a Sabbath evening. The dinner began and ended with prayer and scriptural readings, and the bread and wine were blessed by the priest. The faithful appear to have believed that the bread and wine were, or represented, the body and blood of Christ; [12] the worshipers of Dionysus, Attis, and Mithras had entertained like beliefs at the banquets where they ate the magic embodiments or symbols of their gods.[13] The final ritual of the *agapé* was the "kiss of love." In some congregations this was given only by men to men, and by women to women; in others this hard restriction was not enforced. Many participants discovered an untheological delight in the pleasant ceremony; and Tertullian and others denounced it as having led to sexual indulgences.[14] The Church recommended that the lips should not be opened in kissing, and that the kiss should not be repeated if it gave pleasure.[15] In the third century the *agapé* gradually disappeared.

Despite such episodes, and the diatribes of preachers calling their congregations to perfection, we may accept the old belief that the morals of the early Christians were a reproving example to the pagan world. After the weakening of the ancient faiths had removed their frail support from the moral life, and the attempt of Stoicism at an almost natural ethic had failed with all but the best of men, a new supernatural ethic accomplished, at whatever cost to the free and dissolvent intellect, the task of regulating the jungle instincts of man into a viable morality. The hope of the coming Kingdom carried with it belief in a Judge who saw every act, knew man's every thought, and could not be eluded or deceived. To this divine surveillance was added mutual scrutiny: in these little groups sin could with difficulty find a hiding place; and the community publicly reprimanded those members who had violated the new moral code with insufficient secrecy. Abortion and infanticide, which were decimating pagan society, were forbidden to Christians as the equivalents of murder; [16] in many instances Christians rescued exposed infants, baptized them, and brought them up with the aid of the community fund.[17] The Church forbade with less success the attendance of Christians at the theater or the public games, and their participation in the festivities of pagan holidays.[18] In general, Christianity continued and exaggerated the moral sternness of the embattled Jews. Celibacy and virginity were recommended as ideal; marriage was tolerated only as a check on promiscuity and as a ridiculous means of continuing the race, but husband and wife were encouraged to refrain from sexual relations.[19] Divorce was allowed only when a pagan wished to annul a marriage with a convert. The remarriage of widows or widowers was discountenanced, and homosexual practices were condemned with an earnestness rare in antiquity. "So far as sex is concerned," said Tertullian, "the Christian is content with the woman." [20]

Much of this difficult code was predicated on the early return of Christ. As that hope faded, the voice of the flesh rose again, and Christian morals were relaxed; an anonymous pamphlet. *The Shepherd of Hermas* (*ca.* 110), inveighed against the reappearance, among Christians, of avarice, dishonesty, rouge, dyed hair, painted eyelids, drunkenness, and adultery.[21] Nevertheless, the general picture of Christian morals in this period is one of piety, mutual loyalty, marital fidelity, and a quiet happiness in the possession of a confident faith. The younger Pliny was compelled to report to Trajan that the Christians led peaceful and exemplary lives.[22] Galen described them as "so far advanced in self-discipline and . . . intense desire to attain moral excellence that they are in no way inferior to true philosophers." [23] The sense of sin took on a new intensity with the belief that all mankind had been tainted by Adam's fall, and that soon the world would end in a judgment of eternal punishment or reward. Many Christians were absorbed in the effort to come clean to that dread assize; they saw a lure of Satan in every pleasure of the senses, denounced the "world and the flesh," and sought to subdue desire with fasts and varied chastisements. They looked with suspicion upon music, white bread, foreign wines, warm baths, or shaving the beard—which seemed to flout the evident will of God.[24] Even for the ordinary Christian, life took on a more somber tint than paganism had ever given it except in the occasional "apotropaic" appeasement of subterranean deities. The serious temper of the Jewish Sabbath was transferred to the Christian Sunday that replaced it in the second century.

On that *dies Domini*, or Lord's Day, the Christians assembled for their weekly ritual. Their clergy read from the Scriptures, led them in prayer, and preached sermons of doctrinal instruction, moral exhortation, and sectarian controversy. In the early days members of the congregation, especially women, were allowed to "prophesy"—i.e., to "speak forth," in trance or ecstasy, words to which meaning could be given only by pious interpretation. When these performances conduced to ritual fever and theological chaos, the Church discouraged and finally suppressed them. At every step the clergy found itself obliged not to generate superstition, but to control it.

By the close of the second century these weekly ceremonies had taken the form of the Christian Mass. Based partly on the Judaic Temple service, partly on Greek mystery rituals of purification, vicarious sacrifice, and participation, through communion, in the death-overcoming powers of the deity, the Mass grew slowly into a rich congeries of prayers, psalms, readings, sermon, antiphonal recitations, and, above all, that symbolic atoning sacrifice of the "Lamb of God" which replaced, in Christianity, the bloody offerings of older faiths. The bread and wine which these cults had considered as gifts placed upon the altar before the god were now conceived as changed by the priestly act of consecration into the body and blood of Christ, and were presented to God as a repetition of the self-immolation of Jesus on the cross. Then, in an intense and moving ceremony, the worshipers partook of the very life and substance of their Saviour. It was a conception long sanctified by time; the pagan mind needed no schooling to receive it; by embodying it in the "mystery of the Mass," Christianity became the last and greatest of the mystery religions. It was a custom lowly in origin [25] and beautiful in development; its adoption was part of the profound wisdom with which the Church adjusted itself to the symbols of the age and the needs of her people; no other ceremony could have so heartened the essentially solitary soul, or so strengthened it to face a hostile world.*

The eucharist, or "blessing" of the bread and wine, was one of the seven Christian "sacraments"—sacred rituals believed to convey divine grace. Here, too, the Church used the poetry of symbols to console and dignify the life of man, to renew at each step in the human odyssey the fortifying touch of deity. In the first century we find only three ceremonies conceived of as sacraments—baptism, communion, and holy orders; but already, in the customs of the congregations, the germs of the rest were present. It was apparently the practice of the early Christians to add to baptism an "imposition of hands," whereby the apostle or priest introduced the Holy Spirit into the believer;[28] in the course of time this action was separated from baptism and became the sacrament of confirmation.[29] As the baptism of adults was gradually replaced by the baptism of infants, men felt the need of some later spiritual cleansing; public acknowledgment of sin passed into private confession to the priest, who claimed to have received from the apostles or their episcopal successors the right to "bind and loose"—to impose penances and pardon sins.[30] The sacrament of penance was an institution capable of abuse through the ease of forgiveness; but it gave the sinner strength to reform, and spared anxious souls the neuroses of remorse. In these centuries marriage was still a civil ceremony; but by adding and requiring her sanction the Church lifted it from the level of a passing contract to the sanctity of an inviolable vow. By the year 200 the laying on of hands took the added form of "holy orders," by which the bishops assumed the exclusive right to ordain priests capable of administering the sacraments validly. Finally the Church derived from the Epistle of James (v, 14) the sacrament of "extreme unction," or last blessing, by which the priest anointed the sense organs and extremities of a dying Christian, cleansed him again of sin, and prepared him to meet his God. It would be the shallowest folly to judge

---

* In the mysteries of Mithras the worshipers were offered consecrated bread and water.[26] The *conquistadores* were shocked to find similar rites among the Indians of Mexico and Peru.[27]

these ceremonies in terms of their literal claims; in terms of human encouragement and inspiration they were the wisest medicaments of the soul.

Christian burial was the culminating honor of the Christian life. Since
the new faith proclaimed the resurrection of the body as well as of the soul,
every care was taken of the dead; a priest officiated at the interment, and
each corpse received an individual tomb. About the year 100 the Christians
of Rome, following Syrian and Etruscan traditions, began to bury their dead
in catacombs—probably not for concealment but for the economy of space
and expense. Workmen dug long subterranean passages at various levels,
and the dead were laid in superimposed crypts along the sides of these
galleries. Pagans and Jews practiced the same method, perhaps as a convenience for burial societies. Some of the passages seem purposely devious,
and suggest their use as hiding places in persecutions. After the triumph of
Christianity the custom of catacomb burial died out; the crypts became
objects of veneration and pilgrimage; by the ninth century they had been
blocked up and forgotten, and only accident discovered them in 1578.

What remains of early Christian art is for the most part preserved in the
frescoes and reliefs of the catacombs. Here, about 180, appear the symbols that
were to be so prominent in Christianity: the dove, representing the soul freed
from the prison of this life; the phoenix, rising out of the ashes of death; the
palm branch, announcing victory; the olive branch, offering peace; and the fish,
chosen because the Greek word for it, *i-ch-th-u-s*, formed the initials of the
phrase *Iesous Christos theou uios soter*—"Jesus Christ, Son of God, Saviour."
Here also is the famous theme of the Good Shepherd, frankly modeled on a
Tanagra statue of Mercury carrying a goat. Occasionally these designs catch a
certain Pompeian grace, as in the flowers, vines, and birds that decorated the
ceiling of St. Domitilla's tomb; usually they are the undistinguished work of
minor craftsmen corrupting with Oriental obscurity the clearness of classic line.
Christianity was in these centuries so absorbed in the other world that it had
little interest in adorning this one. It continued the Judaic aversion to statuary,
confused imagery with idolatry, and condemned sculpture and painting as too
often glorying in the nude; consequently, as Christianity grew, plastic art declined. Mosaic was more popular; the walls and floors of basilicas and baptistries
were inlaid with tesselated foliage and flowers, the Paschal Lamb, and pictures
from the Testaments. Similar scenes were carved in rough relief on sarcophagi.
Meanwhile architects were adapting the Greco-Roman basilica to the needs of
Christian worship. The small temples that had housed the pagan gods could
offer no models for churches designed to enclose whole congregations; the
spacious nave and aisles of the basilica lent themselves to this purpose, and its
apse seemed naturally destined to become the sanctuary. In these new shrines
Christian music inherited diffidently the Greek notation, modes, and scales. Many

theologians frowned upon the singing of women in church, or, indeed, in any public place; for a woman's voice might arouse some profane interest in the ever excitable male.[31] Nevertheless, the congregations often expressed in hymns their hope, thanksgiving, and joy; and music began to be one of the fairest adornments and subtlest servants of the Christian faith.

All in all, no more attractive religion has ever been presented to mankind. It offered itself without restriction to all individuals, classes, and nations; it was not limited to one people, like Judaism, nor to the freemen of one state, like the official cults of Greece and Rome. By making all men heirs of Christ's victory over death, Christianity announced the basic equality of men, and made transiently trivial all differences of earthly degree. To the miserable, maimed, bereaved, disheartened, and humiliated it brought the new virtue of compassion, and an ennobling dignity; it gave them the inspiring figure, story, and ethic of Christ; it brightened their lives with the hope of the coming Kingdom, and of endless happiness beyond the grave. To even the greatest sinners it promised forgiveness, and their full acceptance into the community of the saved. To minds harassed with the insoluble problems of origin and destiny, evil and suffering, it brought a system of divinely revealed doctrine in which the simplest soul could find mental rest. To men and women imprisoned in the prose of poverty and toil it brought the poetry of the sacraments and the Mass, a ritual that made every major event of life a vital scene in the moving drama of God and man. Into the moral vacuum of a dying paganism, into the coldness of Stoicism and the corruption of Epicureanism, into a world sick of brutality, cruelty, oppression, and sexual chaos, into a pacified empire that seemed no longer to need the masculine virtues or the gods of war, it brought a new morality of brotherhood, kindliness, decency, and peace.

So molded to men's wants, the new faith spread with fluid readiness. Nearly every convert, with the ardor of a revolutionary, made himself an office of propaganda. The roads, rivers, and coasts, the trade routes and facilities, of the Empire largely determined the lines of the Church's growth: eastward from Jerusalem to Damascus, Edessa, Dura, Seleucia, and Ctesiphon; southward through Bostra and Petra into Arabia; westward through Syria into Egypt; northward through Antioch into Asia Minor and Armenia; across the Aegean from Ephesus and Troas to Corinth and Thessalonica; over the Egnatian Way to Dyrrhachium; across the Adriatic to Brundisium, or through Scylla and Charybdis to Puteoli and Rome; through Sicily and Egypt to north Africa; over the Mediterranean or the Alps to Spain and Gaul, and thence to Britain: slowly the cross followed the fasces, and the Roman eagles made straight the way for Christ. Asia

Minor was in these centuries the stronghold of Christianity; by 300 the majority of the population in Ephesus and Smyrna were Christians.[32] The new faith fared well in north Africa: Carthage and Hippo became leading centers of Christian learning and dispute; here rose the great Fathers of the Latin Church—Tertullian, Cyprian, Augustine; here the Latin text of the Mass, and the first Latin translation of the New Testament, took form. In Rome the Christian community numbered some 100,000 by the end of the third century; it was able to send financial aid to other congregations; long since it had claimed for its bishop the supreme authority in the Church. Altogether we may count a fourth of the population in the East as Christian by 300, and a twentieth in the West. "Men proclaim," said Tertullian (*ca.* 200), "that the state is beset with us. Every age, condition, and rank is coming over to us. We are only of yesterday, but already we fill the world."[33]

II. THE CONFLICT OF CREEDS

It would have been surprising if, in the multitude of relatively independent centers of Christianity, subject to different traditions and environments, there had failed to develop a diversity of customs and creeds. Greek Christianity in particular was destined to a flood of heresies by the metaphysical and argumentative habits of the Greek mind. Christianity can be understood only in the perspective of these heresies, for even in defeating them it took something of their color and form.

One faith united the scattered congregations: that Christ was the son of God, that he would return to establish his Kingdom on earth, and that all who believed in him would at the Last Judgment be rewarded with eternal bliss. But Christians differed as to the date of the second advent. When Nero died and Titus demolished the Temple, and again when Hadrian destroyed Jerusalem, many Christians hailed these calamities as signs of the second coming. When chaos threatened the Empire at the close of the second century, Tertullian and others thought that the end of the world was at hand; [34] a Syrian bishop led his flock into the desert to meet Christ halfway, and a bishop in Pontus disorganized the life of his community by announcing that Christ would return within a year.[35] As all signs failed, and Christ did not come, wiser Christians sought to soften the disappointment by reinterpreting the date of his return. He would come in a thousand years, said an epistle ascribed to Barnabas;[36] he would come, said the most cautious, when the "generation" or race of the Jews was quite extinct, or when the Gospel had been preached to all gentiles; or, said the Gospel of John, he would send in his stead the Holy Spirit or Paraclete. Finally the Kingdom was transferred from earth to heaven, from the years of our life to a paradise beyond the grave. Even the belief in the millennium—in the return of Jesus after a thousand years—was discouraged by the Church, and was ultimately condemned. The faith in the second advent had established Christianity; the hope of heaven preserved it.*

Aside from these basic tenets, the followers of Christ, in the first three centuries, divided into a hundred creeds. We should misjudge the function of history—which is to illuminate the present through the past—were we to detail the varieties of religious belief that sought and failed to capture the growing Church, and which the Church had to brand, one after another, as disintegrating heresies. Gnosticism—the quest of godlike knowledge (*gnosis*) through mystic means —was not a heresy so much as a rival; it antedated Christianity, and had proclaimed theories of a *Soter*, or Savior, before Christ was born.[37] That same Simon Magus of Samaria, whom Peter rebuked for "simony," was probably the author of a *Great Exposition* which gathered together a maze of Oriental notions about the complicated steps that could lead the human mind to a divine comprehension of all things. In Alexandria the Orphic, Neo-Pythagorean, and Neoplatonist traditions, fusing with the Logos philosophy of Philo, stirred Basilides (117), Valentinus (160), and others to form weird systems of divine emanations and personified "aeons" of the world. In Edessa Bardesanes (200) created literary Syriac by describing these aeons in prose and verse. In Gaul the Gnostic Marcus offered to reveal to women the secrets of their guardian angels; his revelations were flattering, and he accepted their persons as his reward.[38]

The greatest of the early heretics was not quite a Gnostic, but was influenced by their mythology. About 140 Marcion, a rich youth of Sinope, came to Rome vowing to complete Paul's work of divorcing Christianity from Judaism. The Christ of the Gospels, said Marcion, had described as his father a God of tenderness, forgiveness, and love; but the Yahveh of the Old Testament was a harsh god of unrelenting justice, tyranny, and war; this Yahveh could not be the father of the gentle Christ. What good god, asked Marcion, would have condemned all mankind to misery for eating an apple, or desiring knowledge, or loving woman? Yahveh exists, and is the creator of the world; but he made the flesh and bones of man from matter, and therefore left man's soul imprisoned in an evil frame. To release the soul of man a greater god sent his son to earth; Christ appeared,

---

* Thousands of Christians, including many who actually practice Christianity, interpret the disturbances of our time as the predicted portents of Christ's early return. Millions of Christians, non-Christians, and atheists still believe in an imminent earthly paradise where war and wickedness will cease. Historically the belief in heaven and the belief in utopia are like compensatory buckets in a well: when one goes down the other comes up. When the classic religions decayed, communistic agitation rose in Athens (430 B.C.), and revolution began in Rome (133 B.C.); when these movements failed, resurrection faiths succeeded, culminating in Christianity; when, in our eighteenth century, Christian belief weakened, communism reappeared. In this perspective the future of religion is secure.

already thirty years of age, in a phantasmal, unreal body, and by his death won for good men the privilege of a purely spiritual resurrection. The good, said Marcion, are those who, following Paul, renounce Yahveh and the Jewish Law, reject the Hebrew Scriptures, shun marriage and all sensual enjoyment, and overcome the flesh by a stern asceticism. To propagate these ideas Marcion issued a New Testament composed of Luke's Gospel and the letters of Paul. The Church excommunicated him, and returned to him the substantial sum that he had presented to it on coming to Rome.

While the Gnostic and Marcionite sects were spreading rapidly in both East and West, a new heresiarch appeared in Mysia. About 156 Montanus denounced the increasing worldliness of Christians and the growing autocracy of bishops in the Church; he demanded a return to primitive Christian simplicity and austerity, and a restored right of prophecy, or inspired speech, to the members of the congregations. Two women, Priscilla and Maximilla, took him at his word and fell into religious trances; and their utterances became the living oracles of the sect. Montanus himself prophesied with such eloquent ecstasy that his Phrygian followers—with the same religious enthusiasm that had once begotten Dionysus—hailed him as the Paraclete promised by Christ. He announced that the Kingdom of Heaven was at hand, and that the New Jerusalem of the Apocalypse would soon descend from heaven upon a neighboring plain. To the predestined spot he led so large a host that some towns were depopulated. As in early Christian days, marriage and parentage were neglected, goods were communistically shared, and an absorbed asceticism anxiously prepared the soul for Christ.[39] When, about 190, the Roman proconsul Antonius persecuted Christianity in Asia Minor, hundreds of Montanists, eager for paradise, crowded before his tribunal and asked for martyrdom. He could not accommodate them all; some he executed; but most of them he dismissed with the words: "Miserable creatures! If you wish to die are there not ropes and precipices?" [40] The Church banned Montanism as a heresy, and in the sixth century Justinian ordered the extinction of the sect. Some Montanists gathered in their churches, set fire to them, and let themselves be burned alive.[41]

Of minor heresies there was no end. The Encratites abstained from meat, wine. and sex; the Abstinents practiced self-mortification and condemned marriage as a sin; the Docetists taught that Christ's body was merely a phantom, not human flesh; the Theodotians considered him only a man; the Adoptionists and the followers of Paul of Samosata thought that he had been born a man, but had achieved divinity through moral perfection; the Modalists, Sabellians, and Monarchians recognized in the Father and the Son only one person, the Monophysites only one nature, the Monothelites only one will. The Church overcame them by its superior organization, its doctrinal tenacity, and its better understanding of the ways and needs of men.

In the third century a new danger rose in the East. At the coronation of Shapur I (242) a young Persian mystic, Mani of Ctesiphon, proclaimed himself a Messiah sent upon earth by the True God to reform the religious and moral life of mankind. Borrowing from Zoroastrianism, Mithraism, Judaism, and Gnosticism, Mani divided the world into rival realms of Darkness and Light; the earth belonged to the kingdom of Darkness, and Satan had created man. Nevertheless, the angels of the God of Light had surreptitiously introduced some elements of light into humanity—mind, intelligence, reason. Even woman, said Mani, has in her some sparks of light; but woman is Satan's masterpiece, his chief agent in tempting man to sin. If a man will refrain from sex, idolatry, and sorcery, and lead an ascetic life of vegetarianism and fasting, the elements of light in him can overcome his Satanic impulses, and lead him, like a kindly light, to salvation. After thirty years of successful preaching Mani was crucified at the suggestion of the Magian clergy, and his skin, stuffed with straw, was hung from one of Susa's gates. Martyrdoms enflamed the faith to wild enthusiasm; Manicheism spread into western Asia and north Africa, won Augustine for ten years, survived the persecutions of Diocletian and the conquests of Islam, and maintained a declining life for a thousand years till the coming of Genghis Khan.

The old religions still claimed a majority of the Empire's population. Judaism gathered its impoverished exiles into scattered synagogues, and poured its piety into its Talmuds. The Syrians continued to worship their Baals under Hellenistic names, and the Egyptian priests tended faithfully their zoological pantheon. Cybele, Isis, and Mithras retained their addicts till the close of the fourth century; under Aurelian a modified Mithraism captured the Roman state. Votive offerings to the classical divinities still came to the temples, initiates and candidates journeyed to Eleusis, and throughout the Empire aspiring citizens performed the motions of the imperial cult. But life had gone out of the classic creeds. They no longer aroused, except here and there, the warm devotion that makes a religion live. It was not that the Greeks and the Romans abandoned these faiths, once so lovely or austere; they abandoned rather the will to live, and by excessive family limitation, or physiological exhaustion, or devastating wars, so reduced their own number that the temples lost their cultivators step by step with the farms.

About the year 178, while Aurelius fought the Marcomanni on the Danube, paganism made a lusty attempt to defend itself against Christianity. We know of it only through Origen's book *Against Celsus,* and the quotations recklessly made there from Celsus' *True Word.* This second Celsus in our story was a gentleman of the world rather than a speculative philosopher; he felt that the civilization which he enjoyed was bound up with the old Roman faith; and he resolved to defend that faith by attacking the Christianity that was now its most challenging enemy. He made so intimate a study of the new religion that the learned Origen was astounded by his erudition. Celsus assailed the credibility of the Scriptures, the character of Yahveh, the importance of Christ's miracles, the incompatibility of Christ's death with his omnipotent divinity. He ridiculed the Christian belief in a final conflagration, the Last Judgment, and the resurrection of the body:

> It is silly to suppose that when God, like a cook, brings the fire, the rest of mankind will be roasted, and only the Christians will remain—not merely the living ones, but those who died long ago, rising from the earth with the identical flesh they had before. Really, it is the hope of worms! . . . It is only the simpletons, the ignoble, the senseless—slaves and women and children—whom Christians can persuade—wool-dressers, and cobblers and fullers, the most uneducated and common men, whoever is a sinner . . . or a godforsaken fool.[42]

Celsus was alarmed by the spread of Christianity, by its scornful hostility to paganism, military service, and the state; how was the Empire to protect itself from the barbarians prowling on every frontier if its inhabitants succumbed to so pacifistic a philosophy? A good citizen, he thought, should conform to the religion of his country and his time without public criticism of its absurdities; these did not much matter; what counted was a unifying faith supporting moral character and civic loyalty. Then, forgetting the insults he had heaped upon them, he appealed to the Christians to come back to the old gods, to worship the guardian *genius* of the emperor, and to join in the defense of the imperiled state. No one paid much attention to him; pagan literature does not mention him; he would have been quite forgotten had not Origen undertaken to refute him. Constantine was wiser than Celsus, and knew that a dead faith could not salvage Rome.

III. PLOTINUS

Moreover, Celsus was out of step with his time; he asked men to behave like gentlemen skeptics when they were withdrawing from a society that enslaved so many of them into a mystic world that made every man a god. That consciousness of supersensible powers which is the foundation of religion was prevailing universally over the materialism and determinism of a prouder age. Philosophy was abandoning the interpretation of that sense experience which is the realm of science, and was devoting itself to a study of the unseen world. Neo-Pythagoreans and Neoplatonists developed Pythagoras' theory of transmigration, and Plato's contemplation of the Divine Ideas, into an asceticism that sought to sharpen spiritual perception by starving the physical senses, and to reclimb by self-purification the steps by which the soul had been degraded from heaven into man.

Plotinus was the culmination of this mystic theosophy. Born at Lycopolis in 203, he was a Coptic Egyptian with a Roman name and a Greek education. In his twenty-eighth year he discovered philosophy, passed unsatisfied from teacher to teacher, and found at last, in Alexandria, the man he sought. Ammonius Saccas, a Christian converted to paganism, was attempting to reconcile Christianity and Platonism, as his pupil Origen would do. After studying under Ammonius for ten years, Plotinus joined a Persia-bound army in the hope of learning the wisdom of the Magi and the Brahmans at first hand. He reached Mesopotamia, turned back to Antioch, went to Rome (244), and remained there till his death. His school of philosophy became so fashionable that the Emperor Gallienus made him a court favorite, and agreed to help him establish in Campania an ideal Platonopolis, to be governed on the principles of the *Republic*. Gallienus later withdrew his consent, perhaps to spare Plotinus an ignominious failure.

Plotinus restored the repute of philosophy by living like a saint amid the luxuries of Rome. He had no care for his body; indeed, says Porphyry, "he was ashamed that his soul had a body." [43] He refused to sit for his portrait, on the ground that his body was the least important part of him—a hint to art to seek the soul. He ate no meat and little bread, was simple in his habits, kindly in his ways. He avoided all sexual relations, but did not condemn them. His modesty befitted a man who saw the part in the perspective of the whole. When Origen attended his class, Plotinus blushed and wished to end his lecture, saying, "The zest dies down when the speaker feels that his hearers have nothing to learn from him." [44] He was not an eloquent speaker, but his devotion to his subject, and his absorbed sincerity, were good substitutes for oratory. Reluctantly, and only late in life, he put his doctrines into writing. He never revised his first draft, and despite Porphyry's editing, the *Enneads* remain among the most disorderly and difficult works in the history of philosophy.*

Plotinus was an idealist who graciously recognized the existence of matter. But matter by itself, he argued, is only the formless possibility of form. Every form that matter takes is given it by its inward energy or soul (*psyche*). Nature is the total of energy or soul, producing the totality of forms in the world. The lower reality does not produce the higher; the higher being, soul, produces the lower—embodied form. The growth of the individual man from his beginnings in the womb, through the slow formation of organ after organ to full maturity is the work of the psyche

---

* Porphyry arranged the fifty-four treatises into groups of nine (*ennea*) on the ground that in Pythagoras' theory nine is the perfect number, since it is the square of three, which is the trinity of complete harmony.[45]

or vital principle within him; the body is gradually molded by the longings and directives of the soul. Everything has soul—an inward energy creating outward form. Matter is evil only insofar as it has not received mature form; it is an arrested development; and evil is the possibility of good.

We know matter only through idea—through sensation, perception, thought; what we call matter is (as Hume would say) only a bundle of ideas; at most it is an elusive hypothetical something pressing against our nerve ends (Mill's "permanent possibility of sensation"). Ideas are not material; the notion of extension in space is obviously inapplicable to them. The capacity to have and use ideas is reason (*nous*); this is the peak of the human triad of body, soul, and mind. Reason is determined insofar as it depends upon sensation; it is free insofar as it is the highest form of the creative, molding soul.

The body is both the organ and the prison of the soul. The soul knows that it is a higher kind of reality than the body; it feels its kinship with some vaster soul, some cosmic creative life and power; and in the perfection of thought it aspires to join again that supreme spiritual reality from which it appears to have fallen in some primeval catastrophe and disgrace. Plotinus here surrenders discursively to the Gnosticism that he professes to reject, and describes the descent of the soul through various levels from heaven to corporeal man; generally he prefers the Hindu notion that the soul transmigrates from lower to higher, or from higher to lower, forms of life according to its virtues and vices in each incarnation. Sometimes he is playfully Pythagorean: those who have loved music too much will become songbirds in their next avatar, and overspeculative philosophers will be transformed into eagles.[46] The more developed the soul is the more persistently it seeks its divine source, like a child strayed from its parent, or a wanderer longing for home. If it is capable of virtue, or true love, or devotion to the Muses, or patient philosophy, it will find the ladder down which it came, and will climb it to its God. Let the soul, then, purify itself, let it desire the unseen essence passionately, let it lose the world in meditation; suddenly, perhaps in some moment when all the noise of the senses is stilled, and matter ceases to pound on the gates of mind, the soul will feel itself absorbed in the ocean of being, the spiritual and final reality. ("Sometimes," wrote Thoreau, idly drifting on Walden Pond, "I ceased to live, and began to be.") "When this takes place," says Plotinus,

> The soul will see divinity as far as it is lawful. . . . And she will see herself illuminated, full of intellectual light; or, rather, she will perceive herself to be a pure light, unburdened, agile, and becoming god.[47]

But what is God? "He" too is a triad—of unity (*hen*), reason (*nous*), and soul (*psyche*). "Beyond Being there is the One": [48] through the seeming chaos of mundane multiplicity runs a unifying life. We know almost nothing of it except its existence; any positive adjective or prejudiced pronoun applied to it would be an unwarrantable limitation; we may only call it One and First, and Good as the object of our supreme desire. Emanating from this Unity is the World Reason, corresponding to Plato's Ideas, the formative models and ruling laws of things; they are, so to speak, the thoughts of God, the Reason in the One, the order and rationality of the world. Since these Ideas persist while matter is a kaleidoscope of passing shapes, they are the only true or enduring reality. But Unity and Reason, though they hold the universe together, do not create it; this function is performed by the third aspect of the godhead—the vitalizing principle that fills all things and gives them their power and predestined form. Everything, from atoms to planets, has an activating soul, which is itself a part of the World-Soul; every *Atman* is *Brahman*. The individual soul is eternal only as vitality or energy, not as a distinct character. [49] Immortality is not the survival of personality; it is the absorption of the soul in deathless things. [50]

Virtue is the movement of the soul toward God. Beauty is not mere harmony and proportion, as Plato and Aristotle thought, but the living soul or unseen divinity in things; it is the predominance of soul over body, of form over matter, of reason over things; and art is the translation of this rational or spiritual beauty into another medium. The soul can be trained to rise from the pursuit of beauty in material or human forms to seeking it in the hidden soul in Nature and her laws, in science and the subtle order that it reveals, finally in the divine Unity that gathers all things, even striving and conflicting things, into a sublime and marvelous harmony. [51] In the end beauty and virtue are one—the unity and co-operation of the part with the whole.

> Withdraw into yourself and look. And if you do not find yourself beautiful, yet act as does the creator of a statue . . . he cuts away here, he smooths there, he makes this line lighter, the other purer, until a lovely face has grown upon his work. So do you also: cut away all that is excessive, straighten all that is crooked . . . and never cease chiseling your statue until . . . you see the perfect goodness established in the stainless shrine. [52]

We feel in this philosophy the same spiritual atmosphere as in contemporary Christianity—the withdrawal of tender minds from civic interest to religion, a flight from the state to God. It was no accident that Plotinus and Origen were fellow pupils and friends, and that Clement developed a

Christian Platonism at Alexandria. Plotinus is the last of the great pagan philosophers; and like Epictetus and Aurelius, he is a Christian without Christ. Christianity accepted nearly every line of him, and many a page of Augustine echoes the ecstasy of the supreme mystic. Through Philo, John, Plotinus, and Augustine, Plato conquered Aristotle, and entered into the profoundest theology of the Church. The gap between philosophy and religion was closing, and reason for a thousand years consented to be the handmaiden of theology.

IV. THE DEFENDERS OF THE FAITH

The Church now won to its support some of the finest minds in the Empire. Ignatius, Bishop of Antioch, began the powerful dynasty of the post-apostolic "Fathers," who gave a philosophy to Christianity, and overwhelmed its enemies with argument. Condemned to be thrown to the beasts for refusing to abjure his faith (108), Justin composed on his way to Rome several letters whose hot devotion reveals the spirit in which Christians could go to their death:

> I give injunctions to all men that I am dying willingly for God's sake, if you do not hinder it. I beseech you, be not an unseasonable kindness to me. Suffer me to be eaten by the beasts, through whom I can attain to God. . . . Rather entice the wild beasts that they may become my tomb, and leave no trace of my body, that when I fall asleep I be not burdensome to any. . . . I long for the beasts that are prepared for me. . . . Let there come upon me fire and cross [crucifixion], struggles with wild beasts, cutting and tearing asunder, rackings of bones, mangling of limbs, crushing of my whole body, and cruel tortures of the devil, if so I may attain to Jesus Christ! [53]

Quadratus, Athenagoras, and many others wrote "Apologies" for Christianity, usually addressed to the emperor. Minucius Felix, in an almost Ciceronian dialogue, allowed his Caecilius to defend paganism ably, but made his Octavius answer him so courteously that Caecilius was almost persuaded to be a Christian. Justin of Samaria, coming to Rome in the reign of Antoninus, opened there a school of Christian philosophy, and, in two eloquent "Apologies," sought to convince the Emperor, and "Verissimus the Philosopher," that Christians were loyal citizens, paid their taxes promptly, and might, under friendly treatment, become a valuable support to the state. For some years he taught unmolested; but the sharpness of his tongue made him enemies, and in 166 a rival philosopher prodded the authorities to arrest him and six of his followers, and put them all to death. Twenty years later Irenaeus, Bishop of Lyons, struck a powerful blow for the unity of the Church in his *Adversus Haereses,* a blast at all heretics. The only way of preventing Christianity from disintegrating into a thousand sects, said Irenaeus, was for all Christians to accept humbly one doctrinal authority—the decrees of the episcopal councils of the Church.

The doughtiest fighter for Christianity in this period was Quintus Septimius Tertullianus of Carthage. Born there about 160, the son of a Roman centurion, he studied rhetoric in the same school that trained Apuleius; then for years he practiced law at Rome. Midway in life he was converted to Christianity, married a Christian, renounced all pagan pleasures, and (says Jerome) was ordained a priest. All the arts and tricks that he had learned from rhetoric and law were now put at the service of Christian apologetics, enhanced by a convert's ardor. Greek Christianity was theological, metaphysical, mystical; Tertullian made Latin Christianity ethical, juristic, practical. He had the vigor and virulence of Cicero, the satirical scurrility of Juvenal, and sometimes he could rival Tacitus in concentrating acid in a phrase. Irenaeus had written in Greek; with Minucius and Tertullian Christian literature in the West became Latin, and Latin literature became Christian.

In the year 197, while Roman magistrates in Carthage were trying Christians on charges of disloyalty, Tertullian addressed to an imaginary court the most eloquent of his works—the *Apologeticus.* He assured the Romans that Christians "are always praying for all emperors, for . . . a safe dynasty, brave armies, a faithful Senate, and a quiet world." [54] He extolled the grandeur of monotheism, and found premonitions of it in pre-Christian writers. *O testimonium animae naturaliter Christianae!* he cried in a happy phrase—"Behold the witness of the soul, by its very nature Christian!" [55] A year later, passing with strange celerity from persuasive defense to ferocious attack, he issued *De Spectaculis,* a scornful description of the Roman theaters as citadels of obscenity, and of the amphitheaters as the acme of man's inhumanity to man. And he concluded with a bitter threat:

> Other spectacles will come—that last eternal Day of Judgment
> . . . when all this old world and its generations shall be consumed in
> one fire. How vast the spectacle will be on that day! How I shall
> marvel, laugh, rejoice, and exult, seeing so many kings—supposedly
> received into heaven—groaning in the depths of darkness!—and the
> magistrates who persecuted the name of Jesus melting in fiercer flames
> than they ever kindled . . . against the Christians!—sages and phi-
> losophers blushing before their disciples as they blaze together! . . .
> and tragic actors now more than ever vocal in their own tragedy, and

players lither of limb by far in the fire, and charioteers burning red
on the wheel of flame! [56]

Such unhealthy intensity of imagination does not make for orthodoxy.
As Tertullian aged, the same energy that in his youth had courted pleasure
now turned into a fierce denunciation of every consolation but those of
faith and hope. He addressed woman in the coarsest terms as "the gate by
which the demon enters," and told her that "it is on your account that Jesus
Christ died." [57] Once he loved philosophy, and had written works like *De
Anima*, applying Stoic metaphysics to Christianity; now he renounced all
reasoning independent of revelation, and rejoiced in the incredibility of his
creed. "God's son died: it is believable precisely because it is absurd
[*ineptum*]. He was buried and rose again: it is certain because it is impossible." [58] Sinking into a morose puritanism, Tertullian in his fifty-eighth
year rejected the orthodox Church as too sullied with worldly ways, and
embraced Montanism as a more outright application of the teachings of
Christ. He condemned all Christians who became soldiers, artists, or state
officials; all parents who did not veil their daughters; all bishops who restored
repentant sinners to communion; finally he called the pope *pastor moec-
horum*—"shepherd of adulterers." [59]

Despite him the Church prospered in Africa. Able and devoted bishops
like Cyprian made the diocese of Carthage almost as rich and influential as
Rome's. In Egypt the growth of the Church was slower, and its early stages
are lost to history; suddenly, late in the second century, we hear of a
"Catechetical School" in Alexandria, which wedded Christianity to Greek
philosophy, and produced two major fathers of the Church. Both Clement
and Origen were well versed in pagan literature, and loved it after their
own fashion; if their spirit had prevailed there would have been a less
destructive break between classical culture and Christianity.

When Origenes Adamantius was seventeen (202) his father was arrested
as a Christian, and condemned to death. The boy wished to join him in
prison and martyrdom; his mother, failing to deter him by other means, hid
all his clothes. Origen sent his father letters of encouragement: "Take
heed," he bade him, "not to change your mind on our account."[60] The
father was beheaded, and the youth was left to care for the mother and
six young children. Inspired to greater piety by the many martyrdoms he
saw, he adopted the ascetic life. He fasted much, slept little and on bare
ground, wore no shoes, and subjected himself to cold and nakedness; finally,
in rigorous interpretation of Matthew xix, 12, he emasculated himself.* In

* "As it was Origen's general practice to allegorize Scripture," says Gibbon, "it seems unfortunate that, in this instance only, he should have adopted the literal sense." [61]

203 he succeeded Clement as head of the Catechetical School. Though he was only eighteen, his learning and eloquence drew many students, pagan as well as Christian, and his fame spread throughout the Christian world.

Some ancients reckoned his "books" at 6000; many, of course, were brief brochures; even so Jerome asked, "Which of us can read all that he has written?" [62] In love with the Bible, which through boyhood memorizing had become part of his mind, Origen spent twenty years, and employed a corps of stenographers and copyists, collating in parallel columns the Hebrew text of the Old Testament, a Greek transliteration of that text, and Greek translations of it by the Septuagint, Aquila, Symmachus, and Theodotion.* By comparing these diverse renderings, and using his knowledge of Hebrew, Origen offered to the Church a corrected Septuagint. Insatiate, he added commentaries, sometimes of great length, on every book in the Bible. In *Peri archon*, "First Principles," he achieved the first orderly and philosophical exposition of Christian doctrine. In a "Miscellany" (*Stromateis*) he undertook to demonstrate all Christian dogmas from the writings of the pagan philosophers. To lighten his task he availed himself of that allegorical method by which pagan philosophers had made Homer accord with reason, and Philo had reconciled Judaism with Greek philosophy. The literal meaning of Scripture, argued Origen, overlay two deeper layers of meaning— the moral and the spiritual—to which only the esoteric and educated few could penetrate. He questioned the truth of Genesis as literally understood: he explained away as symbols the unpleasant aspects of Yahveh's dealings with Israel; and he dismissed as legends such stories as that of Satan taking Jesus up to a high mountain and offering him the kingdoms of the world.[63] Sometimes, he suggested, scriptural narratives were invented in order to convey some spiritual truth.[64] "What man of sense," he asked,

> will suppose that the first and the second and the third day, and the evening and the morning, existed without a sun or moon or stars? Who is so foolish as to believe that God, like a husbandman, planted a garden in Eden, and placed in it a tree of life . . . so that one who tasted of the fruit obtained life? [65]

As Origen proceeds it becomes apparent that he is a Stoic, a Neo-Pythagorean, a Platonist, and a Gnostic, who is nonetheless resolved to be a Christian. It would have been too much to ask of a man that he should abandon the faith for which he had edited a thousand volumes and flung away his manhood. Like Plotinus he had studied under Ammonius Saccas, and sometimes it is hard to distinguish his philosophy from theirs. God, in Origen, is

---

* Of this *Hexapla* (sixfold) only fragments remain. Lost, too, is the *Tetrapla*, containing the four Greek translations.

not Yahveh, he is the First Principle of all things. Christ is not the human figure described in the New Testament, he is the Logos or Reason who organizes the world; as such he was created by God the Father, and is subordinate to him.[66] In Origen, as in Plotinus, the soul passes through a succession of stages and embodiments before entering the body; and after death it will pass through a like succession before arriving at God. Even the purest souls will suffer for a while in Purgatory; but in the end all souls will be saved. After the "final conflagration" there will be another world with its long history, and then another, and another. . . . Each will improve on the preceding, and the whole vast sequence will slowly work out the design of God.[67]

We cannot wonder that Demetrius, Bishop of Alexandria, looked with some doubt upon the brilliant philosopher who adorned his diocese and corresponded with emperors. He refused to ordain Origen to the priesthood, on the ground that emasculation disqualified him. But while Origen was traveling in the Near East two Palestinian bishops ordained him. Demetrius protested that this infringed his rights; he convened a synod of his clergy; it annulled Origen's ordination, and banished him from Alexandria. Origen removed to Caesarea, and continued his work as a teacher. There he wrote his famous defense of Christianity *Contra Celsum* (248). With magnanimous spirit he admitted the force of Celsus' arguments; but he replied that for every difficulty and improbability in Christian doctrine there were worse incredibilities in paganism. He concluded not that both were absurd, but that the Christian faith offered a nobler way of life than could possibly come from a dying and idolatrous creed.

In 250 the Decian persecution reached Caesarea. Origen, now sixty-five, was arrested, stretched on the rack, loaded with chains and an iron collar, and kept in prison for many days. But death caught up with Decius first, and Origen was released. He lived only three years more; torture had fatally injured a body already weakened by unremitting asceticism. He died as poor as when he had begun to teach, and the most famous Christian of his time. As his heresies ceased to be the secret of a few scholars, the Church found it necessary to disown him; Pope Anastasius condemned his "blasphemous opinions" in 400, and in 553 the Council of Constantinople pronounced him anathema. Nevertheless, nearly every later Christian savant for centuries learned from him, and depended upon his work; and his defense of Christianity impressed pagan thinkers as no "apology" had done before him. With him Christianity ceased to be only a comforting faith; it became a full-fledged philosophy, buttressed with Scripture but proudly resting on reason.

V. THE ORGANIZATION OF AUTHORITY

The Church might be excused for condemning Origen: his principle of allegorical interpretation not only made it possible to prove anything, but at one blow it did away with the narratives of Scripture and the earthly life of Christ; and it restored individual judgment precisely while proposing to defend the faith. Faced with the hostility of a powerful government, the Church felt the need of unity; it could not safely allow itself to be divided into a hundred feeble parts by every wind of intellect, by disloyal heretics, ecstatic prophets, or brilliant sons. Celsus himself had sarcastically observed that Christians were "split up into ever so many factions, each individual desiring to have his own party." [68] About 187 Irenaeus listed twenty varieties of Christianity; about 384 Epiphanius counted eighty. At every point foreign ideas were creeping into Christian belief, and Christian believers were deserting to novel sects. The Church felt that its experimental youth was ending, its maturity was near; it must now define its terms and proclaim the conditions of its membership. Three difficult steps were necessary: the formation of a scriptural canon, the determination of doctrine, and the organization of authority.

The literature of Christianity in the second century abounded in gospels, epistles, apocalypses, and "acts." Christians differed widely in accepting or rejecting these as authoritative expressions of the Christian creed. The Western churches accepted the Book of Revelation, the Eastern churches generally rejected it; these accepted the Gospel according to the Hebrews and the Epistles of James, the Western churches discarded them. Clement of Alexandria quotes as sacred scripture a late first-century treatise, The Teaching of the Twelve Apostles. Marcion's publication of a New Testament forced the hand of the Church. We do not know when the books of our present New Testament were determined as canonical—i.e., as authentic and inspired; we can only say that a Latin fragment discovered by Muratori in 1740, named after him, and generally assigned to *ca.* 180, assumes that the canon had by that time been fixed.

Ecclesiastical councils or synods met with increasing frequency in the second century. In the third they were limited to bishops; and by the close of that century they were recognized as the final arbiters of "Catholic"—i.e., universal—Christian belief. Orthodoxy survived heresy because it satisfied the need for a definite creed that could moderate dispute and quiet doubt, and because it was supported by the power of the Church.

The problem of organization lay in determining the center of that power. After the weakening of the mother church at Jerusalem, the individual congregations, unless established or protected by other communities, appear to have exercised an independent authority. The church of Rome, however, claimed to have been founded by Peter, and quoted Jesus as saying: "Thou art Peter" (Heb. *Cephas*, Gk. *Petros*), "and upon this rock" (Heb. *cephas*, Gk. *petra*) "I will build my church, and the gates of Hell shall not prevail against it. I will give you the keys of the Kingdom of Heaven; and whatsoever thou shalt bind on earth shall be bound in heaven; and whatsoever thou shalt loose on earth shall be loosed in heaven." [69] The passage has been challenged as an interpolation, and as a pun to which only Shakespeare would stoop; but the likelihood remains that Peter, if he did not establish the Christian colony in Rome, preached to it, and appointed its bishop.[70] Irenaeus (187) wrote that Peter "committed to the hands of Linus the office of the episcopate"; Tertullian (200) confirmed this tradition; and Cyprian (252), bishop of Rome's great rival, Carthage, urged all Christians to accept the primacy of the Roman see.[71]

The earliest occupants of "Peter's throne" left no mark upon history. The third, Pope * Clement, stands out as the author of an extant letter written about 96 to the church of Corinth, appealing to its members to maintain harmony and order; [72] here, only a generation after Peter's death, the bishop of Rome speaks with authority to the Christians of a distant congregation. The other bishops, while acknowledging the "primacy"of the Roman bishop as the lineal successor of Peter, repeatedly challenged his power to overrule their own decisions. The Eastern churches celebrated Easter on the fourteenth day of the Jewish month of Nisan, whatever day of the week this might be; the Western churches postponed the feast to the following Sunday. Polycarp, Bishop of Smyrna, visiting Rome about 156, tried and failed to persuade Anicetus, Bishop of Rome, to have the Eastern date observed in the West; and on his return he rejected the Pope's suggestion that the Eastern churches should accept the Western date. Pope Victor (190) rephrased Anicetus' request as a command; the bishops of Palestine obeyed, those of Asia Minor refused. Victor sent out letters to the Christian congregations, excommunicating the recalcitrant churches; many bishops, even in the West, protested against so severe a measure, and apparently Victor did not insist.

His successor Zephyrinus (202-18) was "a simple and unlettered man." [73] To aid him in administering the spreading episcopate of Rome, Zephyrinus raised to the archdeaconate a man whose intelligence was less questioned than his morals. Callistus, said his enemies, had begun his career as a slave, had become a banker, had embezzled the funds deposited with him, had been sentenced to hard labor, had been released, had started a riot in a synagogue, had been condemned to the mines of Sardinia, had escaped by having his name surreptitiously inserted into a list of pardoned prisoners, and had then lived for ten years at Antium in painful peace. When Zephyrinus placed him in charge of the papal cemetery he transferred it to the Via Appia, in the catacomb that bears his name. When Zephyrinus died, and Callistus was chosen pope, Hippolytus and some

---

* The term *papa*, "father," which became in English *pope*, was applied in the first three centuries to any Christian bishop.

other priests denounced him as unfit, and set up a rival church and papacy (218). Doctrinal differences accentuated the schism: Callistus believed in readmitting to the Church those who, after baptism, had committed a mortal sin (adultery, murder, apostasy), and who professed their penitence. Hippolytus considered such lenience ruinous, and wrote a *Refutation of All Heresies,* with special attention to this one. Callistus excommunicated him, gave the Church a competent administration, and vigorously asserted the supreme authority of the Roman see over all Christendom.

The schism of Hippolytus ended in 235; but under Pope Cornelius (251-53) his heresy was revived by two priests—Novatus at Carthage and Novatian at Rome—who set up schismatic churches dedicated to the unrelenting exclusion of postbaptismal sinners. The Council of Carthage under Cyprian, and the Council of Rome under Cornelius, excommunicated both groups. Cyprian's appeal for Cornelius' support strengthened the papacy; but when Pope Stephen I (254-57) ruled that converts from heretical sects need not be rebaptized, Cyprian led a synod of African bishops in rejecting the decree. Stephen, like another Cato, excommunicated them in an ecclesiastical Punic War; his providentially early death allowed the quarrel to lapse, and averted the secession of the powerful African Church.

Despite overreachings and setbacks, the Roman see increased its power with almost every decade. Its wealth and ecumenical charities exalted its prestige; it was consulted by the Christian world on every issue of gravity; it took the initiative in repudiating and combating heresies, and in defining the canon of the Scriptures. It was deficient in scholars, and could not boast a Tertullian, an Origen, or a Cyprian; it gave its attention to organization rather than to theory; it built and governed and let others write and talk. Cyprian rebelled; but it was he who, in his *De Catholicae Ecclesiae Unitate,* acclaimed the see or seat of Peter (*cathedra Petri*) as the center and summit of Christendom, and proclaimed to the world those principles of solidarity, unanimity, and persistency which have been the essence and mainstay of the Catholic Church.[74] By the middle of the third century the position and resources of the papacy were so strong that Decius vowed he would rather have a rival emperor at Rome than a pope.[75] The capital of the Empire naturally became the capital of the Church.

As Judea had given Christianity ethics, and Greece had given it theology, so now Rome gave it organization; all these, with a dozen absorbed and rival faiths, entered into the Christian synthesis. It was not merely that the Church took over some religious customs and forms common in pre-Christian Rome—the stole and other vestments of pagan priests, the use of incense and holy water in purifications, the burning of candles and an everlasting light before the altar, the worship of the saints, the architecture of the basilica, the law of Rome as a basis for canon law, the title of *Pontifex Maximus* for the Supreme Pontiff, and, in the fourth century, the Latin language as the noble and enduring vehicle of Catholic ritual. The Roman gift was above all a vast framework of government, which, as secular authority failed, became the structure of ecclesiastical rule. Soon the bishops, rather than the Roman prefects, would be the source of order and the seat of power in the cities; the metropolitans, or archbishops, would support, if not supplant, the provincial governors; and the synod of bishops would succeed the provincial assembly. The Roman Church followed in the footsteps of the Roman state; it conquered the provinces, beautified the capital, and established discipline and unity from frontier to frontier. Rome died in giving birth to the Church; the Church matured by inheriting and accepting the responsibilities of Rome.

CHAPTER XXIX

The Collapse of the Empire

A.D. 193-305

I. A SEMITIC DYNASTY

ON January 1, 193, a few hours after the assassination of Commodus, the Senate met in a transport of happiness, and chose as emperor one of its most respected members, whose just administration as prefect of the city had continued the finest traditions of the Antonines. Pertinax accepted with reluctance a dignity so exalted that any fall from it must be fatal. He "demeaned himself as an ordinary man," says Herodian,[1] attended the lectures of the philosophers, encouraged literature, replenished the treasury, reduced taxes, and auctioned off the gold and silver, the embroideries and silks and beautiful slaves, wherewith Commodus had filled the imperial palace; "in fact, he did everything," says Dio Cassius, "that a good emperor should do." [2] The freedmen who had lost their perquisites through his economy conspired with the Praetorian Guard, which disliked his restoration of discipline. On March 28, 300 soldiers forced their way into the palace, struck him down, and carried his head upon a spear to their camp. The people and the Senate mourned and hid.

The leaders of the Guard announced that they would bestow the crown upon that Roman who should offer them the largest donative. Didius Julianus was persuaded by his wife and daughter to interrupt his meal and enter his bid. Proceeding to the camp, he found a rival offering 5000 drachmas ($3000) to each soldier in return for the throne. The agents of the Guard passed from one millionaire to the other, encouraging higher bids; when Julianus promised each man 6250 drachmas the Guard declared him emperor.

Aroused by this crowning indignity, the people of Rome appealed to the legions in Britain, Syria, and Pannonia to come and depose Julianus. The legions, angered by exclusion from the donative, hailed their respective generals with the imperial title, and marched toward Rome. The Pannonian commander, Lucius Septimius Severus Geta, gained the Principate by boldness, expedition, and bribery. He pledged himself to give each soldier 12,000 drachmas upon his accession; he led them from the Danube to within seventy miles of Rome in a month; he won over to himself the troops sent to halt him, and subdued the Praetorians by offering them pardon in return for the surrender of their leaders. He violated precedent by entering the capital with all his troops in full armor, but he himself appeased tradition by wearing civilian dress. A tribune found Julianus in tears and terror in the palace, led him into a bathroom, and beheaded him (June 2, 193).

Africa, which was at this time providing Christianity with its ablest defenders, gave birth (146) and early schooling to Septimius. Brought up in a family of Punic-speaking Phoenicians, he studied literature and philosophy in Athens and practiced law in Rome. Despite the Semitic accent of his Latin, he was among the best-educated Romans of his time, and liked to surround himself with poets and philosophers. But he did not allow philosophy to impede his wars, or poetry to soften his character. He was a man of handsome features, strong physique, and simple dress, hardy in hardship, clever in strategy, fearless in battle, ruthless in victory. He conversed with wit, judged with penetration, lied without scruple, loved money more than honor, and governed with cruelty and competence.[3]

The Senate had made the mistake of declaring for his rival Albinus; Septimius, surrounded with 600 guards, persuaded it to confirm his own accession; then he put scores of senators to death, and confiscated so many aristocratic estates that he became landlord to half the peninsula. The decimated Senate was replenished by imperial nomination with new members chiefly from the monarchical East. The great lawyers of the age—Papinian, Paulus, Ulpian—accumulated arguments in defense of absolute power. Septimius ignored the Senate except when he sent it commands; he assumed full control of the various treasuries, based his rule frankly upon the army, and made the Principate an hereditary military monarchy. The army was increased in size; the pay of the soldiers was raised, and became an exhausting drain upon the public purse. Military service was made compulsory, but was forbidden to the inhabitants of Italy; henceforth provincial legions would choose emperors for a Rome that had lost the fortitude to rule.

This realistic warrior believed in astrology, and excelled in the interpretation of portents and dreams. When, six years before his accession, his first wife died, he offered his hand to a rich Syrian whose horoscope had pledged her a throne. Julia Domna was the daughter of a rich priest of the god Elagabal at Emesa. There, long since, a meteorite had fallen, had been enshrined in a gaudy temple, and was worshiped as the symbol, if not the embodiment, of the deity. Julia came, bore Septimius two sons, Caracalla and Geta, and rose to her promised throne. She was too beautiful to be monogamous, but Septimius was too busy to be jealous. She gathered around her a salon of literary men, patronized the arts, and persuaded Philostratus to write and adorn the life of Apollonius of Tyana. Her strong character and influence accelerated that orientation of the monarchy toward Eastern ways which culminated morally under Elagabalus, and politically under Diocletian.

Of his eighteen years as emperor Septimius gave twelve to war. He destroyed his rivals in swift and savage campaigns; he razed Byzantium after a four years' siege, thereby lowering a barrier to the spreading Goths; he invaded Parthia, took Ctesiphon, annexed Mesopotamia, and hastened the fall of the Arsacid kings. In his old age, suffering from gout but fretful lest his army deteriorate through five years of peace, he led an expedition into Caledonia. After expensive victories against the Scots he withdrew into Britain, and retired to York to die (211). "I have been everything," he said, "and it is worth nothing." [4] Caracalla, says Herodian, "was much vexed that his father's decease was so lingering . . . and solicited the physicians to dispatch the old man by any means that might come to hand." [5] Septimius had blamed Aurelius for yielding the Empire to Commodus; now he bequeathed it to Caracalla and Geta, with cynical advice: "Make your soldiers rich, and do not bother about anything else." [6] He was the last emperor, for eighty years, who died in bed.

Caracalla,* like Commodus, seemed made to prove that a man's quota of energy seldom allows him to be great in both his life and his seed. Attractive and obedient in boyhood, he became in manhood a barbarian infatuated with hunting and war. He captured wild boars, fought a lion singlehanded, kept lions always near him in his palace, and had one as occasional table companion and bedfellow.[7] He particularly enjoyed the company of gladiators and soldiers, and would keep senators cooling their heels in his antechambers while he prepared food and drink for his companions. Unwilling to share the imperial power with his brother, he had Geta assassinated in 212; the youth was slaughtered in his mother's arms, and covered her garments with his blood. We are told that Caracalla condemned to execution 20,000 of Geta's following, many citizens, and four Vestal Virgins whom he accused of adultery.[8] When the army murmured at the killing of Geta, he silenced it with a donative equal to all the sums that Septimius had gathered into all the treasuries. He favored the soldiers and the poor against the business classes and the aristocracy; possibly the stories we read about him in Dio Cassius are a senator's revenge. Anxious to raise more revenue, he doubled the inheritance tax to ten per cent; and noting that the tax applied only to Roman citizens, he extended the Roman franchise to all free male

* He called himself so from the long Gallic tunic that he wore; his real name was Bassianius; as emperor he styled himself Marcus Aurelius Antoninus Caracalla.

adults in the Empire (212); they achieved citizenship precisely when it brought a maximum of obligations and a minimum of power. He added to the adornment of Rome an arch to Septimius Severus, which still stands, and public baths whose gigantic ruins attest their ancient grandeur. But for the most part he left the civil government to his mother, and absorbed himself in campaigns.

He had made Julia Domna secretary both *a libellis* and *ab epistulis*—of petitions and correspondence. She joined or replaced him in greeting high members of the state or foreign dignitaries. Gossip whispered that she controlled him by incestuous means; the wits of Alexandria maddened him by referring to her and him as Jocasta and Oedipus. Partly in revenge against these insults, partly because he feared that Egypt might revolt while he was fighting Parthia, he visited the city and superintended (we are assured) the massacre of all Alexandrians capable of bearing arms.[9]

Nevertheless, the founder of Alexandria was his model and envy. He organized 16,000 troops into what he called "Alexander's phalanx," equipped them with ancient Macedonian arms, and dreamed of subduing Parthia as Alexander had conquered Persia. He tried hard to be a good soldier, sharing the food and toil and marches of his army, helping it to dig ditches and build bridges, bearing himself bravely in action, and often challenging the enemy to single combat. But his men were not as eager for the Parthian campaign as he was; they loved spoils more ardently than battle; and at Carrhae, where Crassus had been defeated, they stabbed him to death (217). Macrinus, prefect of the Guard, acclaimed himself emperor, and ordered the reluctant Senate to make Caracalla a god. Julia Domna, banished to Antioch, and bereft, within six years, of empire, husband, and sons, refused food until she died.[10]

She had a sister, Julia Maesa, as capable as herself. Returning to Emesa, this second Julia found there two promising grandsons. One, by her daughter Julia Soaemias, was a young priest of Baal; his name was Varius Avitus, and would be Elagabalus—"the creative god." * The other, by Maesa's daughter Julia Mamaea, was a boy of ten called Alexianus, and would be Alexander Severus. Though Varius was the son of Varius Marcellus, Maesa spread the rumor that he was the natural son of Caracalla, and gave him the name Bassianus; the Empire was worth her daughter's reputation, and Marcellus was dead. The Roman soldiers in Syria were already half won to Syrian cults, and felt a pious respect for the fourteen-year-old priest; moreover, Maesa suggested that if they would make Elagabalus emperor she would distribute a substantial donative among them. The soldiers were convinced,

---

* Wrongly transformed by Latin writers into Heliogabalus—"the sun-god."

and complied. Maesa's gold brought over to her cause the army that Macrinus sent against them. When Macrinus himself appeared with a substantial force, the Syrian mercenaries wavered; but Maesa and Soaemias sprang from their chariots, and led the softened army to victory. The men of Syria were women, and the women were men.

In the spring of 219 Elagabalus entered Rome dressed in robes of purple silk embroidered with gold, his cheeks stained with vermilion, his eyes artificially brightened, costly bracelets on his arms, a string of pearls around his neck, a jeweled crown on his pretty head. Beside him his grandmother and his mother rode in state. On his first appearance in the Senate he demanded that his mother should be allowed to sit beside him and attend the deliberations. Soaemias had the sense to withdraw, and contented herself with presiding over that *Senaculum*, or little Senate, of women, which Hadrian's Sabina had founded, and which dealt with questions of feminine dress, jewelry, precedence, and etiquette. Grandmother Maesa was left to govern the state.

The young emperor had some elements of charm. He made no reprisals against the supporters of Macrinus. He loved music, sang well, played the pipes, the organ, and the horn. Being too young to rule the Empire, he only asked permission to enjoy it. Pleasure, not Baal, was his god, and he was resolved to worship it in all its genders and forms. He invited every class of the free population to visit his palace; at times he would eat and drink and make merry with them; often he would distribute among them lottery prizes ranging from a furnished home to a handful of flies. He loved to play jokes upon his guests: to seat them on inflated cushions that would suddenly burst; to stupefy them with wine and let them wake up amid harmless leopards, bears, and lions. Lampridius assures us that Elagabalus never spent less than 100,000 sesterces ($10,000)—and sometimes 3,000,000—on a banquet to his friends. He would mix gold pieces with peas, onyx with lentils, pearls with rice, amber with beans; he would present horses, or chariots, or eunuchs, as favors; often he bade each guest take home the silver plate and goblets in which the dinner had been served. As for himself, he would have nothing but the best. The water in his swimming pools was perfumed with essence of roses; the fixtures in his bathrooms were of onyx or gold; his food had to be of costly rarities; his dress was studded with jewelry from crown to shoes; and gossip said that he never wore the same rings twice. When he traveled, 600 chariots were needed to carry his baggage and his bawds. Told by a soothsayer that he would die a violent death, he prepared worthy means of suicide if occasion required: cords of purple silk, swords of gold, poisons enclosed in sapphires or emeralds.[11] He was slain in a latrine.

Probably his enemies of the Senatorial class invented or exaggerated some of these tales; certainly the stories of his sexual depravity are beyond belief. In any case he perfumed his lust with piety, and schemed to spread among the Romans some worship of his Syrian Baal. He had himself circumcized, and thought of emasculating himself in honor of his god. He brought from Emesa the conical black stone which he worshiped as the emblem of Elagabal; he raised an ornate temple to house it; the stone, encrusted with gems, was carried to it on a chariot drawn by six white horses, while the young emperor walked backward before it in dumb adoration. He was willing to recognize all other religions; he patronized Judaism, and proposed to legalize Christianity. He merely insisted, with admirable loyalty, that his stone was the greatest of gods.[12]

His mother, absorbed in amours, looked with indulgence upon this Priapic farce; but Julia Maesa, failing to control it, resolved to forestall a debacle that would end this remarkable dynasty of Syrian women. She persuaded Elagabalus to adopt his cousin Alexander as successor and Caesar. She and Mamaea trained the boy in the duties of his office, and by every art drew the Senate and the people to look upon him as a desirable alternative to the priestly satyr who had offended Rome not by his extravagance or obscenity, but by his subordination of Jupiter to a Syrian Baal. Soaemias discovered the plot, and stirred up the Praetorians against her sister and nephew; Maesa and Mamaea offered richer arguments; and the Guard slew Elagabalus and his mother, dragged his corpse through the streets and around the Circus, and flung it into the Tiber. The Guard proclaimed, the Senate accepted, Alexander as emperor (222).

Marcus Aurelius Severus Alexander, like his predecessor, mounted the throne at the age of fourteen. His mother had given herself with singular consecration to the training of his body, mind, and character. He strengthened his frame with labor and exercise, swam in a cold pool for an hour every day, drank a pint of water before each meal, ate sparingly and of the simplest foods. He grew into a handsome youth, tall and strong, skilled in every sport and in the arts of war. He studied Greek and Latin literature, and only moderated his love for them on the insistence of Mamaea, who quoted to him those verses of Virgil that called upon Romans to yield the graces of culture to others, and form themselves to organize a world state and rule it in peace. He painted and sang "with distinction," and played the organ and the lyre, but never allowed any but his own household to witness these performances. He dressed and behaved with modest simplicity, "was temperate in the enjoyment of love, and would have nothing to do with catamites." [13] He showed high respect for the Senate, treated its members as his equals, entertained them in his palace, and often joined them in their homes. Kindly and affable, he visited the sick without distinction of class, gave ready audience to any citizen of decent repute, quickly forgave opponents, and shed no civilian blood in the fourteen years of his reign.[14] His mother reproved his amiability, saying, "You have made your rule too gentle, and the authority of the Empire less respected"; to which he answered, "Yes, but I have made it more lasting and secure." [15] He was a man of gold, without the alloy required to withstand the rough usage of this world.

He recognized the absurdity of his cousin's effort to replace Jove with Elagabal, and he co-operated with his mother in restoring the Roman temples and ritual. But to his philosophic mind it seemed that all religions were diverse prayers to one supreme power; he wished to honor all honest faiths; and in his private chapel, where he worshiped every morning, he had icons of Jupiter, Orpheus, Apollonius of Tyana, Abraham, and Christ. He quoted frequently the Judaeo-Christian counsel: "What you do not wish a man to do to you, do not do to him"; he had it engraved on the walls of his palace and on many a public building. He recommended the morals of the Jews and the Christians to the Roman people. The unimpressed wits of Antioch and Alexandria referred to him as "Head of the Synagogue." His mother favored the Christians, protected Origen, and summoned him to explain to her his flexible theology.

Julia Maesa having died soon after Alexander's accession, Mamaea, with his tutor Ulpian, determined the policies, and conceived the reforms, of Alexander's administration. She ruled with wisdom and restraint, caring more for the success of the dynasty than for the pageantry of power; she yielded to the great lawyer and the young emperor the credit for the achievements of his reign. She and Ulpian chose sixteen outstanding senators to serve as an imperial council, without whose approval no major measures were carried out. She could control everything except her love for her son. When he married and showed an affectionate partiality for his wife, Mamaea had her banished, and Alexander, forced to choose, surrendered to his mother. As he grew older he took a more active part in administration. "He would give his attention to public business even before dawn," says his ancient biographer, "and would continue at it to an advanced hour, never growing weary or irritated, but always cheerful and serene." [16]

His basic policy was to weaken the disruptive dominance of the army by restoring the prestige of the Senate and the aristocracy; rule by birth seemed to him the only actual alternative to rule by money, myth, or the sword. With the co-operation of the Senate he effected a hundred economies in administration, dismissed the supernumeraries in his palace, in governmental offices, and in provincial rule. He sold most of the imperial jewelry, and deposited the proceeds in the treasury. Perhaps with less Senatorial approval he legalized, encouraged, and reorganized the workers' and tradesmen's associations, and "allowed them to have advocates chosen from their own numbers." [17] Assuming a severe censorship over public morals, he ordered the arrest of prostitutes and the deportation of homosexuals. While reducing taxes, he restored the Colosseum and the Baths of Caracalla, built a public library, a fourteen-mile aqueduct, and new municipal baths, and financed the construction of baths, aqueducts, bridges, and roads throughout the Empire. To force down interest rates that were harassing debtors, he lent public money at four per cent, and advanced funds to the poor, without any interest charge, for the purchase of agricultural land. All the Empire prospered and applauded; the godly Aurelius, it seemed, had returned to earth and to power.

But as the Persians and the Germans had taken advantage of the philosopher king, so now they took advantage of the emperor saint. In 230 Ardashir, founder of the Sassanid dynasty in Persia, invaded Mesopotamia and threatened Syria. Alexander sent him a philosophical epistle reproving his violence, and arguing that "everyone ought to rest content with his own domain." [18] Ardashir judged him a weakling, and replied by demanding all Syria and Asia Minor. Accompanied by his mother, the young emperor took the field, and waged with more courage than subtlety an indecisive campaign. History is obscure as to his victories and defeats; in any case Ardashir withdrew from Mesopotamia, perhaps to meet attacks on his eastern front; and the Roman coins of 233 pictured Alexander crowned by Victory and having the Tigris and Euphrates at his feet.

Meanwhile the Alemanni and the Marcomanni, noting that the Rhine and Danube garrisons had been depleted to reinforce the legions in Syria, broke through the Roman *limes* and ravaged eastern Gaul. After celebrating his Persian triumph, Alexander, again with Mamaea at his side, rejoined his army, and led it to Mainz. On his mother's advice he negotiated with the enemy, offering them an annual sum to keep the peace. His troops condemned his weakness, and mutinied; they had never forgiven his economy, his discipline, and his subordination of them to the Senate and a woman's rule. They acclaimed as emperor C. Julius Maximinus, commander of the Pannonian legions. The soldiers of Maximinus forced their way into Alexander's tent, and slew him, his mother, and his friends (235).

II. ANARCHY

It was no whim of history that made the army supreme in the third century; internal causes had weakened the state and left it exposed on every front. The cessation of expansion after Trajan, and again after Septimius Severus, was the signal for attack; and as Rome had conquered nations by dividing them, so now the barbarians began to conquer her by uniting in simultaneous assaults. The necessity of defense exalted the power of arms and the prestige of soldiery; generals replaced philosophers on the throne, and the last reign of the aristocracy yielded to the revived rule of force.

Maximinus was a good soldier and no more, the robust son of a Thracian peasant; history assures us that he was eight feet tall, and had a thumb of such circumference that he could wear his wife's bracelet on it as a ring. He had no education, scorned it, and envied it. In his three years as emperor he never visited Rome, but preferred the life of his camp on the Danube or the Rhine. To support his campaigns and appease his troops, he laid such taxes upon the well to do that an upper-class revolt soon formed against his rule. Gordianus, the wealthy and learned proconsul of Africa, accepted the nomination of his army as a rival emperor; being eighty years old, he associated his son with him in the lethal office; they failed to withstand the forces sent against them by Maximinus; the son was killed in battle, the father killed himself. Maximinus revenged himself by proscriptions and confiscations that almost destroyed the aristocracy. "Every day," says Herodian, "one could see the richest men of yesterday turned beggars today." [19] The Senate, which had been reconstituted and reinvigorated by Severus, fought back valiantly; it declared Maximinus an outlaw, and chose two of its members, Maximus and Balbinus, as emperors. Maximus led an improvised army to meet Maximinus, who came down across the Alps and besieged Aquileia. Maximinus was the better general, and had the superior forces; the fate of the Senate and the propertied classes seemed sealed; but a group of Maximinus' soldiers, who had suffered from his savage punishments, killed him in his tent. Maximus returned in triumph to Rome, and was assassinated, along with Balbinus, by the Praetorian Guard. The Praetorians made a third Gordian emperor, and the Senate confirmed the choice.

We shall not repeat in bloody detail the names and battles and deaths of these emperors of anarchy. In the thirty-five years between Alexander Severus and Aurelian, thirty-seven men were proclaimed emperors. Gordian III was slain by his troops while fighting the Persians (244); his successor, Philip the Arab, was defeated and killed at Verona by Decius (249), an Illyrian of wealth and culture whose devotion to Rome well deserved a name so honorable in ancient story. Between campaigns against the Goths he laid out an ambitious program for the restoration of Roman religion, morals, and character, and gave orders for the destruction of Christianity; then he returned to the Danube, met the Goths, saw his son slain beside him, told his wavering army that the loss of any one individual was of little importance, pressed on against the enemy, and was himself struck down in one of the worst defeats in Roman history (251). He was succeeded by Gallus, who was murdered by his troops (253), and then by Aemilianus, who was murdered by his troops (253).

The new emperor, Valerian, already sixty, and facing war at once with the Franks, the Alemanni, the Marcomanni, the Goths, the Scythians, and the Persians, made his son Gallienus ruler of the Western Empire, kept the East for himself, and led an army into Mesopotamia. He was too old for his tasks, and soon succumbed. Gallienus, now thirty-five, was a man of courage, intelligence, and a culture that seemed almost out of place in this century of barbaric war. He reformed the civilian administration in the West, led his armies to victory against one after another of the Empire's enemies, and yet found time to enjoy and patronize philosophy and literature, and promote a transient revival of classic art. But even his varied genius was overwhelmed by the accumulating evils of the time.

In 254 the Marcomanni raided Pannonia and north Italy. In 255 the Goths invaded Macedonia and Dalmatia, Scythians and Goths invaded Asia Minor, the Persians invaded Syria. In 257 the Goths captured the fleet of the Bosporan kingdom, ravaged the Greek cities on the Black Sea coasts, burned Trapezus and enslaved its people, and raided Pontus. In 258 they took Chalcedon, Nicomedia, Prusa, Apamea, Nicaea; in the same year the Persians conquered Armenia, and Postumus declared himself the independent ruler of Gaul. In 259 the Alemanni broke into Italy, but were defeated by Gallienus at Milan. In 260 Valerian was overwhelmed by the Persians at Edessa, and died in captivity at a time and place unknown. Shapur I and his clouds of cavalry advanced through Syria to Antioch, surprised the population in the midst of its games, sacked the city, killed thousands, and led more thousands into slavery. Tarsus was taken and devastated, Cilicia and Cappadocia were overrun, and Shapur returned to Persia laden with spoils. Within a decade three ignominious tragedies had overtaken Rome: a Roman emperor had for the first time fallen in defeat, another had been captured by the enemy, and the unity of the Empire had been sacrificed to the necessity of meeting simultaneous attacks on many fronts. Under the force of these blows, and the disorderly elevation and assassination of emperors by troops, the imperial prestige collapsed; those psychological forces which time consecrates into habitual and unquestioned authority lost their hold upon Rome's enemies, even upon her subjects and citizens. Revolts broke out everywhere: in Sicily and Gaul the oppressed peasantry flared up in wild *jacqueries;* in Pannonia Ingenuus proclaimed himself sovereign of the eastern provinces. In 263 the Goths sailed down the Ionian coast, sacked Ephesus, and burned down the great Temple of Artemis. All the Hellenistic East was in terror.

An unexpected ally saved the Empire in Asia. Odenathus, who governed Palmyra as a vassal of Rome, drove the Persians back across Mesopotamia, defeated them at Ctesiphon (261), and declared himself king of Syria, Cilicia, Arabia, Cappadocia, and Armenia. He was assassinated in 266; his youthful son succeeded to his titles, his widow to his power. Like Cleopatra, from whom she claimed descent, Zenobia combined beauty of person with statesmanly capacity and many accomplishments of mind. She studied Greek literature and philosophy, learned Latin, Egyptian, and Syriac, and wrote a history of the East. Apparently connecting chastity with vigor, she allowed herself only such sexual relations as were needed for motherhood.[20] She inured herself to hardship and fatigue, enjoyed the dangers of the chase and marched on foot for miles at the head of her troops. She governed with sternness and wisdom, made the philosopher Longinus her premier, gathered scholars, poets, and artists at her court, and beautified her capital with Greco-Roman-Asiatic palaces whose ruins startle the desert traveler today. Feeling that the Empire was breaking up, she planned a new dynasty and realm, brought Cappadocia, Galatia, and most of Bithynia under her control, fitted out a great army and fleet, conquered Egypt, and took Alexandria after a siege that destroyed half the population. The subtle "Queen of the East" pretended that she was proceeding as the agent of the Roman power; but all the world knew that her victories were an act in the spacious drama of Rome's collapse.

Seeing the wealth and weakness of the Empire, the barbarians poured down into the Balkans and Greece. While the Sarmatians pillaged again the cities on the Black Sea, a branch of the Goths sailed in 500 ships through the Hellespont into the Aegean, took isle after isle, anchored in the Piraeus, and sacked Athens, Argos, Sparta, Corinth, and Thebes (267). While their navy brought some of the marauders back to the Black Sea, another group fought its way overland towards its Danube home. Gallienus met them at the river Nestus in Thrace, and won a costly victory; but a year later he was murdered by his troops. In 269 another Gothic horde descended into Macedonia, besieged Thessalonica, and pillaged Greece, Rhodes, Cyprus, and the Ionian coast. The Emperor Claudius II rescued Thessalonica, drove the Goths up the Vardar valley, and defeated them with great slaughter at Naissus, the modern Nish (269). If he had lost that battle no army would have intervened between the Goths and Italy.

III. THE ECONOMIC DECLINE

Political anarchy accelerated economic disintegration, and economic decline promoted political decay; each was the cause and effect of the other. Roman statesmanship had never found a healthy economic life for Italy; and perhaps the narrow plains of the peninsula have never provided an adequate base for the soaring aims of the Italian state. The production of cereals was discouraged by the competition of cheap grains from Sicily, Africa, and Egypt, and the great vineyards were losing their markets to provincial wines. Farmers complained that high taxes consumed their precarious profits and left them too little to keep the drainage and irrigation canals in repair; the canals filled up, the marshes spread, and malaria weakened the population of the Campagna and Rome. Large tracts of fertile land had been withdrawn from cultivation for residential estates. The absentee owners of the latifundia exploited labor and the soil to the limit of tolerance, and absolved themselves by philanthropies in the towns; urban architecture and games profited while the countryside grew desolate. Many peasant proprietors and free rural workers abandoned the farms for the cities, leaving Italian agriculture for the most part to latifundia manned by listless slaves. But the latifundia themselves were ruined by the *Pax Romana*, the dearth of wars of conquest in the first and second centuries, and the consequent fall in the supply, and rise in the cost, of slaves. Compelled to lure free labor back to the land, the great landlords divided their holdings into units which they leased to *coloni*, "cultivators"; they required from these tenants a small money rent or a tenth of the produce, and a period of unpaid labor in the owner's villa or on his private domain. In many cases landlords found it profitable to emancipate their slaves and change them into *coloni*. In the third century the owners, harassed by invasion and revolution in the cities, took more and more to living in their villas; these were fortified into castles, and were gradually transformed into medieval châteaux.*

The lack of slaves strengthened for a time the position of free labor in industry as well as in agriculture. But while the resources of the rich were

---

* The "colonate" probably had a major beginning when Aurelius settled captive Germans on imperial estates (172), and gave them hereditary possession on condition of an annual tax, military service at call, and an agreement not to leave their allotment without permission of the state. Similar conditions were laid upon Roman veterans receiving frontier lands, especially in the *agri decumates*—"tithe-paying fields"—along the Danube and Rhine.[21] A great extension of this imperial colonate occurred under Septimius Severus, who divided the lands he had appropriated into parcels tilled by tenants paying taxes in money or kind. As Septimius imitated the Ptolemies, so private landowners imitated him; the colonate began with monarchs, and produced a feudalism that undermined monarchy.

consumed by war and government, the poverty of the poor did not de-crease.[22] Wages were from six to eleven, prices some thirty-three, per cent of comparative wages and prices in the United States of the early twentieth century.[23] The class struggle was becoming more violent, for the army, recruited from the provincial poor, often joined in the attack upon wealth, and felt that its services to the state justified confiscatory taxation for dona-tives, or more direct pillaging of the well to do.[24] Industry suffered as commerce declined. The export trade of Italy fell as the provinces graduated from customers to competitors; barbarian raids and piracy made trade routes as unsafe as before Pompey; depreciated currencies and uncertain prices discouraged long-term enterprise. The extension of the frontier having ceased, Italy could no longer prosper by supplying or exploiting an expand-ing realm. Once Italy had collected the bullion of conquered lands and grown rich on the robbery; now money was migrating to the more indus-trialized Hellenistic provinces, and Italy grew poorer while the rising wealth of Asia Minor forced the replacement of Rome with an Eastern capital. Italian industry was thrown back upon its domestic market, and found the people too poor to buy the goods they could make.[25] Internal commerce was hampered by brigands, rising taxes, and the deterioration of roads through lack of slaves. The villas became more self-sufficient in industry, and barter competed with money trade. Large-scale production gave way year by year to small shops supplying chiefly a local demand.

Financial difficulties entered. The precious metals were running low: the gold mines of Thrace and the silver mines of Spain had reduced their yield, and Dacia, with its gold, would soon be surrendered by Aurelian. Much gold and silver had been consumed in art and ornament. Faced with this dearth when war was almost continuous, the emperors from Septimius Severus onward repeatedly debased the currency to pay for state expenses and military supplies. Under Nero the alloy in the denarius was ten per cent, under Commodus thirty, under Septimius fifty. Caracalla replaced it with the *antoninianus*, containing fifty per cent silver; by 260 its silver content had sunk to five per cent.[26] The government mints issued unprece-dented quantities of cheap coin; in many instances the state compelled the acceptance of these at their face value instead of their actual worth, while it insisted that taxes should be paid in goods or gold.[27] Prices rose rapidly; in Palestine they increased one thousand per cent between the first and third centuries;[28] in Egypt inflation ran out of control, so that a measure of wheat that had cost eight drachmas in the first century cost 120,000 drachmas at the end of the third.[29] Other provinces suffered much less; but in most of them inflation ruined a large part of the middle class, nullified trust funds and charitable foundations, rendered all business discouragingly precarious, and destroyed a considerable portion of the trading and investment capital upon which the economic life of the Empire depended.

The emperors after Pertinax were not displeased by this attrition of the aristocracy and the *bourgeoisie*. They felt the hostility of the Senatorial class and the great merchants to their alien origin, their martial despotism, and their exactions; the war of Senate and emperor, interrupted from Nerva to Aurelius, was renewed; and by donatives, public works, and doles, the rulers deliberately based their powers upon the favor of the army, the proletariat, and the peasantry.

The Empire suffered only less than Italy. Carthage and north Africa, farthest from the invaders, flourished; but Egypt decayed under destructive factionalism, Caracalla's massacre, Zenobia's conquest, high taxes, listless forced labor, and Rome's annual exaction of grain. Asia Minor and Syria had borne invasion and pillaging, but their ancient and patient industries had survived all tribulations. Greece, Macedonia, and Thrace had been devastated by the barbarians, and Byzantium had not recovered from Septimius' siege. As war brought Roman garrisons and supplies to the German frontier new cities rose along the rivers—Vienna, Karlsburg, Strasbourg, Mainz. Gaul had been disordered and discouraged by German attacks; sixty of her cities had been sacked; most of her towns and cities were shrinking within new walls, and were abandoning the broad straight streets of Roman design for the more easily defended irregular alleys of early antiquity and the Middle Ages. In Britain, too, the cities were becoming smaller, the villas larger; [30] class war and high taxation had destroyed wealth or driven it into rural concealment. The Empire had begun with urbanization and civilization; it was ending in reruralization and barbarism.

IV. THE TWILIGHT OF PAGANISM

The cultural graph of the third century follows loosely the curve of declining wealth and power. Nevertheless, in these tragic years we have the rise of notational algebra, the highest names in Roman jurisprudence, the finest example of ancient literary criticism, some of Rome's most majestic architecture, the oldest romantic novels, the greatest of mystic philosophers.

The *Greek Anthology* summarizes the life of Diophantus of Alexandria (A.D. 250) with algebraic humor: his boyhood lasted one sixth of his life, his beard grew after one twelfth more, he married after another seventh, his son was born five years later and lived to half his father's age, and the father died four years after his son—therefore at the age of eighty-four.[31] Of his works the chief survivor is the *Arithmetica*—a treatise on algebra. It solves determinate equations of the first degree, determinate quadratic equations, and indeterminate equations up to the sixth degree. For the unknown quantity which we denote by *x*, and which he called *arithmos* (the number)—he used a Greek sigma; and for the other powers he used the letters of the Greek alphabet. An algebra without symbols had existed before him: Plato had recommended, for training and amusing the youthful mind, such problems as the distribution of apples in certain proportions among several persons; [32] Archimedes had propounded like puzzles in the third century B.C.; and both the Egyptians and the Greeks had solved geometrical problems by algebraic methods without algebraic notation. Probably Diophantus systematized methods already familiar to his contemporaries; [33] the accident of time has preserved him; and to him, through the Arabs, we trace that bold and esoteric symbolism which aspires to formulate all the quantitative relations of the world.

Papinian, Paulus, and Ulpian, the culminating trio of Roman law, all rose to power under Septimius Severus; all, as prefects of the Praetorian Guard, were the prime ministers of the realm; and all justified absolute monarchy on the ground that the people had delegated their sovereignty to the emperor. Papinian's *Quaestiones* and *Responsa* were so distinguished by clarity, humanity, and justice that Justinian's collections leaned heavily on these works. When Caracalla killed Geta, he bade Papinian write a legal defense of the act; Papinian refused, saying that it was "easier to commit fratricide than to justify it." Caracalla ordered him beheaded, and a soldier performed the deed with an ax in the presence of the Emperor. Domitius Ulpianus continued Papinian's labors as jurist and humanitarian. His legal opinions defended slaves as by nature free, and women as endowed with the same rights as men. [34] Like most landmarks in the history of law, his writings were essentially a co-ordination of his predecessors' work; but his judgments were so definitive that nearly a third of them survive in the *Digest* of Justinian. "It was because Alexander Severus ruled chiefly in accord with Ulpian's advice," says Lampridius, "that he was so excellent an emperor." [35] However, Ulpian had had some of his opponents put to death; and in 228 his enemies in the Guard killed him in turn, with less legality and equal effect. Diocletian encouraged and financed schools of law, and commissioned the codification of post-Trajanic legislation in the *Codex Gregorianus*. Thereafter the science of jurisprudence hibernated till Justinian.

The third century continued the art of painting on Pompeian and Alexandrian lines; its meager remains are Oriental and crude, and almost effaced by time. Sculpture flourished, for many emperors had to be carved; it stiffened into a primitive frontality, but no later age has surpassed this one in portraits of startling veracity. It is a credit to Caracalla, or a testimony to his dullness, that he allowed a sculptor to transmit him to us as the curlyheaded scowling brute of the Naples Museum. Two sculptural colossi date from this period: the *Farnese Bull* and the *Farnese Hercules,* both of them exaggerated and unpleasantly tense, but showing undiminished technical mastery. That sculptors could still work in the classic style appears from the chaste reliefs on the sarcophagus of Alexander Severus, and on the *Ludovisi Battle Sarcophagus*. But the reliefs on the Arch of Septimius Severus at Rome frankly rejected Attic simplicity and grace for a coarse and picturesque virility that almost foreshadowed the rebarbarization of Italy.

Architecture at Rome now carried to completion the Roman flair for sublimity through size. Septimius raised on the Palatine the last of its imperial palaces, with an eastern wing seven stories high—the "Septizonium." Julia Domna provided funds for the Atrium Vestae, and the pretty Temple of Vesta that still stands in the Forum. Caracalla built for Isis' consort Serapis an immense shrine of which some handsome fragments survive. The Baths of Caracalla, finished under Alexander Severus, are among the world's most impressive ruins. They added nothing to architectural science, following essentially the lines of Trajan's Baths; but their frowning mass well expressed the murderer of Geta and Papinian. The main block, of brick and concrete, covered 270,000 square feet—more than the Houses of Parliament and Westminster Hall combined. A winding stairway led to the top of the walls; perched there Shelley wrote *Prometheus Unbound*. The interior was garrisoned by a multitude of statues, and upheld by 200 columns of granite, alabaster, and porphyry; the marble floors and walls were inlaid with mosaic scenes; water poured from massive mouths of silver into pools and basins where 1600 persons could bathe at once. Gallienus and Decius raised similar baths; in the latter case the Roman engineers rested a circular dome upon a decagonal edifice, and supported it with buttresses in the angles of the decagon—an expedient with little past and much future. In 295 Maximian began the most enormous of the eleven imperial *thermae*, and named it with singular modesty the Baths of Diocletian. Here were bathing facilities for 3600 persons at one time, gymnasiums, concert and lecture halls; out of one room, the tepidarium, Michelangelo fashioned Santa Maria degli Angeli—with the exception of St. Peter's the largest church in Rome. Structures only less monumental rose in the provinces. Diocletian built extensively in Nicomedia, Alexandria, and Antioch; Maximian adorned Milan, Galerius Sirmium, Constantius Trèves.

Literature prospered less, for it could seldom tap the wealth that gathered in imperial hands. Libraries grew in number and size; a third-century physician had a collection of 62,000 volumes, and the Bibliotheca Ulpiana was renowned for its historical archives. Diocletian sent scholars to Alexandria to transcribe classical texts there and bring copies to the libraries of Rome. Scholars were plentiful and popular; Philostratus memorialized them well in his *Lives of the Sophists*. Porphyry continued Plotinus, attacked Christianity, and called the world to vegetarianism. Iamblichus tried to harmonize Platonism and pagan theology, and succeeded sufficiently to inspire the Emperor Julian. Diogenes Laertius put together the lives and opinions of the philosophers in fascinating excerpt and anecdote. Athenaeus of Naucratis, having consumed the libraries of Alexandria, poured his chyme into the *Deipnosophists*, or "Sophists of the Dinner Table"

—a dreary dialogue on foods, sauces, courtesans, philosophers, and words, brightened here and there by some revelation of ancient custom or some reminiscence of great men. Longinus, perhaps of Palmyra, composed a polished essay *Peri hypsus*, "On the Sublime"; the peculiar pleasure given by literature (runs the argument) is due to the "lifting up" (*ekstasis*) of the reader by the eloquence that comes to a writer from strength of conviction and sincerity of character.* Dio Cassius Cocceianus of Bithynian Nicaea, after a life spent in the *cursus honorum*, began at fifty-five to write his *History of Rome* (210?); in his seventy-fourth year he completed it, having carried the story down from Romulus to himself. Of its eighty "books" less than half remain, but they fill eight substantial volumes. It is a work of noble scope rather than high quality. It has vivid narratives, revealing speeches, and philosophical asides that are not always platitudinous and conservative. But, like Livy, it is disfigured with "portents"; like Tacitus it is a long brief for the Senatorial opposition; and like all Roman histories it cleaves narrowly to the vicissitudes of politics and war—as if life for a thousand years had been nothing but taxes and death.

More significant than these honorable men for the historian of the mind is the appearance, in this century, of the romantic novel. It had had a long preparation in the *Cyropaideia* of Xenophon, the love poems of Callimachus, the legends that had accumulated about Alexander, and the "Milesian Tales" told by Aristides and others in the second century B.C. and afterward. These stories of adventure and love pleased an Ionian populace so classic in tradition but so Oriental in mood, perhaps now Oriental in blood. Petronius in Rome, Apuleius in Africa, Lucian in Greece, Iamblichus in Syria, developed the picaresque romance in varied ways, with no special accent on love. In the first Christian centuries, possibly responding to an increasing audience of women readers, the novel of adventure merged with the romance of love.

Our oldest extant example is the *Aethiopica*, or "Egyptian Tales," of Heliodorus of Emesa. Of its date there is much dispute, but we may provisionally assign it to the third century. It begins in a style honorable with age:

> The day had begun to smile cheerily, and the sun was already brightening the tops of the hills, when a band of men, in arms and appearance pirates, having ascended the summit of a slope that overlooks the Heracleotic mouth of the Nile, paused and surveyed the sea. Finding no sail there to promise them booty, they turned their eyes to the shore beneath them; and this is what they saw.[37]

At once we meet the rich and handsome youth Theagenes, and the lovely and tearful princess Chariclea; they have been captured by pirates; and there

---

* The oldest mss. assign the essay in one case to "Dionysius Longinus," in the other to "Dionysius or Longinus," without further clue. The only literary Longinus known to us from antiquity is Cassius Longinus, Zenobia's premier. He was famous throughout the Empire for his learning; Eunapius called him "a living library," and Porphyry ranked him "the first of critics." [36]

befalls them such a medley of mishaps, misunderstandings, battles, murders, and reunions as might supply a season's fiction today. Whereas in Petronius and Apuleius the chastity of maidens is a matter of swiftly passing concern, it is here the essence and pivot of the tale: Heliodorus preserves Chariclea's virginity through a score of narrow escapes, and writes persuasive homilies on the beauty and necessity of feminine virtue. There may be here some Christian influence; indeed, tradition made the author become the Christian bishop of Thessalonica. The *Aethiopica* unwittingly fathered an endless chain of imitations: here is the model for Cervantes' *Persiles y Sigismunda,* the story of Clorinda in Tasso's *Jerusalem Delivered,* and the vast romances of Mme de Scudéry; here are the love potions, signs, moans, faintings, and happy endings of a million pleasant tales; here is *Clarissa Harlowe* 1500 years before Richardson.

The most famous love story in ancient prose was *Daphnis and Chloë.* Of its author we know only the name Longus; and we merely guess at the third century as his time. Daphnis is exposed at birth, is rescued and reared by a shepherd, and becomes a shepherd in turn. Excellent passages of rural description suggest that Longus, like his poetic model Theocritus, had discovered the country after long residence in the city. Daphnis falls in love with a peasant girl who has also been rescued from infant exposure; they tend their flocks in charming comradeship, bathe together in innocent nudity, and intoxicate each other with an unprecedented kiss. An old neighbor explains their fever to them, and describes from his own youth the sickness of romantic love. "I thought not of my food, I cared not for my drink. I could take no rest, and sleep deserted me. My soul was heavy with sadness, my heart beat quickly, my limbs felt a deadly chill." [38] In the end their fathers, now wealthy, discover and enrich them; but they ignore their wealth and return to their modest pastoral life. The tale is told with the simplicity of finished art. Translated into supple French by Amyot (1559), it became the model for Saint-Pierre's *Paul and Virginia,* and the inspiration of countless paintings, poems, and musical compositions.

Akin to it is a fragment of poetry known as *Pervigilium Veneris,* "The Eve of Venus." No one knows who wrote it, or when; probably it belongs to this century.[39] The theme is that of Lucretius' apostrophe and Longus' romance— that the goddess of love, by inflaming all living things with reckless desire, is the real creator of the world:

> Tomorrow let him love who never loved;
> Tomorrow let him love who loved before.
> Fresh spring has come, and sings her amorous song;
> The world is born anew, and vernal love
> Drives birds to mate, and all the waiting woods
> Unloose their tresses to the showers of spring.
> Tomorrow let him love who never loved,
> And let him love who loved before.

So the limpid verse flows on, finding the work of love in the fertilizing rain, in the forms of flowers, in the songs of merry festivals, in the awkward tentatives of desirous youth, in timid trysts amid woodland haunts; and after each stanza the pithy promise returns: *Cras amet qui numquam amavit, quique amavit cras amet*. Here, in the last great lyric poem of the pagan soul, we hear the trochaic cadence of medieval hymns, and a melodious premonition of the troubadours.

V. THE ORIENTAL MONARCHY

When Claudius II died of a pestilence that was decimating Goths and Romans alike (270), the army chose as his successor the son of an Illyrian peasant. Domitius Aurelianus had risen from the lowest ranks by strength of body and will; his nickname was *Manu ad ferrum*—"hand on sword." It was a sign of reawakened good sense in the army that it chose a man who exacted as hard a discipline from others as from himself.

Under his lead the enemies of Rome were repulsed at every point except the Danube. There Aurelian ceded Dacia to the Goths, hoping that they would stand as a barrier between the Empire and ulterior hordes. Perhaps encouraged by this surrender, the Alemanni and the Vandals invaded Italy; but Aurelian in three battles overcame and dispersed them. Meditating distant campaigns, and fearing an assault upon Rome during his absence, he persuaded the Senate to finance, and the guilds to erect, new walls around the capital. Everywhere in the Empire city walls were being built, signifying the weakening of the imperial power and the end of the Roman peace.

Preferring offense to defense, Aurelian determined to restore the Empire by attacking Zenobia in the East, and then Tetricus, who had succeeded Postumus as the usurper of sovereignty in Gaul. While his general Probus recovered Egypt from Zenobia's son, Aurelian marched through the Balkans, crossed the Hellespont, defeated the Queen's army at Emesa, and besieged her capital. She tried to escape and enlist Persia's aid, but was captured; the city surrendered and was spared, but Longinus was put to death (272). While the Emperor was leading his army back to the Hellespont, Palmyra revolted and slew the garrison he had left there. He turned about with the speed of Caesar, again besieged and soon took the city; now he abandoned it to pillage by his troops, razed its walls, rerouted its trade, and let it lapse into the desert village that it had been before and is today. Zenobia graced in golden chains Aurelian's triumph in Rome, and was allowed to spend her remaining years in comparative freedom at Tibur.

In 274 Aurelian defeated Tetricus at Châlons, and returned Gaul, Spain, and Britain to the Empire. Happy at the resumption of its mastery, Rome

hailed the victor as *restitutor orbis*, restorer of the world. Turning to
the tasks of peace, he re-established some economic order by reforming the
Roman coinage; and reorganized the government by applying to it the
same severe discipline that had regenerated the army. Ascribing Rome's
moral and political chaos in some degree to religious disunity, and impressed by the political services of religion in the East, he sought to unite
old faiths and new in a monotheistic worship of the sun-god, and of the
Emperor as the vicar of that deity on earth. He informed a skeptical army
and Senate that it was the god, and not their choice or confirmation, that
had made him Emperor. He built at Rome a resplendent Temple of the Sun,
in which, he hoped, the Baal of Emesa and the god of Mithraism would
merge. Monarchy and monotheism were advancing side by side, each seeking to make the other its aide. Aurelian's religious policy suggested that the
power of the state was falling, that of religion rising; kings were now kings
by the grace of God. This was the Oriental conception of government, old
in Egypt, Persia, and Syria; in accepting it Aurelian advanced that Orientalization of the monarchy which had begun with Elagabalus and would complete itself in Diocletian and Constantine.

In 275, as Aurelian was leading an army across Thrace to settle matters
with Persia, a group of officers, misled into thinking that he planned to
execute them, assassinated him. Shocked by its own accumulated crimes, the
army asked the Senate to appoint a successor. None wanted an honor that
so regularly heralded death; finally Tacitus, being seventy-five years old,
consented to serve. He claimed descent from the historian, and illustrated
all the virtues preached by that laconic pessimist; but he died of exhaustion
six months after taking the crown. The soldiers, repenting their repentance,
resumed the prerogative of force, and saluted Probus as emperor (276).

It was an excellent choice and a merited name, for Probus stood out in
courage and integrity. He expelled the Germans from Gaul, cleared the
Vandals from Illyricum, built a wall between the Rhine and the Danube,
frightened the Persians with a word, and gave peace to the whole Roman
realm. Soon, he pledged his people, there would be no arms, no armies, and
no wars, and the reign of law would cover the earth. As a prelude to this
utopia he compelled his troops to clear wastelands, drain marshes, plant
vines, and perform other public works. The army resented this sublimation,
murdered him (282), mourned him, and built a monument to his memory.

It now hailed as imperator one Diocles, the son of a Dalmatian freedman.
Diocletian, as he henceforth called himself, had risen by brilliant talents
and flexible scruples to the consulate, a proconsulate, and command of the
palace guards. He was a man of genius, less skilled in war than in statesman-

ship. He came to the throne after a period of anarchy worse than that which had prevailed from the Gracchi to Antony; like Augustus, he pacified all parties, protected all frontiers, extended the role of government, and based his rule on the aid and sanction of religion. Augustus had created the Empire, Aurelian had saved it; Diocletian reorganized it.

His first vital decision revealed the state of the realm and the waning of Rome. He abandoned the city as a capital, and made his emperial headquarters at Nicomedia in Asia Minor, a few miles south of Byzantium. The Senate still met in Rome, the consuls went through their ritual, the games roared on, the streets still bore the noisome pullulation of humanity; but power and leadership had gone from this center of economic and moral decay. Diocletian based his move on military necessity: Europe and Asia must be defended, and could not be defended from a city so far south of the Alps. Hence he appointed a capable general, Maximian, as his coruler (286), charging him with defense of the West; and Maximian made not Rome but Milan his capital. Six years later, to further facilitate administration and defense, each of the two *Augusti* chose a "Caesar" as his aide and successor: Diocletian selected Galerius, who made his capital at Sirmium (Mitrovica on the Save), and was responsible for the Danube provinces; and Maximian appointed Constantius Chlorus (the Pale), who made his capital at Augusta Trevirorum (Trèves). Each *Augustus* pledged himself to retire after twenty years in favor of his Caesar, who would then appoint a "Caesar" to aid and succeed him in turn. Each *Augustus* gave his daughter in marriage to his "Caesar," adding the ties of blood to those of law. In this way, Diocletian hoped, wars of succession would be avoided, government would recapture continuity and authority, and the Empire would stand on guard at four strategic points against internal rebellion and external attack. It was a brilliant arrangement, which had every virtue but unity and freedom.

The monarchy was divided, but it was absolute. Each law of each ruler was issued in the name of all four, and was valid for the realm. The edict of the rulers became law at once, without the sanction of the Senate at Rome. All governmental officials were appointed by the rulers, and a gigantic bureaucracy spread its coils around the state. To further fortify the system, Diocletian developed the cult of the Emperor's *genius* into a personal worship of himself as the earthly embodiment of Jupiter, while Maximian modestly consented to be Hercules; wisdom and force had come down from heaven to restore order and peace on earth. Diocletian assumed a diadem—a broad white fillet set with pearls—and robes of silk and gold; his shoes were studded with precious gems; he kept himself aloof in his palace, and required visitors to pass the gantlet of ceremonious eunuchs and titled chamberlains, and to kneel and kiss the hem of his robe. He was a man of the world, and doubtless smiled in private at these myths and forms; but his throne lacked the legitimacy of time, and he hoped to buttress it, to check the turbulence of the populace and the revolts of the army, by enduing himself with divinity and awe. "He had himself called *dominus*," says Aurelius Victor, "but he behaved like a father." [40] This adoption of Oriental despotism by the son of a slave, this identification of god and king, meant the final failure of republican institutions in antiquity, the surrender of the fruits of Marathon; it was a reversion, like Alexander's, to the forms and theories of Achaemenid and Egyptian courts, of Ptolemaic, Parthian, and Sassanid kings. From this Orientalized monarchy came the structure of Byzantine and European kingdoms till the French Revolution. All that was needed now was to ally the Oriental monarch in an Oriental capital with an Oriental faith. Byzantinism began with Diocletian.

VI. THE SOCIALISM OF DIOCLETIAN

He proceeded with Caesarian energy to remake every branch of the government. He transformed the aristocracy by raising to it many civil or military officials, and making it a hereditary caste with an Oriental gradation of dignities, profusion of titles, and complexity of etiquette. He and his colleagues redivided the Empire into ninety-six provinces grouped into seventy-two dioceses and four prefectures, and appointed civil and military rulers for each division. It was a frankly centralized state, which considered local autonomy, like democracy, a luxury of security and peace, and excused its dictatorship by the needs of actual or imminent war. Wars were waged, and with brilliant success; Constantius recovered revolted Britain, and Galerius defeated the Persians so decisively that they surrendered Mesopotamia and five provinces beyond the Tigris. For a generation Rome's enemies were held at bay.

In years of peace Diocletian, with his aides, faced the problems of economic decay. To overcome depression and prevent revolution he substituted a managed economy for the law of supply and demand.[41] He established a sound currency by guaranteeing to the gold coinage a fixed weight and purity which it retained in the Eastern Empire till 1453. He distributed food to the poor at half the market price or free, and undertook extensive public works to appease the unemployed.[42] To ensure the supply of necessaries for the cities and the armies, he brought many branches of industry under complete state control, beginning with the import of grain; he persuaded the shipowners, merchants, and crews engaged in this trade to accept such control in return for governmental guarantee of security in employment and returns.[43] The state had long since owned most quarries, salt deposits, and mines; now it forbade the export of salt, iron, gold, wine, grain, or oil from Italy, and strictly regulated the importation of these articles.[44] It went on to control establishments producing for the army, the bureaucracy, or the court. In munition factories, textile mills, and bakeries the government required a minimum product, bought this at its own price, and made the associations of manufacturers responsible for carrying out orders and specifications. If this procedure proved inadequate, it completely nationalized these factories, and manned them with labor bound to the job.[45] Gradually, under Aurelian and Diocletian, the majority of industrial establishments and guilds in Italy were brought under the control of the corporate state. Butchers, bakers, masons, builders, glass blowers, ironworkers, engravers, were ruled by detailed governmental regulations.[46] The "various corporations," says Rostovtzeff, "were more like minor supervisors of their own concerns on behalf of the state than their owners; they were themselves in bondage to the officials of the various departments, and to the commanders of the various military units."[47] The associations of tradesmen and artisans received various privileges from the government, and often exerted pressure upon its policies; in return they served as organs of national administration, helped to regiment labor, and collected taxes for the state from their membership.[48] Similar methods of governmental control were extended, in the late third and early fourth centuries, to provincial armament, food, and clothing industries. "In every province," says Paul-Louis, "special *procuratores* superintended industrial activities. In every large town the state became a powerful employer . . . standing head and shoulders above the private industrialists, who were in any case crushed by taxation."[49]

Such a system could not work without price control. In 301 Diocletian and his colleagues issued an *Edictum de pretiis*, dictating maximum legal prices or wages for all important articles or services in the Empire. Its preamble attacks monopolists who, in an "economy of scarcity," had kept goods from the market to raise prices:

> Who is . . . so devoid of human feeling as not to see that immoderate prices are widespread in the markets of our cities, and that the passion for gain is lessened neither by plentiful supplies nor by fruitful years?—so that . . . evil men reckon it their loss if abundance comes. There are men whose aim it is to restrain general prosperity . . . to seek usurious and ruinous returns. . . . Avarice rages throughout the world. . . . Wherever our armies are compelled to go for the common safety, profiteers extort prices not merely

four or eight times the normal, but beyond any words to describe. Sometimes the soldier must exhaust his salary and his bonus in one purchase, so that the contributions of the whole world to support the armies fall to the abominable profits of thieves.* [50]

The Edict was until our time the most famous example of an attempt to replace economic laws by governmental decrees. Its failure was rapid and complete. Tradesmen concealed their commodities, scarcities became more acute than before, Diocletian himself was accused of conniving at a rise in prices,[52] riots occurred, and the Edict had to be relaxed to restore production and distribution.[53] It was finally revoked by Constantine.

The weakness of this managed economy lay in its administrative cost. The required bureaucracy was so extensive that Lactantius, doubtless with political license, estimated it at half the population.[54] The bureaucrats found their task too great for human integrity, their surveillance too sporadic for the evasive ingenuity of men. To support the bureaucracy, the court, the army, the building program, and the dole, taxation rose to unprecedented peaks of ubiquitous continuity. As the state had not yet discovered the plan of public borrowing to conceal its wastefulness and postpone its reckoning, the cost of each year's operations had to be met from each year's revenue. To avoid returns in depreciating currencies, Diocletian directed that, where possible, taxes should be collected in kind: taxpayers were required to transport their tax quotas to governmental warehouses, and a laborious organization was built up to get the goods thence to their final destination.[55] In each municipality the *decuriones* or municipal officials were held financially responsible for any shortage in the payment of the taxes assessed upon their communities.[56]

Since every taxpayer sought to evade taxes, the state organized a special force of revenue police to examine every man's property and income; torture was used upon wives, children, and slaves to make them reveal the hidden wealth or earnings of the household; and severe penalties were enacted for evasion.[57] Towards the end of the third century, and still more in the fourth, flight from taxes became almost epidemic in the Empire. The

---

* Some of the "ceilings" established in the Edict reveal the level of prices and wages in A.D. 301. Wheat, lentils, peas, $3.50 a bu.; barley, rye, beans, $2.10 a bu.; wine, 21-26 cents a pint; olive oil, 10.5 cents a pint; pork, 10.5 cents a lb., beef or mutton, 7 cents; chickens, 2 for 52.5 cents; dormice, 10 for 35 cents; best cabbage or lettuce, 5 heads for 3.5 cents; green onions, 25 for 3.5 cents; best snails, 20 for 3.5 cents; large apples or peaches, 10 for 3.5 cents; figs, 25 for 3.5 cents; hair, 5 cents a lb.; shoes, 62 cents to $1.38 a pair. Wages of farm labor, 23-46 cents, plus keep, per day; stonemasons, carpenters, blacksmiths, bakers, 46 cents plus keep; barbers, $1.75 cents per man; scribes, 23 cents per 100 lines; elementary teachers, 46 cents per pupil per month; teachers of Greek or Latin literature, or geometry, $1.84 per pupil per month; lawyers for pleading a case, $7.36.[51]

well to do concealed their riches, local aristocrats had themselves reclassified as *humiliores* to escape election to municipal office, artisans deserted their trades, peasant proprietors left their overtaxed holdings to become hired men, many villages and some towns (e.g., Tiberias in Palestine) were abandoned because of high assessments; [58] at last, in the fourth century, thousands of citizens fled over the border to seek refuge among the barbarians.[59]

It was probably to check this costly mobility, to ensure a proper flow of food to armies and cities, and of taxes to the state, that Diocletian resorted to measures that in effect established serfdom in fields, factories, and guilds. Having made the landowner responsible, through tax quotas in kind, for the productivity of his tenants, the government ruled that a tenant must remain on his land till his arrears of debt or tithes should be paid. We do not know the date of this historic decree; but in 332 a law of Constantine assumed and confirmed it, and made the tenant *adscriptitius*, "bound in writing" to the soil he tilled; he could not leave it without the consent of the owner; and when it was sold, he and his household were sold with it.[60] He made no protest that has come down to us; perhaps the law was presented to him as a guarantee of security, as in Germany today. In this and other ways agriculture passed in the third century from slavery through freedom to serfdom, and entered the Middle Ages.

Similar means of compelling stability were used in industry. Labor was "frozen" to its job, forbidden to pass from one shop to another without governmental consent. Each *collegium* or guild was bound to its trade and its assigned task, and no man might leave the guild in which he had been enrolled.[61] Membership in one guild or another was made compulsory on all persons engaged in commerce and industry; and the son was required to follow the trade of his father.[62] When any man wished to leave his place or occupation for another, the state reminded him that Italy was in a state of siege by the barbarians, and that every man must stay at his post.

In the year 305, in impressive ceremonies at Nicomedia and Milan, Diocletian and Maximian abdicated their power, and Galerius and Constantius Chlorus became *Augusti*, emperors respectively of the East and the West. Diocletian, still but fifty-five years of age, lost himself in his immense palace at Spalato, spent there the remaining eight years of his life, and saw without interference the breakdown of his tetrarchy in civil war. When Maximian urged him to return to power and end the strife, he replied that if Maximian could see the excellent cabbages he was growing in his garden he would not ask him to sacrifice such content for the pursuit and cares of power.[63]

He deserved his cabbages and his rest. He had ended a half century of anarchy, had re-established government and law, had restored stability to industry and security to trade, had tamed Persia and stilled the barbarians, and, despite a few murders, had been, all in all, a sincere legislator and a just judge. It is true that he had established an expensive bureaucracy, had ended local autonomy, had punished opposition harshly, had persecuted the church that might have been a helpful ally in his healing work, and had turned the population of the Empire into a caste society with an unlettered peasantry at one end and an absolute monarch at the other. But the conditions that Rome faced would not permit liberal policies; Marcus Aurelius and Alexander Severus had tried these and failed. Confronted by enemies on every side, the Roman state did what all nations must do in crucial wars; it accepted the dictatorship of a strong leader, taxed itself beyond tolerance, and put individual liberty aside until collective liberty was secured. Diocletian had, with more cost but under harder circumstances, repeated the achievement of Augustus. His contemporaries and his posterity, mindful of what they had escaped, called him the "Father of the Golden Age." Constantine entered the house that Diocletian built.

CHAPTER XXX

The Triumph of Christianity

A.D. 306-325

I. THE WAR OF CHURCH AND STATE

A.D. 64-311

IN pre-Christian days the Roman government had for the most part allowed to the rivals of orthodox paganism a tolerance which they in turn had shown to the official and imperial cults; nothing was demanded from the adherents of new faiths except an occasional gesture of adoration to the gods and head of the state. The emperors were piqued to find that of all the heretics under their rule only the Christians and the Jews refused to join in honoring their *genius*. The burning of incense before a statue of the emperor had become a sign and affirmation of loyalty to the Empire, like the oath of allegiance required for citizenship today. On its side the Church resented the Roman idea that religion was subordinate to the state; it saw in emperor-worship an act of polytheism and idolatry, and instructed its followers to refuse it at any cost. The Roman government concluded that Christianity was a radical—perhaps a communist—movement, subtly designed to overthrow the established order.

Before Nero the two forces had found it possible to live together without blows. The law had exempted the Jews from emperor-worship, and the Christians, at first confused with the Jews, were granted the same privilege. But the execution of Peter and Paul, and the burning of Christians to light up Nero's games, turned this mutual and contemptuous tolerance into unceasing hostility and intermittent war. We cannot wonder that after such provocation the Christians turned their full armory against Rome—denounced its immorality and idolatry, ridiculed its gods, rejoiced in its calamities,[1] and predicted its early fall. In the ardor of a faith made intolerant by intolerance, Christians declared that all who had had a chance to accept Christ and had refused would be condemned to eternal torments; many of them foretold the same fate for all the pre-Christian or non-Christian world; some excepted Socrates. In reply, pagans called the Christians "dregs

646

of the people" and "insolent barbarians," accused them of "hatred of the human race," and ascribed the misfortunes of the Empire to the anger of pagan deities whose Christian revilers had been allowed to live.[2] A thousand slanderous legends arose on either side. Christians were charged with demonic magic, secret immorality, drinking human blood at the Paschal feast,[3] and worshiping an ass.

But the conflict was profounder than mere pugnacity. Pagan civilization was founded upon the state, Christian civilization upon religion. To a Roman his religion was part of the structure and ceremony of government, and his morality culminated in patriotism; to a Christian his religion was something apart from and superior to political society; his highest allegiance belonged not to Caesar but to Christ. Tertullian laid down the revolutionary principle that no man need obey a law that he deemed unjust.[4] The Christian revered his bishop, even his priest, far above the Roman magistrate; he submitted his legal troubles with fellow Christians to his church authorities rather than to the officials of the state.[5] The detachment of the Christian from earthly affairs seemed to the pagan a flight from civic duty, a weakening of the national fiber and will. Tertullian advised Christians to refuse military service; and that a substantial number of them followed his counsel is indicated by Celsus' appeal to end this refusal, and Origen's reply that though Christians will not fight for the Empire they will pray for it.[6] Christians were exhorted by their leaders to avoid non-Christians, to shun their festival games as barbarous, and their theaters as stews of obscenity.[7] Marriage with a non-Christian was forbidden. Christian slaves were accused of introducing discord into the family by converting their masters' children or wives; Christianity was charged with breaking up the home.[8]

The opposition to the new religion came rather from the people than from the state. The magistrates were often men of culture and tolerance; but the mass of the pagan population resented the aloofness, superiority, and certainty of the Christians, and called upon the authorities to punish these "atheists" for insulting the gods. Tertullian notes "the general hatred felt for us." [9] From the time of Nero Roman law seems to have branded the profession of Christianity as a capital offense; [10] but under most of the emperors this ordinance was enforced with deliberate negligence.[11] If accused, a Christian could usually free himself by offering incense to a statue of the emperor; thereafter he was apparently allowed to resume the quiet practice of his faith.[12] Christians who refused this obeisance might be imprisoned, or flogged, or exiled, or condemned to the mines, or, rarely, put to death. Domitian seems to have banished some Christians from Rome; but "being in some degree human," says Tertullian, "he soon stopped what he had begun, and restored the exiles." [13] Pliny enforced the law with the officiousness of an amateur (111), if we may judge from his letter to Trajan:

> The method I have observed toward those who have been denounced to me as Christians is this: I interrogated them whether they were Christians; if they confessed it I repeated the question twice again, adding the threat of capital punishment; if they still persevered, I ordered them to be executed. . . . The temples, which had been almost deserted, begin now to be frequented . . . and there is a general demand for sacrificial animals, which for some time past have met with but few purchasers.

To which Trajan replied:

> The method you have pursued, my dear Pliny, in sifting the cases of those denounced to you as Christians is eminently proper. . . . *No search should be made for these people;* when they are denounced and found guilty they must be punished; but where the accused party denies that he is a Christian, and gives proof . . . by adoring our gods, he shall be pardoned. . . . Information without the accuser's name subscribed must not be admitted in evidence against anyone.[14]

The passage here italicized suggests that Trajan only reluctantly carried out a pre-existing statute. Nevertheless, we hear of two prominent martyrs in his principate: Simeon, head of the church of Jerusalem, and Ignatius, Bishop of Antioch; presumably there were others of less fame.

Hadrian, a skeptic open to all ideas, instructed his appointees to give the Christians the benefit of every doubt.[15] Being more religious, Antoninus allowed more persecution. At Smyrna the populace demanded of the "Asiarch" Philip that he enforce the law; he complied by having eleven Christians executed in the amphitheater (155). The bloodthirst of the crowd was aroused rather than assuaged; it clamored for the death of Bishop Polycarp, a saintly patriarch of eighty-six years, who was said in his youth to have known Saint John. Roman soldiers found the old man in a suburban retreat, and brought him unresisting before the Asiarch at the games. Philip pressed him: "Take the oath, revile Christ, and I will let you go." Polycarp, says the most ancient of the *Acts of the Martyrs*, replied: "For eighty-six years have I been his servant, and he has done me no wrong; how then can I blaspheme my King who saved me?" The crowd cried out that he should be burned alive. The flames, says the pious document, refused to burn him, "but he was within them as bread that is being baked; and we perceived such a fragrant smell as might come from incense or other costly spices. At length the lawless men commanded an executioner to stab him. When he did this there came out a dove, and so much blood that the fire was quenched, and all the crowd marveled." [16]

The persecutions were renewed under the saintly Aurelius. When famine, flood, pestilence, and war overwhelmed a once happy reign, the conviction spread that these evils were due to neglect and denial of the Roman gods. Aurelius shared the public terror, or yielded to it. In 177 he issued a rescript ordering the punishment of sects that caused disturbances by "exciting the ill-balanced minds of men" with new winds of doctrine. In that same year, at Vienne and Lyons, the pagan populace arose in fury against the Christians, and stoned them whenever they dared to stir from their homes. The imperial legate ordered the arrest of the leading Christians of Lyons. Bishop Pothinus, ninety years old, died in jail from the effects of torture. A messenger was sent to Rome to ask the advice of the Emperor as to the treatment of the remaining prisoners. Marcus replied that those who denied Christianity should be freed, but those who professed it should be put to death according to the law.

The annual festival of the Augustalia was now to be celebrated in Lyons, and delegates from all Gaul crowded the provincial capital. At the height of the games the accused Christians were brought to the amphitheater and were questioned. Those who recanted were dismissed; forty-seven who persisted were put to death with a variety and barbarity of tortures equaled only by the Inquisition. Attalus, second to Pothinus in the Christian community, was forced to sit on a chair of red-hot iron and roast to death.[17] Blandina, a slave girl, was tortured all day, then bound up in a bag, and thrown into the arena to be gored to death by a bull. Her silent fortitude led many Christians to believe that Christ made his martyrs insensitive to pain; the same result might have come from ecstasy and fear. "The Christian," said Tertullian, "even when condemned to die, gives thanks." [18] *

Under Commodus the persecutions waned. Septimius Severus renewed them, even to the point of making baptism a crime. In 203 many Christians suffered martyrdom in Carthage. One of them, a young mother named Perpetua, left a touching account of her days in prison, and her father's prostrate pleas that she should renounce Christianity. She and another young mother were tossed and gored by a bull; we have an indication of the anesthetic effect of fear and trance in her later query, "When are we to be tossed?" Story tells how she guided to her throat the dagger of the reluctant gladiator who had to kill her.[19] The Syrian empresses who followed Septimius had little concern for the Roman gods, and gave Christianity a careless

---

* Our knowledge of the Lyons persecutions comes from a letter of "the servants of Christ at Lugdunum and Vienna in Gaul, to the brethren in Asia and Phrygia," preserved in Eusebius, *Ecclesiastical History*, v, 1. Some exaggeration may have crept into the report.

toleration. Under Alexander Severus peace seemed established among all the rival faiths.

The renewal of the barbarian attacks ended this truce. To understand the persecution under Decius (or Aurelius) we must imagine a nation in the full excitement of war, frightened by serious defeats, and expecting hostile invasion. In 249 a wave of religious emotion swept the Empire; men and women flocked to the temples and besieged the gods with prayers. Amid this fever of patriotism and fear the Christians stood apart, still resenting and discouraging military service,[20] scorning the gods, and interpreting the collapse of the Empire as the prophesied prelude to the destruction of "Babylon" and the return of Christ. Using the mood of the people as an opportunity to strengthen national enthusiasm and unity, Decius issued an edict requiring every inhabitant of the realm to offer a propitiatory act of homage to the gods of Rome. Apparently Christians were not asked to abjure their own faith, but were commanded to join in the universal *supplicatio* to the deities who, the populace believed, had so often saved imperiled Rome. Most Christians complied; in Alexandria, according to its Bishop Dionysius, "the apostasy was universal";[21] it was likewise in Carthage and Smyrna; probably these Christians considered the *supplicatio* a patriotic formality. But the bishops of Jerusalem and Antioch died in jail, and the bishops of Rome and Toulouse were put to death (250). Hundreds of Roman Christians were crowded into dungeons; some were beheaded, some were burned at the stake, a few were given to the beasts in holiday festival. After a year the persecution abated; and by Easter of 251 it was practically at an end.

Six years later Valerian, in another crisis of invasion and terror, ordered that "all persons must conform to the Roman ceremonials," and forbade any Christian assemblage. Pope Sixtus II resisted, and was put to death with four of his deacons. Bishop Cyprian of Carthage was beheaded, the bishop of Tarragona was burned alive. In 261, after the Persians had removed Valerian from the scene, Gallienus published the first edict of toleration, recognizing Christianity as a permitted religion, and ordering that property taken from Christians should be restored to them. Minor persecutions occurred in the next forty years, but for the most part these were for Christianity decades of unprecedented calm and rapid growth. In the chaos and terror of the third century men fled from the weakened state to the consolations of religion, and found them more abundantly in Christianity than in its rivals. The Church made rich converts now, built costly cathedrals, and allowed its adherents to share in the joys of this world. The *odium theologicum* subsided among the people; Christians intermingled more freely with pagans, even married them. The Oriental monarchy of Diocletian seemed destined to consolidate religious as well as political security and peace.

Galerius, however, saw in Christianity the last obstacle to absolute rule, and urged his chief to complete the Roman restoration by restoring the Roman gods. Diocletian hesitated; he was averse to needless risks, and estimated more truly than Galerius the magnitude of the task. But one day, at an imperial sacrifice, the Christians made the sign of the cross to ward off evil demons. When the augurs failed to find on the livers of the sacrificed animals the marks that they had hoped to interpret, they blamed the presence of profane and unbelieving persons. Diocletian ordered that all in attendance should offer sacrifice to the gods or be flogged, and that all soldiers in the army should similarly conform or be dismissed (302). Strange to say, Christian writers agreed with the pagan priests: the prayers of the Christian, said Lactantius,[22] kept the Roman gods at a distance; and Bishop Dionysius had written to the same effect a generation before. Galerius at every opportunity argued the need of religious unity as a support to the new monarchy; and at last Diocletian yielded. In February, 303, the four rulers decreed the destruction of all Christian churches, the burning of Christian books, the dissolution of Christian congregations, the confiscation of their property, the exclusion of Christians from public office, and the punishment of death for Christians detected in religious assembly. A band of soldiers inaugurated the persecution by burning to the ground the cathedral at Nicomedia.

The Christians were now numerous enough to retaliate. A revolutionary movement broke out in Syria, and in Nicomedia incendiaries twice set fire to Diocletian's palace. Galerius accused the Christians of the arson; they accused him; hundreds of Christians were arrested and tortured, but the guilt was never fixed. In September Diocletian ordered that imprisoned Christians who would worship the Roman gods should be freed, but that those who refused should be subjected to every torture known to Rome. Infuriated by scornful resistance, he directed all provincial magistrates to seek out every Christian, and use any method to compel him to appease the gods. Then, probably glad to leave this miserable enterprise to his successors, he resigned.

Maximian carried out the edict with military thoroughness in Italy. Galerius, become *Augustus*, gave every encouragement to the persecution in the East. The roll of martyrs was increased in every part of the Empire except Gaul and Britain, where Constantius contented himself with burning a few churches. Eusebius assures us, presumably with the hyperbole of indignation, that men were flogged till the flesh hung from their bones, or their flesh was scraped to the bone with shells; salt or vinegar was poured upon the wounds; the flesh was cut off bit by bit and fed to waiting animals; or bound to crosses, men were eaten piecemeal by starved beasts. Some victims had their fingers pierced with sharp reeds under the nails; some had their eyes gouged out; some were suspended by a hand or a foot; some had molten lead poured down their throats; some were beheaded, or crucified, or beaten to death with clubs; some were torn apart by being tied to the momentarily bent branches of trees.[23] We have no pagan narrative of these events.

The persecution continued for eight years, and brought death to approximately 1500 Christians, orthodox or heretic, and diverse sufferings to countless more. Thousands of Christians recanted; tradition said that even Marcellinus, Bishop of Rome, denied his faith under duress of terror and pain. But most of the persecuted stood firm; and the sight or report of heroic fidelity under torture strengthened the faith of the wavering and won new members for the hunted congregations. As the brutalities multiplied, the sympathy of the pagan population was stirred; the opinion of good citizens found courage to express itself against the most ferocious oppression in Roman history. Once the people had urged the state to destroy Christianity; now the people stood aloof from the government, and many pagans risked death to hide or protect Christians until the storm should pass.[24] In 311 Galerius, suffering from a mortal illness, convinced of failure, and implored by his wife to make his peace with the undefeated God of the Christians, promulgated an edict of toleration, recognizing Christianity as a lawful religion and asking the prayers of the Christians in return for "our most gentle clemency."[25]

The Diocletian persecution was the greatest test and triumph of the Church. It weakened Christianity for a time through the natural defection of adherents who had joined it, or grown up, during a half century of unmolested prosperity. But soon the defaulters were doing penance and pleading for readmission to the fold. Accounts of the loyalty of martyrs who had died, or of "confessors" who had suffered, for the faith were circulated from community to community; and these *Acta Martyrum*, intense with exaggeration and fascinating with legend, played a historic role in awakening or confirming Christian belief. "The blood of martyrs," said Tertullian, "is seed."[26] There is no greater drama in human record than the sight of a few Christians, scorned or oppressed by a succession of emperors, bearing all trials with a fierce tenacity, multiplying quietly, building order while their enemies generated chaos, fighting the sword with the word, brutality with hope, and at last defeating the strongest state that history has known. Caesar and Christ had met in the arena, and Christ had won.

II. THE RISE OF CONSTANTINE

Diocletian, peaceful in his Dalmatian palace, saw the failure of both the persecution and the tetrarchy. Seldom had the Empire witnessed such confusion as followed his abdication. Galerius prevailed upon Constantius to let him appoint Severus and Maximinus Daza as "Caesars" (305). At once the principle of heredity asserted its claims: Maxentius, son of Maximian, wished to succeed his father's authority, and a like resolution fired Constantine.

Flavius Valerius Constantinus had begun life at Naissus in Moesia (272?) as the illegitimate son of Constantius by his legal concubine Helena, a barmaid from Bithynia.[27] On becoming a "Caesar," Constantius was required by Diocletian to put away Helena and to take Maximian's stepdaughter Theodora as his wife. Constantine received only a meager education. He took up soldiering early, and proved his valor in the wars against Egypt and Persia. Galerius, on succeeding Diocletian, kept the young officer near him as a hostage for the good behavior of Constantius. When the latter asked Galerius to send the youth to him Galerius procrastinated craftily; but Constantine escaped from his watchers, and rode night and day across Europe to join his father at Boulogne and share in a British campaign. The Gallic army, deeply loyal to the humane Constantius, came to love his handsome, brave, and energetic son; and when the father died at York (306), the troops acclaimed Constantine not merely as "Caesar" but as *Augustus*—emperor. He accepted the lesser title, excusing himself on the ground that his life would be unsafe without an army at his back. Galerius, too distant to intervene, reluctantly recognized him as a "Caesar." Constantine fought successfully against the invading Franks, and fed the beasts of the Gallic amphitheaters with barbarian kings.

Meanwhile in Rome the Praetorian Guard, eager to restore the ancient capital to leadership, hailed Maxentius as emperor (306). Severus descended from Milan to attack him; Maximian, to confound the confusion, returned to the purple at his son's request, and joined in the campaign; Severus was deserted by his troops and put to death (307). To help himself face the growing chaos, the aging Galerius appointed a new *Augustus*—Flavius Licinius; hearing which, Constantine assumed a like dignity (307). A year later Maximinus Daza adopted the same title, so that in place of the two *Augusti* of Diocletian's plan there were now six; no one cared to be merely "Caesar." Maxentius quarreled with his father; Maximian went to Gaul to seek Constantine's aid; while the latter fought Germans on the Rhine, Maximian tried to replace him as commander of the Gallic armies; Constantine marched across Gaul, besieged the usurper in Marseilles, captured him, and granted him the courtesy of suicide (310).

The death of Galerius (311) removed the last barrier between intrigue and war. Maximinus plotted with Maxentius to overthrow Licinius and Constantine, who conspired to overthrow them. Taking the initiative, Constantine crossed the Alps, defeated an army near Turin, and advanced upon Rome with a celerity of movement, and a restraining discipline of his troops, that recalled the march of Caesar from the Rubicon. On October 27, 312, he met the forces of Maxentius at Saxa Rubra (Red Rocks) nine miles north of Rome; and by superior strategy compelled Maxentius to fight with his back to the Tiber, and no retreat possible except over the Mulvian Bridge. On the afternoon before the battle, says Eusebius,[28] Constantine saw a flaming cross in the sky, with the Greek words *en toutoi nika*—"in this sign conquer." * Early the next morning, according to Eusebius and Lactantius,[31] Constantine dreamed that a voice commanded him to have his soldiers mark upon their shields the letter X with a line drawn through it and curled around the top—the symbol of Christ. On arising he obeyed, and then advanced into the forefront of battle behind a standard (known henceforth as the *labarum*) carrying the initials of Christ interwoven with a cross. As Maxentius displayed the Mithraic-Aurelian banner of the Unconquerable Sun, Constantine cast in his lot with the Christians, who were numerous in his army, and made the engagement a turning point in the history of religion. To the worshipers of Mithras in Constantine's forces the cross could give no offense, for they had long fought under a standard bearing a Mithraic cross of light.[32] In any case Constantine won the battle of the Mulvian Bridge, and Maxentius perished in the Tiber with thousands of his troops. The victor entered Rome the welcomed and undisputed master of the West.

Early in 313 Constantine and Licinius met at Milan to co-ordinate their rule. To consolidate Christian support in all provinces, Constantine and Licinius issued an "Edict of Milan," confirming the religious toleration proclaimed by Galerius, extending it to all religions, and ordering the restoration of Christian properties seized during the recent persecutions. After this historic declaration, which in effect conceded the defeat of paganism, Constantine returned to the defense of Gaul, and Licinius moved eastward to overwhelm Maximinus (313). The death of Maximinus shortly afterward left Constantine and Licinius the unchallenged rulers of the Empire. Licinius

---

* Usually handed down by tradition in a Latin form: *in hoc vince*, or *in hoc signo vinces*— "in this sign thou shalt conquer." Eusebius, our sole authority for this vision, is confessedly [29] prone to edification; "but seeing," he pleads, "that the Emperor did with an oath confirm it to be true when he related it to me who intended to write his history . . . who can doubt his relation?" [30]

married Constantine's sister, and a war-weary people rejoiced at the prospect of peace.

But neither of the *Augusti* had quite abandoned the hope of undivided supremacy. In 314 their mounting enmity reached the point of war. Constantine invaded Pannonia, defeated Licinius, and exacted the surrender of all Roman Europe except Thrace. Licinius revenged himself upon Constantine's Christian supporters by renewing the persecution in Asia and Egypt. He excluded Christians from his palace at Nicomedia, required every soldier to adore the pagan gods, forbade the simultaneous attendance of both sexes at Christian worship, and at last prohibited all Christian services within city walls. Disobedient Christians lost their positions, their citizenship, their property, their liberty, or their lives.

Constantine watched for an opportunity not only to succor the Christians of the East, but to add the East to his realm. When barbarians invaded Thrace, and Licinius failed to move against them, Constantine led his army from Thessalonica to the rescue of Licinius' province. After the barbarians were driven back Licinius protested Constantine's entry into Thrace; and as neither ruler desired peace, war was renewed. The defender of Christianity, with 130,000 men, met the defender of paganism, with 160,000 men, first at Adrianople and then at Chrysopolis (Scutari), won, and became sole emperor (323). Licinius surrendered on a promise of pardon; but in the following year he was executed on the charge that he had resumed his intrigues. Constantine recalled the Christian exiles, and restored to all "confessors" their lost privileges and property. While still proclaiming liberty of worship for all, he now definitely declared himself a Christian, and invited his subjects to join him in embracing the new faith.

III. CONSTANTINE AND CHRISTIANITY

Was his conversion sincere—was it an act of religious belief, or a consummate stroke of political wisdom? Probably the latter.[33] His mother Helena had turned to Christianity when Constantius divorced her; presumably she had acquainted her son with the excellences of the Christian way; and doubtless he had been impressed by the invariable victory that had crowned his arms under the banner and cross of Christ. But only a skeptic would have made so subtle a use of the religious feelings of humanity. The *Historia Augusta* quotes him as saying, "it is *Fortuna* that makes a man emperor"[34]—though this was a bow to modesty rather than to chance. In his Gallic court he had surrounded himself with pagan scholars and philosophers.[35] After his conversion he seldom conformed to the ceremonial requirements of Christian worship. His letters to Christian bishops make it clear that he cared little for the theological differences that agitated Christendom—though he was willing to suppress dissent in the interests of imperial unity. Throughout his reign he treated the bishops as his political aides; he summoned them, presided over their councils, and agreed to enforce whatever opinion their majority should formulate. A real believer would have been a Christian first and a statesman afterward; with Constantine it was the reverse. Christianity was to him a means, not an end.

He had seen in his lifetime the failure of three persecutions; and it was not lost upon him that Christianity had grown despite them. Its adherents were still very much in the minority; but they were relatively united, brave, and strong, while the pagan majority was divided among many creeds, and included a dead weight of simple souls without conviction or influence. Christians were especially numerous in Rome under Maxentius, and in the East under Licinius; Constantine's support of Christianity was worth a dozen legions to him in his wars against these men. He was impressed by the comparative order and morality of Christian conduct, the bloodless beauty of Christian ritual, the obedience of Christians to their clergy, their humble acceptance of life's inequalities in the hope of happiness beyond the grave; perhaps this new religion would purify Roman morals, regenerate marriage and the family, and allay the fever of class war. The Christians, despite bitter oppression, had rarely revolted against the state; their teachers had inculcated submission to the civil powers, and had taught the divine right of kings. Constantine aspired to an absolute monarchy; such a government would profit from religious support; the hierarchical discipline and ecumenical authority of the Church seemed to offer a spiritual correlate for monarchy. Perhaps that marvelous organization of bishops and priests could become an instrument of pacification, unification, and rule?

Nevertheless, in a world still preponderantly pagan, Constantine had to feel his way by cautious steps. He continued to use vague monotheistic language that any pagan could accept. During the earlier years of his supremacy he carried out patiently the ceremonial required of him as *pontifex maximus* of the traditional cult; he restored pagan temples, and ordered the taking of the auspices. He used pagan as well as Christian rites in dedicating Constantinople. He used pagan magic formulas to protect crops and heal disease.[36]

Gradually, as his power grew more secure, he favored Christianity more openly. After 317 his coins dropped one by one their pagan effigies, until by 323 they bore only neutral inscriptions. A legal text of his reign, questioned but not disproved, gave Christian bishops the authority of judges in their dioceses;[37] other laws exempted Church realty from taxation,[38] made

Christian associations juridical persons, allowed them to own land and receive bequests, and assigned the property of intestate martyrs to the Church.[39] Constantine gave money to needy congregations, built several churches in Constantinople and elsewhere, and forbade the worship of images in the new capital. Forgetting the Edict of Milan, he prohibited the meetings of heretical sects, and finally ordered the destruction of their conventicles.[40] He gave his sons an orthodox Christian education, and financed his mother's Christian philanthropies. The Church rejoiced in blessings beyond any expectation. Eusebius broke out into orations that were songs of gratitude and praise; and all over the Empire Christians gathered in festal thanksgiving for the triumph of their God.

Three clouds softened the brilliance of this "cloudless day": the monastic secession, the Donatist schism, the Arian heresy. In the interval between the Decian and the Diocletian persecution the Church had become the richest religious organization in the Empire, and had moderated its attacks upon wealth. Cyprian complained that his parishioners were mad about money, that Christian women painted their faces, that bishops held lucrative offices of state, made fortunes, lent money at usurious interest, and denied their faith at the first sign of danger.[41] Eusebius mourned that priests quarreled violently in their competition for ecclesiastical preferment.[42] While Christianity converted the world, the world converted Christianity, and displayed the natural paganism of mankind. Christian monasticism arose as a protest against this mutual adjustment of the spirit and the flesh. A minority wished to avoid any indulgence of human appetite, and to continue the early Christian absorption in thoughts of eternal life. Following the custom of the Cynics, some of these ascetics renounced all possessions, donned the ragged robe of the philosopher, and subsisted on alms. A few, like Paul the Hermit, went to live as solitaries in the Egyptian desert. About 275 an Egyptian monk, Anthony, began a quarter century of isolated existence first in a tomb, then in an abandoned mountain castle, then in a rock-hewn desert cell. There he struggled nightly with frightful visions and pleasant dreams, and overcame them all; until at last his reputation for sanctity filled all Christendom, and peopled the desert with emulating eremites. In 325 Pachomius, feeling that solitude was selfishness, gathered anchorites into an abbey at Tabenne in Egypt, and founded that cenobitic, or community, monasticism which was to have its most influential development in the West. The Church opposed the monastic movement for a time, and then accepted it as a necessary balance to its increasing preoccupation with government.

Within a year after Constantine's conversion the Church was torn by a schism that might have ruined it in the very hour of victory. Donatus, Bishop of

Carthage, supported by a priest of like name and temper, insisted that Christian bishops who had surrendered the Scriptures to the pagan police during the persecutions had forfeited their office and powers; that baptisms or ordinations performed by such bishops were null and void; and that the validity of sacraments depended in part upon the spiritual state of the ministrant. When the Church refused to adopt this stringent creed, the Donatists set up rival bishops wherever the existing prelate failed to meet their tests. Constantine, who had thought of Christianity as a unifying force, was dismayed by the chaos and violence that ensued, and was presumably not unmoved by the occasional alliance of Donatists with radical movements among the African peasantry. He called a council of bishops at Arles (314), confirmed its denunciation of the Donatists, ordered the schismatics to return to the Church, and decreed that recalcitrant congregations should lose their property and their civil rights (316). Five years later, in a momentary reminiscence of the Milan edict, he withdrew these measures, and gave the Donatists a scornful toleration. The schism continued till the Saracens overwhelmed orthodox and heretic alike in the conquest of Africa.

In those same years Alexandria saw the rise of the most challenging heresy in the history of the Church. About 318 a priest from the Egyptian town of Baucalis startled his bishop with strange opinions about the nature of Christ. A learned Catholic historian describes him generously:

> Arius . . . was tall and thin, of melancholy look, and an aspect that showed traces of his austerities. He was known to be an ascetic, as could be seen from his costume—a short tunic without sleeves, under a scarf that served as a cloak. His manner of speaking was gentle; his addresses were persuasive. The consecrated virgins, who were numerous in Alexandria, held him in great esteem; and he counted many stanch supporters among the higher clergy.[43]

Christ, said Arius, was not one with the Creator, he was rather the Logos, the first and highest of all created beings. Bishop Alexander protested, Arius persisted. If, he argued, the Son had been begotten of the Father, it must have been in time; the Son therefore could not be coeternal with the Father. Furthermore, if Christ was created, it must have been from nothing, not from the Father's substance; Christ was not "consubstantial" with the Father.[44] The Holy Spirit was begotten by the Logos, and was still less God than the Logos. We see in these doctrines the continuity of ideas from Plato through the Stoics, Philo, Plotinus, and Origen to Arius; Platonism, which had so deeply influenced Christian theology, was now in conflict with the Church.

Bishop Alexander was shocked not only by these views but by their rapid spread even among the clergy. He called a council of Egyptian bishops at

Alexandria, persuaded it to unfrock Arius and his followers, and sent an account of the proceedings to other bishops. Some of these objected; many priests sympathized with Arius; throughout the Asiatic provinces clergy as well as laity divided on the issue, and made the cities ring with such "tumult and disorder . . . that the Christian religion," says Eusebius, "afforded a subject of profane merriment to the pagans, even in their theaters." [45] Constantine, coming to Nicomedia after overthrowing Licinius, heard the story from its bishop. He sent both Alexander and Arius a personal appeal to imitate the calm of philosophers, to reconcile their differences peaceably, or at least to keep their debates from the public ear. The letter, preserved by Eusebius, clearly reveals Constantine's lack of theology, and the political purpose of his religious policy.

> I had proposed to lead back to a single form the ideas which all people conceive of the Deity; for I feel strongly that if I could induce men to unite on that subject, the conduct of public affairs would be considerably eased. But alas! I hear that there are more disputes among you than recently in Africa. The cause seems to be quite trifling, and unworthy of such fierce contests. You, Alexander, wished to know what your priests were thinking on a point of law, even on a portion only of a question in itself entirely devoid of importance; and you, Arius, if you had such thoughts, should have kept silence. . . . There was no need to make these questions public . . . since they are problems that idleness alone raises, and whose only use is to sharpen men's wits . . . these are silly actions worthy of inexperienced children, and not of priests or reasonable man.[46]

The letter had no effect. To the Church the question of the "consubstantiality" (*homoousia*) as against the mere similarity (*homoiousia*) of the Son and the Father was vital both theologically and politically. If Christ was not God, the whole structure of Christian doctrine would begin to crack; and if division were permitted on this question, chaos of belief might destroy the unity and authority of the Church, and therefore its value as an aide to the state. As the controversy spread, setting the Greek East aflame, Constantine resolved to end it by calling the first ecumenical—universal—council of the Church. He summoned all bishops to meet in 325 at Bithynian Nicaea, near his capital Nicomedia, and provided funds for all their expenses. Not less than 318 bishops came, "attended" says one of them, "by a vast concourse of the lower clergy": [47] the statement reveals the immense growth of the Church. Most of the bishops were from the Eastern provinces; many Western dioceses ignored the controversy; and Pope Silvester I, detained by illness, was content to be represented by some priests.

The Council met in the hall of an imperial palace. Constantine presided and opened the proceedings by a brief appeal to the bishops to restore the unity of the Church. He "listened patiently to the debates," reports Eusebius, "moderated the violence of the contending parties," [48] and himself joined in the argument. Arius reaffirmed his view that Christ was a created being, not equal to the Father, but "divine only by participation." Clever questioners forced him to admit that if Christ was a creature, and had had a beginning, he could change; and that if he could change he might pass from virtue to vice. The answers were logical, honest, and suicidal. Athanasius, the eloquent and pugnacious archdeacon whom Alexander had brought with him as a theological sword, made it clear that if Christ and the Holy Spirit were not of one substance with the Father, polytheism would triumph. He conceded the difficulty of picturing three distinct persons in one God, but argued that reason must bow to the mystery of the Trinity. All but seventeen of the bishops agreed with him, and signed a statement expressing his view. The supporters of Arius agreed to sign if they might add one iota, changing *homoousion* to *homoiousion*. The Council refused, and issued with the Emperor's approval the following creed:

> We believe in one God, the Father Almighty, maker of all things visible or invisible; and in one Lord Jesus Christ, the Son of God, begotten . . . not made, being of one essence (*homoousion*) with the Father . . . who for us men and our salvation came down and was made flesh, was made man, suffered, rose again the third day, ascended into heaven, and comes to judge the quick and the dead. . . .* [49]

Only five bishops, finally only two, refused to sign this formula. These two, with the unrepentant Arius, were anathematized by the Council and exiled by the Emperor. An imperial edict ordered that all books by Arius should be burned, and made the concealment of such a book punishable with death.†

Constantine celebrated the conclusion of the Council with a royal dinner to all the assembled bishops, and then dismissed them with the request that they should not tear one another to pieces. [51] He was mistaken in thinking that the controversy was ended, or that he himself would not change his view of it, but he was right in believing that he had struck a great blow for the unity of the Church. The Council signalized the conviction of the eccle-

---

* This differs from the "Nicene Creed" now in use, which is a revision made in 362.

† The Council also decreed that all churches should celebrate Easter on the same day, to be named in each year by the Bishop of Alexandria according to an astronomical rule, and to be promulgated by the Bishop of Rome. On the question of clerical celibacy the Council inclined to require continence of married priests; but Paphnutius, Bishop of Upper Thebes, persuaded his peers to leave unchanged the prevailing custom, which forbade marriage after ordination, but permitted a priest to cohabit with a wife whom he had married before ordination. [50]

siastical majority that the organization and survival of the Church required a certain fixity of doctrine; and in final effect it achieved that practical unanimity of basic belief which gave the medieval Church its Catholic name. At the same time it marked the replacement of paganism with Christianity as the religious expression and support of the Roman Empire, and committed Constantine to a more definite alliance with Christianity than ever before. A new civilization, based on a new religion, would now rise over the ruins of an exhausted culture and a dying creed. The Middle Ages had begun.

IV. CONSTANTINE AND CIVILIZATION

A year after the Council Constantine dedicated, amid the desolation of Byzantium, a new city which he termed Nova Roma, and which posterity called by his name. In 330 he turned his back upon both Rome and Nicomedia, and made Constantinople his capital. There he surrounded himself with the impressive pomp of an Oriental court, feeling that its psychological influence upon army and people would make its expensive pageantry a subtle economy in government. He protected the army with able diplomacy and arms, tempered despotism with humane decrees, and lent his aid to letters and the arts. He encouraged the schools at Athens, and founded at Constantinople a new university where state-paid professors taught Greek and Latin, literature and philosophy, rhetoric and law, and trained officials for the Empire.[52] He confirmed and extended the privileges of physicians and teachers in all provinces. Provincial governors were instructed to establish schools of architecture, and to draw students to them with divers privileges and rewards. Artists were exempted from civic obligations, so that they might have time to learn their art thoroughly and transmit it to their sons. The art treasures of the Empire were drawn upon to make Constantinople an elegant capital.

In Rome the architectural works of this period were inaugurated by Maxentius. He began (306), and Constantine finished, an immense basilica that marked the climax of classical architecture in the West. Adapting the structure of the great baths, this edifice covered an area 330 by 250 feet. Its central hall, 114 by 82 feet, was roofed by three cross vaults of concrete 120 feet high, partly supported by eight broad piers faced with fluted Corinthian columns sixty feet tall. Its pavement was of colored marble; its bays were peopled with statuary; and the walls of these bays were prolonged above their roofs to serve as elevated buttresses for the central vaults. Gothic and Renaissance architects found much instruction in these vaults and buttresses. Bramante, designing St. Peter's, planned to "raise the Pantheon over the Basilica of Constantine" [53]—i.e., to crown a spacious nave with a massive dome.

The first Christian emperor built many churches in Rome, probably including the original form of San Lorenzo outside the Walls. To celebrate his victory at the Mulvian Bridge he raised in 315 the arch that still towers over the Via dei Trionfi. It is one of the best preserved of Rome's remains; and its majesty is not visibly injured by the diverse pilferage of its parts. Four finely proportioned shafts, rising from sculptured bases, divide the three arches, and support an ornate entablature. The attic story bears reliefs and statues taken from monuments of Trajan and Aurelius; while the medallions between the columns are from some building of Hadrian's reign. Two of the reliefs appear to be the work of Constantine's artists. The crude squat figures, the awkward quarrel of profile faces with frontal legs, the rude piling of heads upon heads as a substitute for perspective, betray a coarsening of technique and taste; but the deep drilling produces, in the play of light and shade, an impressive effect of depth and space; and the episodes are presented with a rough vitality as if Italian art had resolved to return to its source. The colossal figure of Constantine in the Palazzo dei Conservatori carries this primitiveness to a repellent extreme; it seems incredible that the man who presided so graciously over the Council of Nicaea should have resembled this dour barbarian—unless the artist had a mind to illustrate in advance the cynical summary of Gibbon: "I have described the triumph of barbarism and religion." [54]

Early in this fourth century a new art took form—the "illumination" of manuscripts with miniature paintings. Literature itself was now predominantly Christian. Lucius Firmianus Lactantius expounded Christianity eloquently in *Divinae Institutiones* (307), and in *De Mortibus Persecutorum* (314) described the final agonies of the persecuting emperors with Ciceronian elegance and venom. "Religion," wrote Lactantius, "must by its very nature be untrammeled, unforced, free" [55]—a heresy which he did not live to expiate. More famous was Eusebius Pamphili, bishop of Caesarea. He began his literary career as a priestly scribe and librarian for his episcopal predecessor, Pamphilus, whom he loved so well that he adopted his name. Pamphilus had acquired Origen's library, and had built around it the largest Christian collection of books yet known. Living among these volumes, Eusebius became the most erudite cleric of his time. Pamphilus lost his life in the Galerian persecution (310), and Eusebius was much plagued by later queries as to how he himself had survived. He made diverse enemies by taking a middle position between Arius and Alexander; nevertheless, he became the Bossuet of Constantine's court, and was commissioned to write the imperial biography. Part of his scholastic harvest was gathered into a *Universal History*—the most complete of ancient chronologies. Eusebius arranged sacred and profane history in parallel columns divided by a synchronizing row of dates, and tried to fix the time of every important event from Abraham to Constantine. All later chronologies rested on this "canon."

Putting flesh upon these bones, Eusebius issued in 325 an *Ecclesiastical History* describing the development of the Church from its beginnings to the Council of Nicaea. Here in the first chapter, again serving as a model for Bossuet, was the earliest philosophy of history—portraying time as the battleground of God and Satan, and all events as advancing the triumph of Christ. The book was poorly arranged but well written. The sources were critically and conscientiously examined, the statements are as accurate as in any ancient work of history; and at every turn Eusebius put posterity in his debt by quoting important documents that would otherwise have been lost. The bishop's learning is enormous, his style is warmed with feeling and rises to eloquence in moments of theological odium. He frankly excludes such matters as might not edify his Christian readers or support his philosophy, and he manages to write a history of the great Council without mentioning either Arius or Athanasius. The same honest dishonesty makes his *Life of Constantine* a panegyric rather than a biography. It begins with eight inspiring chapters on the Emperor's piety and good works, and tells how he "governed his empire in a godly manner for more than thirty years." One would never guess from this book that Constantine had killed his son, his nephew, and his wife.

For like Augustus, Constantine had managed well everything but his family. His relations with his mother were generally happy. Apparently by his commission she went to Jerusalem, and leveled to the ground the scandalous Temple of Aphrodite that had been built, it was said, over the Saviour's tomb. According to Eusebius the Holy Sepulcher thereupon came to light, with the very cross on which Christ had died. Constantine ordered a Church of the Holy Sepulcher to be built over the tomb, and the revered relics were preserved in a special shrine. As in classical days the pagan world had cherished and adored the relics of the Trojan War, and even Rome had boasted the *Palladium* of Troy's Athene, so now the Christian world, changing its surface and renewing its essence in the immemorial manner of human life, began to collect and worship relics of Christ and the saints. Helena raised a chapel over the traditional site of Jesus' birth at Bethlehem, modestly served the nuns who ministered there, and then returned to Constantinople to die in the arms of her son.

Constantine had been twice married: first to Minervina, who had borne him a son Crispus; then to Maximian's daughter Fausta, by whom he had three daughters and three sons. Crispus became an excellent soldier, and rendered vital aid to his father in the campaigns against Licinius. In 326 Crispus was put to death by Constantine's order; about the same time the Emperor decreed the execution of Licinianus, son of Licinius by Constantine's sister Constantia; and shortly thereafter Fausta was slain by her husband's command. We do not know the reasons for this triple execution. Zosimus assures us that Crispus had made love to Fausta, who accused him to the Emperor; and that Helena, who loved Crispus dearly, had avenged him by persuading Constantine that his wife had yielded to his son.[57] Possibly Fausta had schemed to remove Crispus from the path of her sons' rise to imperial power, and Licinianus may have been killed for plotting to claim his father's share of the realm.

Fausta achieved her aim after her death, for in 335 Constantine bequeathed the Empire to his surviving sons and nephews. Two years later, at Easter, he celebrated with festival ceremonies the thirtieth year of his reign. Then, feeling the nearness of death, he went to take the warm baths at near-by Aquyrion. As his illness increased, he called for a priest to administer to him that sacrament of baptism which he had purposely deferred to this moment, hoping to be cleansed by it from all the sins of his crowded life. Then the tired ruler, aged sixty-four, laid aside the purple robes of royalty, put on the white garb of a Christian neophyte, and passed away.

He was a masterly general, a remarkable administrator, a superlative statesman. He inherited and completed the restorative work of Diocletian; through them the Empire lived 1150 years more. He continued the monarchical forms of Aurelian and Diocletian, partly out of ambition and vanity, partly, no doubt, because he believed that absolute rule was demanded by the chaos of the times. His greatest error lay in dividing the Empire among his sons; presumably he foresaw that they would fight for sole supremacy as he had done, but surmised that they would fight even more certainly if he chose another heir; this, too, is a price of monarchy. His executions we cannot judge, not knowing their provocation; burdened with the problems of rule, he may have allowed fear and jealousy to dethrone his reason for a while; and there are signs that remorse weighed heavily upon his declining years. His Christianity, beginning as policy, appears to have graduated into sincere conviction. He became the most persistent preacher in his realm, persecuted heretics faithfully, and took God into partnership at every step. Wiser than Diocletian, he gave new life to an aging Empire by associating it with a young religion, a vigorous organization, a fresh morality. By his aid Christianity became a state as well as a church, and the mold, for fourteen centuries, of European life and thought. Perhaps, if we except Augustus, the grateful Church was right in naming him the greatest of the emperors.

Epilogue

I. WHY ROME FELL

"THE two greatest problems in history," says a brilliant scholar of our time, are "how to account for the rise of Rome, and how to account for her fall." [1] We may come nearer to understanding them if we remember that the fall of Rome, like her rise, had not one cause but many, and was not an event but a process spread over 300 years. Some nations have not lasted as long as Rome fell.

A great civilization is not conquered from without until it has destroyed itself within. The essential causes of Rome's decline lay in her people, her morals, her class struggle, her failing trade, her bureaucratic despotism, her stifling taxes, her consuming wars. Christian writers were keenly appreciative of this decay. Tertullian, about 200, heralded with pleasure the *ipsa clausula saeculi*—literally the *fin de siècle* or end of an era—as probably a prelude to the destruction of the pagan world. Cyprian, towards 250, answering the charge that Christians were the source of the Empire's misfortunes, attributed these to natural causes:

> You must know that the world has grown old, and does not remain in its former vigor. It bears witness to its own decline. The rainfall and the sun's warmth are both diminishing; the metals are nearly exhausted; the husbandman is failing in the fields.[2]

Barbarian inroads, and centuries of mining the richer veins, had doubtless lowered Rome's supply of the precious metals. In central and southern Italy deforestation, erosion, and the neglect of irrigation canals by a diminishing peasantry and a disordered government had left Italy poorer than before. The cause, however, was no inherent exhaustion of the soil, no change in climate, but the negligence and sterility of harassed and discouraged men.

Biological factors were more fundamental. A serious decline of population appears in the West after Hadrian. It has been questioned, but the mass importation of barbarians into the Empire by Aurelius, Valentinian, Aurelian, Probus, and Constantine leaves little room for doubt.[3] Aurelius, to replenish his army, enrolled slaves, gladiators, policemen, criminals; either the crisis was greater, or the free population less, than before; and the slave population had certainly fallen. So many farms had been abandoned, above all in Italy, that Pertinax offered them gratis to anyone who would till them.

A law of Septimius Severus speaks of a *penuria hominum*—a shortage of men.[4] In Greece the depopulation had been going on for centuries. In Alexandria, which had boasted of its numbers, Bishop Dionysius calculated that the population had in his time (250) been halved. He mourned to "see the human race diminishing and constantly wasting away."[5] Only the barbarians and the Orientals were increasing, outside the Empire and within.

What had caused this fall in population? Above all, family limitation. Practiced first by the educated classes, it had now seeped down to a proletariat named for its fertility;[6] by A.D. 100 it had reached the agricultural classes, as shown by the use of imperial *alimenta* to encourage rural parentage; by the third century it had overrun the western provinces, and was lowering man power in Gaul.[7] Though branded as a crime, infanticide flourished as poverty grew.[8] Sexual excesses may have reduced human fertility; the avoidance or deferment of marriage had a like effect, and the making of eunuchs increased as Oriental customs flowed into the West. Plantianus, Praetorian Prefect, had one hundred boys emasculated, and then gave them to his daughter as a wedding gift.[9]

Second only to family limitation as a cause of lessened population were the slaughters of pestilence, revolution, and war. Epidemics of major proportions decimated the population under Aurelius, Gallienus, and Constantine. In the plague of 260-65 almost every family in the Empire was attacked; in Rome, we are told, there were 5000 deaths every day for many weeks.[10] The mosquitoes of the Campagna were winning their war against the human invaders of the Pontine marshes, and malaria was sapping the strength of rich and poor in Latium and Tuscany. The holocausts of war and revolution, and perhaps the operation of contraception, abortion, and infanticide, had a dysgenic as well as a numerical effect: the ablest men married latest, bred least, and died soonest. The dole weakened the poor, luxury weakened the rich; and a long peace deprived all classes in the peninsula of the martial qualities and arts. The Germans who were now peopling north Italy and filling the army were physically and morally superior to the surviving native stock; if time had allowed a leisurely assimilation they might have absorbed the classic culture and reinvigorated the Italian blood. But time was not so generous. Moreover, the population of Italy had long since been mingled with Oriental strains physically inferior, though perhaps mentally superior, to the Roman type. The rapidly breeding Germans could not understand the classic culture, did not accept it, did not transmit it; the rapidly breeding Orientals were mostly of a mind to destroy that culture; the Romans, possessing it, sacrificed it to the comforts of sterility. Rome was conquered not by barbarian invasion from without, but by barbarian multiplication within.

Moral decay contributed to the dissolution. The virile character that had been formed by arduous simplicities and a supporting faith relaxed in the sunshine of wealth and the freedom of unbelief; men had now, in the middle and upper classes, the means to yield to temptation, and only expediency to restrain them. Urban congestion multiplied contacts and frustrated surveillance; immigration brought together a hundred cultures whose differences rubbed themselves out into indifference. Moral and esthetic standards were lowered by the magnetism of the mass; and sex ran riot in freedom while political liberty decayed.

The greatest of historians held that Christianity was the chief cause of Rome's fall.[11] For this religion, he and his followers [12] argued, had destroyed the old faith that had given moral character to the Roman soul and stability to the Roman state. It had declared war upon the classic culture—upon science, philosophy, literature, and art. It had brought an enfeebling Oriental mysticism into the realistic stoicism of Roman life; it had turned men's thoughts from the tasks of this world to an enervating preparation for some cosmic catastrophe, and had lured them into seeking individual salvation through asceticism and prayer, rather than collective salvation through devotion to the state. It had disrupted the unity of the Empire while soldier emperors were struggling to preserve it; it had discouraged its adherents from holding office, or rendering military service; it had preached an ethic of nonresistance and peace when the survival of the Empire had demanded a will to war. Christ's victory had been Rome's death.

There is some truth in this hard indictment. Christianity unwillingly shared in the chaos of creeds that helped produce that medley of mores which moderately contributed to Rome's collapse. But the growth of Christianity was more an effect than a cause of Rome's decay. The breakup of the old religion had begun long before Christ; there were more vigorous attacks upon it in Ennius and Lucretius than in any pagan author after them. Moral disintegration had begun with the Roman conquest of Greece, and had culminated under Nero; thereafter Roman morals improved, and the ethical influence of Christianity upon Roman life was largely a wholesome one. It was because Rome was already dying that Christianity grew so rapidly. Men lost faith in the state not because Christianity held them aloof, but because the state defended wealth against poverty, fought to capture slaves, taxed toil to support luxury, and failed to protect its people from famine, pestilence, invasion, and destitution; forgivably they turned from Caesar preaching war to Christ preaching peace, from incredible brutality to unprecedented charity, from a life without hope or dignity to a faith that consoled their poverty and honored their humanity. Rome was not destroyed by Christianity, any more than by barbarian invasion; it was an empty shell when Christianity rose to influence and invasion came.

The economic causes of Rome's decline have already been stated as prerequisite to the understanding of Diocletian's reforms; they need only a reminding summary here. The precarious dependence upon provincial grains, the collapse of the slave supply and the latifundia; the deterioration of transport and the perils of trade; the loss of provincial markets to provincial competition; the inability of Italian industry to export the equivalent of Italian imports, and the consequent drain of precious metals to the East; the destructive war between rich and poor; the rising cost of armies, doles, public works, an expanding bureaucracy, and a parasitic court; the depreciation of the currency; the discouragement of ability, and the absorption of investment capital, by confiscatory taxation; the emigration of capital and labor, the strait jacket of serfdom placed upon agriculture, and of caste forced upon industry: all these conspired to sap the material bases of Italian life, until at last the power of Rome was a political ghost surviving its economic death.

The political causes of decay were rooted in one fact—that increasing despotism destroyed the citizen's civic sense and dried up statesmanship at its source. Powerless to express his political will except by violence, the Roman lost interest in government and became absorbed in his business, his amusements, his legion, or his individual salvation. Patriotism and the pagan religion had been bound together, and now together decayed.[13] The Senate, losing ever more of its power and prestige after Pertinax, relapsed into indolence, subservience, or venality; and the last barrier fell that might have saved the state from militarism and anarchy. Local governments, overrun by imperial *correctores* and *exactores*, no longer attracted first-rate men. The responsibility of municipal officials for the tax quotas of their areas, the rising expense of their unpaid honors, the fees, liturgies, benefactions, and games expected of them, the dangers incident to invasion and class war, led to a flight from office corresponding to the flight from taxes, factories, and farms. Men deliberately made themselves ineligible by debasing their social category; some fled to other towns, some became farmers, some monks. In 313 Constantine extended to the Christian clergy that exemption from municipal office, and from several taxes, which pagan priests had traditionally enjoyed; the Church was soon swamped with candidates for ordination, and cities complained of losses in revenue and senators; in the end Constantine was compelled to rule that no man eligible for municipal position should be admitted to the priesthood.[14] The imperial police pursued fugitives from political honors as it hunted evaders of taxes or conscription;

it brought them back to the cities and forced them to serve; [15] finally it decreed that a son must inherit the social status of his father, and must accept election if eligible to it by his rank. A serfdom of office rounded out the prison of economic caste.

Gallienus, fearing a revolt of the Senate, excluded senators from the army. As martial material no longer grew in Italy, this decree completed the military decline of the peninsula. The rise of provincial and mercenary armies, the overthrow of the Praetorian Guard by Septimius Severus, the emergence of provincial generals, and their capture of the imperial throne, destroyed the leadership, even the independence, of Italy long before the fall of the Empire in the West. The armies of Rome were no longer Roman armies; they were composed chiefly of provincials, largely of barbarians; they fought not for their altars and their homes, but for their wages, their donatives, and their loot. They attacked and plundered the cities of the Empire with more relish than they showed in facing the enemy; most of them were the sons of peasants who hated the rich and the cities as exploiters of the poor and the countryside; and as civil strife provided opportunity, they sacked such towns with a thoroughness that left little for alien barbarism to destroy.[16] When military problems became more important than internal affairs, cities near the frontiers were made the seats of government; Rome became a theater for triumphs, a show place of imperial architecture, a museum of political antiquities and forms. The multiplication of capitals and the division of power broke down the unity of administration. The Empire, grown too vast for its statesmen to rule or its armies to defend, began to disintegrate. Left to protect themselves unaided against the Germans and the Scots, Gaul and Britain chose their own *imperatores*, and made them sovereign; Palmyra seceded under Zenobia, and soon Spain and Africa would yield almost unresisting to barbarian conquest. In the reign of Gallienus thirty generals governed thirty regions of the Empire in practical independence of the central power. In this awful drama of a great state breaking into pieces, the internal causes were the unseen protagonists; the invading barbarians merely entered where weakness had opened the door, and where the failure of biological, moral, economic, and political statesmanship had left the stage to chaos, despondency, and decay.

Externally the fall of the Western Roman Empire was hastened by the expansion and migration of the Hsiung-nu, or Huns, in northwestern Asia. Defeated in their eastward advance by Chinese armies and the Chinese Wall, they turned westward, and about A.D. 355 reached the Volga and the Oxus. Their pressure forced the Sarmatians of Russia to move into the Balkans; the Goths, so harassed, moved again upon the Roman frontiers. They were admitted across the Danube to settle in Moesia (376); maltreated there by Roman officials, they revolted, defeated a large Roman army at Adrianople (378), and for a time threatened Constantinople. In 400 Alaric led the Visigoths over the Alps into Italy, and in 410 they took and sacked Rome. In 429 Gaiseric led the Vandals to the conquest of Spain and Africa, and in 455 they took and sacked Rome. In 451 Attila led the Huns in an attack upon Gaul and Italy; he was defeated at Chalons, but overran Lombardy. In 472 a Pannonian general, Orestes, made his son emperor under the name of Romulus Augustulus. Four years later the barbarian mercenaries who dominated the Roman army deposed this "little Augustus," and named their leader Odoacer king of Italy. Odoacer recognized the supremacy of the Roman emperor at Constantinople, and was accepted by him as a vassal king. The Roman Empire in the East would go on until 1453; in the West it had come to an end.

II. THE ROMAN ACHIEVEMENT

It is easier to explain Rome's fall than to account for her long survival. This is the essential accomplishment of Rome—that having won the Mediterranean world she adopted its culture, gave it order, prosperity, and peace for 200 years, held back the tide of barbarism for two centuries more, and transmitted the classic heritage to the West before she died.

Rome has had no rival in the art of government. The Roman state committed a thousand political crimes; it built its edifice upon a selfish oligarchy and an obscurantist priesthood; it achieved a democracy of freemen, and then destroyed it with corruption and violence; it exploited its conquests to support a parasitic Italy, which, when it could no longer exploit, collapsed. Here and there, in East and West, it created a desert and called it peace. But amid all this evil it formed a majestic system of law which through nearly all Europe gave security to life and property, incentive and continuity to industry, from the Decemvirs to Napoleon. It molded a government of separated legislative and executive powers whose checks and balances inspired the makers of constitutions as late as revolutionary America and France. For a time it united monarchy, aristocracy, and democracy so successfully as to win the applause of philosophers, historians, subjects, and enemies. It gave municipal institutions, and for a long period municipal freedom, to half a thousand cities. It administered its Empire at first with greed and cruelty, then with such tolerance and essential justice that the great realm has never again known a like content. It made the desert blossom with civilization, and atoned for its sins with the miracle of a lasting peace. Today our highest labors seek to revive the *Pax Romana* for a disordered world.

Within that unsurpassed framework Rome built a culture Greek in origin,

Roman in application and result. She was too engrossed in government to create as bountifully in the realms of the mind as Greece had done; but she absorbed with appreciation, and preserved with tenacity, the technical, intellectual, and artistic heritage that she had received from Carthage and Egypt, Greece and the East. She made no advance in science, and no mechanical improvements in industry, but she enriched the world with a commerce moving over secure seas, and a network of enduring roads that became the arteries of a lusty life. Along those roads, and over a thousand handsome bridges, there passed to the medieval and modern worlds the ancient techniques of tillage, handicraft, and art, the science of monumental building, the processes of banking and investment, the organization of medicine and military hospitals, the sanitation of cities, and many varieties of fruit and nut trees, of agricultural or ornamental plants, brought from the East to take new root in the West. Even the secret of central heating came from the warm south to the cold north. The south has created the civilizations, the north has conquered and destroyed or borrowed them.

Rome did not invent education, but she developed it on a scale unknown before, gave it state support, and formed the curriculum that persisted till our harassed youth. She did not invent the arch, the vault, or the dome, but she used them with such audacity and magnificence that in some fields her architecture has remained unequaled; and all the elements of the medieval cathedral were prepared in her basilicas. She did not invent the sculptural portrait, but she gave it a realistic power rarely reached by the idealizing Greeks. She did not invent philosophy, but it was in Lucretius and Seneca that Epicureanism and Stoicism found their most finished form. She did not invent the types of literature, not even the satire; but who could adequately record the influence of Cicero on oratory, the essay, and prose style, of Virgil on Dante, Tasso, Milton, . . . of Livy and Tacitus on the writing of history, of Horace and Juvenal on Dryden, Swift, and Pope?

Her language became, by a most admirable corruption, the speech of Italy, Rumania, France, Spain, Portugal, and Latin America; half the white man's world speaks a Latin tongue. Latin was, till the eighteenth century, the Esperanto of science, scholarship, and philosophy in the West; it gave a convenient international terminology to botany and zoology; it survives in the sonorous ritual and official documents of the Roman Church; it still writes medical prescriptions, and haunts the phraseology of the law. It entered by direct appropriation, and again through the Romance languages (*regalis, regal, royal; paganus, pagan, peasant*), to enhance the wealth and flexibility of English speech. Our Roman heritage works in our lives a thousand times a day.

When Christianity conquered Rome the ecclesiastical structure of the pagan church, the title and vestments of the *pontifex maximus*, the worship of the Great Mother and a multitude of comforting divinities, the sense of supersensible presences everywhere, the joy or solemnity of old festivals, and the pageantry of immemorial ceremony, passed like maternal blood into the new religion, and captive Rome captured her conqueror. The reins and skills of government were handed down by a dying empire to a virile papacy; the lost power of the broken sword was rewon by the magic of the consoling word; the armies of the state were replaced by the missionaries of the Church moving in all directions along the Roman roads; and the revolted provinces, accepting Christianity, again acknowledged the sovereignty of Rome. Through the long struggles of the Age of Faith the authority of the ancient capital persisted and grew, until in the Renaissance the classic culture seemed to rise from the grave, and the immortal city became once more the center and summit of the world's life and wealth and art. When, in 1936, Rome celebrated the 2689th anniversary of her foundation, she could look back upon the most impressive continuity of government and civilization in the history of mankind. May she rise again.

THANK YOU, PATIENT READER.

Bibliographical Guide

to books mentioned in the Notes

(Books marked with an asterisk are recommended for further study.)

ABBOTT, F., The Common People of Ancient Rome, N. Y., 1911.

ACTON, LORD, The History of Freedom, London, 1907.

ALCIPHRON, Letters, London, n.d.

ANDERSON, W., and SPIERS, R., The Architecture of Greece and Rome, London, 1902.

APOCRYPHA AND PSEUDEPIGRAPHA OF THE OLD TESTAMENT, Oxford, 1913. 2v.

APPIAN, Roman History, Loeb Classical Library. 4v.

APULEIUS, The Golden Ass, tr. W. Adlington, N. Y., 1927.

ARISTOTLE, Physics, Loeb Library. 2v.

*   Politics, Everyman Library.

ARNOLD, W., Roman System of Provincial Administration, Oxford, 1914.

ARRIAN, Anabasis of Alexander, London, 1893.

ATHENAEUS, The Deipnosophists, London, 1854, 3v.

AUGUSTINE, ST., The City of God, London, 1934.

                Select Letters, Loeb Library.

AUGUSTUS, *Res gestae*, Loeb Library.

BAILEY, C., The Legacy of Rome, Oxford, n.d.

BALL, W. W., Short History of Mathematics, London, 1888.

BALSDON, J., The Emperor Gaius, Oxford, 1934.

*BARNES, H. E., History of Western Civilization, N. Y., 1935. 2v

BARON, S., Social and Religious History of the Jews, N. Y., 1937. **3v.**

BATTIFOL, L., The Century of the Renaissance, N. Y., 1935.

BEARD, M., History of the Business Man, N. Y., 1938.

BEVAN, E., The House of Seleucus, London, 1902, 2v.

            The Legacy of Israel, Oxford, 1927.

*BIBLE, Revised Version of the King James Translation.

BIEBER, M., History of the Greek and Roman Theater, Princeton, 1939.

BIGG, C., Neo-Platonism, London, 1935.

BOISSIER, G., L'Afrique romaine, Paris, 1935.

*   Cicero and His Friends, N. Y., n.d.

            La fin du paganisme, Paris, 1894.

            L'opposition sous les Césars, Paris, 1875.

            La réligion romaine, Paris, 1909. 2v.

            Rome and Pompeii, London, 1896.

            Tacitus and Other Roman Studies, London, 1906.

BOOKS OF ENOCH AND WISDOM, cf. Apocrypha.

BOUCHIER, E., Life and Letters in Roman Africa, Oxford, 1913.

BREASTED, J., Ancient Times, Boston, 1916.

            Oriental Forerunners of Byzantine Painting, Chicago, 1924.

BRECCIA, E., Alexandrea ad Aegyptum, Bergamo, 1922.

BRITTAIN, A., Roman Women, Philadelphia, 1907.
BUCHAN, J., Augustus, N. Y., 1937.
BUCKLAND, W., Textbook of Roman Law, Cambridge U.P., 1921.
BURCKHARDT, J., Die Zeit Constantins des Grossen, Phaidon Verlag, Wien, n.d.
BURY, J., History of the Roman Empire, N. Y., n.d.
          History of Freedom of Thought, N. Y., n.d.

CAESAR, J., De bello civili, Loeb Library.
          De bello Gallico, Loeb Library.
CAMBRIDGE ANCIENT HISTORY, N. Y., 1924f. 12v.
CAMBRIDGE MEDIEVAL HISTORY, N. Y., 1924f. 8v.
CAPES, W., University Life in Ancient Athens, N. Y., 1922.
CARPENTER, EDW., Pagan and Christian Creeds, N. Y., 1920.
CARTER, T., The Invention of Printing in China, N. Y., 1925.
*CASTIGLIONE, A., History of Medicine, N. Y., 1941.
CATHOLIC ENCYCLOPEDIA, N. Y., 1913. 16v.
CATO, M., De agri cultura, Loeb Library.
CATULLUS, Poems, tr. Horace Gregory, N. Y., 1931.
*CATULLUS, Tibullus, and Pervigilium Veneris, Loeb Library.
CHARLESWORTH, M., Trade Routes and Commerce of the Roman Empire, Cam-
          bridge U.P., 1926.
CICERO, Academica, Loeb Library.
          De divinatione, Loeb Library.
          De finibus, Loeb Library.
          De legibus, Loeb Library.
          De natura Deorum, Loeb Library.
          De officiis, Everyman Library.
          De re publica, Loeb Library.
          De senectute and De amicitia, Loeb Library.
          Disputationes Tusculanae, Loeb Library.
          Letters, tr. Melmoth; cf. Middleton.
          Pro Milone and Other Speeches, Loeb Library.
CLEMENT OF ALEXANDRIA, Writings and Opinions, ed. Kaye, London, n.d.
COLLINGWOOD, R., and MYRES, N., Roman Britain, Oxford, 1937.
COLUMELLA, De re rustica, Loeb Library.
CONYBEARE, W. J., and HOWSON, J. S., Life, Times, and Travels of St. Paul,
          N. Y., 1869. 2v.
COULANGES, F. DE, The Ancient City, Boston, 1901.
CUMONT, F., Oriental Religions in Roman Paganism, Chicago, 1911.
CUNNINGHAM, W. C., Western Civilization in Its Economic Aspects, Cambridge
          U.P., 1900. 2v.

DAVIS, W. S., Influence of Wealth in Imperial Rome, N. Y., 1913.
DAVIS, W. S., and WEST, W. M., Readings in Ancient History, Boston, 1912.
DECLAREUIL, J., Rome the Law-Giver, N. Y., 1926.
DENNIS, G., Cities and Cemeteries of Etruria, Everyman Library. 2v.
*DILL, SIR S., Roman Society from Nero to Marcus Aurelius, London, 1911.
DIO CASSIUS, History of Rome, Troy, N. Y., 1905. 8v.

Dio Chrysostom, Orations, Loeb Library. 3v.
Diodorus Siculus, Library of History, Loeb Library. 10v.
Dionysius of Halicarnassus, Roman Antiquities, London, 1758. 4v.
Doughty, G., Travels in Arabia Deserta, N. Y., 1923. 2v.
Duchesne, Mon. L., Early History of the Christian Church, London, 1933. 3v.
Duff, J., Literary History of Rome, London, 1909.
       Literary History of Rome in the Silver Age, N. Y., 1930.
Duruy, V., History of the Roman People, Boston, 1883. 8v.

Edersheim, A., Life and Times of Jesus the Messiah, N. Y., n.d. 2v.
Encyclopaedia Britannica, 14th ed. 24v.
*Epictetus, Works, Loeb Library. 2v.
       Encheiridion, Girard, Kan., n.d.
Eusebius Pamphilus, Ecclesiastical History, N. Y., 1839.
       Historical View of the Council of Nice, in preceding.
       Life of Constantine, in Ancient Ecclesiastical Histories, London,
         1650.
       Praeparatio evangelica, Oxford, 1843.

Fattorusso, J., Wonders of Italy, Florence, 1930.
Ferrero, G., Ancient Rome and Modern America, N. Y., 1914.
*   Greatness and Decline of Rome, N. Y., 1909. 5v.
       The Ruin of Ancient Civilization, N. Y., 1921.
       The Women of the Caesars, N. Y. n.d.
Finkelstein, L., Akiba, N. Y., 1936.
*Flaubert, G., Salammbo, Modern Library.
Flick, A. C., Rise of the Medieval Church, N. Y., 1909.
Foakes-Jackson, F., and Lake, K., Beginnings of Christianity, London, 1920. 5v.
Fowler, W. W., Religious Experience of the Roman People, London, 1933.
       Roman Festivals of the Period of the Republic, N. Y., 1899.
       Social Life at Rome, N. Y., 1927.
Frank, T., Economic History of Rome, Baltimore, 1927.
       Roman Imperialism, N. Y., 1914.
       Economic Survey of Ancient Rome, Baltimore, 1933f. 5v.
Frazer, Sir J., Adonis, Attis, and Osiris, London, 1907.
       The Magic Art, N. Y., 1935. 2v.
       The Scapegoat, N. Y., 1935.
       Spirits of the Corn and Wild, N. Y., 1935. 2v.
*Friedlander, L., Roman Life and Manners under the Roman Empire, London,
       1928. 4v.
Frontinus, Stratagems and Aqueducts, Loeb Library.
Fronto, M., Correspondence, Loeb Library.

Gaius, Elements of Roman Law, ed. Poste, Oxford, 1875.
Galen, On the Natural Faculties, Loeb Library.
Gardiner, E., Athletics of the Ancient World, Oxford, 1930.
Gellius, Aulus, Attic Nights, Loeb Library. 3v.
Garrison, F., History of Medicine, Phila., 1929.

GATTESCHI, G., Restauri della Roma Imperiale, Rome, 1924.
GEST, A., Roman Engineering, N. Y., 1930.
GIBBON, E., Decline and Fall of the Roman Empire, Everyman Library. 6v.
        Ed. Bury, J. B., London, 1900. 7v. Only when so specified.
GLOVER, T. R., The Conflict of Religions in the Early Roman Empire, London,
        1932.
GOGUEL, M., Life of Jesus, N. Y., 1933.
GOODSPEED, E. J., The New Testament, an American Translation, Univ. of
        Chicago, 1937.
GRAETZ, H., History of the Jews, Phila., 1891. 6v.
GREEK ANTHOLOGY, Loeb Library.
GUHL, E., and KONER, W., Life of the Greeks and the Romans, N. Y., 1876.
GUIGNEBERT, C., Christianity Past and Present, N. Y., 1927.
        Jesus, N. Y., 1935
GUMMERE, R., Seneca the Philosopher, Boston, 192?

HADZSITS, G., Lucretius and His Influence, London, 1935.
HAGGARD, H., Devils, Drugs, and Doctors, N. Y., 1929.
HALLIDAY, W. R., The Pagan Background of Early Christianity, London, 1925.
HAMMERTON, J., Universal History of the World, London, n.d. 8v.
HARRISON, JANE, Prolegomena to the Study of Greek Religion, Cambridge
        U.P., 1922.
HASKELL, H., The New Deal in Old Rome, N. Y., 1939.
HASTINGS, J., Encyclopedia of Religion and Ethics, N. Y., 1928. 12v.
HATCH, E., Influence of Greek Ideas and Usages upon the Christian Church,
        London, 1890.
HAVERFIELD, F., The Romanization of Roman Britain, Oxford, 1923.
        The Roman Occupation of Britain, Oxford, 1924.
HEATH, SIR T., History of Greek Mathematics, Oxford, 1921. 2v.
HEINE, H., Memoirs, London, 1910. 2v.
HEITLAND, W., Agricola, Cambridge U.P., 1921.
HELIODORUS, Longus, etc., Greek Romances, London, 1901.
HENDERSON, B., Life and Principate of the Emperor Hadrian, N. Y., n.d.
        Life and Principate of the Emperor Nero, Phila., 1903.
HERODIAN, History of Twenty Caesars, London, 1629.
*HERODOTUS, History, ed. Rawlinson, London, 1862. 4v.
HIMES, N., Medical History of Contraception, Baltimore, 1936.
HISTORIAE AUGUSTAE, Loeb Library, 2v.
HOLMES, T. R., The Architect of the Roman Empire, Oxford, 1928. 2v.
HOMO, L., Primitive Italy, London, 1927.
        Roman Political Institutions, N. Y., 1930.
*HORACE, Odes and Epodes, Loeb Library.
        Satires and Epistles, Loeb Library.
HOWARD, C., Sex Worship, Chicago, 1909.

INGE, DEAN W. R., The Philosophy of Plotinus, London, 1929. 2v.
IRENAEUS, Adversus haereses, Oxford, 1872.

JEROME, Select Letters, Loeb Library.
JONES, A., Cities of the Eastern Roman Provinces, Oxford, 1937.
JONES, H., Companion to Roman History, Oxford, 1912.
JONES, W., Malaria and Roman History, Manchester U.P., 1909.
JOSEPHUS, Works, tr. Whiston, Boston, 1811, 2v.
JULLIAN, C., Histoire de la Gaule, Paris, 1908. 6v.
JUSTINIAN, Digest; cf. Scott, S. P.
*JUVENAL AND PERSIUS, Satires, Loeb Library.
JUVENAL, PERSIUS, SULPICIA, AND LUCILIUS, Satires, tr. Gifford, London, 1852.

KALTHOFF, A., Rise of Christianity, London, 1907.
KAUTSKY, K., Ursprung des Christentums, Vienna, 1908.
KLAUSNER, J., From Jesus to Paul, N. Y., 1943.
        Jesus of Nazareth, N. Y., 1929. ·
KOHLER, C., History of Costume, N. Y., 1928.

LACTANTIUS, Works, in Ante-Nicene Christian Library, vols. XXI-II, London,
        1881.
LAKE, K., ed., The Apostolic Fathers, Loeb Library. 2v.
LANCIANI, R., Ancient Rome, Boston, 1899.
LANG, P., Music in Western Civilization, N. Y., 1941.
LEA, H. C., Historical Sketch of Sacerdotal Celibacy, Boston, 1884.
LECKY, W., History of European Morals, N. Y., 1926. 2v.
LESLIE SHANE, The Greek Anthology, N. Y., 1929.
LIVINGSTONE, R. W., The Legacy of Greece, Oxford, 1924.
LIVY, T., History of Rome, Everyman Library. 6v.
LONGINUS ON THE SUBLIME, Loeb Library.
LOT, FERDINAND, End of the Ancient World, N. Y., 1931.
LUCAN, Pharsalia, Loeb Library.
*LUCIAN, Works, tr. Fowler, Oxford, 1905, 4v.
*LUCRETIUS, De rerum natura, Loeb Library.

MACGREGOR, R., The Greek Anthology, London, n.d.
MACKENNA, STEPHEN, The Essence of Plotinus, N. Y., 1934.
MACROBIUS, Works, French tr., Paris, 1827. 2v.
        Opera, London, 1694.
MAHAFFY, J., The Silver Age of the Greek World, Chicago, 1906.
MAINE, SIR H., Ancient Law, Everyman Library.
MAIURI, A., Les fresques de Pompeii, Paris, n.d.
        Pompeii, Rome, n.d.
MANTZIUS, K., History of Theatrical Art, N. Y., 1937. 6v.
*MARCUS AURELIUS, Meditations, tr. Long, Boston, 1876.
MARTIAL, Epigrams, Loeb Library. 2v.
MATTHEWS, B., Development of the Drama, N. Y., 1921.
MAU, A., Pompeii, N. Y., 1902.
MERIVALE, C., History of the Romans under the Empire, London, 1865. 8v.
MIDDLETON, C., Life of Marcus Tullius Cicero, London, 1877.
MINUCIUS, FELIX, Octavius, in Tertullian, Apologeticus, Loeb Library.

MOMIGLIANO, A., Claudius, Oxford, 1934.
*MOMMSEN, T., History of Rome, London, 1901. 5v.
        The Provinces of the Roman Empire, N. Y., 1887. 2v.
MONROE, P., Source Book of the History of Education for the Greek and Roman
        Period, N. Y., 1932.
MONTESQUIEU, CHARLES DE, Grandeur et Décadence des Romains, Paris, 1924.
MOORE, G. F., Judaism in the First Centuries of the Christian Era, Cambridge,
        Mass., 1932. 2v.
MULLER-LYER, F., Evolution of Modern Marriage, N. Y., 1930.
MURRAY, G., Five Stages of Greek Religion, Oxford, 1930.

NEPOS, CORNELIUS, Lives, N. Y., 1895.

OVID, Ars amatoria, Loeb Library.
    Fasti, Loeb Library.
    Heroides and Amores, Loeb Library.
    Love Books of, tr. May, N. Y., 1930.
    Metamorphoses, Loeb Library. 2v.
    Tristia and Ex Ponto, Loeb Library.
OWEN, JOHN, Evenings with the Sceptics, London, 1881. 2v.

PATER, WALTER, Marius the Epicurean, N. Y., n.d.
PAUL-LOUIS, Ancient Rome at Work, N. Y., 1927.
PFUHL, E., Masterpieces of Greek Drawing and Painting, London, 1926.
PHILO, Works, Loeb Library. 9v.
PHILOSTRATUS, Life of Apollonius of Tyana, Loeb Library. 2v.
PHILOSTRATUS AND EUNAPIUS, Lives of the Sophists, Loeb Library.
PLAUTUS, Comedies, London, 1889.
PLINY THE ELDER, Natural History, London, 1855. 6v.
*PLINY THE YOUNGER, Letters, Loeb Library.
PLOTINUS, Select Works, London, 1912.
PLUTARCH, De Iside et Osiride, French tr., Paris, 1924.
        De tranquillitate animi, tr. Harvard U.P., 1931.
        Lives, Everyman Library. 3v.
        Moralia, Loeb Library.
        Quaestiones Romanae, tr. Holland, London, 1892.
POLYBIUS, Histories, Loeb Library. 6v.
POPE, A. U., Survey of Persian Art, London, 1938. 6v.
PORPHYRY, Life of Plotinus, in MacKenna, S., The Essence of Plotinus, N. Y,
        1934.
PROPERTIUS, Poems, Loeb Library.

QUINTILIAN, Institutes of Oratory, Loeb Library. 4v.

RAMSAY, W. M., The Church in the Roman Empire, N. Y., 1893.
RANDALL-MACIVER, D., The Etruscans, Oxford, 1927.
RAWLINSON, G., The Sixth Great Oriental Monarch, N. Y., n.d.
REID, J., Municipalities of the Roman Empire, Cambridge U.P., 1913.

REINACH, S., Apollo, a History of Art, N. Y., 1917.
    A Short History of Christianity, N. Y., 1922.
RENAN, E., Antichrist, London, n.d.
    The Apostles, London, n.d.
    The Christian Church, London, n.d.
    Lectures on the Influence of Rome on Christianity, London, 1884.
    Life of Jesus, N. Y., n.d.
    Marc Aurèle, Paris, n.d.
    St. Paul, Paris, n.d.
ROBERTSON, J. M., Short History of Freethought, London, 1914. 2v.
RODENWALDT, G., Die Kunst der Antike: Hellas und Rom, Berlin, 1927.
ROSTOVTZEFF, M., History of the Ancient World, Oxford, 1928, 2v.
    Mystic Italy, N. Y., 1927.
    Social and Economic History of the Hellenistic World, N. Y.,
      1942. 3v.
    Social and Economic History of the Roman Empire, Oxford,
      1926.

SACHAR, A., History of the Jews, N. Y., 1932.
SALLUST, Works, Loeb Library.
SANDYS, SIR J., Companion to Latin Studies, Cambridge U.P., 1925.
SARTON, G., Introduction to the History of Science, Baltimore, 1930. Vol. I.
SCHÜRER, E., History of the Jewish People in the Times of Jesus, N. Y., 1890. 6v.
*SCHWEITZER, A., The Quest of the Historical Jesus, London, 1926.
SCOTT, E. F., First Age of Christianity, N. Y., 1935.
SCOTT, S. P., The Civil Law of Rome, Cincinnati, 1932. 17v.
SENECA, Epistulae Morales, Loeb Library. 2v.
    Moral Essays, Loeb Library. 3v.
    Quaestiones naturales, tr. in Clarke, Physical Science in the Time of
      Nero, London, 1910.
    Tragedies, Loeb Library. 2v.
SEXTUS EMPIRICUS, Works, Loeb Library. 3v.
    Opera, Leipzig, 1840. 2v.
SHOTWELL, J., Introduction to the History of History, N. Y., 1936.
SHOTWELL, J., and LOOMIS, L., The See of Peter, Columbia U.P., 1927.
SIDONIUS APOLLINARIS, Poems, Loeb Library.
SIMPSON, F., History of Architectural Development, London, 1921. Vol. I.
SMITH, R. B., Carthage and the Carthaginians, N. Y., 1908.
SMITH, WM., Dictionary of Greek and Roman Antiquities, Boston, 1859.
SELLAR, W., Horace and the Elegiac Poets, Oxford, 1937.
    Roman Poets of the Augustan Age: Virgil, Oxford, 1877.
    Roman Poets of the Republic, Oxford, 1881.
SOCRATES, Ecclesiastical History, London, 1892.
STATIUS, Poems, Loeb Library. 2v.
STRABO, Geography, Loeb Library. 8v.
STRONG, E., Art in Ancient Rome, N. Y., 1928. 2v.
SUETONIUS, Works, Loeb Library. 2v.

*SUMNER, W. G., Folkways, Boston, 1906.
             War and Other Essays, Yale U.P., 1911.
SYME, R., The Roman Revolution, Oxford, 1939.
SYMONDS, J. A., Studies of the Greek Poets, London, 1920.

*TACITUS, Annals, Loeb Library.
*   Histories, Loeb Library.
          Works, tr. Murphy, London, 1830.
TAINE, H., Essai sur Tite Live, Paris, 1874.
          Modern Regime, N. Y., 1890. 2v.
TALMUD, Babylonian, tr., London, 1935f. 24v.
TARN, W. W., Hellenistic Civilization, London, 1927.
TAYLOR, H., Cicero, Chicago, 1916.
TERENCE, Comedies, London, 1898.
TERTULLIAN, Apologeticus, etc., Loeb Library.
THIERRY, A., Histoire de la Gaule sous l'administration romaine, Paris, 1840. 3v
THOMPSON, SIR E., Introduction to Greek and Latin Paleography, Oxford, 1912
THORNDIKE, L., History of Magic and Experimental Science, N. Y., 1929. 2v.
THUCYDIDES, History of the Peloponnesian War, Everyman Library.
TIBULLUS, Poems, cf. Catullus.
TOUTAIN, J., Economic Life of the Ancient World, N. Y., 1930.
TOYNBEE, A. J., A Study of History, Oxford, 1935. 3v.
TRENCH, R., Plutarch, London, 1874.

UEBERWEG, F., History of Philosophy, N. Y., 1871. 2v.
USHER, A., History of Mechanical Inventions, N. Y., 1929.

VALERIUS MAXIMUS, Factorum et dictorum, Berlin, 1854.
VARRO, M., Rerum rusticarum, Loeb Library.
*VIRGIL, Poems, Loeb Library. 2v.
VITRUVIUS, De architectura, Loeb Library.
VOGELSTEIN, H., Rome, Phila., 1940.
VOLTAIRE, Philosophical Dictionary, N. Y., 1901.

WARD, C. O., The Ancient Lowly, Chicago, 1907. 2v.
WATSON, P. B., Marcus Aurelius Antoninus, N. Y., 1884.
WEIGALL, A., The Paganism in Our Christianity, N. Y., 1928.
WEISE, O., Language and Character of the Roman People, London, 1909.
WESTERMARCK, E., Origin and Development of the Moral Ideas, London,
          1917. 2v.
WHITE, E. L., Why Rome Fell, N. Y., 1927.
WICKHOFF, F., Roman Art, London, 1900.
WILLIAMS, H., History of Science, N. Y., 1909. 5v.
WINCKELMANN, J., History of Ancient Art, Boston, 1880. 2v.
WRIGHT, F., History of Later Greek Literature, N. Y., 1932.

ZEITLIN, S., The Jews, Phila., 1936.
          The Pharisees and the Gospels, N. Y., 1938.

Notes

Capital Roman numerals, except at the beginning of a note, will usually indicate volumes, followed by page numbers; small Roman numerals will usually indicate "books" (main divisions) of a classical text, followed by chapter or verse numbers, and sometimes additionally by section or paragraph numbers.

CHAPTER I

1. Pliny, *Natural History*, xxxvii, 77.
2. Virgil, *Georgics*, ii, 149.
3. Ibid., ii, 198.
4. Strabo, *Geography*, v, 4. 8.
5. Polybius, *History*, i, 2. 15.
6. In Taine, *Modern Regime*, 17.
7. Aristotle, *Physics*, 1329b.
8. Thucydides, *Peloponnesian War*, vi, 18. 2.
9. Homo, *Primitive Italy*, 32; Toutain, *Economic Life of the Ancient World*, 207.
10. Dennis, *Cities and Cemeteries of Etruria*, I, 36.
11. Herodotus, *Histories*, v, 94; Strabo, v, 1. 2; Tacitus, *Annals*, iv, 55; Appian, *Roman History*, viii, 9. 66; etc. Dionysius of Halicarnassus, i, 30, regarded the Etruscans as indigenous to Italy; so did Mommsen, *History of Rome*, I, 155. Dennis, I, 17, Frank, *Economic History of Rome*, 16, Randall-MacIver, *Etruscans*, 23, and Rostovtzeff, *History of the Ancient World*, II, 180, accept the tradition.
12. Dennis, I, 39.
13. Paul-Louis, *Ancient Rome at Work*, 66; Toutain, 211.
14. Dennis, I, 329.
15. Athenaeus, *Deipnosophists*, xii, 3.
16. Garrison, *History of Medicine*, 119.
17. Castiglione, *History of Medicine*, 192.
18. Aristotle in Athenaeus, i, 19; Dennis, I, 321.
19. Ibid., 21.
20. *Cambridge Ancient History*, IV, 415.
21. Frazer, Sir J., *Magic Art*, II, 287.
22. Scholiast on Juvenal, vi, 565.
23. Frazer, l. c.
24. CAH, IV, 420-1; Mommsen, I, 232-3; Dennis, II, 168.
25. *Enc. Brit.*, VIII, 787.
26. Anderson and Spiers, *Architecture of Greece and Rome*, 121; Strong, E., *Art in Ancient Rome*, 21; CAH, VII, 386.
27. Pliny, xxxv, 6.
28. Rodenwaldt, G., *Die Kunst der Antike: Hellas*, 509.

29. Ovid, *Fasti*, iii, 15.
30. Livy, *History of Rome*, i, 9-13.
31. Frazer, II, 289.
32. Livy, i, 19.
33. Tacitus, *Annals*, iii, 26.
34. Cicero, *De re publica*, ii, 14.
35. Livy, i, 22.
36. Ibid., 27.
37. Dio Cassius, *History of Rome*, fragment vii.
38. Strabo, v, 2. 2.
39. Livy, i, 35.
40. Pais, E., *Ancient Legends of Roman History*, 38.
41. Cicero, *Republica*, ii, 21.
42. Livy, i, 46.
43. Pais, 137-8.
44. Dio, iii, 7, and frag. x, 2.
45. Livy, i. 56-7.
46. Syme, R., *The Roman Revolution*, 85n.
47. Cicero, *Republica*, i, 39; Coulanges, F., *The Ancient City*, 384.
48. Tacitus, *Histories*, iii, 72.
49. Mommsen, I, 414.
50. Dennis, I, 26.
51. Duff, J. W., *Literary History of Rome*, 6; CAH, IV, 407.
52. Livy, i, 8; Strabo, v, 2. 2; Dennis, II, 166.
53. CAH, VII, 384.
54. Livy, i, 8.
55. CAH, VIII, 387; Hammerton, J., *Universal History of the World*, II, 1158.
56. Strabo, v, 2. 2.

CHAPTER II

1. Livy, i, 8.
2. Aulus Gellius, *Attic Nights*, vi, 13.
3. Livy, ii, 56; CAH, VII, 456.
4. Aulus Gellius, xx, 1. 45-51; Dio, frag. xvi, 4.
5. Livy, ii, 23-30; Dio, iv, 7 and frag. xvi, 6; Dionysius, vi, 45; Plutarch, "Coriolanus."
6. Livy, iv, 13; Dio, vi, 7.
7. Livy, iii, 52.
8. Dio, v, 7.
9. Ibid.
10. Livy, i, 43.

11. Frank, *Economic History*, 20; Smith, W., *Dictionary of Greek and Roman Antiquities*, s. v. *exercitus*.
12. Mommsen, III, 60.
13. Plutarch, "Pyrrhus."
14. Coulanges, 244.
15. Dio, iv, 7.
16. Twelve Tables, iv, 1-3, in Monroe, P., *Source Book*, 337.
17. Twelve Tables, iii, 1-6.
18. Ibid., viii, 3.
19. Ibid., 21-26.
20. Cicero, *Pro Roscio Amerino*, 25-6.
21. Polybius, iii, 6.
22. Livy, vii, 24.
23. Vitruvius, *De Architectura*, ii, 12.
24. Polybius, vi, 37.
25. Frontinus, *Stratagems and Aqueducts*, iv, 1.
26. Frank, *Economic History*, 338; Id., *Economic Survey of Ancient Rome*, V, 160; Fowler, W. W., *Social Life at Rome*, 32; Edwards, H. J., Appendix A to Caesar, *Gallic War*.
27. Dio, vi, 95.
28. Livy, ii, 34; Dionysius, vii, 50; Dio, v, 7 and frag. xvii, 2; Appian, *Roman History*, ii, 5; Plutarch, "Coriolanus."
29. Polybius, ii, 15-20.
30. Livy, v, 42.
31. Dio, vii, 7.
32. Coulanges, 494.
33. Plutarch, "Sayings of Great Commanders," in *Moralia*, 184C.

CHAPTER III

1. Mommsen, II, 138.
2. Smith, R. B., *Carthage*, 29.
3. Appian, viii, 95.
4. Polybius, vi, 56.
5. Plutarch, *De re publica ger.*, iii, 6.
6. Frazer, *Adonis, Attis, Osiris*, I, 114.
7. Diodorus Siculus, *Library of History*, xx, 14.
8. St. Augustine, *Letters*, xvii, 2.
9. Appian, viii, 127.
10. Aristotle, *Politics*, 1272b.
11. Ibid., 1273a.
12. Polybius, iii, 22.
13. Strabo, xvii, 1. 19.
14. Polybius, i, 20-1.
15. Cicero, *De Officiis*, iii, 26; *In Pisonem*, 43.
16. Gellius, vii, 4.
17. Polybius, i. 80.
18. Smith, R. B., *Carthage*, 151.
19. Polybius, i, 87. Flaubert has told the story with perfect art in *Salammbo*.
20. Mommsen, ii, 223.

21. Dio, frag. lii, 2.
22. Livy, xxi, 4.
23. Mommsen, II, 243.
24. Livy, xxi, 22.
25. Plutarch, *Moralia*, 195D.
26. Livy, xxii, 57.
27. Polybius, ii, 75, 118.
28. Livy, xxii, 50.
29. Livy, xxviii, 12.
30. Diodorus, xxvii, 9; Appian, vii, 59.
31. Ibid., viii, 134.
32. Livy, xxxix, 51.

CHAPTER IV

1. Twelve Tables, iv, 1.
2. St. Augustine, *City of God*, vi, 9.
3. Horace, *Satires*, i, 8, 35; Müller-Lyer, F., *Evolution of Modern Marriage*, 55; Castiglione, 195; Howard, C., *Sex Worship*, 65, 79; *Enc. Brit.*, 11th ed., XVII, 467; XXI, 345.
4. Pliny, xxviii, 19.
5. Livy, xxiii, 31.
6. Virgil, *Georgics*, ii, 419; Horace, *Odes*, i, 1.25.
7. Frazer, *Magic Art*, II, 190; the derivation is questioned by Fowler, W. W., *Roman Festivals of the Republic*, 99.
8. Virgil, *Aeneid*, vii, 761; Ovid, *Fasti*, vi, 753; *Metamorphoses*, xv, 497; Strabo, v, 3.12; Pliny, xxx, 12-13; Frazer, *Magic Art*, I, 11.
9. Boissier, G., *La réligion romaine*, I, 27.
10. Livy, v, 21-2; vi, 29; Coulanges, 199.
11. Ovid, *Metam.*, xv, 626.
12. Livy, viii, 15; Lanciani, R., *Ancient Rome*, 143.
13. Fowler, W. W., *Religious Experience of the Roman People*, 337.
14. Mommsen, III, 11.
15. Cicero, *Pro Archia*, 4; Fowler, op. cit., 30. The derivation is not certain; Cicero gives another in *De natura deorum*, ii, 28.
16. Reinach, S., *Apollo*, 109.
17. Livy, vii, 5.
18. Pliny, xxviii, 10.
19. Harrison, J., *Prolegomena to the Study of Greek Religion*, 35.
20. Plautus, *Curculio*, 33-8.
21. Ovid, *Fasti*, iii, 523.
23. Howard, 66.
24. Athenaeus, xiv, 44.
25. Westermarck, E., *Origin and Development of the Moral Ideas*, I, 430; Cicero, *Pro Caelio*, 20.
26. Brittain, A., *Roman Women*, 135-6.
27. Coulanges, 63.
28. Plutarch, "Numa and Lycurgus."

29. Gellius, x, 23.
30. Abbott, F., *Common People of Ancient Rome*, 87.
31. Catullus, *Poems*, xxv.
32. Pliny, xxxiii, 16.
33. Fowler, W. W., *Social Life at Rome*, 50-1, 270.
34. Polybius, xxxi, 26.
35. Ibid., vi, 56.
36. Cf. Appian, vi, *passim*.
37. Polybius, vi, 58.
38. Plutarch, *Quaestiones Romanae*, 59.
39. Livy, iii, 38.
40. Heine, H., *Memoirs*, I, 12.
41. Thompson, Sir E., *Greek and Latin Paleography*, 5.
42. Schlegel, A. W., *Lectures on Dramatic Art and Literature*, 202.
43. Livy, vii, 2; Bieber, N., *History of the Greek and Roman Theater*, 307.
44. In Duff, J., *Literary History of Rome*, 130.
45. Castiglione, 196.
46. Lanciani, R., *Ancient Rome*, 53.
47. Glover, T. R., *Conflict of Religions in the Early Roman Empire*, 13; Friedländer, L., *Roman Life and Manners under the Early Empire*, III, 141.
48. Twelve Tables, x, 9.
49. Pliny, xxix, 6.
50. Frank, *Economic Survey*, I, 12; CAH, VII, 417; for the contrary cf. Mommsen, *History*, I, 193, 238.
51. Pliny, xviii, 3.
52. Virgil, *Georgics*, i, 299.
53. Guhl, E., and Koner, W., *Life of the Greeks and Romans*, 503.
54. Cato, *de agri cultura*, viii; Varro, *Rerum rusticarum libri tres*, pref.
55. Cicero, *Letters*, vii, 1.
56. Pliny, xxxiii, 13.
57. CAH, VIII, 345.
58. Mommsen, *History*, III, 75.
59. CAH, X, 395; Frank, *Economic History of Rome*, 340. For other comparative prices cf. ibid., 66.
60. Twelve Tables, viii, 18; Tacitus, *Annals*, vi, 16.
61. Livy, vii, 19-21, 42.
62. Paul-Louis, 118.
63. Frank, *Economic History*, 119; for a contrary view cf. Ward, C. O., *The Ancient Lowly*, 208-9.
64. Livy, viii, 12; Dionysius of Halicarnassus, ix, 43.
65. Mommsen, *History*, I, 248-9; Paul-Louis, 47.
66. 77% between 200 and 150 B.C.—Frank, *Economic Survey*, I, 146.

67. Ibid., 41; CAH, VIII, 344; Paul-Louis, 102; Mommsen, *History*, II, 55.
68. Pliny, xxxvi, 24.
69. *Enc. Brit.*, XIX, 466.
70. Rickard, T., *Man and Metals*, I, 280.
71. Twelve Tables, x, 4.
72. E.g. in Plautus' *Captives*, 998.
73. Lucian, *Dialogues of the Dead*, xxv.

CHAPTER V

1. Livy, iv, 302.
2. Plutarch, "Flamininus."
3. Livy, xliv, 22.
4. Appian, vi, 9-10; Mommsen, *History*, III, 220.
5. Livy, xxxix, 7; Mommsen, 201.
6. Polybius, vi, 17.
7. Davis, W. S., *Influence of Wealth in Imperial Rome*, 74, 77; Mommsen, III, 83.
8. Polybius, xxxi, 25; Mommsen, III, 127; Sellar, W. Y., *Roman Poets of the Republic*, 234.
9. Mommsen, III, 40.
10. Polybius, xxxi, 25.
11. Guhl, 490.
12. Plutarch, "Cato the Elder."
13. Livy, xxxiv, 1.
14. Brittain, 95.
15. Polybius, xxx, 14.
16. Mommsen, III, 21, 127.
17. Ibid., 44, 294, 301-2.
18. CAH, VIII, 359.
19. Plutarch, "Marcellus."
20. Anderson, 137.
21. Cicero, *De divinatione*, ii, 24.52.
22. Polybius, vi, 56.
23. Livy, xxxix, 8.
24. Cicero, *De re publica*, ii, 19.
24a. Horace, *Epistles*, ii, 1.156.
25. Cicero, *De senectute*, viii, 26.
26. Cf. Bk. II of the *Republic*.
27. Appian, vi, 9.53.
28. Ennius, *Telamo*, frag. in Duff, 141.
29. Cicero, *De div.*, ii, 50.
30. Ennius, frag. in Gellius, xii, 4.
31. Ennius in Cicero, *Disp. Tusc.*, ii, 1.1.
32. Collins, W. L., *Plautus and Terence*, 33-4; Matthews, B., *Development of the Drama*, 98.
33. Cicero, *De re publica*, iv, 10.
34. Collins, 45.
35. Plautus, *Amphitryon*, iii, 2, 4.
36. Batiffol, L., *Century of the Renaissance*, 164.
37. Suetonius, *On Poets*, "Terence," ii.
38. Terence, *Heauton Timoroumenos*, prologue.

39. Terence, *Adelphi*, prologue.
40. Suetonius, l. c.
41. Plutarch, *Moralia*, 198E, 199C.
42. Pliny, vii, 28.
43. Livy, xxxix, 42; Plutarch, "Cato the Elder."
44. Fowler, *Social Life*, 191.
45. Pliny, viii, 11.
46. Plutarch, l. c.
47. Ibid., Pliny, xxix, 7.
48. Appian, viii, 14.
49. Strabo, xvii, 3.15.

CHAPTER VI

1. Mommsen, *History*, III, 306.
2. Livy, xli, 28; xlv, 34.
3. Ibid., xxxix, 29.
4. Heitland, W., *Agricola*, 161; Ward, I, 121.
5. Dio Cassius, xxxiv, frag. ii, 23; Livy, Epitome of Book xc.
6. Plutarch, "Tiberius Gracchus."
7. Ibid.
8. Appian, *Civil Wars*, i, 1.
9. Pliny, xxxiii, 14.
10. Appian, *Civil Wars*, i, 3.
11. Julius Philippus in Cicero, *De off.*, ii, 21.
12. Appian, *Civil Wars*, i, 4.
13. Plutarch, "Marius."
14. Sallust, *Jugurthine War*, xiii, xx-xxviii.
15. Plutarch, l. c.
16. Ibid.
17. Plutarch, "Sylla."
18. Sallust, xcv.
19. Ibid., xcvi.
20. Mommsen, IV, 142.
21. Appian, *Civil Wars*, i, 8.
22. Plutarch, l. c.
23. Ibid.
24. Ibid.

CHAPTER VII

1. Plutarch, "Caesar."
2. Davis, 13-14.
3. Cicero, *Ad Atticum*, iv, 15.
4. Plutarch, "Pompey."
5. Cicero, *Ad Quintum*, ii, 5.
6. Cicero, *Letters*, iii, 29.
7. Cicero, *Ad Quintum*, iii, 2.
8. Mommsen, V, 349.
9. Plutarch, "Cicero."
10. Cicero, *I In Verrem*, 13.
11. Frank, *Economic History*, 295.
12. Mommsen, IV, 173.
13. Frank, 289.
14. Cicero, *De off.*, i, 8.
15. Plutarch, l. c.
     of *History*, 238.

16. Nepos, "Atticus."
17. Plutarch, "Lucullus."
18. Frank, *Economic Survey*, I, 354.
19. Macrobius, *Saturnalia*, iii, 13.
20. Varro, iii, 16; Cicero, *Letters*, ix, 18; Mommsen, V, 387.
22. Cicero, *Letters*, vii, 26.
23. Pliny, xxxvi, 24.
24. L. c.
25. *Historiae Augustae*, "Alex. Severus," 33; Livy, xxxix, 8f; Mommsen, V, 384; Ward, I, 406.
26. In Boissier, G., *Cicero and His Friends*, 164.
27. Cicero, *Pro Caelio*.
28. Plutarch, "Cato the Younger."
29. Cicero, *Ad Atticum*, ii, 1; Plutarch, l. c., and "Phocien."
30. Appian, *Roman History*, vi, 16.
31. Plutarch, "Crassus."
32. Ibid.
33. Plutarch, "Sertorius."
34. Plutarch, "Pompey."
35. Cicero, *De lege Manilia*, vii, 18-19.
36. Cicero, *Pro Caelio*, 16.
37. Cicero, *Pro Sexto Roscio*.
38. Sallust, *The War of Catiline*, xv.
39. Ibid.; Plutarch, "Cicero."
40. Haskell, H., *The New Deal in Old Rome*, 125.
41. Sallust, *Catiline*, xx, 7-13.
42. Cicero, *III In Catilinam*, vii.
43. Haskell, 167.
44. Sallust, xxxiii, 1.
45. Cicero, op. cit., viii.
46. Ibid., i.
47. Cicero, *In Pisonem*, vi-vii.

CHAPTER VIII

1. Lucretius, *De rerum natura*, iii, 1053f; tr. W. D. Rouse.
2. Ibid., iv, 1045-71.
3. Mommsen, IV, 207.
4. Fowler, *Religious Experience of the Roman People*, 391.
5. Lucretius, i, 1-40.
6. Ibid., i, 101.
7. V, 1202.
8. I, 73.
9. II, 646.
10. II, 1090.
11. VI, 35.
12. I, 430.
13. II, 312.
14. IV, 834.
15. V, 419.
16. V, 837.
17. II, 8.

18. V, 1116.
19. II, 29.
20. IV, 1052.
21. V, 925f.
22. II, 79.
23. II, 1148.
24. II, 576.
25. Shotwell, *Introduction*, 221.
25a. Appian, ii, 2.
26. Lucretius, v, 564.
27. VI, 1093.
28. In Eusebius, *Chronicles* in Hadzsits, G., *Lucretius and His Influence*, 5.
29. Sellar, *Poets of the Republic*, 277.
30. Voltaire, *Lettres de Memmius à Ciceron*, in Hadzsits, 327.
31. Apuleius, *Apology*, in Sellar, 411.
32. Catullus, *Poems*, li.
33. Id., ii.
34. V.
35. XI.
36. LXXXV.
37. LXX.
38. CI.
39. XXXI.
40. XXXVIII.
41. XCVIII.
42. Varro, pref.
43. Ibid., ii, 10.
44. St. Augustine, *City of God*, iv, 27.
45. Ibid., vii, 5.
46. Sallust, *Jug. War*, lxxxv.
46a. Gellius, xvii, 18.1.
46b. Pliny, xiv, 17.
47. In Weise, O., *Language and Character of the Roman People*, 86.
48. Nepos, "Atticus," xvi.
49. Cf. the letter to Trebatius, in Cicero, vii, 10.
50. Cf. the letter to Lentulus in Cicero, i, 7 with the speech *Pro Balbo*, 27.
51. *Ad Atticum*, vii, 1.
52. *Letters*, xv, 4, to Cato.
53. Boissier, *Cicero*, 84; Frank, *Economic Survey*, I, 395.
54. *Ad Atticum*, i, 18.
55. Ibid., i, 7.
56. *Pro Archia*, vii.
57. *De div.*, i, 2.1; ii, 2.4-5.
58. *De off.*, ii, 17.
59. *De natura deorum*, i, 2, 8.
60. *De div.*, ii, 12.28.
61. *Academica*, ii, 41.
62. *De natura deorum*, i, 5.
63. *De div.*, ii, 47.97.
63a. *De natura deorum*, iii, 16.
64. Ibid., ii, 37.
65. Ibid., i, 1; *De legibus*, ii, 7; *De off.*, ii, 72.148.

66. *De legibus*, i, 7.
67. *De re publica*, i, 2.
68. Ibid., i, 44.
69. III, 22.
70. *De legibus*, i, 15.
71. *De amicitia*, xii, 40.
72. *De senectute*, xi, 38.
73. *Disp. Tusc.*, i.
74. *De legibus*, i, 2.

CHAPTER IX

1. Suetonius, Supplement, i, 3.
2. Suetonius, "Julius," 49.
3. Ibid., 4; Plutarch, "Caesar."
4. Suetonius, "Julius," 52.
5. Plutarch, "Cato the Younger."
6. Quintilian, *Institutes*, x, 1.114.
7. Sallust, *Cataline*, ii.
8. Appian, *Civil Wars*, ii, 2.
9. Ferrero, G., *Greatness and Decline of Rome*, I, 261.
10. Boissier, *Tacitus*, 215f.
12. Mommsen, V, 132.
13. Caesar, *Gallic War*, i, 44.
14. Mommsen, V, 34.
15. Ibid., 38.
16. Cicero, l. c., 81.
17. Mommsen, V, 100.
18. Plutarch, "Pompey," "Crassus," "Cato the Younger."
19. Homo, L., *Roman Political Institutions*, 184; Mommsen, V, 166.
20. Ibid., 385.
21. Appian, *Civil Wars*, ii, 3.
22. Cicero, *Pro Sextio*, 35; Mommsen, V, 108f, 370; Ferrero, I, 313; Boissier, *Cicero*, 213; Fowler, *Social Life*, 58.
23. Dio Cassius, xl, 57.
24. Plato, *Republic*, 562f.
25. Suetonius, "Julius," 77.
26. Appian, *Civil Wars*, ii, 5; Ferrero, II, 187.
27. Suetonius, "Julius," 32; Appian, l.c.
28. Syme, 89.
29. Cicero *ad Atticum*, vⅰⅰ, 16.
30. Ferrero, II, 212.
31. Cicero, *Letters*, xvi, 12, to Tiro, 49 B.C.
32. Cf., e.g., *De bello civile*, i, 43-52.
33. Ibid., i, 53; Appian, ii, 15.
34. Caesar, *Bello civile*, iii, 1.
35. Plutarch, "Caesar"; Appian, ii, 8.
36. Caesar, iii, 10.
37. Ibid., iii, 53.
38. Cicero, *Letters*, vii, 3 to Marcus Marius, 46 B.C.; *ad Atticum*, xi, 6.
39. Appian, ii, 10.
40. Plutarch, "Pompey."
41. Plutarch, "Marcus Brutus."
42. Caesar, iii, 88.

43. Plutarch, "Pompey."
44. Appian, ii, 13.
45. Mahaffy, J., *Silver Age of the Greek World*, 199.
46. CAH, X, 37; Buchan, *Augustus*, 117.
47. Suetonius, "Julius," 52.
48. Ibid.
49. Plutarch, "Caesar."
50. Dio Cassius, xlii, 49.
51. Appian, ii, 13.
52. Suetonius, "Julius," 80.
53. Pliny, xxviii, 2.
55. Frank, *Economic History*, 351.
56. Plutarch, "Caesar."
57. Cicero *Pro Marcello*, 6-10.
58. Cf. *ad Familiares*, viii, 14, 22-5; ix, 11.
59. In Cicero, *ad Atticum*, xiv, 1.
60. Dio Cassius, ii, 44.
61. Plutarch, "Brutus."
62. Appian, ii, 16.
63. Plutarch, l.c.
64. From a doubtful letter of Brutus in Boissier, *Cicero and His Friends*, 334.
65. Cicero, *ad Atticum*, v, 21; vi, 1-9.
66. Appian, ii, 16.
67. Suetonius, "Julius," 79.
68. Ibid., 81-87; Plutarch, "Caesar"; Appian, ii, 16-21.
69. Suetonius, 82.
70. Appian, l.c.

CHAPTER X

1. Ferrero, II, 226.
2. Boissier, *Cicero*, 192.
3. Appian, *Civil Wars*, ii, 2; Dio, xlv, 2.
4. Appian, iv, 11.
5. Ibid., 2-6; Plutarch, "Antony."
6. Brutus to Cicero, *ad Familiares*, xi, 20.
7. Plutarch, "Cicero."
8. Appian, iv, 4; Plutarch, "Antony."
9. Philo, *Quod omnis probus*, 118-20; Appian, iv, 8-10.
10. Plutarch, "Antony"; Appian, v, 1.
11. Ibid.; Athenaeus, iv, 29.
13. CAH, X, 79.
14. Suetonius, 17. Rostovtzeff, *Social and Economic History of the Roman Empire*, 29, thinks the will a forgery; CAH, X, 97, accepts it as genuine.
15. Dio, li, 35.
16. Ibid., 6.
17. Ibid.
18. Ibid., Suetonius, 17.

CHAPTER XI

1. Suetonius, "Augustus," 33.
2. Dio, liv, 17.
3. Ibid., lv, 4.

4. Suetonius, 40.
5. Gibbon, E., *Decline and Fall of the Roman Empire*, ed. Bury, I, 65.
6. Suetonius, 23; Dio, lvi, 17.
7. Plutarch, *Moralia*, 207D.
8. Charlesworth, M., *Trade Routes and Commerce of the Roman Empire*, 8.
9. Suetonius, 41.
9a. Dio, liv, 18.
9b. Suetonius, 28.
10. Ibid., 42.
12. Augustus, *Res gestae*, iii, 21.
13. Dio, lv, 25.
14. Suetonius, 58.
16. Pliny, xiv, 5.
18. Cf. Himes, N., *Medical History of Contraception*, 85f and 188.
19. Dio, liv, 19.
20. Tacitus, *Annals*, xv, 19.
21. Ibid., iii, 25.
22. Horace, *Odes*, iii, 24.
23. Davis, *Influence of Wealth*, 304.
24. Gellius, x, 2.2.
25. Ibid.
26. Dio, lvi, 1.
27. Ovid, *Ars Amatoria*, 637.
28. Augustus, *Res gestae*, ii, 10.
29. Buchan, 286.
30. Suetonius, 76-83.
31. Ibid., 81; Dio, lii, 30.
32. Suetonius, 76.
33. Ibid., 84.
34. Ibid., 90-2.
35. Ferrero, IV, 175.
36. Plutarch, *Moralia*, 207C.
37. Suetonius, 53.
38. Dio, lvii, 2.
39. Suetonius, 64.
40. Macrobius, *Saturnalia*, ii, 5, *ad finem*: "I never take on a passenger unless the vessel is already full."
41. Seneca, *Moral Essays*, III, vi, 32.1.
42. Suetonius, 99.

CHAPTER XII

1. Macrobius, ii, 4.
2. Horace, *Epistles*, ii, 1.117.
3. Juvenal, *Satires*, i, 2; iii, 9.
4. Martial, *Epigrams*, i, 67, 118; Friedländer, III, 37.
4a. Lanciani, *Ancient Rome*, 183.
5. Ovid., *Tristia*, i, 1.105.
6. Tacitus *De oratoribus*, 13.
8. Virgil, *Eclogues*, i, 46.
9. Ibid., i, ix.
10. Suetonius, *On Poets*, "Virgil," 9.
11. Virgil, *Georgics*, iii, 284.
12. Ibid., i, 145.

13. II, 490.
14. In Duff, *Literary History of Rome*, 455.
15. *Georgics*, iii, 46.
16. *Aeneid*, vi, 860f; Suetonius, "Virgil," 31.
17. *Aeneid*, ii, 293.
18. Ibid., iv, 331-61.
19. VI, 126.
20. VI, 852.
21. IV, 508.
22. Suetonius, 23.
23. Ibid., 43.
24. Voltaire, *Philosophical Dictionary*, art. *Epic Poetry*.
25. Suetonius, *On Poets*, "Horace."
26. Horace, *Odes*, iii, 2.
27. *Epodes*, ii, 2.41.
28. *Satires*, i, 1.
28a. *Epistles*, i, 16; Rostovtzeff, *Social and Economic of the Roman Empire*, 61.
29. Horace, *Satires*, ii, 5.
30. Ibid., ii, 7.105.
31. Ibid., 23.
32. I, 1.69.
33. *Odes*, ii, 10.
34. *Satires*, i, 1.105.
35. Ibid., ii, 1.1.
36. *Odes*, iii, 29.12.
37. *Satires*, ii, 6.60.
39. *Odes*, iii, 16.29.
40. *Epodes*, ii, 1.
41. Petronius, *Satyricon*, 118.
42. *Odes*, ii, 11.
43. I, 9.
44. I, 28.
45. I, 35.
46. III, 30.
47. *Ars poetica*, 139.
48. Ibid., 343.
49. Ibid., 102.
50. *Epistles*, i, 6.1.
51. *Odes*, ii, 3.
52. Ibid., ii, 10.
53. *Satires*, ii, 7.83.
54. *Odes*, iii, 3.
55. *Epistles*, i, 4.16; cf. i, 17.
56. *Satires*, ii, 6.93.
57. *Epistles*, ii, 2.55.
58. *Odes*, ii, 14.
59. *Satires*, i, 1.117.
60. *Epistles*, ii, 2.214.
61. *Odes*, ii, 17.
63. Taine, H., *Essai sur Tite Live*, 1.
64. Pliny, *Natural History*, dedication.
65. Taine, l.c., 10.
66. E.g., Livy, ii, 48.
67. E.g., cf. Livy, xlv, 12 with Polybius, xxix, 27; or Livy, xxiv, 34 with Polybius, viii, 5.
68. Pliny, *Letters*, ii, 3.

69. Tibullus, i, 1.
70. Ibid., i, 6.
71. I, 3, 10.
72. Propertius, ii, 34, 57.
73. Ibid., ii, 6.
74. I, 8.
75. Ovid, *Tristia*, iv, 10.
76. Ovid, *Ars amatoria*, 157.
77. Ibid., 99.
78. Ibid., 171.
79. *Amores*, ii, 4.
80. Ibid., i, 1; ii, 18.
81. II, 1.
82. I, 4.
83. II, 5.
84. II, 10.
85. III, 7; ii, 10.
86. *Ars amatoria*, 97.
90. *Remedia amoris*, 183.
91. Ibid., 194.
92. *Heroides*, iv.
93. *Tristia*, ii, 103.
94. *Ex Ponto*, iv, 6.41.
95. *Tristia*, i, 1; iii, 8.
96. Ibid., iii, 3.15; *Ex Ponto*, i, 4.47.

CHAPTER XIII

1. In Holmes, *Architect of the Roman Empire*, 108.
2. Suetonius, "Tiberius," 68.
3. Ibid., 69.
4. Tacitus, *Annals*, i, 11.
5. Suetonius, 23.
6. Dio, lvii, 18.
7. Ibid., 6; Suetonius, 30; Tacitus, *Annals*, iv, 6.
8. Suetonius, 27.
9. Tacitus, l.c.
10. Suetonius, 32.
11. Ferrero, G., *Women of the Caesars*, 136.
12. Tacitus, ii, 50.
13. Ibid., iv, 57.
14. Dio, lvii, 11.
15. Ferrero, *Women*, 140.
16. Tacitus, iv, 57; Suetonius, 42-4.
17. CAH, X, 638.
18. Tacitus, iv, 58.
19. Suetonius, 60.
20. Tacitus, iv, 70.
21. Ibid., vi, 50.
22. Mommsen, T., *Provinces of the Roman Empire*, II, 187.
23. Josephus, *Antiquities*, xix, 1.15.
24. Suetonius, "Gaius," 50-1.
25. Ibid.
26. Dio, lix, 5.
27. Suetonius, "Gaius," 29, 32.
28. Dio, lix, 26.

29. Suetonius, 24.
30. Ibid.
31. Seneca *Ad Helviam,* x, 4.
32. Suetonius, 40.
33. Ibid., 38.
34. Ibid., 30.
35. Dio, lix, 3.
36. Suetonius, 27.
37. For a defense of Caligula cf. Balsdon, *The Emperor Gaius,* 33 etc.
39. Dio, lix, 28.
40. Balsdon, 161.
41. Ibid., 168.
42. Dio, lix, 29.
43. Suetonius, "Claudius," 29.
44. Dio, lx, 10.
45. Suetonius, 21.
46. Seneca, *Apocolocyntosis,* 3.
47. Tacitus, xii, 53.
48. Suetonius, 28.
49. Brittain, 244.
50. Suetonius, 37; Dio, lx, 14.
51. Suetonius, 50.
52. Dio, lx, 18.
53. Tacitus, xi, 12.
54. Ibid., 25.
55. Dio, lxi, 31.
56. Ferrero, *Women,* 226.
57. Buchan, 247.
58. Tacitus, xi, 25.
59. Pliny, *Nat. Hist.,* ix, 117.
60. Tacitus, xiii, 43.
61. Dio, lxi, 34.
62. Ibid., 2.
63. Suetonius, "Nero," 52.
64. Dio, lxi, 3.
65. Tacitus, xiii, 4.
66. Henderson, B., *Life and Principate of the Emperor Nero,* 75.
67. Tacitus, xv, 48.
68. Suetonius, 56.
69. Ibid., 27.
70. Tacitus, xvi, 18.
71. Dio, lxii, 15; lxi, 7; Suetonius, 26.
72. Dio, lxii, 14; Tacitus, xiv, 5, adds that some writers question the story.
73. Tacitus, xiv, 10.
74. Ibid., xiii, 3.
75. Suetonius, 20.
76. Ibid., 41; Dio, lxiii, 26.
77. Suetonius, 52.
78. Ibid., 11.
79. Tacitus, xiv, 60.
80. CAH, X, 722.
81. Tacitus, xv, 44.
82. Ibid., xvi, 6; Suetonius, 25.
83. Dio, lxii, 27; Suetonius, 27.
84. Tacitus, xvi, 18.
85. Suetonius, 22.

86. Ibid.
87. Dio, lxiii, 23.
88. Suetonius, 43.
89. Ibid., 57.
90. Suetonius, "Galba," 23.
91. Tacitus, *Histories,* i, 49.
92. Suetonius, "Otho," 5.
93. Tacitus, *Hist.,* iii, 67.
94. Suetonius, "Vitellius," 17.
95. Suetonius, "Vespasian," 13.
96. Ibid., 16.
97. Dio, lxv, 14.
98. Suetonius, 18.
99. Ibid., 21.
100. Tacitus, *Hist.,* ii, 2.
101. Suetonius, 23-4.
102. Suetonius, "Titus," 8.
103. Suetonius, "Domitian," 18.
104. Dio, lxvi, 26.
105. Suetonius, 22; Dio, lxvii, 6.
106. Frank, *Economic Survey,* V, 56.
107. Dio, lxvii, 14.
108. Suetonius, 10.

CHAPTER XIV

1. Lucan, *Pharsalia,* ii, 67.
2. Ibid., i, 128.
3. Petronius, *Epigrams,* frag. 22 in Robertson, J. M., *Short History of Freethought,* I, 211.
4. Petronius, *Satyricon,* 11.
5. Ibid., 48.
6. 71.
7. 35, 40, 47.
8. 74.
9. Seneca in Boissier, G., *La réligion romaine,* II, 204.
10. Tacitus, *Annals,* xiv, 59; xvi, 34.
11. Lucian, *Icaromenippus,* 4.
12. Seneca, *Epistulae Morales,* xii; *Moral Essays,* III, vii, 11.1.
13. Monroe, *Source Book,* 401.
14. Quintilian, *Institutes,* x, 1.125.
15. Dio, lxii, 2.
16. Friedländer, III, 238.
17. Tacitus, *Annals,* xiii, 42.
18. Seneca, *De vita beata,* xvii-xviii.
19. Davis, *Influence of Wealth,* 154.
20. Seneca, *Epist.* xv.
21. *De vita beata,* xviii.
22. *De clementia,* i, 3.
24. *Epist.,* vii.
25. Tacitus, *Annals,* xiii, 2.
27. Boissier, *Tacitus,* 11.
28. Seneca, *Epist.,* lxxvi.
30. Seneca, *Epist.,* lxxv.
31. Ibid., vii.
32. XXVI.

33. *De providentia*, ii, 6.
34. *Epist.*, xli.
36. *De providentia*, v, 8.
37. *Epist.*, xxxi.
38. Ibid., cii; *ad Marciam*, xxiv, 3.
39. In Henderson, *Nero*, 309.
40. *Epist.*, lxxii and iii.
41. Ibid., lxxii.
44. XXXIII.
45. *De brevitate vitae*, xiv.
46. *Epist.*, lxix.
47. Ibid., ii.
48. VII; XXV.
49. XXIII.
50. LXX.
51. *De ira*, v, 15.
52. *Epist.*, lviii.
53. Ibid., lxi.
54. *De ira*, ii, 34.
55. *Epist.*, i, lxi.
56. Tertullian, *De anima*, xx.
57. In Acton, Lord, *History of Freedom*, 25.
58. *Epist.*, xxxi.
59. Gummere, R. M., *Seneca the Philosopher*, 131.
60. Seneca, *Medea*, 364.
61. *Quaestiones naturales*, vii, 30-33.
62. Ibid., vii, 25, 30.
63. Pliny, xxxvi, 15.
64. Ibid., ii, 5.
65. Plutarch, "Sertorius."
66. Pliny's *Letters*, iii, 5.
67. Pliny, *Nat. Hist.*, iii, 6.
68. Ibid., ii, 5.
69. II, 30.
70. II, 33.
71. II, 6, 64.
72. II, 90-92.
73. II, 63.
74. XXXIV, 39.
75. XXXVII, 27.
76. XIX, 4.
77. XVIII, 76.
78. XXV, 110.
79. XXXVIII, 52.
80. XXVIII, 80.
81. VII, 5.
82. XXVIII, 16.
83. VII, 3.
84. XXV, 13.
85. Castiglione, 214.
86. Pliny, ii, 5, 117.
87. XXXIII, 13.
88. II, 5.
89. VII, 56.
90. XXVIII, 7.
91. VIII, 67.
92. VII, 13.
93. XVIII, 78f.

94. II, 57.
95. Jones, W. H. S., *Malaria and Greek History*, 61.
96. Pliny's *Letters*, i, 12.
97. Castiglione, 237.
98. Tacitus, *Hist.*, iv, 81; Suetonius, "Vespasian," 7.
99. Dill, Sir S., *Roman Society from Nero to Marcus Aurelius*, 92.
100. Pliny, *Nat. Hist.*, xxix, 8.
101. Lucian, "To an Illiterate Book-Fancier," 29.
102. Pliny, xxvi, 7-8; Castiglione, 200; Garrison, *History of Medicine*, 106.
103. Castiglione, 233, 240.
104. Ibid., 226.
105. Soranus in Friedländer, I, 171.
106. Castiglione, 237; Garrison, 118.
107. Bailey, C., *Legacy of Rome*, 291; Williams, H. S., *History of Science*, I, 274.
108. Pliny, xxix, 5.
109. Ibid., 8.
110. Garrison, 119.
111. Pliny, xxxv, 94.
112. Ibid., xxix, 5.
113. Friedländer, I, 180-1.
114. Castiglione, 234; Friedländer, I, 178; Duff, J., *Literary History of Rome in the Silver Age*, 121; Pliny, xxviii, 2.
115. Frank, *Economic Survey*, I, 381.
116. Bailey, 284.
117. Quintilian, vi, pref.
118. I, 12.17.
119. I, 10.36.
120. X, 3.9, 19.
121. X, 4.1.
122. II, 12.7.
123. II, 5.21.
124. Juvenal, vii, 82.
126. Martial, xi, 43, 104.
127. II, 53.
128. IV, 49.
129. I, 16.
130. X, 4.
131. IV, 4.
132. IX, 37.
133. I, 32; III, 65.
134. I, 32.
135. E.g., ix, 27.
136. XI, 16.
137. III, 69.
138. Pliny's *Letters*, iii, 21.

CHAPTER XV

1. Columella, *De re rustica*, i, 3.12.
2. In Davis, *Influence of Wealth*, 144.
3. Pliny, *Nat. Hist.*, xviii, 4; Heitland, 224; Frank, *Economic Survey*, V, 175.

4. Columella, iii, 3.
5. Strabo, v, 4.3.
6. Frank, V, 158.
7. Pliny, xv, 68-83.
8. Columella, iii, 8.
9. Rostovtzeff, *Roman Empire*, 182-3.
10. Suetonius, "Domitian," 7.
11. Cato, *De agri cultura*, 144.
12. Pliny, xix, 2.
13. Paul-Louis, 274-6.
14. Tacitus, *Agricola*, 12.
15. Pliny, ii, 108-9.
15a. Ammianus Marcellinus, xxiii, 4.15.
16. *Encyclopaedia Britannica*, V, 868.
17. Paul-Louis, 287.
18. Frank, V, 229.
19. Rostovtzeff, *Roman Empire*, 252.
20. Haskell, H. J., *New Deal in Old Rome*, 24-6.
21. Scott, S. P., *Civil Law*, Fragments of Ulpian in Justinian, *Digest*, iii, 2.4.
22. Friedländer, I, 289-91.
23. Gibbon, Everyman Lib. ed., I, 50; Bailey, C., *Legacy of Rome*, 158.
24. Seneca *Ad Helviam*, vi.
25. Plutarch, *Moralia*, "On Exile," 604A.
26. Halliday, W. R., *Pagan Background of Early Christianity*, 88.
27. Juvenal, xiv, 287.
29. Athenaeus, ii, 239.
30. Josephus, *Life*, p. 511.
31. Mommsen, *Provinces*, II, 278.
32. Friedländer, I, 286.
33. Pliny, xix, 1, 4.
34. Ibid., ii, 57.
35. Cf. the crane pictured on the tomb of the Haterii in the Lateran Museum, Rome, in Wickhoff, E., *Roman Art*, p. 50; cf. also Gest, 60, and Bailey, 462.
36. Reid, *Municipalities*, 28.
37. Gest, 110-131.
38. Pliny, xxxvi, 24.
39. Bailey, 290.
40. Frontinus, *Stratagems*, iii, 1.
41. Frontinus, *Aqueducts*, ii, 75.
42. Ibid., i, 16.
43. In Friedländer, I, 13.
44. Carter, T. F., *Invention of Printing*, 86; Gibbon, Everyman ed., I, 55.
45. Tarn, W. W., *Hellenistic Civilization*, 206.
46. CAH, X, 417.
47. Strabo, xvii, 1.3.
48. Pliny, vi, 26, computes Rome's annual payment to India at 550,000,000 sesterces; but this is probably an exaggeration, for elsewhere (xii, 41) he estimates the yearly loss of Rome to India, China, and Arabia at 100,000,000 sesterces each.

49. Halliday, 97.
50. Tacitus, *Annals*, vi, 16-17; Suetonius, "Tiberius," 48; Davis, *Influence of Wealth*, 1. Renan, in *Lectures on the Influence of Rome on Christianity*, 25, and *The Apostles*, 170, compares Tiberius' relief measures to the Crédit Foncier of France in 1852; and Haskell compares the situation with the "easy money" period in the United States, 1923-9, the crisis of 1929, and the Reconstruction Finance Corporation (*The New Deal in Old Rome*, 183, 188).
51. Ovid, *Fasti*, i, 191.
52. In Toynbee, A., *Study of History*, I, 41n.
53. Davis, 242.
54. Beard, M., *History of the Business Man*, 47.
55. Athenaeus, vi, 104.
56. Seneca *De clementia*, i, 24.
56a. Sandys, Sir J., *Companion to Latin Studies*, 354.
57. Pliny, vii, 40.
58. Friedländer, II, 221.
59. Boissier, *La réligion romaine*, II, 330.
59a. Seneca *De ira*, iii, 3.
60. Juvenal, vi, 474.
61. Ovid, *Ars amatoria*, 235; *Amores*, i, 14.
62. In Holmes, *Architect of the Roman Empire*, 132.
63. Dill, 116.
64. Statius, *Silvae*, ii, 6.
65. Seneca, *Epist.*, xlvii, 13.
66. Dill, 117.
68. Rostovtzeff, *Roman Empire*, 105; Reid, 323, 521.
69. Toutain, 304.
70. Frank, *Economic History*, 280.
71. Frank, *Economic Survey*, V, 235.
72. Petronius, 44.
73. Rostovtzeff, 172; Declareuil, J., *Rome the Law-Giver*, 269.
74. Pliny, xiii, 23.

CHAPTER XVI

1. Seneca in Friedländer, II, 321.
2. Livy, xxiv, 9; Pliny's *Letters*, viii, 17; Tacitus, *Annals*, i, 70.
3. Strabo, v, 3.8.
4. Juvenal, iii, 235-244.
5. Ibid., v, 268.
6. Martial, cxvii, 7.
7. Friedländer, I, 5.
8. Pliny, xxxv, 45.
9. Friedländer, II, 317, 330.
10. Mau, A., *Pompeii*, 231; Rostovtzeff, *Roman Empire*, 135; Gest, 96.

15. Suetonius, "Nero," 39.
16. In Boissier, *Rome and Pompeii*, 119.
17. Pliny, *Nat. Hist.*, xxxiii, 45.
18. Boissier, *Tacitus*, 223.
18a. N. Y. *Times*, Apr. 27, 1943.
19. Mau, 414.
20. Pliny, xxxv, 66; Strabo, xvi, 25.
21. Winckelmann, J., *History of Ancient Art*, II, 312.
22. Reid, 278.
23. Cf. Strong, *Art in Ancient Rome*, II, fig. 341.
24. Valerius Maximus, *Factorum et dictorum*, viii, 14.
25. Pliny, xxxv, 37.
26. Cf. Maiuri, A., *Les fresques de Pompeii*, Table XXXIII.
27. Cf. Rostovtzeff, *Mystic Italy, passim.*
27a. Pliny, xxxv, 40.
28. Duff, *Literary History of Rome*, 632.
29. Vitruvius, ii, 4.
30. Ibid., i, 1.
31. Ibid., x, 9.
32. Friedländer, II, 191.
32a. Seneca, *Epistles*, lxxxviii.
32b. Kirstein, L., *The Dance*, 49.
32c. Lucretius, ii, 416; Ovid, *Ars*, i, 103.
33. Pliny, xxxvi, 24.

CHAPTER XVII

1. Juvenal, v, 141.
2. Petronius in Henderson, *Nero*, 326.
3. Seneca *Ad Marciam*, xix, 2.
4. Juvenal, vi, 367.
5. Friedländer, I, 238.
6. Cf. Pliny, xxiv, 11: "They say that if the male organ is rubbed with [oil or gum of] cedar just before coitus, it will prevent impregnation." Cr. also Himes, 85f, 186.
7. Juvenal, vi, 592.
10. Gatteschi, G., *Restauri della Roma Imperiale*, 64.
11. Gibbon, I, 42; Friedländer, I, 17; Sandys, 355-7; Davis, 195; Paul-Louis, 15, 227.
12. Tacitus, *Annals*, xiii, 27.
13. Vogelstein, H., *Rome*, 10.
14. Cicero, *Pro L. Flacco*, 28.
15. Edersheim, A., *Life and Times of Jesus the Messiah*, I, 67.
16. Tacitus, *Annals*, ii, 85; Suetonius, "Tiberius," 36.
17. Dio, lvii, 18; Schürer, *History of the Jewish People*, Div. II, Vol. II, 234.
18. Vogelstein, 17.
19. Ibid., 31, 33; Renan, *Lectures*, 50.
20. Tacitus, *Annals*, ii, 85; Ammanianus, M., xxii, 5.
21. Dill, 83-4.
22. Dio, lx, 33
23. Martial, vii, 30.

24. Juvenal, iii, 62.
25. In Bailey, 143.
26. Tacitus, xiv, 42, 60.
27. Juvenal, xiv, 44.
28. Gellius, xii, 1.
29. *Enc. Brit.*, X, 10.
30. Horace, *Satires*, i, 6.75.
31. Pliny's *Letters*, ii, 3.
32. Petronius, 1.
33. Pliny's *Letters*, iv, 3.
34. Ovid, *Ars amatoria*, 98.
35. Juv., ix, 22.
36. Minucius Felix, *Octavius*, 67; Tertullian, *Apology*, 15.
37. Horaces, *Epodes*, xi.
38. Martial, viii, 44; xi, 70, 88, etc.; Juv., ii, vi, ix.
39. In Friedländer, I, 234.
40. Seneca the Elder, *Controversiae*, in Friedländer, I, 241.
41. Seneca, *Ad Helviam*, xvi, 3; *Ad Marciam*, xxiv, 3.
42. Ovid, *Amores*, i, 8.43; iii, 4.37.
43. Friedländer, I, 241.
44. Juv., vi, 228.
45. Ibid., 281.
46. I, 22.
47. Boissier, *La réligion romaine*, II, 197.
48. Juv., vi, 248.
49. Martial, *De spectaculis*, vi.
50. Statius, *Silvae*, i, 6.
51. Seneca, *Moral Essays*, i, 9.4.
52. Ovid, *Ars amatoria*, 113.
53. Martial, x, 35.
54. Ibid., i, 14.
55. Tacitus, *Annals*, xvi, 10.
56. Friedländer, I, 265.
57. Tacitus, xiv, 5.
58. Martial, vi, 57.
59. Catullus, lxxxvi.
60. Ovid, *Ars*, 158; Kohler, K., *History of Costume*, 118; Pfuhl, E., *Masterpieces of Greek Drawing*, fig. 117.
61. Tibullus, i, 8.
62. Juv., vi, 502.
63. Pliny, xxviii, 12.
64. Guhl and Konar, 498.
65. Martial, ix, 37.
66. Ovid, *Ars*, 160.
67. Pliny, ix, 63.
68. Ibid., xxxviii, 12.
69. IX, 58.
70. Friedländer, II, 181.
71. Pliny, xxxiii, 18.
72. Seneca, *Epist.*, lxxxvi.
73. Pliny, viii, 74.
74. Quintilian, vi, 3.
75. Galen in Friedländer, II, 227. The remainder of this chapter is particularly indebted to Friedländer's devoted accumulation of Roman mores.

76. Juv., vii, 178.
77. Jones, H. S., *Companion to Roman History*, 116; Friedländer, I, 12.
78. Seneca, *Epist.*, lxxxvi.
79. Ker, W. C., in Martial, I, 244n.
80. Gardiner, E. N., *Athletics of the Ancient World*, 230.
81. Pliny, xxviii, 51.
82. *Journal of the American Medical Association*, Aug. 1, 1942, 1089.
83. Ovid, *Ars*, 165; *Tristia*, ii, 477-80.
84. Pliny, viii, 51, 77.
85. Ibid., ix, 30, 31.
86. Ibid., 39.
87. VIII, 82.
88. VIII, 77.
89. Seneca *Ad Helviam*, x, 9.
90. Ibid., 3.
91. Sandys, 502.
92. Mantzius, K., *History of Theatrical Art*, I, 217.
93. Suetonius, "Vespasian," 19.
94. Mantzius, I, 218.
95. Boissier, *La réligion romaine*, II, 215.
96. Cicero *Pro Murena*, 6.
97. Lang, P. N., *Music in Western Civilization*, 35.
98. Ammianus, xiv, 6.
99. Martial, v, 78.
100. Ammianus, xiv, 6.
101. Seneca, *Epist.*, lxxxviii.
102. Philostratus, *Life of Apollonius of Tyana*, v, 21.
103. Lang, 33.
104. Virgil, *Aeneid*, v, 362f.
105. Friedländer, II, 30.
106. Dio, lxi, 33.
107. Lecky, W. E., *History of European Morals*, I, 280.
108. Friedländer, II, 72.
109. Pliny, viii, 70.
110. Friedländer, II, 5.
111. Boissier, *Tacitus*, 246.
112. Martial, *De spectaculis*, vii.
113. Friedländer, II, 43.
114. Ibid., 49.
115. Epictetus, *Discourses*, i, 29.37.
116. Seneca, *Epist.*, lxx.
117. Friedländer, II, 61.
118. Juv., iii, 36.
119. Pliny II, *Panegyricus*, xxxiii.
120. Tacitus, *Annals*, xiv, 44.
121. Cicero, *Letters*, vii, 1, to Marcus Marius, 55 B.C.
122. Seneca, *Epist.*, vii, xcv.
123. In St. Augustine, *City of God*, vi, 10.
124. Tertullian, *Apology*, 15.
125. Juv., xiii, 35.
126. Abbott, *Common People of Ancient Rome*, 88; Dill, 498.
127. Friedländer, III, 283.

CHAPTER XVIII

1. Bury, J. B., *History of the Roman Empire*, 527.
2. Justinian, *Digest*, i, 1, in Scott, *The Civil Law*.
3. Gaius, *Institutes*, i, 8.
4. Maine, Sir H., *Ancient Law*. This generalization has been questioned, but seems substantially true.
5: Justinian, *Codex*, vii, 16.1.
6. Gaius, i, 144.
7. Ibid., 145, 194.
8. Buckland, W. W., *Textbook of Roman Law*, 113.
9. Gaius, i, 114.
10. Friedländer, I, 236.
11. Suetonius, "Vespasian," 3; *Hist. Aug.*, "Antoninus," 8; "Aurelius," 29.
12. Castiglione, 227.
13. Gaius, commentary, p. 66.
14. Ibid., p. 64.
15. Gaius, i, 56.
16. Davis, *Influence of Wealth*, 211.
17. Tacitus, xiv, 41.
18. Renan, *Marc Aurèle*, 24.
19. Ulpina, in *Digest*, L, 17.32.
20. Lecky, I, 295.
21. Gaius, iii, 40-1.
22. Cicero *Ad Familiares*, viii, 12, 14.
23. Gaius, ii, 157; iii, 2.
24. Maine, 117.
25. Buckland, 64.
26. Gaius, iii, 189; iv, 4.
27. Ibid., iv, 11.
28. In Friedländer, I, 165.
29. Ammianus, xxx, 4.
30. Ulpian in *Digest*, L, 13.1.
31. Quintilian, xii, 1.25.
32. Pliny's *Letters*, v, 14.
33. Martial, vii, 65.
34. Pliny's *Letters*, ii, 14.
35. Tacitus, *Annals*, xi, 5.
36. David, 125.
37. Pliny's *Letters*, vi, 33.
38. Juv., xvi, 42.
39. Apuleius, *Golden Ass*, p. 245.
40. Psalms, cxvi, 11; St. Paul, Epistle to the Romans, iii, 4.
41. In Taylor, H., *Cicero*, 77.
42. Quintilian, v, 7.26.
43. Ibid., vi, 1.47.
44. *Codex Theodosius*, ix, 35, in Gibbon, II, 120.
45. Gellius, xx, 1.13.

46. Sallust, *Catiline*, 55.
47. Cicero, *De re publica*, iii, 22; cf. *De officiis*, i, 23; *De legibus*, i, 15.
48. Gaius, i, 1.

CHAPTER XIX

1. Ker, W., in Martial, II, 54n.
2. Dio, lxviii, 13.
3. Renan, *Marc Aurèle*, 479.
4. Dio, lxviii, 15.
5. Mahaffy, J., *Silver Age of the Greek World*, 307.
6. In CAH, XI, 201, 855.
7. Pliny II, *Panegyricus*, 50.
8. Justinian, *Digest*, xlviii, 19.5.
9. Bury, *Roman Empire*, 437.
10. Brittain, 366.
11. Wickhoff, 113.
12. Dio, lxix, 1.
13. *Hist. Aug.*, "Hadrian," i, 4.
14. Ibid, xxvi, 1.
15. Ibid.
16. XIV, 1.
17. Martial, viii, 70; ix, 26.
18. *Hist. Aug.*, "Hadrian," xv, 10.
19. Ibid., xx, 7.
20. Henderson, *Hadrian*, 207.
21. Eusebius, *Ecclesiastical History*, iv, 9.
22. Dio, lxix, 6.
23. Fronto, M., *Correspondence*, A.D. 162; II, 4.
24. *Hist. Aug.*, "Hadrian," x, 1.
25. Winckelmann, I, 327.
26. Bevan, E. R., *House of Seleucus*, II, 15.
27. *Hist. Aug.*, viii, 3.
29. Simpson, F. M., *History of Architectural Development*, 123.
30. Dio, lxix, 4; cf. Henderson, 247.
31. Dio, lxix, 8.
32. *Hist. Aug.*, xxiv, 8.
33. Merivale, C., *History of the Romans under the Empire*, VIII, 255.
34. Marcus Aurelius, *Meditations*, 16.
35. *Hist. Aug.*, "Antoninus," iv, 8.
36. Ibid., viii, 1.
37. IX, 10.
38. Appian, preface, 7.
39. Bury, 566.
40. Renan, *The Christian Church*, 159.
41. Renan, *Marc Aurèle*, 2.
42. Gibbon, I, 76.
43. Marcus, i, 17.
44. Ibid., 1.
45. I, 14.
46. I, 15.
47. I, 14.
48. VII, 70.
49. *Hist. Aug.*, "Marcus," xxiii, 4.

50. Friedländer, III, 191.
51. Watson, P., *Marcus Aurelius Antoninus*, 297.
52. Castiglione, 244.
53. Galen, in Friedländer, I, 28.
54. Dio, lxii, 14.
55. Ammianus, xxv, 4.
56. Williams, H., I, 280.
57. Renan, *Marc*, 469.
58. Marcus, i, 17.
59. Bury, 547.
60. *Hist. Aug.*, "Marcus," xix, 7.
61. Marcus, x, 10.
62. Mommsen, *Provinces*, I, 253.

CHAPTER XX

1. Boissier, *Tacitus*, 2.
2. Tacitus, *Agricola*, 9.
3. Pliny's *Letters*, ii, 1; vi, 16.
4. *Agricola*, end.
5. *Germania*, 25, 27.
6. *Annals*, iii, 65.
7. *Historiae*, i, 1.
8. *Agricola*, 4.
9. *Germania*, 34.
10. *Annals*, xvi, 33.
11. Ibid., iii, 18; vi, 22.
12. *Germania*, i, 33.
13. *Agricola*, 46.
14. *Annals*, vi, 17.
15. *Agricola*, 3.
16. *Dialogue on Orators*, 40.
17. *Historiae*, iii, 12, 64.
18. *Agricola*, 18.
19. *Historiae*, i, 16.
20. Ibid.
21. Juvenal, i, 147.
23. X, 81.
24. VI, 652.
25. 434.
26. 448.
27. III.
28. XIV, 316.
29. X, 356.
30. Seneca, *De beneficiis*, i, 10; *Epist.*, xcvii.
31. Pliny's *Letters*, iii, 19.
32. V, 3.
33. 8.
34. I, 17.
35. VI, 32.
36. V, 16.
37. I, 16.
38. VII, 19.
39. VII, 20; IX, 23.
40. Boissier, *Tacitus*, 19.
41. Gibbon, I, 57.
42. Pliny's *Letters*, iii, 12.
43. Strong, II, fig. 435.

44. Marcus, ii, 11.
45. VII, 75.
46. Ibid., 9; iv, 40, 27.
47. IV, 10.
48. II, 17.
49. III, 2.
50. X, 8.
51. IV, 23.
52. II, 17.
53. VII, 12.
54. XI, 1.
55. VIII, 10.
56. IV, 42, 48; viii, 21.
57. VII, 3.
58. II, 1.
59. IX, 38; vii, 26.
60. VI, 48.
61. 44.
62. XI, 18.
63. IV, 49; viii, 61; ii, 5.
64. IV, 21; viii, 18; ii, 17.
65. IV, 14, 48; ix, 3.
66. Dio, lxxii, 2-3.
67. *Hist. Aug.*, "Commodus," 2, 14, 15.
68. Dio, lxxiii, 19.
69. *Hist. Aug.*, 13.
70. Ibid., 2, 10, 11.
71. Paul-Louis, 215.

CHAPTER XXI

1. Pliny, *Nat. Hist.*, iii, 6.
2. Dill, 239.
3. Fattorusso, J., *Wonders of Italy*, 473.
4. Herodotus, i, 196.
5. Strabo, v, 1.7.
6. Varro, *Rerum rust.*, i, 2.
7. Pliny, iii, 6.
8. Strabo, v, 4.5.
9. Varro, *Sat. Men.*, frag. 44, in Friedländer, I, 338.
10. Boissier, *Cicero*, 168.
11. Seneca, *Epist.* li.
12. Strabo, v, 4.3.
13. Reid, 3.
14. Dio, lxvi, 22.
15. Pliny's *Letters*, vi, 16.
16. Ibid., 20.
17. Rostovtzeff, *Mystic Italy*, 52.
18. Mau, 491; Boissier, *Rome and Pompeii*, 430.
19. Id., *La réligion romaine*, II, 296.
20. Mau, 226, 148.
21. Ibid., 16.
22. Rostovtzeff, *Roman Empire*, 142; Dill, 194; Frank, *Economic Survey*, V, 98; Friedländer, II, 254.
23. CAH, XI, 587; Friedländer, II, 228.
24. As at Antium, Lanuvium, Tibur, Aricia.

CHAPTER XXII

1. Cicero, *II, In Verren*, iii, 207.
2. Tacitus, *Annals*, xii, 31.
3. Cicero, *Pro lege Manilia*, 6.
4. Plutarch, *De reip. ger.*, 32.
5. Mommsen, *History*, II, 205.
6. Livy, xxv, 29.
7. Reid, 288.
8. Toutain, 269.
9. Bouchier, E., *Life and Letters in Roman Africa*, 73.
10. St. Augustine, *Letters*, 185.
11. Friedländer, I, 312.
12. Boissier, *L'Afrique romaine*, 181-2; Davis, 200.
13. Bouchier, 33.
14. Juvenal, vii, 148.
15. Apuleius, 41; a fine example of Adlington's delectable translation (1566).
16. Book XI.
17. Books IV-VI.
18. Strabo, iii, 4.16.
19. Ibid., 3.7.
20. Ibid., 4.16-18.
21. Buchan, 310.
22. Gest, 201.
23. Caesar, *Bello Gallico*, ii, 30.
24. Pliny, xxxviii, 5.
25. Appian, iv, 7.
26. Strabo, iv, 4.5.
27. Ibid.
28. Caesar, v, 34.
29. Ammianus, xv, 12.
30. Caesar, vi, 14; Val. Max; ii, 6; Hammerton, J., *Universal History of the World*, III. 1524.
31. Caesar, vi, 14.
33. Arnold, W. P., *The Roman System of Provincial Administration*, 142.
34. Pliny, xviii, 72.
35. Frank, *Economic Survey*, V, 133f.
36. Pliny, xxxiv, 18.
37. Ibid., iii, 5.
38. Sidonius Apollinaris, *Poems*, xxiii, 37.
40. Jullian, C. *Histoire de la Gaule*, V, 35n.
41. In Mommsen, *Provinces*, I, 118.
43. See the statement of their case in Barnes, H. E., *History of Western Civilization*, I, 434.
44. Mommsen, *History*, V, 100.
45. Caesar, V, 12.
46. Tacitus, *Annals*, xiv, 29.
47. Tacitus, *Agricola*, 21.
48. Haverfield, F., *The Roman Occupation of Britain*, 213.
49. Id., *The Romanization of Britain*, 62; Collingwood and Myres, *Roman Britain*, 197; Home, G., *Roman London*, 93.

50. Strabo, iv, 5.2.
51. CAH, XII, 289.
52. *Time*, Mar. 17, 1941.
53. Tacitus, *Germania*, 14.
54. Strabo, vii, 1.2.
55. Seneca, *De ira*, v, 10.
56. *Germania*, 22.
57. Sumner, W. G., *Folkways*, 380.
58. Ibid., 316.
59. *Germania*, 20.

CHAPTER XXIII

1. Dio Chrysostom, *Orat.*, vii.
2. Plutarch, "Demosthenes."
3. In Trench, R. C., *Plutarch*, 40.
4. Ibid., 41.
5. In Glover, T. R., *Conflict of Religions in the Early Roman Empire*, 85.
6. Plutarch, *Quaestiones Romanai; De Isise et osiride*.
7. Plutarch, *Moralia*, introd., I, 15.
8. Ibid., 37.
9. Ibid., vol. II, pp. 123, 128, 131-2, 173.
10. Ibid., 140B.
11. *De tranq. an.*, ix, 20.
12. Dio Chr., *Orat.*, xii.
13. Epictetus, *Discourses*, i, 6.26.
14. Lucian, "Of Pantomime," 2.
15. Id., "Demonax," 57.
16. Apuleius, book X.
17. Alciphron, *Letters*, vi, p. 175.
18. Dio. Chr., *Orat.*, lxxii.
19. Philostratus, *Lives of the Sophists*, 223f.
20. Renan, *Christian Church*, 167.
21. Our sole source for Demonax is an essay uncertainly ascribed to Lucian, and possibly colored with fiction.
22. Lucian, "Peregrinus Proteus."
23. Renan, *Christian Church*, 166.
24. Lucian, "Demonax," 55; Epictetus, *Discourses*, iii, 22.
25. Id., frag. 1.
27. I, 12, 21; vi, 25.
28. IV, 1.
29. I, 24.
30. II, 5.
31. I, 2.
32. *Encheiridion*, 8.
33. *Discourses*, i, 6.
34. Ibid., 9.
35. 3, 9; ii, 8.
36. I, 29.
37. III, 24; ii, 6.
38. I, 16.
39. I, 18, 19; frag. 43.
40. III, 10.
41. Frag. 42.
42. *Encheir.*, 33.

43. *Discourses*, ii, 10.
44. III, 12.
45. 13.
46. Frags. 54, 94.
47. *Discourses*, ii, 16.
48. I, 9.
49. Ibid., introd., xxviif.
50. In Sextus Empiricus, *Hypotyposes Pyrr.*, 1, 36f, and Gellius, xi, 5.6. For details cf. Owen, J., *Evenings with the Sceptics*, I, 323-5.
51. Sextus, *Hyp. Pyrr.*, ii, 204.
52. III, 29; i, 135-8.
53. III, 210.
54. *Adv. Dogmaticos*, i, 148; *Hyp. Pyrr.*, iii, 9-11.
55. Ibid., i, 7.
56. Ibid., i, 8, 25.
57. III, 235; *Adv. Dogm.*, i, 49.
58. CAH, XII, 449.
59. Lucian, "Icaromenippus," 25.
60. "Zeus Cross-Examined," 2-18.
61. "Zeus Tragoedus," 53.
62. *Dialogues of the Dead*, x.
63. "Hermotimus," end.
64. "Charon," 2.
65. "Icaromenippus," 17.
66. "Charon," 24.
67. "Menippus," 21.
68. Inge, W., *Philosophy of Plotinus*, I, 82.

CHAPTER XXIV

1. Josephus, *Against Apion*, ii, p. 480.
2. Charlesworth, 26; Frank, *Economic Survey*, II, 330.
3. Ibid., 337.
4. 445; Rostovtzeff, *Social and Economic History of the Hellenistic World*, 1288.
5. Josephus, *Wars*, ii, 16.4; Frank, V, 245.
6. Breccia, E., *Alexandria ad Aegyptum*, 41.
8. Dio Chr., xxxii, 69.
9. In Frank, V, 247; Mommsen, *Provinces*, II, 177.
10. Baron, S. W., *Social and Religious History of the Jews*, I, 196-7.
11. Edersheim, I, 61.
12. Josephus, *Against Apion*, ii, p. 489.
13. Eusebius, *Ecclesiastical History*, ii, 4.
14. Graetz, H., *History of the Jews*, II, 186.
15. Philo, *Quod Deus sit immutabilis*, 12.
16. Philo, *De mundi opificio*, i, 4; Inge, I, 98.
17. Philo, *De confusione linguarum*, 28.
18. In Sachar, A., *History of the Jews*, 110.
19. Philo, *De vita contemplativa*.
20. Usher, A., *History of Mechanical Inventions*, 40.
21. Bailey, 314.

22. Sarton, G., *Introduction to the History of Science*, I, 274.
23. Ibid., 202; Heath, Sir, T., *History of Greek Mathematics*, II, 306.
24. Ammianus, xxii, 16-19.
25. Philostratus, in Friedländer, I, 171.
26. Bailey, 283.
27. Sarton, 283.
28. Himes, 86.
29. Garrison, 30, 110.
30. Sarton, 282; Castiglione, 202.
31. Ibid.; Himes, 90.
32. Haggard, H., *Devils, Drugs, and Doctors*, 23.
33. Galen, *On the Natural Faculties*, introd., xv.
34. Galen in Thorndike, L., *History of Magic and Experimental Science*, I, 117, 152.
35. Ibid., 143.
36. Williams, I, 278.
37. In Friedländer, I, 174.
38. Castiglione, 225.
39. Thorndike, I, 171.
40. Strabo, xvi, 4.
41. Doughty, C., *Travels in Arabia Deserta*, I, 40.
42. Josephus, *Antiquities*, xv, 9.
43. MacGregor, R., *Greek Anthology*, v, 171.
44. Tr. by Goldwyn Smith in Symonds, J. A., *The Greek Poets*, 521.
45. Leslie, S., *Greek Anthology*, vii, 476.
46. Ibid., p. 17.
47. Ibid., ix, 489.
48. *Greek Anthology*, ix, 570.
49. Strabo, xv, 2.23.
50. Frank, IV, 158.
51. Rostovtzeff, *Roman Empire*, 135; CAH, II, 634.
52. Breasted, J. H., *Oriental Forerunners of Byzantine Painting*, pref.
53. CAH, XI, 638.
54. Ibid., 646.
55. In Mahaffy, *Silver Age*, 211.
59. Philostratus, *Apollonius*, iv, 7.
60. Aelius Aristides, *Orat.*, xvii, 8, in Frank, IV, 750.
61. Philostratus, *Lives of the Sophists*, i, 25.
62. Ibid.
63. Longus, *Daphnis and Chloe, ad init.*, in Heliodorus, *Greek Romances*.
64. Dio Cassius, lxx, 4.
65. Appian, *Roman History*, xiv, 16.
66. Ibid.
67. Pliny, xxv, 3.
68. Ibid., xxxiii, 14.
69. Appian, xii, 4.
70. Ibid., 7.

71. Ferrero, I, 83.
72. Arrian, *Anabasis of Alexander*, i, 12.
73. Reid, 376.
74. Williams, I, 255.
75. Strabo, i, 1.22-3.
76. Ibid., 3.5.
77. Dio. Chr., xlvi, 3.
78. Ibid., x, 21.
79. In Bigg, C., *Neoplatonism*, 70.
80. Ibid., 73.
81. Dio. Chr., xii, 10; xiii, 28; xiv, 18; xxiii, 7.
82. Friedländer, III, 299.
83. Frazer, *Adonis, Attis, and Osiris*, 157.
84. Cumont, F., *Oriental Religions in the Roman Empire*, 53.
85. Ibid., 55.
86. Frazer, 306; Boissier, *La réligion romaine*, I, 383; Dill, 549f.
87. Plutarch, *De Iside;* Dill, 577; Halliday, W., *Pagan Background of Early Christianity*, 240.
88. Tarn, 296; Dill, 582.
89. Cumont, 41, 93.
90. Breasted, J., *Ancient Times*, 660; Weigall, A., *The Paganism in Our Christianity*, 129.
91. Dill, 610.
92. Ibid., 601, 623.
93. Cumont, 158.
94. Guignebert, C., *Christianity, Past and Present*, 71.
95. Hatch, E., *Influence of Greek Ideas upon the Christian Church*, 283.
96. Frazer, *Adonis*, 229; Halliday, 317.
97. Hatch, 147.
98. Philo, *De vita contemplativa*, 18-40.
99. Lucian, "Alexander the Oracle-Monger."
100. Philostratus, *Apollonius*, i, 14.
101. Ibid., 19; iv, 45.
102. I, 33-4.
103. Apollonius, epistles xliii and xiv in Philostratus.
104. Philostratus, iv, 3.
105. Ibid., viii, 29-31.

CHAPTER XXV

1. Appian, *Roman History*, xii, 15.
2. Frank, IV, 197.
2a. In the State Museum, Berlin; reproduced in Pope, A., *Persian Art*, IV, 134A.
3. Rawlinson, G., *Sixth Great Oriental Monarchy*, 423.
4. Plutarch, "Crassus."
5. Sachar, 105.
6. Josephus, *Antiquities*, xiv, 2.9; Strabo, xvi, 2.40.
7. Josephus, xiv, 11.
8. Id., *Wars*, i, 21.

9. *Antiquities*, xv, 7; xvi, 5.
10. Ibid., xv, 8.
11. Ibid., 11.
12. Ibid.; *Wars*, v, 5; Foakes-Jackson and Lake, *Beginnings of Christianity*, I, 5-7; Schürer, Div. I, Vol. I, 280.
13. *Antiquities*, xvi, 7.
14. Our sole authority for this is Josephus, *Ant.*, xv, 8.1.
15. Ibid., 10.
16. XVII, 5.
17. Klausner, J., *Jesus of Nazareth*, 145.
18. Moore, G., *Judaism*, I, 23.
19. Baron, I, 131.
20. Ibid., 192-3.
21. *Antiquities*, iv, 10.
22. *Against Apion*, p. 456.
23. Finkelstein, L., *Akiba*, 33.
24. Schürer, Div. II, Vol. I, 162; Moore, I, 82; Goguel, M., *Life of Jesus*, 471; Graetz, II, 54-5.
25. Zeitlin, S., *The Jews*, 43; id., *The Pharisees and the Gospels*, 237; CAH, IX, 408.
26. Josephus, *Wars*, i, 8.14.
27. Philo, *Quod omnis homo*, 86; *Hypothetica*, 11.4 and 12; Josephus, *Antiquities*, xviii, 1.
28. Josephus, *Wars*, ii, 8.
29. Ibid., 9.
30. Graetz, II, 29; Ueberweg, F., *History of Philosophy*, I, 228.
31. Klausner, 231; Graetz, II, 145.
32. Josephus, *Wars*, ii, 8.
33. In Moore, I, 313.
34. Hastings, J., *Encyclopedia of Religion and Ethics*, s.v. Hillel.
35. Philo, in Eusebius, *Praeparatio evangelica*, viii, 7.
36. Babylonian Talmud, Abot, i, 42, Shab, 31a.
37. Abot, ii, 4.
38. Foakes-Jackson, 134; CAH, IX, 420.
39. Book of Wisdom, ii.
40. Ibid., v.
41. Isaiah, ix, 6.
42. Book of Wisdom, xviii, 13f.
43. Isaiah, liii.
44. Daniel, ii, 44; vii, 13f; Song of Solomon, xvii.
45. Sibylline Oracles, iii, 767f in Klausner, *From Jesus to Paul*, 159.
46. Isaiah, ii, 4; xi, 6; Book of Enoch, i-xxvi; Sib. Or., ii, 303f in Klausner, 150.
47. Book of Wisdom, iv; Enoch, cviii.
48. Book of Wisdom, ii-iii.
49. Finkelstein, 263.
50. Tacitus, *Histories*, v, 9.
51. Josephus, *Wars*, ii, 14.

52. Graetz, II, 239.
53. Josephus, l.c.
54. Ibid., v, 1f; Tacitus, **v, 12.**
55. Josephus, ii, 14.
56. Ibid., ii, 18.
57. Tacitus, v, 13.
58. Josephus, v, 11.
59. Dio Cassius, lxv, 4.
60. Josephus, ix, 3; Tacitus, v, 13.
61. Strabo in Josephus, *Antiquities*, xiv, 7.
62. Philo, *Legatio ad Caium*, 36.
63. Baron, I, 132-3; Bevan, E. R., *Legacy of Israel*, 29.
64. Josephus, *Against Apion*, ii, 3.
65. Josephus, *Life of Flavius Josephus*, p. 540.
66. Finkelstein, 141.
67. Baron, I, 191.
68. Dio Cassius, lxix, 12f; Renan, *The Christian Church*, 106.
69. Moore, *Judaism*, I, 93.
70. Finkelstein, 276.

CHAPTER XXVI

1. Reinach, S., *Short History of Christianity*, 22; Guignebert, *Jesus*, 63.
2. Josephus, *Antiquities*, xviii, 3.
3. Scott, E., *First Age of Christianity*, 46; Schürer, I, 143. This conclusion applies also to the Slavonic version of Josephus; cf. Guignebert, op. cit., 148.
4. Klausner, *Jesus*, 46; Goguel, 71.
5. Pliny the Younger, v, 8.
6. Tacitus, *Annals*, xv, 44.
7. Goguel, 94; Klausner, 60.
8. Suetonius, "Nero," 16.
9. Id., "Claudius," 25.
10. Acts of the Apostles, xviii, 2. Quotations from the New Testament are in most cases from the translation of E. J. Goodspeed.
11. In Goguel, 9, 184.
12. E.g., Galatians, i, 19; I Corinthians, ix, 5.
13. I Cor., xi, 23-6.
14. Ibid., xv, 3; Gal., ii, 20.
15. Eusebius, *E.H.*, iii, 39.
16. E.g., vi, 30-45; viii, 1-13, 17-20.
17. Klausner, *From Jesus to Paul*, 260.
18. Schweitzer, A., *Quest of the Historical Jesus*, 335.
19. Irenaeus, *Contra Haereses*, ii, 1.3.
20. Guignebert, *Jesus*, 30; CAH, XI, 260.
21. Guignebert, 467.
22. Foakes-Jackson and Lake, *Beginnings of Christianity*, I, 268.
23. *Enc. Brit.*, X, 537.
24. Ibid., XIV, 477.
25. Partially listed in *Enc. Brit.*, XIII, 95.

26. Scott, *First Age*, 217; *Enc. Brit.*, XIII, 98; Goguel, 150; CAH, XI, 261.
27. Matthew, ii, 1; Luke, i, 5.
27a. Luke, iii, 1, 23.
28. Josephus, *Wars*, ii, 8.
29. Tertullian, *Adv. Marcionem*, iv, 19.
30. *Enc. Brit.*, V, 642; III, 525.
31. Matt. xiii, 55; Mark, vi, 2.
32. Guignebert, *Jesus*, 127; Klausner, 23.
33. John, vii, 15; Mark, vi, 2.
34. Thorndike, 471.
35. *Enc. Brit.*, XIII, 26.
36. Guignebert, *Christianity*, 58.
37. Josephus, *Antiquities*, xiii, 5. On the authenticity of the passage cf. Foakes-Jackson and Lake, I, 101.
38. Graetz, II, 145.
39. Matt., iii, 11-12.
40. Ibid., 23.
41. John, iv, 2.
42. Josephus, *Antiquities*, xviii, 5.
43. Mark, vi, 14-29.
44. Matt., xiv, 1-12.
45. Mark, i, 14; Matt., iv, 12.
46. Luke, iv, 14.
47. Isaiah, lxi, 1-2.
48. Luke, iv, 19.
49. Luke, vi, 14.
50. Mark, ix, 48; Matt., xiii, 37.
51. Luke, xvi, 25.
52. Mark, xi, 12-14.
53. Matt., xii, 46; Luke, viii, 19.
54. Mark, i, 7; Matt., v, 40; Luke, vi, 29.
55. Guignebert, *Jesus*, 186.
56. Klausner, 69.
57. Luke, vii, 36-59.
58. Mark, x, 16.
59. Cf. Robertson, J. M., *Christianity and Mythology*.
60. Matt., xiii, 57.
61. Mark, v, 35f.
62. Matt., xix, 28.
63. Luke, x, 1-4.
64. Guignebert, *Jesus*, 52, 253; Goguel, 282, 287.
65. E.g., Matt., xx, 1-16.
66. Matt., xxiv, 30.
67. John, xviii, 36.
68. Mark, iv, 11, 30; xii, 34.
69. Luke, xvii, 20.
70. Matt., xix, 29.
71. Cf. Schweitzer, 212; Guignebert, 341.
72. Mark, xiv, 25.
73. Matt., x, 23.
74. Matt., xvi, 28.
75. Luke, xiii, 30.
76. Mark, xiii, 32.
77. Matt., xxiv, 6-12.

78. E.g., Kautsky, K., *Ursprung des Christentums;* Kalthoff, A., *Rise of Christianity.*
79. Mark, x, 23; Matt., vi, 25; xix, 24; Luke, xvi, 13.
80. Matt., xix, 15.
81. Acts, ii, 44-5.
82. Matt., xxii, 21.
83. Matt., xxv, 14.
84. Luke, xix, 26.
85. Matt., xx, 15.
86. Matt., xxiv, 46; Luke, xvii, 7-10.
87. Matt., xi, 12.
88. Mark, i, 14-15; vi, 12; Matt., x, 7.
89. Luke, xviii, 29; xiv, 26; Matt., viii, 21f; x, 34; xix, 12.
90. Leviticus, xix, 17-18, 34.
91. Exodus, xxiii, 4-5.
92. Jeremiah, iii, 30.
93. Isaiah, i, 6.
94. Ibid., i, 2.
95. Hosea, ii, 1.
96. Matt., x, 5.
97. Acts, x-xi.
98. John, iv, 22.
99. Matt., xv, 24f; Mark, vii, 27.
100. Matt., viii, 4.
101. Matt., xxiii, 1.
102. Matt., v, 17.
103. Luke, xvi, 17; Matt., v, 18.
104. Foakes-Jackson and Lake, I, 316.
105. Matt., v, 31-2.
106. Matt., v, 21-2.
107. Mark, ii, 25.
108. Luke, xvi, 16; Matt., v, 18.
109. Matt., xxiii, 1-34; xxi, 31.
110. Cf. Mark, xxii, 32-3, and Klausner, *Jesus*, 113.
111. Luke, xiii, 31-3.
112. Acts, i, 6.
113. Mark, xii, 35-7.
114. Matt., xix, 17.
115. Matt., xvi, 39.
116. Daniel, vii, 13.
117. Matt., xii, 8.
118. Matt., xi, 27; Luke, x, 22.
119. Matt., xvi, 16f.
120. Luke, xix, 37.
121. John, xii, 13.
122. Mark, xiv, 49; Luke, xxi, 1; xxi, 37.
123. John, xi, 50.
124. Mark, x, 45; xiv, 24.
125. E.g., Guignebert, *Jesus*, 454; Brandes, G., *Did Jesus Exist?*, 104.
126. Cf. Goguel, 497.
127. Mark, xiv, 26; Klausner, 326.
128. John, xiii, 33.
129. Mark, xiv, 43.
130. Mark, xiv, 61; Matt., xxvi, 63.

131. Philo, *Legatio*, 38.
132. Matt., xxvii, 11.
133. John, xviii, 38.
134. Tacitus, *Annals*, xv, 44.
135. Luke, xxiii, 26.
136. Cicero, *V in Verrem*, 64.
137. Mark, xv, 32.
138. Luke, xxiii, 39-43.
139. John, xix, 25; Mark, xv, 37.
140. Justinian, *Digest*, xlviii, 20.6.
141. Luke, xxiii, 48.
142. Luke, xxiv, 13-32.
143. Matt., xxviii, 16-17.
144. John, xxi, 4.
145. Luke, xxiv, 52.

CHAPTER XXVII

1. Foakes-Jackson and Lake, II, *passim*, and especially, 305-6; Scott, *First Age*, 110; CAH, XI, 257-8; Klausner, *From Jesus to Paul*, 215; Ramsay, W. M., *The Church in the Roman Empire*, 6-8; Renan, *Apostles*, p. v.
2. Shotwell, J., and Loomis, L., *The See of Peter*, 56-7.
3. I Peter, iv, 7.
4. I John, ii, 18.
5. Acts, ii, 16.
6. Ibid., xi, 8.
7. V, 20.
8. Mark, vi, 13.
9. Acts, iv, 32-6; ii, 44-5.
10. IV, 4.
11. VI, 11.
12. VII, 51-3.
13. VIII, 2-3.
14. XI, 19.
15. I Cor., ix, 5; Clement of Alexandria, *Stromata*, vii, 11; Eusebius, *E.H.*, iii, 30.
16. I Peter, i, i-iv, 8.
17. Shotwell and Loomis, 64-5.
18. Lactantius, *De Mortibus Persecutorum*, 2.
19. Eusebius, ii, 25.
20. Ibid., iii, 1.
21. Renan, *Antichrist*, 93.
22. Acts, xiii, 9; Coneybeare and Howson, *Life, Times, and Travels of St. Paul*, I, 46, 150.
23. Guignebert, Christianity, 75-6; Livingstone, R. W., *The Legacy of Greece*, 33, 54.
24. Acts, xxi, 3.
25. Renan, *Jesus*, 167.
26. II Cor., x, 9.
27. Ibid., xii, 7.
28. Gal., v, 12.
29. II Cor., xi, 1.

30. Acts, ix, 1.
31. IX, 3-9.
32. IX, 18.
33. XV, 1.
34. XV, 27-9. The account in Acts harmonizes sufficiently well, *pace* Renan and others, with Paul's report in Gal. ii.
35. Gal. ii, 10.
36. Ibid., ii, iii.
37. Acts, xvii, 18.
38. XVII, 22.
39. XVIII, 12.
40. II Cor., ii, 16.
41. Acts, xxi, 21-4.
42. XXVIII, 28.
43. Guignebert, *Christianity*, 65; Goguel, 105; CAH, XI, 257; Klausner, *Jesus*, 63.
44. Coloss., iii, 15.
45. II Cor., iii, 6.
46. I Cor., xv, 33.
47. Titus, i, 15.
48. I Timothy, vi, 10. The letters to Titus and Timothy, however, are of doubtful authenticity.
49. I Cor., ix, 19; x, 33.
50. Romans, v, 12.
51. Frazer, Sir J., *The Scapegoat*, 210, 413; Weigall, 70f.
52. Guignebert, *Christianity*, 88.
53. I Cor., xv, 51.
54. Ibid., i, 24.
55. Coloss., i, 15-17.
56. Rom., ix, 11, 18; xi, 5.
57. Hebrews, xi, 1. Probably not Paul's.
58. Gal. ii, 24f.
59. I Cor., xiii.
60. Ibid., ix, 5.
61. VII, 8.
62. Rom., xiii, 14.
63. Ibid., i, 26.
64. I Cor., vi, 15.
65. Ibid., vii, 20f.
66. Rom., xiii, 1.
66a. II Tim., iv, 9, 6.
67. Philippians, iii, 20.
68. I Cor., vii, 29; cf. I Thessalonians, iv, 15.
69. II Thess., ii, 1-5.
70. Acts, xvii, 7.
71. Eusebius, *E.H.*, iii, 1.
72. Cf. Revelation, xvii, 10.
73. Renan, *Antichrist*, 95; CAH, X, 726.
74. Duchesne, Mon. L., *Early History of the Christian Church*, I, 99.
75. Eusebius, iii, 25.
76. Ibid., iii, 33.
77. Rev., vii, 4; xiv, 1.
78. Ibid., vi, 2-8.
79. VII, 14.

80. XX, 15; xxi, **8**.
81. XIX, 18.
82. XXI.
83. Proverbs, viii, 22-31.
84. John, i, 5.
85. Justin, *Apology*, i, 66; Tertullian, *De Baptismo*, 5; Halliday, 9.

CHAPTER XXVIII

1. Duchesne, I, 38.
2. Tertullian, *Contra Marcionem*, v, 8.
3. Jerome, *Letters*, xciii.
4. Clement of Alexandria, *Paedagogus*, iii, 11.
5. Paul, I Cor., xi, 3.
6. Lucian, *Peregrinus Proteus*.
7. Tertullian, *Apologeticus*, xxxix, 11-12.
8. Ibid., 5.
9. Renan, *Marc Aurèle*, 600.
10. James, v, 1; ii, 5.
11. Ibid., i, 10.
12. Renan, *St. Paul*, 402.
13. Klausner, *From Jesus to Paul*, 113-4.
14. Tertullian, *De jejuniis*, i, 17; Duchesne, II, 253; Renan, *Christian Church*, 211; Robertson, *History of Freethought*, I, 244.
15. Clement of Alex., *Paedag.*, iii, 11; Renan, *Marc Aurèle*, 520.
16. Tertullian, *Apol.*, ix, 8.
17. Gibbon, I, 480.
18. Tertullian, *De spectaculis*, 1, 3.
19. Sumner, W. G., *War and Other Essays*, 54-5.
20. Tertullian, *Apol.*, xlvi, 10.
21. Friedländer, III, 204; Tertullian, *De exhort. castitatis*, 13; Lea, H. C., *Historical Sketch of Sacerdotal Celibacy*, 41; Robertson, *History of Freethought*, I, 244.
22. Pliny the Younger, x, 97.
23. Galen in Hammerton, IV, 2179.
24. Tertullian, *De spect.*, 23.
25. Perhaps anthropophagic; cf. Sumner, *Folkways*, 451.
26. Renan, *St. Paul*, 268.
27. Frazer, Sir J., *Spirits of the Corn and Wild*, II, 92-3; Carpenter, Edw., *Pagan and Christian Creeds*, 65-7.
28. Acts, viii, 14-17; xix, 1-6.
29. *Catholic Encyclopedia*, IV, 217-8.
30. Matt., xvi, 18; John, xx, 23.
31. Friedländer, II, 364.
32. Renan, *Marc Aurèle*, 449.
33. Tertullian, *Apol.*, xxxvii, 4.
34. Id., *Ad uxorem*, i, 5; Renan, *Marc*, 551; Glover, *Conflict of Religions*, 341.
35. CAH, XII, 456.
36. Lake, K., *Apostolic Fathers*, I, 395.

37. Murray, Sir G., *Five Stages of Greek Religion*, 196.
38. Renan, *Marc*, 292.
39. Duchesne, I, 196.
40. Friedländer, III, 192.
41. CAH, XII, 459.
42. Origen, *Contra Celsum*, in Glover, 252; Carpenter, 220.
43. Plotinus, *Enneads*, xliii.
44. Porphyry, *Life of Plotinus*, 14.
45. MacKenna, Stephen, *Essence of Plotinus*, 11n.
46. Plotinus, *Enneads*, iii, 4.
47. Ibid., vi, 9.
48. V, 1.
49. IV, 1; Inge, *Philosophy of Plotinus*, II, 21-4, 92.
50. Plotinus, v, 1; iii, 7.
51. Ibid., v, 11.
52. MacKenna, introd., xx.
53. In Lake, *Apostolic Fathers*, I, 23
54. Tertullian, *Apol.*, xxx, 4.
55. Ibid., xvii, 6.
56. Id., *De spect.*, 30.
57. Id., *De cultu feminarum.*
58. In Ueberweg, I, 303.
59. CAH, XII, 593.
60. Eusebius, vi, 2.
61. Gibbon, I, 467.
62. Jerome, *Letters*, xxxiii.
63. Shotwell, *Introduction*, 292.
64. Origen, *De principiis*, i, 15-16, in Hatch, 76.
65. Origen, op. cit., iv, 1, in Hatch, 76.
66. Duchesne, I, 255f.
67. Inge, *Plotinus*, II, 19, 102.
68. In Watson, *Marcus Aurelius*, 305.
69. Matt., xvi, 18.
70. Shotwell and Loomis, 64-5.
71. Ibid., 60-1, 84-6.
72. Lake, I, 121.
73. Duchesne, I, 215.
74. CAH, XII, 198, 600.
75. Cyprian's Letters in Inge, *Plotinus*, I, 62.

CHAPTER XXIX

1. Herodian, *History of Twenty Caesars*, II, 83.
2. Dio Cassius, lxxiv, 5.
3. Herodian, II, 100, 103; III, 155.
4. *Historia Augusta*, "Septimius Severus," xviii, 11.
5. Herodian, III, 139.
6. Lot, F., *End of the Ancient World*, 10.
7. Dio, lxxix, 7.
8. Ibid., lxxviii, 16.
9. Herodian, IV, 210; Dio, lxxviii, 22.
10. Dio, lxxix, 23.

11. *Historia Augusta*, "Elagabalus," 19-32; Dio, lxxx, 13; Herodian, IV, 253.
12. Dio, lxxix, 14; Gibbon, I, 141.
13. *Historia Augusta*, "Severus Alexander" 30, 39.
14. Herodian, VI, 5.
15. *Hist. Aug.*, "Severus Alexander," 20.
16. Ibid., 29.
17. Ibid., 33.
18. Herodian, VI, 8.
19. In Rostovtzeff, *Social and Economic History of the Roman Empire*, 399.
20. Gibbon, I, 294.
21. Maine, *Ancient Law*, 177.
22. West, L., "Economic Collapse of the Roman Empire," in *Classical Journal*, 1932, p. 106.
23. Abbott, *Common People*, 174.
24. Rostovtzeff, op. cit., 424, 442-3.
25. Ibid., 305.
26. Frank, *Economic History*, 489.
27. Ferrero, *Ruin of Ancient Civilization*, 58; Rostovtzeff, *History of the Ancient World*, II, 317.
28. Frank, *Economic Survey*, IV, 220.
29. Rostovtzeff, *Roman Empire*, 419.
30. Collingwood and Myres, 206.
31. Heath, II, 448.
32. Plato, *Laws*, 819.
33. Ball, W. W., *Short History of Mathematics*, 96.
34. Justinian, *Digest*, i, 1.4.
35. *Hist. Aug.*, "Severus Alexander," 51.
36. Roberts, W. R., introd. to *"Longinus" on the Sublime*, Loeb Library.
37. Heliodorus, *Greek Romances*, 1.
38. Ibid., 289.
39. In *Catullus, Tibullus*, etc., p. 343.
40. In Burckhardt, J., *Die Zeit Constantins*, 54.
41. CAH, XII, 273; Frank, *Economic Survey*, III, 633.
42. Ferrero, *Ancient Rome and Modern America*, 88.
43. Toutain, 326.
44. West, l. c., 102.
45. Rostovtzeff, *Ancient World*, II, 329.
46. Toutain, 326; CAH, XII, 271; *Cambridge Medieval History*, I, 52.
47. Rostovtzeff, *Roman Empire*, 474.
48. Cunningham, W. C., *Western Civilization in Its Economic Aspects*, I, 191-2.
49. Paul-Louis, 283-5.
50. Translation based on that of Elsa Glaser in Frank, *Economic Survey*, V, 312.
51. Ibid., The prices are calculated on the valuation of gold at $35 per oz. in the United States of 1944.
52. Frank, *Survey*, III, 612.
53. Lactantius, *De Mortibus Persecutorum*, vii.
54. Ibid., vii, 3.
55. Charlesworth, 98.
56. West, 105; Ferrero, *Ruin of Ancient Civilization*, 106.
57. Cunningham, I, 188.
58. Frank, *Survey*, II, 245; IV, 241.
59. Reid, *Municipalities*, 492; Arnold, 265.
60. Heitland, 382.
61. Davis, W. S., 233.
62. Frank, *Economic History*, 404; Rostovtzeff, *Roman Empire*, 409.
63. Gibbon, I, 377.

CHAPTER XXX

1. Renan, *Marc*, 592.
2. Tertullian, *Apol.*, xl, 1.
3. Minucius Felix, *Octavius*, ix, 5, in Tertullian, *Apol.*
4. Guignebert, *Christianity*, 164.
5. I Cor., vi, 1; Renan, *Marc*, 597.
6. Origen *Contra Celsum*, viii, 69, in Halliday, 27.
7. Tertullian, *Apol.*, xv, 1-7; Duchesne, I, 34.
8. Friedländer, III, 186.
9. Tertullian, *Apol.*, iv, 1.
10. Ramsay, 253; CAH, X, 503.
11. Duchesne, I, 82.
12. Bury, J., *History of Freedom of Thought*, 42.
13. Tertullian, *Apol.*, v, 4; Eusebius, iii, 17.
14. Pliny the Younger, x, 96-7.
15. Rescript of Hadrian in Eusebius, iv, 9. For a defense of its authenticity cf. Ramsay, 320.
16. From an account said to have been sent to the Christian churches by the elders of the church at Smyrna, in Lake, *Apostolic Fathers*, II, 321.
17. Renan, *Marc*, 331.
18. Tertullian, *Apol.*, xlv, 14.
19. *Memoirs of St. Perpetua*, in Davis and West, *Readings in Ancient History*, 287.
20. Rostovtzeff, *Ancient World*, II, 349.
21. Duchesne, I, 267.
22. Lactantius, *De Mortibus Persecutorum*, x.
23. Eusebius, viii, 1f.
24. Gibbon, II, 57.
25. Eusebius, viii, 17.
26. Tertullian, *Apol.*, i, 13.
27. Ambrose in *Enc. Brit.*, VI, 297.
28. Eusebius, *Life of Constantine*, i, 28.
29. Eusebius, *E.H.*, viii, 2.
30. Id., *Life of Constantine*, i, 28.
31. Lactantius, *De Mortibus*, xliv, 5.

32. *Cambridge Medieval History*, I, 4.
33. For the detailed evidence cf. Burckhardt, 252f.
34. *Hist. Aug.*, "Elagabalus," xxxiv, 4.
35. Lot, 29.
36. Flick, A. C., *Rise of the Medieval Church*, 123-4.
37. Duruy, V., *History of the Roman People*, VII, 510.
38. Kalthoff, 172; Lot, 98.
39. Eusebius, *Life*, ii, 36.
40. Ibid., iii, 62f.
41. Duchesne, I, 290.
42. Eusebius, *E.H.*, viii, 1.
43. Duchesne, II, 99.
44. Eusebius, *Historical View of the Council of Nice*, 6.
45. Ibid.
46. Eusebius, *Life*, ii, 63, 70.
47. Eusebius, *Nice*, 6.
48. Ibid., 15.
49. *Cambridge Medieval History*, I, 121.
50. Socrates, *Ecclesiastical History*, i, 8.
51. Duchesne, II, 125.
52. Ferrero, *Ruin*, 170.
53. Gatteschi, 24; Reinach, *Apollo*, 89.
54. Gibbon, VI, 553.
55. Lactantius, *Divinae Institutiones*, v, 19.
56. Eusebius, *Life*, i, 1.
57. *Cambridge Medieval History*, I, 15.

EPILOGUE

1. Reid, J. S., in *Cambridge Medieval History*, I, 54.
2. Cyprian, *Ad Demetrium*, 3, in Inge, *Plotinus*, I, 25.
3. Cf. West, op. cit., 103.
4. Frank, *Survey*, III, 575.
5. In Eusebius, *E. H.*, vii, 21.
6. Rostovtzeff, *Roman Empire*, 424.
7. Frank, *Survey*, III, 74.
8. Gibbon, I, 421.
9. Davis, *Influence of Wealth*, 214.
10. Gibbon, I, 274.
11. Id., chap. xvi, etc.
12. Renan, *Marc*, 589; Ferrero, *Ruin*, 7, 74; White, E. L., *Why Rome Fell, passim*.
13. Montesquieu, *Grandeur et décadence des Romains*, 36.
14. *Cambridge Medieval History*, I, 10.
15. Abbott, 201.
16. Rostovtzeff, *Roman Empire*, 445.

Index

I am indebted for this index to the careful scholarship of Mr. Arnold Canell.—W. D.

A

Abeona, 59
abortion, 211, 222, 313, 363-364, 396-397, 479, 505, 598, 666
About Nature, see *Physeos, Peri*
Abraham, 626, 662
absentee landlordism, 77, 233, 311, 631
Abstinents, 605
Abtolim, Jewish rabbi (fl. 1st century B.C.), 538
Ab Urbe Condita (Livy), 250-252
Academic, see Platonic
Academica (Cicero), 163*
Academy, Plato's, 421, 489, 495, 497
Acca Larentia (Lupa), nurse of Romulus and Remus, 12
Accius, tragic dramatist (170-? B.C.), 98
Achaea, 216, 424, 482
Achaean League, 86
Achaemenids, 507, 528, 529, 641
Acheron, 147, 238, 389
Achillas, Egyptian general (fl. 1st century B.C.), 187
Achilleid (Statius), 316
Achilles, 37, 100, 353, 354, 381
Acropolis, 487
Acta Diurna, 172, 382, 435, 447
Acta Senatus, 435
Acte, Claudia, mistress of Nero (1st century), 277, 284
acting, in Etruria, 18; in Rome, 18, 73-74, 83, 99, 223, 265-266, 278-279, 283, 378-379, 428
Actium (naval battle, 31 B.C.), 128, 139, 207, 208, 217, 218, 219, 241, 358, 434, 442, 465, 482
Acts of the Apostles, The, 403, 554, 556, 573, 575-595
Acts of the Martyrs, 648, 652
Adam, 588-589, 599
Addison, Joseph, English essayist and poet (1672-1719), 304
Adelphi (Terence), 101
Aden (*anc.* Adena), 325, 508
Adige (*anc.* Athesis), 454
administration, of Caesar, 190-194; of Augustus, 215-217; of Claudius, 270-271; of Nero, 275-276; of Vespasian, 287-288; of Domitian, 291; under the Principate, 293, 328, 330, 344, 391, 434; of Trajan, 409, 441; of Hadrian, 414-416, 419-420; of Antoninus Pius, 422-424; of Commodus, 447-448; of Alexander Severus, 626-627; of Gallienus, 629; of Diocletian, 639-645; of Constantine, 664; monarchic, 668-669
Adonis, 256, 523, 553, 595
Adoptionists, 605

Ad Pisones (Horace), 249
Adramyttium, 518
Adria (*anc.* Hadria, or Atria), 11, 414
Adrian of Tyre, Greek rhetorician (ca. 112-ca. 192), 488-489
Adrianople (*anc.* Adrianopolis), 483, 655, 670
Adriatic Sea, 37, 47, 50, 157, 183, 184, 203, 207, 232, 324, 325, 414, 455, 480, 496, 602
Aduatici, 175
adultery, 69, 134-135, 144, 157, (Caesar's) 168-169, 202, 211, 222-224, 229, 230-232, 248, 253, 255, 272-273, 274, 279, 290, 293, 297-298, 302, 312, 363, 369-370, 396, 424, 430, 438, 479, 485, 495, 529, 562, 599, 618, 621, 622
Adversus Haereses (Irenaeus), 612
Aebutia, lex, 401
Aedes Vestae, 359
aediles, 22, 28, 29*, 74, 82, 99, 328, 336, 369
Aedui, 174-175, 177
Aegatean (Aegadean) Isles, 45
Aegean Sea, 139, 157, 429, 514, 592, 602, 630
Aelia Capitolina, see Jerusalem
Aelianus, Claudius, historian (fl. 2nd century), 442
Aelius, see Aristides, Publius Aelius
Aelius, Pons, 422
Aemilia, stepdaughter of Sulla and wife of Pompey (fl. 1st century B.C.), 134
Aemilian (Marcus Julius Aemilius Aemilianus), Roman emperor (?-253), 629
Aemilian Way, 78
Aemilii, Roman clan, 21, 364
Aemilius, Pons, 340, 438
Aeneas, 12,61,98,148,167,237,239-241,382,456
Aeneid (Virgil), 225, 239-244, 254, 456
Aenesidemus of Cnossus, Greek Skeptic (1st century), 494
Aequi, 36
aerarium, 220
Aeschines, Athenian orator (389-314 B.C.), 95
Aeschylus, Greek dramatist (525-456 B.C.), 258
Aesculapius, 62, 75, 311, 487, 526
Aesopus, Claudius, tragic actor (fl. 1st century B.C.), 133, 160, 378
Aethiopica (Heliodorus), 636-637
Aetna, 265
Aetolian League, 85
Afranius, politician (?-46 B.C.), 129, 185
Africa, 38, 39, 40, 53, 54, 78, 85, 105, 106-107, 111, 112, 119, 123, 138, 183, 189, 190, 203, 216, 237, 246, 297, 308, 313, 320, 322, 326, 328-329, 336, 346, 347, 356, 366, 413, 417, 418, 431, 441, 442, 455, 464-466, 468, 470, 475, 499, 513, 523,

Africa (*continued*)
602, 603, 606, 613, 618, 621, 628, 631, 633, 636, 658, 659, 669-670
Africanus, Sextus Julius, Christian historian (?-232), 555
Against Apion (Josephus), 500, 546
Against Catiline (Cicero), 142
Against Celsus (Origen), 606, 615
1gape, 386, 597-598
Agathocles, Tyrant of Syracuse (361?-289 B.C.), 42
ager publicus, 76, 113-114, 116, 121, 171, 287, 320, 336
Aglibol, 511
Agnus Dei, 578-579
Agricola, Cnaeus Julius, governor (37-93), 288, 291, 433-434, 435-436, 476
Agricola (Tacitus), 433-434, 435-436
agriculture, Carthaginian, 39-40, 42; under Rome, 54, 76-77, 103-104, (agrarian revolt) 111-127, 190, 192, 211, 235, 237-239, 311, 319-321, 338, 348, 410-411, 448, 464, 473, 474, 476, 478, 483, 498, 522, 528-529, 535, 631-633, 644, 665, 668, 671
Agrigentum (Girgenti), 52, 112, 464
Agrippa, King of Chalcis (30-100), 586-587
Agrippa, Herod, King of the Jews (reigned 41-44), 543
Agrippa, Marcus Vipsanius, general (63-12 B.C.), 205, 207, 212, 214, 215, 219-220, 230-232, 263*, 308, 340, 359, 375, 420, 474
Agrippa, Baths of, 290, 340, 359, 375
Agrippina, wife of Germanicus (?-33 A.D.), 262-265, 273
Agrippina the Younger, mother of Nero (?-59), 263*, 272, 273-275, 277, 279, 280, 302, 479
Ahenobarbi, Domitii, Roman family, 274
Ahenobarbus, Cnaeus Domitius, father of Nero (fl. 1st century), 273, 274, 282, 334
Ahriman, 524
Ahura-Mazda, 524, 529
Aisne (*anc.* Axona), 175
Akiba ben Joseph, Jewish rabbi (40-138), 547-549
Alalia, battle of (535 B.C.), 7
Alaric, King of the Visigoths (376?-410), 670
Alba Longa, 11, 12, 241, 344
Alban hills, 77, 82
Albania, in Asia, 413
Alban poetry contest, 316
Albinus, procurator of Judea (fl. 1st century), 543
Albinus, Clodius, rival of Septimius Severus for emperorship (?-192), 621
Alcaeus, Greek lyric poet (620-580 B.C.), 247
Alcibiades, Athenian politician and general (450-404 B.C.), 147
Alciphron, Greek letter writer (fl. 180), 488
Alcmaeon, 278
Alcmena, 93, 100
Alcon, surgeon (fl. 1st century), 312
Aldobrandini, Villa, 454*

"*Aldobrandini*" *Wedding*, 354
Alemanni, 175, 627, 629, 638
Alesia (Alise Ste.-Reine), 177
Alexander the Great, King of Macedon (356-323 B.C.), 28, 37, 39, 169, 194, 208, 218, 226, 302, 413, 500, 557*, 623, 636, 641
Alexander, Bishop of Alexandria (fl. 4th century), 658-660, 662
Alexander, son of Herod the Great (?-6 B.C.), 534
Alexander of Abonoteichus, Greek worker of miracles (fl. 1st century), 525-526
Alexander Severus (Marcus Alexianus Bassianus Aurelius Severus Alexander), Roman emperor (208?-235), 375, 623, 625-627, 628, 634, 635, 645, 650
Alexander Severus, Baths of, 375
Alexandria, 93, 155, 158, 159, 186, 187-188, 190, 204, 206, 207, 211, 218, 234, 253, 266, 280, 291, 299, 312, 323, 325, 326, 329, 331, 339, 347, 352, 355, 356, 368, 374, 378, 380, 386, 389, 419, 431, 465, 494, 498-506, 508, 516, 521-522, 544, 545, 546, 604, 608, 611, 613, 615, 623, 626, 630, 634, 635, 650, 658-659, 660*, 666
Alexandria, library of, 188, 291, 516, 635
Alexandria, Museum of, 415, 419
Alexandria Issi (Alexandretta), 513
Alexandrian style, 361
Alexandria Troas, 516, 583, 602
Alfieri, Vittorio, Count, Italian dramatist (1749-1803), 3
algebra, 633-634
Alighieri, Dante, Italian poet (1265-1321), 8, 240, 243, 422, 437, 671
alimenta, 407, 411, 427, 461, 666
Allia (battle, 390 B.C.), 36
alphabet, Latin, 73, 269
Alps, 3, 5, 6, 11, 36, 47, 48-49, 53, 87, 118, 119, 137, 175, 178, 324, 429, 454, 474, 602, 628, 640, 654, 670
Altamira, 468
Altar of the Augustan Peace, *see Ara Pacis Augustae*
Altinum, 461
Amasea (Amasia), 520
Amastris (Amasra), 157, 520
Ambarvalia (Feast of the Arval Brotherhood), 59, 66
Ambiani, 175, 471*
Ambracia (Arta), 92
Ambracian Gulf (Gulf of Arta), 207
America, 132, 307, 352
America, Latin, 671
American Revolution, 192, 670
Amhaarez, 562
Amicitia, De (Cicero), 163*
Amiens (*anc.* Samarobriva, *later* Ambiani), 471*
Amisus (Samsun), 520
Amiternum, 455
Ammianus Marcellinus, historian (fl. 4th century), 322*, 365, 380, 402, 471, 504

Amores (Ovid), 254
amphitheaters, 82, 90, 111, 133, 277, 355, 359-361, 362, 378, 383-387, 410, 454, 455, 456, 459, 460-461, 465, 466, 474, 508, 512, 532, 612-613, 648, 649, 653
Amphitryon (Plautus), 100
Ampurias (*anc.* Emporium), 47
amulets, 60, 62, 373
Amulius, legendary usurper to the throne of Latium (8th century B.C.), 12
Amulius, painter (fl. 1st century), 352
Amyot, Jacques, French savant, and Bishop of Auxerre (1513-1593), 637
Anabasis of Alexander (Flavian), 520
Anacreon, Greek lyric poet (560?-475? B.C.), 158, 235, 247, 509
Analogy, On (Caesar), 162
Anastasius I, Roman Pope (?-401), 615
ancestor worship, 56, 59, 83-84, 226
Anchises, 240-241, 382
Ancona, 410
Ancus Marcius, fourth King of Rome (fl. 7th century B.C.), 14
Ancyra (Angora), 513
Andrew, apostle, 563
Andria (Terence), 101
Androcles, slave (dates uncertain), 385
Andromeda, 256
anesthetics, 313, 505
Anger, On (Seneca), 302
Anglo-Saxon, 477
Anicetus, Roman Pope (ca. 157-ca. 168), 617
Anicetus, courtier of Nero (fl. 1st century B.C.), 279
Anima, De (Tertullian), 613
animals, feeling for, in Lucretius, 147; in Virgil, 238; Pliny on, 310; Hadrian's, 414
animism, 60
Anio, 22
Anio Novus Aqueduct, 270
Anna, daughter of Phanuel, 542
Annales (Ennius), 98, 164
Annales (Tacitus), 434-437, 442
Anna Perenna, 65
Annas, priest (in the Bible), 571
Annona, 388
Annunciation, 558
Anthony, Saint, Egyptian founder of monachism (251-356?), 445, 657
anthropology, Lucretius on, 152-153
Antibes (*anc.* Antipolis), 78, 474
Anti-Cato (Caesar), 195
Antichrist, 575, 593
Antigonus, King of Judea (fl. 43 B.C.), 531
Anti-Lebanon Mountains, 511
Antinoöpolis, 419
Antinoüs, Greek favorite of Hadrian (?-122), 419, 442, 523
Antioch (Antakia), 54, 205, 280, 329, 413, 418, 428, 495, 504, 534, 546, 576, 582-583, 585, 588, 602, 608, 611, 623, 626, 629, 635, 650
Antioch (in Pisidia), 582

Antiochus III the Great, King of Syria (reigned 223-187 B.C.), 55, 86, 88, 91, 528
Antiochus IV Epiphanes, King of Syria (200?-164 B.C.), 107, 418, 487, 534, 540
Antiochus of Ascalon, Greek Platonic philosopher (fl. 1st century B.C.), 489
Antipater, son of Herod the Great (?-4 B.C.), 534-535
Antipater the Idumean, father of Herod and procurator of Judea (?-43 B.C.), 531
Antiquities of the Jews, The (Josephus), 546, 554
anti-Semitism, 546, 595
Antium (Anzio), 280, 340, 453
Antonia, mother of Germanicus and Claudius (1st century B.C.-1st century A.D.), 262, 264, 265, 266, 267, 268, 269, 274, 371
Antonines, 324, 392, 405, 411, 437, 442, 449, 516, 620
Antoninus Pius (Titus Aurelius Fulvius Boionius Arrius Antoninus Pius), Roman emperor (86-161), 345, 368, 392, 395, 396, 398, 408, 421-425, 426, 427, 428, 430, 444, 511, 549, 611, 648
Antoninus, Wall of, 476
Antonius, governor (fl. ca. 190), 605
Antonius, Lucius, governor (fl. 1st century B.C.), 204-205
Antonius, Marcus (Mark Antony), Roman general (83-30 B.C.), 70, 155, 160, 161, 169, 181, 185, 188, 191, 195-208, 211, 226, 228, 229, 230, 231, 232, 236, 239, 261, 265, 268, 273, 274, 309, 312, 329, 371, 372, 373, 412, 413, 418, 448, 482, 512, 516, 531, 583, 640
Antonius, Marcus, Roman general, father of Antony (fl. 1st century B.C.), 144, 160
Antonius Primus, general of Vespasian (fl. 1st century), 285, 301
Antyllus, ophthalmologist (fl. 1st century), 505
Anubis, 390
Apamea, 512, 514, 629
Apamea Celaenae, 513
Apelles, Greek painter (fl. 330 B.C.), 352, 355
Apennines, 3, 11, 50, 121, 141, 236, 253, 270, 344
Aphrodite, 512, 516
Aphrodite, Temple of (Jerusalem), 663
Aphrodite Pandemos, Temple of, 487
Apicata, divorced wife of Sejanus (?-31 A.D.), 264
Apicius, famous epicure (fl. reign of Tiberius), 376-377
Apion, Greek grammarian (fl. 1st century), 546
apocalypse, 540-542, 564-570, 575, 590-591, 592-595, 605, 616
Apocolocyntosis or *Pumpkinification* (Seneca), 275, 350
Apocrypha, 539-540, 559, 575*
Apollinaris Sidonius, Caius Sollius, Saint, bishop and poet (430?-482?), 473
Apollo, 8, 62, 64, 236-237, 240, 280, 351, 358, 381, 458, 513

Apollo the Healer, 62
Apollo, Temple of, 358
Apollo, Temple of (Pompeii), 459
Apollo the Healer, Temple of, 62
Apollo Belvedere, 349, 453
Apollodorus, Greek architect (fl. reign of Trajan), 411, 421
Apollodorus, attendant of Cleopatra (1st century B.C.), 187
Apollonia (*near* Valona), 200, 480, 482
Apollonia (*in* Palestine), 508
Apollonius of Athens, Greek sculptor in Rome (fl. ca. birth of Christ), 349
Apollonius of Rhodes, Greek poet and grammarian (fl. 222-181 B.C.), 241
Apollonius of Tyana, Greek philosopher (fl. 1st century), 515, 526, 622, 626
Apollonius, Life of (Philostratus), 526, 622
Apollonius Molo of Alabanda, Greek rhetorician (fl. 1st century B.C.), 141, 514
Apollo of Veii, 10
Apollo Room, 132
Apologeticus (Tertullian), 612
Apologia (Apuleius), 467
"Apologies," 611
apostles, 556,557,563-565,567,571,572,575-595
Appian (Appianus), historian (fl. 2nd century), 189, 196, 197, 424, 442, 471, 518, 519
Appian Aqueduct, 29, 81, 340
Appian Way (*via Appia*),29,77-78,138,340,617
Apuleius, satirist and philosopher (fl. 2nd century), 155, 299, 402, 442, 465, 466-468, 485, 487, 525, 612, 636, 637
Apulia, 50, 53, 112, 139, 244, 455
Aquae Aureliae (Baden-Baden), 480
Aquae Salis (Bath), 477
Aquae Sextiae (Aix), battle in 102 B.C., 119
Aqua Virgo Aqueduct, 327*
aqueducts, 81, 92, 103, 220, 270, 326-328, 340, 343,356,410,411,418-419,464,470,474,509,627
Aquila, *called* Ponticus, Greek-Jewish translator of the Old Testament (fl. 117-138), 614
Aquileia (Aquileja), 322, 324, 347, 429, 455, 628
Aquilia, lex, 312
Aquilius, Manius, general (?-88 B.C.), 121, 518
Aquincum, 480, *see also* Budapest
Aquinum, 437, 453
Aquis Urbis Romae, De (Frontinus), 328
Aquitania (Gallia Aquitanica), 472, 473
Aquyrion, 664
Arabia, 204, 217, 325, 329, 337, 346, 366, 419, 507-508, 546, 581, 602, 630
Arabia Deserta, 508
Arabia Felix (Yemen), 508
Arabia Petrea, 413, 508
Arabic, 504, 507
Arabs, 464, 470, 500, 503, 504, 507, 508, 529, 634
Aramaic, 508, 512, 529, 535, 556, 572
Ara Pacis Augustae, 225, 229, 346, 348, 349
Aratus of Soli, Greek didactic poet (315-245 B.C.), 238, 308, 584*
Arausio (Orange), 118, 119, 474

Arcadia, 101
Arcadius, Roman emperor in the East (?-408), 412
Arcesilaus, Greek sculptor in Rome (fl. 1st century B.C.), 342, 349
arch, 92, 327, 339, 340, 348, 349, 355-361, 443, 454, 455, 466, 470, 473, 474, 511, 529, 623, 635, 662, 671
Archagathus the Peloponnesian (Carnifex), physician (fl. 219 B.C.), 75-76
Archelaus, King of the Jews (reigned 4 B.C.-A.D. 6), 535, 542-543
Archias, Aulus Licinius, Greek poet in Rome (ca. 120-? B.C.), 141, 163
Archilochus, Greek lyric poet (714?-676 B.C.), 158, 244, 246, 247
Archimedes, Greek mathematician and scientist (287?-212 B.C.), 72, 77, 503, 634
Architectural (Second) Style (painting), 353
architecture, Etruscan, 8-9, 18; Carthaginian, 40-41, 42; Byzantine, 421; Parthian, 529; under Rome, 18, 75, 81, 92-93, 133, 281, 287, 338-354 *passim*, 355-362, 410, 411-413, 418-421, 442-443, (Pompeian) 458-459, 464, 465, 477, 511, 514, 515, 516, 532-533, 631, 633, 635, 661-662, 669, 671
Architecture, On (Vitruvius), 356
Archon, Peri (Origen), 614
archon basileus, 13
Ardashir I (*or* Artaxerxes), King of Persia (reigned 227-240), 530, 627
Ardea, 10, 16, 35
Arellius, painter (fl. end of 1st century B.C.), 352
Areopagus (Hill of Mars), 487, 584
Arescon, hermaphrodite mentioned by Pliny, 310
Aretas IV, King of Saba (9 B.C.-A.D. 40), 508
Arethusa, 256
Areus, Greek philosopher in Rome (fl. reign of Augustus), 299
Arezzo (*anc.* Arretium, *q.v.*), 9
Argentoratum (Strasbourg), 480, 633
Argiletum, The, 234
Argonautica (Apollonius of Rhodes), 241
Argos, 139, 310, 487, 630
Ariadne, 157, 256, 352
Aricia, 35, 61
Aries, 298
Ariminum (Rimini), 11, 78, 182, 455
Ariovistus, German chief (fl. 1st century B.C.), 174-175
Aristarchus of Samos, Greek astronomer (fl. 280-264 B.C.), 502
Aristides, Greek writer of romance (fl. 2nd century B.C.), 636
Aristides, Publius Aelius, surnamed Theodorus, Greek rhetorician (117-187), 328, 424, 515, 516
Aristippus, Greek philosopher (435?-356? B.C.), 494

Aristobulus II, King of Judea (reigned 67-63 B.C.), 530
Aristobulus, grandson of Hyrcanus II (1st century B.C.), 532, 534
Aristobulus, son of Herod the Great (?-6 B.C.), 534
aristocracy, in Etruria, 6, 17; in Carthage, 40-43, 46; under Rome, 16-17, 21-31, 34, 64, 69, 70, 76, 77, 81, 82, 85, 88, 90, 91, 92, 93, 95, 98, 103, 104, 111-208, 212, 215-216, 222, 234, 243, 251-252, 258, 260, 267, 270, 271, 279, 282, 286-287, 292, 296, 297, 313, 319, 332, 335, 348, 351, 363-364, 372, 373, 384, 409, 433, 434-435, 440, 441, 446, 449, 460, 622, 626, 628, 633, 641, 644, 670; Cicero on, 165
Aristonicus, pretender to throne of Pergamum (?-129 B.C.), 516
Aristophanes, Greek comic dramatist (448?-380? B.C.), 74, 99
Aristotelian (Peripatetic) philosophy, 95, 432, 489-490
Aristotle, Greek philosopher (384-322 B.C.), 4, 25, 42, 79, 123, 302, 308, 311, 421, 490, 497, 506, 507, 610, 611
arithmetic, 72, 75
Arithmetica (Diophantus of Alexandria), 634
Arius, Greek priest of Alexandria, and founder of Arianism (280?-336),658-660,662,663
Ark of the Covenant, 533
Arles (anc. Arelate or Arelas), 192, 474, 658
Arles, Council of, 658
Armageddon, 593
Armenia, 132, 179, 206, 217, 231, 275, 280, 320, 366,413,414,517,528,602,629,630;Lesser,188
Arminius, chief of German tribe of Cherusci (18 B.C.-A.D. 19), 218
army, of Pyrrhus, 38; of Carthage, 43, 46, 48, 50-51, 53, 106; under the Republic, 33-34, 46, 49, 50-51, 53, 80, 87, 116, 118-120, 126, 178-179; under the Principate, 216-217, 220, 232, 260, 268, 269, 271, 284-285, 292, 293-294, 330, 336, 340, 417, 429, 620-621; under the monarchy, 621-622, 626, 628-629, 632, 633, 638-639, 641, 661, 669, 670
Arnus (Arno), 454
Arpinum (Arpino), 118, 141, 162, 453
Arretium (Arezzo), 6, 77, 322, 328, 346, 454
Arrian (Flavius Arrianus), Greek historian and philosopher (100?-170?), 418, 490, 520
Arsaces, King of Parthia (fl. ca. 248 B.C.), 528
Arsacids, 528-529, 622
Ars Amatoria (Ovid), 255
Arsinoë, 499
art, Etruscan, 5, 8-11, 18, 149, 339, 350, 359, 443; Campanian, 37; Greek, 92-93, 95-96, 338-339, 349, 351-361; German, 479; Byzantine, 512, 529; Parthian, 529; Christian, 601; under the Republic, 18, 77, 92-93, 95, 102, 108, 123, 125, 132; under the Principate, 215, 225, 233-234, 269, 277-279, 280, 291, 310, 338-362, 376, 415, 421, 442-443, 456, 459-460, 461, 511-512; under the monarchy, 621, 629,

630, 632, 634-635, 661; of Rome, 671, 672
Artabanus IV, King of Parthia (?-227), 529, 530
Artaxata, 528
Artemis, 63, 514, 515, 585
Artemis, Festival of, 515
Artemis,Temple of (Ephesus),515,518,585,630
Artemis, Temple of (Magnesia), 514
Artes Liberales, 342
Artibus, De (Celsus), 313
artisans, see craftsmen
"Art of Poetry, The" (Horace), see Ad Pisones
Art Poétique, L' (Boileau), 249*
Arval Brotherhood, 59, 66, 73, 388
Ascalon, 508
Ascanius (Iulus), 167, 240-241
asceticism, 303, 426, 445, 490, 497, 502, 525-526, 527, 537-538, 560, 562, 577, 580, 605, 606, 607-609, 613, 615, 657, 658, 667
Asclepiades of Prusa, Greek physician in Rome (fl. 1st century B.C.), 312, 507
Asclepieum of Pergamum, 516, 518
Asclepius, see Aesculapius
Ascyltos, 297
Ashoka, Indian ruler and religious teacher (reigned 273-232 B.C.), 559*
Ashur (city), 529
Asia, 40, 60, 86, 88, 89, 91, 92, 94, 112, 117, 124, 134, 139, 140, 147, 157, 167, 171, 207, 211, 225, 226, 308, 324, 347, 355, 359, 366, 389, 392, 412, 423, 431, 433, 483, 508, 514, 516, 517, 518, 519, 524, 526, 540, 578, 590, 592, 606, 630, 640, 649*, 655, 659, 669
Asia Minor, 5, 8, 116, 130, 187, 216, 262, 320, 329, 364, 381, 418, 429, 431, 483, 513-516, 518, 520, 522, 578, 583, 585, 588, 592, 602-603, 605, 617, 627, 629, 632, 633, 640
"Asianic" style, 161, 169
Asiatic style, 361
Asiaticus, freedman of Vitellius (fl. 1st century), 285
Asisium (Assisi), 455
Aspasia of Miletus, consort of Pericles (470?-410 B.C.), 187, 487
Aspendus, 513
assassination as a political method, 260
Assembly, Centurial, 23-30, 33, 34, 44, 50, 52, 85, 91-92, 107, 116-117, 119, 139-140, 200, 232, 260, 265, 269, 393
Assembly, Curial, 25-26, 393, 395
Assembly, Tribal, 24, 26-28, 30, 34, 47, 91, 113-115, 121-122, 123, 126, 145, 171, 173, 179, 180, 181, 188, 191, 201, 213, 223, 232, 260, 340, 393
Assyria, 413, 414, 511
Astarte, 41
Astraea, 237*; see also Virgin
astrology, 75, 147, 164, 231, 259, 278, 292, 308, 311,388,415,425,435,503,512,514,525,559,621
astronomy, 75, 307-308, 309, 367-368, 472, 488, 502-503, 514

Asturae (Astura), 162
Atalanta, 256
Atargatis (dea Syria), 390, 522
Atella (Aversa), 237
Athanasius, St., Greek father of the Church (296?-373), 660, 663
atheism, in Lucretius, 147-154; 388, 485, 490, 497, 522
Athenaeum, 415
Athenaeus of Naucratis, Greek grammarian (fl. 3rd century), 325, 334, 635-636
Athenagoras, Greek philosopher (fl. 168), 611
Athene, see Pallas Athene
Athenion, leader of slave rebellion (?-101 B.C.), 121
Athenodorus Cananites of Tarsus, Greek Stoic philosopher (fl. 1st century B.C.), 228
Athens, 13, 40, 68, 79, 87, 95, 96, 98, 99, 100, 104, 123, 124, 131, 141, 186, 203, 205, 207, 228, 234, 239, 244, 254, 300, 325, 349, 368, 389, 418, 428, 431, 432, 462, 465, 466, 482, 483, 484, 486, 487-490, 495, 504, 514, 515, 519, 520, 534, 546, 579, 583-584, 585, 604*, 621, 630, 661
athletics, in Etruria, 7; under Rome, 72, 223, 277-279, 314, 340, 351, 360, 375, 377, 382, 430, 438, 510, 532, 625
Atlantic Ocean, 175, 217, 252, 307, 325, 326, 466, 470, 475, 514, 521
Atlas Mountains, 464
Atman, see soul
atomic philosophy, of Lucretius, 150-154; 164
Atreus, 293
atrium, 343-344
Atrium Vestae, 359, 635
Attalids, 516
Attalus, King of Perganum (reigned 241-197 B.C.), 94
Attalus III Philometor, King of Pergamum (reigned 138-133 B.C.), 114, 516
Attalus, Gallic Christian martyr (?-177), 649
Attalus, Stoic philosopher (fl. 1st century), 301
Attianus, Caelius, guardian of Hadrian (fl. end of 1st century), 414
Attica, 4, 487
Attic Nights (Aulus Gellius), 442
Attic style (art), 348, 349, 361, 635
"Attic" style (literature), 161
Atticus, Titus Pomponius, scholar and philosopher (109-32 B.C.), 130, 131-132, 159, 163, 169, 189, 202
Atticus Herodes, Tiberius Claudius, Greek rhetorician and millionaire (104?-180), 487, 515
Attila, King of the Huns (406?-453), 670
Attis, 94, 385, 523, 553, 588, 598
"Atys" (Catullus), 157
Aude (anc. Atax), 470
Auditoria, 312
Augsburg (anc. Augusta Vindelicorum), 324, 480
augury, 63-64, 93, 388, 435, 651

Augustales, 226
Augustalia, 649
Augustan Age, 188, 211-258, 271, 295, 297, 338, 361, 454, 533
Augusta Rauricorum (Augst), 480
Augusta Taurinorum, see Turin
Augusta Trevirorum (Trèves), 474, 635, 640
Augusta Vindelicorum, see Augsburg
Augustine, Saint, Bishop of Hippo and father of the Church (354-430), 42, 60, 307, 465, 493, 494, 603, 606, 611
Augustonemetum (Clermont-Ferrand), 473
Augustus (Caius Julius Caesar Octavianus), Roman emperor (63 B.C.-14 A.D.), 111, 121, 128, 154, 159, 199-258, 259, 260, 262, 265, 266, 269, 270, 273, 274, 285, 286, 288, 290, 294, 299, 308, 309, 312, 319, 323, 325, 326†, 331, 335, 338, 340, 341, 344, 345, 346, 347, 348, 350, 352, 356, 357, 358, 360, 363, 365*, 381, 383, 387, 388, 391, 394, 396, 397, 398, 407, 410, 411, 413, 414, 417, 419, 432, 434, 454, 455, 460, 464, 465, 469, 472, 473, 474, 478, 482, 487, 499, 508, 511, 514, 516, 528, 530, 531, 532, 543, 558, 640, 645, 663, 664
Aulis, 149
Aulularia (Plautus), 100
aurea mediocritas, 245-246, 249
Aurelia, mother of Caesar (2nd and 1st centuries B.C.), 167
Aurelian (Lucius Domitius Aurelianus), Roman emperor (212?-275), 606, 628, 632, 638-639, 640, 642, 654, 664, 665
Aurelian Way, 78
Aurelius, Marcus (Marcus Annius Aurelius Antoninus), Roman emperor and philosopher (121-180), 13, 28, 97, 108, 159, 299, 322, 329, 330, 331, 335, 346, 349, 396, 398, 412, 422, 423, 424, 425-432, 442, 443-446, 447, 448-449, 460, 465,.469, 478, 480, 489, 490, 492, 495, 505, 507, 606, 611, 622, 627, 631*, 633, 645, 649, 650, 662, 665, 666
Aurelius, Severus, brother of Marcus Aurelius (fl. 2nd century), 426
Aurelius, Column of, 412, 443
Aurelius Imperator, 443
aureus, 192
Aurignacian man, 470-471
Aurora, 241, 255
Austria, 471
Austria-Hungary, 480
autobiography, Hadrian's, 415
Autun (anc. Augustodunum), 175, 474
Auvergne, 176
Avare, L' (Molière), 100
Avaricum (Bourges), 177, 471*, 473
Aventine, 12*, 74, 81, 117, 339-340, 360
Avernus, Lacus (Lake Averno), 220, 240, 456
Avignon (anc. Avenio), 417, 474
Aviola, Marcus Acilius, consul (fl. 1st century B.C.), 311
Aziz, 390

B

Baal (Bel), 45, 390, 511, 606, 623-625, 639; Baal-Haman, 41, 42, 47; Baal-Moloch, 41

Baalbek, see Heliopolis

Babylonia or Babylon, 7, 9, 88, 133, 308, 322, 374, 538, 540, 546, 549, 588

Babylon, whore of, 593

Babylonian Captivity, 545

Bacchae (Euripides), 178, 529

Baachanalia, 94

Bacchantes, 204

Bacchus,94,164,347,354,511;see also Dionysus

bachelors, 68, 224, 237, 250, 363

Bacon, Francis, Baron Verulam, Viscount St. Albans, English philosopher and statesman (1561-1626), 304

Baedeker, Karl, German publisher of guidebooks (1801-1859), 324

Baetica (Andalusia), 216, 470

Bagradas (Medjerda) River, 39, 464-465

Baiae (Baja),133,135,185,266,370,377,422,456

Balbinus (Decimus Caelius Balbinus), Roman emperor (?-238), 628

Balbus, Lucius Cornelius, consul (fl. 1st century B.C.), 191, 192, 195, 333, 340, 360

Balbus and Ollius, banking firm, 331

Balearic Islands, 40, 42, 470

Balkans, 431, 483, 519, 630, 638, 669

ballet, 378-379, 487

Baltic Sea, 478

Balzac, Honoré de, French novelist (1799-1850), 412

banking, 79-80, 88, 111, 130, 169, 323, 331-332, 336, 499, 514, 515, 536, 671

bankruptcy, 58, 79, 111, 192, 331-332, 396

baptism, 558,560,577,598,600,618,649,658,664

barbarian invasions, 174-178, 188, 294, 406, 424, 428-429, 431, 448-449, 480-481, 507, 627-633, 638-639, 644, 650, 665-670

Barcino (Barcelona), 470

Bar Cocheba, Simeon, Jewish rebel leader (?-135), 542, 548, 549

Bardesanes, Syrian heretic (fl. 200), 604

Barnabas, Joses, apostle, 582-583, 590, 603

Basilica Aemilia, 92

Basilica Julia, 267

Basilica Porcia, 92

basilicas, 92-93, 130, 219, 340, 345, 355, 362, 465, 466,476,477,480,511,601,618-619,661-662,671

Basilica Ulpia, 411

Basilides, Alexandrian heretic (fl. 117), 604

Bassa, 317

Batanea, 535

Bath, see Aquae Salis

bathing, 81, 343, 344, 345, 374-375, 459, 477, 599, 624; see also watering places

baths, public, Carthaginian, 40, 465; Roman, 81, 219, 220, 277, 289, 290-291, 317, 327, 343, 355, 356-357, 359-360, 362, 363, 374-376, 412, 418, 440, 459, 460-461, 465, 466, 473, 474, 476, 477,480,509,511,512,515,548,623,627,635,661

Bathyllus of Alexandria, artist in pantomime (fl. end of 1st century B.C.), 378

Baucalis, 658

Baucis, 256

Bauer, Bruno, German theologian (1809-1882), 554

Baur, Ferdinand Christian, German Protestant theologian (1792-1860), 553-554

beards, 415, 471, 529

Beaumarchais, de (Pierre Auguste Caron), French dramatist (1732-1799), 101

Beauvais (anc. Caesaromagus), 471*, 474

Beersheba, 535

Beethoven, Ludwig van, German composer (1770-1827), 381

Behistun inscription, 528

Belgae, 175

Belgica, see Gaul, Belgic

Belgium, 36, 329

Belgrade (anc. Singidunum), 480

Bellerophon, 10

Bellona, 62, 447

Bellovaci, 471*

Beloch, Karl Julius, German historian in Italy (1854-1929), 333, 364

Benacus, Lacus, see Garda, Lago di

Benedicta, 426

Benefits, On (Seneca), 302

Beneventum (Benevento), 37, 38, 78, 410, 440, 455

Ben-Giora, Simon, Jewish hero (fl. 1st century), 404

Berenice, Jewish queen (28?-?), 288

Berenice (Benghazi), 499

Berkeley, George, Bishop of Cloyne, Irish philosopher (1685-1753), 310

Berlin, 350

Beroea (Aleppo), 512

Beroea (Verria), 583, 585

Berytus (Beirut), 510, 511, 534, 545

Bethar, 548

Bethlehem, 535, 558, 663

Bethsaïda, 535

betrothal, 68, 369, 374

Bible, 539-542, 553, 555, 578, 598, 599, 606, 613*, 614, 615, 616, 618, 658

bibliotheca, 343, 344

Bibliotheca Ulpiana, 635

Bibracte (near Autun), 175

Bibulus, Marcus Calpurnius, politician (?-48 B.C.), 171-172, 196

Bilbilis (Bámbola), 316, 318

biography, 160, 269, 433-434, 442, 483-484, 635, 662-663

birth control, 56, 88, 90, 132, 134, 158, 193, 211, 222-225, 232, 286, 363-364, 438, 483, 487, 505, 606, 666

bisexuality, 132, (Caesar's) 168, (Antony's) 199, 246, 253, (Domitian's) 290, (Martial's) 317-318, (Horace's) 369, (Commodus') 447, (Meleager's) 509, (Greek Anthology) 510

Bithynia, 55, 120, 140, 155, 157, 167, 170, 216, 276, 366, 441, 516, 518-519, 521, 578, 630, 636, 653, 659; Bithynia-Pontus, 520

Bicuriges, 471*

Black (Euxine) Sea (anc. Pontus Euxinus), 112, 157, 194, 217, 232, 256-257, 275, 291, 329, 418, 480, 483, 516, 517, 518, 520, 528, 629, 630

Black Stone of Pessinus, 513

Blandina, Gallic Christian martyr (?-177), 649

Blissful Groves, 241

Blossius, Caius, Greek philosopher (fl. 2nd century B.C.), 113, 516

Blue Glass Vase, 347

Boadicea or Boudicca, Queen of the Iceni in Britain (?-61), 476

Boccaccio, Giovanni, Italian novelist (1313-1375), 258

Boeotia, 310, 483

Bohemia, 406, 431, 432

Boii, 49

Boileau-Despréaux, Nicolas, French poet, satirist, and critic (1636-1711), 249*

Boissier, Marie Louis Gaston, French historian, critic, and archaeologist (1823-1908), 441

Bolingbroke, Henry Saint-John, Viscount, English statesman and political writer (1678-1751), 553

Bologna (anc. Felsina, later Bononia), 5, 11, 78, 455

Bona Dea, 59, (feast of) 65, 172

books, 158, 234, 267, 269, 333, 346

bookshops, 234, 342

Bordeaux (anc. Burdigala), 324, 470, 473

Borghese Gladiator, 453

Borysthenes (Dnieper), 521

Boscoreale, 346, 459

Bosporus, kingdom of, 219, 413, 629

Bosporus (strait), 483, 518-519

Bossuet, Jacques Bénigne, French Bishop of Meaux, and pulpit orator (1627-1704), 662, 663

Boston Museum, 259

Bostra (Basra), 508, 535, 602

Botticelli, Sandro (Alessandro Filipepi), Italian painter (1447?-1510), 354

Boulogne (anc. Gesoriacum), 324, 653

bourgeoisie, 88, 89, 116, 171, 286, 343, 633

Bourges, see Avaricum

boxing, in Etruria, 7; in Rome, 90, 99, 377, 382

Boy, 351

Brahman, 610

Brahmans, 526, 536, 608

Brahmanism, 537

Bramante, Donato d'Agnolo, Italian architect and painter (1444-1514), 661

bread, see grain

Brenner Pass, 454, 480

Brevity of Life, On the (Seneca), 302

bridges, 17, 77, 176, 266-267, 324, 326, 336, 410, 411, 455, 470, 473, 474, 627, 671

Briseis, 354

Britain, 40, 176, 234, 270-271, 288, 291, 302, 322, 324, 326, 327, 329, 366, 413, 417, 428, 470, 471, 472, 475-477, 479, 602, 620, 622, 633, 638, 641, 651, 669

Britanni, 475

Britannicus, son of Claudius and Messalina (42-55), 273-275

British Empire, 406

British Museum, 347, 350, 351

Britons, 176

Bronze, Age of, 471

bronzework, 9-10, 18, 82, 227, 346, 349-351, 359, 420, 443, 457, 459-460, 469, 510

brothels, see prostitution

Brothers Pettius, banking firm, 332

Brumalia, 512

Brundisium (Brindisi), 78, 97, 125, 170, 173, 183, 184, 200, 205, 239, 244, 325, 326, 410, 455, 602

Bruttians, 35, 37, 51

Bruttium, 53

Brutus, Decimus Junius, commander (?-43 B.C.), 177, 197, 200, 201

Brutus, Lucius Junius (fl. 6th century B.C.), consul, 16, 17, 196, 197

Brutus, Marcus Junius, politician (85-42 B.C.), 130, 161, 185-186, 189, 194, 196-204, 211, 244, 426, 448, 482, 484, 513, 583

Brutus (in Martial), 318

Bubastis, 498

Budapest, 480

Buddhism, 537, 559

building materials, 356-357, 420, 477, 533, 635

building trades, 322

Bulgaria, 480

bullfights, in Etruria, 6; in Crete and Thessaly, 384; in Rome, 385

bureaucracy, 191, 215, 220, 270-271, 275, 409, 416, 448, 498, 640, 642-645, 665, 668

Burgundy, 473

Burrus, prefect of the Praetorian Guard (fl. 1st century), 273, 275, 276

Bury, John Bagnell, Irish historian (1861-1927), 273*

business, see trade

buttress, 635, 661

Byblus, 39, 534

Byron, George Gordon, sixth Baron, English poet (1788-1824), 249*

Byrsa, 41, 465

Byzantine Empire, 419, 641

Byzantinism, 641

C

Cabala, 538

Cabillonum (Chalon-sur-Saône), 474

Cádiz, see Gades

Cadmea, 483

Caecilius (in Octavius, by Minucius Felix), 611

Caecilius Statius, comic dramatist (?-168 B.C.), 101

Caelian hill, 12*, 340, 361

Caelius, Marcus Caius Rufus, orator (fl. 1st century B.C.), 135, 155, 184, 188-189

Caenis, mistress of Vespasian (1st century), 288

Caepiones, Roman family, 76

Caere (Cervetri), 7, 8, 10, 11, 121

Caesar, Caius Julius, Roman general, statesman, and historian (100-44 B.C.), 3, 23, 27, 31, 34, 48, 66, 70, 73, 102, 116, 118, 119, 123, 128, 129, 133, 134, 136, 139, 140, 143, 144, 145, 146, 147, 155, 159, 160, 161, 162, 163, 165, 166, 167-202, 204, 205, 208, 211, 212, 213, 219, 225, 226, 227, 228, 229, 231, 235, 242, 256, 260, 270, 271, 283, 291, 293, 296, 303, 312, 319, 323, 324, 326, 329, 330, 335, 340, 341, 346, 349, 350, 354, 356, 360, 361, 364, 365, 372, 383, 385, 386, 391, 392, 400, 412, 414, 419, 431, 448, 456, 457, 462, 465, 466, 469, 471-476, 482, 487, 500, 508, 514, 516, 523, 528, 557*, 562, 638, 641, 654

Caesarea (Kaisaria), 508, 534, 535, 544, 577, 586, 615, 662

Caesarea (Cherchel), 466

Caesarean birth, 167

Caesarea Philippi, or Paneas (Banias), 545, 569

Caesarion, Egyptian prince, son of Cleopatra 47-30 B.C.), 188, 189, 195, 206, 208

Caesarodunum (Tours), 474

Caesars, the, 175, 362, 460, 593

Caesonia, fourth wife of Caligula (?-41 A.D.), 266, 268

Caiaphas, Jewish high priest (fl. 18-36), 571

Cairo, 350

Caius Caesar, grandson of Augustus (?-4 A.D.), 230-231, 473

Calagurris (Calahorra), 313

Caledonia, see Scotland

calendar, Roman, 66-67, 75, 193; Julian, 193; Druidic, 472

Calidus, Quintus, politician (fl. 1st century B.C.), 129

Caligula (Caius Caesar Germanicus), Roman emperor (12-41), 264-268, 269, 270, 273, 279, 293, 300, 301, 304, 344, 345, 365*, 378, 380, 384, 388, 390, 434, 456, 466, 482, 500, 501, 543

Callimachus, Greek grammarian and poet (320-?—240-? B.C.), 155, 158, 636

Callistus, Roman Pope (reigned 217-222), 617-618

Callistus, secretary of Claudius (fl. 1st century), 270

Calpurnia, last wife of Caesar (1st century B.C.), 172, 189, 195, 197, 198

Calpurnia, third wife of Pliny the Younger (1st-2nd centuries), 440

Calvin, John, French Protestant reformer at Geneva (1509-1564), 592

Calvus, Licinius, poet (fl. 1st century B.C.), 146, 161, 174

cameos, 346

Camillus, Marcus Furius, general and patrician leader (?-365 B.C.), 24, 36, 68, 120

Campagna di Roma, 320, 631, 666

Campania, 11, 18, 37, 62, 74, 77, 171, 213, 231, 265, 303, 326, 328, 339, 346, 455-456, 608

Campus Martius, see Field of Mars

Camulodunum (Colchester), 476, 477

Canaan, 567

canals, 77, 410, 464, 499, 500, 631

Canary Islands, 308

Candia, 247

Cannae (battle of, 216 B.C.), 34, 50-51, 70, 71, 86, 93, 164

Cannus, musician (fl. 1st century), 381

canonization, 226

canon law, 406, 619

Canopus (Abukir on site of), 500

Cantii, 476

Canuleius, Caius, tribune (fl. 445 B.C.), 24

Canusium (Canosa), 51

Capernaum, 563

capital, 90, 323, 333, 633, 668

Capitol, 36, 52, 60, 82, 83, 169, 198, 206, 263, 280, 291, 358, 388, 419, 443

Capitol, in Washington, 421

Capitolias, 535

Capitoline, 12*, 13, 36, 61, 81, 82, 316, 340, 341, 358

Capitoline games, 291, 381

Capitoline Museum, 349, 351, 443

Cappadocia, 140, 147, 188, 357, 366, 418, 462, 490, 496, 513, 517, 520, 523, 524, 528, 578, 629, 630

Capri (anc. Capreae), 263, 265, 344, 456

Captivi (Plautus), 100

Capua, 11, 37, 51, 52, 78, 116, 137, 138, 181, 194, 322, 346, 457, 546

Caracalla (Marcus Aurelius Antoninus Bassianus Caracallus), Roman emperor (188-217), 331, 375, 621-623, 632, 633, 634, 635

Caracalla, Baths of, 375, 627, 635

Caractacus, king of the Silures in Britain (fl. 1st century), 271

Carales (Cagliari), 464

Carcer Tullianum, 404

Care of the Hair, On the (Domitian), 289

Caria, 513, 514, 518

carmen saeculare, 225, 248, 380

Carneades, Greek philosopher and orator (213-129 B.C.), 95-96, 489, 497

Carnutes, 471*

Carpathian Mountains, 431

Carrara, 10, 357, 454

Carrhae (Harran), 131, 178, 529, 623

Carrinas Secundus, rhetorician (fl. 1st century A.D.), 267

Carteia (Algeciras), 470

Carthage, 25, 34, 38, 39-54, 57, 70, 76, 77, 80, 82, 85, 86, 87, 88, 91, 101, 105-108, 116, 117, 118, 192, 194, 240, 269, 326, 332, 418, 454, 465, 466, 467, 468, 469, 472, 482, 546, 603, 612, 613, 617, 633, 649, 650, 671

Carthage, Council of, 618

Casanova de Seingalt, Giovanni Jacopo, Italian adventurer (1725-1798), 487
Casinum, 461
Caspian Sea, 528
Cassius, Avidius, general and rebel (fl. 2nd century), 428, 431
Cassius, Spurius, consul (?-486 B.C.), 23
Cassius Longinus, Caius, general and conspirator (?-42 B.C.), 168, 186, 194, 196-204, 211, 448
Cassius Longinus Varus, Caius, governor (fl. 1st century B.C.), 137
Cassivelaunus, British chief (fl. 1st century B.C.), 176
Castel Gandolfo, 11
Castor, 35, 62
Castor and Pollux, Temple of, 268, 358, 359
castration, see emasculation
catacombs, 601
Catana (Catania), 66, 464
Catechetical School, 613, 614
Catholicae Ecclesiae Unitate, De (St. Cyprian), 618
Catiline (Lucius Sergius Catilina), conspirator (108?-62 B.C.), 126, 142-144, 147, 168, 169, 170, 172, 184, 189, 202, 395
Catiline (Sallust), 160
Cato, Marcus Porcius (the Elder), general and patriot (234-149 B.C.), 4, 68, 69, 70, 73, 87, 88-90, 91, 92, 93, 95, 96, 97, 102-105, 106-108, 136, 160, 238, 312, 315, 370, 396, 399, 415, 454, 456, 618
Cato, Marcus Porcius, son of Cato Uticensis (?-42 B.C.), 190, 203
Cato Uticensis, Marcus Porcius (the Younger), philosopher and patriot (95-46 B.C.), 56, 75, 108, 131, 133, 134, 135-136, 144-145, 168, 171, 173, 174, 180, 181, 183, 186, 189-190, 195, 196, 203, 282, 296, 426
Catoptrica (Hero), 504
cattle raising, 104, 131, 238, 319-321, 455, 464, 478, 483, 513
Catullus, Caius Valerius, poet (87-54 B.C.), 69, 102, 135, 154, 155-158, 174, 225, 235
Catulus, Quintus Lutatius, aristocratic leader (fl. 1st century B.C.), 145, 146
Caucasus, 329, 448, 517, 528
Caudine Forks (battle of, 321 B.C.), 37
Caunus, 518
Celer, architect (fl. 1st century), 345
Celer, Asinius, epicure (fl. 1st century), 376
celibacy, 132, 134, 222-224, 237, 250, 363, 524, 526, 537, 566, 598; clerical, 660†
Cellini, Benvenuto, Italian artist (1500-1571), 9, 349
Celsus, general of Trajan (?-118), 414
Celsus, Antichristian philosopher (fl. 2nd century), 559, 596, 606-607, 615, 616, 647
Celsus, Aurelius Cornelius, writer on science (fl. 1st century), 295, 308, 313
Celtiberians, 87
Celtic languages, 73, 477

Celts, 36, 49, 118-120, 126, 174-177, 235, 468, 471, 472, 475, 477
cena, 70
Cenabum (Orléans), 177, 474
Cena Trimalchionis, 297-298
censors, 24,28,29,191,214-215,270,272,286,290
censorship, 74, 99, 229, 300
census, 193, 214, 333, 463, 558
central heating, 343, 344, 477, 671
Centum Cellae (Civita Vecchia), 410, 461
ceramics, Etruscan, 9; Carthaginian, 42; Roman, 77, 322-323, 336, 346-347, 454, 473, 474, 477, 498
Cerberus, 389
Ceres, 59, 62, 84, 164, 381
Cervantes Saavedra, Miguel de, Spanish novelist (1547-1616), 637
Cethegus, Caius Cornelius, conspirator (?-64 B.C.), 143-144
Cévennes mountains (anc. Cebenna), 176
Ceylon, 329, 406
Chaerea, Caius Cassius, tribune of Praetorian Guard (?-41 A.D.), 268
Chaeremon, Greek Stoic philosopher (fl. 1st century), 274
Chaeronea, 124, 483, 484
Chalcedon (Kadiköi), 133, 629
Chalcis, 73, 483
Chaldaic, 537
Chaldea, 64
Châlons-sur-Marne, 638, 670
Champollion, Jean François, French Egyptologist (1790-1832), 5
Chance, 349
Chariclea, 636-637
chariot races, in Etruria, 7; in Rome, 265, 267, 274, 278-279, 377, 382-383, 447, 465
charity, 71
Charmion, Egyptian handmaiden of Cleopatra (?-30 B.C.), 208
Charmis of Marseilles, physician in Rome (fl. 1st century), 313
charms, 60, 64, 388
Charon, 387, 496-497
Charondas, Sicilian lawgiver (ca. 500 B.C.), 32
Chartres, 471*
Charybdis, 602
Chasidim, 536-537
Chastity, 349
Châtelet, Marquis du, Florent-Claude (1695-?), 135
Chatti, 291, 428, 429, 431
Chaucer, Geoffrey, English poet (1340?-1400), 258
Chephren, 350
chess, 375
Chester (anc. Deva or Devana Castra), 477
Chichester (anc. Cissaceaster), 477
Chimera, 9
China, 134, 329, 529, 669
Chinese Wall, 669
Chiusi (anc. Clusium q.v.), 9

Chloe, 247

Christ, 72, 75, 154, 160, 235, 281, 347*, 390, 449, 466, 475, 493-494, 502, 509, 510, 527, 529, 535, 537, 541*, 550-619, 626, 646-664, 667

Christianity, 63, 65, 95, 165, 307, 335, 358, 404, 405, 406, 465, 467-468, 489, 490, 493-494, 497, 510, 520, 523, 524, 527, 538, 549, 550-619, 621, 625, 626, 628, 635, 637, 646-664, 667-668, 671-672

Christians, 281, 292, 308, 365, 366, 386, 416, 423,442,447,507,529,554-619,626,646-664,665

Chrysoloras, Manuel, reviver of Greek in Italy (1355?-1415), 96

Chrysopolis (Scutari), 655

Chrysostom, Saint John, Greek father of the Church (347?-407), 494

Church, early, 557, 558, 575, 577, 588, 591-595, 596-619, 646-664, 668

Church, Roman Catholic, 475, 554, 592, 617-619, 671-672

churches, 662, 663

Cicero, Marcus Tullius, orator and man of letters (106-43 B.C.), 11, 13, 14, 32, 68, 70, 73, 82, 95, 96-97, 98, 102, 108, 115, 118, 128, 129, 130, 131, 132, 133, 135, 136, 140-145, 146, 154, 160, 161-166, 167, 168, 169, 171, 172-174, 178, 179, 180, 181, 182, 183, 185, 188, 189, 193, 194, 195, 196, 197, 198, 201, 202, 212, 216, 228, 258, 307, 308, 313, 315, 324, 325, 356, 365, 368, 378, 379, 387, 391, 393, 398, 403, 405, 415, 439, 453, 454, 456, 457, 462, 463, 464, 489, 510, 513, 514, 516, 557, 572, 587, 612, 662, 671

Cicero, Quintus Tullius, governor, brother of M. Tullius Cicero (ca. 102-43 B.C.),143*,173

Cilicia, 129, 139, 140, 167, 180, 196, 203, 204, 205, 378, 413, 500, 505, 513, 579, 629, 630

Cimbri, 118-120, 472

Cinara, 247

Cincian law (204 B.C.), 32, 132, 402

Cincinnatus, Lucius Quinctius, dictator (519?-439? B.C.), 31

Cineas, Greek philosopher (fl. 280 B.C.), 28, 37

Cinna, Helvius, poet (?-44 B.C.), 155

Cinna, Lucius Cornelius, dictator (?-84 B.C.), 123-125, 167, 519

circumcision, 530, 546, 548, 559, 577, 580, 582-583, 585, 586, 587, 625

circuses, see games

Circus Flaminius, 82, 340, 360

Circus Maximus,18,82,280,360-361,382-383,625

Ciris, 270

Cirta (Constantine), 105, 466

citizenship, Roman, 25-27, 58, 99, 100, 114, 115, 116, 118, 121, 122, 126, 182, 193-194, 216, 235, 270-271, 283, 394-395, 398, 460, 462, 473, 476, 546, 586, 591, 622-623

city-states, in Etruria, 6; in Greece, 6, 86, 482; in Latium, 11; Rome, 35, 81, 212; Tarentum, 455; in the Roman Empire, 460-461

Civilis, Julius, Batavian rebel leader (fl.71),473

Civil War in Rome, 122-126, 168, 169, 177, 180-208, 211, 220, 225, 252, 283-286, 293-294, 296, 301, 514, 644

civitates, 324

clan (gens), 56, 69

clan council, in the early Republic, 57

clan name (nomen,) 56-57

Clarissa Harlowe (Richardson), 637

classicism, 249, 258, 302, 338-339, 381, 442, 635

class war, in Greece, 86, 87, 482; in Rome, 23-24, 38, 47, 51, 77, 108, 111-208, 242, 632, 633, 656, 665, 668, 669

Claudia, first wife of Augustus (fl. 1st century B.C.), 229

Claudia or Clodia, Vestal Virgin (3rd century B.C.), 94

Claudian Aqueduct, 270, 340

Claudii, Roman clan, 21,35,155,172,205,259,364

Claudius I (Tiberius Claudius Drusus Nero Germanicus), Roman emperor (10 B.C.-A.D. 54), 216, 267, 268-275, 293, 295, 301, 302, 312, 322, 326, 336, 350, 365*, 371, 383, 384, 390, 397, 402,410,419,434,456,466,473,476,501,543,554

Claudius II (Marcus Aurelius Claudius Gothicus), Roman emperor (214-270), 630, 638

Claudius, Caius, naval commander (fl. 3rd century), 44

Claudius Caecus, Appius, politician and writer (fl. 312 B.C.), 29, 32, 37, 77-78, 81

Claudius Regillensis Sabinus, Appius, lawmaker (fl. 450 B.C.), 23-24, 29, 72

Cleander, Praetorian prefect (?-190), 447-448

Cleanthes, Greek Stoic philosopher (300?-220? B.C.), 584*

Cleisthenes, Athenian statesman (fl. 510 B.C.), 15

Clemency, On (Seneca), 302

Clemens, Flavius, relative of Domitian (?-95), 292

Clement I, or Clemens Romanus, Roman Pope (30?-100?), 588, 617

Clement of Alexandria (Titus Flavius Clemens) Christian father and writer (150?-220?), 558, 610-611, 613, 614, 616

Clementia, De (Seneca), 275

Cleopatra VII, Queen of Egypt (69-30 B.C.), 70, 168, 187-190, 195, 204-208, 228, 237, 247, 329, 344, 347, 512, 531, 630

clepsydra (water clock), 66, 308, 356

clientes, 22

climate, 455, 476

Clitias, Greek potter, 9

Clivus Victoriae, 341

Cloaca Maxima, 81

Clodia, wife of Caius Caecilius Metellus Celer (fl. 1st century B.C.), 135, 155-157, 172, 235

Clodius Pulcher, Publius, politician (?-52 B.C.), 132, 135, 171-174, 180, 202, 219

Clorinda, 637

clothing, in Etruria, 6, 18; in Carthage, 40, 41; in Rome, 18, 70, 76, 89, 108, 132, 134, 215, 223, 321-322, 328-329, 372-373, 624; in Spain,

clothing (*continued*)
468; in Gaul, 471; in Egypt, 499; in Parthia, 529
Clusium (Chiusi), 17, 36
Clyde, 476; Firth of, 476
Clytie, 351
Cnidus, 513
Code (Justinian), 394, 406
Codex Gregorianus, 634
Coele-Syria, 204
coinage, Etruscan, 6, 17; Carthaginian, 40; Roman, 17, 78-79, 87, 192-193, 195, 275, 291, 329, 330-331, 346, 358, 372, 627, 632, 639, 641, 656; British, before Caesar, 476; Pontic, 517
coitus interruptus, see birth control
Colchis, 413
Collatinus, Lucius Tarquinius, friend of Sextus Tarquin (fl. 6th century B.C.), 16
collegia, of priests, 63, 225; of workers, 80, 128, 173, 192, 335, 371, 427, 627, 644; of physicians, 312
Colline Gate, battle of (82 B.C.), 125
Cologne (*anc.* Oppidum Ubiorum; *later* Colonia Agrippinensis), 175*, 176, 324, 408, 479-480
coloni, see tenant farmers
colonization, Etruscan, 11; Latin, 12, 38; Greek, 35; Roman, 24, 38. 47, 116-117, 120, 192, 194, 218, 410, 419, 457, 465
Colonna, Piazza, 443
Colosseum, 287, 289, 345, 351, 356, 361, 383-387, 455, 627
Colossians, The Epistle of Paul the Apostle to the, 587*, 588
Colossus of Rhodes, 514
Columbus, Christopher, Genoese discoverer of America (1446?-1506), 308, 325, 329, 503
Columella, Lucius Junius Moderatus, writer on agriculture (fl. 1st century), 319, 320, 473
column, 355-361, 411-413, 420, 427*, 443, 453, 465, 466, 474, 499, 500, 508, 509, 511, 512, 515, 516, 533, 661-662
Columna Lactaria, 364*
Comana Pontica, 517
comedy, 73-74, 93, 95, 98, 99-102, 232, 269, 378
Comedy of Errors, 100
comites, 479
comitia centuriata, see Centurial Assembly
comitia curiata, see Curial Assembly
comitia populi tribuna, see Tribal Assembly
Commagene, 322, 495, 513
Commentaries (Caesar), 146, 169, 178
Commentarii (Sulla), 126
commerce, *see* trade
Commodus (Lucius Aurelius Commodus), Roman emperor (161-192), 214, 221, 323, 330, 390, 396, 430, 432, 446-448, 505, 620, 622, 632, 649
communication, 271, 323-324
communion, 525, 598, 599-600, 613
communism, in *Saturnia Regna*, 61; 526, 537-538, 565, 576, 597, 604*, 605, 646

Como (*anc.* Comum), 322, 368, 411, 439, 440, 454
Como, Lake (Lacus Larius), 4, 344, 454
Compitalia (Feast of the Crossroads), 59
Composite order (architecture), 338, 357
Comum, *see* Como
concilium principis, 215
Concord, 358; Temple of, 24, 358
concubinage, 134, 204, 222, 272, 288, 290, 300-301, 396, 423, 516, 529, 653
confession, 525, 600
confirmation, 600
Confucius, Chinese philosopher (551-479 B.C.), 567
conquistadores, 600*
conscription, 34, 51, 87, 90, 111, 114, 118, 178, 179, 182, 222, 429, 482, 621, 631*, 647, 650, 667, 668
Conservatori, Museo de', 443*
Conservatori, Palazzo dei, 662
consolatio, 301
Consolatio ad Helviam (Seneca), 301
Consolatio ad Polybium (Seneca), 301
Consolatione, De (Cicero), 163*
Constancy of the Sage, On the (Seneca), 302
Constantia, sister of Constantine I (2nd and 3rd centuries), 663
Constantine I the Great (Flavius Valerius Constantinus), Roman emperor (272-337), 331, 349, 375, 426, 483, 607, 639, 643, 644, 645, 653-664, 665, 666, 668
Constantine, Arch of, 443*
Constantine, Basilica of, 661-662
Constantine, Baths of, 375
Constantine, Life of (Eusebius), 663
Constantine, *anc.* Cirta, q.v.
Constantinople (Byzantium, Istanbul), 95, 332, 354, 406, 410, 412, 482, 483, 509*, 518, 529, 622, 633, 640, 656, 657, 661, 663, 670
Constantinople, Council of, 615
Constantius I (Flavius Valerius Constantius Chlorus), Roman emperor (reigned 305-306), 635, 640-641, 644, 651, 653, 655
constitution of Rome, 670; under the Republic, 25-35, 51, 114, 123, 125, 126, 139, 174; under the Principate, 212-217, 285, 292, 391
consulship, 23-25, 27, 29-31, 34, 126, 180-181, 191, 213, 216
Contra Celsum (Origen), *see Against Celsus*
contraception, *see* birth control
contracts, in the early Republic, 57
Copenhagen, 350
Copernicus, Nikolaus, Polish astronomer (1473-1543), 502, 503
Coponius, Caius, senator (fl. 1st century B.C.), 202
Corbulo, Cnaeus Domitius, general (fl. 1st century), 271, 275
Corcyra (Corfu), 383
Corduba (Cordova), 296, 425, 470
Cordus, Aulus Cremutius, historian (?-25), 301
Corfinium, 78, 122, 182, 184
Corinna, 254-255

Corinth, 87, 107, 192, 193, 194, 283, 332, 374, 383, 487, 546, 584-585, 602, 617, 630; Isthmus of, 283, 487

Corinthian order (architecture), 338, 345, 355, 357, 420, 427*, 465, 474, 511, 533, 661

Corinthians, The First Epistle of Paul the Apostle to the, 554, 580, 587*, 589, 591

Corinthians, The Second Epistle of Paul the Apostle to the, 554, 587*

Coriolanus, Caius (or Cneius) Marcius, hero (banished 491 B.C.), 35

Corioli, 35

corn, see grain

Corneille, Pierre, French dramatist (1606-1684), 302, 412

Cornelia, mother of the Gracchi (fl. 2nd century B.C.), 113, 115, 117

Cornelia, lex, 312

Cornelia, sister of the Gracchi and wife of Scipio Aemilianus (fl. 2nd century B.C.), 113, 115

Cornelia, second wife of Caesar (?-68 B.C.), 167, 168

Cornelian Laws, 126

Cornelii, Roman clan, 21, 91, 364

Cornelius, Roman Pope (?-253), 618

Corneto (anc. Tarquinii, q.v.), 11

corporations, 78-80, 88, 340

Corsica, 38, 40, 43, 46, 52, 301, 302, 463-464

Coruncanius, Tiberius, consul (fl. 280 B.C.), 32

Corvini, Roman family, 255

Corvus, Marcus Valerius, consul and dictator (fl. 350, B.C.), 71

Cos, 312, 329, 504, 514

cosmetics, 89, 187, 255, 329, 372-373, 465, 596, 599, 624, 657

Cossutia, first wife of Caesar (1st century B.C.), 167

Costoboii, 431

Cotta, Aurelius, political leader (fl. 241 B.C.), 78

Cotta, Lucius, friend of Caesar (fl. 1st century B.C.), 197

Cottian Alps, 454

Country Life, On (Varro), 159

courtesans, in Etruria, 7; under Rome, 62, 68, 132, 138, 199, 204, 244, 254, 255, 366, 369, 636

court life, 235, 303, 640-641, 643, 655, 661, 662, 668

courts, 129, 160, 180, 216, 220, 231, 261, 270, 275, 340, 397-398, 401-403, 448

crafts, 80, 111, 243, 321-323, 333, 335, 338, 365, 373, 479, 510, 513, 528, 536, 642-644, 671

Crassus, Lucius Licinius, orator (fl. 1st century B.C.), 160

Crassus Dives, Marcus Licinius, general and triumvir (112-53 B.C.), 126, 130-131, 137-139, 168-169, 170-179, 192, 194, 217, 312, 529, 531, 623

Crates of Mallus, Stoic philosopher (fl. 2nd century B.C), 95

cremation, 84, 232, 443, 472

Cremona, 47, 87, 236, 285, 454, 461

Crescens, colleague who forsook St. Paul (1st century), 590

Crete or Candia (anc. Creta), 17*, 55, 200, 216, 505

Crimea, 517, 519

criminals, in labor, 78, 322; in games, 383-387; law and, 398; in the army, 665

Crispus, son of Constantine I (?-326), 663-664

Crispus, Caius, husband of Agrippina the Younger (fl. 1st century), 273

Critolaus, Greek philosopher (fl. 2nd century B.C.), 95-96

Croesus, King of Lydia (fl. 560 B.C.), 516

Cronus, 62-63, 588*

Crotona, (Cotrone), 35, 37, 51, 363

Crucifixion, 555, 559, 572-574

crucifixion, 112, 138, 168, 281, 385, 397, 404, 469, 543, 544, 545, 572-573, 578, 591, 606, 652

Ctesiphon, 413, 428, 528, 529, 531, 602, 605, 622

Cuba, 59

cults, see religion

culture, Italian, 3-5; Villanovan, 5; Etruscan, 5-11, 17-18, 36; Celtic, 36; Latin, 38; Carthaginian, 40-42; Greek, 95, 96; German, 479; under the Republic, 75, 177; under the Principate, 234-235, 287, 311, 379, 419-420, 449, 455, 459, 461, 474, 478, 481, 625; under the monarchy, 661, 666-667; of Rome, 670-672

Cumae, 17, 35, 37, 64, 73, 113, 121, 126, 240, 346, 347, 456

cuneiform, 529

Cupid, 255, 352-353, 468

Curio, Caius Scribonius, orator and consul (?-53 B.C.), 168

Curio, Caius Scribonius, general (?-49 B.C.), 133, 168, 181, 183, 361

Curius, Marcus Dentatus, hero and consul (fl. 275 B.C.), 71

currency, see mediums of exchange

cursus honorum, 28-29, 636

cursus publicus, see post

Curtius, Marcus, legendary hero, 64

Cutilia, Lake (Pozzo di Ratignano), 288

Cybele, 94, 157, 276, 358, 513, 523, 524-525, 526, 527, 606; see also Magna Mater

Cybele, Temple of, 358

Cyclades, 519

Cydnus, 204

Cynicism, 136, 286, 292, 300, 489-490, 493, 509, 537, 657

Cynoscephalae (battle, 197 B.C.), 85

Cynthia, 253

Cyprian, St. (Thascius Caecilius Cyprianus), Latin father of the Church and Bishop of Carthage (200?-258), 603, 613, 617, 618, 650, 657, 665

Cyprus, 173, 174, 196, 204, 206, 216, 310, 322, 505, 513, 548, 582, 583, 630

Cyrenaica, 40, 328, 364

Cyrene, 200, 216, 413, 548, 559*

Cyropaideia (Xenophon), 636
Cyzicus, 418, 516; Temple of, 418

D

Dacia (Rumania), 291, 322, 330, 366, 410, 412, 414, 424, 429, 434*, 480, 632, 638
Daedalus, 256, 352
Daily Doings, see Acta Diurna
Dalmatia, 217, 366, 455, 480, 629, 639, 653
damage suits, 58, 396
Damascus, 78, 320, 508, 511, 530, 534, 544, 577, 581, 602
Damis the Epicurean (in Lucian), 496
dancing, in Etruria, 7, 11; under Rome, 83, 135, 204, 266, 314, 354, 367, 377-379, 430, 437, 470, 500
Dancing Faun, 459
dancing girls (*puellae Gaditanae*), 470
Daniel, Book of, 539, 540, 541, 559, 564, 569, 593
Dante, *see* Alighieri
Danube (*anc.* Danubius *or* Ister), 112, 194, 217, 257, 291, 329, 410, 411, 412, 414, 417, 429, 431, 432, 441, 446, 448, 475, 478, 480, 523, 606, 620, 627, 628, 630, 631*, 638, 639, 640, 669
Daphne, park in Antioch, 512
Daphnis, grammarian of slave class (fl. 1st century B.C.), 334
Daphnis and Chloë (Longus), 637
Dardanelles, *see* Hellespont
Dares, 382
Darius I Hystaspis, King of Persia (558?-486? B.C.), 528
Dark Ages, 470
David, King of the Jews (reigned 1010-974 B.C.), 534, 541, 557, 558*, 559, 569
Dawn, 241, 340
Day of Atonement, 533
Dead Sea (*anc.* Lacus Asphaltites), 537
death masks, 350
debts, 184, 192, 213, 331, 399-400, 514, 536, 644
Decapolis, 535
Decebalus, King of the Dacians (?-106), 291, 410, 412
Decemvirs, 23, 31, 399, 670
decimal system, 75
Decius (Caius Messius Quintus Traianus Decius), Roman emperor (200?-251), 615, 628-629, 635, 650, 657
Decius Mus, Publius, consul (?-340 B.C.), 37*, 64
Decius Mus, Publius, son of preceding, consul (?-295 B.C.), 64
deforestation, 77, 270, 487, 665
Deianeira, 354
deification, 226-227, 256, 260, 266, 268, 269, 274, 280, 291-292, 309, 316, 388, 430, 432, 523, 623, 640-641, 646
Deipnosophists (Athenaeus of Naucratis), 635-636
delatores, 262, 264, 269, 279, 289, 290, 292, 302-303, 438, 447

Delia, 253
Delos, 80, 86, 92*, 112, 139, 330, 519, 546
Delphi (Kastri), 64, 124, 472, 517
Delphic oracle, 64, 484
Demas, colleague who forsook St. Paul (1st century), 590
Demeter, 62, 511; Feast of, 525
Demetrius, Cynic philosopher (fl. 1st century), 300
Demetrius, Bishop of Alexandria (fl. 3rd century), 615
Demetrius, Greek image-maker (at time of Saint Paul), 515, 585
demigods, 241
democracy, in Carthage, 54; Cicero on, 165; under Rome, 34, 54, 91, 116, 122, 128, 136, 160, 179-180, 208, 212, 251, 260, 335, 340, 395, 406, 449, 460, 641, 670
Democritus, Greek philosopher (460?-362? B.C.), 150, 153, 164, 497
Demonax, Greek Cynic philosopher (50-150), 487, 490
Demosthenes, Athenian orator and statesman (384?-322 B.C.), 95, 161
dentistry, Etruscan, 6; Roman, 75, 313
Derbe, 513, 582
Deuteronomy, 536
Dialogue on Orators (Tacitus), 433
Dialogues of the Dead (Lucian), 496-497
Dialogues of the Hetairai (Lucian), 495-496
Diana, 61, 62, 63, 81, 389, 459
Diatribai (Epictetus), *see Discourses*
dice, in Etruria, 7; in Rome, 269, 375, 403
dictatorship, in Rome, 30-31, 34, 119, 124, 126, 128, 136, (Cicero on), 165, 179-184, 189-197, 208, 213, 214, 645
Didius, general (fl. 1st century B.C.), 136
Didius Julian (Marcus Didius Salvius Julianus Severus), Roman emperor (133?-193), 620-621
Dido (Elissa), daughter of King Belus of Tyre, 39, 42, 240-241, 256
Didyma, 514
Diels, Hermann, German classical philologist (1848-1922), 504*
Digest (Justinian), 393, 406, 409, 634
Digesta (Salvius Julianus), 392
di indigetes, 61; *di novensiles*, 62
Dio Cassius, *see* Dion Cassius Cocceianus
Dio Chrysostom, *see* Dion Chrysostomus
Diocletian (Caius Aurelius Valerius Diocletianus Jovius), Roman emperor (245-313), 359, 367, 375, 426, 474, 480, 520, 606, 622, 634, 635, 639-645, 651, 653, 657, 664, 668
Diocletian, Baths of, 359, 375, 635
Diodorus Siculus, Greek historian (1st century B.C.), 42, 234
Diogenes of Seleucia (the Babylonian), Stoic philosopher (fl. 2nd century B.C.), 95-96, 491
Diogenes Laertius, Greek historian of philosophy (2nd century), 635

Diognetus, Stoic philosopher (fl. 2nd century), 425

Dion Cassius Cocceianus (Dio Cassius), Bithynian historian of Rome (155-240?), 14, 24, 207, 212, 219, 225, 262, 267, 268, 272, 280*, 290, 302, 414, 442, 516, 545, 548, 620, 622, 636

Dion Chrysostomus, Greek rhetorician (fl. reign of Trajan), 408-409, 483, 486, 487, 488, 500, 521-522

Dionysian Artists, 80

Dionysian cult, 94, 354, 458

Dionysius, Bishop of Alexandria (fl. 3rd century), 650, 651, 666

Dionysius of Halicarnassus, Greek historian 54?-7 B.C.), 234, 513

Dionysus, 62, 94, 204, 352, 353, 523, 525, 553, 588, 595, 598, 605; see also Bacchus

Dionysus, Theater of, 487

Diophantus of Alexandria, Greek algebraist (fl. 250), 633-634

Dioptra (Hero), 504

Dioscorides of Cilicia, Greek writer on medicine (40-90 A.D.), 505

Dioscurides, gem cutter (fl. reign of Augustus), 346

Discourses (Epictetus), 490-494

Dispersion, the (Diaspora), 545-549, 577, 579

Disputationes Tusculanae (Cicero), 163*, 454

dissection, 313, 504, 506

Divinae Institutiones (Lactantius), 662

divination, see soothsaying

Divinatione, De (Cicero), 163*

Divine Antiquities (Varro), 159

divorce, 69, 89, 134-136, 167, 223-224, 229, 230, 254, 266, 272, 279, 370, 438, 479, 529, 539, 560, 568, 590, 598

Docetists, 605

Dolabella, Cnaeus Cornelius, governor (fl. 1st century B.C.), 169

Dolabella, Publius Cornelius, consul and governor (?-43 B.C.), 188-189, 191, 200

dole, see grain

Doliche (Kakava), 390

dome, 355-361, 420, 421, 635, 662, 671

Domitia, wife of Domitian (1st century), 292

Domitia, Via, 473

Domitian (Titus Flavius Domitianus Augustus), Roman emperor (51-96), 234, 287, 289-293, 311, 316, 317, 320, 336, 340, 344, 345, 348, 351, 365*, 372, 390, 398, 399, 407, 412, 415, 433, 434, 437, 440, 476, 490, 521, 526, 547, 575, 592, 647; Domitii, Roman clan, 284

Domitilla, St. (?-100), 601

Domitius, Lucius, politician (fl. 1st century B.C.), 174, 176, 184

Domna, Julia, wife of Septimius Severus (?-217), 621-623, 635

Domus Aurea, see Golden House

Domus Flavia, 290, 316, 345

Domus Gaiana, 344

Domus Tiberiana, 344

Domus Transitoria, 280

Donar (Tor), 479

Donatists, 658

Donatus, Bishop of Carthage and founder of the Donatists (fl. 4th century), 657-658

Dorchester (anc. Durnovaria)

Doric order (architecture), 338, 355, 357, 411

Doryphoros (Polycleitus), 350

dowry, in Etruria, 7; in Rome, 57, 68, 69, 89, 134, 141, 167, 223, 230, 370, 396, 440

drainage, 81, 103, 193, 326, 410, 454, 461, 466, 473, 511, 631, 639

drama, 74-75, 97-102, 235, 255, 269, 277, 301-302, 307, 314, 378-379, 461; Horace on, 249

drawings, in Varro's Imagines, 159

dream analysis, 388, 485, 507, 525, 621

"Dream of Scipio" (Cicero), 165

Drepana (Trapani), battle in 249 B.C., 45

Drews, Arthur, German philosopher (1865-1935), 554

drinking, in Etruria, 7; in Carthage, 41; under Rome, 65, 71, 88-89, 94, 123, 196, 199, 200, 204, 220, 247, 263, 267, 269, 297-298, 320, 324, 334, 342, 354, 372, 377, 408, 423, 447, 458, 512, 562, 599; in Gaul, 471; in Germany, 478; in Parthia, 529

drugs, 310, 312-313, 329, 342, 505, 506-507

Druids, 472, 473, 479

Drunken Satyr, 459

Drusi, Roman family, 122

Drusilla, sister of Caligula (?-38 A.D.), 266

Drusus, Marcus Livius, statesman (fl. 2nd century B.C.), 117, 121

Drusus, Marcus Livius, statesman, son of preceding (?-91 B.C.), 121-122

Drusus Caesar, son of Tiberius (?-23), 263, 264

Drusus Senior, Nero Claudius, general, stepson of Augustus, (38-9 B.C.), 217, 229, 230, 248, 259, 261, 269, 299, 323, 371

Dryden, John, English poet and dramatist (1631-1700), 239, 671

Duchesne, Louis Marie Olivier, French Roman Catholic prelate and scholar (1843-1922), 658

Dura, 602

Dura-Europus, 512, 529

Dürer, Albrecht, German painter and engraver (1471-1528), 580

Duties, On (Panaetius), 97

dyeing, 322-323, 329, 331, 342, 373, 471, 510

Dyrrhachium (Durazzo), 184-185, 480, 482, 602

E

East, the, 78, 86, 94, 95, 121, 124, 125, 129, 138, 139, 147, 154, 157, 161, 170, 171, 178, 186, 188, 195, 203, 204, 206, 208, 213, 226, 251, 253, 262, 292, 320, 323, 329, 330, 331, 335, 364, 373, 378, 389, 406, 410, 413, 419, 420, 442, 455, 463, 471, 482, 507, 511-512, 524, 525, 564, 576, 603, 605, 616-617, 621, 622, 629, 630, 638, 639, 644, 651, 655, 659, 666, 670, 671

Easter, 617, 647, 660†, 664

Ebionim, 577
Eboracum, *see* York
Ebro (*anc.* Iberus), 47, 48, 215, 469
Eburones, 176
Ecbatana (Hamadan), 528
Ecclesiastes, 540
Ecclesiastical History (Eusebius), 649*, 663
Ecclesiasticus, 539
Eclogues (Virgil), 205, 236, 243
Ecnomus (naval battle off, 256 B.C.), 44
Eden, Garden of, 614
Edessa (in Greece), 483
Edessa (Urfa), 513, 602, 604, 629
Edictum de Pretiis (Diocletian), 642-643
Edom, 530
education, Etruscan, 7; Carthaginian, 48;
    Athenian, 487-488; Roman, 70, 72, 75, 90, 95,
    137, 141, 217, 259, 265, 314, 367-368, 424, 440,
    477, 509, 511, 513, 661, 671
education, state, 287, 368, 424, 461, 466, 476,
    661, 671
effeminacy, 132, 215, 251, 438, 442
Egeria, 13, 63, 365*
Egnatia, Via, 324, 482, 602
Egypt, 5, 6, 8, 10, 71, 77, 91, 92*, 107, 159, 168,
    170, 186-188, 193, 203, 204, 206, 207-208, 211,
    212, 213, 216, 217, 218, 225, 233, 247, 266, 284,
    301, 308, 313, 322, 323, 324, 325, 327, 329, 331,
    336, 342, 347*, 349, 352, 355, 357, 359, 364-365,
    366, 374, 381, 389, 390, 413, 424, 429, 431, 437,
    482, 483, 484, 487, 495, 498-507, 508, 514, 523,
    525, 526, 530, 532, 548, 559, 588, 595, 602, 606,
    613, 623, 630, 631, 632, 633, 634, 638, 639, 641,
    653, 655, 657, 658, 671
Egyptian, 187, 630
Egyptian Tales (Heliodorus), see *Aethiopica*
Eighth Legion, 182
Elagabal, 621, 625, 626
Elagabalus (Marcus Varius Avitus Bassianus
    Aurelius Antoninus Heliogabalus), Roman
    emperor (205?-222), 390, 622, 623-625, 626,
    639
Elba, 6, 322
Elbe (*anc.* Albis), 217, 432
Elders (*presbyteri*), 579, 582, 586
Elea, *see* Velia
Eleusinian mysteries, 418, 487, 525
Eleusis, 431, 487, 525, 606
Elijah, Jewish prophet, 574
Elis, 482
Elizabeth, mother of John the Baptist, 560
Elizabethan Age, 258, 510
Elysian Fields, 84, 241
emancipation, 57, 112, 221-222, 335, 363, 365,
    384, 398, 631
emasculation, 94, 157, 282, 290, 385, 512, 515,
    523, 567, 580, 613, 614, 615, 625, 666
embalming, 282
Emerita (Mérida), 470
Emerson, Ralph Waldo, American essayist,
    poet, and philosopher (1803-1882), 307, 367
Emesa, 621, 623, 625, 638, 639

emetics, 377
emigration, 117, 118, 482, 487
Emmaus (Kuloniyeh), 535, 573
Empedocles, Greek philosopher (500-430?
    B.C.), 148, 153
emperor-worship, *see* deification
emphyteusis, 416
Empire, growth of, 87, 95, 107, 108, 177-178,
    206, 217-218, 248
Emporiae, 470
Emporium, 339, 342
Encheiridion, of Epictetus (Arrian), 490*, 494
Encolpius, 297-298
Encratites, 605
Engadi, 537
engineering, Etruscan, 6, 18; Roman, 75, 81,
    176, 193, 219-220, 266-267, 270, 326-328, 356,
    359-361, 410, 418-421, 464, 465, 470, 473, 474,
    480, 511, 635
England, 249*, 258, 302, 346, 406, 475, 535
English, 671
English Channel, 176, 470, 475, 476
engraving, 278, 346
Enna (Castrogiovanni), 112
Enneads (Plotinus), 608-611
Ennius, Quintus, poet and dramatist (239-169
    B.C.), 67, 97-98, 148, 155, 159, 164, 234, 241,
    315, 442, 667
Enoch, 574; Book of, 540, 541, 559, 564, 593
Entellus, 382
Epaphroditus, freedman of Nero (fl. 1st cen-
    tury), 284, 292, 490
Ephesians, The Epistle of Paul the Apostle to
    the, 587*
Ephesus (Ayasoluk), 204, 312, 329, 417-418,
    504, 513, 515, 518, 546, 577, 585, 592, 602, 603, 630
Epicharis, conspirator (?-65), 371
epic poetry, 74, 98, 239-244, 278, 296, 316, 317
Epictetus, Stoic philosopher (60?-120?), 295,
    301, 307, 415, 424, 425, 482, 486, 490-494, 520, 611
Epicureanism, 95, 131, 132, 148, 154, 164, 236,
    249, 304, 370, 432, 485, 489-490, 491, 496, 602, 671
epicureanism, 68, 98, 147, 154, 215, 230, 244,
    247, 253, 260, 276, 279, 282, 285, 286, 300, 304,
    373, 388, 456, 487, 522, 540-541
Epicurus, Greek philosopher (342?-270 B.C.),
    95, 132, 148, 149, 153, 154*, 250, 304, 305, 307,
    346, 388, 490
Epidaurus, 62, 124, 139, 482, 487, 563
epigram, 135, 155, 160, 174, 234, 247, 290, 295-
    296, 302, 316-318, 369, 389, 398, 436, 437, 509-510
Epiphanius, Christian writer (fl. 4th century),
    616
Epirus, 37, 38, 112, 131, 184, 482
Epistles (Horace), 248-249
Epistolae Morales (Seneca), 304
Epodes (Horace), 246
equites (equestrians), 15, 21, 22, 24, 26, 27, 32,
    80, 121, 126, 139, 142, 191, 286, 332-333, 363-
    364, 384, 433, 440, 622, 633
Eratosthenes, Greek geometer and astron-
    omer (276?-195? B.C.), 521

Eretria, 483
Ergotimus, Greek potter, 9
Eros, 353
Eros, 461
erosion, 339, 487, 665
Esdraela, 535
espionage, Hannibal's, 48
Eshmun, 41, 42
Esperanto, 671
Esquiline, 12*, 215, 253, 312, 340, 342, 354
essay, 241, 304, 671; Cicero, 163-166; Seneca, 302-304; Plutarch, 485-486
Essay on Criticism (Pope), 249*
Essenes, 537-538, 559, 560, 562, 568, 577, 597
Etesian winds, 325
ethics, of Lucretius, 148-154; of Zeno, 196; of Marcus Aurelius, 444-446; of Epictetus, 491-494; Jewish, 548, 591, 618; of Christ, 566-567, 602, 618, 667
Ethiopia, 188, 217, 328, 364, 366, 500, 546
Etna, Mt., 418
Etruria (or Tuscia), 3-18, 35, 36, 37, 50, 51, 64, 73, 112, 113, 139, 143-144, 269, 339, 350, 440, 454, 601
Etruscan Federation, 5-6, 17*
Etruscans, 5-18, 35, 36, 37, 52, 122
Etruscan style, *see* Tuscan style
Euboea, 73, 310, 357, 483, 519
eucharist, *see* communion
Eucopion, slave, 334
Eudoxus of Cnidus, Greek astronomer (409?-353? B.C.), 165
Euhemerus, Greek mythologist (fl. 300 B.C.), 98
Eumenes II, King of Pergamum (reigned 197-159 B.C.), 516
Eunapius, Greek sophist and historian (fl. end of 4th century), 636*
Eunoe, Queen of Numidia (1st century B.C.), 168
Eunuch, The (Terence), 101
eunuchs, 329, 334, 363, 515, 624, 640, 666
Eunus, Sicilian slave leader (fl. 2nd century B.C.), 112
Euphrates, Greek Stoic philosopher (?-138), 422
Euphrates, 178,194,217,414,495,511,512,513,627
Euripides, Athenian dramatist (480-406 B.C.), 98, 154, 178, 258, 302, 513
Europe, 78, 86, 95, 132, 154, 166, 178, 308, 320, 322, 324, 421, 475, 478, 497, 507, 524, 583, 640, 641, 653, 655, 664, 670
Eurydice, 94, 256
Eusebius Pamphili, Bishop of Caesarea, ecclesiastical historian (260?-340?), 501, 592, 649*, 651, 654, 657, 659-660, 662-663
Euxine Sea, *see* Black Sea
evil eye, 60
evolution, Lucretius on, 150-153
excommunication, among Jews, 547; Church, 554, 605, 618
Exodus, 567

expansion, *see* Empire, growth of
Ex Ponto (Ovid), 257-258
extreme unction, 600

F

Fabia, third wife of Ovid (fl. 1st century), 256, 257, 258
Fabian strategy, 50, 185
Fabii, Roman clan, 21, 76, 255, 364
Fabius (Quintus Fabius Maximus Verrucosus, Cunctator), general and dictator (?-203 B.C.), 50, 68
Fabius Pictor, Caius, painter (fl. 303 B.C.), 82, 352
Fabius Pictor, Quintus, general and historian (fl. end of 3rd century B.C.), 71, 73
Fabricius, Pons, 327
Fabulina, 59
factories, 321-323, 333, 342, 477, 498, 642, 644
fairs, 78, 328
Faith, 358; Temple of, 358
Falernian wine, 456
family, in Etruria, 7; in Germany, 479; in early Rome, 56-59, 67, 72, 88, 91; in the later Republic, 134, 147; under the Principate, 222-225, 300, 321, 334, 348, 363-364, 366, 371, 441; under the monarchy, 656
family name (*cognomen*), 56-57
Fannia, wife of Helvidius Priscus (1st century), 371, 441
Far East, 84, 529
Farnese Bull, 634
Farnese Hercules (Glycon), 349, 634
Farnese Juno, 349
Farnese Palace, 351
Fasti (Ovid), 256-257
Fate, 242, 304
father, the (*paterfamilias*), in the Republic, 56, 57, 59, 68-69, 226; under the Principate and Empire, 395
Fathers of the Church, 308, 524, 603, 611-615
Fato, De (Cicero), 163*
Faunus, 59, 65
Fausta, second wife of Constantine I (4th century), 663-664
Faustina Senior, wife of Antoninus Pius (2nd century), 423, 427, 430
Faustina Junior, wife of Marcus Aurelius (?-175), 423, 425, 427-428, 430, 442
Faventia (Faenze), 455
Favorinus of Gaul, philosopher at Hadrian's court (fl. 2nd century), 367, 415
feasting, Etruscan, 6, 7; Carthaginian, 41; under Rome, 65-66, 68, 69, 71, 82, 88-89, 90, 132, 133, 147, 186, 190, 202, 223, 245, 266, 276, 285, 296, 297-298, 334, 335, 372, 376-377, 386, 461, 476, 515, 562, 624
Feast of Tabernacles, 65
Febris, 75
februa, 67

Felix, Antonius, procurator of Judea (fl. 1st century A.D.), 271, 543, 586
Feralia, 65
feriae (holy days), 65
Ferrara (*anc.* Forum Alieni), 454
Ferrero, Guglielmo, Italian historian (b. 1872), 273*
fertility, 56, 59, 60, 61, 65, 66, 67, 159, 193, 212, 221-222, 224-225, 232, 363-366, 431, 449, 479, 480-481, 515, 525, 545, 666
fertilizers, 76, 320-321
festivals, 59, 63, 65-67, 71, 74, 76, 98, 223, 225-226, 239, 256, 334, 335, 347, 377-379, 381, 390, 423,461,484,512,515,523,542-543,579,598,672
Festus, procurator of Judea (fl. 62), 543, 586
fetiales, 63
fetishism, 60
feudalism, 631*
Fidenae (Castel Giubileo), 11
Field of Mars, 65, 128, 143, 173, 192, 232, 280, 291, 308, 340, 348, 360, 362, 365, 390
Figaro, 101
Fimbria, Caius Flavius, politician and general (?-84 B.C.), 124-125
finance, 190, 192-193, 330-332, 336, 411
Finibus, De (Cicero), 163*, 165
fire brigade, Crassus', 131
first name (*praenomen*), 56-57
First Principles (Origen), see *Peri Archon*
fisci, 221*
fiscus, 221-222
fishing, 321, 336, 423, 470, 483, 515, 520, 563, 573
Flaccus, Avillius, governor (fl. 1st century), 500-501
Flaccus, Lucius Valerius, consul (?-86 B.C.), 124
Flaccus, Valerius, senator (fl. 3rd century B.C.), 102
flaggelation, 354
flamines, 63
Flaminian Way, 78, 455
Flaminius, Caius, political leader (?-217 B.C.), 47, 49, 78, 340
Flaminius, Titus Quinctius, general (fl. 200 B.C.), 85, 96, 382
Flanders, 174
Flaubert, Gustave, French novelist (1821-1880), 239
Flaviales, 291-292
Flavian Amphitheater, *see* Colosseum
Flavian Dynasty, 285-293, 351, 407, 412, 442
fleet, *see* navy
floods, 159, 193, 339, 365, 429, 649
Flora (goddess), 65, 381
Flora, courtesan (fl. 1st century B.C.), 138-139
Floralia, 65, 378, 381
Florence (*anc.* Florentia), 9, 348*, 454
Florus, Lucius Annaeus, historian (fl. 1st century), 473
Florus, procurator of Judea (fl. 1st century), 543-544
flute, 379-381

Fontana dei Trevi, 327*
food, in the Roman army, 34; in Carthage, 40, 41; under Rome, 38, 54, 70-71, 76, 88-89, 133, 215, 227, 245, 247, 298, 320-321, 328-330, 373, 376-377, 636
forgery, in art, 342
Formiae (Formia), 162, 202
Fornax, 59
Forth, 476; Firth of, 476
Fortuna Primigenia, Temple of, 454
Fortuna Virilis, Temple of, 358
Fortune (Fortuna), 358, 388, 424, 655
Fortune, Temple of, 340, 358
fortunetelling, *see* soothsaying
Forum, 23, 24, 27, 47, 64, 66, 72, 79, 84, 89, 115, 123, 125, 126, 136, 141, 146, 160, 161, 166, 169, 179, 189, 192, 198, 199, 202, 228, 231, 239, 280, 284, 340, 341, 342, 352, 358, 362, 378, 393, 394, 402, 421, 423, 427*, 429, 635
Forum Boarium, 340, 342, 358
Forum Holitorium, 342
Forum Iulii (Fréjus), 474
Forum Iulium, 192, 341
Forum Piscatorium, 342
Forum Traianum, 411
forums, 464, 466, 473, 477
fountains, 343-345, 348, 384, 515
Fourth Gospel, *see* John, Gospel of Saint
Fracastaro, Girolamo, Italian astronomer, poet, and physician (1483-1553), 154
Fragonard, Jean Honoré, French painter and engraver (1732-1806), 351
France, 174-175,234,302,369,406,470-475,484,671
Francis, Saint, Italian founder of Franciscan order (1182-1226), 455
François Vase, 9
Franks, 175, 629, 653
Frascati, 454*
Frazer, Sir James George, Scottish anthropologist (1854-1941), 588*
free cities, 462, 474, 482
freedmen, status of, 270, 271, 287, 290, 292, 298, 333, 334, 338, 415, 543, 620, 639
French, 73, 295, 475, 637
French civilization, 177-178, 470, 475
French Revolution, 192, 641, 670
frescoes, in Etruria, 10; in Pompeii, 74, 352-354; under Rome, 82, 338, 352-354, 372, 512; Christian, 601
Freya, 479
friendship, Cicero on, 165-166; Horace on, 247, 250; in Rome, 441
From Jesus to Paul (Klausner), 557*
From the Pontus (Ovid), see *Ex Ponto*
Frontinus, Sextus Julius, engineer and statesman (fl. 1st century), 327-328
Fronto, Marcus Cornelius, rhetorician (110?-180?), 108,302,315,417,425,430,442,443,466
frumentaria, lex, 116
Fucinus, Lake (Lago di Celano), 193, 270, 326, 410
fuels, 76, 77, 322-323, 343, 477

Fufia Caninia, lex, 222, 398
Fulvia, wife of Antony (?-40 B.C.), 202, 204-205, 206, 208
Fulvius, general (fl. 3rd century B.C.), 92
Fulvius, Aulus, conspirator (1st century B.C.), 395
Funck-Brentano, Frantz, French historian (b. 1862), 475
Fundamentalism, 592
funeral rites, 83-84, 98, 101, 157, 180, 190, 199, 232, 282, 335, 378, 379, 381-382, 568, 601
furniture, 88, 92, 133, 303, 345-346, 352, 373, 459, 532

G

Gabinian Law, 139-140
Gabinius, Aulus, politician (?-48 B.C.), 139, 172, 174, 186, 211
Gabriel, 289
Gadara (Katra), 297, 509, 530, 535
Gades (Cádiz), 40, 133, 169, 252, 325, 469, 470, 514
Gaiseric, King of the Vandals (fl. 429-455), 670
Gaius, jurist (fl. 2nd century), 392, 394, 396, 397, 399, 401, 405
Galatia (Anatolia), 86, 218, 513, 578, 583, 585, 630
Galatians, The Epistle of Paul the Apostle to, 554, 571*, 585, 587*
Galba (Servius Sulpicius Galba), Roman emperor (3 B.C.-A.D. 69), 283-285, 323, 434, 436
Galba, Servius Sulpicius, statesman (fl. 2nd century B.C.), 87
Galen (Claudius Galenus), Greek physician (130-200?), 313, 334, 375, 428, 430, 505-507, 513, 516, 599
Galerius (Caius Galerius Valerius Maximianus), Roman emperor (ca. 250-311), 635, 640-641, 644, 651, 652, 653, 654, 662
Galicia, Danubian, 432
Galilee, 530, 535, 543, 544, 557, 558, 560, 563, 573, 577
Galla, 317
Gallia Lugdunensis, 472, 474
Gallic War, 169, 174-178, 179
Gallienus (Publius Licinius Valerianus Egnatius Gallienus), Roman emperor (reigned 253-268), 608, 629-630, 635, 650, 666, 669
Gallio, *see* Novatus, Marcus Annaeus
Gallus (Caius Vibius Trebonianus Gallus), Roman emperor (ca. 207-253), 629
Gallus, Aelius, general (fl. 1st century B.C.), 336-337, 508
Gamaliel II, Jewish Patriarch (fl. ca. 100), 547
Gamaliel, a Pharisee, and president of the Sanhedrin (fl. 1st century), 576, 579-580
gambling, in Etruria, 7; under Rome, 62, 269, 383, 447, 456, 458, 488
games, in Etruria, 6-7; under Rome, 82, 90, 99, 111, 121, 133-134, 168-169, 171, 212-213, 219, 220, 223, 224, 225, 260, 265, 270, 274, 277-279, 289, 290-291, 302, 316, 319, 332, 340, (children's) 367, 372, 375, 376, 377-378, 379, 380, 381-387, 388, 389, 410, 415, 423, 427, 428, 438,
443, 447, 456, 458-459, 461, 486-487, 500, 515, 532, 545, 598, 629, 631, 640, 646, 647, 649, 668
Ganymede, 510
Gard, Pont du, 474
Garda, Lago di (*anc.* Lacus Benacus), 4, 155, 158, 454
gardens, 76, 132-133, 141, 160, 185, 199, 215, 245*, 266, 272, 278, 280, 319, 327, 340, 343, 344, 353, 354, 362, 421, 440, 454, 459, 500, 532
Gargantua, 299
Garonne (*anc.* Garumna), 470
Gassendi, Pierre, French philosopher and savant (1592-1655), 154
Gaul, 43, 48, 53, 73, 89, 107, 112, 118, 119, 129, 144, 167, 168, 174-178, 180-181, 183, 184, 188, 191, 192, 217, 219, 231, 270, 283, 320, 322, 326, 329, 330, 331, 348, 366, 417, 429, 431, 468, 470-475, 476, 478, 479, 481, 495, 513, 514, 602, 604, 627, 629, 633, 638, 639, 649, 651, 653-654, 666, 669-670
Gaul, Belgic (Gallia Belgica), 176, 431, 433, 472, 474
Gaul, Cisalpine (northern Italy), 36, 47, 49, 51, 87, 88, 155, 172, 174-175, 182, 189, 193, 196, 200, 201, 235, 236, 454
Gaul, Narbonese (Gallia Narbonensis), 172, 174-177, 216, 472, 473
Gaul, Transalpine, 49, 271, 454
Gauls, 12, 23, 24, 35, 36, 37, 47, 48-51, 86, 124, 130, 174-177, 191, 235, 271, 340, 375, 454, 471-475, 478, 513
Gaza, 508, 530, 535
Gazith, 536
Gellius, Aulus, Latin grammarian (ca. 117-ca. 180), 368, 442
Gemala, Lucilius, millionaire (fl. 1st century), 461
Gemma Augusta, 346
generalship, of Hannibal, 48-54; of Scipio Africanus, 52-54; of Caesar, 174-178, 182-189; of Antony, 199, 203, 206-207; of Tiberius, 217-218, 231, 259-260; under Claudius, 271; of Marcus Aurelius, 428-429, 431-432; of Septimius Severus, 622; of Constantine, 664
Genesis, 444, 540, 614
Geneva, 175
Genghis Khan, Asiatic conqueror (1162?-1227), 606
Genoa (*anc.* Genua), 78, 454
Geographical Outline (Ptolemy), 503
geography, 220, 308, 503, 514, 520-521
Geography (Strabo), 520
geometry, 75, 314, 368, 503, 507, 634
Georgics (Virgil), 215, 225, 237-239
Gerasa (Djerasch), 508-509, 530, 535
Gergovia, 177
Gerizim (Jebel et Tôr), 535
Germanicus Caesar, general (15 B.C.-A.D. 19), 224, 261-262, 263*, 273, 291, 301, 371
Germans, 174-178, 217, 428-431, 434, 446, 475, 478-481, 627, 631*, 639, 653, 666, 669

Germans, On the Situation and Origin of the (Tacitus), 434

Germany, 36, 112, 118, 176, 178, 194, 217-218, 231, 248, 261, 284, 285, 308, 320, 326, 329, 366, 406, 410, 417, 424, 428, 430, 431, 432, 471, 472, 473, 475, 478-481, 633, 644; Upper Germany, 291, 439, 479-480; Lower Germany, 479

Gesco, Carthaginian general (3rd century B.C.), 46

Geta (Publius Septimius Geta), Roman emperor (?-211), 621-622, 634, 635

Getae, 257

Gethsemane, 569, 571

Gibbon, Edward, English historian (1737-1794), 364, 425, 613*, 662, 667

Gibraltar (*anc.* Calpe), 39, 40, 43, 194

Gil Blas (Lesage), 299

Gilgamesh, 428

Giorgione da Castelfranco (Giorgio Barbarelli), Venetian painter (1478?-1511), 355

Giton, 297

gladiators, Etruscan, 7; Roman, 52, 90, 131, 133-134, 137, 173, 179-180, 198, 223, 265, 267, 274, 279, 303, 313, 351, 370, 377, 382, 383-387, 410, 428, 429, 430, 447, 453, 456, 459, 465, 487, 532, 545, 622, 649, 665; schools for, 385-386, 447, 505

glass, 322, 328, 329, 342, 347, 361, 374-375, 456, 473, 474, 499-500, 510; *see also* murrhine glass

Glevum (Gloucester), 477

Gloria, De (Cicero), 163*

Glycera, 247

Glycon, Athenian sculptor in Rome (fl. 1st century B.C.), 349

Gnosticism, 502, 556, 595, 604-605, 606, 609, 614

God, Seneca on, 304; Marcus Aurelius on, 444-445; Plutarch on, 484-485, 486; Panaetius on, 490; Epictetus on, 491-494; Philo on, 501-502; Galen on, 507; Poseidonius on, 514; Dion Chrysostomus on, 522; Apollonius of Tyana on, 526; Plotinus on, 610; Origen on, 614-615

gods, in Etruria, 7; in Carthage, 41-42; under Rome, 58-67, 69, 75, 76, 81-82, 84, 93-94, 104, 164, 214, 225-227, 235, 238-239, 240, 242, 243, 248, 251, 256, 259, 265, 268, 274, 280, 293, 300, 316, 335, 340, 343, 349, 352, 371, 372, 377, 388-390, 427, 429, 430, 438, 444, 449, 457, 489, 510, 512, 522-526, 557, 588, 601, 607, 625, 646-651, 655; Lucretius on, 147-153; Cicero on, 162; in the *Aeneid*, 242, 243; Horace on, 248-249; Pliny on, 309; Sextus Empiricus on, 495; Lucian on, 495-497

Goethe, Johann Wolfgang von, German writer (1749-1832), 354

Golden Age, Saturn's, 61, 225, 236; Augustus', 233-258, 346; Diocletian's, 645

Golden Ass, The (Apuleius), 299, 442, 467-468

Golden Bough, 62

Golden Horn, 483

Golden House, 280, 282, 283, 344-345, 352, 358, 361

golden mean, *see aurea mediocritas*

Golden Milestone, *see* Millenarium Aureum

Golden Thoughts (Marcus Aurelius), see *Meditations*

Golgotha, 572-573, 581

Good Goddess, *see* Bona Dea

Gorboduc (Sackville and Norton), 302

Gordian I (Marcus Antonius Gordianus), Roman emperor (158-238), 628

Gordian II (Marcus Antonius Gordianus), Roman emperor (?-238), 628

Gordian III (Marcus Antonius Gordianus), Roman emperor (226-244), 628

Gospels, 553-574, 591

Gothic architecture, 661

Gothic letters, 479

Goths, 316, 480, 622, 628, 629-630, 638, 669-670

gout, 311, 389, 622

government, in Etruria, 6; in Latium, 11-17; in Carthage, 42-43; under the Republic, 21-35, 57, 89, 93-94, 99, 113, 128-130, 136, 146, 174, 180-208; Cicero on, 165; under the Principate, 212-217, 227, 266, 270-271, 285-294, 328, 336, 338, 405, 415-416, 418-420, 422-424, 425, 436, 447-449; under the monarchy, 623, 626-627, 632, 639, 640-645, 647, 664, 668-669; of Rome, 670, 672

governors, 87, 129, 155, 174, 194, 198-199, 215, 216-217, 261, 462-463, 661

Gracchi, 23, 47, 91, 111, 113-117, 122, 126, 140, 165, 171, 192, 194, 319, 363, 391, 469, 516, 640

Gracchus, Caius Sempronius, statesman (153?-121 B.C.), 113, 115-117, 465

Gracchus, Tiberius Sempronius, statesman, father of the Gracchi (fl. 2nd century B.C.), 87, 92, 113

Gracchus, Tiberius Sempronius, statesman (162?-133 B.C.), 113-115

grace, 589

Graecia Magna, 37, 38

graffiti, 458-459

Graii, 4

grain, 111, 116, 117-118, 120, 126, 139-140, 173, 174, 179, 183, 184, 186, 189, 190, 192, 212-213, 214, 219, 220, 221, 237, 260, 265, 267, 270, 320-321, 325, 328-329, 333, 336, 339, 348, 362, 376, 388, 411, 423, 427-428, 429, 438, 446, 453, 461, 463, 464, 483, 498, 513, 631, 633, 641-642, 666, 668

grammar, 29, 72, 95, 146, 234, 295, 308, 367, 415

Grand Central Terminal (in New York), 360*

Granna (Gran), 431

Great Exposition (Simon Magnus?), 604

Great Leptis, *see* Leptis Magna

Great Mother, *see* Magna Mater *and* Cybele

Greece, 5, 6, 8, 10, 23, 34, 38, 47, 48, 51, 54, 57, 62, 68, 70, 75, 76, 77, 78, 84, 85-87, 89, 92, 93, 94, 95-102, 104-105, 108, 112, 113, 125, 130, 141, 147, 154, 158, 163, 164, 173, 178, 183, 186, 187, 192, 203, 211, 233, 235, 239, 240, 241, 246, 256, 259, 269, 278-279, 282-283, 287, 311, 317, 320, 323, 324, 328, 329, 330, 331, 333, 338-339,

Greece (*continued*)
342, 344, 347†, 349, 351-361, 364, 371, 379-381, 391, 392, 406, 414, 419, 420, 429, 431, 442, 455, 456, 459, 468, 472, 474, 480, 481, 482-527, 532, 542, 579, 588, 594-595, 602, 618, 630, 633, 636, 666, 667, 670-671; *see also* Hellenistic

Greek, 72-73, 95, 97, 104, 135, 141, 167, 187, 196, 233, 244, 259, 269, 274, 308, 312, 313, 365, 393, 415, 432, 440, 442, 443, 455, 479, 535, 556, 560, 563, 571, 572, 579, 582, 594-595, 596, 601, 612, 614, 634, 661; *see also* Hellenistic

Greek Anthology, 509, 633

Greek Asia, 482, 486, 490, 512, 518, 542, 630, 659

Greeks, 4, 17, 18, 35, 37, 38, 39, 43, 44, 51, 52, 58, 59, 62, 71, 72, 74, 76, 78, 82, 86-87, 89, 92, 94-95, 99, 104-105, 121, 132, 152, 164, 240, 242, 249, 253, 255, 256, 263, 277, 311, 312, 326, 328, 348, 352, 356, 364-365, 366, 367, 370, 388, 438, 457, 468, 469, 480, 482-527, 529, 532, 535, 544, 554, 558, 579, 582, 595, 634; *see also* Hellenistic

Guadalquivir, 39, 470

guilds, 499, 536, 642, 644; *see also collegia*

gymnastics, *see* athletics

gynecology, 313, 505

H

Hadad, 522

Hades, 63, 84, 94, 240, 242, 389, 509, 525

Hadrian (Publius Aelius Hadrianus), Roman emperor (76-138), 4, 220, 234, 322, 344, 351, 359, 361, 368, 379, 392, 394, 395, 396, 398, 403, 408, 411, 413-422, 423, 425, 426, 427, 428, 437, 442, 454, 455, 476, 482, 487, 489, 491, 499, 512, 516, 548, 549, 603, 624, 648, 662, 665

Hadrian's Villa, 421, 454

Hadrian's Wall, 476, 524

Hadrumetum (Sousse), 39, 465

Haggada, 547

Halacha, 547

Halicarnassus (Budrum), 234, 513

Halstatt iron culture, 471

Hamburg, 553

Hamilcar Barca, Carthaginian general and father of Hannibal (?-229 B.C.), 44-47, 48

Hammurabi, King of Babylon (ca. 1950 B.C.), 405, 557

Hannibal, Carthaginian general (247-183 B.C.), 39, 47-55, 57, 70, 71, 81, 85, 90, 91, 93-94, 105, 118, 120, 121, 252, 429, 457, 469

Hanno, Carthaginian navigator (ca. 490 B.C.), 40, 42

Happy Life, On the (Seneca), 302-303

harbors, 78, 193, 220, 270, 324, 325, 326, 328, 410, 454, 455, 456, 465, 480, 483, 499, 508, 512, 513, 514, 515, 516, 534

harems, 199, 447, 517

haruspicy, in Etruria, 7, 18; in Rome, 18, 60, 63-64, 93, 164, 228, 651, 656

Harvey, William, English anatomist and physician (1578-1657), 506

Hasdrubal, Carthaginian general, son-in-law of Hamilcar (?-221 B.C.), 47, 48

Hasdrubal, Carthaginian general, brother of Hannibal (?-207 B.C.), 47, 50, 52-53

Hasdrubal, Carthaginian general in the Third Punic War (2nd century B.C.), 107

Hasmoneans, Jewish family, 530-532, 536

Hatra, 529

Haverfield, 477*

Head of Caesar, 350

Health, 358

Health, Temple of, 82, 352, 358

hearth, 58

Heath, Sir Thomas Little, English mathematician (1861-1940), 504*

Heauton Timoroumenos (Terence), 101

heaven, 241-242, 243, 485

Hebrew language, 41, 501, 533, 535, 556, 579, 614

Hebrews, The Gospel according to the, 616

Hebron, 535

Hecatompylus, 528

Hector, 240

Hecyra (Terence), 101

Heiberg, Johan Ludvig, Danish classical philologist (1854-1928), 504*

Heine, Heinrich, German poet (1797-1856), 72, 484, 583

Helen, 256, 354, 516

Helena, concubine of Constantius I (fl. 3rd century), 653, 655, 663

Heliodora (in Meleager), 509

Heliodorus of Emesa, Greek writer of romance (fl. 3rd century B.C.), 636-637

Heliogabalus, *see* Elagabalus

Heliopolis (Baalbek), 498, 511

Hell, belief in, 8, 84, 147, 149, 241-242, 485, 542, 561, 593-594

Hellas, *see* Greece

Hellenism, 37, 85, 92, 101, 108, 339, 367, 417, 420, 442, 472, 495, 502, 534, 535, 549, 579-580

Hellenistic age and culture, 78, 79, 84, 86, 92*, 95, 96, 107, 113, 121, 125, 158, 233, 297, 323, 339, 343, 344, 348, 349, 352, 378, 419, 442, 443, 482-527, 530, 532, 534, 540, 576, 577, 579, 581, 584†, 585, 594-595, 606, 630, 632

Hellespont (Dardanelles), 124, 518, 630, 638

Helvetii, 175

Helvidius, *see* Priscus, Helvidius

Hephaestus, 63, 352

Hera, 418, 516

Heraclea (battle, 280 B.C.), 37

Heraclea, in Egypt, 636

Heracleitus, Greek philosopher (fl. 500 B.C.), 484, 502

Heracles, 63, 226, 278, 385

Herculaneum, 354, 456, 457-460

Hercules, 62, 63, 286, 354, 447, 479, 513, 640

Hercynian Mountains, 431

Herder, Johann Gottfried von, German philosopher, poet, and critic (1744-1803), 553

heresy, 577, 592, 595, 603-606, 612, 615, 616, 618, 646, 657-661, 662, 664

hermaphrodites, 310, 334
Hermes, 63, 352, 496, 525
Hermogenes, Greek architect (fl. 2nd century B.C.), 514
Hernici, 36
Hero *or* Heron, Alexandrian mathematician and inventor (fl. 3rd century), 503-504
Hero, 256
Herod the Great, King of the Jews (62?-4 B.C.), 487, 508, 512, 531-535, 536, 539, 542, 545, 546, 557
Herod Antipas, King of the Jews (fl. 1st century), 535, 560, 568
Herodes, *see* Atticus Herodes
Herodian, Greek writer on Roman history (180-238), 620, 622, 628
Herodias, wife of Herod Antipas (1st century), 560
Herod Philip, half brother of Herod Antipas (fl. 1st century), 560
Herodotus, Greek historian (484?-425 B.C.), 454-455, 486, 513
Heroides (Ovid), 256, 258
Hertha, 479
Hesiod, Greek epic poet (ca. 800 B.C.), 238, 495
hetairai, 7, 68
Heywood, Jasper, English translator of Seneca (1535-1598), 302
Hexapla (Origen), 614
Hierapolis, 390, 490, 522
Hiero II, King of Syracuse (324?-216 B.C.), 44, 51
Higher Criticism, 553-557
Hillel, Jewish rabbi, President of Sanhedrin (60 B.C.?-A.D. 10?), 536, 538-539, 542, 547, 567, 580
Himilco, Carthaginian navigator (ca. 450 B.C.), 40
Himly, Karl, German professor of medicine (1772-1837), 310
Hinduism, 444, 525, 609
Hippalus, Greek navigator (fl. 1st century), 325
Hipparchus of Nicaea, Greek astronomer (160?-125? B.C.), 503
Hippocrates, Greek physician and writer on medicine (460-357 B.C.), 313, 505, 507, 514
Hippodamus of Miletus, Greek architect (fl. 5th century B.C.), 356
Hippo Diarrhytus (Bizerte), 39, 465, 603
Hippolytus, Christian schismatic (?-ca. 230), 617-618
Hippolytus, 254
Hippo Regius (Bone), 39, 465
Hirtius, Aulus, Roman consul (?-43 B.C.), 201
Hispalis, *see* Seville
Hissarlik, *see* Troy
Historia Augusta, 655
Historiae (Tacitus), 434-437, 442
Historia Naturalis (Pliny the Elder), 296, 308-311, 439

Histories (Appian), 442
Histories (Sallust), 160
historiography, 83, 290, 295-296, 500, 671; Varro, 159-160; Sallust, 160; Caesar, 178; Livy, 250-252; Claudius, 269; Pliny the Elder, 308-311; (art) Pasiteles, 349; Tacitus, 433-437; Suetonius, 442; Plutarch, 483-484; Nicolaus of Damascus, 512-513; Arrian, 520; Josephus, 546; Dion Cassius Cocceianus, 636; Eusebius, 662-663
history (in schools), in Carthage, 48; in Rome, 72, 367
History of Rome (Q. Fabius Pictor), 73
Hittites, 513, 516, 528
holidays, *see* festivals
Holland, Philemon, English classical scholar (1552-1637), 167, 442
Holland, 479
holy orders, 600, 658, 660†
Holy Sepulcher, Church of the, 663
Holy Spirit, 576, 582, 590, 600, 604, 605, 658, 660
Homer (fl. 9th century B.C.), 98, 147, 213, 241, 242, 243, 254, 441, 495, 522, 614
homosexuality, 65, 89, 94, 132, 144, 158, 167-168, 199, 237, 246-247, 266, 276, 279, 282, 290, 297-298, 317-318, 369, 408, 438, 447, 456, 509*, 598, 625, 627; *see also* bisexuality
Homs (*anc.* Emesa), 511
honestiores, 332
Honor, 358; Temple of, 358
Horace (Quintus Horatius Flaccus), Latin poet (65-8 B.C.), 60, 61, 73, 95*, 98, 154, 155, 158, 215, 224, 225, 233, 234, 235, 243, 244-250, 252, 258, 367, 369, 380, 437, 455, 509, 546, 671
Horatii, Roman clan, 21
Horatius (Horatius Cocles), hero (fl. 6th century B.C.), 17
horse racing, 277, 377, 382-383, 500
Hortensia, lex, 24
Hortensius, Quintus, orator (114-50 B.C.), 131, 132, 136, 141, 160, 161, 185, 213
Hortensius Hortalus, Quintus, noble (?-42 B.C.), 203
horticulture, 308
Horus, 523
Hosea, 567
hospitals, 312
housing, 341-345, 362, 373, 465, 477, 510
Huan-ti, Emperor of China (fl. 2nd century), 329
Hugo, Victor Marie, Viscount, French writer (1802-1885), 249*
human sacrifice, 588*; in Etruria, 7-8; in Carthage, 42, 465, 588*; in Rome, 51, 64, 65, 94, 149; in Gaul, 472; in Germany, 479; in Antioch, 512
Hume, David, Scottish philosopher and historian (1711-1776), 494, 609
humiliores, 332, 644
Hungary, 406
Huns, 480, 669, 670

hunting, 96, 321, 408, 414, 415, 423, 425, 428, 430, 446-447, 478, 529, 531, 622, 630
hydrotherapy, 312-313
Hymettus, 322
hymns, 73, 82, 226, 588, 601, 638
Hypsus, Peri (Longinus), see *Sublime, On the Hymn to Zeus* (Cleanthes), 584 *
Hyrcanus II, King of Judea (?-30 B.C.), 530-531, 534

I

Iamblichus, Syrian Neoplatonic philosopher in Alexandria (?-333?), 635, 636
Iazyges, 429, 431
Iberia, in Asia, 413
Iberians, 468, 472, 475
Icarus, 256, 385
Iconium (Konia), 513, 582
Ides of March, 197
Idumea, 530, 535
ientaculum, 70
Ignatius, Saint, *called* Theophorus, Bishop of Antioch (?-107?), 588, 611, 648
Iliad, 240, 241, 516
Ilium, *see* Troy
illuminated manuscripts, 662
Illyria, 47, 51, 52, 200, 217, 454, 628, 638
Illyricum, 639
Imagines (Varro), 159
immigration into Rome, under the Republic, 81, 94, 95, 121, 126, 179; under the Principate, 221, 364-366
immortality, 527; Cicero on, 165; Caesar on, 170; Virgil on, 242; Horace and, 250; Seneca on, 305; in religion, 429; Tacitus on, 435-436; Marcus Aurelius on, 446; Plutarch on, 485; Jews on, 536, 575; Christian, 592, 595, 599, 602, 603, 656, 657; Plotinus on, 610
imperator, 191, 213, 268, 350
imperialism, Roman, 54, 85, 90, 105, 107, 175, 242, 252, 261, 409-410, 414
impressionism (art), 339, 353, 355
Inacha, 247
incest, 172, 266, 274, 290, 495, 623
Incitatus, 267
Incrustation (First) Style (painting), 353
indeterminacy, principle of, 151*
India, 134, 325, 326, 329, 337, 338, 346, 413, 499, 500, 508, 512, 514, 521, 526
Indian Ocean, 325, 413, 499
Indians, 600*
Indica (Arrian), 520
Indies, 503
Indo-European languages, 73
Indo-Europeans, 36, 60, 528
Indus, 413
Industrial Revolution, 477
industry, Etruscan, 6; Carthaginian, 40; under Rome, 77-81, 88, 190, 310, 321-323, 328, 330, 332-334, 336-337, 342, 370, 448, 455, 456, 457, 463, 473, 477, 482, 498-499, 510, 529, 631-633, 641-642, 644, 668, 671

infanticide, in Greece, 42; in Rome, 56, 222, 363-364, 396, 434, 666; forbidden among Jews and Christians, 546, 598
Inferno (Dante), 8
inflation, 211, 330-331, 632-633
informers, *see Delatores*
Ingenuus, ruler of eastern provinces (fl. 258), 629
inheritance, 57, (taxes) 58, 222-224, 245, 267, 301, 363, 396, 397, 399, 438, 479, (tax), 622, 657
initiation, 524-525, 606
Innocenza, 351
In Pisonem (Cicero), 161
"In Praise of Nero" (Lucan), 296
Inquisition, 649
insanity, 312
inscriptions, Etruscan, 5; Roman, 73, 271, 293; Pompeian, 458; Italian, 461
Institutes (Justinian), 406
Institutiones (Gaius), 392
Institutio Oratoria (Quintilian), 314-315
insulae, 341-342
interest, 79, 88, 129-130, 131, 169, 170, 184, 192, 211, 212, 219, 302, 310, 331-332, 336, 627, 657
intermarriage, of Phoenicians with natives, 39; in Rome, 221-224, 395
international law, 48
interregnum, 30
Intricate (Fourth) Style (painting), 353
invention, 287-288, 323, 328*, 503-504
Ionia, 86, 125, 132, 133, 158, 204, 513, 514, 523, 594, 629, 630, 636
Ionian Sea, 206
Ionic order (architecture), 338, 355, 357
Iphigenia, 149, 353
Iranians, 471, 516, 529
Ireland, 36, 73, 471, 472
Irenaeus, St., Greek Bishop of Lyons (130?-202?), 556, 611-612, 616, 617
Iris, Egyptian handmaiden of Cleopatra (?-30 B.C.), 208
Iron, Age of, 236
irrigation, Etruscan, 6; Roman, 320, 464, 631, 665
Isaeus, Greek rhetorician in Rome (end of 1st century), 368
Isaiah, 540, 541, 560-561, 567, 574
Isiac cult, *see* Isis
Isis, 193, 266, 358, 390, 447, 467-468, 523-524, 525, 526, 527, 596, 606, 635
Isis, Temple of, 291, 358, 369, 390
Islam, 666
Isocrates, Athenian orator and rhetorician (436-338 B.C.), 103, 166
Israel, *see* Jews
Isthmian games, 85, 283, 486-487
Istria, 73, 455
Istrus, 480
Italian, 73, 295
Italica (Sevilla la Vieja), 414, 470
Italus, King of the Sicels, 4

Italy, 3-5; city-states, 6; art, 10; Roman conquest, 34-38; Second Punic War, 49-52, 54; soil, 76-77; trade, 78; population, 81; music, 82; northern boundary, 87; farming, 104, 111; Celtic attack, 119, 472; Social War, 122; slave revolt, 137-138; troops in, 172; saved by Caesar, 177-178; supports Caesar, 182; chaotic state in 45 B.C., 190; citizenship, 193; Augustus in, 205-206; exhaustion, 211-212; agriculture, 237, 319-321; industry, 323; trade, 328-330; lack of grain, 336; water of, 356; law, 404-406; plague in, 429; in the 2nd century, 448-449; under the Principate, 453-461; religion, 522-523, 542; barbarian invasions, 629, 638; economic and political condition under the monarchy, 632, 666-669

Ithaca, 241

Iucundus, Lucius Caecilius, Pompeian auctioneer, 459-460

Iulus, *see* Ascanius

ius civile, 393-404, 405

ius gentium, 393, 404-406

Ixion, 352

J

Jairus, father of girl awakened by Christ (1st century), 563

James, Christ's brother, 558

James, son of Alphaeus, *called* the Just, apostle (?-62), 555, 577, 583, 597

James, son of Zebedee, apostle (?-41?), 563, 577, 592

James, The General Epistle of, 600, 616

James I, King of England (1566-1625), 555

Jamnia, 535, 547-548

Janiculum, 12, 340

Janus, 58-59, 61, 67, 82, 358

Janus, Temple of, 211, 285, 358

Japan, 295, 374, 421

javelin, 308

Jeremiah, Hebrew prophet, 567

Jericho, 535

Jerome, Saint (Hieronymus, Sophronius Eusebius), Latin father of the Church (340?-420), 154, 392, 578, 596, 612, 614

Jerusalem, 288, 349, 358, 365, 404, 419, 508, 530, 531, 532, 535, 537, 538, 542-549, 558, 559, 562, 569-571, 574, 576, 577, 579, 581-583, 585, 586, 587, 602, 603, 616, 650, 663

Jerusalem, Temple of, 268, 349, 365, 530-531, 533, 536, 537, 538, 539, 542-545, 548, 560, 568, 570-571, 574, 575, 577, 583, 586, 599, 603

Jerusalem Delivered (Tasso), 637

Jesus, *see* Christ

Jesus, Life of (Renan), 554

Jesus, Life of (Strauss), 553

jewelry, in Etruria, 6; in Carthage, 41, 42; under Rome, 70, 89, 132, 134, 193, 215, 223, 273, 328-329, 345, 346, 373, 429, 465, 471, 489, 529, 578, 596, 624-625, 640

Jewish Commonwealth, Second, 530

Jews, 41, 65, 66, 192, 193, 199, 225, 288, 292, 365-366, 390, 394, 407, 413, 419, 421, 423, 438, 487, 500-502, 507, 512, 525, 529-549, 554, 556, 559, 563-595, 598, 601, 614, 626, 646

Job, 540

Jocasta, 623

Johanan ben Zakkai, Jewish rabbi (fl. 1st century), 547

John, St., apostle and evangelist, 555, 556, 559, 561-562, 563, 571-572, 575*, 577, 592-595, 611, 648

John, The Epistles of, 557, 575*, 592; First, 575

John, The Gospel of St., 502, 553, 559, 561-562, 565, 570, 571-572, 575*, 592-595, 603

John the Baptist, 558, 560-561, 562, 563, 564, 568, 569, 570

John the Elder, early Christian, 555

joint-stock companies, 79-80, 323

Joppe *or* Joppa (Jaffa), 508, 535, 577

Jordan, 535, 560, 577

Joseph, Christ's brother, 558

Joseph, husband of Mary, mother of Christ, 559

Josephus, Flavius, Jewish historian (37-95?), 325, 498, 500, 531, 536, 537, 538, 543, 544-545, 546, 554, 558, 560

Joshua, son of Sirach, 539

Jotopata, 544

Jove, *see* Jupiter

Juba I, King of Numidia (?-46 B.C.), 189, 466

Juba II, King of Numidia and historian (?-ca. 19 A.D.), 42, 466

Judah, Jewish Patriarch (fl. ca. 200), 547

Judaism, 63, 366, 501-502, 529, 549, 575-595, 597-599, 601, 602, 604-605, 606, 614, 625, 626

Judas, Christ's brother, 558

Judas the Gaulonite, Jewish rebel leader (fl. beginning of 1st century), 543

Judas Iscariot (of Kerioth) apostle, 563-564, 571

Judea, 140, 203, 204, 268, 281, 283, 285, 390, 508, 530-549, 557, 558, 560, 569, 570, 577, 618

Judgment, Last, 243, 542, 553, 559, 560, 563, 567, 593-594, 595, 597, 599, 603, 607, 612

Jugurtha, King of Numidia (?-104 B.C.), 118-119, 404

Jugurthine War, 118-119

Jugurthine War (Sallust), 160

Julia, sister of Caesar (1st century B.C.), 200

Julia, daughter of Caesar and fourth wife of Pompey (?-54 B.C.), 134, 171, 179

Julia, daughter of Augustus (?-14 A.D.), 220, 229-232, 235, 257, 259, 262, 263*, 265

Julia, granddaughter of Augustus (1st century A.D.), 232, 235

Julia, daughter of Germanicus (1st century), 301

Julian (Flavius Claudius Julianus), called the Apostate, Roman emperor (331-363), 18, 474, 635

Julian Aqueduct, 220

Julian Laws, of Caesar, 171-173; of Augustus, 223-224, 230, 235, 255, 256, 290

Julianus, *see* Didius Julian

Julianus, Salvius, jurist (fl. 2nd century), 392, 394, 416

Julii, Roman clan, 21, 167

Julio-Claudian dynasty, 211-285, 286, 289, 293, 349

Jullian, Camille, French historian (1859-1933), 475

Juno, 61, 67, 81, 82, 83, 349, 358; of Veii, 62

Juno Moneta, Temple of, 358

Jupiter (Jove), 61, 63, 67, 81, 82, 83, 93, 100, 144, 151, 167, 242, 256, 268, 284, 306, 317, 349, 350, 357-358, 388, 389, 419, 458, 496, 548, 625, 626, 640; Jupiter Optimus Maximus, 358; Jupiter Pluvius, 61; Jupiter Stator, 358; Jupiter Tonans, 61, 357; planet, 309

Jupiter, Temple of, 92, 341

Jupiter, Temple of (Pompeii), 459

Jupiter Heliopolitanus, Temple of, 511

Jupiter, Juno, and Minerva, Temple of, 81, 83, 287, 289, 290, 358

Jupiter Stator, Temple of, 358

Jupiter Tonans, Temple of, 61, 357

juries, 114, 116-117, 121, 126, 178, 192, 403

jurisprudence, *see* law

Justice, *see* Astraea

Justin, Christian martyr (?-108), 611

Justin Martyr (Justinus Flavius), Church father in Palestine (100?-166), 592, 611

Justinian I the Great (Flavius Anicius Justinianus), Byzantine emperor (483-565), 392, 393, 394, 399, 406, 409, 416, 605, 634

Juvenal (Decimus Junius Juvenalis), satirical poet (ca. 60-ca. 140), 67, 73, 234, 272, 295, 312, 314, 319, 325, 332, 334, 341, 343, 363, 364, 365, 366, 367, 369, 370, 371, 372-373, 376, 381, 387, 388, 389, 402, 433, 436, 437-439, 440, 453, 466, 546, 612, 671

Karlsburg, 633

Keats, John, English poet (1795-1821), 147, 157

Kent, 476

Kerasous, *or* Cerasus (Kerasun), 320

Kerch, *see* Panticapaeum

Kerch, Strait of, 517

Kingdom of Heaven, 538, 540-542, 557, 559, 560, 562, 564-570, 575, 582, 593, 594-595, 596, 597, 602, 603-604, 605, 617

Klausner, Joseph, Jewish scholar (b. 1874), 557*

"knucklebones," 354

Krishna, 553

Kuban River, 517

L

labarum, 654

Labeo, Antistius, jurist (?-42B.C.),203,391-392

Labienus, Quintus, general (?-39 B.C.), 205

Labienus, Titus, politician and soldier (?-45 B.C.), 182, 186, 189, 205

Lactantius Firmianus, Lucius Caelius, father of the Latin church, in Africa (260?-325?), 578, 643, 651, 654, 662

Lady of Elche, The, 469

Laelius Sapiens, Caius (ca. 186-? B.C.), 96-97, 101, 102, 107, 114

Laenas, Caius Popilius, consul and ambassador (fl. 172-168 B.C.), 107

Laetus, Praetorian prefect (fl. reign of Commodus), 448

Lais (*Greek Anthology*), 510

Lake Garda, *see* Garda, Lago di

Lake Regillus, Battle of (496 B.C.), ...

Lalage, 247

Lambaesis (Lambèse), 466

Lamia, Lucius Aelius, consul and patron (fl. 1st century B.C. and 1st century A.D.), 233

Lampridius, Aelius, Latin historian (fl. early 4th century), 624, 634

land distribution, in Greece, 86; in Rome, 47, 87, 113-117, 119, 120, 121, 126, 128, 136, 171, 174, 184, 192-193, 213, 218, 287, 319, 336, 407, 465, 627, 631*

landownership, 57, 76-77, 90, 111-118, 192, 213, 219, 319-320, 333, 336, 483, 631, 644, 657

landscape, *see* painting

language, Etruscan, 5, 17; Celtic, 36; Carthaginian, 41; Latin, 17, 38, 72-73

Lanuvium (Civita Lavinia), 35, 371, 423

Laocoön, 345

Laodicea (Latakia), 512, 513, 516

lararium, 343

Lares, 7, 58, 69, 226

lares compitales, 81

Larissa, 186

Larius, Lacus, *see* Lake Como

Lasa (*or* Mean), Etruscan goddess, 7

Last Supper, 555

La Tène iron culture, 471, 472

Lateran Museum, 350

latifundia, 77, 104, 105, 107, 111-114, 118, 130, 190,297,319,336,411,464,465,473,498,631,668

Latin, 72-74, 97, 98, 101, 102, 103-104, 156, 158-162, 164, 166, 167, 177, 233, 258, 259, 295, 304, 312, 313, 319, 365, 393, 410, 415, 441, 442, 443, 455, 469, 474, 476, 477, 507, 514, 517, 572, 612, 619, 630, 661, 671

Latina, Via, 77

Latin Language, On the (Varro), 159

Latin League, 35, 37, 38

Latins, 5, 11, 21, 35, 36, 39, 241

Latinus, 240-241

Latium, 11, 12, 14, 18, 21, 35, 37, 43, 51, 61, 200, 240-241, 344, 437, 453, 666

laurel, 83, 191

Laurentum, 344, 440

Laureolus, robber, crucified (1st century), 385

Lavinia, 12, 241

Law, *see* Torah

law, under the Republic, 22-33, 57, 67, 70, 71, 72, 73, 79, 83, 89, 99, 104-105, 113-118, 126,

law, under the Republic (*continued*)
133, 138, 139-140, 144, 171-173, 174, 176, 179,
182, 189, 191-194, 198; Cicero on, 165-166;
under the Principate, 213-217, 219, 221-225,
230-231, 250, 261, 262, 264, 269, 270-271, 293,
312, 323, 324, 331-332, 335, 338, 340, 341, 364,
369, 391-406, 416, 418, 420, 424, 427-428, 443,
448, 465, 473, 474, 477, 481, 488, 510, 619, 646;
under the monarchy, 633-634, 642-652, 656-
657, 661; of Rome, 670
law, practice of, 141, 160, 316, 317, 466,
(Ovid's) 254, (Seneca's) 301, 401-403, (Juvenal's) 437, (Pliny's) 439-441, (Apuleius')
467-468, (Lucian's) 495, (Tertullian's) 612,
(L. Septimius Severus') 621
Law of the Nations, *see ius gentium*
Laws (Cicero), see *Legibus, De*
lays, 73
Lebanon (Libanus), 329
Lebanon (*anc.* Libanus) Mountains, 511
lectures, 135, 443, 465, 483-485, 488-490, 495,
505, 511, 514, 521-522, 635
legates, 216
legend, in Livy, 251, 256, 308
Legibus, De (Cicero), 141, 163*
Leicester (*anc.* Ratae Coritanorum), 477
Leiden (*anc.* Lugdunum Batavorum), 324
leisure, 235
Lemures, 59-60; Feast of, 65
Lentuli, Roman family, 76
Lentulus, Gnaeus, senator (fl. 1st century),
332
Lentulus Batiates, trainer of gladiators (fl. 1st
century B.C.), 137
Lentulus Crus, Lucius Cornelius, consul (?-48
B.C.), 181, 183, 185
Lentulus Sura, Publius Cornelius, conspirator
(?-63 B.C.), 129, 143-144, 202
Leochares, Athenian sculptor (fl. 4th century
B.C.), 349
Leonardo, *see* Vinci, Leonardo da
Lepidus, Marcus Aemilius, consul (?-216 B.C.),
382
Lepidus, Marcus Aemilius, triumvir (?-13
B.C.), 201, 203, 225
Leptis Magna (Lebda), 39, 105, 465
Leptis Minor, 40, 465
Lesbia, 135, 155-157
Lesbos, 253
Lessing, Gotthold Ephraim, German critic
and dramatist (1729-1781), 100, 553
letters, Cornelia's, 113; Cicero's, 162-163, 165,
195; Marcus Aurelius', 425, 430; Pliny the
Younger's, 440-441; Fronto's, 442
Leucas (*lt.* Santa Maura), 139
Leuce Come, 508
Leviticus, 539, 567
lex talionis, 32, 398
Liber, 62, 65-66
Libera, 65-66
Liberalia, 66
Libra, 298

libraries, in Carthage, 42; in Athens, 418; un-
der Rome, 96, 131, 132, 159, 219, 234, 343,
459, 635, 662
libraries, public, 159, 193, 219, 234, 257, 291,
358, 360, 376, 411, 421, 440, 461, 466, 515, 627
Libya, 43, 46, 48, 413, 500
Licinian laws, 24, 114
Licinianus, son of Licinius and nephew of
Constantine I (?-326), 663-664
Licinius (Caius Flavius Valerius Licinianus
Licinius), Roman emperor (?-325), 653-655,
656, 659, 663
Licinius Calvus (Stolo), Caius, tribune and
consul (fl. 376-361 B.C.), 24
Liége, 176
Life of the Roman People (Varro), 160
lighthouses, 325
Ligurians, 4, 35, 468
limes, 417, 480, 627
Limonum (Limoges), 473
Lindum (Lincoln), 477
Linus, Bishop of Rome (fl. 1st century), 617
Lisbon, *see* Olisipo
literary criticism, 315, 513, 633, 636
literature, Etruscan, 5; Greek, 95-96, 104, 123,
259, 630; under the early Republic, 5, 73-75,
97-105, 108, 113, 123; under the Revolution,
144-146, 174, 178; under the Principate, 215,
225, 233-258, 259, 263, 287, 291, 293, 295-319,
367-368, 408, 415, 433-446, 456, 464, 467-468,
477, 483-486, 490-497, 509-510, 539-542, 555-
595, 603, 606-616, 618, 620, 621; under the
monarchy, 621, 625, 629, 635-638, 661, 662-
663; of Rome, 671
Liternum (Patria), 92, 347
Lives of Illustrious Men (Suetonius), 442
Lives of the Sophists (Philostratus), 635
Livia, third wife of Augustus (1st century
B.C. and 1st century A.D.), 205, 223, 229-232,
262, 264, 268, 286, 299, 348, 350, 354
Livia Orestilla, wife of Caligula (1st century
A.D.), 266
Livias, 508
Livilla, daughter of Antonia and wife of Dru-
sus (?-31 A.D.), 264, 268
Livius Andronicus, earliest Roman poet (fl.
240 B.C.), 74
Livy (Titus Livius), historian (59 B.C.-A.D. 17),
13, 14, 15, 21, 36*, 48, 53, 60, 72, 89, 94, 112,
225, 233, 250-252, 434, 636, 671
Lixus, 39
Locri, 35, 37, 51
Logia (sayings of Christ), 556
logic, 164, 425
Logos, 501-502, 540, 541, 556, 589, 594-595, 604,
615, 658
Loire (*anc.* Liger), 470
Loisy, Alfred Firmin, French Orientalist and
Biblical scholar (1857-1940), 554
Lollia Paulina, wife of Caligula (1st century
A.D.), 266, 273, 373

Lollius, governor of Britain (fl. 2nd century), 476

Lombards, 431

Lombardy, 670

London (anc. Londinium), 324, 476, 477, 523-524

Longinus, Caius Cassius, jurist (fl. 1st century), 282

Longinus, Dionysius Cassius, Greek philosopher and critic (213?-272), 630, 636

Longinus, Lucius Cassius, governor of Syria (?-42 B.C.), 531

Longobardi, see Lombards

Longus, Greek sophist and novelist (fl. 3rd century), 516, 637

lotteries, 219, 624

Louis XIV, King of France (1638-1715), 258

Lourdes, 563

Louvre, 348*

love feast, see agape

Luca (Lucca), 175

Lucan (Marcus Annaeus Lucanus), poet (39-65), 282, 295, 296, 316, 319, 408, 435, 470

Lucanians, 35, 37, 51, 519

Lucanus, Publius Terentius, senator (2nd century B.C.), 101

Lucian, Greek satirical author (120?-200?), 60, 84, 299, 304, 312, 428, 487, 489, 494-497, 513, 597, 636

Lucifer, 241, 289

Lucilius, Caius, satirist (180-103 B.C.), 73, 97, 245, 437, 509

Lucilius Junior, governor and Epicurean (fl. 1st century), 304, 306

Lucilla, daughter of Marcus Aurelius (2nd century), 426

Lucilla, sister of Marcus Aurelius (2nd century), 447

Lucina, 60, 236

Lucius (in Apuleius' Golden Ass), 467-468

Lucius Caesar, grandson of Augustus (?-2 A.D.), 230-231, 473

Lucretia, wife of Collatinus (6th century B.C.), 16, 23

Lucretia (in Martial), 318

Lucretius Carus, Titus, poet (99?-55? B.C.), 61, 73, 95, 98, 102, 146-154, 155, 164, 225, 234-235, 238, 241, 243, 245, 258, 296, 308, 388, 637, 667, 671

Lucrinus, Lacus, 220

Lucullus, Lucius Licinius, general and patron (?-57? B.C.), 129, 130, 132, 138, 139, 140, 171, 211, 265, 272, 322, 342, 353, 373, 508, 519

Lucullus, Lucius Licinius, proconsul (fl. 2nd century B.C.), 87

ludi (games), 74, 377-378, 381-387; ludi iuvenales, 277; ludi saeculares, 225-226, 248, 387; ludi scenici, 74, 377-378

Ludovisi Battle Sarcophagus, 635

Ludovisi Juno, 349

Lugdunum (Lyons), 234, 269, 271, 283, 324, 332, 470, 473, 474, 504, 611, 649

Luke, St., evangelist (fl. 1st century), 553, 555-574, 575*, 583, 590

Luke, The Gospel of St., 555-574, 575*, 583, 605

Luna (Luni), 322, 357, 454

Lupanaria, see prostitution

Lupercalia, 63, 65, 195-196, 388

Luperci (Brotherhood of the Wolf), 63, 65, 388

Lusitania (Portugal), 87, 277, 311, 322, 470, 671

lustrum, 29, 63

Lutetia, see Paris

Luther, Martin, leader of German Reformation (1483-1546), 592

luxury, under the Republic, 54, 70-71, 88-89, 92, 97, 103, 128, 132, 136, 160, 185, 186, 204; under the Principate, 211, 213, 219, 223, 224, 232, 248, 251, 256, 297, 303, 305, 308, 311, 328-330, 331, 333, 337, 342, 364, 373-377, 438, 456, 465, 474, 478, 522, 608, 666, 667

Lycaonia, 513

Lyce, 247

Lyceum, Aristotle's, 421, 489-490

Lycia, 203, 218

Lyciscus, 369

Lycopolis, 608

Lycurgus, Spartan lawgiver (9th century B.C.), 32, 226

Lydda, 548

Lydia, 5, 6†, 9, 125, 513, 514-515, 523

Lydia (Horace), 247

Lyons, see Lugdunum

lyre, 379-381

lyric poetry, 82, 155-158, 244-250, 252-254, 278, 315-318, 379, 509-510, 637-638

Lysias, Athenian orator (450?-380? B.C.), 95

Lystra, 513, 582, 583

M

Ma, 147, 523

Maccabee, Judas, Jewish patriot (fl. 167 B.C.), 542

Maccabee, Simon, King of Judea (fl. 142 B.C.), 530

Maccabees, see Hasmoneans

Macedon or Macedonia, 51, 52, 85-87, 88, 90, 91, 94, 96, 136, 200, 203, 212, 216, 482, 483, 519, 583, 585, 623, 630, 633

Macedonian Wars, 85-87, 482

Macellum, 342

machinery, 323, 356

Macrina, Caelia, millionaire (2nd century), 411

Macrinus (Marcus Opellius Severus Macrinus), Roman emperor (164?-218), 529, 623-624

Madaura (Medaura), 466, 467

Madeira, 40, 308

Madonna della Febbre, La (Our Lady of the Fever), 75

Maeander (Menderez), 514

Maecenas, Caius Cilnius, statesman and patron (?-8 B.C.), 212, 215, 219, 224, 225, 234, 237, 239, 244, 246, 250, 253, 280, 454

Maelius, Spurius, politician (?-439 B.C.), 23

Maesa, Julia, sister of Julia Domna (?-222), 623-626

Maggiore, Lago (*anc.* Lacus Verbanus), 4, 454

Magi, 525, 526, 529, 559, 606, 608

magic, 60, 64, 75, 94, 308, 311-312, 388, 415, 419, 466-467, 485, 507, 512, 525-526, 537-538, 559, 656

Magna Mater (Great Mother), 94, 147, 381, 390, 523, 595, 672; *see also* Cybele

Magnesia (Manissa), battle in 190 B.C., 55, 86, 208, 514

Magnificat, 558

Mago, Carthaginian general, brother of Hannibal (fl. end of 3rd century B.C.), 47

Mago, Carthaginian writer in agriculture, 40, 42, 464

Maia, 60, 67

maiestate, lex Iulia de, 262, 264, 269, 279, 416, 591

Maimonides, Spanish Jewish rabbi and philosopher (1135-1204), 548

Mainz (*anc.* Magontiacum), 291, 324, 627, 633

Maison Carrée, 357, 473

Malaga (*anc.* Malaca), 469, 470

malaria, 193, 311, 312, 326†, 631, 666

Malchus, Tyrian dyeing firm, 331

Mallonia, critic of Tiberius, and suicide (1st century), 371

Mallus, 95

Malta, 40, 587

Mamaea, Julia, daughter of Julia Maesa and mother of Alexander Severus (?-235), 623-627

Mamertines, 43-44

Mammon, 340, 597

Manes, 59

Man, Isle of (*anc.* Monapia *or* Monarina), 476, 477

Manchester (*anc.* Mancumium), 477

Mani of Ctesiphon, Persian mystic (215-273), 605-606

Mania, 7

Manicheism, 606

manifest destiny, 43

Manilian Law, 140

Manilius, senator (fl. 2nd century B.C.), 103

Manilius, Caius, Roman tribune (fl. 66 B.C.), 140

Manlii, Roman clan, 21

Manlius, Lucius, conspirator (fl. 1st century B.C.), 144, 157

Manlius, Marcus, general (?-384 B.C.), 23

manners, 70-72, 90, 101, 102, 108, 134-135, 234-235, 286, 310, 316, 335

mansio, 324

mansions, 88, 92, 132, 133, 160, 162, 190, 195, 202, 213, 223, 245*, 290, 297, 326, 327, 328, 339, 340, 343-345, 351, 355, 362, 373-374, 421, 453, 456, 508, 635

Mantua, 3, 8, 11, 235, 454

Mantus, 7

manumission, *see* emancipation

manuscripts, 280, 662

maps, 220, 308

Marathon, battle in 490 B.C., 208, 442, 641

Marcellinus, Roman Pope (reigned 296-304), 652

Marcellus, Marcus Claudius, consul and conqueror of Syracuse (268?-208 B.C.), 50, 52, 82, 92

Marcellus, Marcus Claudius, son-in-law of Augustus (43-23 B.C.), 219, 230, 239, 357

Marcellus, Marcus Claudius, consul (?-46 B.C.), 181, 195

Marcellus, Varius, father of Elagabalus (fl. 2nd century), 623

Marcellus, For (Cicero), 195

Marceotis, Lake, 525

Marcia, wife of Cato, the Younger and Hortensius (fl. 1st century B.C.), 136

Marcia, daughter of Cremutius Cordus (1st century), 301

Marcia, Christian mistress of Commodus (2nd century), 447-448

Marcian Aqueduct, 220, 340

Marcion, Gnostic of Sinope (fl. 2nd century), 604-605, 616

Marcomanni, 346, 429, 431, 432, 606, 627, 629

Marcomannic Wars, 428-432, 443, 505

Marcus, Gallic Gnostic (fl. 2nd century), 604

Mariaba, 508

Mariamne, wife of Herod the Great (fl. end of 1st century B.C.), 534

Marinus of Alexandria, famous surgeon (fl. 1st and 2nd centuries), 505

Maritime Alps, 474

Marius, Caius, general and consul (157-86 B.C.), 3, 26, 27, 116, 118-120, 122-126, 128, 144, 146, 160, 167, 169, 391, 453

Marius, Caius, consul, son of preceding (109?-82 B.C.), 125

Mark, St., evangelist (fl. 1st century), 553, 555-574, 576

Mark, The Gospel of St., 555-574, 576

markets, 78, 342

Marquardt, Joachim, German antiquarian (1812-1882), 364

marriage, in Etruria, 7; under the Republic, 57, 67, 68-69, 132, 134, 204; under the Principate, 222-224, 262, 266, 301, 363-364, 369-371, 396, 397, 438, 441, 443, 599, 605; under the monarchy, 656, 666; ancient concept of, 240, 369-370; St. Paul and the Church on, 590, 598, 600, 647

Mars, 12, 59, 61, 63, 65, 66-67, 82, 193, 211, 346, 353, 388, 479; Ultor (the Avenger), 358

Mars (planet), 309

Mars Ultor, Temple of, 358, 383

Marseilles (*anc.* Massalia), 43, 49, 119, 180, 184, 231, 313, 326, 470, 474, 504, 654

Marsians, 270

Marsyas, 298

Martial (Marcus Valerius Martialis), Latin epigrammatist (40?-102?), 158, 234, 289, 290, 291, 295, 296, 312, 315-318, 319, 341, 342, 366, 369,370,371,380,385,389,398,403,408,437,441

Mary, mother of Christ, 527, 558-559, 560, 572

Mary, aunt of Christ, 572-573

Mary Magdalene, cured by Christ (1st century), 563, 572-573, 577

Masada, 544

Masinissa, King of Numidia (238-148 B.C.), 53, 105-106, 107, 118, 166, 464

Mass, Catholic, 578-579, 595, 599, 602, 603

Massalia, see Marseilles

Materia Medica (Dioscorides), 505

Mater Matuta, Temple of

materialism, in Lucretius, 146-154; in Seneca, 304

mathematics, 414, 488, 503-504, 507

Mathematiké Syntaxis (Ptolemy), 502-503

Matho, Libyan rebel leader (fl. 241-237 B.C.), 46

Matius, citizen and friend of Caesar (fl. 1st century B.C.), 191, 195

Matthas, Dutch biblical scholar, 554

Matthew, St., evangelist and apostle, 553, 555-574

Matthew, The Gospel of St., 555-574, 613

Mauretania (Morocco), 268, 413, 417, 466

Mauretania Caesariensis, 466

Mauretania Tingitana, 466

Mauri, see Moors

Mausoleum of Hadrian (Castel Sant' Angelo), 4, 422

Maxentius (Marcus Aurelius Valerius Maxentius), Roman emperor (reigned 306-312), 653-654, 656, 661

Maximian (Marcus Aurelius Valerius Maximianus Herculius), Roman emperor (240?-310), 635, 640, 644, 651, 653-654, 663

Maximilla, Montanist heretic (2nd century), 605

Maximinus (Caius Julius Verus Maximinus "Thrax"), Roman emperor (172?-238), 627-628

Maximinus Daza, Roman emperor (reigned 308-314), 653-654

Maximus Tyrius, Greek philosopher (fl. 2nd century), 426

Maximus and Vibo, banking firm, 332

measures, 78

Mechanica (Hero), 504

Medea, 256, 353, 385

Medea (painting), 354

Medea (Ovid), 255

Medea (Seneca), 307

Media, 413

Medicamina Faciei Feminineae, De (Ovid), 255

Medici, Lorenzo de', Florentine poet, patron, and scholar (1448-1492), 131

Medicina, De (Celsus), 313

medicine, in Etruria, 6; under Rome, 75-76, 104, 135, 227, 308, 310, 311-313, 324, 368, 414, 465, 467, 488, 504-507, 510, 512, 514, 515, 516, 517, 661, 671

Mediolanum, see Milan

Meditations (Marcus Aurelius), 425-426, 430, 431, 442, 443-446, 449

Mediterranean, 3, 6, 18, 25, 29, 34, 38, 39, 40, 43, 54, 76, 78, 80, 81, 85, 105, 107, 112, 139, 169, 170, 177, 187, 188, 212, 218, 221, 241, 251, 266, 310, 320, 324, 325, 328, 337, 339, 355, 367, 419, 453, 462, 464, 465, 466, 468, 469, 470, 474, 484, 498, 499, 500, 508, 512, 513, 518, 523-524, 527, 535-536, 545, 547, 596, 602, 670

mediums of exchange; in Etruria, 6, 17; in Carthage, 40, 46; under Rome, 17, 78-79, 184, 192, 205, 218, 287*, 330-332, 336, 448, 632, 641, 643, 668

Megalesia (Feast of the Great Goddess), 94

Megara, 239, 300, 487

Meir, Jewish rabbi (fl. 2nd century), 547

Mela, Lucius Annaeus, father of Lucan and brother of Seneca (?-65), 282

Mela, Pomponius, geographer (fl. 1st century), 308

Meleager, Greek epigrammatist (fl. 1st century B.C.), 509-510

Melkart, 42, 45, 465

Memmius, Caius, statesman (?-100 B.C.), 120

Memmius, Caius Gemellus, politician and man of letters (fl. first century B.C.), 148, 155, 157

memoirs, 123, 159, 275

Memoirs (Agrippina the Younger), 275

Memoirs (Sulla), 123

Memphis, 498

Menaechmi (Plautus), 100

Menander, Greek comic dramatist (342-291 B.C.), 99, 100, 102, 513

Menippus, Syrian Cynic philosopher (fl. 60 B.C.), 297, 509

Menippus (in Lucian), 495, 497

Mephitis, 75

mercenaries, 43, 46, 48, 53, 106, 207, 429, 517, 624, 669, 670

Mercury, 62, 63, 93, 342, 387, 473, 479, 601

Mesopotamia, 342, 349, 413, 414, 428, 528, 530, 548, 608, 622, 627, 629, 630, 641

Messala, Marcus Valerius, consul (fl. 1st century B.C.), 129

Messala, Marcus Valerius Corvinus, general and patron (fl. 1st century B.C.), 221, 233-234, 252-253

Messalina, Valeria, wife of Claudius (?-48), 272-273, 302

Messana (Messina), 44, 464

Messene, 329, 413

Messiah, 226, 243, 538, 540-542, 548, 554, 558*, 559, 560, 564-570, 577, 581, 582, 585, 588-589, 591, 593, 595, 603, 604, 605

metallurgy, 77, 322-323, 328, 469, 479

Metamorphoseon Libri XI (Apuleius), see Golden Ass

Metamorphoses (Ovid), 256, 257, 258
metaphysics, 95, 147, 154, 164, 196, 300, 304, 591, 613
Metapontum, 35, 51
Metaurus (Metauro) River (battle of, 207 B.C.), 53
Metellus, Lucius Caecilius, politician (fl. 1st century B.C.), 183
Metellus Celer, Caius Caecilius, husband of Clodia (fl. 1st century B.C.), 135
Metellus Macedonicus, Quintus Caecilius, general (fl. 1st century B.C.), 134
Metellus Numidicus, Quintus Caecilius (fl. 109-99 B.C.), 119
Metellus Pius, Caecilius (?-63 B.C.), general, 137
Metellus Pius Scipio, Quintus Caecilius, general (?-46 B.C.), 186, 189, 194
meteorology, 308
Metrodora, Alexandrian woman physician (fl. 1st century), 505
Metrodorus, Greek Epicurean philosopher (?-277 B.C.), 133
Metronax, philosopher (fl. 1st century), 303
Metropolitan Museum of Art, 347, 351
Mexico, 469, 600*
Michael, Archangel, 593
Michelangelo (Buonarroti), Italian artist (1475-1564), 4, 356, 443, 635
Middle Ages, 178, 243, 249*, 258, 307, 308, 310, 311, 312, 313, 503, 507, 592, 633, 644, 661, 672
midwives, 312
migrations, Celtic, 118; into towns, 190
Milan (*anc.* Mediolanum), 236, 454, 629, 635, 640, 644, 653, 654
Milan, Edict of, 654, 657, 658
Miles Gloriosus (Plautus), 100
Milesian Tales, 297, 514, 636
Miletus, 168, 312, 329, 513-514, 546
military science, 327-328
millefiori, 347
Mill, John Stuart, English philosopher (1806-1873), 609
Millenarium Aureum, 340-341
millennium, *see* Kingdom of Heaven
Milo, Pyrrhus' general, 38
Milo Papinianus, Titus Annius, politician (?-48 B.C.), 169, 173, 180, 184, 188, 189
Milton, John, English poet (1608-1674), 243, 671
mimes, 378, 389, 430
Minas de Rio Tinto, 469
Mincio (*anc.* Mincius), 235
Minerva, 61, 81, 83, 311, 358; Pallas Minerva, 61; *see also* Pallas Athene
Minerva, Temple of, 74
Minervina, first wife of Constantine I (fl. 4th century), 663
mining, Etruscan, 6; Carthaginian (in Spain), 40, 47, 469; Roman (in Spain), 54, 346, 469; Roman, 77, 80, 131, 218, 310, 320, 322, 330, 336, 448, 455, 477, 483, 513, 632, 665

Minos, 284
Minotaur, 354
Minturnae, 113, 322
Minucius, Quintus, proconsul (fl. 2nd century B.C.), 87
Minucius Felix, Latin Christian writer (fl. 2nd century), 611, 612
Minucius Rufus, Marcus, dictator (fl. 216 B.C.), 50
miracles, 60, 75, 93, 435, 442, 466, 512, 525-526, 553, 556, 557, 559, 562-563, 576, 580, 585, 607
Miranda (*anc.* Continum Lusitanorum), 427*
Misenum (Miseno), 132, 265, 325, 326, 457
Mithraism, *see* Zoroastrianism
Mithras, 280, 390, 524, 529, 540, 553, 598, 600*, 606, 639, 654; *see also* Zoroastrianism
Mithridates I, King of Pontus (fl. ca. 302, B.C.), 517
Mithridates VI the Great, King of Pontus (132?-63 B.C.), 122-125, 132, 140, 188, 347, 482, 507, 517-519, 528
Mithridatic Wars, 122-125, 132, 140, 188, 516-519
Mnester, dancer (fl. 1st century), 272
Moab, 530
Modalists, 605
Modena, *see* Mutina
Modernism, 554
Moesia, 218, 291, 480, 653, 670
Moguntiacum (Mayence), 480
Molière (Jean Baptiste Poquelin), French dramatist (1622-1673), 100
Mommsen, (Christian Matthias) Theodor, German historian (1817-1903), 48, 88, 175, 178, 265, 432, 475
Monarchians, 605
monarchy, in Etruria, 6; in Rome, 13-16, 34, 139, 190, 193-197, 198, 208, 670; Cicero on, 165; the Principate, 209-549; the later monarchy, 621-670
monasticism, 595, 657, 668
Mondragone, Villa, 454*
money-changers, 533, 570
moneylending, 79, 88, 103, 129-130, 131, 140, 169-170, 192, 196, 219, 246, 302, 303, 331-332, 336, 482, 500, 539, 627, 657
Monophysites, 605
monopolies, 80, 642
monotheism, 365-366, 390, 502, 507, 578, 582, 612, 639, 656
Monothelites, 605
Montaigne, Michel Eyquem de, French philosopher and essayist (1533-1592), 304, 307, 440, 466, 484
Montanism, 613
Montanus, Phrygian heretic (fl. ca. 156), 605
months of the Roman year, 66-67; Quinctilis renamed Julius, 193
Montignac, 470-471
Moors, (*anc.* Mauri), 387, 417, 431
Moralia (Plutarch), 483, 485-486
morals, in Etruria, 7; in Carthage, 41; in Capua, 52; in Germany, 479; in Corinth,

morals (*continued*)
487; under the Republic, 54, 57, 58, 67-69,
71, 72, 84, 89, 90, 92, 95, 97, 102, 104, 108,
112, 132-133, 134, 146, 155, 159, 160, 164, 205,
211; under the Principate and monarchy,
221-225, 232, 235, 239, 247-248, 251, 253-257,
260, 274, 276, 286, 293, 296-299, 300-301, 305,
307, 308, 315, 316, 363-366, 368, 369-371, 373,
443, 456, 500, 522, 593, 598-599, 602, 626-627,
628, 646, 656, 665-667; Caesar's, 167-169;
Clodius', 172-173; Antony's, 199-200, 204-
206; Julia's, 230-232; Horace on, 247-250;
Livy on, 251; Tiberius', 263; Caligula's, 266-
267; Claudius', Messalina's, and Agrippina's,
272-273; Nero's, 276-277, 279; Galba's, 284;
Vespasian's, 288; Titus', 288, 289; Domitian's, 290; Juvenal on, 438-439; Marcus Aurelius', 444-446; Commodus', 446; Herod's,
532; Christ's moral ideas, 566-567; Elaga-
balus', 624-625; Alexander Severus', 625-627
Morgantia, 121
Mortibus Persecutorum, De (Lactantius), 662
mosaic, 343, 345, 442, 459, 477, 601, 635
Mosaic Code, 537, 538, 542, 567, 585
Moses, 536, 567, 574, 576, 582, 586
Moslems, 507
Mosul, 529
mother, the, in the Republic, 58, 59
Mt. Alban, 11
Mt. Moriah, 533
Mount of Olives, 570
Mucianus, Licinius, general and historian (fl.
1st century), 310
Mulvian Bridge, 654, 662
Mummius Achaicus, Lucius, general (fl. 2nd
century B.C.), 87, 297
Munda, battle in 45 B.C., 190, 470
murals, *see* painting
Muratori, Ludovico Antonio, Italian archae-
ologist (1672-1750), 616
Murena, Lucius Licinius, propraetor in Asia
(fl. 83-81 B.C.), 519
murrhine glass, 347, 374
Musa, Antonius, physician (fl. end of 1st cen-
tury B.C.), 227, 313
Musa Paidiké (Strabo of Sardis), 509*
Muses, 150, 247, 510, 609
Museum (Alexandria), 500
music, in Etruria, 7, 11, 18; under Rome, 18,
69, 74, 82, 83, 90, 99, 133, 135, 159, 204, 226,
277-279, 282-283, 291, 302, 314, 335, 354-355,
367, 376, 377, 379-381, 384, 414, 421, 430, 440,
456, 487, 500, 511, 512, 523, 532, 599, 624, 625,
635; Christian, 601-602
Musica, De (Varro), 379
Mutina, (Modena, *q.v.*), 11,78, 87, 201, 322, 455
Mycale, 514
Myos Hormos, 499
Myrlea, 520
Myron, Greek sculptor (fl. ca. 450 B.C.), 338,
358
Myrtale, 247

Mysia, 513, 605
mysteries, *see* Eleusinian mysteries, Orphic
doctrine, Pythagoreanism
Mysteries, Temple of the, 431
mysticism, 468, 501-502, 514, 522, 524-525, 537,
547, 549, 553, 582, 589, 594-595, 604-611, 614-
615, 633, 667; *see also* pantheism
mythology, 75, 84, 94, 165, 241, 248, 251, 256,
316, 317, 353, 367, 522-525, 604
Mytilene, 186, 516

N

Naber, Dutch biblical scholar, 554
Naevius, Cnaeus, dramatist and poet (?-ca.
202 B.C.), 74-75, 98, 155, 241
Naissus (Nish), 630, 653
names, 56-57, 76
Naples (*anc.* Neapolis), 4, 35, 37, 52, 141, 236,
237, 278, 316, 356, 455, 456, 457, 461; Bay of,
11, 133, 325
Naples Museum, 349, 350, 351, 352, 354, 459-
460, 634
Napoleon I (Bonaparte), Emperor of the
French (1769-1821), 412, 416, 484, 553, 670
Narbo (Narbonne), 116, 473
Narcissus, secretary of Claudius (?-54 A.D.),
270-273
Narcissus (or *Dionysus*), 459
Nativity, 558-559
Natura Deorum, De (Cicero), 163*
Natural History (Pliny the Elder), see *Historia Naturalis*
nature, love of, in Lucretius, 147; in Virgil,
238; in Horace, 246; in Rome, 343; in Pliny
the Younger, 440; Christ's, 559
Nature of Things, On the (Lucretius), see
Rerum Natura, De
Naucratis, 498, 499
naumachia, 270, 377, 383, 470
naval battles, sham, *see naumachia*
navigation, 308, 324-326
navy, Carthaginian, 43, 44, 45, 54, 106, 107;
under the Republic, 44-45, 80, 106, 107, 139-
140, 183-185, 206-207, 518; under the Princi-
pate, 217, 219, 220, 308, 325, 337, 413, 455
Nazarenes, 559-560, 576
Nazareth, 535, 554, 558, 560, 562, 563
Neaera, 247
Neapolis, *see* Naples
Near East, 5, 211, 254, 559, 615
Nebuchadrezzar II, King of Babylon (reigned
605-562 B.C.), 39
Nemean games, 283, 486-487
Nemi (Aricia), 61, 351
Neoplatonism, 502, 514, 595, 604, 607
Neo-Pythagoreans, 497, 594, 604, 607, 614
Nepos, Cornelius, historian and biographer
(100-29 B.C.), 146, 160, 162
Neptune, 60, 63
Nero (Nero Claudius Caesar Drusus Ger-
manicus. *Originally* Lucius Domitius
Ahenobarbus), Roman emperor (37-68),

Nero (continued)
56, 68, 81, 92, 159, 263ᵛ, 273, 274-285, 286, 289, 293, 295-296, 298, 299, 300, 301, 302, 303, 304, 306, 307, 323, 324, 326†, 330, 334, 336, 339, 344-345, 347, 350-351, 352, 358, 359, 361, 363, 366, 371, 372, 374, 375, 379, 380, 384, 388, 397, 418, 434, 443, 456, 479, 482, 483, 485, 490, 491, 525, 528, 554, 575, 578, 587, 591, 593, 594, 603, 632, 633, 646, 647, 667
Nero, Baths of, 359, 375
Nero, Circus of, 578
Nero, son of Agrippina the Elder (fl. 1st century A.D.), 262, 263*, 264
Nero, Tiberius Claudius, noble, father of Tiberius (fl. 1st century B.C.), 205
Neronia, 277, 296, 381
Nerva (Marcus Cocceius Nerva), Roman emperor (32-98), 307, 365*, 371, 407-408, 425, 433, 434, 521, 633
Nerva, 407, 442, 547
Nervii, 175
Nestus, 630
Neumagen, 474
New Academy, 164, 308
New Babylon, 260
New Carthage, see Nova Carthago
New Comedy (in Athens), 99
New Jerusalem, 594, 605
Newman, John Henry, Cardinal, English writer (1801-1890), 493
newspapers, Caesar's, 172
New Testament, 553-595; 601, 603, 605, 615, 616
New Year, 65, 221
New York, 81, 100, 325, 337, 340, 360*
Nicaea (Is-nik), 418, 516, 520, 629, 636, 659
Nicaea, Council of, 659-661, 662, 663
Nice (anc. Nicaea), 474
Nicene Creed, 660*
Nicias, (Greek Anthology), 510
Nicodemus, Jewish Pharisee (1st century), 569
Nicolaus of Damascus, Greek historian (fl. 1st century B.C.), 512-513, 532, 534
Nicomedes II Epiphanes, King of Bithynia (reigned 142-91 B.C.), 120, 518
Nicomedes III Philopator, King of Bithynia (reigned 91-74 B.C.), 167, 518-519
Nicomedia (Is-nikmid), 418, 490, 516, 520, 629, 635, 640, 644, 651, 655, 659, 661
Nicopolis, 482, 490
Niebuhr, Barthold Georg, German historian and philologist (1776-1831), 16*, 392
Nietzsche, Friedrich Wilhelm, German philosopher (1844-1900), 104
Nigrinus, general of Trajan (?-118), 414
Nike, 461
Nile, 188, 419, 498, 499, 502, 636
Nile, Battle of the, 188
Nîmes (anc. Nemausus), 357, 417, 422, 473
Nineveh, 9*
Nisibis (Nisibin), 530
Nisida (anc. Nesis), 122

Noah, 528
Nola (Nola), 37, 122, 232
Nomentum, 316
Norba Caesarina (Alcantara), 470
Noreia (Neumarkt), 118
Noricum, 218, 429, 480
North, the, 481
North Sea, 470, 478
Nova Carthago, or New Carthage (Cartagena), 47, 49, 53, 112, 470
Novatian, Christian schismatic (fl. 3rd century), 618
Novatus, Christian schismatic (fl. 3rd century), 618
Novatus, Marcus Annaeus (Gallio), governor (?-65), 282, 470, 584
Nova Via, 340, 341
novel, the, 295, 296-299, 514, 633, 636-637
Nubians, 366, 500
Numa Pompilius, second King of Rome (fl. 8th and 7th centuries B.C.), 13, 66, 80, 167*
Numantia, 87, 115, 118
Numbers, 536
Numidia, 49, 53, 105-106, 118, 160, 168, 190, 357, 366, 462, 466
numina, 59-60
Numitor, legendary King of Latium (8th century B.C.), 12
nursing of children, in the Republic, 58; under the Principate, 367
Ny Carlsberg Glyptotek, 350
nymphaea, see fountains
Nymphs, 238-239

O

obelisk, 308
obscenity, in Catullus, 158; in Horace, 246; Caligula's, 268; in Petronius, 299; in Martial, 316-318; in mimes, 378; in Hadrian, 415; in Pliny the Younger, 440; in graffiti, 458; in Roman theater, 612, 647
obstetrics, 313, 505
Ocean, On the (Poseidonius), 514
Octavia, sister of Augustus (?-11 B.C.), 179, 205-206, 208, 230, 239, 268, 269, 274, 371
Octavia, wife of Nero (40-62), 273, 277, 279-280
Octavian, see Augustus
Octavius (Minucius Felix), 611
Octavius, Caius, see Augustus
Octavius, Cnaeus, consul (?-87 B.C.), 123-124
Octavius, Marcus, tribune (fl. 2nd century B.C.), 114
Odenathus, ruler of Palmyra (?-266), 630
Odes (Horace), 215, 246-250, 252
Odessus (Varna), 480
Odoacer, first barbarian ruler of Italy (434?-493), 670
Odysseus, 240, 353
Odyssey, 74, 240
Oea (Tripoli), 465, 466
oecus, 343

Oedipus, 278, **623**
Oenotria, 4
Officiis, De (Cicero), 163*, 165
old age, 83; Cicero on, 165-166; Seneca on, 304, 306
Old Comedy (in Athens), 99
Old Testament, 501-502, 540, 541* 555, 556, 557, 559, 578, 601, 604-605, 614
oligarchy, in Etruria, 6; in Carthage, 54; in Rome, 91, 119, 139-140, 190, 208, 212, 214, 460, 670; Cicero on, 165
Olisipo (Lisbon), 470
Olympia, 124, 277, 486, 489, 521-522
Olympic games, 277, 282-283, 486
Olympieum, 418, 487
Olympus, 35, 60, 92, 242, 275, 357, 495-496
omens, 60, 73, 93, 147, 171-172, 197, 228, 251, 311, 388, 435, 442, 525, 621
ophthalmology, 313, 505
Oppian Law, 89
Oppius, Caius, tribune (fl. end of 3rd century B.C.), 89
Oppius, Caius, citizen and friend of Caesar (fl. 1st century B.C.), 191
Ops, 62; Temple of, 200
Optica (Ptolemy), 503
oracles, 64, 164, 197, 243, 251, 415, 429, 454, 459, 485, 513, 525-526, 540
Orator, 9, 10
oratory, 73, 95, 103-104, 108, 115, 132, 141, (Cicero's) 160-162, 163*, 167, (Caesar's) 169, 250, (Livy's) 251-252, 265, 277, 295, 302, 304, 308, 314-315, 317, 356, 362, 367-368, 425, 433, 487, 488, (Dion Chrysostomus') 521-522, 671
Orchomenus, 124
Orcus, 84, 147
Orestes, 278
Orestes, Pannonian general (?-476), 670
organ, 380-381
Oriental civilization, 366
Orientals, 78, 364, 366, 438
Origen (Origines Adamantius), Christian Alexandrian teacher (185?-254?), 578, 591, 606-607, 608, 610, 613-615, 616, 618, 626, 647, 658, 662
Origines (Cato the Elder), 104, 160
Ornate (Third) Style (painting), 353
Orontes, 366, 512
Orpheus, 94, 256, 385, 525, 626
Orphic doctrine, 241, 242, 525, 604
Oscans, 457
Osiris, 468, 523, 553, 588
Osrhoene (Diar Modhar), 413, 513
Osroes, King of Parthia (fl. 2nd century), 413
Ostheim, 175
Ostia, 78, 94, 193, 257, 270, 272, 283, 325, 326, 339, 389, 410, 411, 453, 456, 461
Ostia, Via, 591
Otho (Marcus Salvius Otho), Roman emperor (32-69), 277, 284-285, 390
Otricoli (*anc.* Oriculum), 461

outlines, 159, 305
Ovid (Publius Ovidius Naso), poet (43 B.C.-A.D. 17), 61, 68, 154, 155, 224, 225, 229, 232, 234, 235, 245, 252, 253-258, 301, 332, 334, 369, 370, 373, 388-389, 404, 455
Oxus (Amu Darya), 669
Oxyrhynchus (Behnesa), 498

P

Pachomius, St., Egyptian founder of first monastery (292?-346?), 657
pacifism, 538
Pacuvius, Marcus, tragic dramatist (220-130 B.C.), 98
Padua (*anc.* Patavium), 11, 78, 250, 455
Padus, *see* Po
Paestum (Pesto), 3, 35, 455
Paeta, Arria, wife of Caecina Paetus (1st century), 371
Paetus, Caecina, aristocrat (?-42), 371
Pahlavi, 529
painting, Etruscan, 6, 10-11; under Rome, 82, 92, 233, 278, 310, 338, 339, 345, 349, 351-355, 358, 359, 374, 376, 386, 414, 418, 442, (Pompeian), 459, 477, 511-512, 625, 634, 662; Christian, 601
Pais, Ettore, Italian historian (b. 1856), 15†
palaces, *see* mansions
Palatine, 12, 13, 65, 162, 173, 263, 280, 340, 341, 344, 358, 359, 360, 361, 635
Pales, 59
Palestine, 170, 505, 508-509, 510, 522, 530, 532, 533, 535, 537, 543, 544, 546, 547-549, 559, 587, 615, 617, 632, 644
Palladio, Andrea, Italian architect (1518-1580), 356
Palladium, 61, 240, 663
Pallas, treasurer of Claudius (fl. 1st century), 270-273, 543
Pallas Athene, 240, 663
Palma, Aulus Cornelius, general of Trajan (?-118), 414
Palma, 470
Palmyra (*Bib.* Tadmor), 329, 419, 454, 508, 511-512, 529, 636, 638, 669
Pamphilus, Bishop of Caesarea (?-310), 662
pamphlets, 159
Pamphylia, 218, 582
Pan, 238-239, 353
Panaetius of Rhodes, Stoic philosopher (ca. 180-ca. 110 B.C.), 97, 164, 490, 514
Pandateria (Vandotena), 231, 264, 279
Panathenaic games, 487
Panegyric (Pliny the Younger), 433
Panhellenia, 487
Pannonia, 217, 218, 231, 429, 480, 620, 627, 629, 655, 670
Panormus (Palermo), 45, 464
Pansa, Caius Vibius, consul (?-43 B.C.), 201
Pantagruel, 299
Panthea, beauty of Antioch (2nd century), 428

pantheism, Marcus Aurelius', 444; in Stoicism, 490, 497

Pantheon, 220, 290, 356, 359, 361, 420-421, 661

Panticapaeum (Kerch), 518

pantomime,74,99,290,378-379,380,381,437,489

paper, 159, 498, 499

paper currency, equivalent of in Carthage, 40

Paphlagonia, 418, 519

Paphnutius, Egyptian Bishop of Upper Thebes (fl. 4th century), 660†

Paphos, 582

Papia Poppaea, lex, 224

Papias, Bishop of Hierapolis and writer (fl. 2nd century), 555-556, 592

Papinian (Aemilius Papinianus), jurist (?-212), 392, 510, 621, 634, 635

papyrus, 159, 498

Paraclete, *see* Holy Spirit

paradise, *see* heaven

Paradise Lost (Milton), 244

Parallel Lives (Plutarch), 483-484

parchment, 159, 529

Paré, Ambroise, father of French surgery (1517-1590), 505

Parentalia, 65

Paris, 278, 487, 516

Paris, famous pantomime actor (fl. 1st century), 437

Paris (*anc.* Lutetia), 100, 324, 412, 471*, 474

Parisii, 471*, 474

Parliament, Houses of, 635

Parma, 11, 455

Parmenides of Elea, Greek philosopher (fl. 6th century B.C.), 455

Paros, 322, 411

Parousia (Second Appearance), 591, 603-604

Parseeism, *see* Zoroastrianism

Parthenius, Roman freedman (fl. 1st century), 316

Parthenon, 328, 348, 359

Parthia, 131, 178-179, 181, 194, 197, 205-206, 217, 253, 275, 322, 329, 337, 350*, 366, 390, 412-413, 414, 428, 448, 508, 512, 513, 528-530, 531, 546, 622, 623, 641

Pasiphaë, 284, 352, 385

Pasiteles, Greek artist in Rome (fl. 60-30 B.C.), 349

Passover, Feast of the, 542, 559, 570-571, 579, 588*

pastoral poetry, 235, 236

Patavium, *see* Padua

paterfamilias, see father

pater patriae, 221

Patmos, 592

Patrae (Patras), 125, 325, 486, 546

patricians, *see* aristocracy

patriotism, 67, 72, 74, 85, 242, 251-252, 300, 650, 668

Patroclus, 381

patronage, 233-234, 316-317, 333, 335, 339, 374, 415, 423, 621, 661

patronus, 22

Paul, St. (Saul), apostle to the Gentiles (10?-64?), 271, 282, 325, 404, 470, 492, 513, 515, 554-556, 559, 568†, 570*, 571, 573, 575, 576, 578, 579-592, 604, 605, 646

Paul, Epistles of St., 553, 555, 579, 585, 587-591, 592, 605

Paul of Samosata, Syrian heretic (fl. 2nd century), 605

Paul the Hermit, Egyptian Christian monk (fl. 3rd and 4th centuries), 657

Paul-Louis, 642

Paul and Virginia (Saint-Pierre), 637

Paulina, Pompeia, wife of Seneca (1st century), 301, 306-307, 371

Paulinus, Caius Suetonius, governor and general (fl. 1st century), 271, 476

Paulus, Heinrich Eberhard Gottlob, German Protestant theologian (1761-1851), 553

Paulus, Julius, jurist (fl. 2nd and 3rd centuries), 392, 621, 634

Paulus, Lucius Aemilius, consul and general (?-216 B.C.), 50, 86, 92

Paulus Macedonicus, Lucius Aemilius, general (229-160 B.C.), 86, 92, 96, 101

Pauly, August, German classical philologist (1796-1845), 504*

Pausanias, Greek traveler and topographer (fl. 2nd century), 324

Pausanias, Greek sophist (fl. 2nd century), 506

Pavia (*anc.* Ticinum), 49

Pax, 287, 348

Pax Augusta, 232

Pax Romana, 194, 217, 218, 232, 325, 424, 473, 631, 670

Peace, Goddess of, *see* Pax

Peace, Temple of, 358

Pedanius Secundus, prefect (fl. 1st century), 366, 397

pederasty, 158, 282, 369, 398, 408

Pedius, Quintus, painter (fl. reign of Augustus), 352

Pedum (Gallicano), 252

Peel, Sir Robert, English statesman (1788-1850), 324

Peisistratus, Athenian tyrant (605-527 B.C.), 418

Peleus, 157

"Peleus and Thetis" (Catullus), 157

Pelicitas, 342

Pella, 483, 530, 577

Peloponnesian War, 383

Peloponnesus, 322, 454, 486, 497

penalties, legal, 403-404

penance, 600, 652

Penates, 7, 58, 69

Penelope, 256

Pennsylvania Station (in New York), 360*

Pentateuch, 535, 547

Pentecost, 543, 579, 585

Pentelicus, 487

Pentheus, 178, 531

Pera, Brutus, aristocrat (?-264 B.C.), 382

Peraea, 535, 560

Peregrinus, Greek Cynic philosopher (?-165), 489

Perennis, Praetorian Prefect (?-185), 447

perfumes, in Carthage, 41; under Rome, 132, 134, 144, 266, 286, 298, 328-329, 337, 342, 345, 376, 377, 438, 498

Perga (Murtana), 582

Pergamum (Bergama), 86, 94, 95, 114, 312, 334, 348, 418, 430, 504, 505, 515, 516, 518, 534, 592

Pergamum, library of, 635

Periclean Age, 258, 351, 370, 418, 522

Pericles, Athenian statesman (495?-429 B.C.), 214, 428, 442

Perinthus, 483

Peripatetic, see Aristotelian

Periplus of the Erythrean Sea, 326

peristylium, 343, 345

Perpenna (or Perperna) Vento, Marcus, general (?-72 B.C.), 137

Perpetua, Carthaginian Christian martyr (?-203), 649

Perpetual Edict, see Praetorian Perpetual Edict

Persephone, 525; Temple of, 516

Perseus, last King of Macedon (reigned 178-168 B.C.), 86, 88, 96

Perseus (mythology), 256

Perseus and Andromeda, 349

Persia, 77, 92*, 212, 320, 323, 329, 500, 524, 526, 528-530, 540, 595, 605, 608, 623, 627, 628, 629, 638, 639, 641, 644, 650, 653

Persian Gulf, 413

Persiles y Sigismunda (Cervantes), 637

Persius Flaccus, Aulus, satirical poet (34-62), 437

Pertinax (Publius Helvius Pertinax), Roman emperor (?-193), 333, 620, 633, 665, 668

Peru, 409, 600*

Perusia (Perugia), 6, 205, 454

perversion, see abortion, birth control, bisexuality, homosexuality, incest, pederasty

Pervigilium Veneris, 637-638

Pessinus, 94, 513

Peter, St., also called Simon or Simon Peter, apostle (?-64?), 404, 555, 557, 563, 569, 575-579, 581-582, 583, 587, 590, 591-592, 604, 617, 618, 646

Peter, The First Epistle General of, 575, 577-578

Petra, 508, 602

Petrarch (Francesco Petrarca), Italian poet (1304-1374), 307

Petronia, lex, 397

Petronius Arbiter, Gaius, author (?-66), 60, 247*, 276, 282, 295, 296-299, 312, 317, 319, 333, 336, 347, 363, 368, 401, 435, 466, 636, 637

Phaedo (Plato), 190

Phaedra, 256

Phaëthon, 256

Phainomena (Aratus), 584*

phallic worship, 60, 66, 458

Phanuel, 542

Phaon, freedman (fl. 1st century), 283

Pharaohs, 5, 226, 266, 507

Pharisees, 530, 532, 536-539, 545, 547, 562, 566, 567-570, 576, 579-580, 586

Pharnaces, King of Pontus (?-47 B.C.), 188, 519

Pharos, 188, 207

Pharsalia (Lucan), 296

Pharsalus (Pharsala), battle in 48 B.C., 185-186, 189, 208

Pheidias, Greek sculptor (ca. 490-432 B.C.), 96, 338, 354, 412, 442, 459, 486, 522

Philadelphia, 508, 535

Phile, municipal officer of Priene (fl. 1st century B.C.), 514

Philemon, Greek comic dramatist (361-263 B.C.), 99

Philemon, The Epistle of Paul to, 587*

Philemon (mythology), 256

Philip II, King of Macedon (382-336 B.C.), 483

Philip V, King of Macedon (220-179 B.C.), 51, 85, 86

Philip, Asiarch (fl. 155), 648

Philip, King of the Jews (fl. 1st century), 535

Philip the Arab (Marcus Julius Philippus "Arabs"), Roman emperor (reigned 244-249), 628

Philippi, battle in 42 B.C., 203, 221, 358, 546, 583, 585

Philippians, The Epistle of Paul the Apostle to the, 587*, 591

"Philippics," Cicero's, 201, 202

Philippopolis, 483

Philo Judaeus, Jewish Hellenistic philosopher (ca. 20 B.C.-ca. 54 A.D.), 424, 500, 546, 589, 594-595, 604, 611, 614, 658

Philodemus of Gadara, Epicurean philosopher and poet (fl. 1st century B.C.), 510

Philosophus Platonicus, 467

philosophy, 93, 95-97, 102, 104, 108, 113, 133, 135, 136, 141, 144, 146-154, 163-166, 168, 190, 196, 200, 203, 205, 231, 233, 244, 250, 251, 259, 267, 269, 274, 286, 292, 295-296, 297-298, 299-307, 308, 310, 314, 324, 356, 367-368, 370, 373, 376, 388-389, 392, 393, 406, 415, 417, 421, 424, 425-428, 431, 432, 435, 438, 441, 443, 449, 465, 467, 485-497, 500-502, 505-506, 509, 512, 513, 514, 515, 521-522, 584, 594-595, 604, 607-615, 620, 621, 629, 630, 633, 635-636, 661, 671; Lucretius', 146-154; Cicero's, 163-166; Horace's, 248-250; Ovid's, 256; Pliny's, 310-311; Marcus Aurelius', 425, 431, 443-446; Plutarch's, 485-486; Epictetus', 490-494; Sextus Empiricus', 494-495; Lucian's, 495-497; Plotinus', 607-611

Philostratus, Flavius, Greek rhetorician and biographer (fl. first half of 3rd century), 488, 504, 513, 515, 526, 621

Phoceans, 7

Phoebe, servant of Julia (1st century B.C.), 231

Phoebus, see Apollo

Phoenicia, 39, 41, 48, 105, 204, 240, 465, 468, 488, 500, 505, 510-511, 546, 621

Phormio (Terence), 101

Phrygia, 94, 133, 147, 366, 472, 490, 513, 523, 528, 583, 595, 605, 649

Phyllis, 247

Physeos, Peri, 148

physical characteristics, of Etruscans, 6; of Romans, 69-70, 349-351, 372, 415

physicians, *see* medicine

physics, 504

Picenum, 182

Pictones, 471*

Pierson, Dutch biblical scholar, 554

piety (*pietas*), 57, 58, 59, 60, 61, 64, 67, 148, 149, 162, 238-242, 250, 251, 265, 357, 366, 371, 390, 423, 425, 444, 447, 467, 484, 492-494, 497, 526, 530, 537, 599, 625, 663

Pilate, Pontius, Procurator of Judea (fl. first half of 1st century), 281, 571-573

Pillars of Hercules, 40

pinacotheca, 343

Pincian hill, 132, 340

piracy, 43, 47, 78, 112, 139-140, 167-168, 170, 211, 219, 275, 325, 632

Piraeus, 630

Pisa (*anc.* Pisae), 78, 454

Pisa, in the Peloponnesus, 454

Pisidia, 513, 582

Piso family, 249

Piso, Caius Calpurnius, conspirator (?-65), 266, 282, 296, 306, 316, 371

Piso, Cnaeus Calpurnius, governor (?-20 A.D.), 262

Piso, Lucius Calpurnius, politician and governor (fl. 1st century B.C.), 161, 172, 174

Pistoia (*anc.* Pistoria), 144

Placentia (Piacenza), 47, 78, 454, 455

Place Vendée, 412

plague, 428-429, 432, 448, 638, 649, 666, 667

Plancus, Lucius Munatius, governor (fl. 1st century B.C.), 233

Plantianus, Praetorian Prefect (fl. 3rd century), 666

plastic surgery, 313

Plataea, 482, 483

Plato, Greek philosopher (427-347 B.C.), 72, 96, 136, 164, 165, 180, 196, 208, 243, 304, 389, 421, 427, 485, 489, 494, 497, 501-502, 541, 607, 608, 610, 611, 634, 658

Platonic (Academic) philosophy, 95, 432, 489, 540, 588, 608, 611, 614, 635, 658

Platonopolis, 608

Plautus, Titus Maccius, comic dramatist (ca. 254-184 B.C.), 7, 65, 70, 90, 93, 98, 99-101, 102, 234, 455

Plebeian Games, 381

plebeians, 21-31, 35, 37, 44, 80, 90, 93, 95, 98, 99, 102, 111-208, 216, 243, 252, 282, 286, 297, 332-333, 335, 339-340, 341-342, 351, 384, 438, 446

Pliny the Elder (Caius Plinius Secundus), naturalist and encyclopedist (23-79), 3, 10, 60, 269, 295, 308-311, 312, 313, 319, 320, 325, 327, 328, 337, 347, 373, 439, 453, 456, 457, 473, 507, 516

Pliny the Younger (Caius Plinius Caecilius Secundus), author and orator (61-114?), 252, 289, 295, 309, 311, 314, 315, 318, 320, 344, 368, 371, 387, 402, 409, 411, 433, 435, 437, 438, 439-441, 442, 454, 463, 520, 521, 554, 599, 648

Plotina, Pompeia, wife of Trajan (fl. 1st and 2nd centuries), 409, 414, 442

Plotinus, Egyptian Neoplatonist (203-270?), 497, 501, 514, 608-611, 614-615, 635, 658

plumbing, 343

Plutarch, Greek biographer (46?-120?), 41, 72, 85, 113, 119-120, 124, 126, 127, 137, 140, 185, 196, 197*, 304, 324, 367, 403, 424, 463, 483-486, 487, 497, 546

Pluto, 63, 84

Pneumatica (Hero), 504

Po (*anc.* Padus), 4, 36, 37, 49, 120, 158, 235, 250, 320, 454, 455

"Poem of Consolation to Flavius Ursus" (Statius), 335

Poetelia, lex, 400

poetry, 74-75, 82, 97-102, 135, 146-158, 159, 233-250, 252-258, 277-279, 289, 291, 295-296, 315-318, 354, 369, 370, 376, 379, 386, 388-389, 415, 422, 437-439, 440, 456, 486-487, 509-510, 621, 637-638; Horace on, 249; *see also* comedy, drama, epic poetry, lyric poetry, pastoral poetry, satire, tragedy

Poggio Bracciolini, Gian Francesco, Italian scholar (1380-1459), 154

pogroms, 544, 546, 548

Poitiers (*anc.* Limonum), 471*

Pola, 455

Poland, 406

Polemo (Polemon), Antonius, Greek sophist and rhetorician (fl. 2nd century), 515-516

police, 216, 220, 429, 668-669

Politta, suicide in Nero's reign (1st century), 371

Pollentia (Pollensa, Spain), 470

Pollentia (Pollenza, Italy), 322

pollice verso, 386-387

Pollio, Asinius, orator, poet, and historian (76 B.C.-A.D. 4), 159, 161, 236

Pollio, Vedius, friend of Augustus (?-15 B.C.), 376

Pollux, 35, 62

Polybius, Greek historian (204?-122? B.C.), 3, 25, 34, 36, 41, 44, 46, 51, 71, 86, 90, 93, 96, 97, 160, 251, 514, 520, 521

Polycarp, Saint, Bishop of Smyrna and martyr (69?-155), 588, 617, 648

Polycleitus, Greek sculptor (fl. 452-412 B.C.), 96, 350, 355

polygamy, in Parthia, 529; in Judea, 534

Polygnotus, Greek painter (fl. 465 B.C.), 351

Pomona, 59

Pompeia, third wife of Caesar (1st century B.C.), 168, 172

Pompeii, 10, 35, 162, 289, 321-322, 338, 347, 352-354, 367, 370, 455, 456, 457-460, 546, 601, 634

Pompey, Sextus (Sextus Pompeius Magnus), commander (?-35 B.C.), 189, 194, 205, 219, 237

Pompey the Great (Cnaeus Pompeius Magnus), general and triumvir (106-48 B.C.), 125, 128, 129, 130, 132, 133, 134, 136, 137-140, 163, 168, 170-186, 188-190, 194-195, 197, 199, 205, 211, 212, 214, 278, 293, 296, 340, 346, 347, 349, 350, 360, 365, 373, 391, 419, 448, 482, 508, 514, 517, 519, 524, 528, 530-531, 632

Pomponii, Roman clan, 255

Pontia (Ponza), 264

pontifex maximus, 63, 388, 619, 672; Caesar as, 147, 170, 172, 191, 193; Augustus as, 225-227; Hadrian as, 415; Constantine as, 656

pontiffs, 63, 66

Pontine marshes, 193, 311†, 410, 666

Pontus, 122, 124, 132, 140, 170, 188, 216, 320, 516-519, 520, 528, 578, 603, 629

Pope, the, 11, 613, 617-619, 672

Pope, Alexander, English poet (1688-1744), 249*, 671

Popilia, Via, 78

Popilius, see Laenas, Caius Popilius

Poppaea, see Sabina, Poppaea

population, of Rome, in 560 B.C., 15; of Carthage, 40; of Italy south of Rubicon, 81; of Rome, in 2nd and 1st centuries B.C., 81, 90, 126, 159, 193; under the Principate, 221-222, 363-366, 436; under the monarchy, 665-666; of Italy, 461; of Sicily, 464; of Germany, 218; of Egypt, 499-500; of Syria, 510, 512; in Asia Minor, 513, 515, 520; of Palestine, 535

Populonia, 6

populus Romanus, 21

Porch, the, 75

Porphyry, Syrian Neoplatonist philosopher (233-304?), 608, 635, 636*

Porsena, Lars, chief magistrate of Clusium (fl. 6th century B.C.), 17, 35

Porta Capena, 340

Porta Nigra, 474

portents, see omens

Portia, wife of Brutus (1st century B.C.), 196, 197

Portia (in The Merchant of Venice), 303

Portico of Octavia, 290

Portland, third Duke of, Wm. Henry Cavendish-Bentinck (1738-1809), 347†

Portland, sixth Duke of, Wm. John Cavendish-Bentinck (1857-1943), 347†

Portland Vase, 347

ports, see harbors

Portugal, see Lusitania

Portuguese (language), 73

Portus Romanus, 270, 325, 453

Poseidon, 63, 500

Poseidonia, see Paestum

Poseidonius, Greek Stoic philosopher (135?-51? B.C.),141,164,308,471,472,490,503,514,521

post, 271, 323-324

Postumian Way, 78

Postumius, Aulus, dictator (496 B.C.), 35

Postumus, pretender in Gaul (reigned 258-267), 629, 638

Postumus (in Horace), 250

Postumus (in Juvenal), 438

Pothinus, vizier of Ptolemy XII (fl. 1st century B.C.), 186, 187

Pothinus, Bishop of Lyons (87-177), 649

Poussin, Nicolas, French painter (1594-1665), 353

praefectus urbi, 216

Praeneste (Palestrina), 11, 121, 125, 454

Praetorian Guard, 29*, 216, 263-264, 268, 269, 272-273, 275, 283-285, 286, 293, 340, 384, 407-408, 427, 620-621, 625, 628, 634, 639, 653, 669

Praetorian Perpetual Edict, 392, 416

praetors, 24, 28, 29, 32, 125, 191; praetorian law, 57

prandium, 70

Praxiteles, Greek sculptor (385-ca. 320 B.C.), 96, 338, 355, 459

prayer, 64, 67, 75, 311, 444, 495-496, 523, 525, 537, 547, 568, 598, 599, 650, 651, 667

predestination, 592

prefects, 216-217

Priam, 12

Priapeia, 369

Priapus, 60, 254, 354, 625

prices, 184, 331, 632, 642-643

Priene, 514

priests, 63-64, 94, 226, 268, 291-292, 348, 349, 388, 390, 425, 498-499, 522-526, 527, 531, 532, 533, 535-539, 545, 547, 567, 568, 570-571, 576, 581, 586, 588*, 596, 598, 600-601, 606, 615, 651, 656, 657, 660†, 669, 670

Prima Porta, 350, 354

princeps senatus, 214, 216, 260

Principate, the, 34, 209-621

printing, 346-347

Priscilla, Montanist heretic (2nd century), 605

Priscus, Helvidius, Stoic philosopher (fl. 1st century), 279, 282, 286, 371, 426, 441

Priscus, Marius, governor in Africa (fl. 1st and 2nd centuries), 441

Probus (Marcus Aurelius Probus), Roman emperor (reigned 276-282), 638-639, 665

proconsuls, see governors

procurators, 216-217, 271, 281

Prodicus, Greek philosopher (fl. 5th century B.C.), 486

proletariat, 77, 90, 111, 113, 116-118, 119, 130, 142-145, 180, 189-192, 287, 333, 465, 596, 622, 633, 666

Prometheus Unbound (Shelley), 635

promiscuity, in Carthage, 41; under Rome, 54, 65, 94, 147, (Caesar's) 168, (Julia's) 230-231, 232, 254, 288, 290, 369, 590, 599

Propertius, Sextus, poet (49-15 B.C.), 155, 234, 235, 252, 253, 455 property, 57, 58, 68, 76-77, 113, 118, 125, 126, 130, 160, 172, 189, 205, 211, 212, 220-221, 257, 269, 370, 396, 397, 398, 399-400, 407, 479, 487, 650, 651, 654-655, 657, 658, 670

prophecy, see soothsaying

prophets, 559, 562, 564, 567, 568, 576

propitiation, 64, 65

Propontis (Sea of Marmara), 516

proscriptions, 125-126, 128, 130, 132, 141, 146-147, 167, 170, 185, 201-202, 212, 371, 373, 447-448, 628

prose, 103-104, 108, 113, 158, 160-166, 234, 250-252, 258, 295-315, 319, 433-437, 439-446, 467-468, 483-486, 490-497, 505-507, 514, 520-522, 546, 555-595, 606-616, 635-637, 662-663, 671

Proserpina, 84; Rape of, 256

prostitution, in Etruria, 7; under Rome, 68, 89, 134, 135, 222-223, 244, 245, 267, 272, 276, 285, 290, 297, 313, 317, 324, 328, 342, 352, 354, 369,378,382,458,487,488,512,522,562,569,627

prostration, 269, 280

Protagoras, Greek philosopher (481?-411 B.C.), 494

Protestantism, 592

Protogenes, Greek painter (fl. 330-300 B.C.), 338, 352, 355

Provence, 472

Proverbs, 540, 541

Providence, Cicero on, 164; Seneca on, 304; Marcus Aurelius on, 444; see also God

Providence, On (Seneca), 302

provinces, 87-88, 90, 107, 112, 114, 116, 118, 121, 125, 126, 129-130, 132, 140, 142, 171, 175, 177-178, 179, 190, 192, 193-194, 196, 200, 201, 205-206, 208, 211, 213, 214, 215, 216-217, 220-221, 226, 228, 235, 261, 270-271, 275, 285-288, 293, 302-303, 319, 320, 322, 330, 333, 350*, 373, 377, 380, 404-406, 408, 410, 411, 413, 417-420, 423-424, 427, 434, 438, 441, 448-449, 453, 462-549, 619, 621, 626-627, 632-633, 635, 640-645, 651, 659, 661, 666, 668-669, 672

Prusa (Brusa), 516, 521, 629

Psalms, 559, 572-573

Psalms of Solomon, 540

Psyche, 353, 468

Ptolemais (Menchieh), 498, 502

Ptolemies, 186, 187, 208, 226, 327, 344, 498, 500, 507, 631*, 641

Ptolemy VI Philometor, King of Egypt (181-146 B.C.), 186

Ptolemy XI Auletes or Neos Dionysos, King of Egypt (reigned 80-51 B.C.), 186-187

Ptolemy XII, King of Egypt (reigned 51-47 B.C.), 186-188

Ptolemy XIII, King of Egypt (reigned 47-43 B.C.), 188, 189

Ptolemy, Claudius, Greco-Egyptian astronomer, geographer, and geometer (fl. 127-151), 502-503, 507

publicans, 126, 129, 139, 140, 141, 171, 192, 196, 340, 463, 556, 562, 563, 569

public debt, 79, 220, 287, 330, 337

public lands, see ager publicus

Publicola, Publius Valerius, consul (?-503 B.C.), 16

public urinals, 287

public works, 88, 103, 111, 176, 192, 213, 216, 219-220, 225, 270, 274, 287, 290-291, 326, 336, 409, 410, 418-419, 423, 461, 499, 627, 633, 639, 641, 668

Publilia, wife of Cicero (fl. 1st century B.C.), 163

Pumpkinification (Seneca), see Apocolocyntosis

Punchinello (Punch), 74

Punic, 621

Punic Wars, 43, 91, 218, 618; First, 43-46, 70, 74, 78, 330, 469; Second, 48-54, 70, 80, 105, 252, 455, 469; Third, 105-108

punishment, in the early Republic, 57

Pupienus (Marcus Clodius Pupienus Maximus), Roman emperor (?-238), 628

purgatory, 241-242, 243, 485, 497, 615

purification, 29, 63, 64, 65, 67, 524-525, 527, 560, 586, 599, 607, 609, 618; see also baptism

Puritans, 535

Puteoli (Pozzuoli), 78, 162, 218, 322, 324, 325, 326, 330, 346, 389, 456, 457, 546, 602

Pydna (battle, 168 B.C.), 86, 96

Pylades of Cilicia, artist in pantomime (fl. end of 1st century B.C.), 378

Pyramids, 328, 499

Pyramus, 256

Pyrenees, 49, 119, 470

Pyrrha, 247

Pyrrho, Greek philosopher (365-275 B.C.), 494, 495

Pyrrhus, King of Epirus (318-272 B.C.), 28, 29, 37, 38, 71, 92, 98, 104

Pythagoras, Greek philosopher (fl. 540-510 B.C.), 98, 165, 246, 390, 497, 507, 525, 607, 608*

Pythagoreanism, 242, 301, 343, 390, 525-526, 537, 609

Pytheas, Greek navigator (fl. ca. 350 B.C.), 475-476

Pythian games, 283, 486-487

Q

quacks, 312

Quadi, 429, 431, 432

Quadratus, Christian apologist (fl. 2nd century), 611

Quaestiones (Papinian), 634

Quaestiones Naturales (Seneca), 303, 307-308, 311

quaestors, 28, 29*, 191

Quebec, 406

Quietus, Quintus Lusius, general of Trajan (?-118), 413, 414

Quintilian (Marcus Fabius Quintilianus), rhetorician (ca. 40-118?), 103, 295, 299, 302, 313-315, 316, 319, 356, 367, 380, 403, 439, 440

Quirinal, 12*, 317, 340, 411

Quirinius, Publius Sulpicius, governor of Syria (?-21 A.D.), 558
Quirinus, 13
Quirites, 13

R

rabbis, 537-539, 545, 547-548, 564
Rabelais, François, French writer (1490?-1553), 69, 100
Rabirius, architect (fl. 1st century), 345
Racine, Jean Baptiste, French dramatist, (1639-1699), 302, 412
Raetia, 217-218, 429, 480
Ram, 298
Raphia (Rafa), 508, 530
Ravenna, 11, 78, 325, 326, 410, 455
readings, 234, 296
real estate, see property
realism (art), 339, 349, 350, 351, 353, 361, 412, 442-443, 459-460, 634-635, 671
Reate (Rieti), 102, 286, 288
Red Sea (anc. Sinus Arabicus), 325, 413, 499, 507, 508, 516, 529
Reformation, 592
Refutation of All Heresies (Hippolytus), 618
Regulus, Marcus Atilius, general (?-ca. 250 B.C.), 44-45, 183
Regulus (in Pliny), 438
Reid, James Smith, English classical scholar (1846-1926), 665
Reimarus, Hermann Samuel, German scholar (1694-1768), 553
reincarnation, 242, 390, 497, 525, 526, 609
reliefs, 229, 338, 347-349, 361, 412, 427, 442-443, 453, 455, 474, 601, 635, 662
religion, in Etruria, 7-8, 18; in Carthage, 41-42; in Germany, 479; before the Principate, 13, 18, 30, 31, 56, 58-67, 72, 93-97, 102, 104, 108, 157, 163-165, 193, 214; under the Principate, 222, 225-227, 238-239, 248, 251, 256-257, 259, 266, 269, 291-292, 299, 335, 354, 365-366, 371, 372, 388-390, 426, 429, 443, 449, 486, 488, 497, 512, 515, 522-527, 535-542, 550-619; under the monarchy, 625, 628, 639, 640, 646-664, 667-668; Judaism, 535-542; Christianity, 550-619, 646-664, 667-668; Lucretius on, 147-154; Varro on, 159-160; Cicero on, 161, 164-165; Caesar and, 193; in Virgil, 242-243; in Horace, 248-250; in Livy, 251, 256-257; Nero's, 276; Domitian's, 292; Hadrian's, 415; Antoninus Pius', 423; Marcus Aurelius', 425-426, 444; Tacitus', 435-436; in The Golden Ass, 467-468; Plutarch's, 484-485; Demonax on, 489; Epictetus', 492-494; Philo's 501-502; Dion Chrysostomus on, 522
Rembrandt van Rijn (Rembrandt Harmenszoon van Rijn), Dutch painter (1606-1669), 355
Remedia Amoris (Ovid), 255
Remi, 471*
Remus, twin of Romulus (8th century B.C.), 12, 82, 241

Renaissance, 4, 95, 243, 258, 307, 352, 353, 356, 406, 505, 661, 672
Renan, Ernest, French Orientalist and critic (1823-1892), 425, 554, 556
Republic, the Roman, 15-208, 213, 214, 242, 251, 260, 261, 264, 286, 330, 335, 352, 373, 374, 379, Chap. XVIII, passim, 436, 442, 462, 469
Republic (Cicero), see Republica, De
Republic (Plato), 608
Republic, Plato's, 427
Republica, De (Cicero), 163*, 165
republicanism, of Cato the Younger, 135, 136
Rerum Natura, De (Lucretius), 148-154, 239
Re Rustica, De (Cato the Elder), 103-104
Re Rustica, De (Columella), 319
Re Rustica, De (Varro), see Country Life, On
Resemblances, 243
Responsa (Papinian), 634
Resting Mercury, 459
resurrection, 94, 523-526, 573-574, 575, 585, 592, 595, 601, 604*, 605, 607
Revelation of St. John the Divine, The, 592-595, 616
revolution, 108, 111-208, 391, 604*, 631, 666
Rhea Silvia, mother of Romulus and Remus (8th century B.C.), 12
Rhegium (Reggio), 35, 44, 231, 377, 455
Rheims (anc. Durocortorum), 324, 471*
rhetoric, 29, 95, 103, 141, 160-162, 167, 168, 169, 236, 244, 250, 251, 258, 287, 295-296, 301, 313, 317, 324, 367-368, 423, 425, 434, 436, 437, 438, 441, 465, 467, 470, 486-490, 510, 512, 514, 515, 521-522, 612, 661
Rhine (anc. Rhenus), 6, 118, 174-176, 178, 179, 194, 217-218, 291, 417, 431, 441, 470, 474, 475, 478, 479, 480, 523, 627, 628, 631*, 639, 653
Rhineland, 479, 480
Rhodes, 86, 96, 97, 105, 133, 139, 141, 168, 187, 203, 231, 259, 329, 368, 388, 418, 462, 490, 512, 514, 516, 534, 588*, 630
Rhone (anc. Rhodanus), 6, 470, 474
Richardson, Samuel, English novelist (1689-1761), 637
Rimini, see Ariminum
Rio Tinto, see Minas de Rio Tinto
ritual, 64, 65, 67, 94, 147-148, 149, 226, 242, 354, 388, 389, 425, 523-525, 527, 536, 548, 575, 578-579, 582, 595, 599, 602, 618-619, 626, 656
roads, 77-78, 116, 193, 219, 291, 324, 326-327, 340-341, 343, 410, 411, 417, 453, 464, 465, 466, 469, 473, 477, 480, 499, 512, 579, 602, 627, 632, 671
Robertson, John Mackinnon, British journalist and scholar (1856-1933), 554
Roland de la Platière, Marie Jeanne, French Girondist (1754-1793), 484
Roma, 381, 388, 389
Roman Catholics, 66
Romance languages, 73, 671
Romanesque architecture, 421
Roman Games, 381
Romans, The Epistle of Paul the Apostle to the, 554, 587*

Romanticism, 249, 258

Rome, founding of, 11-13; city of, in 2nd and 3rd centuries B.C., 81-82, 92-93; under Augustus, 219-220; burning and rebuilding, 280-281; fire and plague, 289; Flavian Rome, 338-362; under Hadrian, 420-421

Rome, Council of, 618

Rome, History of (Dion Cassius Cocceianus), 636

Romeo, 255

Romulus, first King of Rome (8th century B.C.), 12, 13, 15†, 18, 21, 82, 120, 136, 145, 233, 241, 359, 636

Romulus, House of, 4, 359

Romulus Augustulus (Flavius Momyllus Romulus Augustus), Roman emperor in the West (?-476), 670

Roscius Gallus, Quintus, comedian (?-62 B.C.), 160, 378

Rostovtzeff, Michael, American historian (b. 1870), 642

rostrum, 340

rotation of crops, 76, 320

Rothschild, Meyer Anselm, Jewish banker (1743-1812), 131

Rouen (*anc.* Rotomagus), 324

Rousseau, Jean Jacques, French philosopher (1712-1778), 152, 367, 440

Rubens, Peter Paul, Flemish painter (1577-1640), 354

Rubicon (Fiumicino), 48, 81, 163, 182, 654

Rufus, Caesetius, proscribed by Antony (?-43 B.C.), 202

Rufus, Corellius, friend of Pliny the Younger (?-96?), 311

Rufus, Musonius, Stoic philosopher (fl. 1st century), 282, 300-301, 490, 521

Rufus, Virginius, governor and guardian of Pliny the Younger (14-97), 439

Rufus of Ephesus, Greek physician (fl. 98-117), 505

Ruins of Empire (Volney), 553

Rumania, 410, 480

Rumanian, 73

Russia, 112, 218, 326, 448, 478, 520, 528, 669

Rusticus, Quintus Junius, Stoic philosopher (fl. 2nd century), 425

Rutuli, 15, 240

S

Saba (*Bib.* Sheba), 508

Sabbath, 598, 599

Sabellians, 605

Sabidius, 318

Sabina, Poppaea, wife of Nero (?-65), 277, 279-282, 366, 372-373

Sabina, Vivia, wife of Hadrian (?-138), 414, 419, 442, 624

Sabine (language), 274

Sabines, 5, 12, 13, 14, 21, 35, 244, 246, 254, 286, 288; rape of women, 13

Sabinus, Poppaeus, accused of conspiracy (?-27 A.D.), 264

Sabrata, 465

Saccas, Ammonius, Alexandrian Neoplatonist (fl. 3rd century), 608, 614

sacraments, seven, 600, 602, 658

Sacra Via (Sacred Way), 341

Sacred History (Euhemerus), 98

Sacred Mount, 22

sacrifice, in Etruria, 7; under Rome, 52, 59, 60, 63-64, 65, 76, 83, 100, 104, 149, 164, 197, 239, 265, 290, 292, 354, 381, 388, 429, 444, 522, 524-525, 526, 531, 533, 547, 570, 583, 588, 599-600, 648, 651

Sadducees, 536-538, 545, 562, 576

sadism, Caligula's, 267

Saguntum (Sagunto), 47, 48

Sahara, 40, 217, 448, 464, 466

St. Barbara, Baths of, 474

St. Mark's, in Venice, 351

St. Peter's, in Rome, 18, 420, 421, 578, 635, 661

Saint-Pierre, Jacques Henri Bernardin de, French writer of romance (1737-1814), 637

St. Quentin (*anc.* Augusta Veromanduorum), 474

Sais, 498

Salamis (in Cyprus), 196

Salamis (island), naval battle in 480 B.C., 383

Salaria, Via, 283

Salernum (Salerno), 456

Salii, 63

Sallust (Caius Sallustius Crispus), historian (86-35 B.C.), 42, 123, 142-144, 146, 160, 190, 233, 340, 436, 455, 557

"Sallust, House of," 353

Salome, daughter of Herodias (1st century), 560

Salome, visitor at the tomb of Jesus, 573

Salome Alexandra, Queen of the Jews (reigned 78-69 B.C.), 530

Salona (Spalato), 480

salons, 113, 131-132, 135, 230, 234, 279, 621

Salvius, leader of slave rebellion (end of 2nd century B.C.), 121

Samaria, 530, 576, 577, 604, 611

Samaria-Sebaste (Sebustieh), 508

Samaritans, 535, 567

Samaritis, 535

Samnites, 35, 37, 38, 43, 51, 125, 519

Samnium, 455

Samos, 133, 139

Samosata, 322, 495, 513

Samothrace, 139

sanctuary, 398, 518

Sanhedrin, 536, 539, 545, 547-548, 568, 570-571, 576, 580, 586

sanitation, *see* sewage system

San Lorenzo, Church of, 427*

San Lorenzo outside the Walls, Church of, 662

San Paolo fuori le Mura, Basilica of, 591

Sanskrit, 73

Santa Maria degli Angeli, Church of, 635
Saône (*anc.* Arar), 470, 474
Sappho, Greek poet (fl. 7th century B.C.), 155, 156, 158, 247, 256
Saracens, 658
Saragossa (*anc.* Caesaraugusta), 504
Sardinia, 38, 40, 43, 46, 52, 53, 97, 111, 112, 279, 365*, 447, 463-464
Sardis, 516, 546, 592
Sarmatians, 431, 432, 480, 630, 669
Sarmizegetusa, 410, 431, 480
Sarsina, 455
Sassanids, 530, 627, 641
Satan, 524, 540, 589, 591, 593, 595, 599, 606, 614, 663
satire, 73, 74, 97, 99, 235, 241, 245-246, 248, 250, 275, 295, 296-299, 312, 317-318, 333, 369, 437-439, 509, 671
Satires (Horace), 245-246, 248, 250
Saturn, 59, 61, 63, 66, 205, 225, 237, 242, 253, 358, 500
Saturn (planet), 309
Saturn, Temple of, 341, 358
Saturnalia, 66
Saturnian verse, 74, 98
Saturnia regna, 61, 66, 205, 225, 236-237, 242, 253
Saturninus, Antoninus, governor (fl. 1st century), 291, 292
Saturninus, Caius Sentius, governor of Syria (fl. 1st century B.C.), 558
Saturninus, Lucius Appuleius, radical leader (?-100 B.C.), 120, 519
Saturninus, Pompeius, friend of Pliny the Younger (fl. 1st and 2nd centuries), 441
Satyricon (Petronius), 296-299, 466
Save, 410, 480, 640
Saviour, *see* Messiah
Saxa Rubra, 654
Scaevola, Caius Mucius, hero (fl. 6th century B.C.), 385
Scaevola, Publius Mucius, statesman and lawyer (fl. second half of 2nd century B.C.), 391
Scaevola, Quintus Mucius, jurist (?-82 B.C.), 391, 406
Scaevola, Quintus Mucius, jurist (2nd-1st centuries B.C.), 141, 159, 391, 406
Scaliger, Joseph Justus, French critic and scholar (1540-1609), 302
Scandinavia, 326
Scandinavians, 475
Scantinia, lex, 398
Scaurus, Marcus Aemilius, general and governor (fl. 1st century B.C.), 133, 334, 482
schism, 618, 657-658
Schola Medicorum, 312
scholarship, 158-161, 234, 250, 252, 269, 272, 415, 635-636
Scholasticism, 548
schools, *see* education
Schweitzer, Albert, Alsatian philosopher, theologian, physician, and musician (b. 1875), 556

science, 75, 102, 108, (in Lucretius) 148-154, 233, 269, 307-313, 314, 356, 392, 393, 406, 500, 502-507, 514, 520-521, 671
Scipio, Publius Cornelius, general, father of Scipio Africanus Major (?-211 B.C.), 49, 52, 91
Scipio Aemilianus Africanus Minor, Publius Cornelius, general (ca. 185-129 B.C.), 41, 57, 87, 91, 96-97, 101, 107, 113, 114, 115, 379, 490
Scipio Africanus, Publius Cornelius, son of Scipio Africanus (2nd century B.C.), 96
Scipio Africanus Maior, Publius Cornelius, general (234-183 B.C.), 51, 52-55, 57, 82, 85, 86, 91, 92, 94, 96, 97, 104, 113, 424
Scipio Asiaticus, Lucius Cornelius, general (fl. 190 B.C.), 86, 91, 104, 113
Scipio, Calvus Cneius Cornelius, general (?-211 B.C.), 52
Scipio Nasica Corculum, Publius Cornelius (fl. 158 B.C.), 66
Scipio Nasica Serapio, Publius Cornelius, senator (fl. 133 B.C.), 115
Scipionic circle, 96-97, 101, 104, 113
Scipios, patrician family, 85, 86, 97, 372, 469
Scopas, Greek sculptor (400-ca. 340 B.C.), 96, 351, 358
Scotland (*anc.* Caledonia), 36, 291, 406, 448, 476, 622, 669
Scribes, 536, 538, 567, 568, 662
Scribonia, second wife of Augustus (fl. 1st century B.C.), 205, 229
Scriptures, *see* Bible
Scudéry, Madeleine de, French novelist (1607-1701), 637
sculpture, Etruscan, 9-10, 18; Carthaginian, 41, 42; Pompeian, 459-460; Italian, 461; Sicilian, 464, 465; Christian, 601; under Rome, 18, 71, 82, 92, 133, 141, 227, 233, 278, 291, 293, 310, 338-346 *passim*, 347-351, 352-362 *passim*, 372, 376, 384, 386, 412, 414, 418, 442-443, 453, 480, 511-512, 514, 532, 634-635, 661-662, 671
Scylla, 602
Scythia, 194, 218, 429, 483, 496, 500, 520, 528, 629
Secular Games, *see ludi saeculares*
Secundini Family, Tomb of the, 474
Segovia, 470
Seine (*anc.* Sequana), 175, 470, 523
Sejanus, Lucius Aelius, prefect of the Praetorian Guard (?-31 A.D.), 263-264, 365*, 447
Seleucia, 96, 428, 528, 529, 546, 602
Seleucia Pieria, 512
Seleucids, 507, 511, 528-530, 536
Seleucus IV Philopator, King of Syria (187-175 B.C.), 86
Selinus, 413
semaphores, 324
Semites, 41, 245, 530
Sempronian Law, 144
Senaculum, 624
Senate, 13, 21-31, 34, 37, 44, 45, 49-52, 70, 71, 76, 85, 86, 89, 90-91, 93-94, 95, 96, 103, 105-

Senate (*continued*)
107, 111, 114-118, 120-126, 129, 130, 136-140, 143-145, 160, 165, 170-175, 180, 181-184, 186, 190-191, 193-201, 205, 206, 212-216, 221, 226, 232, 250, 260-264, 265, 266, 268-271, 273, 275-277, 279, 280, 283-287, 289, 291-293, 301, 331, 332, 336, 348, 364, 393, 395, 397, 407, 409, 413, 414-415, 416, 423, 427, 433, 446, 447, 449, 463, 519,620,621,623-628,633,636,638-640,668-669

Seneca, 351

Seneca, Lucius Annaeus, Stoic philosopher (4? B.C.-A.D. 65), 95, 97, 154, 239, 260, 267, 273, 274, 275-279, 282, 295, 296, 299, 301-308, 311, 315, 316, 319, 324, 333, 334, 335, 338, 343, 350, 351, 363, 367, 369, 370, 371, 377, 379, 380, 387,388,408,435,436,439,456,469,470,478,671

Seneca, Marcus Annaeus, rhetorician (fl. 1st century B.C.), 295, 296, 301, 319, 369, 379, 470

Senectute, De (Cicero), 108, 163*

Senlis (*anc.* Augustomagus), 474

Senones, 471*

Sens (*anc.* Agendicum, *later* Senones), 471*

sententiae, 296

Sentinum (battle, 295 B.C.), 37

Sepphoris, 543

Septimius Severus (Lucius Septimius Severus), Roman emperor (146-211), 330, 336, 465, 620-622, 623, 628, 631*, 632, 633, 635, 649, 666, 669

Septimius Severus, Arch of, 623, 635

Septimontium, 12-13

"Septizonium," 635

Septuagint, 541, 614

Serapis, 635

Serapis, Temple of (Rome), 291, 635

Serapis, Temple of (Serapeum), 500

Serbia, 480

Serdica (Sofia), 483

serfdom, 6, 39, 319, 473, 479, 529, 644, 668-669

sermones, 245

Sertorius, Quintus, general (?-72 B.C.), 136-137

Servian census, 27

Servian constitution, 123

Servile Wars, 141; First, 80, 112; Second, 120-121

Servilia, mistress of Caesar and mother of Brutus (1st century B.C.), 168, 196

Servilian Gardens, 283

Servius Tullius, sixth King of Rome (fl. 6th century B.C.), 14-15, 340

Seuthes and Son, Alexandrian banking firm, 331

Seven against Thebes, 316

Severus (Flavius Valerius Severus), Roman emperor (?-307), 653

Severus, architect (fl. 1st century), 345

Seville (*anc.* Hispalis), 192, 470

sewage system, 81, 220, 326, 356, 439, 671

Sextius, Lucius, tribune and consul (fl. 376-366 B.C.), 24

Sextus of Chaeronea, Greek Stoic philosopher (fl. 2nd century), 425-426

Sextus Empiricus, Greek philosopher (fl. end of 2nd century), 494-495

sexual intercourse, recommended by Pliny, 310; among the Essenes, 537

sexual life, *see* abortion, adultery, betrothal, birth control, bisexuality, celibacy, concubinage, courtesans, divorce, effeminacy, emasculation, eunuchs, hermaphrodites, hetairai, homosexuality, incest, marriage, morals, pederasty, polygamy, promiscuity, prostitution, venereal disease

Shakespeare, William (1564-1616), 16*, 100, 147, 241, 302, 435, 484, 617

Shalmaneser III, King of Assyria (reigned 859-824 B.C.), 39

Shammai, Jewish rabbi (fl. 1st century B.C.), 539, 547

Shansi, 329

Shaosyant, *see* Mithras

Shapur I, King of Persia (reigned 242-271), 605, 629

share-croppers, 104

shaving, in Carthage, 41; in Rome, 70, 372; Christians and, 599

Shelley, Percy Bysshe, English poet (1792-1822), 147, 311, 635

Shemaya, Jewish rabbi (fl. 1st century B.C.), 538

Shepherd of Hermas, The, 599

shipbuilding, 220, 325, 513, 516

ships, 324-326, 329, 516

shrines, 75, 79, 335

Sibyl, Cumean, 64, 236-237, 240-241

Sibylline Books, 64, 94, 236

Sibylline oracle, 197

Sicels, 4

Sicily, 4, 38, 40, 43, 44, 45, 52, 54, 62, 66, 77, 92, 106, 107, 111, 112, 120, 138, 141, 183, 216, 234, 237, 254, 297, 310, 322, 325, 328, 339, 418, 455, 464, 518, 523, 602, 629, 631

Sidon, 39, 329, 347, 510, 511, 534

Sidonius, *see* Apollinaris Sidonius

Silanus, senator (fl. 1st century B.C.), 144

Silanus, Marcus Junius, poisoned by Agrippina (14-54), 273

Silas, colleague of St. Paul (1st century), 583

Silchester (*anc.* Calleva Atrebatum), 477

Silenus, 354

Silius, Caius, lover of Messalina (?-48), 272

silk, 329, 373, 510, 514, 624, 640

Silvae (Statius), 316

Silvanus, 60, 238-239

Silver Age, 235, 295-318, 319

silverware, 346, 349, 373, 529, 624

Silvester I, Roman Pope (reigned 314-335), 659

Simeon (New Testament), 542

Simeon, Bishop of Jerusalem and martyr (87 B.C. ?-A.D. 107?), 648

Simon, Christ's brother, 558

Simon Magus, Samaritan sorcerer (1st century), 577, 604

simony, 604
Singidunum, *see* Belgrade
Sinope (Sinob), 517, 518, 520, 604
Sinuessa (Rocca di Mandragone), 113
Sirach, 539
Sirmio (Sirmione), 158
Sirmium (Mitrovica), 480, 635, 640
Siro the Epicurean, philosopher in Naples (fl. 1st century B.C.), 236
Sixtus II, Roman Pope (257-258), 650
skepticism, 308, 388-389, 489, 494-497, 500, 522; Cicero's, 164-165; Augustus', 225-228; Horace's, 248; Ovid's, 256; Vespasian's, 287, 311; Hadrian's, 415, 418, 648; Lucian's, 495-497; Constantine's, 655-656
slavery, in Etruria, 6; in Carthage, 39, 52; in Greece, 86; in Germany, 479; under Rome, 22, 57, 58, 63, 66, 71, 76, 77, 80, 81, 87, 88, 95, 99, 103-104, 105, 107, 111-113, 117, 120-121, 124, 130, 133, 134, 137-138, 143, 170, 175, 177, 184, 189, 190, 192, 202, 203-204, 205, 211, 215, 220, 221-222, 245*, 255, 261, 267, 270, 279, 290, 297-298, 301, 319, 320, 322, 323, 324, 326, 328-329, 332, 333-335, 336, 338, 342, 364, 366, 374-375, 380, 385-387, 395, 397-398, 400, 403, 412, 424, 429, 441, 448, 462-463, 464, 465, 469, 473, 476, 490, 493, 499, 513, 515, 516, 522, 529, 531, 536, 543, 545, 548, 566, 589, 590, 596, 631-632, 634, 644, 665, 667, 668; barbarian and foreign, 629
slums, 90, 111, 132, 280, 342, 366, 465, 481, 510
Smith, William Benjamin, American educator (1850-1934), 554
Smyrna, *see* Tralles
Soaemias, Julia, daughter of Julia Maesa and mother of Elagabalus (?-222), 623-625
soap, 375
social service, 371
Social War, 79, 122, 125, 146, 182
Socrates, Athenian philosopher (469-399 B.C.), 104, 258, 306, 491, 557, 646
Socrates, brother of Nicomedes III (fl. 1st century B.C.), 518
soil, 76, 77, 238, 319-321, 339, 456, 457, 464, 476, 482, 511, 513, 631, 665
Soissons (*anc.* Noviodunum), 177, 471*, 474
solarium, 343
Solomon, King of the Jews (reigned 974-937 B.C.), 530
Solon, Athenian lawgiver (638?-559? B.C.), 23, 32, 83, 392, 405
Solway Firth, 417, 476
soothsaying, 60, 63-64, 147, 164, 197, 243, 278, 292,308,311,388,419,429,485,514,537,559,624
Sophistic, Second, 488-489
Sophists, 497, 515
Sophists of the Dinner Table (Athenaeus of Naucratis), *see Deipnosophists*
Soranus of Ephesus, Greek writer on medicine (fl. 98-138), 505
Sorrento, *see* Surrentum
Sorrows (Ovid), see *Tristia*

Sotion, Pythagorean philosopher (fl. 1st century), 301
soul, Lucretius on, 152; Seneca on, 304-305; Plotinus on, 608-610; Origen on, 615
South Africa, 406
Spain, 36, 39, 40, 43, 46, 47, 48, 50, 52-53, 54, 82, 86, 87-88, 96, 107, 111, 112, 113, 119, 126, 129, 136-137, 138, 169, 170, 176, 179, 183-184, 188, 189, 190, 192, 200, 217, 218, 219, 252, 283, 285, 308, 318, 319, 322, 323, 329, 330, 346, 348, 366, 406, 408, 410, 414, 417, 431, 468-470, 471, 472, 473, 475, 481, 513, 514, 521, 585, 590, 602, 632, 638, 669-670, 671
Spalato (*anc.* Spalatum), 644
Spanish, 73, 295
Sparta, 87, 200, 387, 482, 487, 519, 534, 630
Spartacus, slave leader (?-71 B.C.), 137-138
Spartianus, Aelius, biographer (fl. 4th century), 414, 416, 419
Spectaculis, De (Tertullian), 612-613
speedometers, 356
Spendius, Campanian slave and rebel leader (fl. 241-237 B.C.), 46
Spenser, Edmund, English poet (1552?-1599), 258
spinning, 58, 77, 213, 230, 321-322, 371
Spinoza, Baruch, Dutch Jewish philosopher (1632-1677), 580
Spinther, Publius, senator (fl. 1st century), 331
spoils, 82-83, 87, 88, 90, 92, 94, 96, 103, 120, 123, 125, 129-130, 141, 169-170, 175-177, 183, 194, 196, 205, 211, 213, 219, 261, 287, 288, 293, 331, 349, 365, 410, 482, 543, 546, 623, 629
sports, *see* athletics, games
Sporus, youth married by Nero (1st century), 282
Spring, 354
Spurinna Vestritius, soothsayer (fl. 1st century B.C.), 197
Stabiae (Castellammare di Stabia), 354
stadiums, 360, 362, 378, 382, 487
stage, *see* theater
statio, 324
Statius, Publius Papinius, poet (ca. 61-ca. 96), 289, 291, 295, 315-318, 335, 370, 456
statuary, *see* sculpture
Statue of Liberty, 351*
Steele, Sir Richard, English essayist and dramatist (1672-1729), 304
stenography, 466
Stephanos (Meleager), 509
Stephen I, Roman Pope (reigned 254-257), 618
Stephen, first Christian martyr (?-30?), 576, 580
Sterculus, 59
sterility, 212, 229, 366, 449, 480, 482, 666
Stertinius, Quintus, physician (fl. 1st century), 312
Stilicho, general (?-408), 358
Stoa, Zeno's, 421, 490, 497

Stoicism, 63, 95, 97, 135, 141, 144, 154*, 164, 165, 166, 190, 196, 249, 250, 274, 279, 286, 292, 300-307, 335, 370, 389, 392, 405, 409, 415, 422, 425-427, 431, 432, 449, 485, 489-494, 496, 497, 502, 514, 521-522, 541, 588, 594, 598, 602, 613, 614, 658, 671

stoicism, 57, 68, 88, 133, 154*, 225, 230, 251, 260, 274, 282, 301, 307, 408, 426, 468, 667

Stone Age, New, 4, 11, 471

Stone Age, Old, 4, 468, 471

Strabo, Greek geographer (63 B.C.?-A.D. 24?), 321, 329, 347, 424, 455, 468, 471, 477, 478, 483, 513, 514, 516, 520-521, 546

Strabo of Sardis, Greek anthologist (fl. 50 B.C.), 509*

Strasbourg, see Argentoratum

Strategamata (Frontinus), 328

Strauss, David Friedrich, German rationalistic theologian (1808-1874), 553

streets, Roman, 81, 281, 341-342, 477, 633; of Italy, 461; of Petra, 508; of Antioch, 512; of Rhodes, 514; of Ephesus, 515

strikes, 80, 499

Stromateis (Origen), 614

Styx, 522

Sublicius, Pons, 327

Sublime, On the (Longinus), 636

Subura, the, 167, 341-342

Succubo, 425

Suessiones, 175, 471*

Suetonius Tranquillus, Caius, historian (70?-121?), 167, 188, 197, 212, 215, 218, 221, 227, 228, 261, 264, 266, 267, 272, 275, 280*, 283, 286, 287, 293, 350, 414, 441, 554

Suez, 521

Sufetula, 465

suicide, 190, 203, 207-208, 218, 240, 262, 264, 282, 284, 296, 300, 301, 306-307, 311, 371, 386, 398-399, 422, 478, 489, 516, 623, 654

Suilius, Publius, delator (fl. 1st century), 302-303

Sulla, Lucius Cornelius (Felix), dictator (138-78 B.C.), 31, 91, 92, 119, 122-127, 128, 130, 131, 132, 134, 138, 139-140, 141, 142, 167, 168, 169, 170, 189, 195, 211, 391, 448, 457, 483, 519

Sulmo (Soloma), 253-254, 257, 455

Sulpicia, poetess (fl. end of 1st century), 370

Sulpicius Rufus, Publius, orator (124-88 B.C.), 122-123, 160

Sun, Temple of the, 511-512, 639

sundial, 66, 308

suovetaurilia, 64

superstition, 60, 61, 93-94, 118, 123, 147-148, 228, 251, 269, 292, 308, 311, 368, 388, 415, 425, 442, 485, 500, 515, 517, 522, 599

Sura, Lucius Licinius, aristocrat (fl. 1st and 2nd centuries), 408

Surena, Parthian general (fl. 54 B.C.), 529

surgery, in Etruria, 6; under Rome, 75-76, 104, 312-313, 412, 505

Surrentine wine, 456

Surrentum (Sorrento), 322, 456, 457

Susa, 606

Susannah, 539

Swift, Jonathan, English satirist (1667-1745), 671

Switzerland, 175, 471, 474

Symmachus, Samaritan Bible translator (fl. late 2nd century), 614

syphilis, 311

Syracuse, 38, 44, 51, 52, 92, 107, 141, 464, 546

Syria, 88, 89, 107, 130, 131, 140, 170, 176, 178, 187, 200, 204, 205, 247, 297, 298, 310, 320, 326, 328, 329, 330, 331, 333, 347*, 364-365, 366, 381, 390, 413, 428, 431, 487, 495, 500, 510-513, 522-523, 531, 532, 535, 543, 544-545, 546, 558, 577, 588, 595, 601, 602, 603, 606, 620, 623-625, 627, 629, 630, 633, 636, 639, 651

Syriac, 187, 495, 604, 630

"Syrian Athens" (Meleager), 509

T

Tabenne, 657

Tabitha, raised from death by Peter (1st century), 577

taboos, 60

Tacapae (Gabes), 465

Tacitus (Marcus Claudius Tacitus), Roman emperor (ca. 200-276), 639

Tacitus, Caius Cornelius, historian (ca. 55-ca. 120), 15‡, 160, 224, 261-265, 267, 272, 273*, 275, 276, 277, 279, 280*, 281, 285, 289, 291, 292, 293, 295, 296, 303, 306, 314, 315, 322, 365, 366, 387, 433-437, 439, 440, 441, 442, 447, 463, 476, 478-479, 543, 544, 545, 546, 554, 557, 572, 612, 636, 639, 671

Tacitus, Cornelius, procurator and father of Tacitus (fl. 1st century), 433

Tagus, 318, 469, 470

Taine, Hippolyte Adolphe, French historian and critic (1828-1893), 251

Talleyrand-Périgord, Charles Maurice de, Prince de Bénévent, French statesman (1754-1838), 195

Talmud, 548, 549, 554, 580, 606

Tammuz, 523

Tanagra, 601

Tanaquil, wife of the first Tarquin (fl. 6th century B.C.), 7, 14

Tangier (anc. Tingis), 39, 464, 466, 468

Tanith, 41-42

tanning, 322

Tantalus, 245

Tarentum (Taranto), 35, 37, 38, 74, 78, 97, 116, 133, 188, 297, 377, 455

tariffs, 80-81

Tarpeia, daughter of governor (8th century B.C.), 13

Tarpeian Rock, 13, 199, 400

Tarquin (Lucius Tarquinius Priscus), fifth King of Rome (fl. 7th and 6th centuries B.C.), 7, 14, 18, 82, 358

Tarquin, Sextus, son of Tarquin the Proud (fl. 6th century B.C.), 16

Tarquin the Proud (Lucius Tarquinius Superbus), seventh King of Rome (fl. 6th century B.C.), 15-17

Tarquinii (Corneto), 5, 8, 14, 35, 461

Tarracina (Terracina), 411

Tarraco, see Tarragona

Tarraconensis, 470

Tarragona (anc. Tarraco), 417, 470, 650

Tarsus, 203, 204, 329, 513, 546, 579, 581, 582, 629

Tartarus, 147, 240, 456

Tartessus, 39, 40, 469

Tasso, Torquato, Italian poet (1544-1595), 258, 637, 671

Tatius, Titus, King of the Sabines (8th century B.C.), 13

Taurini, 454

Tauromenium (Taormina), 464

Taurus, Statilius, general (fl. end of 1st century B.C.), 361

Taurus, 298

Taurus Mountains, 513

taverns, see drinking

taxation, in Carthage, 54; in Judea, 532; under Rome, 51, 58, 68, 80-81, 89, 91, 103, 116-117, 120, 126, 129, 139-141, 170, 192-194, 203-204, 205, 207, 211, 213, 217, 220-221, 224, 227, 261, 265, 267, 269, 275-276, 287-288, 290, 330, 336, 337, 368, 373, 398, 407, 409, 415, 416, 423, 427, 432, 448, 462-463, 464, 482, 483, 487, 498, 499, 532, 543, 547, 548, 620, 622, 627, 628, 631-633, 642-645, 656, 665, 667-668

Teiresias, 497

Telamon, 47

Telephus, 354

Tellus (Terra Mater), 59, 348, 350*; feast for, 59

tempera, 352

temples, Etruscan, 9; Carthaginian, 40, 41, 42, 465, 469; under Rome, 62, 64, 79, 81-82, 92, 193, 219, 225, 226, 268, 269, 279, 280, 287, 290-291, 335, 339, 340, 347, 351, 352, 357-359, 362, 363, 369, 371, 381, 388, 418-421, 423, 425, 426-427, 440, 453, 455, 456, 458, 459, 460-461, 464, 465, 466, 470, 473, 476, 477, 480, 498-500, 508-509, 511-512, 513, 515, 516, 519, 522, 601, 606, 621, 625, 626, 648, 650, 656

tenant farmers, 77, 104, 111, 319-320, 631, 644

tenuiores, 332

Terence (Publius Terentius Afer), comic dramatist (190?-159? B.C.), 90, 97, 98, 99, 101-102

Terentia, wife of Cicero (fl. 1st century B.C.), 141, 163

Tergeste (Trieste), 455

Terme, Museo delle, 348*, 349, 350, 351

Terminus, 59

Terpnos, Nero's musician (fl. 1st century), 278

Terracina (anc. Anxur), 297

terra cottas, 18, 82, 347-348

terramaricoli, 4-5

Terra Mater, see Tellus

Tertia, wife of Cassius and daughter of Servilia, q.v. (1st century B.C.), 168

Tertia, sister of Publius Clodius Pulcher and wife of Lucullus (1st century B.C.), 172-173

Tertulla, wife of Crassus (1st century B.C.), 168

Tertullian (Quintus Septimius Florens Tertullianus), Latin father of the Church (160?-230?), 307, 385, 465, 524, 558, 591, 597, 598, 603, 612-613, 617, 618, 647-649, 652, 665

Tetrabiblios (Ptolemy), 503

Tetricus, Caius Pesuvius, pretender in Gaul (274), 638

Teutones, 118-119, 472

textbooks, 159

textiles, 77, 92, 473, 486, 510

Thallus, secretary to Augustus, 229

Thallus, pagan commentator on Christ (fl. 1st century), 555

Thames (anc. Tamesis), 176, 179, 441, 477

Thamugadi (Timgad), 466

Thapsacus, 512

Thapsus, battle in 46 B.C., 54, 189, 465, 466

Theagenes, 636

theater, 98-99, 133, 193, 219, 266-267, 274, 278, 296, 302, 316, 317, 319, 340, 352, 357, 360, 362, 363, 369, 371, 377-379, 381, 418-419, 421, 456, 458-459, 464, 466, 470, 473, 474, 480, 499, 508-509, 513, 515, 532, 548, 598, 612-613

Thebaid, 445

Thebaid (Statius), 316

Thebes (anc. Thebae), 316, 483, 498, 499, 630

Theocritus, Greek pastoral poet (fl. 3rd century B.C.), 235, 236, 637

Theodora, wife of Constantine (4th century), 653

Theodosius I the Great (Flavius Theodosius), Roman emperor (346?-395), 486

Theodotians, 605

Theodotion, Bible translator (fl. 2nd century), 614

theology, 304, 308, 501-502, 522-525, 547-548, 553-554, 556, 562, 575, 582, 586-590, 594-595, 601, 603-615, 618, 626, 635, 656, 658-661

Theophila, philosopher and friend of Martial, 370

Theophrastus, Greek philosopher (?-287 B.C.), 310, 311, 490

Theopompus, Greek historian (ca. 378-? B.C.), 7

Therapeutae, 525

thermae, see baths, public

Thermus, Marcus Minucius, general (fl. 1st century B.C.), 167

Theseus, 354

Thessalonians, The First Epistle of Paul the Apostle to the, 587*

Thessalonians, The Second Epistle of Paul the Apostle to the, 587*, 591

Thessalonica (Salonika), 78, 324, 483, 546, 583, 585, 591, 602, 630, 637, 655

Thessaly, 184, 185, 467, 483, 519

Third Legion, 466

Thirteenth Legion, 182

Thisbe, 256

Thoreau, Henry David, American philosopher and writer (1817-1862), 609

Thrace, 203, 366, 482, 483, 516, 519, 595, 630, 632, 633, 639, 655

Thrasea, Publius Paetus, Stoic philosopher and senator (?-66), 279, 282, 300, 426, 441

Thrasymachus, Greek Sophist and rhetorician (fl. 5th century B.C.), 96

Thucydides, Greek historian (471?-400? B.C.), 4

Thugga (Dougga), 465

Thurii (Terra Nuova), 37, 51, 138

Thysdrus (El. Djem), 465

Tiber, 5, 11, 17, 36, 62, 65, 78, 81, 94, 115, 117, 159, 179, 193, 253, 265, 270, 278, 280, 283, 285, 325, 326, 327, 339, 365, 366, 378, 410, 422, 439, 453, 625, 654

Tiberias (Tabariah), 535, 644

Tiberius (Tiberius Claudius Nero Caesar), Roman emperor (42 B.C.-A.D. 37), 215, 217, 229, 230-231, 232, 234, 248, 259-265, 266, 268, 270, 275, 281, 290, 291, 292, 293, 323, 329, 331-332, 344, 347, 350, 358, 365*, 371, 373, 386, 434, 436, 478, 543, 558, 560

Tibullus, Albius, poet (54-19 B.C.), 60, 155, 234, 235, 252-253, 370, 407

Tibur (Tivoli), 35, 78, 121, 155, 252, 344, 421, 454, 638

Ticino, 49

Tigellinus, Sophonius, favorite of Nero (?-69), 279, 282

Tigranes, King of Armenia (fl. end of 1st century B.C.), 217

Tigranes the Great, King of Armenia (reigned 94-56 B.C.), 528

Tigranocerta (Sert), 528

Tigris, 546, 627, 641

time, measurement of, 66-67

Timocles the Stoic (in Lucian), 496

Timomachus of Byzantium, Greek painter (fl. 1st century B.C.), 354

Timothy, colleague of St. Paul (1st century), 583, 590

Timothy, The Second Epistle of Paul the Apostle to, 590

Tingis, see Tangier

Tinia, 7

Tiridates, King of Armenia (fl. 1st century), 280

Tiro, Marcus Tullius, writer and secretary to Cicero (fl. 1st century B.C.), 163

Titus (Titus Flavius Sabinus Vespasianus), Roman emperor (40-81), 287, 288-289, 290, 291, 345, 348-349, 351, 359, 361, 365, 375, 383, 404, 419, 535, 538, 544-545, 546, 577, 603

Titus, Arch of, 348-349, 357, 412

Titus, Baths of, 291, 345, 359, 375

Titus, colleague who forsook St. Paul (1st century), 590

Tiu (Tyr), 479

toga, 70

Toletum (Toledo), 470

Tolosa (Toulouse), 473

Tolstoy, Count Leo Nikolaevich, Russian novelist (1828-1910), 301, 537

Tomb of the Lioness (at Corneto), 11

tombs, in Etruria, 6, 7, 8, 339, 443; under Rome, 57, 69, 84, 226, 243, 284, 298, 334, 348, 389, 414, 443, 474; in Saba, 508; Christian, 601

Tomi (Constanta), 232, 256-257, 301, 480

Tom Jones (Fielding), 299

Torah, 535-542, 547-549, 560, 567-568, 576-577, 579, 580, 581, 585-589, 591, 595, 605

Torlonia, Villa, 454*

Torquatus, Manlius (Caius Nonius Asprenas?), friend of Horace (fl. 1st century B.C.), 233

Torquatus, Titus Manlius Imperiosus, dictator (fl. 363-340 B.C.), 37*

Torso Belvedere (Apollonius of Athens), 349

torture, 267, 270, 285, 292, 334, 395, 403, 424, 529, 534, 615, 643, 649, 651-652

totemism, 60

Toulouse (anc. Tolosa), 650

town planning, 356

trade, Etruscan, 6; Carthaginian, 40-41, 54, 105, 106, 107; under Rome, 38, 54, 77-81, 88, 90, 92, 107, 111, 116, 118, 139-140, 170, 190, 205, 211-212, 215, 218-219, 233, 321-322, 324-326, 328-331, 332-334, 336-337, 340-342, 362, 364-365, 399, 411, 432, 448, 454, 455, 456, 465, 466, 470-471, 473, 474, 476, 477, 480, 482-483, 486, 487, 499, 508, 510, 514, 520, 528-529, 532, 535, 579, 632-633, 642-644, 665, 668, 671

trade routes, 413, 455, 508, 511-512, 529, 602, 632

tragedy, 74-75, 98, 301-302, 378

Traiana, Via, 410

Trajan (Marcus Ulpius Nerva Trajanus), Roman emperor (52-117), 28, 97, 234, 275, 291, 299, 307, 322, 326, 330, 335, 341, 345, 349, 361, 368, 371, 375, 387, 395, 408-413, 414, 433, 434, 436, 439, 441, 442, 455, 456, 457, 470, 480, 499, 508, 510, 520, 521, 528, 554, 599, 628, 634, 648, 662

Trajan, Arch of, 411

Trajan, Baths of, 345, 375, 635

Trajan, Column of, 411-412, 413, 442-443

Trajan, Temple of, 411

Tralles (Smyrna), 312, 329, 431, 504, 515, 546, 592, 603, 617, 648, 650

Tranquillity of the Soul, On the (Seneca), 302

Transjordania, 530

transport, 77-78, 271, 323-6, 328, 339, 341, 411, 473, 477, 499, 668

Transylvania, 410

Trapezus (Trebizond), 418, 518, 520, 629

Trasimene, Lake (anc. Trasimenus, It. Trasimeno or Perugia), battle in 217 B.C., 49

travel, 323-326

treaties, violation of, 90

Trebia (battle, 218 B.C.), 91

Trebonius, Caius, governor and conspirator (?-43 B.C.), 197

Trèves, see Augusta Trevirorum

tribunes, 22-25, 27, 30, 85, 114, 126, 139, 191, 213, 216

tribute, see taxation

tributum capitis, 220

tributum soli, 220

triclinium, 343, 376

Trimalchio, 297-298, 333, 380

Trinity, 595, 660

Trionfi, Via dei, 662

Tripoli (*anc.* Tripolis), 464, 465

Tripoli, see Oea

Tristia (Ovid), 257-258

Tristram Shandy (Sterne), 299

triumphs, 82-83, 86, 119, 121, 136, 138, 170, 171, 177, 190, 206, 208, 211, 219, 271, 272, 283, 288, 291, 348-349, 365, 381, 413, 428, 432, 466, 545, 546, 669

Triumvirate, First, 134, 171, 174, 175-176

Triumvirate, Second, 201-208, 531

Troad, the, 157

Troas, see Alexandria Troas

Troesmis (Iglitza), 480

Trojan War, 663

troubadours, 255, 638

Troy (*anc.* Troia, *now* Hissarlik), 12, 61, 74, 190, 239-240, 278, 280, 516, 522, 663

True Word (Celsus), 606-607

tuberculosis, 313, 504, 506

Tullia, daughter of Cicero (fl. 1st century B.C.), 163, 165

Tullus, Desumius, millionaire (fl. 1st century), 461

Tullus Hostilius, third King of Rome (fl. 7th century B.C.), 13-14

Tunis, 39, 42

Tunisia, 105, 465

Turanians, 528

Turbo, Marcius Livianus, general of Trajan (fl. 2nd century), 413

Turin, 254, 654

Turkestan, 528

Turkey, 513

Turnus, 240-241, 278

Tuscan (Etruscan) style (architecture), 18, 81, 92, 357

Tuscany, 5, 6, 11, 666

Tusculan Disputations (Cicero), see *Disputationes Tusculanae*

Tusculum, 11, 35, 132, 162, 454

Tutumus, 60

Twelfth Legion, 182

Twelve Great Gods, 7

Twelve Tables, 23, 31-33, 72, 75, 79, 83, 99, 393, 398, 400, 401, 403

Tyndaris, 247

Tyne, 417, 476

typhus, 227

Tyre, 39, 329, 331, 373, 469, 509, 510, 534

Tyrrha (Tireh), 6†

Tyrrhenian (Etruscan) Sea, 6, 453

U

Uffizi Gallery, 348*

Ulpian (Domitius Ulpianus), jurist (?-228), 392, 398, 405, 510, 621, 626, 634

Umbria, 99, 253, 455

Umbrians, 5, 12, 35, 37, 51, 122

unemployment, under Rome, 38, 116, 176, 180, 192, 205, 213, 288, 290, 323, 326, 336, 410, 641; in Athens, 418

United States, 79, 218, 372, 546, 632

unities, Horace on, 249

Universal History (Eusebius), 662

Universal History (Poseidonius), 514

universities, 465, 474, 487-489, 500, 504, 510, 515, 661

Urals, 218

Urban VIII (Maffeo Barberini), Pope (1568-1644), 420

urbanization, under the Republic, 90, 111, 113, 118; under the Principate, 222, 237, 286, 319, 481, 498, 508-509, 510, 516; under the monarchy, 631, 633, 667

urology, 313, 318

Ursus, Flavius, friend of Statius (fl. 1st century), 335

Ustica, 244

usury, see moneylending

Utica (Utique), 39, 40, 80, 106, 107, 186, 188, 189-190, 325, 418, 465

Utrecht (*anc.* Trajectus), 324

V

Valentia (Valencia), 470

Valentinian I (Flavius Valentinianus), Roman emperor in the West (321-375), 665

Valentinus, Alexandrian heretic (fl. 160), 604

Valerian (Caius Publius Licinius Valerianus), Roman emperor (?-260), 340, 629, 650

Valerian Way, 78

Valerii, Roman clan, 21, 364

Valerius Maximus, historian (fl. 1st century), 352, 471-472

Vandals, 358, 638, 639, 670

Van Dyke, Sir Anthony, Flemish painter (1599-1641), 354

Van Gogh, Vincent (1853-1890), 355

Vardar (*anc.* Axius), 630

Varro, Caius Terentius, consul and general (fl. 216 B.C.), 50

Varro, Marcus Terentius, scholar and writer (116-26 B.C.), 60, 146, 159-160, 193, 238, 308, 379, 456, 509

Varus, Publius Quintilius, governor (?-9 A.D.), 218, 543

Varus, Quintilius, noble (?-42 B.C.), 203

Vasari, Giorgio, Italian artist and biographer of artists (1511-1574), 349

vases, see ceramics

Vatican (hill), 12, 340, 578

Vatican, the, 348*, 349, 350, 407

vault, 339, 355-361, 529, 661, 671

vehicles, 323, 341

Veii (Isola Farnese), 6, 10, 17; war with (405-396 B.C.), 24, 36, 62, 344

Velia, 455

Velitrae (Veletri), 200

venereal disease, 268, 313

Veneti, 454-455

Venetia, 454, 461

Venice, 429, 455, 516

Venus, 12, 61, 82, 148-149, 152, 167, 193, 204, 239, 241, 253, 254, 255, 256, 346, 468, 487, 510, 511, 548; Venus Genitrix, 349; Venus Pompeiana, 458

Venus, Temple of, 196

Venus and Mars, Temple of, see Pantheon

Venus and Roma, Temple of, 421

Venusia (Venosa), 78, 244, 455, 546

Veratius, Lucius, slaveowner (2nd century), 404

Verbanus, Lacus, see Maggiore, Lago

Vercellae (Vercelli), battle in 101 B.C., 120

Vercingetorix, Gallic chief of the Arverni (?-45 B.C.), 176-177

Verona, 11, 78, 154, 155, 410, 429, 454, 628

Verres, Caius Cornelius, governor (?-43 B.C.), 92, 141, 462, 464

Versailles, 345

versification, 74, 98, 99, 155, 295; of Lucretius, 148, 154; of Catullus, 155-158; of Virgil, 236, 238, 243; of Horace, 244-248; of Tibullus, 253; of Ovid, 254, 256-258; of Statius, 316; of Martial, 317, 318; of Juvenal, 439

Verulamium (St. Albans), 476

Verus, Lucius Aurelius (Lucius Ceionius Commodus Verus), Roman emperor (127-169), 422, 426-428, 430

Verus, Lucius, friend of Hadrian (?-138), 421, 422

Vespasian (Titus Flavius Sabinus Vespasianus), Roman emperor (9-79), 234, 271, 284-288, 290, 301, 309, 311, 312, 313, 322, 336, 337, 341, 345, 348, 351, 358, 361, 365, 368, 378, 383, 396, 402, 407, 409, 461, 489, 516, 544, 546, 575

Vespillo, Quintus Lucretius (fl. 1st century), 370

Vesta, 12, 58, 61, 518; House of, see Aedes Vestae; Temple of, 4, 635

Vestal Virgins, 61, 63, 94, 133, 142, 199, 202, 206, 290, 348, 351, 370, 388, 397, 622; Palace of, see Atrium Vestae

Vesuvius, 137, 289, 346, 352, 456, 457

veterinarians, 313

Vettii, House of, 352-353

Vetulonia, 17*

viaducts, 326

Victor I, Roman Pope (ca. 190-198), 617

Victor, Sextus Aurelius, writer (fl. 4th century), 641

Victory, 627; Temple of, 94

Victory Hill, see Clivus Victoriae

Vicus Lorarius, 342

Vicus Margaritarius, 342

Vicus Sandalarius, 342

Vicus Vitrarius, 342

Vienna (anc. Vindobona), 78, 324, 346, 432, 480, 633

Vienne, 49, 649

Villa Item, 354

Villanova, 5; culture, 5, 9; migrants from, 11

villas, see mansions

Viminal, 12*, 340, 342

Viminal Gate, 263

Vinci, Leonardo da, Italian artist (1452-1519), 220, 232, 356

Vindex, Caius Julius, legate of Gallia Lugdunensis (fl. 1st century), 283, 473

Vindobona, see Vienna

Vindonissa (Windisch), 480

vineyards, 320, 344, 456, 464, 473, 535, 631, 639

Vipsania Agrippina, daughter of Agrippa (fl. 1st century B.C.), 230, 259

Virbius ("King of the Woods"), 62

Virgil (Publius Vergilius [or Virgilius] Maro), poet (70-19 B.C.), 3, 8, 60, 61, 74, 98, 102, 154, 155, 157, 158, 205, 215, 225, 233, 234, 235-244, 245, 248, 250, 251, 252, 258, 278, 283, 307, 348, 382, 438, 441, 454, 456, 625, 671

Virgin, 236-237

Virginia, daughter of Lucius Virginius (5th century B.C.), 23, 72

Virginius, Lucius, plebeian (5th century B.C.), 23

Virgo, 298

Viriathus, Lusitanian leader (fl. 2nd century B.C.), 87

Viroconium (Wroxeter), 477

Virtue, 358; Temple of, 358

Virtutibus, De (Cicero), 163*

Visigoths, 670

Vistula, 478

vitalism, 507

Vitellius (Aulus Vitellius Germanicus), Roman emperor (15-69), 268, 284-285, 287

Vitruvius Pollio, Marcus, architect and engineer (1st century B.C.), 9, 343*, 356

vivisection, 504-505, 506

Voconia, lex, 224, 399

Volga (anc. Rha), 669

Volney, Comte de, Constantin François de Chasseboeuf, French skeptical author (1757-1820), 553

Vologases III, King of Parthia (fl. 2nd century), 428

Vologases IV, King of Parthia (?-209), 530

Vologases V, King of Parthia (?-227?), 530

Volscians, 15, 35, 36, 37, 326†

Voltaire, François Marie Arouet de, French writer (1694-1778), 99, 131, 154, 225, 244, 304, 495, 497, 553

vote buying, 128-129, 192

vows, 64-65, 311, 606

Vulcan, 59, 63
Vulci, 9
Vulso, Cnaeus Manlius, general (fl. 2nd century B.C.), 88

W

wages, 111, 112, 632, 642-643
Walden Pond, 609
Wales, 36, 73, 475, 477
Wall Street, 340
war, 24, 80, 81, 83, 85, 86, 90, 91, 96, 193, 198, 232, 233, 242, 253, 255, 261, 301, 310, 330, 336-337, 387, 424, 478, 602, 622, 632, 636, 641, 650, 665, 666, 667
War of the Mercenaries, 46
Wars of the Jews, The (Josephus), 546
Washington, D. C., 356
water clock, see clepsydra
watering places, 133, 324, 377, 456, 477, 664
water supply, of Rome, 220, 281, 326-328, 343; in Italian cities, 461; in Syria, 511, 512; in Smyrna, 515
Watt, James, Scottish inventor (1736-1819), 504
Watteau, Jean Antoine, French painter (1684-1721), 351
wealth, 88-89, 90, 91, 95, 108, 118, 128, 130-134, 212, 221, 337, 339, 391, 399, 448, 483, 510-512, 514, 631-633, 657, 667
weapons, 33, 77, 106-107, 322, 328*
weddings, 223, 379
weights, 78
West, the, 154, 188, 203, 208, 234, 251, 283, 329, 331, 366, 389, 392, 406, 420, 463, 473, 475, 481, 512, 529, 603, 605, 612, 616-617, 629, 640, 644, 654, 657, 661, 665, 666, 669, 670, 671
Westminster Hall, 635
Wieland, Christopher Martin, German poet and novelist (1733-1813), 553
Winchester (anc. Venta Belgarum), 477
Winckelmann, Johann Joachim, German archeologist and art historian (1717-1768), 349
Wisdom of Solomon, Book of the, 540, 541, 589
Wissowa, George, German classical philologist (1859-1931), 504*
witchcraft, 526, 559
Wodin (Odin), 479
Wolfenbüttel Fragments (Reimarus), 553
Wolf of the Capitol, 82
woman, in Etruria, 7, 18; in Carthage, 41; in early Rome, 18, 57-58, 89-90, 99; in the later Republic, 134-135; under the Principate, 222-224, 300-301, 313, 368, 369-373, 378, 395-396, 399-400, 438, 485, 505, 596-597; under the monarchy, 634, 636; in Germany, 478-

479; in Parthia, 529; Paul and Christianity on, 590, 596-597, 601
Wordsworth, William, English poet (1770-1850), 147
works, good, 589, 663
wrestling, in Etruria, 7; in Rome, 382
writing materials, 73

X

Xanten (anc. Colonia Trajana), 176
Xantho (in Philodemus), 510
Xanthus, 203, 513
Xenophon, Athenian historian and general (435?-355?), 132, 520, 636

Y

Yabne, see Jamnia
Yahveh, 390, 529, 533, 534, 535, 540, 543, 558, 567, 604, 605, 607, 614, 615
Yarhibol, 511
Yemen, see Arabia Felix
York (anc. Eboracum), 78, 477, 622, 653
Youth Games, see ludi iuvenales
Yugoslavia, 480

Z

Zadok, Jewish founder of the Sadducees, 536
Zaleucus, Greek lawgiver (fl. 660 B.C.), 32
Zama (battle of, 202 B.C.), 49, 53, 85, 91, 92, 105
Zebedee, father of apostles James and John (1st century), 563, 577
Zela, battle in 47 B.C., 188
Zeno, Greek Stoic philosopher (336?-264? B.C.), 154*, 196, 249, 304, 346, 421, 455, 514
Zenobia, Septimia, Queen of Palmyra (?-after 272), 454, 630, 633, 636*, 638, 669
Zenodorus, Greek sculptor (fl. 1st century), 342, 351, 473
Zenophila (in Meleager), 509
Zephyrinus, Roman Pope (ca. 198-ca. 218), 617
Zerubbabel, Hebrew prince (fl. 520 B.C.), 533
Zeugma, 512
Zeus, 61, 63, 353, 390, 487, 495-496; Zeus Panhellenicos, 418; Zeus the Olympian, 418
Zeus, 461
Zeus (Pheidias), 486
Zeuxis, Greek painter (fl. 430 B.C.), 351
Zion, 535
zodiac, 298
Zola, Emile, French novelist (1840-1902), 412
zoological gardens, 384
Zoroastrianism, 524-525, 529-530, 537, 540, 558, 595, 596, 600*, 606, 639, 654; see also Mithras
Zosimus, Greek historian (fl. 5th century), 663

About the Author

WILL DURANT was born in North Adams, Massachusetts, in 1885. He was educated in the Catholic parochial schools there and in Kearny, New Jersey, and thereafter in St. Peter's (Jesuit) College, Jersey City, New Jersey, and Columbia University, New York. For a summer he served as a cub reporter on the New York *Journal*, in 1907, but finding the work too strenuous for his temperament, he settled down at Seton Hall College, South Orange, New Jersey, to teach Latin, French, English, and geometry (1907–11). He entered the seminary at Seton Hall in 1909, but withdrew in 1911 for reasons which he has described in his book *Transition*. He passed from this quiet seminary to the most radical circles in New York, and became (1911–13) the teacher of the Ferrer Modern School, an experiment in libertarian education. In 1912 he toured Europe at the invitation and expense of Alden Freeman, who had befriended him and now undertook to broaden his horizons.

Returning to the Ferrer School, he fell in love with one of his pupils, resigned his position, and married her (1913). For four years he took graduate work at Columbia University, specializing in biology under Morgan and Calkins and in philosophy under Woodbridge and Dewey. He received the doctorate in philosophy in 1917, and taught philosophy at Columbia University for one year. In 1914, in a Presbyterian church in New York, he began those lectures on history, literature, and philosophy which, continuing twice weekly for thirteen years, provided the initial material for his later works.

The unexpected success of *The Story of Philosophy* (1926) enabled him to retire from teaching in 1927. Thenceforth, except for some incidental essays, Mr. and Mrs. Durant gave nearly all their working hours (eight to fourteen daily) to *The Story of Civilization*. To better prepare themselves they toured Europe in 1927, went around the world in 1930 to study Egypt, the Near East, India, China, and Japan, and toured the globe again in 1932 to visit Japan, Manchuria, Siberia, Russia, and Poland. These travels provided the background for *Our Oriental Heritage* (1935) as the first volume in *The Story of Civilization*. Several further visits to Europe prepared for Volume II, *The Life of Greece* (1939) and Volume III, *Caesar and Christ* (1944). In 1948, six months in Turkey, Iraq, Iran, Egypt, and Europe provided perspective for Volume IV, *The Age of Faith* (1950). In 1951 Mr. and Mrs. Durant returned to Italy to add to a lifetime of gleanings for Volume V, *The Renaissance* (1953); and in 1954 further studies in Italy, Switzerland, Germany, France, and England opened new vistas for Volume VI, *The Reformation* (1957).

Mrs. Durant's share in the preparation of these volumes became more and more substantial with each year, until in the case of Volume VII, *The Age of Reason Begins* (1961), it was so pervasive that justice required the union of both names on the title page. The name Ariel was first applied to his wife by Mr. Durant in his novel *Transition* (1927) and in his *Mansions of Philosophy* (1929)—now reissued as *The Pleasures of Philosophy*.

Volume VIII of the series will be published in 1963, as *The Age of Louis XIV*. It will be followed by *The Age of Voltaire* (Volume IX), and by *Rousseau and Revolution*, the tenth and final volume, which will include a special section on "The Lessons of History," summing up the message and the conclusions of this vast panorama of history.

North
W
E
S
RAETIA
NORICUM
HELVETII
SEDUNI
VENONETES
ALPES CARN
PANNONIA
LIBURNIA
DALMATIA
HISTRIA
VENETIA
GALLIA TRANSPADANA
CENOMANI
LIGURIA
LINGONES
APPENNINUS
SENONES
UMBRIA
PICENUM
ETRURIA
SABINI
AEQUI
PAELIGNI
LATINI
VOLSCI
SAMNIUM
CORSICA
ILVA
RHENUS F.
ARNUS F.
TIBERUS
Tridentum
Forum Julii
Augusta Praetoria
Comum
Mediolanium
Novaria
Verona
Patavium
Aquileia
Tergeste
Augusta Taurinorum
Ticinum
Placentia
Cremona
Mantua
Atria
Iria
Fidentia
Parma
Pollentia
Mutina
Spina
Pola
Genua
Bononia
Ravenna
Savo
Portus Veneris
Lima
Forum Clodii
Ariminum
Pisaurum
Pistoria
Faesulae
Luca
Florentia
Pisae
Monoecus
Nicaea
Antipolis
Sena Gallica
Ancona
Arretium
Volaterrae
Saena
Cortona
MONS
Firmum
L. TRASIMENUS
Perusia
Clusium
Asculum
CastrumNovum
Volsinii
Spoletium
Hadria
Vetulonia
Portus Traianus
Rusellae
Narnia
Reate
Horta
Falerii
Tarquinii
Caere
Corfinium
Tibur
Antinum
ROMA
Portus Augusti
Ostia
Lavinium
Praeneste
Fregellae
Teanum
Arpi
Luceria
Sipontum
Salapia
Cannae
Canusium
Turenum
Ausculum
Barium
Gnatia
APU
Beneventum
Volturnum
Capua
Mariana
Aleria
Alista
Palla
FRETUM GALLICUM
Salonae
LISSA
CORCYRA NIGRA
Epidaurum
Mare Adriaticum
S. Superum
Sinus Ligusticus